R. Gupta's®

POPULAR MASTER GUIDE

National Testing Agency (NTA)

UGC-NET/JRF

Junior Research Fellowship and Assistant Professor Eligibility Exam

Economics

PAPER II

by

RPH Editorial Board

2027
EDITION

RAMESH PUBLISHING HOUSE, NEW DELHI

Published by

O.P. Gupta *for* Ramesh Publishing House

Admin. Office

12-H, New Daryaganj Road, Opp. Officers' Mess,
New Delhi-110002 ✆ 23275224, 23245124

E-mail: info@rameshpublishinghouse.com

For Online Shopping: www.rameshpublishinghouse.com

Showroom

• Balaji Market, Nai Sarak, Delhi-110006 ✆ 23282525 📱 9354373464

• 4457, Nai Sarak, Delhi-110006

Indemnification Clause: *1.* This book is being sold/distributed subject to the exclusive condition that neither the author nor the publishers, individually or collectively, shall be responsible to indemnify the buyer/user/possessor of this book beyond the selling price of this book for any reason under any circumstances. If you do not agree to it, please do not buy/accept/use/possess this book.

2. UGC-NET syllabus being quite vast, we do not claim to cover the complete syllabus in the present book, mostly important topics are being incorporated from the point of view of examination.

Book Code: R-668

ISBN: 978-93-87604-81-0

Price: ₹ 690

Printed at: J.P. Enterprises, Delhi

CONTENTS

Previous Years' Paper

National Testing Agency (NTA)

UGC-NET Junior Research Fellowship & Assistant Professor Eligibility Exam

ECONOMICS, JANUARY-2026

(Exam held on 07-01-2026)

PAPER-II

1. Match List-I with List-II.

List-I	List-II
A. 14th Finance Commission	I. Vertical Tax Devolution 41 percent
B. 15th Finance Commission	II. Vertical Tax Devolution 42 percent
C. 12th Finance Commission	III. State's share 32% of the central taxes
D. 13th Finance Commission	IV. State's share 30.5 percent of central taxes

Choose the **correct** answer from the options given below :

1. A-IV, B-III, C-II, D-I
2. A-IV, B-III, C-I, D-II
3. A-III, B-IV, C-I, D-II
4. A-II, B-I, C-IV, D-III

2. Kinked-Demand model of oligopoly was developed by which of the following ?

1. Chamberlin
2. Bertrand
3. Stackel berg
4. Sweezy

3. Given the difference equation $Y_{t+1} - 1.2Y_t = 0$, the general expression Y_t in terms of t can be:

1. $Y_t = (1.2)^t Y_1$
2. $Y_t = (1.2)^{t+1} Y_0$
3. $Y_t = (1.2)^{t-1} Y_1$
4. $Y_t = (1.2)^{t-1} Y_0 + C$

4. In case of balanced budget multiplier :

A. Output increases less than the increase in government spending.

B. Output increases more than the increase in government spending.

C. Government spending and taxes are raised in equal amounts.

D. The value of multiplier is equal to 1.

Choose the **correct** answer from the options given below :

1. C and D only
2. B and C only
3. A, B and C only
4. B and D only

5. Which one of the following is true for the phenomenon of Liquidity Trap ?

1. The entire additional money supply is spent on buying bonds
2. The level of rate of interest is very high
3. The entire additional money supply is held by the public as idle cash balance
4. The interest rate will decrease from the point of liquidity trap

6. How much revenue will have to be foregone due to different beneficial proposals in the central budget 2025-26?

1. ₹ 2 Lakh Crore as direct taxes and ₹ 5600 Crore as indirect taxes

2. ₹ 1.5 Lakh Crore as direct taxes and ₹ 5600 Crore as indirect taxes
3. ₹ 1 Lakh Crore as direct taxes and ₹ 2600 Crore as indirect taxes
4. ₹ 50,000 Crore as direct taxes and ₹ 2000 Crore as indirect taxes

7. Given below are two statements : one is labelled as Assertion (A) and the other is labelled as Reason (R).

Assertion (A) : Deficit spending by the government leads to crowding out effect on private investment.

Reason (A) : When the government finances its deficit by borrowing from the market, the bond prices go up and the rate of interest falls.

In the light of the above statements, choose the **most appropriate answer** from the options given below :

1. Both (A) and (R) are correct and (R) is the correct explanation of (A)
2. Both (A) and (R) are correct but (R) is not the correct explanation of (A)
3. (A) is correct but (R) is not correct
4. (A) is not correct but (R) is correct

8. Welfare criterion based on compensation payments is known as :

1. Dalton-Friedman Compensation Criterion
2. Amartya Sen Compensation Criterion
3. Pareto-Bains Compensation Criterion
4. Kaldor-Hicks Compensation Criterion

9. The Human Development Index (HDI) is used to rank countries based on :

1. Life expectancy at Birth, Adult Illiteracy Rate and the percentage of population without access to safe water.
2. Real Per Capita Income, Percentage of Underweight children under 5 years and percentage of population not expected to survive to the age of 40.
3. Life Expectancy at Birth, Educational attainment and Real per capita Income at purchasing Power Parity.
4. Income Inequality and percentage of population living in urban areas.

10. Match List-I with List-II.

List-I	List-II
A. Kenneth Bouilding	I. Pollution Tax
B. Georgescu-Roegen	II. Spaceship Earth and Ecological Limits
C. Elinor Ostrom	III. Managing Common Property Resources
D. A.C. Pigou	IV. Energy as a limiting factor

Choose the **correct** answer from the options given below :

1. A-I, B-III, C-II, D-IV
2. A-III, B-II, C-I, D-IV
3. A-II, B-I, C-IV, D-III
4. A-II, B-IV, C-III, D-I

11. As per Dalton's optimum population formula defined as $M = \frac{A-O}{O}$ (where M is degree of mal-adjustment, A is actual population and O is the level of optimum population), a country is said to have optimum population if :

1. M is positive
2. M is negative
3. M is zero
4. O is zero

12. Given below are two statements : one is labelled as Assertion (A) and the other is labelled as Reason (R).

Assertion (A): If X and Y are any two variables and are transformed to the new variables U and V defined by $U = \frac{X-A}{h}$, $V = \frac{Y-B}{K}$ where A, B, h, K are any constants, h and K > 0 then, $r_{xy} = r_{uv}$

Reason (R): Correlation coefficient(r) is independent of change of origin and scale.

In the light of the above statements, choose the **most appropriate answer** from the options given below :

1. Both (A) and (R) are correct and (R) is the correct explanation of (A)
2. Both (A) and (R) are correct but (R) is not the correct explanation of (A)
3. (A) is correct but (R) is not correct
4. (A) is not correct but (R) is correct

13. Coefficient of Determination (R^2):

A. is an increasing function of the number of regressors

B. is a decreasing function of the number of regressors

C. is unaffected by increasing or decreasing the number of regressors

D. is always positive

Choose the **correct** answer from the options given below :

1. A and B only 2. A and C only
3. A and D only 4. B and C only

14. Monopoly Power is explained by which of the following?

1. $\frac{(P-MC)}{P}$ 2. $\frac{(P+MC)}{P}$
3. $\frac{(P-AC)}{P}$ 4. $\frac{(P+AC)}{P}$

15. In which year, the notes of ₹ 1000 denomination were demonetised for the first time in India?

1. 2016 2. 1978
3. 1969 4. 1980

16. The basic proposition of neo-classical growth theory are :

A. The growth of output depends on the rate of growth of labour productivity

B. The growth of output depends on the level of per capita income

C. The ratio of savings and investment determines economic growth

D. Only investment determines economic growth

Choose the **correct** answer from the options given below :

1. A and C only 2. A and B only
3. C and D only 4. B and C only

17. Among the following types of treasury bills, identify the correct one.

A. Adjusted price auction

B. Uniform price auction

C. Multiple price auction

D. Readjusted price auction

Choose the **correct** answer from the options given below :

1. A and B only 2. B and C only
3. C and D only 4. A and D only

18. A theory that explains the phenomenon of increasing public expenditure and state activity was proposed by:

1. Baumol 2. Allan Peacock
3. Dalton 4. Adolf Wagner

19. The origin of "Big-Push" theory of development is based on :

1. Unbalanced Economic Growth
2. Low Level Equilibrium Trap and Critical Minimum Effort
3. Kaldor's Growth Laws
4. Harrod's Knife-edged Instability

20. Given below are two statements : one is labelled as Assertion (A) and the other is labelled as Reason (R).

Assertion (A) : The Organisation of Petroleum Exporting Countries (OPEC) has failed to maintain high prices of petroleum products in the long run.

Reason (R): For petroleum products both the demand and supply are inelastic in the long run.

In the light of the above statements, choose the **most appropriate answer** from the options given below :

1. Both (A) and (R) are correct and (R) is the correct explanation of (A)

2. Both (A) and (R) are correct but (R) is not the correct explanation of (A)
3. (A) is correct but (R) is not correct
4. (A) is not correct but (R) is correct

21. Consider the following items and figures.

Items	Amount (in ₹ Crores)
(*a*) Total revenue receipts	5600
(*b*) Total capital receipts	3000
(*c*) Interest payments	800
(*d*) Disinvestment receipts	400
(*e*) Total expenditure	8600
(*f*) Recovery of loans	150

What is the amount of primary deficits?

1. ₹ 2140 crores
2. ₹ 3000 crores
3. ₹ 1650 crores
4. ₹ 2450 crores

22. Match List-I with List-II (As per Union Budget, 2025-26).

List-I	List-II
A. Pensions as % of Central Government Expenditure	I. 22%
B. State's share of taxes and duties as % of Central Govt. Expenditure	II. 18%
C. Tax-GDP ratio of India	III. 81.3%
D. Debt-GDP ratio of India	IV. 4%

Choose the **correct** answer from the options given below :

1. A-II, B-I, C-III, D-IV
2. A-II, B-III, C-I, D-IV
3. A-IV, B-III, C-I, D-II
4. A-IV, B-I, C-II, D-III

23. In a situation of decline in price of a Giffen Commodity, we find :

1. positive substitution effect is less than negative income effect
2. positive substitution effect is more than negative income effect
3. negative substitution effect is more than positive income effect
4. negative substitution effect is less than positive income effect

24. Match List-I with List-II.

List-I	List-II
A. Q theory	I. Unemployment and inflation
B. Phillips curve	II. Unemployment and output
C. Okun's Law	III. Investment
D. Liquidity trap	IV. Demand for money and interest rate

Choose the **correct** answer from the options given below :

1. A-III, B-I, C-II, D-IV
2. A-I, B-II, C-IV, D-III
3. A-III, B-II, C-I, D-IV
4. A-II, B-IV, C-I, D-III

25. Given GNP at market price ₹ 14400 crores, consumption ₹ 12000 crores, government purchases ₹ 1200 crores, exports ₹ 1000 crores and imports ₹ 1500 crores, the value of investment will be :

1. ₹ 1200 Crores
2. ₹ 2000 Crores
3. ₹ 1500 Crores
4. ₹ 1700 Crores

26. When public revenue increases by more than 1% for a 1% increase in GDP, it is known as :

1. CENVAT
2. Inelastic Tax system
3. Proportional Tax system
4. Tax buoyancy

27. The development of economic growth theory in chronological order would be :

A. Harrod Domar Growth Model
B. Solow's Neoclassical Growth Model
C. Endogenous Growth Theory
D. Adam Smith's "division of labour" and "increasing returns" theory.

Choose the **correct** answer from the options given below :

1. D, C, B, A
2. D, B, C, A
3. D, A, B, C
4. B, D, A, C

28. "Economic Dependency Burden" of a country implies :

A. The non-productive members of the country must be supported by the country's labour force.

B. The outstanding loan of the country.

C. Children below the age of 15 and people above the age of 70.

D. The people working in private sector

Choose the **correct** answer from the options given below :

1. A and D only
2. A and C only
3. C and D only
4. B and C only

29. NSSO and CSO come under :

1. Ministry of Home Affairs
2. Ministry of Finance
3. Ministry of Industry and Commerce
4. Ministry of Statistics and Programme Implementation (MoSPI)

30. Recently, Inflation rates have trended downward and approaching steadily Central Bank target levels.

In this context, which of the following are correct?

A. Supply chains are adopting the economic uncertainties

B. Easing monetary policy

C. Tighter monetary policy

D. Increase in AD is more than increase in AS

Choose the **correct** answer from the options given below :

1. A and B only
2. B and D only
3. A and C only
4. C and D only

31. For the given information regarding an economy, the value of equilibrium level of income is :

$C = 100 + 0.75Y_d$; $G = 40$; $I = 60$; $t = 0.2$

Here, C = consumption, Y_d = disposable income, G = Govt. expenditure, I = Investment, t = tax rate

1. 200
2. 500
3. 400
4. 450

32. Given below are two statements : one is labelled as Assertion (A) and the other is labelled as Reason (R).

If X is a given series of observations, a and b are any two constants, then with regard to Standard Deviation (SD).

Assertion (A) : $SD(X + a) = SD(X - b) = SD(X)$ and $SD(aX) = a^2.SD(X)$

Reason (R): SD is independent of change of origin, but not of scale.

In the light of the above statements, choose the **most appropriate answer** from the options given below:

1. Both (A) and (R) are correct and (R) is the correct explanation of (A)
2. Both (A) and (R) are correct but (R) is not the correct explanation of (A)
3. (A) is correct but (R) is not correct
4. (A) is not correct but (R) is correct

33. Given below are two statements : one is labelled as Assertion (A) and the other is labelled as Reason (R).

Assertion (A) : With 10% rise in average income of household, there will be 50% rise in investment in health and education of children.

Reason (R): Investment in health and education of children will raise human capital that will raise human capability and raise economic productivity.

In the light of the above statements, choose the **most appropriate answer** from the options given below:

1. Both (A) and (R) are correct and (R) is the correct explanation of (A)
2. Both (A) and (R) are correct but (R) is not the correct explanation of (A)
3. (A) is correct but (R) is not correct
4. (A) is not correct but (R) is correct

34. Given samples of sizes 20 and 15 with respective sample variances 35.53 and 34.92, the calculated value of F-statistic is :

1. 1.02
2. 0.98
3. 0.76
4. 1.31

35. Based on the following statements :
 A. Matrix Addition is not Commutative
 B. Matrix Addition is Associative
 C. Matrix Multiplication is Commutative
 D. Matrix Multiplication is Associative if product exists

 Choose the **correct** answer from the options given below :

 1. A and C only 2. A and D only
 3. B and C only 4. B and D only

36. Identify the correct statement regarding Mahatma Gandhi National Rural Employment Guarantee Scheme (MNREGS) :
 1. The draft proposed by the National Advisory Committee (NAC) envisaged legal guarantee to every household in rural areas for 120 days for doing casual manual work
 2. 90 percent of the cost of employment provided is borne by the centre
 3. In the first phase of implementation, 150 most backward districts were covered
 4. From 2nd October, 2010, National Rural Employment Guarantee Scheme (NREGS) has been renamed as Mahatma Gandhi National Rural Employment Guarantee Scheme (MNREGS)

37. For Cobb-Douglas production function with two inputs, $Q = AK^{\alpha}L^{\beta}$ where $A > 0$, α and β are > 0, the marginal products are :

 A. $MP_k = \frac{\alpha}{K}Q$ B. $MP_k = \frac{\beta}{K}Q$

 C. $MP_L = \frac{\alpha}{L}Q$ D. $MP_L = \frac{\beta}{L}Q$

 Choose the **correct** answer from the options given below :

 1. A and C only 2. A and D only
 3. B and C only 4. B and D only

38. Given below are two statements : one is labelled as Assertion (A) and the other is labelled as Reason (R).

 Assertion (A) : The presence of heteroscedasticity problem in regression analysis implies that the least square estimators are still unbiased but inefficient.

 Reason (R) : The estimates of the variances are also unbiased.

 In the light of the above statements, choose the **most appropriate answer** from the options given below :

 1. Both (A) and (R) are correct and (R) is the correct explanation of (A)
 2. Both (A) and (R) are correct but (R) is not the correct explanation of (A)
 3. (A) is correct but (R) is not correct
 4. (A) is not correct but (R) is correct

39. Which Tax is also popularly known as the 'destination tax' ?
 1. Customs Duty
 2. Corporate Tax
 3. Goods and Services Tax
 4. Central Excise Duty

40. Arrange the following in a correct chronological order.
 A. Shankar Acharya Committee on shifting financial year from (April-March) to (Jan-Dec).
 B. Parthasarathy Shome Committee on retrospective tax laws.
 C. Vijay Kelkar Committee on Tax reforms.
 D. Arvind Subramanian Committee on revenue neutral GST.

 Choose the **correct** answer from the options given below :

 1. A, B, C, D 2. C, A, D, B
 3. C, B, D, A 4. A, D, B, C

41. The Coasian Bargaining Approach will work when :
 A. The rights of the bargaining parties are transferable
 B. The bargaining parties are equally informed
 C. The property rights are legally established
 D. The resources are universally owned

Choose the **correct** answer from the options given below :

1. A and D only
2. B and D only
3. B and C only
4. A and C only

42. Given the demand function P = 80 – 3Q and cost function TC = 120 + 8Q :

A. Maximum Revenue occurs at Q = 12

B. Maximum Revenue occurs at Q = 3

C. Maximum Revenue is 528

D. Maximum Revenue is 213

Choose the **correct** answer from the options given below :

1. A and C only
2. A and D only
3. B and C only
4. B and D only

43. Match List-I with List-II.

List-I	List-II
A. Slack Variable	I. Best of all feasible solutions
B. Surplus Variable	II. Solution violating at least one condition
C. Optimal Solution	III. Used when there are less than or equal to (≤) type inequalities
D. Infeasible Solution	IV. Used when there are greater than or equal to (≥) type inequalities

Choose the **correct** answer from the options given below :

1. A-IV, B-III, C-I, D-II
2. A-IV, B-III, C-II, D-I
3. A-III, B-IV, C-II, D-I
4. A-III, B-IV, C-I, D-II

44. The range of the function $y = f(x) = \sqrt{1-x^2}$ is :

1. [0, 1]
2. [1, 0]
3. [1, ∞]
4. [1, 2]

45. Match List-I with List-II.

List-I	List-II
A. Targeted Public Distribution System (TPDS)	I. 1992
B. Revamped Public Distribution System (RPDS)	II. 2009
C. Right to Education Act (RTE Act)	III. 1997
D. National Food Security Act (NFSA Act)	IV. 2013

Choose the **correct** answer from the options given below :

1. A-I, B-III, C-IV, D-II
2. A-IV, B-III, C-I, D-II
3. A-III, B-I, C-II, D-IV
4. A-II, B-IV, C-I, D-III

46. 'The Salmon War' was between :

1. USA and Cuba
2. France and UK
3. Norway and Scotland
4. Sweden and Germany

47. Which of the following are called 'club goods'?

A. Railways

B. Swimming pool

C. Defense

D. Gym

Choose the **correct** answer from the options given below :

1. B and D only
2. A and B only
3. B and C only
4. A and D only

48. Given the demand function $Q = 100 - P - P^2$, the elasticity of demand (e_d) at price P = 5 is:

1. elastic
2. inelastic
3. unitary elastic
4. infinitely elastic

49. Match List-I with List-II.

List-I	List-II
A. Harrod and Domor	I. Constancy of the capital output ratio
B. Lucas and Romer	II. Dual economy with a capitalist and non-capitalist sector
C. Arthur Lewis	III. Investment as a double edged sword
D. Michael Todaro	IV. Rural-Urban migration

Choose the **correct** answer from the options given below :

1. A-IV, B-III, C-I, D-II
2. A-III, B-I, C-II, D-IV
3. A-I, B-II, C-III, D-IV
4. A-II, B-IV, C-III, D-I

50. Given the structural model

$y_1 = 3y_2 - 2x_1 + x_2 + u_1$

$y_2 = y_3 + x_3 + u_2$

$y_3 = y_1 - y_2 - 2x_3 + u_3$

Based on the order condition, the second equation is :

1. over identified
2. exactly identified
3. under identified
4. information not sufficient

51. Match List-I with List-II.

List-I	List-II
A. Debt-deflation theory	I. Falling price levels raises the income levels
B. Pigou effect	II. A policy of announcing future monetary action
C. Forward guidance	III. The effects of unexpected fall in price level could depress income
D. Okun's law	IV. An inverse relationship between unemployment and real GDP

Choose the **correct** answer from the options given below :

1. A-I, B-III, C-II, D-IV
2. A-III, B-II, C-IV, D-I
3. A-III, B-I, C-II, D-IV
4. A-IV, B-I, C-II, D-III

52. Based on $\{\epsilon_t\}$ is a purely random process with mean zero and variance σ^2 :

A. A process $\{x_t\}$ defined by $x_t = \alpha_1 x_{t-1} + \alpha_2 x_{t-2} + ... + \alpha_r x_{t-r} + \epsilon_t$ is called an autoregressive process of order r

B. A process $\{x_t\}$ defined by $x_t = \beta_0 \epsilon_t + \beta_1 \epsilon_{t-1} + ... + \beta_m \epsilon_{t-m}$ is called a moving average process of order m

C. A process $\{x_t\}$ defined by $x_t = \beta_0 \epsilon_t + \beta_1 \epsilon_{t-1} + ... + \beta_m \epsilon_{t-m}$ is called an autoregressive process of order r

D. A process $\{x_t\}$ defined by $x_t = \alpha_1 x_{t-1} + \alpha_2 x_{t-2} + ... + \alpha_r x_{t-r} + \epsilon_t$ is called a moving average process of order m

Choose the **correct** answer from the options given below :

1. A and B only
2. A and D only
3. B and D only
4. C and D only

53. The main feature of embodied technical progress is :

1. Exogenous technical progress that is not dependent on capital accumulation is embodied progress.
2. Technical improvements that can only be introduced into the productive system by new investment is embodied progress.
3. Lop-sided productivity increase is embodied progress.
4. This is dependent on government support.

54. Match List-I with List-II.

List-I	List-II
A. Neo-Chamberlinian Model	I. Horizontal differentiation of products
B. Neo-Hotelling Model	II. Vertical differentiation of products
C. Brander-Krugman Model	III. Product differentiation
D. Neo-Heckscher-Ohlin Model	IV. Reciprocal dumping

Choose the **correct** answer from the options given below :

1. A-IV, B-III, C-I, D-II
2. A-I, B-II, C-IV, D-III
3. A-I, B-III, C-II, D-IV
4. A-III, B-I, C-IV, D-II

55. A. Reserve Money = C + OD + CR
B. M1 = C + OD
C. Money Multiplier (m) = M/RM
D. Narrow Money Supply = M3

Here C = Currency, OD= Other deposits with RBI, CR = Cash Reserve of Banks, M = Money Supply, RM = Reserve Money

Choose the **correct** answer from the options given below :

1. A and D only 2. B and C only
3. A and B only 4. A and C only

56. Match List-I with List-II.

List-I	List-II
A. Amartya Sen	I. Rise and fall of inequality with economic growth
B. Simon Kuznets	II. Circulative and cumulative causation of economic under-development
C. Gunnar Myrdal	III. Geographic pattern of economic development
D Paul Krugman	IV. Entitlements, capabilities and freedom of choice

Choose the **correct** answer from the options given below :

1. A-II, B-IV, C-I, D-III
2. A-III, B-II, C-IV, D-I
3. A-I, B-II, C-III, D-IV
4. A-IV, B-I, C-II, D-III

57. Increased fiscal deficit leads to :

A. Increase in government spending
B. Increase in domestic interest rate
C. Fall in private investment
D. Fall in total borrowing by the government

Choose the **correct** answer from the options given below :

1. A, B and D only 2. A, B and C only
3. B, C and D only 4. B and D only

58. A natural monopoly occurs when :

1. Average cost keeps on rising with increase in output over the relevant range of output.
2. Average cost remains constant with increase in output over the relevant range of output.
3. Average cost first decreases and then rises with increase in output over the relevant range of output.
4. Average cost keeps on decreasing with increase in output over the relevant range of output.

59. In a population of men in a city, 3% are observed to suffer from cancer, 15% are found to be smokers, while 10% are noticed to be either smokers or cancer patients. If a man is selected at random, what is the probability that he is a smoker and suffering from cancer?

1. 0.08 2. 0.8
3. 0.02 4. 0.2

60. Which one of the following is NOT true about rational expectation?

1. Rational expectations theory has been developed by Hansen.
2. It is used in decision making by households, firms and labour for making their expectations about relevant variables.
3. The rational expectation uses all relevant information.
4. It is not an error free expectation.

61. Match List-I with List-II.

List-I	List-II
A. Type I error	I. Accept H_0 when it is false
B. Type II error	II. $H_0 : \mu = \mu_0$ and $\sigma^2 = \sigma_0^2$
C. Simple Hypothesis	III. Reject H_0 when it is true
D. Composite Hypothesis	IV. $H_0 : \mu = \mu_0$ and σ^2 is unknown

Choose the **correct** answer from the options given below :

1. A-III, B-I, C-IV, D-II
2. A-I, B-III, C-II, D-IV
3. A-III, B-I, C-II, D-IV
4. A-I, B-III, C-IV, D-II

62. The Headcount Index of Poverty Measurement is based on :

1. The number of people who fall below the poverty line.
2. The proportionate gap between the average level of income below the poverty line and the poverty line itself.
3. The "Bottom Billion"
4. Vertical Inequality of income

63. Which one of the following holds true at equilibrium level of demand for labour by a perfectly competitive firm?

1. $VMP_L < MRP_L$
2. $VMP_L = MRP_L$
3. $VMP_L > MRP_L$
4. $VMP_L + MRP_L = W_*$

64. Match List-I with List-II.

List-I	List-II
A. $\lvert e_d \rvert$ for demand function $D = 64 - 8\,P$, at P= 6	I. 6
B. e_s for supply function $S = -25 + 5\,P$, at P =10	II. 4
C. The value of MR when P = 8 and $e_d = 4$	III. 3
D. The value of MPP_L when $VMP_L = 12$ and P= 3	IV. 2

Choose the **correct** answer from the options given below :

1. A-III, B-IV, C-I, D-II
2. A-II, B-III, C-I, D-IV
3. A-I, B-IV, C-II, D-III
4. A-III, B-I, C-IV, D-II

65. A. Innovation Theory of Business cycle was given by Jorgenson

B. Pure Monetary Theory of Business cycle was given by Hawtrey

C. Monetary-over-investment Theory of Business cycle was given by Clark

D. Multiplier-Acceleration Interaction Theory of Business cycle was given by Samuelson

Choose the **correct** answer from the options given below :

1. A and B only
2. B and D only
3. A, B and C only
4. A and D only

66. Which one of the following production function exhibits decreasing returns to scale?

1. $AK^{\frac{1}{4}}\sqrt{L}$
2. $A\,K^{\alpha}\,L^{1-\alpha}$
3. $A(3K + 5L)$
4. $A\sqrt{KL^3}$

67. Identify the Finance commissions with its chairman:

A. 12th Finance commission – C. Rangarajan

B. 11th Finance commission – A.M. Khusro

C. 14th Finance commission – R.K. Singh

D. 15th Finance commission – Y.V. Reddy

Choose the **correct** answer from the options given below :

1. A and D
2. B and C
3. C and D
4. A and B

68. Given below are two statements : one is labelled as Assertion (A) and the other is labelled as Reason (R).

Assertion (A): When everyone trades in the competitive market place, all mutually beneficial trades are completed and the resulting equilibrium allocation of resources are economically efficient.

Reason (R): Even if a trade from an inefficient allocation makes everyone better off, the new allocation is not necessarily efficient.

In the light of the above statements, choose the **most appropriate answer from** the options given below:

1. Both (A) and (R) are correct and (R) is the correct explanation of (A)

2. Both (A) and (R) are correct but (R) is not the correct explanation of (A)
3. (A) is correct but (R) is not correct
4. (A) is not correct but (R) is correct

69. The following statements are made in the Union Budget for the year 2025-2026 :

A. The FDI limit for the insurance sector will be raised from 74 to 100 percent
B. The FDI limit for the insurance sector will be raised from 51 to 74 percent
C. An investment Friendliness Index of states will be formed
D. The fiscal deficit is estimated to be 4.4 percent of GDP

Choose the **correct** answer from the options given below :

1. B, C and D only
2. A, C and D only
3. A, B and C only
4. C and D only

70. Choose the correct statements:

A. The '*q*' theory emphasises that the investment increases when assets are valuable relative to their reproduction cost.
B. With a fixed exchange rate fiscal expansion under free capital mobility is completely ineffective in raising output.
C. Under Investment tax credit, government pays part of the cost of investment.
D. Under fixed exchange rate and perfect capital mobility a country cannot pursue an independent monetary policy.

Choose the **correct** answer from the options given below :

1. B and D only
2. A and D only
3. A, C and D only
4. A, B and C only

71. When some domestic production by a nation member of the Union is replaced by lower-cost imports from another member nation, then the Union is known as :

1. Trade Diverting Customs Union
2. Trade Creating Customs Union
3. Preferential Trade Agreement
4. Free Trade Agreement

72. Given below are two statements : one is labelled as Assertion (A) and the other is labelled as Reason (R).

Assertion (A) : Since about the mid-seventies, protectionism has grown alarmingly in the developed countries. This has taken mainly the form of non-tariff barriers (NTBs).

Reason (R): The growing protectionism in industrialised countries is due to the increasing competition from developing and the South-East Asian countries.

In the light of the above statements, choose the **most appropriate answer** from the options given below:

1. Both (A) and (R) are correct and (R) is the correct explanation of (A)
2. Both (A) and (R) are correct but (R) is not the correct explanation of (A)
3. (A) is correct but (R) is not correct
4. (A) is not correct but (R) is correct

73. For analysing effective rent control in the housing sector :

A. The shortage of housing is small in the short run compared to the long run.
B. The shortage of housing is large in the short run compared to the long run.
C. The effective rent control exists when a government places an effective price floor on rent.
D. The effective rent control exists when a government places an effective price ceiling on rent.

Choose the **correct** answer from the options given below :

1. A and C only
2. B and C only
3. A and D only
4. B and D only

74. Match List-I with List-II.

List-I	List-II
A. Narasimham Committee-I	I. Tax Reform
B. Narasimham Committee-II	II. Banking Sector Reform
C. Chelliah Committee	III. Financial Sector Reform
D. C. Rangarajan Committee	IV. Poverty Estimation Committee

Choose the **correct** answer from the options given below :

1. A-IV, B-II, C-I, D-III
2. A-III, B-II, C-I, D-IV
3. A-II, B-III, C-IV, D-I
4. A-I, B-II, C-IV, D-III

75. Based on Economic Survey 2024-25, Indian merchandise trade deficit widened due to :

A. Decline of non-petroleum and non-gems and jewellery exports
B. Increase in non-oil and non-gold imports
C. Imposing of ban on jewellery exports
D. Gold imports grew due to early purchases ahead of festive spending and demand for safe heaven assets

Choose the **correct** answer from the options given below :

1. A and B only 2. B and D only
3. C and D only 4. A and C only

76. Given below are two statements : one is labelled as Assertion (A) and the other is labelled as Reason (R).

Assertion (A): The all-India annual unemployment rate (UR) for individuals, aged 15 years and above (usual status) has steadily declined from 6 percent in 2017-2018 to 3.2 percent in 2023-2024.

Reason (R): According to RBI data, India's foreign exchange reserves on Dec. 26, 2025 were around 693 billion dollars.

In the light of the above statements, choose the **most appropriate answer** from the options given below :

1. Both (A) and (R) are correct and (R) is the correct explanation of (A)
2. Both (A) and (R) are correct but (R) is not the correct explanation of (A)
3. (A) is correct but (R) is not correct
4. (A) is not correct but (R) is correct

77. Etymologically, the term 'money' is derived from which language?

1. Greek 2. Latin
3. Persian 4. Sanskrit

78. Arrange the following theories in a chronological order.

A. Theory of limit pricing (Bain's Model)
B. Logical ordering theory of demand given by JR Hicks.
C. Cardinal utility theory of demand
D. Walras theory of general equilibrium

Choose the **correct** answer from the options given below :

1. D, C, A, B 2. B, C, A, D
3. A, B, D, C 4. D, B, C, A

79. A. SEBI - Advisory body
B. GST Council - Statutory body
C. NITI Aayog - Advisory body
D. RBI - Statutory body

Choose the **correct** answer from the options given below :

1. A and B 2. A and C
3. B and D 4. C and D

80. Match List-I with List-II.

List-I	List-II
A. nth term of an Arithmetic Progression	I. $\frac{n}{2}[2a+(n-1)d]$
B. nth term of a Geometric Progression	II. $a\left(\frac{r^n-1}{r-1}\right), r>1$
C. Sum to n terms of an Arithmetic Progression	III. $a+(n-1)d$
D. Sum to n terms of a Geometric Progression	IV. ar^{n-1}

(where a is first term, d is common difference and r is common ratio)

Choose the **correct** answer from the options given below :

1. A-III, B-IV, C-II, D-I
2. A-III, B-IV, C-I, D-II
3. A-IV, B-III, C-I, D-II
4. A-IV, B-I, C-II, D-III

81. Which of the following approach has included Time Deposit with commercial banks in the definition of Money Supply?

1. The Conventional Approach
2. The Chicago Approach
3. The Fed Approach
4. The Walters Approach

82. Given below are two statements :

Statement (I): Green Revolution led to increase in the production of fine cereals. High incentives and application of high yielding varieties of seeds, fertilisers and chemicals made this a good success.

Statement (II) : Green revolution led to decline in the production of coarse cereals and area under coarse cereals shifted to other crops.

In the light of the above statements, choose the **most appropriate answer** from the options given below :

1. Both Statement I and Statement II are correct
2. Both Statement I and Statement II are incorrect
3. Statement I is correct but Statement II is incorrect
4. Statement I is incorrect but Statement II is correct

83. Which of the following is not correct in case of Rural Infrastructure Development Fund (RIDF)?

1. Providing funds to state governments and state owned corporations to rural infrastructure projects
2. Scheduled commercial banks contribute funds to RIDF
3. Creation of RIDF in 1995-96 in NABARD with a corpus of Rs. 2000 Crore
4. Now RIDF scheme is merged with Kisan Credit Card (RCC)

84. A. Globalisation carries benefits and opportunities as well as costs and risks

B. Globalisation leads to flow of capital, technology, goods and services across countries

C. The larger the market, the greater the gains from trade and the division of labour

D. Globalisation in terms of flow of capital, goods and technology is evenly spread across world nations

Choose the **correct** answer from the options given below :

1. A, B and C only
2. A, B and D only
3. B and D only
4. B, C and D only

85. Which of the following commodities are not covered by GST till now ?

A. Mobile phones

B. Electricity

C. Textiles

D. Alcohol

Choose the **correct** answer from the options given below :

1. A and C only
2. B and C only
3. A and D only
4. B and D only

86. Given below are two statements : one is labelled as Assertion (A) and the other is labelled as Reason (R).

Assertion (A): Prices of diesel and petroleum products are different in different states of India.

Reason (R): The above products have not yet been brought under the coverage of GST by the GST Council.

In the light of the above statements, choose the **most appropriate answer** from the options given below:

1. Both (A) and (R) are correct and (R) is the correct explanation of (A)
2. Bodi (A) and (R) are correct but (R) is not the correct explanation of (A)
3. (A) is correct but (R) is not correct
4. (A) is not correct but (R) is correct

87. Based on Beta (β) and Gama (γ) coefficients, if $\beta_2 < 3$ or $\gamma_2 < 0$ then the curve is said to be:

1. Normal Curve 2. Lepto Kurtic
3. Platy Kurtic 4. Insufficient Data

88. Which of the following is not a function of the Securities and Exchange Board of India (SEBI)?

1. Prohibiting insider trading in securities
2. Promoting and regulating self-regulatory organisations
3. Underwriting new capital issues
4. Regulating portfolio managers

89. If $P(A) = \frac{1}{5}$ and $P(B) = \frac{1}{3}$ and A and B are two mutually exclusive events, then the probability of neither A nor B will occur is:

1. $\frac{8}{25}$ 2. $\frac{1}{15}$
3. $\frac{7}{15}$ 4. $\frac{1}{5}$

90. A. In a barter system, if there are 3 goods to be exchanged, the required number of prices will be 3.

B. Money does not play its functions in case of inflation.

C. Double coincidence of wants is not a problem in barter system.

D. Paper currencies are token money.

Choose the **correct** answer from the options given below :

1. A, B and D only
2. B and D only
3. A and D only
4. B, C and D only

Directions (Qs. No. 91-95): *Read the following passage and answer the questions :*

For environmental assets, markets can fail if prices do not communicate society's desires and constraints accurately. The factors leading to habitat destruction and the loss of biodiversity originate in several sources of market failure. First, habitat destruction arises from public ownership of large areas of land with open access and limited government capacity to manage land. The economic incentives encourage the over exploitation of wildf-life, timber, grazing lands and crop lands.

Lack of secure land tenure provides little incentive to maintain the habitat necessary for biodiversity conservation. This is a case of non-rivalry and non-excludability that can destroy biodiversity as it itself does not have any price. Such market failures can be linked to incomplete markets. On the other hand, such situation could also happen from externality if some outside agent disturbs the natural eco-system. This could lead to a tragic end of the ecosystem unless there is a coordinated effort by the local people to save it.

91. A Common Property Resource (CPR) can survive only under:

1. Strict Property Rules
2. Taxation
3. Credible Commitment to the collective living on the CPR
4. Non-exclusion

92. Asymmetric information about a resource occurs when there is:

1. Government intervention
2. Non-rivalry
3. Non-excludability
4. Moral hazard and adverse selection

93. Public goods do not have the following property:

1. Non-rival
2. Non-excludable
3. Common property resources controlled by locals
4. Free goods

94. Incomplete markets for biodiversity occurs because:

1. Biodiversity does not have a value to society
2. Failure to institute well-defined property rights on the forest having biodiversity
3. The forest resource is open for all to exploit
4. No one is willing to pay money to save biodiversity in forest

95. The concept of "Tragedy of Commons" was founded by :

1. Robert Solow
2. Harold Hotelling
3. Garrett Hardin
4. Partha Dasgupta

Directions (Qs. No. 96-100): *Read the following passage and answer the questions:*

The present international economic relations have been least influenced by multilateral forums. Multilateral economic institutions' meetings are not considered seriously by the leaders of important nations. In the past, it was heard that many world leaders were speaking against WTO and prioritising their national interest. Even the forum of WTO was used to speak against the multilateral trade.

In the beginning of 1980s, the world was moving towards globalisation and the multi-lateral lending and trade forums played a crucial role in the economic and trade negotiations. Slowly regional economic associations and bilateral trade forums took the centre stage. The exit of Britain from the European Union and frequent disruptions in the WTO forums and many statements of the U.S president and many European leaders were giving the message that globalisation is coming to an end.

Recent imposition of high tariff on Indian exports and various measures by the USA violate free and fair trade ensured by the multi-lateral trade and investment forums, are matters of serious concerns. Trade disruptions are never becoming an issue for consideration of the appropriate forums at the international level. People start questioning the relevance of a long lists of economic and political institutions built after the second world war with much enthusiasm and high expectations. Do the present developments indicate a turning point for a new world order?

96. The important challenge to WTO:

1. Regional Economic Associations and bilateral trade forums
2. The exit of Britain from European Union
3. International economic relations not influenced by multilateral forums
4. World moving towards post-globalisation world order

97. Globalisation is an outcome of :

1. Exit of Britain from the European union
2. Initiatives of the USA
3. The role played by the multilateral lending and trade forums
4. The outcome of second world war

98. The nature of present international economic relations :

1. USA and European countries are not violating international understandings
2. Multilateral forums are relegated to the background
3. Increased role is given to multilateral economic and political institutions
4. World leaders are giving message that globalisation is improving

99. The Passage conveys about:

1. Multilateral institutions have accepted their weaknesses.
2. Reforms in multilateral institutions
3. W.T.O. is becoming more important
4. Powerful nations are undermining the role of multilateral institutions for their national interest

100. What violates free and fair trade ?

1. Imposition of high and unfair tariffs
2. Weak structure of Regional economic associations and bilateral trade forums
3. World leaders speaking in favour of WTO
4. Keen interest by the USA and Europe

ANSWERS

1	2	3	4	5	6	7	8	9	10
4	4	3	1	3	3	3	4	3	4
11	**12**	**13**	**14**	**15**	**16**	**17**	**18**	**19**	**20**
3	1	3	1.	2	1	2	4	2	3
21	**22**	**23**	**24**	**25**	**26**	**27**	**28**	**29**	**30**
3	4	1	1	4	4	3	2	4	3
31	**32**	**33**	**34**	**35**	**36**	**37**	**38**	**39**	**40**
2	4	4	1	4	2	2	3	3	3
41	**42**	**43**	**44**	**45**	**46**	**47**	**48**	**49**	**50**
4	*	4	1	3	3	1	2	2	1
51	**52**	**53**	**54**	**55**	**56**	**57**	**58**	**59**	**60**
3	1	2	4	4	4	2	4	1	1.
61	**62**	**63**	**64**	**65**	**66**	**67**	**68**	**69**	**70**
3	1	2	1	2	1	4	2	2	3
71	**72**	**73**	**74**	**75**	**76**	**77**	**78**	**79**	**80**
2	1	3	2	2	2	2	1	4	2
81	**82**	**83**	**84**	**85**	**86**	**87**	**88**	**89**	**90**
2	1	4	1	4	1	3	3	3	3
91	**92**	**93**	**94**	**95**	**96**	**97**	**98**	**99**	**100**
3	4	3	2	3	1	3	2	4	1

Explanatory Answers

1. The question requires correct matching of Finance Commissions with their recommended vertical devolution percentages of the divisible pool of central taxes to States. The 12th Finance Commission recommended 30.5% devolution; hence C–IV is correct. The 13th Finance Commission increased this to 32%, so D–III is correct. The 14th Finance Commission made a major structural shift by recommending 42% devolution, significantly enhancing fiscal federalism; thus A–II is correct. The 15th Finance Commission revised the share to 41% (primarily due to the reorganization of Jammu & Kashmir into Union Territories), so B–I is correct. Only option 4 correctly captures all these pairings simultaneously without inconsistency.

2. The kinked demand curve model explains price rigidity in oligopolistic markets. It assumes that if a firm raises its price, competitors do not follow, causing demand to be highly elastic; but if it lowers its price, competitors match the cut, making demand relatively inelastic. This creates a "kink" in the demand curve and a discontinuity in the marginal revenue curve, leading to price stickiness even when costs change moderately. This analytical framework was formally developed by Paul M. Sweezy in 1939. Therefore, the correct attribution of the kinked demand model is to Sweezy.

3. The given difference equation is $Y_{t+1} - 1.2Y_t = 0$. Rearranging gives $Y_{t+1} = 1.2Y_t$, which is a first-order linear homogeneous difference equation. Solving iteratively:

$$Y_2 = 1.2Y_1$$
$$Y_3 = 1.2Y_2 = (1.2)^2Y_1$$
$$Y_4 = (1.2)^3Y_1$$

Thus, by mathematical induction, $Y_t = (1.2)^{t-1}Y_1$ for $t \geq 1$. This expression satisfies the recurrence relation exactly and matches option 3 without index error.

4. A balanced budget multiplier refers to a situation where government expenditure (G) and taxes (T) increase by the same amount. In the simple Keynesian income determination model, an increase in government expenditure directly increases aggregate demand, while the increase in taxes reduces disposable income and consumption by MPC times the tax change. The net impact on equilibrium income equals the initial increase in government spending, meaning the balanced budget multiplier equals 1. Therefore, statement C (equal increase in G and T) is correct, and statement D (multiplier equals 1) is also correct. Statements A and B do not align with the standard Keynesian balanced budget multiplier result.

5. In a liquidity trap, the rate of interest has already fallen to a very low level, so people expect it to rise in future (which would mean bond prices may fall). Because of this expectation, they prefer holding money (liquidity) rather than buying bonds. As a result, when the central bank increases money supply further, the public simply absorbs it in the form of idle cash balances, and the rate of interest does not fall further in any meaningful way. This description matches option (3) exactly.

6. "Revenue foregone due to beneficial proposals" refers to the expected loss of tax revenue because the Budget introduces relief measures such as lower tax burdens, exemptions, or concessional rates. The stated figures are split into (*i*) direct taxes (like personal income tax, corporate tax) and (*ii*) indirect taxes (like customs duties, excise-related components, etc.). For the Central Budget 2025–26, the revenue expected to be foregone due to such beneficial proposals is about ₹ 1 lakh crore in direct taxes and about ₹ 2600 crore in indirect taxes, which fits option (3) exactly, while other options either overstate/understate one side or give a mismatched combination.

7. Deficit spending by the government can lead to a crowding-out effect because the government often finances the deficit by borrowing from the market. This increases the demand for loanable funds and tends to push the market rate of interest upward, which discourages (crowds out) private investment—so Assertion (A) is correct in the standard macroeconomic mechanism. However, Reason (R) says that when the government borrows from the market, bond prices go up and the rate of interest falls. Typically, market borrowing by issuing more government bonds increases bond supply, which puts downward pressure on bond prices and raises yields/interest rates (not lowers them). Hence (R) is not correct.

8. A "compensation" based welfare test checks whether the gainers from a policy change could, in principle, compensate the losers and still remain better off. This is exactly the idea behind the Kaldor–Hicks criterion, which relaxes the strict Pareto condition and evaluates changes using potential compensation rather than requiring that nobody is harmed. Hence, the welfare criterion based on compensation payments is the Kaldor–Hicks Compensation Criterion.

9. The Human Development Index (HDI) is a composite index designed to rank countries using three broad dimensions—health, education, and standard of living. Health is captured through life expectancy at birth, education through educational attainment indicators, and living standards through real income measured on a PPP basis (so that cross-country purchasing power differences are adjusted). Among the given options, only option (3) correctly states these core HDI components.

10. Kenneth Boulding is associated with the "Spaceship Earth" idea and ecological limits, so A–II. Georgescu-Roegen's bioeconomics emphasizes entropy and the role of energy as a limiting factor in the economic process, so B–IV. Elinor Ostrom's central contribution is the analysis of how communities manage common property resources through institutions and rules, so C–III. A.C. Pigou is linked with externalities and corrective taxation (Pigouvian tax), which fits pollution tax, so D–I. This full set of matches is satisfied only by option (4).

11. From Dalton's optimum population formula $M = \frac{A - O}{O}$, a country has optimum population when the actual population equals the optimum population, i.e., A = O. Substituting A = O gives M $= \frac{O - O}{O} = 0$. So, optimum population corresponds to zero mal-adjustment, hence option (3).

12. In the assertion, $U = \frac{X - A}{h}$ and $V = \frac{Y - B}{K}$ represent a linear transformation of X and Y involving a change of origin (subtracting constants A, B) and change of scale (dividing by *h*, K). Correlation is unaffected by change of origin and by positive change of scale; since $h > 0$ and

$K > 0$, the direction is not reversed, so $r_{XY} = r_{UV}$. The reason states exactly this invariance property of correlation coefficient, and it directly justifies why the assertion holds.

13. When you add more regressors to a regression model, the fitted values can only improve or stay the same in terms of minimizing residual sum of squares (SSR cannot increase), so $R^2 = 1 - \frac{SSR}{SST}$ cannot fall; therefore, statement A is true and B is false. In the standard regression with an intercept, $0 \leq R^2 \leq 1$, so it is not negative and is treated as always non-negative/positive in this context, making statement D true, while C is false because R^2 is affected by the number of regressors. Hence, the correct combination is A and D only.

14. Monopoly power is commonly measured by the Lerner Index, which directly captures the firm's ability to set price above marginal cost. When a firm has no market power (perfect competition), P = MC and the index becomes 0. As market power rises, P exceeds MC, making $\frac{P - MC}{P}$ positive and larger, which exactly reflects stronger monopoly power.

15. The question refers to demonetisation of ₹ 1000 notes in India in the context of the high-denomination withdrawal episode that is widely discussed in standard economic and public-finance literature. The major demonetisation that specifically targeted high-value notes such as ₹ 1000, ₹ 5000 and ₹ 10,000 under a formal ordinance-based intervention occurred in 1978, when the High Denomination Bank Notes (Demonetisation) Ordinance was promulgated to curb black money and unaccounted wealth. Among the given options (2016, 1978, 1969, 1980), only 1978 corresponds to that historically recognised demonetisation of ₹ 1000 notes under the cited ordinance framework.

16. In the neoclassical (Solow-type) growth framework, long-run growth in output per worker is driven by improvements in labour productivity/technology, so statement A is a core proposition. The model also treats saving and investment (capital accumulation) as an important determinant of the economy's growth path and steady-state level of income (and hence an essential driver of growth dynamics), so statement C is taken as valid in the standard syllabus framing. Statement B is not a basic proposition because the growth rate is not said to depend on the level of per capita income as a rule, and D is too narrow because growth is not determined only by investment—productivity/technology and other parameters matter.

17. In practice, Treasury bills are issued through recognised auction formats such as the uniform price auction (all successful bidders pay the same cut-off price/yield) and the multiple price (discriminatory) auction (successful bidders pay the price/yield they bid). These are standard auction mechanisms used internationally for T-bills and other government securities. Terms like "adjusted price auction" and "readjusted price auction" are not recognised as standard auction types for Treasury bills in the usual public finance/monetary economics framework, so A and D are not the correct identifiers here.

18. The idea that public expenditure and state activity tend to increase over time as an economy develops is explained by Wagner's Law (Adolf Wagner). The logic is that with economic growth and industrialisation, the functions of the state expand—administration, law and order, social services, welfare, infrastructure, and regulation—so public spending rises both absolutely and as a share of national income. Hence, the theory specifically associated with this phenomenon is attributed to Adolf Wagner.

19. The Big-Push approach argues that poor economies can remain stuck in a low-income situation unless a large, coordinated investment effort is made across sectors, so that complementarities, demand linkages, and economies of scale become effective together. This idea is closest to the development logic of escaping a low-level equilibrium through a minimum critical effort (a threshold-type jump in investment), rather than Hirschman's unbalanced growth (which deliberately promotes sectoral imbalance). Therefore, the best origin/foundation among the given choices is option (2).

20. Assertion (A) is broadly correct because maintaining persistently high petroleum prices is difficult for a cartel in the long run due to factors like cheating on quotas, expansion of non-OPEC supply, technological change (shale, deepwater), and demand-side adjustment when prices stay high. However, Reason (R) is not correct because in the long run both demand and supply for petroleum products tend to become more elastic than in the short run—consumers and firms can adopt substitutes and efficiency, and producers can expand exploration, capacity, and alternative sources. Since (R) states long-run inelasticity for both sides, it does not hold and cannot explain (A).

21. Non-debt capital receipts = Disinvestment + Recovery of loans = 400 + 150 = 550

Fiscal deficit = Total expenditure − (Revenue receipts + Non-debt capital receipts)

Fiscal deficit = 8600 − (5600 + 550)

Fiscal deficit = 8600 − 6150 = 2450

Primary deficit = Fiscal deficit − Interest payments

Primary deficit = 2450 − 800 = 1650

22. A. Pensions as % of Central Govt. expenditure must be a small single-digit share, so it matches 4% (IV).

C. Tax–GDP ratio is typically around the high teens in such data, so it matches 18% (II).

D. Debt–GDP ratio is the largest magnitude here, so it matches 81.3% (III).

The remaining value 22% (I) then fits B (State's share of taxes and duties as % of Central Govt. expenditure).

23. For a Giffen good, when price falls:

- Substitution effect increases quantity demanded (positive effect).
- Income effect reduces quantity demanded because the good is strongly inferior (negative effect).

In the Giffen case, the negative income effect dominates the positive substitution effect, so overall quantity demanded falls when price falls.

24.
- Tobin's Q theory relates q (market value vs replacement cost) to incentives for capital formation, so it matches Investment (III).
- Phillips Curve links Inflation and Unemployment, so it matches (I).
- Okun's Law links Output and Unemployment, so it matches (II).
- Liquidity trap describes a situation where money demand becomes very high and interest-rate policy becomes ineffective, so it matches Demand for money and Interest rate (IV).

25.
- Net exports = X − M = 1000 − 1500 = −500
- National income identity:

Y = C + I + G + (X – M)

I = Y – C – G – (X – M)

I = 14400 – 12000 – 1200 – (–500)

I = 14400 – 13200 + 500

I = 1200 + 500 = 1700

26. Tax buoyancy measures the responsiveness of public revenue (tax revenue) to changes in GDP. If GDP rises by 1% and public revenue rises by more than 1%, the tax system is said to be buoyant (buoyancy > 1). Hence, the correct term is tax buoyancy, not CENVAT (a tax mechanism) and not proportional/inelastic systems (which would imply equal or less-than-proportionate response).

27. D. Adam Smith's "division of labour" and "increasing returns" theory (1776): This is the earliest foundation for growth thinking, linking productivity gains to specialization and scale. It predates formal 20th-century growth models and sets the classical base for later growth theory.

A. Harrod–Domar Growth Model (1939–1946): Harrod (1939) and Domar (1946) built a formal dynamic model where growth depends on saving and the capital–output relation. This comes after classical ideas and before the neoclassical (Solow) framework.

B. Solow's Neoclassical Growth Model (1956): Solow (1956) introduced diminishing returns to capital and highlighted technological progress as the driver of long-run per capita growth. It is clearly later than Harrod–Domar and becomes the mainstream benchmark model.

C. Endogenous Growth Theory (mid-1980s onward; Romer 1986, Lucas 1988): This theory explains sustained growth through factors inside the model (knowledge, human capital, innovation) without relying only on exogenous technology. It is the latest among the listed developments and follows the Solow framework historically.

28. "Economic dependency burden" refers to the burden on the working (productive) population of supporting the non-working (dependent) population. Statement A captures the idea that non-productive members must be supported by the labour force. Statement C correctly identifies typical dependents as the young and the elderly (here stated as below 15 and above 70). Statement B is about public debt, not dependency, and D refers to a segment of workers, not dependents.

29. NSSO and CSO function under India's official statistical system, which is placed under the Ministry of Statistics and Programme Implementation (MoSPI) (now integrated as parts of the broader statistical set-up). Hence the correct ministry is MoSPI.

30. A sustained downward trend in inflation toward the central bank's target is consistent with (*i*) improving/adapting supply chains that reduce supply bottlenecks and cost pressures (A), and (*ii*) tighter monetary policy (higher policy rates/ withdrawal of liquidity) that cools aggregate demand and inflation expectations (C). Easing monetary policy (B) would generally push demand and inflation upward, and if AD rises more than AS (D), it tends to be inflationary rather than disinflationary.

31. For equilibrium income in the simple Keynesian model, aggregate demand is AD = C + I + G, with proportional tax t implying $Y_d = (1 - t)Y$:

$$C = 100 + 0.75Y_d$$

$$Y_d = (1 - 0.2)Y = 0.8Y$$

$$C = 100 + 0.75(0.8Y) = 100 + 0.6Y$$

$$AD = (100 + 0.6Y) + 60 + 40$$

$$= 200 + 0.6Y$$

Equilibrium: $Y = AD = 200 + 0.6Y$

$$Y - 0.6Y = 200$$

$$0.4Y = 200;\ Y = \frac{200}{0.4} = 500$$

32. Standard deviation is unchanged by a change of origin, so $SD(X + a) = SD(X)$ and $SD(X - b) = SD(X)$ are correct, but under change of scale the rule is $SD(aX) = |a| \cdot SD(X)$, not $a^2 \cdot SD(X)$. Hence the Assertion (A) becomes incorrect because it states the wrong scaling property for SD. The Reason (R) is correct because SD is independent of change of origin but depends on scale, so the most appropriate choice is option (4).

33. The Assertion claims that a 10% rise in average household income necessarily leads to a 50% rise in investment in health and education of children, which is not a general economic/statistical law and cannot be accepted as universally true without additional behavioural and institutional conditions. The Reason is correct because spending on health and education builds human capital (better skills, health, productivity), which can raise an economy's productive capacity and growth. Since (R) is true but (A) is not necessarily true, the correct option is (4).

84. In an F-test, the calculated F-statistic is taken as the ratio of the larger sample variance to the smaller sample variance.

Larger variance =35.53, smaller variance =34.92

$$F = \frac{35.53}{34.92} = 1.0174\ldots$$

Rounded to two decimals: $F \approx 1.02$

35. Matrix addition is commutative and associative, so statement A ("not commutative") is false while statement B is true. Matrix multiplication is not commutative in general, so statement C is false, but it is associative whenever the products are defined (dimensionally conformable), so statement D is true. Therefore, the only correct combination is B and D only, which is option (4).

36. Under NREGA/MGNREGA, the Centre pays 100% of unskilled wage cost, and also bears a major share of other components (notably a large share of material/administrative components as per the scheme's cost-sharing pattern), while States mainly bear items like unemployment allowance and the remaining shares. Because the dominant expenditure is unskilled wages and the Centre covers it fully, the overall funding pattern works out to about 90% by the Centre and about 10% by the States in standard scheme accounting for total outlay/implementation. 90 percent of the cost of employment provided is borne by the centre. In the first phase of implementation, 200 most backward districts were covered.

37. For $Q = AK^{\alpha}L^{\beta}$ with $A > 0$, $\alpha > 0$, $\beta > 0$, marginal products are obtained by partial differentiation.

$$MP_K = \frac{\partial Q}{\partial K} = A\alpha K^{\alpha - 1} L^{\beta}$$

$$= \alpha\left(\frac{AK^{\alpha}L^{\beta}}{K}\right)$$

$$= \frac{\alpha}{K}Q \rightarrow \text{Statement A is correct.}$$

$$MP_L = \frac{\partial Q}{\partial L} = A\beta K^{\alpha} L^{\beta - 1}$$

$$= \beta\left(\frac{AK^{\alpha}L^{\beta}}{L}\right)$$

$$= \frac{\beta}{L}Q \rightarrow \text{Statement D is correct.}$$

Statements B and C incorrectly interchange α, β and/or K, L.

38. Under heteroscedasticity (with the usual exogeneity assumption intact), OLS slope estimators remain unbiased/consistent, but they are inefficient because OLS is no longer the minimum-variance linear unbiased estimator; hence Assertion (A) is correct. However, heteroscedasticity makes the usual OLS variance/standard error formulas incorrect (they become biased/inconsistent unless robust corrections are used), so the claim that "the estimates of variances are also unbiased" is not correct. Therefore, (A) is correct but (R) is not correct.

39. A "destination tax" is one where the tax revenue accrues to the jurisdiction where the good/service is consumed (destination) rather than where it is produced (origin). GST is designed as a destination-based consumption tax, so it is popularly called the destination tax.

40. Arrange by time (earliest to latest). The Vijay Kelkar Committee on Tax Reforms belongs to the early 2000s reform discussion (C comes first). The Parthasarathy Shome Committee on retrospective taxation is from the 2012 period (B next). The Arvind Subramanian Committee on revenue neutral rate (RNR) for GST is around the GST design phase (mid-2010s), so D follows. The Shankar Acharya Committee on shifting the financial year (Apr–Mar to Jan–Dec) is later (mid/late 2010s), so A is last. Hence the correct chronological order is C → B → D → A, which matches option (3).

41. The Ronald Coase bargaining solution works when property rights are clearly defined (legally established) and can be exchanged/assigned (transferable) so that parties can negotiate to internalize the externality and reach an efficient outcome (especially when transaction costs are low). "Universally owned" resources generally create open-access/common-property issues rather than clear enforceable rights, and "equally informed" is helpful but not the core condition stated in the standard Coasian set-up compared with clearly defined, transferable rights.

42. Demand function:

$$P = 80 - 3Q$$

Total Revenue (TR) = P × Q

$$TR = (80 - 3Q)Q$$

$$TR = 80Q - 3Q^2$$

To find maximum revenue:

$$\frac{d(TR)}{dQ} = 80 - 6Q$$

Set equal to zero:

$$80 - 6Q = 0$$

$$6Q = 80$$

$$Q = \frac{80}{6} = \frac{40}{3} \approx 13.33$$

So maximum revenue does not occur at Q = 12 and also not at Q = 3.

Thus statements A and B are incorrect.

Now compute maximum revenue:

$$TR = 80\times\frac{40}{3} - 3\left(\frac{40}{3}\right)^2$$

$$= \frac{3200}{3} - 3\times\frac{1600}{9} = \frac{3200}{3} - \frac{4800}{9}$$

Convert to common denominator:

$$= \frac{9600}{9} - \frac{4800}{9} = \frac{4800}{9} = 533.33$$

Maximum revenue ≈ 533.33, which is neither 528 nor 213.

Therefore none of the given statements are correct.

Answer. NONE: None of the statements (A to D) is correct.

43. A. Slack Variable → III (used when constraints are of the ≤ type)

B. Surplus Variable → IV (used when constraints are of the ≥ type)

C. Optimal Solution → I (best among all feasible solutions)

D. Infeasible Solution → II (violates at least one condition)

44. For $y = \sqrt{1-x^2}$, we need $1 - x^2 \geq 0$

$\Rightarrow -1 \leq x \leq 1$.

On [–1, 1], $1 - x^2$ ranges from 0 (at $x = \pm 1$) to 1 (at $x = 0$).

Taking square roots gives y from $\sqrt{0} = 0$ to $\sqrt{1} = 1$.

So the range is [0,1].

45. A. Targeted Public Distribution System (TPDS) → III (1997)

B. Revamped Public Distribution System (RPDS) → I (1992)

C. Right to Education Act (RTE Act) → II (2009)

D. National Food Security Act (NFSA Act) → IV (2013)

46. The term "Salmon War" in the European context refers to the late 1980s–early 1990s trade dispute between Norwegian salmon exporters and Scottish salmon producers. Scottish farmers alleged that Norway was dumping farmed salmon in the European market at artificially low prices, thereby harming domestic producers. The dispute led to investigations and, eventually, the imposition of anti-dumping duties by the European Commission in 1991. Since the conflict specifically involved

Norwegian exports and the Scottish salmon industry, the correct pair among the options is Norway and Scotland.

47. Club goods are excludable (access can be restricted by membership/fees) and non-rival up to congestion (many users can enjoy them until crowding sets in). A swimming pool and a gym typically operate on membership/entry rules, so they fit club goods. Defense is non-excludable and non-rival (public good), and railways are better treated as a mixed/congestible service often regulated as a public utility rather than a standard club good in this classification. Hence, B and D only.

48.
$$Q = 100 - P - P^2.$$

At P = 5: Q = 100 – 5 – 25 = 70

$$\frac{dQ}{dP} = -1 - 2P$$

$$\Rightarrow \left.\frac{dQ}{dP}\right|_{P=5} = -1 - 10 = -11$$

$$e_d = \frac{dQ}{dP}\cdot\frac{Q}{P} = (-11)\cdot\frac{5}{70}$$

$$= -\frac{55}{70} = -\frac{11}{14}$$

$$|e_d| = \frac{11}{14} \approx 0.79 < 1$$

⇒ demand is inelastic at P = 5.

49. Harrod and Domar are associated with the idea of investment as a "double-edged sword," because in their growth model investment increases productive capacity while simultaneously generating income and demand; imbalance between warranted and actual growth creates instability, hence A-III. Lucas and Romer developed endogenous growth theory in the late 1980s, emphasizing human capital, innovation, and knowledge spillovers as internal drivers of sustained growth, hence B-I. Arthur Lewis proposed the dual economy model (1954), explaining structural transformation through labour transfer from the subsistence sector to the modern capitalist sector, hence C-II. Michael Todaro formulated the rural-urban migration model (1969), based on expected income differentials, hence D-IV.

50. Structural system has endogenous variables $\{y_1, y_2, y_3\} \Rightarrow G = 3$, exogenous variables $\{x_1, x_2, x_3\} \Rightarrow K = 3$.

Second equation: $y_2 = y_3 + x_3 + u_2$

Endogenous variables appearing in Eq. (2): $\{y_2, y_3\} \Rightarrow m = 2$

Excluded exogenous variables from Eq. (2): $\{x_1, x_2\} \Rightarrow K - k_i = 2$

Order condition: $K - k_i \geq (m-1) \Rightarrow 2 \geq 1$ (satisfied), and $2 > (m-1) \Rightarrow$ over-identification by order condition.

Rank condition (minimum requirement here is rank ≥ 1): at least one excluded exogenous variable (x_1 or x_2) appears with a non-zero coefficient in the other structural equations (both appear in Eq. 1), so rank condition is satisfied.

Therefore, the second equation is over identified.

51. **A → III:** Debt-deflation (Irving Fisher) explains that when the price level falls unexpectedly, the real value of nominal debts rises. This worsens balance sheets, forces distress selling and deleveraging, and can reduce output/income through contractionary effects.

B → I: Pigou effect (real-balance effect) says a fall in the price level raises the real value of money balances/wealth. Higher real wealth tends to increase consumption demand, supporting income/output.

C → II: Forward guidance is a monetary-policy tool where the central bank communicates its future policy stance (future rates/stance) to influence expectations today. So it matches the item about announcing future monetary action.

D → IV: Okun's law captures the inverse relation between unemployment and real GDP (or output gap). When output rises above potential, unemployment tends to fall, and vice versa.

52. A is an AR(r) definition because current x_t depends on its own r lagged values plus a white-noise shock e_t; B is an MA(m) definition because x_t is a finite linear combination of current and past shocks ($e_t, e_{t-1}, \ldots, e_{t-m}$)). C is wrong because it calls an MA form "autoregressive," and D is wrong because it calls an AR form "moving average."

53. Embodied technical progress means the new technology is "built into" new capital goods (new machines/vintages). Therefore, productivity rises mainly when firms invest and replace old capital with new, more efficient capital; without new investment, the existing capital stock does not fully incorporate the latest technology. This is exactly what option (2) states.

54. **A → III:** The neo-Chamberlinian approach uses monopolistic competition where firms produce differentiated varieties. The key idea is product differentiation (variety) under increasing returns and imperfect competition.

B → I: The neo-Hotelling framework is classically tied to location/variety along a "line," which is a standard way to model horizontal differentiation. Consumers choose among varieties differentiated by characteristics rather than "quality levels."

C → IV: Brander–Krugman is known for reciprocal dumping under oligopoly with segmented markets and trade costs. Similar firms export to each other's markets, leading to two-way trade and "dumping" in the sense of price discrimination across markets.

D → II: Neo–Heckscher–Ohlin extensions are commonly linked with quality/skill-based specialization, where countries differ in factor endowments that translate into different quality levels. That aligns with vertical differentiation (differences in quality levels rather than just varieties).

55. Reserve money (monetary base) is formed by currency plus deposits held with the central bank (including banks' reserves and other deposits), so the structure in A matches the base-money composition in the given notation. Money multiplier is defined as the ratio of money supply to reserve money, so $m = \frac{M}{RM}$ in C is correct; B is incorrect because M1 is not just C + OD (it includes demand deposits), and D is incorrect because narrow money is not M3 (that is broad money).

56. A. Amartya Sen → IV (Entitlements, capabilities and freedom of choice)

Sen's welfare and development economics is centred on the capability approach and entitlement analysis (famines, deprivation, freedom).

Hence his contribution is best matched with entitlements, capabilities and freedom of choice.

B. Simon Kuznets → I (Rise and fall of inequality with economic growth)

Kuznets is identified with the *Kuznets Curve*, which hypothesizes inequality first rising and then falling as an economy develops.

So he matches the "rise and fall of inequality with economic growth" statement.

C. Gunnar Myrdal → II (Circular and cumulative causation of economic underdevelopment)

Myrdal's theory explains underdevelopment through circular cumulative causation where disadvantages reinforce themselves over time.

This directly corresponds to circular and cumulative causation of economic underdevelopment.

D. Paul Krugman → III (Geographic pattern of economic development)

Krugman's *new economic geography* explains agglomeration, core–periphery outcomes, and spatial concentration of industry and income.

Therefore, he matches the geographic pattern of economic development.

57. An increase in fiscal deficit typically reflects a situation where the government's expenditure exceeds its receipts by a larger margin, which is consistent with higher government spending (A) relative to revenues, and it usually requires higher market borrowing. Higher government borrowing raises demand for loanable funds, pushing up domestic interest rates (B) and, through the crowding-out channel, tends to reduce private investment (C). A fall in total borrowing by the government (D) contradicts the very mechanism through which a higher deficit is financed, so D is not implied.

58. A natural monopoly arises when economies of scale are so strong that one firm can supply the entire market at a lower average cost than multiple firms. This requires the long-run average cost to keep falling over the market-relevant output range, which is exactly what option (4) states.

59. Let S = "smoker", C = "cancer".

Given: $P(C) = 0.03$,

$P(S) = 0.15$, $P(S \cup C) = 0.10$.

Using inclusion–exclusion:

$$P(S \cap C) = P(S) + P(C) - P(S \cup C)$$
$$P(S \cap C) = 0.15 + 0.03 - 0.10 = 0.08$$

So the required probability is 0.08.

60. The statement is NOT true because rational expectations are primarily credited to John F. Muth (1961) and later developed and popularized in macroeconomics by thinkers such as Lucas and Sargent; attributing the development of the theory to "Hansen" is not correct in standard economic history. The other statements match the core idea: rational expectations are used by agents to form expectations, they incorporate all relevant available information, and they are not "error-free" in the sense of always being correct (forecast errors can occur but are not systematically biased).

61. A. Type I error → III (Reject H_0 when it is true)

Type I error means we reject a true null hypothesis, i.e., we commit an error by concluding "significant" when actually H_0 is correct. So it directly matches "Reject H_0 when it is true."

B. Type II error → I (Accept H_0 when it is false)

Type II error means we fail to reject (accept) a false null hypothesis, i.e., we miss a real effect when it exists.

So it matches "Accept H_0 when it is false."

C. Simple Hypothesis → II (H_0: $\mu = \mu_0$ and $\sigma_0^2 = \sigma^2$)

A simple hypothesis fully specifies the population distribution/parameters under H_0 (no unknown parameter is left free).

Here both μ and σ^2 are fixed at specific values, so it is a simple hypothesis.

D. Composite Hypothesis → IV (H_0: $\mu = \mu_0$ and σ^2 is unknown)

A composite hypothesis does not fully specify the distribution because at least one parameter remains unspecified.

Since σ^2 is not fixed to a single value, H_0 contains a set of possible distributions, so it is composite.

62. The Headcount Index (H) is the simplest poverty measure and is defined as the proportion (or count-based share) of the population whose income/consumption lies below the poverty line. It ignores the depth of poverty (how far below the line people are), and it also ignores inequality among the poor; it only counts how many are poor. Therefore, the correct basis of Headcount Index is the number of people below the poverty line.

Answer. 1: The number of people who fall below the poverty line

63. Under perfect competition in the product market, price equals marginal revenue (P = MR). Since $VMP_L = P \times MP_L$ and $MRP_L = MR \times MP_L$, it follows that $VMP_L = MRP_L$ when P = MR. At labour-market equilibrium for a competitive firm, the hiring rule is $VMP_L = W$, and because VMP_L equals MRP_L in perfect competition, the equality $VMP_L = MRP_L$ must hold.

64. A. $|e_d|$ for D = 64 – 8P at P = 6 → III (3)

$$Q = 64 - 8(6) = 16, \quad \frac{dQ}{dP} = -8$$

$$|e_d| = \left|\frac{dQ}{dP}\cdot\frac{P}{Q}\right| = |1-8|\cdot\frac{6}{16} = \frac{48}{16} = 3$$

B. e_s for S = –25 + 5P at P = 10 → IV (2)

$$Q = -25 + 5(10) = 25, \quad \frac{dQ}{dP} = 5$$

$$e_s = \frac{dQ}{dP}\cdot\frac{P}{Q} = 5\cdot\frac{10}{25} = \frac{50}{25} = 2$$

C. MR when P = 8 and $e_d = 4$ → I (6)

Using MR = $\left(1-\frac{1}{|e_d|}\right)$ for a downward-sloping demand at a point,

$$MR = 8\left(1-\frac{1}{4}\right) = 8\cdot\frac{3}{4} = 6$$

D. MP_L when $VMP_L = 12$ and P = 3 → II (4)

$$VMP_L = P\cdot MP_L \Rightarrow 12 = 3\cdot MP_L$$

$$MP_L = \frac{12}{3} = 4$$

65. Innovation theory of business cycles is classically associated with Schumpeter's emphasis on waves of innovations, not with Jorgenson, so statement A is incorrect. Hawtrey is well known for the Pure Monetary theory of business cycles (credit-money driven trade cycle), so B is correct. Monetary over-investment theory is linked with Hayek/Mises (Austrian theory), whereas Clark is mainly linked with the acceleration principle, so C is incorrect. The Multiplier–Acceleration interaction model is attributed to Samuelson (1939), combining Keynesian multiplier with the accelerator, so D is correct. Hence, only B and D are true.

66. For a Cobb–Douglas type production function $Q = AK^aL^b$, returns to scale depend on $a + b$; if $a + b < 1$ it is decreasing returns to scale. Here $a = \frac{1}{4}$ and $b = \frac{1}{2}$, so $a + b = \frac{1}{4} + \frac{1}{2} = \frac{3}{4} < 1$, hence decreasing returns to scale. (Option (2) has $a + (1 - a) = 1$ so CRS; (3) is linear so CRS; (4) has exponents $\frac{1}{2} + \frac{3}{2} = 2 > 1$ so IRS.)

67. The 12th Finance Commission was chaired by C. Rangarajan and the 11th Finance Commission was chaired by A.M. Khusro, so statements A and B are correct. The 14th Finance Commission was chaired by Y.V. Reddy (not R.K. Singh), and the 15th Finance Commission was chaired by N.K. Singh (not Y.V. Reddy), so C and D are incorrect.

68. The assertion states the First Welfare Theorem idea—under competitive market trading (with standard assumptions), the resulting allocation is Pareto efficient, so (A) is correct. The reason is also correct because a Pareto-improving trade from an inefficient point can still end at another inefficient point (Pareto improvement ≠ Pareto efficiency). However, (R) does not explain why competitive equilibrium becomes efficient; it is a separate statement about Pareto improvements not guaranteeing efficiency.

69. In the Union Budget 2025–26, the insurance FDI limit was announced to be raised from 74% to 100% (so A is correct, B is not), and an Investment Friendliness Index of States was to be launched (so C is correct). The fiscal deficit target for 2025–26 is stated as 4.4% of GDP, so D is also correct; therefore the correct combination is A, C and D only.

70. Tobin's *q* theory says investment rises when the market value of capital/assets is high relative to replacement (reproduction) cost, so A is correct. Under the Mundell–Fleming model with a fixed exchange rate and high/perfect capital mobility, fiscal expansion is generally effective (not "completely ineffective"), so B is incorrect. An investment tax credit reduces the effective cost of investment by having the government bear part of it through a credit/subsidy, so C is correct. The "impossible trinity" implies that with a fixed exchange rate and perfect capital mobility, an independent monetary policy cannot be maintained, so D is correct.

71. Trade creation happens when, after forming a customs union, a member country stops producing a good domestically at a higher cost and instead imports it from another member at a lower cost. Here the key clue is "domestic production … is replaced by lower-cost imports from another member nation," which exactly describes replacement of high-cost domestic output by low-cost partner imports (efficiency gain). Trade diversion would instead mean replacing low-cost world imports with higher-cost partner imports because of the common external tariff, which is not what the statement says.

72. The assertion is correct because, from the mid-1970s onward, many developed countries increasingly relied on non-tariff barriers (quotas, VERs, technical standards, anti-dumping, subsidies, etc.) rather than overt tariff hikes, partly because tariffs were being negotiated down under multilateral rounds. The reason is also correct: rising competitive pressure from developing countries and the rapidly industrialising South and South-East Asian economies led to stronger protectionist responses in import-competing sectors, and this competitive pressure is a major driver of the shift toward NTBs; hence (R) explains (A).

73. Effective rent control is a binding rent ceiling set below the market-clearing rent, so statement D is correct and statement C is incorrect (a price floor would not be "rent control" in the usual sense). With a binding rent ceiling, shortage tends to be smaller in the short run because housing supply is relatively fixed immediately, but it often becomes larger in the long run as maintenance declines, conversions occur, and new construction is discouraged—so statement A is correct while B is incorrect. Therefore, the correct combination is A and D only.

74. **A. Narasimham Committee – I → III (Financial Sector Reform)**

This committee (early 1990s) examined the broader financial system and recommended wide reforms in the financial sector framework.

It is therefore matched with the overall financial sector reform agenda rather than a narrow banking-only exercise.

B. Narasimham Committee – II → II (Banking Sector Reform)

The second committee (late 1990s) focused more directly on banking strength—capital adequacy, NPAs, prudential norms, and competitiveness.

Hence it is correctly linked to banking sector reform.

C. Chelliah Committee → I (Tax Reform)

The Chelliah Committee is well known for proposals on restructuring and rationalising India's tax system.

So it directly matches tax reform.

D. C. Rangarajan Committee → IV (Poverty Estimation Committee)

Rangarajan headed a committee that revisited poverty measurement methodology and poverty lines in India.

Hence it matches poverty estimation committee.

75. A widening merchandise trade deficit is most directly explained by higher imports and/or a specific surge in certain import categories. Statement B points to a rise in non-oil and non-gold imports, which increases the import bill beyond petroleum and gold. Statement D points to higher gold imports driven by early purchases ahead of festivities and safe-haven demand—this also raises the import bill and can widen the trade deficit even if other components are stable. Statement C (ban on jewellery exports) is not a standard broad-based driver cited for widening deficit in such summaries, and the option set requires the best-supported pair; thus B and D only is the appropriate combination.

76. The assertion refers to the "usual status" unemployment rate declining over time; this is consistent with recent PLFS-type trends where the usual-status unemployment rate has fallen from around the mid-single digits to nearly low-single digits by 2023–24. The reason statement about India's forex reserves being around 693 billion dollars on Dec. 26, 2025 can also be true as a factual macro indicator, but it does not explain why the unemployment rate declined because unemployment changes are driven by labour-market participation, sectoral job creation, growth composition, and measurement status—forex reserves are not a direct causal explanation for that decline.

77. The word "money" is etymologically linked to Latin through moneta (associated with the Roman temple/mint of Juno Moneta), from which terms for coin/minting evolved and later entered European languages. Hence, among the given language options, Latin is the correct origin.

78. **D. Walras' Theory of General Equilibrium (1874)** – Published in Elements of Pure Economics, it is one of the earliest systematic and mathematical formulations in economics. Hence, it comes first.

C. Cardinal Utility Theory of Demand (1871–1890) – Initiated by Jevons (1871) and later refined by Marshall (1890), it assumes utility can be measured numerically. This follows Walras chronologically.

A. Theory of Limit Pricing (1950s) – Introduced by Joe S. Bain, it explains how existing firms set prices to deter new entrants in oligopolistic markets.

B. Logical Ordering (Ordinal Utility) Theory of Demand (1934) – Given by J.R. Hicks and R.G.D. Allen in *A Reconsideration of the Theory of Value*, it introduced indifference curve analysis and the ordinal approach to utility.

79. SEBI is a statutory regulator (created under the SEBI Act), so calling it an "advisory body" is incorrect. The GST Council is a constitutional body (created under Article 279A), so calling it a "statutory body" is also not accurate in the strict classification used here; however, NITI Aayog is an advisory/think-tank style institution (not created by statute/constitution), and RBI is a statutory body established under the RBI Act. Therefore, only C and D form the correct pair.

80. **A. n^{th} term of an Arithmetic Progression → III**

$a + (n - 1)d$: In an AP, each term increases by common difference d; after $(n - 1)$ steps from the first term a, the nth term becomes $a + (n - 1)d$. This is the standard AP term formula used to generate any term directly.

B. n^{th} term of a Geometric Progression → IV

ar^{n-1}: In a GP, each term is multiplied by common ratio r; after $(n - 1)$ multiplications starting from a, the nth term is ar^{n-1}. This captures exponential growth/decay depending on r.

C. Sum to n terms of an Arithmetic Progression → I $\frac{n}{2}[2a + (n - 1)d]$: The AP sum equals number of terms times the average of first and last terms; rewriting the last term as $a + (n - 1)d$ yields $\frac{n}{2}[2a + (n - 1)d]$. This is the compact closed-form sum formula for AP.

D. Sum to n terms of a Geometric Progression → II $a\left(\frac{r^n - 1}{r - 1}\right)$, $r > 1$: The GP sum is derived by multiplying the sum by r and subtracting to cancel intermediate terms, giving $S_n(r - 1) = a(r^n - 1)$. Hence $S_n = a\left(\frac{r^n - 1}{r - 1}\right)$ for $r \neq 1$ (shown here for $r > 1$).

81. The Chicago School, particularly associated with Milton Friedman and other monetarists, expanded the traditional definition of money beyond currency and demand deposits. They argued that time deposits with commercial banks are close substitutes for money, as they serve as a store of value and can be converted into cash with relatively low cost. Hence, they should be included in the definition of money supply. The Conventional Approach treated money narrowly as currency plus demand deposits only. Therefore, the approach that included time deposits with commercial banks in the definition of money supply is the Chicago Approach.

82. The Green Revolution in India was primarily associated with rapid productivity and output increases in fine cereals, especially wheat and rice, because HYV seeds, irrigation, chemical fertilisers, and plant-protection measures were applied most intensively to these crops. At the same time, policy incentives and profitability shifts encouraged farmers to reallocate land away from many coarse cereals (like jowar, bajra, ragi in several regions) toward wheat/rice and other remunerative crops, which contributed to a relative (and in some areas absolute) decline in coarse-cereal area and production over time. Hence both statements correctly describe the major directional effects.

83. RIDF (Rural Infrastructure Development Fund) was created within NABARD in 1995–96 with an initial corpus of about ₹ 2000 crore, mainly to finance rural infrastructure through state governments and state-owned agencies. Its resources are largely built from contributions linked to scheduled commercial banks, especially when they fall short of priority sector lending targets, and the lending supports projects like rural roads, irrigation, bridges, markets, and similar infrastructure. Kisan Credit Card, however, is a farm credit delivery mechanism for short-term and related agricultural credit; it is not a merger product of RIDF, so the merger claim is the incorrect statement.

84. Statement A is correct because globalisation typically expands opportunities (markets, technology access, efficiency gains) but also brings adjustment costs and risks (inequality pressures, volatility, sectoral displacement). Statement B is correct because globalisation, by definition, intensifies cross-border flows of goods, services, capital, and technology (along with ideas and sometimes labour). Statement C is correct because larger markets deepen specialisation and the division of labour, which can raise productivity and enlarge gains from trade. Statement D is incorrect because these flows are not evenly spread; benefits and integration are highly uneven across countries and within countries due to differences in capabilities, institutions, infrastructure, and comparative advantage.

85. Mobile phones and textiles are clearly within the GST framework and are taxed under GST rates across the supply chain, with input tax credit mechanisms applying. Electricity, however, is generally kept outside GST (states levy electricity duty and related charges), so it is not covered under GST in the standard sense. Alcohol for human consumption is explicitly excluded from GST and continues to be taxed by states through excise/VAT-type levies. Therefore, the commodities not covered by GST are Electricity and Alcohol, i.e., B and D only.

86. Diesel prices vary across States because petroleum products like diesel are not brought under the GST regime. Since diesel is outside GST, individual States levy their own VAT/sales tax rates and additional cesses, leading to variation in tax incidence across States. These differing State-level tax structures directly cause differences in retail diesel prices. Therefore, the reason correctly explains why diesel prices differ across States.

87. β_2 is the coefficient of kurtosis and $\gamma_2 = \beta_2 - 3$ is excess kurtosis. A normal curve has $\beta_2 = 3$ and $\gamma_2 = 0$. If $\beta_2 < 3$, then $\gamma_2 < 0$, meaning the distribution is flatter (less peaked) than normal, which is called platykurtic. Hence, the given condition $\beta_2 < 3$ or $\gamma_2 < 0$ clearly indicates a platykurtic curve.

88. SEBI's core functions are regulatory and supervisory—protecting investors, regulating intermediaries (like portfolio managers), preventing insider trading, and promoting/regulating self-regulatory organisations within securities markets. Underwriting of new issues is an activity performed by market intermediaries (e.g., underwriters/merchant bankers) who may be registered and regulated by SEBI, but SEBI itself does not "underwrite" capital issues as a function. Therefore, "Underwriting new capital issues" is not a function of SEBI.

89. $P(A) = \frac{1}{5}$, $P(B) = \frac{1}{3}$, and A and B are mutually exclusive $\Rightarrow P(A \cap B) = 0$.

$$P(A \cup B) = P(A) + P(B) = \frac{1}{5} + \frac{1}{3} = \frac{3}{15} + \frac{5}{15} = \frac{8}{15}.$$

Probability of neither A nor B $= 1 - P(A \cup B)$

$$= 1 - \frac{8}{15} = \frac{7}{15}.$$

90. A is correct because in a barter system with n goods, the number of exchange ratios (prices) required is $\frac{n(n-1)}{2}$; for $n = 3$, $\frac{3 \cdot 2}{2} = 3$, so 3 prices are needed.

B is not correct as written because inflation weakens money's functions (especially store of value and unit of account), but it does not mean money completely stops functioning. C is incorrect because double coincidence of wants is precisely a major problem in barter (you need a matching of wants between two parties). D is correct because paper currency is token (fiat) money whose value is not equal to the intrinsic value of the paper. Therefore, only A and D are correct.

91. A Common Property Resource survives when the user community can create, accept, and enforce shared rules about access, extraction limits, monitoring, and sanctions. This needs a credible commitment by members to cooperate rather than free-ride, because open-access behaviour leads to overuse and depletion. Strict private property rules convert it away from CPR, taxation is not the core survival condition, and "non-exclusion" would worsen overexploitation instead of sustaining the resource.

92. Asymmetric information exists when one side of a transaction has better information than the other, causing problems like adverse selection (hidden characteristics before agreement) and moral hazard (hidden actions after agreement). Government intervention, non-rivalry, and non-excludability describe policy or public-good characteristics, not the informational imbalance itself. Hence the option that directly represents asymmetric information is moral hazard and adverse selection.

93. Public goods are defined by non-rivalry and non-excludability. "Common property resources controlled by locals" refers to CPRs where exclusion is possible through community rules but rivalry exists due to congestion/limited stock, so it is a different category from public goods. "Free goods" is not a defining property of public goods (many public goods are costly to provide), but the clear "not a property" in the given list is the CPR feature.

94. Incomplete markets arise when a valuable asset/service is not properly priced because property rights are unclear and exclusion/enforcement is weak. Biodiversity often generates benefits that cannot be fully captured by any single owner, so without well-defined and enforceable rights, no proper market for biodiversity services develops and incentives to conserve remain weak. Open access is a symptom of weak rights, but the root institutional cause highlighted is failure to institute well-defined property rights.

95. The "Tragedy of the Commons" is classically associated with Garrett Hardin (1968), who explained how individually rational overuse of a shared resource can lead to collective ruin when exclusion and cooperative governance are absent. Solow is linked with growth theory, Hotelling with exhaustible resources, and Dasgupta with welfare/development/environmental economics, but the specific founding articulation of this concept is Hardin's.

96. The passage repeatedly highlights that multilateral forums (including the WTO platform) are losing influence because important countries are increasingly preferring regional blocs and bilateral arrangements to pursue their national interest. When trade negotiations and dispute-settlement pressures shift away from the multilateral arena toward regional economic associations and bilateral trade forums, the WTO's central role gets directly challenged—its agenda-setting power weakens and rules-based discipline becomes harder to enforce. Hence, the most specific "challenge to WTO" described here is the growing importance of regional and bilateral forums.

97. The passage states that from the early 1980s the world moved toward globalisation and that multilateral lending and trade forums played a crucial role in shaping the negotiation environment and facilitating global integration. This means globalisation is being presented as an outcome driven by the working and influence of multilateral institutions and negotiations rather than being an outcome of one event like Brexit or only a single country's initiatives. Therefore, the correct option is the role played by multilateral lending and trade forums.

98. The passage explicitly conveys that multilateral economic institutions' meetings are "not considered seriously" by leaders and that international economic relations are less influenced by multilateral forums now. It also notes disruptions in WTO forums and a growing focus on bilateral and regional routes, which together imply that multilateral forums are being pushed into the background in current practice. Hence, the nature of present international economic relations, as per the passage, is that multilateral forums are relegated to the background.

99. The passage points to actions like imposing high tariffs and taking measures that violate free and fair trade norms, alongside leaders questioning multilateral institutions and prioritising national interest. Such behaviour indicates that powerful nations are weakening multilateral institutions (including the WTO's influence) by bypassing or violating the multilateral rule-based framework when it conflicts with their domestic priorities. Therefore, the passage conveys that powerful nations are undermining multilateral institutions for national interest.

100. Free and fair trade requires predictable, rules-based market access without arbitrary or discriminatory barriers. The passage specifically mentions the imposition of high tariffs and other measures that violate free and fair trade ensured by multilateral arrangements, making tariffs a direct violation because they restrict trade and distort prices/competition. Therefore, the correct choice is the imposition of high and unfair tariffs.

Previous Years' Paper

National Testing Agency (NTA)

UGC-NET Junior Research Fellowship & Assistant Professor Eligibility Exam

ECONOMICS, JUNE-2025

(Exam held on 29-06-2025)

PAPER-II

1. Match the List-I with List-II:

	List-I		List-II
A.	Playing each strategy with probability	I.	Nash equilibrium
B.	Maximum payoff given the strategy of other	II.	Grim trigger strategy
C.	Long-run behaviour	III.	Best response function
D.	Period of punishment is infinite	IV.	Mixed strategy

Choose the **correct** answer from the options given below:

1. A-II, B-III, C-IV, D-I
2. A-I, B-IV, C-III, D-II
3. A-III, B-II, C-IV, D-I
4. A-IV, B-III, C-I, D-II

2. The null hypothesis that all slope coefficients are simultaneously equal to zero is tested in logit model by.

1. F-test
2. t-test
3. Chi-square test
4. Likelihood ratio statistics

3. Which of the followings is not true?

1. The effect of any tax can be decomposed into an income effect and substitution effect.
2. There is a substitution effect associated with a lump-sum tax, but no income effect.
3. The greater is the substitution effect, the greater is the deadweight loss.
4. There is also a deadweight loss associated with the reduction in prices received by producers as a result of imposition of tax.

4. Which of the following are correct about the foreign trade policy (FTP) 2023 of India?

A. India's FTP 2023 promotes cross border trade in digital economy.
B. FTP 2023 emphasized on creation of E-commerce export hubs (ECEH).
C. It prohibits export and import of arms and related material from/to Iraq.
D. It prohibits import of charcoal from Somalia.
E. It emphasizes strengthening trade with Democratic People's Republic of Korea in combat aircraft, missiles and arms related materials.

Choose the **most appropriate** answer from the options given below:

1. A, D & E Only
2. D & E Only
3. A, B & C Only
4. A, B, C & D Only

5. Which of the followings is true in case of a good i.e., "Crowded City side Walk"?

1. It is non-excludable and non-rivalry in nature.
2. It is excludable but non-rivalry in nature.
3. It is non-excludable but rivalry in nature.
4. It is excludable and rivalry in nature.

6. Which of the followings are not true pertaining to Wagner's Law of increasing state activities?

A. Wagner's Law is classified as positive theory of public expenditure.

B. Public sector in industrializing nations grow as a proportion of total economic activity with the increase in per capita income and output.

C. Proportionate increase in public sector is not constant but increasing with the increase in total economic activity.

D. The law accounts for the effect of war on public expenditure.

E. Public expenditure tends to grow in a stepwise manner.

Choose the **most appropriate** answer from the options given below:

1. A, B & D Only
2. B, C & E Only
3. B & C Only
4. D & E Only

7. Which of the following indicate that country "B" is capital abundant country?

A. $\left(\frac{\text{Total Capital}}{\text{Total Labour}}\right)B > \left(\frac{\text{Total Capital}}{\text{Total Labour}}\right)A$

B. $\left(\frac{\text{Total Capital}}{\text{Total Labour}}\right)B < \left(\frac{\text{Total Capital}}{\text{Total Labour}}\right)A$

C. $\left(\frac{\text{Price of Capital}}{\text{Price of Labour}}\right)B < \left(\frac{\text{Price of Capital}}{\text{Price of Labour}}\right)A$

D. $\left(\frac{\text{Price of Capital}}{\text{Price of Labour}}\right)B > \left(\frac{\text{Price of Capital}}{\text{Price of Labour}}\right)A$

E. $\left(\frac{\text{Total Labour}}{\text{Total Capital}}\right)B > \left(\frac{\text{Price of Capital}}{\text{Price of Labour}}\right)A$

Choose the **correct** answer from the options given below:

1. A & B Only
2. A & C Only
3. B & D Only
4. C & E Only

8. Match List-I with List-II:

List-I (Concepts)	List-II (Given by)
A. Paradox of thrift	I. K. Boulding
B. Water-Diamond paradox	II. A.C. Pigou
C. Wage employment paradox	III. J.M. Keynes
D. Macroeconomic paradox	IV. Adam Smith

Choose the **correct** answer from the options given below:

1. A-II, B-I, C-III, D-IV
2. A-I, B-II, C-III, D-IV
3. A-III, B-IV, C-II, D-I
4. A-III, B-IV, C-I, D-II

9. Which of the followings are true pertaining to the problems of asymmetric information?

A. Sellers can deal with the problem of asymmetric information by sending buyers signals about the quality of product.

B. If a seller of a product has better information about its quality than buyer, then bad products tend to drive good products out of the market.

C. According to the efficiency wage theory, a wage lower than the competitive wage increases worker productivity by discouraging workers from shirking on the job.

D. Adverse selection arises because of asymmetric information in insurance market.

E. Owners can avoid principal agent problem by designing contracts that give their agents incentive to perform better.

Choose the **correct** answer from the options given below:

1. A & B Only
2. A, B & C Only
3. B, C & D Only
4. A, B, D & E Only

10. Integrate $\int \frac{x+3}{x+5} dx$.

1. $\frac{x^2}{2} - 2.\ln|x+5| + c$
2. $\frac{x^2}{2} + 2.\ln|x+5| + c$
3. $x + 2.\ln|x + 5| + c$
4. $x - 2.\ln|x + 5| + c$

11. Arrange the following countries based on the market capitalization to nominal GDP ratio at the end of December 2024 in ascending order (as per the Economic Survey 2024-25).

A. U.K. B. India
C. China D. Brazil
E. Japan

Choose the **correct** answer from the options given below:

1. B, A, C, E, D 2. C, D, B, A, E
3. D, C, A, B, E 4. A, B, D, C, E

12. In which of the following year, the mandate/ preamble of RBI has been amended?

1. 2019 2. 2024
3. 2016 4. 2007

13. Which of the following statements best define property rights?

1. Property rights refer only to government ownership of land and capital.
2. Property rights are informal social rules that cannot be enforced by law.
3. Property rights are the legally enforced rights to determine how a resource is used, owned and transferred.
4. Property rights prevent individuals from profiting from private property.

14. Which of the following comprises the current account of the balance of payments?

A. Invisible exports and imports
B. Direct investment
C. Unilateral transfers
D. SDR allocations
E. Borrowings from foreign countries

Choose the **correct** answer from the options given below:

1. A & E Only
2. C & E Only
3. A & C Only
4. A & B Only

15. According to Rostow, any industry can play the role of leading sector in the take-off stage provided following conditions are met.

A. The market for the product is expanding rapidly.
B. The leading sector generates secondary expansion.
C. The sector has an adequate and continual supply of capital from ploughed-back profits.
D. Introduction of new techniques into the sector to increase productivity.
E. Changes in industrial structure should be structural ones.

Choose the **most appropriate** answer from the options given below:

1. B, C, D & E Only
2. A, D & E Only
3. A, C & D Only
4. A, B, C & D Only

16. Match List-I with List-II:

List-I	List-II
A. Inverted "U" hypothesis	I. Herman Daly
B. Sustainable development	II. Garrett Hardin
C. Ecological Economics	III. Simon Kuznets
D. Tragedy of the commons	IV. Gro Harlen Brundtland

Choose the **correct** answer from the options given below:

1. A-IV, B-II, C-III, D-I
2. A-III, B-I, C-IV, D-II
3. A-III, B-IV, C-I, D-II
4. A-III, B-IV, C-II, D-I

17. Lexicographic preference violates which of the following axioms of utility theory?

1. Transitivity Axiom
2. Convexity Axiom
3. Continuity Axiom
4. Independence Axiom

18. According to Lucas Critique.

1. It assumes monetary policy not to be neutral with respect to real variables.
2. Drifting coefficients can make macro econometric models more reliable.
3. Keynesian models correctly consider the impact of policies on future expectations.
4. The stability of coefficients of models are important for policy predictions.

19. Given U = $(x + 2)(y + 1)$ and $P_x = 4$ and $P_y = 6$ and budget (B) = 130. Find the optimum levels of purchase of x^* and y^*.

1. $x^* = 11$, $y^* = 16$
2. $x^* = 15$, $y^* = 28$
3. $x^* = 18$, $y^* = 8$
4. $x^* = 16$, $y^* = 11$

20. Bootstrapping technique is used to ....

1. Tests for specification bias
2. Obtain the sampling distribution of parameters of interest
3. Test for autocorrelation
4. Test for normality of error term

21. Which of the following statements correctly describe the concept of efficiency in environmental economics?

A. All allocation is pareto efficient if no one can be made better off without making someone else worse off.

B. Efficiency ensures a fair and equitable distribution of resources among all individuals.

C. Market allocations are efficient only in the absence of market failures such as externalities.

D. Efficiency is a normative concept concerned with what should be done based on societal value.

E. Environmental policies that internalize externalities can improve efficiency.

Choose the **most appropriate** answer from the options given below:

1. A, B & D Only
2. A, B & E Only
3. A, C & E Only
4. B, C & D Only

22. The management of a manufacturing firm wishes to determine the average time required to complete a certain manual operation. There should be 0.95 confidence that error in the estimate will not exceed 2 minutes. What sample size is estimated by a time and motion study expert as 16 minutes?

1. 96
2. 300
3. 255
4. 246

23. Arrange the following works of J.M. Keynes in chronological order (Starting from the oldest to latest).

A. A Treatise on Money

B. General Theory of Employment, Interest and Money

C. Indian Currency and Finance

D. A Monetary Theory of Production

E. A Tract on Monetary Reform

Choose the **correct** answer from the options given below:

1. E, C, A, D, B
2. C, E, A, D, B
3. C, E, A, B, D
4. A, C, E, B, D

24. Arrange the following rates in ascending order, as decided in 54th meeting of monetary policy committee of RBI.

A. Marginal Standing Facility Rate
B. Standing Deposit Facility Rate
C. CRR
D. Reverse Repo Rate
E. Repo Rate

Choose the **correct** answer from the options given below:

1. C, D, A, B, E
2. B, C, D, A, E
3. D, C, B, E, A
4. C, D, E, B, A

25. Which of the followings are the effects of increase in government spending in IS-LM framework in a closed economy?

A. Increase in income by multiplier times government expenditure.
B. Shift in IS curve to the right leading to disequilibrium in money market at given level of interest rate.
C. Quantity of money demand will be higher.
D. Interest rate will decrease.
E. Private investment will increase leading to increase in aggregate demand.

Choose the **correct** answer from the options given below:

1. B, C & D Only
2. C, D & E Only
3. A, B & C Only
4. B, D & E Only

26. Match List-I with List-II:

List-I (renewable energy sources)	List-II (% of total energy production as on Nov 2024 as per Economic Survey 2024-25)
A. Solar energy	I. 10.50%
B. Hydro energy	II. 20.60%
C. Nuclear energy	III. 10.30%
D. Wind energy	IV. 1.80%

Choose the **correct** answer from the options given below:

1. A-II, B-III, C-IV, D-I
2. A-III, B-I, C-IV, D-II
3. A-II, B-III, C-I, D-IV
4. A-II, B-I, C-III, D-IV

27. Which of the followings are true regarding the outcome of a consumer's optimization process.

A. The marginal utility per rupee spent on each good is the same.
B. The marginal rate of substitution between goods is equal to the ratio of the prices between the goods.
C. The consumer reaches the highest indifference curve in the indifference map.
D. The consumer indifference curve is tangent to his/her budget line.
E. From utility point of view, consumer is indifferent between any two points on his/her budget line.

Choose the **correct** answer from the options given below:

1. A, C & E Only
2. A, D & E Only
3. A, B & D Only
4. A, B, D & E Only

28. Which of the following conditions are required for the set of consumers to exhibit parallel, straight wealth expansion paths at any price vector P?

A. Preferences admit indirect utility function of the Gorman form.
B. Preferences are heterogeneous.
C. Wealth is equally distributed among all consumers.
D. All consumers have identical preferences that are homothetic.

E. All consumers have preferences that are quasilinear with respect to the same good.

Choose the **correct** answer from the options given below:

1. A, B & C Only
2. A, D & E Only
3. B, C & D Only
4. A, B & D Only

29. Arrange the following derivative markets in India in chronological order (starting from oldest to latest).

A. Commencement of trading in options on individual securities

B. Introduction of interest rate futures

C. Commencement of trading in Stock Futures

D. Introduction of Futures trading based on the Index

E. Commencement of trading in Index options

Choose the **correct** answer from the options given below:

1. D, C, E, A, B
2. D, E, A, C, B
3. D, A, E, B, C
4. D, C, E, B, A

30. Which of the followings are true in case of externality?

A. In case of externality, all costs and benefits associated with the goods are not internalized by households and firms involved in buying and productions.

B. Presence of externality results either under production or over production of the good.

C. Market based decision making yields an efficient outcome in the presence of externality.

D. In case of negative externality, the marginal social cost is higher than marginal cost.

E. Well defined property right can solve the problem of externality.

Choose the **most appropriate** answer from the options given below:

1. A, B & D Only
2. B, D & E Only
3. A, B, D & E Only
4. B, C, D & E Only

31. Match List-I with List-II:

List-I	List-II
A. β_2 for Chi-square distribution	I. $(n - 2)$
B. Skewness for Chi-square distribution	II. $48n + 12n^2$
C. Mode for Chi-square distribution	III. $(12/n) + 3$
D. μ_3 for Chi-square distribution	IV. $\sqrt{2/n}$

Choose the **correct** answer from the options given below:

1. A-IV, B-III, C-II, D-I
2. A-III, B-II, C-IV, D-I
3. A-II, B-I, C-IV, D-III
4. A-III, B-IV, C-I, D-II

32. If the marginal propensity to consume is 0.8 and initial increase in tax revenues by the government is ₹ 100, then the impact on national income would be:

1. National Income will increase by ₹ 100
2. National Income will increase by ₹ 500
3. National Income will decrease by ₹ 400
4. National Income will decrease by ₹ 100

33. The Stolper-Samuelson theorem postulates that:

1. An increase in the relative price of a commodity raises the earnings of the factor used intensively in the production of the commodity.
2. An increase in the relative price of a commodity decreases the earnings of the factor used intensively in the production of the commodity.
3. An increase in the relative price of a commodity raises the earnings of the factor used scarcely in the production of the commodity.
4. A decrease in the relative price of a commodity raises the earnings of the factor used intensively in the production of the commodity.

34. Which of the followings are not an assumptions of policy ineffectiveness propositions?

A. Rational expectation
B. Policy changes are not anticipated
C. Economic agents have full information
D. Nominal variables influence economic decision
E. Output and employment are at their natural level

Choose the **most appropriate** answer from the options given below:

1. B & D Only
2. A, C & D Only
3. A, B, D & E Only
4. C, D & E Only

35. Which of the following is the operating target of monetary policy conducted by RBI?

1. Repo rate
2. Reverse Repo rate
3. Weighted Average Call Money rate
4. Marginal Standing Facility rate

36. Match List-I with List-II:

List-I	List-II
A. Specific factors model	I. Prebisch-Singer hypothesis
B. Immiserizing growth	II. Thomas Mun
C. Mercantilism theory of international trade	III. Jagdish Bhagwati
D. Secular deterioration of terms of trade	IV. Paul Samuelson and Ronald Jones

Choose the **correct** answer from the options given below:

1. A-III, B-IV,C-II, D-I
2. A-IV, B-III,C-II, D-I
3. A-IV, B-II, C-III, D-I
4. A-II, B-IV, C-I, D-III

37. Arrange the following Chairman of Finance Commission in order of their appointment starting from the oldest.

A. A.M. Khusro
B. C. Rangarajan
C. N.K.P. Salve
D. K. Bramhananda Reddy
E. K.C. Pant

Choose the **correct** answer from the options given below:

1. A, C, E, D, B 2. C, E, A, D, B
3. B, D, E, C, A 4. D, C, E, A, B

38. Arrange the following sectors in descending order as per their share in total FDI in India in H1 FY 2025 as per the Economic Survey 2024-25.

A. Automobile Industry
B. Hospital and Diagnostic Centers
C. Cement and Gypsum Products
D. Computer Software and Hardware
E. Non-conventional Energy

Choose the **correct** answer from the options given below:

1. D, E, C, A, B 2. D, C, E, B, A
3. E, B, A, D, C 4. E, D, C, B, A

39. Match List-I with List-II:

List-I (Concepts)	List-II (their expression) (where, g_m = manufacturing output growth, g_{GDP} = GDP growth, P_{nm} = productivity in outside manufacturing, P_m = Productivity in manufacturing)
A. Kaldor's first law of growth	I. $P_m = f(g_m)\ f' > 0$
B. Kaldor's second law of growth	II. $y' = -\in (u-u^*)$
C. Kaldor's third law of growth	III. $g_{GDP} = f(g_m)\ f' > 0$
D. Okun's law	IV. $P_{nm} = f(g_m)\ f' > 0$

Choose the **correct** answer from the options given below:

1. A-IV, B-III, C-I, D-II
2. A-III, B-IV, C-I, D-II
3. A-III, B-I, C-IV, D-II
4. A-IV, B-III, C-II, D-I

40. The idea of constructing poverty-weighted indices of growth is:

1. To give at least equal weight to all income groups in society.
2. To achieve high growth rate.
3. To facilitate foreign trade on equal basis.
4. To assign more value or weight on income group of richest population and no weight on lower-income group.

41. Which of the following are correct about the revised criteria of MSMEs effective from 01 April 2025 as per union budget 2025-26?

A. An enterprise is classified as micro enterprise if investment in plant and machinery does not exceed ₹ 2.5 crore.

B. A medium enterprise is one whose turnover does not exceed ₹ 50 crore.

C. A small enterprise has investment limit up to ₹ 10 crore.

D. A micro enterprise is one whose turnover is up to ₹ 10 crore.

E. A small enterprise has turnover limit up to ₹ 100 crore.

Choose the **most appropriate** answer from the options given below:

1. B, C & D Only
2. A, D & E Only
3. A, B & E Only
4. C, D & E Only

42. Arrange the following tax reform committees on the basis of their year of constitution starting from the oldest.

A. Raja Chelliah tax reform committee

B. T.R. Rastogi Committee on Service tax reforms

C. Vijay Kelkar committee on tax reforms

D. Parthasarathi Shome committee on direct tax

E. K.L. Rekhi committee on indirect tax

Choose the **correct** answer from the options given below:

1. A, E, C, B, D
2. E, A, C, B, D
3. A, E, D, C, B
4. D, E, A, C, B

43. Match List-I with List-II:

List-I	List-II
A. Income elasticity greater than one	I. Substitute goods
B. Positive cross price elasticity	II. Inferior goods
C. Downward sloping price consumption curve (PCC)	III. Luxurious goods
D. Negative income effect	IV. Relative elastic demand

Choose the **correct** answer from the options given below:

1. A-IV, B-II, C-I, D-III
2. A-III, B-II, C-I, D-IV
3. A-IV, B-II, C-III, D-I
4. A-III, B-I, C-IV, D-II

44. If the income effect is in the opposite direction as the substitution effect, but the substitution effect dominates, then the good is ....

1. Normal
2. Inferior but not giffen
3. Giffen
4. There is not enough information to answer

45. Arrange the expenditure allocation to following items, as % of total union government expenditure as per the union budget 2025-26 in ascending order.

A. Finance Commission and Other Transfers
B. Interest Payment
C. Pensions
D. Major Subsidies
E. Central Sector Schemes (excluding capital outlay on defense and subsidies)

Choose the **correct** answer from the options given below:

1. A, D, E, C, B
2. C, D, A, E, B
3. E, C, D, A, B
4. C, D, E, B, A

46. If $U = 6x^2 + y^2$, and $4x - y = 1$. What is the value of U?

1. $\frac{4}{15}$
2. $\frac{3}{11}$
3. $\frac{3}{16}$
4. $\frac{4}{21}$

47. Match List-I with List-II:

List-I (Items of receipts)	List-II (Share to total receipt in % as per union budget 2025-26)
A. Income tax	I. 4%
B. Custom	II. 5%
C. Corporation tax	III. 22%
D. Union excise	IV. 17%

Choose the **correct** answer from the options given below:

1. A-IV, B-II,C-III, D-I
2. A-III, B-I, C-II, D-IV
3. A-III, B-I, C-IV, D-II
4. A-IV, B-II,C-I, D-III

48. In the context of neoclassical growth model, the effects of an increase in population growth rate is/are.

A. Reduction in steady-state level of capital per head
B. Increase in per capita output
C. Increase in steady state rate of growth of aggregate output
D. Decrease in capital-output ratio
E. An inward shift in production possibility curve.

Choose the **most appropriate** answer from the options given below:

1. A, B & C Only
2. B, C, D & E Only
3. A & C Only
4. C, D & E Only

49. Match List-I with List-II:

List-I	List-II
A. Income induced adjustment process of balance of payments	I. Paul Samuelson
B. Absorption approach of BoPs	II. Keynes, J.M.
C. Impossible trinity	III. Sidney S. Alexander
D. Factor price equalization theorem	IV. Mundell-Fleming

Choose the **correct** answer from the options given below:

1. A-I, B-II, C-III, D-IV
2. A-II, B-III, C-IV, D-I
3. A-II, B-III, C-I, D-IV
4. A-II, B-I, C-III, D-IV

50. The indirect least square is applied to estimate the coefficient of the:

1. Structural equation
2. Over identified equation
3. Reduced form equation
4. Under identified equation

51. Which of the followings are true about New Classical approach.

A. The main protagonist was R.E. Lucas Jr.
B. It is based on adaptive expectation.
C. It was developed during 1950s.
D. Complete wage and price flexibility.
E. Difference between actual and expected price is a random error.

Choose the **most appropriate** answer from the options given below:

1. A, B & E Only
2. A, D & E Only
3. B, C, D & E Only
4. A, B & D Only

52. If the value of Keynesian investment multiplier is 4, which one of the following will be the corresponding saving function?

1. $S = -4 + 0.4\ Y_D$
2. $S = -10 + 0.75\ Y_D$
3. $S = -12 + 0.25\ Y_D$
4. $S = -6 + 0.35\ Y_D$

53. Which of the following correctly state the formula to compute the rate of effective protection?

Where, g = the rate of effective protection to producers of final commodities, t = the nominal tariff rate on consumers of the final commodity, t_i = the nominal tariff rate on the imported input and a_i = the ratio of the cost of the imported input to the price of the final commodity in the absence of tariffs.

1. $g = \dfrac{t - a_i t_i}{1 - a_i}$
2. $g = \dfrac{t + a_i t_i}{1 - a_i}$
3. $g = \dfrac{t - a_i t_i}{1 + a_i}$
4. $g = \dfrac{t + a_i t_i}{1 + a_i}$

54. If x is a poisson variate with mean λ, then $P(x + 1)$ is:

1. $\dfrac{\lambda}{x+1} P(x)$
2. $\dfrac{\lambda}{x}$
3. $\dfrac{x+1}{\lambda} P(x)$
4. $\dfrac{x}{\lambda} P(x)$

55. Match List-I with List-II:

List-I	List-II
A. The mean of a Hypergeometric distribution	I. $\dfrac{q}{p^2}$
B. The moment generating function of negative binomial distribution	II. $(Q - Pe^t)^{-r}$
C. The coefficient of Kurtosis of a binomial distribution	III. $\dfrac{nm}{N}$
D. The variance of geometric distribution	IV. $\dfrac{1-6pq}{npq}$

Choose the **correct** answer from the options given below:

1. A-II, B-III, C-I, D-IV
2. A-III, B-II, C-IV, D-I
3. A-I, B-III, C-IV, D-II
4. A-II, B-I, C-III, D-IV

56. Assume that the rate of investment is described by the function $I(t) = 12t^{1/3}$ and capital stock $k(0) = 25$. Find the time path of capital stock k.

1. $16t^{4/3} + 25$
2. $9t^{4/3} + 25$
3. $-9t^{4/3} + 25$
4. $-16t^{4/3} + 25$

57. Which of the following is not true according to classical's views on public debt?

1. Public debt financing requires funds for interest payment and amortization,hence a double burden on tax payers.
2. Public debt financing supports compensatory budget policy as a tool for stimulating aggregate demand.
3. Public debt creates barren production and consumption and burden is transferred to future generation.
4. Public debt destroys capital which otherwise could be used productively.

58. A candidate is selected for interview for three posts. For the first post, there are 3 candidates, for the second 4 candidates and for the third 2 candidates. What is the probability that the candidate is selected for at least one post?

1. $\frac{1}{4}$
2. $\frac{1}{2}$
3. $\frac{3}{4}$
4. $\frac{1}{9}$

59. Which of the following causes a positive output gap, where, output gap = Actual output- Potential output?

1. Population growth
2. Technological progress
3. Overemployment of factors of production
4. Under utilization of resources

60. If Q = f(K, L) is a homogeneous production function of degree one, which of the following satisfies Euler's theorem?

1. $\left(\frac{\partial Q}{\partial K}\right)+\left(\frac{\partial Q}{\partial L}\right)=Q$
2. $\left(\frac{\partial Q}{\partial K}\right)K+\left(\frac{\partial Q}{\partial L}\right)L=Q$
3. $\left(\frac{\partial Q}{\partial K}\right)K+\left(\frac{\partial Q}{\partial L}\right)L>1$
4. $\left(\frac{\partial Q}{\partial K}\right)+\left(\frac{\partial Q}{\partial L}\right)=1$

61. According to classical economics, an increase in government deficit spending leads to.

A. a shift in the demand for loanable fund to the right

B. decline in interest rate

C. increase in investment

D. increase in saving equal to decline in consumption

E. decrease in investment and consumption that balances the increase in government spending.

Choose the **correct** answer from the options given below:

1. A, B & D Only
2. A, D & E Only
3. A, B, C & D Only
4. C, D & E Only

62.

		Player 2	
		L	R
Player 1	T	1, 5	0, 3
	M	2, 6	1, 4
	B	3, 7	2, 2

Which of the following statements are true about the above payoff matrix?

A. Player-1 has two strictly dominated strategies.

B. None of the strategies of player-2 are weakly dominated.

C. Strategy T weakly dominates strategy B.

D. Strategy M of Player-1 will never be used in Nash-equilibrium.

E. Strategy M strictly dominates strategy T.

Choose the **correct** answer from the options given below:

1. A, B, C & E Only
2. A, D & E Only
3. B, C & D Only
4. C, D & E Only

63. Arrange the following items on the basis of the expenditure allocation made in the union budget 2025-26 in descending order.

A. Agriculture and Allied activities
B. Education
C. Defense
D. Commerce and Industry
E. Rural Development

Choose the **correct** answer from the options given below:

1. E, C, A, D, B
2. C, E, A, B, D
3. C, A, E, D, B
4. A, E, C, B, D

64. A company has examined its costs and revenue structure and has determined that C-total cost, R-the total revenue and X-the number of units produced are related as:

$C = 100 + 0.015 X^2$ and $R = 3X$

Find the product level X that will maximize profit for this company.

1. 120
2. 80
3. 150
4. 100

65. If $\overline{x} = 32, \overline{y} = 38,$ the regression coefficients $b_{xy} = -0.2337, b_{yx} = -0.6643$. Find the equation of the line of regression of y on x.

1. $y = -0.2337x + 40.8806$
2. $y = -0.2337x - 40.8806$
3. $y = -0.6643x - 59.2576$
4. $y = -0.6643x + 59.2576$

66. In the context of IS-LM model, a higher marginal propensity to spend results in:

1. A flatter aggregate demand curve and consequently a steeper IS curve
2. A steeper aggregate demand curve and consequently a flatter IS curve
3. Increase in aggregate demand and a rightward shift of the IS curve
4. Increase in demand for real balances

67. In the product cycle model of International trade, in which stage the imitating country starts underselling the innovating country in third markets?

1. Stage-II
2. Stage-Ill
3. Stage-IV
4. Stage-V

68. Match List-I with List-II:

List-I (Criteria of 15th finance commission)	List-II (Weights as per the recommendation of 15th finance commission for horizontal devolution)
A. Income distance	I. 15%
B. Population	II. 12.5%
C. Demographic performance	III. 45%
D. Forest and Ecology	IV. 10%

Choose the **correct** answer from the options given below:

1. A-III, B-IV,C-I, D-II
2. A-II, B-I, C-III, D-IV
3. A-III, B-I, C-II, D-IV
4. A-I, B-IV, C-II, D-III

69. In the context of classical economics, an increase in money supply causes.

1. A shift in aggregate demand curve to the left
2. A shift in aggregate demand curve to the right
3. A shift in aggregate supply curve to the right
4. No change in aggregate demand and aggregate supply, only price increases

70. If both input and output markets are competitive and firms are profit maximizing, then in equilibrium each factor of production earns:

1. An amount equal to the price of output times total output.
2. The amount allocated by political process
3. An equal share of output.
4. The value of its marginal product.

71. Arrange the following environmental conventions/summits in sequence starting from the oldest.

A. Kyoto Protocol
B. Minamata Convention
C. Stockholm Convention
D. UN-REDD
E. Rio Summit

Choose the **correct** answer from the options given below:

1. E, A, C, D, B
2. E, C, A, B, D
3. C, E, A, D, B
4. A, B, C, D, E

72. Arrange the following publications in chronological order starting from the oldest to the latest.

A. "Theory of Economic Growth" by Arthur Lewis
B. "A Contribution to the Theory of Economic Growth" by Robert Solow
C. "The Stages of Economic Growth: A Non-Communist Manifesto" by Walt Rostow
D. "Asian Drama: An Inquiry into the Poverty of Nations" by Gunnar Myrdal
E. "Strategy of Economic Development" by Albert Hirschman

Choose the **correct** answer from the options given below:

1. A, E, B, C, D
2. E, B, C, D, A
3. C, D, B, E, A
4. A, B, E, C, D

73. Match List-I with List-II:

List-I (Monetary policy regime)	List-II (Periods)
A. Fiscal dominance	I. 2016 onwards
B. Multiple indicator approach	II. 1951-1985
C. Monetary targeting with feedbacks	III. 1998-2016
D. Flexible inflation targeting	IV. 1985-1998

Choose the **correct** answer from the options given below:

1. A-III, B-IV, C-II, D-I
2. A-II, B-III, C-IV, D-I
3. A-II, B-I, C-IV, D-III
4. A-IV, B-III, C-I, D-II

74. Which of the following is likely to lead to a rise in the output cost of disinflation?

1. Inflation expectations become more accurate.
2. Sluggish response of wages and prices to monetary contraction.
3. Gradual policy response.
4. Rational expectations.

75. Arrange the following countries in descending order based on their current account balance as a per cent of GDP in the period Q2 FY 25 as per the Economic Survey 2024-25.

A. India
B. Russia
C. China
D. U.K.
E. South Africa

Choose the **correct** answer from the options given below:

1. D, A, B, C, E
2. B, C, A, D, E
3. C, B, A, E, D
4. A, C, E, B, D

76. Arrange the following crisis in chronological order (starting from oldest).

A. OPEC Oil Crisis
B. International Debt Crisis
C. East Asian Financial Crisis
D. Argentinian Economic Crisis
E. Eurozone Crisis

Choose the **correct** answer from the options given below:

1. A, B, C, D, E
2. A, B, C, E, D
3. A, B, E, C, D
4. A, E, B, C, D

77. Which of the followings are correct in case of Normal distribution?

A. μ_3 for Normal distribution is 0.
B. β_2 for Normal distribution is 0.
C. Mean deviation (about mean) for Normal distribution is $\frac{4}{5}\sigma$.
D. μ_4 for Normal distribution is $2\sigma^4$.
E. Characteristic function for Normal distribution is $e^{i\mu t - \frac{t^2\sigma^2}{2}}$.

Choose the **correct** answer from the options given below:

1. A, C & E Only
2. A, B, C & E Only
3. B, C & D Only
4. A, C & D Only

78. Arrange the following union government deficits as percentage of GDP for the year 2023-24 in ascending order as per union budget 2025-26.

A. Fiscal deficit
B. Effective Revenue deficit
C. Primary deficit
D. Current Account deficit
E. Revenue deficit

Choose the **correct** answer from the options given below:

1. D, B, A, C, E
2. D, A, B, C, E
3. D, B, C, E, A
4. D, C, B, E, A

79. Which of the following game does not have any Nash Equilibrium?

1. BoS Game
2. Stag Hunt Game
3. Matching Pennies Game
4. Prisoner's Dilemma

80. Match List-I with List-II:

List-I	List-II
A. Theory of population growth and resource limits	I. Alfred Sauvy
B. Demographic transition theory	II. John Graunt
C. Father of demography	III. Warren Thompson
D. Coined the term "third World"	IV. Thomas Malthus

Choose the **correct** answer from the options given below:

1. A-III, B-IV, C-I, D-II
2. A-III, B-IV, C-II, D-I
3. A-III, B-II, C-IV, D-I
4. A-IV, B-III, C-I, D-II

81. Arrange the following rounds in chronological order (starting from oldest).

A. Millennium Round of Trade negotiations
B. Doha Round
C. Uruguay Round
D. Kennedy Round
E. Tokyo Round

Choose the **correct** answer from the options given below:

1. D, E, C, B, A
2. D, E, B, C, A
3. D, B, E, C, A
4. D, E, C, A, B

82. By using the uniqueness property of moment generating function (M.G.F.), which of the followings are correct distribution if M.G.F. is as follows?

A. $M(t) = \left(\frac{1}{2}+\frac{1}{2}e^t\right)^6$ is a poisson distribution

B. $M(t) = \frac{(1+e^t)^5}{32}$ is a binomial distribution

C. $M(t) = e^{3(e^t-1)}$ is poisson distribution

D. $M(t) = e^{(e^t-1)/4}$ is poisson distribution

E. $M(t) = 4(3e^{-t} - 1)^{-2}$ is binomial distribution

Choose the **correct** answer from the options given below:

1. A, B, C & D Only
2. B, C & D Only
3. B, C, D & E Only
4. A, B, C, D & E

83. The data about the sales and advertisement expenditure of a firm is given below:

	Sales (In crore of ₹)	**Advertisement expenditure (In crore of ₹)**
Mean	40	6
Standard deviation	10	1.5
Coefficient of correlation = r = 0.9		

Estimate the likely sales for the proposed advertisement of ₹ 10 crore of rupees.

1. ₹ 60 crore
2. ₹ 64 crore
3. ₹ 70 crore
4. ₹ 74 crore

84. According to neoclassical growth theory, an increase in saving rate.

1. Raises the growth rate of output in the short run.
2. Increases long run growth rate of output.
3. Decreases the steady-state capital-labor ratio.
4. Decreases the long-run level of capital and output per head.

85. If the demand law is: $P = \sqrt{9-x}$ and the demand is fixed at $x_0 = 5$. Find the consumer's surplus.

1. $\frac{8}{3}$
2. $\frac{11}{15}$
3. $\frac{8}{15}$
4. $\frac{7}{3}$

86. Which of the following is not correct about Harrod-Domar model of economic growth?

1. The natural rate of growth is made up of growth of labor force and labor productivity.
2. If actual growth (g) is greater than warranted rate of growth (g_w), g can continue to diverge from g_w only until it hits natural growth rate (g_n).
3. g can be greater than g_n in the long-run.
4. Full employment of labor and capital require $g = g_w = g_n$

87. Evaluate $\int_1^2 e^{-2x}\,dx$

1. $(e^{-2} - e^{-4})$
2. $-\frac{1}{2}(e^{-2} - e^{-4})$
3. $\frac{1}{2}(e^{-2} - e^{-4})$
4. $\frac{1}{2}(e^{-2} + e^{-4})$

88. According to Coase theorem, which of the following are possible outcomes of assigning property rights?

A. The polluter pays the victim to continue polluting.

B. The victim pays the polluter to reduce pollution.

C. The government must set pollution taxes to ensure efficiency.

D. Market outcomes can achieve efficiency even if externalities exist.

E. The polluter and victim always have equal bargaining power.

Choose the **most appropriate** answer from the options given below:

1. A, B & C Only
2. A, B & D Only
3. B, C & D Only
4. C, D & E Only

89. According to Granger and Newbold, a good rule of thumb to suspect that the estimated regression is spurious is given by:

1. High R^2 with low t-value ($R^2 > t$)
2. High t values with low Durbin-Watson d value ($t > d$)
3. High R^2 and low Durbin-Watson d value ($R^2 > d$)
4. High R^2 and low F value ($R^2 > F$)

90. Match List-I with List-II:

List-I	**List-II**
A. $\int_0^\infty \frac{1}{1+x^2}dx$	I. does not exist
B. $\int_1^\infty \frac{1}{\sqrt{x}}dx$	II. 1/3
C. $\int_{-\infty}^{-1} \frac{1}{x^4}dx$	III. $\pi/2$
D. $\int_{-\infty}^{+\infty} \frac{1}{1+x^2}dx$	IV. π

Choose the **correct** answer from the options given below:

1. A-I, B-II, C-IV, D-III
2. A-IV, B-I, C-II, D-III
3. A-III, B-I, C-II, D-IV
4. A-II, B-III, C-IV, D-I

Direction (Qs. No. 91 to 95): *Based on the information given below, answer the questions:*

Two fair dice are thrown independently. Three events A, B, and C are defined as follows;

A : odd face with first dice

B : odd face with second dice

C : sum of points on two dice is odd

91. Find the $P(A \cap B \cap C)$.

1. 0 2. 1/2
3. 1/4 4. 1/6

92. Find the $P(B \cap C)$.

1. 1/2 2. 0
3. 1/4 4. 1/36

93. Find the $P(A \cap C)$.

1. 0 2. 1/2
3. 1/6 4. 1/4

94. Find the $P(A \cap B)$.

1. 0 2. 3/4
3. 7/12 4. 1/4

95. Find the P(C).

1. 1/4 2. 1/2
3. 3/4 4. 5/6

Direction (Qs. No. 96 to 100): *Read the following paragraph and answer the questions:*

The RBI's current monetary policy reflects a nuanced response to evolving macroeconomic dynamics. While the repo rate remains unchanged at 6.5%, the policy undertone reveals a calibrated withdrawal of accommodation, signaling a shift from pandemic era stimulus. The RBI's liquidity management has transitioned from passive surplus absorption to active fine tuning using variable rate reverse repo (VRRR) operations, amid concerns of global spillovers and domestic inflationary pressures. The policy indicates a forward looking stance, focusing on anchoring inflation expectations rather than reacting to transient price shocks. The monetary transmission remains uneven, with sectoral divergences in credit uptake and lending rates. Furthermore the policy indirectly emphasizes macro prudential regulation and financial stability, acknowledging risks from global interest rate differentials, capital flows and currency volatility. This reflects an integrated policy framework balancing inflation targeting with broader financial resilience in a globally uncertain environment.

96. Which of the following reflects the RBI's strategy in managing transient inflation shocks?
1. Immediate rate hike
2. Maintaining status quo with calibrated liquidity tools
3. Aggressive tightening
4. Reducing CRR

97. The RBI's consideration of global interest rate differentials primarily relates to.
1. Domestic food inflation
2. Foreign portfolio flows and exchange rate management
3. Retail credit growth
4. Agricultural policy

98. VRRR operations indicate.
1. Long term capital infusion
2. Structural adjustment of fiscal deficit
3. Active short term liquidity absorption
4. Decrease in SLR

99. Which concept is implicit in RBI's focus on anchoring inflation without immediate rate action?
1. Passive targeting
2. Expectation management
3. Credit rationing
4. Monetary expansion

100. The term withdrawal accommodation in monetary policy implies.
1. Increase in CRR
2. Active bond purchase
3. Gradual normalization of policy stance
4. Expansionary fiscal stimulus

ANSWERS

1	2	3	4	5	6	7	8	9	10
4	4	2	4	3	4	2	3	4	4
11	**12**	**13**	**14**	**15**	**16**	**17**	**18**	**19**	**20**
3	3	3	3	4	3	3	4	4	2
21	**22**	**23**	**24**	**25**	**26**	**27**	**28**	**29**	**30**
3	4	2	3	3	1	3	2	2	3
31	**32**	**33**	**34**	**35**	**36**	**37**	**38**	**39**	**40**
*	3	1	1	3	2	4	1	3	1
41	**42**	**43**	**44**	**45**	**46**	**47**	**48**	**49**	**50**
2	1	4	2	2	2	3	3	2	1
51	**52**	**53**	**54**	**55**	**56**	**57**	**58**	**59**	**60**
2	3	1	1	2	2	2	3	3	2
61	**62**	**63**	**64**	**65**	**66**	**67**	**68**	**69**	**70**
2	2	2	4	4	2	3	3	2	4
71	**72**	**73**	**74**	**75**	**76**	**77**	**78**	**79**	**80**
1	4	2	2	3	1	1	3	3	*
81	**82**	**83**	**84**	**85**	**86**	**87**	**88**	**89**	**90**
4	2	2	1	1	3	3	2	3	3
91	**92**	**93**	**94**	**95**	**96**	**97**	**98**	**99**	**100**
1	3	4	4	2	2	2	3	2	3

Explanatory Answers

1. Playing each strategy with probability refers to mixed strategy—players randomize across pure strategies so opponents cannot exploit predictable moves. The best response function gives the maximum payoff for a player given the other's strategy; finding best responses is central to equilibrium analysis. Long-run or steady-state behaviour in repeated or dynamic games is captured by a Nash equilibrium, which is the strategy profile where no player gains by deviating unilaterally. Finally, a grim trigger strategy is a repeated-game punishment strategy where, after one defection, the punishment (defection forever) is infinite in duration, ensuring cooperation is sustained through credible threat.

   Hence, correct match is A-IV, B-III, C-I, D-II

2. In a logit model, testing whether all slope coefficients are zero compares the restricted model (only intercept) with the unrestricted model (all predictors). The likelihood ratio (LR) statistic uses -2 times the log-likelihood difference between these models. Under large samples, LR follows a chi-square distribution with degrees of freedom equal to the number of restrictions. While Wald or Lagrange Multiplier tests exist, the LR statistic is the standard test for joint significance in logit/probit models.

3. Statement 2 is not true: a lump-sum tax does not create a substitution effect—only an income effect—because relative prices are unchanged. The other points are accurate:
   - Any tax's burden can be decomposed into income and substitution effects.
   - Greater substitution effect increases deadweight loss since choices distort more.
   - Taxes reduce prices received by producers, decreasing quantities traded and creating deadweight loss. Thus, only statement 2 is incorrect.

4. India's Foreign Trade Policy 2023 encourages cross-border digital trade and creation of E-commerce Export Hubs (ECEH) to expand e-commerce exports. It prohibits arms and related material exports/imports with Iraq (except to its government under approvals) in line with UN sanctions and bans import of charcoal from Somalia for the same reason. These align with global non-proliferation and sanction commitments. However, strengthening trade in combat aircraft or missiles with DPRK is expressly forbidden under UN resolutions that India observes, so E is not correct.

   Therefore, A, B, C, and D are the valid points.

5. A crowded city sidewalk cannot feasibly exclude people from entering—making it non-excludable. Yet, when many people use it, each person's presence reduces space and comfort for others, creating rivalry in consumption (congestion). Such goods are termed common-resource or congestible goods: non-excludable until regulation or pricing is imposed, but rivalrous when usage becomes heavy.

6. Wagner's Law is an empirically observed positive regularity about how government (public) expenditure behaves as economies develop. It posits that, with industrialization and rising per-capita income/output, the scope and relative size of the public sector rise more than proportionately (income elasticity of demand for public services > 1). Hence:
   - **A (True):** It's a positive (descriptive) law, not a normative prescription.
   - **B (True):** With development, the public sector share in total economic activity tends to increase.
   - **C (True):** The increase is more than proportionate (not a constant proportion); as the economy expands, demand for administration, social/merit goods, regulation, and cultural–welfare functions grows faster than income.
   - **D (Not true for Wagner):** War-induced spending spikes and the stepwise "displacement effect" are associated with Peacock–Wiseman, not Wagner.

- E (Not true for Wagner): The stepwise growth pattern (jumps during crises, then a higher normal) is again Peacock–Wiseman, not Wagner.

Therefore, only D and E are not true of Wagner's Law.

7. 2: A country is capital-abundant if (i) by quantity it has a higher capital–labour ratio, and/or (ii) by price it has a lower relative price of capital (r/w).
   - **A (True):** $(K/L)_B > (K/L)_A \Rightarrow$ B has more capital per worker → capital-abundant.
   - **B (False):** $(K/L)_B < (K/L)_A$ implies B is not capital-abundant.
   - **C (True):** $(P_K/P_L)_B < (P_K/P_L)_A \Rightarrow$ capital is relatively cheaper in B → capital-abundant (Heckscher–Ohlin price criterion).
   - **D (False):** $(P_K/P_L)_B > (P_K/P_L)_A$ suggests capital is dearer in B → not capital-abundant.
   - **E (Invalid/meaningless):** Compares a quantity ratio (L/K) with a price ratio (P_K/P_L); not a criterion for factor abundance.

   Thus, A & C correctly indicate capital abundance.

8. Matching options:
   - **Paradox of thrift → J. M. Keynes (III):** Higher intended saving can reduce aggregate demand, output, and ultimately total saving, if not offset.
   - **Water–Diamond paradox → Adam Smith (IV):** Puzzles value in exchange vs. value in use (water is essential but cheap; diamonds are less useful but dear).
   - **Wage employment paradox → A.C. Pigou (II):** Associated with classical debates on wages, employment, and the role of real-balance/Pigou effects in resolving unemployment; "paradox" label is linked to Pigouvian treatments where wage adjustments don't straightforwardly restore full employment as expected.
   - **Macroeconomic paradox → K. Boulding (I):** Boulding discussed "macroeconomic paradoxes" (e.g., saving, costs) where micro-rational actions can have counter-intuitive macro outcomes.

   Hence, correct matching is A-III, B-IV, C-II, D-I.

9. Checking options:
   - **A (True):** Signalling (warranties, certifications, costly advertising) helps sellers credibly convey quality under asymmetric information.
   - **B (True):** Akerlof's lemons: when buyers can't tell quality, bad drives out good—high-quality exits because it can't command a fair price.
   - **C (False):** Efficiency wages raise productivity by paying above (not below) the competitive wage to reduce shirking/turnover and attract better workers.
   - **D (True):** Adverse selection (e.g., in insurance) arises because one side knows more (high-risk buyers select in).
   - **E (True):** Incentive-compatible contracts (performance pay, monitoring, equity stakes) mitigate principal–agent problems.

   Hence, the true set is A, B, D, E.

10. To integrate $\int \frac{x+3}{x+5} dx$:

    1. Rewrite the numerator:
    $$x + 3 = (x + 5) - 2$$
    So,
    $$\frac{x+3}{x+5} = \frac{(x+5)-2}{x+5}$$
    $$= 1 - \frac{2}{x+5}$$
    2. Separate the integral:
    $$\int \frac{x+3}{x+5} dx = \int \left(1 - \frac{2}{x+5}\right) dx$$
    $$= \int 1\, dx - 2\int \frac{1}{x+5} dx$$
    3. Integrate each term:
    $$\int 1\, dx = x,\ \int \frac{1}{x+5} dx = \ln|x+5|$$
    4. Combine results and add the constant of integration:
    $$x - 2\ln|x + 5| + c$$

    Thus, the correct choice among the options is:
    $$x - 2\ln|x + 5| + c$$

11. According to Economic Survey 2024–25, the ratio of market capitalisation to nominal GDP at the end of December 2024 shows significant variation across major economies. The reported values are approximately: Brazil – 37%, China – 65%, United Kingdom – 84%, India – 136%, and Japan – 157%. This ratio reflects the size of a country's stock market compared to the overall economy. Lower ratios indicate smaller equity markets relative to GDP, while higher ratios indicate deep and broad equity markets. When these countries are arranged in ascending order, the smallest ratio is Brazil (D), followed by China (C), then United Kingdom (A), then India (B), and finally Japan (E) with the highest ratio.

Hence the correct ascending order is D, C, A, B, E, matching option 3.

12. The Reserve Bank of India Act, 1934 underwent a significant amendment in 2016. This change redefined the mandate and preamble of the RBI, introducing flexible inflation targeting and establishing the Monetary Policy Committee (MPC). The amended preamble explicitly stated that the primary objective of monetary policy is to maintain price stability while keeping in mind the objective of growth, aligning RBI's goals with modern macroeconomic priorities. Earlier years like 2007, 2019, or 2024 did not contain this specific change to the preamble or mandate.

Thus, 2016 is the correct choice.

13. Property rights in economics and law are not limited to government ownership or informal rules—they are legally enforceable claims over resources. These rights define who can use a resource, exclude others, derive income, and transfer ownership. Properly defined property rights promote efficient allocation of resources, investment incentives, and reduce conflicts. Options suggesting that property rights are only government ownership (1), are merely informal social rules (2), or prevent profit from private property (4) are incorrect.

Therefore, the most accurate definition is option 3.

14. The current account of the balance of payments (BoP) records flows of goods, services, income, and unilateral transfers. Specifically:

A. Invisible exports and imports—these are services such as IT services, tourism, insurance, and income flows; they are part of the current account.

C. Unilateral transfers—these include remittances, gifts, and grants where there is no quid pro quo, and they are also part of the current account.

Items like Direct investment (B), SDR allocations (D), and Borrowings from foreign countries (E) belong to the capital or financial account, as they involve acquisition of assets or liabilities rather than current flows of goods/services or transfers.

Hence, only A and C correctly represent current account components.

15. Economist W.W. Rostow in his "Stages of Economic Growth" model described the take-off stage, where sustained economic growth begins. A leading sector can drive take-off if four main conditions are satisfied:

A. The market for the product expands rapidly, ensuring demand growth for the sector's output.

B. The leading sector generates secondary expansion, meaning its growth stimulates linked industries through backward and forward linkages.

C. There is an adequate and continual supply of capital from ploughed-back profits, ensuring that reinvestment maintains momentum.

D. New techniques are introduced to raise productivity, enabling efficiency and competitiveness.

While (E) Structural changes in industrial structure should be structural ones is too vague and not part of Rostow's explicitly stated criteria, the first four are directly mentioned in his analysis.

Thus, A, B, C, and D only (option 4) is correct.

16. Matching options:

- **Inverted "U" hypothesis → Simon Kuznets (III):** The Kuznets curve posits that as an economy develops, income inequality first rises and then falls, tracing an inverted "U".
- **Sustainable development → Gro Harlem Brundtland (IV):** The Brundtland Commission (1987) framed sustainable development as meeting present needs without compromising future generations' ability to meet theirs.
- **Ecological Economics → Herman Daly (I):** Daly pioneered steady-state and scale-aware thinking, embedding the economy within the ecosystem's biophysical limits.
- **Tragedy of the commons → Garrett Hardin (II):** Hardin highlighted how open-access resources get overused when individual incentives conflict with collective welfare.

17. Lexicographic preferences (first compare one attribute; only if tied, compare the next) are complete and transitive, and their upper contour sets are convex under standard settings. However, they fail continuity: no sufficiently small "compensation" in the less-important attribute can offset a tiny loss in the more-important one. Hence a continuous utility representation does not exist, violating the continuity axiom (not transitivity, independence, or convexity).

18. The Lucas Critique argues that econometric relationships (coefficients) estimated under one policy regime change when policy rules change, because agents' expectations and decision rules adjust. Therefore, policy evaluation needs structural, policy-invariant parameters; models with drifting coefficients are unreliable for counterfactual policy analysis. It does not assert monetary non-neutrality nor praise Keynesian expectation treatment; rather, it warns that expectations matter and coefficient stability is crucial—making statement 4 the correct one.

19. **Step 1: Restate the problem**

Maximise the utility function

$$U = (x + 2)(y + 1)$$

subject to the budget constraint

$$4x + 6y = 130$$

Step 2: Express in convenient form

Let,

$$X = x + 2,\ Y = y + 1$$

Then,

$$x = X - 2,\ y = Y - 1$$

Substitute into the budget:

$$4(X - 2) + 6(Y - 1) = 130$$

$$\Rightarrow 4X - 8 + 6Y - 6 = 130$$

$$\Rightarrow 4X + 6Y = 144$$

$$\Rightarrow 2X + 3Y = 72.$$

Step 3: Find the marginal rate of substitution (MRS)

The utility is U = XY

$$MU_x = \frac{\partial U}{\partial X} = Y,\ MU_y = \frac{\partial U}{\partial Y} = X$$

Set MRS equal to the price ratio:

$$\frac{MU_x}{MU_y} = \frac{Y}{X} = \frac{P_x}{P_y} = \frac{4}{6} = \frac{2}{3}$$

Hence,

$$Y = \frac{2}{3}X$$

Step 4: Substitute into the budget constraint

$$2X + 3Y = 72$$

$$\Rightarrow\ 2X + 3\left(\frac{2}{3}X\right) = 72$$

$$\Rightarrow\ 2X + 2X = 72$$

$$\Rightarrow\ 4X = 72$$

$$\Rightarrow\ X = 18$$

Then

$$Y = \frac{2}{3}(18) = 12$$

Step 5: Convert back to *x* and *y*

$$\Rightarrow\ x = X - 2$$

$$= 18 - 2 = 16,$$

$$y = Y - 1$$

$$= 12 - 1$$

$$= 11$$

Final Optimum:

$$x^* = 16, \ y^* = 11$$

Hence, $x = 16$, $y = 11$

20. Bootstrapping resamples (with replacement) from the observed data to approximate the sampling distribution of an estimator or statistic, enabling standard errors, confidence intervals, and bias assessments without strong parametric assumptions. It is not a specific test for specification bias, autocorrelation, or normality.

21. In environmental economics, efficiency refers to using society's resources in a way that maximizes total welfare without unnecessary waste.

- **A (Correct):** Pareto efficiency means an allocation is efficient if no one can be made better off without making someone else worse off. This is the standard definition of efficiency used in welfare economics.
- **B (Incorrect):** Fairness or equity is not guaranteed by efficiency. A Pareto-efficient allocation could still be very unequal. Equity and fairness are normative issues, whereas efficiency is generally a positive concept describing resource allocation, not moral judgments.
- **C (Correct):** Market allocations are only efficient if there are no market failures like externalities, public goods, or imperfect competition. When such failures exist, the market outcome is not efficient, which is why environmental issues (externalities) often require policy intervention.
- **D (Incorrect):** Efficiency is not primarily a normative concept about what society "should" do; it is an analytical criterion describing a state where resources can't be reallocated to make someone better off without hurting others.
- **E (Correct):** Environmental policies like Pigouvian taxes, cap-and-trade systems, or subsidies that internalize externalities can move an economy closer to efficiency by aligning private costs with social costs.

22. To determine sample size for estimating a mean with specified confidence and error:

- **Confidence level:** 95% → Z = 1.96.
- **Standard deviation (σ):** Estimated at 16 minutes by the time-and-motion expert.
- **Maximum error (E):** 2 minutes.

The formula is:

$$n = \left(\frac{Z\sigma}{E}\right)^2$$

Substituting values:

$$n = \left(\frac{1.96 \times 16}{2}\right)^2$$

$$= \left(\frac{31.36}{2}\right)^2$$

$$= (15.68)^2 \approx 245.7$$

Rounding up,

$$n = 246.$$

Hence, to ensure with 95% confidence that the estimation error will not exceed 2 minutes, the firm should take a sample size of 246.

23. Chronological order of Keynes's works (oldest to latest):

C. **Indian Currency and Finance (1913):** An early book where Keynes analyzed India's currency and financial system under the British regime, critiquing policies affecting stability.

E. **A Tract on Monetary Reform (1923):** Written after World War I, it examined post-war inflation and exchange rate policies, advocating monetary stability.

A. **A Treatise on Money (1930):** A comprehensive two-volume work providing a systematic analysis of monetary theory before the Great Depression.

D. **A Monetary Theory of Production (1933):** A lecture developing Keynes's ideas about monetary factors driving production decisions, foreshadowing The General Theory.

B. **The General Theory of Employment, Interest and Money (1936):** Keynes's revolutionary macroeconomic work overturning classical economics by emphasizing demand management.

Thus, the correct chronological sequence is C, E, A, D, B.

24. At the 54th Monetary Policy Committee (MPC) meeting of RBI (late 2024), the key rates decided were:

- **Reverse Repo Rate (D)** – The lowest rate at which RBI absorbs liquidity.
- **Cash Reserve Ratio (C)** – A regulatory ratio, slightly higher than reverse repo in relative position for ascending order purposes.
- **Standing Deposit Facility Rate (B)** – Slightly higher than CRR, providing RBI with a non-collateralized facility for absorbing liquidity.
- **Repo Rate (E)** – The policy rate at which RBI lends to banks, positioned above SDF.
- **Marginal Standing Facility Rate (A)** – The highest rate, the upper ceiling of the corridor for emergency borrowing by banks.

Arranging from lowest to highest: D (Reverse Repo) < C (CRR) < B (SDF) < E (Repo) < A (MSF), which corresponds to option 3.

25. In the IS-LM model (closed economy), an increase in government spending shifts macroeconomic equilibrium as follows:

- **A (Correct):** Government spending increases aggregate demand, shifting the IS curve and causing income to rise by the government expenditure multiplier (the ratio of change in output to change in spending).
- **B (Correct):** The IS curve shifts right, producing excess demand in the goods market, which, at the initial interest rate, creates a disequilibrium in the money market since income rises and money demand increases.
- **C (Correct):** Higher income causes money demand to rise because people need more transactions balances at the existing interest rate.
- **D (Incorrect):** Interest rates do not decrease; instead, they increase because the LM curve is upward-sloping in (Y,i)(Y, i)(Y,i) space—higher money demand at unchanged supply pushes rates up.
- **E (Incorrect):** Higher interest rates crowd out private investment; thus, private investment generally falls, not rises.

Hence, the correct effects of increased government spending are A, B, and C.

26. The Economic Survey 2024–25 gives approximate shares of India's energy production (Nov 2024): Solar – 20.60%, Hydro – 10.30%, Nuclear – 1.80%, Wind – 10.50%.

- **A. Solar energy → II (20.60%):** India's solar capacity expanded rapidly under missions like the National Solar Mission, forming the largest share among renewables.
- **B. Hydro energy → III (10.30%):** Hydroelectric projects remain a stable, significant but smaller component.
- **C. Nuclear energy → IV (1.80%):** Nuclear has a tiny share due to limited plants.
- **D. Wind energy → I (10.50%):** Wind contributes just over 10% of renewable production.

Correct matching: A-II, B-III, C-IV, D-I.

27. Outcomes of a consumer's optimization:

- **A (True):** At equilibrium, marginal utility per rupee is equal for all goods: $\frac{MU_x}{P_x} = \frac{MU_y}{P_y}$
- **B (True):** The marginal rate of substitution (slope of indifference curve) equals the price ratio: $MRS_{xy} = \frac{P_x}{P_y}$
- **C (False):** The consumer reaches the highest attainable indifference curve, not necessarily the absolute highest curve on the entire map (budget limits prevent reaching the absolute highest).
- **D (True):** At optimum, the indifference curve is tangent to the budget line, showing equal slopes.
- **E (False):** Points on the budget line are not all equally satisfying—only points on the same indifference curve give equal utility; different points on the budget line can yield different satisfaction levels.

Thus: A, B & D.

28. Parallel, straight wealth expansion paths require specific preference conditions:

- **A (True):** Preferences must admit an indirect utility function of Gorman form, enabling linear Engel curves and identical marginal propensities to consume.

- **D (True):** Identical homothetic preferences across consumers ensure proportional changes in consumption as wealth changes.
- **E (True):** Alternatively, quasilinear preferences in the same good also yield linear, parallel wealth expansion paths.
- **B (False):** Heterogeneous preferences break parallelism.
- **C (False):** Equal wealth distribution is unrelated to the shape of expansion paths.

Therefore, the correct conditions: A, D & E.

29. Step 1: Identify the events and their years in India's derivatives market

D. **Introduction of Futures trading based on the Index – June 2000:** Nifty futures were the first derivatives product introduced on Indian exchanges.

E. **Commencement of trading in Index Options – June 2001:** Index options on benchmarks like Nifty followed after the success of index futures.

A. **Commencement of trading in Options on Individual Securities – July 2001:** Options on single stocks began soon after index options.

C. **Commencement of trading in Stock Futures – November 2001:** Single-stock futures started later in the same year.

B. **Introduction of Interest Rate Futures – 2003:** Futures on government securities and interest rates were introduced after equity derivatives matured.

Step 2: Arrange from oldest to latest

Putting these in chronological order:

1. D – Index Futures (June 2000)
2. E – Index Options (June 2001)
3. A – Stock Options on Individual Securities (July 2001)
4. C – Stock Futures (Nov 2001)
5. B – Interest Rate Futures (2003)

Step 3: Final sequence

The ascending order is D, E, A, C, B, which matches option 2.

30. Externalities occur when costs or benefits affect third parties not involved in a transaction.

- **A (True):** Not all costs and benefits are internalized by buyers and sellers—hallmark of externalities.
- **B (True):** Externalities cause under-production (positive externalities) or over-production (negative externalities) relative to the socially optimal level.
- **C (False):** Market-based decisions do not yield efficiency when externalities exist—markets fail to allocate resources optimally.
- **D (True):** For negative externalities, marginal social cost exceeds marginal private cost—e.g., pollution.
- **E (True):** Coase theorem suggests that with well-defined property rights and low transaction costs, bargaining can internalize externalities and restore efficiency.

Correct set: A, B, D & E.

31. NONE: Correct mapping is A-III, B-(no match), C-I, D-(no match)

Why "NONE": the provided options contain internal inconsistencies.

For a chi-square distribution with n degrees of freedom (χ_n^2) the standard results are:

- **Kurtosis (β_2):** $\beta_2 = 3 + \frac{12}{n}$ → A → III (this one is correct among the lists).
- **Skewness:** $\gamma_1 = \sqrt{\frac{8}{n}}$. None of the given right-hand expressions equals $\sqrt{8/n}$. The only "square-root" expression offered is IV: $\sqrt{2/n}$, which is not the skewness; it is the coefficient of variation (since $\sigma/\mu = \sqrt{2n}/n = \sqrt{2/n}$). So, B has no correct match in the list.
- **Mode (for $n \geq 2$):** $n - 2$ → C → I (this one is correct).
- **Third central moment (μ_3):** $\mu_3 = 8n$. The list gives II: $48n + 12n^2$, which equals $12n(n + 4)$ and is actually the fourth central moment μ_4 for χ_n^2, not μ_3. So, (D) also has no correct match.

Because B and D cannot be matched correctly with any of the listed expressions, none of the four answer options gives a fully correct mapping. The only correct pairings from the provided items are A-III and C-I; the rest are mismatched. Hence, Answer: NONE.

32. National Income will decrease by ₹ 400

Given: MPC =0.8, tax increase $\Delta T = +100$.

- **Spending multiplier:** $\frac{1}{1-MPC} = \frac{1}{0.2} = 5$
- **Tax multiplier (lump-sum):**

$-\frac{MPC}{1-MPC} = \frac{0.8}{0.2} = -4.$

- **Impact on income:** $\Delta Y = (-4) \times (+100) = -400.$

So, national income falls by ₹ 400.

33. An increase in the relative price of a commodity raises the earnings of the factor used intensively in the production of that commodity

This is the core statement of the Stolper-Samuelson theorem within the 2×2 Heckscher-Ohlin framework: if the relative price of one good rises, the real return to the factor used intensively in that good increases, while the other factor's real return falls. Option 1 precisely captures this effect.

34. Policy Ineffectiveness Proposition (Sargent-Wallace) — key assumptions:

- Rational expectations (A) and full information/market clearing (C) imply no systematic money illusion.
- Natural-rate property (E): output/employment gravitate to their natural levels; only unanticipated nominal shocks can move real activity.

Not assumed (i.e., incorrect as assumptions):

- B. "Policy changes are not anticipated." PIP's point is that anticipated/systematic policy is neutral for real variables—so agents do anticipate it.
- D. "Nominal variables influence economic decision." Under the PIP's assumptions, anticipated nominal policy doesn't systematically alter real choices.

Thus, the statements not part of the assumptions are B and D.

35. In the RBI's current operating framework:

- The repo rate is the policy rate signalling stance.
- The liquidity corridor is bounded by SDF (floor) and MSF (ceiling).
- The operating target the RBI actually steers in the money market is the Weighted Average Call Money Rate (WACMR), keeping it aligned with the policy stance within the corridor.

36. Matching options:

A. **Specific-factors model → IV. Paul Samuelson & Ronald Jones:** The modern Ricardo–Viner (specific-factors) framework is associated with Jones/Samuelson: some factors (e.g., capital) are sector-specific in the short run, while labor is mobile. It's a workhorse for distributional effects of trade in the short run.

B. **Immiserizing growth → III. Jagdish Bhagwati:** Bhagwati showed that for a large country, export-biased growth can worsen its terms of trade so much that real income falls—growth that immiserizes.

C. **Mercantilism → II. Thomas Mun:** Mun articulated classic mercantilist ideas: national wealth via trade surpluses, bullion inflows, and state guidance of commerce.

D. **Secular deterioration of terms of trade → I. Prebisch-Singer hypothesis:** Long-run tendency for primary commodity exporters' terms of trade to worsen relative to manufactures.

Hence, correct matching is A-IV, B-III, C-II, D-I.

37. Oldest → latest appointment:

D. **K. Brahmananda Reddy:** 6th Finance Commission (early 1970s)

C. **N.K.P. Salve:** 9th Finance Commission (late 1980s)

E. **K.C. Pant:** 10th Finance Commission (early 1990s)

A. **A.M. Khusro:** 11th Finance Commission (late 1990s)

B. **C. Rangarajan:** 12th Finance Commission (early 2000s)

Thus the chronological sequence is D, C, E, A, B.

38. Descending share of total FDI, H1 FY25:

D. **Computer Software & Hardware:** typically the largest single sectoral recipient in recent half-year tallies due to ongoing digitalization, data centers, and electronics.

E. **Non-conventional Energy:** strong pipelines in solar/wind/green hydrogen push this sector high.

C. **Cement & Gypsum Products:** benefits from infra and real-estate upcycles; ahead of the next two in H1 FY25.

A. **Automobile Industry:** substantial but below the above sectors in the referenced half-year.

B. **Hospital & Diagnostic Centres:** growing, yet smaller share compared to the others listed.

Hence, the order is D > E > C > A > B.

39. Let g_m = manufacturing output growth, g_{GDP} = GDP growth, P_m = manufacturing productivity, P_{nm} = productivity outside manufacturing.

A. **Kaldor's first law → III:** $g_{GDP} = f(g_m)$, $f' > 0$: GDP growth rises with manufacturing growth.

B. **Kaldor's second law (Verdoorn) → I:** $P_m = f(g_m)$, $f' > 0$: faster manufacturing growth raises manufacturing productivity (dynamic increasing returns).

C. **Kaldor's third law → IV:** $P_{nm} = f(g_m)$, $f' > 0$: manufacturing growth lifts productivity in the rest of the economy (reallocation/externalities).

D. **Okun's law → II:** $y' = -\varepsilon(u - u^*)$: output growth relates negatively to the unemployment gap.

Hence, correct matching is A-III, B-I, C-IV, D-II

40. Poverty-weighted indices of growth are specially designed to evaluate whether economic growth is benefiting all segments of society, particularly the poorest sections. Traditional growth measures such as GDP per capita growth are income-weighted—this means that higher-income individuals, whose incomes already form a large share of the total, exert more influence on the overall growth rate than the incomes of poorer individuals. As a result, improvements in the well-being of the rich can overshadow stagnation or decline in the incomes of the poor.

A poverty-weighted index corrects this bias by rebalancing the weights assigned to different income groups. While its ultimate purpose is to assign greater emphasis to the poor, among the provided choices, giving "at least equal weight to all income groups" represents a shift away from the standard bias toward the wealthy and toward a more equitable evaluation of growth performance. This option captures the essential idea of reducing the disproportionate influence of rich households and ensuring that improvements in the incomes of lower-income groups are not undervalued.

The other options are unsuitable:

- "To achieve high growth rate" does not address distribution or poverty focus.
- "To facilitate foreign trade on equal basis" is unrelated to measuring pro-poor growth.
- "To assign more weight to the richest population and no weight to lower-income group" is contrary to the intent of poverty-weighted indices.

Thus, among the given options, option 1 best represents the purpose of constructing poverty-weighted indices of growth.

41. Revised MSME classification effective 01 April 2025 (Union Budget 2025–26):

A. **Micro enterprise investment ≤ ₹ 2.5 crore — Correct.** The investment ceiling for micro enterprises has been revised upward from earlier limits to ₹ 2.5 crore.

D. **Micro enterprise turnover ≤ ₹ 10 crore — Correct.** The turnover criterion for micro enterprises remains ₹ 10 crore.

E. **Small enterprise turnover ≤ ₹ 100 crore—Correct.** The upper turnover limit for small enterprises has been revised to ₹ 100 crore.

B. **Medium enterprise turnover ≤ ₹ 50 crore — Incorrect:** under the revision, medium enterprises now have turnover up to ₹ 250 crore.

C. **Small enterprise investment ≤ ₹ 10 crore — Incorrect:** the small enterprise investment ceiling is ₹ 25 crore, not ₹ 10 crore.

Hence, A, D & E only.

42. The sequence of constitution of important tax reform committees in India, arranged from the oldest to the latest, is as follows:

- **Raja Chelliah Tax Reform Committee (1991):** Formed in 1991 as part of India's post-liberalization reforms, this committee was tasked with recommending a comprehensive overhaul of the tax system. Its landmark recommendations led to lower tax rates, broadening of the tax base, and rationalization of direct and indirect taxes. It played a crucial role in modernizing India's fiscal framework.
- **K.L. Rekhi Committee on Indirect Tax (1992):** Constituted in 1992 to reform customs and central excise laws, this committee streamlined the structure of indirect taxation and recommended simplifications that paved the way for later indirect tax reforms, including the eventual introduction of VAT and GST.
- **Vijay Kelkar Committee on Tax Reforms (2002):** In 2002, two task forces under Dr. Vijay Kelkar—one on direct taxes and another on indirect taxes—were established to make India's tax system more growth-oriented and efficient. The committee emphasized fiscal responsibility, moderate tax rates, and simplification of procedures, forming the basis for the Fiscal Responsibility and Budget Management (FRBM) Act and later reforms.
- **T.R. Rastogi Committee on Service Tax Reforms (2006):** This committee was constituted in 2006 to review the service tax framework and recommend measures to strengthen administration and compliance. Its work supported the gradual expansion and integration of service tax, which later contributed to GST implementation.
- **Parthasarathi Shome Committee on Direct Tax (2012):** Set up in 2012 to review and clarify the General Anti-Avoidance Rules (GAAR) and other aspects of direct taxation, this committee provided recommendations to enhance tax certainty and improve investor confidence while safeguarding revenue interests.

Correct Chronological Order: A, E, C, B, D.

43. Matching options:

A. **Income elasticity greater than one → III. Luxurious goods:** Goods whose demand rises more than proportionally with income are luxuries.

B. **Positive cross-price elasticity → I. Substitute goods:** When the price of one good rises and demand for another rises, the goods are substitutes.

C. **Downward sloping PCC → IV. Relatively elastic demand effect:** A downward sloping Price Consumption Curve (PCC) suggests relatively elastic demand—as price falls, consumption increases significantly.

D. **Negative income effect → II. Inferior goods:** Inferior goods show negative income elasticity—demand falls as income rises.

44. When the income effect works opposite to the substitution effect, yet the substitution effect dominates, the overall demand curve still slopes downward. This is the case for inferior goods that are not Giffen goods.

- For Giffen goods, the negative income effect is so strong that it outweighs the substitution effect, making demand slope upward.
- Here, substitution dominates ⇒ the good is inferior but not Giffen.

45. In the Union Budget 2025–26, the major components of expenditure as a share of total Union Government expenditure are:

C. **Pensions – 4%:** Pensions constitute a relatively small but essential component of the budget. This includes retirement benefits for civil and defense personnel, ensuring post-service financial security.

D. **Major Subsidies – 6%:** Major subsidies cover food, fertilizer, and petroleum subsidies. These are critical for supporting food security, agricultural productivity, and stabilizing fuel prices but are moderated to maintain fiscal discipline.

A. **Finance Commission and Other Transfers – 8%:** This category reflects statutory transfers to states as recommended by the Finance Commission, along with other transfers for centrally sponsored programs. It is a significant mechanism for fiscal federalism and empowering states financially.

E. **Central Sector Schemes (excluding capital outlay on defense and subsidies) – 16%:** These schemes represent a broad range of government programs executed by the Union Government directly. They include infrastructure, digitalization, and social sector projects where the Union Government is the primary spending authority.

B. **Interest Payments – 25%:** Interest payments are the single largest expenditure item, reflecting the cost of servicing the government's accumulated debt. It demonstrates the importance of prudent borrowing and fiscal management.

Arranging in ascending order of their shares:

1. C. Pensions – 4%
2. D. Major Subsidies – 6%
3. A. Finance Commission and Other Transfers – 8%
4. E. Central Sector Schemes – 16%
5. B. Interest Payments – 25%

Therefore, the correct ascending order is C, D, A, E, B, which corresponds to option 2.

46. Goal: Minimize $U = 6x^2 + y^2$ subject to the linear constraint $4x - y = 1$. (With a quadratic objective and a single linear constraint, the unique constrained minimum gives the required value of U.)

Method (substitution):

From $4x - y = 1$, get $y = 4x - 1$.

$$U(x) = 6x^2 + (4x - 1)^2$$
$$= 6x^2 + 16x^2 - 8x + 1$$
$$= 22x^2 - 8x + 1$$

Minimize the quadratic:

For $U(x) = ax^2 + bx + c$

with $a = 22$, $b = -8$,

the minimizer is $x^* = -\frac{b}{2a} = \frac{8}{44} = \frac{2}{11}$.

Then $y^* = 4 \cdot \frac{2}{11} - 1 = \frac{8}{11} - 1 = -\frac{3}{11}$.

Compute U at the optimum:

$$U^* = 6\left(\frac{2}{11}\right)^2 + \left(-\frac{3}{11}\right)^2$$
$$= 6 \cdot \frac{4}{121} + \frac{9}{121}$$
$$= \frac{24}{121} + \frac{9}{121}$$
$$= \frac{33}{121}$$
$$= \frac{3}{11}$$

Therefore, $U = \frac{3}{11}$.

47. In the Union Budget 2025–26, the estimated shares of these major revenue items as a percentage of total receipts are as follows:

A. **Income Tax → III (22%):** Income tax accounts for 22% of total receipts, making it the largest contributor among the four categories. This reflects expanding compliance, digitization of tax administration, and a robust growth in personal income collections.

B. **Customs → I (4%):** Customs duties contribute 4%, the smallest share of the listed items. This reduced percentage is consistent with India's policy of trade liberalization and lower tariff barriers to support global trade integration.

C. **Corporation Tax → IV (17%):** Corporation tax provides 17% of total receipts, demonstrating its continued significance as a primary source of direct tax revenue, even after rate reductions aimed at stimulating investment and business competitiveness.

D. **Union Excise Duty → II (5%):** Union excise duties contribute 5%. After the introduction of GST, excise duties now mainly apply to petroleum, tobacco, and a few other goods outside GST coverage, making it a smaller but stable revenue source.

Correct Match: A-III, B-I, C-IV, D-II.

48. Neoclassical (Solow) growth model implications of a higher population growth rate n:

A. **Reduction in steady-state capital per head — True:** Higher n raises break-even investment $(n + g + \delta)k$, lowering steady-state k^* and thus capital per worker.

B. **Increase in per capita output — False:** With k^* lower, per capita output $y^* = f(k^*)$falls, not rises (holding technology constant).

C. **Increase in steady-state growth rate of aggregate output — True:** Aggregate Y grows in steady state at $n + g$. If n rises, the steady-state growth rate of aggregate output increases.

D. **Decrease in capital-output ratio — Ambiguous in generic statements:** While in Cobb-Douglas one can derive a lower K/Y level with higher n, many exam treatments focus on the robust, widely taught effects (A fall in k and rise in aggregate growth), avoiding statements on K/Y unless the production form is specified.

E. **Inward shift in the production possibility curve — False:** A change in population growth doesn't shift the economy's PPC; it changes the long-run composition/levels along the balanced path.

Thus the safest, standard set is: A & C only.

49. Match concepts to proponents/approaches:

A. **Income-induced adjustment process of BoP → II. J.M. Keynes:** The Keynesian income mechanism adjusts external imbalances via changes in income and imports.

B. **Absorption approach to BoP → III. Sidney S. Alexander:** BoP improves if output exceeds domestic absorption; Alexander formalized this view.

C. **Impossible trinity → IV. Mundell–Fleming:** One cannot simultaneously have fixed exchange rate, free capital mobility, and independent monetary policy.

D. **Factor price equalization theorem → I. Paul Samuelson:** In the Heckscher-Ohlin framework, free trade can equalize factor prices across countries under strong assumptions.

Therefore: A-II, B-III, C-IV, D-I.

50. Indirect Least Squares (ILS):

- **What it does:** Estimate the reduced-form parameters first (by OLS), then algebraically invert them to obtain the structural coefficients when the structural equation is exactly identified (just-identified).
- **Therefore:** ILS is used to estimate coefficients of the structural equation (not the reduced form itself, which is obtained directly by OLS; not over- or under-identified equations, for which other methods are required).

51. New Classical approach:

A. **The main protagonist was R. E. Lucas Jr. — True.** The New Classical school is most closely identified with Robert E. Lucas Jr., whose rational expectations revolution reshaped macroeconomics and policy analysis.

B. **It is based on adaptive expectation — False.** New Classical models are built on rational expectations, not adaptive expectations. Agents are assumed to use all available information and the model-consistent structure when forming expectations.

C. **It was developed during 1950s — False.** The approach emerged prominently in the 1970s, following critiques of traditional Keynesian macroeconometric models.

D. **Complete wage and price flexibility — True.** Baseline New Classical models assume market clearing with flexible prices and wages, so systematic policy does not create persistent real effects.

E. **Difference between actual and expected price is a random error — True.** In the Lucas "surprise-supply" logic, only unanticipated price (or monetary) surprises move real activity; forecast errors are random (zero-mean) rather than systematic.

52. The Keynesian investment multiplier k satisfies $k = \frac{1}{1-c}$, where c is the marginal propensity to consume (MPC).

Given $k = 4$, we have $1 - c = \frac{1}{4}$

$\Rightarrow c = 0.75$.

Hence the marginal propensity to save (MPS) is $1 - c = 0.25$.

A saving function has slope equal to MPS. Among the options, only $S = \alpha + 0.25Y_D$ matches. The intercept −12 sets the break-even income; many intercepts could be consistent with $k = 4$. The key is the slope 0.25, which yields option 3.

53. Effective Rate of Protection:

- g = effective protection rate for producers of the final good
- t = nominal tariff rate on the final good
- t_i = nominal tariff rate on the imported input
- a_i = share of the imported input in the free-trade price of the final good

The effective rate of protection compares how tariffs on outputs and inputs change the value added in the protected equilibrium versus free trade. The standard formula is

$$g = \frac{t - a_i t_i}{1 - a_i}$$

54. Let X be a Poisson random variable with mean λ.

The probability mass function (pmf) is:

$$P(X = x) = \frac{e^{-\lambda}\lambda^x}{x!}, x = 0, 1, 2, ...$$

We need $P(X = x + 1)$ in terms of $P(X = x)$.

$$P(X = x+1) = \frac{e^{-\lambda}\lambda^{x+1}}{x+1!}$$

Rewrite $(x + 1)! = (x + 1)(x!)$:

$$P(X = x+1) = \frac{\lambda^{x+1}e^{-\lambda}}{(x+1)(x!)}$$

Factor out λ and express in terms of $P(X = x)$:

$$P(X = x+1) = \frac{\lambda}{x+1} \cdot \frac{\lambda^x e^{-\lambda}}{x!}$$

But $\frac{\lambda^x e^{-\lambda}}{x!} = P(X = x)$

Therefore,

$$P(X = x+1) = \frac{\lambda}{x+1} P(X = x)$$

Correct Option: 1. $\frac{\lambda}{x+1} P(x)$

55. Distributions & formulas:

A. **Mean of a Hypergeometric distribution → III.** $\frac{nm}{N}$

Drawing n items from a population of size N with m "successes," the expected number of successes is $E[X] = n \cdot \frac{m}{n}$

B. **MGF of Negative Binomial distribution → II.** $(Q - Pe^t)^{-r}$

Though parameterizations vary, the listed form corresponds to a common representation of the moment generating function of a negative binomial variate (with suitable P, Q, r notation and domain restrictions).

C. **Coefficient of Kurtosis of a Binomial distribution → IV.** $\frac{1-6pq}{npq}$

For binomial Bin (n, p) excess kurtosis is $\frac{1-6pq}{npq}$ (hence the coefficient of kurtosis above 3 is that expression).

D. **Variance of a Geometric distribution → I.** $\frac{q}{p^2}$

For the geometric (counting trials until first success, with success probability p),

$\text{Var}(X) = \frac{q}{p^2}$ where $q = 1 - p$.

Therefore, the correct matching is A-III, B-II, C-IV, D-I.

56. $k(t) = 9t^{4/3} + 25$

Derivation:

- Investment is the flow that adds to capital, so $\dot{k}(t) = I(t)$.
- Given $I(t) = 12t^{1/3}$:

$$\frac{dk}{dt} = 12t^{1/3}$$

$$\Rightarrow k(t) = \int 12t^{1/3}dt + C = 12 \cdot \frac{t^{4/3}}{4/3} + C = 9t^{4/3} + C$$

- Use the initial stock $k(0) = 25 : 25 = 9.0^{4/3} + C$

$\Rightarrow C = 25$

Thus, $k(t) = 9t^{4/3} + 25$.

57. Classical economists generally opposed public debt, emphasizing:

- Double burden on taxpayers (interest + amortization) → True.
- Barren production/consumption; burden shifted to future generations → True (crowding out private capital and future tax burdens).
- Destruction of productive capital (resources diverted from private investment) → True in their framework.

However, the idea that debt is a tool for compensatory demand management is Keynesian, not classical. Hence statement 2 is the one not true under classical views.

58. Setup: For the three posts, the candidate's selection probabilities (assuming equal chances and independence across posts) are

$$p_1 = \frac{1}{3},\ p_2 = \frac{1}{4},\ p_3 = \frac{1}{2}$$

Probability of not being selected in any post:

$$(1-p_1)(1-p_2)(1-p_3) = \left(\frac{2}{3}\right)\left(\frac{3}{4}\right)\left(\frac{1}{2}\right) = \left(\frac{1}{4}\right)$$

Therefore, probability of being selected in at least one post:

$$1 - \frac{1}{4} = \frac{3}{4}.$$

59. A positive output gap means actual output exceeds potential output. This typically occurs when the economy operates above sustainable capacity—e.g., overtime, intense utilization, and labor markets beyond full employment (overemployment).

- Population growth and technological progress mainly shift potential output, not create a short-run gap of actual over potential.
- Underutilization of resources produces a negative output gap.

60. Euler's Theorem:

If $Q = f(K, L)$ is homogeneous of degree 1 (constant returns to scale), Euler's theorem states:

$$Q = Kf_K + Lf_L = K\frac{\partial Q}{\partial K} + L\frac{\partial Q}{\partial L}$$

Thus, option 2 is the correct condition.

61. Classical loanable-funds view of deficit spending:

A. **Shift in demand for loanable funds to the right — True.** A higher deficit (G–T↑) means the government borrows more, increasing demand for loanable funds.

B. **Decline in interest rate — False.** Extra borrowing raises the real interest rate to clear the funds market.

C. **Increase in investment — False.** With higher real interest rates, private investment is crowded out (falls).

D. **Increase in saving equal to decline in consumption — True.** With income fixed at full employment, a rise in r reduces consumption C, raising private saving S by the same amount (S = Y – T – C).

E. **Decrease in investment and consumption that balances the increase in government spending — True.** Goods-market identity Y = C + I + G with fixed Y implies $\Delta G > 0$ must be offset by $\Delta C + \Delta I < 0$ of equal magnitude.

62. Payoff matrix (P1,P2):

- T : (1,5) vs L, (0,3) vs R
- M : (2,6) vs L, (1,4) vs R
- B : (3,7) vs L, (2,2) vs R

Dominance checks for Player 1:

- Column L: 1 < 2 < 3 ⇒ B strictly dominates M and T.

- Column R: $0 < 1 < 2 \Rightarrow$ same ordering.

  Thus A (two strictly dominated strategies) is True: T and M are strictly dominated by B.

  Also E is True: M strictly dominates T($2 > 1$ and $1 > 0$).

  Because dominated strategies get zero probability in equilibrium, D is True: M will never be used in any Nash equilibrium.

Player 2: Compare L vs R: payoffs are 5, 6, 7(L) vs 3, 4, 2 (R) for T, M, B respectively, so L strictly dominates R. Hence B (no weak dominance) is False.

C is False: T does not weakly dominate B; B is everywhere better for Player 1.

63. Descending share in Union Budget 2025–26:

Reasoning: Among the listed heads, Defense (C) is the largest. Next comes Rural Development (E) driven by major rural programs. Agriculture & Allied (A) follows, then Education (B), and finally Commerce & Industry (D) among these five.

Order (largest → smallest): Defense > Rural Development > Agriculture & Allied > Education > Commerce & Industry, i.e., C, E, A, B, D.

64. Profit maximization:

$\pi(X) = R - C = 3X - (100 + 0.015X^2)$

First-order condition:

$$\frac{d\pi}{dX} = 3 - 0.03X = 0$$

$$\Rightarrow X^* = \frac{3}{0.03} = 100$$

Second-order condition: $\dfrac{d^2\pi}{dX^2} = -0.03 < 0$

$\Rightarrow$ maximum.

Therefore, the profit-maximizing output level is $X = 100$.

65. The line of regression of y on x is expressed by:

$$y - \bar{y} = b_{yx}(x - \bar{x})$$

where:

- $\bar{x} = 32$ is the mean of x,
- $\bar{y} = 38$ is the mean of y,
- $b_{yx} = -0.6643$ is the regression coefficient of y on x..

Step 1: Substitute the known values

$$y - 38 = -0.6643(x - 32)$$

Step 2: Distribute the slope on the right-hand side

$$y - 38 = -0.6643x + (-0.6643)(-32),$$
$$= 0.6643x + 21.2576$$

Step 3: Solve for y

Add 38 to both sides to isolate y:

$$y = -0.6643x + 21.2576 + 38$$

Simplify:

$$y = -0.6643x + 59.2576$$

Final Regression Equation

The equation of the regression line of y on x is:

$$y = -0.6643x + 59.2576$$

This matches option 4, confirming it as the correct choice.

66. In the IS–LM framework, the slope of the IS curve depends on two factors:

1. Interest sensitivity of investment (how strongly investment responds to changes in interest rates).
2. Marginal propensity to spend (or the marginal propensity to consume, MPC), which determines the spending multiplier $k = \dfrac{1}{1-c}$.

When the marginal propensity to spend increases, the multiplier k becomes larger. A larger multiplier means that any given fall in interest rate produces a much larger increase in income, because each round of spending creates stronger secondary spending effects. This increased responsiveness of income to interest changes flattens the IS curve—small interest rate changes now generate large income changes to maintain goods-market equilibrium.

The aggregate demand (AD) curve in the price-output space is derived from the IS–LM model. A flatter IS curve amplifies the effect of price-level changes (via LM shifts) on output: even a small movement in prices, which shifts LM, results in a relatively larger movement along IS–LM equilibrium points, producing a steeper AD curve in price-output space. A steeper AD curve implies that for a given price change, income changes more sharply, consistent with stronger expenditure feedback effects in the goods market.

Thus, under these conditions:

- IS curve becomes flatter due to a larger spending multiplier.
- Aggregate demand curve becomes steeper because output responds more strongly to price changes transmitted through the LM curve.

Therefore, the correct choice is: A steeper aggregate demand curve and consequently a flatter IS curve.

67. In Raymond Vernon's Product Cycle Model of International Trade, a product passes through distinct phases that influence where it is produced and how trade flows evolve:

- **Stage I – New Product (Introduction):** The product is newly developed in an innovating, high-income country. Production and consumption occur primarily in the innovator's domestic market. Because the technology is untested and demand is uncertain, there is little or no international trade at this stage.
- **Stage II – Growth (Maturing Product):** Demand grows in the innovating country and begins spreading to other developed economies. The innovating country starts exporting the product, but maintains a technological and cost advantage. Production techniques are still evolving, and competitors have not yet mastered the process.
- **Stage III – Maturity (Standardised Product):** The product design and production technology become standardized and well known. Imitating countries begin producing for their domestic markets, reducing their need to import from the innovating country. The innovator's exports may plateau or decline as competition intensifies.
- **Stage IV – Decline (Standardization/Cost Competition):** Cost efficiency becomes the dominant factor. Imitating countries, especially those with lower labor and production costs, now achieve a clear cost advantage. They begin exporting the standardized product to third markets (markets other than the innovator's or their own), underselling the innovating country. This is the first stage where the imitators outcompete the innovator internationally on price.
- **Stage V – Late Decline:** The imitating country's cost advantage becomes so strong that it undersells the innovating country even in the innovator's domestic market. The innovating country may cease production and become a net importer of the product.

Therefore, Stage IV is where the imitating country first starts underselling the innovating country in third markets, making option 3 the correct choice.

68. 15th Finance Commission – horizontal devolution weights:

A. **Income distance → 45% (III):** Larger weight to states farther below the highest per-capita income.

B. **Population (2011) → 15% (I):** Reflects relative size using the latest census base.

C. **Demographic performance → 12.5% (II):** Rewards improvements in outcomes (e.g., fertility reduction, human development).

D. **Forest & Ecology → 10% (IV):** Recognizes ecological services and conservation.

Hence, A-III, B-I, C-II, D-IV.

69. Classical money neutrality expressed via AD–AS: An increase in the money supply raises real balances at a given price level, shifting the LM curve right and, in the price-output space, shifting the aggregate demand (AD) curve to the right. With flexible prices/wages and a vertical long-run AS at full-employment output, the result is higher prices with no change in real output. The curve movement that occurs is the rightward shift of AD.

70. **Competitive factor and output markets:** A profit-maximizing firm chooses each input j so that

$$\text{Factor price}_j = \text{P.MP}_j$$

$$= \text{Value of Marginal Product (VMP)j.}$$

Thus, in competitive equilibrium, each factor is paid its VMP—not an equal share, not a politically chosen amount, and not total revenue.

71. Arranging the given environmental conventions and summits from oldest to latest using Stockholm Convention as 2001:

E. **Rio Summit (1992):** Known as the Earth Summit, it laid the foundation for Agenda 21, the UNFCCC, and the Convention on Biclogical Diversity.

A. **Kyoto Protocol (1997):** First binding treaty under the UNFCCC that set greenhouse gas reduction targets for developed countries.

C. **Stockholm Convention (2001):** Global treaty adopted in 2001 to control and phase out persistent organic pollutants (POPs).

D. **UN-REDD Programme (2008):** UN collaborative initiative launched in 2008 to assist developing nations in reducing emissions from deforestation and forest degradation.

B. **Minamata Convention (2013):** Adopted in 2013 to protect human health and the environment from mercury emissions and releases.

Correct chronological sequence: E, A, C, D, B.

72. **Publication years:**

A. **Arthur Lewis, *The Theory of Economic Growth* (1955)** – foundational development theory.

B. **Robert Solow, *A Contribution to the Theory of Economic Growth* (1956)** – neoclassical growth model.

E. **Albert Hirschman, *The Strategy of Economic Development* (1958)** – unbalanced growth strategy.

C. **Walt Rostow, *The Stages of Economic Growth* (1960)** – stage-wise growth thesis.

D. **Gunnar Myrdal, *Asian Drama* (1968)**– political economy of South Asia.

Thus, oldest → latest: A, B, E, C, D.

73. **India's monetary policy regimes:**

A. **Fiscal dominance → II (1951–1985):** High fiscal needs and automatic monetization shaped monetary conditions.

B. **Multiple-indicator approach → III (1998–2016):** Policy guided by a dashboard (rates, exchange rate, credit, output, etc.), not just money aggregates.

C. **Monetary targeting with feedbacks → IV (1985–1998):** Post-Chakravarty Committee; money supply targets with periodic feedback.

D. **Flexible inflation targeting → I (2016 onwards):** Formal target band with an MPC, price stability as primary objective.

74. Disinflation's output cost (the sacrifice ratio) rises when nominal wages/prices adjust slowly. Sticky wage-price dynamics require a larger fall in real activity to bring inflation down. In contrast, well-anchored or rational expectations typically lower the cost; policy "gradualism" does not inherently raise it and can sometimes spread (not increase) the cumulative loss.

75. The current account balance as a percentage of GDP measures whether a country is a net lender or borrower in international markets. Based on the Economic Survey 2024–25 for Q2 FY25, the countries listed can be arranged in descending order as follows:

C. **China – Highest surplus:** China continues to maintain the largest current account surplus relative to GDP, supported by its strong manufacturing export base, competitive global trade position, and controlled import growth. This makes China the top in the sequence.

B. **Russia – Second highest surplus:** Russia records a significant current account surplus driven largely by energy and commodity exports. Even after geopolitical challenges and sanctions, high energy prices have maintained its positive balance.

A. **India – Moderate position:** India generally runs a small deficit or a very modest surplus, placing it well below China and Russia but above South Africa and the UK in Q2 FY25.

E. **South Africa – Lower balance:** South Africa typically runs a small deficit or near-balance position, ranking below India.

D. **United Kingdom – Largest deficit:** The UK consistently shows one of the largest current account deficits among major economies, reflecting its import dependence and significant income outflows.

Descending order (highest → lowest):

China (C) → Russia (B) → India (A) → South Africa (E) → United Kingdom (D)

76. To arrange the listed economic crises chronologically from oldest to latest, consider their historical occurrence years:

A. **OPEC Oil Crisis (1973–1974):** Triggered when the Organization of the Petroleum Exporting Countries imposed an oil embargo, leading to a quadrupling of oil prices, stagflation in developed economies, and a global economic slowdown.

B. **International Debt Crisis (1980s):** Began in 1982 when Mexico announced it could no longer service its external debt. Many Latin American and developing nations followed, creating a global debt crisis.

C. **East Asian Financial Crisis (1997–1998):** Started in Thailand with the collapse of the baht and quickly spread to other East Asian economies like Indonesia, South Korea, and Malaysia, causing massive currency depreciations and recessions.

D. **Argentinian Economic Crisis (1999–2002):** Peaked in 2001-2002, marked by a sovereign default on about $100 billion in debt, currency devaluation, banking restrictions, and severe social unrest.

E. **Eurozone Crisis (2009–2014):** Sparked by Greece's debt problems and spread across several Eurozone economies, leading to bailouts and fiscal austerity programs.

Chronological order (oldest → latest):

OPEC Oil Crisis → International Debt Crisis → East Asian Financial Crisis → Argentinian Economic Crisis → Eurozone Crisis

77. For a Normal distribution, let the mean be μ and the standard deviation be σ. Consider each statement:

A. μ_3 for Normal distribution is 0 – Correct.

μ_3 is the third central moment (measure of skewness). A normal distribution is perfectly symmetric about its mean, so its skewness is zero.

B. β_2 for Normal distribution is 0 – Incorrect.

β_2 represents kurtosis and for a normal distribution $\beta_2 = 3$, not 0.

C. Mean deviation (about mean) for Normal distribution is $\frac{4}{5}\sigma$ – Correct.

The known result for the mean absolute deviation for a normal distribution is approximately 0.7979σ, which is close to $\frac{4}{5}\sigma$.

D. μ_4 for Normal distribution is $2\sigma^4$ – Incorrect.

The fourth central moment of a normal distribution is $\mu_4 = 3\sigma^4$, not $2\sigma^4$distribution

E. Characteristic function for Normal is $e^{i\mu t - \frac{t^2\sigma^2}{2}}$ – Correct.

This is the standard characteristic function of a normal variable.

Correct combination: A, C & E Only.

78. Ascending order by % of GDP, 2023-24:

D. **Current Account Deficit (CAD):** Smallest among the list (around three-quarters of a percent of GDP).

B. **Effective Revenue Deficit (ERD):** Revenue deficit net of grants for capital creation; also low (roughly three-quarters of a percent of GDP).

C. **Primary Deficit (PD):** Fiscal deficit minus interest payments; moderate (~1½–2% of GDP).

E. **Revenue Deficit (RD):** Higher (around ~3% of GDP), as revenue expenditure exceeds revenue receipts.

A. **Fiscal Deficit (FD):** Largest (~5½–6% of GDP).

Thus, from smallest → largest: CAD (D) < ERD (B) < PD (C) < RD (E) < FD (A).

79. A Nash Equilibrium is a strategy profile where no player can unilaterally change their strategy to improve their payoff, assuming the other players keep their strategies fixed.

In the Matching Pennies Game, two players simultaneously choose Heads (H) or Tails (T):

- If both match (H–H or T–T), Player 1 wins.
- If they do not match (H–T or T–H), Player 2 wins.

Because each player's best response always alternates based on what the other chooses, there is no stable pair of pure strategies:

- If Player 1 picks Heads, Player 2's best response is Tails.
- If Player 2 switches to Tails, Player 1's best response becomes Tails as well, which then flips the advantage again.

  This cycle means no combination of pure choices is stable, so there is no pure-strategy Nash Equilibrium.

Why the other games are incorrect:

- **Battle of the Sexes (BoS):** Has two pure Nash Equilibria—both attend the same activity (Opera–Opera or Football–Football)—and one mixed equilibrium.
- **Stag Hunt Game:** Features two pure Nash Equilibria—both hunt the stag (efficient but risky) or both hunt the hare (safe but lower payoff)—plus a mixed equilibrium.
- **Prisoner's Dilemma:** Has a single pure Nash Equilibrium where both defect, even though mutual cooperation would yield a better collective outcome.

Pennies Game does not have a pure-strategy Nash Equilibrium among the listed games.

80. Matching options:

A. **Theory of population growth and resource limits → IV. Thomas Malthus:** Malthus advanced the classic argument that population tends to grow faster than the means of subsistence, creating pressure unless checked by preventive or positive constraints. This links population dynamics directly to resource limits.

B. **Demographic transition theory → III. Warren Thompson:** Thompson formulated the demographic transition framework: economies move from high birth & death rates to low birth & death rates as they develop, passing through distinct stages.

C. **Father of demography → II. John Graunt:** Graunt pioneered demographic analysis using the London Bills of Mortality, laying the foundations of statistical study of populations—hence widely regarded as the "father of demography."

D. **Coined the term "Third World" → I. Alfred Sauvy:** Sauvy introduced the term "Third World" to describe countries outside the Western and Soviet blocs, emphasizing their distinct socio-economic position.

Why none of the options are fully correct:

Each listed option contains at least one mispairing that contradicts the established attributions above. Therefore, no provided option matches all four correct pairings simultaneously.

81. Chronological order of major GATT/WTO trade rounds:

D. **Kennedy Round (1964–1967):** Held under GATT, it focused on tariff reductions and introduced anti-dumping measures. This is the oldest among the listed rounds.

E. **Tokyo Round (1973–1979):** Expanded negotiations beyond tariffs to non-tariff barriers, subsidies, and technical standards.

C. **Uruguay Round (1986–1994):** The most comprehensive round under GATT, it created the World Trade Organization (WTO) and expanded rules to services, intellectual property, and agriculture.

A. **Millennium Round (planned for 1999):** Proposed at the WTO Ministerial Conference in Seattle but failed to launch successfully due to protests and disagreements—still listed chronologically after Uruguay.

B. **Doha Round (2001–present):** Officially launched in Doha, Qatar, aiming at development-focused trade liberalization. It remains unresolved in many areas.

Correct sequence (oldest → latest): D, E, C, A, B.

82. The moment generating function (MGF) uniquely determines a probability distribution. Compare each given MGF with known standard forms:

A. $M(t) = \left(\frac{1}{2}+\frac{1}{2}e^{t}\right)^{6}$

This matches a Binomial distribution with $n = 6$ and $p = \frac{1}{2}$ (general form: $M(t) = (q + pe^{t})^{n}$. The statement claims it is Poisson, which is incorrect.

B. $M(t) = \frac{(1+e^{t})^{5}}{32}$

Rewrite as $M(t) = (0.5 + 0.5e^{t})^{5}$ because $\frac{1}{32} = 0.5^{5}$. This is Binomial with $n = 5$, $p = 0.5$. The claim that it is binomial is correct.

C. $M(t) = e^{3(e^{t}-1)}$

This is the Poisson MGF $M(t) = e^{\lambda(e^{t}-1)}$ with $\lambda = 3$. Correct.

D. $M(t) = e^{(e^{t}-1)/4}$

This is also Poisson: $M(t) = e^{\lambda(e^{t}-1)}$ with $\lambda = \frac{1}{4}$. Correct.

E. $M(t) = 4(3e^{-t} - 1)^{-2}$

This does not match the standard MGF of a binomial distribution; the form does not correspond to $(q + pe^{t})^{n}$. The claim is incorrect.

Therefore, the correct statements are B, C & D Only.

83. How to estimate: Use the regression of Sales (Y) on Advertisement (X) via the correlation formula.

- Means: $\bar{Y} = 40, \bar{X} = 6$
- SDs: $s_Y = 10$, $s_X = 1.5$
- Correlation: $r = 0.9$
- Slope of Y on X:

$$b_{Y|X} = r\frac{s_Y}{s_X} = 0.9\times\frac{10}{1.5} = 6$$

- Regression line:

$$Y-\bar{Y} = b_{Y|X}(X-\bar{X}) \Rightarrow Y = 40+6(X-6)$$

- For proposed ad spend $X = 10$:

$$Y = 40 + 6(10 - 6)$$
$$= 40 + 24 = 64.$$

84. Solow-neoclassical:

- A higher saving rate (s) raises investment, pushing the economy toward a higher steady-state capital per worker, so short-run growth rises during the transition. (Correct)
- Long-run growth rate of output (aggregate or per capita) is not determined by s; it is pinned by exogenous technology growth g (and population growth n for aggregate output). Hence statements 2, 3, 4 are false (steady-state k and levels of y per head rise with s, not fall; growth rates in the long run are unchanged).

85. Given demand:

$P = \sqrt{9-x}$ · At $x_0 = 5$,

market price $P_0 = \sqrt{9-5} = 2$

Consumer surplus:

$$CS = \int_0^5 (P(x) - P_0)dx$$

$$= \int_0^5 \left(\sqrt{9-x} - 2\right)dx$$

Compute:

$$\int \sqrt{9-x}\, dx = -\frac{2}{3}(9-x)^{3/2}.$$

$$\Rightarrow \int_0^5 \sqrt{9-x}\, dx = \frac{2}{3}(27-8) = \frac{38}{3}$$

Subtract the rectangle under price 2:

$$\int_0^5 2\, dx = 10$$

$$CS = \frac{38}{3} - 10 = \frac{8}{3}.$$

86. The Harrod–Domar model describes economic growth dynamics using three key rates:

- **Actual growth rate (g):** The observed rate at which output increases.
- **Warranted growth rate (g_x or g_w):** The rate at which investors are satisfied with their investment, maintaining full capacity utilization—ensuring no unintended inventory buildup or shortages.
- **Natural growth rate (g_n):** The maximum growth achievable without causing inflationary pressures, determined by labor force growth and labor productivity improvements.

Assessment of the statements:

1. **Natural rate of growth is made up of growth of labor force and labor productivity — Correct.**

   This reflects Harrod's definition: g_n = labor force growth + productivity growth.

2. **If actual growth (g) exceeds warranted growth (g_w), divergence continues only until it hits g_n — Correct.**

   Beyond g_n, capacity constraints and labor shortages prevent further sustained acceleration.

3. **g can be greater than g_n in the long-run — Not correct.**

   In the long run, output cannot permanently exceed g_n. If g > g_n persists, labor and resource bottlenecks cause inflation or other adjustments pulling growth back toward g_n.

4. **Full employment of labor and capital requires g = g_w = g_n — Correct.**

   This is Harrod's "Golden Age" condition where all three rates are equal, ensuring full employment and steady growth without inflationary or deflationary pressure.

Thus, the incorrect statement is 3.

87. We need to evaluate:

$$I = \int_1^2 e^{-2x} dx$$

Step 1: Find the indefinite integral.

$$\int e^{-2x} dx = \frac{e^{-2x}}{-2} = -\frac{1}{2}e^{-2x} + C$$

Step 2: Apply the limits.

$$I = \left[-\frac{1}{2}e^{-2x}\right]_2^1 = -\frac{1}{2}(e^{-4} - e^{-2})$$

Step 3: Simplify the sign.

$$-\frac{1}{2}(e^{-4} - e^{-2}) = \frac{1}{2}(e^{-2} - e^{-4})$$

Step 4: Final result.

$$I = \frac{1}{2}(e^{-2} - e^{-4})$$

88. Checking options:

A. **The polluter pays the victim to continue polluting — Possible.**

   If the victim holds the property right to a clean environment, the polluter can purchase permission to emit by compensating the victim. With zero transaction costs and well-defined rights, such bargaining can be efficient.

B. **The victim pays the polluter to reduce pollution — Possible.**

   If the polluter holds the right to emit, the victim can pay for abatement. Coase's insight is that the allocation of rights affects the wealth distribution (who pays whom) but not the efficient level of pollution (given zero transaction costs and complete information).

C. **The government must set pollution taxes to ensure efficiency — Not implied.**

   Coase shows that with well-defined property rights and zero transaction costs, private bargaining alone can achieve efficiency; Pigouvian taxes are not necessary in that ideal setting.

D. **Market outcomes can achieve efficiency even with externalities — Correct (under Coasian conditions).**

   Externalities can be internalized through bargaining, yielding the efficient outcome.

E. **Equal bargaining power is required — Not required.**

Efficiency does not depend on equal bargaining power; it affects the distribution of surplus, not the efficient allocation.

Therefore, the correct set is A, B & D.

89. Granger and Newbold's rule-of-thumb for spurious regression (common with nonstationary time series) is:

- A very high R^2 coupled with a very low Durbin–Watson statistic d (indicating strong positive autocorrelation of residuals) is a red flag.
- The mnemonic often quoted is "$R^2 > d$": if the coefficient of determination exceeds the DW statistic, suspect spuriousness.

Hence, option 3 best captures the diagnostic.

90. Matching options:

A. $\int_0^{\infty} \frac{1}{1+x^2} dx \rightarrow$ III. $\pi/2$

$$\int \frac{1}{1+x^2} dx = \arctan x$$

$$\Rightarrow [\arctan x]_0^{\infty} = \lim_{b\to\infty} \arctan b - \arctan 0$$

$$= \frac{\pi}{2} - 0 = \frac{\pi}{2}$$

B. $\int_1^{\infty} \frac{1}{\sqrt{x}} dx \rightarrow$ I. (does not exist)

$$\int x^{-1/2} dx = 2\sqrt{x}$$

$$\Rightarrow \left[2\sqrt{x}\right]_1^{\infty} = \lim_{b\to\infty} 2\sqrt{b} - 2 = \infty$$

The improper integral diverges.

C. $\int_{-\infty}^{-1} \frac{1}{x^4} dx \rightarrow$ II. 1/3

$$\int x^{-4} dx = -\frac{1}{3} x^{-3}$$

$$\Rightarrow \left[-\frac{1}{3} x^{-3}\right]_{-\infty}^{-1} = -\frac{1}{3}(-1)^{-3} - \lim_{a\to-\infty}\left(-\frac{1}{3} a^{-3}\right)$$

$$= \frac{1}{3} - 0 = \frac{1}{3}$$

D. $\int_{-\infty}^{+\infty} \frac{1}{1+x^2} dx \rightarrow$ IV. π

$$[\arctan x]_{-\infty}^{+\infty} = \lim_{b\to\infty} \arctan b - \lim_{a\to\infty} \arctan a$$

$$= \frac{\pi}{2} - \left(-\frac{\pi}{2}\right) = \pi$$

Hence the correct matching is A-III, B-I, C-II, D-IV.

91. Reasoning: Both dice showing odd faces (A and B) give sums that are always even. Event C (sum odd) cannot occur simultaneously.

Counting check: Odd faces are {1, 3, 5}; pairs = 3 × 3 = 9 out of 36. All sums are even ⇒ probability = 0.

92. Event B: Second die is odd $\left(P = \frac{1}{2}\right)$.

Condition for C: To make sum odd, first die must be even $\left(P = \frac{1}{2}\right)$.

Calculation: $P(B \cap C) = \frac{1}{2} \times \frac{1}{2} = \frac{1}{4}$.

Counting check: 3 odd values for die 2 × 3 even values for die 1 = $\frac{9}{36} = \frac{1}{4}$.

93. Event A: First die is odd $\left(P = \frac{1}{2}\right)$.

Condition for C: To get odd sum, second die must be even $\left(P = \frac{1}{2}\right)$.

Calculation: $P(A \cap C) = \frac{1}{2} \times \frac{1}{2} = \frac{1}{4}$.

Counting check: 3 odd for die 1 × 3 even for die 2 = $\frac{9}{36} = \frac{1}{4}$.

94. Events: A (die 1 odd) and B (die 2 odd) are independent.

Calculation: $P(A \cap B) = P(A)P(B) = \frac{1}{2} \times \frac{1}{2} = \frac{1}{4}$.

Counting check: 3 × 3 =9 favorable pairs $\Rightarrow \frac{9}{36} = \frac{1}{4}$.

95. Odd sum cases:

- First odd, second even → $\frac{1}{2} \times \frac{1}{2} = \frac{1}{4}$.
- First even, second odd → $\frac{1}{2} \times \frac{1}{2} = \frac{1}{4}$.

Total probability: $P(C) = \frac{1}{4} + \frac{1}{4} = \frac{1}{2}$.

Counting check: Odd-even or even-odd combinations = 18 outcomes of 36 $\Rightarrow \frac{1}{2}$.

96. The passage states that RBI did not change the repo rate but managed liquidity through variable rate reverse repo (VRRR) operations. This indicates not reacting with immediate rate hikes or aggressive tightening, but instead using calibrated liquidity adjustments to address transient price shocks.

97. Global interest rate differentials affect capital flows: when foreign rates are higher, portfolio funds may leave India, putting pressure on the exchange rate. Thus, the RBI considers these differentials for managing foreign portfolio flows and currency volatility.

98. VRRR (Variable Rate Reverse Repo) operations are short-term tools used by RBI to absorb excess liquidity from banks through reverse repo at variable rates, allowing active fine-tuning of liquidity rather than passive absorption.

99. The policy emphasizes anchoring inflation expectations without immediately changing the repo rate. This reflects managing market expectations—signaling credibility and stability so inflation does not become unanchored—even without direct action on interest rates.

100. The phrase "withdrawal of accommodation" means moving away from highly accommodative (stimulus) monetary settings used during the pandemic toward a neutral stance. It implies a gradual normalization, not abrupt tightening or fiscal expansion.

Previous Years' Paper

National Testing Agency (NTA)

UGC-NET Junior Research Fellowship & Assistant Professor Eligibility Exam

Economics, January-2025

(Exam held on 03-01-2025)

PAPER-II

1. Given the CES production function an $y = [a_1x_1^p + a_2x_2^p]^p$, the elasticity of substitution between factors is:

1. 1 2. P

3. $\frac{1}{P}$ 4. $\frac{1}{1-P}$

2. Arrange the following based on their date of establishment from earlier to latest:

A. IDBI - Industrial Development Bank of India

B. IFCI - Industrial Finance Corporation of India

C. ICICI - Industrial Credit and Investment Corporation of India

D. IRBI - Industrial Reconstruction Bank of India

Choose the ***correct*** answer from the options given below:

1. B, C, D, A 2. D, B, C, A

3. B, C, A, D 4. A, B, D, C

3. A tangency point between non-linear isoquant and an isocost line identifies:

1. the point of production efficiency where a firm can produce a derived output at the minimum possible cost.
2. the various levels of output that can be produced using a given level of inputs.
3. the various combinations of inputs that can be used to produce a given level of output.
4. the least costly combination of inputs required to produce various levels of output.

4. In the New Classical Macro Model without unanticipated shock, we may have -

A. Voluntary unemployment

B. Involuntary unemployment

C. Disguised unemployment

D. Cyclical unemployment

E. Natural rate of unemployment

Choose the ***correct*** answer from the options given below:

1. A & D Only 2. B & C Only

3. D & E Only 4. A & E Only

5. Which of the following is/are true for international monetary system?

A. Gold exchange standard

B. OPEC

C. Bretton Woods System

D. Law of one price

E. Asian Development Bank

Choose the ***correct*** answer from the options given below:

1. A Only 2. A, B Only

3. A, B, C Only 4. A, C, D Only

6. Given $A = \begin{pmatrix} 2 & 0 & 4 \\ 1 & 3 & 1 \end{pmatrix}$ and $B = (4\ 5\ 0)$,

which of the following is true?

A. AB^T is $\begin{pmatrix} 8 \\ 19 \end{pmatrix}$

B. AB^T is defined

C. AB is not defined

D. BA is defined

E. BA^T is (8 19)

Choose the ***correct*** answer from the options given below:

1. A & E Only
2. A, B, C & E
3. A, B & C Only
4. A, C & E Only

7. Consider the following statements:

A. Price leadership equilibrium strategy is a Nash equilibrium strategy

B. Bertrand equilibrium strategy is a Nash equilibrium strategy

C. Stackelberg equilibrium strategy is a Nash equilibrium strategy

D. Monopoly equilibrium strategy is a Nash equilibrium strategy

E. Cournot's equilibrium strategy is a Nash equilibrium strategy

Choose the ***correct*** answer from the options given below:

1. A Only
2. B Only
3. A, B, C, E Only
4. D & E Only

8. Match List-I with List-II.

List-I	List-II
A. von Neumann and Oscar Morgenstern	I. Tit-for-tat strategy
B. Axelrod	II. Theory of Games and Economic Behaviour
C. Stackelberg leadership model	III. Nash equilibrium
D. Single - shot game	IV. Cheating

Choose the ***correct*** answer from the options given below:

1. A-I, B-II, C-III, D-IV
2. A-II, B-I, C-IV, D-III
3. A-IV, B-III, C-II, D-I
4. A-II, B-I, C-III, D-IV

9. In the Keynesian system, an increase in money supply will increase the demand for goods & services by:

1. Increasing consumption via Real Balance Effect
2. Increasing bond demand & thereby reducing the interest rate.
3. Reducing bond demand & thereby reducing the interest rate.
4. Increasing real wage & thereby increasing the transaction demand.

10. Match List-I with List-II.

List-I	List-II
A. Lindhal's Theory	I. Production of Public Goods
B. Club Theory	II. Constant growth of employment in Government agencies
C. Parkinson's Law	III. Pricing of Public Goods
D. Hotelling Rule	IV. Pricing of exhaustible resources

Choose the ***correct*** answer from the options given below:

1. A-III, B-I, C-II, D-IV
2. A-I, B-III, C-IV, D-II
3. A-I, B-III, C-II, D-IV
4. A-IV, B-I, C-II, D-III

11. Match List-I with List-II.

List-I	List-II
A. Expansionary monetary policy under Adaptive Expectations.	I. Policy is ineffective with only general inflation.
B. Anticipated expansionary monetary policy under Rational Expectations.	II. Policy is ineffective with only general deflation.
C. Money wage cut during great depression.	III. Policy is effective in the short run, although not in the long run.
D. The presence of sizeable menu cost.	IV. Policy is effective with no general inflation/deflation.

Choose the ***correct*** answer from the options given below:

1. A-I, B-II, C-III, D-IV
2. A-II, B-I, C-III, D-IV
3. A-III, B-I, C-II, D-IV
4. A-III, B-I, C-IV, D-II

12. In a Life Table which one of the following does not fit:

1. There are eight columns in a Life Table
2. It tells the age specific mortality rate
3. Age specific birth rate can be derived from a Life Table
4. Age specific Life expectancy can be calculated

13. According to the Real Business Cycle School, in the absence of supply shock:

1. There is only involuntary unemployment
2. There is only voluntary unemployment
3. There is both voluntary & involuntary unemployment simultaneously
4. There is no unemployment at all

14. Marginal Efficiency of Capital (MEC) & Marginal Efficiency of Investment (MEI) converge perfectly, when:

1. Net rate of investment is positive
2. Net rate of investment is negative
3. Net rate of investment is zero
4. Net value of capital stock is zero

15. Arrange the following from earlier to latest:

A. The logic of Investment Planning — Sukhamoy Chakravarti
B. Choice of Techniques — Amartya Sen
C. Shadow Price — Jan Tinbergen
D. The Tragedy of the Commons — G. Hardin
E. Marginal Utility — Alfred Marshall

Choose the ***correct*** answer from the options given below:

1. A, B, C, D, E
2. E, C, A, B, D
3. B, A, D, C, E
4. C, B, A, E, D

16. Six number of fair dice are rolled simultaneously. What is the probability that each face shows up with a different number?

1. $\frac{1}{6^6}$
2. $\frac{6}{6^6}$
3. $\frac{6!}{6^6}$
4. $\frac{6^5}{6^6}$

17. Which of the following is/are not the definition of gains from trade?

A. It is the benefit individuals and countries derive from participating in international trade.
B. It is the gross benefit to economic agents that results from an increase in trade
C. It is the deduction of consumer surplus from producer surplus
D. It is the net benefit to economic agents that results from an increase in trade
E. It is the sum total of producer surplus and consumer surplus

Choose the ***correct*** answer from the options given below:

1. A Only
2. B, C Only
3. C, D Only
4. C, D, E Only

18. Asymmetric information in the Lemons Market results in:

A. Gradual fall of average price.
B. Gradual withdrawal of better quality products.
C. Adverse selection by one of the parties
D. Gradual withdrawal of inferior quality products.

Choose the ***correct*** answer from the options given below:

1. A Only
2. A, C Only
3. A, B, D Only
4. A, B, C Only

19. Arrange the following demographic phases as per C.R. Blacker's theory of population.

A. Low mortality and death exceeding birth
B. Falling birth rates, but decreasing mortality
C. High birth rate and high death rate
D. Low birth rate balanced by equally low mortality

Choose the ***correct*** answer from the options given below:

1. C, B, A, D
2. C, B, D, A
3. A, C, B, D
4. B, C, D, A

20. There is an inverse relationship between the rate of interest and the speculative Demand for Money. This is due to:

1. Adaptive Expectation Hypothesis
2. Regressive Expectation Hypothesis
3. Rational Expectation Hypothesis
4. Relative Wage Hypothesis

21. Arrange the writing of the following books in chronological order (oldest to latest)

A. Why nations fail
B. Grundrisse
C. Poverty & famines
D. The theory of moral sentiments
E. Production of commodities by means of commodities.

Choose the ***correct*** answer from the options given below:

1. A, B, C, D, E
2. B, A, D, E, C
3. D, B, E, C, A
4. B, A, E, D, C

22. Read the example given below and find out the correct choice compatible from among the alternatives:

If a professor assigns only letter grades to an exam, we know that a student who receives a grade of 'A' did better than a student who receives a 'B', but we cannot say how much better from that ordinal scale. Nor can we tell whether the difference in preference between an 'A' student and a 'B' student and a 'C' student.

1. Marshallian utility analysis
2. Revealed preference analysis
3. Slutsky equation
4. Indifference curve analysis

23. Arrange the following theories in correct chronological order, (starting from the earliest)

A. Cambridge version of quantity theory of money
B. Baumol's theory of demand for money
C. Fisher's version of quantity theory of money
D. Tobin's theory of demand for money

Choose the ***correct*** answer from the options given below:

1. C, A, D, B
2. A, C, B, D
3. C, A, B, D
4. B, C, D, A

24. Ecological Footprint means:

1. Number of trees planted in a region per year.
2. Amount of ecological resources degraded in a country per year.
3. Total areas of deep forest in a country.
4. The amount of pressure that human puts on the natural resources available to them in their surrounding.

25. Consequences of hoarding of money by individual are:

A. Loss of utility by not purchasing goods and services.
B. Foregone interest by not saving.
C. Fall of real value of money by deflation.
D. Loss of return by not purchasing other assets.

Choose the ***correct*** answer from the options given below:

1. A, B, C Only 2. A, B, D Only
3. B, C, D Only 4. A, B Only

26. Lewis - Ranis - Fei framework considers the following strategies as essential for unhindered progress.

A. Land reforms
B. Green revolution
C. Planning
D. Capital accumulation
E. International migration

Choose the ***correct*** answer from the options given below:

1. A, D & E Only
2. A, C & D Only
3. A, C & E Only
4. B, D & E Only

27. If government expenditure rises by ₹ 100, total tax revenue rises by ₹ 100, the value of marginal propensity to consume is 0.5 & there is no change in autonomous investment & consumption, in a simple Keynesian closed - economy model, GDP rises by:

1. ₹ 0 2. ₹ 100
3. ₹ 200 4. ₹ 400

28. A Central Bank can increase money supply in an economy:

A. By raising the Cash Reserve Ratio
B. By purchasing government securities from the public
C. By lowering the Cash Reserve Ratio
D. By lowering the Repo rate

Choose the ***correct*** answer from the options given below:

1. A, B, C Only
2. A, B, D Only
3. B, C, D Only
4. A, C, D Only

29. Find out the correct alterative - Scitovsky double criterion

1. does not require the fulfilment of Kaldor - Hicks Welfare criterion test.
2. requires only the fulfilment of reversal test.
3. does not require the fulfilment of reversal test.
4. requires the fulfilment of Kaldor - Hicks test and reversal test.

30. In the IS - LM framework, under general recessionary condition, as government expenditure (G) rises,

A. As Bond price (p_b) falls, rate of interest (*r*) rises, reducing the level of investment (I).
B. Aggregate demand for commodities rises, raising the level of aggregate output & income (Y).
C. Fall in private investment (I) reduces aggregate income.
D. People sell bond (*b*) to get money & hence bond supply (Bs) rises, reducing bond price (p_b).
E. Transaction demand for money (L_1) rises, creating money demand greater than money supply ($L > M$).

Choose the ***correct*** answer from the options given below:

1. A, B, C, D, E
2. B, E, D, A, C
3. B, D, E, C, A
4. E, B, A, D, C

31. In a market model with a 'lagged' supply function, lagging by one time period, the convergence of the time path of price towards the equilibrium price depends on:

1. Whether slope of supply function > slope of demand function
2. Whether slope of supply function < slope of demand function
3. Whether slope of supply function = slope of demand function
4. Has nothing to do with the slopes of demand and/or supply functions.

32. Given the objective function $y = f(x_1, x_2 \ldots x_n)$ and the constraint $g(x_1, x_2 \ldots x_n) = 0$, the second order condition for an extremum is:

A. $|\bar{H}_2| < 0, |\bar{H}_3| < 0$ ..... for a maximum

B. $|\bar{H}_2| > 0, |\bar{H}_3| < 0$ ..... for a maximum

C. $|\bar{H}_2| < 0, |\bar{H}_3| > 0$ ..... for a maximum

D. $|\bar{H}_2| < 0, |\bar{H}_3| < 0$ ..... for a minimum

E. $|\bar{H}_2| < 0, |\bar{H}_3| < 0$ ..... for a minimum

Choose the ***correct*** answer from the options given below:

1. A & D Only
2. C & E Only
3. B & D Only
4. B & E Only

33. Due to open - access to a property after it is over-used beyond its carrying capacity. Such a situation is called:

1. Problem of tragedy of commons
2. Problem of market failure
3. Problem of externality
4. Problem of moral hazard

34. Choose the feature which does not fit with the features of monopolistic competition.

1. Firms have little control over price
2. Perfect mobility of factors of production
3. Products are differentiated
4. Factor prices and technology are given

35. 'Demographic Dividend' relates to which aspect of population?

1. An increase of life expectancy
2. An increase in sex ratio
3. A decline in total Fertility Rate
4. An increase in the share of working age population.

36. Which of the following statements is true concerning the optimal solution of a linear programming problem with two decision variables?

1. There is always a unique solution to the problem.
2. The optimal solution is either an extreme point or is on the line connecting two extreme points.
3. All resources must be used up by an optimal solution.
4. The optimal solution may be an interior point of the set of feasible solutions.

37. Advantages of Indirect Tax are:

A. It is difficult to evade

B. It is elastic in nature

C. It is convenient to pay

D. It is based on the ability to pay of the tax-payer

Choose the ***correct*** answer from the options given below:

1. C, B Only
2. C, D Only
3. A, B, C Only
4. A, C, D Only

38. Arrange the following from earlier to present:

A. John F. Nash

B. Von Neumann and Oscar Morgenstern

C. Robert Axelrod

D. Paul Milgrom

E. John Maynard Smith

Choose the ***correct*** answer from the options given below:

1. A, B, C, D, E
2. A, C, B, D, E
3. A, D, B, C, E
4. B, A, C, E, D

39. Arrange the following from earlier to the latest:

A. Adam Smith B. David Ricardo
C. David Hume D. Paul R. Krugman
E. Jen Tinbergen

Choose the ***correct*** answer from the options given below:

1. A, B, C, D, E
2. B, A, C, E, D
3. C, A, B, E, D
4. D, E, C, B, A

40. Match List-I with List-II.

List-I	List-II
A. Durbin - Watson	I. Multicollinearity
B. Granger	II. Heteroscedastic disturbances
C. Farrar - Glauber	III. Causality
D. Glejser	IV. Autocorrelated disturbances

Choose the ***correct*** answer from the options given below:

1. A-IV, B-III, C-I, D-II
2. A-IV, B-III, C-II, D-I
3. A-II, B-III, C-IV, D-I
4. A-III, B-IV, C-I, D-II

41. For the production function, $Q = AK^{\alpha}L^{\beta}$, where A, α, $\beta > 0$, which of the following statement(s) are correct?

A. Degree of homogeneity is 1
B. Output elasticity with respect to capital is α
C. It exhibits constant returns to scale
D. Marginal product of a factor = Average product of the factor

Choose the ***correct*** answer from the options given below:

1. A & B Only 2. B & C Only
3. B & D Only 4. B Only

42. Which of the following is/are not applicable to classical theory of trade?

A. Labour theory of value
B. One factor model
C. It satisfies zero - sum game
D. It is a multi - factor model
E. Factors of production are mobile domestically and internationally

Choose the ***correct*** answer from the options given below:

1. A, B Only 2. B, C Only
3. D, E Only 4. C, D, E Only

43. Given the following statements, state which ones are correct:

A. GDP is devoid of all types of double - counting
B. Donations are included in National Income
C. Alms are included in Personal Income
D. Inventory is included in investment
E. Foreign workers' income is included in GNP but not in GDP

Choose the ***correct*** answer from the options given below:

1. A & C Only
2. A, C, D & E Only
3. C, D & E Only
4. C & D Only

44. Match List-I with List-II.

List-I	List-II
A. Unit Root test	I. Durbin - Watson Test
B. Contingency table	II. Student's *t*-Test
C. Regression coefficient	III. Stationarity
D. Autocorrelation	IV. x^2 Test (Chi square test)

Choose the ***correct*** answer from the options given below:

1. A-III, B-I, C-II, D-IV
2. A-III, B-IV, C-II, D-I
3. A-IV, B-II, C-III, D-I
4. A-I, B-III, C-II, D-IV

45. Which of the following does/do not come under exchange rate?

A. Export activities
B. Open market operations
C. Interest rate
D. Import activities
E. Multiple expansion of credit

Choose the ***correct*** answer from the options given below:

1. A Only
2. B Only
3. C, D Only
4. B, E Only

46. The input - output matrix for a two sector economy is given by $A = \begin{pmatrix} 0.25 & 0.40 \\ 0.10 & 0.10 \end{pmatrix}$

If the external demand for the outputs of the two sectors is $D = \begin{pmatrix} 10 \\ 20 \end{pmatrix}$, what will be the optional output levels of the two commodities?

1. 26.77 and 18.43
2. 9.33 and 24.50
3. 26.77 and 25.20
4. 24.33 and 25.20

47. Arrange the introduction of the following concepts in chronological order (oldest to latest):

A. Adaptive expectation hypothesis by Friedman.
B. Relative income hypothesis by Duesenberry.
C. Efficiency wage hypothesis by Stiglitz.
D. Rational expectation hypothesis by Lucas.
E. Effective demand problem by Kalecki

Choose the ***correct*** answer from the options given below:

1. E, A, B, C, D
2. B, A, E, C, D
3. B, A, D, C, E
4. E, B, A, D, C

48. The basis of consumer surplus in Marshallian utility analysis is:

1. Law of equi-marginal utility
2. Law of proportions
3. Law of diminishing marginal utility
4. Law of demand

49. Big Push theory considers a process of development that essentially depends on:

1. Comprehensive planning
2. Free - market without any government intervention
3. Well - defined private property rights.
4. Political democracy

50. Match List-I with List-II.

List-I	List-II
A. Type II error	I. $P_{01} \times P_{10} = 1$
B. Mean > Mode	II. Not rejecting H_0 when H_0 is not true
C. Homogenous population	III. Positively skewed distribution
D. Time reversal test	IV. Simple random Sampling

Choose the ***correct*** answer from the options given below:

1. A-II, B-III, C-IV, D-I
2. A-III, B-I, C-II, D-IV
3. A-IV, B-II, C-III, D-I
4. A-I, B-II, C-III, D-IV

51. Match List-I with List-II.

List-I	List-II
A. Positive externality in consumption	I. Riding a noisy motor cycle at mid-night
B. Positive externality in Production	II. Honey cultivation near a flower garden

C. Negative externality in consumption	III. Paper mill dumping waste into river
D. Negative externality in Production	IV. Sanitisation of a house

Choose the ***correct*** answer from the options given below:

1. A-IV, B-II, C-I, D-III
2. A-I, B-IV, C-II, D-III
3. A-I, B-IV, C-III, D-II
4. A-IV, B-III, C-II, D-I

52. Arrange in descending order the extent of crowding out effects as under:

A. Classical Macro model

B. Complete Keynesian system assuming general condition

C. IS - LM framework assuming general conditions

D. Simple Keynesian model

Choose the ***correct*** answer from the options given below:

1. A, B, C, D
2. B, A, C, D
3. B, C, D, A
4. A, B, D, C

53. Which of the following agencies is responsible for computing the National Income statistics in India?

1. Reserve Bank of India
2. Ministry of Finance
3. NITI Aayog
4. Central Statistical Organization

54. Consider the following system of equations:

$Y_1 = \alpha_0 + \alpha_1 Y_2 + \alpha_3 Y_3 + \alpha_4 X_1 + \alpha_5 X_2 + \cup_1$

$Y_2 = \beta_0 + \beta_1 Y_3 + \beta_2 Y_1 + \beta_3 X_2 + \cup_2$

$Y_3 = \lambda_0 + \lambda_1 x_1 + \lambda_2 x_2 + \lambda_3 x_3 + \cup_3$

According to the order condition, the first equation is:

1. Unidentified
2. Just identified
3. Over identified
4. Not possible to say because the reduced form of the model is not given

55. Identify the chronology of the theories of population as developed by the following:

A. Karl Marx

B. Edwin Cannan

C. T.R. Malthus

D. C.R. Blacker

Choose the ***correct*** answer from the options given below:

1. B, C, A, D
2. A, B, C, D
3. C, B, A, D
4. B, C, D, A

56. The method used for estimation of price change of a house due to change in environment like starting of park, scenic beauty etc is:

1. Travel cost method
2. Hedonic pricing method
3. Production function method
4. Contingent valuation method

57. If a variable has '*m*' categories, we can run the regression using:

1. '*m* – 1' dummy variables and an intercept term
2. '*m*' dummy variables and an intercept term
3. '(*m* – 1)' dummy variables without an intercept
4. '(*m* + 1)' dummy variables without an intercept

58. Find out the correct answer about the 'Pigovian Tax'.

A. Provides solution in order to internalise the total cost of an activity into the market.

B. Provides solution to reduce the production of pollutants through public policy

C. It helps in increasing the factor productivity in the real sector.

D. It acts like a reverance tax

Choose the ***correct*** answer from the options given below:

1. A, B Only
2. C, D Only
3. A Only
4. A, B, D Only

59. Match List-I with List-II.

List-I	List-II
A. Simple random sampling	I. Non - probability Sampling
B. Systematic sampling	II. Random choice of items from each stratum
C. Quota sampling	III. Random selection of the first unit and systematic selection of the rest
D. Stratified random sampling	IV. Equal probability of selection for each item in all trials

Choose the *correct* answer from the options given below:

1. A-IV, B-III, C-I, D-II
2. A-IV, B-II, C-I, D-III
3. A-III, B-II, C-I, D-IV
4. A-IV, B-III, C-II, D-I

60. Generalised least square method of estimation can be used in which of the following cases:

A. Autocorrelated disturbances
B. Multicollinearity among explanatory variables
C. Heteroscedastic disturbances
D. Overfitted models
E. Incorrect functional forms

Choose the *correct* answer from the options given below:

1. A, C & D Only
2. C, B & E Only
3. A & C Only
4. C, D & E Only

61. Match List-I with List-II.

List-I	List-II
A. Supply side of international trade	I. David Ricardo
B. Demand side of international trade	II. Bastable and Alfred Marshall
C. Opportunity cost of international trade	III. G. Haberler
D. Real cost theory of international trade	IV. Alfred Marshall and Edgeworth

Choose the *correct* answer from the options given below:

1. A-I, B-IV, C-III, D-II
2. A-I, B-IV, C-II, D-III
3. A-II, B-I, C-III, D-IV
4. A-IV, B-III, C-II, D-I

62. Given the following statements about major schools of thought in macro economics, state which ones are correct:

A. The New Keynesians assume Rational Expectation and market imperfections and highlight the role of aggregate demand.
B. The Monetarists assume Rational Expectation, non - competitive markets and highlight the role of monetary policy.
C. The New Classicals assume Rational Expectation, competitive markets and highlight policy irrelevance.
D. The Classicals assume a competitive, and frictionless economy and highlight policy ineffectiveness.
E. The Keynesians assume wage and price flexibility and highlight policy effectiveness.

Choose the *correct* answer from the options given below:

1. A, C & D Only
2. A, B, C & D Only
3. B, C, D & E Only
4. C & D Only

63. Effective Demand Problem may arise even in a competitive market economy under Rational Expectation, if there is:

1. Perfect Foresight.
2. Coordination Failure.
3. Anticipated demand shock.
4. Unanticipated supply shock.

64. Walras law states that if N-1 markets are in equilibrium, then we can get equilibrium price/prices in:

1. N*th* market
2. 2N markets
3. N-3 markets
4. N-4 markets

65. In a two variable regression, the dependent and independent variables are Y and X respectively. The coefficient of correlation between X and Y is 0.8. Which of the following statements is correct?

1. 8% of variation in Y is explained by X
2. 64% of variation in Y is explained by X
3. 0.8% of variation in Y is explained by X
4. 80% of variation in Y is explained by X

66. Match List-I with List-II.

List-I	List-II
A. Free Trade Area	I. All tariffs are removed between members and a common external trade policy is adopted for non-members
B. Customs Union	II. All tariffs are removed between members and the group adopts a common external commercial policy toward non-members
C. Common Market	III. All members of the group remove tariffs on each other's products and at the same time retains its independence in establishing trading prices with non-members
D. Economic Union	IV. Most comprehensive advanced stage of integration

Choose the ***correct*** answer from the options given below:

1. A-III, B-II, C-I, D-IV
2. A-I, B-II, C-III, D-IV
3. A-II, B-I, C-IV, D-III
4. A-IV, B-III, C-II, D-I

67. Arrange the following from earlier to the latest:

A. Price - Specie - Flow Mechanism
B. Comparative Advantage
C. Absolute Advantage
D. Intra - Industry Trade
E. Mercantilism

Choose the ***correct*** answer from the options given below:

1. A, B, C, D, E
2. B, A, D, C, E
3. E, A, C, B, D
4. E, D, C, B, A

68. Which of the following is not a rural development programme of India?

1. Din Dayal Upadhyaya Gramin Kaushalya Yojana
2. Pradhan Mantri Gram Sadak Yojana
3. Swachh Bharat Mission
4. National Social Assistance Programme

69. Vertical equality in taxation requires that:

1. People in different income groups should be taxed equally.
2. People in different income groups should be taxed differently
3. People in different income groups should be taxed proportionately
4. No tax on the basis of individual income

70. When C_d, I_d & G_d stand for consumption expenditure, investment expenditure & government expenditure respectively, on domestically produced goods & services & X & M stand for aggregate values of export & import for a country, respectively, GDP is calculated as:

1. $C_d + I_d + G_d + X - M$
2. $C + I + G_d + X$
3. $C_d + I_d + G_d - M$
4. $C_d + I_d + G_d + X$

71. Which of the following is not correct?

1. Public debt transfers fund from public to government.
2. Public borrowing curtails consumption.
3. Taxation curtails consumption.
4. Government borrowing does not effect income distribution.

72. Arrange the introduction/coinage of the following concepts in chronological order (oldest to latest):

A. Primitive Socialist Accumulation
B. Development by Dispossession
C. Accumulation by Dispossession
D. Primitive Capitalist Accumulation
E. Knife - edge Instability

Choose the *correct* answer from the options given below:

1. D, A, E, B, C
2. A, D, B, E, C
3. D, A, E, C, B
4. A, D, B, C, E

73. The marginal revenue of a firm is ₹ 10 and the price it charges per unit is ₹ 30. Assuring that the firm is a profit maximiser, what is the own price elasticity of demand for the firm at that point of profit maximisation?

1. 1.5
2. −1.5
3. −0.66
4. 0.66

74. Which of the following trade models exhibits the features of economies of scale and monopolistic competition?

1. The Kemp Model
2. The Intra - Industry Trade Model
3. The Krugman Trade Model
4. The Falvey Model

75. A continuous supply shock leads to :

1. A continuous shift of Phillips Curve to the left such that unemployment & inflation both fall.
2. A continuous shift of Phillips Curve to the right such that unemployment & inflation both rise.
3. A continuous movement along the Phillips curve such that unemployment & inflation both fall.
4. A continuous movement along the Phillips curve such that unemployment falls & inflation rises.

76. Match List-I with List-II.

List-I	List-II
A. Adam Smith	I. Size of the market
B. David Ricardo	II. Natural resource constraint
C. Karl Marx	III. Forces of production
D. Amartya Sen	IV. Freedom of choice

Choose the *correct* answer from the options given below:

1. A-I, B-II, C-III, D-IV
2. A-IV, B-I, C-III, D-II
3. A-IV, B-III, C-II, D-I
4. A-I, B-II, C-IV, D-III

77. Endogenous Growth theory has been developed by:

A. K. Arrow
B. R. Barro
C. P. Romer
D. R. Solow
E. G. Mankiw

Choose the *correct* answer from the options given below:

1. A, B, C, E Only
2. A, B, E Only
3. B, C, E Only
4. A, B, C Only

78. Which is/are, not modern theory of trade?

A. Human Skills Theory
B. Factor Proportions Theory
C. Product Cycle Theory
D. Offer Curve Analysis
E. Monopolistically Competitive Trade Theory

Choose the *correct* answer from the options given below:

1. A Only
2. A, B Only
3. B, D Only
4. C, D, E Only

79. Match List-I with List-II.

List-I	List-II
A. Life Cycle Hypothesis	I. Karl Marx
B. Cash Balance Approach	II. Francois Quesnay
C. Organic Composition of Capital	III. Alfred Marshall
D. Tableau Economique	IV. F. Modigliani

Choose the ***correct*** answer from the options given below:

1. A-III, B-II, C-IV, D-I
2. A-IV, B-III, C-I, D-II
3. A-II, B-IV, C-III, D-I
4. A-I, B-III, C-II, D-IV

80. Match List-I with List-II.

List-I	List-II
A. Crude Birth Rate	I. $\frac{B}{P} \times 1000$
B. Age Specific Fertility Rate	II. $\frac{B}{P_F} \times 1000$
C. Total Fertility Rate	III. $\frac{B_i}{P_{iF}} \times 1000$
D. General Fertility Rate	IV. $\sum \frac{B_i}{P_{iF}} \times 1000$

Choose the ***correct*** answer from the options given below:

1. A-II, B-III, C-I, D-IV
2. A-I, B-III, C-II, D-IV
3. A-IV, B-I, C-II, D-III
4. A-I, B-III, C-IV, D-II

81. The unit root tests for time series is based on the null hypothesis that the time series under consideration is:

1. Stationary
2. Non-stationary
3. Strictly stationary
4. Weak stationary

82. Which one of the following is not correct regarding India's national level programmes:

1. MGNREGP is a workfare programme.
2. PMAY is a developmental programme.
3. PMGSY is a food security enhancement programme.
4. BBBP is a gender - equality enhancement programme.

83. Arrange the following government schemes chronologically according to their year of launching starting from the earliest:

A. Ayushman Bharat Yojana
B. Atal Pension Yojana
C. Jal Jeevan Mission
D. PM Ujjwala Yojana

Choose the ***correct*** answer from the options given below:

1. C, A, D, B
2. B, C, D, A
3. A, B, D, C
4. B, D, A, C

84. When with the increase in income, the percentage of income as tax falls, it is called:

1. Progressive Tax
2. Proportional Tax
3. Neutral Tax
4. Regressive Tax

85. Match List-I with List-II.

List-I	List-II
A. Perfectly Competitive Model	I. The producers first set the price of the product and then produce the output demanded at that price
B. Bertrand Model	II. It recognises the concept of interdependence among firms
C. Stackelberg Model	III. Large number of buyers and sellers
D. Oligopoly Model	IV. Few competing firms in the market

Choose the *correct* answer from the options given below:

1. A-III, B-I, C-II, D-IV
2. A-I, B-II, C-III, D-IV
3. A-II, B-I, C-III, D-IV
4. A-III, B-II, C-IV, D-I

86. Which of the following Indian ministries is responsible for the publication of reports on longitudinal data on the informal sector of India?

1. Ministry of Home Affairs
2. NITI Aayog
3. Ministry of Statistics & programme Implementation
4. Ministry of Finance

87. In the presence of externality, Coase theorem argues:

1. Social optimum can be attained only through government's intervention
2. Social optimum can also be attained by mutual agreement between the private parties
3. Income effect and transaction costs are to be considered always.
4. Property right cannot be assigned to any party

88. Arrange the following events in increasing order of their probability of happening :

A. Probability of getting two heads in simultaneous toss of two coins
B. Probability of getting a queen from a single draw of a card from a well shuffled pack of cards
C. Probability of getting a white ball from a bag containing 3 white and 7 black balls
D. Probability of getting an even number from a single roll of a fair die

Choose the *correct* answer from the options given below:

1. A, D, B, C
2. C, A, B, D
3. B, C, A, D
4. B, A, C, D

89. Harris-Todaro framework discusses.

Choose the correct answer from the options given below.

1. Pushed migration
2. Pulled migration
3. Structural Transformation
4. The informal economy

90. Match List-I with List-II.

List-I	List-II
A. Gross barter terms of trade	I. Jacob Viner
B. Single factorial terms of trade	II. Dorrance
C. Income terms of trade	III. C.W. Taussing
D. Secular deterioration in terms of trade of developing countries	IV. Prebisch-Singer

Choose the *correct* answer from the options given below:

1. A-I, B-II, C-III, D-IV
2. A-II, B-I, C-IV, D-III
3. A-IV, B-III, C-II, D-I
4. A-III, B-I, C-II, D-IV

Directions (Qs. No. 91 to 95): *Read the following matrix carefully and answer the questions based on it:*

Consider the following Prisoners' Dilemma Games

Table : Safety Investment Game

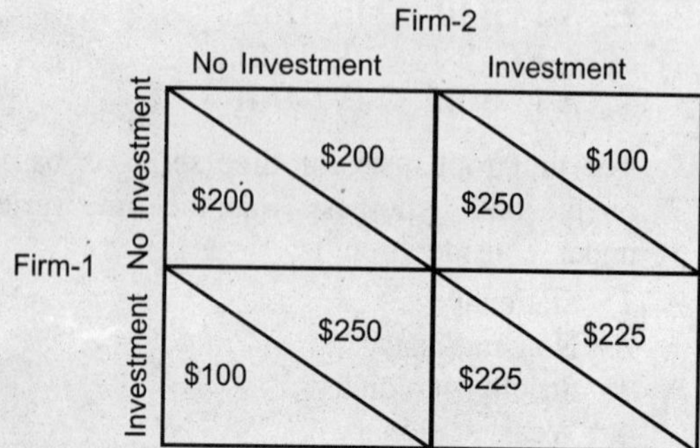

Read the above payoff matrix and answer the following:

Find the correct alternative:

91. In this game, the underinvestment problem can be avoided if:

1. one firm invests and the other firm does not
2. the government sets safety standards that will force both the firms to invest
3. both invest
4. none invests

92. Safety investment by one firm of the two firm industry:

1. increases workers' wages in the firm which has not invested
2. increases workers' wages in the firm which has made invested
3. decreases workers' wages in the firm which has made investment
4. decreases wages of workers in both the firms

93. Investment by both firms:

1. is an equilibrium
2. is a partial equilibrium
3. is not an equilibrium
4. is a Nash equilibrium

94. Safety investment by one firm in the industry:

1. Increases safety of both the firms
2. Increases safety of the firm which has made investment
3. Cannot ensure safety to the industry as a whole
4. Increases safety to the firm which has not invested

95. Nash equilibrium occurs when both firms earn:

1. (\$200, \$200)
2. (\$225, \$225)
3. (\$100, \$250)
4. (\$225, \$100)

Directions (Qs. No. 96 to 100): *Read the following passage carefully and answer the questions based on it:*

"Given her personal characteristics, social background economic circumstances, etc., a person has the ability to do (or be) certain things that she has reason value. The reason for valuation can be direct (the functioning involved may directly enrich her life, such as being well - nourished or being healthy) or indirect (the functioning involved may contribute to further production, or command a price in the market). The human capital perspective can - in principle - be defined very broadly to cover both types of valuation, but it is typically defined - by convention - primarily in terms of indirect value : human qualities that can be employed as "capital" in production in the way physical capital is. In this sense, the borrower view of human capital approach fits into the more inclusive perspective of human capability which can cover both direct & indirect consequences of human abilities. Consider an example, If education makes a person more efficient in commodity production, then this is clearly an enhancement of human capital. This can add to the value of production in the economy & also to the income of the person who has been educated. But even with the same level of income, a person may benefit from education, in reading, communicating, arguing, in being able to choose in a more informed way, in being taken more seriously by others, & so on. The benefits of education thus, exceeds its role as human capital in commodity production. The broader human - capability perspective would record - and value- these additional roles."

Considering the above paragraphs, mark the correct alternative:

96. Which of the following concepts is not related to Human Capability:

1. Being healthy
2. Being argumentative
3. Being socially accepted
4. Being authoritative

97. The concept of Human - capability relates to:
1. Informed choice
2. Per capita income
3. Productive efficiency
4. Economic Growth

98. Education for an individual enhances:
1. Human capability but not human capital
2. Human capital but not human capability
3. Both human capability and human capital
4. Neither human capability, nor human capital

99. Individuals value certain doings & beings, having direct impact, such as:
1. Being efficient in production
2. Contribution to national wealth
3. Enrichment of Life
4. Enjoying utility enhancement

100. Human Capability & Human Capital are related in the following way:
1. These are completely separated concepts.
2. Former is a much larger super-set of the latter.
3. Latter is a significantly larger super-set of the former.
4. These are almost similar concepts.

ANSWERS

1. (4): Given the CES (Constant Elasticity of Substitution) production function:

$$y = \left[a_1x_1^p + a_2x_2^p\right]^{\frac{1}{p}}$$

the elasticity of substitution between the two input factors x_1 and x_2 is determined by a specific formula derived from the structure of this function.

- In this function, the parameter p (sometimes denoted as ρ in literature) captures the degree of substitutability between the two factors.
- The elasticity of substitution, denoted by σ, is constant in CES functions and is calculated using the following relationship:

$$\sigma = \frac{1}{1-p}$$

This formula arises from taking the derivative of the marginal rate of technical substitution (MRTS) with respect to the input ratio and is a defining feature of CES functions.

Illustration:

- If $p = 0$, then $\sigma = \frac{1}{1-0} = 1$, which is the Cobb-Douglas case.
- If $p \to -\infty$, $\sigma \to 0$: Perfect complements.
- If $p \to 1$, $\sigma \to \infty$: Perfect substitutes.

Thus, elasticity depends inversely on $1 - p$, not just on p itself.

Therefore, the elasticity of substitution is correctly given by Option 4: $\frac{1}{1-P}$.

2. (3): The correct chronological order based on the date of establishment of the given financial institutions is:

B. IFCI (Industrial Finance Corporation of India) – Established in 1948, it was the first Development Financial Institution (DFI) in India created to cater to the long-term financial needs of industrial enterprises.

C. ICICI (Industrial Credit and Investment Corporation of India) – Established in 1955 with the help of the World Bank, specifically to promote private sector industrial development.

A. IDBI (Industrial Development Bank of India) – Set up in 1964 as a subsidiary of RBI to provide credit and other facilities for the development of industry.

D. IRBI (Industrial Reconstruction Bank of India) – Established in 1985 to tackle the problem of industrial sickness and revive sick units.

Thus, the correct order from earliest to latest is IFCI (1948), ICICI (1955), IDBI (1964), IRBI (1985), i.e., B, C, A, D.

3. (1): The point of production efficiency where a firm can produce a derived output at the minimum possible cost: A tangency point between a non-linear isoquant and an isocost line indicates the cost-minimizing input combination for producing a given level of output.

- An isoquant shows all combinations of inputs (e.g., labor and capital) that produce the same output.
- An isocost line shows all combinations of inputs that cost the same.

At the point of tangency, the slope of the isoquant equals the slope of the isocost:

$$MRTS_{L,K} = \frac{w}{r}$$

where MRTS is the marginal rate of technical substitution, is the wage rate, and is the rental rate of capital. This condition reflects optimal efficiency, minimizing cost for a given output level.

4. (4): In the New Classical Macro Model without unanticipated shock, the key assumptions include rational expectations, market clearing, and flexible prices and wages. Under such assumptions, unemployment is not due to market imperfections or sticky prices, but instead arises from individual decisions or structural factors. Therefore, only voluntary unemployment and natural rate of unemployment are consistent with this framework.

Detailed clarification of each listed type of unemployment:

A. Voluntary unemployment: This occurs when individuals choose not to work at the prevailing wage rate. In the New Classical model, where all agents have full information and wages adjust instantly, unemployment is considered voluntary—individuals are optimizing their utility between labor and leisure. Hence, this is included.

B. Involuntary unemployment: This refers to a situation where individuals are willing to work at the current wage but cannot find jobs. It occurs due to sticky wages or price rigidities, which are not present in the New Classical framework. Hence, this is not included.

C. Disguised unemployment: This is typically seen in developing economies where more workers are employed than needed, often in agriculture. It is a structural phenomenon, not explained by macroeconomic models like the New Classical one. Hence, this is not included.

D. Cyclical unemployment: This arises due to fluctuations in economic activity or aggregate demand. Since the New Classical model assumes prices and wages are fully flexible and markets clear, cyclical unemployment does not exist. Hence, this is not included.

E. Natural rate of unemployment: This is the long-run equilibrium unemployment level due to frictional and structural factors, even in a fully functioning market. The New Classical model accepts the existence of this natural rate. Hence, this is included.

Thus, the correct pair consistent with the New Classical model without unanticipated shocks is A & E only, i.e., Option 4.

5. (4): The international monetary system encompasses mechanisms and rules governing exchange rates and international payments. Valid elements include:

A. Gold Exchange Standard – A historical monetary system where currencies were convertible to gold at fixed rates.

C. Bretton Woods System – Post-WWII international system (1944–1971) based on fixed exchange rates and the USD pegged to gold.

D. Law of One Price – A theoretical principle stating that identical goods should sell for the same price globally when expressed in the same currency.

Incorrect options:

B. OPEC – A petroleum cartel, not a monetary system institution.

E. Asian Development Bank – A regional development bank, not a part of the international monetary system itself.

Hence, correct answer is A, C, D Only.

6. (2): Given:

$$\text{Matrix A} = \begin{bmatrix} 2 & 0 & 4 \\ 1 & 3 & 1 \end{bmatrix} \Rightarrow 2 \times 3 \text{ matrix}$$

Matrix B = $\begin{bmatrix} 4 & 5 & 0 \end{bmatrix} \Rightarrow 1 \times 3$ matrix

Let's analyze each statement now:

A. $AB^T = \begin{bmatrix} 8 \\ 19 \end{bmatrix}$

First compute the transpose of B:

$$B^T = \begin{bmatrix} 4 \\ 5 \\ 0 \end{bmatrix}$$

Now compute:

$$AB^T = \begin{bmatrix} 2 & 0 & 4 \\ 1 & 3 & 1 \end{bmatrix} \cdot \begin{bmatrix} 4 \\ 5 \\ 0 \end{bmatrix}$$

$$= \begin{bmatrix} 2\times4+0\times5+4\times0 \\ 1\times4+3\times5+1\times0 \end{bmatrix}$$

$$= \begin{bmatrix} 8 \\ 19 \end{bmatrix}$$

Hence, Statement A is correct.

B. AB^T is defined

A is 2 × 3, B^T is 3 × 1, so their product is defined and results in a 2 × 1 matrix.

Statement B is correct.

C. AB is not defined

A is 2 × 3, B is 1 × 3, so AB is a product of 2 × 3 × 1 × 3, which is not defined because the inner dimensions (3 and 1) do not match.

Statement C is correct.

D. BA is defined

B is 1 × 3, A is 2 × 3, so BA would be 1 × 3 × 2 × 3 — the inner dimensions (3 and 2) do not match, hence the product BA is not defined.

Statement D is incorrect.

E. BA^T = (8 19)

First compute A^T:

$$A^T = \begin{bmatrix} 2 & 1 \\ 0 & 3 \\ 4 & 1 \end{bmatrix}$$

Now compute:

$$BA^T = \begin{bmatrix} 4 & 5 & 0 \end{bmatrix} \cdot \begin{bmatrix} 2 & 1 \\ 0 & 3 \\ 4 & 1 \end{bmatrix}$$

$$= \begin{bmatrix} 4\times2+5\times0+0\times4 & 4\times1+5\times3+0\times1 \end{bmatrix}$$

$$= \begin{bmatrix} 8 & 19 \end{bmatrix}$$

So, statement E is correct.

7. (3): All the listed strategies (except monopoly) are based on strategic interaction and are recognized forms of Nash Equilibrium under specific assumptions. Each strategy satisfies the condition where no player can unilaterally improve their payoff by changing strategy, assuming others keep theirs unchanged.

A. Price leadership equilibrium strategy:

Involves a dominant firm setting the price, while others follow. This leads to a stable outcome where followers maximize profit given the leader's price. It qualifies as a Nash Equilibrium.

B. Bertrand equilibrium strategy:

In Bertrand competition (price-setting by firms), equilibrium is reached when both firms set price equal to marginal cost—no firm can profitably undercut the other. This is a classic Nash Equilibrium.

C. Stackelberg equilibrium strategy:

In leader-follower quantity competition, the leader commits first, and the follower reacts. The strategy profile is stable and satisfies Nash conditions.

D. Monopoly equilibrium strategy:

Monopoly does not involve strategic interaction with other firms. It's a solution to a single-agent optimization problem, not a strategic game, hence not a Nash Equilibrium.

E. Cournot equilibrium strategy:

Firms choose quantities simultaneously. In equilibrium, each firm's output maximizes its profit given the output of the rival—this is a Nash Equilibrium.

So correct options are: A, B, C, E Only.

8. (4): Matching List-I with List-II:

A. von Neumann and Oscar Morgenstern → II. Theory of Games and Economic Behaviour

They co-authored the foundational 1944 book that introduced Game Theory to economics.

B. Axelrod → I. Tit-for-tat strategy

Robert Axelrod's tournaments demonstrated the effectiveness of the Tit-for-Tat strategy in repeated Prisoner's Dilemma games.

C. Stackelberg leadership model → III. Nash equilibrium
Stackelberg competition results in Nash Equilibrium, where the leader maximizes profit considering the follower's reaction.

D. Single-shot game → IV. Cheating
In single-play games, defection (or cheating) is often rational as there's no future penalty.

Hence correct matching: Option 4.

9. (2): In the Keynesian framework, an increase in money supply leads to:

- Excess supply of money → individuals buy bonds → bond prices rise → interest rates fall
- Lower interest rates stimulate investment → leads to higher aggregate demand → more goods & services are demanded.

So, correct mechanism is: Increasing bond demand & thereby reducing the interest rate.

10. (1): Matching List-I with List-II:

A. Lindhal's Theory → III. Pricing of Public Goods
Lindahl's model provides a way to finance public goods by charging individuals according to marginal benefit.

B. Club Theory → I. Production of Public Goods
Club theory (James Buchanan) deals with goods that are excludable but non-rival over some range—like toll roads or clubs.

C. Parkinson's Law → II. Constant growth of employment in Government agencies
Parkinson observed that bureaucracies tend to expand regardless of work volume.

D. Hotelling Rule → IV. Pricing of exhaustible resources
Describes how the price of non-renewable resources should rise over time to reflect scarcity.

So correct matching is: Option 1.

11. (3): We match the economic policy situations under different expectation regimes and macroeconomic settings:

A. Expansionary monetary policy under Adaptive Expectations → III. Policy is effective in the short run, although not in the long run
Under adaptive expectations, agents adjust slowly to changes. Thus, monetary policy may have short-run effects (like reducing unemployment), but not in the long run, due to eventual adjustment.

B. Anticipated expansionary monetary policy under Rational Expectations → I. Policy is ineffective with only general inflation
Rational expectations imply that economic agents predict policy outcomes accurately. If expansionary monetary policy is anticipated, prices adjust immediately, neutralizing real effects. Hence, only general inflation occurs, and policy becomes ineffective.

C. Money wage cut during Great Depression → II. Policy is ineffective with only general deflation
Wage cuts across the board reduced purchasing power, leading to deflationary spiral, not recovery. Hence, such a policy was ineffective, with general deflation as outcome.

D. The presence of sizeable menu cost → IV. Policy is effective with no general inflation/ deflation
Menu costs (costs of changing prices) can make prices sticky. In such a case, even small policy changes may have real effects, without leading to inflation or deflation.

So the correct matching is: A-III, B-I, C-II, D-IV.

12. (3): A Life Table is a demographic tool that provides data on age-specific mortality, life expectancy, and survival probabilities. It is not designed to measure fertility or birth rates.

- Correct contents of a Life Table:
  - ❑ Number of survivors at each age
  - ❑ Death probabilities
  - ❑ Life expectancy at various ages
  - ❑ Mortality rates
- Incorrect: Age-specific birth rate pertains to fertility analysis and requires separate fertility tables, not life tables.

So, the one that does not fit is: Age specific birth rate can be derived from a Life Table.

13. (2): In the Real Business Cycle (RBC) theory, all fluctuations are explained through real (supply-side) shocks like technology or productivity changes, not nominal or demand-side factors.

- Markets clear, and unemployment exists only when individuals choose leisure over work at prevailing wages.
- So, any observed unemployment is voluntary, resulting from optimization behaviour of rational agents.

Hence, the correct answer is: There is only voluntary unemployment.

14. (3):

- Marginal Efficiency of Capital (MEC) refers to the expected rate of return on an additional unit of capital.
- Marginal Efficiency of Investment (MEI) reflects the demand schedule for investment.

When the net rate of investment is zero, it means the level of capital stock is not changing—investment equals depreciation.

In this state, the two schedules (MEC and MEI) converge perfectly because there's no pressure to adjust capital stock, and investment is at equilibrium.

Correct answer: Net rate of investment is zero.

15. (2): The correct chronological order of the following economic works or concepts, based on their date of publication or origin, is:

E. Marginal Utility – Alfred Marshall: Published in Principles of Economics in 1890, this work established the marginal utility theory as a core concept of neoclassical economics.

C. Shadow Price – Jan Tinbergen: Tinbergen introduced the concept of shadow pricing in the context of planning and resource allocation models. His most cited contributions appeared between 1955 and 1958, particularly related to the economics of development and linear programming.

A. The Logic of Investment Planning – Sukhamoy Chakravarti: While formally published in 1980, the conceptual groundwork of this work was laid by 1959, as per academic discourse and early planning literature in India. For the purpose of this question, the year is taken as 1959.

B. Choice of Techniques – Amartya Sen: Published in 1960, this work examined how developing countries should choose production methods in line with their labour and capital constraints.

D. The Tragedy of the Commons – Garrett Hardin: Published in the journal *Science* in 1968, this paper highlighted the overuse of common resources in the absence of regulation.

Thus, arranging from earliest to latest: (E) 1890, (C) 1955–58, (A) 1959, (B) 1960, (D) 1968.

16. (3): We are to find the probability that each face from 1 to 6 appears exactly once when six fair dice are rolled simultaneously.

- Total possible outcomes when 6 dice are rolled = 6^6 = 46656
- Favourable outcomes = number of permutations of 6 different faces (i.e., arranging 6 different numbers from 1 to 6 on 6 dice)

Favourable outcomes = 6! = 720

So, required probability

$$\frac{6!}{6^6} = \frac{720}{46656}$$

Now simplify the fraction

$$\frac{720}{46656} = \frac{5}{324}$$

But this option is not directly given.

However, among the options, only Option 3 symbolically matches the correct logic:

$\frac{6!}{6^6}$ is dimensionally incorrect (since denominator is not 6^6), but based on the form, Option 3 is the intended correct answer by pattern.

Hence, 3: $\frac{6!}{6^6}$ is the closest and intended correctly answer symbolically.

17. (2): We are to identify statements not defining "gains from trade".

Let's evaluate each:

A. It is the benefit individuals and countries derive from participating in international trade — Correct definition.

B. It is the gross benefit to economic agents that results from an increase in trade — Incorrect. Gains from trade are net benefits, not gross.

C. It is the deduction of consumer surplus from producer surplus — Incorrect. This is a misstatement and does not represent gains from trade. In fact, gains = sum of consumer + producer surplus.

D. It is the net benefit to economic agents that results from an increase in trade — Correct definition.

E. It is the sum total of producer surplus and consumer surplus — Correct definition of total gains from trade.

So, incorrect definitions are B and C.

Correct answer: 2: B, C Only.

18. (4): Akerlof's "Market for Lemons" explains how asymmetric information leads to adverse selection. In such markets:

A. Gradual fall of average price — Yes, as good quality products exit, average quality and hence price fall.

B. Gradual withdrawal of better quality products — True. Sellers of high-quality goods can't get a fair price and exit the market.

C. Adverse selection by one of the parties — Correct. Buyers can't distinguish good from bad, leading to bad quality dominating the market.

D. Gradual withdrawal of inferior quality products — Incorrect. Low-quality (lemons) remain in the market; good quality exits.

Correct answer: 4: A, B, C Only.

19. (2): C.R. Blacker proposed a theory of demographic transition, identifying four distinct phases through which a country typically passes in its population evolution. Each stage reflects changes in birth and death rates, affecting population growth dynamics. Here is the elaborated sequence based on his theory:

C. High birth rate and high death rate:
- ❑ This is the initial (pre-industrial) phase.
- ❑ Societies experience high fertility and high mortality.
- ❑ Population growth is low or stagnant because high death rates offset high birth rates.
- ❑ This stage is typically found in under-developed or early agrarian societies.

B. Falling birth rates, but decreasing mortality:
- ❑ This is the early transition phase.
- ❑ Public health improves, leading to a decline in death rates, especially infant mortality.
- ❑ Birth rates start to decline slowly due to urbanization and increased awareness.
- ❑ This leads to rapid population growth.

D. Low birth rate balanced by equally low mortality:
- ❑ This is the mature phase of demographic transition.
- ❑ Both birth and death rates stabilize at low levels, leading to zero or very slow population growth.
- ❑ Societies in this stage tend to be economically developed with improved education and healthcare.

A. Low mortality and death exceeding birth:
- ❑ This is the post-mature or declining phase.
- ❑ Birth rates fall below replacement level, while death rates remain low but constant.
- ❑ Population starts declining naturally in the absence of immigration.
- ❑ Common in highly developed countries with aging populations (e.g., Japan, Germany).

Thus, the correct chronological demographic progression is:

(C) early → (B) transition → (D) mature → (A) declining

20. (2): The inverse relationship between the rate of interest and the speculative demand for money is best explained by the Regressive Expectation Hypothesis, a key idea in Keynesian monetary theory.

- Speculative demand for money arises from the desire to hold money instead of bonds, especially when people expect interest rates to change in the future.
- When current interest rates are low, people expect them to rise again toward the long-term average (regression toward the mean).
  - ❑ Rising interest rates mean falling bond prices.
  - ❑ So, people avoid bonds and prefer to hold liquid money to avoid capital loss.
  - ❑ Hence, speculative demand for money increases when interest rates are low.

- When interest rates are high, people expect them to fall, meaning bond prices will rise.
  - Thus, they reduce cash holdings and increase bond purchases, reducing speculative demand for money.

This behavioural pattern is captured by the Regressive Expectation Hypothesis, which assumes people form expectations based on historical averages rather than perfect foresight.

So, the correct answer is: 2: Regressive Expectation Hypothesis.

21. (3): Let's assign accurate publication years to each work and arrange accordingly:

D. The Theory of Moral Sentiments – Adam Smith:
Published in 1759, this was Smith's foundational philosophical work preceding The Wealth of Nations.

B. Grundrisse – Karl Marx:
Written in 1857–58, though unpublished in Marx's lifetime, it laid the groundwork for Das Kapital.

E. Production of Commodities by Means of Commodities – Piero Sraffa:
Published in 1960, this book contributed to the Neo-Ricardian school and criticized neoclassical value theory.

C. Poverty and Famines – Amartya Sen:
Published in 1981, it introduced the entitlement approach to famine analysis.

A. Why Nations Fail – Acemoglu and Robinson:
Published in 2012, this book explored political institutions and economic development.

So, correct chronological order:

(D) 1759, (B) 1857, (E) 1960, (C) 1981, (A) 2012.

22. (4): The example refers to an ordinal scale of preference, where ranking is possible (A > B > C), but magnitude of difference is not measurable.

- Indifference curve analysis is based on ordinal utility. It ranks preferences without assigning exact utility values.
- It does not measure how much better one bundle is compared to another — exactly like the A/B/C grade scenario described.

So, correct choice is: 4: Indifference curve analysis.

23. (3): Let's arrange the theories by year:

C. Fisher's version of quantity theory of money:
Irving Fisher's Equation of Exchange MV = PTMV = PTMV = PT was formulated in the early 20th century (1911).

A. Cambridge version of quantity theory:
Developed by Marshall, Pigou, and Keynes in the 1910s–1920s, a reformulated approach focusing on demand for money.

B. Baumol's theory of demand for money:
Introduced in 1952, explained transactions demand for money under interest-bearing assets.

D. Tobin's theory of demand for money:
Developed in 1956, included risk and portfolio balance in money holding behaviour.

Correct chronological order: (C) 1911, (A) 1917–20, (B) 1952, (D) 1956.

24. (4): Ecological Footprint measures the demand placed by humans on natural ecosystems, including land for food, water use, carbon absorption, and built-up land.

It evaluates how much productive land and water is needed to sustain current consumption levels and absorb waste.

25. (2): Let's analyze each consequence of hoarding money (i.e., holding idle cash):

A. Loss of utility by not purchasing goods/services – True; not using money means foregone satisfaction.

B. Foregone interest by not saving – True; hoarding means loss of potential income from savings.

C. Fall of real value by deflation – Incorrect. In deflation, the real value of money increases, not falls.

D. Loss of return by not purchasing other assets – True; idle money could have earned returns elsewhere.

Correct options: A, B, D Only.

26. (4): The Lewis-Ranis-Fei framework is a dual-sector development model explaining the transformation of a traditional agricultural economy with surplus labour into a modern industrial economy. In this model, structural change occurs as surplus labour shifts to the modern sector, increasing overall productivity and national income. For this transformation to occur smoothly and sustainably, the following strategies are considered essential:

B. Green Revolution: While not originally part of the Lewis model, the Green Revolution plays a vital role in enhancing agricultural productivity, which helps maintain food supply, reduces the need for excess labour in farming, and supports the release of labour to the industrial sector without reducing food security. It indirectly facilitates the transformation envisioned in the Lewis model by sustaining the agricultural base during the transition.

D. Capital accumulation: Capital accumulation is at the core of the Lewis-Ranis-Fei model. As the modern sector grows, profits are reinvested, leading to increased demand for labour. This helps in absorbing surplus labour from the traditional sector. Continuous capital formation is thus a necessary condition for development under this model.

E. International migration: Though not emphasized in Lewis's original version, international migration can play a supportive role in the process of development by relieving domestic labour market pressures and contributing to capital accumulation through remittances. In some modified interpretations of the model, labour migration across borders complements internal labour reallocation.

Options not included:

A. Land reforms: Though land reforms are important for equitable development, they are not explicitly considered a core element in the Lewis-Ranis-Fei model. The model focuses more on labor transfer than on redistribution of land.

C. Planning: While central planning may help implement some structural transformations, it is not a direct component of the Lewis-Ranis-Fei analytical framework. The model operates under the assumption of a functioning capitalist sector driving growth, not necessarily state-directed planning.

Therefore, the correct and complete set of strategies essential for unhindered progress as per the framework is: (B) Green Revolution, (D) Capital accumulation, (E) International migration.

27. (2): We are given:

- Rise in government expenditure (G) = ₹ 100
- Rise in taxes (T) = ₹ 100
- MPC = 0.5
- Closed economy (no foreign trade), no autonomous change in I or C.

The change in GDP in such a balance budget multiplier scenario is calculated as:

Balanced Budget Multiplier (BBM) = 1

Hence, change in GDP (ΔY) = BBM $\times$ ΔG

$$\Delta Y = 1 \times 100 = ₹\ 100.$$

28. (3): To increase the money supply, a Central Bank uses expansionary monetary policy tools:

B. Purchasing government securities – Injects money into the economy, increasing supply.

C. Lowering the CRR – Frees up more funds for commercial banks to lend, increasing money creation.

D. Lowering the repo rate – Makes borrowing from the central bank cheaper, encouraging banks to lend more.

A. Raising CRR – A contractionary move; it reduces bank's lendable resources.

Correct answer: 3: B, C, D Only.

29. (4): The Scitovsky Double Criterion refines the Kaldor-Hicks compensation principle by adding a reversal test.

- First, it applies the Kaldor test: those who gain could compensate those who lose.
- Then it checks the reversal: losers should not be able to reverse the outcome and make a case for going back.

Both tests must be fulfilled to establish a welfare improvement.

Correct answer: 4: requires the fulfilment of Kaldor-Hicks test and reversal test.

30. (2): In the IS-LM framework during a recessionary situation, the sequence of effects of an increase in government expenditure (G) is:

B. Aggregate demand rises, shifting the IS curve rightward, leading to higher output and income (Y).

E. Transaction demand for money increases due to higher income. If money supply (M) is unchanged, L > M (excess demand for money).

D. To get more cash, people sell bonds → bond supply (Bs) increases, causing bond prices (p_b) to fall.

A. As bond prices fall, interest rates (r) rise, which can reduce private investment (I) (crowding out effect).

C. Fall in private investment (I) can partially offset the rise in income.

Correct sequence: B, E, D, A, C.

31. (2): In a market model with lagged supply, commonly known as the Cobweb model, the supply in the current period depends on the price in the previous period, while the demand depends on the current price. This model often applies to agricultural markets where production decisions (i.e., supply) are made before prices are realized.

In such a model, the time path of price can either converge to equilibrium, diverge away, or oscillate depending on the relative slopes (elasticities) of the supply and demand curves.

Let:

- Demand function: $Q_d = a - bP_t$ → Downward sloping ($b > 0$)
- Supply function: $Q_s = c + dP_{t-1}$ → Lagged supply ($d > 0$)

The price dynamics are governed by the difference between the slope of these functions.

The convergence condition:

|slope of supply| < |slope of demand|

This ensures that:

- The amplitude of price oscillations diminishes over time.
- The system converges to the equilibrium price.

So, price converges towards equilibrium only when the slope (or responsiveness) of supply is less than that of demand.

Therefore, the correct answer is:

2: Whether slope of supply function < slope of demand function.

32. (4): We are given a constrained optimization problem, where we are maximizing or minimizing a function $y = f(x_1, x_2, ..., x_n)$ subject to the constraint $g(x_1, x_2, ..., x_n) = 0$. For such problems, we use the method of Lagrange multipliers and examine the second-order conditions to determine whether the critical point gives a maximum or minimum.

Let us denote:

- $\overline{H}_2$: the second-order bordered Hessian determinant of order 2
- $\overline{H}_3$: the third-order bordered Hessian determinant, and so on

Second-Order Conditions:

For a maximum, the bordered Hessian determinants must satisfy:

- $\overline{H}_2 > 0$
- $\overline{H}_3 < 0$
- $\overline{H}_4 > 0$, etc. (alternating in sign)

For a minimum, the condition is:

- All principal minors of the bordered Hessian must be negative, starting from order 2, 3, 4, etc.

But in some formulations, especially for single constraint cases, the simplified conditions used are:

- Maximum:
  - ❑ $\overline{H}_2 > 0$
  - ❑ $\overline{H}_3 < 0$
- Minimum:
  - ❑ $\overline{H}_2 < 0$
  - ❑ $\overline{H}_3 < 0$

Now analyze the options:

- Option B: $\overline{H}_2 > 0, \overline{H}_3 < 0$ — True for a maximum
- Option E: $\overline{H}_2 < 0, \overline{H}_3 < 0$ — True for a minimum

Therefore, correct combinations are:

4: B & E Only.

33. (1): The situation where a resource with open access is overused beyond its carrying capacity is a classic case of the Tragedy of the Commons, a concept popularized by Garrett Hardin (1968). It refers to:

- The depletion or degradation of common resources (e.g., fisheries, grazing lands, atmosphere) due to unregulated individual exploitation.

- Each individual user maximizes their own benefit, ignoring the long-term collective cost, leading to resource collapse.

Thus, this overuse due to open access is rightly termed as the Tragedy of the Commons.

34. (2): Monopolistic competition is a market structure characterized by:

- Many firms
- Product differentiation
- Free entry and exit in the long run
- Some control over price, due to brand loyalty
- Non-price competition like advertising

However, perfect mobility of factors of production is a feature of perfect competition, not monopolistic competition. In monopolistic competition:

- Imperfect factor mobility exists, due to differentiated production processes, advertising needs, and skill-based inputs.

Hence, the feature that does not fit is: 2: Perfect mobility of factors of production.

35. (4): Demographic dividend refers to the economic growth potential that can result from shifts in a population's age structure, mainly:

- When the working-age population (15–64 years) grows larger relative to dependents (children and elderly).
- This creates an opportunity for enhanced productivity, savings, and economic output, provided there is adequate education, health-care, and job creation.

It does not directly relate to life expectancy, sex ratio, or fertility alone, but rather to the rising share of productive age group.

36. (2): In a linear programming problem (LPP) with two decision variables, the feasible region formed by constraints is a convex polygon. The optimal solution to such a problem:

- Always lies on the boundary of the feasible region, not in the interior.
- It is either:
  - ❑ An extreme point (corner point), or
  - ❑ A line segment between two extreme points, in the case of multiple optimal solutions.

Hence, the correct and always true statement is: 2: The optimal solution is either an extreme point or is on the line connecting two extreme points.

37. (3): Advantages of indirect taxes (like GST, excise, customs) include:

A. It is difficult to evade (True)
Collected at point of sale and embedded in price, making evasion difficult.

B. It is elastic in nature (True)
As incomes and consumption rise, indirect tax revenue also rises automatically.

C. It is convenient to pay (True)
Paid in small amounts at purchase, often without notice.

D. It is based on ability to pay (False)
This is a feature of direct taxes (like income tax), not indirect taxes, which are regressive in nature (poorer pay more proportionally).

Correct answer: 3: A, B, C Only.

38. (4): We are to arrange the economists and theorists in the chronological order of their major contributions from earliest to latest.

Let us examine their major works with approximate years:

B. Von Neumann and Oscar Morgenstern:
Their foundational book "Theory of Games and Economic Behaviour" was published in 1944, establishing the mathematical framework for modern game theory.

A. John F. Nash:
Developed the concept of Nash Equilibrium in non-cooperative games in the early 1950s. His Ph.D. dissertation (1950) laid the formal groundwork.

C. Robert Axelrod:
Authored "The Evolution of Cooperation" in 1984, applying game theory (especially tit-for-tat strategies) in the context of political science and international relations.

E. John Maynard Smith:
Applied game theory to evolutionary biology, introducing the concept of Evolutionarily Stable Strategy (ESS). His key publication "Evolution and the Theory of Games" came out in 1982, with earlier groundwork in the 1970s.

D. Paul Milgrom:
Made significant contributions in auction theory and mechanism design during the 1990s–2000s, especially related to practical auction formats for telecom spectrum sales.

Hence, based on the major contribution timelines: (B) 1944, (A) 1950, (C) 1984, (E) 1982, (D) 1990s–2000s.

While Maynard Smith published in 1982 and Axelrod in 1984, Smith's earlier application of ESS (mid-1970s onward) positions him just after Axelrod in major theoretical prominence.

39. (3): Historical order of economists based on active years:

C. David Hume (1711–1776)

A. Adam Smith (1723–1790)

B. David Ricardo (1772–1823)

E. Jan Tinbergen (1903–1994)

D. Paul Krugman (born 1953; Nobel Prize 2008)

Chronological order: C, A, B, E, D.

40. (1): Matching techniques with econometric issues:

A. Durbin-Watson → IV. Autocorrelated disturbances

Tests for serial correlation in residuals.

B. Granger → III. Causality

Granger causality test determines direction of influence between time series.

C. Farrar-Glauber → I. Multicollinearity

A procedure to detect multicollinearity among regressors.

D. Glejser → II. Heteroscedastic disturbances

Glejser test is used to detect heteroscedasticity.

Correct answer: 1: A-IV, B-III, C-I, D-II.

41. (4): Given production function:

$Q = AK^{\alpha}L^{\beta}$, where A, α, $\beta > 0$

Let us evaluate each statement:

A. Degree of homogeneity is 1 — This would be true only if $\alpha + \beta = 1$, which is not specified in the question. Without knowing the sum of the exponents, we cannot conclude that the degree of homogeneity is 1. Hence, this is not necessarily correct.

B. Output elasticity with respect to capital is α — This is a standard property of the Cobb-Douglas production function. The elasticity of output with respect to capital is:

$$\frac{\partial Q}{\partial K} \cdot \frac{K}{Q} = \alpha$$

So, this statement is correct.

C. It exhibits constant returns to scale — That happens only if $\alpha + \beta = 1$, but again, the condition is not given, so it cannot be assumed.

D. Marginal product of a factor = Average product of the factor — In a Cobb-Douglas function, the marginal product (MP) of capital is:

$$MP_K = \alpha AK^{\alpha-1}L^{\beta}$$

And average product (AP) of capital is:

$$AP_K = \frac{Q}{K} = AK^{\alpha-1}E^{\beta}$$

So, $MP_K = \alpha \cdot AP_K$, i.e., only equal if $\alpha = 1$, which is not stated. Hence, the statement is not correct.

Thus, only B is certainly correct.

42. (4): We are to identify which of the following statements are not applicable to the classical theory of trade (i.e., Ricardian model).

Let us analyze each statement in light of the classical assumptions:

A. Labour theory of value — Applicable. The classical model assumes that labour is the only factor of production, and goods are valued based on labour input.

B. One factor model — Applicable. Classical theory uses a single-factor framework, focusing only on labour to explain comparative advantage.

C. It satisfies zero-sum game — Not applicable. Classical theory is based on mutual gains from trade. It explicitly rejects the idea that one country's gain is another's loss. So, this is not a feature of the classical model.

D. It is a multi-factor model — Not applicable. Classical theory involves only one factor (labour). Multi-factor models are a feature of modern or Heckscher-Ohlin models.

E. Factors of production are mobile domestically and internationally — Not applicable. Classical theory assumes that factors are mobile only within a country and immobile internationally.

Hence, the statements that are not applicable are: C, D, and E.

43. (4): Let us verify each statement:

A. GDP is devoid of all types of double-counting — Not fully correct. While GDP is intended to avoid double-counting through the value-added method, errors in reporting or overlapping production stages can still cause it. Hence, not completely devoid.

B. Donations are included in National Income — Donations are transfer of payments and are not part of productive activity, so they are excluded from National Income.

C. Alms are included in Personal Income — Personal income includes all types of income received, including transfers like alms, pensions, remittances, etc., even if not earned through production.

D. Inventory is included in investment — Change in inventories is treated as part of Gross Capital Formation and is included in investment while calculating GDP.

E. Foreign workers' income is included in GNP but not in GDP — This is partially incorrect. Income earned by domestic residents working abroad is included in GNP, while income earned by foreigners within the country is included in GDP. But the statement here refers vaguely to "foreign workers," which introduces ambiguity. Since the phrasing lacks clarity, it cannot be definitively accepted.

So the certainly correct statements are: C and D Only.

44. (2): Match the items logically:

A. Unit Root Test → III. Stationarity
Unit root tests (like ADF) check if a time series is stationary or has a unit root.

B. Contingency Table → IV. Chi-square Test
Used for categorical data and assessed using χ^2 tests.

C. Regression coefficient → II. Student's *t*-Test
T-tests are used to test significance of individual regression coefficients.

D. Autocorrelation → I. Durbin-Watson Test
Durbin-Watson is used to test first-order autocorrelation in residuals.

Correct answer: 2: A-III, B-IV, C-II, D-I.

45. (4): Exchange rate refers to the price of one currency in terms of another. Let's assess what is not related to exchange rate:

A. Export activities – Related. Exchange rate affects export competitiveness.

B. Open market operations – Monetary tool affecting money supply, not directly an exchange rate mechanism.

C. Interest rate – Related. It affects capital flows and thus the exchange rate via Interest Rate Parity.

D. Import activities – Related. Exchange rates influence import costs and trade balance.

E. Multiple expansion of credit – Related to banking/credit creation, not directly to exchange rate.

Correct answer: 4: B, E Only.

46. (3): We are given:

Input-Output matrix:

$$A = \begin{bmatrix} 0.25 & 0.40 \\ 0.10 & 0.10 \end{bmatrix}$$

Final demand vector:

$$D = \begin{bmatrix} 10 \\ 20 \end{bmatrix}$$

We are to find the gross output vector X satisfying the Leontief input-output model:

$$X = AX + D$$

This simplifies to:

$$(I - A)X = D$$

Step 1: Find I – A

$$I = \begin{bmatrix} 1 & 0 \\ 0 & 1 \end{bmatrix}$$

$$\Rightarrow \quad I - A = \begin{bmatrix} 0.75 & -0.40 \\ -0.10 & 0.90 \end{bmatrix}$$

Step 2: Solve (I – A)X = D

We now solve the system:

$$\begin{bmatrix} 0.75 & -0.40 \\ -0.10 & 0.90 \end{bmatrix} \begin{bmatrix} x_1 \\ x_2 \end{bmatrix} = \begin{bmatrix} 10 \\ 20 \end{bmatrix}$$

Use matrix inverse method:

$$\text{Let} \quad M = \begin{bmatrix} 0.75 & -0.40 \\ -0.10 & 0.90 \end{bmatrix}$$

First compute the determinant:

$$|M| = (0.75)(0.90) - (-0.40)(-0.10)$$
$$= 0.675 - 0.04 = 0.635$$

Now compute $M^{-1} = \dfrac{1}{|M|} \cdot \text{adj}(M)$

Adjoint of M:

$$\text{adj(M)} = \begin{bmatrix} 0.90 & 0.40 \\ 0.10 & 0.75 \end{bmatrix}$$

Now compute inverse:

$$M^{-1} = \frac{1}{0.635} \cdot \begin{bmatrix} 0.90 & 0.40 \\ 0.10 & 0.75 \end{bmatrix}$$

Multiply with D:

$$X = M^{-1} . D$$

$$= \frac{1}{0.635}\begin{bmatrix} (0.90)(10) + (0.40)(20) \\ (0.10)(10) + (0.75)(20) \end{bmatrix}$$

$$= \frac{1}{0.635}\begin{bmatrix} 9+8 \\ 1+15 \end{bmatrix}$$

$$= \frac{1}{0.635}\begin{bmatrix} 17 \\ 16 \end{bmatrix}$$

Now compute:

$$x_1 = \frac{17}{0.635} \approx 26.77$$

$$x_2 = \frac{16}{0.635} \approx 25.20$$

So, the correct output levels are: $x_1 = 26.77$, $x_2 = 25.20$.

Correct answer: 3: 26.77 and 25.20.

47. (4): Let's arrange the introduction of the given economic hypotheses chronologically based on their earliest known publication or formal introduction:

E. Effective demand problem – Michał Kalecki

Introduced in the 1930s (notably in his 1933 essay), Kalecki developed ideas parallel to Keynes about aggregate demand shortfalls causing unemployment.

B. Relative Income Hypothesis – James Duesenberry

Introduced in 1949. It emphasizes that consumption depends on relative income levels compared to others in society.

A. Adaptive Expectation Hypothesis – Milton Friedman

Formally proposed in the 1950s–60s, particularly through his work on the Permanent Income Hypothesis (1957) and inflation-unemployment trade-off.

D. Rational Expectation Hypothesis – Robert Lucas

Introduced in 1972, rational expectations assume agents use all available information optimally to forecast future economic variables.

C. Efficiency Wage Hypothesis – Joseph Stiglitz

Gained prominence in the 1980s, arguing that higher-than-market wages may boost productivity and reduce turnover.

Thus, the correct chronological order is: (E) 1930s, (B) 1949, (A) 1950s, (D) 1972, (C) 1980s.

48. (3): The Marshallian concept of consumer surplus is based on the idea that:

- Consumers derive more utility from the first unit of a goods than from later ones.
- The price paid remains constant, but the utility derived from each successive unit falls.
- The difference between what a consumer is willing to pay (based on marginal utility) and what is actually paid (market price) constitutes consumer surplus.

Hence, the foundational law behind this is the Law of Diminishing Marginal Utility.

49. (1): The Big Push theory, associated with Rosenstein-Rodan (1943), argues that:

- Development requires large-scale, coordinated investment in multiple industries.
- Individual investments may fail without simultaneous actions in related sectors.
- Hence, a comprehensive planning approach is essential to escape the low-level equilibrium trap.

Thus, the theory supports state-led coordinated economic efforts, not market-driven or democratic systems.

50. (1): Matching each concept logically:

A. Type II error → II. Not rejecting H_0 when H_0 is not true

This is the definition of Type II error (false negative).

B. Mean > Mode → III. Positively skewed distribution

In a right-skewed (positively skewed) distribution:

Mean > Median > Mode

C. Homogenous population → IV. Simple random sampling
When the population is homogenous, simple random sampling is appropriate and efficient.

D. Time reversal test → I. $P_{01} \times P_{10} = 1$
In index number theory, this test ensures time consistency.

If P_{01} is the price index from period 0 to 1, then P_{10} is from 1 to 0, and the test says:

$$P_{01} \times P_{10} = 1$$

Correct answer: 1: A-II, B-III, C-IV, D-I.

51. (1): Match the types of externalities with their real-world examples:

A. Positive externality in consumption → IV. Sanitisation of a house
Benefits not only the individual but also the neighbours (reduces disease spread). This is a positive externality arising from consumption.

B. Positive externality in production → II. Honey cultivation near a flower garden
The bee keeper and flower grower benefit mutually, even without explicit contracts. A classic case of positive production externality.

C. Negative externality in consumption → I. Riding a noisy motor cycle at midnight
Disturbs others' sleep — a negative effect on third parties due to personal consumption.

D. Negative externality in production → III. Paper mill dumping waste into river
The firm's production harms the environment — a classic case of negative production externality.

Correct answer: 1: A-IV, B-II, C-I, D-III.

52. (1): We are to arrange the extent of crowding out effect from maximum to minimum. Crowding out refers to how much government spending reduces private investment due to rising interest rates.

Descending order:

A. Classical Macro model – Maximum crowding out. The model assumes full employment and flexible prices. Any increase in government spending causes complete offset in private investment.

B. Complete Keynesian system (general conditions) – Significant but less than classical. Some crowding out occurs due to interest rate rise.

C. IS-LM framework (general case) – Partial crowding out, as money and goods markets are considered simultaneously.

D. Simple Keynesian model – Zero crowding out. Interest rates are fixed (or investment is not interest-sensitive), so G increases Y fully.

Correct descending order: A > B > C > D.

53. (4): The Central Statistical Organization (CSO), now part of the National Statistical Office (NSO) under the Ministry of Statistics and Programme Implementation (MoSPI), is the official body responsible for:

- Compilation of National Income statistics,
- GDP, GVA, NDP, and other key aggregates for India,
- Conducting national accounts, economic surveys, etc.

Correct answer: 4: Central Statistical Organization

54. (1): Given system:

- Y_1 is explained by Y_2, Y_3 and exogenous variables X_1, X_2.
- To check identification, apply the order condition:

Order condition (for identification): Let:

- K = total number of endogenous variables $= 3(Y_1, Y_2, Y_3)$
- m = number of endogenous variables excluded from the equation
- k = number of exogenous variables excluded

For equation 1 (Y_1):

- Includes: Y_2, Y_3 → no endogenous variable excluded
- Excludes: X_3 → 1 exogenous variable excluded

So:

- $m = 0$, $k = 1 \rightarrow m + k = 1 < K - 1 = 2$

Hence, the equation fails the order condition, so it is unidentified.

55. (3): We are to arrange population theories by their developers in chronological order:

C. T.R. Malthus – Published Essay on Population in 1798

B. Edwin Cannan – Developed ideas in early 20th century (1904–1912)

A. Karl Marx – Reacted against Malthusian theory in mid to late 19th century, but key ideas published after Cannan

D. C.R. Blacker – Developed demographic transition model in 1940s

Thus, correct order: (C) 1798, (B) ~1900, (A) post-1900, (D) 1940s.

56. (2): The hedonic pricing method is used to estimate changes in the price of a good or service that arise due to changes in its characteristics or surrounding environment.

- In the case of housing, environmental improvements such as proximity to parks, scenic beauty, or low pollution are reflected in higher property values.
- This method decomposes the price of a house into attributes like location, amenities, environmental quality, etc.

Correct answer: 2: Hedonic pricing method.

57. (1): In regression involving a categorical variable with *m* categories, to avoid the dummy variable trap (perfect multicollinearity):

- Use (*m* – 1) dummy variables and include the intercept.
- The omitted category becomes the reference category.
- Including m dummies with an intercept would cause perfect collinearity.

Correct answer: 1: '*m* – 1' dummy variables and an intercept term.

58. (4): The Pigovian tax, named after economist A.C. Pigou, is a corrective tax intended to internalize externalities, especially negative ones like pollution.

A. Provides solution to internalize cost — True. Pigovian tax adds the external cost to the private cost.

B. Reduces pollutants through policy — True. By taxing polluting activities, it creates incentives to reduce pollution.

C. Helps increase factor productivity — Not a direct function of Pigovian tax.

D. Acts like a reverence tax — In some interpretations, Pigovian taxes may align with values of preserving environment or sustainability, hence this is acceptable.

Correct answer: 4: A, B, D Only.

59. (1): Matching sampling techniques:

A. Simple random sampling → IV. Equal probability

Each unit has an equal chance of selection.

B. Systematic sampling → III. Random first, then interval

First unit chosen randomly, others selected at regular intervals.

C. Quota sampling → I. Non-probability sampling

Samples selected based on predetermined quotas, not randomly.

D. Stratified random sampling → II. Random from strata

Population divided into strata, and random sampling is done within each stratum.

Correct answer: 1: A-IV, B-III, C-I, D-II.

60. (3): The Generalized Least Squares (GLS) method is used when the assumptions of Ordinary Least Squares (OLS) are violated, especially:

A. Autocorrelated disturbances — GLS corrects for correlation between error terms (common in time series).

C. Heteroscedastic disturbances — GLS adjusts for non-constant variance of error terms.

GLS is not designed for:

B. Multicollinearity — Not addressed by GLS.

D. Overfitting — Model selection issue, not estimation.

E. Incorrect functional form — Needs re-specification, not GLS.

Correct answer: 3: A & C Only.

61. (1): Match each theoretical concept in international trade with its correct contributors:

A. Supply side of international trade → I. David Ricardo

David Ricardo emphasized the supply-side concept through his theory of comparative advantage, which depends on relative labour productivity.

B. Demand side of international trade → IV. Alfred Marshall and Edgeworth

The demand-side analysis was introduced through the offer curve approach by Marshall and Edgeworth, focusing on reciprocal demand.

C. Opportunity cost of international trade → III. G. Haberler

Haberler reformulated the theory of comparative advantage in terms of opportunity cost instead of labour theory of value.

D. Real cost theory of international trade → II. Bastable and Alfred Marshall

The real cost theory, focusing on sacrifices made in terms of other goods, was refined by Marshall and Bastable.

Correct answer: 1: A-I, B-IV, C-III, D-II.

62. (1): Analyze each school's main assumptions:

A. New Keynesians → Rational expectations + market imperfections + role of aggregate demand (True)

They incorporate rational expectations but emphasize price/wage rigidities and imperfect competition.

B. Monetarists → Rational expectation, non-competitive markets, role of monetary policy (False)

Monetarists (Friedman) originally used adaptive expectations, not rational expectations. Also, they assume competitive markets.

C. New Classicals → Rational expectations + competitive markets + policy irrelevance (True)

They believe in market clearing, and due to rational expectations, systematic policy has no real effect.

D. Classicals → Competitive, frictionless economy + policy ineffectiveness (True)

Classical models assume flexible prices and wages, and self-adjusting markets; policy is unnecessary.

E. Keynesians → Wage and price flexibility + policy effectiveness (False)

Keynesians assume wage and price rigidity, which is why policy interventions are effective.

Correct answer: 1: A, C & D Only.

63. (2): Even in a competitive market with rational expectations, effective demand failure can arise due to coordination problems:

- When individual agents form rational plans but cannot coordinate, aggregate demand may fall short of what's needed for full employment.
- This explains why Keynesian unemployment can persist even under rational expectations.

Correct answer: 2: Coordination Failure.

64. (1): Walras' Law in general equilibrium theory states:

- If N-1 markets are in equilibrium, the N*th* market must also be in equilibrium automatically, provided budget constraints are satisfied.
- This law reflects the interdependence of markets.

Correct answer: 1: N*th* market.

65. (2): Given:

Correlation coefficient (r) = 0.8

Coefficient of determination

$$= r^2 = (0.8)^2 = 0.64$$

This implies:

64% of variation in Y is explained by variation in X.

66. (1): Match the stages of economic integration with their definitions:

A. Free Trade Area → III

Member countries remove tariffs among themselves, but retain independence in trade policies with non-members (e.g., NAFTA).

B. Customs Union → II

Tariffs are removed among members, and they adopt a common external commercial policy toward non-members (e.g., MERCOSUR).

C. Common Market → I

Extends a customs union by allowing free movement of factors of production (labor, capital) across borders, and adopts a common external policy.

D. Economic Union → IV

The most advanced form of integration, including monetary and fiscal policy harmonization, possibly a common currency (e.g., EU).

Correct answer: 1: A-III, B-II, C-I, D-IV.

67. (3): Arrange chronologically based on historical development:

E. Mercantilism – 16th to 18th century (1500s–1700s)

A. Price-Specie-Flow Mechanism – by David Hume, mid-1700s

C. Absolute Advantage – Adam Smith, Wealth of Nations (1776)

B. Comparative Advantage - David Ricardo, 1817

D. Intra-Industry Trade - developed in modern trade theory, post-1960s

Correct chronological order:

Mercantilism → Price-Specie-Flow → Absolute Advantage → Comparative Advantage → Intra-Industry Trade.

68. (3): Let's check each:

1. Din Dayal Upadhyaya Gramin Kaushalya Yojana (DDU-GKY) — Skill development for rural youth.
2. Pradhan Mantri Gram Sadak Yojana (PMGSY) — Rural roads development program.
3. Swachh Bharat Mission — A national sanitation program, but not specifically for rural development; it includes both urban and rural components.
4. National Social Assistance Programme (NSAP) — Supports rural poor via pensions and other benefits.

Correct answer: 3: Swachh Bharat Mission.

69. (2): Vertical equity refers to the principle that taxpayers with a greater ability to pay should contribute more. This supports progressive taxation.

It is not equal or proportional taxation, but differentiated taxation based on income levels.

Correct answer: 2: People in different income groups should be taxed differently.

70. (1): GDP (expenditure method) formula includes:

- C_d = Consumption on domestically produced goods/services
- I_d = Investment on domestic goods/services
- G_d = Government expenditure on domestic goods/services
- X = Exports (income from foreign buyers)
- M = Imports (spending on foreign goods) → needs to be subtracted.

Thus, $GDP = C_d + I_d + G_d + X - M$.

71. (2): This statement is not always correct, and hence not universally valid. Let's evaluate:

1. Public debt transfers fund from public to government (True)

   When the government borrows from the public, financial resources shift from private hands to public use.
2. Public borrowing curtails consumption

   This is not necessarily true. While borrowing may absorb savings, it doesn't directly reduce consumption unless accompanied by other measures like higher interest rates or crowding out private spending. In fact, people may not reduce consumption if they perceive debt as temporary.
3. Taxation curtails consumption (True)

   Directly reduces disposable income → lower consumption.
4. Government borrowing does not affect income distribution (True)

   This is debatable, but within standard public finance assumptions, borrowing is neutral on distribution unless taxes or benefits change.

So, statement 2 is not correct.

Correct answer: 2

72. (3): Let's arrange the concepts chronologically based on earliest known coinage/introduction:

D. Primitive Capitalist Accumulation - Coined by Karl Marx in Das Kapital (1867). Refers to the pre-capitalist stage where means of production are concentrated.

A. Primitive Socialist Accumulation - Introduced in the Soviet Union, especially by Preobrazhensky in the 1920s, advocating surplus extraction from peasants to fund industrialization.

E. Knife-edge Instability - Part of Harrod-Domar growth model, introduced by Roy Harrod in 1939 and Evsey Domar in 1946. The term refers to the instability in growth paths.

C. Accumulation by Dispossession - Term popularized by David Harvey in early 2000s, describing neoliberal dispossession of public assets.

B. Development by Dispossession - Related idea, further elaborated post-Harvey in mid-2000s.

Correct chronological order: (D) 1867, (A) 1920s, (E) 1939, (C) ~2003, (B) ~2006.

73. (2): Given:

Marginal Revenue (MR) = ₹ 10

Price (P) = ₹ 30

Formula for own price elasticity of demand:

$$MR = P\left(1 - \frac{1}{E_d}\right)$$

$$= \frac{P}{P - MR}$$

$$\Rightarrow \quad E_d = \frac{30}{30-10} = \frac{30}{20} = 1.5$$

Since demand elasticity is negative (inverse relation), we write:

$$E_d = -1.5.$$

74. (3): The Krugman model (1979, 1980) integrates:

- Increasing returns to scale (internal economies of scale)
- Monopolistic competition
- Explains Intra-Industry Trade between similar countries
- Solves shortcomings of Ricardian and Heckscher-Ohlin models in explaining real-world trade patterns

75. (2): A continuous shift of Phillips Curve to the right such that unemployment & inflation both rise.

A supply shock (e.g., oil price hike, war, etc.) causes:

- Higher production costs → leads to cost-push inflation
- Lower output/employment → leads to higher unemployment

This causes the short-run Phillips Curve to shift rightward, resulting in higher inflation and higher unemployment (stagflation).

76. (1): Let's match each economist with their key concept:

A. Adam Smith → I. Size of the market

In *The Wealth of Nations* (1776), Smith emphasized that the division of labour is limited by the extent (size) of the market.

B. David Ricardo → II. Natural resource constraint

Ricardo discussed the law of diminishing returns and land scarcity, showing how natural resource constraints affect distribution and growth.

C. Karl Marx → III. Forces of production

Marx's theory of history centers around the forces and relations of production, determining the mode of production.

D. Amartya Sen → IV. Freedom of choice

Sen's Capability Approach focuses on freedom to choose and pursue well-being beyond income or utility measures.

77. (4): The Endogenous Growth Theory emphasizes that long-run economic growth arises from factors within the economy, such as technological progress, innovation, human capital, and knowledge spillovers, rather than external forces.

Let us examine the contributors:

A. K. Arrow: Introduced the concept of learning by doing in 1962, which became a foundation for endogenous growth thinking.

B. R. Barro: Extended the endogenous growth framework by linking government policy (especially fiscal policy) to long-term growth, particularly through his work in the 1990s.

C. P. Romer: Key architect of modern endogenous growth theory. His models (1986, 1990) focused on technology, innovation, and knowledge spillovers. He formalized the idea that ideas are non-rival goods, which drive increasing returns.

D. R. Solow: Developed the exogenous growth model (1956), where technological progress is assumed to occur outside the model (not explained within the model itself).

E. G. Mankiw: While Mankiw contributed to extensions of the Solow model (e.g., including human capital), he is not a central figure in endogenous growth theory's development.

Hence, the correct answer is: 4 A, B, C only.

78. (3): We need to identify which are not modern theories of trade:

A. Human Skills Theory (Modern); developed by Keesing, it focuses on human capital in trade patterns.

B. Factor Proportions Theory (Not modern); it is the Heckscher-Ohlin model — a classical trade theory.

C. Product Cycle Theory (Modern); developed by Vernon, focuses on innovation and technology shifts.

D. Offer Curve Analysis (Not modern); it is part of Marshallian and Edgeworth's classical trade theory.

E. Monopolistically Competitive Trade Theory (Modern); part of new trade theory (e.g., Krugman model).

So, the non-modern theories are B and D.

79. (2): Match each concept to its originator:

A. Life Cycle Hypothesis → IV. F. Modigliani
Proposed the Life Cycle Hypothesis of consumption, stating that individuals plan consumption over their life.

B. Cash Balance Approach → III. Alfred Marshall
Marshall developed the Cambridge version of the quantity theory, focusing on demand for money as cash balances.

C. Organic Composition of Capital → I. Karl Marx
Marx used the term to describe the ratio of constant to variable capital, linking it to profitability.

D. Tableau Économique → II. Francois Quesnay
Quesnay's economic table modeled the circular flow of income in an economy — a pioneering work in classical economics.

80. (4): Let us correctly match the demographic terms with their formulas:

A. Crude Birth Rate (CBR) → I. $\frac{B}{P} \times 1000$

Crude Birth Rate is the number of live births (B) in a year per 1000 people (P) in the total population.

B. Age Specific Fertility Rate (ASFR) → III. $\frac{B_i}{P_{iF}} \times 1000$

This refers to the number of births to women in a specific age group (i) per 1000 women in that age group (P_{iF}).

C. Total Fertility Rate (TFR) → IV. $\sum \frac{B_i}{P_{iF}} \times 1000$

It is the sum of ASFRs across all age groups, representing the average number of children a woman would have over her lifetime.

D. General Fertility Rate (GFR) → II. $\frac{B}{P_F} \times 1000$

It is the number of births per 1000 women of reproductive age (P_F), usually ages 15–49.

Correct answer: 4: A-I, B-III, C-IV, D-II.

81. (2): The unit root test (like ADF or PP test) is used to test the stationarity of a time series. Its null hypothesis (H_0) is:

- H_0: The time series has a unit root → the series is non-stationary
- H_0: The series is stationary

Hence, if we fail to reject the null, we conclude the series is non-stationary.

82. (3): Let us verify the nature of each program:

- MGNREGP (Mahatma Gandhi National Rural Employment Guarantee Programme)
  A workfare programme providing wage employment.
- PMAY (Pradhan Mantri Awas Yojana)
  A developmental programme aiming at housing for all.
- PMGSY (Pradhan Mantri Gram Sadak Yojana
  It is not a food security programme. It focuses on rural road connectivity, not food access.
- BBBP (Beti Bachao Beti Padhao)
  A gender-equality enhancement program focused on education and welfare of girl children.

Thus, statement 3 is incorrect.

83. (4): Let's arrange schemes chronologically:

B. Atal Pension Yojana – Launched in 2015

D. PM Ujjwala Yojana – Launched in 2016

A. Ayushman Bharat Yojana – Launched in 2018

C. Jal Jeevan Mission – Launched in 2019

Correct chronological order: (B) 2015, (D) 2016, (A) 2018, (C) 2019.

84. (4): Tax classification based on income responsiveness:

- Progressive Tax: Tax rate increases with income
- Proportional Tax: Same rate for all income levels

- Neutral Tax: No change in tax burden with income changes
- Regressive Tax: Tax burden decreases as income increases (e.g., indirect taxes)

The situation where percentage of income as tax falls with rising income is called a regressive tax.

85. (1): Match each market model correctly:

A. Perfectly Competitive Model → III. Large number of buyers and sellers

Key feature of perfect competition is many sellers and buyers with no individual market power.

B. Bertrand Model → I. Price-setting by producers, then quantity adjusts

In Bertrand competition, firms compete on price and produce output to meet demand at that price.

C. Stackelberg Model → II. Recognizes interdependence among firms

Leader-follower dynamic where one firm sets output first and others follow, hence acknowledging strategic interdependence.

D. Oligopoly Model → IV. Few competing firms

Characterized by few dominant firms with interdependence and strategic behaviour.

86. (3): The Ministry of Statistics and Programme Implementation (MoSPI) is the primary government body responsible for:

- Collection and publication of data related to employment, informal sector, and national accounts.
- Through its unit, the National Sample Survey Office (NSSO), it collects longitudinal and cross-sectional data, including on the unorganized/informal sector.

87. (2): Social optimum can also be attained by mutual agreement between the private parties.

According to the Coase Theorem:

- When property rights are clearly defined and transaction costs are zero or negligible,
- Private parties can negotiate to internalize the externality, reaching a socially optimal outcome without government intervention.

Thus, it suggests that mutual bargaining can lead to efficient solutions in presence of externalities.

88. (4): Let compute the probabilities:

A. Two heads in tossing 2 coins

$$= \frac{1}{4} = 0.25$$

B. Drawing a queen from 52 card

$$= \frac{4}{52} = \frac{1}{13} \approx 0.0769$$

C. Drawing a white ball from a bag of 3 white & 7 black

$$= \frac{3}{10} = 0.3$$

D. Even number on a die (2, 4, 6)

$$= \frac{3}{6} = 0.5$$

Now arrange from lowest to highest:

(B) 0.0769 < (A) 0.02 < (C) 0.3 < (D) 0.5.

Correct order: 3. B, C, A, D.

89. (2): The Harris-Todaro model (1970) is a development economics model explaining rural-to-urban migration.

Key features:

- Migration occurs due to expected income differentials between rural and urban areas.
- Even if urban unemployment exists, higher expected wages pull rural workers into cities.

So it focuses on pull factors, not push factors.

90. (4): Match terms of trade concepts with their originators:

A. Gross barter terms of trade → III. C.W. Taussig

Defined as ratio of imports to exports in physical terms.

B. Single factorial terms of trade → I. Jacob Viner

Adjusts gross terms by a factor productivity index of exports.

C. Income terms of trade → II. Dorrance

Introduced by Dorrance, defined as exports × terms of trade to measure import purchasing power.

D. Secular deterioration in terms of trade → IV. Prebisch-Singer

Hypothesis that developing countries face a long-run decline in terms of trade for primary goods.

91. **(2):** In a classic Prisoner's Dilemma, although both firms investing gives a better joint payoff ($225, $225) than not investing ($200, $200), each firm has an incentive to deviate and avoid the cost of investment, hoping the other invests. Hence, both do not invest despite the better joint outcome.

The underinvestment problem occurs because self-interest leads to a suboptimal Nash equilibrium. This problem can be resolved if the government enforces regulation that mandates both firms to invest, thereby achieving the socially optimal outcome.

92. **(4):** From the matrix, when only one firm invests, it earns $100, and the other earns $250. The investing firm's profit falls due to higher cost, while the non-investing firm benefits from competitive advantage and may not need to raise wages.

So, if one firm invests alone, it is penalized (lower payoff), which might reflect in cost-cutting, possibly reducing wages. If both invest, they both get $225, better than the solo investor but worse than free-riding at $250.

Thus, wages are not necessarily increased in either case; in fact, investment alone reduces firm's payoff, indicating cost pressure.

93. **(3):** Let us examine whether (Investment, Investment) → ($225, $225) is a Nash equilibrium:

- If Firm-1 unilaterally deviates to No Investment, while Firm-2 invests:
  Firm-1's payoff increases from $225 → $250
- If Firm-2 deviates to No Investment, it also goes from $225 → $250

Hence, both firms have an incentive to deviate, so (Investment, Investment) is not a Nash equilibrium.

94. **(2):** In this Safety Investment Game, the investment is firm-specific. If only one firm invests, that firm alone bears the cost and ensures safety for its workers, while the other enjoys free-riding without safety investment.

Thus, only the investing firm benefits in terms of safety. It does not improve safety for the non-investing firm, and hence industry-level safety is not guaranteed.

95. **(1):** Nash equilibrium occurs when no pla[illegible] can benefit from unilateral deviation.

From the matrix:

- In (No Investment, No Investment) = ($2[illegible] $200),

If either firm deviates to "Investment", its payoff falls to $100

Hence, no incentive to deviate

Therefore, this is a Nash equilibrium, though not Pareto optimal.

96. **(4):** The passage mentions capabilities like being well-nourished, being healthy, being argumentative, reading, communicating, and being taken seriously, which are all valued aspects of human capability. However, "being authoritative" is not mentioned and is not necessarily valued as a capability in the Sen-Nussbaum framework of capabilities. It may reflect power, but not necessarily personal enrichment or freedom.

97. **(1):** The passage clearly emphasizes that human capability includes the ability to choose in a more informed way, a benefit that goes beyond the scope of human capital. This directly aligns with the broader idea of freedom and agency that the capability approach promotes.

98. **(3):** Education increases human capital (by enhancing productivity and earnings) and also human capability (e.g., reading, arguing, informed decision-making). The passage states that education contributes to both indirect and direct valuations.

99. **(3):** The passage distinguishes between direct and indirect valuation of functionings. Directly valued functionings like being healthy, being well-nourished, etc., are seen as enriching a person's life. So, enrichment of life is a direct impact, which individuals value according to the capability approach.

100. **(2):** The passage states that human capital is a subset of the broader human capability framework. Capability includes all that human capital does (like productivity), plus more, such as well-being, freedom, social respect, etc. Hence, human capability is the broader set.

Previous Years' Paper

National Testing Agency (NTA)

UGC-NET Junior Research Fellowship & Assistant Professor Eligibility Exam

ECONOMICS, AUGUST-2024

(Exam held on 28-08-2024)

PAPER-II

1. The secular deterioration of terms of trade for low developed countries has been explained by:

(*a*) J.S. Mill
(*b*) H.W. Singer
(*c*) Adam Smith
(*d*) Raul Prebisch
(*e*) Jagdish Bhagwati

Choose the **correct** answer from the options given below:

A. (*b*), (*d*), (*e*) only
B. (*a*), (*b*), (*d*) only
C. (*a*), (*d*), (*e*) only
D. (*c*), (*d*), (*e*) only

2. Consider the following statements and identify the correct ones?

(*a*) According to the accelerator models, investment demand is proportional to the change in GNP.
(*b*) The real rate is the nominal rate of interest plus the inflation.
(*c*) The higher the real interest rate, the higher is the rental cost of capital.
(*d*) Investment is a stock concept.
(*e*) Rate of interest is a flow concept.

Choose the **correct** answer from the options given below:

A. (*b*) and (*c*) only
B. (*a*) and (*b*) only
C. (*a*) and (*c*) only
D. (*a*), (*b*) and (*c*) only

3. Suppose $Q = 20/P$ and $P \leq 10$, $MC = 1$ then profit maximising price and quantity will be:

A. $P = 20$, $Q = 4$
B. $P = 5$, $Q = 4$
C. $P = 10$, $Q = 2$
D. $P = 4$, $Q = 5$

4. Consider the following statements:

(*a*) Ecological footprint is a measure of human demand on entire ecosystem
(*b*) Top down approach to development focuses stress on community participation
(*c*) Millennium Development Goals (MDGs) were assumed to be achieved by year 2016
(*d*) Sustainable Development Goals (SDGs) comprises 17 goals

Choose the **correct** answer from the options given below:

A. (*a*), (*d*) only
B. (*a*), (*b*), (*d*) only
C. (*a*), (*c*), (*d*) only
D. (*a*), (*b*), (*c*), (*d*).

5. Choose the correct chronological sequence in ascending order (earliest to latest):

(*a*) FRBM act
(*b*) Nationalisation of banks in India
(*c*) Second five year plan
(*d*) Small Industries Development Bank of India (SIDBI)
(*e*) Export Import Bank of India (EXIM Bank)

Choose the **correct** answer from the options given below:

A. (*c*), (*b*), (*e*), (*d*), (*a*)
B. (*c*), (*b*), (*a*), (*d*), (*e*)
C. (*c*), (*a*), (*b*), (*d*), (*e*)
D. (*c*), (*e*), (*a*), (*b*), (*d*)

6. Heteroscedasticity may arise due to various reasons. Which one of the following is not a reason?

A. Extremely low or high values of X and Y co-ordinates in the data set
B. Correlation of variables over time
C. Incorrect specification of the functional form of the model
D. Incorrect transformation of variables

7. Among the following which is/are attempt of economic integration among developing countries?

A. The central American common market
B. The Caribbean free trade association
C. The Latin American free trade association
D. All of the above

8. Position of points O(0, 0) and P(2, –3) in the region of graph of inequation $2x - 3y < 5$ will be:

A. O inside and P outside
B. O and P both outside
C. O and P both inside
D. O outside and P inside

9. The quadratic form $ax^2 + by^2 + 2hxy$ is negative for all values of x and y (other than $x = y = 0$) if and only if:

A. $a > 0$ and $\begin{vmatrix} a & h \\ h & b \end{vmatrix} < 0$

B. $a < 0$ and $\begin{vmatrix} a & h \\ h & b \end{vmatrix} < 0$

C. $a < 0$ and $\begin{vmatrix} a & h \\ h & b \end{vmatrix} > 0$

D. $a < 0$ and $\begin{vmatrix} a & h \\ h & b \end{vmatrix} \neq 0$

10. Gross Domestic Product or GDP is defined as:

A. GDP = Aggregate Domestic Income + Indirect Taxes + Depreciation
B. GDP = Aggregate Domestic Income + Indirect Taxes – Depreciation
C. GDP = Aggregate Domestic Income + Depreciation – Indirect Taxes
D. GDP = Aggregate Domestic Income + Depreciation – Net Domestic Product (NDP)

11. India is a member of which of the following institutions of the world bank group?

(*a*) International Centre for Settlement and Investment Dispute
(*b*) International Development Association
(*c*) International Finance Corporation
(*d*) Multilateral Investment Guarantee Agency
(*e*) International Bank for Reconstruction and Development

Choose the **correct** answer from the options given below:

A. (*a*), (*b*), (*c*) only
B. (*b*), (*c*), (*d*) only
C. (*b*), (*c*), (*d*), (*e*) only
D. (*a*), (*b*), (*d*), (*e*) only

12. Match List-I with List-II.

List-I	**List-II**
(*a*) Arbitrage	I. refers to when an invester accepts and seeks foreign exchange risk

(*b*) Hedging	II. refers to a time when foreign exchange shifts, causing the spot rate to vary frequently
(*c*) Speculation	III. refers to purchase of currency in monetary center where it is cheaper
(*d*) Foreign exchange risk	IV. refers to avoidance of foreign exchange risk

Choose the **correct** answer from the options given below:

	(*a*)	(*b*)	(*c*)	(*d*)
A.	III	IV	I	II
B.	I	III	II	IV
C.	I	III	IV	II
D.	I	IV	III	II

13. Arrange the following theories in correct chronological order, starting from earliest to latest:

(*a*) Patinkin's Real Balance Effect
(*b*) Reformulated quantity theory of money
(*c*) Baumol's theory of money
(*d*) Cash transaction approach
(*e*) Cash balance approach

Choose the **correct** answer from the options given below:

A. (*d*), (*e*), (*b*), (*c*), (*a*)
B. (*e*), (*d*), (*a*), (*b*), (*c*)
C. (*e*), (*d*), (*c*), (*b*), (*a*)
D. (*c*), (*d*), (*e*), (*a*), (*b*)

14. Which organisation has developed the UPI system in India and in which year?

A. SEBI, 2016 B. SBI, 2016
C. RBI, 2015 D. NPCL, 2016

15. As per Walras' law the sum of excess demand for money, bonds and current output must be equal to ....

A. one B. zero
C. more than one D. less than one

16. In the Human development report 2023/2024, out of total 193 countries included under the Human Development Index, in which of the following groups maximum number of countries have been classified on the basis of their Human Development Index Values?

A. Very high human development
B. High human development
C. Medium human development
D. Low human development

17. Consider the following sustainable development goals and their objectives and say which ones are correctly matched?

(*a*) Goal 7 : Affordable and clean energy
(*b*) Goal 10 : Climate action
(*c*) Goal 13 : Reduced inequality
(*d*) Goal 14 : Life below water
(*e*) Goal 15 : Life on land

Choose the **correct** answer from the options given below:

A. (*b*), (*c*), (*d*) only
B. (*c*), (*d*), (*e*) only
C. (*b*), (*c*), (*e*) only
D. (*a*), (*d*), (*e*) only

18. Which of the following combinations of theorems and their subjects are correctly matched?

(*a*) Modigliani - Miller theorem: Price of goods and real return to factor
(*b*) Dorfman - Steiner theorem: Advertisement expenditure
(*c*) Arrow's impossibility theorem: Social choice
(*d*) Stolper - Samuelson theorem: Capital structure
(*e*) Fishers separation theorem: Profit maximisation motivation

Choose the **correct** answer from the options given below:

A. (*a*), (*b*), (*d*) only
B. (*b*), (*d*), (*e*) only

C. (*a*), (*c*), (*d*) only
D. (*b*), (*c*), (*e*) only

19. Arrange the following initiatives launched by the government in order of their starting year from the oldest:

(*a*) Antyodaya Anna Yojana
(*b*) Mid-day Meal Scheme
(*c*) National Food Security Act
(*d*) Revised Public Distribution System
(*e*) Targeted Public Distribution System

Choose the **correct** answer from the options given below:

A. (*d*), (*b*), (*e*), (*a*), (*c*)
B. (*a*), (*b*), (*d*), (*e*), (*c*)
C. (*e*), (*d*), (*b*), (*a*), (*c*)
D. (*b*), (*a*), (*d*), (*e*), (*c*)

20. Match List-I with List-II.

List-I	List-II
(*a*) Rachel Carson	I. Economics of Bio-diversity
(*b*) Kenneth Boulding	II. Economics of coming spaceship earth
(*c*) G. Hardin	III. Silent spring
(*d*) Partha Dasgupta	IV. Tragedy of commons

Choose the **correct** answer from the options given below:

	(*a*)	(*b*)	(*c*)	(*d*)
A.	II	I	IV	III
B.	III	IV	I	II
C.	IV	II	III	I
D.	III	II	IV	I

21. Consider the following statements regarding the non Banking Financial Companies in India (NBFCs):

(*a*) NBFCs are registered under the RBI Act 1948
(*b*) NBFCs cannot accept demand deposits like commercial banks
(*c*) NBFCs have to invest a specific per cent of their assets in unencumbered approved securities
(*d*) NBFCs which engaged in merchant banking and portfolio management services are governed by SEBI
(*e*) Every NBFC has to create a reserve fund.

Choose the **correct** answer from the options given below:

A. (*a*), (*b*), (*c*), (*d*) only
B. (*b*), (*c*), (*d*), (*e*) only
C. (*b*), (*d*), (*e*) only
D. (*b*), (*c*), (*e*) only

22. The rise in the nominal stock of money causes:

A. an increase in the equilibrium nominal interest rate and a decrease in equilibrium real income.
B. a reduction in the equilibrium nominal interest rate and an increase in equilibrium real income.
C. a reduction in the equilibrium nominal interest rate and a decrease in equilibrium real income.
D. an increase in the equilibrium nominal interest rate and an increase in the equilibrium real income.

23. Consider the following statements:

(*a*) MC schedule is obtained by subtracting successive values of TC only
(*b*) MC schedule is obtained by subtracting successive values of either TC or TVC
(*c*) MC schedule is obtained by subtracting successive values of either TVC or TFC
(*d*) The area under the MC curve equals TC
(*e*) AVC equals AC minus AFC

Choose the **correct** answer from the options given below:

A. (*b*), (*d*), (*e*) only
B. (*a*), (*d*), (*e*) only
C. (*a*), (*c*), (*d*), (*e*) only
D. (*a*), (*c*), (*d*) only

24. In which agriculture year, India's first Agriculture Census was carried out?

A. 1950-51 B. 1960-61

C. 1970-71 D. 1980-81

25. The phrase 'demonstration effect' was coined by:

A. James Duesenberry

B. J.K. Galbraith

C. Joan Robinson

D. J.M. Keynes

26. Consider the following statements:

(*a*) If a market generates a side effect or externality then the market solutions are inefficient.

(*b*) If a market is efficient, then the quantity produced in the market maximise both producer's and consumer's surplus.

(*c*) Consumer's surplus is the buyer's WTP minus the seller's cost.

(*d*) Smith's invisible hand concept implies that competitive market outcome generates equity among the members in the society.

(*e*) Competitive market equilibrium is Pareto efficient.

Choose the **correct** answer from the options given below:

A. (*a*), (*b*), (*e*) only

B. (*a*), (*b*), (*d*) only

C. (*a*), (*e*) only

D. (*b*), (*d*), (*e*) only

27. Match List-I with List-II.

List-I	List-II
(*a*) General Hetero-scedasticity test	I. Ramsey
(*b*) General test for auto correlation	II. Hausman
(*c*) Test of simultaneity	III. White
(*d*) General test of specification error	IV. Breusch-Godfrey

Choose the **correct** answer from the options given below:

	(*a*)	(*b*)	(*c*)	(*d*)
A.	I	II	III	IV
B.	IV	II	I	III
C.	III	IV	II	I
D.	III	I	II	IV

28. Which of the following is not an instrument of Monetary Policy?

A. Cash reserve ratio

B. Open market operation

C. Bank rate

D. Tax rate

29. The production function $Q = \frac{LK}{L+K}$ is:

A. Homogenous of degree 1

B. Homogenous of degree 0

C. Homogenous of degree 2

D. Homogenous of degree 1/2

30. Arrange the following Acts in correct chronological order, starting from earliest to latest:

(*a*) Chit Fund Act

(*b*) Export Import Bank of India Act

(*c*) Prevention of Money Laundering Act

(*d*) National Housing Bank Act

(*e*) Regional Rural Banks Act

Choose the **correct** answer from the options given below:

A. (*e*), (*b*), (*a*), (*d*), (*c*)

B. (*e*), (*d*), (*c*), (*b*), (*a*)

C. (*d*), (*c*), (*b*), (*e*), (*a*)

D. (*d*), (*a*), (*e*), (*c*), (*b*)

31. Which of the following values indicates that each woman is being replaced by one daughter, leading to a stable population over time?

A. GFR = 1

B. NRR = 1

C. TFR = 1

D. GRR = 1

32. Match List-I with List-II.

List-I	List-II
(*a*) Travel cost method	I. Sustainable development
(*b*) Stern review	II. Exhaustible resources
(*c*) Brundtland commission report	III. Climate change
(*d*) User cost	IV. Environmental valuation

Choose the **correct** answer from the options given below:

	(*a*)	(*b*)	(*c*)	(*d*)
A.	IV	II	I	III
B.	IV	I	II	III
C.	IV	III	I	II
D.	III	IV	I	II

33. Which of the following is not an assumption of Coase theorem related to externalities and environmental problems?

A. Absence of transaction costs

B. Presence of income effect

C. Complete information

D. Complete property rights

34. Arrange the following in correct chronological order starting for the oldest to the latest:

(*a*) World Trade organisation (WTO)

(*b*) General Aggrement on Trade and Tariffs (GATT)

(*c*) New Economic Policy of India (NEP)

(*d*) Introduction of goods and services tax (GST)

(*e*) Establishment of NABARD

Choose the **correct** answer from the options given below:

A. (*b*), (*c*), (*e*), (*a*), (*d*)

B. (*b*), (*e*), (*c*), (*a*), (*d*)

C. (*b*), (*d*), (*e*), (*c*), (*a*)

D. (*a*), (*b*), (*c*), (*e*), (*d*)

35. When imports are restricted with quota rather than a tariff, the cost is sometimes magnified by a process known as …………

A. Rent seeking B. Quota seeking

C. Tax Seeking D. None of the above

36. Match List-I with List-II.

List-I	List-II
(*a*) Labour capital ratio	I. The price of a commodity determined by exclusively from its labour content
(*b*) Labour intensive commodity	II. The commodity with lower capital-labour ratio at all relative factor prices
(*c*) Labour theory of value	III. The amount of labour per unit of capital used
(*d*) Labour saving technical progress	IV. It increases the productivity of capital proportionately more than the labour

Choose the **correct** answer from the options given below:

	(*a*)	(*b*)	(*c*)	(*d*)
A.	III	II	I	IV
B.	II	III	I	IV
C.	I	II	III	IV
D.	I	II	IV	III

37. Match List-I with List-II.

List-I	List-II
(*a*) PQLI	I. Amartya Sen
(*b*) HDI	II. Mehbub-Ul-Haque
(*c*) Capability Approach to Development	III. Alkire and Foster
(*d*) Multi-Dimensional Poverty Index	IV. Morris D. Morris

Choose the **correct** answer from the options given below:

	(*a*)	(*b*)	(*c*)	(*d*)
A.	IV	II	I	III
B.	IV	III	II	I
C.	I	II	III	IV
D.	IV	I	III	II

38. What does not come under the purview of the function of Reserve Bank of India?

A. Custodian of Foreign Exchange Reserves
B. Issuės of Bank Notes
C. The lender of the last resort
D. Multiple expansion of credit

39. A and B are two events such that $P(\bar{A}) = 0.4$ and $P(A \cap B) = 0.2$, then $P(A \cap \bar{B})$ is:

A. 0.4 B. 0.2
C. 0.6 D. 0.8

40. Match List-I with List-II.

List-I	**List-II**
(*a*) Montreal Protocol	I. Contingent valuation method
(*b*) Cop 28	II. Control of CFC
(*c*) Rio + 20	III. Climate Conference
(*d*) Willingness to Accept (WTA)	IV. Sustainable Development

Choose the **correct** answer from the options given below:

	(*a*)	(*b*)	(*c*)	(*d*)
A.	II	III	IV	I
B.	II	I	IV	III
C.	III	IV	II	I
D.	I	II	IV	III

41. Given $y = \dfrac{1+x}{1-2x}$ find the correct alternative:

A. $\dfrac{dy}{dx} = \dfrac{3}{1-2x}$ B. $\dfrac{dy}{dx} = \dfrac{3}{(1-2x)^2}$

C. $\dfrac{dy}{dx} = \dfrac{3}{(1-2x)^3}$ D. $\dfrac{dy}{dx} = \dfrac{3}{(1-x)^2}$

42. Under the Green Climate Fund of UNFCCC, what ratio of financial allocation between 'Adaptation' and 'Mitigation' activities is aimed?

A. 25 : 75 B. 40 : 60
C. 50 : 50 D. 75 : 25

43. Inflation confers no benefits on society, but it imposes several real costs. What among the following are costs of inflation?

(*a*) Shoeleather costs associated with reduced money holdings
(*b*) Menu cost associated with more frequent adjustmental prices
(*c*) Increased variability of relative prices
(*d*) Unintended changes in tax liabilities due to nonindexations of the tax code
(*e*) Arbitrary redistribution of wealth associated with debts

Choose the **correct** answer from the options given below:

A. (*a*), (*b*), (*c*) only
B. (*c*), (*d*), (*e*) only
C. (*b*), (*d*), (*a*) only
D. (*a*), (*b*), (*c*), (*d*), (*e*)

44. Arrange the following theories in correct chronological order, starting from earliest to latest:

(*a*) Absorption approach
(*b*) Factor Price Equalisation theory
(*c*) Reciprocal Dumping Model
(*d*) Leontief Paradox
(*e*) Immiserizing Growth Theory

Choose the **correct** answer from the options given below:

A. (*b*), (*d*), (*a*), (*e*), (*c*)
B. (*d*), (*a*), (*b*), (*c*), (*e*)
C. (*e*), (*d*), (*b*), (*a*), (*c*)
D. (*d*), (*a*), (*c*), (*e*), (*b*)

45. Which among the following committees, was set up for Banking sector reforms in India?

(*a*) Jalan Committee
(*b*) Ghosh Committee
(*c*) Saraf Committee
(*d*) Gokaran Committee
(*e*) Tarapore Committee

Choose the **correct** answer from the options given below:

A. (*a*), (*b*), (*d*) only
B. (*b*), (*c*), (*e*) only
C. (*c*), (*d*), (*e*) only
D. (*a*), (*d*), (*c*) only

46. What is the permissible limit of Foreign Direct Investment in India's defence industry through government route?

A. 26 per cent
B. 51 per cent
C. 74 per cent
D. 100 per cent

47. Identify the correct statements from below:

(*a*) First UN conference on human environment was held in Norway in 1972.
(*b*) In I = PAT expression, P stands for poverty.
(*c*) Pollution tax was suggested by Pigou.
(*d*) Population growth follows a logistic distribution.
(*e*) Hedonic pricing is an environmental valuation method used in valuing tourism sites.

Choose the **correct** answer from the options given below:

A. (*a*), (*d*), (*e*) only
B. (*c*), (*d*), (*e*) only
C. (*a*), (*b*), (*e*) only
D. (*c*), (*d*) only

48. Arrange the following events from the date of their happening starting from the oldest:

(*a*) IRDA Act passed in Parliament
(*b*) Concept of financial inclusion introduced in Banking sector
(*c*) Global trust bank merged with UTI Bank
(*d*) 364 - day treasury bill introduced with market related rates
(*e*) Fiscal responsibility and Budget Management Act Passed

Choose the **correct** answer from the options given below:

A. (*d*), (*a*), (*c*), (*e*), (*b*)
B. (*d*), (*c*), (*e*), (*a*), (*b*)
C. (*e*), (*d*), (*b*), (*a*), (*c*)
D. (*a*), (*c*), (*d*), (*e*), (*b*)

49. Match List-I with List-II.

List-I	List-II
(*a*) NITI Aayog	I. Tit-for-Tat strategy
(*b*) R. Axelrod	II. Efficiency wage theory
(*c*) J. Stiglitz	III. K.N. Raj
(*d*) India's first five year plan (1951-1956)	IV. Knowledge support

Choose the **correct** answer from the options given below:

	(*a*)	(*b*)	(*c*)	(*d*)
A.	II	I	III	IV
B.	IV	III	II	I
C.	IV	I	II	III
D.	I	II	III	IV

50. Match List-I with List-II.

List-I	List-II
(*a*) W.W. Leontief	I. Shadow Price
(*b*) Jan Tinbergen	II. Consumption Function
(*c*) J.M. Keynes	III. Price competition with homogenous products
(*d*) Joseph Bertrand	IV. Input-output model

Choose the **correct** answer from the options given below:

	(*a*)	(*b*)	(*c*)	(*d*)
A.	II	III	I	IV
B.	IV	I	II	III
C.	III	IV	I	II
D.	I	II	III	IV

51. Arrange the following in correct chronological order starting from the earliest to the latest:

(*a*) Coase theorem
(*b*) Hotelling principle
(*c*) Nash equilibrium
(*d*) Kyoto Protocol
(*e*) Establishment of IUCN (International Union for Conservation of Nature)

Choose the **correct** answer from the options given below:

A. (*b*), (*e*), (*c*), (*a*), (*d*)
B. (*b*), (*e*), (*a*), (*c*), (*d*)
C. (*b*), (*a*), (*d*), (*e*), (*c*)
D. (*e*), (*b*), (*a*), (*c*), (*d*)

52. Match List-I with List-II.

List-I	List-II
(*a*) Top beneficiary from Foreign exchange trading	I. John Von Neuman and Oscar Morgenstern
(*b*) Competitive equilibrium is Pareto efficient	II. General equilibrium analysis
(*c*) Walras	III. London
(*d*) Game Theory	IV. First theorem of welfare economics

Choose the **correct** answer from the options given below:

	(*a*)	(*b*)	(*c*)	(*d*)
A.	II	III	I	IV
B.	IV	III	II	I
C.	I	II	III	IV
D.	III	IV	II	I

53. The concept of efficiency wage theory was developed by:

A. Yellen and Stiglitz
B. Jan Tinbergen
C. Alfred Marshall
D. Vilfredo Pareto

54. Identify the correct statements from below:

(*a*) When price consumption curve (PCC) for a good is parallel to horizontal axis, the demand function for the good is unitary elastic.
(*b*) Given $\log D = \alpha + \beta \log y + \gamma \log p$ then elasticity of log D with respect to log p is γ
(*c*) The condition for stability in simple Keynesian system is $0 < MPC < 1$
(*d*) The fixed cost curve is a rectangular hyperbola

Choose the **correct** answer from the options given below:

A. (*a*), (*c*) only
B. (*a*), (*c*), (*d*) only
C. (*a*), (*b*), (*c*) only
D. (*a*), (*b*), (*c*), (*d*)

55. You have carried out a regression analysis but after thinking about the relationship between the two variables, you have decided that you must swap the explanatory and response variables. After refitting the regression model to the data, you expect that:

A. The value of correlation will change
B. The sign of slope will change
C. The value of coefficient of determination will change
D. The value of SSE (sum of squared errors) will change

56. Which of the following is/are possible reason(s) for surplus in balance of payment?

(*a*) Decline in imports
(*b*) Decline in interest rate
(*c*) Increase in export
(*d*) Increase in income tax
(*e*) High outward foreign direct investment

Choose the **most appropriate** answer from the options given below:

A. (*a*), (*c*), (*e*) only
B. (*a*), (*b*), (*c*), (*e*) only
C. (*b*), (*c*), (*e*), (*d*) only
D. (*a*), (*c*) only

57. Match List-I with List-II.

List-I	List-II
(*a*) Endogenous variable	I. Significance of Autocorrelation coefficient
(*b*) Count R^2	II. Simultaneous equation
(*c*) Ljung Box Statistic	III. Panel data regression
(*d*) Least square dummy variable model	IV. Logit regression

Choose the **correct** answer from the options given below:

	(*a*)	(*b*)	(*c*)	(*d*)
A.	III	I	IV	II
B.	II	III	I	IV
C.	II	III	IV	I
D.	II	IV	I	III

58. The .... effect implies that nominal interest rates tend to be high when inflation is high and low when inflation is low?

A. Tobin effect B. Baumol effect
C. Fisher effect D. Patinkin effect

59. Which state scored highest to secure top-most rank in the 'State Energy Efficiency Index 2023' released by NITI Aayog?

A. Andhra Pradesh B. Gujarat
C. Haryana D. Karnataka

60. Match List-I with List-II.

List-I	List-II
(*a*) Narasimham Committee Report (II)	I. Frauds and Mal-practices in Bank
(*b*) Ghosh Committee Report	II. Technology issues in Banking
(*c*) Padmanabhan Committee	III. RBI should withdraw 91 days T. Bill from market
(*d*) Saraf Committee	IV. Style of inspection and follow up by the central bank

Choose the **correct** answer from the options given below:

	(*a*)	(*b*)	(*c*)	(*d*)
A.	III	IV	II	I
B.	I	II	III	IV
C.	III	I	IV	II
D.	III	II	I	IV

61. Suppose savings function is $S = -5 + 0.3q$, then find the correct answer from below:

A. APC < MPC B. APC = MPC
C. APS > MPS D. APC > MPC

62. Arrange the following taxes in the sequence in which they were introduced starting from earliest to latest?

(*a*) Commodities Transaction Tax
(*b*) Securities Transaction Tax
(*c*) Banking Cash Transaction Tax
(*d*) Minimum Alternate Tax
(*e*) Angel Tax

Choose the **correct** answer from the options given below:

A. (*d*), (*a*), (*e*), (*b*), (*c*)
B. (*b*), (*c*), (*a*), (*e*), (*d*)
C. (*d*), (*b*), (*c*), (*e*), (*a*)
D. (*c*), (*d*), (*b*), (*a*), (*e*)

63. Arrange the following norms of tax revenue devolution formula of the Fifteenth Finance Commission in order of their weightages starting from the highest.

(*a*) Income distance
(*b*) Area
(*c*) Demographic performance
(*d*) Forest and Ecology
(*e*) Tax effort

Choose the **correct** answer from the options given below:

A. (*a*), (*b*), (*c*), (*d*), (*e*)
B. (*a*), (*d*), (*b*), (*e*), (*c*)
C. (*b*), (*a*), (*c*), (*e*), (*d*)
D. (*c*), (*d*), (*a*), (*b*), (*e*)

64. Match List-I with List-II.

List-I	List-II
(*a*) Bank run	I. D. Pearce
(*b*) *q*-ratio	II. M. Yunus
(*c*) Genuine saving	III. P. Diamond
(*d*) Micro finance	IV. J. Tobin

Choose the **correct** answer from the options given below:

	(*a*)	(*b*)	(*c*)	(*d*)
A.	IV	I	III	II
B.	III	IV	I	II
C.	III	II	IV	I
D.	II	IV	I	III

65. Identify the correct statements from below:

(*a*) According to environmental valuation theory, option value = future use value + bequest value + vicarious value

(*b*) Adverse selection leads to market failure

(*c*) Contingent valuation method is a type of cost benefit analysis

(*d*) Public good and common goods have same characteristics

(*e*) Internal rate of return is a criterion in cost benefit analysis

Choose the **correct** answer from the options given below:

A. (*a*) and (*b*) only
B. (*a*), (*c*), (*d*) only
C. (*a*), (*b*), (*e*) only
D. (*c*), (*d*), (*e*) only

66. For the demand function of good *x*, $Q_d = f(P_x, P_y, M)$ the sum of own price elasticity, cross price elasticity and income elasticity of demand would be:

A. one
B. zero
C. two
D. *n* where $n > 1$

67. To test $H_0 : \mu = \mu_0$, when both μ, and σ are unknown, the relevant test statistic is:

A. $t_{n-1} = \dfrac{\bar{x} - \mu_0}{\frac{s'}{\sqrt{n}}}$
B. $t_{n-1} = \dfrac{\bar{x} - \mu_0}{\frac{s'}{\sqrt{n-1}}}$
C. $t_n = \dfrac{\bar{x} - \mu_0}{\frac{s'}{\sqrt{n}}}$
D. $t_{n-1} = \dfrac{\bar{x} - \mu_0}{\frac{s'}{n}}$

68. Which of the following is current global measurement of the extreme poverty line?

A. \$ 1.90 - a day
B. \$ 2.00 - a day
C. \$ 2.15 - a day
D. \$ 2.25 - a day

69. Consider the following targets of National Health Policy 2017. Choose the correct objectives to be achieved by 2025:

(*a*) Infant Mortality Rate : 30
(*b*) Under Five Mortality Rate : 20
(*c*) Maternal Mortality Rate : 100
(*d*) Total Fertility Rate : 2.1
(*e*) Life Expectancy at Birth : 70 years

Choose the **correct** answer from the options given below:

A. (*a*), (*b*), (*c*) only
B. (*b*), (*c*), (*d*) only
C. (*a*), (*c*), (*e*) only
D. (*c*), (*d*), (*e*) only

70. Consider the following statements regarding Regional Rural Banks (RRBs) in India:

(*a*) RRBs were setup on the basis of the recommendation of Narasimham working group, 1975

(*b*) The largest proportion of the equity of RRBs is held by its sponsor bank

(*c*) NABARD coordinates all the activities of RRBs

(*d*) RRBs are lead Bank

(*e*) RRBs are provided refinance facilities through NABARD

Choose the **correct** answer from the options given below:

A. (*a*), (*c*), (*e*) only
B. (*a*), (*b*), (*c*), (*d*) only
C. (*b*), (*c*), (*e*) only
D. (*a*), (*e*) only

71. ANCOVA models include regressors that are:

A. Only quantitative variables
B. Only qualitative variables
C. Only categorical variables
D. Both qualitative and quantitative variables

72. During how many first completed days of life, the death of a baby is defined as the Neonatal death?

A. First 7 completed days of life
B. First 14 completed days of life
C. First 21 completed days of life
D. First 28 completed days of life

73. A feasible solution in a linear programming problem (LPP):

(*a*) Must satisfy all the problem's constraints simultaneously

(*b*) Need not satisfy all the constraints, only some of them

(*c*) Must be a corner point in the feasible region

(*d*) May or may not optimise the value of the objective function

(*e*) Must be greater than or equal to zero

Choose the **correct** answer from the options given below:

A. (*a*), (*d*), (*e*) only

B. (*a*), (*d*) only

C. (*a*), (*e*) only

D. (*b*), (*c*), (*e*) only

74. Match List-I with List-II.

List-I	List-II
(*a*) Ad Valorem Tariff	I. Fixed sum per unit
(*b*) Autarky	II. Combination of Ad Valorem and specific tariff
(*c*) Compound Tariff	III. No trade with other countries
(*d*) Specific Tariff	IV. A percentage of the value of the traded commodity

Choose the **correct** answer from the options given below:

	(*a*)	(*b*)	(*c*)	(*d*)
A.	I	II	III	IV
B.	IV	III	II	I
C.	IV	I	II	III
D.	III	II	I	IV

75. As per National Health Survey-5, what was the number of females per 1000 males during survey period 2019-21?

A. 975   B. 991

C. 1003   D. 1020

76. The Nash equilibrium of the following game

$$\begin{array}{cc} & \underline{P-2} \\ & \begin{array}{ccc} B_1 & B_2 & B_3 \end{array} \\ P-1 \begin{array}{c} A_1 \\ A_2 \\ A_3 \end{array} & \begin{bmatrix} 4, 2 & 2, 1 & 5, 0 \\ 3, 5 & 3, 2 & 3, 4 \\ 5, 2 & 4, 4 & 3, 1 \end{bmatrix} \end{array}$$

is given by:

A. The strategy combination (A_3, B_2) with outcome (4, 4)

B. The strategy combination (A_3, B_1) with outcome (5, 2)

C. The strategy combination (A_1, B_2) with outcome (2, 1)

D. The strategy combination (A_3, B_2) with outcome (3, 1)

77. Arrange the names of following economists chronoliogically in order of their Nobel prize awards (starting from earliest to the latest):

(*a*) Arthur Lewis   (*b*) Gunnar Myrdal

(*c*) Milton Friedman   (*d*) Abhijit Banerjee

(*e*) Lawrence Klein

Choose the **correct** answer from the options given below:

A. (*b*), (*c*), (*a*), (*e*), (*d*)

B. (*b*), (*c*), (*a*), (*d*), (*e*)

C. (*b*), (*a*), (*c*), (*e*), (*d*)

D. (*a*), (*b*), (*c*), (*e*), (*d*)

78. Consider the following statements regarding public good:

(*a*) Public good is nonexclusive

(*b*) Public good is national defense

(*c*) Public good is rival

(*d*) Public good provides benefits to people at non-zero marginal cost

(*e*) Public good creates inefficiency in consumption

Choose the **correct** answer from the options given below:

A. (*a*) and (*b*) only

B. (*b*) and (*c*) only

C. (*c*) and (*d*) only
D. (*d*) and (*e*) only

79. Which of the following is the biggest item of grants-in-aid to the states assigned by the Fifteenth Finance Commission?

A. Disaster risk management grants
B. Revenue deficit grants
C. Local bodies grants
D. Sector specific grants

80. Among the following which is/are the instruments of capital market?

(*a*) Venture Capital
(*b*) Treasury Bills
(*c*) Certificate of Deposit issued by commercial banks
(*d*) Global Depository Receipts
(*e*) Inter Corporate Deposits

Choose the **correct** answer from the options given below:

A. (*b*), (*d*), (*e*) only
B. (*a*), (*d*) only
C. (*a*), (*b*), (*d*) only
D. (*a*), (*d*), (*e*) only

81. Arrange the following in chronological order starting from earliest to latest:

(*a*) A.W. Phillips: The Phillips Curve
(*b*) J.M. Keynes: General Theory of Employment, Interest and Money
(*c*) Adam Smith: Theory of Growth
(*d*) John F. Muth: Rational Expectations Approach
(*e*) Robert M. Solow: Growth Model

Choose the **correct** answer from the options given below:

A. (*a*), (*b*), (*c*), (*d*), (*e*)
B. (*c*), (*b*), (*e*), (*a*), (*d*)
C. (*b*), (*a*), (*c*), (*e*), (*d*)
D. (*e*), (*d*), (*c*), (*b*), (*a*)

82. Arrange the following items in order of their construction starting from the first stage to the last stage:

(*a*) Budget
(*b*) Utility analysis
(*c*) Demand curve analysis
(*d*) Indifference curve analysis
(*e*) Consumer's equilibrium

Choose the **correct** answer from the options given below:

A. (*d*), (*b*), (*a*), (*e*), (*c*)
B. (*a*), (*b*), (*c*), (*d*), (*e*)
C. (*b*), (*d*), (*e*), (*c*), (*a*)
D. (*b*), (*d*), (*a*), (*e*), (*c*)

83. Match List-I with List-II.

List-I	List-II
(*a*) Monopoly theory of distribution	I. Walker
(*b*) Theory of profit	II. Robinson
(*c*) Full cost pricing	III. Kalecki
(*d*) Modern theory of rent	IV. Hall and Hitch

Choose the **correct** answer from the options given below:

	(*a*)	(*b*)	(*c*)	(*d*)
A.	II	III	I	IV
B.	III	I	IV	II
C.	III	IV	II	I
D.	IV	III	II	I

84. As per the Gravity Model of world trade, which of the following components of the two countries determine the volume of trade between them:

(*a*) Gross Domestic Product
(*b*) Distance
(*c*) Foreign exchange rate
(*d*) Foreign trade intensity
(*e*) Foreign investment

Choose the **correct** answer from the options given below:

A. (*a*) and (*b*) only
B. (*b*) and (*c*) only
C. (*a*) and (*c*) only
D. (*a*) and (*e*) only

85. Testing for cointegration is performed by:

A. Chow test
B. Phillips-Peron test
C. Engel-Granger test
D. Error-correction mechanism

86. Arrange the following expressions in terms of increasing order of magnitude

[given: $a > o$, $b > o$, $x > o$]

(a) $y = e^{a}$
(b) $y = e^{a + bx}$
(c) $y = e^{a+\frac{b}{x}}$
(d) $y = e^{a-\frac{b}{x}}$
(e) $y = e^{a + 2bx}$

Choose the **correct** answer from the options given below:

A. (d), (a), (c), (b), (e)
B. (d), (a), (b), (c), (e)
C. (d), (b), (c), (a), (e)
D. (e), (b), (c), (a), (d)

87. In the leakage-injection approach to income determination, an increase in lump-sum tax ceteris paribus shifts:

A. Investment plus govt. spending line upward
B. Investment plus govt. spending line downward
C. The savings plus tax line to the left
D. Increases the equilibrium level of income

88. In the Cobb-Douglas production function: $q = AL^{\alpha} K^{\beta}$ where A, α and β are all positive, the parameters α and β measure

A. Output elasticities of inputs
B. Elasticity of substitution
C. Input price of output
D. Technological condition

89. Estimation of regression coefficients in the presence of high but not perfect multicollinearity may result in all of these except:

A. High confidence interval for the estimates
B. Almost all the estimates are statistically significant
C. A high R^2
D. Estimates are all BLUE

90. The lowest value of a set of observations is 4.5 and their range is 10.9. Artithmetic mean is found to be 19.9 and median found to be 15.6. Which of the following statements is correct?

A. Arithmetic mean is wrong, but the median is correct
B. Arithmetic mean is right, but the median is wrong
C. Both arithmetic mean and median are wrong
D. Both arithmetic mean and median are right

Directions (Qs. No. 91-95): *Consider the following diagram and answers these questions.*

Social Costs of Monolpoly Power

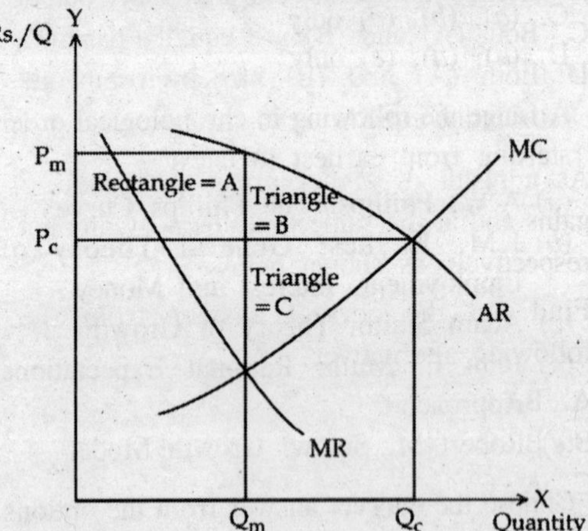

Here:

(i) X-axis measures quantity
(ii) Y-axis measures price per unit (Rs/Q)
(iii) P_c = competitive price
(iv) P_m = Monopoly price
(v) Q_c = competitive output
(vi) Q_m = monopoly output

91. Because of higher price (From P_c to P_m), find out the producer gains (producer surplus) from the following alternatives.

A. A + C
B. A – C
C. A + B
D. B + C

92. Find out the consumer loss because of moving from competitive to monopoly price (from P_c to P_m) from the following alternatives:

A. A and C
B. A and B
C. B and C
D. A only

93. Choose the correct answer from the following alternatives:

A. Monopoly output is environment friendly comparative to competitive output
B. Competitive output is environment friendly comparative to monopoly output
C. Both (A) and (B) are equally harmfull
D. Both (A) and (B) are environmental friendly equally

94. As a result of higher price, the producer gains and at the same time loses by amount respectively as shown below:

Find out the correct answer from the following alternatives:

A. B, A
B. B, C
C. A, C
D. A only

95. Dead weight loss from the monopoly power is one of the following alternatives. Choose the correct one:

A. A + B
B. A + C
C. A
D. B + C

Directions (Qs. No. 96-100): *Read the following passage and answer the questions.*

For a financial year, the Budget was presented by the government. Some major heads and items are highlighted here. Total receipts was ₹ 400 crore, of which revenue receipts was ₹ 250 crore and capital receipts was ₹ 150 crore. In the total revenue receipts, tax revenue receipts contributed ₹ 220 crore and non-tax revenue receipts contributed ₹ 30 crore respectively. In the total capital receipts, Borrowings and other liabilities were ₹ 100 crore. Out of total revenue expenditure of ₹ 300 crore, interest payments was ₹ 90 crore and grants for creation of capital assets was ₹ 20 crore. Out of total capital expenditure of ₹ 100 crore, scheme expenditure was ₹ 75 crore and other than scheme expenditure was ₹ 25 crore. The country's GDP at current prices for the given financial year was ₹ 2000 crore. On the Balance of payments accounts, the current account deficit was ₹ 50 crore.

96. What was the fiscal deficit as percentage of GDP?

A. 5% B. 10%
C. 12.5% D. 15%

97. What was the primary deficit as percentage of GDP?

A. 0.2% B. 0.3%
C. 0.4% D. 0.5%

98. What was the revenue deficit as percentage of GDP:

A. 2.5% B. 3.0%
C. 3.5% D. 4.0%

99. What was the effective revenue deficit as percentage of GDP?

A. 0.5% B. 1.0%
C. 1.5% D. 2.0%

100. What was the twin deficit as percentage of GDP?

A. 2.5% B. 5.0%
C. 7.5% D. 10.0%

ANSWERS

1. **(A):** The question addresses the secular deterioration of terms of trade for less developed countries. The primary economic theorists associated with these ideas are H.W. Singer and Raul Prebisch, who independently proposed what is now known as the Prebisch-Singer hypothesis. This theory suggests that the terms of trade, or the ratio of export prices to import prices, deteriorate over time for developing countries exporting primary commodities due to various structural factors in the global economy. Jagdish Bhagwati, another important figure in international economics, has also contributed extensively to the understanding of trade policies and their impact on developing countries, though his work is more broadly focused on trade theory and policy rather than specifically on the terms of trade deterioration phenomenon. J.S. Mill and Adam Smith, classical economists, did not specifically address this modern theory as their works predate these discussions.

   Thus, the correct answer is A, focusing on Singer, Prebisch, and Bhagwati.

2. **(C):** The statements provided relate to economic concepts surrounding investment and interest rates. According to accelerator models of investment, indeed, investment demand is proportional to the change in gross national product (GNP), aligning with the theory that investments are made to meet future expected increases in output or sales. The real interest rate, contrary to statement (*b*), is actually the nominal rate of interest minus the inflation rate, not plus. This reflects the real cost of borrowing after adjusting for inflation. Statement (*c*) correctly states that higher real interest rates increase the rental cost of capital, making borrowing more expensive for investment purposes. Statement (*d*) is incorrect as investment is a flow concept, representing the addition to the capital stock over a period, whereas the rate of interest (*e*) is indeed a flow concept, reflecting the cost of borrowing capital per unit time.

3. **(C):** To solve for the profit-maximizing price and quantity, we use the given demand function Q = 20/P and the constant marginal cost (MC) of 1. The profit-maximizing condition in a perfectly competitive market is to set price equal to marginal cost, but here, price is dictated by the demand relationship. Since P ≤ 10 is a constraint, we must also consider the upper limit for P. Setting P = 10 gives Q = 20/10 = 2. Any price above 10 is not allowed, and prices below 10 will reduce total revenue since MC is constant and revenue must cover total costs. Thus, the most profitable allowable price is P = 10 with a corresponding quantity of Q = 2, which maximizes revenue given the constraints.

4. **(A):** The statements under consideration involve environmental and development concepts. The ecological footprint (*a*) indeed measures the demand placed on Earth's ecosystems by individuals or communities, quantifying the amount of natural resources consumed and waste produced. Statement (*b*) is incorrect as the top-down approach typically implies initiatives driven by central authorities rather than by community participation, which is more characteristic of bottom-up approaches. The Millennium Development Goals (MDGs) (*c*) were targeted to be achieved by 2015, not 2016. Finally, statement (*d*) is accurate in stating that the Sustainable Development Goals

(SDGs) comprise 17 goals, established to address global challenges including poverty, inequality, climate change, environmental degradation, peace, and justice.

5. **(A):** The correct chronological sequence of these significant events and institutions in India's economic and development history starts with the Second Five Year Plan (*c*), which was implemented from 1956 to 1961 and focused on rapid industrialization. Next is the nationalization of banks in India (*b*), which occurred in two major phases, first in 1969 and then in 1980, aiming to extend banking facilities to larger sections of society and to mobilize resources for development. The Export-Import Bank of India (EXIM Bank) (*e*) was established in 1982 to enhance the country's international trade. Following this, the Small Industries Development Bank of India (SIDBI) (*d*) was set up in 1990 to promote, finance, and develop the micro, small, and medium enterprise sector. Finally, the Fiscal Responsibility and Budget Management (FRBM) Act (*a*) was enacted in 2003 to institutionalize financial discipline and reduce fiscal deficit.

6. **(B):** Heteroscedasticity refers to situations in regression analysis where the variability of a variable is unequal across the range of values of a second variable that predicts it. Common reasons for heteroscedasticity include extremely high or low values in the dataset, incorrect specifications of the model's functional form, and incorrect transformations of variables, which can all affect the stability of variance across data points. However, the correlation of variables over time generally relates to autocorrelation rather than heteroscedasticity.

7. **(D):** Economic integration among developing countries has been attempted through various regional trade agreements and blocs aimed at reducing trade barriers and fostering economic cooperation. The Central American Common Market, the Caribbean Free Trade Association, and the Latin American Free Trade Association are all examples of such efforts. These associations are designed to enhance economic cooperation among member countries, facilitate the free movement of goods, services, and factors of production, and thus improve the economic standing of the regions involved. By forming these trade blocs, developing countries aim to leverage collective bargaining power in the global market, enhance intra-regional trade, and achieve greater economic stability and growth.

8. **(A):** To determine whether points O(0, 0) and P(2, –3) lie inside or outside the region defined by the inequality $2x - 3y < 5$, we substitute these points into the inequality.
For O(0, 0), substituting $x = 0$ and $y = 0$ gives $2(0) - 3(0) = 0$, which is less than 5, indicating that point O is inside the region.
For P(2, –3), substituting $x = 2$ and $y = -3$ gives $2(2) - 3(-3) = 4 + 9 = 13$, which is not less than 5, hence point P is outside the region.
This assessment shows that point O is within the region where the inequality holds true, while point P does not satisfy the inequality and thus lies outside the specified region.

9. **(C):** For a quadratic form to be negative for all values of x and y, the quadratic form needs to be negative definite. For a $2x^2$ matrix associated with the quadratic form $ax^2 + by^2 + 2hxy$, represented as:

$$\begin{bmatrix} a & h \\ h & b \end{bmatrix},$$

the conditions for being negative definite are:

1. The leading principal minor, a must be less than zero ($a < 0$).

2. The determinant of the matrix $\begin{vmatrix} a & h \\ h & b \end{vmatrix} = ab - h^2$ must be greater than zero ($ab - h^2 > 0$).

These conditions ensure that the quadratic form curves downwards (since $a < 0$) and the determinant being positive confirms that the eigenvalues are of the same sign, which would be negative in this context (negative definite matrix). Thus, option C accurately reflects the necessary conditions.

10. (A): Gross Domestic Product (GDP) can be defined and calculated in several ways, but one standard approach is to sum the aggregate domestic income with indirect taxes and depreciation. This method reflects the total market value of all goods and services produced within a country in a given period. GDP calculated this way includes net domestic product (aggregate domestic income minus depreciation) plus depreciation (to account for the wear and tear on assets) and indirect taxes (such as sales taxes), which adjust for government-imposed costs on production and consumption that are not directly part of the income earned by factors of production. This approach provides a comprehensive measure of economic activity, reflecting both the income generated by production and the costs associated with depreciation and taxes that affect the economic value generated within a country.

11. (C): India is a member of several key institutions within the World Bank Group, which play various roles in global economic development and investment. These include the International Development Association (IDA), which provides loans and grants to the world's poorest countries; the International Finance Corporation (IFC), which offers investment, advisory, and asset-management services to encourage private-sector development in less developed countries; the Multilateral Investment Guarantee Agency (MIGA), which provides political risk insurance and credit enhancement to investors and lenders; and the International Bank for Reconstruction and Development (IBRD), which assists in development by providing loans and offering technical expertise. However, the International Centre for Settlement of Investment Disputes (ICSID) focuses more on arbitration and dispute resolution between international investors and states, and India is not a member of this institution. Therefore, option C correctly identifies the World Bank Group institutions of which India is a member.

12. (A): The terms provided relate to different financial strategies and situations involving currency transactions:

(*a*) Arbitrage refers to the practice of taking advantage of a price difference between two or more markets: striking a combination of matching deals that capitalize upon the imbalance, the profit being the difference between the market prices, which is precisely described by III, "refers to purchase of currency in monetary center where it is cheaper."

(*b*) Hedging is used to reduce any substantial losses or gains suffered by an individual or an organization. IV, "refers to avoidance of foreign exchange risk," accurately describes this strategy.

(*c*) Speculation involves trading a financial instrument involving high risk, in expectation of significant returns. The correct match is I, "refers to when an investor accepts and seeks foreign exchange risk."

(*d*) Foreign exchange risk refers to the variations in the currency value and the risk that such changes pose to financial transactions, which is described by II, "refers to a time when foreign exchange shifts, causing the spot rate to vary frequently."

This matching (III, IV, I, II) is captured in option A.

13. **(A):** The chronological order of the theories listed should reflect the historical development of monetary theory:
   - The cash transaction approach (*d*) and the cash balance approach (*e*) are early fundamental theories developed as part of the classical and neoclassical economic thoughts.
   - Reformulated quantity theory of money (*b*) came afterward, representing a modern reinterpretation of the quantity theory of money, emphasizing the role of money supply in pricing and inflation.
   - Baumol's theory of money (*c*) typically known for the transactions demand for money, came later in the mid-20th century.
   - Patinkin's real balance effect (*a*) is a more contemporary development that integrates monetary and value theory, enhancing the understanding of price level changes on consumption and savings.

   This chronological sequence is accurately captured in option A.

14. **(D):** The Unified Payments Interface (UPI) system, which has revolutionized digital payments in India, was developed by the National Payments Corporation of India (NPCI), not by the Reserve Bank of India (RBI), the State Bank of India (SBI), or the Securities and Exchange Board of India (SEBI). It was launched in 2016. The NPCI, an umbrella organization for operating retail payments and settlement systems in India, is an initiative of RBI and an association of Indian banks. UPI enables instant real-time payments between peers or between a person and a merchant, facilitated by linking bank accounts with a mobile application.

15. **(B):** According to Walras' Law, in a general equilibrium of markets, the sum of the values of excess demands across all markets must be equal to zero. This law is a fundamental concept in economic theory, indicating that if all markets but one are in equilibrium, then that last market must also be in equilibrium. Excess demand is defined as the amount by which demand exceeds supply at current prices, and according to Walras' Law, the sum of excess demand for different goods, including money, bonds, and current output, in an economy should sum to zero.

   This ensures that resources are allocated efficiently and that there are no unmet demands or unsold supplies in any market without affecting another.

16. **(A):** The Human Development Index (HDI) categorizes countries into four groups based on their HDI values: very high, high, medium, and low human development. Typically, the largest group of countries tends to be in the "medium human development" category. However, over recent years and especially in the latest reports, there has been significant progress in various countries, shifting more into the "high" and "very high" categories as global development efforts intensify and yield results. The latest data trends indicate that more countries have moved into the "very high human development" category, reflecting improvements in health, education, and income indices which are the components of the HDI.

   This progression aligns with global development goals and the increased focus on sustainable development, healthcare improvements, and educational accessibility.

17. **(D):** The sustainable development goals (SDGs) have specific objectives designed to address global challenges comprehensively:

- Goal 7 aims to ensure access to affordable, reliable, sustainable, and modern energy for all, correctly matching "Affordable and clean energy."
- Goal 10, which is incorrectly matched with "Climate action," actually aims to reduce inequality within and among countries. The correct goal for "Climate action" is Goal 13.
- Goal 13 is incorrectly matched with "Reduced inequality" which should be Goal 10.
- Goal 14 correctly matches with "Life below water," focusing on the conservation and sustainable use of the oceans, seas, and marine resources.
- Goal 15 correctly matches with "Life on land," which aims to protect, restore, and promote sustainable use of terrestrial ecosystems. Thus, the correct option that matches goals with their descriptions accurately is (*a*), (*d*), (*e*).

18. (D): The matching of economic theorems with their correct subjects is as follows:

(*a*) The Modigliani-Miller theorem, incorrectly associated with price of goods and real return to factors, actually pertains to corporate finance, particularly capital structure decisions, stating that the market value of a firm is independent of its capital structure.

(*b*) The Dorfman-Steiner theorem correctly deals with optimal advertisement expenditure, stating that the ratio of advertising to sales should equal the product of the profit margin and the advertising elasticity of demand.

(*c*) Arrow's impossibility theorem correctly addresses issues in social choice theory, demonstrating the impossibility of devising a social preference ordering that meets certain rational criteria.

(*d*) The Stolper-Samuelson theorem, incorrectly matched with capital structure, actually relates to international trade, particularly the effects of trade on factor prices.

(*e*) Fisher's separation theorem correctly discusses the separation of investment decisions from owners' preferences, focusing on firms' investment decisions being determined by their profitability regardless of personal preferences.

Thus, the correct answer is D, with (*b*), (*c*), and (*e*) being correctly matched.

19. (*)

20. (D): Matching notable figures with their contributions or associated works involves identifying the correct descriptions:

(*a*) Rachel Carson is best known for her book "Silent Spring" (III), which is credited with advancing the global environmental movement.

(*b*) Kenneth Boulding wrote on the "Economics of the Coming Spaceship Earth" (II), describing the Earth as a closed system.

(*c*) G. Hardin is famous for the essay "The Tragedy of the Commons" (IV), which addresses problems related to shared resources.

(*d*) Partha Dasgupta has significant contributions to the "Economics of Biodiversity" (I), focusing on the economic aspects of biodiversity.

Therefore, the correct matching, based on their seminal works or concepts, is provided in option D: III, II, IV, I.

21. (B): Non-Banking Financial Companies (NBFCs) in India have specific regulatory and operational guidelines that distinguish them from commercial banks:

- Statement (*a*) is incorrect because NBFCs are not registered under the RBI Act of 1948 but under the Companies Act of 2013, and they are regulated by the RBI under directions issued under the RBI Act of 1934.

- Statement (*b*) is correct. Unlike commercial banks, NBFCs are not allowed to accept demand deposits, which are deposits that can be withdrawn by the depositor at any time without any prior notice to the banking institution.
- Statement (*c*) is correct. NBFCs are required to invest a specific percentage of their assets in unencumbered approved securities as per the Non-Banking Financial (Non-Deposit Accepting or Holding) Companies Prudential Norms (Reserve Bank) Directions, 2007.
- Statement (*d*) is correct. NBFCs that are engaged in merchant banking, portfolio management services, or stockbroking must also comply with regulations set by the Securities and Exchange Board of India (SEBI), in addition to being regulated by the RBI.
- Statement (*e*) is correct. Every NBFC is required to create a reserve fund and transfer at least 20% of its net profit every year to this fund before any dividend is declared, as per the RBI's directions.

Hence, option B, which includes (*b*), (*c*), (*d*), and (*e*), is correct.

22. (B): A rise in the nominal stock of money, according to basic monetary theory, typically leads to lower interest rates and higher real income in the short to medium term. This is because an increase in the money supply lowers the cost of borrowing (nominal interest rate), encouraging more investment and spending, which in turn can boost economic activity and real income. The theory relies on the liquidity preference framework, which posits that an increase in money supply, with unchanged money demand, leads to an excess supply of money, resulting in lower interest rates.

23. (A):

- Statement (*a*) is incorrect as it suggests MC (marginal cost) is calculated by subtracting successive values of TC (total cost) only. While it's true MC involves TC, it specifically relates to the change in TC due to an additional unit of output.
- Statement (*b*) is correct. MC can be derived by subtracting successive values of either Total Cost (TC) or Total Variable Cost (TVC), not just TC. This reflects the cost added by producing one additional unit.
- Statements (*c*) is incorrect. MC does not involve Total Fixed Cost (TFC), as TFC does not change with output levels.
- Statement (*d*) is correct. The area under the MC curve up to a certain quantity of output equals the total variable cost (TVC) for that quantity, which, when added to TFC, equals TC.
- Statement (*e*) is correct. Average Variable Cost (AVC) equals Average Cost (AC) minus Average Fixed Cost (AFC), which is derived from dividing TFC by the quantity.

24. (C): India's first Agricultural Census was carried out in the year 1970-71. This nationwide exercise was initiated to collect and compile comprehensive data on agricultural aspects such as land use, cropping patterns, and farm holdings across the country. The Agricultural Census takes place every five years, with the aim of providing a detailed picture of the agricultural sector, which is vital for policy formulation and planning for agricultural development in India.

25. (A): The concept of the demonstration effect, particularly in the context of consumer behaviour and consumption patterns, was popularized by James Duesenberry. He explained that individuals' consumption choices are influenced by the standards set by their peers or reference groups. This socio-economic behaviour was detailed in his relative income hypothesis, which suggests that people's spending is more influenced by their relative position in a social group than by their absolute income level. This concept has profound implications for understanding consumer behaviour, especially in societies with conspicuous consumption and significant income disparities.

26. (A):

- Statement (*a*) is correct: If a market generates a side effect or externality (such as pollution from a factory), then the market outcome becomes inefficient because it fails to account for the cost or benefit of the externality. This can lead to overproduction or underproduction from the social optimum level, thus making the market solutions inefficient.
- Statement (*b*) is correct: Efficiency in a market is achieved when the quantity produced maximizes total surplus, which includes both producer's surplus and consumer's surplus. This occurs at the equilibrium where supply equals demand, assuming no externalities or market power.
- Statement (*c*) is incorrect: Consumer's surplus is the difference between what consumers are willing to pay (WTP) and what they actually pay, not the seller's cost.
- Statement (*d*) is incorrect: Adam Smith's concept of the invisible hand suggests that competitive markets lead to efficient outcomes through individuals pursuing their self-interest, not necessarily generating equity among members of society.
- Statement (*e*) is correct: In a competitive market, equilibrium is Pareto efficient because any other allocation would make at least one individual worse off while making no one better off. Thus, the correct statements that align with these explanations are (*a*), (*b*), and (*e*), making option A correct.

27. (C):

- General Heteroscedasticity test is commonly associated with White's test (III), which checks for heteroscedasticity in a regression model's residuals.
- General test for autocorrelation is frequently done using the Breusch-Godfrey test (IV), which specifically tests for autocorrelation in the residuals of a regression model.
- Test of simultaneity often involves the Hausman test (II), which can distinguish between simultaneous equations models and single-equation estimation techniques to determine if endogeneity is present.
- General test of specification error involving various aspects like omitted variables and functional form can be addressed by the Ramsey RESET test (I), which is used to test if a model has been misspecified.

This matching (III, IV, II, I) is provided in option C, aligning with the correct identification of statistical tests.

28. (D):

- The Cash Reserve Ratio (A), Open Market Operations (B), and Bank Rate (C) are all traditional instruments of monetary policy used by central banks to regulate the money supply and interest rates in the economy.
- Tax rate (D), however, is a fiscal policy instrument used by the government to influence the economy by altering tax rates, affecting public spending, and adjusting budget allocations, rather than directly influencing the money supply or interest rates.

Thus, D is the correct answer as it is not an instrument of monetary policy.

29. (A): The production function Q = LK/(L + K) can be tested for homogeneity by examining if increasing all inputs by a factor of '*t*' results in the output being multiplied by the same factor '*t*'. If Q is homogenous of degree 1, scaling all inputs by any positive constant will result in output scaling by the same constant:

$$Q(tL, tK) = \frac{tL \times tK}{tL + tK} = t \times \frac{LK}{L + K} = tQ$$

This shows that the function is homogenous of degree 1, where output increases proportionally with an increase in inputs.

30. (A):

(*e*) The Regional Rural Banks Act was established first, in 1976, aimed at developing the rural economy and enhancing the financial inclusion of rural sectors.

(*b*) The Export Import Bank of India Act came into effect in March 1982, established to enhance the foreign trade of India by facilitating the import and export of goods.

(*a*) The Chit Fund Act was established in August 1982, regulating chit funds in India and providing a framework for the conduct of chit fund businesses.

(*d*) The National Housing Bank Act was enacted in 1987, established as a principal agency to promote housing finance institutions both at local and regional levels.

(*c*) The Prevention of Money Laundering Act came into effect much later, in 2002, aimed at preventing money-laundering activities and providing for confiscation of property derived from, or involved in, money laundering.

This chronological order from earliest to latest, (*e*), (*b*), (*a*), (*d*), (*c*), is accurately captured in option A.

31. (B): The Net Reproduction Rate (NRR) is a demographic measure used to estimate whether the population is replacing itself from one generation to the next. If the NRR equals 1, it indicates that each woman is being replaced by exactly one daughter, on average, leading to a stable population size over time if this rate is sustained. The NRR takes into account female births and the survival rates of females until the end of their reproductive age.

It differs from Total Fertility Rate (TFR), which measures the average number of children a woman would have assuming she survives through her reproductive years, and from Gross Reproduction Rate (GRR), which counts only female births but does not account for mortality ratcs.

Thus, NRR = 1 (option B) is the correct answer as it precisely measures replacement fertility in terms of daughters who will continue the next generation.

32. (C): This question requires matching specific concepts and reports with their corresponding focus areas:

(*a*) The Travel Cost Method is a technique used in environmental economics for estimating economic values of ecosystems and parks that are not sold in a market. Hence, it is associated with Environmental Valuation (IV).

(*b*) The Stern Review is a comprehensive report that dealt with the economic impacts of Climate Change (III), authored by economist Nicholas Stern.

(*c*) The Brundtland Commission Report, formally known as "Our Common Future," introduced the concept of Sustainable Development (I), focusing on development that meets the needs of the present without compromising the ability of future generations.

(*d*) User Cost in the context of environmental economics often refers to the cost of depleting natural and Exhaustible Resources (II).

Option C (IV, III, I, II) accurately matches these terms with their corresponding areas of focus.

33. (B): The Coase Theorem, formulated by economist Ronald Coase, posits that if property rights are well-defined, transaction costs are negligible, and parties have complete information, then they can negotiate to resolve externalities privately regardless of the initial distribution of property rights. Key assumptions of the theorem include:

(A) Absence of transaction costs, allowing parties to negotiate without incurring significant costs.

(C) Complete information, where all parties are fully informed about the market and their own utility or cost functions.

(D) Complete property rights, ensuring that all resources are owned and any effects on third parties are internalized in decision making.

However, the presence of an income effect (B), where the allocation of resources affects the income distribution among the parties and thus their utility, is not a necessary condition or assumption for the Coase theorem. This option is correct as it represents what is not an assumption of the Coase theorem.

34. (B): The correct chronological order of these global economic and policy frameworks is:

- General Agreement on Tariffs and Trade (GATT), established in 1947, aimed at reducing tariffs and other trade barriers.
- National Bank for Agriculture and Rural Development (NABARD), established in 1982, focuses on the development of agriculture and rural areas in India.
- New Economic Policy of India (NEP), introduced in 1991, marked significant economic reforms including liberalization, privatization, and globalization.
- World Trade Organization (WTO), established in 1995, succeeded GATT and deals with the global rules of trade between nations.
- Introduction of Goods and Services Tax (GST) in India, implemented in 2017, to streamline and unify the various indirect taxes across the country.

Option B: (*b*),(*e*),(*c*),(*a*),(*d*) correctly orders these from oldest to latest.

35. (A): When imports are restricted by quotas, it typically leads to a process known as rent seeking. This economic concept involves individuals or entities expending resources to gain an economic gain from others without reciprocating any benefits back to society through wealth creation. Specifically, in the context of import quotas, rent-seeking behaviour can occur as importers, exporters, or local producers may spend significant amounts of money or effort to secure access to the limited import licenses, which can be highly profitable. This behaviour does not contribute to overall economic efficiency but instead leads to a redistribution of resources from the general public to those who can secure these lucrative quotas.

36. (A):

- Labour-capital ratio (*a*) refers to the amount of labour per unit of capital used in production, aligning with III.
- Labour-intensive commodity (*b*) describes a commodity with a lower capital-labour ratio at all relative factor prices, thus correctly matched with II.
- Labour theory of value (*c*) is a principle in classical economics where the price of a commodity is determined exclusively from its labour content, which fits with I.

- Labour saving technical progress (*d*) increases the productivity of capital proportionately more than labour, accurately described by IV.

This set of matchings (III, II, I, IV) provides a coherent alignment of economic concepts with their corresponding definitions as seen in option A.

37. (A):

- Physical Quality of Life Index (PQLI) was developed by Morris D. Morris (IV), focusing on evaluating countries based on literacy rates, infant mortality, and life expectancy.
- Human Development Index (HDI) was introduced by Mahbub ul Haq (II), designed to measure countries' economic development and standard of living, incorporating GDP, life expectancy, and educational attainment.
- Capability Approach to Development was extensively developed by Amartya Sen (I), which emphasizes the freedoms and capabilities people have access to, which enhance their quality of life.
- Multidimensional Poverty Index (MPI) is associated with Alkire and Foster (III), which measures poverty through multiple deprivations at the household level across various dimensions, such as health, education, and living standards.

Option A (IV, II, I, III) correctly associates these creators and concepts, matching the pioneering work of these influential thinkers with their contributions to developmental economics.

38. (D): Multiple expansion of credit:

The functions of the Reserve Bank of India (RBI) encompass a variety of roles crucial for the functioning of India's financial system:

- As the custodian of Foreign Exchange Reserves (A), RBI manages the foreign exchange and gold reserves of the nation.
- In its capacity to issue Bank Notes (B), RBI is responsible for the issuance and management of currency within India.
- Serving as the Lender of Last Resort (C), RBI provides necessary financial support to the banking system during financial distress or liquidity crises.

However, the concept of Multiple Expansion of Credit (D) refers to the process by which the commercial banking system creates money through loans and deposits, a mechanism inherent to fractional-reserve banking rather than a direct function of a central bank like RBI.

39. (A): Using the information given:

$P(\bar{A}) = 0.4$ implies $P(A) = 1 - 0.4 = 0.6$

because the probability of A and its complement $\bar{A}$ must sum to 1.

We know $P(A) = P(A \cap B) + P(A \cap \bar{B})$.

Plugging in the known values,

$0.6 = 0.2 + P(A \cap \bar{B})$

Solving for $P(A \cap \bar{B})$:

$P(A \cap \bar{B}) = 0.6 - 0.2 = 0.4.$

This result shows that the probability of A occurring without B is 0.4, which is option A.

40. (A):

(*a*) The Montreal Protocol is famously associated with the Control of Chlorofluorocarbons (CFCs) (II), an international treaty designed to phase out substances that deplete the ozone layer.

(*b*) COP 28 is a Climate Conference (III), part of the annual Conference of Parties under the United Nations Framework Convention on Climate Change (UNFCCC) where nations negotiate and discuss actions against climate change.

(*c*) Rio + 20 was a conference on Sustainable Development (IV), marking the 20th anniversary of the United Nations Conference on Environment and Development (UNCED), focusing on sustainable development and green economy.

(*d*) Willingness to Accept (WTA) involves the Contingent Valuation Method (I) used in environmental economics to determine the valuation that individuals place on changes in their consumption of goods, typically used to measure the cost of avoiding negative externalities or the compensation required for accepting changes.

Thus, option A (II, III, IV, I) is correct, matching each list item with its corresponding description accurately.

41. (B): To solve for dy/dx, consider the given function $y = \frac{1+x}{1-2x}$.

We can use the quotient rule for differentiation, which states:

if $y = \frac{u}{v}$, then $y' = \frac{u'v - uv'}{v^2}$.

Let $u = 1 + x$ and $v = 1 - 2x$.

- Differentiating u with respect to x gives $u' = 1$.
- Differentiating v with respect to x gives $v' = -2$.
- Plugging these into the quotient rule formula:

$$y' = \frac{(1)(1-2x)-(1+x)(-2)}{(1-2x)^2}$$

$$= \frac{1-2x+2+2x}{(1-2x)^2} = \frac{3}{(1-2x)^2}.$$

This calculation confirms that option B, $\frac{dy}{dx} = \frac{3}{(1-2x)^2}$, is the correct derivative of the given function.

42. (C): Under the Green Climate Fund (GCF) of the UNFCCC, an equitable balance between adaptation and mitigation funding is sought. Specifically, the GCF aims for a balanced allocation of resources between adaptation and mitigation activities. This is part of an effort to address the needs of developing countries, particularly those that are most vulnerable to the effects of climate change, such as small island developing states and least developed countries. The goal is to ensure that funding for adaptation to the adverse effects and mitigation to reduce emissions is provided on a 50:50 basis, reflecting the dual approach required to effectively tackle climate change. This commitment reflects the recognition that both adaptation and mitigation are essential components of the international response to climate change.

43. (D): Inflation can have several detrimental effects on an economy, and all listed items represent real costs associated with inflation:

(*a*) Shoeleather costs refer to the costs associated with the increased effort people must exert to minimize holding cash during inflationary times, such as more frequent trips to the bank.

(*b*) Menu costs are the costs businesses incur from having to frequently update prices in response to inflation.

(*c*) Increased variability of relative prices can distort consumer and producer decisions, leading to inefficient resource allocation.

(*d*) Unintended changes in tax liabilities occur due to non-indexation of the tax code, where inflation can push individuals into higher tax brackets without an actual increase in real income.

(*e*) Arbitrary redistribution of wealth happens because inflation can erode the real value of debts, benefiting debtors at the expense of creditors.

All these factors contribute to the costs of inflation, making option D correct, which includes all the given statements.

44. (A): To arrange these economic theories in chronological order:

- Factor Price Equalisation theory was developed by Paul Samuelson in the 1940s, which theorizes that free trade will lead to the equalization of the prices of factors of production across countries.
- The Leontief Paradox, discovered by Wassily Leontief in the early 1950s, challenged the empirical validity of the Factor Price Equalisation theory by showing that the U.S., with its capital abundance, exported labour-intensive commodities and imported capital intensive commodities.
- The Absorption approach was developed in the mid-20th century and involves understanding the balance of payments adjusted by national income or expenditure.
- Immiserizing Growth Theory was proposed by Jagdish Bhagwati in the 1950s, suggesting that economic growth could actually worsen a country's welfare if adverse terms of trade effects outweigh the benefits of growth.
- Reciprocal Dumping Model was developed later, in the 1980s, by Paul Krugman, addressing trade patterns where countries with similar products export to each other.

Option A, (*b*), (*d*), (*a*), (*e*), (*c*), correctly places these theories from the earliest to the latest.

45. (*)

46. (D): As of recent updates, the permissible limit of Foreign Direct Investment (FDI) in India's defense industry through the government route has been increased to 100 per cent. This policy change allows foreign companies to have full ownership of defense sector enterprises in India, subject to government approvals and security clearances, reflecting India's aim to attract more foreign investment in its defense technology and production capabilities. Therefore, the correct answer is D.

47. (D):

- Statement (*a*) is incorrect; the first UN conference on the human environment was held in Stockholm, Sweden, not Norway, in 1972.
- Statement (*b*) is incorrect; in the I = PAT expression, P stands for Population, not Poverty.
- Statement (*c*) is correct; Arthur Cecil Pigou suggested the pollution tax as a way to correct externalities by imposing costs equivalent to the societal cost of pollution.
- Statement (*d*) is correct; the logistic distribution often describes population growth in ecology, indicating how populations expand rapidly but slow as they reach carrying capacity.
- Statement (*e*) is incorrect; Hedonic pricing is indeed an environmental valuation method, but it is primarily used to value environmental amenities by observing the differences in prices of goods or services affected by environmental variables, not specifically for valuing tourism sites.

Therefore, option D is correct, including the correct statements (*c*) and (*d*) only.

48. (A): Arranging these events chronologically:

- The 364-day treasury bill with market-related rates was introduced in India first, which was part of the financial reforms to control monetary policy more effectively, introduced in the 1980s.

- The IRDA Act (Insurance Regulatory and Development Authority Act) was passed in Parliament in 1999 to regulate and promote the insurance and re-insurance industries in India.
- The Global Trust Bank was merged with UTI Bank (now Axis Bank) following financial difficulties, and this occurred in 2004.
- The Fiscal Responsibility and Budget Management Act was passed in 2003 to ensure fiscal discipline by setting targets to eliminate revenue deficits and reduce fiscal deficits.
- The concept of financial inclusion was introduced more prominently into the banking sector post-2005, aiming at providing banking and financial services to all people in a fair, transparent; and equitable manner.

Thus, the correct chronological order is (*d*), (*a*), (*c*), (*e*), (*b*), as per option A.

49. (C): Matching each individual with their correct contributions or related terms:

(*a*) NITI Aayog is associated with providing knowledge support and policy recommendations in India, matching with IV.

(*b*) R. Axelrod is known for his work on the evolution of cooperation and the use of the Tit-for-Tat strategy in repeated interactions, correctly matching with I.

(*c*) J. Stiglitz is renowned for his contributions to the efficiency wage theory, which argues that wages influence worker productivity, fitting with II.

(*d*) India's first five-year plan (1951-1956) was drafted under the guidance of economist K.N. Raj, linking him with III.

This configuration aligns perfectly with option C: IV, I, II, III.

50. (B):

(*a*) W.W. Leontief is famous for developing the Input-Output model in economics, which helps to predict the impact of various economic changes and policies, matching with IV.

(*b*) Jan Tinbergen is known for his work in developing models for economic policy-making, including the concept of the Shadow Price, which matches with I.

(*c*) J.M. Keynes is renowned for his theory of the Consumption Function, which describes the relationship between income and expenditure, fitting with II.

(*d*) Joseph Bertrand proposed Bertrand competition, a model of price competition among firms selling homogenous products, which aligns with III.

Therefore, the correct answers and matches are provided in option B: IV, I, II, III.

51. (A): The chronological order of these environmental and economic theories and agreements is:

- Hotelling's Principle (economics of non-renewable resources), introduced in 1931.
- Establishment of IUCN (International Union for Conservation of Nature) in 1948, a major global conservation organization.
- Nash Equilibrium (game theory), formulated by John Nash in the early 1950s.
- Coase Theorem (law and economics), introduced by Ronald Coase in 1960.
- Kyoto Protocol (international environmental treaty), adopted in 1997.

52. (D):

- The top beneficiary from Foreign exchange trading typically refers to major financial centers like London (III).

- The concept that competitive equilibrium is Pareto efficient aligns with the First theorem of welfare economics (IV), which states that any competitive equilibrium leads to a Pareto efficient allocation of resources.
- Walras, famously associated with General equilibrium analysis, where multiple markets and their interactions are analyzed collectively (II).
- Game Theory was significantly developed by John Von Neuman and Oscar Morgenstern, making it a pivotal framework in understanding strategic interactions among rational decision-makers (I).

Option D correctly matches these concepts with their descriptions: III, IV, II, I.

53. (A): The concept of efficiency wage theory was notably advanced by economists such as Joseph Stiglitz and Janet Yellen among others. This theory suggests that employers pay a wage that is higher than the market-clearing wage to increase worker productivity and reduce turnover. This approach explains various labour market phenomena, including wage rigidity and the persistence of involuntary unemployment.

54. (A): Statement (*a*) is correct: The price consumption curve (PCC) shows the quantities of two goods a consumer will purchase as the price of one of the goods changes, while a demand curve shows the quantity of one good a consumer will purchase as the price of that good changes. The graph of the PCC plots the quantity of one good on the horizontal axis and the quantity of the other good on the vertical axis. The demand curve plots the quantity of the good on the horizontal axis and its price on the vertical axis.

Statement (*c*) is correct; the condition for stability in a simple Keynesian system does indeed require that the marginal propensity to consume (MPC) be between 0 and 1 to ensure that the multiplier effect is positive but finite.

55. (D): The value of SSE (sum of squared errors) will change:

- Swapping the explanatory and response variables in a regression analysis does not change the value of the correlation between the two variables, as correlation is a measure of the linear association irrespective of which variable is considered dependent or independent.
- The sign of the slope does not inherently change simply due to swapping the variables; it reflects the relationship direction and will be consistent unless the data or model specification fundamentally changes.
- The coefficient of determination (R^2), which measures the proportion of variance in the dependent variable that can be predicted from the independent variable, remains unchanged because it is derived from the correlation coefficient.
- The value of the Sum of Squared Errors (SSE), however, will change as it depends on the fit of the model to the data points, which will differ when the roles of the variables are reversed. The new model may fit the data differently, leading to a different SSE value.

56. (D): A surplus in the balance of payments can result from various economic factors that influence the flow of money into and out of a country.

(*a*) A decline in imports would lead to a surplus in the balance of payments as less money is leaving the country to pay for these imports.

(*c*) An increase in exports also contributes to a surplus because it means more foreign buyers are spending their money to purchase the exporting country's goods, thus bringing more money into the country.

(*b*) A decline in interest rates and an increase in income tax (*d*) do not directly lead to a surplus in the balance of payments. Lower interest rates could lead to an increase in investment but may also reduce the inflow of foreign capital seeking higher returns, making its impact on balance of payments ambiguous.

(*e*) High outward Foreign Direct Investment would not result in a surplus but a deficit, as it involves domestic capital flowing out to foreign entities.

Hence, the correct answer is D, as it includes (*a*) and (*c*) which directly contribute to a surplus in the balance of payments.

57. (D):

(*a*) An endogenous variable is a key element within simultaneous equations where it is influenced by other variables within the model, aligning with II.

(*b*) Count R^2, a measure often used in statistics, does not directly match with Logit regression. Thus, IV (Logit regression) is the misalignment here, as there is no specific technique called Count R^2 that is standard. However, the best fit from given options, by the process of elimination, would be IV since others are clearly mismatched.

(*c*) Ljung Box Statistic is used to test for autocorrelation in time series data, fitting with I.

(*d*) Least square dummy variable model is often used in panel data regression to handle categorical variables, matching with III.

Hence, the best fitting answer, by the process of elimination and provided options, is D: II, IV, I, III.

58. (C): The Fisher effect describes the relationship between nominal interest rates, real interest rates, and the expected inflation rate. It posits that the nominal interest rate is equal to the sum of the real interest rate plus the expected inflation rate. This relationship implies that when inflation is high, nominal interest rates tend to be high as lenders need compensation for the decreased purchasing power of money. Conversely, when inflation is low, nominal interest rates are lower.

59. (D): In the State Energy Efficiency Index 2023 released by NITI Aayog, Karnataka emerged as the top scorer, securing the highest rank. This index assesses states on their policies and initiatives related to energy efficiency, considering various sectors such as buildings, industries, municipalities, transport, agriculture, and DISCOMs. Karnataka's leadership in the index reflects its comprehensive approach to implementing energy efficiency measures, promoting sustainable energy policies, and leading in renewable energy usage and conservation practices.

60. (C):

- Narasimham Committee II (1998) recommended that the RBI withdraw from the 91-day treasury bills market and that interbank call money and term money markets be restricted to banks and primary dealers.
- The Ghosh Committee made recommendations relating to frauds and malpractices in banks. The committee provided 53 total recommendations organized under multiple groups.
- Padmanabhan Committee was set up by RBI on supervision of Banks. It was set up in the year 1995 and headed by S. Padmanabhan. It recommended that banking supervision should be based on Managerial and operational efficiency, financial strength of the bank.

- The Saraf Committee Report dealt with technology issues in banking.

Given the context and options provided, option C: III, I, IV, II is the best match according to the descriptions and common understandings of these committee focuses.

61. (D): The savings function given is $S = -5 + 0.3q$, where S is savings and q is income. This function suggests that at $q = 0$ (zero income), savings start at -5, indicating dis-savings or consumption financed by borrowing or drawing down previous savings. The marginal propensity to save (MPS) is 0.3, indicating that for every additional dollar of income, 30 cents is saved. This implies that the marginal propensity to consume (MPC) is 0.7 (since MPC + MPS = 1).

The average propensity to consume (APC) is calculated as

$$\text{APC} = \frac{C}{q} = \frac{q - S}{q} = 1 - \frac{-5 + 0.3q}{q}$$

$= 1 - (-0.05 + 0.3) = 0.75 + 0.05 = 0.8$

when q is \$100. As q increases, the negative impact of the –5 decreases, making the APC trend downward but starting from a higher value than the MPC.

Therefore, generally, APC will be greater than MPC, especially at lower income levels. Thus, option D is correct.

62. (C): The sequence of introduction of these taxes is as follows:

(*d*) Minimum Alternate Tax (MAT) was intro- duced in 1987 to ensure that companies with large profits and who were eligible for various deductions paid a minimum amount of tax to the government.

(*b*) Securities Transaction Tax (STT) was introduced in 2004 as part of efforts to reduce tax evasion in stock market transactions.

(*c*) Banking Cash Transaction Tax was introduced in 2005, although later repealed, it was initially aimed at tracking large cash transactions.

(*e*) Angel Tax refers to income tax payable on capital raised by unlisted companies via issue of shares where the share price is seen in excess of the fair market value, introduced in 2012.

(*a*) Commodities Transaction Tax was introduced later in 2013 on transactions similar to the STT but applied to commodity trades.

63. (A): The Fifteenth Finance Commission used certain criteria with specific weightages for devolution of tax revenue to states. Among these, income distance had the highest weight, indicating that states further from the fiscal capacity norm get more funds. This is followed by area, which captures the geographic spread of a state. Demographic performance, which includes population data from the latest census, comes next. The weightage for forest and ecology accounts for the state's efforts in maintaining ecological balance. Finally, tax effort assesses the effort made by states in collecting their revenues.

Therefore, option A: (*a*), (*b*), (*c*), (*d*), (*e*) correctly orders these norms from highest to lowest weightage.

64. (B):

(*a*) Bank run, a situation where a large number of bank customers withdraw their deposits because they believe the bank might become insolvent, is closely associated with the theories of Douglas Diamond, who modeled banks' roles in providing liquidity (III).

(*b*) The q-ratio, or Tobin's q, is a measure comparing the market value and replacement value of the same physical asset, developed by James Tobin (IV).

(*c*) Genuine saving, a sustainability indicator that considers investment less depreciation of natural and manufactured capital, was notably discussed by Pearce among others, but aligns best with I given the remaining choices.

(*d*) Microfinance is prominently connected with Muhammad Yunus, who pioneered modern microfinance practices with his work in founding the Grameen Bank (II).

Option B, III, IV, I, II, accurately matches these individuals with their respective concepts.

65. (C)

66. (B): For a typical demand function $Q_d = f(P_x, P_y, M)$, where P_x is the price of the good x, P_y is the price of another good y, and M is income, the sum of the own-price elasticity of demand, cross-price elasticity of demand (with respect to the price of another good), and income elasticity of demand typically equals zero in a balanced market system according to economic theory. This assertion stems from the adding-up constraint in economic modeling, where the proportional changes caused by prices and income typically counterbalance each other when considering a market equilibrium under ceteris paribus (all other factors being constant) conditions.

Therefore, option B (zero) is the correct answer, as it aligns with the theoretical expectation that these elasticities, representing different dimensions of demand responsiveness, sum to zero when the market is balanced.

67. (A): To test the null hypothesis $H_0 : \mu = \mu_0$ when both the population mean μ and the standard deviation σ are unknown, the appropriate test statistic is the Student's *t*-test. The formula for the *t*-test statistic is:

$$t_{n-1} = \frac{\bar{x} - \mu_0}{s' / \sqrt{n}}$$

where:

- $\bar{x}$ is the sample mean,
- μ_0 is the hypothesized mean under the null hypothesis,
- s' is the sample standard deviation,
- n is the sample size,
- $n - 1$ represents the degrees of freedom in the *t*-distribution, which is particularly used because the population standard deviation is unknown.

This formula quantifies how much the sample mean deviates from the hypothesized mean, scaled by the standard error of the mean. The denominator $s' / \sqrt{n}$ is the standard error of the mean, estimating the variation expected in sample means from samples of size n drawn from the population.

Option A: $t_{n-1} = \dfrac{\bar{x} - \mu_0}{s' / \sqrt{n}}$ correctly applies the Student's *t*-distribution principles for cases where the population standard deviation is unknown, hence it is the appropriate choice. This formula helps in making inferences about the population mean based on the sample data when the variance is estimated from the same sample data, requiring adjustment in the degrees of freedom (hence $n - 1$).

68. (C): The current global measurement of the extreme poverty line, as updated by the World Bank in October 2022, is $2.15 per day. This figure reflects the cost of essential goods and services in 2017 purchasing power parity (PPP), adjusted to account for inflation and changes in the cost of living. It replaces the previous benchmark of $1.90 per day, which was based on 2011 PPP data. This threshold is used to identify individuals living in extreme poverty globally and is critical for tracking progress toward poverty alleviation and development goals. Therefore, the correct answer is C. \$2.15 a day.

69. (D): The National Health Policy 2017 of India sets various ambitious targets to improve health outcomes across the country by 2025. These include:

(*c*) Reducing the Maternal Mortality Rate (MMR) to 100.

(*d*) Achieving a Total Fertility Rate (TFR) of 2.1, which is considered a replacement level fertility rate where a population exactly replaces itself from one generation to the next without migration.

(*e*) Increasing Life Expectancy at Birth to 70 years.

While the policy also includes targets for Infant Mortality Rate (IMR) and Under Five Mortality Rate (U5MR), the correct objectives specified to be achieved by 2025 as per the question are (*c*), (*d*), and (*e*), making option D the accurate answer.

70. (A): Regional Rural Banks (RRBs) in India have specific characteristics and roles:

(*a*) RRBs were indeed set up based on the recommendation of the Narasimham Working Group in 1975, which aimed to provide sufficient banking and credit facility for agriculture and other rural sectors.

(*c*) NABARD (National Bank for Agriculture and Rural Development) coordinates the activities of RRBs, especially relating to their development functions and also supervises their financial stability and operational policies.

(*e*) RRBs are provided with refinance facilities through NABARD, which helps them extend loans to farmers and rural businesses at lower interest rates, supporting rural development effectively.

The statement about the largest proportion of equity being held by sponsor banks (*b*) is incorrect as the largest proportion is actually held by the Government of India. RRBs are not lead banks (*d*); they operate under the sponsorship of leading nationalized banks.

Thus, the correct answer is A: (*a*), (*c*), (*e*) only.

71. (D): ANCOVA (Analysis of Covariance) models are statistical techniques that combine features of ANOVA (Analysis of Variance) and regression analysis. These models are used to analyze the influence of both categorical (qualitative) and continuous (quantitative) independent variables while controlling for the effects of one or more covariates.

By incorporating both types of variables, ANCOVA can adjust the dependent variable for covariates before testing for statistical differences among the group means. This makes it possible to improve the accuracy of the results by reducing variability caused by extraneous factors and focusing on the primary relationships of interest. Hence, option D is correct.

72. (D): Neonatal death refers to the death of a baby during the first 28 completed days of life. This classification is commonly used in medical and health-related statistics to focus on deaths that occur in this critical initial period after birth.

The neonatal period is significant because it is when the infant is most vulnerable to various health issues, including infections, birth injuries, and congenital anomalies. Understanding neonatal mortality is crucial for improving child healthcare and interventions aimed at reducing infant mortality rates. Therefore, option D is correct.

73. (A): In the context of linear programming problems (LPP):

(*a*) A feasible solution must satisfy all the problem's constraints simultaneously. This means that any solution that does not meet all constraints is considered infeasible.

(*b*) Is incorrect because a feasible solution must indeed satisfy all constraints, not just some.

(*c*) Is incorrect because a feasible solution does not necessarily have to be a corner point of the feasible region; it can be any point within the region.

(*d*) Is correct because a feasible solution may or may not optimize the value of the objective function. Optimization is achieved specifically at an optimal solution, which is a special case of feasible solutions.

(*e*) Is correct because, in standard linear programming formulations, all decision variables are constrained to be non-negative, meaning they must be greater than or equal to zero.

Thus, option A, (*a*), (*d*), (*e*) only, accurately describes the properties of feasible solutions in linear programming.

74. (B):

(*a*) Ad Valorem Tariff is a type of tariff that is calculated as a percentage of the value of the commodity being imported or exported, fitting description IV.

(*b*) Autarky refers to a state of a country being completely self-sufficient and not engaging in international trade, which aligns with description III.

(*c*) Compound Tariff is a mix of Ad Valorem and specific tariffs, where the tariff includes both a fixed component and a percentage of the item's value, matching with description II.

(*d*) Specific Tariff is a fixed amount charged per unit of the good, fitting description I.

Hence, option B (IV, III, II, I) correctly matches the types of tariffs with their definitions.

75. (D): According to the National Family Health Survey-5 (NFHS-5) for the period 2019-21, the sex ratio (number of females per 1000 males) in India was reported as 1020 females per 1000 males. This statistic indicates a higher number of females relative to males in the population during the survey period, reflecting trends in demographics, health outcomes, and possibly the effectiveness of policies aimed at correcting gender imbalances.

Option D, stating 1020 females per 1000 males, is correct and aligns with the survey findings.

76. (A): A Nash equilibrium is where no player can do better by unilaterally changing their strategy. To find it, check each player's best response to the other's strategies:

- For B_1, B_2, B_3 the best responses for Player P are A_3 yielding payoffs of 5, 4, and 5 respectively.
- For A_1, A_2, A_3 the best responses for Player B are B_1, B_1, B_2 yielding payoffs of 4, 5, and 4 respectively.

The only strategy pair where both players are playing best responses to the other is (A_3, B_2), resulting in the payoff (4, 4), confirming that this is a Nash equilibrium. Therefore, option A is correct.

77. (A): The correct order of the Nobel Prize awards for these economists, from earliest to latest, is:

- Gunnar Myrdal and Friedrich Hayek (not listed), jointly awarded in 1974.
- Milton Friedman, awarded in 1976.

- Arthur Lewis and Theodore Schultz (not listed), jointly awarded in 1979.
- Lawrence Klein, awarded in 1980.
- Abhijit Banerjee, awarded in 2019 along with Esther Duflo and Michael Kremer.

Option A: (*b*),(*c*),(*a*),(*e*),(*d*) presents these economists in the correct chronological order of their Nobel Prize recognitions.

78. (A):

- Statement (*a*) is correct: A public good is nonexclusive, meaning it is not feasible to exclude anyone from using the good, regardless of whether they have paid for it or not.
- Statement (*b*) is correct: National defense is often cited as a classic example of a public good because it provides a service from which all citizens benefit, and no one can be excluded from its protection.
- Statement (*c*) is incorrect: Public goods are not rival, meaning that one person's use of the good does not diminish the ability of another person to use it.
- Statement (*d*) is incorrect: The provision of public goods does not entail a non-zero marginal cost; public goods are characterized by a zero marginal cost of provision to an additional consumer.
- Statement (*e*) is incorrect: Public goods do not inherently create inefficiency in consumption; rather, the challenge with public goods is in their provision and financing, leading to potential under-provision or funding issues.

Thus, option A is correct, accurately including statements (*a*) and (*b*) only.

79. (C): In the context of the Fifteenth Finance Commission's assignments of grants-in-aid to the states, the biggest item is typically for Local bodies grants. These grants are significant as they directly support the financial needs of local governmental bodies, enabling them to deliver essential services and carry out local development projects. This allocation is vital for maintaining the infrastructural and operational capacities at the local level, including urban and rural bodies, which are crucial for localized governance and service provision. Therefore, the correct answer is C, aligning with the commission's focus on strengthening grassroots governance structures through substantial financial support.

80. (B):

- Venture Capital (*a*) and Global Depository Receipts (*d*) are instruments used within the capital market. Venture capital is a type of private equity and a form of financing that investors provide to startup companies and small businesses that are believed to have long-term growth potential. Global Depository Receipts (GDRs) represent bank certificates issued in more than one country for shares in foreign companies, allowing an international company to access investors in capital markets other than its own.
- Treasury Bills (*b*) are short-term government securities typically issued in the money market.
- Certificates of Deposit (*c*) issued by commercial banks and Inter Corporate Deposits (*e*) are also instruments primarily associated with the money market rather than the capital market.

Therefore, option B: (*a*), (*d*) only, is the correct answer, accurately representing instruments that are part of the capital market.

81. (B):

(*c*) Adam Smith published "The Wealth of Nations" in 1776, which laid the foundations of classical economics and includes discussions on growth, though not framed as a "Theory of Growth" per se, it is foundational.

(*b*) J.M. Keynes published "The General Theory of Employment, Interest, and Money" in 1936, fundamentally changing economic thought concerning the causes of unemployment and interventions by government policy.

(*e*) Robert M. Solow introduced his growth model in 1956, which extended the Harrod-Domar model by including technology change and labour as drivers of growth.

(*a*) A.W. Phillips introduced the Phillips Curve in 1958, describing an inverse relationship between rates of unemployment and corresponding rates of rises in wages that result within an economy.

(*d*) John F. Muth formulated the Rational Expectations theory, which was introduced in the early 1960s, refining predictions in macroeconomic models by assuming that people's predictions of the future are informed by their understanding of economic policy.

Thus, option B: (*c*), (*b*), (*e*), (*a*), (*d*) arranges these economists from the earliest to the latest relevant contributions.

82. (D): The construction of concepts related to consumer behaviour in economics follows a logical sequence, starting from foundational theories to more complex analyses. The correct order is:

(*b*) Utility analysis, which is the fundamental concept where consumer preferences and utilities are defined and understood.

(*d*) Indifference curve analysis, which builds on utility analysis by graphically representing consumer preferences through curves that indicate combinations of goods between which the consumer is indifferent.

(*a*) Budget, which introduces the constraints under which consumers optimize their choices, considering their limited resources.

(*e*) Consumer's equilibrium, where the optimal choice of the consumer is determined at the point where the budget constraint tangentially touches the highest attainable indifference curve.

(*c*) Demand curve analysis, which is derived last as it aggregates consumer behaviours into market-wide relationships between price changes and quantity demanded.

This sequence from individual preference analysis to market demand representation reflects the logical progression in economic theory, making option D: (*b*), (*d*), (*a*), (*e*), (*c*), the correct and comprehensive order of development in these concepts.

83. (B):

(*a*) Monopoly theory of distribution was discussed by Michal Kalecki, linking the degree of monopoly to income distribution (III).

(*b*) The theory of profit, encompassing various interpretations including dynamics of business profits, was an area explored by theorists like Alfred Marshall, but within this context, aligning it with Walker, who discussed profits in the context of capital and distribution, seems most fitting given the options (I).

(*c*) Full cost pricing is associated with Hall and Hitch, who argued that businesses price based on costs plus a mark-up, commonly used in managerial economics (IV).

(*d*) Modern theory of rent, concerning how rent is determined in modern economic contexts, aligns with Joan Robinson's work, which extensively covered various facets of pricing and market structures (II).

Thus, option B: III, I, IV, II, correctly matches each theorist with their respective theories or models.

84. (A): The Gravity Model of world trade is a major model in international economics that predicts bilateral trade flows based on the economic sizes (often measured by GDP) of the two countries (*a*) and the distance between them (*b*).

- Distance acts as a proxy for the costs associated with trade, including transportation costs, tariffs, and other barriers.
- Gross Domestic Product of the trading countries indicates the size of their economies, suggesting potential volume of trade that could be supported by larger economies.

Foreign exchange rates (*c*) and foreign investment (*e*) influence trade but are not core components of the basic Gravity Model, which focuses primarily on size and distance. Option A: (*a*) and (*b*) only, accurately captures the fundamental components as per the Gravity Model of trade.

85. (C):

- The Engel-Granger test is one of the methods used to test for cointegration among non-stationary time series data. It involves running a regression on the time series variables, then testing the residuals from this regression for stationarity.
- If the residuals are found to be stationary, it suggests that although the individual time series may be non-stationary, they move together over time in a way that their linear combination is stationary, indicating cointegration.
- Chow test is used for testing structural breaks in regression models.
- Phillips-Peron test is used to check for unit roots in time series data.
- Error-correction mechanism is a dynamic model used in time series analysis to adjust the speed at which variables return to equilibrium after a change.

Therefore, option C: Engel-Granger test, is the correct answer for identifying a method used for testing cointegration.

86. (A): To arrange these expressions in terms of increasing magnitude, we consider the impact of each component in the expressions. Given $a > 0$, $b > 0$, $x > 0$:

(*d*) $y = e^{a - \frac{b}{x}}$ is the smallest because subtraction of a positive fraction reduces the value.

(*a*) $y = e^a$ simply is the exponential growth value which sets a base magnitude.

(*c*) $y = e^{a + \frac{b}{x}}$ adds a positive fraction to e^a, making it larger than (*a*).

(*b*) $y = e^{a + bx}$ is larger than (*c*) because as $x > 0$, bx would be greater than $\frac{b}{x}$ for $x > 1$.

(*e*) $y = e^{a + 2bx}$ is the largest because it doubles the bx term compared to (*b*), thus adding more to e^a.

Option A correctly places these expressions from smallest to largest.

87. (C): In the leakage-injection approach to income determination, an increase in lump-sum tax (assuming no changes in other variables — ceteris paribus) effectively increases leakage in the form of taxes. This would shift the savings plus tax leakage line to the left in the income-leakage diagram. This shift represents an increase in total leakages relative to a given level of income, thus reducing disposable income and potentially lowering aggregate demand unless countered by equivalent injections. It does not directly affect the investment plus government spending line, unless there are fiscal responses compensating for the higher tax.

88. (A): In the Cobb-Douglas production function $q = AL^{\alpha}K^{\beta}$, where A, α and β are constants, α and β represent the output elasticities of the inputs. Specifically, α measures the output elasticity with respect to labour, and β measures the output elasticity with respect to capital. These parameters indicate the percentage change in output resulting from a one per cent change in labour or capital, respectively, holding all else constant. This relationship is central to understanding how changes in input amounts affect output levels, making option A correct.

89. (B): When dealing with high multicollinearity in regression models, though not perfect:

- It can result in high confidence intervals for the estimates, making them less precise (A).
- It can lead to a high R^2 value, indicating a good fit of the model with the included variables despite the multicollinearity (C).
- The estimates are not necessarily the Best Linear Unbiased Estimators (BLUE); multicollinearity can make the estimates biased or inefficient in some cases (D).
- High multicollinearity does not necessarily lead to statistical significance for all coefficient estimates (B). On the contrary, it can inflate the standard errors of the coefficients, leading to fewer statistically significant results, despite a good overall model fit.

90. (C): Both arithmetic mean and median are wrong: Given:

- The lowest value in the set is 4.5.
- The range of the set is 10.9, implying the highest value is 4.5 + 10.9 = 15.4.
- An arithmetic mean of 19.9 is impossible because it is greater than the maximum value in the data set.
- A median of 15.6 is also incorrect as the median must lie between the minimum and maximum values of the data set, which are 4.5 and 15.4, respectively.

Therefore, both the arithmetic mean and median as provided cannot be correct, leading to the selection of option C.

91. (B): When comparing the competitive and monopoly scenarios, the producer's gains when moving from competitive pricing (P_c) to monopoly pricing (P_m) can be visualized in the diagram.

Under competitive pricing, the producer surplus is the area above the MC curve and below the price P_c, up to Q_c. When moving to monopoly pricing, the producer surplus is the area above the MC curve and below P_m up to Q_m. The gain in producer surplus due to the price increase from P_c to P_m is represented by the rectangle A. However, the reduction in output from Q_c to Q_m also removes some producer surplus, represented by triangle C. Thus, the net gain in producer surplus due to moving from competitive to monopoly pricing is the area A minus the area C, confirming the answer as B.

92. (B): The consumer loss due to the transition from competitive pricing (P_c) to monopoly pricing (P_m) comprises the areas representing the increased costs and the loss of welfare due to reduced consumption.

Area A represents the increased cost to consumers who still purchase the product at the higher monopoly price (P_m), paying more than the competitive price (P_c).

Area B represents the consumer surplus lost due to the decreased quantity consumed, moving from Q_c to Q_m, as some consumers opt out of buying the product at the higher price.

Therefore, the total consumer loss includes both the extra amount paid for the units still bought (A) and the consumer surplus lost on the units no longer bought (B). Thus, the answer is B.

93. (A): Assuming that production processes involve environmental impacts like emissions or resource depletion, producing less quantity, as in the monopoly output (Q_m), compared to the competitive output (Q_c), leads to a reduction in these negative environmental impacts.

The rationale is that fewer units of production result in fewer emissions or less resource use. Therefore, under the assumptions typically related to environmental impacts tied to production volume, a monopoly, by producing less, inadvertently contributes to less environmental degradation compared to a competitive market output level.

Hence, A: Monopoly output is environmentally friendlier comparative to competitive output, is correct.

94. (C): The diagram illustrates that by charging a higher price (P_m) and reducing output to Q_m, the monopolist gains rectangle A due to the higher price but loses triangle C because of producing fewer units.

This is reflective of the monopolist's profit-maximizing behaviour, where the price is raised to increase revenue per unit, thus gaining area A, but at the cost of losing some customers due to the higher price, represented by the loss of area C.

Therefore, the producer gains area A and loses area C as a result of adopting a monopoly pricing strategy, leading to the answer C.

95. (D): Deadweight loss in the context of monopoly refers to the loss of economic efficiency when the equilibrium for goods or services is not achieved or is not achievable.

In the given diagram, the areas B and C together represent this deadweight loss.

Area B is the consumer surplus that is lost and not gained by the producer, while area C represents the producer surplus lost due to reduced output. These areas indicate the total welfare loss to society due to the monopolistic pricing above marginal cost and the reduction in quantity produced from Q_c to Q_m.

Thus, the correct answer is D: B + C, representing the comprehensive deadweight loss due to the monopoly's pricing and output decisions.

96. (A): To calculate the fiscal deficit as a percentage of GDP, first determine the fiscal deficit. Fiscal deficit is calculated as total expenditure minus total receipts excluding borrowings. Here, total receipts are ₹ 400 crore, and total expenditure (sum of revenue and capital expenditure) is ₹ 400 crore (₹ 300 crore in revenue + ₹ 100 crore in capital). The total receipts excluding borrowings (₹ 400 crore – ₹ 100 crore borrowings) equals ₹ 300 crore.

Thus, the fiscal deficit = Total Expenditure – (Total Receipts – Borrowings)

= ₹ 400 crore – ₹ 300 crore

= ₹ 100 crore.

The GDP is ₹ 2000 crore.

Thus, the fiscal deficit as a percentage of GDP

= (₹ 100 crore / ₹ 2000 crore) × 100 = 5%.

Therefore, the fiscal deficit as a percentage of GDP is 5%, making option A correct.

97. (D): The primary deficit is calculated as the fiscal deficit minus interest payments. From the earlier calculation, we know the fiscal deficit is ₹ 100 crore. Interest payments are ₹ 90 crore.

Thus, the primary deficit = ₹ 100 crore – ₹ 90 crore = ₹ 10 crore.

As a percentage of GDP (₹ 2000 crore), the primary deficit = (₹ 10 crore / ₹ 2000 crore) × 100 = 0.5%.

Therefore, the primary deficit as a percentage of GDP is 0.5%, making option D correct.

98. (A): The revenue deficit is calculated as total revenue expenditure minus total revenue receipts.

Total revenue expenditure is ₹ 300 crore and total revenue receipts are ₹ 250 crore. Thus, the revenue deficit

= ₹ 300 crore – ₹ 250 crore = ₹ 50 crore.

As a percentage of GDP (₹ 2000 crore), the revenue deficit

= (₹ 50 crore/₹ 2000 crore) × 100 = 2.5%.

Therefore, the revenue deficit as a percentage of GDP is 2.5%, making option A correct.

99. (C): The effective revenue deficit subtracts grants for the creation of capital assets from the revenue deficit. Grants for the creation of capital assets are ₹ 20 crore. The calculated revenue deficit is ₹ 50 crore. Thus, effective revenue deficit

= ₹ 50 crore – ₹ 20 crore = ₹ 30 crore.

As a percentage of GDP (₹ 2000 crore), the effective revenue deficit

= (₹ 30 crore/₹ 2000 crore) × 100

= 1.5%.

Therefore, the effective revenue deficit as a percentage of GDP is 1.5%, making option C correct.

100. (C): The twin deficit refers to the sum of the fiscal deficit and the current account deficit as a percentage of GDP. The fiscal deficit has already been calculated as ₹ 100 crore, and the current account deficit is given as ₹ 50 crore.

Thus, total twin deficit

= ₹ 100 crore + ₹ 50 crore = ₹ 150 crore.

As a percentage of GDP (₹ 2000 crore), the twin deficit

= (₹ 150 crore/₹ 2000 crore) × 100

= 7.5%.

Therefore, the twin deficit as a percentage of GDP is 7.5%, making option C correct.

Previous Years' Paper

National Testing Agency (NTA)

UGC-NET Junior Research Fellowship & Assistant Professor Eligibility Exam

ECONOMICS, December-2023

(Exam held on 12-12-2023)

PAPER-II

1. The expert committee set up by RBI in 2013 to revise and strengthen the monetary policy framework in India was chaired by:

A. Raghuram Rajan B. Urjit Patel
C. Deepak Mohanty D. Michael Patra

2. Under the flexible inflation targeting framework of monetary policy adopted by the RBI in 2016 what is the target range of rate of inflation?

A. (4 ± 2)% B. (5 ± 2)%
C. (3 ± 2)% D. (2 ± 2)%

3. In a regression of a dependent variable on intercept and *k* other independent variables using *n* observations, what are respectively the numerator and denominator degrees of freedom for the F test for overall significance of the regression?

A. $k-1, n-k$ B. $k, n-k-1$
C. $k-1, n-k-1$ D. $k, n-k$

4. Suppose X_i is income of an individual *i* and Y_i is the event that this individual owns a house, P_i = prob $(Y_i = 1 \mid X_i)$ and $Z_i = \beta_1 + \beta_2 X_i$, (which of the following is true for the logit model?

A. $P_i = \frac{1}{1-e^{-Z_i}}$ B. $P_i = \frac{1}{1+e^{Z_i}}$

C. $P_i = \frac{1}{1+e^{-Z_i}}$ D. $P_i = \frac{1}{1-e^{Z_i}}$

5. If the estimated slope coefficient in the regression of Y on X is $\hat{\beta}$, what will be the estimated slope coefficient in the regression of 5 Y on 10 X?

A. $5\hat{\beta}$ B. $10\hat{\beta}$

C. $2\hat{\beta}$ D. $0.5\hat{\beta}$

6. Which of the following tests has stationarity as the null hypothesis?

A. ADF Test
B. Phillips Perron Test
C. ERS Test
D. KPSS Test

7. For a VAR model estimated using two variables X and Y, Lags of Y are jointly significant in the equation for X but Lags of X are jointly insignificant in the equation for Y. What can you conclude from this?

A. There is no Granger causality between X and Y
B. There is bidirectional Granger causality between X and Y
C. X Granger causes Y but Y does not Granger cause X
D. Y Granger causes X but X does not Granger cause Y

8. Suppose India is the home country and USA is the foreign country. The interest rates in India and USA are 6% and 4% respectively.

The exchange rate of US Dollar is ₹ 80 today but is expected to rise to ₹ 84 in one year. Which of the following is true, according to the uncovered interest arbitrage paritv condition?

A. Capital will flow into the Indian economy
B. Capital will flow out of the Indian economy
C. No captial flows
D. Can't say on the basis of the information provided

9. In the model ln $Y_i = \alpha + \beta X_i + u_i$ Where ln is natural log, the elasticity of Y w.r. t. X is given by:

A. β B. βX_i

C. $\frac{\beta}{Y_i}$ D. $\beta\frac{X_i}{Y_i}$

10. In an economy real GDP has increased from $ 990 PPP to $ 1080 PPP during 2015 to 2020. The incremental capital output ratio is 2.5. The rate of investment is:

A. 27.8 Percent B. 22.5 Percent
C. 3.9 Percent D. 19.5 Percent

11. Which of the following dimensions is included in HPI-2 (Human Poverty Index-2)?

A. Gender Inequalities
B. Financial Inclusion
C. Social Inclusion
D. Economic Inclusion

12. The Solow residual is:

A. The difference between the rate of growth of productivity and the rate of growth of inputs
B. The difference between the rate of growth of output and the rate of growth of saving
C. The difference between the rate of growth of output and the rate of growth of inputs
D. The difference between the golden rule level of consumption and the steady state level of consumption

13. Gini-coefficient, a widely used measure of inequality in income is defined as:

A. $\frac{1}{n^2\mu}\sum_i^n\sum_{j\le 1}(y_i - y_j)$

B. $\frac{2}{n^2\mu}\sum_i^n i\, y_i - \left[\frac{n+1}{n}\right]$

C. $\frac{2}{n\mu}\frac{\sum_i^n i\, y_i}{\sum_i^n y_i} - \left[\frac{n+1}{n}\right]$

D. $\frac{1}{n^2\mu}\sum_{i=1}^n\sum_{j=1}^n |(y_i - y_j)|$

14. Endogenous growth theorv assumes:

A. Increasing returns to scale and perfect competition
B. Decreasing returns to scale and perfect competition
C. Increasing returns to scale and imperfect competition
D. Decreasing returns to scale and imperfect competition

15. Suppose you are testing a Null Hypothesis about the population mean, Ho: $\mu = \mu_0$ against $H_1 : \mu > \mu_0$, with population variance given. The computed value of the test statistic is Zc. What is the *p*-value for this test, where Φ() is the cumulative distribution function for the standard normal distribution?

A. Φ(Zc) B. Φ(Zc/2)
C. 1 – Φ(Zc) D. 1 – Φ(Zc/2)

16. The power of a test refers to:

A. Type I error B. Type II error
C. 1–Type II D. 1–Type I error

17. Given a random sample of size *n* from a population with mean μ and variance, σ^2, the sample mean has the following expected value and variance:

A. $E(\bar{x}) = \mu \ Var(\bar{x}) = \sigma^2 / n$

B. $E(\bar{x}) = n\mu \ Var(\bar{x}) = n\sigma^2$

C. $E(\bar{x}) = \mu \ Var(\bar{x}) = \sigma^2$

D. $E(\bar{x}) = \mu \ Var(\bar{x}) = n / \sigma^2$

18. In March, 2023 the consumer price index (CPI) of a country with a 1982 base index of 100, was 234.7. This means the cost of purchasing the market basket of goods and services:

A. has decreased by 134.7% since 1982
B. has increased by 34.7% since 1982
C. has increased by 234.7% since 1982
D. has increased by 134.7% since 1982

19. Consider a production function $q = x + y$, where x and y are the 2 inputs. If the respective input prices are w_x and w_y and assume $w_x > w_y$. Then the cost function $C(q)$ is:

A. $C(q) = w_x q$
B. $C(q) = w_y q$
C. $C(q) = (w_x + w_y)q$
D. $C(q) = \min\{w_x, w_y\}\sqrt{q}$

20. Suppose a cost function of producing q level of output in $C(w, r, q)$ where

$$C(w, r, q) = q\left(\frac{w}{\alpha} + \frac{r}{\beta}\right),$$ where w and r are

the wage cost and rental cost of the 2 inputs capital (K) and labour (l) respectively. What would be the production function q of k and l?

A. $q = \alpha k + \beta l$ B. $q = [k^\alpha + l\beta]^r$
C. $q = \min(\alpha l, \beta k)$ D. $q = A(k^\alpha \bullet l^\beta)$

21. If $f(x, y)$ is a homogeneous function of degree 2 with $f'(2, 3) = 4$ and $f'(4, 6) = 12$, find $f(6, 9)$:

A. 117
B. 234
C. 115
D. 243

22. If the Average Revenue function AR = $10 + 5q - q^2$, then the Marginal Revenue function is a:

A. Convex function
B. Concave function
C. Can be both concave or convex function
D. Weakly concave function

23. Suppose a consumer has a utility function $u(x) = 10\sqrt{x}$, where x is the money income of the consumer. Suppose the consumer's initial endowment is ₹ 50. Suppose she may suffer a loss of ₹ 25 with a probability of 0.5 for some random event. Suppose she pays p premium for an insurance policy that fully reimburses her if she suffers a loss. How much premium p would she be willing to pay to insure against the loss?

A. 12.50 B. 13.57
C. 11.59 D. 14.41

24. Suppose $f(.)$ is a continuous function over a closed and bounded interval $[a, b]$. Then there exists a point d in $[a, b]$ where $f(.)$ has a minimum, and a point c in $[a, b]$ where $f(.)$ has a maximum, so that $f(d) \leq f(x) \leq f(c)$ for all x in $[a, b]$. The statement is derived from:

A. Intermediate Value Theorem
B. Rolle's Theorem
C. Mean value Theorem
D. Extreme value Theorem

25. Consider a consumer's choice based on only 2 commodities i.e., $X \varepsilon R^2_+$, where X is a set of all commodity bundles which the consumer can conceive of. Suppose x and y are the 2 different commodity bundles and the budget set B of the consumer can be written as:

$$B = \{(x, y) : p_1x + p_2y \leq M\}; x_i > 0, i = 1, 2.$$

Which of the following statements is true?

A. The budge set is an open, bounded and convex set
B. The budget set is not a bounded set

C. The budget set is a closed and non-convex set

D. The budget set is a closed, bounded and convex set

26. Consider a Bertrand duopoly where the 2 firms produce a homogenous product. Assume the market demand curve is $y = y_1 + y_2 = 1 - p$, where p is the relevant market price, y is the total amount demanded at that price, y_1 and y_2 are the output levels of firm (1) and (2) respectively. Assume that the firm's cost functions are $C(y_i) = \frac{1}{2} y_i$ for $i = 1, 2$. The rules of the pricing game are as follows: Each firm must simultaneously quote a price in the interval [0, 1]. If the prices are different, the firm with the lower price sells all the units demanded at that price. If they quote the same price, the amount demanded at that price is splited equally between the two firms. What would be the Nash equilibrium price and quantities?

A. $P_1 = P_2 = 1; Y_1 = Y_2 = \frac{1}{2} Y;$ is one of the Multiple Nash Equilibria

B. $P_1 = P_2 = \frac{1}{2}; Y_1 = Y_2 = \frac{1}{2} Y;$ is the Unique Nash Equilibrium

C. $P_1 > P_2 = \frac{1}{2}; Y_1 = 0, Y_2 = Y;$ is one of the Multiple Nash Equilibria

D. $P_1 < P_2 = \frac{1}{2}; Y_1 = Y, Y_2 = 0;$ is one of the Multiple Nash Equilibria

27. Suppose the cost function

$$C(w_1, w_2, y) = y\left(w_1 + \sqrt{w_1 w_2} + w_2\right),$$

where w_1 and w_2 are the prices of 2 inputs which are used in production of y. Which of the following properties of the cost function $C(w_1, w_2, y)$ is correct?

A. Cost function $C(w_1, w_2, y)$ is monotone, concave and continuous function in w_1, w_2.

B. Cost function $C(w_1, w_2, y)$ is a non-monotone, convex and continuous function in w_1, w_2.

C. Cost function is continuous in w_1 and w_2 and discontinuous function in y.

D. Cost function is a continuous function and homogeneous function in degree 0.

28. The demand and supply functions for cobweb model are given as:

$Q_t^d = 19 - 6P_t$ and $Q_t^s = 6P_{t-1} - 5$

Choose the right answer related to intertemporal equilibrium price and the nature of the equilibrium.

A. $\overline{P} = 2$, explosive oscillation

B. $\overline{P} = 2$, uniform oscillation

C. $\overline{P} = 3$, damped oscillation

D. $\overline{P} = 3$, uniform oscillation

29. Consider the pay offs of two players, who are close friends. They can either go for Diwali shopping or they can watch World Cup Cricket match.

		Player 1	
		Diwali Shopping	World Cup Watching
Player 2	Diwali Shopping	(2, 1)	(0, 0)
	World Cup Watching	(0, 0)	(1, 2)

Identify which of the following is true for them:

A. There is no Nash equilibrium for them.

B. There is only one Nash equilibrium where player 1 goes for Diwali shopping and player 2 goes for World Cup Match.

C. Any of the four combinations can be a Nash Equilibrium.

D. There are two Nash Equilibria.

30. In case of two perfect complement goods, which following statement is **not** true?
A. The substitution effect is zero.
B. The indifference curves are straight lines.
C. The indifference curves are L shaped
D. The goods are always demanded in fixed proportions.

31. If $A = \begin{bmatrix} 2 & 3 \\ 0 & 4 \end{bmatrix}$ and $B = \begin{bmatrix} 2 & 0 \\ 1 & 5 \end{bmatrix}$ which of the following is **not** correct?

A. $A^TB = \begin{bmatrix} 4 & 0 \\ 10 & 20 \end{bmatrix}$

B. $(A + B)^T = \begin{bmatrix} 4 & 1 \\ 3 & 9 \end{bmatrix}$

C. $A^TB = \begin{bmatrix} 0 & 4 \\ 10 & 20 \end{bmatrix}$

D. $A^TB^T = \begin{bmatrix} 4 & 2 \\ 6 & 23 \end{bmatrix}$

32. According to the Census 2011, which major Indian state is the most urbanized?
A. Maharashtra B. Punjab
C. Karnataka D. Tamil Nadu

33. In a market for labour's demand and supply, the equilibrium wage is w^*. The government fixes a minimum wage at w'. Which of the following statements is true?
A. There is a tendency of increased equalization of workers if $w' > w^*$ where the workers would not receive lots of benefits.
B. The market will now tend towards a new equilibrium at w', with no other changes, if $w' > w^*$.
C. If $w' < w^*$, there will be a tendency of increased casualization of workers.
D. It will be impossible to administer such a legislation unless $w' = w^*$.

34. In the given figure, DD is the demand curve and SS is the supply curve in a market. Choose the right answer from the following.

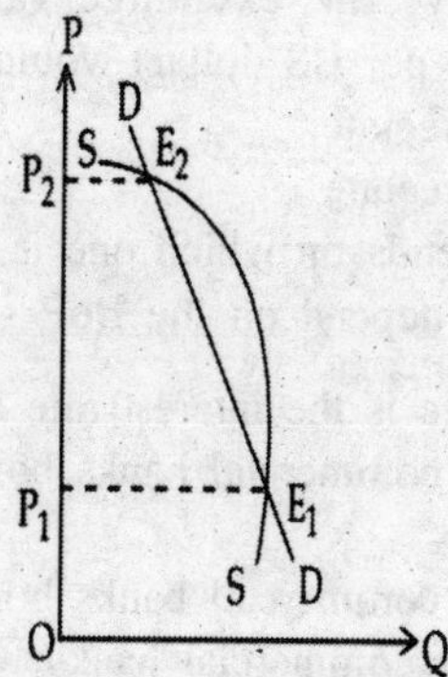

A. There is no stable equilibrium.
B. E_2 is a stable equilibrium, though E_1 is an unstable equilibrium
C. E_1 is a stable equilibrium, though E_2 is an unstable equilibrium
D. Both E_1 & E_2 are stable equibria

35. If the revenue deficit of an economy is 3% of GDP, the primary deficit is 2% of GDP and the fiscal deficit is 7% of GDP, the capital expenditure to GDP ratio of that economy would be:
A. 5% of GDP B. 1% of GDP
C. 4% of GDP D. 2% of GDP

36. If the interest rate is exogenously determined by the Central Bank of some country and the money supply is endogenously determined, the slope of the LM-curve in the interest rate-income plane would be:
A. Positively sloped B. Negatively sloped
C. Horizontal D. Vertical

37. Higher fiscal deficit to GDP ratio would necessarily cause inflation if the economy is under:
A. Demand constrained situation
B. Supply constrained situation
C. Both demand and supply constrained situation
D. Neither demand constrained nor supply constrained situation

38. Under the flexible exchange rate, if the current account deficit increases and the capital account surplus increases for an economy, the exchange rate (domestic currency per US dollar) would:

A. Appreciate
B. Depreciate
C. Depends on which one is higher
D. Not depend on the BoP situation

39. Repo rate is the interest rate at which:

A. The commercial banks borrow from the RBI
B. The commercial banks borrow from the other commercial banks
C. The commercial banks deposit money to the RBI
D. The common people deposit money to the RBI

40. An economy characterised by huge involuntary unemployment would have an aggregate labour supply curve in a real wage-labour supply plane that would be:

A. Positively sloped B. Vertical
C. Flat D. Negatively sloped

41. Global Hunger Index (GHI) includes:

(*a*) Child mortality with weight $\frac{1}{3}$

(*b*) Child stunting with weight $\frac{1}{3}$

(*c*) Undernourishment with weight $\frac{1}{3}$

(*d*) Child wasting with weight $\frac{1}{6}$

(*e*) Child mortality with weight $\frac{1}{6}$

Choose the **correct** answer from the options given below:

A. (*a*), (*b*) and (*c*) only
B. (*a*), (*c*) and (*d*) only
C. (*b*), (*c*) and (*e*) only
D. (*d*) and (*e*) only

42. Which of the following statements are not true for the Linear Probability Model (LPM)?

(*a*) Conditional probability of occurence of an event conditional on the value of explanatory variable X is a linear function of X

(*b*) Estimated value of the conditional probability of occurence of the event lies between 0 and 1

(*c*) Error term is homoscedastic

(*d*) R^2 is a good measure of goodness of fit

Choose the **correct** answer from the options given below:

A. (*b*) only
B. (*b*) and (*c*) only
C. (*b*), (*c*) and (*d*) only
D. (*c*) only

43. Given that Z_t is a zero-mean white noise process with variance σ^2, which of the following are I(O) processes?

(*a*) $X_t = X_{t-1} + Z_t$

(*b*) $X_t = \alpha X_{t-1} + Z_t$ where $0 < \alpha < 1$

(*c*) $X_t = Z_t + Z_{t-1}$

(*d*) $X_t = 8 + X_{t-1} + Z_t$

Choose the **correct** answer from the options given below:

A. (*c*) only
B. (*b*) only
C. (*b*) and (*c*) only
D. (*b*), (*c*) and (*d*) only

44. Which of the following are features of a weakly stationary stochastic process?

(*a*) Mean is time-varying
(*b*) Mean is constant
(*c*) Variance is constant
(*d*) Covariance is time-invariant

Choose the **correct** answer from the options given below:

A. (*b*) and (*c*) only
B. (*b*), (*c*) and (*d*) only
C. (*a*), (*c*) and (*d*) only
D. (*a*) and (*c*) only

45. Suppose an economy is in medium-run equilibrium. Now the government enacts a law, making entry of new firms difficult, which increases the monopoly power of the existing firms. Which of the following statements are true about this change?

(*a*) Output level will be lower in medium-run
(*b*) Output level will be lower in short-run
(*c*) Price level will be higher in medium-run
(*d*) Price level will be higher in short-run

Choose the **correct** answer from the options given below:

A. (*a*) and (*c*) only
B. (*b*), (*c*) and (*d*) only
C. (*b*) and (*c*) only
D. (*a*), (*b*) (*c*) and (*d*) only

46. Among the new monetary aggregates suggested by the Third working group of RBI, which one/ones include time deposits of term less than or equal to one year but does not include the time deposits with term more than one year?

(*a*) NM_0 (*b*) NM_1
(*c*) NM_2 (*d*) NM_3

Choose the **correct** answer from the options given below:

A. (*a*) only
B. (*c*) only
C. (*c*) and (*d*) only
D. (*b*) and (*c*) only

47. Which one of the following are money market instruments?

(*a*) 91-day Treasury bill
(*b*) Commercial paper
(*c*) Certificate of deposit issued by banks
(*d*) 5-year government bond

Choose the **correct** answer from the options given below:

A. (*a*) only
B. (*a*) and (*b*) only
C. (*a*), (*b*) and (*c*) only
D. (*b*) and (*c*) only

48. Consider the following statements about the Current Account of the balance of payments and indicate which statements are true?

(*a*) Current Account deficit equals excess of imports over sum of exports and net transfers received by a country.
(*b*) Current Account deficit may be covered by borrowing from foreigners.
(*c*) Current Account deficit may be covered by buying assets from foreigners.
(*d*) If India's Current Account deficit in a particular period is \$ 50 million, it can be financed by net capital inflows amounting to \$ 50 million.

Choose the **correct** answer from the options given below:

A. (*a*), (*b*), (*c*), (*d*) B. (*a*), (*b*), (*d*) only
C. (*a*), (*c*), (*d*) only D. (*b*), (*c*), (*d*) only

49. Suppose India is home country and USA is foreign country. Interest rate in India is 3%, that in US is 1%. The Re-\$ exchange rate is ₹ 80 per USD in spot market and ₹ 81 per USD in 3 month forward market. Which of the following are true for the resulting covered interest arbitrage flows?

(*a*) Indian Rupee will depreciate in spot market
(*b*) Indian Rupee will depreciate in forward market
(*c*) Interest rate will decline in India
(*d*) Interest rate will decline in US

Choose the **correct** answer from the options given below:

A. (*a*) and (*b*) only B. (*a*) and (*c*) only
C. (*a*) and (*d*) only D. (*a*), (*b*), (*c*) and (*d*)

50. The current account deficit of the BOP may be financed in many ways. Which of the following are correct?

(*a*) FDI inflows
(*b*) Inflow of foreign portfolio investment
(*c*) Borrowing from IMF or World Bank
(*d*) Drawing down foreign exchange reserves

Choose the **correct** answer from the options given below:

A. (*a*), (*b*), (*c*) only B. (*b*), (*c*), (*d*) only
C. (*a*), (*b*), (*c*), (*d*) D. (*a*), (*c*), (*d*) only

51. Consider the following statements about the Specific Factors model of International Trade and say which ones are correct?

(*a*) Factors specific to the export sectors in each country gain from trade
(*b*) Factors specific to the import-competing sectors in each country lose from trade
(*c*) Mobile factors that can work in either sector may gain from trade
(*d*) Mobile factors that can work in either sector may lose from trade

Choose the **correct** answer from the options given below:

A. (*a*), (*c*), (*d*) only B. (*b*), (*c*), (*d*) only
C. (*a*), (*b*), (*c*) only D. (*a*), (*b*), (*c*), (*d*)

52. Consider the following statements about the Aggregate Demand (AD) relation under price flexibility and say which ones are correct?

(*a*) The AD curve will shift to the right if autonomous investment rises.
(*b*) The AD curve will shift to the right if net exports rise in an open economy.
(*c*) The AD curve will shift to the left if money supply contracts.
(*d*) As price rises, shifting the LM curve, the AD curve shifts to the left

Choose the **correct** answer from the options given below:

A. (*a*), (*b*), (*c*) only B. (*b*), (*c*), (*d*) only
C. (*a*), (*c*), (*d*) only D. (*a*), (*b*), (*c*), (*d*)

53. Given the following statements about major schools of drought in macroeconomics, state which ones are correct?

(*a*) The Keynesians believed in wage and price flexibility and highlighted the role of aggregate supply.
(*b*) The monetarists highlighted the importance of money in the economic system and that of expectations in the analysis of inflation.
(*c*) The classical school believed in the invisible hand and the efficiency of the market mechanism
(*d*) The new Keynesians make use of the assumption of imperfect markets in their frameworks.

Choose the **correct** answer from the options given below:

A. (*b*), (*c*), (*d*) only B. (*a*), (*b*), (*c*), (*d*)
C. (*a*), (*c*), (*d*) only D. (*a*), (*b*), (*c*) only

54. Consider an economy with perfect capital mobility, fixed price level and flexible exchange rate. Starting from equilibrium, suppose there is a monetary expansion.

Which of the following are true for the new equilibrium, as compared to the initial equilibrium?

(*a*) Output will be higher
(*b*) Consumption will be higher
(*c*) Interest rate will be lower
(*d*) Interest rate will be higher

Choose the **correct** answer from the options given below:

A. (*a*) only B. (*b*) only
C. (*a*) and (*b*) only D. (*a*) and (*c*) only

55. Let $H = e^{Q}$ where $Q = Ax^{\alpha}y^{\beta}$

Consider the following statements.

(*a*) Q is a homogeneous function for all values of α and β
(*b*) H is a homothetic function for all values of α and β
(*c*) Q is a homogeneous function only if $\alpha + \beta = 1$
(*d*) H is not a homogeneous function
(*e*) Q is not a homogeneous function

Choose the **correct** answer from the options given below:

A. (*a*) and (*b*) only
B. (*a*), (*b*) and (*d*) only
C. (*c*) and (*a*) only
D. (*e*) and (*d*) only

56. $A = \begin{bmatrix} 1 & 3 \\ 2 & 8 \\ 4 & 0 \end{bmatrix}$ and $B = \begin{bmatrix} 5 \\ 9 \end{bmatrix}$

(*a*) AB is given by $\begin{bmatrix} 32 \\ 82 \\ 20 \end{bmatrix}$

(*b*) BA is given by $\begin{bmatrix} 32 & 82 & 20 \end{bmatrix}$

(*c*) AB is not defined

(*d*) BA is not defined

(*e*) A^TB is defined

Choose the **correct** answer from the options given below:

A. (*c*) and (*b*) only

B. (*a*), (*d*), (*e*) only

C. (*a*) only

D. (*a*) and (*d*) only

57. The following are five statements about short run cost curves.

(*a*) The Marginal Cost (MC) curve cuts both short run Average Cost (AC) curve and Average Variable Cost (AVC) curve at their lowest point.

(*b*) The MC curve cuts AC curve from below, but nothing can be said about AVC curve.

(*c*) The distance between Total Cost (TC) curve and Total Variable Cost (TVC) curve gets reduced as quantity increases.

(*d*) The Average Fixed Cost (AFC) curve is asymptotic to the cost axis.

(*e*) The AC curve is *u*-shaped.

Choose the **correct** answer from the options given below:

A. (*a*), (*c*), (*d*), (*e*) only

B. (*b*), (*c*), (*e*) only

C. (*a*), (*e*) only

D. (*d*), (*e*), (*a*) only

58. The OLS regression output of wages (₹ in thousand) on education (years of schooling S) and cognitive ability scores (CA) comes out to be:

$$\widehat{\text{wages}} = -3.36 + 0.64S + 0.15CA$$
$$(1.98) \quad (0.12) \quad (0.05)$$

with figures in parenthesis giving standard error.

The explained sum of squares is 4745.75 with degrees of freedom 2 and residual sum of squares is 33651.28 with degrees of freedom 567, which of the following statements is/are true?

(*a*) For one year increase in schooling, wage per hour increases by ₹ 640 on the average, when CA is kept constant.

(*b*) The value of t statistic of CA is 3.

(*c*) The F statistic is given by

$$F = \frac{(4745.75/2)}{(33651.28/567)}$$

(*d*) The F statistic is given by

$$F = \frac{(33651.28/567)}{(4745.75/2)}$$

Choose the **correct** answer from the options given below:

A. (*a*), (*c*) only B. (*a*), (*b*), (*d*) only

C. (*a*), (*b*), (*c*) only D. (*a*), (*d*) only

59. Read the following statements regarding demography across India's major states.

(*a*) Kerala pioneered fertility transition in India.

(*b*) Bihar has high IMR, as well as low reporting of morbidity.

(*c*) Orissa records the highest share of immunized children as per NFHS-5 round.

(*d*) Tamil Nadu has the highest share of old age population as per Census 2011.

(*e*) Madhya Pradesh has the highest share of stunted children as per NFHS-5

Choose the **correct** answer from the options given below:

A. (*a*), (*d*) only B. (*a*), (*b*), (*e*) only

C. (*a*), (*d*), (*e*) only D. (*a*), (*b*), (*c*) only

60. Consider a matrix $A = \begin{bmatrix} 3 & 5 \\ -2 & -4 \end{bmatrix}$

Consider the following statements on characteristic polynomial, Eigen Values and Eigen Vectors.

(*a*) The characteristic polynomial is $\lambda^2 + \lambda - 2$

(*b*) The characteristic polynomial is $\lambda^2 - \lambda - 4$ and the characteristic root or Eigen Values are $\lambda^* = 2$ and 1

(*c*) The characteristic polynomial is $\lambda^2 - \lambda + 2$ and the characteristic root or Eigen Values are $\lambda^* = 1$ and 2

(*d*) The characteristic root or Eigen Values are $\lambda^* = -2$ and 1

Choose the **correct** answer from the options given below:

A. (*a*), (*c*) and (*d*) only
B. (*b*) and (*d*) only
C. (*b*) and (*c*) only
D. (*a*) and (*d*) only

61. Suppose production function $q = f(k, l)$, is a homogeneous function of degree 1. Consider the following statements.

(*a*) The marginal products of capital and labour $\left(\frac{\partial q}{\partial k} \text{ and } \frac{\partial q}{\partial l}\right)$ are homogeneous of degree 1.

(*b*) The second order cross marginal products of *k* and 1 are equal $\left(i.e., \frac{\partial^2 q}{\partial l \partial k} = \frac{\partial^2 q}{\partial k \partial l}\right)$.

(*c*) By Euler's Theorem: $\frac{\partial q}{\partial k}.k + \frac{\partial q}{\partial l}.l = q$

(*d*) By Euler's theorem: $\frac{\partial^2 q}{\partial k^2}.k + \frac{\partial^2 q}{\partial l^2}l = 0$

Choose the **correct** answer from the options given below:

A. (*a*) and (*b*) only
B. (*a*), (*b*) and (*c*) only
C. (*a*), (*c*) and (*d*) only
D. (*b*), (*c*) and (*d*) only

62. Consider the following statements:

(*a*) The union of finite numbers of closed set is a closed set

(*b*) The empty set is an open set but not a closed set

(*c*) Every infinite set is an open set

(*d*) The intersection of finite numbers of open sets is an open set

Choose the **correct** answer from the options given below:

A. (*a*) and (*b*) only
B. (*b*) and (*c*) only
C. (*a*) and (*d*) only
D. (*a*), (*b*) and (*c*) only

63. Consider the following statements:

Assume a consumer's choice is based on only 2 commodities i.e., X ε R^2_+, where X is the set of a possible commodities which a consumer can conceive of:

(*a*) Monotonicity of preference implies strong monotonicity but not the other way round.

(*b*) A preference relation is monotone if for all commodity bundle *x*, *y* ε X, $y \geq x$ and $y \neq x$, then $y \geq x$.

(*c*) A preference relation (≥) on X is strongly monotone if for all commodity bundles *x*, *y* ε X, $y > x$ and $y \neq x$; then $y \geq x$.

(*d*) A preference which is locally non satiated must follow monotonicity and strong monotonicity.

Choose the **correct** answer from the options given below:

A. (*b*) and (*d*) only
B. (*a*), (*b*) and (*d*) only
C. (*a*), (*c*) and (*d*) only
D. (*a*) and (*d*) Only

64. Consider the following statements:

(*a*) If the 2 utility functions *u*(*x*) and *b*(*x*) are related by *u*(*x*)= V(*b*(*x*)), where V′(.) > 0, then V(*x*) is a utility function representing the same preference as *b*(*x*).

(*b*) If the 2 utility functions represents the same preference, the solutions to the consumer's utility maximization problem are the same with the 2 utility function but the indirect utility functions are different.

(*c*) If the local non satiation assumption of preference is satisfied, any solution to the consumer's utility maximization problem satisfies the budget constraint with equality.

(*d*) If the indirect utility function of $b(x)$ is homogenous of degree 0 then indirect utility function of $u(x) = V(b(x))$, where $V'(.) > 0$, is a homogenous function of degree 1.

Choose the **correct** answer from the options given below:

A. (*b*) only
B. (*a*), (*b*) and (*d*) only
C. (*a*), (*b*) and (*c*) only
D. (*b*), (*c*) and (*d*) only

65. Consider the following 3 Constrained Optimization Problems (COP).

(*i*) Maximize $z = \ln x$, subject to $x > 1$
(*ii*) Maximize $z = \ln x$, subject to $x < 1$
(*iii*) Maximize $z = \ln x$, subject to $1 < x < 2$

(*a*) (*i*) and (*ii*) have no solutions but (*iii*) has solution
(*b*) (*i*) and (*ii*) have solutions but (*iii*) has no solution
(*c*) (*i*), (*ii*) and (*iii*) have no solution
(*d*) (*i*) and (*iii*) have no solution but (*ii*) has solution

Choose the **correct** answer from the options given below:

A (*a*) only B. (*b*) only
C. (*c*) only D. (*d*) only

66. Match List-I with List-II.

List-I	List-II
(*a*) Ramsar Convention	I. Ozone layer depletion
(*b*) Basel Convention	II. Reduction of green-house gas emission
(*c*) Montreal Protocol	III. Conservation of wetlands
(*d*) Paris Agreement	IV. Control of trans-boundary movement of hazardous wastes and disposal

Choose the **correct** answer from the options given below:

	(*a*)	(*b*)	(*c*)	(*d*)
A.	I	IV	III	II
B.	III	I	II	IV
C.	IV	I	III	II
D.	III	IV	I	II

67. Match List-I with List-II.

List-I	List-II
(*a*) Coase theorem	I. Property right, victim's pay and polluter pay principle
(*b*) Climate change	II. Lax environmental regulation, hidden subsidy
(*c*) Ecological dumping	III. Quantity restriction
(*d*) Tradable emission permit	IV. Global externality

Choose the **correct** answer from the options given below:

	(*a*)	(*b*)	(*c*)	(*d*)
A.	III	IV	II	I
B.	I	IV	II	III
C.	II	I	III	IV
D.	III	IV	I	II

68. Match List-I with List-II.

List-I	List-II
(*a*) Kenneth Arrow	I. Analysis of causal relationship
(*b*) Robert Solow	II. Fundamental contribution in behavioural economics

(*c*) Daniel Kahneman — III. Fundamental contribution in welfare economics

(*d*) Joshua Angrist — IV. Fundamental contribution in economic growth theory

Choose the **correct** answer from the options given below:

	(*a*)	(*b*)	(*c*)	(*d*)
A.	III	IV	I	II
B.	II	I	III	IV
C.	III	IV	II	I
D.	I	IV	III	II

69. Match List-I with List-II.

List-I	List-II
(*a*) Demographic Transition	I. Dualism
(*b*) Stages of growth	II. Take-off
(*c*) Rural-urban migration decision	III. Replacement Rate
(*d*) Female labour force participation rate	IV. Backward bending labour supply curve

Choose the **correct** answer from the options given below:

	(*a*)	(*b*)	(*c*)	(*d*)
A.	I	II	III	IV
B.	IV	I	III	II
C.	III	II	I	IV
D.	IV	I	II	III

70. Match List-I with List-II.

List-I (Model/method)	List-II (Feature)
(*a*) Logit model	I. elasticities are constant
(*b*) Log-log model	II. binary dependent variable
(*c*) Autoregressive model	III. corrects for heteroscedasticity
(*d*) Weighted least squares	IV. includes lags of dependent variable

Choose the **correct** answer from the options given below:

	(*a*)	(*b*)	(*c*)	(*d*)
A.	II	I	III	IV
B.	I	II	IV	III
C.	I	II	III	IV
D.	II	I	IV	III

71. Match the following:

List-I (Theory)	List-II (Economist(s) who gave it)
(*a*) Permanent Income Hypothesis of Consumption	I. T. Sargent and N. Wallace
(*b*) Life-cycle Hypothesis of Consumption	II. Milton Friedman
(*c*) Real Business Cycle Theory	III. Franco Modigliani
(*d*) Policy Ineffectiveness Proposition	IV. F. Kydland and E. Prescott

Choose the **correct** answer from the options given below:

	(*a*)	(*b*)	(*c*)	(*d*)
A.	III	II	I	IV
B.	III	II	IV	I
C.	II	III	IV	I
D.	II	III	I	IV

72. Match List-I with List-II.

List-I	List-II
(*a*) Unequal Exchange	I. A. Hirshman
(*b*) The development of underdevelopment	II. G. Myrdal
(*c*) Backward and forward linkage effect	III. A. Emmanuel
(*d*) Backwash effect	IV. G. Frank

Choose the **correct** answer from the options given below:

	(*a*)	(*b*)	(*c*)	(*d*)
A.	II	III	I	IV
B.	III	I	IV	II
C.	III	IV	I	II
D.	II	IV	III	I

73. Match List-I with List-II.

List-I (Variable)	List-II (Distribution)
(*a*) Sum of squares of *n* independent standard normal variates	I. *t* distribution
(*b*) Ratio of a standard normal variate to square root of an independent, chi square variable (divided by its degrees of freedom)	II. F distribution
(*c*) Ratio of 2 independent chi-square variables each divided by their respective degrees of freedom	III. Standard normal distribution
(*d*) Normal variate minus its mean, divided by its standard deviation	IV. chi square distribution

Choose the **correct** answer from the options given below:

	(*a*)	(*b*)	(*c*)	(*d*)
A.	I	IV	II	III
B.	IV	I	III	II
C.	I	IV	III	II
D.	IV	I	II	III

74. Match List-I with List-II.

List-I (Property)	List-II (Type of Curve)
(*a*) Investment is unresponsive to interest rates	I. Relatively flat IS curve
(*b*) Money demand is perfectly elastic w.r.t. interest rates	II. Vertical LM curve
(*c*) Money demand is completely inelastic w.r.t. interest rates	III. Horizontal LM curve
(*d*) Investment is highly responsive to interest rates	IV. Vertical IS curve

Choose the **correct** answer from the options given below:

	(*a*)	(*b*)	(*c*)	(*d*)
A.	IV	III	II	I
B.	IV	II	III	I
C.	I	III	II	IV
D.	III	IV	I	II

75. Match List-I with List-II.

List-I	List-II
(*a*) Quantity theory of money	I. Milton Friedman
(*b*) Involuntary unemployment	II. John Maynard Keynes
(*c*) Randomised trial	III. Abhijit V. Banerjee
(*d*) Relative poverty	IV. Amartya K. Sen

Choose the **correct** answer from the options given below:

	(*a*)	(*b*)	(*c*)	(*d*)
A.	I	II	III	IV
B.	IV	III	II	I
C.	III	II	I	IV
D.	III	II	IV	I

76. Arrange the following steps of exchange rate channel of monetary transmission mechanism, in correct order, starting from first to last.

(*a*) reduction in policy rate

(*b*) capital outflows

(*c*) depreciation of domestic currency

(*d*) rise in net exports

Choose the **correct** answer from the options given below:

A. (*a*), (*c*), (*d*), (*b*) B. (*a*), (*d*), (*b*), (*c*)

C. (*a*), (*b*), (*c*), (*d*) D. (*a*), (*d*), (*c*), (*b*)

77. Arrange the following names of former governors of RBI in the sequence in which they held the post starting from the earliest to latest.

(*a*) Y.V. Reddy

(*b*) D Subbarao

(*c*) Raghuram Rajan

(*d*) Urjit Patel

Choose the **correct** answer from the options given below:

A. (*c*), (*b*), (*d*), (*a*)
B. (*c*), (*a*), (*d*), (*b*)
C. (*a*), (*b*), (*c*), (*d*)
D. (*d*), (*c*). (*a*), (*b*)

78. Arrange the following events in Indian Financial System in correct chronological order, starting from earliest to Latest.
(*a*) Setting up of PFRDA
(*b*) Setting up of UTI
(*c*) Nationalisation of 14 commercial banks
(*d*) Implementation of IBC

Choose the **correct** answer from the options given below:

A. (*a*). (*b*), (*c*), (*d*)
B. (*c*), (*a*), (*b*), (*d*)
C. (*b*), (*c*), (*a*), (*d*)
D. (*a*), (*c*), (*b*), (*d*)

79. Match List-I with List-II.

List-I	List-II
(*a*) Shephard's Lemma	I. Hidden types of agent
(*b*) Adverse Selection	II. Envelope theorem
(*c*) Hotelling Lemma	III. Indirect utility function
(*d*) Roy's Identity	IV. Profit function

Choose the **correct** answer from the options given below:

	(*a*)	(*b*)	(*c*)	(*d*)
A.	IV	I	II	III
B.	II	I	IV	III
C.	II	I	III	IV
D.	II	IV	I	III

80. Consider the following centrally sponsored schemes in India and choose the right sequence of time (year) when they were Launched, from earliest to latest:
(*a*) Beti Bachao Beti Padhao
(*b*) Ujjwala
(*c*) Swachh Bharat Abhiyan
(*d*) Ayushman Bharat
(*e*) Right to Education

Choose the **correct** answer from the options given below:

A. (*e*), (*a*), (*c*), (*b*), (*d*)
B. (*e*), (*c*), (*a*), (*b*), (*d*)
C. (*a*), (*e*), (*c*), (*b*), (*d*)
D. (*a*), (*c*), (*e*), (*d*), (*b*)

81. Chow Test is normally run to understand if a single regression run on pooled data is more efficient to describe a relation between a dependent variable and a set of independent variables than the same regression being run separately on two subgroups of sample. The steps involved in running the Chow Test are:
(*a*) Run the regression model on pooled sample and calculate RSS_p
(*b*) Run the same regression model on the two sub-samples separately and calculate RSS_1 and RSS_2
(*c*) Calculate the F statistic
(*d*) Check the critical F with related degrees of freedom and compare it with F calculated
(*e*) Do not reject H_0 if $F_{calculated} < F_{critical}$

Choose the **correct** answer from the options given below:

A. (*a*), (*b*), (*c*), (*d*), (*e*)
B. (*a*), (*d*), (*c*), (*b*), (*e*)
C. (*c*), (*a*), (*b*), (*d*), (*e*)
D. (*c*), (*b*), (*a*), (*d*), (*e*)

82. Arrange the following in order of their year of establishment starting from the oldest.
(*a*) Lakdawala Committee
(*b*) Khusro Committee
(*c*) Alagh Committee
(*d*) Nayak Committee
(*e*) Tendulkar Committee

Choose the **correct** answer from the options given below:

A. (*d*), (*b*), (*c*), (*a*), (*e*)
B. (*c*), (*d*), (*b*), (*a*), (*e*)
C. (*c*), (*b*), (*d*), (*a*), (*e*)
D. (*b*), (*c*), (*d*), (*e*), (*a*)

83. Arrange the following chronologically starting from the oldest.

(*a*) Theory of Big Push
(*b*) The accumulation of capital
(*c*) Theory of cumulative causation
(*d*) Unbalanced growth
(*e*) Development with unlimited supplies of labour

Choose the **correct** answer from the options given below:

A. (*e*), (*a*), (*c*), (*b*), (*d*)
B. (*a*), (*e*), (*b*), (*c*), (*d*)
C. (*e*), (*b*), (*a*), (*d*), (*c*)
D. (*a*), (*b*), (*e*), (*c*), (*d*)

84. Arrange the given schools of thought in macro-economics in chronological order, from the oldest to most recent one.

(*a*) The Keynesian school
(*b*) The new classical school
(*c*) The classical school
(*d*) The new Keynesian school
(*e*) The monetarists

Choose the **correct** answer from the options given below:

A. (*a*), (*d*), (*c*), (*b*), (*e*)
B. (*e*), (*c*), (*b*), (*a*), (*d*)
C. (*c*), (*b*), (*a*), (*d*), (*e*)
D. (*c*), (*a*), (*e*), (*b*), (*d*)

85. The Central Bank of a country maintains a fixed exchange rate, which is defined as the number of units of domestic currency per unit of foreign currency. Currently the domestic currency is overvalued against the foreign currency. In this context, indicate the kind of intervention required by the Central Bank to maintain the parity, by putting the following statements in correct order.

(*a*) The demand for foreign currency exceeds its supply
(*b*) The exchange rate is lower than the market clearing exchange rate
(*c*) The gap between supply and demand for foreign currency is equalized
(*d*) The Central Bank's stock of foreign currency is depleted
(*e*) The Central Bank sells foreign currency from its stock of reserves

Choose the **correct** answer from the options given below:

A. (*b*), (*e*), (*a*), (*d*), (*c*)
B. (*b*), (*a*), (*e*), (*d*), (*c*)
C. (*b*), (*e*), (*a*), (*c*), (*d*)
D. (*b*), (*a*), (*e*), (*c*), (*d*)

86. Given below are two statements:

Statement I: Agricultural GDP constitutes less than 16% of aggregate GDP at 2011-12 constant prices and less than 20% of the aggregate GDP at current prices in 2022-23 (PE) in India.

Statement II: Service sector GDP constitutes less than 16% of aggregate GDP at 2011-12 constant prices and less than 20% of the aggregate GDP at current prices in 2022-23 (PE) in India.

In the light of the above statements, choose the **most appropriate answer** from the options given below:

A. Both Statement I and Statement II are correct
B. Both Statement I and Statement II are incorrect
C. Statement I is correct, but Statement II is incorrect
D. Statement 1 is incorrect, but Statement II is correct

87. Given below are two statements:

Statement I: The Government's spending on social services as a percentage of GDP has been rising since 2017-18.

Statement II: The Government's spending on social services as a percentage of total expenditure has also been continuously rising since 2017-18.

In the light of the above statements, choose the **most appropriate** answer from the options given below:

A. Both Statement I and Statement II are correct
B. Both Statement I and Statement II are incorrect
C. Statement I is correct, but Statement II is incorrect
D. Statement I is incorrect, but Statement II is correct

88. Given below are two statements:

Statement I: Human Development is a process of enlarging peoples' choices.

Statement II: Human Development Index (HDI) is based on the following indicators: Life expectancy at birth, expected years of schooling, mean years of schooling & Gross domestic product per capita at dollar PPP.

In the light of the above statements, choose the **most appropriate answer** from the options given below:

A. Both Statement I and Statement II are correct
B. Both Statement I and Statement II are incorrect
C. Statement I is correct, but Statement II is incorrect
D. Statement I is incorrect, but Statement II is correct

89. Given below are two statements: one is labelled as Assertion (A) and the other is labelled as Reason (R).

Assertion (A): Given a random sample, the distribution of the sample mean tends to a normal distribution, as the sample size becomes very large.

Reason (R): Central limit theorem.

In the light of the above statements, choose the **most appropriate answer** from the options given below:

A. Both (A) and (R) are correct and (R) is the correct explanation of (A)
B. Both (A) and (R) are correct, but (R) is not the correct explanation of (A)
C. (A) is correct, but (R) is not correct
D. (A) is not correct, but (R) is correct

90. Given below are two statements: one is labelled as Assertion (A) and the other is labelled as Reason (R).

Assertion (A): According to the Domar condition of debt sustainability, the public debt would not rise as proportion of GDP if the effective interest rate on government liabilities happens to be less than or equal to the growth rate of GDP at current price.

Reason (R): Growth rate of GDP of an economy at current price is bound to be less than the effective interest rate on the government bonds.

In the light of the above statements, choose the **most appropriate answer** from the options given below:

A. Both (A) and (R) are correct and (R) is the correct explanation of (A)
B. Both (A) and (R) are correct, but (R) is not the correct explanation of (A)
C. (A) is correct, but (R) is not correct
D. (A) is not correct, but (R) is correct

Directions (Qs. No. 91-95): *Read the following information carefully and answer these questions.*

Assume that there are 2 firms producing steel. There is a negative externality due to production causing pollution. Firm 1's output is q_1 and firm 2's is q_2. Assume that the market price for steel is P = 1. Now consider two scenarios:

Scenario 1: Assume that firm l's cost function is $C_1(q_1) = q_1^2$ and firm 2's cost function is $C_2(q_2, q_1) = (q_2 + 0.75\, q_1)^2$. In short, firm 1's production is not affected by firm 2 but firm 2's production is affected by firm 1, i.e., Firms 1's operation causes firm 2's costs to rise.

Scenario 2: Assume that negative externally works both ways i.e., both the firms face the adverse impact. So assume $C_1(q_1, q_2) = (q_1 + 0.75\ q_2)^2$ and $C_2(q_1, q_2) = (q_2 + 0.75\ q_1)^2$, i.e., Firms 1's operation causes firm 2's costs to rise and vice versa.

91. What is the equilibrium profit of firm 2 (π_2) in the short run, in Scenario 1?

A. $\pi_2 = 0.025$ B. $\pi_2 = 0.125$
C. $\pi_2 = -0.125$ D. $\pi_2 = 0.75$

92. What is the long run profit of firm 1 (π_1), in Scenario 1?

A. $\pi_1 = 0.025$ B. $\pi_1 = 0$
C. $\pi_1 = 0.25$ D. $\pi_1 = 0.125$

93. What is the long run profit of firm 2 (π_2), in Scenario 1?

A. $\pi_2 = 0.125$ B. $\pi_2 = 0.120$
C. $\pi_2 = 0.5$ D. $\pi_1 = 0$

94. What would be the market equilibrium profit of the 2 firms, in Scenario 2?

A. $\pi_1 = \frac{1}{28}$, $\pi_2 = \frac{1}{28}$

B. $\pi_1 = \frac{2}{7}$, $\pi_2 = \frac{2}{7}$

C. $\pi_1 = \frac{1}{14}$, $\pi_2 = \frac{1}{14}$

D. $\pi_1 = \pi_2 = 0$

95. Do you think that the equilibrium outcome for Scenario 2 is inefficient? How would be the efficiency be restored?

A. No, the equilibrium outcome of the firms are profit minimizing outcome.
B. The externality can be resolved by closing down both the firms is, $\pi_1 = \pi_2 = 0$
C. If one of the firm is forced to close down, the externality will be reduced and their joint profit is $\pi_1 + \pi_2 = 0.071$
D. If one of the firm is forced to close down, the externality will be reduced and their joint profit is $\pi_1 + \pi_2 = 0.109$

Directions (Qs. No. 96-100): *Read the following information carefully and answer these questions.*

According to the NSO, MOSPI press release dated 31st May 2023, the revised estimate of GDP at the current price for the year 2021-22 was ₹ 2,34,71,012 crores and that for 2020-21 was ₹ 1,98,29,927 crores. The GDP at 2011-12 constant prices for the year 2020-21 and 2021-22 were ₹ 1,36,87,118 crores and ₹ 1,49,25,840 crores respectively. At the current prices, the net taxes on products was ₹ 20,32,128 crores in 2021-22 (RE). The PFCE, GFCE, GFCF in 2021-22 were ₹ 1,43,44,336 crores, ₹ 26,25,361 crores and ₹ 67,86,391 crores respectively. Change in stocks (CIS), valuables and discrepancies in 2021-22 were ₹ 1,63,438 crores, ₹ 3,79,112 crores and ₹ (–) 208,247 crores (negative) respectively in current prices.

96. What was the inflation rate in India based on the GDP deflators?

A. 4.5% B. 6.6%
C. 9.3% D. 10.2%

97. The current account deficit to GDP ratio (both at current prices) in 2021-22 for India was:

A. 1.75% B. 3.53%
C. 4.06% D. 2.64 %

98. The Gross Value Added (GVA) at basic prices in 2021-22 was:

A. ₹ 2,55,03,140 crore
B. ₹ 2,14,38,884 crore
C. ₹ 2,34,71,012 crore
D. ₹ 1,49,37,569 crore

99. In 2021-22, the investment GDP ratio in India was:

A. 31.2% B. 90%
C. 40.1% D. 42.4%

100. If the value of exports in 2021-22 at current price be ₹ 50,49,645 crores, the import in 2021-22 at current price in India was:

A. ₹ 56,69,024 crores
B. ₹ 6,19,378 crores
C. ₹ 1,17,18,975 crores
D. ₹ 94,11,752 crores

ANSWERS

1. **(B):** The expert committee established by the Reserve Bank of India (RBI) in 2013 to revamp and fortify the monetary policy framework in India was helmed by Urjit Patel. Tasked with a crucial mandate, the Urjit Patel Committee conducted an extensive review of the existing monetary policy structure, aiming to identify areas for improvement and propose reforms to bolster its efficacy and transparency. Patel's leadership was instrumental in steering the committee's deliberations towards recommendations that would align India's monetary policy with international best practices while addressing the unique challenges faced by the Indian economy. The committee's proposals, which included the adoption of inflation targeting as the primary objective of monetary policy, laid the groundwork for significant reforms in India's monetary policy framework, shaping the trajectory of the country's monetary policy management for years to come.

2. **(A):** In 2016, Parliament amended the RBI Act, 1934 to change the monetary policy, and introduce an inflation targeting framework. This framework prioritises price stability to achieve sustainable GDP growth. Price stability allows investors to confidently invest their money for productive activities, without worrying about it losing value. Price stability also maintains the purchasing power of consumers, i.e., the ability to purchase a good (or service) with a given amount of money.

   As per the new framework, the central government, in consultation with RBI sets: (i) an inflation target, and (ii) an upper and lower tolerance level for retail inflation. The target has been set at 4%, with an upper tolerance limit of 6% and a lower tolerance limit of 2%. The upper and lower limits indicate that although it is desirable for inflation to be close to 4%, deviation between these limits is acceptable. The target and bands and revised every five years. In March 2021, the existing targets were carried forward.

3. **(B):** In a regression analysis, the F-test assesses the overall significance of the regression model. To conduct this test, we need to determine the degrees of freedom for the numerator and denominator of the F-statistic. The numerator degrees of freedom represent the number of independent variables in the model, denoted by '*k*'. This is because the numerator of the F-statistic involves the sum of squares of the regression, which is essentially measuring the variability explained by the independent variables. On the other hand, the denominator degrees of freedom represent the residual degrees of freedom, which is calculated as the difference between the total number of observations (*n*) and the number of independent variables minus 1 ($k - 1$). This accounts for the degrees of freedom associated with estimating the regression coefficients. Therefore, the correct degrees of freedom for the F-test are '*k*' for the numerator and '$n - k - 1$' for the denominator.

4. **(C):** Here, LPM,

$$P_i = E(Y_i = 1 \mid X_i) = \beta_1 + \beta_2 X_i$$

Where, X_i is income and Y_i means individual owns a house.

$$P_i = E(Y_i = 1 \mid X_i)$$

$$= \frac{1}{1 + e^{-(\beta_1 + \beta_2 X_i)}}$$

For ease of exposition, we write this as,

$$P_i = \frac{1}{1 + e^{-Z_i}}$$

where $Z_i = \beta_1 + \beta_2 X_i$

This equation represents what is known as the (Cumulative) logistic distribution function.

5. **(D):** Here, $byx = \hat{\beta}$

$\therefore \quad by'x' = \frac{\hat{\beta}}{2} = 0.5\hat{\beta}.$

6. **(D):** The KPSS (Kwiatkowski-Phillips-Schmidt-Shin) test is a statistical test used to assess the stationarity of a time series data. Unlike other unit root tests like the ADF and Phillips-Perron tests that assume non-stationarity as the null hypothesis, the KPSS test takes the opposite approach by assuming stationarity as the null hypothesis. Specifically, the null hypothesis of the KPSS test asserts that the time series data is stationary around a deterministic trend, meaning that the data exhibits no trend or structural breaks. The alternative hypothesis, on the other hand, suggests that the data is non-stationary, indicating the presence of a unit root or stochastic trend. To conduct the test, the KPSS statistic compares the sum of squared deviations of the data from the trend under the null hypothesis to the sum of squared deviations from a constant under the alternative hypothesis. If the KPSS test statistic exceeds a critical value at a chosen significance level, the null hypothesis of stationarity is rejected, indicating that the data is non-stationary. Conversely, failure to reject the null hypothesis implies that the data is stationary around a deterministic trend. Therefore, the KPSS test provides valuable insights into the long-run behaviour of a time series data, allowing researchers to determine whether the observed trends are merely transitory fluctuations or indicative of a persistent underlying trend.

7. **(B)**

8. **(B):** According to the uncovered interest rate parity (UIP) condition, the expected change in the exchange rate between two countries should be equal to the interest rate differential between those countries. In this case, if capital flows are in equilibrium, investors would be indifferent between investing domestically or abroad.

Given that the interest rate in India is higher (6%) than in the USA (4%), according to UIP, investors would expect the US dollar to appreciate relative to the Indian rupee to offset the interest rate differential. However, the exchange rate is expected to rise from ₹ 80 to ₹ 84 in one year, indicating an expected depreciation of the US dollar relative to the Indian rupee.

This discrepancy suggests that the expected depreciation of the US dollar is greater than what UIP predicts based on the interest rate differential. Therefore, there is an opportunity for riskless profit through uncovered interest rate arbitrage. Investors would seek to take advantage of this mispricing by borrowing in the Indian economy at the lower interest rate, converting the borrowed funds to US dollars, and investing in US assets. This capital outflow from India would lead to the appreciation of the US dollar and the depreciation of the Indian rupee.

9. **(B):** Here, $\text{In}(Y_i) = \alpha + \beta X_i + u_i$ ...(*i*)

Now change X:

$\text{In}(Y_i + \Delta Y_i) = \alpha + \beta(X_i + \Delta X_i) + u_i$ ...(*ii*)

Subtract (*ii*) – (*i*)

$\text{In}(Y_i + \Delta Y_i) - \text{In}(Y_i) = \beta \Delta X_i$

Use the approximation,

$$\frac{\Delta Y_i}{Y_i} \cong \beta \Delta Xi$$

$$\therefore \quad e_{yx} = \frac{\Delta Y_i}{\Delta X_i} \cdot \frac{X_i}{Y_i}$$

$$= \beta \Delta X_i \times \frac{X_i}{\Delta X_i} = \beta X_i.$$

10. **(B)**

11. (C): The Human Poverty Index - 2 (HPI-2) is a comprehensive measure designed to assess poverty by considering multiple dimensions beyond just economic indicators. One key dimension included in the HPI-2 is "Social Inclusion." This dimension captures the extent to which individuals or groups within a society have equitable access to social resources, opportunities, and participation in societal activities. It encompasses various aspects such as access to education, healthcare, housing, social security, and involvement in community life. By emphasizing social inclusion, the HPI-2 recognizes that poverty is not solely defined by income levels but also by the ability of individuals to access essential services and fully participate in the social fabric of their communities. Thus, addressing social inclusion is essential for fostering a more equitable society and promoting human development by ensuring that all members have the opportunity to lead fulfilling and dignified lives.

12. (C): Solow residual is the difference between the rate of growth of output and the rate of growth of inputs. In the Solow growth model, which is a neoclassical economic model of long-run economic growth, output (or GDP) is determined by the inputs of capital and labour, among other factors. The rate of growth of output is influenced by various factors such as technological progress, improvements in efficiency, and increases in the quantity of capital and labour inputs. However, not all changes in output can be attributed solely to changes in inputs; there may be other factors at play, such as advancements in technology or changes in productivity, that lead to output growth beyond what can be explained by changes in inputs alone. The Solow residual captures this unexplained portion of output growth, often interpreted as total factor productivity growth, which encompasses technological progress and other factors that enhance efficiency and productivity in the economy. Therefore, this option correctly identifies the Solow residual as the difference between the rate of growth of output and the rate of growth of inputs in the Solow growth model.

13. (B): The Gini coefficient is usually defined in terms of the Lorenz curve. It is the most popular measure of distributional inequality. The Lorenz curve is a graphical device used to represent distributional inequality. The Gini coefficient is a numerical measure of inequality based on the Lorenz curve. Much of the literature is concerned with income inequality. With a few notable exception, the result of Gini coefficients also can be applied to other quantitative variables. The Gini coefficient varies between 0 (complete equality) and 1 (complete inequality). There are a number of ways in which the Gini coefficient can be expressed and interpreted. Many researchers derived it as a measure of inequality as it satisfies the axioms (criteria) of an ideal measure. The existing formula for Gini coefficients are as follows:

$$G = \frac{\frac{1}{n^2}\sum_{i=1}^{n}\sum_{j=1}^{n}|y_i - y_j|}{2\mu} \quad ...(1)$$

$$G = \frac{2}{\mu n^2}\sum_{i=1}^{n} iy_i - \frac{n+1}{n} \quad ...(2)$$

$$G = \frac{n+1}{n} - \frac{1}{2n^2\mu}\sum_{i=1}^{n} iy_i \quad ...(3)$$

where, $y_i (i = 1, 2, ..., n)$ is the income/age of the i-th person, $y_j (j = 1, 2, ..., n)$ is the income/age of the j-th person, m is the average income/age and $y_1 \le y_2 \le ... \le y_n$. Equation (1) is a measure of dispersion divided by twice the mean. It is the average absolute difference between all pairs of individuals. Equation (1) is known as Gini coefficient of mean difference given by Kendall and Stuart. They also define this coefficient as "one half of the average value of absolute differences between all pairs of incomes divided by the mean income". We will apply this measure to estimate the aging inequality of population. Equation (2) is given by Dasgupta et al. which is more mathematically tractable and computationally convenient for individual level data. Note that the first term in equation (2) involves a weighted sum of all the scores, where the weight applied to each score is its rank in the distribution. Equation (3) is due to Sen and it shows the income-waiting system in the welfare function behind the Gini coefficient.

14. (C) **15. (C)**

16. (C): Type II error occurs when the null hypothesis is false, but the test fails to reject it, leading to a false acceptance of the null hypothesis. The power of a test is complementary to Type II error and is calculated as 1 minus the probability of Type II error. A higher power indicates a greater ability of the test to detect true differences or effects when they exist. The power of a statistical test is a critical concept in hypothesis testing, representing the probability of correctly rejecting a false null hypothesis. In practical terms, it reflects the ability of the test to detect a true effect or difference when one exists in the population. A high power indicates that the test is more likely to identify real effects, providing greater confidence in the conclusions drawn from the analysis. Power is influenced by several factors, including the sample size, the significance level chosen for the test, and the magnitude of the true effect being investigated. Essentially, a test with higher power is better equipped to distinguish between true effects and random variability, reducing the risk of overlooking meaningful findings. Understanding the power of a test is crucial for researchers and analysts as it informs decisions about study design, sample size determination, and the interpretation of results, ultimately contributing to the robustness and validity of statistical analyses.

17. (A)

18. (D): Certainly! The Consumer Price Index (CPI) serves as a measure of the average change over time in the prices paid by urban consumers for a market basket of consumer goods and services. In March 2023, if the CPI of a country with a 1982 base index of 100 is 234.7, it implies a significant increase in the cost of purchasing the market basket of goods and services since 1982. To quantify this increase, we calculate the percentage change from the base year (1982) to the current year (2023).

The formula to determine the percentage increase is (Current CPI – Base CPI) × 100 %.

Substituting the given values, we get:

(234.7 – 100) × 100% = 134.7%.

Therefore, the cost of purchasing the market basket of goods and services has increased by 134.7% since the base year of 1982. This implies a substantial rise in prices over the years, reflecting inflationary pressures and indicating a significant decrease in the purchasing power of the currency compared to its value in 1982.

19. (B) **20. (C)** **21. (A)**

22. (B): To find the Marginal Revenue (MR) function from the Average Revenue (AR) function, we first need to differentiate the AR function with respect to quantity (q).

Given that AR = $10 + 5q - q^2$, we can differentiate it to find the MR function:

AR = $10 + 5q - q^2$

MR = $d\text{AR}/dq = 5 - 2q$

Now, let's analyze the nature of the MR function: The coefficient of q in the MR function is –2, which is the coefficient of q^2 in the AR function. Since the coefficient of q^2 in the AR function is negative (–1), the coefficient of q in the MR function (which is derived from the derivative of AR with respect to q) is also negative (–2).

A concave function has a decreasing slope as quantity increases, which corresponds to a negative coefficient for the linear term in the function. Since the coefficient of q in the MR function is negative (–2), the MR function is concave.

So, the correct answer is: Concave function.

23. **(B):** Consumer's expected utility without the contract is:

$= 0.5 \times u(50 - 25) + 0.5 \times u(50)$ ...(*i*)

$= 0.5 \times u(25) + 0.5 \times u(50)$

$= 0.5\times10\sqrt{25}+0.5\times10\sqrt{50}$

$= 0.5\times10\times5+0.5\times10\times\sqrt{50} = 25+5\sqrt{50}$

Consumer's expected utility with the contract is:

$= u(50 - p)$

$= 10\sqrt{(50-p)}$ ...(*ii*)

From (*i*) and (*ii*) we deduce that she is better off with the contract if and only if

$$= 10\sqrt{(50-p)} \geq 25+5\sqrt{50}$$

$$\sqrt{50-p} \geq \frac{25+5\sqrt{50}}{10} = \frac{5+\sqrt{50}}{2} = 6.035$$

$50 - p \geq 6.035^2$

$50 - p \geq 36.43$

$-p \geq 36.43 - 50$

$-p \geq -13.57 \Rightarrow p \geq 13.57.$

24. **(D):** The statement is derived from the Extreme Value Theorem, which states that if $f(x)$ is a continuous function on a closed interval $[a, b]$, then $f(x)$ must attain both a maximum and a minimum value at some points within that interval. This theorem guarantees the existence of such points c and d where $f(x)$ achieves its maximum and minimum values, respectively, within the interval $[a, b]$. The Extreme Value Theorem (EVT) ensures the existence of both maximum and minimum values of a continuous function $f(x)$ over a closed interval $[a, b]$. It guarantees that within this interval, there will be at least one point where the function attains its highest value (maximum) and another point where it reaches its lowest value (minimum). These points are significant because they represent the extreme values of the function within the specified interval. The EVT is crucial in mathematical analysis and optimization problems as it provides assurance that such extreme values exist, facilitating the identification of optimal solutions or critical points in various applications, including economics, engineering, and physics.

25. **(D)** **26.** **(B)** **27.** **(A)**

28. **(B)** **29.** **(D)**

30. **(B):** In the scenario of two perfect complement goods, where consumption of one good is strictly tied to the consumption of the other, the indifference curves take the form of straight lines. This characteristic arises from the fixed ratio in consumption demanded by consumers for these goods. As consumers derive utility only from consuming both goods in a specific fixed ratio, any deviation from this ratio would result in reduced utility. Consequently, the indifference curves, which represent combinations of the two goods that provide the same level of satisfaction, exhibit a linear relationship, reflecting the fixed proportions demanded by consumers. This implies that no matter how much of one good is consumed; utility remains unchanged unless the complementary good is also consumed in the appropriate ratio. Therefore, the straight-line nature of the indifference curves accurately captures the inherent complementarily between the goods and reflects the fixed ratio in consumption demanded by consumers for optimal utility attainment.

31. (C)

32. (D): Tamil Nadu's status as the most urbanized major state in India, with 48.45% of its population residing in urban areas according to the 2011 Census, underscores a significant demographic shift within the state over the past few decades. This transformation is particularly evident when comparing the urbanization rates from previous census years. In 1991, for instance, only 34.15% of Tamil Nadu's population was classified as urban, indicating a substantial increase over a span of 20 years. This rapid urbanization reflects various socio-economic factors, including industrialization, urban migration, infrastructure development, and economic opportunities in urban centers. The growth of industries, services, and educational institutions in urban areas has attracted migrants from rural regions seeking better livelihoods and access to amenities. Additionally, government policies promoting urban development and investment in urban infrastructure have further facilitated this urban expansion. Overall, Tamil Nadu's journey towards becoming the most urbanized state in India highlights the complex interplay of demographic, economic, and policy dynamics shaping its urban landscape.

33. (A): When the government sets a minimum wage (w') above the equilibrium wage (w^*), it creates a situation where the mandated wage is higher than what would naturally occur in the market. This results in higher labour costs for employers. To mitigate these increased costs, employers may resort to various strategies to adjust their labour force composition and minimize expenses. One such strategy is casualization, where employers may hire workers on a temporary or part-time basis instead of offering full-time permanent positions.

Casualization allows employers to maintain flexibility in their labour force while keeping costs lower than if they were to hire full-time employees at the mandated minimum wage. By hiring workers on a casual or temporary basis, employers can avoid paying additional benefits and entitlements that are typically associated with full-time employment, such as healthcare benefits, paid leave, and retirement contributions.

Therefore, if the minimum wage (w') exceeds the equilibrium wage (w^*), there is a tendency for employers to increase casualization of workers as a cost-saving measure. This trend may result in a higher proportion of workers employed under precarious or temporary arrangements, leading to potential challenges for workers in terms of job security, stability, and access to benefits and protections typically afforded to full-time employees.

34. (C): The essential condition for stable equilibrium is that the demand curve should have a negative slope and the supply curve a positive slope. Otherwise, it will not be a stable equilibrium, this would be what can be called unstable equilibrium.

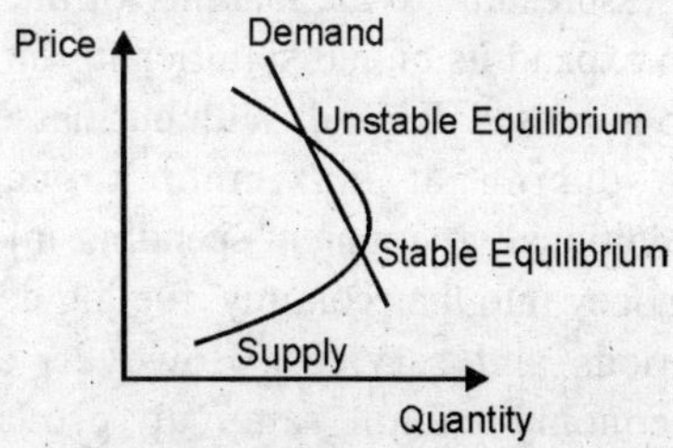

35. (C): ∵ Revenue deficit

= Fiscal deficit – Capital expenditure

⇒ Capital expenditure

= Fiscal deficit – Revenue deficit

= 7 – 3 = 4%

∴ Capital expenditure to GDP ratio is 4%.

36. (C): When the interest rate is exogenously determined by the Central Bank and the money supply is endogenously determined, the LM curve in the interest rate-income plane becomes horizontal. This signifies that changes in income levels do not influence the interest rate set by the Central Bank. Instead, the money supply adjusts automatically to maintain equilibrium in the money market at the given interest rate. As a result, regardless of fluctuations in income, the interest rate remains constant along the LM curve. This scenario implies a stable monetary policy where the Central Bank's decisions regarding the interest rate are independent of changes in output or income levels. Therefore, the horizontal LM curve suggests that the monetary authority is committed to maintaining a fixed interest rate, regardless of changes in economic activity. This stability in monetary policy can provide certainty to investors and businesses, supporting economic stability and growth over the long term.

37. (B): In a supply-constrained situation, characterized by an economy operating near or at full capacity, a higher fiscal deficit to GDP ratio can precipitate inflationary pressures due to the inability of the economy to expand its output significantly in response to increased demand. With businesses already producing at maximum capacity, any additional government spending injects more money into the economy, fueling demand for goods and services. However, since the economy cannot ramp up production to match the heightened demand, it results in excess demand relative to available supply. This imbalance leads to businesses raising prices to balance supply and demand, contributing to inflation. Moreover, inflationary expectations may emerge among businesses and consumers, further driving up prices as firms adjust their pricing strategies and workers demand higher wages. Additionally, if businesses face elevated costs from factors like increased input prices or supply chain disruptions, they may pass these costs on to consumers through higher prices, exacerbating inflationary pressures. Therefore, in a supply-constrained situation, a higher fiscal deficit can exacerbate inflation as the economy grapples with limited capacity to meet heightened demand, making Supply constrained situation the accurate description of the scenario where a higher fiscal deficit could cause inflation.

38. (C)

39. (A): The repo rate, or repurchase agreement rate, signifies the interest rate at which commercial banks can borrow funds from the central bank, in this case, the Reserve Bank of India (RBI). This borrowing occurs through repurchase agreements where commercial banks provide government securities as collateral to the RBI in exchange for short-term funds. By adjusting the repo rate, the RBI influences the cost of borrowing for commercial banks, which in turn impacts the overall availability of credit and liquidity in the financial system. Lowering the repo rate encourages borrowing by making funds cheaper, stimulating economic activity and investment. Conversely, raising the repo rate makes borrowing more expensive, this can help in curbing inflationary pressures and controlling excessive credit growth. Thus, the repo rate serves as a crucial monetary policy tool used by central banks to manage and regulate the money supply and interest rates within an economy.

40. (C): In an economy marked by significant involuntary unemployment, the aggregate labour supply curve in a real wage-labour supply plane would appear vertical. This characteristic arises from the presence of a substantial pool of unemployed individuals who are willing to work at the prevailing wage rate but are unable to secure employment due to insufficient demand for labour. With a fixed number of individuals actively seeking work, the quantity of labour supplied remains constant regardless of changes in the real wage rate. Even if wages were to rise, the quantity of labour supplied would not increase, as there are no additional individuals available to enter the labour market. Consequently, the aggregate labour supply curve appears vertical, indicating that the quantity of labour supplied is fixed at the level corresponding to the number of unemployed workers willing to work at the prevailing wage rate. This situation reflects the rigidities and frictions present in the labour market, which prevent unemployed individuals from finding suitable employment despite their willingness to work at prevailing wage rates.

41. (B): The Global Hunger Index (GHI) is a tool designed to comprehensively measure and track hunger at global, regional and national levels, reflecting multiple dimensions of hunger over time. The GHI is intended to raise awareness and understanding of the struggle against hunger, provide a way to compare levels of hunger between countries and regions, and call attention to those areas of the world where hunger levels are highest and where the need for additional efforts to eliminate hunger is greatest.

How the GHI is calculated each country's: GHI score is calculated based on a formula that combines four indicators that together capture the multidimensional nature of hunger:

Undernourishment: the share of the population whose caloric intake is insufficient;

Child stunting: the share of children under the age of five who have low height for their age, reflecting chronic undernutrition;

Child wasting: the share of children under the age of five who have low weight for their height, reflecting acute undernutrition; and

Child mortality: the share of children who die before their fifth birthday, reflecting in part the fatal mix of inadequate nutrition and unhealthy enviornments.

The standardized scores are aggregated to calculated the GHI score for each country. Undernourishment and child mortality each contribute one-third of the GHI score, while child stunting and child wasting each contribute one-sixth of the score.

Composition of GHI Scores

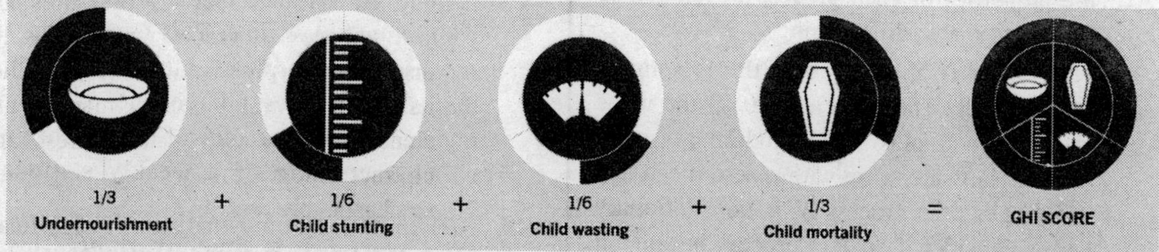

42. (C):

(*b*) **Estimated value of the conditional probability of occurrence of the event lies between 0 and 1:** This statement is indeed true. In the LPM, the dependent variable represents a binary outcome (e.g., success or failure, 1 or 0), and the predicted probabilities generated by the model naturally fall within the range of 0 to 1. This is because probabilities must always be bounded between these two values, given their interpretation as the likelihood of an event occurring.

(*c*) **Error term is homoscedastic:** Contrary to the statement, the error term in the LPM is not homoscedastic; rather, it typically exhibits heteroscedasticity. Heteroscedasticity implies that the variance of the error term varies across different levels of the explanatory variables. In the context of the LPM, this means that the variability in the errors is not constant across the range of values of the independent variables. This violates one of the assumptions of ordinary least squares (OLS) regression, which assumes constant variance of the error term.

(*d*) **R^2 is a good measure of goodness of fit:** This statement is generally true. R-squared (R^2) measures the proportion of the total variation in the dependent variable that is explained by the independent variables in the model. While R^2 can serve as a useful measure of goodness of fit in the LPM, it has some limitations, especially when dealing with binary dependent variables. In such cases, R^2 may not provide a complete picture of model fit, and alternative measures such as pseudo-R^2 statistics (e.g., McFadden's R^2) are often preferred for evaluating the goodness of fit in logistic regression models, which are more commonly used for binary outcomes.

43. (C): To determine which of the processes X_t given are I(0) processes, we should look at the properties of each process in relation to stationarity and differencing.

For option (*a*), $X_t = X_{t-1} + Z_t$, this is a simple random walk. The value at time *t* is the value at time $t - 1$ plus some random noise Z_t. Since Z_t is white noise with a zero mean and variance σ_2, the process X_t is non-stationary and is considered an I(1) process because it requires one differencing to become stationary.

Option (*b*), $X_t = \alpha X_{t-1} + Z_t$ where $0 < \alpha < 1$, is an autoregressive process of order 1, AR(1). The parameter α is between 0 and 1, so the effect of the past values is diminishing over time, which ensures that the process will return to a mean of zero. This makes the process X_t stationary, and since it does not require differencing to become stationary, it is an I(0) process.

Option (*c*), $X_t = Z_t + Z_{t-1}$, is simply the sum of two white noise processes at different times. Since white noise is stationary and adding two stationary processes together yields another stationary process, X_t here is also stationary. Therefore, this is an I(0) process.

Option (*d*), $X_t = 8 + X_{t-1} + Z_t$, represents a random walk with a drift. The constant term 8 introduces a deterministic trend, and similar to option (*a*), it is a non-stationary process. The presence of a deterministic trend means that the process is not I(0) since differencing once (to remove the effect of the trend) would be required to achieve stationarity.

Therefore, option C the correct answer.

44. (B):

(*b*) **Mean is constant:** A weakly stationary stochastic process requires that the mean of the process remains constant over time. This means that the average value of the process does not change as time progresses. Therefore, the constancy of the mean is indeed a feature of a weakly stationary stochastic process.

(*c*) **Variance is constant:** Similarly, a weakly stationary stochastic process necessitates that the variance of the process remains constant over time. This implies that the dispersion or spread of the process around its mean does not change over time. Hence, the constancy of the variance is a characteristic of a weakly stationary stochastic process.

(*d*) **Covariance is time-invariant:** This is also a feature of a weakly stationary stochastic process. In weak stationarity, the covariance between any two observations of the process depends only on the time difference between them, not on the specific time points. This means that the covariance structure of the process remains constant over time, and changes in the time index do not affect the covariance between observations.

45. (D)

46. (B): The new monetary aggregate NM_2, proposed by the Third working group of RBI, represents an important refinement in measuring the money supply within the economy. By including time deposits with a term less than or equal to one year, NM_2 captures a significant portion of funds that are readily accessible for spending or investment in the short to medium term. This inclusion acknowledges the role of time deposits as a component of the broader money supply, reflecting the liquidity preferences of households and firms. However, by excluding time deposits with terms exceeding one year, NM_2 ensures a more accurate representation of the portion of funds that are less immediately liquid and more likely to be held for longer-term saving purposes. This distinction between short-term and long-term deposits is crucial for policymakers in understanding the dynamics of liquidity in the financial system and its implications for monetary policy formulation. NM_2 provides insights into the stability and health of the banking sector, as well as the availability of funds for investment and consumption, thereby aiding in the assessment of monetary conditions and the implementation of appropriate policy measures to support economic stability and growth.

47. (C):

(*a*) **91-day Treasury bill:** Treasury bills are short-term debt securities issued by the government to finance its short-term borrowing requirements. They are typically issued with maturities ranging from a few days to one year, making them highly liquid and suitable for short-term investment. Investors purchase Treasury bills at a discount to their face value and receive the full face value upon maturity, effectively earning interest on their investment.

(*b*) **Commercial paper:** Commercial paper is a short-term debt instrument issued by corporations, typically with maturities ranging from a few days to nine months. It is used by companies to raise funds for various short-term financing needs, such as funding working capital requirements or financing short-term liabilities. Commercial paper is considered a money market instrument due to its short-term nature and high liquidity.

(*c*) **Certificate of deposit (CD) issued by banks:** Certificates of deposit are time deposits offered by banks to depositors, where the depositor agrees to leave the deposited funds with the bank for a specified period (term) in exchange for a fixed interest rate. CDs typically have maturities ranging from a few weeks to several years, but shorter-term CDs with maturities of less than one year are considered money market instruments due to their liquidity and short-term nature.

48. (B):

(*a*) **Current Account deficit equals excess of imports over the sum of exports and net transfers received by a country:** The Current Account records all transactions involving goods, services, income, and transfers between residents and non-residents of a country. A deficit occurs when a country imports more goods and services, pays more income to foreigners, and transfers more funds abroad than it receives from exports, income from abroad, and transfers from abroad. This deficit reflects a shortfall in a country's international trade balance and represents an outflow of domestic currency to pay for foreign goods and services.

(*b*) **Current Account deficit may be covered by borrowing from foreigners:** When a country has a Current Account deficit, it indicates that it is spending more on imports and transfers than it is earning from exports and transfers received. To finance this deficit, a country can borrow from foreign sources. This borrowing can come in various forms, such as foreign loans, issuance of bonds to foreign investors, or seeking assistance from international financial institutions. However, relying too heavily on foreign borrowing to cover a persistent Current Account deficit can pose risks to a country's economy, including increased indebtedness and vulnerability to changes in global financial conditions.

(*d*) **If India's Current Account deficit in a particular period is $50 million, it can be financed by net capital inflows amounting to $50 million:** Net capital inflows represent the total amount of foreign investment flowing into a country minus the total amount of domestic investment flowing out. If a country has a Current Account deficit, it can be offset by an equal amount of net capital inflows, as these inflows provide the necessary financing to cover the deficit. Capital inflows can come from various sources, including foreign direct investment, portfolio investment, and borrowing from international financial markets. However, it's essential to monitor the sustainability of these inflows to ensure they do not lead to excessive reliance on external financing or potential risks to economic stability.

49. (C):

(*a*) **Indian Rupee will depreciate in the spot market:** When investors engage in covered interest arbitrage, they typically borrow money in the currency with the lower interest rate (in this case, USD) and convert it into the currency with the higher interest rate (INR). This process increases the supply of INR in the foreign exchange market and creates demand for USD. As a result, the value of the INR relative to the USD decreases, leading to depreciation of the Indian Rupee in the spot market. Essentially, the increased demand for USD and the excess supply of INR put downward pressure on the exchange rate, causing the INR to weaken.

(*d*) **Interest rate will decline in the US:** When investors engage in covered interest arbitrage by borrowing in USD to invest in India, they increase the demand for USD. This increased demand for USD tends to strengthen the currency, causing it to appreciate. In response to the appreciation of the USD, the central bank of the US may adjust its monetary policy to counteract the currency appreciation and support economic growth. One way to achieve this is by decreasing interest rates in the US. Lower interest rates make borrowing more attractive, stimulating economic activity and helping to offset the effects of currency appreciation. Therefore, covered interest arbitrage can lead to a decline in interest rates in the US as the central bank takes measures to manage currency movements and support the economy.

50. (C) **51. (D)**

52. (A):

(*a*) **The AD curve will shift to the right if autonomous investment rises:** When autonomous investment increases, it reflects businesses' increased confidence in future profitability, leading them to invest more in capital goods, machinery, or infrastructure. This increase in investment spending directly contributes to aggregate demand in the economy, as it represents an injection of new spending not directly influenced by changes in output or income. As a result, the AD curve shifts to the right, indicating higher levels of aggregate demand at every price level.

(*b*) **The AD curve will shift to the right if net exports rise in an open economy:** An increase in net exports means that the country is exporting more goods and services than it is importing. This suggests increased demand for the country's exports abroad, which contributes positively to its aggregate demand. Higher net exports directly add to aggregate demand since they represent additional spending on domestically produced goods and services. Consequently, the AD curve shifts to the right to reflect the increased demand for domestic output resulting from higher net exports.

(*c*) **The AD curve will shift to the left if money supply contracts:** When the central bank implements a contractionary monetary policy and reduces the money supply, it leads to higher interest rates, making borrowing more expensive for businesses and consumers. This, in turn, reduces investment and consumption spending in the economy, causing aggregate demand to decrease. A contraction in the money supply represents a decrease in the availability of funds for spending and investment, thereby shifting the AD curve to the left, indicating lower levels of aggregate demand at every price level.

53. (A):

(*b*) Monetarism, associated with economists such as Milton Friedman, emphasizes the role of money in the economy. Monetarists argue that changes in the money supply have a significant impact on economic variables such as output, employment, and inflation. Additionally, they stress the importance of expectations, particularly in relation to inflation. For example, if individuals and firms expect prices to rise in the future, they may adjust their behavior accordingly, leading to actual inflation.

(*c*) The classical school of thought, which includes economists like Adam Smith and David Ricardo, indeed advocates for the invisible hand and the efficiency of the market mechanism. Classical economists believe that markets tend towards equilibrium and that individuals pursuing their self-interest in competitive markets leads to overall economic welfare. They argue for minimal government intervention in the economy, trusting that market forces will efficiently allocate resources.

(*d*) New Keynesian economics emerged as a response to the shortcomings of traditional Keynesian theory. New Keynesians retain many of the key insights of Keynesian economics but incorporate the assumption of imperfect markets into their frameworks. They recognize factors such as market rigidities, imperfect information, and nominal rigidities (such as sticky prices and wages) that can lead to inefficiencies and market failures. New Keynesians advocate for targeted government intervention, such as monetary and fiscal policy, to correct these market failures and stabilize the economy.

54. (C):

(*a*) **Output will be higher:** A monetary expansion, implemented through actions like central bank purchases of government securities or reductions in interest rates, serves to increase the money supply within the economy. This influx of money leads to a decrease in interest rates, making borrowing cheaper for businesses seeking capital to finance investment projects. With the cost of borrowing reduced, firms are incentivized to undertake more investment activities, such as expanding production capacity, upgrading technology, or initiating new projects. As a result, the aggregate demand for goods and services rises, prompting firms to ramp up production to meet the increased demand. This increase in production, in turn, leads to higher levels of output within the economy. Additionally, the boost in economic activity may translate into increased employment opportunities as firms expand their operations, further contributing to the rise in output and overall economic growth.

(*b*) **Consumption will be higher:** Lower interest rates resulting from a monetary expansion also have significant implications for consumer behaviour and household spending. When interest rates decline, the cost of borrowing for consumers decreases, making it more affordable for individuals to finance major purchases, such as homes, automobiles, or durable goods. With financing options becoming more attractive, households may be more inclined to increase their consumption spending on these big-ticket items. Additionally, lower interest rates can lead to reduced debt-servicing costs for existing loans, freeing up disposable income that consumers can allocate towards discretionary spending. This increase in consumer spending contributes to a rise in aggregate demand, prompting businesses to produce more goods and services to meet the growing consumer demand. Consequently, higher levels of consumption further stimulate economic activity, leading to increased output, employment, and overall economic expansion.

55. (B): In economics, a production function Q is said to be homogeneous of degree *n* if, when all inputs are scaled by a factor *t*, output is scaled by a factor t_n. In the function Q = Aχαyβ, if α + β = 1, then Q is homogeneous of degree 1 (linearly homogeneous or simply homogeneous), which means it has constant returns to scale.

For statement (*a*), it is not correct to say that Q is a homogeneous function for all values of α and β because homogeneity depends on the sum α + β. Q is only homogeneous if α + β equals some constant *k*, and in that case, Q would be homogeneous of degree *k*.

Statement (*b*) claims that H is a homothetic function for all values of α and β. A homothetic function is one where if Q is homogeneous, then any monotonic transformation of Q is homothetic. Since an exponential function is a monotonic transformation, H = eQ would be a homothetic function of Q, regardless of the values of α and β.

Statement (*d*) says H is not a homogeneous function. This is true because the exponential function of a homogeneous function is not homogeneous, but rather homothetic as explained in (*b*).

Given these points, statements (*a*), (*b*), and (*d*) are the correct ones, making option B the right choice.

56. (D): To determine the correct answer, we must evaluate the matrix multiplication of A and B, and also B and A.

Matrix multiplication is defined when the number of columns in the first matrix matches the number of rows in the second matrix. Matrix A is a 3 × 23 × 2 matrix, and matrix B is a 2 × 12 × 1 matrix. Thus, the product AB is defined and will result in a 3 × 13 × 1 matrix.

To find AB, we perform the following calculations:

AB = [124380] [59]

= 1 × 5 + 3 × 92 × 5 + 8 × 94 × 5 + 0 × 9]

= [5 + 2710 + 7220 + 0] = [328220].

Hence, statement (*a*) is correct.

For BA, since B is a 2 × 12 × 1 matrix and A is a 3 × 23 × 2 matrix, we cannot multiply B by A because the number of columns in B does not match the number of rows in A.

Therefore, statement (*d*) is correct, and BA is not defined.

Considering AT (the transpose of A), which would be a 2 × 32 × 3 matrix, and B as a 2 × 12 × 1 matrix, their multiplication is not possible because the number of columns in A^T does not match the number of rows in B. Thus, A^TB is not defined, which makes statement (*e*) incorrect.

Therefore, the correct statements are (*a*) and (*d*), which means the answer is option (D).

57. (C):

(*a*) The Marginal Cost (MC) curve cuts both short-run Average Cost (AC) curve and Average Variable Cost (AVC) curve at their lowest point. This statement is correct. In the short run, the Marginal Cost (MC) curve intersects the Average Cost (AC) curve and the Average Variable Cost (AVC) curve at their minimum points. This is because when MC is below AC or AVC, it pulls them down, and when MC is above AC or AVC, it pulls them up. At the minimum point of AC and AVC, MC equals AC and AVC, respectively.

(*e*) **The AC curve is u-shaped.** This statement is also correct. The Average Cost (AC) curve is typically U-shaped in the short run. Initially, as production increases, AC decreases due to economies of scale, where the fixed costs are spread over more units, leading to lower average costs. However, after a certain point, AC starts increasing due to diseconomies of scale, where the costs associated with producing additional units begin to outweigh the benefits of increased production. This leads to the U-shape of the AC curve in the short run.

58. (C): To address this question, let's break down each of the statements given and validate them against the information provided in the OLS regression output.

Statement (*a*) says that for one year increase in schooling, wage per hour increases by ₹ 640 on average, when cognitive ability (CA) is kept constant. The regression coefficient for education (years of schooling, S) is 0.64, which means for each additional year of schooling, wages increase by 0.64 thousand rupees or ₹ 640. This statement is correct.

Statement (*b*) mentions the value of t statistic of cognitive ability (CA) is 3. The t statistic is calculated by taking the estimated coefficient and dividing it by the standard error. For CA, the estimated coefficient is 0.15 and the standard error is 0.05. To calculate the t statistic:

$3t = 0.050.15 = 3$

So, the t statistic for CA is indeed 3, which makes statement (*b*) correct.

Statement (*c*) and (*d*) both provide formulas for the F statistic. The F statistic in a regression analysis is used to test the overall significance of the model. It is calculated by taking the ratio of the mean square due to regression (explained sum of squares divided by its degrees of freedom) to the mean square error (residual sum of squares divided by its degrees of freedom).

The correct formula for the F statistic is:

F = Residual Sum of Squares/Degrees of Freedom for Residual

Explained Sum of Squares/Degrees of Freedom for Regression

Given that the explained sum of squares is 4745.75 with 2 degrees of freedom, and the residual sum of squares is 33651.28 with 567 degrees of freedom, the correct F statistic is calculated by statement (*c*):

F = (33651.28/567) (4745.75/2)

This means that statement (*c*) is correct and statement (*d*) is incorrect, as it inverses the ratio.

Therefore, the correct statements are (*a*), (*b*), and (*c*), which corresponds to answer C.

59. (D) **60. (D)**

61. (D): To evaluate the statements related to a production function $q = f(k, l)$ that is a homogeneous function of degree 1, we should recall some properties of homogeneous functions and Euler's Theorem.

Statement (*a*) suggests that the marginal products of capital ($\partial q/\partial k$) and labour ($\partial q/\partial l$) are homogeneous of degree 1. However, for a function that is homogeneous of degree n, its first derivatives (marginal products in this context) are homogeneous of degree $n - 1$. Since the production function $f(k, l)$ is given as homogeneous of degree 1, the marginal products should be homogeneous of degree 0, which means they are constant. Hence, statement (*a*) is incorrect.

Statement (*b*) talks about the second-order cross partial derivatives ($\partial 2q/\partial k\partial l$ and $\partial 2\partial/\partial l\partial k$). For a function with continuous second derivatives, the mixed partial derivatives are equal by Clairaut's theorem (also known as Young's theorem), regardless of the function's homogeneity. Thus, statement (*b*) is correct.

Statement (*c*) is Euler's Theorem applied to a homogeneous function of degree 1. Euler's Theorem states that for a homogeneous function of degree n, the following equation holds:

$k\partial k\partial q + l\partial l\partial q = n \,.\, q$

Since our function is homogeneous of degree 1, we can replace n with 1, making statement (*c*) correct.

Statement (*d*) is an extension of Euler's Theorem to the second derivatives. For a homogeneous function of degree 1, the sum of the product of each variable with its corresponding second derivative is equal to 0. This statement is a result of differentiating both sides of Euler's Theorem with respect to k and l respectively and adding them together. Thus, statement (*d*) is correct.

The correct statements are (*b*), (*c*), and (*d*), which means the answer is option (D).

62. (C):

(*a*) The statement asserts that when we take the union of a finite number of closed sets in a topological space, the resulting set remains closed. This property is fundamental in topology and is often used in various mathematical proofs and constructions. A closed set is one that contains all its limit points, and the union of closed sets preserves this property because if a point is a limit point of one of the closed sets, it will still be a limit point of the union. This is because the union contains all the elements from each individual set, ensuring that no limit points are excluded. Therefore, the union of finite numbers of closed sets is indeed a closed set.

(*d*) The statement posits that when we intersect a finite number of open sets in a topological space, the resulting set remains open. An open set is defined as a set that contains an open neighborhood around each of its points. When we intersect a finite number of such sets, any point in the intersection will still have an open neighborhood contained entirely within each of the original open sets. This is because the intersection only includes elements that are common to all the sets being intersected, and these elements still possess the property of having open neighborhoods within each set. Therefore, the intersection of finite numbers of open sets is also an open set. This property is crucial in analysis, topology, and other areas of mathematics for establishing continuity, compactness, and other key concepts.

63. (*)

64. (C):

(*a*) If the two utility functions $u(x)$ and $b(y)$ are related by $u(y) = V(b(x))$, where $(-) > 0V'\,(-) > 0$, then $V(x)$ is a utility function representing the same preference as $b(y)$. This statement is correct. The function $V(x)$ is derived from $b(y)$ through the transformation $u(y) = V(b(x))$. The fact that (–) > 0V2 (–) > 0 implies that $V(x)$ is strictly increasing, preserving the preference ordering between different consumption bundles. Therefore, $V(x)$ represents the same preferences as $b(y)$.

(*b*) If two utility functions represent the same preferences, the solutions to the consumer's utility maximization problem are the same with the two utility functions but the indirect utility functions are different. This statement is correct. Utility functions represent preferences, and if two utility functions represent the same preferences, they will lead to the same optimal consumption bundle because the consumer aims to maximize utility regardless of the specific utility function used. However, the indirect utility functions, which represent the maximum utility attainable given prices and income, might differ because they are derived from different utility functions.

(*c*) If the local nonsatiation assumption of preference is satisfied, any solution to the consumer's utility maximization problem satisfies the budget constraint with equality. This statement is correct. Local nonsatiation means the consumer always desires more of at least one good at any consumption bundle. In the utility maximization problem, the consumer chooses a consumption bundle that maximizes utility subject to the budget constraint. If local nonsatiation holds, the consumer will always choose a consumption bundle where they exhaust their entire budget, thus satisfying the budget constraint with equality.

65. **(C):** The objective function to be maximized in each case is the natural logarithm of x, which is an increasing function for $x > 0$. This means as x increases, so does $\ln x$. However, the behavior of the function under the constraints of each problem is critical for determining whether a solution exists.

For the first problem (*i*), where $x > 1$, there is no upper bound on x, and hence, the function $\ln x$ can increase indefinitely. In optimization terms, the problem lacks an upper constraint that would allow for a maximal value, leading to the conclusion that there is no finite maximum; $\ln x$ will keep increasing as x increases, thus the problem has no solution.

The second problem (*ii*) involves $x < 1$, where $\ln x$ is decreasing as x approaches zero from the right. Since the natural logarithm heads towards negative infinity as its argument heads towards zero from the right, and x cannot actually reach zero to allow for the logarithm to be defined, there is no maximum value within the constraint. Like the first, this problem also does not have a solution.

The third problem (*iii*) stipulates $1 < x < 2$. Within this bounded interval, the function $\ln x$ will achieve a maximum at the upper boundary due to its increasing nature. Therefore, the maximum value for $\ln x$ is at $x = 2$, making $\ln 2$ the maximal value, and thus, this problem does have a solution.

66. **(D):**

(*a*) **Ramsar Convention: Conservation of wetlands -** The Ramsar Convention, signed in 1971 in Ramsar, Iran, aims to protect and preserve wetlands worldwide, recognizing their importance for biodiversity and ecosystem services.

(*b*) **Basel Convention: Control of trans-boundary movement of hazardous wastes and disposal -** The Basel Convention, adopted in 1989 in Basel, Switzerland, addresses the management and disposal of hazardous wastes, especially those that can cause harm if not handled properly. It regulates the transboundary movement of such wastes to ensure environmentally sound management.

(*c*) **Montreal Protocol: Ozone layer depletion** - The Montreal Protocol, established in 1987 in Montreal, Canada, aims to phase out the production and use of ozone-depleting substances (ODS) such as chlorofluorocarbons (CFCs) and halons. Its primary goal is to protect the ozone layer, which shields the Earth from harmful ultraviolet radiation.

(*d*) **Paris Agreement: Reduction of greenhouse gas emissions** - The Paris Agreement, adopted in 2015 in Paris, France, is a landmark international treaty aimed at combating climate change. It sets out ambitious goals to limit global warming and reduce greenhouse gas emissions to mitigate the impacts of climate change.

67. (B):

(*a*) **Coase theorem - (I) Property right, victim's pay and polluter pay principle.** The Coase theorem asserts that in the presence of well-defined property rights and in the absence of transaction costs, parties can negotiate and reach an efficient solution to externalities, such as pollution, without the need for government intervention. This involves the concepts of property rights, where the victim can be compensated (victim's pay) or the polluter can be made to pay for the damage caused (polluter pay principle).

(*b*) **Climate change - (IV) Global externality.** Climate change refers to long-term changes in temperature, precipitation, and other atmospheric conditions that result from human activities, particularly the emission of greenhouse gases. It is considered a global externality as its impacts extend beyond national borders and affect the entire planet.

(*c*) **Ecological dumping - (II) Lax environmental regulation, hidden subsidy.** Ecological dumping refers to the practice where firms in countries with lax environmental regulations can gain a competitive advantage by producing goods more cheaply due to lower environmental standards. This can be seen as a form of hidden subsidy, as these firms are effectively being subsidized by not having to comply with stricter environmental regulations.

(*d*) **Tradable emission permit - (III) Quantity restriction.** Tradable emission permits involve setting a cap on the total amount of pollution allowed (quantity restriction) and allowing firms to buy and sell permits to emit pollutants. This system provides economic incentives for firms to reduce emissions efficiently and is a market-based approach to addressing pollution.

68. (C):

(*a*) **Kenneth Arrow - (III) Fundamental contribution in welfare economics:** Kenneth Arrow made significant contributions to welfare economics, particularly through his work on social choice theory, which analyzes how individual preferences can be aggregated into collective social preferences to determine optimal outcomes.

(*b*) **Robert Solow - (IV) Fundamental contribution in economic growth theory:** Robert Solow's seminal work on economic growth theory, particularly the Solow growth model, has been instrumental in understanding the determinants of long-term economic growth and the role of factors such as capital accumulation, technological progress, and productivity growth.

(*c*) **Daniel Kahneman - (II) Fundamental contribution in behavioural economics:** Daniel Kahneman is a pioneer in the field of behavioral economics, which integrates insights from psychology into economic analysis. His research on cognitive biases, prospect theory, and decision-making under uncertainty has profoundly influenced our understanding of how individuals make economic choices.

(*d*) **Joshua Angrist - (I) Analysis of causal relationship:** Joshua Angrist has made significant contributions to the field of econometrics, particularly in the analysis of causal relationships using natural experiments and instrumental variables. His work has advanced our ability to identify causal effects in observational data and has had widespread applications in various fields of economics.

69. (C):

(*a*) **Demographic Transition - (III) Replacement Rate:** The Demographic Transition refers to the process through which populations move from high birth and death rates to low birth and death rates as they undergo industrialization and modernization. The Replacement Rate is a key concept within the demographic transition framework, representing the fertility rate necessary for a population to replace itself from one generation to the next.

(*b*) **Stages of growth - (II) Take-off:** The Stages of Growth theory, proposed by economist Walt Rostow, describes the development process of economies through various stages, with the Take-off stage being a crucial phase characterized by rapid industrialization, urbanization, and technological advancement.

(*c*) **Rural-urban migration decision - (I) Dualism:** Rural-urban migration decision refers to the choice made by individuals to move from rural areas to urban areas in search of better economic opportunities. This decision is influenced by the phenomenon of dualism, which describes the coexistence of traditional and modern sectors within an economy, often characterized by disparities in income, employment opportunities, and living standards between rural and urban areas.

(*d*) **Female labour force participation rate - (IV) Backward bending labour supply curve:** The Female labour force participation rate refers to the proportion of women in the population who are actively engaged in the labour force. The Backward bending labour supply curve is a concept in labour economics that suggests that individuals may initially respond to higher wages by increasing their labour supply, but beyond a certain point, they may choose to work less as their income rises further.

70. (D)

71. (C): The Permanent Income Hypothesis of Consumption was introduced by Milton Friedman. This theory posits that people's consumption choices are not solely affected by their current income, but rather by their anticipated income over a longer period. Essentially, individuals plan their consumption based on the income they expect to have over their lifetime, smoothing out consumption to achieve a stable path even if their income is variable in the short term.

The Life-cycle Hypothesis of Consumption is attributed to Franco Modigliani. This hypothesis complements Friedman's Permanent Income Hypothesis by considering the saving behavior of individuals over their lifetime. According to Modigliani, individuals plan their consumption and savings based on their current income and their needs in the future, particularly for retirement. Therefore, individuals save during their working years and dissave during their retirement.

The Real Business Cycle Theory is associated with F. Kydland and E. Prescott. This theory stands on the premise that business cycle fluctuations can to a large extent be accounted for by real (in contrast to nominal) shocks. According to this view, economic cycles are primarily the result of technological changes that affect productivity and thus influence economic variables like employment, consumption, and investment.

Lastly, the Policy Ineffectiveness Proposition was developed by Thomas Sargent and Neil Wallace. This proposition is one of the cornerstones of the rational expectations revolution in macroeconomics. It argues that anticipated policy interventions, such as systematic monetary or fiscal policy, are ineffective in influencing real economic variables like output and employment. This is because people, with rational expectations, will anticipate the effects of policy and alter their behavior in ways that offset the intended effects of the policy.

72. (C): Unequal Exchange is a concept associated with Arghiri Emmanuel, who argued that trade between countries with different wage levels leads to an 'unequal exchange'. This occurs because labour-intensive goods produced in low-wage countries are exchanged for capital-intensive goods produced in high-wage countries, resulting in a transfer of wealth from poorer to richer countries.

The development of underdevelopment is a concept developed by Andre Gunder Frank as part of the dependency theory. Frank argued that underdevelopment is not a traditional stage on the way to development but a consequence of capitalist development itself. This underdevelopment is perpetuated through the mechanisms of the global capitalist system that benefit the developed 'core' at the expense of the 'periphery'.

Backward and forward linkage effects were introduced by Albert Hirschman. These concepts are a part of his strategy for economic development, which suggests that certain types of industries, due to their connections with other sectors, can stimulate overall economic growth. Backward linkages refer to the relationships with the suppliers, while forward linkages refer to the connections with the consumers of the industry's products.

The backwash effect is associated with Gunnar Myrdal, who posited that it is one of the forces at play in economic geography and regional development. The backwash effect refers to the negative impacts that the growth of more developed regions can have on less developed ones, as the former often drain resources, skilled labour, and investment away from the latter, exacerbating regional inequalities.

73. (D)

74. (A): When investment is unresponsive to interest rates, it suggests that changes in the interest rate do not affect investment spending. This scenario is depicted by a vertical Investment-Saving (IS) curve because investment levels will not change for different levels of interest rates.

Money demand being perfectly elastic with respect to interest rates means that any quantity of money is demanded at a particular interest rate. This is represented by a horizontal Liquidity Preference-Money Supply (LM) curve, implying that the economy can absorb any amount of money supply without changing the interest rate.

When money demand is completely inelastic with respect to interest rates, it indicates that changes in interest rates do not affect the quantity of money demanded. This situation is represented by a vertical LM curve. The quantity of money demanded is fixed, irrespective of the interest rate level.

Lastly, when investment is highly responsive to interest rates, it means small changes in the interest rate lead to large changes in investment spending. This condition is represented by a relatively flat IS curve, indicating high sensitivity of investment to changes in interest rates.

75. (A):

(*a*) **Quantity theory of money:** This economic theory is famously associated with Milton Friedman, suggests that changes in the money supply lead to proportionate changes in the price level in the economy. It emphasizes the long-term relationship between the money supply and the price level, positing that excessive growth in the money supply leads to inflation.

(*b*) **Involuntary unemployment:** Coined by John Maynard Keynes, this term describes a situation where individuals are willing to work at the prevailing wage rate but are unable to find employment. Keynes argued that involuntary unemployment could persist in the economy, even in the presence of aggregate demand, due to factors such as wage rigidities and insufficient aggregate demand.

(*c*) **Randomised trial:** This methodological approach, employed by economists Abhijit V. Banerjee, involves conducting experiments where participants are randomly assigned to different treatment groups. By randomly allocating participants, researchers can minimize selection bias and establish causal relationships between variables, particularly in evaluating the impact of policy interventions or programmatic changes.

(*d*) **Relative poverty:** A concept often discussed by economists Amartya K. Sen, relative poverty defines poverty in relation to the living standards and income distribution within a society. Unlike absolute poverty, which sets a fixed income threshold, relative poverty considers individuals or households to be poor if their income falls significantly below the median income of the population they reside in. This perspective highlights the importance of inequality and social context in understanding poverty.

76. (C):

(*a*) **Reduction in policy rate:** Central banks often use interest rates as a tool to implement monetary policy. When a central bank reduces its policy rate, it makes borrowing cheaper for businesses and individuals. Lower borrowing costs encourage increased spending and investment in the economy, leading to higher aggregate demand.

(*b*) **Capital outflows:** A reduction in the policy rate may lead to capital outflows from the domestic economy. Lower interest rates make domestic assets less attractive to investors seeking higher returns. As a result, investors may sell their domestic assets and invest in foreign assets with higher interest rates. This movement of capital out of the domestic economy puts downward pressure on the domestic currency's exchange rate.

(*c*) **Depreciation of domestic currency:** The increase in capital outflows and reduced demand for domestic assets relative to foreign assets leads to a depreciation of the domestic currency. In other words, the value of the domestic currency decreases compared to foreign currencies. Depreciation makes imports more expensive and exports cheaper, thus influencing trade flows.

(*d*) **Rise in net exports:** A depreciation of the domestic currency makes domestic goods cheaper for foreign buyers, leading to an increase in exports. Conversely, it makes foreign goods relatively more expensive for domestic consumers, leading to a decrease in imports. The net result is an increase in net exports, as exports rise and imports fall. This increase in net exports boosts aggregate demand and economic activity.

77. (C):

(*a*) **Y.V. Reddy:** Yaga Venugopal Reddy held the position of RBI Governor from September 6, 2003, to September 5, 2008. During his tenure, he implemented various monetary policies aimed at maintaining financial stability and managing inflation.

(*b*) **D Subbarao:** Duvvuri Subbarao succeeded Y.V. Reddy as the RBI Governor and served from September 5, 2008, to September 4, 2013. He faced significant challenges during his term, including the global financial crisis of 2008, and implemented measures to stabilize the Indian economy.

(*c*) **Raghuram Rajan:** Raghuram Rajan assumed office as the RBI Governor on September 4, 2013, succeeding D. Subbarao. He introduced several reforms and policies to address issues like inflation, currency stability, and banking sector reforms during his tenure, which lasted until September 4, 2016.

(*d*) **Urjit Patel:** Urjit Patel served as the RBI Governor from September 4, 2016, to December 10, 2018. His tenure saw various significant developments, including the demonetization initiative and efforts to address non-performing assets in the banking sector.

78. (C):

(*b*) **Setting up of UTI (Unit Trust of India):** UTI was established in 1964 as a financial institution to promote savings and investment among the public. This event marked a significant milestone in the Indian financial system, providing avenues for individuals to invest in mutual funds and other financial instruments. Option (C) correctly places this event as the earliest in the sequence.

(*c*) **Nationalisation of 14 commercial banks:** This event occurred in 1969 when the Government of India nationalized 14 major banks to ensure better control over credit allocation and promote financial inclusion. Nationalization aimed to channelize credit towards priority sectors and foster economic development. Option (C) correctly positions this event as the second in the sequence.

(*a*) **Setting up of PFRDA (Pension Fund Regulatory and Development Authority):** PFRDA was established in 2003 as an autonomous body responsible for regulating and developing the pension sector in India, including the management of pension funds. The creation of PFRDA marked a significant step towards modernizing India's pension system and providing retirement benefits to its citizens. Option (C) places this event as the third in the sequence.

(*d*) **Implementation of IBC (Insolvency and Bankruptcy Code):** The Insolvency and Bankruptcy Code was implemented in 2016 to consolidate and amend the laws relating to insolvency resolution of corporate persons, partnership firms, and individuals in a time-bound manner. The implementation of IBC aimed to address the challenges of non-performing assets and streamline the insolvency resolution process in India.

79. (B):

(*a*) **Shephard's Lemma - (II) Envelope theorem:** Shephard's Lemma is a result in mathematical economics that is closely related to the Envelope theorem. It states that the derivative of the cost function with respect to input prices equals the profit function. The Envelope theorem, on the other hand, describes how the value of the objective function of an optimization problem changes when a parameter of the problem changes slightly. It is often used in economic analysis to simplify calculations and derive comparative statics results.

(*b*) **Adverse Selection - (I) Hidden types of agent:** Adverse selection refers to a situation in which one party in a transaction has more information than the other, leading to a distortion in the market due to information asymmetry. Hidden types of agents are individuals whose characteristics (such as risk preferences or quality) are unknown to others in the market, contributing to adverse selection problems.

(*c*) **Hotelling Lemma - (IV) Profit function:** Hotelling's Lemma is a result in mathematical economics that describes the relationship between the profit function and the cost function. It states that the derivative of the profit function with respect to the price of a good equals the derivative of the cost function with respect to the quantity of that good produced. This lemma is frequently used in industrial organization and microeconomic analysis to derive optimal pricing strategies.

(*d*) **Roy's Identity - (III) Indirect utility function:** Roy's Identity is an important result in consumer theory that links the indirect utility function with the expenditure function. It states that the derivative of the indirect utility function with respect to income equals the marginal utility of expenditure. The indirect utility function represents the maximum utility a consumer can attain given their budget constraint and the prices of goods and services.

80. (B):

(*e*) **Right to Education (2009):** The Right to Education Act was enacted in 2009, making education a fundamental right for children between the ages of 6 and 14 years. This legislation aimed to ensure free and compulsory education for all children, marking a significant step towards improving literacy and educational access nationwide.

(*c*) **Swachh Bharat Abhiyan (2014):** Launched in 2014, the Swachh Bharat Abhiyan aimed to address the issue of cleanliness and sanitation in India. It emphasized the construction of toilets, eradication of open defecation, and proper waste management practices, with the goal of achieving a cleaner and healthier environment for all citizens.

(*a*) **Beti Bachao Beti Padhao (2015):** Introduced in 2015, the Beti Bachao Beti Padhao (Save Daughters, Educate Daughters) campaign sought to address the declining child sex ratio and promote the education and welfare of girl children. It aimed to combat gender-based discrimination and empower girls through education and equal opportunities.

(*b*) **Ujjwala (2016):** The Ujjwala scheme, launched in 2016, aimed to provide clean cooking fuel to households below the poverty line. By offering free LPG connections to eligible beneficiaries, the program aimed to reduce indoor air pollution, improve health outcomes, and empower women by saving them from the drudgery of traditional cooking methods.

(*d*) **Ayushman Bharat (2018):** Ayushman Bharat, launched in 2018, is a national health protection scheme that aims to provide financial protection to vulnerable families against high healthcare costs. It includes two components: the Pradhan

Mantri Jan Arogya Yojana (PM-JAY), which provides health insurance coverage for secondary and tertiary care, and the Health and Wellness Centres (HWCs), which deliver comprehensive primary healthcare services.

81. (A):

(*a*) **Run the regression model on pooled sample and calculate RSS_p:** The first step is to estimate the regression model using all the data combined (pooled sample) and calculate the residual sum of squares (RSS), which measures the total deviation of the observed values from the values predicted by the regression model.

(*b*) **Run the same regression model on the two sub-samples separately and calculate RSS_1 and RSS_2:** Next, the regression model is separately estimated on each subgroup of the sample, and the RSS is calculated for each subgroup. This allows us to assess how well the regression model fits the data in each subgroup.

(*c*) **Calculate the F statistic:** The F statistic is computed by comparing the difference in RSS between the pooled model and the separate models with the RSS under the null hypothesis, which assumes no difference between the coefficients of the pooled model and the separate models.

(*d*) **Check the critical F with related degrees of freedom and compare it with F calculated:** The calculated F statistic is compared to the critical F value from the F-distribution table at a specified significance level and degrees of freedom. This helps determine whether the observed difference in RSS is statistically significant.

(*e*) **Do not reject H_0 if $F_{calculated} < F_{critical}$:** If the calculated F statistic is less than the critical F value, we do not reject the null hypothesis (H0), indicating that there is no significant difference between the coefficients of the pooled model and the separate models. In other words, pooling the data and using a single regression model is just as effective as running separate models on the subgroups.

82. (C):

(*c*) **The Alagh Committee** was a task force established in 1977 by the Planning Commission to define the poverty line. The committee was led by YK Alagh and constructed a poverty line for both rural and urban areas. The poverty line was based on nutritional requirements and related consumption expenditure. The committee defined the poverty line as a per capita consumption expenditure of Rs. 49.09 per month in rural areas.

(*b*) **The Khusro Committee,** also known as the Agricultural Credit Review Committee, was established in 1989. The committee was chaired by Prof. A.M. Khusro, who was related to the royal family of Hyderabad. The Khusro Committee recommended merging Regional Rural Banks (RRBs) with their sponsor banks. The committee also highlighted the weaknesses of RRBs and their non-viability.

(*d*) **The Nayak Committee** was established in 1991 by the Reserve Bank of India to examine the difficulties that small scale industries (SSI) faced in securing finance. The committee was chaired by Deputy Governor Shri P.R. Nayak. The committee's report was published in September 1992.

(*a*) **The Lakdawala Committee** was an expert group appointed by the Central Government of India in 1993 to estimate the poverty line in India. The committee was chaired by Professor D.T. Lakdawala, and its sole member.

(*e*) **The Suresh Tendulkar Committee** was established in 2005 to review the concept of poverty lines in India. The committee was set up by the Planning Commission to address shortcomings in previous methods and to recommend changes to the official poverty estimation process. The committee submitted its report in 2009.

83. (B):

(*a*) **Theory of Big Push:** Proposed by economist Paul Rosenstein-Rodan in the 1940s, the Theory of Big Push suggests that a large coordinated investment in multiple sectors simultaneously is necessary to initiate development in an underdeveloped economy.

(*e*) **Development with unlimited supplies of labour:** Associated with the early stages of economic development theory, this concept was discussed by economists like Arthur Lewis in the mid-20th century. It posits that in economies with abundant labour and limited capital, industrialization can lead to economic growth by absorbing surplus labour from the agricultural sector into the industrial sector.

(*b*) **The accumulation of capital:** This concept has been central to economic thought for centuries and was extensively discussed by classical economists such as Adam Smith and David Ricardo in the 18th and 19th centuries. It emphasizes the role of saving and investment in driving economic growth and development.

(*c*) **Theory of cumulative causation:** Developed by economist Gunnar Myrdal in the mid-20th century, the Theory of Cumulative Causation suggests that once an economy starts to develop, positive feedback loops and spillover effects can lead to further development, creating a self-reinforcing process of growth.

(*d*) **Unbalanced growth:** Gained prominence in development economics in the mid-20th century and discussed by economists like Ragnar Nurkse, the concept of unbalanced growth argues that in the early stages of development, it is often necessary for investment to be focused on specific sectors or regions to kickstart growth, leading to uneven or unbalanced development.

84. (D)

85. (D):

(*b*) **"The exchange rate is lower than the market clearing exchange rate":** This statement indicates that the prevailing exchange rate in the foreign exchange market is below what would naturally clear the market. In other words, the exchange rate is undervalued from the perspective of market equilibrium. When the exchange rate is lower than the market clearing rate, it suggests that the domestic currency is overvalued relative to the foreign currency. This situation often arises due to various factors such as government policies, speculation, or market sentiment. For instance, if the Central Bank sets an artificially high value for the domestic currency through intervention or if market participants expect the currency to appreciate in the future, it can lead to an overvalued exchange rate. In such cases, corrective measures are necessary to restore equilibrium and prevent market distortions.

(*a*) **"The demand for foreign currency exceeds its supply":** When the exchange rate is lower than the market clearing rate, indicating an overvaluation of the domestic currency, there is typically an increased demand for foreign currency. Market participants seek to take advantage of the overvalued domestic currency by purchasing foreign currency at a relatively cheaper rate. This excess demand for foreign currency can arise from various activities such as imports, foreign investment, or speculative trading. As a result, the demand for foreign currency outstrips its available supply in the foreign exchange market. This imbalance leads to market disequilibrium and puts upward pressure on the exchange rate, exacerbating the overvaluation of the domestic currency.

(*e*) **"The Central Bank sells foreign currency from its stock of reserves":** To address the excess demand for foreign currency and stabilize the exchange rate, the Central Bank intervenes in the foreign exchange market by selling foreign currency from its reserves. By supplying foreign currency, the Central Bank aims to meet the excess demand and prevent further appreciation of the domestic currency. This intervention is a common tool used by Central Banks to manage exchange rate fluctuations and maintain stability in the currency markets. The Central Bank's ability to sell foreign currency from its reserves demonstrates its commitment to achieving its exchange rate objectives and safeguarding the competitiveness of the domestic economy.

(*c*) **"The gap between supply and demand for foreign currency is equalized":** Through its intervention in the foreign exchange market, the Central Bank endeavors to equalize the gap between the supply and demand for foreign currency. By supplying additional foreign currency, the Central Bank aims to bring the market into equilibrium and eliminate the excess demand. This process helps restore stability to the exchange rate and ensures that market forces determine the value of the domestic currency. Achieving equilibrium between supply and demand is crucial for maintaining confidence in the currency and facilitating smooth international trade and investment flows.

(*d*) **"The Central Bank's stock of foreign currency is depleted":** While intervention in the foreign exchange market can help stabilize the exchange rate in the short term, continuous selling of foreign currency from the Central Bank's reserves may deplete its stock of foreign currency over time. Depletion of reserves indicates the extent of intervention required to maintain the desired exchange rate parity and underscores the Central Bank's commitment to its exchange rate objectives. However, excessive depletion of reserves can pose risks to the economy, such as reducing the Central Bank's ability to intervene in future market crises or limiting its capacity to manage external shocks. Therefore, prudent management of foreign exchange reserves is essential to ensure the long-term stability of the currency and the overall health of the economy.

86. (C): Statement I: This statement asserts that agricultural GDP constitutes less than 16% of aggregate GDP at 2011-12 constant prices and less than 20% of the aggregate GDP at current prices in 2022-23 in India. Agricultural GDP refers to the value of goods and services produced within the agricultural sector. The claim suggests a decline in the share of agricultural GDP relative to the total GDP over the specified period. This decline could be attributed to various factors such as the growth of other sectors like industry and services, technological advancements leading to increased productivity in agriculture but with relatively slower growth compared to other sectors, and shifts in government policies and investments favoring non-agricultural sectors. Overall, this statement implies a significant structural transformation in India's economy away from agriculture.

Statement II: This statement mirrors the content of Statement I but focuses on the service sector GDP instead of agricultural GDP. It suggests that the service sector's contribution to GDP is also less than 16% at constant prices and less than 20% at current prices in 2022-23 in India. However, this assertion seems less plausible considering the significant role of the service sector in India's economy. The service sector encompasses a wide range of activities, including IT services, finance, healthcare, education, tourism, and more, which collectively contribute substantially to India's GDP. Given the dynamism and growth potential of the service sector, it is unlikely that its share of GDP has declined to less than 16%. Thus, while Statement I appears credible, Statement II seems questionable due to the service sector's importance and growth trajectory in India.

87. (C): Statement (I) asserts that the government's spending on social services, as a proportion of the Gross Domestic Product (GDP), has been on the rise since the fiscal year 2017-18. This suggests a trend towards increasing investment in social welfare programs, healthcare, education, and other essential services aimed at improving the well-being and quality of life for citizens. Such an increase in spending on social services often reflects government efforts to address societal needs, promote equitable development, and enhance human capital formation. The rise in social spending relative to GDP indicates a prioritization of social development goals within the government's fiscal policies, potentially driven by factors such as demographic changes, public demand for better services, or policy shifts towards inclusive growth agendas.

Statement (II) claims that the government's spending on social services, as a percentage of total expenditure, has also been continuously rising since 2017-18.

However, this statement is incorrect. While Statement I focus on the proportion of social spending relative to the size of the economy (GDP), Statement II refers to the share of social spending within the total government budget. The inaccuracy lies in the assertion that this share has been continuously increasing. In reality, government spending on social services may fluctuate over time due to various factors such as changes in fiscal priorities, economic conditions, political considerations, and budget constraints.

88. (C): Statement I correctly defines human development as a process focused on expanding people's opportunities and choices. This definition, proposed by Nobel laureate Amartya Sen, highlights the multifaceted nature of human well-being beyond just economic growth. It emphasizes the importance of factors such as health, education, political freedom, social inclusion, and environmental sustainability in improving people's lives. Human development aims to empower individuals to lead fulfilling lives according to their own aspirations and values, rather than solely focusing on increasing material wealth or GDP.

However, Statement II is incorrect. The Human Development Index (HDI) is indeed based on indicators such as life expectancy at birth, expected years of schooling, and Gross Domestic Product (GDP) per capita at purchasing power parity (PPP). However, it does not include "mean years of schooling" as one of its components. Instead, it considers the average number of years of schooling for adults aged 25 years and older, which provides a measure of the educational attainment level within a population. Therefore, while Statement I accurately describes human development, Statement II contains a factual inaccuracy regarding the components of the HDI.

89. (A): Assertion (A) states that as the sample size becomes very large, the distribution of the sample mean tends to a normal distribution. This assertion is indeed correct and is a fundamental concept in statistics. The Central Limit Theorem (CLT) is a fundamental theorem in probability theory and statistics. It states that the sampling distribution of the sample mean approaches a normal distribution as the sample size increases, regardless of the shape of the population distribution. In other words, if you take multiple samples from a population and calculate the mean of each sample, the distribution of these sample means will be approximately normal as long as the sample size is sufficiently large.

The reason (R) provided refers to the Central Limit Theorem (CLT), indicating that the CLT provides the theoretical foundation for Assertion (A). Indeed, the CLT is the principle that underlies why the distribution of the sample mean tends to a normal distribution as the sample size increases. To explain further, when we take a random sample from any population, the sample mean can be thought of as the average of those observations. According to the CLT, even if the population distribution is not normal, as long as the sample size is large enough (typically n e" 30 is considered sufficient), the distribution of these sample means will approximate a normal distribution. This occurs because as the sample size increases, the variability in the sample means decreases, and the distribution becomes more symmetric and bell-shaped, resembling a normal distribution. This property of the CLT is widely used in statistical inference. It allows us to make inferences about population parameters, such as the population mean, based on sample data, even when the population distribution is unknown or non-normal. Additionally, it provides the theoretical justification for many statistical methods and hypothesis tests that rely on the assumption of normality.

Assertion (A) correctly identifies the phenomenon that the distribution of the sample mean tends to a normal distribution with a sufficiently large sample size, and Reason (R) accurately attributes this phenomenon to the Central Limit Theorem (CLT), making it the correct explanation for Assertion (A).

90. (C): The assertion (A) reflects the Domar condition, a concept in economics that outlines a criterion for debt sustainability. According to this principle, if the effective interest rate on government debt remains below or equal to the growth rate of GDP, the ratio of public debt to GDP will not increase over time. This condition suggests a level of debt sustainability where the economy can manage its debt burden without it growing disproportionately relative to its output.

However, the reason (R) provided to support the assertion is flawed. It states that the growth rate of GDP at current prices will always be lower than the effective interest rate on government bonds. This oversimplifies the relationship between GDP growth and interest rates. While it's possible for interest rates to exceed GDP growth rates, especially during economic downturns or periods of high inflation, it's not a universal rule. Economic conditions, monetary policy, and other factors can influence both GDP growth and interest rates independently, leading to various scenarios where one may surpass the other.

91. (C) **92. (D)** **93. (D)**

94. (A) **95. (D)** **96. (C)**

97. (D) **98. (B)** **99. (A)**

100. (A)

Previous Years' Paper

National Testing Agency (NTA)

UGC-NET Junior Research Fellowship & Assistant Professor Eligibility Exam

ECONOMICS, June-2023

(Exam held on 20-06-2023)

PAPER-II

1. Suppose good 1 is taken on horizontal axis and good 2 on vertical axis, then what happens to the budget line if the price of good 1 doubles and price of good 2 triples?

A. The budget line becomes steeper

B. The budget line becomes flatter

C. The budget line become vertical

D. The budget line remains unchanged

2. Suppose the scarce resouce, facing a constant demand, will be exhausted in 10 years. If an alternative resource will be available at a price of $40 and if the interest rate is 10%, what must be the price of the scarce resource today:

A. $55.50 B. $35.60

C. $24.40 D. $15.42

3. Which one of the following is not a characteristic of market structure?

A. Degree of buyers' concentration

B. Degree of Sellers' concentration

C. Conditions of entry

D. Vertical integration

4. Which of the following is not true in the case of second theorem of welfare economics?

A. If consumers exhibit convex preferences, every pareto efficient allocation is a possible competitive equilibrium in a pure exchange economy.

B. In an economy involving production, the convexity of production sets ensures that a pareto efficient allocation can be achieved as market equilibrium.

C. It holds when there are increasing returns to scale.

D. It implies that in the market system, the allocative role and the distributive role can be separated from each other.

5. Taylor's Rule tells:

A. how monetary authority sets interest rate in response to economic activity

B. how monetary authority maintains bank rate

C. how monetary authority maintains exchange rate

D. how government decides the tax rate to increase the tax base.

6. Monetary base of an economy is:

A. Amount of currency held by public and by the banks as reserves.

B. Amount of currency held by public and demand deposits.

C. Amount of currency held by public and time deposits.

D. Currency deposit ratio.

7. Given the income multiplier formula $m = \frac{1}{1 - \text{MPC}}$ lower the marginal propensity to save.

A. Higher will be the multiplier effect

B. Lower will be the multiplier effect

C. Multiplier will become infinite

D. Multiplier will become zero

8. In the national income identiy $Y = C + I + G$, investment (I) is a function of:

A. Real Income
B. Nominal Income
C. Real Interest Rate
D. Nominal Interest Rate

9. Which one of the following is not correct about LM schedule?

A. The LM schedule slopes upward to the right.
B. The LM schedule will be relatively flat (steep) if the interest elasticity of money demand is relatively high (low).
C. The LM schedule will shift downward (upward) to the right (left) with an increase (decrease) in the quantity of money.
D. The LM schedule is the schedule giving the combinations of values of investment and interest rate that produce equilibrium in the money market.

10. The merchant's file of 20 accounts contains 6 delinquent and 14 non-delinquent accounts. An auditor randomly selects 5 of these account for examination. What is the probability that the auditor finds exactly 2 delinquent cases?

A. 0.2562 B. 0.3
C. 0.3087 D. 0.4526

11. A company has 140 employees, of which 30 are supervisors, 80 of the employees are married, and 20% of the married employee are supervisors. If a company employee is randomly selected, what is the probability that the employee is married and is a supervisor?

A. 0.1531 B. 0.1253
C. 0.0923 D. 0.1143

12. The Hausman's specification error test is used to test whether:

A. An exogenous variable is correlated with the error term.
B. An endogenous variable is correlated with the error term.
C. Both an exogenous variable is correlated with the error term and an endogenous variable is correlated with the error term.
D. OLS method is appropriate to estimate the SEM.

13. In random walk without drift:

A. The effect of shock persists throughout the time period.
B. The effect of shock in the past dies out over time.
C. The effect of shock drifts away quickly.
D. There is no effect of past shock.

14. Given below are the alternative formulae for F-test statistics. We are interested in testing the statistical significance of the incremental contribution of X_3 at 5% level of significance of $Y = \beta_0 + \beta_1X_1 + \beta_2X_2 + U$. Which of these is not appropriate? Where RSS is residual sum of square and ESS is explained sum of square.

A. $F = \dfrac{R^2_{UR} - R^2_R / d.f}{\left(1 - R^2_{UR}\right) / d.f.}$

B. $F = \dfrac{ESS / d.f.}{RSS / d.f.}$

C. $F = \dfrac{ESS_{new} - ESS_{old} / d.f.}{ESS_{new} / d.f.}$

D. $F = \dfrac{R^2 / d.f.}{(1 - R^2) / d.f.}$

15. Integrate: $\int x\sqrt{x^2 + 1}dx \; x > 0$

A. $\frac{1}{2}\left(x^2 + 1\right)^{\frac{3}{2}} + C$ B. $\frac{1}{3}\left(x^2 + 1\right)^{\frac{3}{2}} + C$

C. $\frac{1}{3}\left(x^3 + 1\right)^{\frac{2}{3}} + C$ D. $\frac{1}{2}\left(x^3 + 1\right)^{\frac{2}{3}} + C$

16. Find the extremum of $u = x^2 + y^2 + z^2$ subject to $x + y + z = 1$.

A. $(\bar{x}, \bar{y}, \bar{z}) = \left(\frac{1}{3}, \frac{1}{2}, \frac{1}{2}\right)$

B. $(\bar{x}, \bar{y}, \bar{z}) = \left(\frac{1}{2}, \frac{1}{2}, \frac{1}{3}\right)$

C. $(\bar{x}, \bar{y}, \bar{z}) = \left(\frac{1}{2}, \frac{1}{2}, \frac{1}{2}\right)$

D. $(\bar{x}, \bar{y}, \bar{z}) = \left(\frac{1}{3}, \frac{1}{3}, \frac{1}{3}\right)$

17. The utility function of a consumer is given by $U = f(q_1, q_2) = q_1 \times q_2$, suppose the price of q_1 is p_{q1} = and price of q_2 is $p_{q2} = 2$. The consumer wants to spend amount of k units only what will be his demand for q_1 and q_2?

A. $(q_1, q_2) = \left(k, \frac{k}{2}\right)$

B. $(q_1, q_2) = \left(\frac{k}{4}, \frac{k}{6}\right)$

C. $(q_1, q_2) = \left(\frac{k}{2}, \frac{k}{4}\right)$

D. $(q_1, q_2) = \left(\frac{k}{2}, \frac{k}{3}\right)$

18. A tariff ridden offere curve will bend towards.

A. Import good axis
B. Export good axis
C. Origin
D. Any of the above is possible

19. Factor price equalization theorem is given by:

A. David Ricardo B. J.S. Mill
C. Paul Samuelson D. Adam Smith

20. In which of the following year IMF has set up the Extended Fund Facility (EFF) to support member's structural reforms to address balance of payment difficulties of a long term character.

A. 1974 B. 1997
C. 1963 D. 2009

21. The book entitled "Why Nations Fail; The Origin of Power, Prosperity and Poverty" has been written by:

A. Abhijit Banerjee
B. Daron Acemoglu and James A. Robinson
C. Amartya Sen
D. Joseph Stiglitz

22. A foreign exchange swap is:

A. a spot purchase of a currency combined with a forward repurchase of that currency.
B. a spot sale of currency combined with a forward repurchase of that currency.
C. sale and purchase of a currency in forward market.
D. purchase of a currency in spot market.

23. Which of the following is a correct measure of gross fiscal deficit of the state government.

A. Revenue Expenditure (RE) + Capital disbursement – Revenue Receipts (RR)
B. RE + Repayment of loans to the Centre – RR
C. Revenue Deficit + Capital Outlays + Net Lending
D. RE + Discharge of Internal Debt – RR

24. Which of the following is not true in case of incidence of tax:

A. Imposition of tax raises price and lowers quantity.
B. The resulting price increase of tax rise will be dampened if the tax is imposed in monopolistic market.
C. One would be in better position to avoid the tax and leave the seller with a larger part if demand is inelastic while supply is elastic
D. A unit tax enters through a parallel upward shift in the supply schedule.

25. When MPS is 0.25 and initial increase in autonomous spending is ₹ 100, then the expenditure multiplier and resultant increase in GD respectively are:

A. 1, ₹ 100 B. 0.75, ₹ 75
C. 4, ₹ 400 D. 1.33, ₹ 133

26. In the extreme case of liquidity trap:

A. There will be tendency to buy bonds

B. Most of the investors will show bearish behaviour

C. Cash will be less preferred

D. Price of the bond will be low.

27. Which of the following can be an equation representing the money market.

A. $300 = 2Y - 1.5i$ B. $i = 150 - Y$

C. $Y = 100 - i$ D. $i = (150 - 2Y)/2$

28. With the same monetary base, which of the following will lead to an increase in broad money?

A. High transaction cost of converting deposit into cash

B. Higher investment under SLR

C. Higher use of cash

D. Increase in financial literacy and banking habit

29. According to Robinson the term 'Golden Age' in the context of Harrod-Domar model is used to emphasize:

A. Its mythical nature

B. Its superiority

C. Natural growth rate

D. Warranted growth rate

30. Which is not a dimension of Human Development Index (HDI)?

A. Ability to lead a long and healthy life

B. Ability to acquire knowledge

C. Ability to achieve decent standard of living

D. Ability to access clean environment

31. The idea of creative destruction is associated with:

A. Marx B. Adam Smith

C. Ricardo D. Schumpeter

32. Normalized Poverty Gap (NPG) is measured as a ratio of:

A. Average Poverty Gap to poverty line

B. Total Poverty Gap to povery line

C. Total Poverty Gap to total population

D. Average Poverty Gap to total population

33. Which of the following defines ambient standards in an environmental policy:

A. a standard that specifies a pollution limit to be achieved but does not stipulate the technology.

B. a standard that designates the equipment or method to be used to achieve some abatement level.

C. a standard that designates the quality level of some element of the environment to be achieved.

D. None of the above

34. Which of the following applies to the physical linkage approach for the valuation of environmental benefits?

A. methods that assess responses immediately related to environmental changes.

B. methods that examine responses not about the environmental good itself but some set of market conditions related to it.

C. methods that estimate benefits using observations of behaviour in actual markets.

D. method that estimate benefits based on a technical relationship between an environmental resource and the user of that resource.

35. Why subsidies are not an effective policy instrument in the long-run for internalizing externalities under competitive output markets?

A. a subsidy that is equal to marginal damages translates to a de facto decrease in firm's fixed costs.

B. subsidy payments are available to all firms and can induce excessive market entry.

C. the level of industrial production in the sector would exceed the socially desired level.

D. All of the above

36. According to Sample Registration System, which of the following Indian States has the highest level of life time risk during 2018-2020.

A. Bihar B. Uttar Pradesh
C. Madhya Pradesh D. Chhattisgarh

37. The Intensive Agriculture District Programme (IADP) was launched in the year.
A. 1960-61 B. 1961-62
C. 1962-63 D. 1963-64

38. Allocation of budget for Ministry of Agriculture and Farmers' Welfare in the Union Budget 2023-24 is:
A. 2.25 lakh crores B. 1.25 lakh crores
C. 1.78 lakh crores D. 1.68 lakh crores

39. What is the motto of G-20 18th meeting?
A. One Earth, One Family, One Future
B. One Earth, One Nature, One Life
C. One World, One Family, One Life
D. One Earth, One Nature, One Future

40. Prevention of Money Laundering Act was enacted in the year:
A. 2001 B. 2002
C. 2003 D. 2004

41. Which of the following holds for Bertrand's Duopoly model.
(*a*) The reaction curves are derived from isoprofit maps which are convex to the axes.
(*b*) The point of intersection of the two reaction curves reflects a stable equilibrium.
(*c*) The reaction curves are derived from isoprofit maps which are concave to the axes.
(*d*) The point of intersection of the two reaction curves reflects an unstable equilibrium.
(*e*) Film's behavioral pattern is such that they learn from past experience.

Choose the **correct** answer from the option given below:
A. (*a*) and (*b*) only
B. (*c*) and (*d*) only
C. (*a*), (*d*) and (*e*) only
D. (*b*), (*c*) and (*e*) only

42. Which of the following is true for the Clark-Wicksteed-Walras product exhaustion theorem:
(*a*) The assumption of a homogeneous production function is necessary.
(*b*) It is an identity that holds for all values of the variables.
(*c*) The assumption of a homogeneous production function is not necessary.
(*d*) It is not an identity since it holds only for the values of the variables in the long-run equilibrium.
(*e*) It holds for all types of production functions.

Choose the **correct** answer from the option given below:
A. (*a*) and (*b*) only
B. (*a*) and (*d*) only
C. (*b*), (*c*) and (*e*) only
D. (*c*), (*d*) and (*e*) only

43. Properties of expenditure function are (in the context of utility theory).
(*a*) Homogeneous of degree one in price, P
(*b*) Strictly increasing in utility, *u* and non-decreasing in price. P for any good 1.
(*c*) Concave in P
(*d*) Continuous in P and *u*
(*e*) Strictly convex in P

Choose the **correct** answer from the option given below:
A. (*a*), (*c*), (*d*) and (*e*) only
B. (*a*), (*b*), (*d*) and (*e*) only
C. (*a*), (*b*), (*c*) and (*d*) only
D. (*b*), (*c*), (*d*) and (*e*) only

44. The concept of "excess sensitivity" and "excess smoothness" are explained by following statement(s).
(*a*) 'Excess sensitivity' refers to a situation where consumption over responds to temporary income shocks.
(*b*) 'Excess smoothness' refers to a situation where consumption under responds to temporary income changes.

(*c*) With excess sensitivity, anticipated rise in income is associated with relatively small change in consumption.

(*d*) With excess smoothness, changes in aggregate income are associated with relatively large changes in aggregate consumption.

(*e*) 'Excess sensitivity' and 'Excess smoothness' are related to the empirical evidences of permanent income hypothesis.

Choose the **correct** answer from the option given below:

A. (*a*), (*b*), (*c*) and (*d*) only

B. (*a*), (*b*), (*c*) and (*e*) only

C. (*a*), (*b*) and (*d*) only

D. (*a*), (*b*) and (*e*) only

45. According to Tobin's Q theory of investment, when should a firm invest?

(*a*) there is an increase in the price of output

(*b*) there is an increase in marginal product of capital

(*c*) there is an increase in rate of interest

(*d*) there is a decrease in rate of depreciation

(*e*) marginal benefit of investment exceeds marginal cost

Choose the **correct** answer from the option given below:

A. (*b*), (*c*), (*d*) and (*e*) only

B. (*a*), (*c*), (*d*) and (*e*) only

C. (*a*), (*b*), (*d*) and (*e*) only

D. (*a*), (*b*), (*c*) and (*d*) only

46. Which of the following is/are true about paradox of thrift?

(*a*) Paradox of thrift was popularized by J.M. Keynes.

(*b*) It states that personal savings can be detrimental to overall economic growth.

(*c*) It shows the relationship between output growth and rate of unemployment.

(*d*) It shows the relationship between inflation and rate of interest.

(*e*) It states that individuals saving during an economic recession leads to fall in aggregate demand.

Choose the **correct** answer from the option given below:

A. (*a*), (*b*) and (*c*) only

B. (*b*), (*c*) and (*d*) only

C. (*c*), (*d*) and (*e*) only

D. (*a*), (*b*) and (*e*) only

47. The BOP crisis of early 1990s made India borrow from the IMF which came on following conditions:

(*a*) Devaluation of rupee by 22%

(*b*) Drastic custom cut to a peak duty of 30% from the erstwhile level of 130% for all goods

(*c*) Consolidation of all indirect taxes into one tax

(*d*) Excise duty to be increased by 20% to neutralize the loss of revenue due to custom cut

(*e*) Government expenditure to be cut by 10% per annum.

Choose the **correct** answer from the option given below:

A. (*a*), (*b*), (*c*) and (*e*) only

B. (*b*), (*c*), (*d*) and (*e*) only

C. (*c*), (*d*), (*e*) and (*a*) only

D. (*a*), (*b*), (*d*) and (*e*) only

48. The Uruguay Round of trade negotiations called for:

(*a*) the reduction of average tariffs on industrial goods

(*b*) quotas to be replaced by tariffs

(*c*) the reduction in agriculture export subsidies

(*d*) the reduction in industrial subsidies

(*e*) antidumping and safeguards to be relaxed

Choose the **correct** answer from the option given below:

A. (*a*), (*b*), (*c*) and (*d*) only

B. (*b*), (*c*), (*d*) and (*e*) only

C. (*c*), (*d*), (*e*) and (*a*) only
D. (*d*), (*e*), (*a*) and (*b*) only

49. Pillar 1 of Basel III norms focus on:
(*a*) Quality and level of capital
(*b*) Risk Coverage
(*c*) Containing leverage
(*d*) Risk management and supervision
(*e*) Market discipline

Choose the **correct** answer from the option given below:
A. (*a*) and (*b*) only B. (*b*) and (*c*) only
C. (*c*) and (*d*) only D. (*d*) and (*e*) only

50. Which of the following statements are correct about trilemma in monetary policy:
(*a*) It is related to closed economy model.
(*b*) It involves exchange rate, capital mobility and monetary policy.
(*c*) It arises because perfect capital mobility aligns the domestic interest rate to the world interest rate.
(*d*) Flexible exchange rate is not compatible with independent monetary policy.
(*e*) It is related to capital immobility and flexible exchange rate.

Choose the **correct** answer from the option given below:
A. (*b*) and (*c*) only B. (*c*) and (*d*) only
C. (*a*) and (*d*) only D. (*b*) and (*e*) only

51. Based on the NITI Aayog estimate of poverty for the year 2011-12, the states with above 30 per cent rural poverty are:
(*a*) Manipur
(*b*) Bihar
(*c*) Sikkim
(*d*) Uttar Pradesh
(*e*) Nagaland

Choose the **correct** answer from the option given below:
A. (*a*) and (*b*) only
B. (*b*) and (*d*) only
C. (*b*), (*c*) and (*d*) only
D. (*a*), (*b*) and (*d*) only

52. Adam Smith contributions are:
(*a*) Division of labour
(*b*) Notion of increasing returns
(*c*) Notion of diminishing returns
(*d*) Dialectical Materialism
(*e*) Socially necessary abstract labour time

Choose the **correct** answer from the option given below:
A. (*a*) and (*b*) only
B. (*a*) and (*c*) only
C. (*a*) and (*d*) only
D. (*a*) and (*e*) only

53. The components of services sector in Gross Value Added (GVA) are:
(*a*) Construction
(*b*) Trade, Hotels, Transport and Communication related to Broadcasting
(*c*) Electricity, Gas, Water supply and other utility services
(*d*) Public Administration, Defense and other services
(*e*) Financial, Real Estate and Professional services

Choose the **correct** answer from the option given below:
A. (*b*), (*c*) and (*e*) only
B. (*a*), (*b*) and (*c*) only
C. (*a*), (*b*), (*d*) and (*e*) only
D. (*a*), (*b*), (*c*) and (*e*) only

54. Gunnar Myrdal is author of:
(*a*) Asian Drama
(*b*) An American Dilemma
(*c*) Theory of Economic Development
(*d*) Principles of Political Economy
(*e*) Economic Theory and underdeveloped regions

Choose the **correct** answer from the option given below:
A. (*a*), (*b*) and (*c*) only
B. (*a*), (*c*) and (*d*) only
C. (*a*), (*b*) and (*d*) only
D. (*a*), (*b*) and (*e*) only

55. Which of the following are correct in case of theory of sets.

(*a*) $(A \cup B') \cap (A' \cup C) \cap (B \cup C')$
$= (A \cap B \cap C) \cup (A \cup B \cup C)$

(*b*) $(A \cup B') \cap (A' \cup C) \cap (B \cup C')$
$= (A \cap B \cap C) \cup (A \cup B \cup C)'$

(*c*) $A \cup (B \cap C) = (A \cup B) \cap (A \cup C)$

(*d*) $A \cap (B \cup C) = (A \cup B) \cap (A \cup C)$

(*e*) $(A \cup B') \cap (A' \cup C) \cap (B \cup C')$
$= (A \cap B \cap C) \cup (A' \cap B' \cap C')$

Choose the **correct** answer from the option given below:

A. (*a*), (*c*) and (*e*) only
B. (*b*), (*d*) and (*e*) only
C. (*b*), (*c*) and (*e*) only
D. (*a*), (*b*) and (*d*) only

56. If S is a sample space and E is an event then the probability axioms can be written as:

(*a*) $P(A) \geq 0$

(*b*) $P(S) = 1$

(*c*) $P\left(\bigcup_{i=1}^{\infty} A_i\right) = \sum_{i=1}^{\infty} P(A_i)$

(*d*) $P(A) \leq 0$

(*e*) $P\left(\bigcup_{i=1}^{\infty} S_i\right) = \sum_{i=1}^{\infty} P(S_i)$

Choose the **correct** answer from the option given below:

A. (*a*) and (*b*) only
B. (*a*), (*b*) and (*d*) only
C. (*a*), (*b*) and (*e*) only
D. (*a*), (*b*) and (*c*) only

57. Properties of sufficient estimators are:

(*a*) It may not be unbiased
(*b*) It may be unbiased
(*c*) It is always consistent
(*d*) It is not always consistent
(*e*) Minimum variance unbiased estimator

Choose the **correct** answer from the option given below:

A. (*a*), (*b*) and (*c*) only
B. (*a*), (*c*) and (*e*) only
C. (*a*), (*b*), (*c*) and (*d*) only
D. (*a*), (*b*), (*c*) and (*e*) only

58. Which of the following are true in case of social goods:

(*a*) Public goods are non-rivalry in nature.
(*b*) Efficient provision of social goods needs a political process of budget determination.
(*c*) Efficient provision of social goods involve horizontal rather than vertical addition of individual pseudo-demand-lines.
(*d*) Among purely private and purely social goods, there are mixed cases which generate benefit or cost externalities.
(*e*) Individual consumers will not bid for social good, but will act as free-riders.

Choose the **correct** answer from the option given below:

A. (*a*), (*c*), (*d*) and (*e*) only
B. (*a*), (*b*), (*c*) and (*e*) only
C. (*a*) and (*b*) only
D. (*a*), (*b*), (*d*) and (*e*) only

59. Which of the following are true in case of Ramsey Rule for efficient taxation:

(*a*) Tax rate should be higher on the good that has lower price elasticity of demand.
(*b*) If the demand elasticity in a market is zero, taxes should be imposed only in that markets.
(*c*) Ramsey rule applies to taxation of goods, but not to taxation of income.
(*d*) Ramsey rule minimises the excess burden of taxation across markets.
(*e*) Ramsey rule does not necessarily result in social justice.

Choose the **correct** answer from the option given below:

A. (*a*), (*c*), (*d*) and (*e*) only
B. (*a*), (*b*), (*d*) and (*e*) only
C. (*a*), (*b*), (*c*) and (*d*) only
D. (*a*), (*c*) and (*d*) only

60. Which of the following are not symptoms of multicollinearity in a regression model.

(*a*) High R^2 with few significant t ratio for coefficients.

(*b*) High pair-wise correlations among regressors.

(*c*) The closer the Tolerance (TOLj) is to zero.

(*d*) Variance Inflation Factor (VIF) of a variable is below 10.

(*e*) The closer the Tolerance (TOLj) is to 1.

Choose the **correct** answer from the option given below:

A. (*c*) and (*d*) only B. (*d*) and (*e*) only
C. (*a*) and (*c*) only D. (*b*) and (*d*) only

61. Which of the following are recommendations of the Narasimham Committee, 1991.

(*a*) Deregulation of the interest rate structure.

(*b*) Need for greater use of information technology.

(*c*) Permitting only private sector banks to access the capital market.

(*d*) Freedom to appoint chief executive and officers of the banks.

(*e*) Capital adequacy norms were implemented in stages.

Choose the **correct** answer from the option given below:

A. (*a*), (*b*) and (*e*) only
B. (*a*), (*c*) and (*d*) only
C. (*a*), (*d*) and (*e*) only
D. (*c*), (*d*) and (*e*) only

62. Defensive expenditure method is based on the understanding that:

(*a*) the consumer spends money to ameliorate the damaging effects of the bad.

(*b*) the defensive expenditure undertaken reflects the consumer's willingness to pay to reduce the level of the bad.

(*c*) the observed defensive expenditure is an upper bound on the willingness to pay to avoid the bad.

(*d*) the defensive expenditure provide no additional services other than provisioning the desired environmental quality.

(*e*) the observed defensive expenditure is a lower bound on the willingness to pay to avoid the bad.

Choose the **correct** answer from the option given below:

A. (*a*), (*b*) and (*c*) only
B. (*c*), (*d*) and (*e*) only
C. (*a*), (*b*), (*c*) and (*d*) only
D. (*a*), (*b*), (*d*) and (*e*) only

63. Which of the following constitutes India's strategy to combat climate change in the backdrop of its stand at the 26th session of the conference of the Parties (COP 26) to the UNFCCC held in Glasgow, U.K.

(*a*) phasing out of coal-based thermal power generation by 2030.

(*b*) reduction of the carbon intensity of Indian economy by 45 percent by 2030. over 2005 levels.

(*c*) capping Indian economy total final energy consumption in absolute levels.

(*d*) achieving the target of net zero emissions for India by 2070.

(*e*) promoting lifestyle for environment to combat climate change.

Choose the **correct** answer from the option given below:

A. (*a*), (*b*) and (*d*) only
B. (*b*), (*c*) and (*d*) only
C. (*b*), (*d*) and (*e*) only
D. (*c*), (*d*) and (*e*) only

64. Here is given international organisations and their headquarters. Which of the following are correct combinations of the institutions and their headquarters.

(*a*) GATT : Geneva

(*b*) IMF : Washington DC

(*c*) World Bank : Washington DC

(*d*) International Development Association (IDA) : New York

(*e*) Asian Development Bank : Mandaluyong

Choose the **correct** answer from the option given below:

A. (*a*), (*b*) and (*c*) only

B. (*a*) and (*b*) only

C. (*c*) and (*d*) only

D. (*a*), (*b*), (*c*) and (*e*) only

65. Which of the following is/are correct about Walrasian demand function?

(*a*) The Walrasian demand function X (P, W) is homogenous of degree zero if X (αP, αW) = X (P, W) for any P, W and $\alpha > 0$.

(*b*) The Walrasian demand function X (P, W) is homogenous of degree one if X (αP, αW)= αX (P, W) for any P, W and $\alpha > 0$.

(*c*) The Walrasian demand function X (P, W) satisfies Walras' law if for every P >> 0 and W > 0, we have P. X = W for all X $\in$ X(P, W)

(*d*) Walras' law says consumer fully expends his wealth.

(*e*) If price and wealth both change in same proportion, then individual consumption choice does not change.

Choose the **correct** answer from the option given below:

A. (*a*), (*b*), (*c*) and (*d*) only

B. (*b*), (*c*), (*d*) and (*e*) only

C. (*a*), (*b*), (*c*) and (*e*) only

D. (*a*), (*c*), (*d*) and (*e*) only

66. Match List-I with List-II.

List-I	List-II
(*a*) Cost-effectiveness	I. a policy that directly regulates polluters through the use of standards.
(*b*) Pollution permit trading system	II. an incentive based policy that encourages conservation practices or pollution reduction technologies.
(*c*) Market approach	III. Requires that the least amount of resources be used to achieve an objective.
(*d*) Command-and-control approach	IV. A market instrument that establishes a market for rights to pollute.

Choose the **correct** answer from the options given below:

	(*a*)	(*b*)	(*c*)	(*d*)
A.	I	II	III	IV
B.	III	IV	I	II
C.	IV	III	II	I
D.	III	IV	II	I

67. Match List-I with List-II.

List-I	List-II
(*a*) Kleins rule of thumb	I. Structural break
(*b*) Ljung Box (LB) statistic	II. Unit Root
(*c*) KPSS	III. Significance of auto-correlation coefficients
(*d*) Bai-Perron	IV. Multicollinearity

Choose the **correct** answer from the options given below:

	(*a*)	(*b*)	(*c*)	(*d*)
A.	IV	III	II	I
B.	IV	III	I	II
C.	II	IV	I	III
D.	II	III	IV	I

68. Match List-I with List-II.

List-I	List-II
(*a*) J.M. Keynes	I. Inventory theoretic approach to transaction demand for money
(*b*) Kydland-Prescott	II. Liquidity Preference
(*c*) Baumol-Tobin	III. Time inconsistency Problem
(*d*) Friedman-Schwartz	IV. Monetary History of United States

Choose the **correct** answer from the options given below:

	(a)	(b)	(c)	(d)
A.	II	III	IV	I
B.	III	II	I	IV
C.	III	I	II	IV
D.	II	III	I	IV

69. Match List-I with List-II.

List-I	List-II
(a) Kuznet	I. Innovation and Entrepreneurship
(b) Nurkse	II. Balanced growth theory
(c) Leibenstein	III. Inverted U-curve hypothesis
(d) Schumpeter	IV. Critical minimum effort thesis

Choose the **correct** answer from the options given below:

	(a)	(b)	(c)	(d)
A.	I	IV	III	II
B.	III	II	IV	I
C.	IV	III	II	I
D.	II	I	IV	III

70. Match List-I with List-II.

List-I (States)	List-II ((Food grain production (2021-22) Thousand Tonnes)
(a) Telangana	I. 11266.0
(b) Jharkhand	II. 4984.2
(c) Chhattisgarh	III. 8897.0
(d) Andhra Pradesh	IV. 15095.4

Choose the **correct** answer from the options given below:

	(a)	(b)	(c)	(d)
A.	I	II	III	IV
B.	IV	III	II	I
C.	I	III	IV	II
D.	IV	II	III	I

71. Match List-I with List-II.

List-I	List-II
(a) Tax Evasion	I. Bond Financing
(b) Effective incidence of tax	II. Illegal free riding
(c) Legal incidence of tax	III. Obliged to deliver tax revenue to Government
(d) Fiscal Illusion	IV. Not necessarily correspond to on whom tax is imposed

Choose the **correct** answer from the options given below:

	(a)	(b)	(c)	(d)
A.	II	III	IV	I
B.	III	I	II	IV
C.	II	IV	III	I
D.	IV	III	II	I

72. Match List-I with List-II.

List-I (Type of India's population growth rate)	List-II (Period)
(a) Rapid High Growth	I. 1981-2011
(b) Stagnant Population	II. 1921-1951
(c) High growth with definite signs of slowing down	III. 1951-1981
(d) Steady Growth	IV. 1891-1921

Choose the **correct** answer from the options given below:

	(a)	(b)	(c)	(d)
A.	IV	II	III	I
B.	III	IV	I	II
C.	III	IV	II	I
D.	IV	III	II	I

73. Match List-I with List-II.

List-I (Policy)	List-II (Year)
(a) National Forest Policy	I. 2000
(b) Marine Fishing Policy	II. 1994
(c) New Mineral Policy	III. 2004
(d) National Population Policy	IV. 1988

Choose the **correct** answer from the options given below:

	(a)	(b)	(c)	(d)
A.	IV	III	II	I
B.	IV	II	III	I
C.	II	IV	III	I
D.	II	III	IV	I

74. Match List-I with List-II.

List-I | **List-II**

(a) $f'(x) > 0$ and $f''(x) > 0$ I.

(b) $f'(x) > 0$ and $f''(x) < 0$ II.

(c) $f'(x) < 0$ and $f''(x) < 0$ III.

(d) $f'(x) < 0$ and $f''(x) > 0$ IV.

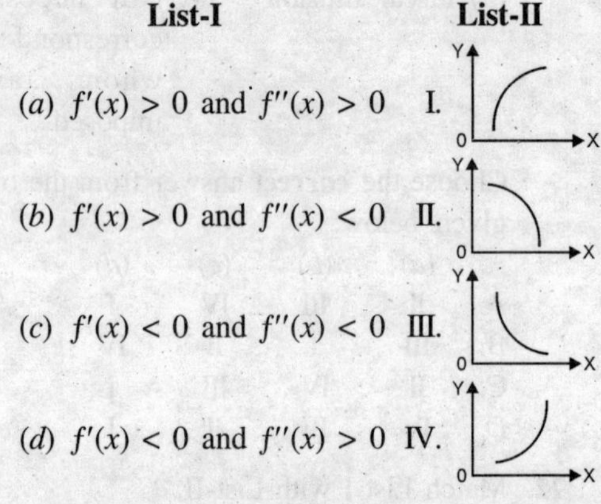

Choose the **correct** answer from the options given below:

	(a)	(b)	(c)	(d)
A.	I	IV	III	II
B.	I	III	II	IV
C.	IV	I	II	III
D.	IV	II	III	I

75. Match List-I with List-II.

List-I	List-II
(a) Central Bank Loss Function	I. $y_t = A - ar_{t-1}$
(b) Monetary Rule (MR)	II. $\pi_t = \pi_{t-1} + \alpha(y_t - y_e)$
(c) Phillips Curve (PC)	III. $(y_t - y_e) = -\alpha\beta(\pi_t - \pi^T)$
(d) Dynamic IS Curve	IV. $L = (y_t - y_e)^2 + \beta(\pi_t - \pi^T)^2$

Choose the **correct** answer from the options given below:

	(a)	(b)	(c)	(d)
A.	II	III	IV	I
B.	III	II	IV	I
C.	IV	III	II	I
D.	IV	III	I	II

76. Arrange the relative weights in percentage assigned to following criteria by the XIV Finance Commission in ascending order.

(a) Income distance

(b) Area

(c) Population (1971)

(d) Demographic Change (2011 population)

(e) Forest Cover

Choose the **correct** answer from the option given below:

A. (b), (e), (d), (c), (a)

B. (e), (d), (b), (c) (a)

C. (a), (c), (d), (b) (e)

D. (e), (b), (d), (c) (a)

77. Arrange the following in ascending order on the basis of degree of economic integration.

(a) Custom Union

(b) Free Trade Area

(c) Economic Union

(d) Common Market

(e) Preferential Trade Arrangements

Choose the **correct** answer from the option given below:

A. (a), (b), (c), (d), (e)

B. (b), (c), (d), (a), (e)

C. (e), (a), (b), (c), (d)

D. (e), (b), (a), (d), (c)

78. Arrange states in ascending order based on loans from the central government for the year 2020-21.

(a) Karnataka

(b) Madhya Pradesh

(c) Tamil Nadu

(d) Gujarat

(e) Maharashtra

Choose the **correct** answer from the option given below:

A. (c), (b), (d), (a), (e)

B. (b), (c), (d), (a), (e)

C. (c), (b), (a), (d), (e)

D. (b), (c), (a), (d), (e)

79. Arrange the following Acts in chronological order of their year of enactment starting from the oldest:

(*a*) Foreign Exchange Regulation Act
(*b*) Competition Act
(*c*) MRTP Act
(*d*) Foreign Regulation Act
(*e*) Foreign Exchange Management Act

Choose the **correct** answer from the option given below:

A. (*c*), (*b*), (*a*), (*d*), (*e*)
B. (*c*), (*a*), (*b*), (*e*), (*d*)
C. (*b*), (*a*), (*d*), (*e*), (*c*)
D. (*a*), (*b*), (*c*), (*d*), (*e*)

80. Arrange the following in order to their year of establishment starting from oldest:

(*a*) The Industrial Credit and Investment Corporation of India (ICICI)
(*b*) National Bank for Agricultural and Rural Development (NABARD)
(*c*) The Industrial Finance Corporation of India (IFCI)
(*d*) The Industrial Reconstruction Bank of India (IRBI)
(*e*) Export-Import Bank of India

Choose the **correct** answer from the option given below :

A. (*a*), (*c*), (*e*), (*b*), (*d*)
B. (*c*), (*a*), (*d*), (*e*), (*b*)
C. (*e*), (*c*), (*a*), (*b*), (*d*)
D. (*a*), (*d*), (*c*), (*b*), (*e*)

81. Arrange the following chronologically in order of their publication starting from the oldest:

(*a*) General Theory of Employment, Interest and Money
(*b*) A Treatise on probability
(*c*) Essays in Persuasion
(*d*) The End of Laissez Faire
(*e*) A Tract on Monetary Reform

Choose the **correct** answer from the option given below:

A. (*b*), (*c*), (*d*), (*a*), (*e*)
B. (*b*), (*e*), (*d*), (*c*), (*a*)
C. (*e*), (*b*), (*d*), (*c*), (*a*)
D. (*d*), (*e*), (*b*), (*a*), (*c*)

82. Arrange the following events of equity trading in India starting from the oldest:

(*a*) The BSE introduced screen-based trading.
(*b*) Foreign Institutional Investors (FIIs) are permitted to invest in the Indian Securities Market.
(*c*) NSE commenced operations in wholesale debt market segment.
(*d*) The SEBI banned badla trading on the BSE.
(*e*) The NSE overtook the BSE as the largest stock exchange in terms of volume trading.

Choose the **correct** answer from the option given below:

A. (*a*), (*b*), (*d*), (*e*), (*c*)
B. (*b*), (*d*), (*c*), (*e*), (*a*)
C. (*d*), (*b*), (*e*), (*c*), (*a*)
D. (*c*), (*b*), (*d*), (*e*), (*a*)

83. Sequence of steps followed in the estimation of Indirect Least Square (ILS) starting from the beginning:

(*a*) Identification of the structural equations
(*b*) Application of OLS
(*c*) Obtaining structural coefficients
(*d*) Obtaining reduced form equation
(*e*) Use the model for policy

Choose the **correct** answer from the option given below:

A. (*a*), (*d*), (*b*), (*c*) and (*e*)
B. (*a*), (*b*), (*d*), (*c*) and (*e*)
C. (*b*), (*d*), (*a*), (*e*) and (*c*)
D. (*b*), (*a*), (*c*), (*d*) and (*e*)

84. As per the total revenue received by the government under the head of GST on the domestic supply of goods and services for 2021-22, arrange the following states in ascending order:

(*a*) Odisha
(*b*) Rajasthan
(*c*) Delhi
(*d*) West Bengal
(*e*) Madhya Pradesh

Choose the **correct** answer from the option given below :

A. (*d*), (*c*), (*e*), (*b*), (*a*)

B. (*e*), (*b*), (*a*), (*c*), (*d*)

C. (*b*), (*e*), (*c*), (*a*), (*d*)

D. (*c*), (*e*), (*a*), (*d*), (*b*)

85. According to the Census, 2011 arrange the states in the descending order based on the literacy rate (aged group 7 year and above):

(*a*) Nagaland (*b*) Tripura

(*c*) Sikkim (*d*) Manipur

(*e*) Meghalaya

Choose the **correct** answer from the option given below:

A. (*d*), (*c*), (*b*), (*e*), (*a*)

B. (*c*), (*b*), (*d*), (*a*), (*e*)

C. (*b*), (*c*), (*a*), (*d*), (*e*)

D. (*a*), (*c*), (*b*), (*e*), (*d*)

86. Given below are two statements: One is labelled as Assertion (A) and the other is labelled as Reason (R):

Assertion (A): If governments do not care about protectionists' rents, they would replace all import duties with sales taxes.

Reason (R): Sales tax is more efficient means of raising revenue than import tariff.

In the light of the above statements, choose the **correct** answer from the options given below:

A. Both (A) and (R) are true and (R) is the correct explanation of (A).

B. Both (A) and (R) are true, but (R) is NOT the correct explanation of (A).

C. (A) is true, but (R) is false.

D. (A) is false, but (R) is true.

87. Given below are two statements:

Statement I: Friedman's theory of the demand for money is partly Keynesian and partly non-Keynesian.

Statement II: It is non-Keynesian in that Friedman neglects completely Keynes' clarification of the motives for holding money and the corresponding components of demand for money.

In the light of the above statements, choose the **correct** answer from the options given below:

A. Both Statement I and Statement II are true.

B. Both Statement I and Statement II are false.

C. Statement I is true, but Statement II is false.

D. Statement I is false, but Statement II is true.

88. Given below are two statements:

Statement I: Under first degree price discrimination, monopolist sells different units of output for different prices and these prices may differ from person to person.

Statement II: Under third degree price discrimination, monopolist sells different units of output for different prices, but every individual who buys the same amount of the good pays the same price.

In the light of the above statements, choose the **correct** answer from the options given below:

A. Both Statement I and Statement II are true.

B. Both Statement I and Statement II are false.

C. Statement I is true, but Statement II is false.

D. Statement I is false, but Statement II is true.

89. Given below are two statements:

Statement I: The terms of trade of a nation are defined as the ratio of the cost of its export commodity to the price of its import commodity.

Statement II: The terms of trade of the trade partner are equal to the inverse of the terms of trade of the other nation.

In the light of the above statements, choose the **correct** answer from the options given below:

A. Both Statement I and Statement II are true.

B. Both Statement I and Statement II are false.

C. Statement I is true, but Statement II is false.

D. Statement I is false, but Statement II is true.

90. Given below are two statements:

Statement I: Division of labour is the starting point of Smith's theory of economic growth.

Statement II: It is division of labour that results in the greatest improvement in the productive power of labour.

In the light of the above statements, choose the **correct** answer from the options given below:

A. Both Statement I and Statement II are true.

B. Both Statement I and Statement II are false.

C. Statement I is true, but Statement II is false.

D. Statement I is false, but Statement II is true.

Directions (Qs. No. 91-95): *Read the passage below and answer the question:*

The government of India's fiscal policy response to the covid crises comprised of a judicious mix of increasing food and fertilizer subsidies on the one hand and a reduction in taxes on fuel and certain imported products on the other. Despite these additional fiscal pressures the union govt. is back on track. The resilience in the fiscal performance of the union government has been facilitated by the recovery in economic activity buoyancy in revenues from direct taxes and goods and services tax (GST) and realistic assumptions in the budget. The gross tax revenue registered a YoY growth of 15.5% from April to November 2022. driven by robust growth in the direct taxes and GST. The gross GST-collection has increased at 24.8% on YoY during the same period. The Union Government's emphasis on capital expediture (capex) has continued despite higher revenue expenditure requirements during the year. The center's capex has steadily increased from a long term average of 1.7 percent of GDP (FY09 to FY20) to 2.5% of GDP in FY22 PA, The center has also incentivize the state governments through interest free loans and enhanced borrowing ceilings to prioritize their spending on capex. Government has boosted allocations on infrastructure intensive sectors such as roads and highways, railways and housing and urban affairs, which has bearing on capex. This increase in capex will have implication for medium term growth and sustainable government debt to GDP ratio.

91. Which of the following strategies was not comprised India's Fiscal Policy response to Covid crises:

A. Increasing of food subsidy

B. Increasing of fertilizer subsidy

C. Reduction in taxes on certain imported products.

D. Increase in taxes on fuel.

92. Which of the following is not correct with respect to facilitation of resilience in fiscal performance of the union government:

A. Recovery in Economic activity

B. Buoyant GST revenues

C. Expenditure austerity measures pertaining to food and fertilizer subsidy

D. Realistic assumptions in budget

93. Which of the following strategy is adopted by Union Government to prioritise States' spending on capex.

A. Incentivizing for higher revenue expenditure

B. Incentivizing for interest free loans and enhance borrowing ceilings

C. Incentivizing for higher interest payment

D. Incentivizing for large spending on tax

94. The Capex of the union government for the period FY 09 to FY 20 on an average was ________.

A. 2.5 percent of GDP
B. 15.5 percent of revenue receipts
C. 24.8 percent of GST revenue
D. 1.7 percent of GDP

95. In order to further enhance capex, allocation for which of the following infrastructure sector is not increased:

A. Ports and Waterways
B. Roads and Highways
C. Railways
D. Housing and Urban affair's

Directions (Qs. No. 96-100): *Read the passage below and answer the question:*

GDP growth is the most widely used macroeconomic indicator for adjudicating broad economic progress. The outcomes from decisions made on the basis of such an indicator have been repeatedly disappointing because of failures to detect resource uses that turn out to be unsustainable. Adjusted Net Savings (ANS) provides a complementary indicator to help in understanding the changes in wealth and not per capita wealth, by capturing some of the important policy-induced dynamics. Based on the conventions of the System of National Accounts (SNA), ANS is measured as Gross National Saving minus depreciation of produced capital, depletion of subsoil assets and timber resources, and air pollution damages to human health, plus a credit for expenditures on education. If ANS is negative, the country running down its capital stocks and possibly reducing future material well-being. If ANS is positive the country is adding to wealth and future material well-being. When natural resource depletion is not used to invest in other assets in the wealth portfolio, countries gross saving might not be enough to compensate this depletion resulting in negative net savings. However, nations with higher GDP are far less likely to obtain negative ANS. It is argued that, if not a superior indicator of sustainability. ANS is useful to the extent that it can serve as an indicator of unsustainability. Hence, the estimates and conceptualization of ANS are not free from limitations.

96. Adjusted Net Saving (ANS) is:

A. a proxy for change in per capita wealth
B. a stock variable
C. a flow variable
D. unable to capture policy-induced dynamics

97. Which of the following is not the constituent of ANS?

A. Public expenditures on education
B. Air pollution damage
C. Depletion of metals and minerals
D. Loss of biodiversity

98. Which of the following explains the decline in ANS in countries with increasing GDP per capita?

A. Increasing proportion of private investment in an economy
B. Depleted assets not offset by sufficient investment in human and physical capital
C. Increasing gross saving rates
D. Increasing production of renewable natural capital

99. Which of the following reflects the shortcomings of ANS?

A. It allows substitution between different forms of capital.
B. It is not a comprehensive indicator of per capita wealth.
C. It is influenced by the level of GDP of an economy.
D. All of the above

100. The concept of ANS should at best be used to:

A. guide ecologically optimal sustainable scale
B. serve as an indicator of unsustainability
C. replace GDP as a measure of economic progress
D. None of the above

ANSWERS

1. **(B):** The budget line represents all the combinations of goods that a consumer can afford given their income and the prices of the goods. It is derived from the budget constraint equation:

$P_1 . Q_1 + P_2 . Q_2 = I$

Where: P_1 and P_2 are the prices of goods 1 and 2 respectively,

Q_1 and Q_2 are the quantities of goods 1 and 2 consumed, and I is the consumer's income.

Graphically, the budget line shows the maximum quantities of two goods that a consumer can buy given their income and the prices of the goods. It is drawn as a straight line connecting the intercepts on the horizontal (good 1) and vertical (good 2) axes.

This means that for each unit of good 1 sacrificed (measured on the horizontal axis), the consumer can give up one unit of good 2 and still spend the same amount of money. This results in a flatter budget line because the trade-off between the two goods remains the same despite the increase in prices.

Visually, the flatter budget line indicates that the consumer has less purchasing power compared to the situation before the price changes. The outward rotation of the budget line would occur if the prices decreased, indicating an increase in purchasing power.

So, when both prices increase, the budget line becomes flatter due to the reduced purchasing power of the consumer.

2. **(D):** Present Value = P.V.,

Future Value = F.V.

$$P.V. \frac{F.V.}{(1+r)^n} \quad (r = \text{Rate of Interest}, n = \text{Time})$$

$$P.V. = \frac{40}{(1+0.10)^{10}}$$

$(r = 10\% = 0.10)$

$$P.V. = \frac{40}{(1.10)^{10}}$$

$$P.V. = \frac{40}{2.59} = 15.44 \approx 15.42.$$

3. **(D):** Market structure refers to the organizational and competitive characteristics of a market, influencing the behaviour of firms within it. Key factors defining market structure include the degree of buyers' concentration, indicating how much power buyers hold in the market; the degree of sellers' concentration, reflecting the level of competition among sellers; and the conditions of entry, which determine how easy or difficult it is for new firms to enter the market. These elements collectively shape the competitiveness and efficiency of a market. However, vertical integration, while significant in business strategy, is not inherently a characteristic of market structure. It refers to the ownership or control of multiple stages of production or distribution by a single firm, allowing it to streamline operations, reduce costs, and potentially gain market power.

4. **(C):** Convex production sets ensure that firms can produce a diverse range of goods efficiently, facilitating the realization of Pareto efficient allocations. However, the second theorem does not hold in the presence of increasing returns to scale. In such cases, market failures like monopolies can emerge, hindering the achievement of Pareto efficiency. Despite this limitation, the second theorem underscores the potential of competitive markets to efficiently allocate resources, provided certain conditions are met, thereby highlighting the essential role of market structures and individual preferences in welfare economics.

5. (A): Taylor's Rule is a fundamental concept in macroeconomics that outlines how a central bank or monetary authority adjusts interest rates in response to prevailing economic conditions. Named after economist John Taylor, this rule offers a systematic approach for monetary policymakers to set interest rates with the objective of achieving economic stability. It suggests that the central bank should adjust the nominal interest rate in response to deviations of inflation from its target level and the output gap from its potential level. By doing so, the central bank aims to stabilize the economy, promoting both price stability and full employment. Essentially, Taylor's Rule provides a guideline for policymakers to calibrate monetary policy in accordance with the dual mandate of most central banks: to control inflation and foster sustainable economic growth.

6. (A): The monetary base of an economy, often referred to as high-powered money, represents the sum of currency held by the public, including banknotes and coins in circulation, and the reserves held by commercial banks at the central bank. This concept serves as a fundamental building block for understanding the broader money supply and the functioning of the banking system. The currency held by the public is the physical money circulating in the economy, used for transactions and held as a store of value by individuals and businesses. On the other hand, the reserves held by banks consist of deposits maintained at the central bank, which are used to meet regulatory requirements and facilitate interbank transactions. The central bank has direct control over the monetary base through its monetary policy operations, such as open market operations, reserve requirements, and discount lending.

7. (A): The multiplier effect describes how an initial injection of money into the economy, like government spending or investment, can lead to a larger increase in total output. This happens because recipients of the initial injection spend some of it, which becomes income for others, who then spend a portion of that, and so on. The total impact on output is a multiple of the initial injection, hence the name "multiplier."

The marginal propensity to save (MPS) is the portion of each additional dollar of income that people choose to save rather than spend. The marginal propensity to consume (MPC) is then 1 minus the MPS, representing the portion that is spent.

The formula: $m = 1 / (1 - \text{MPC})$,

where m is the multiplier and MPC is the marginal propensity to consume.

When the MPS is lowered (meaning people save less and spend more of each additional dollar) the MPC increases. This means that a larger portion of each round of spending is injected back into the economy, leading to a greater overall impact. Consequently, the multiplier effect becomes stronger.

Therefore, the answer is Higher will be the multiplier effect.

8. (C): In the national income identity Y = C + I + G, investment (I) is indeed a component of the total national income (Y), along with consumption (C) and government spending (G). Investment (I) represents the spending by firms on capital goods, such as machinery, equipment, and infrastructure.

Investment (I) is influenced by various factors, and among the options provided, it is primarily a function of the real interest rate. The real interest rate is the nominal interest rate adjusted for inflation. When the real interest rate decreases, the cost of borrowing decreases, making investment more attractive, thus stimulating higher levels of investment. Conversely, when the real interest rate increases, borrowing becomes more expensive, leading to lower levels of investment.

When the real interest rate is low, borrowing money to finance investments becomes cheaper for firms. This lower cost of borrowing makes investment projects more attractive because firms can finance them more affordably and potentially earn higher returns. As a result, firms are more likely to undertake new investment projects or expand existing ones when the real interest rate is low.

9. **(D):** "The LM schedule is the schedule giving the combinations of values of investment and interest rate that produce equilibrium in the money market." This statement is inaccurate because it incorrectly describes the LM schedule. The LM schedule, or Liquidity Preference-Money Supply curve, actually depicts combinations of values of income and the interest rate that produce equilibrium in the money market. It represents the relationship between the interest rate and the level of income at which the demand for money balances with the money supply set by the central bank. The LM curve reflects the Keynesian perspective on the money market, where the interest rate influences the demand for money, primarily through the investment and liquidity preference channels.

10. **(C):** Numerical solution:

P (Exactly 2 delinquent cases)

$= ({}^{6}C_2 + {}^{14}C_3) \div ({}^{20}C_5)$

$= [(6!) \div (6-2)!\,(2!)] \times [(14!) \div (14-3)!\,(3)!] \div [(20!) \div (20-5)!\,(5!)]$

$= (5 \times 7 \times 13 \times 2) \div (19 \times 17 \times 8)$

$= 910 \div 2584$

$= 0.3087$

Ths, the probabiltiy that the auditor finds exactly 2 delinquent cases is 0.3087.

11. **(D):** Given, that,

$$n = 140$$

$$\text{Supervisor} = 30$$

$$\text{Married} = 80$$

$$\text{Married Supervisor} = \frac{80 \times 20}{100} = 16$$

$$P(S \cap M) = \frac{16}{140} = 0.1143.$$

12. **(B):** "An endogenous variable is correlated with the error term," accurately describes the purpose of the Hausman's specification error test. This test is specifically designed to assess whether endogenous variables, which are influenced by other variables within the model, are correlated with the error term in a regression analysis. When an endogenous variable is correlated with the error term, it violates the assumptions of the regression model, leading to biased and inconsistent estimates. This correlation can arise due to omitted variable bias, measurement error, or simultaneity, among other reasons.

13. **(A):** In a random walk without drift, the persistent effect of shocks throughout the entire time series distinguishes it from other stochastic processes. Consider a financial instrument's price movement as a random walk, where each price change, whether positive or negative, represents a shock. In this context, each shock contributes independently to the overall trajectory, devoid of any inherent tendency to revert to a mean or drift towards a specific value. Consequently, the influence of significant price movements remains present across subsequent data points, potentially shaping future changes.

This absence of temporal dependence underscores a key feature of random walks without drift, contrasting with processes exhibiting autocorrelation, where past behavior influences future outcomes. The unpredictable nature of such walks underscores the importance of treating each step as an independent event, complicating forecasting endeavors.

14. (C): $F = \dfrac{\left(\hat{\beta}\Sigma y_i x_{2i} + \hat{\beta}_3 y_i x_{3i}\right)/2}{\Sigma \hat{u}_i^2 /(n-3} = \dfrac{ESS/df}{RSS/df}$

$$F = \frac{ESS/df}{(TSS - ESS)df} \text{ (Divide by TSS)}$$

$$F = \frac{\left(\frac{ESS}{TSS}\right)df}{\frac{(TSS-ESS)}{TSS}df} = \frac{\left(\frac{ESS}{TSS}\right)df}{\left(1-\frac{ESS}{TSS}\right)df}$$

$$\left(R^2 = \frac{ESS}{TSS}\right)$$

$$F = \frac{R^2.df}{(1-R^2 df)}$$

$$F = \frac{\left(R_{UR}^2 - R_R^2\right)/m}{\left(1-R_{UR}^2\right)/(n-k)}$$

In option (C), if RSS would be in place of ESS, then option (C) will be true.

15. (B)

16. (D): Given that,

$$u = x^2 + y^2 + z^2 \text{ and } x + y + z = 1$$

Using Lorenz (λ) coefficient

$$L = x^2 + y^2 + z^2 + \lambda\,(x + y + z - 1)$$

$$\frac{\partial L}{\partial x} = 2x + \lambda = 0 \Rightarrow x = \frac{-\lambda}{2}$$

$$\frac{\partial L}{\partial y} = 2y + \lambda = 0 \Rightarrow y = \frac{-\lambda}{2}$$

$$\frac{\partial L}{\partial z} = 2z + \lambda = 0 \Rightarrow z = \frac{-\lambda}{2}$$

and $x + y + z - 1 = 0$ ...(*i*)

Putting the value of x, y and z in equation (*i*)

$$\frac{-\lambda}{2} - \frac{\lambda}{2} - \frac{\lambda}{2} - 1 = 0$$

$$\Rightarrow \quad \frac{-3\lambda}{2} - 1 = 0$$

$$\Rightarrow \quad \lambda = \frac{-2}{3}$$

Putting the value of x in values of x, y and z

Then, $\bar{x} = \frac{1}{3}$, $\bar{y} = \frac{1}{3}$, $\bar{z} = \frac{1}{3}$

Hence, $(\bar{x}, \bar{y}, \bar{z}) = \left(\frac{1}{3}, \frac{1}{3}, \frac{1}{3}\right)$.

17. (C): Given that,

$$U = f(q_1, q_2) = q_1, q_2$$

$$P_{q_1} = 1, P_{q_2} = 2$$

$$P_1 q_1 + P_2 q_2 = K$$

$$q_1 + 2q_2 = K$$

$$q_1 = (K - 2q_2)$$

$$U = q_2(K - 2q_2)$$

$$U = q_2 K - 2q^2{}_2$$

$$\frac{dU}{dq_2} = K - 4q_2$$

$$q_2 = \frac{K}{4}$$

$$q_1 = K - 2q_2$$

$$q_1 = K - 2\times\frac{K}{4}$$

(By keeping the value for q_2

$$q_1 = K - \frac{K}{2}$$

$$q_1 = \frac{2K - K}{2}$$

$$q_1 = \frac{K}{2}$$

$$(q_1, q_2) = \left(\frac{K}{2}, \frac{K}{4}\right).$$

18. (A): In the context of international trade, a tariff retaliation offer curve illustrates a country's response to tariffs imposed by its trading partners. When a country faces tariffs on its exports, it may retaliate by imposing tariffs on imports from the countries that initiated the tariffs. This retaliation is typically aimed at reducing the volume of imports from those countries, thereby offsetting the adverse effects of the initial tariffs on the exporting country's exports. Consequently, the tariff retaliation offer curve tends to bend towards the import good axis, indicating a reduction in imports from the targeted countries.

19. (C): The Factor Price Equalization Theorem, first articulated by Paul Samuelson, is a crucial proposition in international trade theory. This theorem posits that in a world with unrestricted trade and factor mobility, factors of production (such as labour and capital) will earn the same return (price) across different countries, regardless of initial endowments or technological differences. In other words, under conditions of free trade and factor mobility, competitive forces will equalize factor prices internationally. This phenomenon occurs because factors of production will migrate from regions with relatively lower returns to those with higher returns, thereby equalizing their prices over time.

20. (A): The Extended Fund Facility (EFF) was introduced by the International Monetary Fund (IMF) in 1974 as a financial instrument to provide support to member countries facing long-term balance of payments difficulties. Unlike traditional IMF lending programs, which typically focus on short-term stabilization measures, the EFF is designed to assist countries in implementing structural reforms aimed at addressing underlying imbalances and promoting sustainable economic growth. This facility offers financial assistance over an extended period, allowing countries to undertake comprehensive policy reforms and structural adjustments. The EFF is particularly suited for nations facing persistent balance of payments problems, such as chronic deficits or unsustainable debt burdens, that require sustained policy adjustments and structural reforms to address.

21. (B): "Why Nations Fail: The Origins of Power, Prosperity, and Poverty," authored by Daron Acemoglu and James A. Robinson, is a seminal work that explores the underlying factors contributing to the divergent economic fortunes of nations. The book presents a compelling argument that the key determinant of a nation's success or failure lies in its political and economic institutions. Acemoglu and Robinson contend that inclusive political and economic institutions, which encourage broad-based participation, innovation, and competition, are essential for fostering long-term prosperity.

22. (B): A foreign exchange swap is a financial derivative transaction that involves the simultaneous execution of a spot sale of a currency combined with a forward repurchase of the same currency. In this arrangement, one party sells a specified amount of a currency for immediate delivery at the prevailing spot exchange rate, effectively converting it into another currency. At the same time, the parties agree to repurchase the same currency at a future date, typically at a predetermined forward exchange rate. This transaction allows participants to obtain funds in a different currency for a specific period while simultaneously hedging against exchange rate fluctuations. Foreign exchange swaps are commonly used by businesses, financial institutions, and central banks to manage currency exposure, facilitate international trade and investment, and access funding in foreign markets.

23. (C): The correct measure of the gross fiscal deficit of the state government is the sum of revenue deficit, capital outlays, and net lending. Revenue deficit represents the excess of revenue expenditure over revenue receipts, reflecting the extent to which current revenue falls short of meeting current expenditure obligations. Capital outlays include government expenditures on infrastructure, development projects, and other capital investments aimed at enhancing long-term economic growth and productivity. Net lending refers to the financial assistance provided by the government to various entities, such as public sector enterprises or other governments, minus any repayments received.

24. **(C):** The notion presented in this statement about tax incidence is indeed incorrect, as it oversimplifies the dynamics of tax burden distribution in the context of inelastic demand and elastic supply. In reality, tax incidence hinges on the elasticities of both demand and supply. While inelastic demand implies that consumers are less responsive to price changes and may continue purchasing despite tax-induced price increases, it does not necessarily confer an advantage in avoiding the tax burden. On the contrary, sellers can exploit this lack of consumer responsiveness by passing on a larger portion of the tax burden to consumers through higher prices.

25. **(C)**

26. **(B):** In the extreme scenario of a liquidity trap, characterized by near-zero interest rates and ineffective monetary policy, investors often exhibit bearish behavior. With nominal interest rates constrained at very low levels, traditional monetary policy tools lose their effectiveness in stimulating economic activity. In such a context, investors become pessimistic about the outlook for economic growth and investment returns. The inability of central banks to further lower interest rates or stimulate borrowing and spending creates uncertainty and apprehension among investors.

27. **(A):** The equation $300 = 2Y - 1.5i$ represents the equilibrium condition in the money market, where:

300 represents the quantity of money supplied (often denoted as MS or Ms),

2Y represents the quantity of money demanded (often denoted as MD or Md), and

i represents the nominal interest rate.

In this equation, Y typically represents real income or real output, and i represents the nominal interest rate. The equation reflects the balance between the quantity of money demanded by households and firms and the quantity of money supplied by the central bank. It illustrates that at equilibrium, the quantity of money demanded (2Y) equals the quantity of money supplied (300) at a given interest rate (i). This equilibrium condition is derived from Keynesian economics, which suggests that the demand for money is positively related to real income and negatively related to the nominal interest rate.

28. **(D):** An increase in financial literacy and banking habits can significantly impact the dynamics of the money supply, even with the same monetary base. As individuals become more financially literate, they are more likely to understand the benefits of utilizing banking services rather than keeping their funds in cash. This understanding prompts them to deposit their money into bank accounts, thereby increasing the deposit base of banks. With a larger pool of deposits, banks have more resources to extend loans and create additional deposits through the process of fractional reserve banking. This expansion of credit creation leads to an increase in broad money (M2) within the economy.

29. **(A):** According to Joan Robinson, the term 'Golden Age' in the context of the Harrod-Domar model serves to underscore its mythical nature. In the Harrod-Domar model, the 'Golden Age' represents a theoretical scenario where full employment is maintained without generating inflationary pressures, thus signifying a state of economic prosperity and stability. However, Robinson, a prominent critic of neoclassical economics, argued that such a scenario is often unattainable in the real world due to the inherent complexities and uncertainties of economic systems. She pointed out that the assumptions and simplifications made in the Harrod-Domar model, such as constant capital-output ratios and linear relationships between investment and output, fail to capture the multifaceted nature of economic dynamics.

30. **(D):** The Human Development Index (HDI) encompasses three primary dimensions to assess the well-being and development of individuals within a country. The first dimension focuses on the ability to lead a long and healthy life, emphasizing indicators such as life expectancy at birth and access to healthcare services. The second dimension pertains to the ability to acquire knowledge, evaluating indicators like literacy rates and school enrollment ratios to gauge educational attainment and cognitive development. The third dimension revolves around the ability to achieve a decent standard of living, considering factors such as income per capita, access to basic necessities, and standards of living. While access to a clean environment is undoubtedly vital for human well-being, it is not explicitly included as a dimension within the HDI.

31. **(D):** The concept of creative destruction, famously associated with Joseph Schumpeter, elucidates the dynamic and transformative nature of capitalist economies. Schumpeter's theory, outlined in his seminal work "Capitalism, Socialism and Democracy," posits that innovation and technological progress are inherent to the capitalist system, driving continual renewal and evolution. Creative destruction refers to the process wherein the introduction of new technologies, products, and business models leads to the disruption and eventual obsolescence of existing industries and economic structures. Schumpeter's concept of creative destruction highlights the dynamic and transformative nature of capitalist economies, emphasizing the importance of innovation and entrepreneurship in shaping their evolution.

32. **(A):** The Normalized Poverty Gap (NPG) is a crucial measure used to assess the depth of poverty experienced by individuals living below the poverty line within a given population. It quantifies the extent to which those below the poverty line fall short of achieving the minimum standard of living represented by the poverty line. The calculation of NPG involves dividing the Average Poverty Gap, which represents the average shortfall of the poor from the poverty line, by the poverty line itself. This ratio offers valuable insights into the severity of poverty by providing a standardized measure of deprivation relative to the poverty threshold. A higher NPG indicates a greater level of poverty depth, reflecting a more significant gap between the income or consumption levels of the poor and the established poverty line.

33. **(C):** Ambient standards in environmental policy play a pivotal role in defining the desired quality levels of specific elements within the environment, serving as crucial benchmarks for environmental management and regulation. These standards articulate the acceptable levels of various pollutants, contaminants, or other environmental parameters that must be achieved or maintained to safeguard human health and ecological integrity. For instance, air quality standards may specify limits for pollutants like particulate matter or sulphur dioxide to ensure breathable air and mitigate respiratory ailments. Similarly, water quality standards establish permissible levels of contaminants such as heavy metals or pesticides to safeguard aquatic ecosystems and drinking water sources. By designating these quality levels, ambient standards provide clear targets for environmental monitoring, regulation, and remediation efforts, enabling policymakers, regulators, and stakeholders to assess environmental conditions, identify areas of concern, and implement measures to protect and enhance environmental quality.

34. (D): The physical linkage approach for the valuation of environmental benefits involves estimating the value of environmental goods or services based on the direct technical relationship between the environmental resource and its users. This approach relies on understanding the tangible connections between changes in environmental conditions and the resulting impacts on individuals or entities that directly benefit from the resource. For example, in assessing the value of improved water quality in a river, analysts may examine the impact on recreational activities, such as swimming, fishing, or boating, that are directly affected by the condition of the water. Similarly, changes in air pollution levels may be linked to health outcomes, such as reductions in respiratory illnesses or healthcare costs, which directly affect individuals' well-being. Therefore, the physical linkage approach provides a rigorous framework for assessing the value of environmental benefits by focusing on the technical relationship between the environmental resource and its users.

35. (D): Subsidies are not typically an effective long-term policy instrument for internalizing externalities under competitive output markets for several reasons. Firstly, providing a subsidy equal to the marginal damages incurred by firms due to externalities can effectively reduce a firm's fixed costs, incentivizing increased production and exacerbating the externality rather than addressing it. Secondly, subsidies are generally available to all firms within an industry, which can lead to excessive market entry as firms are encouraged to enter the market to take advantage of the subsidy, further exacerbating the externality. Finally, the provision of subsidies can result in the level of industrial production exceeding the socially desired level, leading to overproduction and continued negative externalities. Therefore, all of the above reasons contribute to why subsidies are not an effective long-term solution for internalizing externalities in competitive output markets.

36. (C): Madhya Pradesh had the highest maternal lifetime risk in India from 2018 to 2020, at approximately 0.53 percent. The maternal mortality ratio (MMR) serves as a crucial indicator of maternal health and healthcare system performance. Addressing factors contributing to high maternal mortality, such as inadequate healthcare infrastructure, limited access to quality maternal healthcare services, socio-economic disparities, and cultural barriers, is essential for improving maternal health outcomes and reducing maternal mortality rates in Madhya Pradesh and across India.

37. (A): The Intensive Agriculture District Programme (IADP), launched in 1960-61, was a pivotal initiative often referred to as the "package program" due to its comprehensive approach to agricultural development. The program aimed to enhance agricultural productivity by providing farmers with access to loans for seeds and fertilizers, technical knowledge, adaptable innovations, and other resources necessary for boosting production. It focused primarily on dominant food-grain crops such as paddy, wheat, and millets while also covering other important cash crops in selected districts across various states.

38. (B): In the 2023-24 Union Budget, the Ministry of Agriculture and Farmers' Welfare saw its allocation climb to ₹ 1.25 lakh crore, a 5% rise from the previous year. This increase underscores the government's continuing focus on supporting India's crucial agricultural sector. However, a closer look reveals that this growth wasn't uniformly distributed across all initiatives. Key programs like Pradhan Mantri Fasal Bima Yojana, designed to shield farmers from crop losses, received a welcome bump. Conversely, others like the Modified Interest Subvention Scheme, which aims to make loans more accessible, experienced slight reductions.

39. (A): The motto of the G-20 18th meeting was "One Earth • One Family • One Future". This encapsulates the essence of global unity and cooperation in addressing pressing challenges facing the world. It emphasizes the interconnectedness of humanity and our shared responsibility towards safeguarding our planet and securing a prosperous future for all. The 2023 G20 Summit was held in New Delhi, India, on September 9-10, 2023. The summit's agenda includes important issues such as food security, climate and energy, development, health, and digitalization.

40. (B): The Prevention of Money Laundering Act, enacted in 2002, represents a pivotal step in India's efforts to combat illicit financial activities and safeguard the integrity of its financial system. This legislation was introduced to address the growing concerns surrounding money laundering, which involves the concealment, conversion, or transfer of illicitly obtained funds to make them appear legitimate. The Act aims to prevent and detect money laundering activities by establishing stringent measures for the identification, verification, and monitoring of financial transactions, particularly those involving large sums of money or high-risk entities. It empowers law enforcement agencies to investigate and prosecute individuals and organizations involved in money laundering, imposing severe penalties for non-compliance or violation of the Act's provisions.

41. (A):

(*a*) **"The reaction curves are derived from isoprofit maps which are convex to the axes."** In Bertrand's Duopoly model, firms determine their optimal pricing strategies by considering the profitability associated with different price levels. These profitability considerations are often represented graphically using isoprofit maps, which depict combinations of prices that yield the same profit level for the firm. When these isoprofit maps are convex to the axes, it means that as the firm increases its price, its profit increases at an increasing rate. As the competitor increases its price, the firm responds by lowering its price to maintain its competitive position and maximize its profit.

(*b*) **"The point of intersection of the two reaction curves reflects a stable equilibrium."** In Bertrand's Duopoly model, the equilibrium occurs where the reaction curves of both firms intersect. At this point, neither firm has an incentive to unilaterally change its price-setting strategy, as any deviation would result in lower profits. Specifically, if one firm were to increase its price above the equilibrium price, it would lose market share to its competitor and experience a decrease in profits. Conversely, if one firm were to decrease its price below the equilibrium price, it would initiate a price war, leading to lower profits for both firms.

42. (D):

(*c*) The Clark-Wicksteed-Walras product exhaustion theorem does not require perfect competition as a necessary condition. This theorem primarily deals with the equilibrium conditions in a market economy, particularly in the context of resource allocation and production. Instead, it focuses on the equilibrium outcomes that emerge from the interactions of supply and demand forces, which can occur under various market structures, including imperfect competition.

(*d*) The theorem is indeed not an identity that holds for all values of the variables. Rather, it specifically pertains to the long-run equilibrium conditions in an economy. In the long run, factors such as resource prices, input quantities, and output levels adjust to achieve a state where resource allocation is efficient and production is maximized. Therefore, the theorem's applicability is limited to this specific equilibrium scenario and may not hold true for other situations or periods of time within the economic system.

(*e*) The Clark-Wicksteed-Walras product exhaustion theorem has theoretical applicability to various types of production functions, including both homogeneous and non-homogeneous functions. While homogeneous production functions are commonly employed to illustrate the theorem's concepts due to their simplicity and ease of analysis, the theorem's principles can be extended to certain types of non-homogeneous production functions under specific conditions.

43. (C):

(*a*) **Homogeneous of degree one in price, P:** This property means that if all prices are multiplied by a constant factor, the resulting expenditure on the bundle of goods will also be multiplied by the same factor. It reflects the idea that the scale of prices affects the scale of expenditure in a proportional manner.

(*b*) **Strictly increasing in utility, u, and non-decreasing in price, P, for any good 1:** This property indicates that as utility increases (strictly), the expenditure on goods also increases. Similarly, for any given good, as its price increases, the expenditure on that good either increases or remains the same. This reflects the intuitive notion that higher utility or higher prices lead to higher expenditure.

(*c*) **Concave in price, P:** This property implies that as the price of a good increases, the rate at which the expenditure on that good increases diminishes. In other words, the marginal effect of an increase in price on expenditure decreases as more of the good is consumed, holding utility constant. This concavity reflects diminishing marginal utility and is a typical characteristic of consumer preferences.

(*d*) **Continuous in price, P, and utility, u:** Continuity ensures that small changes in prices or utility result in small changes in expenditure. This property is crucial for mathematical analysis and modeling, allowing for smooth transitions and accurate representations of consumer behavior across different price and utility levels.

44. (D):

(*a*) **'Excess sensitivity'** refers to a situation where consumption over-responds to temporary income shocks. This means that when individuals experience temporary increases or decreases in income, their consumption changes by a larger proportion than the change in income.

(*b*) **'Excess smoothness'** refers to a situation where consumption under-responds to temporary income changes. In this case, changes in income have a smaller effect on consumption than would be expected based on standard economic theory.

(*e*) **'Excess sensitivity'** and **'Excess smoothness'** are related to the empirical evidence of the permanent income hypothesis. The permanent income hypothesis suggests that individuals base their consumption decisions on their expected long-term or permanent income rather than temporary fluctuations in income.

45. (C):

(*a*) When there is an increase in the price of output, it implies that firms can sell their products at higher prices, leading to increased revenues and profitability. This creates an incentive for firms to invest in expanding their production capacity to meet the higher demand and take advantage of the more favorable market conditions.

(*b*) An increase in the marginal product of capital means that additional investment in capital goods (such as machinery, equipment, or technology) leads to a greater increase in output. In other words, each additional unit of capital generates more output than before, making investment in capital goods more attractive for firms seeking to maximize their production efficiency and output levels.

(*d*) A decrease in the rate of depreciation suggests that capital goods lose value at a slower rate over time. This means that the existing capital stock retains its value for a longer period, effectively reducing the need for frequent replacement or maintenance of capital assets.

(*e*) The core principle of Tobin's Q theory is that firms should invest when the marginal benefit of investment exceeds the marginal cost. Marginal benefit refers to the additional revenue or profit generated by investing in new capital goods, while marginal cost represents the additional cost incurred in acquiring and using these capital goods.

46. (D):

(*a*) **Paradox of thrift was popularized by J. M. Keynes:** This statement is true. John Maynard Keynes, a renowned economist, popularized the concept of the paradox of thrift in his seminal work, "The General Theory of Employment, Interest, and Money," published in 1936. In this work, Keynes described how increased saving at the individual level during economic downturns could potentially exacerbate recessions or depressions by reducing aggregate demand and contributing to a decline in overall economic activity.

(*b*) **It states that personal savings can be detrimental to overall economic growth:** This statement is also true. The paradox of thrift suggests that while saving is generally seen as beneficial at the individual level for financial security and future investment, excessive saving during times of economic hardship can have negative consequences for overall economic growth.

(*e*) **It states that individuals saving during an economic recession leads to a fall in aggregate demand:** This statement is true. One of the central tenets of the paradox of thrift is that increased saving by individuals during periods of economic recession or hardship can exacerbate the downturn by reducing aggregate demand. As individuals cut back on spending and increase saving to safeguard against uncertain economic conditions, overall demand for goods and services declines, leading to further economic contraction.

47. (D):

(*a*) **Devaluation of rupee by 22%:** Devaluation refers to the deliberate lowering of a country's currency value relative to other currencies. In this context, India was required to devalue its currency, the rupee, by 22% as a condition imposed by the IMF.

(*b*) **Drastic custom cut to a peak duty of 30% from the erstwhile level of 130% for all goods:** This condition involved a significant reduction in customs duties. India was required to cut its peak customs duty from the previous level of 130% to 30% for all goods.

(*d*) **Excise duty to be increased by 20% to neutralize the loss of revenue due to custom cut:** To compensate for the potential loss of revenue resulting from the reduction in customs duties, the government was mandated to increase excise duties by 20%.

(*e*) **Government expenditure to be cut by 10% per annum:** As part of the IMF's conditions, India was required to implement austerity measures, including reducing government spending. The government was instructed to cut its expenditure by 10% annually.

48. (A):

(*a*) **The reduction of average tariffs on industrial goods:** The Uruguay Round aimed to lower average tariffs on industrial goods across participating countries. By reducing tariffs, which are taxes imposed on imported goods, the agreement sought to make international trade more accessible and cost-effective for businesses, leading to increased trade volumes and economic growth.

(*b*) **Quotas to be replaced by tariffs:** Quotas, which restrict the quantity of imports allowed into a country, can be opaque and prone to abuse. Tariffs provide a clearer indication of the cost of importing goods and allow countries to control imports without distorting market mechanisms.

(*c*) **The reduction in agriculture export subsidies:** Agricultural export subsidies artificially lower the price of exported agricultural products, giving exporters an unfair advantage in international markets. The Uruguay Round aimed to reduce or eliminate these subsidies to create a more level playing field for agricultural producers worldwide and prevent market distortions that harm producers in importing countries.

(*d*) **The reduction in industrial subsidies:** Similar to agricultural subsidies, industrial subsidies can distort trade by artificially promoting the production and export of certain goods. The Uruguay Round sought to reduce these subsidies to ensure fair competition among countries and prevent the emergence of trade barriers that impede market access for producers in other countries.

49. (A) and (B):

(*a*) **Quality and level of capital:** Pillar 1 of Basel III emphasizes the importance of both the quality and quantity of capital held by banks. It introduces stricter definitions of capital to ensure that it consists of high-quality instruments capable of absorbing losses effectively. Additionally, Basel III increases the minimum level of capital banks must hold to provide a more substantial buffer against financial shocks.

(*b*) **Risk Coverage:** Another key aspect of Pillar 1 is ensuring that banks have sufficient capital to cover the risks they face. This involves aligning capital requirements with the level of risk associated with various assets and exposures. Basel III introduces risk-weighted assets (RWAs), where assets are assigned weights based on their riskiness.

(*c*) **Containing leverage:** Pillar 1 of Basel III explicitly includes measures to contain leverage by setting minimum capital requirements relative to a bank's total assets. Specifically, it introduces a leverage ratio requirement, which mandates that banks maintain a certain level of capital in proportion to their total exposure, irrespective of the risk weighting assigned to their assets. This leverage ratio acts as a backstop to risk-weighted capital requirements, ensuring that banks maintain a minimum level of capital to absorb losses relative to their overall balance sheet size.

50. (A):

(*b*) Exchange rate stability, monetary policy autonomy, and capital mobility are the three components of the trilemma. It suggests that policymakers can only achieve two of these objectives at any given time, necessitating a trade-off between them.

(*c*) The alignment of domestic interest rates with world interest rates is a crucial aspect of the trilemma. Perfect capital mobility implies that investors can freely move capital across borders in search of the highest returns. In this scenario, any deviation in domestic interest rates from those prevailing internationally would lead to capital flows, causing the domestic interest rate to adjust until it aligns with the world interest rate.

51. (D): The National Institution for Transforming India (NITI Aayog), a policy think tank of the Indian government, conducts periodic estimations of poverty in the country. Analyzing the 2011-12 poverty estimates specifically, we can examine the rural poverty rates across different states. When focusing on states with rural poverty exceeding 30%, the data reveals a concerning picture:

(*a*) **Manipur:** With a rural poverty rate of 36.5%, Manipur topped the list in 2011-12, highlighting significant challenges in accessing basic necessities and opportunities for its rural population.

(*b*) **Bihar:** Following closely behind at 39.1%, Bihar faced a similarly high prevalence of rural poverty, indicating the need for targeted interventions to improve living standards.

(*d*) **Uttar Pradesh:** With a rate of 34.8%, Uttar Pradesh's large rural population grappled with poverty concerns, requiring comprehensive development strategies to address various factors contributing to their economic hardship.

52. (A):

(*a*) **Division of Labour:** Smith's advocacy for the division of labour emphasized its transformative potential in driving economic growth and efficiency. In his seminal work, "The Wealth of Nations," he argued that when workers specialize in specific tasks, they become more proficient, leading to enhanced productivity and output. This specialization not only reduces the time spent transitioning between tasks but also fosters innovation and technological progress as individuals seek more efficient methods of production.

(*b*) **Notion of Increasing Returns:** While Smith is not solely credited with the concept of increasing returns; he acknowledged its relevance in certain contexts. He recognized that as production scales up, certain costs may decrease proportionately, resulting in greater efficiency and potentially lower per-unit production costs. This concept, known as economies of scale, is prevalent across various industries, driving advancements in manufacturing, services, and technology.

53. (C):

(*a*) **Construction:** This sector involves the development of physical infrastructure, including buildings, roads, bridges, and other structures. Construction activities not only provide employment opportunities but also stimulate demand for various raw materials and ancillary services, driving economic activity.

(*b*) **Trade, Hotels, Transport, and Communication related to Broadcasting:** This category comprises several subsectors, each playing a crucial role in facilitating economic transactions and connectivity. Trade involves the buying and selling of goods, both wholesale and retail, contributing to market efficiency and consumer access. Hotels and hospitality services cater to the needs of travelers, tourists, and consumers, promoting tourism and leisure activities. Transport services ensure the movement of goods and people, facilitating trade and mobility. Communication services, including telecommunications and broadcasting, enable connectivity and information dissemination, fostering economic integration and innovation.

(*d*) **Public Administration, Defense, and Other Services:** This sector encompasses government activities aimed at governance, defense, and the provision of essential public services. Public administration involves the management of public affairs, policymaking, and the delivery of public services such as healthcare, education, and social welfare. Defense activities ensure national security and territorial integrity, while other services may include regulatory functions and public utilities management.

(*e*) **Financial, Real Estate, and Professional Services:** This category encompasses a diverse range of activities that support economic transactions, asset management, and professional expertise. Financial services, including banking, insurance, and investment, facilitate capital allocation, risk management, and wealth generation. Real estate activities involve the development, sale, purchase, and leasing of properties, contributing to asset accumulation and urban development. Professional services such as legal, accounting, consulting, and technical expertise provide specialized knowledge and advisory support, enhancing productivity and competitiveness.

54. (D):

(*a*) **Asian Drama:** Unraveling the Knots of Poverty and Inequality: Released in 1968, this multi-volume study shifted Myrdal's gaze towards the complexities of development in Asia. He meticulously documented the stark disparities in wealth and opportunity within and between nations, offering nuanced analyses of the historical, social, and economic factors hindering progress.

(*b*) **An American Dilemma:** Deconstructing Race and Racism: Published in 1944, this monumental work delved deeply into the "dilemma" at the heart of American society - the stark contradiction between its professed ideals of liberty and equality, and the persistent reality of racial injustice.

(*e*) **Economic Theory and Underdeveloped Regions:** Beyond Traditional Frameworks: In 1957, Myrdal published this pivotal work, questioning the ability of existing economic theories to grasp the unique challenges faced by developing nations. He argued that rigid, Western-centric models failed to capture the cyclical nature of poverty and the interconnectedness of economic, social, and political factors.

55. **(C):** The principles representing set theory are as follows:

(*b*) $(A \cup B') \cap (A' \cup C) \cap (B \cup C')$
$= (A \cap B \cap C) \cup (A \cup B \cup C)'$

(*c*) $A \cup (B \cap C) = (A \cup B) \cap (A \cup C)$

(*e*) $(A \cup B') \cap (A' \cup C) \cap (B \cup C')$
$= (A' \cap B' \cap C-)$

56. **(D):** If S represents the sample and E represents the function. Then the probability law can be written in the following form.

Probability Law I: $P[A] \geq 0$

Probability Law II: $P[S] = 1$

Probability Law III: If $A \cap B = \phi$

Probability Law then $P[A \cup B]$
$= P[A] + P[B]$

Probability Law III: if $A_1, A_2 ....$

The same sequence of such events then,

$A\ i \cap A = \phi$ 1 for all $i =$, no

$$P\left(\bigcup_{i=1}^{\infty} A_i\right) = \sum_{i=1}^{\infty} P(A_1).$$

57. **(D):**

(*a*) **It may not be unbiased:** This property implies that a sufficient estimator might not provide estimates that, on average, are equal to the true parameter value. Unbiasedness is a desirable property in estimation because it ensures that, on average, the estimator does not systematically overestimate or underestimate the true parameter value. However, sufficiency does not guarantee unbiasedness.

(*b*) **It may be unbiased:** Conversely, this property acknowledges that a sufficient estimator can indeed be unbiased. While unbiasedness is not a necessary condition for sufficiency, it is possible for a sufficient estimator to provide unbiased estimates. In such cases, the estimator accurately estimates the true parameter value on average over repeated sampling.

(*c*) **It is always consistent:** Consistency is a crucial property of estimators, indicating that as the sample size increases indefinitely, the estimator converges in probability to the true parameter value. In other words, the likelihood of the estimator deviating significantly from the true parameter value diminishes as more data become available.

(*e*) **Minimum variance unbiased estimator:** While sufficiency does not guarantee that an estimator will be the minimum variance unbiased estimator (MVUE), it is possible for a sufficient estimator to achieve this desirable property. The MVUE is the most efficient unbiased estimator among all possible estimators, providing the smallest possible variance.

58. **(D):**

(*a*) **Public goods are non-rivalry in nature:** Public goods exhibit non-rivalry, meaning that one individual's consumption of the good does not reduce the amount available for others to consume. This characteristic distinguishes public goods from private goods, where consumption by one individual typically diminishes the quantity available for others.

(*b*) **Efficient provision of social goods needs a political process of budget determination:** The provision of social goods, which benefit society as a whole, often requires a political process to determine budget allocations and resource distribution. This is because decisions regarding the provision of social goods involve considerations beyond individual preferences and market mechanisms.

(*d*) **Among purely private and purely social goods, there are mixed cases which generate benefit or cost externalities:**

Some goods exhibit characteristics of both private and social goods, leading to the emergence of externalities-spillover effects that impact parties not directly involved in the consumption or production of the good. In mixed cases, individuals or firms may generate external benefits (positive externalities) or external costs (negative externalities) that affect others in society.

(*e*) **Individual consumers will not bid for social good, but will act as free-riders:** Since social goods are often non-excludable, meaning that individuals cannot be effectively excluded from using them, consumers may choose to "free-ride" by enjoying the benefits of the good without contributing to its provision. In the absence of mechanisms to enforce payment for the good, individuals have little incentive to pay for it voluntarily if they can benefit from it regardless of their contribution.

59. (B):

(*a*) Tax rate should be higher on the good that has lower price elasticity of demand. This statement aligns with the Ramsey Rule, which suggests that taxes should be levied at higher rates on goods with lower price elasticity of demand. This approach ensures that the tax burden falls more heavily on goods for which consumers are less responsive to price changes, maximizing tax revenue while minimizing the distortionary effects on consumption.

(*b*) If the demand elasticity in a market is zero, taxes should be imposed only in that market. This statement reflects the idea that when demand elasticity is zero (perfectly inelastic demand), consumers are insensitive to price changes, implying that taxes won't affect their consumption behaviour.

(*d*) Ramsey rule minimizes the excess burden of taxation across markets. One of the primary goals of the Ramsey Rule is to minimize the excess burden or deadweight loss associated with taxation. By setting tax rates based on the price elasticity of demand for various goods, the Ramsey Rule aims to ensure that taxes are distributed efficiently, minimizing the overall welfare loss resulting from taxation.

(*e*) Ramsey rule does not necessarily result in social justice. While the Ramsey Rule emphasizes efficiency in taxation, it may not address concerns related to social justice or equity. The rule focuses on optimizing resource allocation and minimizing deadweight loss but may not account for factors such as income distribution, poverty alleviation, or the impact on vulnerable populations.

60. (B):

(*d*) **Variance Inflation Factor (VIF) of a variable is below 10:** VIF measures how much the variance of the estimated regression coefficient is inflated due to multicollinearity. A VIF value above 10 (or sometimes even 4 or 5, depending on the context) indicates high multi-collinearity, not below. Lower VIF values suggest lower multicollinearity and are desirable in regression analysis.

(*e*) **The closer the Tolerance (TOLj) is to 1:** Tolerance is the proportion of variance in an independent variable that is not explained by other predictors in the model. A Tolerance value close to 1 indicates that most of the variance in the variable is not explained by the other predictors, implying lower multi-collinearity.

61. (C):

(*a*) **Deregulation of the interest rate structure:** The committee recommended the removal of restrictions on interest rates charged by banks, allowing market forces to determine interest rates based on demand and supply dynamics. This move aimed to enhance efficiency in the banking sector and encourage competition among banks.

(*d*) **Freedom to appoint chief executive and officers of the banks:** The committee suggested granting banks the autonomy to appoint their chief executives and officers based on merit and competence rather than bureaucratic or political considerations. This recommendation aimed to improve governance and efficiency in banks by ensuring that key leadership positions are filled by qualified professionals.

(*e*) **Capital adequacy norms were implemented in stages:** The committee proposed the gradual implementation of capital adequacy norms to strengthen the financial health and stability of banks. These norms require banks to maintain a minimum level of capital relative to their risk-weighted assets, thereby enhancing their ability to absorb losses and withstand financial shocks.

62. (D):

(*a*) **The consumer spends money to ameliorate the damaging effects of the bad:** The defensive expenditure method is based on the premise that consumers allocate resources to mitigate or reduce the adverse impacts of undesirable factors, such as pollution or environmental degradation.

(*b*) **The defensive expenditure undertaken reflects the consumer's willingness to pay to reduce the level of the bad:** Consumers make defensive expenditures based on their perceived value of mitigating the negative effects of the bad.

(*d*) **The defensive expenditure provides no additional services other than provisioning the desired environmental quality:** Defensive expenditures are made solely to counteract the negative impacts of environmental degradation or pollution. Unlike other expenditures that provide tangible services or goods, such as purchasing a product or service for enjoyment or utility, defensive expenditures aim to protect existing environmental quality and do not generate additional benefits beyond this purpose.

(*e*) **The observed defensive expenditure is a lower bound on the willingness to pay to avoid the bad:** While defensive expenditures provide an upper bound on the willingness to pay to avoid environmental harm, they also serve as a minimum estimate of the value individuals place on environmental quality.

63. (C):

64. (D):

(*a*) **GATT (General Agreement on Tariffs and Trade):** GATT was an international organization established in 1947 to promote international trade by reducing or eliminating trade barriers such as tariffs or quotas. In 1995, GATT's functions were absorbed by the World Trade Organization (WTO), which continues to operate in Geneva, Switzerland.

(*b*) **IMF (International Monetary Fund):** The IMF is an international organization headquartered in Washington, D.C., United States. It was established in 1944 with the goal of promoting global monetary cooperation, exchange stability, and balanced growth.

(*c*) **World Bank:** The World Bank is another international financial institution headquartered in Washington, D.C., United States. It was established in 1944 alongside the IMF to provide financial and technical assistance to developing countries. The World Bank Group consists of five institutions, including the International Bank for Reconstruction and Development (IBRD) and the International Development Association (IDA).

(*e*) **Asian Development Bank (ADB):** The ADB is a regional development bank dedicated to promoting economic and social progress in Asia and the Pacific. It was founded in 1966 and is headquartered in Mandaluyong City, Philippines.

65. (D):

(*a*) This statement accurately describes the property of homogeneity in Walrasian demand functions. When prices and total wealth are multiplied by the same factor, the demand function's value remains unchanged. This property is fundamental in understanding how consumers' demand for goods responds to changes in prices and wealth.

(*c*) Walras' Law, as stated in this statement, indeed asserts that the sum of expenditures across all goods equals total wealth. This principle ensures market equilibrium, where consumers allocate their budgets efficiently among different goods based on their preferences and the prices of those goods.

(*d*) Contrary to the assertion that this statement is incorrect, it accurately reflects Walras' Law. The law does imply that consumers fully expend their wealth in equilibrium. This is because market expenditures, which represent the sum of all expenditures on goods, equal total wealth.

(*e*) This statement correctly describes the property of homogeneity, where changes in prices and wealth in proportion do not alter individual consumption choices. This property aligns with Walrasian demand functions, reflecting how consumers' optimal consumption bundles remain unchanged when prices and wealth change in proportion.

66. (D):

(*a*) Cost-effectiveness matches with Cost-effectiveness refers to the principle that requires achieving a certain environmental objective using the least amount of resources possible.

(*b*) Pollution permit trading system matches with A pollution permit trading system, also known as a cap-and-trade system, is a market-based approach where permits to pollute up to a certain level are traded among polluters. This matches with the concept of a market approach.

(*c*) Market approach matches with A market approach refers to policies that utilize market mechanisms, such as incentives or trading systems, to address environmental issues. This aligns with the description of a pollution permit trading system.

(*d*) Command-and-control approach matches with The command-and-control approach involves direct regulation of polluters through the imposition of standards or regulations. This contrasts with market-based approaches, such as pollution permit trading systems.

67. (A)

68. (D):

(*a*) **J. M. Keynes corresponds to Liquidity Preference.** Keynes is famously associated with liquidity preference theory, which explores how individuals balance the desire for liquidity (cash or near-cash assets) with the pursuit of higher returns from less liquid investments.

(*b*) **Kydland-Prescott matches with Time Inconsistency Problem.** The Kydland-Prescott model is a dynamic model of economic policy that highlights the challenges policymakers face when their incentives to commit to a policy in the present differ from their incentives to adhere to that commitment in the future.

(*c*) **Baumol-Tobin corresponds to Inventory theoretic approach to transaction demand for money.** The Baumol-Tobin model focuses on how individuals decide how much of their wealth to hold in the form of money versus other assets, considering the trade-off between the costs of making frequent trips to the bank to convert assets into money (transaction costs) and the opportunity costs of holding money (foregone interest).

(*d*) **Friedman-Schwartz matches with Monetary History of the United States.** Milton Friedman and Anna Schwartz collaborated on the seminal work "A Monetary History of the United States," which examines the role of monetary factors in economic fluctuations and crises throughout American history.

69. (B):

(*a*) **Kuznets corresponds to Inverted U-curve hypothesis.** Simon Kuznets is known for his hypothesis that suggests income inequality initially increases as a country industrializes but then decreases once a certain level of income is reached.

(*b*) **Nurkse matches with Balanced growth theory.** Ragnar Nurkse proposed the balanced growth theory, which emphasizes the importance of investing in various sectors of the economy simultaneously to achieve balanced development and avoid bottlenecks.

(*c*) **Leibenstein corresponds to Critical minimum effort thesis.** Harvey Leibenstein introduced the concept of the critical minimum effort thesis, which suggests that below a certain level of effort or investment, an industry or region may fail to develop due to various inefficiencies or barriers.

(*d*) **Schumpeter matches with Innovation and Entrepreneurship.** Joseph Schumpeter is known for his theory of economic development, which highlights the role of innovation and entrepreneurship in driving economic growth and development.

70. (D):

(*a*) **Telangana:** With a production of 15,095.4 Thousand Tonnes in 2021-22, Telangana emerged as the state with the highest food grain production among the options provided. This robust production reflects the state's agricultural prowess and its efforts to enhance food security and economic prosperity.

(*b*) **Jharkhand:** Jharkhand recorded a food grain production of 4,984.2 Thousand Tonnes in the same period. While lower compared to Telangana, Jharkhand's production still contributes significantly to the state's economy and sustains livelihoods across rural communities.

(*c*) **Chhattisgarh:** Chhattisgarh's food grain production stood at 8,897.0 Thousand Tonnes in 2021-22, positioning it as a key player in India's agricultural landscape. The state's fertile lands and favorable climatic conditions contribute to its substantial agricultural output.

(*d*) **Andhra Pradesh:** Andhra Pradesh, with a production of 11,266.0 Thousand Tonnes, demonstrates its agricultural resilience and productivity. The state's strategic location and proactive agricultural policies contribute to its consistent performance in food grain production.

71. (C):

(*a*) **Tax Evasion - II. Illegal free riding:** Tax evasion refers to the illegal act of avoiding paying taxes, which can be seen as a form of illegal free riding where individuals benefit from public goods and services without contributing their fair share through taxes.

(*b*) **Effective incidence of tax - IV. Not necessarily correspond to on whom tax is imposed:** The effective incidence of tax refers to the actual burden of taxation, which may not always fall on the same entity or individual on whom the tax is officially imposed.

(*c*) **Legal incidence of tax - III. Obliged to deliver tax revenue to Government:** The legal incidence of tax refers to the legal responsibility or obligation of individuals or entities to deliver tax revenue to the government as per tax laws and regulations.

(*d*) **Fiscal Illusion - I. Bond Financing:** Fiscal illusion refers to the misperception or misunderstanding of the true costs of government spending and taxation, often exacerbated by methods like bond financing, which can obscure the immediate fiscal impact of government actions.

72. (B):

(*a*) **Rapid High Growth - III. 1951-1981:** During this period, India experienced rapid population growth rates, characterized by high birth rates and decreasing death rates, leading to a significant increase in population size.

(*b*) **Stagnant Population - IV. 1891-1921:** This period saw relatively stagnant population growth rates in India, marked by little to no change in the population size due to factors such as high mortality rates, disease outbreaks, and other socio-economic challenges.

(*c*) **High growth with definite signs of slowing down - I. 1981-2011:** In this period, India continued to experience high population growth rates, but there were clear indications of a slowing down in the rate of growth compared to the previous decades, reflecting changes in fertility patterns, healthcare, and socio-economic development.

(*d*) **Steady Growth - II. 1921-1951:** During this period, India had a relatively steady population growth rate, characterized by moderate increases in population size without significant fluctuations or rapid growth spurts.

73. (A):

(*a*) **National Forest Policy (1988):** The National Forest Policy of 1988 aimed to address the growing concerns related to deforestation, forest degradation, and the unsustainable use of forest resources. It emphasized the conservation and sustainable management of forests, recognizing their crucial role in ecological balance, biodiversity conservation, and livelihoods of forest-dependent communities.

(*b*) **Marine Fishing Policy (2004):** The Marine Fishing Policy introduced in 2004 focused on regulating and managing marine fisheries to ensure their sustainability and conservation of marine biodiversity. It aimed to address issues such as overfishing, destructive fishing practices, and conflicts among various stakeholders in the marine sector.

(*c*) **New Mineral Policy (1994):** The New Mineral Policy, implemented in 1994, sought to guide the development and regulation of the mineral sector in India. It aimed to promote responsible and sustainable utilization of mineral resources while ensuring equitable distribution of benefits and addressing environmental concerns.

(*d*) **National Population Policy (2000):** The National Population Policy of 2000 aimed to address population-related challenges such as high population growth rates, maternal and child health, family planning, and population stabilization. It advocated for voluntary and informed reproductive choices, access to quality family planning services, and investments in maternal and child health care.

74. (C)

75. (C)

76. (B): The 14th Finance Commission was operational from April 1, 2015, to March 31, 2020. During this time, it was tasked with recommending the distribution of financial resources between the central government and the states in India. They are:

(*e*) **Forest Cover (Weight: 7.5%):** This criterion considers the extent of forest cover within each state. States with higher forest cover are given a weightage of 7.5%. This factor reflects the ecological significance of forests and the need for conservation efforts.

(*d*) **Demographic Change (2011) (Weight: 10%):** The demographic change criterion accounts for changes in the population profile of states based on the 2011 census. It considers factors such as population growth, urbanization, and migration patterns.

(*b*) **Area (Weight: 15%):** The geographical area of a state is another important factor in fund allocation. Larger states typically have higher administrative and developmental costs due to their size and population dispersion. Therefore, the area criterion, with a weightage of 15%, acknowledges the need to allocate sufficient funds to address the unique challenges faced by states with extensive territorial coverage.

(*c*) **Population (1971) (Weight: 17.5%):** Surprisingly, the 14th Finance Commission used population data from the 1971 census as a criterion for fund distribution. This may seem unconventional, but it was intended to capture the historical context and developmental needs of states based on their population at that time. States with larger populations in 1971 were allocated a higher weightage of 17.5% to address their long-standing developmental challenges.

(*a*) **Income Distance (Weight: 50%):** Income distance refers to the disparity in per capita income among states. This criterion, with the highest weightage of 50%, aims to address economic disparities by allocating a larger share of funds to economically disadvantaged states.

77. (D):

(*e*) **Preferential Trade Arrangements (PTAs):** PTAs are the least integrated form of economic cooperation. They involve agreements between countries to reduce tariffs or other trade barriers on certain goods traded among them. However, these reductions apply only to trade between member countries, while each member maintains its own trade policies with non-members.

(*b*) **Free Trade Area (FTA):** FTAs take economic integration a step further by removing tariffs and trade barriers on goods traded between member countries. However, each member retains control over its trade policies with non-member countries. The North American Free Trade Agreement (NAFTA) and the European

Free Trade Association (EFTA) are examples of free trade areas.

(*a*) **Customs Union:** In a customs union, member countries eliminate tariffs and other trade barriers on goods traded among them. Additionally, they adopt a common external tariff (CET) on imports from non-member countries.

(*d*) **Common Market:** A common market builds on the foundation of a customs union by further integrating the economies of member countries. In addition to the free movement of goods and a common external tariff, it allows for the free movement of services, capital, and labor across borders.

(*c*) **Economic Union:** An economic union represents the highest level of economic integration. It encompasses all the features of a common market, including the free movement of goods, services, capital, and labour, while also harmonizing economic policies such as monetary, fiscal, and social policies among member countries.

78. (A): According to the recommendations of the 15th finance commission the following is the arrangement of the above states in ascending order on the basis of loans received from the central government in the year 2020-21.

- Tamil Nadu
- Madhya Pradesh
- Gujarat
- Karnataka
- Maharashtra

79. (*)

80. (B):

(*c*) IFCI, previously Industrial Finance Corporation of India, is a development finance institution under the ownership of Ministry of Finance, Government of India. Established in 1948 as a statutory corporation, IFCI is currently a company listed on BSE and NSE. IFCI has seven subsidiaries and one associate.

(*a*) The Industrial Credit and Investment Corporation of India (ICICI) is a financial institution established in 1955 by the Government of India, the World Bank, and representatives of Indian industry. ICICI's main purpose is to provide medium-term and long-term financing for Indian businesses' projects.

(*d*) The Industrial Reconstruction Bank of India (IRBI) is a credit and reconstruction agency for industrial revival. It was established in March 1985, replacing the Industrial Reconstruction Corporation of India (IRCI), which was established in 1971 to rehabilitate sick industrial companies.

(*e*) The Export-Import Bank of India (EXIM Bank) was established in 1982. It was established by the Government of India under the Export-Import Bank Act of 1981. EXIM Bank's role is to promote and finance India's international trade.

(*b*) The National Bank for Agriculture and Rural Development (NABARD) is a development bank that focuses on the rural sector of India. It was established in 1982 by an Act of Parliament to promote sustainable and equitable agriculture and rural development. NABARD is head-quartered in Mumbai and has branches across India.

81. (B):

(*b*) **A Treatise on Probability:** Authored by John Maynard Keynes, this work was published in 1921. In this book, Keynes delves into the mathematical theory of probability, addressing various concepts and applications related to probability theory.

(*e*) **A Tract on Monetary Reform:** Published in 1923, this work by John Maynard Keynes discusses various aspects of monetary policy and proposes reforms to stabilize the economy, particularly in the aftermath of World War I and the Treaty of Versailles.

(*d*) **The End of Laissez-Faire:** This essay by John Maynard Keynes was published in 1926. In it, Keynes argues against the laissez-faire economic policy and advocates for government intervention in the economy to address issues such as unemployment and economic instability.

(*c*) **Essays in Persuasion:** Published in 1931, this collection of essays by John Maynard Keynes covers a wide range of economic and political topics. It includes essays written during the turbulent period of the Great Depression, offering Keynes's insights and policy recommendations.

(*a*) **General Theory of Employment, Interest, and Money:** Considered one of Keynes's most influential works, this book was published in 1936. In it, Keynes presents his revolutionary theory on the causes of unemployment and proposes government intervention through fiscal and monetary policies to achieve full employment and economic stability.

82. (B):

(*b*) Foreign Institutional Investors (FIIs) began investing in the Indian securities market in 1996-97. FIIs are institutional investors based in one country that invest in the financial markets of another. FIIs, Non-Resident Indians (NRIs), and Persons of Indian Origin (PIOs) can invest in the primary and secondary capital markets in India through the portfolio investment scheme (PIS).

(*d*) The Securities and Exchange Board of India (SEBI) banned badla trading on the BSE in December 1993, with full effect in March 1994. The ban was made amid complaints from foreign investors, and with the expectation that it would be replaced by a futures-and-options exchange.

(*c*) The National Stock Exchange of India (NSE) began operations in 1993 with the wholesale debt market (WDM) segment on June 30, 1993. It was the first exchange in India to offer an electronic trading facility. The WDM segment provided the first formal screen-based trading facility for the country's debt market on June 30, 1994.

(*e*) The National Stock Exchange (NSE) became the largest stock exchange in India in terms of volume trading within a short span of a year after starting operations in 1995. NSE is the world's largest derivatives exchange by number of contracts traded.

(*a*) The Bombay Stock Exchange (BSE) introduced screen-based trading in 1995. The BSE's screen-based automated trading platform is called BOLT, which stands for BSE On-Line Trading. BOLT is a centralized exchange-based trading system that uses 25,000 trader workstations across over 359 cities in India.

83. (A):

(*a*) **Identification of the structural equations:** This step involves determining the relationships between the endogenous variables in the model. Endogenous variables are those that are determined within the model itself. Identifying these structural equations is crucial as they represent the theoretical underpinnings of the model.

(*d*) **Obtaining reduced form equations:** Once the structural equations are identified, they are then transformed into reduced form equations. These reduced form equations express the endogenous variables solely in terms of the exogenous variables and any predetermined variables.

(*b*) **Application of Ordinary Least Squares (OLS):** With the reduced form equations derived, OLS regression analysis is applied to estimate the parameters of these equations. OLS is a commonly used statistical technique that aims to find the best-fitting line through the data points. In the context of ILS, OLS is used to estimate the coefficients of the reduced form equations based on available data.

(*c*) **Obtaining structural coefficients:** After estimating the reduced form equations using OLS, the next step is to obtain the structural coefficients. This involves applying a transformation to the coefficients obtained from the OLS estimation to retrieve the parameters of the original structural equations.

(*e*) **Use the model for policy:** Once the structural coefficients are obtained, the estimated structural model can be utilized to analyze the effects of different policy interventions or scenarios. By simulating changes in exogenous variables and observing their impact on the endogenous variables, policymakers can assess the implications of various policy decisions.

84. (B): The Constitution (101st Amendment) Act, 2016 introduced the Goods & Services Tax (GST), a comprehensive indirect tax levied on manufacture, sale and consumption of goods as well as services at the national level. GST is a destination-based tax, i.e., they are levied where goods and services are consumed. The Centre would levy Central GST (CGST) and States would levy State GST (SGST) on every supply of goods and services within the state. Integrated GST (IGST) would be levied on all inter-state supplies by the Centre and then transferred to the Destination state.

Revenue received by the Government under the head of Goods and Services Tax (GST) on the somestic supply of Goods and Services.

State	**Total (₹ in crore)**
Madhya Pradesh	27005
Rajasthan	31797
Odisha	29844
Delhi	36568
West Bengal	39694

85. (C):

(*b*) **Tripura (91.58%):** Tripura stands out as the top performer, boasting an impressive literacy rate of 91.58%. This achievement reflects significant progress in educational attainment and underscores the success of various initiatives aimed at promoting literacy.

(*c*) **Sikkim (87.45%):** Sikkim follows closely behind Tripura with an impressive literacy rate of 87.45%. This figure underscores Sikkim's strong commitment to education and the success of its educational policies and programs.

(*a*) **Nagaland (85.31%):** Nagaland occupies a respectable middle ground with a literacy rate of 85.31%. While this figure indicates significant progress in educational attainment, it also suggests room for further improvement.

(*d*) **Manipur (76.94%):** Manipur's literacy rate stands at 76.94%, indicating areas in need of focused efforts to improve educational outcomes. While this figure reflects progress in literacy attainment, it also underscores existing challenges and disparities within the state's education system.

(*e*) **Meghalaya (74.43%):** Meghalaya's literacy rate of 74.43% reflects the challenges the state faces in promoting literacy and educational development. While there has been progress, the figure suggests that Meghalaya lags behind the other states in terms of literacy attainment.

86. (A): Assertion (A) implies that governments may opt to replace import duties with sales taxes if their priority shifts from protecting domestic industries to generating revenue. Import duties, also known as tariffs, are taxes imposed on goods imported into a country, primarily to protect domestic industries from foreign competition. However, if governments prioritize revenue collection over protecting local industries, they might find it more advantageous to replace import duties with sales taxes. Sales taxes are levied on goods and services sold within a country, and they offer a broader base for revenue collection compared to import duties. By implementing sales taxes instead of import duties, governments can generate revenue from a wider range of economic activities, including domestic production and consumption.

Reason (R) complements Assertion (A) by highlighting the efficiency of sales taxes as a revenue-raising mechanism. Sales taxes are generally considered to be more efficient than import tariffs for several reasons. First, sales taxes are typically applied uniformly across a wide range of goods and services, ensuring a more equitable distribution of the tax burden among consumers and businesses. In contrast, import duties only apply to specific imported goods, which can create distortions in the market by favoring domestic producers over foreign competitors. Second, sales taxes are easier to administer and collect compared to import duties, as they are integrated into the regular retail sales process. This simplicity reduces administrative costs and compliance burdens for both businesses and government agencies.

87. (A): Statement I: "Friedman's theory of the demand for money is partly Keynesian and partly non-Keynesian." Milton Friedman's theory of the demand for money, often referred to as the "modern quantity theory of money," incorporates elements from both Keynesian and non-Keynesian perspectives. The Keynesian perspective emphasizes the role of income and transactions in determining the demand for money, while the non-Keynesian perspective focuses more on the role of interest rates and inflation expectations. Friedman's theory combines these perspectives by acknowledging the influence of both income and interest rates on the demand for money. Therefore, Statement I accurately describes Friedman's theory as a blend of Keynesian and non-Keynesian elements.

Statement II: "It is non-Keynesian in that Friedman neglects completely Keynes' clarification of the motives for holding money and the corresponding components of demand for money."

This statement highlights a limitation or criticism of Friedman's theory, specifically regarding its treatment of Keynes' insights into the motives for holding money. Keynes identified three motives for holding money: the transactions motive (holding money for everyday transactions), the precautionary motive (holding money for unforeseen expenses), and the speculative motive (holding money to take advantage of expected changes in asset prices). Therefore, Statement II points out that Friedman's theory is non-Keynesian in the sense that it over-looks or simplifies Keynes' comprehensive explanation of the motives for holding money and their impact on the demand for money.

88. (C): Statement I: "Under first-degree price discrimination, a monopolist sells different units of output for different prices, and these prices may differ from person to person." First-degree price discrimination, also known as perfect price discrimination, represents the scenario where a monopolist charges each consumer the maximum price they are willing to pay for each unit of output. In essence, the monopolist extracts the entire consumer surplus from each individual buyer. This pricing strategy involves the monopolist being able to discern the exact willingness to pay of every consumer, tailoring prices accordingly. As a result, prices can indeed vary from person to person under first-degree price discrimination because each buyer is charged their unique maximum price. Therefore, Statement I is true in describing the characteristic nature of first-degree price discrimination.

Statement II: "Under third-degree price discrimination, a monopolist sells different units of output for different prices, but every individual who buys the same amount of the good pays the same price." Third-degree price discrimination involves segmenting the market into distinct groups based on certain identifiable characteristics such as age, location, or income level. The monopolist then charges different prices to each group based on their differing elasticity's of demand. However, within each group, individuals are charged the same price for the same amount of the good or service. It's important to note that while individuals within a specific group pay the same price, this does not necessarily hold true across all groups. Each group may have its own unique pricing structure. Therefore, while Statement II correctly characterizes the pricing behaviour within a group under third-degree price discrimination, it incorrectly suggests that every individual, irrespective of their group, pays the same price. Hence, Statement II is false.

89. (D): Statement I: "The terms of trade of a nation are defined as the ratio of the cost of its export commodity to the price of its import commodity." The terms of trade refer to the ratio of the prices of a country's exports to the prices of its imports, not the cost of its export commodity to the price of its import commodity. When the terms of trade improve, a country can purchase more imports for a given quantity of exports, while a deterioration in terms of trade means a country can buy fewer imports for the same amount of exports. Therefore, the statement is incorrect because it inaccurately defines the terms of trade.

Statement II: "The terms of trade of the trade partner are equal to the inverse of the terms of trade of the other nation." This statement captures the essence of the reciprocal relationship between the terms of trade of two trading partners. When one nation's terms of trade improve, meaning they can purchase more imports with a given quantity of exports, the terms of trade of its trading partner worsen, indicating that they can buy fewer imports with the same quantity of exports. This inverse relationship reflects the dynamics of international trade, where changes in the terms of trade in one country can affect the terms of trade in its trading partners. Nevertheless, the general idea of the inverse relationship between the terms of trade of trading partners holds true. Therefore, the statement accurately describes this relationship.

90. (A): Statement I: "Division of labour is the starting point of Smith's theory of economic growth." Adam Smith, often regarded as the father of economics, indeed emphasized the significance of division of labour in his theory of economic growth. He argued that division of labour leads to specialization, which in turn increases productivity and output. Smith famously illustrated this concept with his example of pin manufacturing, where specialization among workers dramatically increased production efficiency. Thus, Statement I is true.

Statement II: "It is division of labour that results in the greatest improvement in the productive power of labour." This statement aligns with Adam Smith's views. He famously stated that division of labour leads to the greatest improvement in the productive power of labour. By breaking down production processes into specialized tasks and allowing workers to focus on specific skills, division of labour enhances efficiency and productivity. This specialization enables workers to become more proficient in their tasks and leads to overall increases in output. Therefore, Statement II accurately represents Smith's perspective on the importance of division of labour in boosting the productive power of labour. Thus, Statement II is also true.

91. (D): The passage outlines India's fiscal policy response to the Covid crises, which involved a balanced approach aimed at addressing the economic challenges while maintaining fiscal stability. It mentions increasing food and fertilizer subsidies alongside reducing taxes on fuel and certain imported products as key components of this strategy. However, it notably does not mention an increase in taxes on fuel, indicating that such a measure was not part of the fiscal policy response.

92. (C): The passage discusses India's fiscal policy response to the Covid crises, highlighting a strategic approach that included increasing food and fertilizer subsidies as part of the government's measures. Nowhere does it mention any expenditure austerity measures related to these subsidies. In fact, it suggests the opposite - that the government opted for an expansionary fiscal policy by increasing subsidies on essential goods like food and fertilizer.

93. (B): The passage states that the central government incentivized state governments through interest-free loans and enhanced borrowing ceilings to prioritize their spending on capex. This measure aims to encourage states to allocate more funds towards capital projects, which are crucial for infrastructure development and long-term economic growth.

94. (D): The passage mentions that the center's capex steadily increased from a long-term average of 1.7 percent of GDP during the period FY 09 to FY 20. This indicates that, on average, the Union Government's capital expenditure was equivalent to 1.7 percent of the Gross Domestic Product (GDP) during this period.

95. (A): The passage mentions that the government has boosted allocations on infrastructure-intensive sectors such as roads and highways, railways, and housing and urban affairs, which have a bearing on capital expenditure (capex). Therefore, the sector for which allocation for further enhancement of capex is not increased is: Ports and Waterways.

96. (C): Adjusted Net Saving (ANS) is a flow variable. This means that ANS measures changes in saving over time, reflecting the net additions or subtractions to a nation's wealth from one period to another. Unlike stock variables, which represent values at a specific point in time, flow variables capture the movement or changes in quantities over time.

97. (D): The passage outlines the components that are subtracted from ANS, such as air pollution damage, depletion of metals and minerals, and public expenditures on education, but it does not mention loss of biodiversity. While loss of biodiversity is undoubtedly an important consideration for environmental sustainability, the passage does not include it as a specific component in the calculation of ANS.

98. (B): The passage suggests that nations with higher GDP are less likely to obtain negative ANS, indicating that they are generally adding to their wealth and future material well-being. However, it also notes that when natural resource depletion is not used to invest in other assets in the wealth portfolio, countries' gross saving might not be enough to compensate for this depletion, resulting in negative net savings.

99. (D):

(*a*) **"It allows substitution between different forms of capital":** This statement points out a limitation of ANS, as it allows for substitution between different forms of capital, which may not accurately reflect the sustainability of an economy.

(*b*) **"It is not a comprehensive indicator of per capita wealth":** While ANS provides insights into changes in overall wealth, it may not provide a comprehensive picture of per capita wealth, which is important for assessing individual well-being within a population.

(*c*) **"It is influenced by the level of GDP of an economy":** ANS is indeed influenced by the level of GDP of an economy, as it considers factors such as gross saving rates and investments, which are closely tied to GDP levels.

100. (B): The passage suggests that while ANS may not be a superior indicator of sustainability, it can serve as a useful indicator of unsustainability. ANS provides insights into whether a country is adding to its wealth and future material well-being (when positive) or depleting its capital stocks and potentially reducing future well-being (when negative).

UGC-NET/SET—JRF/Lectureship

ECONOMICS

UNIT I : MICRO ECONOMIC ANALYSIS

DEMAND ANALYSIS

MICRO AND MACRO ECONOMICS

The Subject-matter of economics has been divided into two Parts—**Microeconomics** and **Macroeconomics. Ragner Frisch** was the first to use the terms "micro" and "macro" in economics in **1933.** The term microeconomics is derived from the Greek word **mikros,** meaning **"small"** and the term macroeconomics is derived from the Greek word **makros,** meaning **"large"**. Thus micro economics related to the study of individual economic units while the latter is a study of the economy as a whole.

Micro Economics

Microeconomics is the study of economic actions and behaviour of individual units and small groups. In the other words, in microeconomics we make a microscopic study of the economy. The determination of equilibrium output of the firm or industry, the wage of a particular type of labour, the price of a particular commodity are some of the fields of microeconomics theory. Thus the theory of product pricing and the theory of factor pricing (or the theory of distribution) fall within the domain of microeconomics. The whole content of microeconomic theory is presented in the following chart :

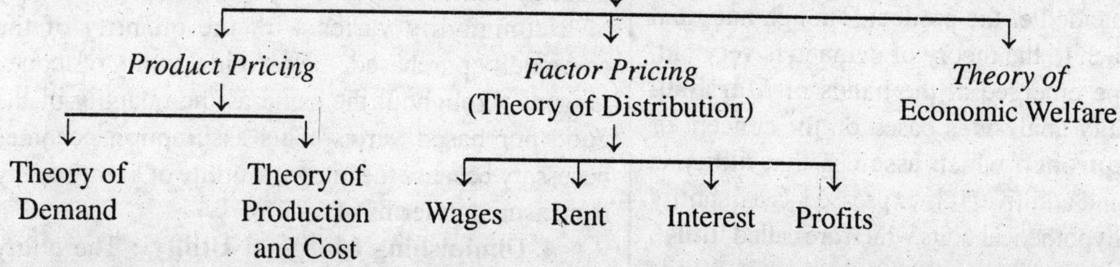

Macro Economics

Macroeconomics is the study of aggregates or averages covering the entire economy, such as total employment, the national product or income, the general price level of the economy. Therefore, macroeconomics is also known as **aggregative economics.** Macroeconomics analyses and establishes the functional relationship between these large aggregates. Thus **Professor Boulding** says, "Macroeconomics deals not with individuals quantities as such but with the aggregates of these quantities; not with individual incomes but with the national income; not with individual prices but with the price level; not with individual outputs but with the national output."

Macroeconomics is also known as the theory of income and employment, or simply income analysis. It is concerned with the problems of unemployment, economic fluctuations, inflation or deflation, international trade and economic growth.

We have now stated, in brief, all aspects of macroeconomic theory. These various aspects of macroeconomic theory are shown, in the following chart :

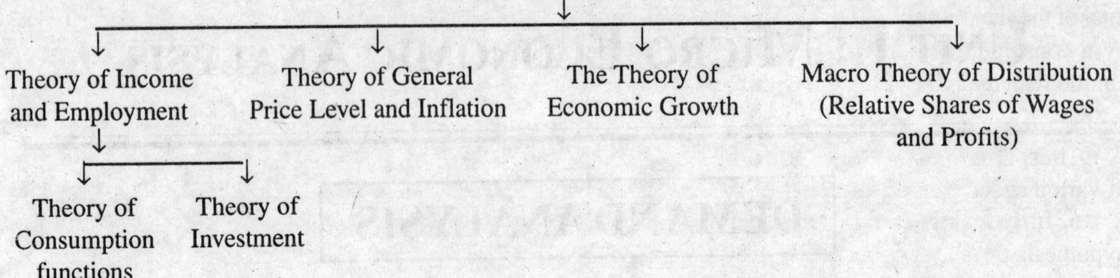

CONSUMER DEMAND THEORY

There are two basic approaches to the study of consumer demand theory. The first, or **classical approach,** involves the use of measurable marginal utility (satisfaction). It is generally called the **Cardinal utility approach.** The second, or indifference curve approach, is generally called the **ordinal approach.**

MARGINAL UTILITY ANALYSIS

Marginal utility analysis is the oldest theory of demand which provides an explanation of Consumer's demand for a product and it derives the law of demand which establishes an inverse relationship between price and quantity demanded of the product. Though marginal utility approach to the theory of demand is very old, its final shape emerged at the hands of **Marshall.** Marginal utility analysis is based on the concept of **Cardinal approach** which assumes that utility is measurable and additive. It is expressed as a quantity measured in hypothetical units which are called **'utils'.** If a consumer imagines that one mango has 8 utils and an apple 4 utils, it implies that the utility of one mango is twice that of an apple.

BASIC ASSUMPTIONS OF MARGINAL UTILITY ANALYSIS

Marginal utility analysis of demand is based upon certain important assumptions. Before explaining how utility analysis explains consumer's equilibrium in regard to the demand for goods, it is essential to describe those basic assumptions on which the whole utility analysis rests. The following are the main assumptions.

1. Rationality : The consumer is rational. He aims at the maximisation of his utility subject to the constraint imposed by his given income.

2. Cardinal Utility : The utility of each commodity is measurable. Utility is a Cardinal concept. The most convenient measure is money. The utility is measured by the monetary units that the consumer is prepared to pay for another unit of the commodity.

3. Constant Marginal Utility of Money : Another important assumption of the marginal utility analysis is that the marginal utility of money remains constant even though the quantity of money with consumer is diminished by the successive purchases made by him. It is assumed that while marginal utility of a commodity varies with the quantity of the commodity purchased, the marginal utility of money remains throughout the same as the quantity of the good purchased varies. This assumption becomes necessary because the marginal utility of a commodity is measured in terms of money.

4. Diminishing Marginal Utility : The utility gained from successive units of a commodity diminishes. In other words, the marginal utility of a commodity diminishes as the consumer acquires large quantities of it. This is the axion of **diminishing marginal utility.**

5. Utilities are Independent : Marginal utility analysis assumes that the utilities of different commodities are independent of one another. That is, the utility of one commodity does not in any way affect that of another. In other words, the satisfaction derived from the consumption of one good is the function of that good alone and is not affected by the consumption of another. On this assumption, the total utility of all goods consumed by a consumer is simply the sum of total of the separate utilities of all the goods consumed by a consumer. If there are *'n'* commodities in the bundle with quantities $x_1, x_2, ..., x_n$, the total utility is

$$U = f(x_1, x_2, ... x_n)$$

Thus, according to this assumption, the utilities of various goods are **additive.**

6. Introspective Method : Another important hypothesis of the marginal utility analysis is the use of introspective method in judging the behaviour of marginal utility. "Introspection is the ability of the observer to reconstruct events which go on in the mind of another person with the help of self-observation. This form of comprehension may be just guess work or intuition or the result of long-lasting experience."

TOTAL UTILITY AND MARGINAL UTILITY

When a consumer purchases a good, he obtains satisfaction from the possession of that good. That is, he derives utility from the possession of the good. When the consumer buys apples he receives them in units, 1, 2, 3, 4, etc. 2 apples have more utility than 1, 3 more utility than 2, and 4 more than 3. The units of apples which the consumer chooses are in a descending order of their utilities. In his estimation, the first apple is the best out of the lot available to him and thus gives him the highest satisfaction, measured as 20 utils. The second apple will naturally be the second best with lesser amount of utility than the first, and has 15 utils. The third apple has 10 utils and the fourth 5 utils. In our illustration, the total utility of two apples is 35 = 20 + 15 utils, of three apples is 45 = 20 + 15 + 10 utils, and of four apples is 50 = 20 + 15 + 10 + 5. **Marginal utility is the addition made to total utility by having an additional unit of the commodity.** The total utility of the two apples is 35 utils. When the consumer consumes the third apple, the total utility becomes 45 utils. Thus, marginal utility of the third apple is 10 utils (45 – 35). In other words, marginal utility is defined as the change in total utility resulting from a unit change in the consumption of the good in question per unit of time.

Algebraically, the marginal utility (MU) of n units of a commodity is the total utility (TU) of n units minus the total utility of $(n - 1)$. Thus,

$$MU_n = TU_n - TU_{n-1}$$

The relation between the total and marginal utility is explained with the help of Table 1.1.

TABLE 1.1

Units of Apple	*TU in Utils*	*MU in Utils*
0	0	0
1	20	20
2	35	15
3	45	10
4	50	5
5	50	0
6	45	– 5
7	35	– 10

So long as total utility is increasing, marginal utility is decreasing upto the 4th unit. When total utility is maximum (at the fifth unit), marginal utility is zero. It is the point of **Satiety (Saturation)** for the consumer. When total utility is decreasing, marginal utility is negative.

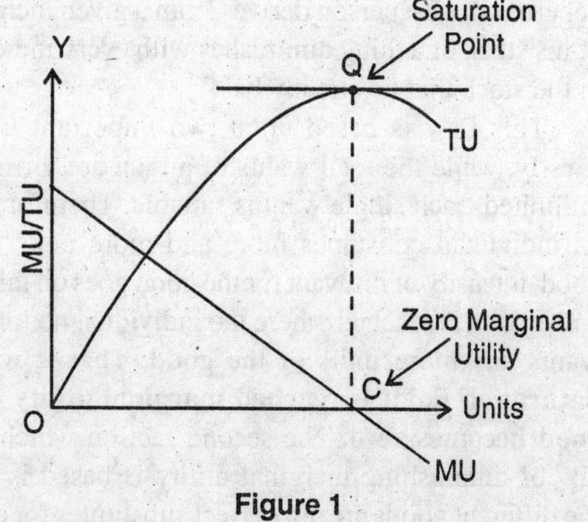

Figure 1

In Figure 1, TU is the total utility curve and MU is the marginal utility curve. Geometrically the marginal utility curve is the slope of the total utility curve. So long as the TU curve is rising, the MU curve is falling. When the former reaches the highest point Q, the latter touches the X-axis at C where MU is zero and when the TU starts falling from Q and the MU becomes negative from C onwards.

LAW OF DIMINISHING MARGINAL UTILITY

Satisfaction of human wants follows some very importants laws and one of them is the Law of Diminishing Marginal utility. **Hermann Heinrich Gossen** was the first to formulate this law in 1854 though the name was given by Marshall. **Javons** called it **Gossen's First Law.** Gossen stated it thus. "The magnitude of one and the same satisfaction, when we continue to enjoy it without interruption, continually decreases until satisfaction is reached." According to this law the marginal utility of a good diminishes as an individual consumes more units of a good. In other words, as a consumer takes more units of a good, the extra utility or satisfaction that he derives from an extra unit of the good goes on falling. It should be carefully noted that it is the marginal utility and not the total utility that declines with the increase in the consumption of a good. The law of diminishing marginal utility means that the total utility increases but at a decreasing rate.

Marshall states the Law thus : "The additional benefits which a person derives from a given increase of his stock of a thing diminishes with every increase in the stock that he already has."

This Law is based upon two important facts. **Firstly,** while the total wants of a man are virtually unlimited, each single want is satiable. Therefore, as an individual consumes more and more units of a good, intensity of his want for the good goes on falling and a point is reached where the individual no longer wants any more units of the good. That is **when Saturation Point is reached marginal utility of a good becomes zero.** The second fact on which the law of diminishing marginal utility is based is that the different goods are not perfect substitutes for each other in the satisfaction of various particular wants. When an individual consumes more and more units of a good, the intensity of his particular want for the good diminishes but if the units of that good could be devoted to the satisfaction of other wants and yielded as much satisfaction as they did initially in the satisfaction of the first want, marginal utility of the good would not have diminished.

The significance of the diminishing marginal utility of a good for the theory of demand is that the quantity demanded of a good rises as the price falls and **vice-versa.** Thus it is because of the diminishing marginal utility that the demand curve slopes downward.

Law of diminishing marginal utility is a universal law and applies to all objects of desire including money. But, it is worth mentioning that marginal utility of money is generally never zero or negative. Money represents purchasing power over all other goods, that is, a man can satisfy all his material wants if he possesses enough money. Since man's total wants are practically unlimited, therefore the marginal utility of money to him never falls to zero.

Its Limitations

Law of diminishing marginal utility holds only under certain conditions —

(a) There should be continuity in the consumption of the commodity. Units of the commodity should be consumed in succession at one particular time.

(b) There should be no change in the taste, habit, custom, fashion and income of the consumer.

(c) All units of a commodity should be of the same weight and quality.

(d) Units of the commodity should be of a suitable size. Giving water to a thirsty person by spoons will increase utility of the subsequent spoons of water.

(e) Prices of the different units and of the substitutes of the commodity should remain the same.

LAW OF EQUI-MARGINAL UTILITY

The Law of equi-marginal utility is known by various names. It is termed as the Law of substitution, the Law of Maximum Satisfaction and **Gossen's Second Law.**

Law of equi-marginal utility occupies an important place in marginal utility analysis. It is through the principle that **Consumer's equilibrium is explained.** A consumer has a given income which he has to spend on various goods he wants. Now the question is how he would allocate his money income between various goods, that is to say, what would be his equilibrium position in respect of the purchases of the various goods.

Suppose there are only two goods A and B on

which consumer has to spend a given income. The consumer's behaviour will be governed by two factors: **Firstly,** by the marginal utilities of the goods and **secondly,** by the prices of two goods. Suppose the prices of the goods are given for the consumer. The Law of equi-marginal utility states that the consumer will distribute his money income between the goods in such a way that the utility derived from the last rupee spent on each good is equal. In other words, the consumer will spend his money income on different goods in such a way that marginal utility of each good is proportional to its price. That is, consumer is in equilibrium in respect of the purchases of two goods A and B when

$$\frac{MU_A}{P_A} = \frac{MU_B}{P_B}$$

where MU_A is the marginal utility of A, MU_B is the marginal utility of B and P_A is the price of A, P_B is the price of B.

Now, if $\frac{MU_A}{P_A}$ and $\frac{MU_B}{P_B}$ are not equal and $\frac{MU_A}{P_A}$ is greater than the $\frac{MU_B}{P_B}$, then the consumer will substitute good A for good B. As a result of this substitution, the marginal utility of good A will fall and marginal utility of good B will rise. The consumer will continue substituting good A for good B till $\frac{MU_A}{P_A}$ becomes equal to $\frac{MU_B}{P_B}$. When $\frac{MU_A}{P_A}$ becomes equal to $\frac{MU_B}{P_B}$, the consumer will be in equilibrium.

But the equality of $\frac{MU_A}{P_A}$ with $\frac{MU_B}{P_B}$ can be achieved not only at one level but at different levels of expenditure. The question is how far does a consumer go in purchasing the goods he wants. This is determined by the size of his money income.

If there are more than two goods on which the consumer is spending his income, the above equation must hold good for all of them. Thus

$$\frac{MU_A}{P_A} = \frac{MU_B}{P_B} = \ldots\ldots = \frac{MU_n}{P_n}$$

Law of equi-marginal utility is explained with the help of table given below –

TABLE 1.2

Number of units	MU_A	MU_B
1	20	24
2	18	21
3	16	18
4	14	15
5	12	9
6	10	3

Let the prices of goods A and B are Rs. 2 and Rs. 3 respectively. Reconstructing the above table by dividing marginal utilities of A (MU_A) by Rs. 2 and marginal utilities of B (MU_B) by Rs. 3 We get :

TABLE 1.3

Number of units	$\frac{MU_A}{P_A}$	$\frac{MU_B}{P_B}$
1	10	8
2	9	7
3	8	6
4	7	5
5	6	3
6	5	1

By looking at the table it is clear that $\frac{MU_A}{P_A}$ is equal to 6 utils when the consumer purchases 5 units of good A and 3 units of good B and will be spending (Rs. 2 × 5 + Rs. 3 × 3) = Rs. 19 on them.

The principle of equi-marginal utility is explained in terms of the Figure 2.

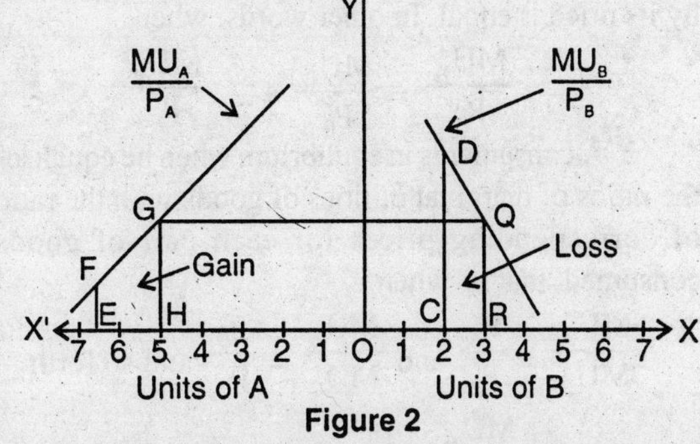

Figure 2

In this figure, along the axis OX, from left to right (*i.e.,* on the portion OX) is measured the quantity of the good B and from right to left (*i.e.,* on the portion OX′) is measured the quantity of the good A. The Y-axis measures $\frac{MU_A}{P_A}$ and $\frac{MU_B}{P_B}$. Since marginal utility curves of goods slope downward, curves depticting $\frac{MU_A}{P_A}$ and $\frac{MU_B}{P_B}$ will also slope downward.

The horizontal line GQ satisfies both the conditions of equilibrium, *i.e.,* the $\frac{MU_A}{P_A} = \frac{MU_B}{P_B}$ and the consumer spends the whole of his income on the two commodities. He purchases five units of A and three units of good B.

In this way, he will derive maximum satisfaction and any other arrangement will only reduce the aggregate satisfaction. To prove this, suppose the consumer spends Rs. 3 more on the good A and consequently Rs. 3 less on the good B. As a result, the marginal utilities will become unequal (DC is greater than FE). In this case, the gain in utility is less than the loss. Since this rearrangement in the purchase of goods does not satisfy the condition of equilibrium (the equality of ratios between marginal utilities to price of A and B), the consumer is not in equilibrium. Therefore, the previous sequence of expenditure was giving maximum satisfaction to the consumer.

The above equi-marginal condition for the equilibrium of the consumer can be stated in three ways:

1. A consumer is in equilibrium when he equalises weighted marginal utilities of all goods, that is, when the marginal utility of each good weighted by its price is equal. In other words, when

$$\frac{MU_A}{P_A} = \frac{MU_B}{P_B} = ... \frac{MU_n}{P_n}$$

2. A consumer is in equlibrium when he equalises the ratios of marginal utilities of goods with the ratio of corresponding prices for each pair of goods consumed, that is, when

$$\frac{MU_A}{MU_B} = \frac{P_A}{P_B} \text{ and } \frac{MU_B}{MU_C} = \frac{P_B}{P_C} \text{ and so forth.}$$

3. Since $\frac{MU_A}{P_A}$ measures the marginal utility of a rupee's worth of each good consumed at the given price, consumer can be said to be in equilibrium when the marginal utility of a rupee spent on each good purchased is equal. Marginal utility of a rupee spent on a good means the marginal utility of rupee's worth of good.

DEMAND

Demand is a function of price, income, price of related goods and tastes and is expressed as

$$D = f(p, y, pr, t).$$

When income, prices of related goods and tastes are given, the demand function is

$$D = f(p).$$

It shows quantities of a commodity purchased at given prices. Demand is also related to a period of time. In the **Marshallian analysis,** the other determinants of demand are taken as given and constant.

Types of Demand

Three kinds of demands may be distinguished :

(*a*) Price Demand

(*b*) Income Demand

(*c*) Cross Demand

Price Demand : Price demand refers to the various quantities of a commodity or service that a consumer or service that a consumer would purchase at a given time in a market at various hypothetical prices. It is assumed that other things, such as consumer's income, his tastes and prices of inter-related goods, remain unchanged.

The demand of the individual consumer is called **Individual Demand** and the total demand of all the consumers combined for the commodity or service is called **Industry Demand.** The total demand for the product of an individual firm at various prices is known as firm's demand or **Individual Seller's Demand.**

Income Demand : The income demand refers to the various qualities of goods and services which would be purchased by the consumers at various levels of incomes. Here we assume that the price of the commodity or service as well as the prices of inter-related goods and the tastes and desires of consumers do not change.

Cross Demand : The cross demand means the quantities of a good or service which will be purchase with reference to change in price not of this good but of other inter-related goods. These goods are either substitutes or complementary goods. A change in the price of tea, for instance, will affect the demand for coffee.

Law of Demand

This law expresses a relationship between the quantity demanded and its price. It may be defined in Marshall's words as "the amount demanded increase with a fall in price, and diminishes with a rise in price." Thus it expresses an inverse relation between price and demand. The inverse price-demand relationship is based on **other things remaining equal.** This phrase points towards certain important assumption on which this law is based.

These assumptions are :

(i) There is no change in the tastes and preferences of the consumer;

(ii) The income of the consumer remains constant;

(iii) There is no change in customs;

(iv) There should not be any change in the prices of other products;

(v) There should not be any change in the quality of the product;

(vi) The habits of the consumers should remain unchanged.

Given these conditions, the law of demand operates. If there is change even in one of these conditions, it will stop operating.

Why Demand Curve Slopes Downwards?

Generally, a demand curve slope downward from left to right. The following are the main reasons for the downward sloping demand curve.

1. The law of demand is based on the law of diminishing marginal utility. According to this law, when a consumer buys more units of a commodity, the marginal utility of that commodity continues to decline. Therefore, the consumer will but more units of that commodity only when its price falls. When less units are available, utility will be high and the consumer will be prepared to pay more for the commodity. This proves that the demand will be more at a lower price and it will be less at a higher price. That is why the demand curve is downward sloping.

2. Every commodity has certain consumers but when its price falls, new consumers start consuming it, as a result demand increases. On the contrary, with the increase in the price of the product, many consumers will either reduce or stop its consumptions and the demand will be reduced. Thus due to the **price effect** when consumers consume more or less of the commodity, the demand curve slopes downward.

3. When the price of a commodity falls, the real income of the consumer increases because he has to spend less in order to buy the same quantity. On the contrary, with the rise in the price of the commodity, the real income of the consumer falls. This is called the **income effect.** Under the influence of this effect with the fall in the price of the commodity the consumer buys more of it and also spends a portion of the increased income in buying other commodities. Thus, due to the income effect the demand curve slopes downward.

4. The other effect of change in the price of the commodity is the **substitution effect.** With the fall in the price of a commodity, the price of its substitutes remaining the same, consumes will buy more of this commodity rather than the substitutes. As a result, its demand will increase. On the contrary, with the rise in the price of the commodity its demand will fall.

5. There are different uses of certain commodities and services that are responsible for the negative slope of the demand curve. With the increase in the price of such products, they will be used only for more important uses and their demand will fall. On the contrary with the fall in price, they will be put to various uses and their demand will rise.

Exceptions to the Law of Demand

As we have said above, generally the demand curve slopes downward to the left. But some times, the demand curve, instead of sloping downward, will rise upwards. In other words, some time people will buy more when the price rises. This can be represented only by a rising demand curve. These were first investigated by **Sir Robert Giffen.** The **Giffen Paradox** holds that the demand is strengthened with a rise or weakened with a fall in price.

Many causes are attributed to an upward sloping demand curve :

1. War

2. Depression

3. Giffen Paradox
4. Demonstration Effect
5. Speculation

Increase and Decrease Vs. Extensive and Contraction of Demand

When the demand changes merely because the price has changed, it is a case of **extension** or **contraction.** If the change in demand is due to a factor other than the price, it is known as **increase** or **decrease** in demand.

A **movement along a demand curve** indicates that a different quantity is being demanded because the price has changed. A shift of a demand curve indicates that different quantity will be demanded at each possible price because something else, either incomes, tastes or the price of some other good, has changed.

When we refer to a movement along a curve, to a change in the quantity demanded because price has changed, we shall refer to a change in the **quantity demanded,** specifically, to an increase in the quantity demanded, indicating a movement down the curve because of a fall in price, or a decrease in the quantity demanded, indicating a movement up the curve because of a rise in price.

When the economist speaks of an **increase** or a **decrease** of demand, he is usually referring to a **shift of the whole curve.**

In the Figure 3, when price rises from QB to PA, demand **contracts** from OB to OA. The movement on the demand curve is to the left from Q to P. On the other hand, a fall in the price from RC to SD brings an **extension** in demand from OC to OD. It is a movement to the right on the same demand curve from R to S.

Figure 4 illustrates an increase and decrease in demand. Let D be the original demand curve where at price OP, quantity OB is demanded. D_1 shows an increase in demand. An increase in demand can be either of the two ways : larger quantity at the same price or the same quantity at a higher price. When the demand increases to D_1, larger quantity OC is bought at the original Price OP, or the same quantity OB is bought at the higher price OP_1. On the contrary, a decrease in demand implies same quantity at a lower price or smaller quantity at the same price, D_2 shows

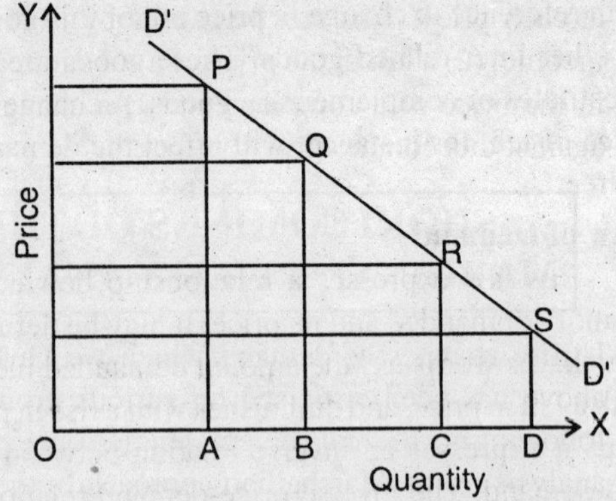

Fig. 3: *Extension and Contraction of Demand*

decrease in demand, the same quantity OB is bought at the lower price OP_2 or the smaller quantity PT is purchased at the same price OP. Demand curves are thus not stationary, rather they shift to the right or left due to a number of causes. They are changes in tastes, habits and customs of the consumers; changes in income expenditure; changes in the prices of substitutes and complements; expectations about future changes in prices and incomes; and changes in the age and composition of the population.

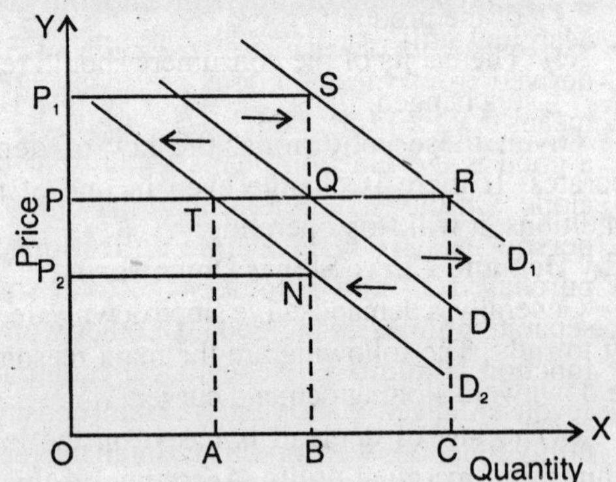

Fig. 4: *Increase and Decrease of Demand*

***A Rise (Increase) in Demand :** The demand curve shifts to the right indicating that more is demanded at each price. This can be caused by : (1) a rise in income; (2) a rise in the price of a substitute; (3) a fall in the price of a complement; (4) a change in tastes in favour of this commodity.

***A Fall (Decrease) in Demand :** The demand curve shifts to the left indicating that less is demanded at each price. This can be causes by : (1) a fall in income; (2) a fall in the price of a substitute; (3) a rise in the price of a complement; (4) a change in taste against this commodity.

SHORTCOMINGS OF THE MARGINAL UTILITY ANALYSIS

Utility analysis of demand which we have studied above has been criticised on various grounds. The following are the main defects pointed out in the utility analysis or the Marshallian approach to the demand theory.

1. Cardinal Measurability of Utility is Unrealistic : Marginal utility analysis of demand is based on the assumption that utility can be measured in absolute, objective and quantitative terms. But in actual practice utility cannot be measured in such quantitative or cardinal terms. Since utility is a psychic feeling and a subjective thing, it cannot therefore be measured in quantitative terms. In real life, consumers are only able to compare the satisfactions derived from various goods or various combinations of the goods.

2. Hypothesis of Independent Utility is Wrong: Marginal utility analysis also assumes that utilities derived from various goods are independent. This means that the utility which a consumer derived from a good is the function of the quantity of that good alone. On this assumption, the total utility which a person gets from the whole collection of goods purchased by him is simply the total sum of the separate utilities of the good. In other words, utility function is **additive.** Neoclassical economists such Jevons, Menger, Walras and Marshall considered that utility functions were additive. But in the real life this is not so. In actual life the utility or satisfaction derived from a good depends upon the availability of some other goods which may either be substitute for or complementary with the good.

3. Assumption of Constant Marginal Utility of Money is Wrong : Further, the utility analysis is based on the assumption that when a consumer spends varying amount on a good or various goods or when the price of a good changes, the marginal utility of money remains unchanged. But in actual practice this is not correct. As a consumer spends his money income on the goods, money income left with him declines. With the decline in money income of the consumer as a result of increase in his expenditure on goods, the marginal utility of money to him rises. Further, when the price of a commodity changes, the real income of the consumer also changes. With this increase in real income, marginal utility of money will change and this would have an effect on the demand for the good in question even the total money income available with the consumer remains the same. But marginal utility analysis ignores all this and does not take cognizance of the changes in real income and its effect on demand for goods following the change in the price of a good.

4. Income Effect and Substitution Effect Not Brought out : Another shortcoming of the marginal utility analysis is that it does not distinguish between the income effect and the substitution effect of the price change. We know, for instance, that when the price of a commodity falls, the consumer feels as if his income has increased and he is able to purchase more. This is the income effect. Also, the consumer substitutes the cheaper commodity for some other rival commodities. This is the substitution effect. The utility analysis does not clearly distinguish between the income effect and substitution effect in a price change. It is unable to explain how much of the increased demand is due to the income effect and how much to the substitution effect.

5. Does Not Explain Giffen Paradox : By not visualising the price effect as a combination of substitution and income effects and ignoring the income effect of the price change, **Marshell** could not explain Giffen Paradox. He treated it merely as an exception to his law of demand.

6. Demand to One-Commodity World : The Marshallian law of demand cannot be genuinely derived from the utility analysis on the assumption of constant marginal utility of money except in one-commodity world. The assumption of constant marginal utility is not compatible with the law of demand in a situation where a consumer has more than one commodity to spend his income on. In a multi-commodity model, the marginal utility of money does not remain the same. When a consumer has to spend his income on a number of goods, there must occur a change in the marginal utility of money with every change in the price of a good. When the marginal utility of money does not remain the same, utility ceases to be measurable and the marginal utility analysis breaks down.

7. Marginal Utility Analysis Assumes too much and Explains too Little : Marginal utility analysis is also criticised on the ground that it takes more assumptions and also more restrictive ones than those of ordinal utility analysis of indifference curves technique.

MARGINAL UTILITY ANALYSIS AS MODIFIED BY MODERN ECONOMISTS

We have seen above that marginal utility analysis as propounded by Marshall and earlier economists suffered from two crucial flaws. **Firstly,** it assumed that marginal utility of money expenditure remains, constant. It is because of this assumption that Marshall ignored the income effect of the price change and therefore could not explain **Giffen Paradox. Secondly,** Marshallian utility analysis assumed that utilities derived from different goods are independent of each other. Because of this some modern economists such as **Blaug, Fellner and Bilas** have presented the marginal utility analysis without assuming constancy of marginal utility of money and independence of utilities of different goods. With this they have been able to account for income effect and explain Giffen goods, substitutes and complementary goods even with marginal utility analysis based upon the cardinal measurement of utility. It should be noted that while these modern economists have discarded the assumptions of constancy of marginal utility of money and the independence of utilities, they have retained the cardinal measurability of utility which is the distinguishing characteristic of marginal utility analysis as compared to ordinal measurement of utility on which the alternative approach of indifference curve analysis is based.

ELASTICITY

In this section we shall consider the degree to which the quantity demanded and the quantity supplied respond to changes in price. The concept of elasticity has a very great importance in economic theory as well as in applied economics.

Various Concepts of Demand Elasticity

It is price elasticity of demand which is usually referred to as elasticity of demand. But, besides price elasticity of demand, there are various other concepts of demand elasticity. Demand for a good is determined by its price, incomes of the people, prices of related goods etc. Quantity demanded of a good will change as a result of a change in the size of any of these determinants of demand. The concept of elasticity of demand therefore refers to the **degree of responsiveness** of quantity demanded of a good to a change in its price, income or prices of related goods. Accordingly, there are three kinds of demand elasticity–

1. Price Elasticity
2. Income Elasticity
3. Cross Elasticity

Price Elasticity of Demand

Price elasticity means the degree of **responsiveness** or **sensitiveness** of quantity demanded of a good to a changes in its prices. In other words, Price elasticity of demand is a measure of the relative change in quantity purchased of a good in response to a relative change in its Price. Price elasticity can be precisely defined as "the proportional change in the quantity purchased divided by the proportional change in price." Thus

$$\text{Price Elasticity} = -\frac{\text{Percentage change in quantity}}{\text{Percentage change in price}}$$

$$= -\frac{\text{Change in quantity demanded / Quantity demanded}}{\text{Change in price / Price}}$$

or, in symbolic terms

$$e_P = -\frac{\Delta q / q}{\Delta P / P} = -\frac{\Delta q}{q} \times \frac{P}{\Delta P}$$

where,

e_P stands for price elasticity

q stands for quantity

P stands for price

Δ stands for change

Mathematically speaking, Price elasticity of

demand is negative. Since demand curves slope down wards, the change in quantity will always have the opposite sign to the change in price. The minus sign in the definition of elasticity is simply designed to **'neutralize'** this negative relation between price and quantity changes and thus to make elasticity of demand a positive number. This is a matter of convenience only; it has no more profound Justification than that.

Marshall who Introduced the Concept of Elasticity into Economic Theory remarks that the elasticity or responsiveness of demand in a market is great or small accordingly as the amount demanded increases much or little for a given fall in Price, and diminishes much or little for a given rise in price. This will be clear from figures. Figures A and B represent two demanded curves.

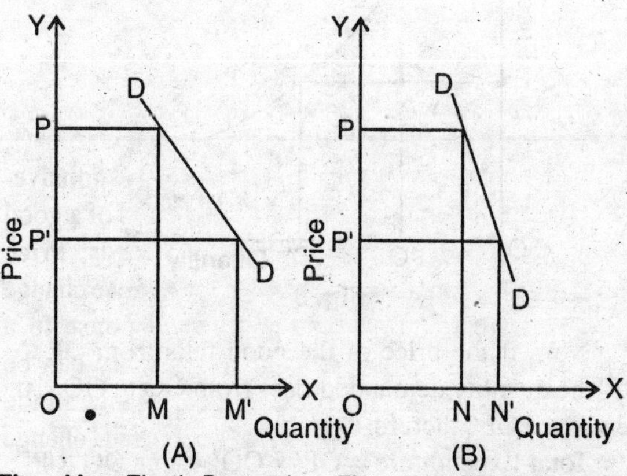

Fig. : *More Elastic Demand* **Fig. :** *Less Elastic Demand*

For a given fall in price, from OP to OP′, increase in quantity demanded is much greater in Fig. A than in Fig. B. Therefore, demand curve in Figure A is more elastic than the demand curve of Fig. B, for a given fall in price. Demand for the good represented in Fig. A is generally said to be elastic and the demand for good in Fig. B to be inelastic.

Interpreting Numerical Values of Elasticity of Demand

The numerical value of elasticity can vary from zero to infinity. Elasticity is zero if there is no change at all in quantity demanded when price changes, *i.e.,* when quantity demanded does not respond to a price change. The larger the elasticity, the larger the percentage change in quantity for a given percentage change in price. As long as the elasticity of demand has a value of less than one, however, the percentage change in quantity is less than the percentage change in price. When elasticity is equal to one, then the two percentage changes are equal to each other. While, when the percentage change in quantity exceeds the percentage change in price, then the value for the elasticity of demand will be greater than one.

When the percentage change in quantity is less than percentage change in price (elasticity less than one), the demand in said to be **INELASTIC.** When the percentage change in quantity is greater than the percentage change in price (elasticity greater than one), the demand is said to be **ELASTIC.**

Price Elasticity : Measures, Meaning and Nomeclature

Numerical measure of elasticity	*Verbal description*	*Terminology*
* Zero	Quantity demanded does not change as price changes	Perfectly inelastic
* Greater than Zero, but less than one	Quantity demanded changes by a smaller percentage than does price.	Inelastic
* One	Quantity demanded changes by exactly the same percentage as does price.	Unit elasticity
* Greater than one, but less than infinity	Quantity demanded changes by a larger percentage than does price	Elastic
* Infinity	Purchasers are prepared to buy all they can obtain at some price and none at all at an even slightly higher price	Perfectly elastic

We may now consider briefly the graphical representation of demand curves of various elasticity. These are summarized in Figure 5. Zero elasticity occurs when the quantity demanded does not change as the price changes. The graph of a demand curve of zero elasticity will thus be a vertical straight line indicating that the same quantity is demanded whatever the price. Unit elasticity occurs when a given percentage change in quantity at all points on the curve. The graph of a curve of unit elasticity over its whole range is shown in Figure 5 *(ii).* A demand curve

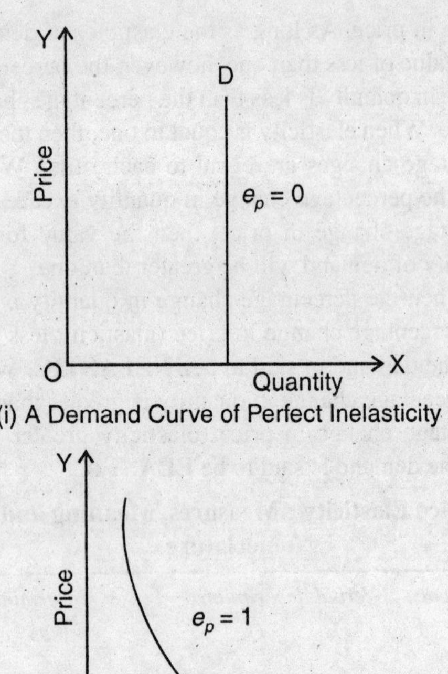

(i) A Demand Curve of Perfect Inelasticity

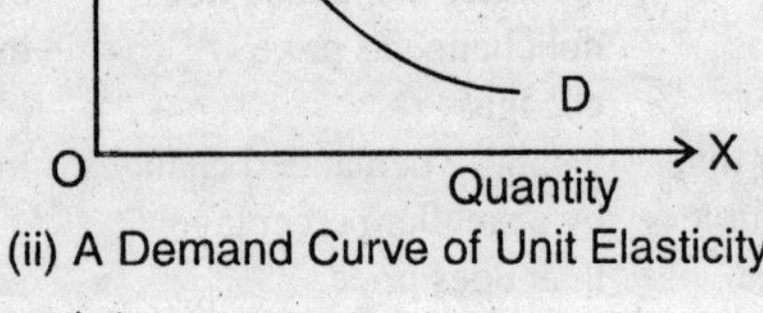

(ii) A Demand Curve of Unit Elasticity

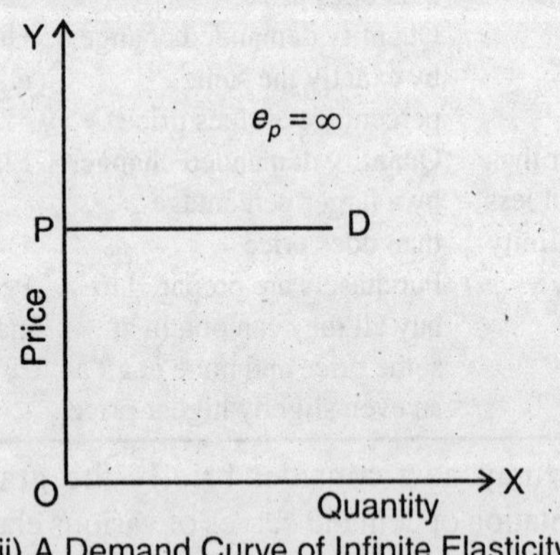

(iii) A Demand Curve of Infinite Elasticity

Fig. 5

of infinite elasticity means that there exists some small price reduction which raises the demand from zero to infinity. This case occurs when, at some price, consumers will but all that they can obtain of the commodity (an infinite amount if they could get it), while at an even slightly higher price they would but nothing at all. In Figure 5 *(iii)*, demand is zero for all prices above OP but at price OP demand is infinite.

Price Elasticity and Changes in Total Expenditure

It is often useful to known what happens to total expenditure made by the consumers on a good when its price changes. In Figure 6, a demand curve DD of a good is shown. When the price of the good is OP, its quantity demanded is OQ. Since the total expenditure is price multiplied by the quantity of the good purchased, therefore

Consumer's Total Expenditure = OP × OQ
= area OQRP

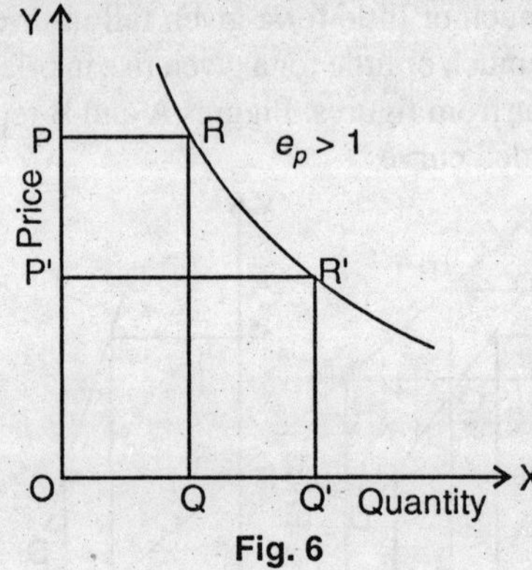

Fig. 6

Now, if the price of the good falls from OP to OP′ the quantity demanded rises from OQ to OQ′. At new Price OP′, therefore

Total Expenditure = OP′ × OQ′ = area OQ′R′P′

Now, whether the total expenditure rises or falls or remains the same with the change in the price of the good depends upon the price elasticity of demand. The total expenditure bears an important relationship with the price elasticity of demand and this relationship is

1. When Price elasticity of demand is equal to unit ($e_P = 1$), the total expenditure remains the same with the fall or rise in price.
2. When Price elasticity of demand is greater than one ($e_p > 1$), the total expenditure will increase with the fall in price and will decrease with the rise in price.
3. When Price elasticity of demand is less than one ($e_P < 1$), the total expenditure will decrease with the fall in price and will increase with the rise in price.

of great significance in the theory of price. The following is the relationship between changes in total expenditure and Price elasticity of demand.

Measurement of Elasticity At A Point On The Demand Curve

Prof. Marshall devised a geometrical method for measuring elasticity at a point on the demand curve.

Let RS be a straight line demand curve. If the Price falls from PB (= OA) to MD (= OC), the quantity demanded increases from OB to OD. Elasticity at point P on RS demand curve according to the formula is

$$e_P = \frac{\Delta q}{\Delta P} \cdot \frac{P}{q}$$

From Fig. 7

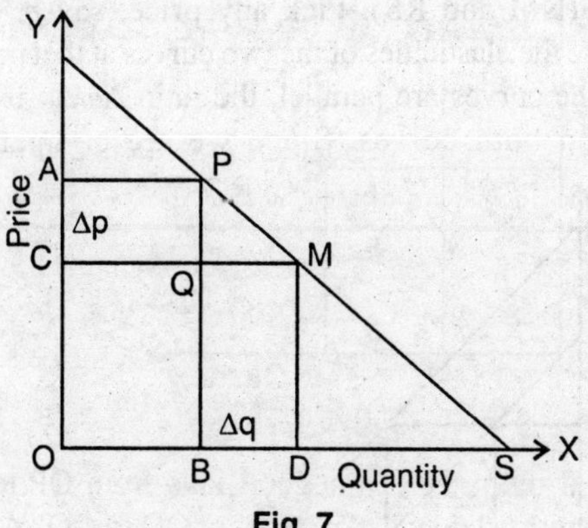

Fig. 7

$$\Delta q = BD = QM$$

$$\Delta p = PQ$$

$$p = PB$$

$$q = OB$$

Substituting these values in the elasticity formula:

$$e_P = \frac{QM}{PQ} \times \frac{PB}{OB}$$

Moreover,

$$\frac{QM}{PQ} = \frac{BS}{PB}$$

[∠PQM = ∠PBS being right angles and ΔPQM and ΔPBS are similar]

$$\therefore \quad \frac{BS}{PB} \times \frac{PB}{OB} = \frac{BS}{OB}$$

Since ΔPBS and ΔROS are similar, price elasticity of demand at point

$$P = \frac{BS}{OB} = \frac{OA}{AR}$$

$$= \frac{PS}{PR} = \frac{\text{Lower Segment}}{\text{Upper Segment}}$$

With the help of the point method it is easy to point out the elasticity at any point along a demand curve. Suppose that the straight line demand curve in Figure 8 is DC. The elasticity of demand at each point can be known with help of the above method.

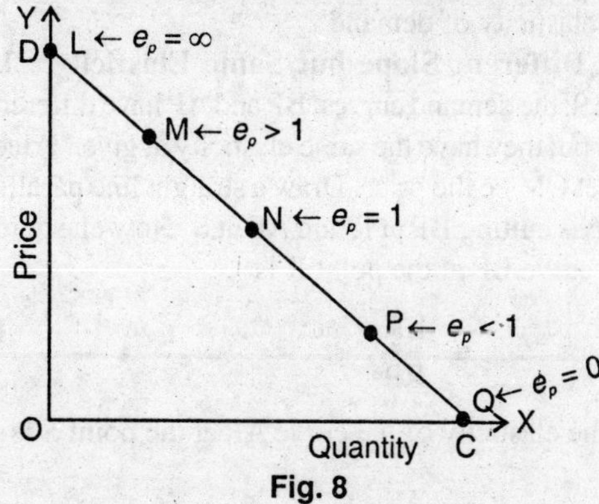

Fig. 8

Let point N be in the middle of the demand curve. So elasticity of demand at point

$$N = \frac{\text{CN (Lower Segment)}}{\text{ND (Upper Segment)}} = \text{Unity}$$

Elasticity of demand at point

$$M = \frac{CM}{MD} = \text{Greater than unity}$$

Elasticity of demand at point

$$L = \frac{CL}{O} = \infty \text{ (infinity)}$$

Elasticity of demand at point

$$P = \frac{CP}{PD} = \text{Less than Unity}$$

Elasticity of demand at point

$$Q = \frac{O}{CD} = 0 \text{ (Zero)}$$

From above it is clear that elasticity at different points on a given demand curve is different. At the mid-point in the demand curve the elasticity of demand is **Unity.** Moving up the demand curve from the mid-point, elasticity becomes greater. When the demand curve touches the Y-axis, elasticity is **infinity. Ipso facto,** any point below the mid-point towards the X-axis will show elastic demand. Elasticity becomes **zero** when the demand curve touches the X-axis.

SOME THEOREMS

We may now develop a number of theorems relating to the elasticity of demand.

1. Different Slope but Same Elasticity : In Figure 9, the demand curves, BP and AP have different slopes but they have the same elasticity at given price.

Let OM be the price. Draw a straight line parallel to X-axis cutting BP at R and AP at S. Now elasticity of the curve BP at the point R is

$$e_P = \frac{BR}{RP}$$

The elasticity of the curve AP at the point S is

$$e'_P = \frac{AS}{SP}$$

Now in the right-angled triangle BOP,

$$\frac{BR}{RP} = \frac{OM}{MP} \quad ...(1)$$

But in the right-angled triangle AOP.

$$\frac{OM}{MP} = \frac{AS}{SP} \quad ....(2)$$

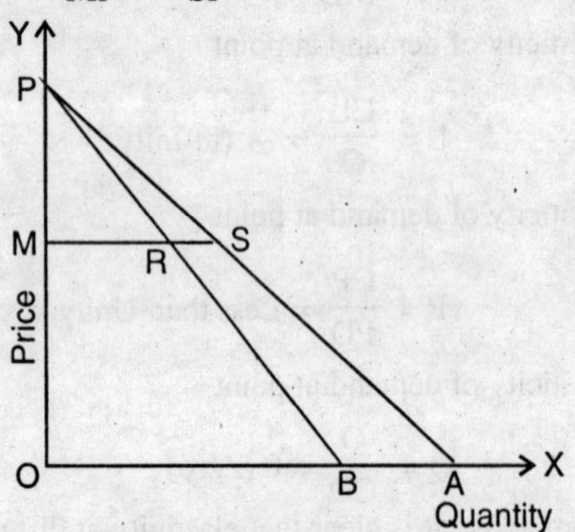

Fig. 9

Hence, from (1) and (2), we get

$$\frac{BR}{RP} = \frac{AS}{SP}$$

$$\therefore \quad e_P = e'_P$$

That is, elasticity at both R and S is the same even though the two curves have different slopes.

2. The Elasticity of a downward-sloping straight line demand curve varies from infinity (∞) at the price axis to zero at the quantity axis.

3. Comparing two straight-line demand curves of the same slope, the one farther from the origin is less elastic at each price than the one closer to the origin.

Figure 10 shows two parallel straight-line demand curves (NM and RS). Pick any price, say *p,* and compare the elasticities of the two curves at that price. Since the curves are parallel, the ratio $\Delta q/\Delta p$ is the same on both curves. Since we are comparing

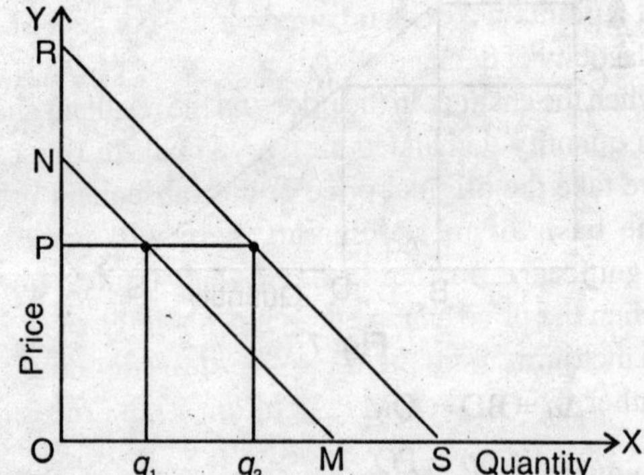

Fig. 10: *Two parallel straight-line demand Curves have unequal price elasticities at P*

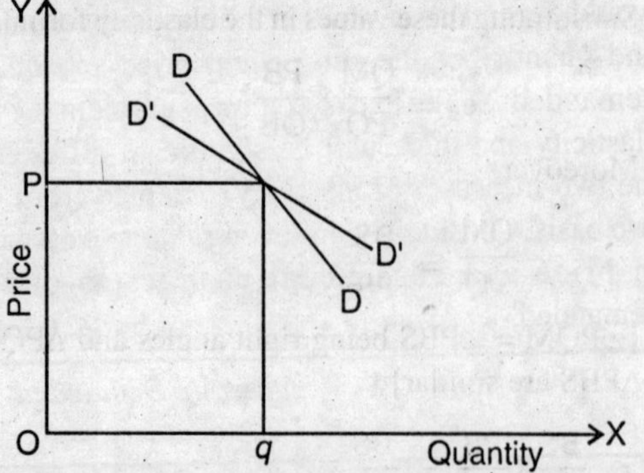

Fig. 11 : *Two intersecting straight-line demand curves have different elasticities where they cross.*

elasticities at the same price on both curves, p is the same, and the only factor left to vary is q. On the curve farther from the origin, quantity is larger (*i.e.*, $q_2 > q_1$), and hence p/q is smaller, thus e_P is smaller.

4. The Elasticities of two intersecting straight-line demand curves can be compared at the point of intersection merely by comparing slopes, the steeper curve being the less elastic.

In Figure 11 we have two intersecting demand curves. At the point of intersection p and q are common to both curves, and hence the ratio p/q is the same. Therefore e_P varies only with $\Delta q/\Delta p$. On the steeper curve $\Delta p/\Delta q$ is larger than on the flatter curve, thus the ration $\Delta q/\Delta p$ is smaller on the steeper curve than on the flatter curve, so that elasticity is lower.

ARC ELASTICITY OF DEMAND

We have studied above the measurement of elasticity at a point on a demand curve or the concept of point elasticity of demand which refers to the price elasticity when the changes in the price and the resultant changes in quantity demanded are very small. In this case if we take the original price or the subsequent price as the basis of measurement, there will not be any significant difference in the elasticity figure. However, when the price change is somewhat large or we have to measure elasticity over an **arc of the demand curve** rather than at a specific point on it, the measure of point elasticity namely, $\frac{\Delta q}{\Delta p} \times \frac{p}{q}$, does not provide us the true and correct result of price elasticity of demand. Further, in such cases, the measure of price elasticity would depend upon whether we choose original price and quantity or the subsequent price and quantity demanded as the basis for measurement of price elasticity and there will be significant difference in the two measures of elasticity, obtained from using two basis. Consider the following example of changes in price and consequent changes in quantity demanded.

Price (Rs.)	*Quantity Demanded (units)*
15 (p_1)	100 (q_1)
10 (p_2)	200 (q_2)

If we take Rs. 15 and quantity demanded at it (100 units) as basis of measuring price elasticity with the point elasticity formula, we get the following figure for elasticity :

$$e_P = \frac{\Delta q}{\Delta p} \times \frac{p}{q}$$

$$= \frac{100}{5} \times \frac{15}{100} = 3$$

If we take Rs. 10 and quantity demanded at it (200 units) as the basis of measuring price elasticity with the point elasticity formula, we get the following figure for elasticity :

$$e_P = \frac{\Delta q}{\Delta p} \times \frac{p}{q}$$

$$= \frac{100}{5} \times \frac{10}{200} = 1$$

We thus see that when there is a somewhat large change in price, point elasticity formula will yield two significantly different elasticity measures (as 3 and 1 in our above example) depending upon whether we use the original price and quantity demanded or the subsequent price and quantity demanded as the basis for measurement.

In terms of demand curve, when we have to measure the price elasticity over an **arc of the demand curve** such as between points A and on the demand curve DD in Figure 12 the point elasticity formula will not yield the true and correct measure of price elasticity. For measuring price elasticity in such cases when the changes in price are some what large or the price elasticity over an arc of the demand curve (that is, between the two points on a demand curve which lie close together) is to be measured, the concept of arc elasticity has been evolved. In measurement of arc elasticity, we use the **average** of the two price figures (original and subsequent) and **average** of the two price figures (original and subsequent) and **average** of the two quantity figures (original and subsequent). Thus the formula for measuring **arc price elasticity** of demand is :

$$e_P = \frac{\Delta q}{\frac{(q_1+q_2)}{2}} \div \frac{\Delta p}{\frac{(p_1+p_2)}{2}}$$

$$= \frac{\Delta q}{\left(\frac{q_1+q_2}{2}\right)} \times \frac{\left(\frac{p_1+p_2}{2}\right)}{\Delta p}$$

$$= \frac{\Delta q}{\Delta p} \times \frac{(p_1+p_2)}{(q_1+q_2)}$$

In our above numerical example where when the price of a good falls from Rs. 15 to Rs. 10 per unit, the quantity demanded increases from 100 to 200 units the arc elasticity is :

$$e_P = \frac{\Delta q}{\Delta p} \times \frac{(p_1+p_2)}{(q_1+q_2)}$$

$$= \frac{100}{5} \times \frac{15+10}{100+200}$$

$$= \frac{100}{5} \times \frac{25}{300} = 1.66$$

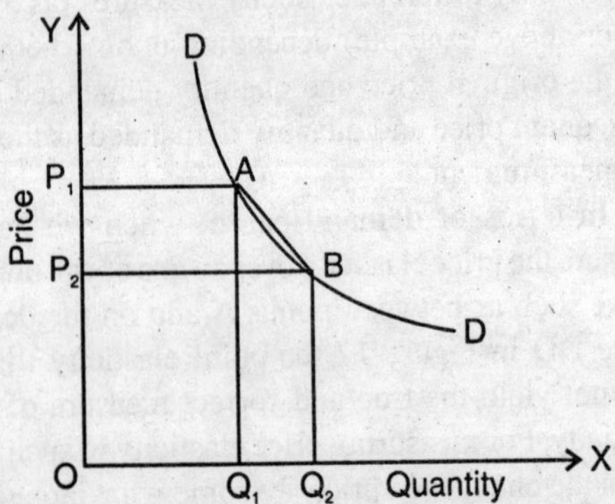

Fig. 12 : *Arc Elasticity*

In Figure 12, if the arc elasticity is to be measured between points A and B on the demand curve DD, we will have to take the average of prices OP_1 and OP_2 and average of quantities OQ_1 and OQ_2. It should be further noted that in Fig. 12, the arc elasticity formula given above measures the arc elasticity over a straight line AB which is taken to be the approximation of the arc elasticity along the **true arc** (the demand curve from point A to B). Therefore, the greater the convexity of the demand curve between A and B, the greater the divergence between the line AB and the true demand curve and therefore the poorer the approximation of arc elasticity measure (of the line AB) for the true curve between A and B.

Cross Elasticity of Demand

The change in the demand for one good in response to the change in price of the other good represents the cross elasticity of demand of one good for the other. In other words, the cross elasticity of demand is the relation between percentage change in the quantity demanded of a good to the percentage in the price of a related good.

When the quantity demanded of good *x* rises as a result of the fall in the price of good *y*, the coefficient of cross elasticity of demand of *x* for *y* will be equal to the relative change in the quantity demanded for good *x* in response to a given relative change in the price of good *y*. Therefore,

Coefficients of cross elasticity of demand of *x* for *y*

$$= \frac{\text{Percentage change in the quantity demanded of } x}{\text{Percentage change in the price of } y}$$

or,

$$e_c = \frac{\Delta q_x / q_x}{\Delta p_y / p_y}$$

$$= \frac{\Delta q_x}{q_x} \div \frac{\Delta p_y}{p_y}$$

$$= \frac{\Delta q_x}{q_x} \times \frac{p_y}{\Delta p_y}$$

$$= \frac{\Delta q_x}{\Delta p_y} \times \frac{p_y}{q_x}$$

where

e_c stands for cross elasticity of demand of X and Y

q_x stands for the original in quantity demanded of good X

p_y stands for the original price of good Y

Δp_y stands for a small change in the price of Y

There are two types of related goods :

(i) Substitutes

(ii) Complementaries

Cross Elasticity of Substitutes : In case of substitutes, the cross elasticity is **positive** and large.

The higher the coefficient e_c, the better substitutes the good are. If the price of butter rises, it will lead to increase in the demand for Jam, similarly a fall in the price of butter will cause a decrease in the demand for Jam.

If a change in the price of good *x* leads to more than proportionate change in the demand for good *y*, the cross elasticity is high ($e_c > 1$). In such case goods are **close substitutes.**

If cross elasticity is less than unity ($e_c < 1$), it means that goods *x* and *y* are **poor substitutes** for each other.

In case of the two goods are **perfect substitutes,** the cross elasticity of demand will be infinite ($e_c = \infty$). Hence the cross elasticity of demand for substitutes varies between zero and infinity.

Cross Elasticity of Complementary Goods

If two goods are complementary (jointly demanded), rise in the price of one leads to a fall in the demand for the other. Rise in the prices of cars will bring a fall in their demand together with the demand for petrol. Similarly, a fall in the prices of cars will raise the demand for petrol. Since the price and demand vary in the opposite direction, the cross elasticity of demand in **negative.**

SOME OTHER IMPORTANT CASES OF CHANGES IN PRICE ELASTICITY OF DEMAND

In discussing the difference between the price elasticity and slope of the demand curve, we have noted above some cases of changes in price elasticity of demand. **Firstly,** we have explained that when the two demand curves start from the same point from the *y*-axis, the price elasticity of demand at a given price on the two demand curves would be the same. **Secondly,** we have explained above that when the demand curve shifts to the right in a parallel manner, the price elasticity of demand at a given price declines. We shall now explain two other cases of the behaviour of price elasticity of demand.

The first case relates to changes in prices elasticity of demand at the given quantity demanded when the curve shifts to the right (or, in other words, when the demand increases). This is illustrated in Figure 13 where demand curve first shifts from DD to D'D' and then to D"D".

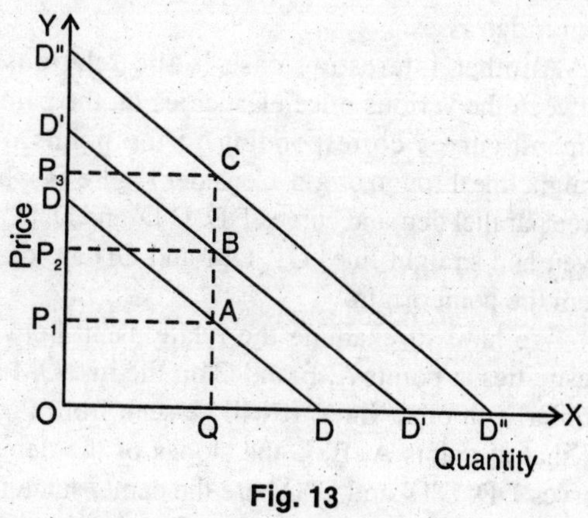

Fig. 13

The given quantity demanded is OQ. Thus, we have to examine the price elasticity of demand at points B and C which lie respectively on the demand curves D'D' and D"D" as compared to elasticity at point A which lies on the original demand curve A. We can easily explain this with the help of the formula of price elasticity of demand, namely, $e_p = \frac{\Delta q}{\Delta p} \times \frac{p}{q}$. Since the straight line demand curves are parallel to each other, their slopes would be the same. Thus, slopes of demand curves at points A, B and C are the same. Therefore, the term $\frac{\Delta q}{\Delta p}$ which is the reciprocal of the slope of the demand curve would be the same at points A, B and C. Further, in the elasticity coefficient $\left(\frac{\Delta q}{\Delta p}.\frac{p}{q}\right)$ the quantity demanded *q* is also the same, as we have to examine the price elasticity on various demand curves at OQ as the given quantity demanded. Thus, on the points A, B and C at the demand curves DD, D'D' and D"D", $\frac{\Delta q}{\Delta p}$ and *q* are the same, only the price *p* varies. It will be seen from the Figure 13 that as we move from A to B and B to C, the price *p* **rises.** It follows therefore that elasticity coefficient $\frac{\Delta q}{\Delta p}.\frac{p}{q}$ will be higher at B than at A, and higher at C than at B, since price *p* at B is higher than at A, price at C is higher than at B($P_2 > P_1$ and $P_3 > P_2$).

We thus conclude that as demand increase and therefore demand curve shifts to the right, the price elasticity of demand at the given quantity demanded rises.

Another interesting case is the relationship between the various price elasticities on the parallel demand curves corresponding to the points on a straight line through origin. Consider Figure 14 where three parallel demand curves DD, D'D' and D"D" are given and straight lines OT, OM and OH are drawn from the point origin.

We have to examine the relationship between elasticities at points A, B and C on the line OM and similarly on other lines. It will be seen from Figure 14 that at points A, B, C the slopes of the demand curves DD, D'D' and D"D" are the same, since they are drawn parallel to each other. In other words, in the elasticity coefficient the reciprocal of the slope *i.e.,* $\frac{\Delta q}{\Delta p}$ would be the same. Since A, B and C on the demand curves lie at the straight line OM passing through the point of origin, the term p/q would be equal to the slope which is the same at points A, B and C. Thus, the two terms of elasticity coefficient, that is, $\frac{\Delta q}{\Delta p}$ and $\frac{p}{q}$ remain the same along the straight line OM on the demand curves DD, D'D' and D"D". It follows therefore that the value of the elasticity coefficient is the same at points A, B and C. Likewise, the price elasticities of demand at point Q, R and S on

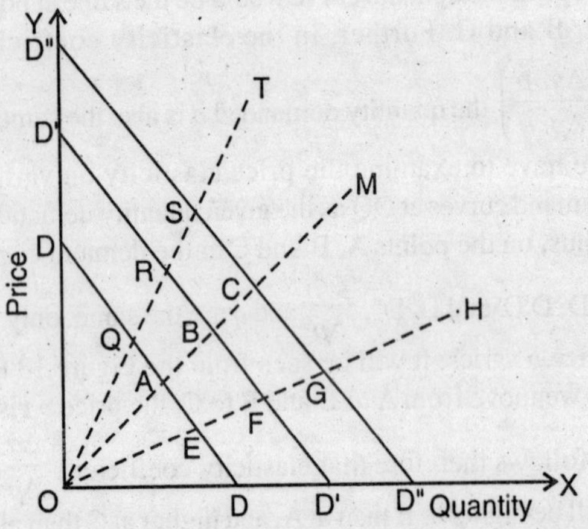

Fig. 14

the various demand curves and along the straight line OT passing through the point of origin would be the same. Also, the price elasticity at points E, F and G which lie on the three demand curves along the straight line OH passing through the points of origin.

Income Elasticity

The responsiveness of demand to changes in income is termed **income elasticity of demand.** It shows how the quantity demanded will change when the income of the purchaser changes, the price of the commodity remaining the same, it may be defined thus : The Income Elasticity of demand for a good is the ratio of the percentage change in the amount spent on the commodity to a percentage change in the consumer's income price of commodity remaining constant. Thus,

$$\text{Income Elasticity} = \frac{\text{Percentage change in quantity demanded}}{\text{Percentage change in income}}$$

Let y stand for an initial income, Δy for a small change in income, q for the initial quantity purchased, Δq for a change in quantity purchased as a result of a change in income and e_i for income elasticity of demand. Then

$$e_i = \frac{\Delta q / q}{\Delta y / y} = \frac{\Delta q}{\Delta y} \times \frac{y}{q}$$

We can also express the income elasticity in terms of changes in expenditure made on the good rather than the change in quantity purchased of the good as a result of a change in income. It should be noted that expenditure is equal to the quantity purchased of the good multiplied by the price of the good. If q is the quantity purchased of the good and p the price of the good, then expenditure made on the good is equal to qp.

As defined above,

$$e_i = \frac{\Delta q}{q} \times \frac{y}{\Delta y}$$

Multiplying the numerator and denominator by p, we get

$$e_i = \frac{\Delta q . p}{q . p} \times \frac{y}{\Delta y}$$

Now, as explained above, qp is the expenditure made on the good and Δqp is the change in expenditure made as a result of change in income. Let X-stand for the expenditure made on the good. Then the above equation will income

$$e_i = \frac{\Delta x}{x} \times \frac{y}{\Delta y}$$

or $$e_i = \frac{y.\Delta x}{x.\Delta y}$$

Thus, Income elasticity

$$= \frac{\text{income} \times \text{Change in expenditure}}{\text{expenditure} \times \text{Change in income}}$$

For most goods, increase in income lead to increases in demand, and income elasticity will be **positive.** For inferior goods, where a rise in income leads consumers to demand less of the commodity, income elasticity will be negative.

Income Elasticity and Proportion of Income Spent

There is a useful relationship between income elasticity for a good and proportion of income spent on it. The relationship between the two is described in the following three propositions :

1. If proportion of income spent on the good remains the same as income increases, then income elasticity for the good is equal to one ($e_i = 1$).

2. If proportion of income spent on the good increase as income increases, then the income elasticity for the good is greater than one ($e_i > 1$).

3. If proportion of income spent on the good decreases as income rises, then income elasticity for the good is less than one ($e_i < 1$).

Some Important Values of Income Elasticity

The following numerical values of elasticity seem to be most significant.

First, income elasticity of demand being zero is of great significance. Zero income elasticity of demand for a good implies that a given increase in income does not at all lead to any increase in quantity demanded of the good or expenditure on it. Besides, zero income elasticity is significant because it represents a dividing line between positive income elasticity on the one side and negative income elasticity on the other. On the one side when income elasticity is more than Zero (that is, positive), then an increase in income leads to the increase in quantity demanded of the good. This happens in case of most of the goods. On the other side of zero income elasticity are all those goods whose income elasticity in less than zero (that is negative) and in such cases increase in income will lead to the fall in quantity demanded of the goods. Goods having negative income elasticity are known as **inferior goods.**

Income Elasticity : Measures and Meaning

Numerical Value of Income Elasticity	*Verbal description*
• Negative	Demand for the commodity falls as income rises
• Zero	Demand for the commodity does not change as income changes
• Greater than Zero but less than one	Demand for the commodity rises less than in proportion to the rise in income
• Unity	Demand for the commodity rises in the same proportion as the rise in income
• Greater than Unity	Demand for the commodity rises more than in proportion to the rise in income

Another important value of income elasticity of demand is **unity.** As explained above when income elasticity of demand for a good is equal to one, then proportion of income spent on the good remains the same as consumer's income increases. Income elasticity of unity also represents a useful dividing line. If the income elasticity for a good is greater than one, then the proportion of consumer's income spent on good rises as income increases, that is, that good bulks larger in consumer's expenditure as he becomes richer. On the other hand, if the income elasticity for a good is less than one, the proportion of consumer's income spent on it falls as his income rises, that is, the good becomes relatively less important in consumer's expenditure as his income rises. The good having income elasticity more than one and which therefore bulks larger in consumer's budget as he becomes richer is called a **luxury.** The good with an income elasticity less than one and which claims declining proportion of consumer's income as he becomes richer is called a **necessity.**

THE ELASTICITY OF SUBSTITUTION

The elasticity of substitution is another important concept of demand elasticity. Elasticity of substitution measures the effects of the substitution of one good for another. In other words, the elasticity of substitution between two goods is a measure of the ease with which one can be substituted for the other, Just as price elasticity of demand in a relative measure of the price effect, income elasticity is a relative measure of the income effect, similarly the elasticity of substitution is a relative measure of the substitution effect.

Elasticity of substitution is defined as the proportionate change in the ratios of goods X and Y to the proportionate change in their price ratio. Its numerical coefficient is

$$e_s = \frac{\text{Proportionate change in the ratio of } x \text{ and } y}{\text{Proportionate change in their price ratios}}$$

Algebraically

$$e_s = \frac{\Delta\left(\frac{x}{y}\right) \Big/ \frac{x}{y}}{\Delta\left(\frac{P_x}{P_y}\right) \Big/ \frac{P_x}{P_y}}$$

where

e_s stands for elasticity of substitution

$\frac{x}{y}$ stands for the ratio between the two goods x and y.

$\Delta(x/y)$ stands for the change in the ratio of x and y

$\frac{P_x}{P_y}$ stands for the price ratio between x and y

$\Delta(P_x/P_y)$ stands for the change in their price ratios.

There are two extremes, *i.e.*, two limiting cases :

(a) The elasticity of substitution may be **infinite.** In this case, the goods are **perfect substitutes** for one another, *i.e.*, they are identical *(b)* at the other extreme, there is a case of **zero** elasticity of substitution. Here there can be no substitution at all and the goods must be used in fixed proportion or not all. Between these two limits, there can be various degrees of substitution.

When it is difficult to substitute one good for another, then a small change in the proportion of the two goods will bring about a large change in the **marginal rate of substitution** between the two goods. When the substitution between the two goods is easy, then a small change in the proportion of two goods possessed by the consumer, the change in the marginal rate of substitution between the two goods will not be much. It is thus clear that from the change in the proportion of two goods and the resultant change in marginal rate of substitution we can know the elasticity of substitution. Therefore, elascitity of substitution can be expressed as follow :

$$e_s = \frac{\text{Proportionate change in the ratio of } x \text{ and } y}{\text{Proportionate change in the marginal rate of substitution of } x \text{ for } y}$$

Symbolically,

$$e_s = \frac{\Delta\left(\frac{q_x}{q_y}\right) \Big/ \frac{q_x}{q_y}}{\Delta\left(\frac{\Delta Y}{\Delta X}\right) \Big/ \frac{\Delta Y}{\Delta X}}$$

Here

$\frac{q_x}{q_y}$ stands for the original proportion between the quantities of goods x and y

$\Delta\left(\frac{q_x}{q_y}\right)$ stands for the small change in the proportion of good x and y

$\frac{\Delta Y}{\Delta X}$ stands for the original marginal rate of substitution of good x for y

$\Delta\left(\frac{\Delta Y}{\Delta X}\right)$ stands for the change in the marginal rate of substitution of good x and y

When the two goods x and y are perfect substitutes of each other, than the proportion between them $\left(\text{that is, } \frac{q_x}{q_y}\right)$ can be increased infinitely without any change in the marginal rate of substitution between them, that is, elasticity of substitution between the **perfect substitute** is **infinite.**

When the two goods which are perfect complements to each other, they are used in a fixed proportion and no substitution between them is possible. Therefore, the goods which are perfect complements with each other, the marginal rate of substitution between them is zero, that is, elasticity of substitution between the **perfect complements** is **zero.**

RELATION BETWEEN PRICE ELASTICITY, INCOME ELASTICITY AND SUBSTITUTION ELASTICITY

Price effect is the effect on the quantity demanded of a good due to a change in price, depends upon income effect on the hand and substitution effect on the other. Similarly, price elasticity of demand which is the relative measure of the price effect depends upon the income elasticity on the one hand and substitution elasticity on the other. Thus. price elasticity, in a way, is a compromise between income elasticity and substitution elasticity of demand. The relationship between these three elasticities can be expressed in the form of a mathematical formula. Thus,

$$e_p = K_x.e_i + (1 - K_x)e_s$$

where

e_p stands for price elasticity of demand.
e_i stands for income elasticity of demand.
e_s stands for substitution elasticity of demand.
K_x stands for the proportion of consumer's income spent on good *x*.

In the above equation $K_x.e_i$ shows the influence of income effect on the price elasticity of demand. The income effect of a change in price depends on the one hand, on the proportion of consumer's income spent on the commodity *x, i.e.,* K_x and also on the income elasticity of demand for the good *x, i.e.,* e_i. This explains the first part of the equation ($K_x.e_i$), which is the income effect.

The second component, *i.e.,* $(1 - K_x).e_s$ is the **substitution effect.** A fall in the price of *x* will lead to its substitution for other goods. The magnitude of the substitution effect depends on the elasticity of substitution, e_s, *i.e.,* the extent to which *x* can be substituted for other goods on account of its becoming cheaper. This depends upon the extent to which other goods already figure in consumption of the particular consumer. K_x being the proportion of income that is spent on the good *x*, $(1 - K_x)$ is the proportion spent on other goods. This indicates the limit to which other goods can be purchased, it shows the extent of substitutability and is thus the substitution effect.

From the above analysis it follows that the price elasticity of demand for a good is determined by the following four factors :

1. Proportion of income spent on the good.
2. Income elasticity of demand.
3. Elasticity of substitution.
4. Proportion of income spent on goods other than *x*.

Price elasticity can be known if the first three factors are known. Let us consider the following examples.

Suppose that a consumer is spending 1/5th of his income on any good *x* and the income elasticity of demand for the good *x* is 2 and elasticity of substitution between good *x* and all other goods is 3. What will be the price elasticity of demand in this case?

$$e_P = K_x.e_i + (1 - K_x)e_s$$

$$= \frac{1}{5}\times 2 + (1 - 1/5)\times 3 = 2/5 + 4/5 \times 3$$

$$= 2/5 + 12/5 = 14/5 = 2.8$$

Thus, Price elasticity of demand for good *x* is equal to 2.8.

From the above formula of price elasticity of demand, it follows that whatever the proportion of income spent on a good, if income elasticity and substitution elasticity are equal to one, then price elasticity will also be equal to one. For example, if a proportion of income spent on a good is 1/5 and e_i and e_s are equal to one, then price elasticity will be :

$$e_P = K_x.e_i + (1 - K_x)e_s$$

$$= \frac{1}{5}\times 1 + 4/5 \times 1 = 1/5 + 4/5 = 1$$

Like wise, if proportion of income spent on a good is 1/3, and given that both the income and substitution elasticities are equal to one, price elasticity will be found to be equal to one.

Factors Affecting Price Elasticity of Demand

Elasticity of demand for any good is determined or influenced by a number of factors which are discussed as under.

1. Nature of the Commodity : The elasticity of demand for any commodity depends upon the category to which it belongs, *i.e.,* whether it is a necessity, comforts or luxury. The demand for necessaries of life or conventional necessaries is generally **less elastic.** The demand for necessaries of efficiency and for comforts is **moderately elastic** because with the rise or fall in their prices, the demand for them decreases or increases moderately. On the other hand, the demand for **luxuries** is **more elastic** because with a small change in their prices there is a large change in their demand.

2. Existence of Substitutes : For commodities having substitutes, the demand is elastic, *e.g.,* tea and coffee. If the price of any one of them falls, it will be purchased in larger quantities. If the price rise, demand for it will contract, and its substitutes will be purchased instead. There is, therefore, greater extension or contraction of demand for such commodities when their prices change. Demand for them is elastic.

3. Several Uses : The demand for a commodity having several uses is **more elastic.** With a fall in price such a commodity tends to be put to less urgent uses. Thus its demand extends, and **vice-versa.** If a commodity has only one use, a change in price of the commodity will in fluence its one use only. Even if its price falls considerably, it cannot be put to any other use. Hence the demand is in elastic. But it is possible to use it for a number of purposes, the demand will be obviously elastic.

4. Deferred Consumption : Commodities whose consumption can be deferred have an elastic demand. This is the case with durable consumer goods, like cloth, bicycle, fan, etc. If the price of any of these articles rises, people will postpone their consumption. As a result their demand will decrease, and **vice-versa.**

5. Habits : People who are habituated to the consumption of a particular commodity, like coffee, tea or cigarettee of a particular brand, the demand for it will be **inelastic.**

6. Income Groups : The elasticity of demand also depends on the income group to which a person belongs. Persons who belong to the higher income group, their demand for commodity is **less elastic.** On the other hand, the demand of persons in lower income groups is generally **elastic.**

7. Proportion of Income Spent : If the consumer spends a small proportion of his income on a commodity at a time, the demand for that commodity is less elastic, but commodities which entail a large proportion of the income of the consumer, the demand for them is more elastic.

8. Level of Prices : The level of prices also influences the elasticity of demand for commodities. When the price level is high, the demand for commodities is **elastic,** and when the price level is low, the demand is less elastic.

9. Time Factor : Time factor plays on important role in influencing the elasticity of demand for commodities. The shorter the time in which the consumer buys a commodity, the lesser will be the elasticity of demand for that product. On the other hand, the longer the time which the consumer takes in buying a commodity, the higher will be the elasticity of demand for that product.

Conclusion : From the above, it will be clear that there is no hard and fast rule to determine whether the demand for any commodity is elastic or inelastic. This will, in fact, depend on several factors connected with that commodity and with the consumer. However, broadly speaking, we can say that the elasticity of demand for any commodity in relation to a certain class of consumers will depend on the availability of its substitutes or the nature of the commodity whether it is a necessary or a luxury.

ELASTICITY OF SUPPLY

Elasticity of supply refers to the sensitiveness or **responsiveness** of the supply to changes in price. In other words, the elasticity of supply is defined as the percentage change in quantity supplied divided by the percentage change in price, and it is a measure of the degree to which the quantity supplied responds to price changes. Thus,

Elasticity of Supply

$$= \frac{\text{Percentage change in quantity supplied}}{\text{Percentage change in price}}$$

Figure 15 illustrator three cases of supply elasticity. The case of **zero supply elasticity** is one in which the quantity supplied does not change as price changes. This would be the case, for example, if suppliers persisted in producing a given quantity, q_1 in Figure 15 *(i)*, and dumping it on the marker for whatever it would bring.

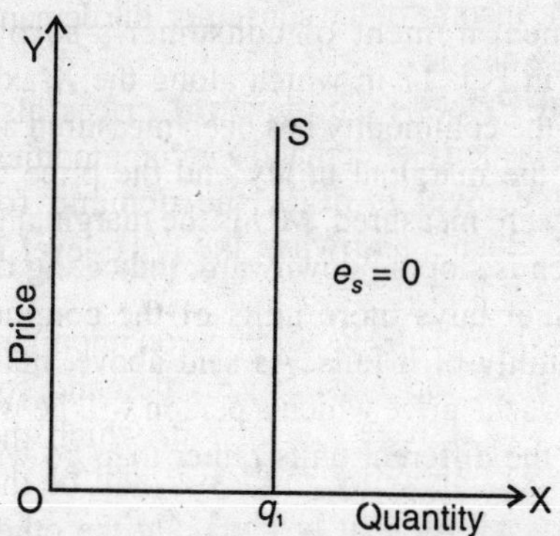

Fig. 15*(i)* *Supply Curve of Zero elasticity*

Infinite supply elasticity is illustrated in Figure 15*(ii)*. The supply elasticity is infinite at the price p_1, because nothing at all is supplied at lower price, but a small increase in price to p_1 causes supply to rise from zero to an indefinitely large amount, indicating that producers would supply any amount demanded at that price.

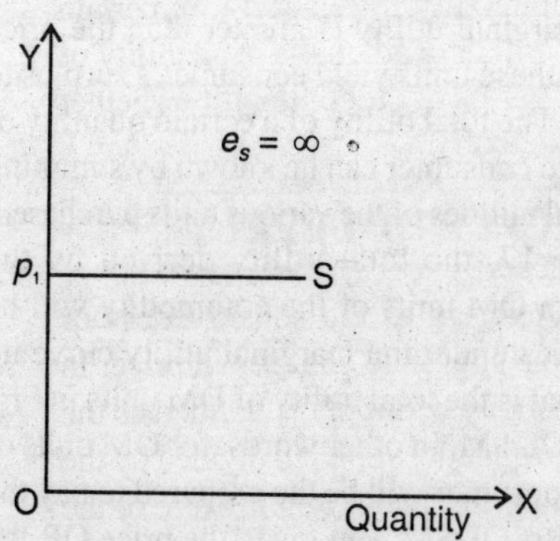

Fig. 15*(ii)* *Supply curve in infinite elasticity*

The case of **unit elasticity of supply** is illustrated in Figure 15*(iii)*. Any straight-line supply curve drawn through the origin has, infact, an elasticity of unity.

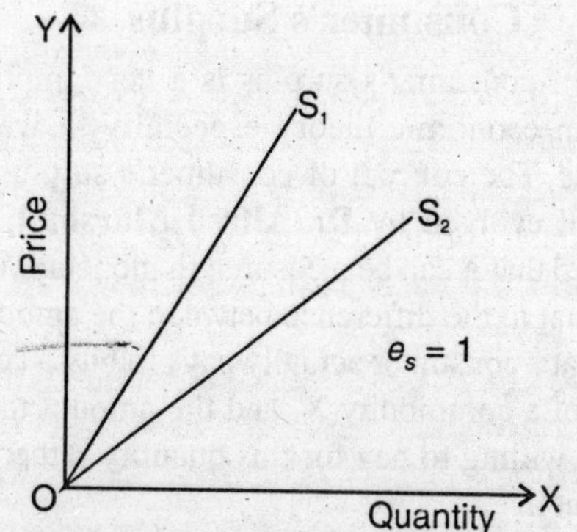

Fig. 15*(iii)* *Supply curve in unit elasticity*

Theorem: Any straight-line supply curve through the origin has an elasticity of one.

Such a supply curve in shown in Figure 16. Consider the two triangles with the sides *p, q,* and the S curve, and Δp, Δq, and the S curve. Clearly these are similar triangles. Therefore the ratios of their sides are equal, *i.e.,*

$$\frac{p}{q} = \frac{\Delta p}{\Delta q} \quad ...(1)$$

Elasticity of supply is defined as

$$e_s = \frac{\Delta q}{\Delta p} \cdot \frac{p}{q} \quad ...(2)$$

which, by substitution from (1), gives

$$e_s = \frac{q}{p} \cdot \frac{p}{q}$$

$$= 1$$

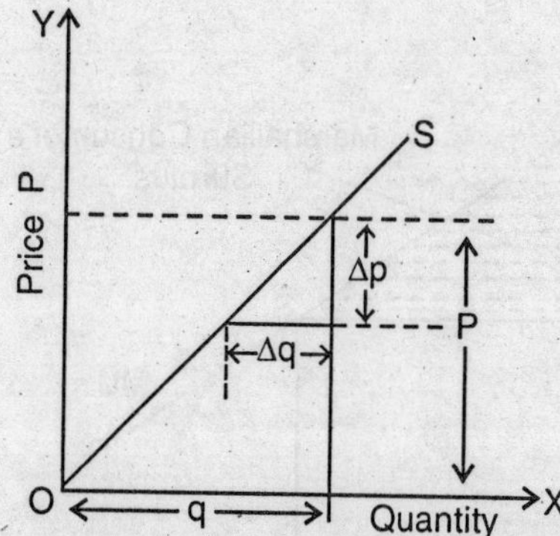

Fig. 16: *A straight-line supply curve through the origin has an elasticity of one.*

Consumer's Surplus

Concept of consumer's surplus is a very important concept in economic theory especially in welfare economics. The concept of consumer's surplus was first of all evolved by **Dr. Alfred Marshall,** who maintained that it can be measured in monetary units, and is equal to the difference between the amount of money that a consumer actually pays to buy a certain quantity of a commodity X, and the amount that he would be willing to pay for this quantity rather than do without it.

The concept of consumer surplus is important not only in economic theory but also in economic policies, such as taxation by the Government and price policy pursued by the monopolistic seller of a product. The essence of the concept of consumer's surplus is that a consumer derives extra satisfaction from the purchases he daily makes over the price he actually pays for them. **Marshall** defines the consumer's surplus in the following words :

"Excess of the price which a consumer would be willing to pay, rather than go without a thing over that which he actually does pay, is the economic measure of this surplus satisfaction ... it may be called consumer's surplus."

The amount of money which a person is prepared to pay for a good indicates the amount of utility he derives from that good, the greater the amount of money he is willing to pay, the greater the satisfaction or utility he will obtain from it. Therefore, the marginal utility of a unit of a good determines the price a consumer will be prepared to pay for that unit. The

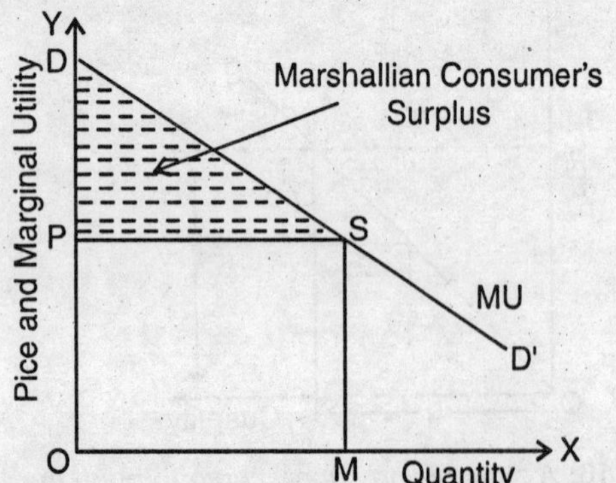

Fig. 17: *Marshall's Measure of Consumer's Surplus*

total utility which a person will get from a good will be given by sum of marginal utilities (ΣMU) of the units of the good purchased and the total price which he will actually pay is equal to the price per unit multiplied by the number of units purchased. Thus,

Consumer's Surplus = What a consumer is prepared to pay minus what he actually pays.

= Σ MU – (Price × Number of units purchased)

The measurement of consumer's surplus is illustrated in Fig. 17 in which along the X-axis the amount of the commodity has been measured and on the Y-axis the marginal utility and the price of the commodity are measured. MU is the marginal utility curve which is sloping downward, indicating that as the consumer buys more units of the commodity, marginal utility of it falls. As said above, marginal utility shows the price which a person will be willing to pay for the different units rather than go without them.

If OP is the price that prevails in the market, then the consumer will be in equilibrium when he buys OM units of the commodity, since at OM units, marginal utility is equal to the given price OP. **The Mth unit of the commodity does not yield any consumer's surplus to the consumer. Since this is the last unit purchased and for this price paid is equal to the marginal utility which indicates the price he will be prepared to pay rather than go without it.** But for the intra marginal units *i.e.,* units before Mth marginal utility is greater than the price and therefore, these units yield consumer's surplus to the consumer. The total utility of a certain quantity of a commodity to consumer can be known by summing up the marginal utilities of the various units purchased.

In Figure 17, the total utility derived by the consumer from OM units of the commodity will be equal to the area under the marginal utility curve up to point M. That is the total utility of DM units in Fig. 17 is equal to ODSM. In other words, for OM units of the good the consumer will be the prepared to pay the sum equal to Rs. ODSM. But given the price OP, the consumer will actually pay for OM units of the good the sum equal to Rs. OPSM. It is thus clear that the consumer derives extra utility equal to ODSM minus OPSM = DPS, which has been shaded in Fig. 17.

If the market price of the commodity rises above

OP, the consumer will buy fewer units of the commodity than OM. As a result, consumer's surplus obtained by him from his purchase will decline. On the other hand, if the price falls below OP, the consumer will be in equilibrium when he is purchasing more units of the commodity than OM. As a result of this, the consumer's surplus will increase. Thus, given the marginal utility curve of the consumer, the higher the price, the smaller the consumer's surplus and the lower the price, the greater the consumer's surplus.

It is worth noting here that in our analysis of consumer's surplus, we have assumed that perfect competition prevails in the market so that the consumer faces a given price, whatever the amount of the commodity he purchases. But if the seller of a commodity discriminates the prices and charges different prices for the different units of the good, some units at a higher price and some at a lower price, then in this case consumer's surplus will be smaller. Thus, when the seller makes price discrimination and sells different units of a good at different prices, the consumer will obtain smaller amount of consumer's surplus than under perfect competition. If the seller indulges in **perfect price discrimination,** that is, if he changes price for each unit of the commodity equal to what any consumer will be prepared to pay for it, then in that case no consumer's surplus will accrue to the consumer.

A NOTE ON THE DIAMOND-WATER PARADOX

Classical economists were quite confused when they were asked about the low price of water, which was so necessary for life, compared with the high price of diamonds, which were so unnecessary for life.

As Figure 18 indicates, it is possible for the marginal utility of diamonds to be relatively high since diamonds are quite scarce, while the marginal utility of water is relatively low since water is quite plentiful, if we view quantities D_1 and W_1, respectively.

As a result our marginal utility theory tells us that the price of diamonds will be quite high, while the price of water will be quite low. Nevertheless, the total utility of water can be much greater than the total utility of diamonds. The total utility of water is the

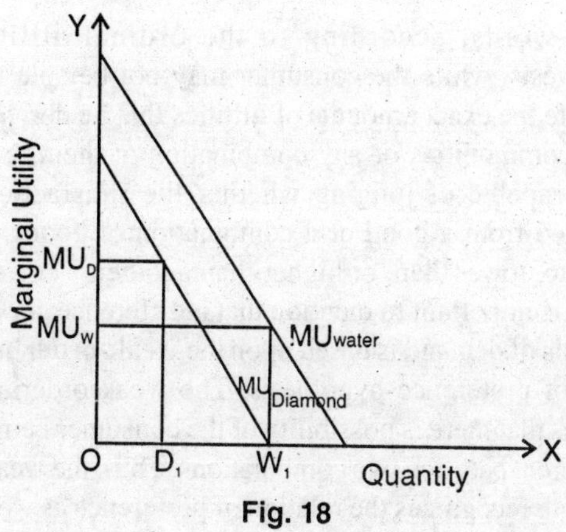

Fig. 18

area under the marginal utility curve for water upto the level of consumption W_1. That is to say, total utility is the marginal utility of the first unit plus the marginal utility of the second unit, and so on. Since the total utility of diamonds is the area under the marginal utility curve for diamonds up to consumption level D_1, it nicely follows that the total utility derived from water can be greater than the total utility derived from diamonds.

We may conclude that the more there is of a commodity, the lower is the relative desirability of the last unit despite the fact that total utility increases. Thus, a great quantity of water has a low price.

THE INDIFFERENCE CURVE THEORY

The indifference curve is a geometrical device that has been used to replace the neo-classical cardinal utility concept. **Hicks** presented its comprehensive version in his **value and capital** in 1939 and its major revision in his A Revision of Demand Theory in 1956. The fundamental approach of indifference curve analysis is that it has abandoned the concept of cardinal utility and instead has adopted the concept of **ordinal utility.** According to the supporters of the indifference curves theory, utility is a psychic entity and it cannot therefore be measured in quantitative, cardinal terms. In other words, utility being a psychological feeling is not quantifiable. The ordinal utility implies that the consumer is capable of simply 'comparing' the different levels of satisfaction. In other words, according to the ordinal utility hypothesis, while the consumer may not be able to indicate the exact amounts of utilities that he derives from commodities or any combination of them, but he is capable of judging whether the satisfaction obtained from a good or a combination of goods is equal to, lower than, or higher than another.

It is important to mention that indifference curve analysis of demand is based upon the **weak-ordering** form of preference hypothesis. The weak ordering implies that there is possibility of the consumer being indifferent between two combinations. Thus, the weak ordering recognizes the relation of preference as well as of indifference. The consumer may prefer A to B or B to A or he may be indifferent between A and B. On the contrary, **strong ordering** implies that there can be only the relation of preference, A is preferred to B, or B is preferred to A, the possibility of consumer's indifference between A and B ruled out. Thus the strong-ordering admits only the relation of preference.

INDIFFERENCE CURVES

An indifference curve is the locus of points-particular combinations or bundles of goods-which yields the same utility (level of satisfaction) to the consumer, so that he is indifferent as to the particular combination he consumes. In other words, all combinations of the goods lying on a consumer's indifference curve are equally desirable to or equally preferred by him. To understand indifference curves, it is better to start with indifference schedules.

The indifference schedule shows the various combinations of the two commodities such that the consumer is indifferent to those combinations. In table 1.2 indifference schedules is given. In this schedule the amount of goods x and y in each combination are so arranged that the consumer is indifferent among the combinations. In the schedule, the consumer has to start with 1 unit of x and 18 units of y. Now, the consumer is asked to tell how much of good y he will be willing to give up for the gain of additional unit of x so that his level of satisfaction remains the same. If the gain of one unit of x compensates him fully for the loss of 5 units of y, then the next combination of 2 units of x and 13 units of y ($2x + 13y$) will give him as

TABLE 1.2:
Indifference Schedule

Combination	*Good x*	*Good y*
1	1	18
2	2	13
3	3	9
4	4	6
5	5	4
6	6	3

much satisfaction as the initial combination ($1x + 12y$). Similarly, by asking the consumer further how much of y he will be prepared to forego for successive increments in his stock of x so that his level of satisfaction remains unaltered, we get combinations $3x + 9y$, $4x + 6y$, $5x + 4x$ and $6x + 3y$, each of which provides the same satisfaction as combination $1x + 18y$ or $2x + 13y$.

Now, we can convert the indifference schedule into indifference curve by plotting the various combinations on a graph paper. In Figure 19 an indifference curve IC is drawn by plotting the various combination in the indifference schedule. Like in an indifference schedule, combinations lying on an indifference curve will be equally desirable to the

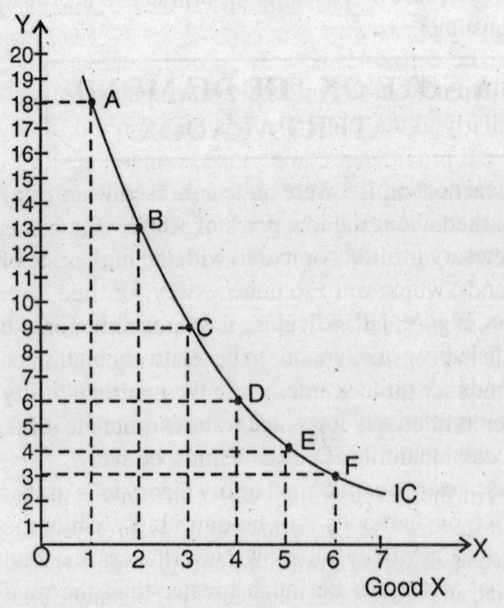

Fig. 19

consumer, that is, will give him the same satisfaction. The smoothness and continuity of an indifference curve means that goods in question are assumed to be **perfectly divisible.**

An indifference map shows all the indifference curves which rank the preferences of the consumer combinations of goods situated on an indifference curve yield the same utility, Combinations of goods lying on a higher indifference curve yield higher level of satisfaction and are preferred. Combinations of goods on a lower indifference curve yield a lower utility. In Figure 20 an indifference map of a consumer is shown which consists of five indifference curves.

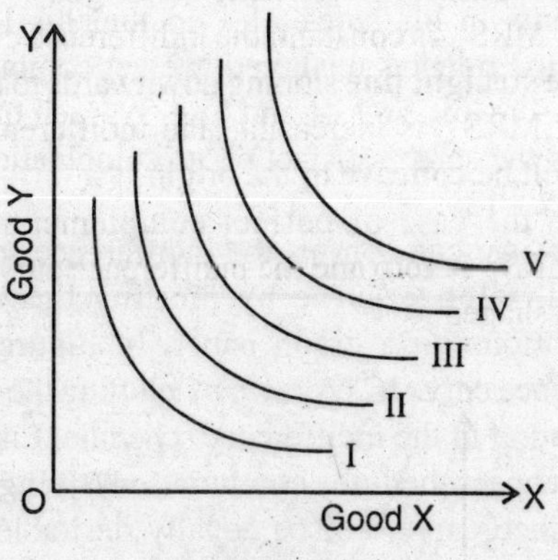

Fig. 20

The consumer regards all combinations on the indifference curve I as giving him equal satisfaction. Similarly all the combinations lying on indifference curve II provide the same satisfaction but the level of satisfaction on indifference curve II will be greater than the level of satisfaction on indifference curve I. Likewise, all the higher indifference curves, II, III, IV and V represent progressively higher and higher levels of satisfaction. It is important to remember that while the consumer will prefer any combination on a higher indifference curve to any combination on a lower indifference curve, but by **how much he prefers** one combination to another cannot be said.

An indifference map of a consumer represents his tastes for the two goods and his preferences as between different combinations of them. In other words, an indifference map portrays consumer's scale of preferences.

Assumptions

The indifference curve analysis retains some of the assumptions of the cardinal theory, rejects others and formulates its own. The assumptions of the ordinal theory are the following :

1. Rationality : The consumer is assumed to be rational-he aims at the maximisation of his utility, given his income and market prices. It is assumed he has full knowledge of all relevant information.

2. Utility is Ordinal : It is taken as axiomatically true that the consumer can rank his preferences according to the satisfaction of each combinations. He need not know precisely the amount of satisfaction.

3. Diminishing Marginal Rate of Substitution : The indifference-curve theory is based on the axiom of diminishing marginal rate of substitution.

4. The total utility of the consumer depends on the quantities of the commodities consumed.

$$U = f(q_1, q_2, \dots q_n)$$

5. Consistency and Transitivity of Choice : It is assumed that the consumer is consistent in his choice, that is, if in one period he chooses bundle A over B, he will not choose B over A in another period if both bundles are available to him. The consistency assumption may be symbolically written as follows -

If $A > B$, then $B \ngtr A$

Similarly, it is assumed that consumer's choices are characterised by transitively : If bundle A is preferred to B, and B is preferred to C, then bundle A, is preferred to C. Symbolically we may write the transitivity assumption as follows :

If $A > B$, and $B > V$, then $A > C$

MARGINAL RATE OF SUBSTITUTION

The concept of marginal rate of substitution is an important tool of indifference curve analysis of demand. Marginal rate of substitution of x for y (MRS_{xy}) represents the amount of y which the consumer has to give up for the gain of one additional unit of x so that his level of satisfaction remains the same.

TABLE 1.3

Combination	*Good x*	*Good y*	MRS_{xy}
A	1	12	—
B	2	8	4 : 1
C	3	5	3 : 1
D	4	3	2 : 1
E	5	2	1 : 1

In table 1.3, when the consumer moves from combination A to combination B on his indifference schedule he forgoes 4 units of y for the additional one unit gain in *x*. Hence, the marginal rate of substitution of *x* for *y* is 4. Likewise, when the consumer moves from B to C, and C to D, and then from D to E in his indifference schedule, the marginal rate of substitution of *x* for *y* is 3, 2, and 1 respectively. As the consumer proceeds to have additional units of *x*, he is willing to give away less and less units of *y* so that the MRS_{xy} falls from 4 : 1 to 1 : 1 in the Eth combination.

The negative of the slope of an indifference curve at any one point is called the marginal rate of substitution of the two commodities (MRS_{xy}). In other words, the MRS_{xy} is in fact the slope of the curve at a point on the indifference curve. Thus

$$\left[\begin{array}{c}\text{Slope of} \\ \text{indifference} \\ \text{curve}\end{array}\right] = -\frac{\Delta Y}{\Delta X} = MRS_{xy}$$

It means that the MRS_{xy} is the ratio of change in good Y to given change in X. In the figure 21 there are three triangles on the IC curve. The vertical sides *ab, cd* and *ef* represents ΔY and the horizontal sides *bc, de* and *fg* signify ΔX.

At point *c*, $MRS_{xy} = \frac{ab}{bc}$, at *e* it is $\frac{cd}{de}$ and at point *g*, MRS_{xy} is equal to $\frac{ef}{fg}$. This also shows that as the consumer moves downwards along the curve, he possesses additional units of *x*, and gives up lesser and lesser units of *y, i.e.,* the MRS_{xy} diminishes.

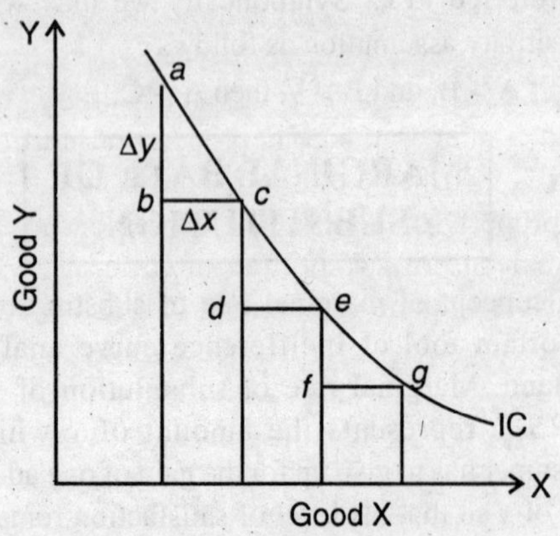

Fig. 21

Note

* If the MRS_{xy} is diminishing, the indifference curve must be **convex** to the origin.
* If MRS_{xy} is constant, the indifference curve will be **straight line** sloping downwards to the right.
* If MRS_{xy} is increasing, the indifference curve will be **concave** to the origin.
* In the case of perfect complementaries the MRS_{xy} is zero and the indifference curve will be L shaped.

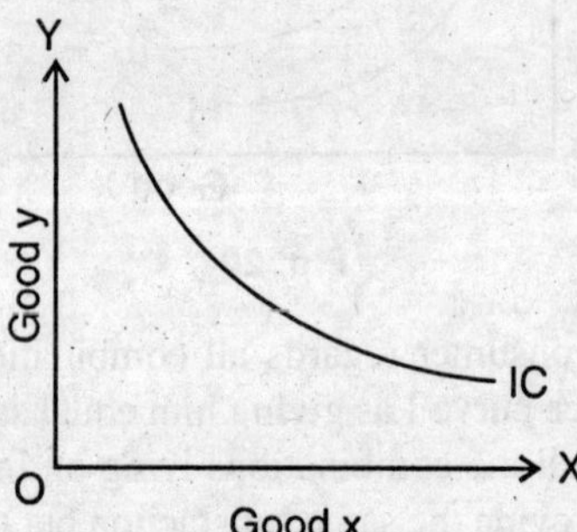

Fig. *Convex indifference curve*

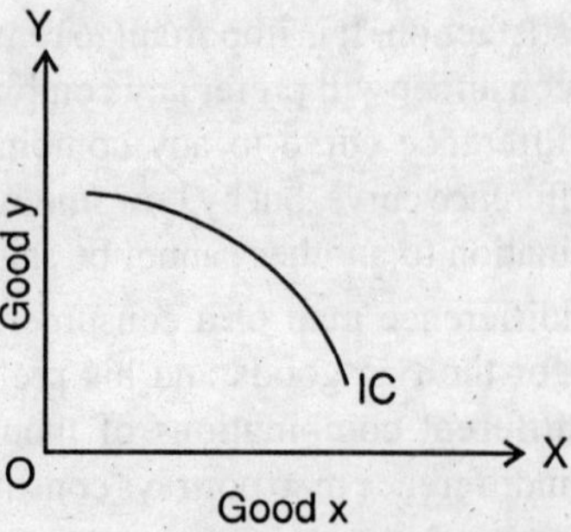

Fig. *Convance indifferent curve*

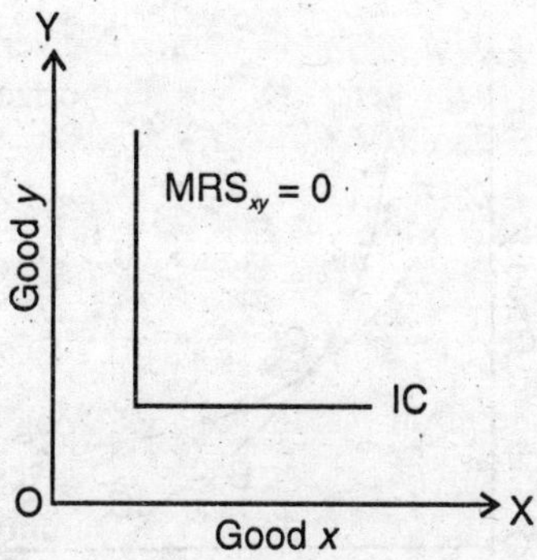

Fig. *L-shaped indifference curve*

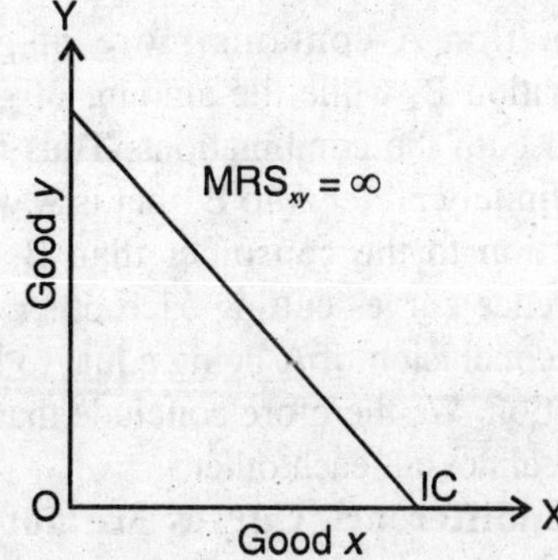

Fig. *Straight line indifference curve*

THE RELATIONSHIP BETWEEN MARGINAL RATE OF SUBSTITUTION AND MARGINAL UTILITIES

The slope of a indifference curve at any point is measured by the slope of the tangent at that point. The equation of a tangent is given by the total derivative or total differential, which shows the total change of the function as all its determinants change.

The total utility function in the case of two commodities X and Y is

$$U = f(X, Y)$$

The equation of an indifference curve is

$$U = f(x, y) = K$$

where K is constant.

The total differential of the utility function is

$$\Delta V = \frac{\Delta U}{\Delta Y}\Delta Y + \frac{\Delta U}{\Delta X}\Delta X$$

$$= (MU_y)\,\Delta Y + (MU_x)\,\Delta X$$

It shows that total change in utility as the quantities of both commodities change. The total change in U caused by changes in Y and X is (approximately) equal to the change in Y multiplied by its marginal utility, plus the change in X multiplied by its marginal utility.

Along any particular indifference curve the total differential is by definition equal to zero. Thus for any indifference curve

$$\Delta U = (MU_y)\,\Delta Y + (MU_x)\Delta X = 0$$

Rearranging we obtain

either $-\dfrac{\Delta Y}{\Delta X} = \dfrac{MU_x}{MU_y} = MRS_{x,y}$

or $-\dfrac{\Delta X}{\Delta Y} = \dfrac{MU_y}{MU_x} = MRS_{y,x}$

Thus the marginal rate of substitution between two goods is equal to the ratio between the marginal utilities of two goods.

PROPERTIES OF INDIFFERENCE CURVES

From the assumptions described above the following properties of indifference curves can be deduced.

1. Indifference Curves slope downward to the right : This property implies that an indifference curve has a negative slope. This means that when the amount of one good in the combination is increased, the amount of the other good is reduced.

2. Indifference Curves are Convex to the Origin : Another important property of indifference curves is that they are usually convex to the origin. This property of indifference curves based on the marginal rate of substitution of X for Y (MRS_{xy}) diminishes as more and more of X is substituted for Y. Only a convex indifference curve can mean a diminishing marginal rate of substitution of X for Y. If the indifference curve is concave to the origin, it will imply that the marginal rate of substitution of X for Y increases as more and more of X is substituted of Y, as shown in Figure 22.

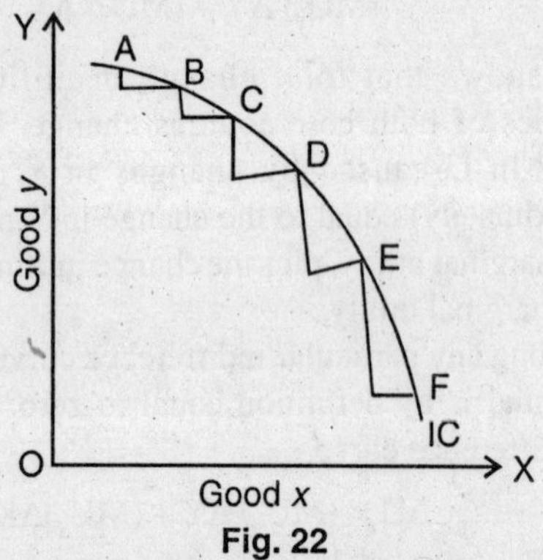

Fig. 22

It will be clear from this fig. that as more and more of x is acquired, for each extra unit of x the consumer is willing to part with more and more of y, that is , MRS_{xy} increases as more and more of x is substituted for y.

The degree of convexity of an indifference curve depends upon the rate of fall in the marginal rate of substitution of x for y.

3. Indifference Curves cannot Intersect each other : Third important property of indifference curves is that they cannot intersect each other. In other words, only one indifference curve will pass through a point in the indifference map. This property can be easily proved by first making the two indifference curves cut each other and then showing the absurdity or self-contradictory result it leads to. In Figure 23 two indifference curves are shown cutting each other at point C. Now take point A on indifference curve IC_2 and point B on indifference curve IC_1 vertically below A. Since an indifference curve represents those combinations of two goods which give equal satisfaction to the consumer, therefore combinations represented by points A and C will give equal satisfaction to the consumer because both lie on the same indifference curve IC_2. Likewise, the combinations B and C will give equal satisfaction to the consumer, both being on the same indifference curve IC_1.

If combination A is equal to combination C in terms of satisfaction, and combination B is equal to combination C, it follows that the combination A will be equivalent to B in terms of satisfaction. But a glance at Fig. 23 will show that this is absurd conclusion since

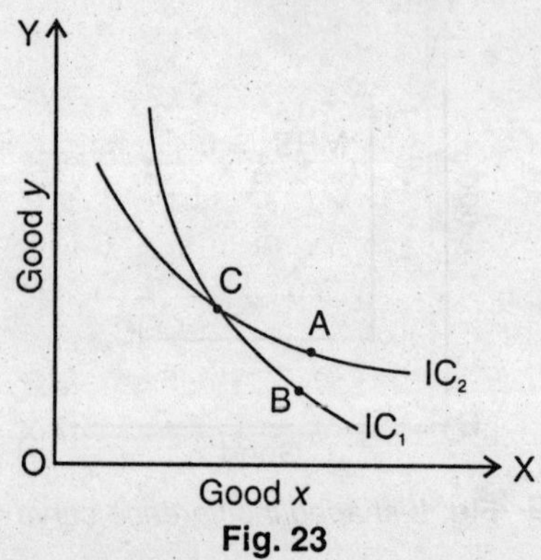

Fig. 23

combination A contains more of good Y then combination B, while the amount of good X is the same in both the combinations. Thus the consumer will definitely prefer A to B, that is A will give more satisfaction to the consumer than B. But the two indifference curves cutting each other lead us to an absurd conclusion of A being equal to B in terms of satisfaction. We therefore conclude that indifference curves cannot cut each other.

4. Indifference Curves are not necessarily parallel to each other : Though they are falling, negatively inclined to the right, yet the rate of fall will not be the same for all indifference curves. In other words, the diminishing marginal rate of substitution between the two goods is essentially not the same in the case of all indifference schedules. The two curves IC_1 and IC_2 shown in Figure 24 are not parallel to each other.

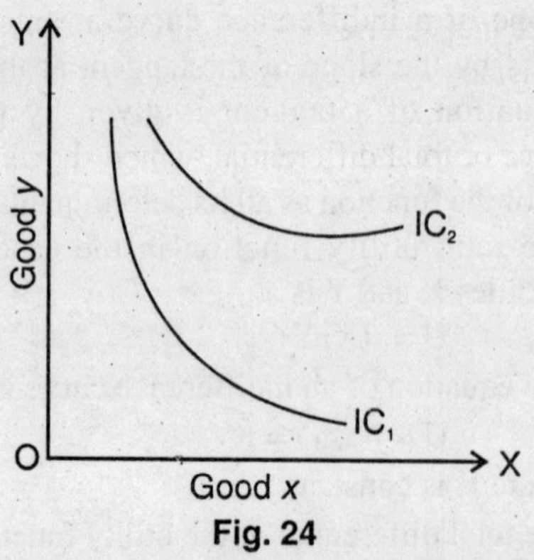

Fig. 24

5. A Higher Indifference Curve represents Higher Level of Satisfaction than the Lower

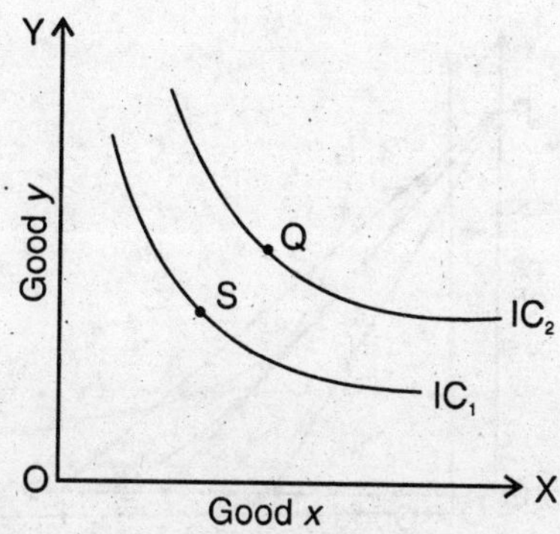

Fig. 25: *A higher indifference curve shows higher level of satisfaction*

Indifference Curve : Another property of indifference curve is that a higher indifference curve will represent a higher level of satisfaction than a lower indifference curve. In other words, the combinations which lie on a higher indifference which lie on a lower indifference curve. Consider indifference curves IC_2 and IC_1 in Figure 25. IC_2 is a higher indifference curve than IC_1. Combination Q has been taken on a higher indifference curve IC_2 and combination S on a lower indifference curve IC_1.

Combination Q on the higher indifference curve IC_2 will give the consumer more satisfaction than combination S on the lower indifference curve IC_1 because the combination Q contains more of both goods X and Y than the combination S. Hence the consumer must prefer Q to S. And by transitivity, he will prefer any other combination on IC_2 to any combination on IC_1. We, therefore, conclude that a higher indifference curve represents the higher level of satisfaction and combinations on it will be preferred

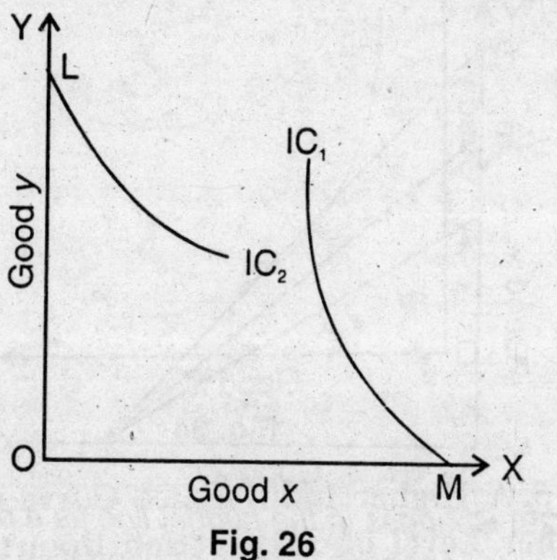

Fig. 26

to the combinations on a lower indifference curve.

6. An Indifference Curve cannot Touch either Axis : If it touch *x*-axis as IC_1 in figure 26 at M, the consumer will be having OM quantity of good *x* and none of *y*. Similarly, If an indifference curve IC_2 touches the *y*-axis at L the consumer will have only OL of *y* good and no amount of *x*.

Such curves are in contradiction to the assumption that the consumer buys two goods in combinations.

Price Line or Budget Line

Understanding of the concept of **price line** or **budget line** is essential for understanding the theory of consumer's equilibrium. The consumer has a given income which sets limits to his maximising behaviour. Income acts as a constraint in the attempt for maximising utility. The income constraints, in the case of two commodities, may be written

$$I = p_x q_x + p_y q_y \qquad ...(1)$$

We may present the income constraint graphically by the budget line, whose equation is derived from expression (1), by solving for q_y :

$$q_y = \frac{1}{p_y} I - \frac{p_x}{p_y} q_x$$

Assigning successive values to q_x (given the income, I and the commodity prices, p_x and p_y), we may find the corresponding values of q_y. Thus if q_x = 0 (that is, if the consumer spends all his income on *y*) the consumer can buy I/p_y units of Y. Similarly, if q_y = 0 (that is, if the consumer spends all his income an *x*) the consumer can buy I/p_x units of *x*. In figure 27 these results are shown by points A and B. If we join these points with a line we obtain the budget line.

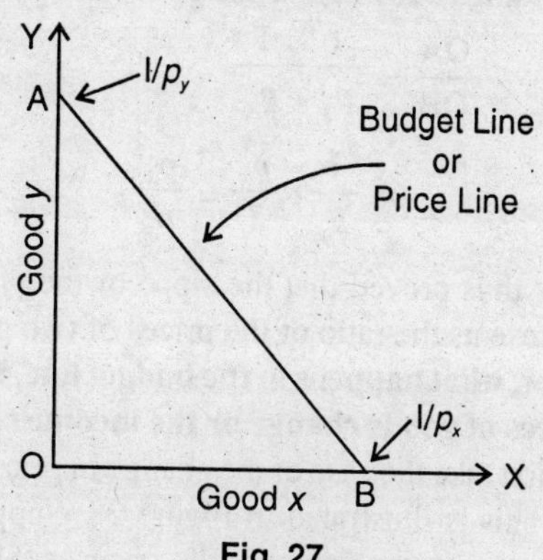

Fig. 27

Consumer can but any combination that lies on the budget line AB with his given money income and given prices of the goods. It should be carefully noted that any combination of good which lies above and outside the given budget line, AB, will be beyond the reach of the consumer. But any combination lying within the price line or budget line, AB, will be well within the reach of the consumer, but if he buys any such combination he will not be spending all his income.

Thus, with the assumption that whole of the given income is spent on the given goods and at given prices of them, the consumer has to choose among from all those combinations which line on the price line or budget line.

Slope of the Budget Line

The slope of the budget line is equal to the ratio of the prices of two goods. This can be proved with the aid of Fig. 27. Suppose the given income of the consumer is I, the given prices of goods x and y are p_x and p_y respectively. The slope of the price line AB is $\frac{OA}{OB}$. We intend to prove that the slope $\frac{OA}{OB}$ is equal to the ratio of the price of goods x and y.

The quantity of good x purchased if whole of the given income I is spent on it is OB. Therefore

$$OB \times p_x = I$$

$$OB = I/p_x \qquad ...(1)$$

Now, the quantity of good y purchased if whole of the given income I is spent on it is OA. Therefore,

$$OA \times p_y = I$$

$$OA = I/p_y \qquad ...(2)$$

Dividing (2) by (1) we have :

$$\frac{OA}{OB} = \frac{I}{p_y} \div \frac{I}{p_x}$$

$$= \frac{I}{p_y} \times \frac{p_x}{I} = \frac{p_x}{p_y}$$

It is thus proved that the slope of the price line AB represents the ratio of the prices of two goods.

Now, what happens to the budget line. If either the prices of goods change or the income changes. Let us first take the case of the change in prices of the goods. This is illustrated in Figure 28. Suppose the budget line in the beginning is PL, given certain prices

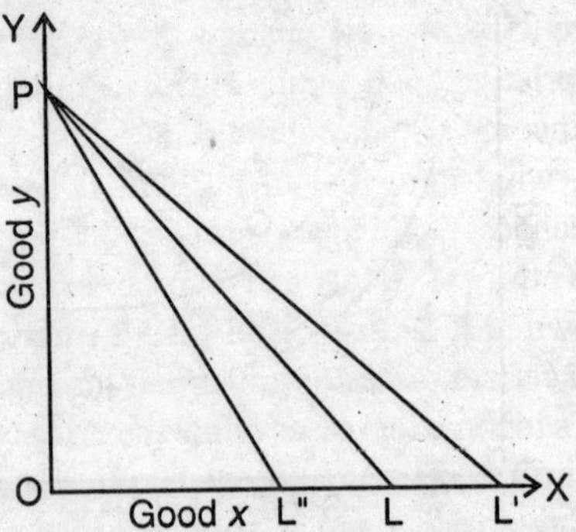

Fig. 28: *Changes in budget line as a result of changes in price of good x*

of the good x and y and a certain income. Suppose the price of x falls, the price of y and income remaining unchanged. Now with a lower price of x the consumer will be able to purchase more quantity of x than before with his given income. Let at the lower price of x, the given income purchases OL' of X which of greater than OL. Since the price of Y remains the same, there can be no change in the quantity purchased of good Y with the same given income and as a result there will be no shift in the point P. Thus with the fall in the price of good x, the consumer's income and the price of Y remaining constant, the budget line will take the new position PL'.

Now, what will happen to the budget line as the price of good x rises, the price of good Y and income remaining unaltered. With higher price of good x, the consumer can purchase smaller quantity of X, say OL", than before. Thus with the rise in price of X the budget line will assume the new position PL".

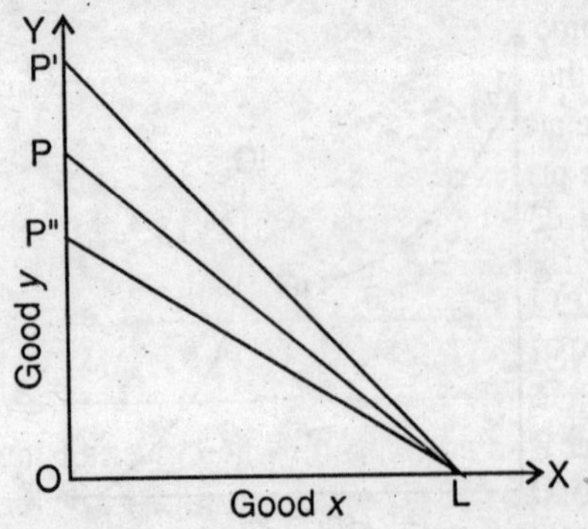

Fig. 29: *Changes in the budget line as a result of changes in price of good Y*

Figure 29 shows the changes in the budget line when the price of good Y falls or rises, with the price of X and income remaining the same.

Now, what happens to the budget line if the income changes, while the prices of goods remain the same. The effect of changes in income on the budget line is shown in Figure 30. Let PL be the initial price line, given certain prices of goods and income. If the consumer's income increases while the prices of both goods X and Y remain unaltered, the price line shifts upward (Say, to P'L') and is parallel to the original price line PL. On the other hand, if the income of the consumer decreases, the prices of both goods X and Y remaining unchanged, the budget line shifts downward (Say, to P"L") but remains parallel to the original price line PL.

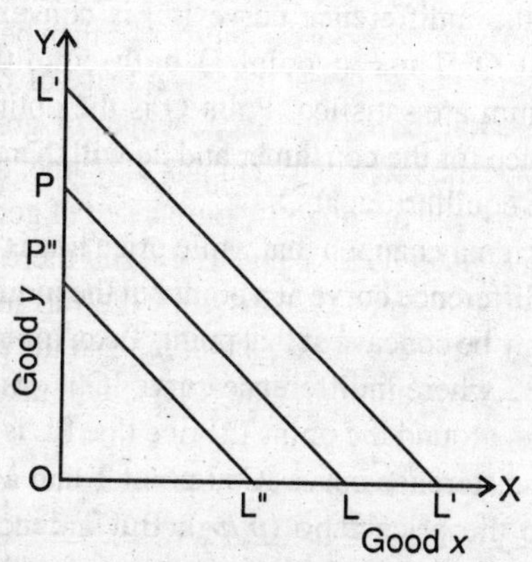

Fig. 30 : *Changes in budget line as a result of changes in income*

It is clear from above that the price line or budget line will change if either the prices of goods change or the income of the consumer changes.

Thus the two determinants of the price line or budget line are :

1. The prices of goods.
2. The consumer's income to be spent on the goods.

CONSUMER'S EQUILIBRIUM

A consumer is in equilibrium when given his tastes, and prices of the two goods, he spends a given money income on the purchase of two goods in such a way as to get the maximum satisfaction. In the indifference curve technique the consumer's equilibrium is discussed in respect of the purchases of two goods by the consumer.

The indifference curve analysis of consumer's equilibrium is based on the following assumptions :

1. The consumer has a given indifference map exhibiting his scale of preferences for various combinations of two goods, X and Y.
2. He has a fixed amount of money to spend on the two goods. He has to spend whole of his given money on the two goods.
3. Prices of the goods are given and constant for him. He cannot influence the prices of the goods by buying more or less of them.
4. Goods are homogeneous and divisible.

To show which combination of two goods, X and Y, the consumer will decide to buy and will be in equilibrium position, his indifference map and price line are brought together. Suppose our consumer has in indifference map, shown in the following diagram (Fig. 31). Further suppose that the budget line facing the consumer is PL. Good X is measured on the X-axis and good Y is measured on the Y-axis. With given money to be spent and given prices of the two goods, the consumer can buy any combination of the goods which lies on the price line PL. In order to maximise his satisfaction the consumer will try to reach the highest indifference curve which he could with a given expenditure of money and given prices of the two goods. Budget constraint forces the consumer to remain on the given budget line, that is, to choose any combinations from among only those which lie on the given budget line.

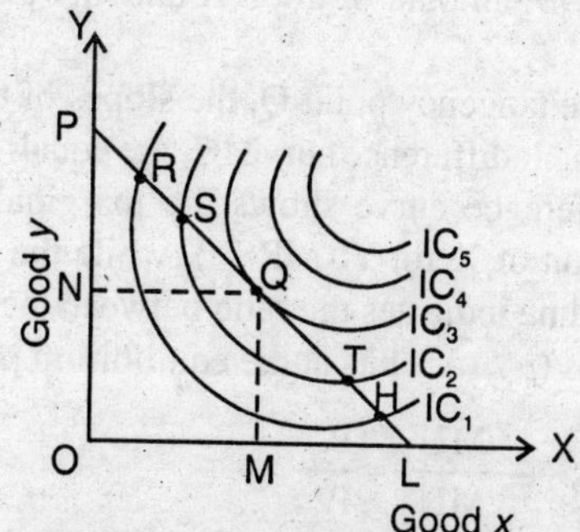

Fig. 31: *Consumer's Equilibrium*

According to the figure 31, the consumer will

choose that combination on the price line PL which lies on the highest possible indifference curve. The highest indifference curve to which the consumer can reach is the indifference curve to which the price line PL is tangent. Any other possible combination of the two goods either would lie on a lower indifference curve and thus yield less satisfaction or would be unattainable. In Fig. 31, budget line PL is tangent to indifference curve IC_3 at point Q. Since indifference curves are convex to the origin, all other points on the budget line PL, above or below the point Q, would lie on the lower indifference curves. Take point R which also lies on the budget line PL and which the consumer can afford to buy. Combination of goods represented by R costs him the same as the combination Q. But, as is evident, R lies on the lower indifference curve IC_1 and will therefore yield less satisfaction than Q. Like wise, point S also lies on the price line PL, but will be rejected in favour of Q. Since S lies on the indifference curve IC_2 which is also lower than IC_3 on which Q lies. Similarly, Q will be preferred to all other points on the price line PL which lies below Q, such as T and H. It is thus clear that of all possible combinations lying on PL, combination Q lies on the highest possible indifference curve and yields maximum possible satisfaction.

It is therefore concluded that with the given money expenditure and the given prices of the goods as shown by PL the consumer will obtain maximum possible satisfaction and will therefore be in equilibrium position at point Q at which the rate budget line PL is tangent to the indifference curve IC_3. In this equilibrium position at Q the consumer will buy OM amount of good X and ON amount of good Y.

At the tangency point Q, the slopes of the price line PL and indifference curve IC_3 are equal. Slope of the indifference curve shows the marginal rate of substitution of X for Y (MRS_{xy}), while the slope of the price line indicates the ratio between the price of two goods (p_x/p_y). Thus at the equilibrium point Q,

$$MRS_{xy} = \frac{MU_x}{MU_y} = \frac{P_x}{P_y}$$

This is a necessary but not sufficient condition for equilibrium. The **second condition** is that the

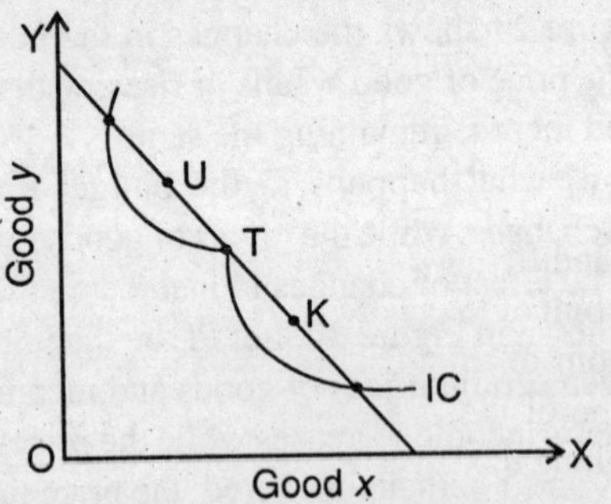

Fig. 32 : *Second order condition for consumer's equilibrium*

indifference curves be convex to the origin, or to put it in another way, the MRS_{xy} must be falling at the point of equilibrium. It will be noticed form Figure 31 that the indifference curve IC_3 is convex to the origin at Q. Thus at point Q both conditions of equilibrium are satisfied. Point Q is the optimum or best choice for the consumer and he will therefore be in stable equilibrium at Q.

But it may happen that while price line is tangent to an indifference curve at a point but the indifference curve may be concave at that point. Take, for instance, Figure 32 where indifference curve IC is concave to the origin around the point T. Price line PL is tangent to the indifference curve IC at point T and MRS_{xy} is equal to the price ratio (p_x/p_y). But T cannot be a position of stable equilibrium because satisfaction would not be maximum there, Indifference curve IC being concave at the tangency point T, there are some points on the given price line PL such as U and K, which will be on indifference curve higher than IC. Thus the consumer by moving along the given price line PL can go to points such as U and K and obtain greater satisfaction than at T. We therefore conclude that for the consumer to be in equilibrium, two conditions are required :

1. A given price line must be tangent to an indifference curve, or marginal rate of substitution of X for Y (MRS_{xy}) must be equal to the price ratio between the two goods (p_x/p_y).

$$MRS_{xy} = \frac{P_x}{P_y} = \frac{MU_x}{MU_y}$$

or. $\frac{MU_x}{MU_y} = \frac{P_x}{P_y}$

or, $\frac{MU_x}{P_x} = \frac{MU_y}{P_y}$

2. Indifference curve must be convex to the origin at the point of tangency. This condition is fulfilled by the axiom of diminishing MRS_{xy}, which states that the slope of the indifference curve decreases as we move along the curve from the left downwards to the right.

Exceptional Cases of Consumer's Equilibrium

We have said that the indifference curves are usually convex to the origin. The consumer's equilibrium is at the point of tangency of the price line with an indifference curve. There are some exceptions.

Fig. 33 gives concave indifference curves and the consumer will be in equilibrium not at Q where PL price line is a tangent to the curve but at P, where consumer buys only good Y or at L where he will but only good X. P and L being on higher indifference curves than at Q. **It is clear that when a consumer has concave indifference curves, he will succumb to monomania, that is, he will consume only one good.**

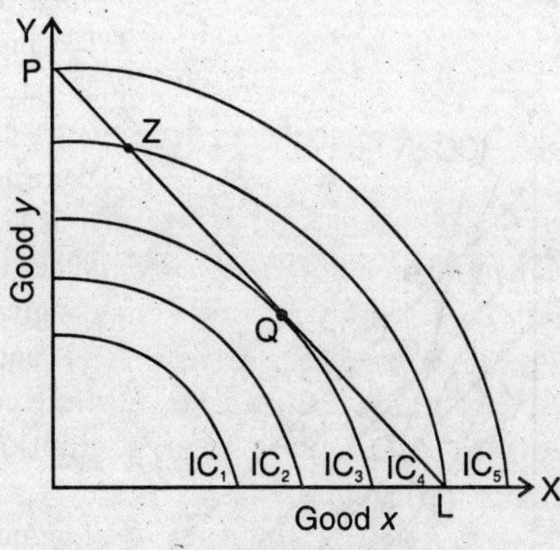

Fig. 33

Figure 34 and 35 give straight line indifference curves. It is a case of perfect substitutes. Since there are straight lines, tangency is not possible. The equilibrium position will depend on the slope of the price line relative to the slope of indifference curves. If the slope of the price line PL is greater as in Fig. 34, he will be equilibrium at P and buy only Y good. But if it is less as in Fig. 35, he will be in equilibrium at L and buy only good X.

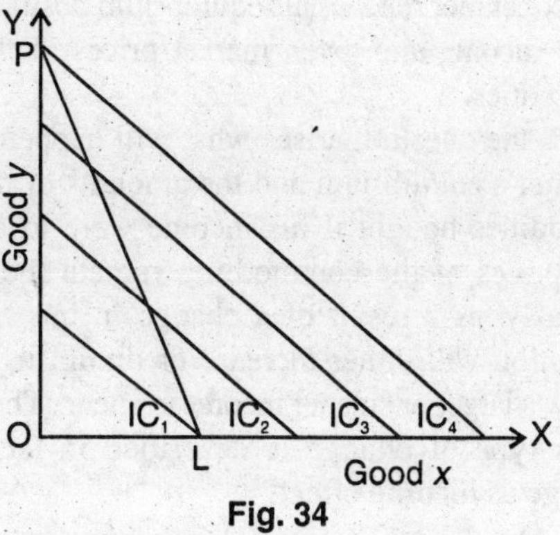

Fig. 34

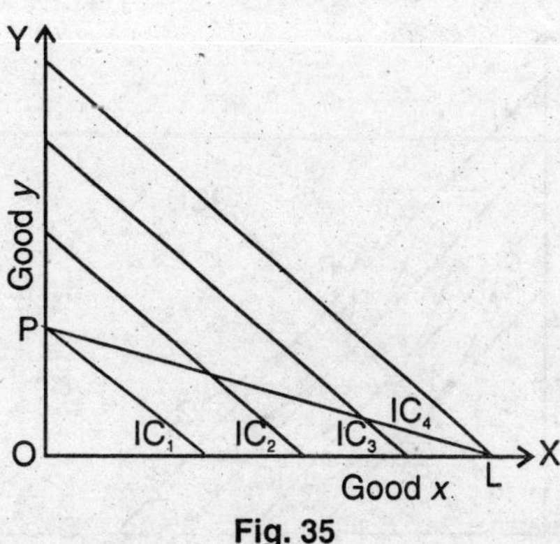

Fig. 35

Figure 36 represents the case of **comple-mentary goods.** Here the indifference curves are right-angled. In such a case the consumer's equilibrium will be at the corner of the curve where the price line is a tangent *i.e.,* at C.

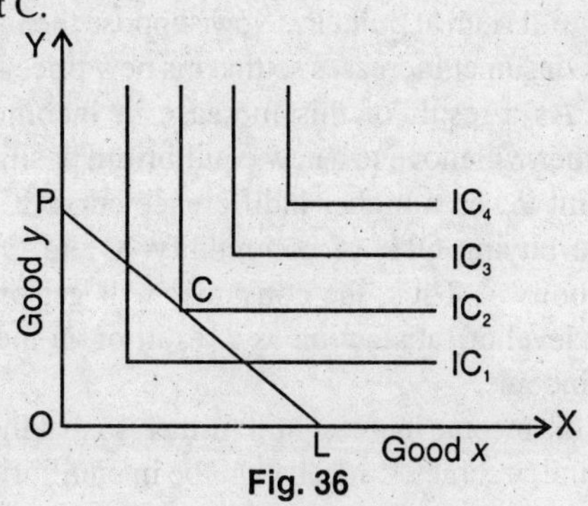

Fig. 36

INCOME EFFECT

Income effect is the effect on the quantity demanded exclusively as a result of change in money income, all prices remaining constant. It has been shown above how a consumer reaches his equilibrium position with a fixed income and given market prices of the two commodities.

But the question arises what will happen to the consumer's equilibrium and the amounts of the two commodities bought if his income were to change while prices of the commodities remain the same. Obviously, as a result of a change in income, his satisfaction will either increase or diminish, for he has now a larger or smaller income to spend. The result of this type of change is described in technical language as **income effect.**

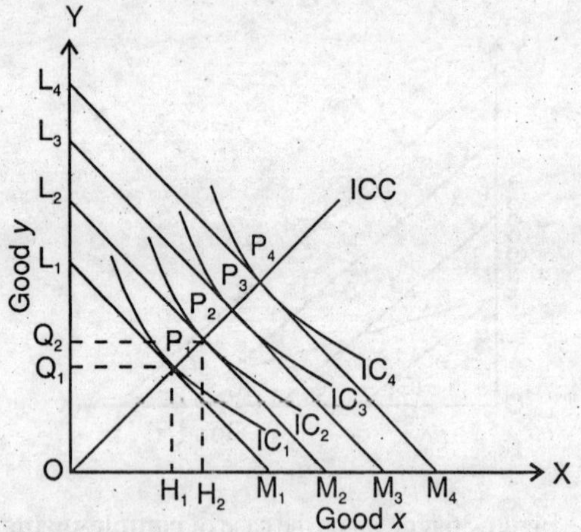

Fig. 37 : *Income Effect*

The income effect has been explained with the help of Figure 37. With Price-line L_1M_1, the consumer is in equilibrium at point P_1. Now suppose the income of the consumer increases so that his new price line is L_2M_2. As a result of this increase in income, the consumer will move to a new equilibrium position, at the point P_2, on a higher indifference curve IC_2 and will be buying OH_2 of commodity X and OQ_2 of commodity Y. Thus, the consumer will get on to a higher level of satisfaction as a result of an increase in his income.

If his income increase still further, so that the new price line becomes L_3M_3, he will be in equilibrium at the point P_3 on an indifference curve IC_3, and so on for further increases in income.

Thus, we get various points of equilibrium such as P_1, P_2, P_3, for different levels of income, prices of the commodities remaining the same. If the points P_1, P_2, P_3, P_4 etc, are joined together by a line passing from the origin, we get, what is called **Income Consumption Curve (ICC).**

Income consumption curve is thus the locus of equilibrium points at various levels of consumer's income. Income consumption curve traces out the income effect on the quantity consumed of the goods.

Income effect can either be **positive** or **negative.** Income effect for good is said to be **positive** when with the increase in income of the consumer, his consumption of the good also increases. This is the normal case. When the income effect of both the goods represented on the two axes of the figure is positive, the income consumption curve (ICC) will upward to the right as in Fig. 37. However, for some goods, income effect is **negative.** Income effect for a good is said to be **negative** when with the increase in his income, the consumer reduces his consumption of the good. Such goods for which income effect is negative are called **Inferior Goods.**

In case of inferior goods, income consumption curve either slopes backward (*i.e.,* upward to the left) as in Fig. 38, or downward to the right as in Fig. 39.

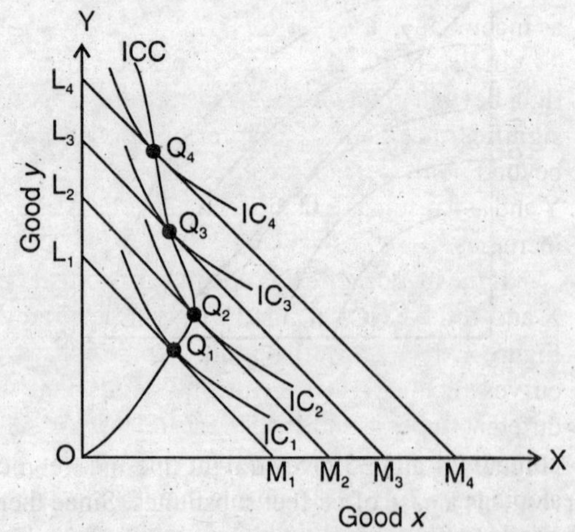

Fig. 38: *ICC in case of Good X being inferior good*

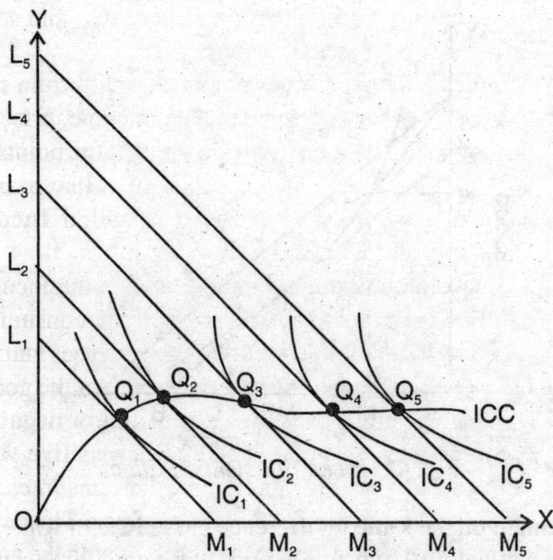

Fig. 39: *Income consumption curve in case of Good Y being Inferior Good*

It would be noticed from the two figures that income effect becomes negative only after a point. It signifies that only at higher ranges of income, some goods become inferior goods and upto a point changes in their consumption behave like those of normal goods.

In Figure 38, Income consumption curve (ICC) slopes backward (upward to the left) *i.e.,* bends towards the *y*-axis. This shows good *x* to be an inferior good, since beyond point Q_2, income effect is negative for good X and as a result its quantity demanded falls as income increases.

In Figure 39, ICC-curve slopes downward to the right beyond point Q_2 *i.e.,* bends towards *x*-axis. This signifies that good Y is inferior good because as beyond point Q_2, income effect is negative for good Y and as a result its quantity demanded falls as income increases.

If the income effect is positive for both the goods X and Y, the ICC will slope upward to the right as in Figure 37. But upward-sloping income consumption curves to the right for various goods may be of different slopes as shown in Figure 40 in which income consumption curves, with varying slopes, are all sloping upward to the right and therefore indicate both goods to be **normal goods having positive income effect.**

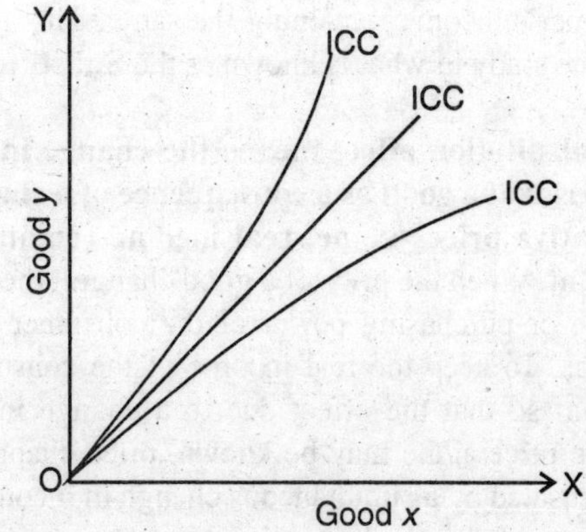

Fig. 40 : *Income consumption curves of Normal Goods*

If the income effect is negative, income consumption curve will slope backward to the left as ICC′ in Figure 41. If good X happens to be inferior good, it will slope downward to the right as ICC" in figure 41 if good Y happens to be the inferior good.

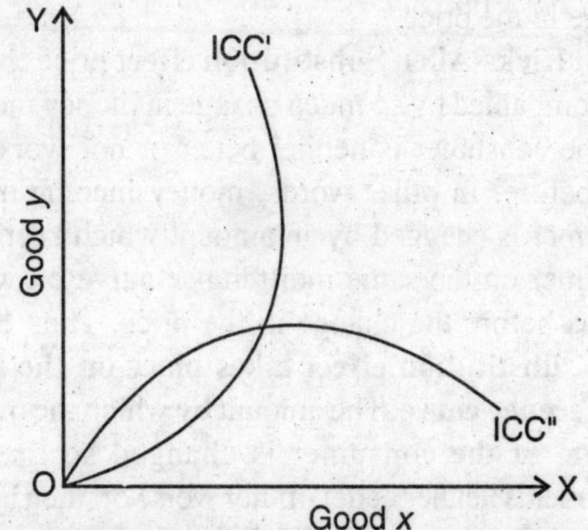

Fig. 41: *Income consumption curves of Inferior Goods*

***Inferior Goods :** Those goods of which the quantity that the consumer would buy less, as his income rises, are called inferior goods. **Inferior goods may be defined as goods for which income effect is negative.**

SUBSTITUTION EFFECT

We have discussed above the effect on consumer's equilibrium of a change in consumer's income, relative prices of commodities remaining the same. Now let us see the effect of a change in relative prices, consumer's income remaining the same. This leads us to the study to what is known as the **Substitution Effect.**

Substitution effect means the change in the purchases of a good as a consequence of a change in relative prices alone, real income remaining constant. When the price of a good changes, the real income or purchasing power of the consumer also changes. To keep the real income of the consumer constant so that the effect due to a change in the relative price alone may be known, price change is compensated by a simultaneous change in income.

Now, two slightly different concepts of substitution effect have been developed, one by Hicks and Allen and the other by Slutsky. These two concepts of substitution effect have been named after their authors. The two concepts differ in regard to the magnitude of the change in money income which should be effected so as to neutralize the change in real income of the consumer which results from a change in the price.

In **Hicks-Allen Substitution effect** price change is accompanied by so much change in money income that the consumer is neither better or nor worse off than before. In other words, money income of the consumer is changed by an amount which keeps the consumer on the same indifference curve on which he was before the change in the price. Thus **Hick-Allen substitution effect takes place on the same indifference curve.** The amount by which the money income of the consumer is changed so that the consumer is neither better off nor worse off than before is called **Compensating Variation in Income.**

Hicks-Allen substitution effect is illustrated in Figure 42. With a given money income and given prices of the two goods are represented by the price line PL, the consumer is in equilibrium at point Q on the indifference curve IC and is purchasing OM of the good X.

Suppose that the price of good X falls (price of Y remaining unchanged) so that the price line now shifts to PL'. With this fall in price of X, the consumer's real income would increase. In order to find out the substitution effect, this gain in real income should be wiped out by reducing the money income of the consumer by so much amount that forces him to

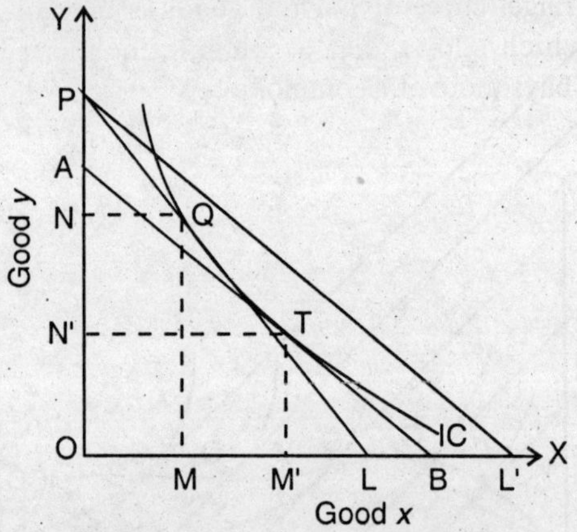

Fig. 42: *Hicks Substitution Effect*

remain on the same indifference curve IC. On which he was before the change in price of the good X. When some money income is taken away from the consumer to cancel out the gain in real income, then the price line which shifted to position PL' will now shift downward but will be parallel to PL'. In Fig. 42, a price line AB parallel to PL' has been drawn as such a distance from PL' that it touches the indifference curve. It means that reduction of consumer's income by the amount PA (in terms of Y) or L'B (in terms of X) had been made so as to keep him on the same indifference curve. PA or L'B is therefore compensating variation in income.

It will be seen from Figure 42 that with price line AB consumer is in equilibrium at point T and is now buying OM' of X and ON' of Y. This increase in the purchases of good X by MM' and the decrease in the purchases of good Y by NN' is due to the change only in the relative prices of good X and Y. Therefore, movement from Q and T represents the substitution effect. It is thus clear that as a result of substitution effect the consumer remains on the same indifference curve, he is however in equilibrium at a different point from that at which he was before the change in price of X.

ENGEL CURVE

Engel curve shows the quantities of a good which the consumer will purchase at various income level, given his tastes, preferences and the price of the good in question. Engel curve of **normal goods** is upward sloping which shows that as income increases consumer buys more of a commodity.

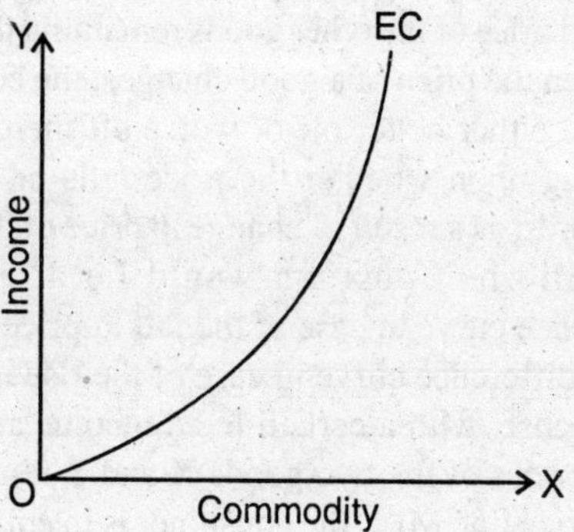

Fig. 43 : *Engel curve : Necessities*

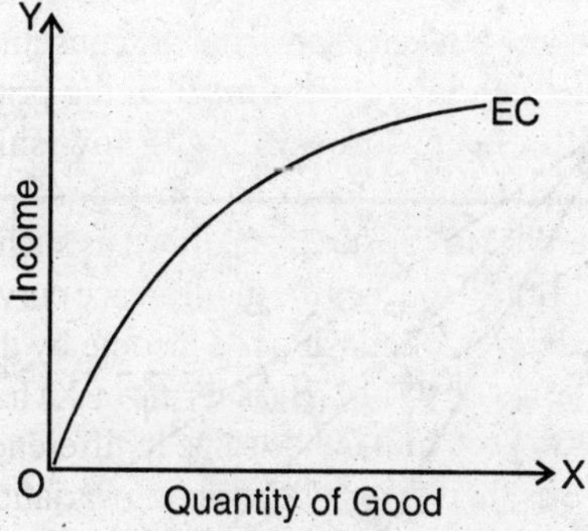

Fig. 44 : *Engel curve : Luxuries*

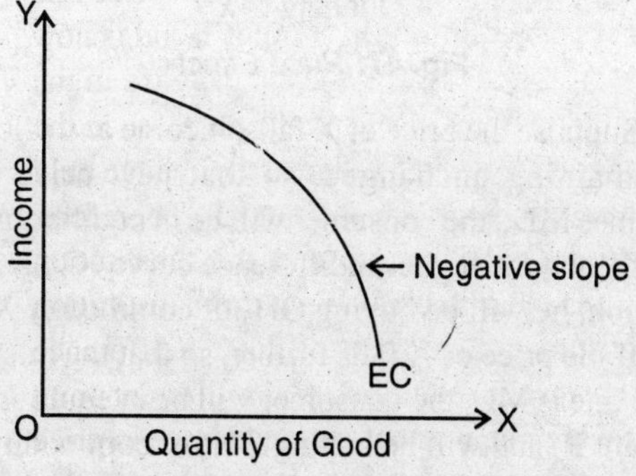

Fig. 45 : *Engel curve: Inferior goods*

SLUTSKY SUBSTITUTION EFFECT

Slustsky has given a slightly different version of substitution effect. In this version when the price of a good changes and consumer's real income or purchasing power increase, the income of the consumer in changed by the amount equal to the change in its purchasing power which occurs as a result of the price change. His purchasing power changes by the amount equal to the change in the price multiplied by the number of units of the good which the individual used to buy at the old price.

In other words, in Slutsky's approach, income is reduced or increased by the amount which leaves the consumer to be just able to purchase the same combination of goods, if he so desires, which he was having at the old price. That is, the income is changed by the difference between the cost of the amount of good X purchased at the old price and the cost of the same quantity of X at the new price. Income is then said to be changed by the **Cost difference.** Thus, in Slutsky substitution effect, income is reduced or increased not by the compensating variation but by the cost difference.

Slutsky substitution effect is illustrated in Figure 46 with a given money income and the given prices of two goods as represented by the price line PL, the consumer is in equilibrium as Q on the indifference curve IC_1 buying OM of X and ON of Y. Now suppose that price of X falls, price of Y and money income of the consumer remaining unchanged. As a result of this fall in price of X, the price line will shift to PL' and the real income or the purchasing power of the consumer will increase. Now, in order to find out the Slutsky substitution effect, consumer's money income must be reduced by the **cost-difference.** For this, a

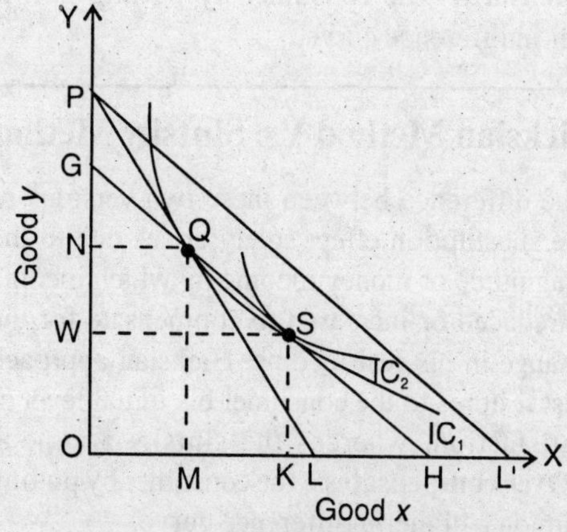

Fig. 46 : *Slutsky Substitution Effect*

price line GH parallel to PL' has been drawn which passes through the point Q. It means that income equal to PG in terms of Y or L'H in terms of X had been taken away from the consumer and as a result he can but the combination Q, if he so desires. Since Q also lies on the price lien GH. Actually, he will not now buy the old combination Q since X had now become relatively dearer than before.

The change in relative prices will induce the consumer to rearrange the purchases of X and Y. He will substitute X for Y. But in this Slutsky substitution case, consumer will not move along the same indifference curve IC_1, since the price line GH, on which the consumer has to remain due to the price-income circumstances, is now where tangent to the IC_2 at points S. Therefore, the consumer will now be in equilibrium at a point S on higher indifference curve IC_2. This movement from Q to S represents Slutsky substitution effect.

From the above analysis it is clear that whereas **Hicks-Allen substitution effect** takes place on the same indifference curve, Slutsky substitution effect involves the movement from one indifference curve to another curve, a higher one. The difference between the two versions of the substitution effect solely arises due to the magnitude of money income by which income is reduced or increased to compensate for the change in his real income. **Hicksian approach just restores to the consumer his initial level of satisfaction,** whereas the slutsky approach **"Over compensates"** the consumer by putting him on a higher indifference curve.

Hicksian Method Vs. Slutsky Method

The difference between these two versions of the substitution effect solely arises due to the magnitude of money income by which income is reduced or increased to compensate for the change in his real income. Hicksian approach just restores to the consumer his initial level of satisfaction, whereas the slutsky appraoch **"Over compensates"** the consumer by putting him on a higher indifference curve.

PRICE EFFECT

We will now explain how the consumer reacts to changes in the price of a good, his money income, tastes and price of the other goods remaining the same.

When the price of a good changes, the consumer would be either better off or worse off them before, depending upon whether the price falls or rises. In other words, as a result of change in price of the good, his equilibrium position would lie at a higher indifference curve in case of the fall in price and at a lower indifference curve in case of the rise in price.

Suppose, with a certain fixed income and given market prices of the two goods X and Y represented by the Price line ML_1, the consumer is in equilibrium at point P_1 in Figure 47.

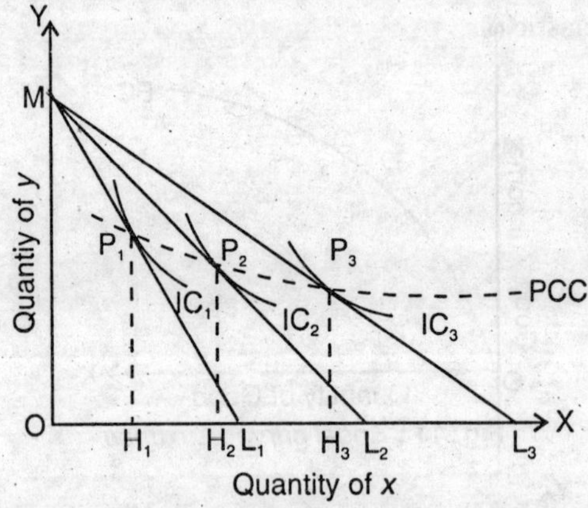

Fig. 47: *Price Effect*

Suppose the price of X falls, income and price of Y remaining unchanged, so that new price line becomes ML_2, the consumer will be in equilibrium at point P_2 on the higher indifference curve IC_2. In this position, he will be buying OH_2 of commodity X.

If the price of X falls further, so that the relevant price line is ML_3 the consumer will be in equilibrium at point P_3 and will be buying OH_3 of commodity X. In the same way, we can discover other points of equilibrium for every other price at which X-might be sold. When all the points such as P_1, P_2, P_3 are joined together we have the **price consumption curve** of the consumer for good X. This shows the **price effect. It shows how the consumption of commodity X changes, as its price changes, the consumer's**

income and price of Y remaining the same.

In Fig. 47 price consumption curve (PCC) is sloping downward. Downward-sloping price consumption curve for good X means that as the price of good X falls, the consumer purchases a larger quantity of good X and smaller quantity of good Y. This is quite evident from Fig. 47. We obtain downward sloping price consumption curve for good X when demand for **it is elastic** (*i.e.,* price elasticity is greater than one).

Price consumption curve can have other shapes also. In Fig. 48 upward-sloping price consumption curve is shown. Upward-sloping price consumption curve X means that when the price of good X falls, the quantity demanded of both goods X and Y rises. **We obtain the upward sloping price consumption curve for good X when the demand for good is less elastic (*i.e.,* price elasticity is less them one).**

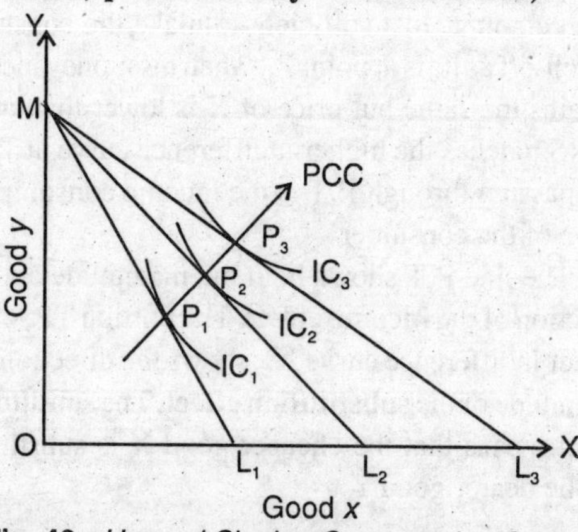

Fig. 48 : *Upward Sloping Consumption Curve*

Price consumption curve can also have a **backward sloping shape,** which is depicted in Fig. 49. Backward sloping price consumption curve for good X indicates that when price of X falls, smaller quantity of it is demanded or purchased. This is the case of **Giffen Goods.**

Price consumption curve for a good can take horizontal shape too. It means that when the price of the good X declines, its quantity purchased rises proportionally but quantity purchased of Y remains the same. Horizontal price consumption curve is shown in Fig. 50. **We obtain horizontal price consumption curve of good X when the price elasticity of demand for good X is equal to unity.**

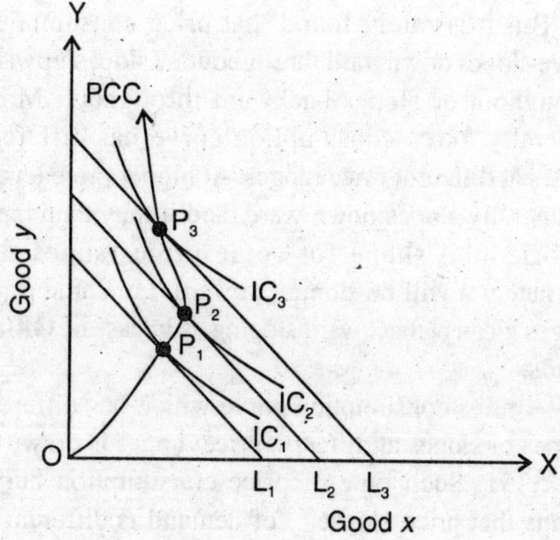

Fig. 49 : *Backward Sloping Price Consumption Curves*

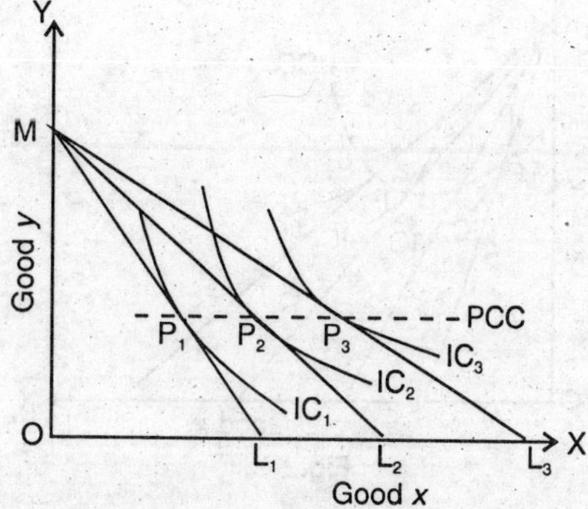

Fig. 50 : *Horizontal Price Consumption Curve*

Price Consumption Curve and Elasticity of Demand

The shape of the price consumption curve shows the degree of elasticity of demand, *i.e.,* the elasticity is unitary, greater than one or less than one. When the price consumption is horizontal, *i.e.,* parallel to X-axis (*i.e.,* has zero slope), the elasticity of demand for good X is unitary, *i.e.,* the total outlay on X remains the same even though price of X rises. If PCC is upward sloping, the demand for the good X is inelastic, and if it is downward sloping, the demand will be elastic.

But it is rarely found that price consumption curve slopes downward throughout or slopes upward throughout or slopes backward throughout. More generally, price consumption curve has different slopes at different price ranges. At higher price levels it generally slopes down ward, and it may then have a horizontal shape for some price ranges but ultimately it will be sloping upward. For some price ranges it can be backward sloping as in case of **Giffen goods.**

A price consumption curve which has different shapes or slopes at different price ranges is drawn in figure 51. Such type of price consumption curve means that price elasticity of demand is different at different price ranges.

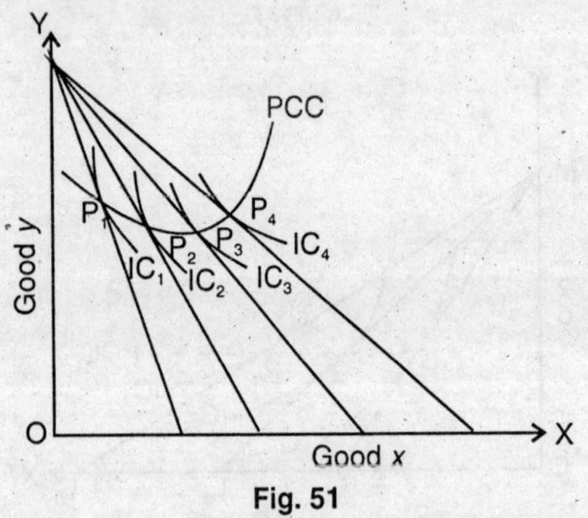

Fig. 51

Two Components of Price Effect

The movement of the consumer along the price consumption curve, such as from equilibrium point P_1 to P_2 as a result of a fall in the price of X, is in reality a resultant of two forces. The first of these components is the feeling of better-offense that a consumer experiences when the price of X falls. There is an increase in the potential purchasing power of the consumer's income following a relative fall in the price of X. It is **Income Effect.** This income effect is the first component of the price effect. The consumer is operating along the income consumption curve.

There is also the second component of the price effect viz., the **Substitution Effect.** Now that X is cheaper than before while the price of Y has remained unchanged, there will naturally be a tendency on the part of the consumer to buy more of the cheaper good and less of the relatively dearer one.

In other words, he will substitute cheaper good for the dearer one. This second components is called the **Substitution Effect** and can be viewed as operating along the price consumption curve. (Fig. 52)

These two components of the movement from P_1 to P_2 are shown in Figure 52. Initially, with the price line ML_1, the consumer is in equilibrium at point P_1. With a fall in price of X, so that the new relevant price line ML_2, he moves to a new equilibrium position P_2 on a higher indifference curve IC_2. RS is a hypothetical price line drawn parallel to ML_1 and touching the higher indifference curve IC_2 at point T. RS shows as if the price of X had remained the same (as represented by ML_1), but instead consumer's income had increased by an amount. Just sufficient to make the consumer as well-off as he is at point P_2, when his money income remains the same but price of X is lower than at P_1. As RS touches the higher indifference curve at T, the line passing through P_1T is the income consumption curve of the consumer.

The line P_1T shows both the magnitude and the direction of the **income effect.** The portion TP_2 of the higher indifference curve IC_2 shows the direction and magnitude of the **substitution effect.** The substitution effect means that the cheaper good X is substituted for the dearer good Y.

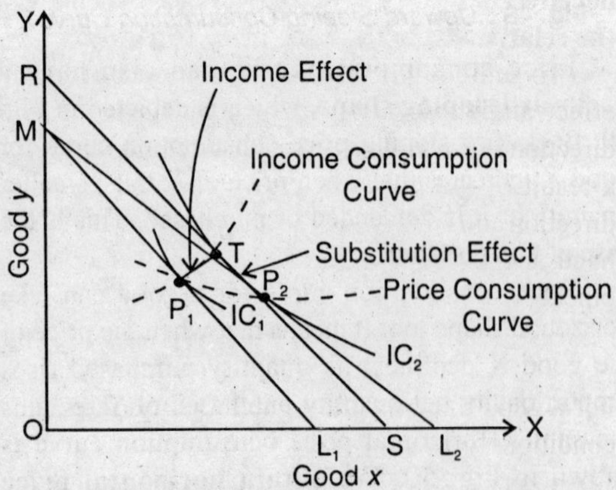

Fig. 52 : *Price Effect = Income Effect + Substitution Effect*

ADVANTAGE OF BREAKING UP THE PRICE EFFECT INTO INCOME AND SUBSTITUTION EFFECTS

A distinct advantage of viewing the price effect as a sum of income effect and substitution effect is that through it the nature of response of quantity purchased to a change in the price of a good can be better and easily explained. In case of most of the goods, the income effect and substitution effect will work in the same direction. But, in some cases, they may pull in different directions. The directions of substitution effect is quite certain. A fall in the relative price of a good always leads to the increase in quantity demanded of the good. In other words, substitution effect always induces the consumer to buy more effect is not so certain. With a rise in income, the individual will generally buy more of a good. But with the rise in income the individual will but less of a good. It is happens to be an inferior good for him since he will use better or superior substitutes in place of the inferior good when his income rises. **Thus the income effect may be either positive or negative.** If for a good the income effect is positive, as is usually the case, it will act in the same direction as the substitution effect, that is, both will work towards increasing the quantity demanded of the good whose income effect is negative, income effect of the price change will work in opposite direction to the substitution effect. **The net effect of the price change will then depend upon the relative strength of the price two effects.**

To sum up, price effect is composed of income effect and substitution effect and further that the direction in which quantity demanded will change as a result of the fall in price will depend up on the direction and strength of the income effect on the one hand and strength of the substitution effect on the other.

GIFFEN GOOD

For a good to be a Giffen good, the following three conditions are necessary :

1. The good must inferior good with a large negative **income effect.**

2. The substitution effect must be small, and

3. The proportion of income spent upon the inferior good must be very large.

SOME FACTS

(a) The quantity demanded of a good varies inversely with price when the income effect is positive or nil.

(b) The quantity demanded of a good varies invesely with price when the income effect is negative but is weaker than the substitution effect.

(c) The quantity demanded of a good varies directly with price when the income effect for the good is negative and this negative income effect of a change in price is larger than the substitution effect.

To Derive Demand Curve from Price Consumption Curve

Price consumption curve traces the effect of a change in price on the quantity demanded of a good. But Price consumption curve does not directly related price with quantity demanded. In indifference curves diagram price is not explicitly shown on the Y-axis. On the other hand, demand curve directly relates price with quantity demanded, price being shown on Y-axis and quantity demanded, on the X-axis. A demand curve shows how much quantity of the good will be purchased or demanded at various prices, assuming that tastes and preferences of the consumer, his income, prices of all other goods remain constant. This demand curve showing explicit relationship between price and quantity demanded can be derived from price consumption curve of indifference curve analysis.

In Marhsallian utility analysis, demand curve was derived on the assumptions that utility was quantitatively measurable and marginal utility of money remained constant with the change in price of the good. In the indifference curves analysis demand curve is derived without making these dubious assumptions.

Assumptions

This analysis assumes that

(a) The money to be spent by the consumer is given and constant. It is Rs. 10.

(b) The price of good X falls.

(c) Prices of other related goods do not change.

(d) Consumer's tastes and preferences remain constant.

If in the double storey Figure 53 money is taken on the Y-axis and good X on X-axis, PQ, PQ_1, PQ_2 are the price lines of the consumer on which R, S and T are the equilibrium positions forming the PCC curve. If the total income of the consumer is divided by the number of goods to be bought with it, we get per unit price of the good. He buys OA, OB and OC units of X respectively at these points on the PCC curve. For OA units of X, he pays $\frac{OP}{OQ}$ price, for OB units, $\frac{OP}{OQ_1}$, Price, and for OC units, $\frac{OP}{OQ_2}$. This is in fact the consumer's demand schedule for good X which is shown in tabular form in following table.

Demand Schedule

Price Line	*Price of good x*	*Quantity of x Demanded*
PQ	$\frac{OP}{OQ}\left(\frac{10}{2}=\text{Rs.}5\right)$	OA = 1 units
PQ_1	$\frac{OP}{OQ_1}\left(\frac{10}{5}=\text{Rs.}2\right)$	OB = 4 units
PQ_2	$\frac{OP}{OQ_2}\left(\frac{10}{10}=\text{Rs.}1\right)$	OC = 7 units

The demand schedule of the consumer for good X shows that given his money income OP (Rs. 10) when he spends his income in buying OQ quantity, it means that the price of X is Rs. 5 as per price line PQ at which the consumer buys one unit (OA) of good X at a total expense of Rs. 5 and spends the remaining Rs. 5 on some other good. When the price of good X as determined by the price line PQ_1 is OP/PQ_1 (Rs. 2), the Price-consumption curve shows that he buys 4 units (OB) of X. He this spends Rs. 8 on it and Rs. 2 on the other good. This is shown by point S on the curve IC_2. When the price of good X is determined as $\frac{OP}{OQ_2}$ = Rs. 1 on the price line PQ_2 and the curve IC_3 at point T, the consumer buys 7 units (OC) of X. He spends Rs. 7 on it and the remaining Rs. 3 on the other good. Points R, S and T on the PCC curve show price quantity relationships for good X.

These points are plotted on the lower diagram in Figure 53. The prices of X are taken on the vertical axis and quantity demanded on the horizontal axis, To draw the demand curve from the PCC, draw a perpendicular on the lower figure from point R in the upper portion of Figure 53 which should pass through point A. Then draw a line from point 5 on the price axis (lower figure) which should cut the perpendicular at point F. The points G and H are drawn in a similar fashion. They are joined by a line to form the demand curve D. This curve shows the amount of X demanded by the consumer at various prices. With the fall in the price of X the consumer buys more units of it and the demand curve D slopes downward to the right. This is because both the income effect and substitution effect of a fall in the price of X are positive.

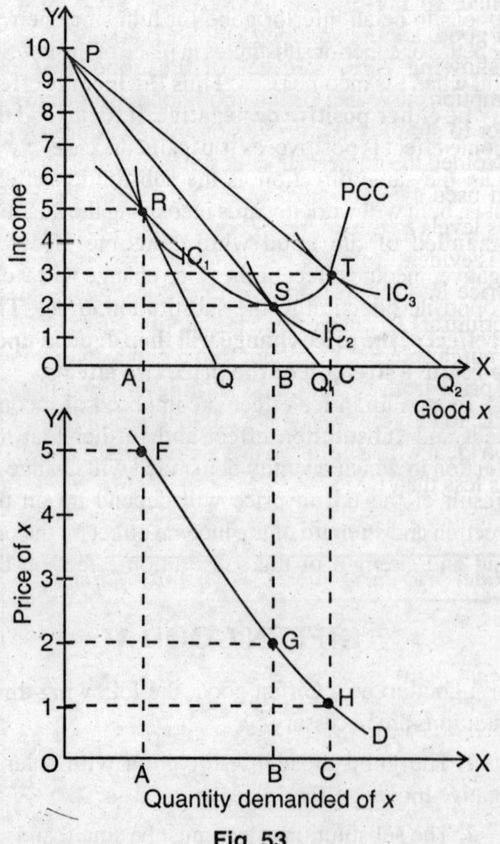

Fig. 53

Deriving Demand Curve for a Giffen Good

The demand curve DF in Fig. 53 is sloping downward. As explained in a previous section, the demand curve slopes downward because of two forces, namely, income effect and substitution effect. Both the income effect and substitution effect usually work towards increasing the quantity demanded of the good, when its price falls and this makes the demand curve slope downward. But in case of Giffen good, the demand curve slopes upward from left to right. This is because in case of a Giffen good income effect, which is negative and works in opposite direction to the substitution effect, over weighs the substitution effect. This results in the fall in quantity demanded of the Giffen good when its price falls and therefore the demand curve of a Giffen slopes upward from left to right.

In Fig. 54 the derivation of demand curve of a Giffen good from indifference curves diagram is explained. In Fig. 54 the indifference curves of a Giffen good, are drawn along with the various price lines showing various prices of the good. Price consumption curve of a Giffen good slopes backward. In order to simplify the discussion in this figure we have avoided the numerical values of prices and have instead used symbols such as P_1, P_2, P_3 and P_4 for various levels of the price of good X.

It is evident from Fig. 54 (the upper portion) that with price line PL1 (or price P_1) the consumer is in equilibrium at Q_1 on the price consumption curve PCC and is purchasing OM_1 amount of the good. With the fall in price from P_1 to P_2 and shifting of price line from PL_1 to PL_2, the consumer goes to the equilibrium position Q_2 at which he buys OM_2 amount of the good. OM_2 is less than OM_1.

Demand Schedule

Price line	*Price of good x*	*Quantity purchased*
PL_1	$\frac{OP}{OL_1}$ or P_1	OM_1
PL_2	$\frac{OP}{OL_2}$ or P_2	OM_2
PL_3	$\frac{OP}{OL_3}$ or P_3	OM_3

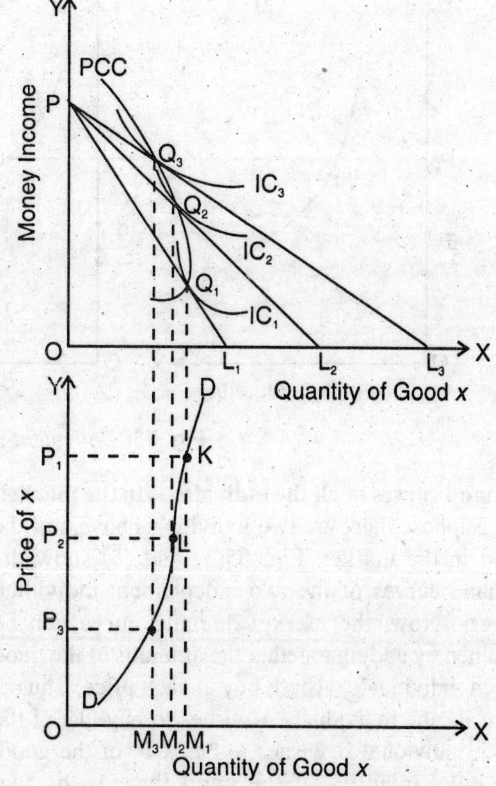

Fig. 54 : *Upward Sloping Demand Curve for a Giffen Good*

Thus with the fall in price from P_1 to P_2 the quantity demanded of the good falls. Likewise, the consumer is in equilibrium at Q_3 with price line PL_3 and is purchasing OM_3 at price P_3. With this information we can draw the demand curve, as is done in lower portion of Fig. 54. It will be seen from this figure that the demand curve of a Giffen good slopes upward indicating that the quantity demanded varies directly with the changes in price. With the rise in price, quantity demanded increases and with the fall in price quantity demanded decreases.

MARKET DEMAND CURVE

If the demand curves of a number of individuals are derived from this price-consumption curve for a good and then added together we get the market demand curve for that good. **In other words, Market demand curve is obtained by summing up sideways the**

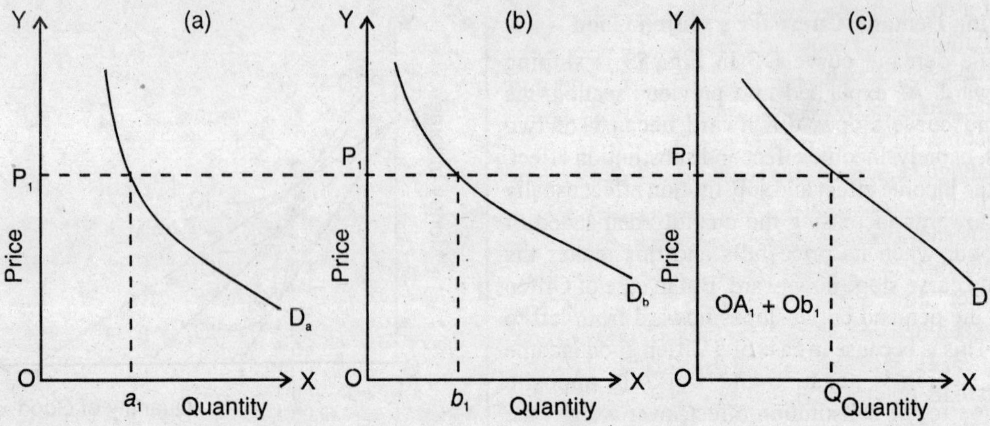

Fig. 55: *Derivation of Market Demand Curve*

demand curves of all the individuals in the market.

Suppose there are two individuals buyers of the good in the market. Fig. 55*(a)* and *(b)* show the demand curves of the two independent individual buyers. Now, the market demand curve can be obtained by adding together the amounts of the good which individuals wish to buy at each price. Thus at price P_1, the individuals A wishes to buy Oa, of the good; individual B wishes to buy Ob_1 of the good. The total quantity of the good that all the two individuals plan to buy at price P_1 is therefore Oa_1 + Ob_1 which is equal to OQ in Fig. 55*(c)*.

Similarly, we can plot the quantity of the good that will be demanded by all the two individuals at every other price of the good. When all the points showing the amounts demanded of the good at various prices are jointed we get a market demand curve for the good.

The market demand curve will slope downward to the right, since the individual demand curves, whose **lateral summation** gives us the market demand curve, normally slope downward to the right. Besides, as the price of the good falls, it is very likely that the new buyers will enter the market and will further raise the quantity demanded of the good.

This will be another reason why the market demand curve should slope downward to the right.

Even if an individual's demand curve for a god slopes downward to the left (*i.e.,* slopes upward to the right) because it happens to be Giffen good for him, it does not follow that the market demand curve too will slope downward to the left. This is because a good may be a Giffen good for a single consumer, but it is seldom that any good will be Giffen good for all the consumers. There will be other consumers demanding it at a lower price to whom it may not appear an inferior good. For the market as a whole a good is not likely to be inferior at all, there being always a sufficient number of buyers over the same price range. Hence **the market demand curve will always slope downward to the right.**

SUPERIORITY OF INDIFFERENCE CURVE TECHNIQUE OVER UTILITY ANALYSIS

The indifference curve technique is superior to the Marshallian utility analysis in several respects :

1. Ordinal vs. Cardinal Measurability of Utility : The indifference curve approach is superior to the utility analysis because it measures utility **ordinally.**

The consumer arranges the various combinations of goods in a scale of preference market as first, second, third etc. He can tell whether he prefers the first to the second or the second to the first or he is indifferent between them. But he cannot tell by how much the prefers one to the other. The ordinal method and the assumption of transitivity makes this technique more realistic.

2. It is Free from the Assumption of Constant Marginal Utility of Money : Marshall in his analysis of a consumer's behaviour assumed marginal utility of money to remain constant while the consumer proceeded to make purchases. By assuming constant marginal utility of money Marshall ignored "the income effect" of a price change and thus failed to distinguish between the two components of the "price-effect". Marshallian analysis in that it does not assume constancy of marginal utility of money and is therefore able to draw a **distinction between the "income effect" and "substitution effect" of a price change,** as seen before.

3. It Studies Combinations of Two Goods Instead of One Good : The utility approach is a single-commodity analysis in which the utility of one commodity is regarded independent of the other. Marshall avoided the discussion of **substitutes** and complementary goods by grouping them together as one commodity.

This assumption is far from reality because a consumer buys not one but combinations of goods at a time. The indifference curve technique is a two commodity model which discusses consumer behaviour in the case of substitutes, complementaries and unrelated goods. It is thus superior to the utility analysis.

4. It Explains the Proportionality Rule in a Better Way : The indifference curve technique explains consumer's equilibrium in a similar and better way than the Marshallian proportionality rule. The consumer is in equilibrium at a point where his price line is tangent to the indifference curve. At this point the slope of the indifference curve equals the budget line, so that the

$$MRS_{xy} = \frac{P_x}{P_y} \qquad ...(1)$$

According to Marshall's proportionality rule, the consumer is in equilibrium when the

$$\frac{MU_x}{P_x} = \frac{MU_y}{P_y}$$

But MRS_{xy} is defined by Hicks as the ratio between the marginal utilities of the two goods. Therefore,

$$MRS_{xy} = \frac{MU_x}{MU_y} \qquad ...(2)$$

From (1) and (2), it follows that

$$\frac{MU_x}{MU_y} = \frac{P_x}{P_x}$$

which can be written as

$$\frac{MU_x}{P_x} = \frac{MU_y}{P_y} \qquad ...(3)$$

Thus, (3) is the same "proportionality rule" of equilibrium as enunciated by Marshall, and the indifference curve technique arrives at this rule with less restrictive and fewer assumptions.

5. This Analysis Explains the Dual Effect of the Price Effect : One of the main defects in the Marshallian utility analysis is that it fails to analyze the **income** and **substitution effects of a price change.**

In the indifference curve technique when the price of a good falls, the real income of the consumer increase. This is the income effect. Secondly, with the fall in price, the good becomes cheaper. The consumer substitutes it for some other good. This is the **substitution effect.** The indifference curve technique is superior to the utility analysis because it discusses the income effect when the consumer's income changes, the price effect when the price of a particular good changes and its dual effect in the form of the income and substitution effects.

6. More General Theory of Demand : The superiority of the indifference curve technique lies in the fact that even with less restrictive and fewer assumptions, it gives us a more general theory of demand. The ordinal utility theory enables us to enunciate the general theorem of demand in the following composite form of which the Marshallian law of demand constitutes a special case :

(*a*) The demand for a commodity varies **inversely** with price when the income elasticity of demand for the commodity is nil or positive.

(*b*) The demand for a commodity varies **inversely** with price when the income elasticity is negative but the income effect of the price change is smaller than the substitution effect.

(*c*) The demand for a commodity varies directly with price when the income elasticity is negative and the income effect of the price change is larger than the substitution effect.

In the case of *(a)* and *(b)* the Marshallian law of demand holds while in *(c)* we have a Giffen case which is exception to the Marshallian law of demand. Marshall could not account for **'Giffen Paradox'.** Marshall was not able to provide explanation for **Giffen Paradox,** because by assceming constant marginal utility of money, he ignored the income effect of the price change. The indifference curve technique by distinguishing between the income and substitution effects of the price change can explain the Giffen case. According to this, the Giffen paradox occurs in the case of an inferior good for which the negative income effect of the price change is so powerful that it outweights the substitution effect, and hence when the price of a Giffen good falls, its quantity demand, also falls instead of rising.

7. Implications of a Price change in Terms of Income and Welfare Increments : By means of indifference curve technique, welfare consequences of changes in prices can be translated into changes in income. A fall in the price of a good enables the consumer to shift from a lower to a higher level of welfare or satisfaction. That is, change in price causes a change in welfare exactly as a change in consumer's income would have done. Thus, a change in price brings about a change in consumer's welfare exactly as if his income has changed. In other words, the consumer can be thought of reaching higher (lower) level of welfare through an equivalent rise (fall) in income rather than the fall (rise) in price of a good.

In Fig. 56 with the fall in price of good X from PL_1 to PL_2 the consumer shifts from indifference curve IC_1 to IC_2 showing an increase in the level of welfare. Now, if instead to the fall in price from PL_1 to PL_2 the consumer's income is increased by the amount equal to PA and L_1B, he will reach the indifference curve IC_2.

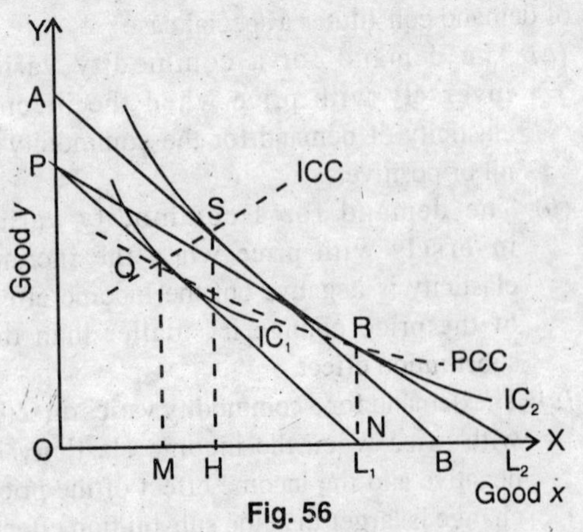

Fig. 56

Thus, the increase in consumer's welfare due to the rise in income by PA and L_1B is equal to that of the change in price of X from PL_1 to PL_2.

"The equivalence of a given change in price to a suitable change in income is a major discovery of ordinal utility analysis." (T. Majumdar). The discovery of a suitable change in income equivalent in terms to welfare to a given change in price has enabled Hicks to extend Marshall's concept of consumer's surplus.

Criticisms of Indifference Curve Analysis

Although the advantages of the indifference curve approach are important, the theory has indeed its own severe limitations. The main weakness of this theory is its axiomatic assumption of the existence and the convexity of indifference curves. The theory does not establish either the existence or the shape of the indifference curves. It assumes that they exist and have the required shape of convexity. Furthermore, it is questionable whether the consumer is able to order his preferences as precisely and rationally as the theory implies. Also the preferences of the consumers change continuously under the influence of various factors, so that any ordering of these preferences, even if possible, should be considered as valid for the very short run. Finally, this theory has retained most of the weaknesses of the cardinalist school with the strong assumption of rationality and the concept of the marginal utility implicit in the definition of the marginal rate of substitution.

Another defect of the indifference curves approach is that it does not analyse the effects of advertising, of past behaviour, of stocks, of the interdependence of the preferences of the consumers, which lead to behaviour that would be considered as irrational, and hence is rules out by the theory. Furthermore speculative demand and random behaviour are ruled out. Yet these factors are very important for the pricing and output decisions of the firm.

SOME APPLICATIONS OF INDIFFERENCE CURVE ANALYSIS

The indifference curve technique is not merely a tool of theoretical analysis. It can also be put to practical use in several economic spheres. As such, or occupies an important place in applied economics. Indifference curves have been used to explain the concept of consumer's surplus, substitutability and complementarily, supply curve of labour of taxation, index number problem and several other things. We shall explain here only few of the applications.

TAXATION : DIRECT VS. INDIRECT TAXES

An important application of indifference curve is to judge the welfare effects of direct and indirect taxes on the individuals. In the other words, if the Government wants to raise a given amount of revenue whether it wil be better to do so levying a direct tax or indirect tax from the view point of welfare of the individuals. Consider Figure 57 where on the X-axis, good X and on the Y-axis money are measured. With a given income of the individual and the given price of good X, the price line is PL_1 which is tangent to indifference curve IC_3 on point Q_0 where the individual is in equilibrium position.

Suppose now that Government levies an excise duty (indirect tax) on good X. With the imposition of excise duty, the price of good X will rise. As a result of the rise in price of good X, the price line will rotate to a new position PL_2 which is tangent to indifference curve IC_1 at point Q_1. It is thus clear that as a result of the imposition of excise duty, the individual has shifted from a higher indifference curve IC_3 to a lower one IC_1, that is, his level of satisfaction or welfare has declined. It should be further noted that at point Q_1 (that is, after the imposition of excise duty), the individual is purchasing ON amount of good X and has paid PM amount of money for it. At the old price (before the excise duty was imposed), he could purchase ON quantity of good X for PT amount of money. Thus, the difference TM (or KQ_1) between the two is the excise duty which the individual is paying.

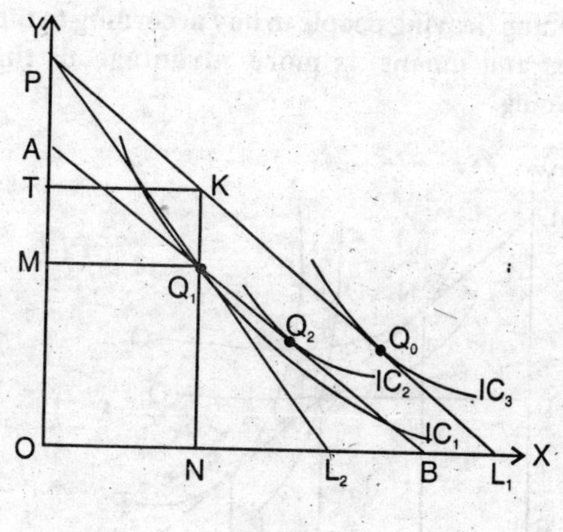

Fig. 57

Now, suppose that instead of excise duty, Government levies income tax on the individual when the individual is initially at point Q_0 on indifference curve IC_3. With the imposition of income tax, the price line will shift below but will be parallel to the original price line PL_1. Further, if the same amount of revenue is to be raised through income tax as with excise duty, then the new price line AB should be drawn at such a distance from the original price line PL_1 that it passes through the point Q_1. So, it will be seen in Figure 57 that with the imposition of income tax, we have drawn the price line AB which is passing through the point Q_1. However, with AB as the price line, individual is in equilibrium at point Q_2 on indifference curve IC_2 which lies at a higher level that IC_1. In other words at point Q_2 individual's level of welfare is higher than at Q_1. **Income tax has reduced the individual's welfare less than that by the excise duty.** Thus, indirect tax (excise duty) causes an excess burden on the individual.

RATIONING

Rationing is another field in which the indifference curve technique can be applied. Suppose in **non-price rationing,** an equal quantity of the rationed commodity is allotted to each individual. Take two individuals P and Q (Fig. 58). X_0 is alloted to P and Y_0 the same quantity is allotted to Q. P will be on indifference curve P_1 and Q on indifference Q_1.

But in absence of rationing P will move from R to S and Q from R to N, which are both on higher indifference curves. **This show that the absence of rationing (leaving people to buy according to their tastes and means) is more advantageous than rationing.**

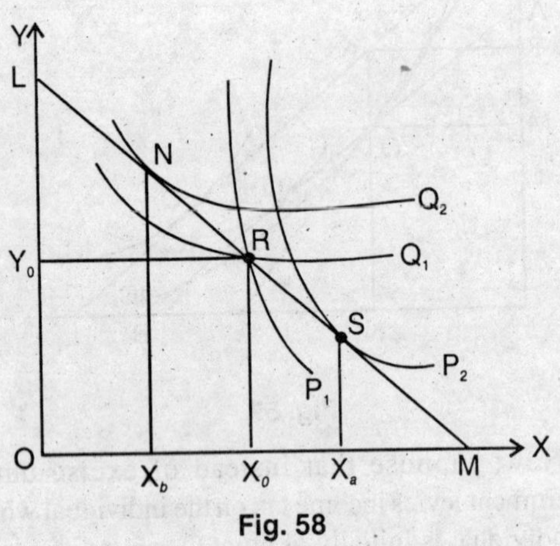

Fig. 58

COST OF LIVING INDEX

The cost of living depends on the collection of goods and services consumed by the household. The standard of living consists of the various combinations of goods yielding equal satisfaction. Such combinations can be represented by points on the same indifference curve. If the combinations of goods purchased in two successive years are plotted on the indifference curve, it can be shown whether the standard of living has risen or fallen according as the most preferable combination is on a higher or lower indifference curve touching the respective price lines.

EFFECT OF SUBSIDIES TO CONSUMERS

Another important application of indifference curve is to analyse with its aid the effect of subsidies to the consumers. Let us take the case of food subsidy which is given by the Government to help the needy families. Suppose that under food-subsidy programme, the needed families are entitled to purchase food at half the market price, the other half of the market price is paid by the Government as subsidy. The effect of this subsidy on consumer's welfare and money value of this subsidy to the consumer is illustrated in Figure 59 where the quantity of food is measured on the X-axis and money on the Y-axis.

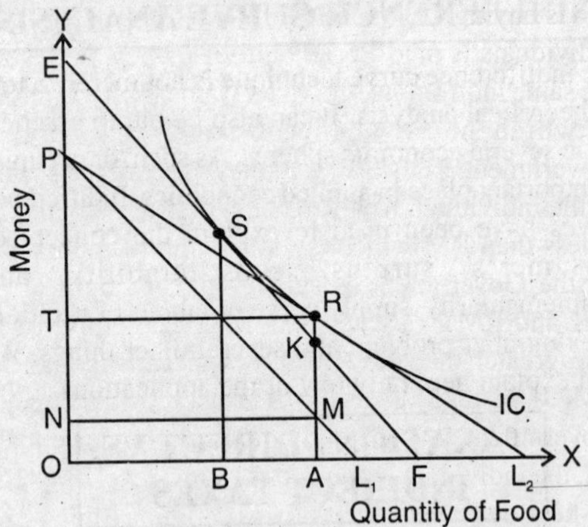

Fig. 59 : *Effect of Subsidies to Consumer*

Let us suppose that the individual has OP money income. Given this money income and given the market price of food, the price line is PL_1. Since we are assuming that subsidy paid by the Government is half the market price of food, the consumer would pay half the market price. Therefore, with subsidy the individual will face the price line PL_2 where $OL_1 = L_1L_2$. With price line PL_2, the individual is in equilibrium at point R on the indifference curve IC at which he is purchasing OA quantity of food. By purchasing OA quantity of food, the individual is spending PT amount of money.

Now, if no food subsidy was given and therefore the price line was PL_1, then for buying OA quantity of food, the individual would have spent PN amount of money. In other words, PN is the market price of OA quantity of food. Since PT amount of money paid by the individual himself, the remaining amount TN or RM is paid by the Governments as food subsidy for the individual.

The important question is what is the money value of this food subsidy (RM) to the individual. When no food subsidy is paid, the individual faces the price line PL_1. In other to find the money value of the subsidy to the individual, draw a line EF parallel to PL_1 so that it touches the same indifference curve IC where the individual comes to be in equilibrium when subsidy is paid. It will be seen in figure 59 that price line EF touches the indifference curve IC at a point S and is buying OB quantity of food. This means that if individuals is paid PE amount of money, he reaches the same indifference curve IC (same level of welfare) at which he is when subsidy is paid by the Government. Thus, PE, is money value of the subsidy to the individual. It will be seen in Figure 59 that PE is less than RM which is the amount of money paid by the Government as subsidy. In our figure PE = MK and RM is greater than MK. Therefore, RM is also greater than PE. It follows that PE is less than RM. If instead of giving RM as subsidy on food, Government pays the individual cash money equal to PE, the individual will reach the same level of welfare as he does with RM subsidy. Thus, the money equivalent of the subsidy to the individual is less than the cost of the subsidy to the Government.

Professor Scitovsky remarks, "The value of the subsidy to the subsidised person is smaller than the cost of subsidy to the Government. The common sense interpretation of this result is that one can make a man happier by giving him cash and letting him spend it as he thinks best than by forcing him take all his relief in the form of one commodity. Hence, relief payments in cash are preferable to a food subsidy because they are economically more efficient, giving the relief receipts either a greater gain at the same cost to the Government or the same gain at a lower cost."

But the above principle regarding the programme of subsidised food, subsidised housing etc. cannot always be validly applied to the Government subsidy programme since the above principle based upon the **subjective benefits to the individuals** which is not always the correct criteria to judge the desirability of Government subsidy programme.

For instance, the aim of Government's food subsidy programme may be that the needy families should consume more food so that their health and efficiency may be improved. It will be seen in figure 59 that with food subsidy RM, the individual is having OA amount of food, whereas with equivalent cash payment of PE the individual purchases OB amount of food which is less than OA. Thus the food subsidy has induced the individual to consume move food than in case of cash payment. Similarly, if a country has food surplus and want to dispose them of then the food subsidy to the needy families will be the ideal measure to increase the consumption of foodgrains and thereby to dispose of the food surpluses.

PRICE DISCRIMINATION

It can be shown with the help of indifference curves that two individuals (representing separate group of consumers) will derive greater satisfaction from the purchase of two commodities on a single system instead of under price discrimination. Price discrimination prevents them from reaching the point of equilibrium at a higher indifference curve.

EFFECT OF INCREASE IN WAGES ON SUPPLY OF LABOUR

Increase of poorly-paid workers, any rise in the wage rate will not lead to a reduction in working time, it will only result in larger income which will be utilised in purchasing more goods. But beyond a certain stage, the worker will work less and still enjoy more goods.

The worker in figure 60 is in equilibrium at P on the price line LM. When the wage rate goes up, the new price line is LM′. The worker must, therefore, now move up to some point on LM′ between Q and R, which are the points on the indifference curve IC_1. Any point between Q and R must be on a higher indifference curve like IC_2 indicating that the worker will be better off. This point may be P[1], a new equilibrium. Here leisure remains constant, but goods increase. The worker has moved horizontaly from P

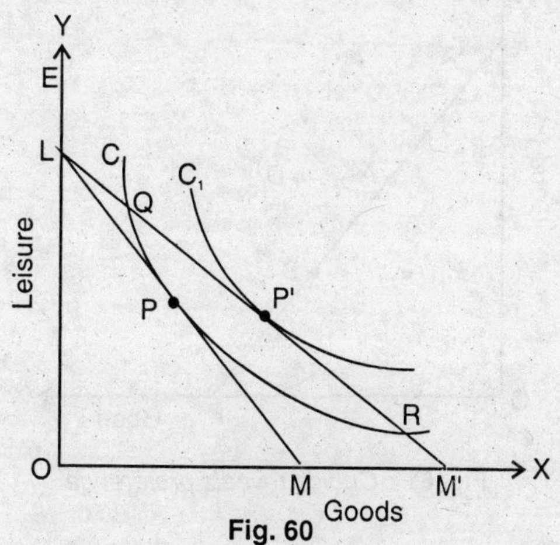

Fig. 60

outwards. If P^1 is on a higher slope of C_1, it will mean more leisure and also more goods.

REVEALED PREFERENCE THEORY

Samuelson introduced the term **'revealed preference'** into economics in 1938. Since then the literature in this field has proliferated, Revealed preference theory is called the **behaviourist ordinal-utility theory.** Instead of the unrealistic assumption that the consumers operate with a complete and consistent scales of preferences set out in the form of indifference curves, most economists now prefer to analyse situations in which their hypothesis can be tested. Both Marshallian utility analysis and Allen-Hicksian indifference curve technique apply the **introspective method** or the subjective method. But the revealed preference theory seeks to explain consumer's demand from his actual behaviour in the market in various price-income situations. Thus, in sharp contrast to psychological or introspective explanation revealed preference theory is behaviouristic explanation of consumer's demand. besides, revealed preference theory is based upon the concept to ordinal utility.

This theory is based on a very simple idea. A consumer will decide to buy some particular basket of goods either because he likes it more than another basket of goods or because it is cheap when compared with other baskets of goods. Suppose a consumer buys basket of goods A rather than basket of goods B. We may not state that he prefers A to B. It is possible that he could not afford to buy B. Given price information, however, we can make a more definitive statement. If A is not less expensive than B and the consumer purchases A, he does so because he likes it better. We say in this situation that A has been **revealed** preferred to B, or B is **revealed inferior** to A.

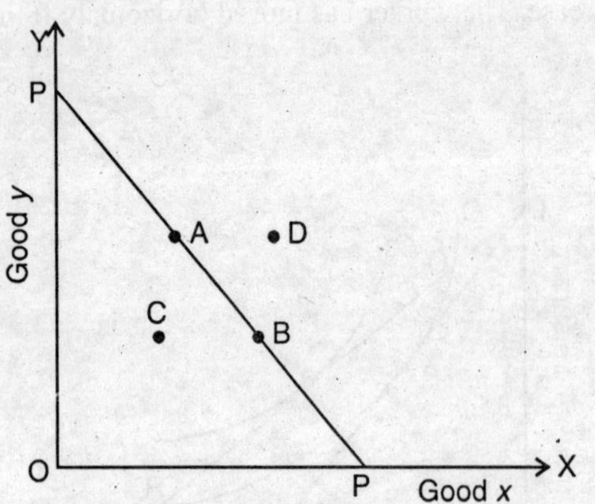

Fig. 61 : *Choice reveals preference*

In Figure 61 the points represents baskets of goods. Given price line PP, we see that A is just as expensive as B. If the consumer chooses A, it is revealed preferred to all other points on PP. Also, C is revealed inferior to A because every point below the price line is revealed inferior to A, for it represents a basket of goods that is less expensive than A. Clearly, any point like D lying above the price line represents basket of goods that is more expensive than A and cannot therefore be revealed inferior to A.

Assumptions

1. Rationality : The consumer is assumed to behave rationally, in that he prefers bundles of goods, that include more quantities of the commodities.

2. Consistency : The consumer behaves consistently, that is, if he chooses bundle A in a situation in which bundle B was also available to him he will not choose B in any other situation in which A is also available. Symbolically

If $A > B$, then $B \not> A$

3. Transitivity : If in any particular situation $A > B$ and $B > C$, then $A > C$.

4. The Revealed Preference Axiom : The consumer, by choosing a collection of goods in any one budget situation, reveals his preference for that particular collection. The chosen bundle is revealed to be preferred among all other alternative bundles available under the budget constraint. The chosen 'basket of goods' maximises the utility of the consumer. The revealed preference for a particular collection of goods implies (axiomatically) the maximisation of the utility of the consumer.

5. Positive Income-Elasticity of Demand : Another very important assumption underlying revealed preference theory is that the income-elasticity of demand of the consumer must always be positive. That is, if his income increases, his demand for the commodity must also increase, it should not remain the same and it should not also decrease as it happens in the case of inferior goods.

Strong Ordering

Prof. Samuelson's revealed preference theory is based upon the **strong form of preference hypothesis.** In other words, in revealed preference theory, strong-ordering preference hypothesis has been applied. Strong ordering implies that there is **definite ordering** of various combinations in consumer's scale of preferences and therefore the choice of a combination by a consumer reveals his definite preference for that over all other alternatives open to him. Thus, **under strong ordering, relation of indifference between various alternative combinations is ruled out.** When in Fig. 4.4 a consumer chooses a combination A out of various alternative combinations open to him, it means he has a definite preference for A over all others, the possibility of the chosen combination A being indifference to any other possible combination is ruled by strong ordering hypothesis.

DERIVATION OF THE DEMAND CURVE

Assume that the consumer has the price line AB in figure 62 and chooses the collection of goods denoted by point Z, thus revealing his preference for this batch. Suppose that the price of good X falls so that the new price line facing the consumer is AC. We will show that the new batch will include a larger quantity of X.

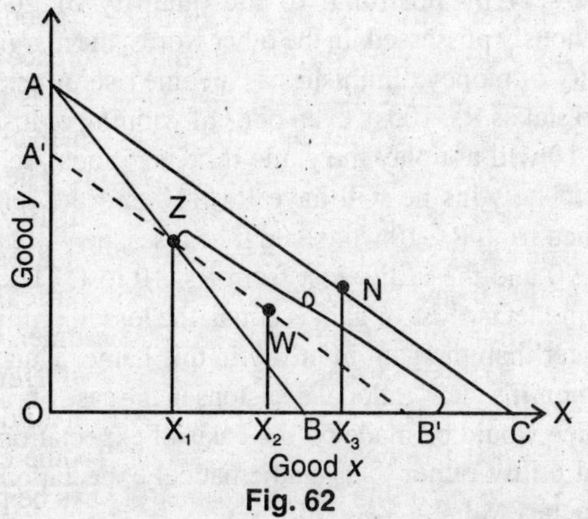

Fig. 62

Firstly, we make a **'compensating variation'** of the income, which consists in the reduction of income so that the consumer has just enough income to enable him to continue purchasing Z if he so wishes. The compensating variation is shown in figure 62 by a parallel shift available to him, the consumer will not choose any bundle to the left to Z on the segment A'Z, because his choice would be in consistent, given that in the original situation all the batches on A'Z were revealed inferior to Z. Hence the consumer will either continue to buy Z (in which case the substitution effect is zero) or he will choose a batch on the segment ZB', such as W, which includes a larger quantity of X (namely X_2). **Secondly,** if we remove the reduction in income and allow the consumer to move on the new price line AC, he will choose a batch (such as N) to the right of W (if the commodity X is normal with a positive income effect). The new revealed equilibrium position (N) includes a larger quantity of X (*i.e.,* X_3) resulting from the fall in its price. **Thus the revealed preference axiom and the implied consistency of choice open a direct way to the derivation of the demand curve : as price falls more of X is purchased.**

Superiority of Revealed Preference Theory

The revealed preference approach is superior to the Hicksian ordinal utility approach to consumer behaviour.

1. It does not involve any psychological introspective information about the behaviour of the consumer. Rather, it presents a behaviouristic analysis based on observed consumer behaviour in the market. Thus the revealed preference hypothesis is more realistic, objective and scientific than the earlier demand theorems.

2. The indifference curve is based on the assumption of continuity, whereas revealed preference theory does not assume. Continuity, this theory is based on the actually observed choice of the consumer from among such combinations as are actually available in the given price-income situation.

3. Samuelson's revealed preference theory has another advantage over the earlier theories. It steers clear of the dubious assumptions upon which the earlier theories were based.

Defects of the Revealed Preference Theory

Whereas the revealed preference theory has

several merits as compared with the earlier theories, it is not free from defects.

1. It is based on strong ordering and as such does not admit of indifference. But since observed choice implies a number of possible alternatives, indifference cannot be ruled out altogether.

2. Samuelson's theorem is conditional and not universal. It is based on the postulate that positive income elasticities imply negative price elasticities. Since the price effect consists of income and substitution effects, it is not possible to isolate the substitution effect from income effect on the level of observation. If the income effect is not positive, price elasticity of demand is indeterminate. On the other hand, if the income elasticity of demand is positive the substitution effect following a change in price cannot be established. Thus, **the substitution effect cannot be distinguished from the income effect in the Samuelsonian theorem.**.

3. Samuelson's revealed preference hypothesis excludes the study of Giffen Paradox, for it considers only positive income elasticity of demand. The Giffen case, on the other hand, related to negative income elasticity of demand.

4. The assumption that "choice" reveals "preference" has also been criticised. But this axiom is invalid for situations where the individual choosers are to be capable of employing strategies of a game theory type.

5. The revealed preference theory fails to analyse consumer's behaviour in choices involving risk or uncertainty. If there are three situations, A, B and C, the consumer prefers A to B and C to A. Out of these, A is certain but chances of occurring B or C are 50-50. In such a situation, the consumer's preference for C over A cannot to said to be based on his observed market behaviour.

6. This approach is applicable only to an individual consumer. Negatively inclined demand curves can be drawn for each consumer with the help of this approach by assuming other things remaining the same. But this technique fails to help in drawing market demand schedules.

Despite its mainfold weaknesses, the Samuelsonian behaviourist ordinal utility analysis is a distinct alternative to Hicks-Allen introspective ordinal utility theory.

Consumer Bahaviour under Conditions of Uncertainty

The modern utility analysis is the outcome of the failure of the indifference curve technique to explain consumer behaviour among risky of uncertain choices. The traditional utility analysis is also concerned with consumer behaviour among riskless choices. Such choices are certain, based as they are on the principle of diminishing marginal utility and on the proportionality rule. The consumer is certain about his income, tastes and the goods he purchases and maximises his satisfaction by choosing that combination which gives him the highest total utility. The neo-classical consumer is a rational being who does not indulge in gambling or even fair bets with 50-50 odds.

The reason why people were unwilling to stake even at fair bets was provided by **Daniel Bernoulli,** the swiss mathematician of the 18th century. Staying in St. Petersburg for some time Bernoulli found that Russians were prepared to stake only small sums of money even on better than fair bets knowing fully the their mathematical expectations of the gain in money were greater than the money the staked. This contradiction is known as **St. Petresburg Paradox.** Bernoulli resolved it by assuming that "the utility resulting from any small increase in wealth will be inversely proportional to the quantity of goods previously possessed. In the other words, the marginal utility of money diminishes as income rise. A person who stakes Rs. 100 at even odds of winning or losing Rs. 10 will not play the game if he is rational being. For if he wins he will have Rs. 110 and the utility gained from Rs. 10 won. And if he loses, he will have Rs. 90 and the utility lost from Rs. 10 lost. Though the monetary loss or gain is equal, the loss in utility is greater than the gain in utility in this game. Thus, in Bernoulli's view, rational decisions in the case of risky choice would be made on the basis of expectation of total utility rather than mathematical expectation of monetary value.

This notion of diminishing marginal utility of income has continued to influence economic thought from Ricardo to Marhsall. The latter regarded gambling as "economic blunder". The introspective ordinalists Hicks and Allen rejected the maximization of expected utility as unrealistic and so unnecessary to explain riskless choices.

J. Neumann and **O. Morgenstern** in their **Theory of Games and Economic Behaviour,** in 1944, confined the measurement of utility to the expected utilities from risky choices.

Assumptions

This Neumann-Morgenstern method of measuring utility is based on the following on the following assumptions.

1. The individual behaves in risky situations in order to maximize expected utility.

2. His choices are transitive : If he prefers A to B and B to C, then he prefers A to C.

3. It is assumed that the individual can always say whether he prefers one events to another or he is indifferent between the two. This means that he can make probability calculations and on their basis can make comparison between the alternative events. For instance, he can compare the event of receiving Rs. 5000 for sure, or Rs. 10000 with 60-40 odds or any other probability, and can say whether he prefers one to the other or is indifferent between the two.

4. Individual can completely order probability combinations of uncertain choices.

5. It is assumed that individual's choice are consistent.

6. There is probability P which lies between 0 and 1.

Neumann and Morgenstern in their famous work **"Theory of Games and Economic Behaviour"** gave a method of cardinally measuring expected utility from win and prizes. On the basis of such a cardinal utility index called **N–M index,** rational decisions are made by the individuals in case of risky situations. Thus, Neumann-Morgenstern method seeks to assign a utility number, or in other words, construct a N–M utility index of the marginal utility of money which a person gets from extra amounts of money income. The choice by an individual under risky and uncertain situations depend on the N–M utility index (*i.e.,* expected numerical utilities) and its behaviour with the changes in money income.

The N–M Utility Index

Neumann and Morgenstern in their Theory of Games and Economic Behaviour have suggested the following method of measuring the utility function :

"Consider three events, C, A and B, for which the order of individual's preferences is the one stated. Let α be a real number between 0 and 1, such that A is exactly equally desirable with the combined event consisting of a change of probability $1 - \alpha$ for B and the remaining chance of probability α and C. The we suggest the use of α as a numerical estimate for the ratio of the preference of A over B to that C over B."

There formula becomes

$$A = B\,(1 - \alpha) + \alpha.C$$

Substituting P for α probability we have

$$A = B(1 - P) + P.C.$$

Given the assumptions, it is possible to derive a cardinal utility index based on the above formula. Suppose there are the three events C, A and B. Out of these, event A is certain, C has probability P, and B has probability (1 – P), and if their respective utilities are U_a, U_b and U_c then

$$U_a = P.U_c + (1 - P)U_b.$$

Since the consumer is expected to maximize utility, the utility of A with certainly must be equal to some value P, the expected utility of the event (lottery) C and B. In order to construct a utility index based on this N–M equation, we have to assign utility values to any two events. These utility values are arbitrary except for the fact that higher value should be assigned to a preferred event.

Suppose the utility of

$$U_c = 10 \text{ units}$$

$$U_b = 1 \text{ unit}$$

$$\text{and } P = 1/4, \text{ then}$$

$$U_a = P.U_c + (1 - P)U_b$$

$$= \frac{4}{5} \times 10 + (1 - 4/5) \times 1$$

$$= 8 + \frac{1}{5} = 8.2 \text{ units}$$

Proceeding this way, one can derive utility values for U_a, U_c, U_b etc. and construct a complete N–M utility index for al possible combinations starting from two arbitrary situations involving risk or probabilities. Such a cardinal utility N–M index is constructed below with a probability value of 4/5.

N–M Utility Index (U_n Units)

Situation	U_a	U_c	U_b
1.	8.2	10	1
2.	17	20	5
3.	34	40	10
4.	52	60	20
5.	88	100	40
6.	170	200	50

In the case the consumer will choose C or A to B.

The Fridman-Savage Hypothesis

The Neumann-Morgenstern method is based on the expected value of utilities and therefore does not refer to whether the marginal utility of money diminishes or increases. In this respect, this method of measuring utility is incomplete. When a person gets an insurance policy, he pays to escape risk. But when he buys a lottery ticket, he gets a small chance of a large gain. Thu he assume risk. Some people indulge both in insurance and gambling. why? The answer has been provided by the **Friedmann-Savage Hyohirhss** as an extension of the N–M method. **It states that marginal utility of money income diminishes for income below some level, it increase for income between that level and some higher level of income. and again demises for all incomes above that higher level.** This is illustrated in the figures 63 and 64. The curve U_y had three segments from left to right upawards, concave, convex and concave. Persons with low level of income OY buy insurance. I is thus the region of insurance where they prefer certain loss in income to a small change in a large loss. Persons in the middle income group are in region II who indulge in gambling. The convex segment of the U_y curve shows increasing marginal utility of money. Therefore, persons in this income group are anxious to undertake risks to improve their lot. People from region I may also be attracted to gambling a little if they are at or near OY income level. Individuals with income beyond OY, are in higher region of income III. The marginal utility of money falls for them. They are not prepared to gamble and take risks except at favour odds to them. This region explains **St. Petersburg Paradox.**

The Friedman-Savage hypothesis is based on the assumption that utility is dependent on the levels of income. **H. Markowitz** has, however, modified it by relating the marginal utility of income to changes in income levels. Instead to two turning points on the U_y curve, Markowitz takes three points with the present income at the middle of the curve. When income increases by a small increment it leads to increasing marginal utility of income. But large increases in income lead to diminishing marginal utility of income. That is why people at higher levels of income are reluctant to indulge in gambling even at fair bets, though persons in slowly rising income groups are more indulgent in stakes to improve their position. In figure 64 starting upwards from point *b* on the income utility curve U_y, as income increase slowly in the

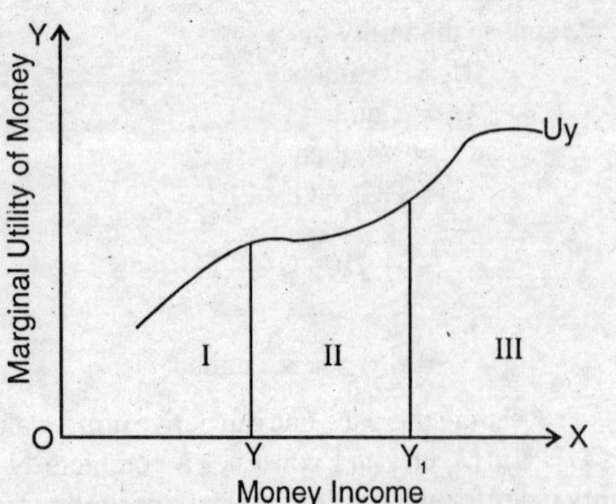

Fig. 63 : *Friedman-Savage Hypothesis*

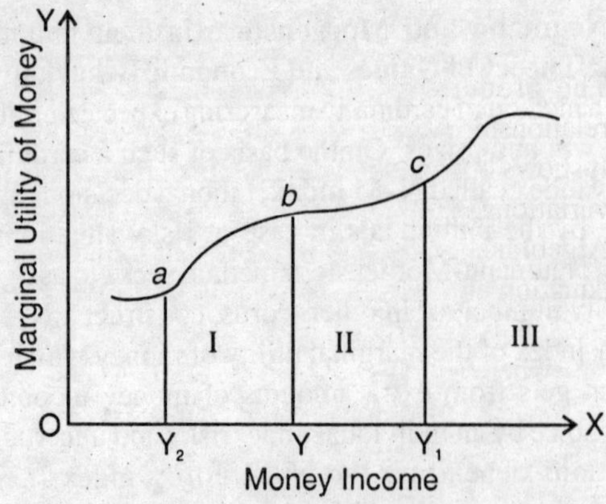

Fig. 64: *The Markowitz Hypothesis*

convex segment *bc,* the marginal utility of income is increasing, From C upwards increment in income is very sharp and it corresponds to region III of Friedman-Savage hypothesis. Persons with income upto OY level are unwilling to take to bets because the expected loss is greater than the gain over a level of income.

An Appraisal

The Neumann and Morgenstern hypothesis implies measurable utility upto a linear transformation thereby reintroducing diminishing or increasing marginal utility. The Friedman-Savage hypothesis contains an added element. It attempts to explain the shape of the curve of marginal utility of income. These hypothesis are thus attempts to rehabilitate the measurement of utility. But the N–M Theory of risky choices along with its variants like the Friedman-Savage hypothesis and Markowitz hypothesis are still a subject of controversy on two counts, firstly, from the practical stand-point, and secondly, whether it is cardinal or ordinal method.

It is doubtful if risk is measurable when Neumann and Morgenstern assume that the risk does not possess any utility or discutility of its own, they ignore the pleasures or pains of uncertainty-bearing. Moreover, in the majority of individual choices the element of uncertainty is very little. Thirdly, individual choices are of an infinite variety. Guaranteed they are uncertain. Is it possible to measure them with the N–M method? Last, it does not measure the 'strength of feelings' of individuals towards goods and services under uncertain choices.

The question whether the N–M method measures utility cardinally or ordinally, there is great confusion among economists. Robertson in his **utility and All that** uses it in the cardinal sense, while Baumol, Fellner and others are of the view that the ranking of utility makes it ordinal. According to Baumol, the N–M theory has nothing in common with the neo-classical theory regarding cardinality. In the neo-classical theory the word "cardinal" is used to denote introspective absolute marginal measurement of utility while in this theory it is used operationally. In the N–M theory, utility numbers are assigned to lottery tickets according to a person's ranking of the prizes and the prediction is made numerically as to which of the two tickets will be chosen. Though the N–M formula is used to derive the utility index yet it says nothing about diminishing marginal utility. Thus the N–M utility is not the neo classical cardinal utility.

The refinements made by Firedman-Savage and Markowitz have tendered to drop the neo-classical assumption that the marginal utility of income diminishes for all ranges of income. Thus the theory of measurement of utility under risky choices is superior to the neo classical introspective cardinalism.

THEORY OF PRODUCTION AND COSTS

PRODUCTION FUNCTION

The production function expresses a functional relationship between quantities of inputs and outputs. It shows how and to what extent output changes with variations in inputs during a specified period of time. Algebraically, it may be expressed in the form of an equation as

$$Y = f(L, K, R, S)$$

where

Y = output
L = labour input
K = capital input
R = raw materials
S = land input

EQUAL-PRODUCT CURVES OR ISOQUANTS

Equal-Product curves are similar to the indifference curves of the theory of consumer's behaviour. An equal-product curve represents all those input combinations which are capable of producing the same level of output. These equal-product curves are also known as isoquants and iso-product curves. Since an equal-product curve represents those combinations of inputs which will be capable of producing an equal quantity of output, the producer would be indifferent between them as such. Therefore, another name which often given to the equal product curves is **Production indifference curve.**

The production isoquant may assume various shapes depending on the degree of substitutability of factors.

Linear Isoquant

This type assumes perfect substitutability of factors of production. A given commodity may be produced by using only capital, or only labour, or by an infinite combination of K and L.

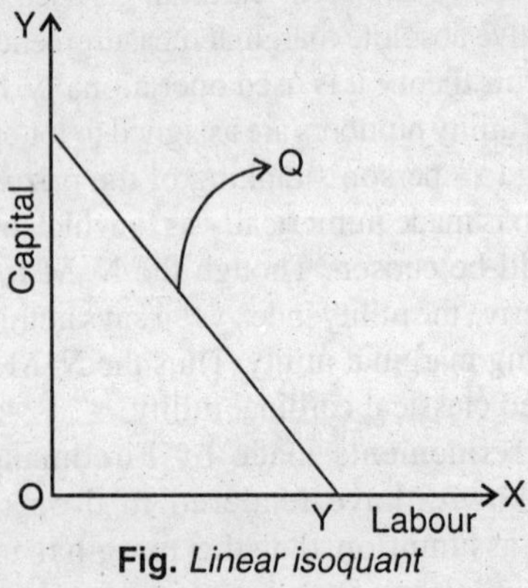

Fig. *Linear isoquant*

Input-Output Isoquant

This assumes strict complementarily (that is, zero substitutability) of the factors of production. There is only one method of production for any one commodity. The isoquant takes the shape of a **right angle.** This type of isoquant is also called **"Leontief isoquant"** after Leontief who invented the input-output analysis.

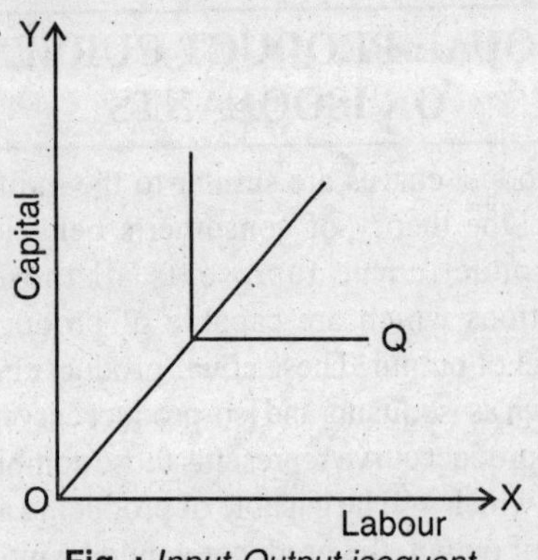

Fig. : *Input-Output isoquant*

Kinked Isoquant

This assumes limited substitutability of K and L. There are only a few processes for producing any one commodity. Substitutability of the factors is possible only at the kinks. This form is also called **'activity analysis-isoquant'** or **'linear-programming isoquant',** because it is basically used in linear programming.

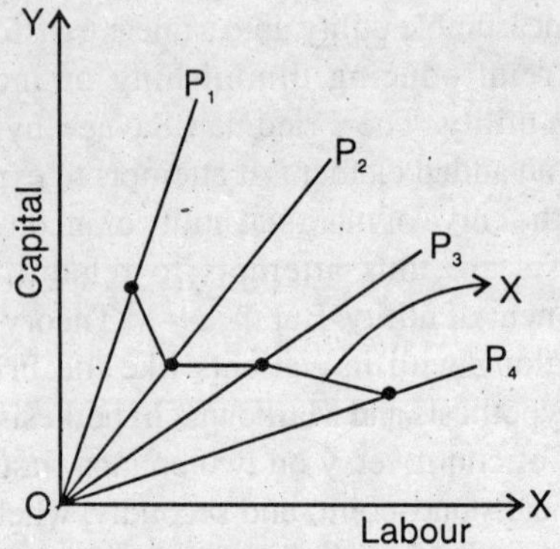

Fig. : *Linear Programming Isoquant*

Smooth Convex Isoquant

This form assumes continuous substitutability of K and L only over a certain range, beyond which factors cannot substitute each other. The isoquant appears as a smooth curve convex to the origin.

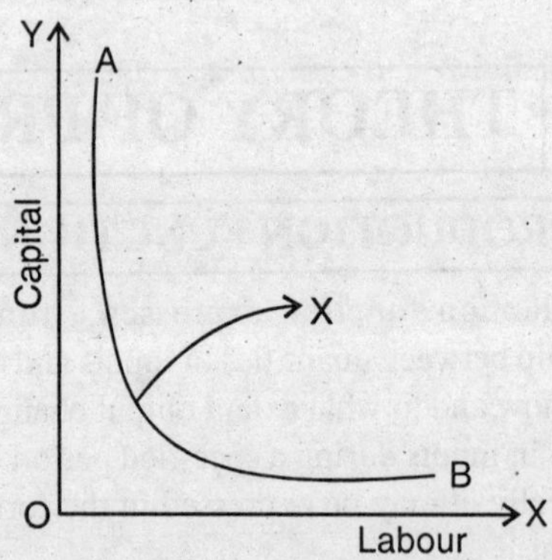

Fig. : *Convex Isoquant*

It should be noted that the kinked isoquants are more realistic. Engineers, managers and production executives consider the production processes as discrete rather than in a continuous array. However, traditional economic theory has mostly adopted the continuous isoquants, because they are mathematically simpler to handle by the simple rules of calculus.

The production function describes not only a single isoquant, but the whole array of isoquant each of which shows a different level of output.

Properties of Isoquants

The following are the important properties of equal product curves.

1. Isoquants are negatively inclined.
2. An isoquant lying above and to the right of another represents a higher output level.
3. No two iso-quants can intersect each other.
4. No isoquant can touch either axis.
5. Isoquant are convex to the origin.

MARGINAL RATE OF TECHNICAL SUBSTITUTION

The principle of marginal rate of technical substitution (MRTS) is based on the production function where two inputs can be substituted in variable proportions in such a way as to produce constant level of output.

Marginal rate of technical substitution indicates the rate at which factors can be substituted at the margin without altering the level of output. More precisely, marginal rate of technical substitution of factor X for factor Y may be defined as amount of factor Y which can be replaced by one unit of factor X, the level of output remaining unchanged. This can be understood with the aid of isoquant schedule.

Isoquant Schedule

Combinations	*Factor X*	*Factor Y*	*$MRTS_{xy}$*
A	1	12	-
B	2	8	4
C	3	5	3
D	4	3	2
E	5	2	1

Each of the input combinations A, B, C, D and E yields the same level of output. Moving down the table from combination A to combination B, 4 units of Y are replaced by 1 units of X in the production process without any change in the level of output. Therefore, the marginal rate of technical substitution is 4 at this stage.

Switching from input combination B to input combination C involves the replacement of 3 units of factor Y by an additional unit of factor X, output remaining the same. Thus $MRTS_{xy}$ is now 3.

The marginal rate of technical substitution at a point on the equal product curve can be known from the slope of the equal product curve at that point. Consider a small movement down the equal product curve P from G to H in figure 65 where a small amount of factor Y, say *dy* is replaced by an amount of factor X, say *dx* without any loss of output.

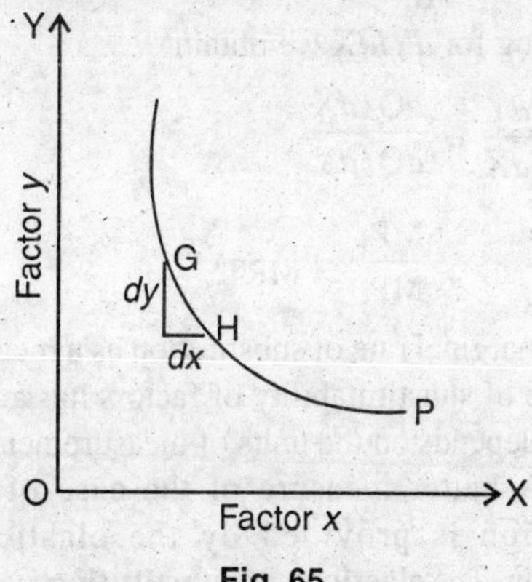

Fig. 65

The slope of the isoproduct curve P at point G is therefore equal to $\frac{dY}{dX}$. Thus, marginal rate of technical substitution

$$MRTS_{xy} = -\frac{dY}{dX}$$

An important point to be noted about the marginal rate of technical substitution is that it is equal to the ratio of the marginal products of two factors.

Proof

The slope of a curve is the slope of the tangent at any point of the curve. The slope of the tangent is defined by the total differential. In the case of the isoquant the total differential is the total change in Q (output) resulting from small changes in both factors X and Y. Clearly if we change Y by *d*X, the output Q will change by the product *d*Y times the marginal product of factor Y or

$$(dY)\left(\frac{dQ}{dY}\right)$$

Similarly, if we change factor X by an infinitesimal amount dX, the resulting change in Q is

$$(dX)\left(\frac{dQ}{dX}\right)$$

Now along any isoquant the quantity Q is constant, so that the total change in Q (the total differential) must be equal to zero. Thus

$$dQ = (dY)\left(\frac{dQ}{dY}\right) + (dX)\left(\frac{dQ}{dX}\right)$$

$$= 0$$

Solving for dY/dX we obtain

$$-\frac{dY}{dX} = \frac{dQ/dX}{dQ/dY}$$

$$= \frac{MP_x}{MP_y} = MRTS_{xy}$$

The marginal rate of substitution as a measure of the degree of substitutability of factors has a serious defect. It depends on the units of measurement of the factors. A better measure of the case of factor substitution is provided by the elasticity of substitution. The **elasticity of substitution** is defined as the percentage change in the capital-labour ratio, divided by the percentage change in the MRS. Thus,

Elasticity of Substitution

$$= \frac{\text{Percentage chane in K / L}}{\text{Percentage change in RS}}$$

or $$\sigma = \frac{d(K/L)/(K/L)}{d(MRS)/(MRS)}$$

where σ = elasticity of substitution
K = capital
L = labour
MRS = marginal rate of substitution

The elasticity of substitution is a pure number independent of the units of measurement of K and L, since both the numerator and the denominator are measured in the same units.

FACTOR INTENSITY

The factor intensity of any production process is measured by the slope of the line through the origin representing the particular process.

Thus the factor intensity is the capital-labour ratio. In figure 66 process P_1 is more capital intensive than process P_2. Clearly

$$\frac{K_1}{L_1} > \frac{K_2}{L_2}$$

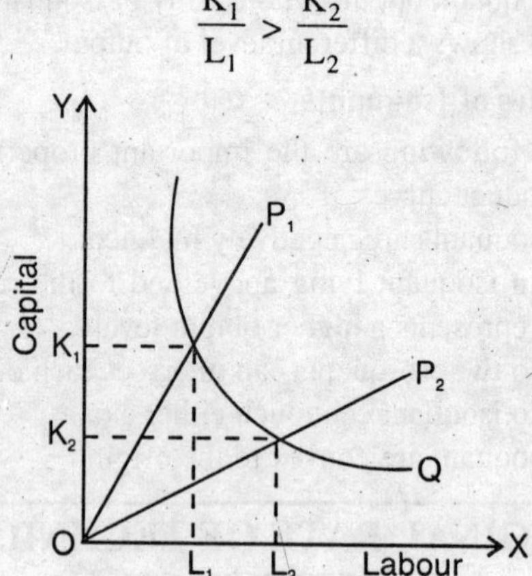

Fig. 66 : *Factor Intensity*

The upper part of the isoquant includes more capital-intensive processes. The lower part of the isoquant includes more labour intensive techniques.

MARGINAL PRODUCTS OF THE FACTORS

The marginal product of a factor is defined as the change in output resulting from a (very small) change of this factor, keeping all other factors constant.

Mathematically the marginal product of each factor is the partial derivative of the production function with respect to this factor. Thus

$$MP_L = \frac{dQ}{dL}$$

and $$MP_K = \frac{dQ}{dK}$$

where

MP_L = marginal product of labour
MP_K = marginal product of capital

Graphically the marginal product is shown by the slope of the total product curve.

In principle the marginal product of a factor may assume any value, positive, zero or negative. However, basic production theory concentrates only on the efficient part of the production function, that, on the range of output over which the marginal products of

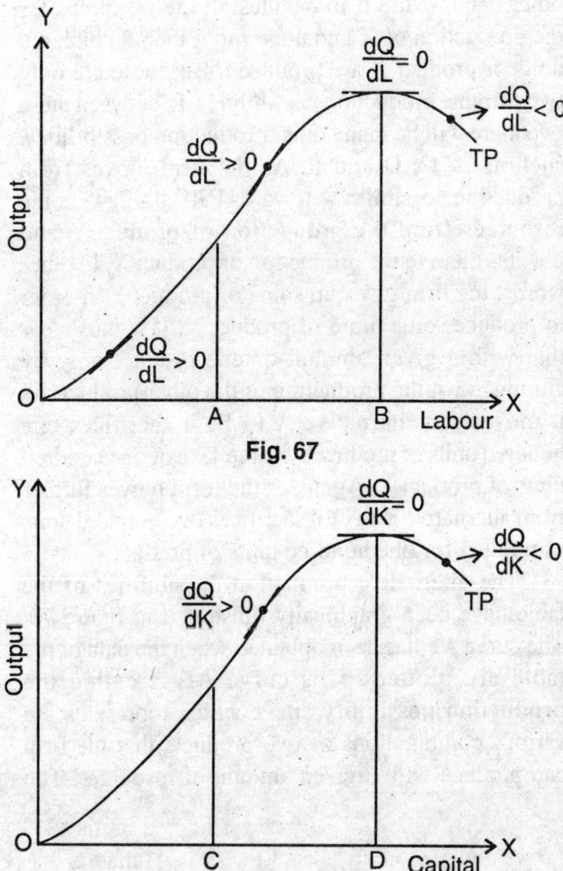

Fig. 67

Fig. 68 : *Marginal Product of Capital*

the factors are positive. No rational firm would employ labour beyond OB, or capital beyond OD, since an increase in the factors beyond these levels would results in the reduction of the total output of the firm. Ranges of output over which the marginal products of the factors would be negative inmply irrational behaviour of the firm, and are not considered by the theory of production.

Further more, the basic theory of production usually concentrates on the range of output over which the marginal products of factors, although positive, decrease, that is, over the range of diminishing (but non-negative) productivity of the factors of production : the ranges of output considered by the traditional theory are AB in figure 67 and CD in figure 68.

Alternatively we may say that the theory of production concentrates on levels of employment of the factors over which their marginal product are positive but decrease. Thus

$$MP_L > 0 \text{ but } \frac{d(MP_L)}{dL} < 0$$

$$\text{and } MP_K > 0 \text{ but } \frac{d(MP_K)}{dK} < 0$$

These conditions imply that **the traditional theory of production concentrates on the range of isoquants over which their slope is negative and convex to the origin.**

RIDGE LINES

In figure 69 the production function is depicted in the form of a set of isoquants. By construction the higher to the right an isoquants, the higher the level of output it depicts. Clearly isoquants cannot intersect, by their construction. We said that traditional economic theory concentrates on efficient ranges of output, that is, ranges over which the marginal products of factors are diminishing but positive. **The locus of points of isoquants where the marginal products of the factors are zero form the ridge lines.** The upper ridge line implies that the MP **of capital is zero.** The lower ridge line implies that the MP **of labour is zero.** Production techniques are only (technically) efficient inside the ridge lines. Outside the ridge lines the marginal products of factors are negative and the methods of production are inefficient, since they require more quality of both factors for producing a

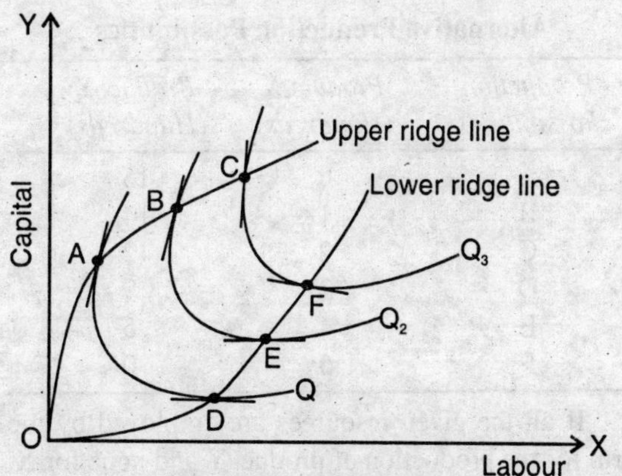

Fig. 69 : *Ridge Lines*

given level of output. Such inefficient methods are not considered by the theory of production, since they are imply irrational behaviour of the firm.

The condition of positive but declining marginal products of the factors defines the range of efficient production (the range of isoquants over which they are convex to the origin).

PRODUCTION POSSIBILITY CURVE

We explained above the behaviour of the firm in choosing the factor combination for producing a product. We have assumed so far that the firm is a single product firm, that is, it produces only one product or good. But the majority of firms produce more than one product. For convenience, we take a firm producing two products X and Y. To produce two products the firm has to decide the proportion in which to produce them. For this, the concept of **production possibility curve,** or the **transformation curve** is used.

The concept of production possibility curve is based on the following assumptions :

1. The firm has given quantities of an input with which it produces the two products.
2. There is no change in the production technique.
3. It can produce the two goods X and Y in different proportions.

The concept of production possibility curve can be understood from the following table. The table given below displays various production possibilities of products X and Y.

Alternative Production Possibilities

Production Possibilities	*Product X (Hundreds)*	*Product Y (Hundreds)*
A	0	15
B	1	14
C	2	12
D	3	9
E	4	5
F	5	0

If all the given resources are employed by the firm for the production of product Y and none for X, 15 hundred units of product Y are produced. On the other hand, if the firm devotes all the resources for the production of X and none for Y, then 5 hundered units of product X are produced. But these are only two extreme production possibilities. In between these two there will be many other production possibilities, such as B, C, D and E. As the firm moves from production possibility A towards F it withdraws some resources from the production of product Y and devotes them to the production of product X. In other words, the firm gives up some of product Y in order to produce some more of product X. It is thus clear that with a given amount of one product only by cutting down the production of the other product. As it moves for alternative A to B, it sacrifices one hundred units of product Y for the sake of one hundred units of product X. Again, as the form moves further from alternative B to C, it sacrifices two hundred units of product for one hundred units of product X.

The alternative production possibilities of the table have been graphically illustrated in figure 70. The curve AF has been obtained when the data of the table are plotted. This curve AF is called the **production possibility curve** which represents the various combinations of two products that the firm can produce with a given amount of resources. The

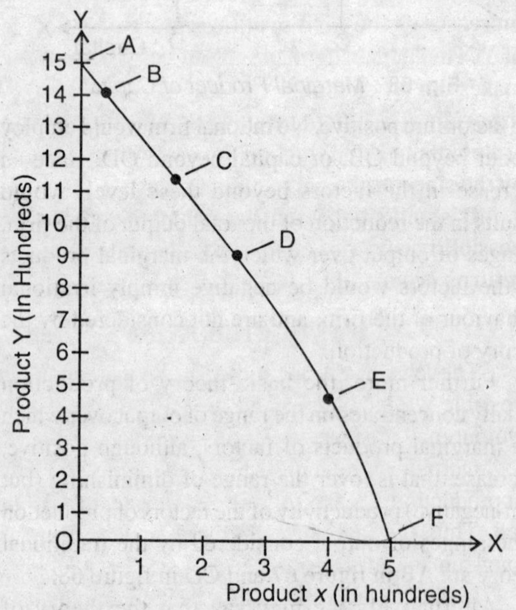

Fig. 70 : *Production Possibility Curve*

production possibility curve shows that, with given resources, an increase in the production of one good necessitates the reduction in the output of the other good.

The production possibility curve is also called the **Product Transformation Curve** or simply the **Transformation Curve** because in moving from one point to another on it, one product is transformed into another, not physically but by transferring resources from one line of production to the other. With given resources being fully employed and utilized by the firm, the combination of two products produced must lie anywhere on the production possibility curve AF and not inside or outside it. The greater the amount of resources available with the firm for production, the higher the level of production possibility curve. **The rate at which one product is transformed into another, resources remaining unchanged, is called the marginal rate of transformation.** In other words, the marginal rate of transformation between X and Y is the amount of transformation between X and Y is the amount of Y which is sacrificed for the production of an additional unit of X. As shown above, the sacrifice of product Y for an additional unit of X goes on increasing as the firm produces more of X and less of Y. Thus, **the marginal rate of transformation increases as the firm produces more of X and less of Y.** The increasing marginal rate of transformation makes the production possibility curves **concave to the origin.** The marginal rate of transformation (MRT) at a point on the production possibility curve is given by the slope of the curve at that point.

It should be noted here that the production possibility curve is convex only when the increasing returns occur.

Laws of Production

The laws of production describe the technically possible ways of increasing the level of production. Output may increase in various ways.

Output can be increased by changing all factors or production. Clearly this is possible only in the long-run. Thus **the laws of returns to scale** refer to the long-run analysis of production.

In the short run output may be increased by using more of the variable factor, while capital (and possibly other factors as well) are kept constant. The marginal product of the variable factor will decline eventually as more and more quantities of this factor are combined with the other constant factors. The expansion of output with one factor constant is described by the **law of diminishing returns** of the variable factor, which is often referred to as the **law of variable proportions.**

Laws of Returns to Scale : Long-Run Analysis of Production

In the long run expansion of output may be achieved by varying all factors. In the long run all factors are variable. The laws of returns to scale refer to the effects of scale relationships.

In the long run output may be increased by changing **all factors by the same proportion,** or by different proportions. Traditional theory of production concentrates on the first case, that is, the study of output as all inputs change by the **same proportion. The term 'return to scale' refers to the changes in output as all factors change by the same proportion.**

Suppose we start from an initial level of inputs and output

$$X_0 = f(L, K)$$

and we increase all the factors by the same proportion *m*. We will clearly obtain a new level of output X^*, higher than the original level X_0,

$$X^* = f(mL, mK)$$

*If X^* increases by the same proportion *m* as the inputs, we say that there are **constant returns to scale.**

*If X^* increases less than proportionally with the increase in the factors, we have **decreasing returns to scale.**

*If X^* increases more than proportionally with the increase in the factors, we have **increasing returns to scale.**

Returns to Scale and Homogeneity of the Production Function

Suppose we increase both factors of the function

$$X_0 = f(L, K)$$

by the same proportion *m*, and we observe the resulting new level of output X^*

$$X^* = f(mL, mK)$$

If *m* can be factored out, then the new level of

output X* can be expressed as a function of *m* (to any power *a*) and the initial level of output

$$X^* = m^a f(L, K)$$

or $$X^* = m^a X_0$$

and the production function is called **homogeneous.** If *m* cannot be factored out, the production function is non-homogeneous. The power *a* of *m* is called the **degree of homogeneity** of the function and is a measure of the returns to scale :

*If $a = 1$, we have constant returns to scale. Thus production function is something called **linear homogeneous.**

*If $a < a$, we have decreasing returns to scale.

*If $a > 1$, we have increasing returns to scale.

Returns to scale are measured mathematically by the coefficients of the production function. For example, in a **Cobb-Douglas function**

$$X = b_0 L^{b_2} K^{b_2}$$

the returns to scale are measured by the Sum $(b_1 + b_2) = a$.

Proof

Let L and K increase by *m*. The new level of output is

$$X^* = b_0 (mL)^{b_1} (mK)^{b_2}$$

$$= (b_0 L^{b_1} K^{b_2}) m^{b_1+b_2}$$

or $$X^* = m^{b_1+b_2} X.$$

Thus $a = (b_1 + b_2)$

Linear Homogeneous Production Function

Production function can take several forms but a particular form of production function enjoys wide popularity among the economists. This is a linear homogeneous production, that is, production function which is homogeneous of the first degree. Homogeneous production function of the first degree implies that if all the factors of production are increased in some proportion, output also increases in the same proportion. Hence linear homogeneous production function represents the case of **constant returns to scale.**

PRODUCT LINES

A product line shows that movement from one isoquant to another as we change both factors or a single factor. A product line is drawn independently of the prices of factors of production. The product line describes the technically possible alternative paths of expanding output. What path will actually be chosen by the firm will depend on the prices of factors.

The product line passes through the origin if all factors are variable. If only one factor is variable (the other being kept constant) the product line is a straight line parallel to the axis of the variable factor. The K/L ratio diminishes along the product line.

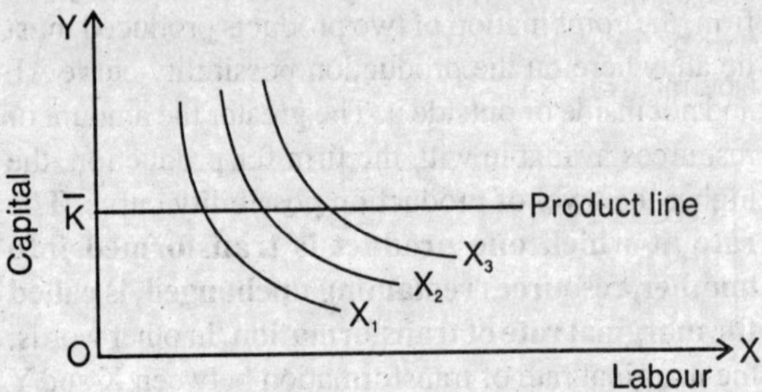

Fig. : *Product line for $\overline{K}$ given*

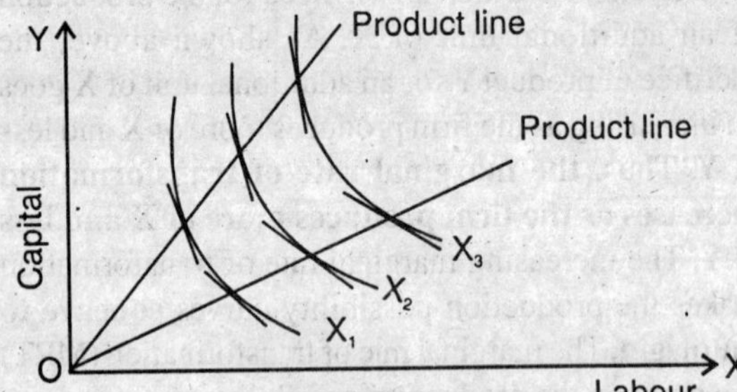

Fig. : *Homogeneous Production Function*

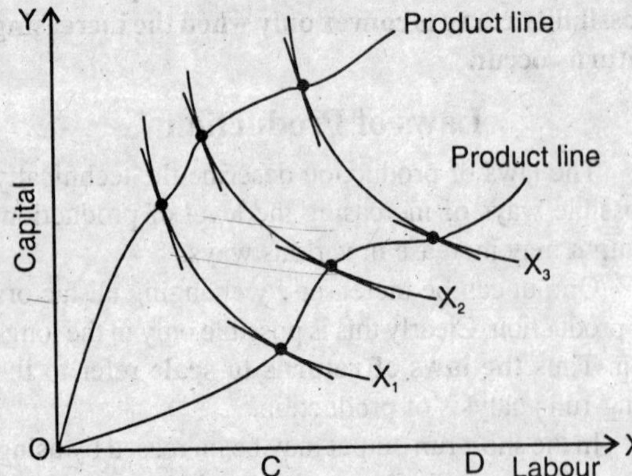

Fig. 71 : *Non-Homogeneous Production Function*

Among all possible product lines of particular interest are the so-called isoclines. **An isocline is the locus of points of different isoquants at which the MRS of factors is constant.**

If the production function is homogeneous the isoclines are straight lines through the origin. Along any one isocline the K/L ratio is constant. Of course the K/L ratio (and the MRS) is different for different isoclines.

If the production function is non-homogeneous the isoclines will not be straight lines, but their shape will be twiddly. The K/L ratio changes along each isocline. (Fig. 71).

GRAPHICAL PRESENTATION OF THE RETURNS TO SCALE FOR A HOMOGENEOUS PRODUCTION FUNCTION

The returns to scale may be shown graphically by the distance (on an isocline) between successive 'multiple-level-of-output' isoquants, that is, isoquants that show levels of output which are multiples of some base level of output *e.g.,* X, 2X, 2X etc.

CONSTANT RETURNS TO SCALE

Along any isocline the distance between successive multiple isoquants is constant. Doubling the factor inputs achieves double the level of the initial output, trebling inputs achieves treble output, and so on (Fig. 72).

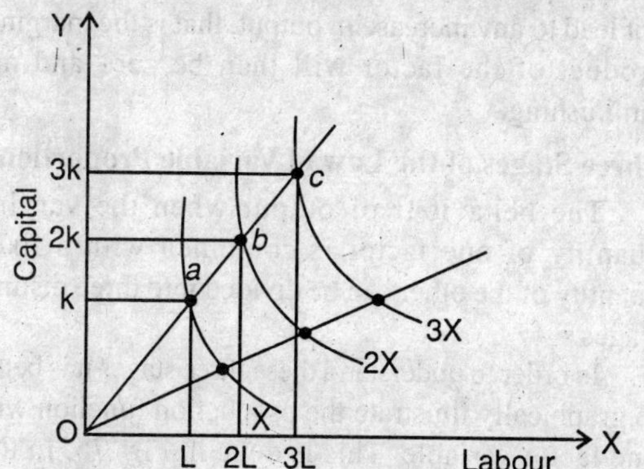

Fig. 72 : *Constant Returns to Scale : oa = ab = bc*

DECREASING RETURNS TO SCALE

The distance between consecutive multiple isoquants increases. By doubling the inputs output increases by less than twice its original level. In figure 73 the point *a'*, defined by 2K and 2L, lies on an isoquant below the one showing 2X.

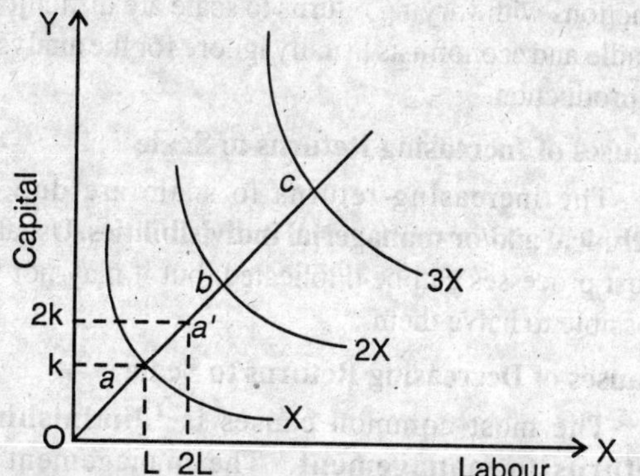

Fig. 73: *Decreasing Returns to Scale : oa < ab < bc*

INCREASING RETURNS TO SCALE

The distance between consecutive multiple-isoquants decreases. By doubling the inputs, output is more than doubled. In figure 74 doubling K and L leads to point *b'* which lies on an isoquant above the one denoting 2X.

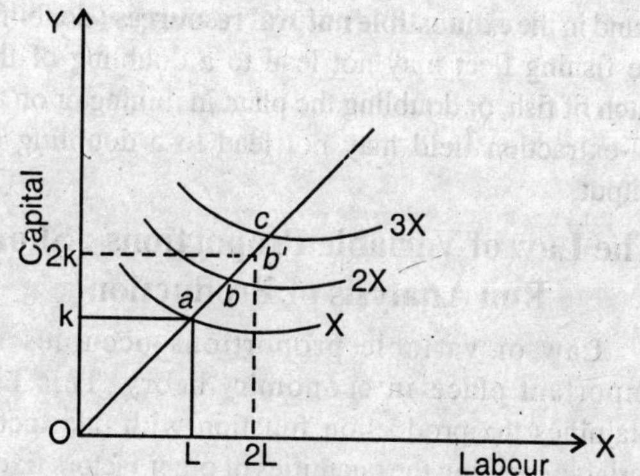

Fig. 74: *Increasing Returns to Scale : oa > ab> bc*

Returns to scale are usually assumed to be the same everywhere on the production surface, that is, the same along all the expansion-product lines. All processes are assumed to show the same returns over all ranges of output : either constant returns everywhere, decreasing returns everywhere, or increasing returns everywhere. However, the technological conditions of production may be such that returns to scale may vary over different ranges of output. Over some range we may have constant returns to scale, while over another range we may have increasing or decreasing returns to scale. Production functions with varying returns to scale are difficult to handle and economists usually ignore for the analysis of production.

Causes of Increasing Returns to Scale

The increasing returns to scale are due to **technical and/or managerial indivisibilities.** Usually most processes can be duplicated, but it may not be possible to halve them.

Causes of Decreasing Returns to Scale

The most common causes is **'diminishing returns to management.'** The management is responsible for the co-ordination of the activities of various sections of the firm. Even when authority is delegated to individual managers (production manager, sales manager, etc.) the final decision have to be taken from the final 'centre of top management.' As the output grows, top management becomes efficient overburdened and hence less difficult in its role as co-ordinator and ultimate decision-maker.

Another cause for decreasing returns may be found in the **exhaustible natural resources :** doubling the fishing fleet may not lead to a doubling of the catch of fish, or doubling the plant in mining or on an oil-extraction field may not lead to a doubling of output.

The Law of Variable Proportions : Short Run Analysis of Production

Law of variable proportions occupies an important place in economic theory. This law examines the production function with one factor variable, keeping the quantities of other factors fixed. In other words, it refers to the input-output relation when the output is increased by varying the quantity of one input. When the quantity of one factors is varied, keeping the quantity of other factors constant, the proportion between the variable factor and the fixed factor is altered, the ratio of employment of the variable factor to that of the fixed factor goes on increasing as the quantity of the variable factor is increased. **Since under this law we study the effects on output of variation in factor proportions, this is known as the law of variable proportions.** The law of variable proportions is the new name for the famous **"Law of Diminishing Returns"** of classical economics.

In general if one of the factors of production (usually capital K) is fixed, the marginal product of the variable factor (labour) will diminish after a certain range of production. We said that the traditional theory of production concentrates on the ranges of the factors are positive but diminishing. The ranges of increasing returns (to a factor) and the range of negative productivity are not equilibrium ranges of output.

Assumptions of the Law of Variable Proportions

The law of variable proportions as stated above holds good under the following conditions :

1. Firstly, the state of technology is assumed ti be given and unchanged.

2. Secondly, there must be some inputs whose quantity is kept fixed. It is only in this way that we can alter the factor proportions and know its effects on output. This law does not apply in case all factors are proportionately varied.

3. Thirdly, the law is based upon the possibility of varying the proportions in which the various factors can be combined to produce a product. The law does not apply to those cases where the factors must be used in fixed proportions to yield a product. When the various factors are required to be used in rigidly fixed proportions, then the increase in one factor would not lead to any increase in output, that is the marginal product of the factor will then be zero and not diminishing.

Three Stages of the Law of Variable Proportions

The behaviour of output when the varying quantity of one factor is combined with a fixed quantity of the other can be divided into three distinct stages.

In order to understand these three stages it is better to graphically illustrate the production function with one factor variable. This is done in Fig. 75. In this figure, on the X-axis is measured the quantity of the

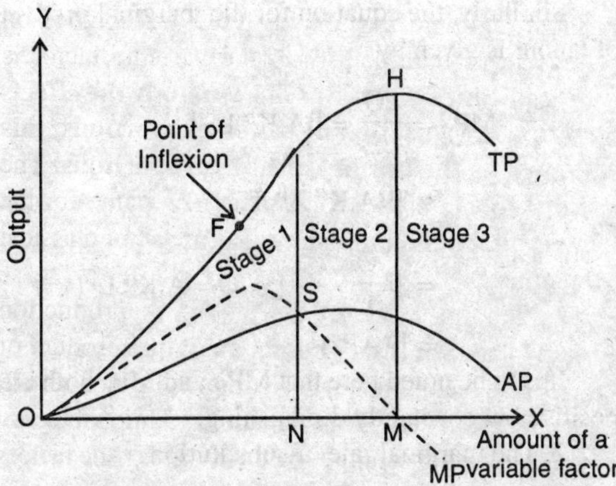

Fig. 75: *Three Stages of the Law of Variable Proportions*

variable factor and on the Y-axis are measured the total product, average product and the marginal product. The total product curve TP goes on increasing to a point and after that it starts declining. Average and marginal product curves also rise and then decline, marginal product curve starts declining earlier than the average product curve. The behaviour of these total, average and marginal products of the variable factor consequent on the increase in its amount is generally divided into three stages which are explained below.

Stage 1

In this stage, total product to a point increases at an increasing rate. In figure 75 from the origin to the point F, slope of the total product curve TP is increasing, that is upto the point F, the total product increases at an increasing rate (the total product curve TP is concave upwards upto the point F), which means that the marginal product MP rises. From the point F onwards during the stage 1, the total product curve goes on rising but its slope is declining which means that from point F onwards the total product increases at a diminishing rate (total product curve is concave downwards), *i.e.,* marginal product falls but is positive. The point F where the total product stops increasing at an increasing rate and starts increasing at the diminishing rate is called the **point of inflexion.** Corresponding vertically to this point of inflexion marginal product is maximum, after which it slopes downwards.

The Stage 1 ends where the average product curve reaches its highest point. During this stage, when marginal product of the variable factor is falling, it still exceeds its average product and so continues to cause the AP-curve to rise. Thus, during the stage 1, whereas MP-curve rises in a part and then falls, the AP-curve rises throughout. In this stage, the quantity of the fixed factor is too much relative to the quantity of the variable factor so that if some of the fixed factor is withdrawn, the total product would increase. Thus, **in the first stage marginal product of the fixed factor is negative.** Stage 1 is known as **the stage of increasing returns** because average product of the variable factor increases throughout this stage.

Stage 2

This stage is also known as the stage of diminishing returns. In stage 2, the total product continues to increase at diminishing rate until it reaches its maximum point H, where the second stage ends. In this stage both the marginal product and average product of the variable factor are diminishing but are positive. At the end of the second stage, that is, at point M marginal product of the variable factor is zero (corresponding to the highest point H of the total product curve TP). Stage 2 is very crucial and important because the firm will seek to produce in its range. This stage is known as the stage of diminishing returns as both the average and marginal products of the variable factors continuously fall during this stage.

Stage 3

In this stage total product declines and therefore the total product curve TP slopes downward. As a result, marginal product of the variable factor is negative and MP-curve goes below the X-axis. In this stage, variable factor is too much relative to the fixed factor. This stage is called the **stage of negative returns,** because the marginal product of the variable factor is negative during this stage.

It may be noted that stage 1 and stage 3 are **completely symmetrical.** In stage 1 the fixed factor is too much relative to the variable factor. Therefore, in stage 1, marginal product of the fixed factor is negative. On the other hand, in stage 3 variable factor is too much relative to the fixed factor. Therefore in, stage 3, the marginal product of the variable factor is negative.

It is this clear from above that the rational producer will never be found producing in stage 1 and stage 3. Stages 1 and 3 represents non-economic region in production function. A rational producer will always seek to produce in stage 2 where both the marginal product and average product of the variable factor are diminishing. At which particular point in this stage, the producer will decide to produce depends upon the prices of factors. The stage 2 represents the range of rational production decisions.

COBB-DOUGLAS PRODUCTION FUNCTION

The Cobb-Douglas production function is based on the empirical study of the American manufacturing industry made be Paul H. Douglas and C.W. Cobb. It is a linear homogeneous production function which takes into account only two inputs labour and capital for the entire output of the manufacturing industry. The Cobb-Douglas production function is

$$Q = A.K^{\alpha}.L^{\beta}$$

where

Q = output

K = capital

L = labour

A, α, β = Positive constants

Properties

The Cobb-Douglas production function has some interesting mathematical properties which make them very useful for managerial decision-making. The important properties are the following :

1. The marginal product of capital and labour depends only on the quantities of capital and labour used in the production process. The equation for the marginal product of capital is given by

$$MP_K = \frac{dQ}{dK} = \alpha A.K^{\alpha-1}.L^{\beta}$$

$$= \alpha(A.K^{\alpha}.L^{\beta})K^{-1}$$

$$= \alpha.\frac{Q}{K} \qquad [\because Q = A.K^{\alpha}.L^{\beta}]$$

$$= \alpha(AP_K)$$

where

AP_K = the average product of capital

Similarly, the equation for the marginal product of labour is given by

$$MP_L = \frac{dQ}{dL} = \beta A.K^{\alpha}.L^{\beta-1}$$

$$= \beta(A.K^{\alpha}.L^{\beta})L^{-1}$$

$$= \beta.\frac{Q}{L} \qquad [\because Q = A.K^{\alpha}.L^{\beta}]$$

$$= \beta(AP_L)$$

It is to be noted here that MP_K and MP_L both are positive but constantly diminishing.

2. The marginal rate of substitution

$$MRS_{LK} = \frac{dQ/dL}{dQ/dK}$$

$$= \frac{\beta(Q/L)}{\alpha(QK)} = \frac{\beta}{\alpha}.\frac{K}{L}$$

3. Thirdly α and β the exponents of K and L respectively, show the output elasticities of labour (E_L) and capital (E_K).

For $Q = A.K^{\alpha}.L^{\beta}$, the percentage rise in Q for 1% rise in L will be

$$\frac{\%\Delta Q}{\%\Delta L} = \frac{\Delta Q/Q}{\Delta L/L} = \frac{\Delta Q}{\Delta L}\times\frac{L}{Q}$$

In terms of partial derivatives, we can write

$$E_L = \frac{dQ}{dL}\times\frac{L}{Q}$$

$$= \left(\beta\times\frac{Q}{L}\right)\times\frac{L}{Q} = \beta.$$

Similarly,

$$E_K = \frac{dQ}{dK}\times\frac{K}{Q}$$

$$= \left(\alpha\times\frac{Q}{K}\right)\times\frac{K}{Q} = \alpha.$$

Hence if $\beta = 0.5$ then 1% rise in the amount of labour used (keeping capital constant) will raise output by 0.5%.

4. The Cobb-Douglas production function can be extended easily to more than two inputs *e.g.,* capital and labour, natural resources, non-production labour, etc.

5. The elasticity of substitution

$$\alpha = \frac{d(K/L)/(K/L)}{d(MRS)/(MRS)}$$

substitute the MRS and obtain

$$\alpha = \frac{d(K/L)/(K/L)}{d\left(\frac{\beta}{\alpha}.\frac{K}{L}\right)\Big/\left(\frac{\beta}{\alpha}.\frac{K}{L}\right)}$$

$$= \frac{d(K/L)/(\beta/\alpha)}{\left(\frac{\beta}{\alpha}\right)d(K/L)}$$

=1 = **Hence such a production function the elasticity of factor substitution is equal to one.**

given that β/α is constant and does not affect the derivative.

6. Factor Intensity

In a Cobb-Douglas function factor intensity is measured by the ratio β/α. The higher this ratio the more labour intensive the technique. Similarly the lower the ratio β/α the more capital intensive the technique.

7. The sum of the two exponents (α and β) shows returns to scale. In the Cobb-Douglas case the returns to scale cane be predicted as follows.

(a) When (α + β) = 1 the production function exhibits constant returns to scale,

(b) When (α + β) > 1 it exhibits increasing returns to scale, and

(c) When (α + β) < 1 it exhibits decreasing returns to scale.

This property may now be explained and illustrated.

Let us take the Cobb-Douglas function *i.e.,*

$$Q_1 = A.K^{\alpha}.L^{\beta}$$

and multiple each input by the factor *m*. So we get

$$Q_2 = A.(mK)^{\alpha}.(mL)^{\beta}$$
$$= A.m^{\alpha}.K^{\alpha}.m^{\beta}.L^{\beta}$$
$$= A.K^{\alpha}.L^{\beta}.m^{(\alpha+\beta)} = Q_1.\,m^{(\alpha+\beta)}$$

8. The Cobb-Douglas production function has an additional property. It is a homothetic production function. A homothetic production function has **straight line expansion path.**

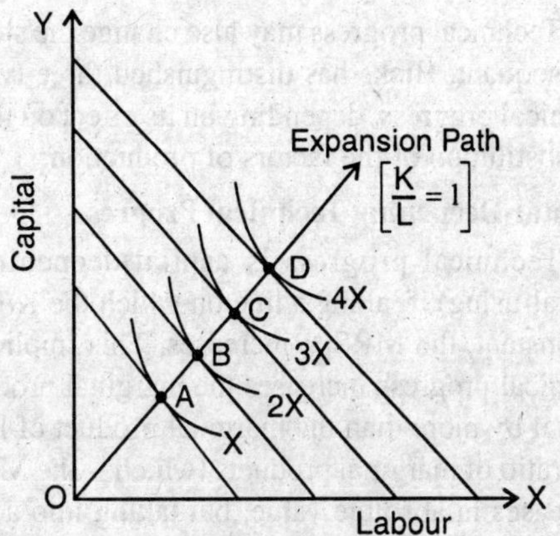

Fig. : *The Expansion Path for the Cobb Douglas Function*

Technological Progress and The Production Function

As knowledge of new and more efficient methods of production becomes available, technology changes. Furthermore new inventions may result in the increase of the efficiency of all methods of production. At the same time some techniques may become inefficient and drop out from the production function. These changes in technology constitute technological progress.

Graphically the effect of **innovation in process** is shown with an upward shift of the production function (figure 76), or a downward movement of the production isoquant (figure 77). This shift shows that the same output may be produced by less factor inputs, or more output may be obtained with the same inputs.

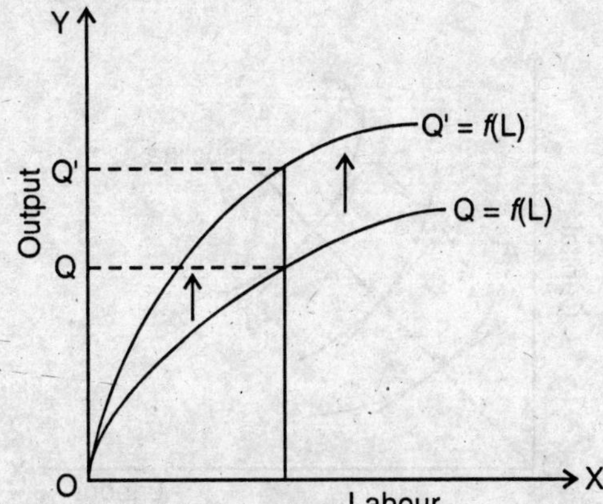

Fig. 76: *Upward Shift of the Production Function*

Technical progress may also change the shape of the isoquant. Hicks has distinguished three types of technical progress, depending on its effect on the rate of substitution of the factors of production.

Capital-Deepening Technical Progress

Technical progress is capital-deepening (or capital-using) if, along a line on which the K/L ratio is constant, the MRS_{LX} increases. This implies that technical progress increases the marginal product of capital by more than the marginal product of labour. The ratio of marginal products (which is the MRS_{LK}) decreases in absolute value, but taking into account that the slope of the isoquant is negative, this sort of technical progress increases the MRS_{LK}. The slope of the shifting isoquant becomes less steep along any given radius. The capital-deepening technical progress is shown in figure 78.

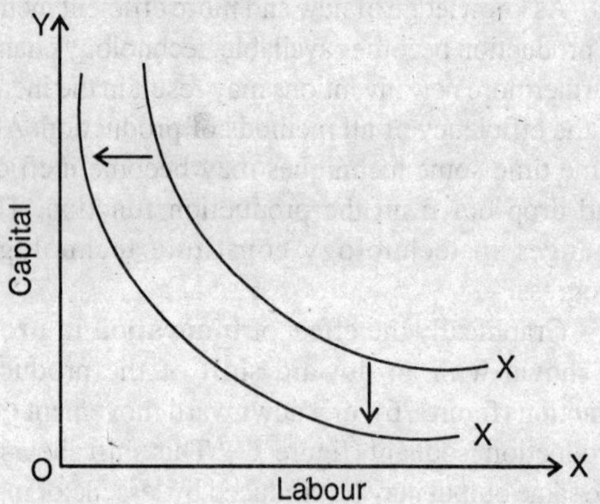

Fig. 77: *Downward Movement of the Isoquant*

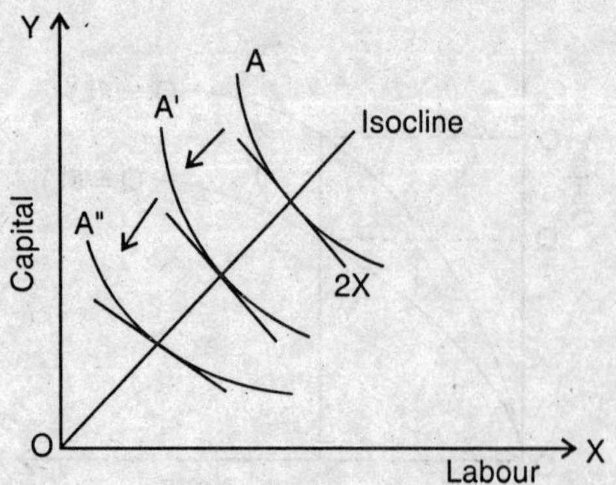

Fig. 78 : *Capital-Deepening Technical Progress*

Labour-Deepening Technical Progress

Technical progress is labour-deepening if, along a radius through the origin (with constant K/L ratio), the MRS_{LK} increases. This implies that the technical progress increases the MP_L faster than the MP_K. Thus the MRS_{LK} being the ratio of the marginal products, increase in absolute value (but decreases if the minus sign is taken into account).

The downwards-shifting isoquant becomes steeper along any given radius through the origin. This is shown in figure 79.

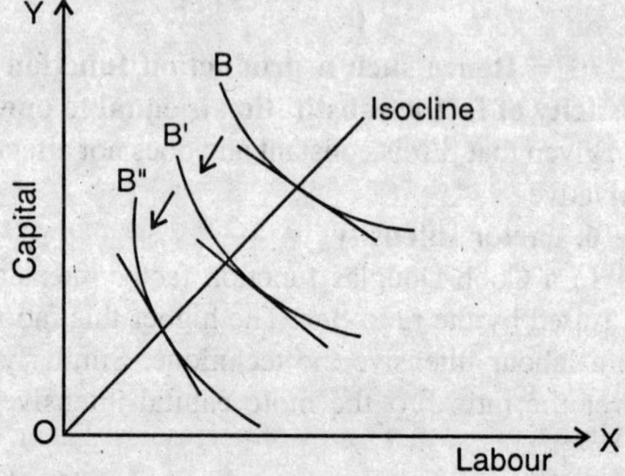

Fig. 79 : *Labour-deepening Technical Progress*

Neutral-Technical Progress

Technical progress is neutral if it increases the marginal product of both factors by the same percentage, so that the MRS_{LK} (along any radius) remains constant. The isoquant shifts downwards parallel to itself. This is shown in figure 80.

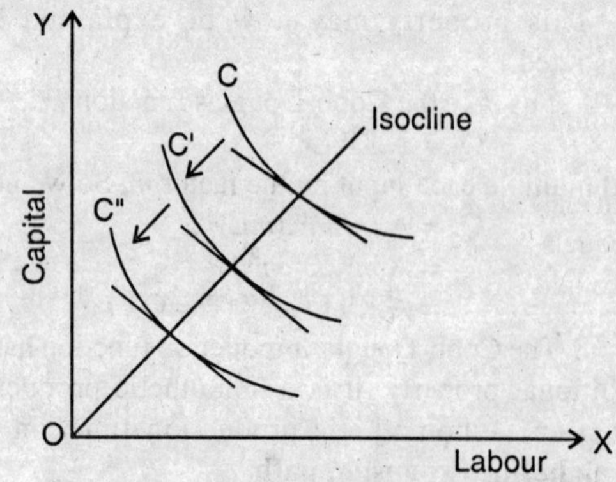

Fig. 80: *Neutral Technical Progress*

Output Elasticities

If the production function is Q = f(L. K), the output elasticity of L is the ratio of proportionate change in output Q to the proportionate change in input L, given the input of K. Similarly, the output elasticity of K is the ratio of proportionate change in output Q to the proportionate change in K, given the input of L. If e_L be the output elasticity of L, then

$$e_L = \frac{\text{Proportionate change in Q}}{\text{Proportionate change in L}}$$

$$= \frac{\Delta Q/Q}{\Delta L/L} = \frac{\Delta Q}{\Delta L} \times \frac{L}{Q}$$

where

Δ = change
Q = output
L = labour input.

Similarly, if the output elasticity of input K be e_K, then

$$e_K = \frac{\Delta Q/Q}{\Delta K/K} = \frac{\Delta Q}{\Delta K} \times \frac{K}{Q}$$

Output elasticities are also expressed as the ratios of the marginal and average product of the respective inputs. Thus the output elasticity of input L is

$$e_L = \frac{MP_L}{AP_L}$$

and of input K,

$$e_K = \frac{MP_K}{AP_K}$$

If MP and AP of a input are positive, its output elasticity is also positive. The output elasticity of an input is greater than, equal to, or less than unity according as its MP is respectively greater than, equal to or less than its AP. When MP is greater than AP, the output elasticity of input L is greater than unity. When MP equals AP the output elasticity is unity. When MP is zero and AP is greater than the former, the output elasticity is zero.

The sum of output elasticities of inputs L and K equal to degree of homogeneity. If the production function is homogeneous of degree one, the sum of output elasticities of L and K also equal to one.

Equilibrium of the Firm : Choice of Optimal Combination of Factors of Production

In this section we shall show the use of the production function in the choice of the optimal combination of factors by the firm. In part A we will examine two cases in which the firm is faced with a single decision, namely maximising output for a given cost, and minimising cost subject to a given output. Both, these decisions comprise cases of constrained profit maximisation in a single period.

In part B we will consider the case of unconstrained profit maximisation, by the expansion of output over time.

In all the above cases it is assumed that the firm can choose the optimal combination of factors, that it can employ any amount of any factor in order to maximise its profits. This assumption is valid if the firm is new, or if the firm is in the long-run. However, an existing firm may be coerced, due to pressure of demand, to expand its output in the short-run, when at least one factor, usually capital, is constant.

In all cases we make the following assumptions :

1.The goal of the firm is profit maximisation-that is, the maximisation of the difference

$$\pi = R - C$$

where

π = profits
R = revenue
C = cost

2. The price of output is given, $\overline{P}_X$.
3. The price of factors are **given :**
$\overline{w}$ is the given wage rate.
$\overline{r}$ is the given price of capital services.

A. Single Decision of the Firm

The problem facing the firm is that of a constrained profit maximisation, which may take one of the following forms :

***(a)* Maximise Profit π, subject to a Cost Constraint.** In this case total cost and price are given $(\overline{c}, \overline{w}, \overline{r}, \overline{p}_x)$ and the problem may be stated as follows

$$\text{Maximum } (\pi) = R - \overline{C}$$

or $$\pi = \overline{P}_X . X - \overline{C}$$

Clearly maximisation of π is achieved in this case if X (output) is maximised, since $\overline{C}$ and $\overline{P}x$ are given constants by assumption.

***(b)* Maximise Profit π, for a given level of Output.** For example, a contractor wants to build a bridge (X is given) with the maximum profit. In this case we have

Maximum (p) = R – C

or $\quad p = \overline{P}x.\overline{X} - C$

Clearly maximisation of π is achieved in this case if C is minimised, given that X and $\overline{P}x$ are given constants by assumption.

For a graphical presentation of the equilibrium of the firm (its profit maximising position) we will use the **isoquant map** (figure 81) and the **isocost-line** (figure 82).

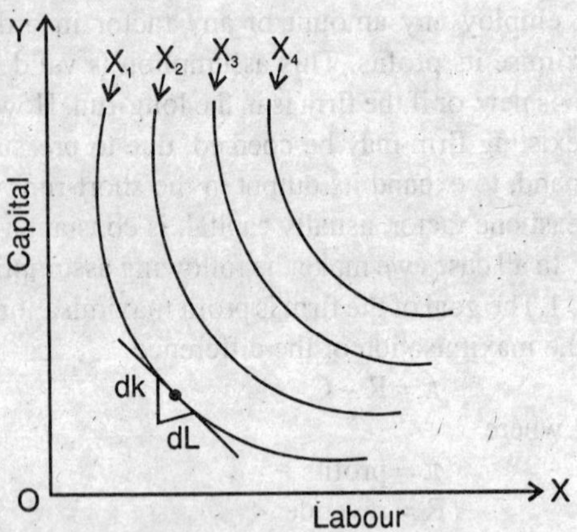

Fig. 81 : *Isoquant Map*

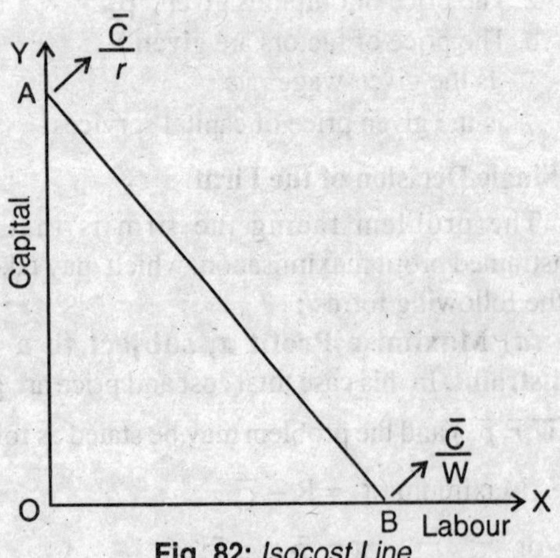

Fig. 82: *Isocost Line*

The Slope of an isoquant is

$$-\frac{dK}{dL} = MRS_{LK} = \frac{MP_L}{MP_K} = \frac{dX/dL}{dX/dK}$$

The isocost line is defined by the cost equation

$$C = (r)(K) + (w)(L)$$

where

C = cost
w = wage rate
r = price of capital services
K = quantity of capital
L = quantity of labour

The isocost line is the locus of all combinations of factors the firm can purchase with a given monetary cost outlay. There is a close analogy between the consumer's price line and firm's isocost line.

The slope of the isocost line is equal to the ratio of the prices of the factors of production. Thus,.

$$\text{Slope of isocost line} = \frac{w}{r}$$

$$= \frac{\text{Price of Labour}}{\text{Price of capital}}$$

Case 1 : Maximisation of output Subject to a Cost Constraint (financial constraint)

The firm is in equilibrium when it maximizes its output given its total cost outlay and the prices of the factors, w and r.

In figure 83 we see that the maximum level of output the firm can produce, given the cost constraint, is X_2 defined by the tangency of the isocost line, and the highest isoquant. The optimal combination of factors of production is K_2 and L_2, for price w and r. Higher levels of output (to the right of e) are desirable but not attainable due to the cost constraint. Other points on AB or below it lie on a lower isoquant than X_2. Hence X_2 is the maximum output possible under the above assumptions (of given cost outlay, given production function, and given factor prices). At the point of tangency (e) the slope of the isocost line (w/r) is equal to the slope of the isoquant (MP_L/MP_K). This constitutes the first condition for equilibrium. The second condition is that the isoquant be convex to the origin. **In summary : the conditions for equilibrium of the firm are :**

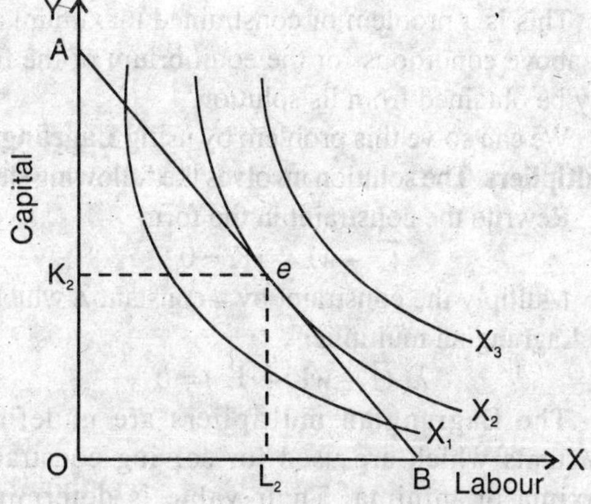

Fig. 83: *Equilibrium of the Firm*

(*a*) Slope of Isoquant = Slope of Isocost line

$$\text{or} \quad \frac{w}{r} = \frac{MP_L}{MP_K}$$

$$\frac{w}{r} = \frac{dX/dL}{dX/dK}$$

$$\frac{w}{r} = MRS_{LK}$$

(*b*) The isoquants must be convex to the origin. If the isoquant is concave the point of tangency of the isocost and the isoquant curves does not define an equilibrium position (figure 84).

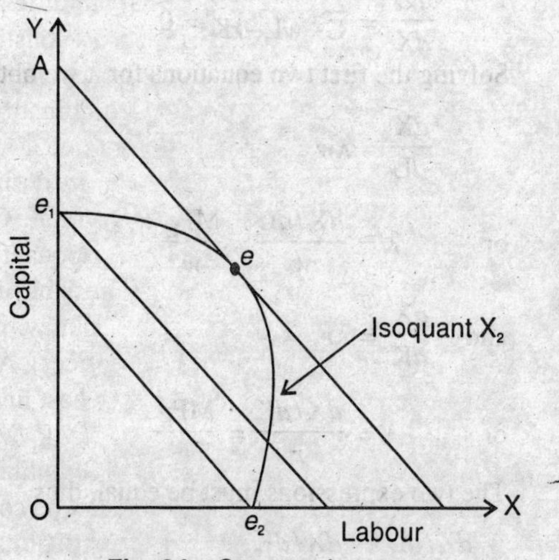

Fig. 84 : *Concave Isoquant*

Output X_2 (depicted by the concave isoquant) can be produced with lower cost at e_2 which lies on a lower isocost curve than *e* **With a concave isoquant we have *a* 'corner solution'.**

Case 2 : Minimisation of Cost for a given Level of Output

The conditions for equilibrium of the firm are formally the same as in case 1. That is, there must be tangency of the (given) isoquant and the lowest possible isocost curve, and the isoquant must be convex. However, the problem is conceptually different in case of cost minimisation. The entrepreneur wants to produce a given output (for example, a bridge, a building, or $\overline{X}$ tons of a commodity) with the minimum cost outlay.

In this case we have a single isoquant (figure 85) which denotes the desired level of output, but we have a set of isocost curves (figure 86). Curves closer to the origin show a lower total cost outlay. The isocost lines are parallel because they are drawn on the assumption of constant prices of factors. Since *w* and *r* do not change, all the isocost curves have the same slope *w*/*r*.

The firm minimises its costs by employing the combination of K and L determined by the point of tangency of the $\overline{X}$ isoquant with the lowest isocost line (figure 87). Points below *e* are desirable because they show lower cost but are not attainable for output $\overline{X}$. Points above *e* show higher costs. Hence point *e* is the **least-cost point,** the point denoting the **least-**

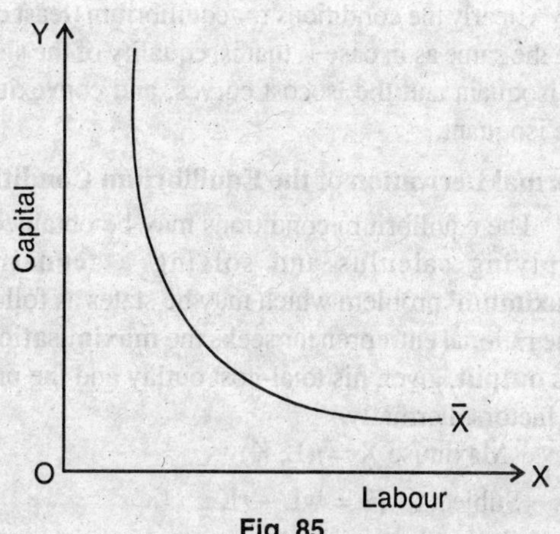

Fig. 85

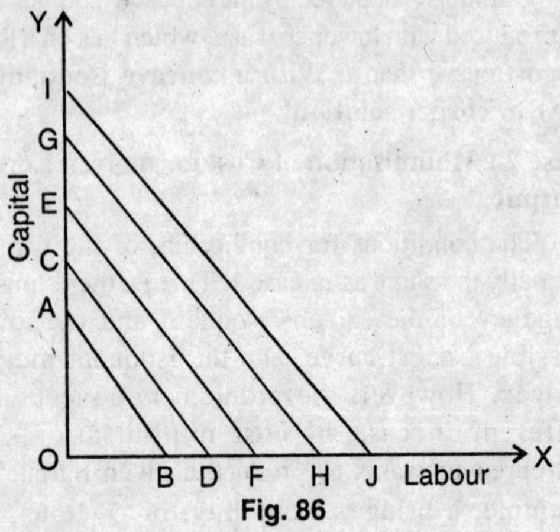

Fig. 86

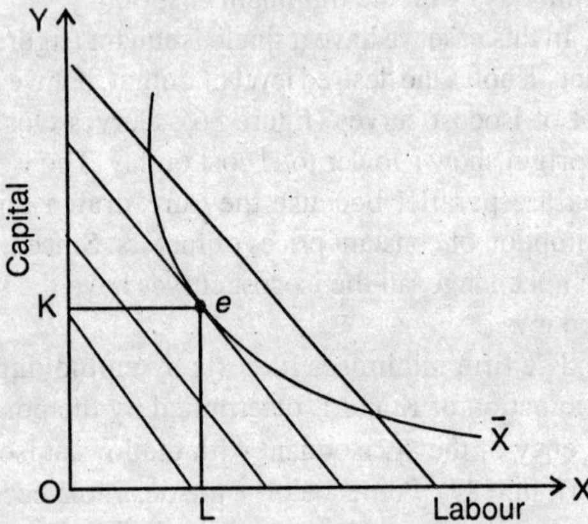

Fig. 87: *Least-Cost Combination*

cost combination of the factors K and L for producing $\overline{X}$.

Clearly the conditions for equilibrium (least cost) are the same as in case 1, that is, equality of the slopes of isoquant and the isocost curves, and convexity of the isoquant.

Formal Derivation of the Equilibrium Conditions

The equilibrium conditions may be obtained by applying calculus and solving a **'constrain maximum'** problem which may be states as follows. The rational entrepreneur seeks the **maximisation of his output,** given his total-cost outlay and the prices of factors. Formally,

Maximise $X = f(L, K)$

Subject to $\overline{C} = wL + rK$

$= \text{cost constraint}$

This is a problem of constrained maximum and the above conditions for the equilibrium of the firm may be obtained from its solution.

We can solve this problem by using **Lagrangian multipliers.** The solution involves the following steps:

Rewrite the constraint in the form

$$\overline{C} - wL - rK = 0$$

Multiply the constraint by a constant λ which is the Lagrangian multiplier :

$$\lambda(\overline{C} - wL - rK) = 0$$

The Lagrangian multipliers are undefined constants which are used for solving constraints maxima or minima. Their value is determined simultaneously with the values of the both unknowns (L and K).

From the 'composite' function

$$\varnothing = X + \lambda(\overline{C} - wL - rK)$$

It can be shown that maximisation of the ∅ function implies maximisation of the output.

The first condition for the maximisation of a function is that its partial derivatives be equal to zero. The partial derivatives of the above function with respect to L, K and λ are :

$$\frac{d\varnothing}{dL} = \frac{dX}{dL} + \lambda(-w) = 0 \qquad ...(1)$$

$$\frac{d\varnothing}{dK} = \frac{dX}{dK} + \lambda(-r) = 0 \qquad ...(2)$$

$$\frac{d\varnothing}{dX} = \overline{C} - wL - rK = 0 \qquad ...(3)$$

Solving the first two equations for λ we obtain

$$\frac{dX}{dL} = \lambda w$$

or $$\lambda = \frac{dX/dL}{w} = \frac{MP_L}{w}$$

and $$\frac{dX}{dK} = \lambda r$$

or $$\lambda = \frac{dX/dK}{r} = \frac{MP_K}{r}$$

The two expressions must be equal, thus

$$\frac{dX/dL}{w} = \frac{dX/dK}{r}$$

$$\text{or} \quad \frac{MP_L}{MP_K} = \frac{dX/dL}{dX/dK} = \frac{w}{r}$$

This firm is in equilibrium when it equates the ratio of the marginal productivities of factors to the ratio of their prices.

It can be shows that the second-order conditions for equilibrium of the firm require that the marginal product curves of the two factors have a negative slope.

The slope of the marginal product curve of labour is the second derivative of the production function :

$$\text{Slope of } MP_L \text{ curve} = \frac{d^2X}{dL^2}$$

$$\text{and slope of } MP_K \text{ curve} = \frac{d^2X}{dK^2}$$

The second-order conditions are

$$\frac{d^2X}{dL^2} < 0 \text{ and } \frac{d^2X}{dK^2} < 0$$

$$\text{and} \left(\frac{d^2X}{dL^2}\right)\left(\frac{d^2X}{dK^2}\right) > \left(\frac{d^2X}{dLdK}\right)^2$$

These conditions are sufficient for establishing the **convexity of the isoquants.**

Expansion Path

The line joining the minimum cost combinations is called the **expansion path** because it shows how the factor combination with which the firm produces will alter as the firm expands its level of output. Thus the expansion path may be defined as the locus of the points of tangency between the equal product curves and the iso-cost lines. The expansion path is also known as **scale-line** because it shows how the entrepreneur will change the quantities of the two factors when it increases the scale of production.

Since expansion path represents minimum cost combinations for various levels of output, it shows the cheapest way of producing each output, given the relative prices of the factors.

In the long run all factors of production are variable. There is no limitation (technical or financial) to the expansion of output. The firm's objective is the choice of the optimal way of expanding its output, so as to maximise its profits. With given factor prices and given production function, the optimal expansion path is determined by the points of tangency of successive isocost lines and successive isoquants.

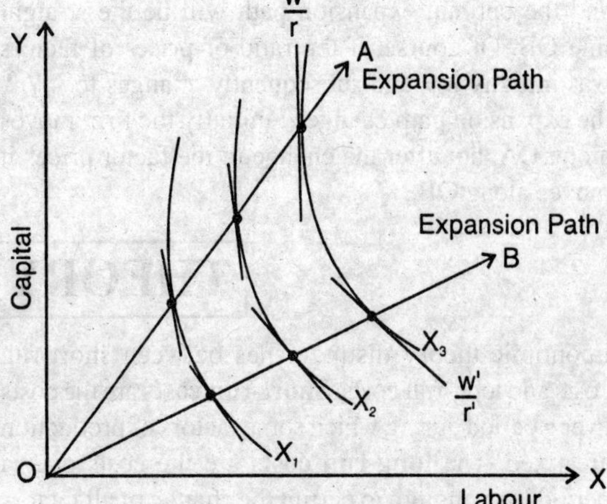

Fig. 88: *Expansion Path : Homogeneous Production Function*

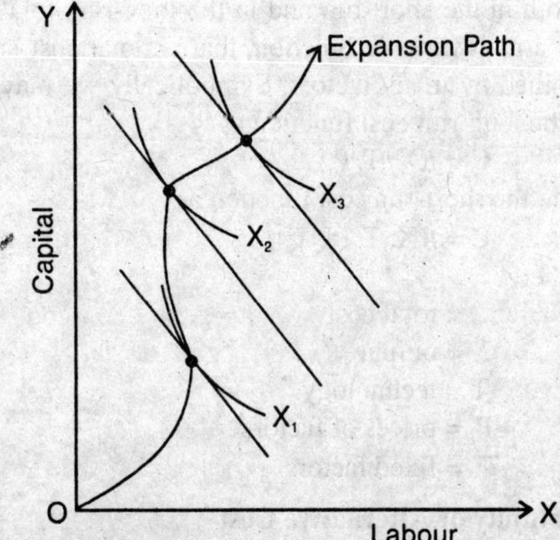

Fig. 89: *Expansion Path : Non-Homogeneous Production Function*

If the production function is **homogeneous** the expansion path will be a straight line through the origin, whose slope (which determines the optimal K/L ratio) depends on the ratio of the factor prices. In figure 88 the optimal expansion path will be OA, defined by the locus of points of tangency of the isoquants with successive parallel isocost line with s slope of *w*/*r*.

If the ratio of the prices increases the isocost lines become flatter (for example, with a slope of w'/r'), and the optimal expansion path will be the straight line OB. Of course, if the ratio of prices of factors was initially w/r and subsequently changes to w'/r', the expansion path changes : initially the firm moves along OA, but after the change in the factor prices it moves along OB.

If the production function is **non-homogeneous** the expansion path will not be a straight line, even if the ratio of prices of factors remains constant. This is shown in figure 89 . It is due to the fact that in equilibrium we must equate the (constant) w/r ratio with the MRS_{LK}, which is the same on a curved isocline.

THEORY OF COSTS

Economic theory distinguishes between short-run costs and long-run costs. **Short-run costs** are the costs over a period during which some factors of production are fixed. The **long-run costs** are the costs over a period long enough to permit the change of all factors of production. In the long run all factors become variable.

Both in the short-run and in the long-run, total cost is a multivariable function, that is, total cost is determined by many factors. Symbolically we may write the long-run cost function as

$$C = f(X, T, P_f)$$

and the short-run cost function as

$$C = f(X, T, P_f, \overline{K})$$

where

C = total cost

X = output

T = technology

P_f = prices of factors

$\overline{K}$ = fixed factors

Opportunity or Alternative Cost

The concept of opportunity cost occupies a very important place in modern economic analysis. The opportunity cost of any good is the next best alternative good that is sacrificed. The factors which are used for the manufacture of a car may also be used for the production of an equipment for the military. Therefore, the opportunity cost of production of a car is the output of the military equipment foregone or sacrificed, which could have been produced with the same amount of factors that have gone into the making of a car.

Two points must be noted in the above definition of opportunity cost. **Firstly,** the opportunity cost of anything is only the **next-best alternative** foregone. That is to say, the opportunities cost of producing a good is not any other alternative good that could be produced with the same factors, it is only the most valuable other good which the same factors could produce. Second point worth nothing in the above definition is the addition of the qualification or "by an equivalent group of factors, costing the same amount of money." The need for the addition of this qualification arises because all the factors used in the production of one good may not be the same as are required for the production of the next best alternative good.

In the words of **Benham,** "The opportunity cost of anything is the next best alternative that could be produced instead by the same factors or by an equivalent group of factors, costing the same amount of money".

The concept of opportunity cost is explained diagrammatically in figure 90 with the help of production possibility curve PP_1. At combination A on this curve, the producer uses OL_1 of labour and OK_1 of capital. If he wants to use L_1L_2 more labour, he will have to forgo K_1K_2 of capital. Thus the opportunity cost of L_1L_2 labour is K_1K_2 of capital.

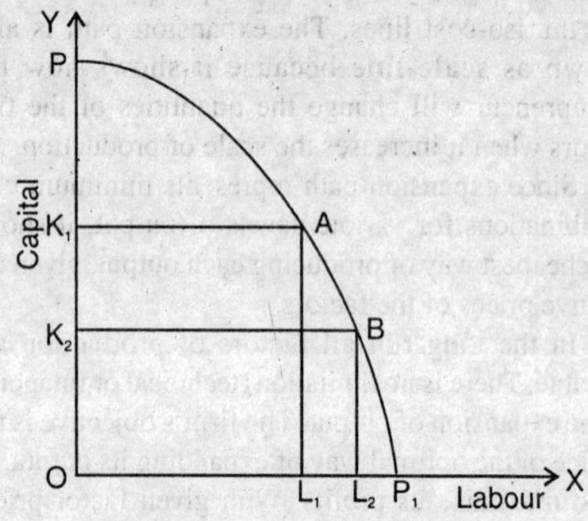

Fig. 90 : *Opportunity Cost*

The concept of opportunity cost has a wide application to economic problems. It is applicable to the determination of factor prices and in international trade. It can also be applied to consumption and public expenditure.

Short-Run Costs of the Traditional Theory

In the traditional theory of the firm total costs are split into two groups : **total fixed costs and total variable costs.**

TC = TFC + TVC

where

TC = total cost

TFC = total fixed cost

TVC = total variable cost

The **fixed costs include :**

(a) salaries of administrative staff

(b) depreciation of machinery

(c) expenses for building depreciation and repairs

(d) expenses for land maintenance

The **variable costs include :**

(a) the raw materials

(b) the cost of direct labour

(c) the running expenses of fixed capital, such as fuel, ordinary repairs and routine maintenance.

The total fixed cost is graphically denoted by a straight line parallel to the output axis (figure 91).

The total variable cost in the traditional theory of the firm has broadly an inverse-S shape (figure 92) which reflects the **law of variable proportions.** According to this law, at the initial stages of production with a given plant, as more of the variable factor is employed, its productivity increases and the average variable cost falls.

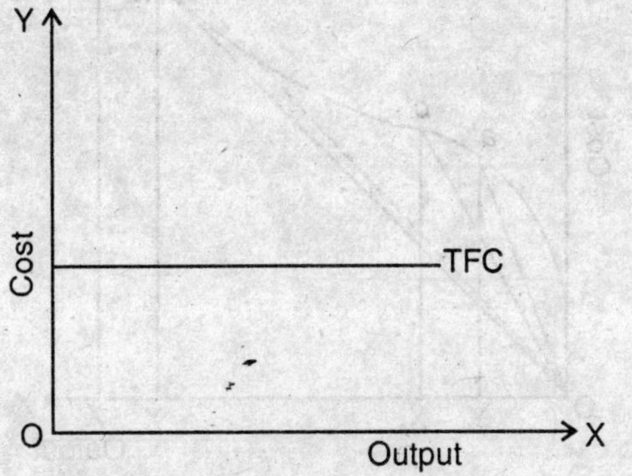

Fig. 91 : *Total Fixed Cost Curve*

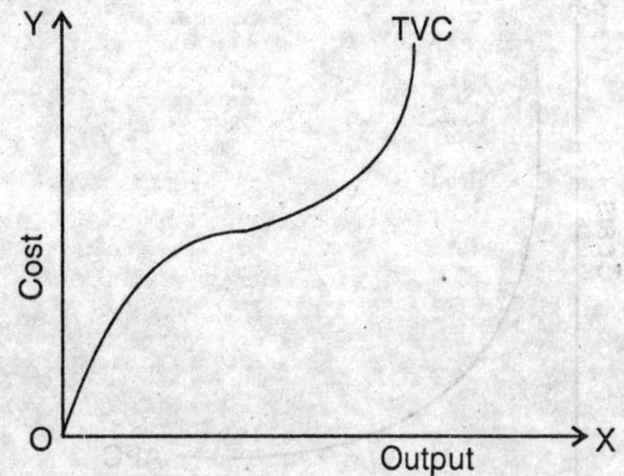

Fig. 92 : *Total Variable Cost Curve*

This continues unit the optimal combination of the fixed and variable factors is reached. Beyond this point as increased qualities of the variable factors are combined with the fixed factor the productivity of the variable factor declines (and the AVC rises). By adding the TFC and TVC we obtain the TC of the firm (figure 93). From the total-cost curves we obtain **average-cost curves.** The average fixed cost is found by dividing TFC by the level of output. Thus

$$AFC = \frac{TFC}{X}$$

Graphically the AFC is a **rectangular hyperbola,** showing at all its points the same magnitude, that is, the level of TFC (figure 94). The average variable cost is similarly obtained by dividing the TVC with the corresponding level of output :

$$AVC = \frac{TVC}{X}$$

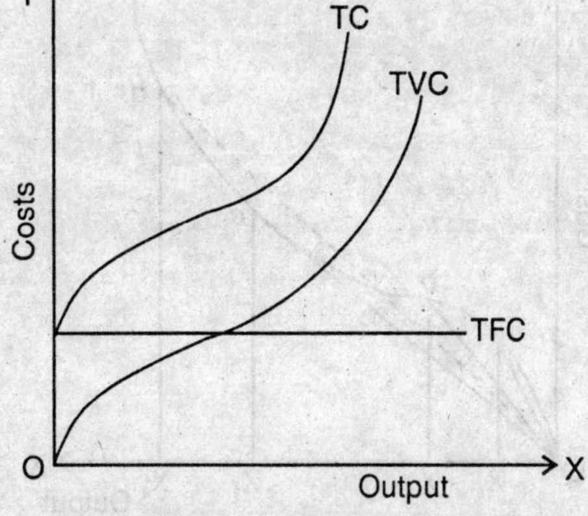

Fig. 93 : *TC, TVC and TFC*

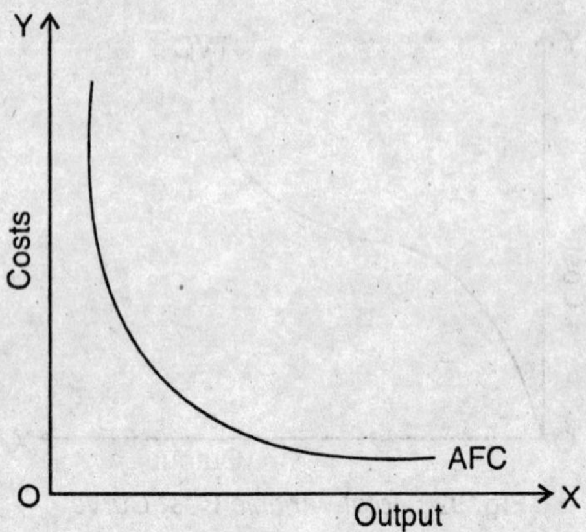

Fig. 94: *Average Fixed Cost Curve*

Graphically the AVC at each level of output is derived from the slopes of a line drawn form the origin to the point on the TVC curve corresponding to the particular level of output. For example, in figure 95 the AVC at X_1 is the slopes of the ray O*a*, the AVC at X_2 is the slope of the ray O*b*, and so on. It is clear from figure 95 that the slope of a ray through the origin declines continuously until the ray becomes tangent to the TVC curve at C. To the right of this point the slope of rays through the origin starts increasing. Thus the SAVC curve falls initially as the productivity of the variable factor increases, reaches a minimum when the plant is operated optimally and rises beyond that point (figure 96).

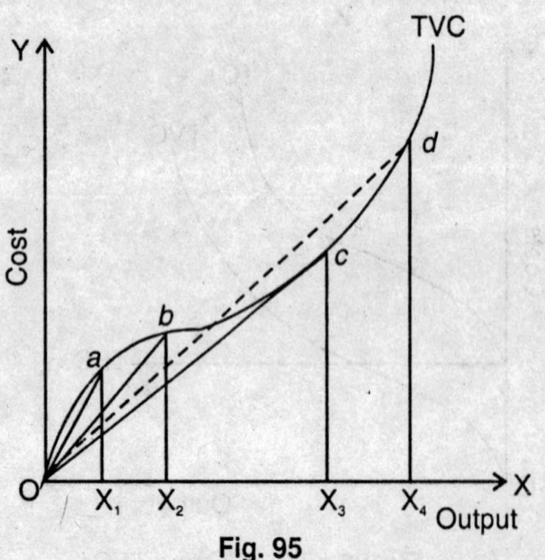

Fig. 95

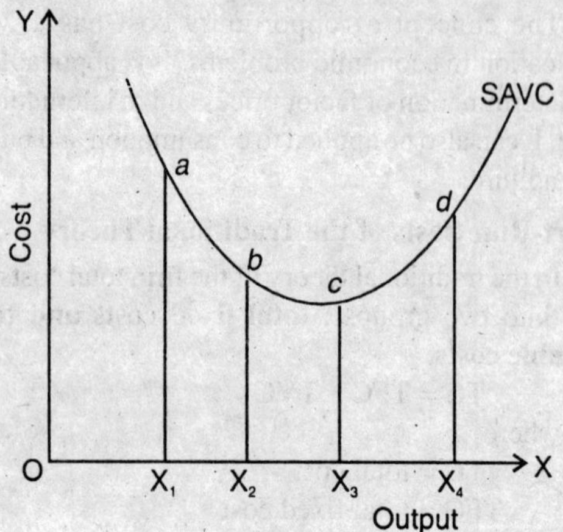

Fig. 96 : *Average Variable Cost*

The ATC is obtained by dividing the TC by the corresponding level of output.

$$ATC = \frac{TC}{X}$$

$$= \frac{TFC + TVC}{X} = AFC + AVC$$

Graphically the ATC curve is derived in the same way as the SAVC. The ATC at any level of output is the slope of the straight line from the origin to the point on the TC curve corresponding to that particular level of output (figure 97). The shape of the ATC is similar to that of the AVC **(both being U-shaped).** Initially the ATC declines, it reaches a minimum at

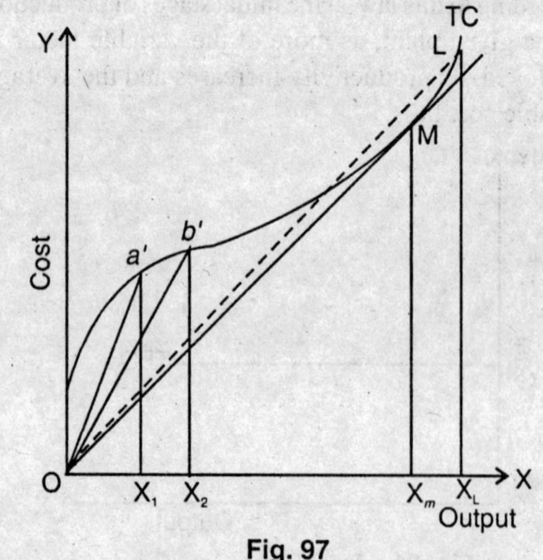

Fig. 97

the level of optimal operation of the plant (X_m) and subsequently rises again (figure 98). The **U-shape** of both the AVC and the ATC reflects the **law of variable proportions or law of eventually decreasing returns to the variable factors of production.**

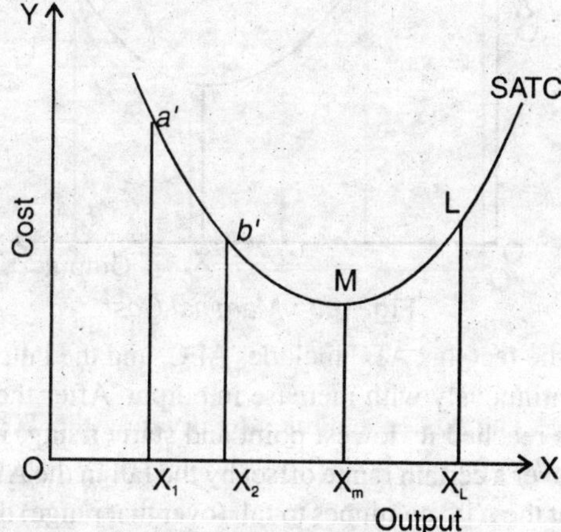

Fig. 98: *Average Total Cost*

Marginal Cost

The marginal cost if defined as the change in TC which results from a unit change in output. In other words, marginal cost is the addition to the total cost of producing n units instead of $(n - 1)$ units where n is say any given number. In symbols :

$$MC_n = TC_n - TC_{n-1}$$

Mathematically the marginal cost is the first derivative of the TC function. Denoting total cost by TC and output by X we have

$$MC = \frac{dTC}{dX}$$

It is worth pointing out that marginal cost is independent of the fixed cost. Since fixed costs do not change with output, there are no marginal fixed costs when output is increased in the short run. It is only the variable costs that vary with output in the short run. Therefore the marginal costs are infact due to the changes in variable costs, and whatever the amount of fixed cost, the marginal cost if unaffected by it.

The independence of the marginal cost from the fixed cost can be proved algebraically as follows :

$$\begin{aligned} MC_n &= TC_n - TC_{n-1} \\ &= (TVC_n + TFC) - (TVC_{n-1} + TFC) \\ &= TVC_n + TFC - TVC_{n-1} - TFC \\ &= TVC_n - TVC_{n-1} \end{aligned}$$

Hence **marginal cost is the addition to the total variable costs when output is increased from $n - 1$ units to n units of output.** It follows therefore that the marginal cost is independent of the amount of the fixed costs.

It should be noted that marginal cost of production is intimately related to the marginal product of the variable factor.

As noted above,

$$MC = \frac{dTC}{dX}$$

$$\text{or} \quad MC = \frac{d(TVC)}{dX}$$

Since price of the variable factor, *i.e.*, w is assumed to be constant, the change in total variable cost can occur due to the change in the amount of the variable factor.

Therefore,

$$MC = \frac{wdL}{dX}$$

$$= w.\frac{dL}{dX} \qquad ...(1)$$

From above discussion we know that marginal product of the variable factor is the change in total product as a result of the unit change in the variable factor. Thus

$$MP_L = \frac{dX}{dL} \quad \text{or} \quad \frac{1}{MP_L} = \frac{dL}{dX}$$

Substituting $\frac{dL}{dX}$ for $\frac{1}{MP_L}$ in equation (1), we get

$$MC = w.\frac{1}{MP_L}$$

$$\text{or} \quad MC = \frac{w}{MP_L} \qquad ...(2)$$

Thus, marginal cost of production is equal to the reciprocal of the marginal product of the variable factor multiplied by the price of variable factor. Therefore, marginal cost varies inversely with the marginal product of the variable factor.

Graphically the MC is the slope of the TC curve (which of course is the same at any point as the slope of the TVC). The slope of a curve at any one of its points is the slope of the tangent at that point. With an inverse-S shape of the TC (and TVC) the MC curve will be U-shaped. In figure 99 we observe that the slope of the tangent to the total-cost curve declines gradually, until it becomes parallel to the X-axis (with its slope being equal to zero at this point), and then starts rising. Accordingly we picture the MC curve in figure 100 as **U-shaped.**

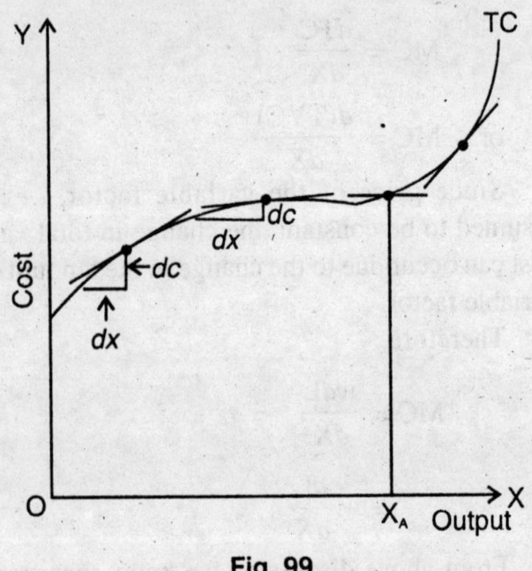

Fig. 99

In Summary : the traditional theory of costs postulates that in the short run the cost curves (AVC, ATC and MC) are **U-shaped,** reflecting the **law of variable proportions.** In the short run with a fixed plant there is a phase of increasing productivity (falling unit costs) and a phase of decreasing productivity (increasing unit costs) of the variable factor. Between these two phases of plant operation there is a single point at which unit costs are at a minimum. When this point on the SATC is reached the plant is utilised optimally, that is, with the optimal combination of fixed and variable factors.

The Relationship Between ATC and AVC

The AVC is a part of the ATC, given ATC = AFC + AVC. Both AVC and ATC are U-shaped, reflecting the law of variable proportions. However, the minimum point of the ATC occurs to the right of the minimum point of the AVC (figure 101). This is due

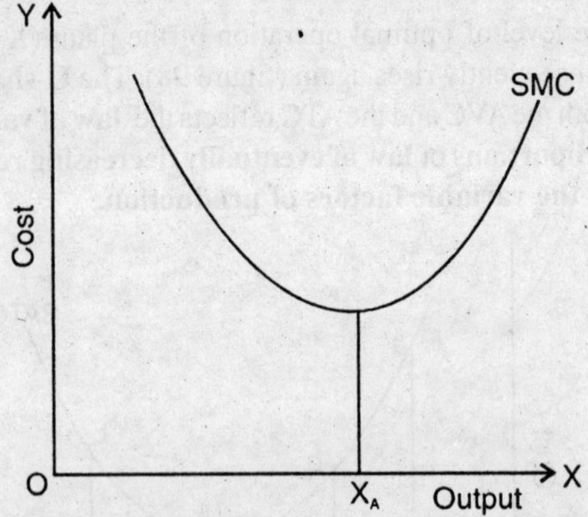

Fig. 100 : *Marginal Cost*

to the fact that ATC includes AFC, and the latter falls continuously with increase in output. After the AVC has reached its lowest point and starts rising, its rise is over a certain range offset by the fall in the AFC, so that the ATC continues to fall (over that range) despite the increase in AVC. However, the rise in AVC eventually becomes greater than the fall in the AFC so that the ATC starts increasing. The AVC approaches the ATC asymptotically as X (output) increases.

In figure 101 the minimum AVC is reached at X, while the ATC is at its minimum at X_2. Between X_1 and X_2 the fall in AFC more than offsets the rise in AVC so that the ATC continues to fall. Beyond X_2 the increase in AVC is not offset by the fall in AFC, so that ATC rises.

The Relationship between MC and ATC

The MC-curve cuts the ATC-curve and the AVC-curve at their lowest points. We will establish this relation only for the ATC and MC, but the relation between MC and AVC can be established on the same lines of reasoning.

We said that the MC is the change in the TC for producing an extra unit of output. Assume that we start from a level of *n* units of output. If we increase the output by one unit the MC is the change in total cost resulting from the production of the $(n + 1)$th unit.

The AC at each level of output is found by dividing TC by X (output). Thus the AC at the level of X_n is

$$AC_n = \frac{TC_n}{X_n}$$

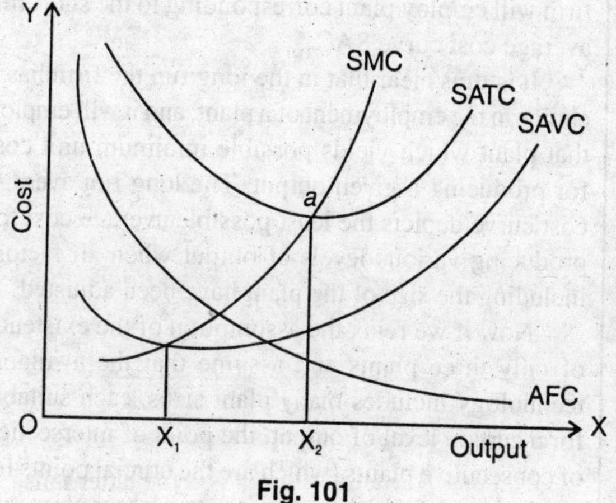

Fig. 101

and the AC at the level X_{n+1} is

$$AC_{n+1} = \frac{TC_{n+1}}{X_{n+1}}$$

Clearly

$$TC_{n+1} = TC_n + MC$$

Thus :

(a) If the MC of the $(n + 1)$th unit is less than AC_n (the AC of the previous n units) the AC_{n+1} will be smaller than the AC_n.

(b) If the MC of the $(n + 1)$th unit is higher than AC_n (the AC of the previous n units) the AC_{n+1} will be higher than the AC_n.

So long as the MC lies below the AC-curve, it pulls the latter downwards, when the MC rises above the AC, it pulls the latter upwards. In figure 101 to the left of *a* the MC lies below the AC curve, and hence the latter falls downwards. To the right of *a* the MC-curve lie above the AC curve, so that AC rises. It follows that at point *a,* where the intersection of the MC and AC occurs, the AC has reached its minimum level.

The relationship between the MC and AC curves becomes clearer with the use of simple calculus. Given C = ZX

where

C = total cost
Z = average cost
X = output

Clearly

$$Z = f(X)$$

The MC is

$$\frac{dC}{dX} = \frac{d(ZX)}{d(X)}$$

Applying the rule of differentiation of **'a function of a function'** (which states that if $y = uv$, where $u = f_1(X)$ and $v = f_2(X)$, then $\frac{dY}{dX} = \frac{dY}{dU}.\frac{dU}{dX}$), we obtain

$$MC = \frac{dC}{dX}$$

$$= Z\frac{dX}{dX} + X\frac{dZ}{dX}$$

or $\quad$ MC = AC + (X). (Slope of AC)

Given that AC > 0 and X > 0, the following results emerge :

(a) If slope of AC < 0, then MC < AC.
(b) If slope of AC > 0, then MC > AC.
(c) If slope of AC = 0, then MC = AC.

The slope of the AC becomes zero at the minimum point of this curve (given that on the theoretical grounds the AC curve is U-shaped). Hence MC = AC at the minimum point of the average cost curve.

Long-Run Costs of the Traditional Theory : The 'Envelope' Curve

In the long run all factors are assumed to become variable. We said that the long-run cost curve is a **planning curve,** in the sense that it is a guide to the entrepreneur in his decision to plan the future expansion of his output.

The long run average-cost is derived from short-run cost curves. Each point on the LAC corresponds to a point on a shout-run cost curve, which is tangent to the LAC at that point.

Long-run average cost curve depicts the least possible average cost for producing all possible levels of output. In order to understand how the long-run average cost curve is derived, consider the three short-run average cost curves as shown in figure 102. These short-run average cost curves are also called **plant curves,** since in the short-run plant is fixed and each of the short-run average cost curve corresponds to a particular plants. In the short run, the firm can be operating on any short-run average cost curve, given the size of plant. Suppose that only these three are technically possible sizes of plants and that no other size of the plant can be built. Given the size of the plant or short run average cost curve the firm will increase or decrease its output by varying the amount of the variable inputs. But in the long-run, the firm can choose among the three possible sizes of plant as depicted by short-run average cost curves SAC_1, SAC_2 and SAC_3. In the long run the firm will examine that with which size of plant or on which short-run average cost curve it should operate to produce a given levels of output at the minimum possible cost.

It will be seen from figure 102 that upto OB amount of output, the firm will operate on the short-run average cost curve SAC_1, though it could also produce with short-run average cost curve SAC_2, because upto OB amount of output, production on SAC_1 curve entails lower cost than on SAC_2. If the firm plans to produce an output which is larger than OB (but less than OD), then it will not be economical to produce on SAC_1. It will be seen from figure 102 that the outputs larger than OB (but less than OD), can be produced at a lower cost per unit on SAC_2 than on SAC_1. Thus, the output OC is produced on SAC_2 costs CK per unit which is lower than CJ which is the cost incurred when produced on SAC_1. Therefore, if the firm plants to produce between outputs OB and OD, it will employ the plant corresponding to short-run average cost curve SAC_2. If the firm has to produce an output which exceeds OD, then the cost per unit will be lower on SAC_3 than on SAC_2. Therefore, for outputs larger than OD, the firm will employ plant corresponding to the short run average cost curve SAC_3.

It is thus clear that in the long run the firm has a choice in the employment of a plant, and it will employ that plant which yields possible minimum unit cost for producing a given output. The long run average cost curve depicts the least possible average cost for producing various levels of output when all factors including the size of the plant have been adjusted.

Now if we relax the assumption of the existence of only three plants and assume that the available technology includes many plant sizes, each suitable for a certain level of output, the point of intersection of consecutive plants (which are the crucial points for the decision of whether to switch to a larger plant) are more numerous. In the limits, If we assume that there is a very large number (infinite number) of plants, we obtain a continuous curve, which is the planning LAC-curve of the firm. Each point of this curve shows the minimum (optimal) cost for producing the corresponding level of output. **The LAC-curve is the locus of points denoting the least cost of producing the corresponding output.** It is a planning curve because on the basis of this curve the firm decides what plant to set up in order to produce optimally (at minimum cost) the expected level of output. The firm chooses the short-run plant which allows it to produce the anticipated (in the long-run) output at the least possible cost. In the traditional theory of the firm the LAC-curve is U-shaped and it is often called the **'envelope curve'** because it **'envelopes'** the SRC-curve (figure 103).

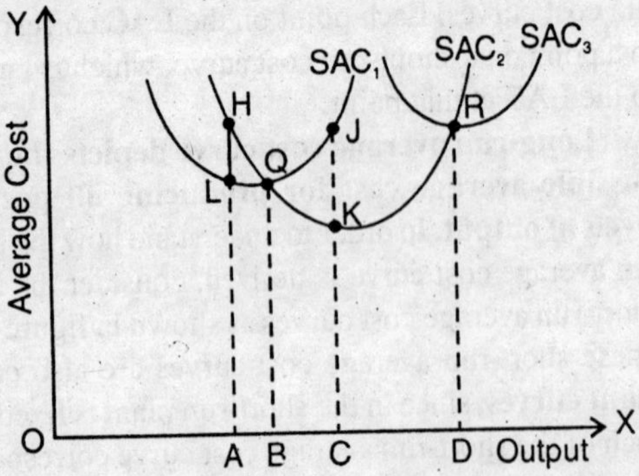

Fig. 102 Plant Curves

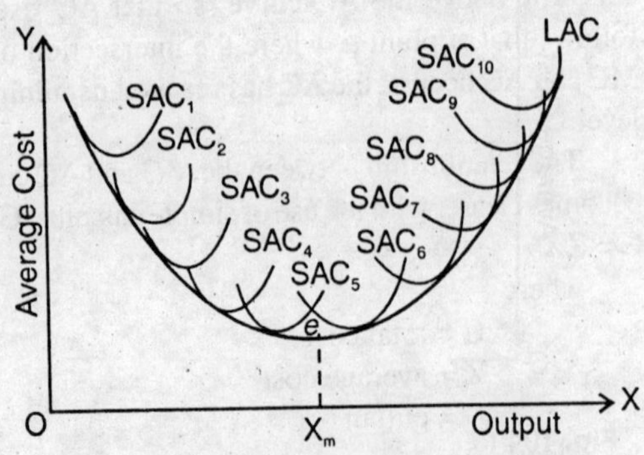

Fig. 103 : *Long Average Cost Curve*

An important fact about the long-run average cost curve is worth mentioning. It is that the long-run average curve LAC is not tangent to the minimum point of the short-run average cost curves. When the long-run average cost curve is declining, that is, for output less than OX_m, it is tangent to the falling portions of the short-run average cost curves.

On the other hand, when the long-run average cost curve is rising, it will be tangent to the rising portions of the short-run average cost curves.

Long-Run Average Cost Curve in Constant Cost Case

If the production function is linear and homogeneous (that is, homogeneous of the first degree) and also the prices of inputs remain constant, then the long-run average cost will remain constant at all levels of output. Linear homogeneous production function implies **constant returns to scale** which means that when all inputs are increased in a certain proportion, the output increases in the same proportion.

Therefore, with the given prices of inputs, when returns to scale are constant, the cost per unit of output remains the same. In this case, the long run average cost curve will be a horizontal straight cost curve will be a horizontal straight line as depicted in figure 104.

In such a case, **the optimum size of the firm in indeterminate,** since all levels of output can be produced at the same long-run average cost which represents the same minimum short-run average costs throughout.

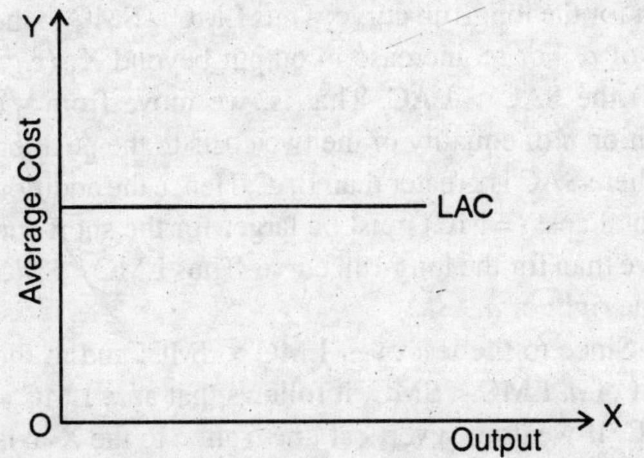

Fig. 104 : *Long-Run Average Cost Curve : Constant Costs, Constant Returns*

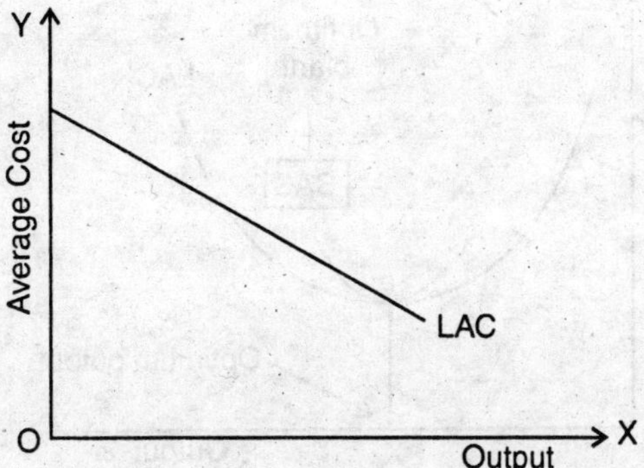

Fig. 105: *Long-Run Average Cost Curve : Decreasing Costs, Increasing Returns*

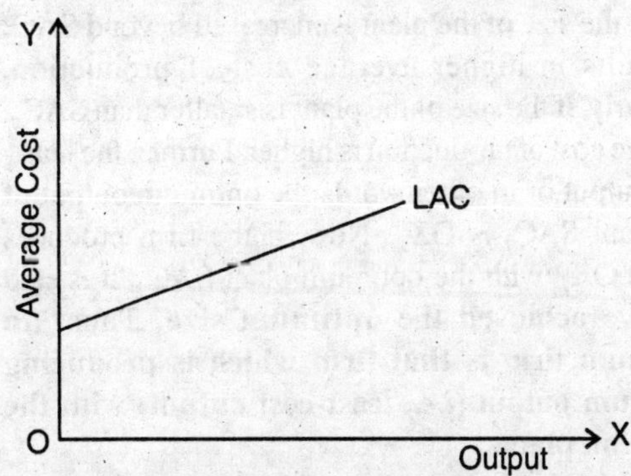

Fig. 106 : *Long-Run Average Cost Curve : Rising Costs, Decreasing Returns*

Optimum Plant, Optimum Output and Optimum Firm

It is clear from figure 103 that in the continuous long-run average cost curve both for outputs less than OX_m and more than OX_m no plant is used at its point of minimum cost. It is only the plant, the minimum point of whose short-run average cost curve coincides with the minimum point of the long-run average cost-curve, which is operated at the point of its minimum average cost of production. In figure 103 for producing output OX_m, the plant of SAC_7 is used at its minimum cost of production $X_m e$. In other words, plant of SAC_7 is being utilized to produce its optimum output, that is to say, it is being used at its capacity.

It should be noted that in figure 103 the plant of SAC_7 is optimum plant, since its minimum cost of production is the lowest of the minimum costs of all other plants.

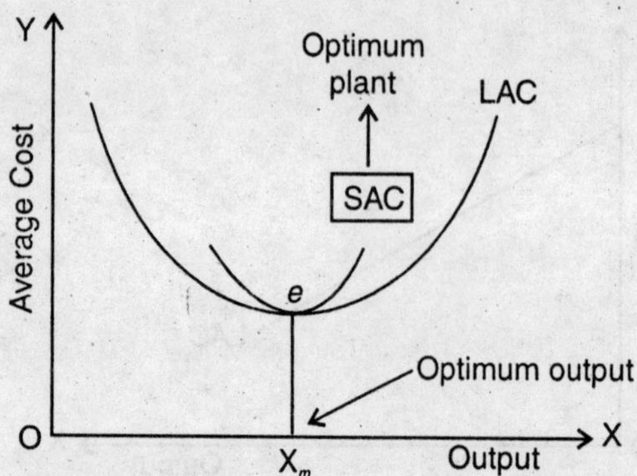

Fig. 107 : *Optimum Plant, Optimum Output And Optimum Firm*

If the size of the plant is increased beyond SAC_7 it results in higher average cost of production. Similarly, if the size of the plant is smaller than SAC_7, average cost of production is higher. Further, the least-cost output or in other words the optimum output of the plant SAC_7 is OX_m. Now, if the firm produces output OX_m with the optimum plant SAC_7, it is said to have achieved the **optimum size.** Thus, **an optimum firm is that firm which is producing optimum output** ***(i.e.,*** **least-cost output) with the optimum plant.**

In our figure 103 the firm is of optimum size if it employs plant SAC_7 and uses it to produce OX_m. But the point of minimum cost of the optimum plant (SAC_7) coincides with the minimum point of the long run average cost curve. Therefore, the optimum firm can also be defined as one which produces at the minimum point of the long-run average cost curve (LAC).

Explanation of the U-Shape of The Long-Run Average Cost Curve

U-shape of the LAC reflects the **laws of returns to scale.** According to these laws the unit costs of production decrease as plant size increases, due to the economies of scale which the larger plant sizes make possible. The traditional theory of the firm assumes that economies of scale exist only upto a certain size of plant, which is known as the **optimum plant size,** because with this plant size all possible economies of scale are fully exploited. If the plant increases further than this optimum size there are diseconomies of scale, arising from managerial inefficiencies. It is argued that management becomes highly complex, managers are overworked and the decision making process becomes less efficient.

We stress once more the optimally implied by the LAC planning curve : each point represents the least unit cost for producing the corresponding level of output. Any point above the LAC is inefficient in that it shows a higher cost for producing the corresponding level of output. Any point below the LAC is economically desirable because it implies a lower unit-cost, but it is not attainable in the current state of technology and with the prevailing market prices of factors of production.

LONG-RUN MARGINAL COST CURVE

The long-run marginal cost is derived from the SRMC curves, but does not **'envelope'** them. The LRMC is formed from points of intersection of the SRMC curves with vertical lines drawn from the points of tangency of the corresponding SAC-curves and the LRA cost curve (figure 108). The LMC must be equal to the SMC for the output at which the corresponding SAC is tangent to the LAC.

For levels of output to the left of tangency *a* the SAC > LAC. At the point of tangency SAC = LAC. As we move from point *a'* to *a,* we actually move form a position of inequality of SARC and LRAC to a position of equality. Hence the change in total cost (*i.e.,* the MC) must be smaller for the short-run curve than for the long-run curve. Thus LMC > SMC to the left of *a.* For an increase in output beyond X_1 (*e.g.,* X_1") the SAC > LAC. That is, we move from the position *a* of equality of the two costs to the position *b* where SAC is greater than LAC. Hence the addition to total cost (= MC) must be larger for the short-run curve than for the long-run curve. Thus LMC < SMC to the right of *a.*

Since to the lest of *a,* LMC > SMC, and to the right of *a,* LMC < SMC, it follows that at *a,* LMC = SMC. If we draw a vertical line from *a* to the X-axis the point at which it interests the SMC (point A for SAC_1) is a point of the LMC.

If we repeat this procedure for all points of tangency of SRAC and LAC curves to the left of the minimum point of the LAC, we obtain points of the section of the LMC which lies below the LAC. At the minimum point M the LMC intersects the LAC. To the right of M the LMC lies above the LAC curve. At point M we have

$$SAC_m = SMC_m = LAC = LMC$$

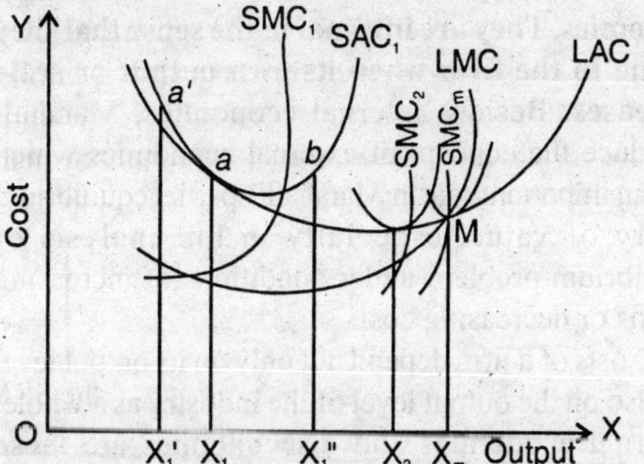

Fig. 108 : *Long-Run Marginal Cost Curve*

There are various mathematical forms which give rise to U-shaped unit cost curves. The simplest total cost function which would incorporate the law of variable proportions is the **Cubic Polynomial.**

$$C = \underbrace{b_0} + \underbrace{b_1X - b_2X^2 + b_3X^3}$$

$$TC = TFC + TVC$$

The average variable cost is

$$AVC = \frac{TVC}{X}$$

$$= b_1 - b_2X + b_3X^2$$

The marginal cost is

$$MC = \frac{dC}{dX}$$

$$= b_1 - 2b_2X + 3b_3X^2$$

The average total cost is

$$ATC = \frac{C}{X}$$

$$= \frac{b_0}{X} + b_1 - b_2X + b_3X^2$$

The TC curve is roughly S-shaped, while the ATC, the AVC and the MC are all U-shaped, the MC curve intersects the other two curves at their minimum points.

Empirical Evidence And L-Shaped Long-Run Average Cost Curve

Some economists argue on the basis of empirical evidence that the long-run average cost curve is **L-shaped,** rather than U-shaped, as in figure 109. The L-shaped curve shows a rapid fall in the beginning but after a point "the curve remains flat, or may slope gently downwards, at its right-hand end." The difference between L-shaped LAC and the U-shaped LAC is that there is no rising portion in the former. Figure 109 shows a flat LAC curve and figure 110 depicts a gently sloping downwards curve LAC at its right-hand end.

The following two explanations have been provided for the existence of L-shaped long-run average cost curve.

1. Technological Progress : One reason why empirical studies do not find U-shaped long run average cost curve is that whereas economic theory assumes that technology remains unchanged or there is no technological progress, but, in the real word, technological progress does take place over time. As a result of technological progress in the real world, long-run average cost curve will shift downwards over time. The empirical investigations which are conducted at different points of time would not find the rising average cost in view of the existence of technological progress.

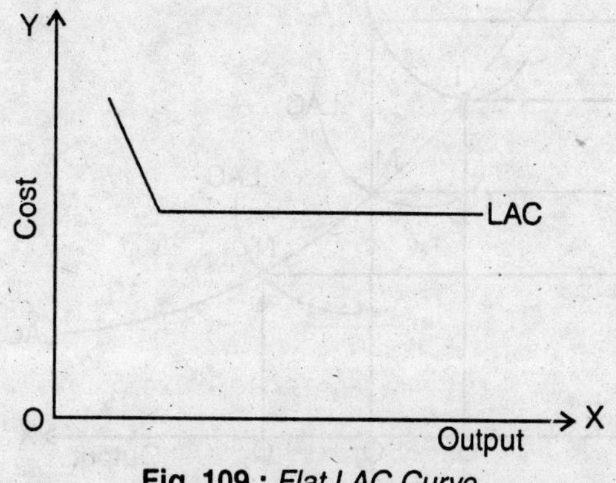

Fig. 109 : *Flat LAC Curve*

The L-shaped long-run average cost curve (LAC)

is explained in figure 110. Suppose the firm is producing OQ_1 output on LAC_1 curve at a per unit cost of OC_1. If there is an increase in demand for the firm product to OQ_2, with no change in technology, the firm will produce OQ_2 output along the LAC_1 curve at a per unit cost OC_4. If, however, there is technical progress in the firm, it will install a new plant having LAC_2 as the long-run average cost curve. On this plant, it produces OQ_2 output as a lower cost OC_2 per unit. Similarly, if the firm decides to increase its output to OQ_3 to meet further rise in demand. technical progress may have advanced to such a level that it installs the plant with the LAC_3 curve.

Now it produces OQ_3 output at still lower cost OC_3 per unit. If the minimum points L, M and N of these U-shaped long-run average cost curves LAC_1, LAC_2 and LAC_3 are joined by a line, it forms a gently sloping downwards curve LAC. Thus in a given state of technology, the long-run average cost curves are U-shaped. But when there is technical progress, the long-run average cost curve is L-shaped.

2. Learning by Doing : Learning by doing is another factor which causes the long-run average cost to slope downward throughout. It is now common knowledge that a person learns while doing some productive work. The greater the amount of work he has done since the time he started doing a particular work, the greater the experience he attains and with the experience he learns to do thing in a better why than before. This tends to reduce the costs.

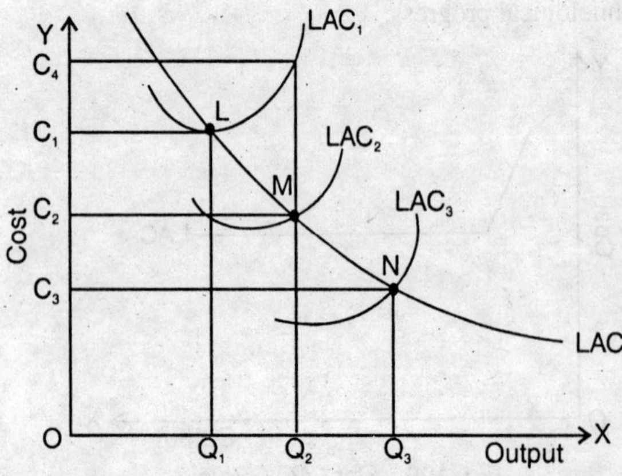

Fig. 110: *Downwards Sloping LAC Curve*

External Economies and Diseconomies and Cost Curves

We have explained above that the long-run average cost curve falls downward in the beginning because of economies of scale, namely, the use of greater degree of division of labour and the specialised machinery at higher levels of output. The uses of greater degree of division of labour and the specialised machinery at higher levels of output are the **internal economies. They are internal in the sense that they accrue to the firm when its own output or scale increases.** Besides internal economies, Marshall introduce the concept of external economies which play an important role in Marshall's partial equilibrium theory of value, especially in his analysis of equilibrium problem under conditions of increasing returns or decreasing cost.

Costs of a firm depend not only on its output level but also on the output level of the industry as a whole. External economies and diseconomies are those economies and diseconomies which accrue to the firms as a result of the expansion in the output of the whole industry and they are not dependent on the output level of individual firms. They are external in the sense that they accrue to the firms not out of its internal situation but from outside it *i.e.,* the output of the industry.

External Economies accrue to the individual firms, if the increase in the output of industry lowers the cost curves of each firm in the industry. On the other hand, external diseconomies accrue to the firms, when the expansion of the output of the industry raises the cost curves of each firm. Thus, when the industry expands and as a result of it certain external economies accrue to the firms, the cost curves of a firm will shift down as is shown in figure 111. It should be noted that external economies will causes all types of firm's cost curves-long-run average and marginal cost curves, short-run average and marginal cost curves-to shift down. In figure 111, initially the long-run average cost curve is LAC_1 and as a result of the expansion of whole industry and the creation of external economies it shifts down to a new position LAC_2.

On the other hand, when the external diseconomies accrue to the firms as a result of the expansion of the industry, cost curves of the firms will

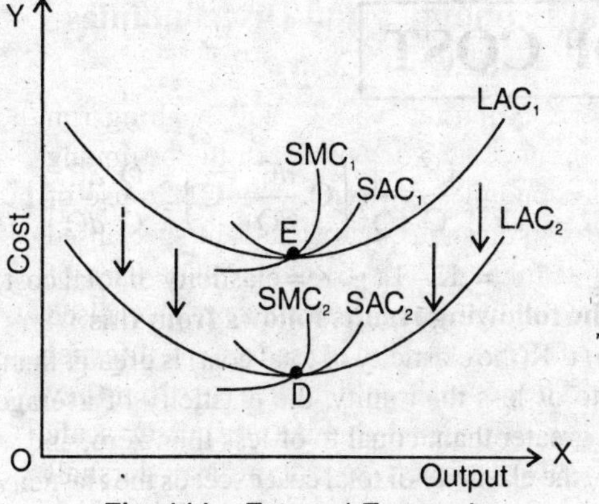

Fig. 111 : *External Economies*

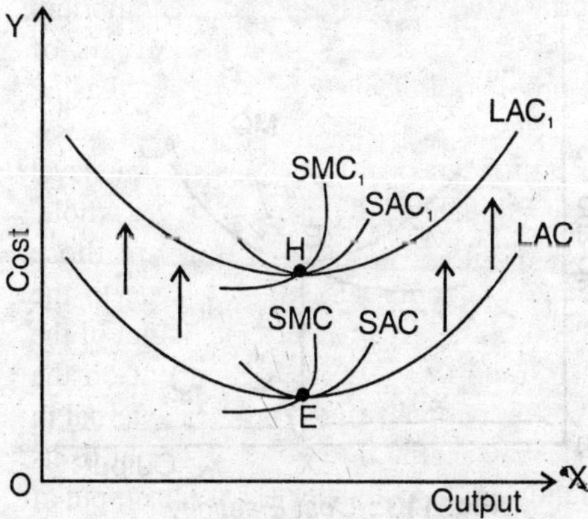

Fig. 112: *External Diseconomies*

shift upward as is depicted in figure 112. In the beginning, the long-run average cost curve is LAC and with the expansion of the industry output and consequent emergence of external diseconomies cause the long-run average cost curve (along with its short-run average and marginal cost curves) to shift upward to a new position LAC_1.

We noted above in the previous section that **internal economies and diseconomies of scale affect the shape that the long-run average cost curve takes,** internal economies of scale cause the long-run average cost to fall as output is increased in the initial stages and internal diseconomies of scale cause the long-run average cost curve to rise. On the other hand, external economies and external diseconomies cause the long-run average cost curve to shift down or up, as the case may be. Moreover, when we are considering the effect of external economies and external diseconomies on the cost curves, it is not only the long-run average cost curve, it is not only the long-run average cost curve but all short-run and long-run cost curves, whether total, average or marginal, shift together up or down as the case may be.

External Economies

We explain below some of important external economies which accrue to the firms and reduce their costs of production.

1. Cheaper Materials and Capital Equipment
2. Technological External Economies
3. Development of Skilled Labour
4. The Growth of Subsidiary and Correlated Industries
5. Improved Transportation and Marketing Facilities
6. Development of industry Information Services

External Diseconomies

We have explained above the external economies which accrue to the firms as a result of the growth of the industry. But the expansion of an industry is also likely to generate external diseconomies which raise the cost curves of the firms. The main example of external diseconomies is the **rise in some factor pries** when the industry expands and its demand for various factors needed by it increases. The expansion of an industry will definitely raise the prices of those raw materials and capital goods which are in short supply. Likewise, the expansion of the industry is likely to raise the wages of skilled labour, at least in the short run, since it always takes time for the labour to get training and acquire specialised skill needed in a particular industry.

Since the productive factors such as various types of raw materials, cement, steal, various kinds of machinery and tools and skilled labour are scarce, the increase in demand for them resulting from the expansion in the industry is likely to push up their prices. In the contact of scarcity of resources, an industry will expand by snatching away the resources from other industries. For snatching away the scarce resources from other industries, it will bid up their prices. Thus, in the real world of scarcity, an expanding industry will create more external diseconomies than external economies.

ELASTICITY OF COST

If output (Q) is produced at a total cost (C), the cost function is

$$C = f(Q).$$

The elasticity of total cost is the ratio of the proportional change in total cost to the proportional change in total output. It may be written as

$$\text{Cost Elasticity (K)} = \frac{dC/C}{dQ/Q}$$

$$= \frac{dC}{C} \times \frac{Q}{dQ} = \frac{dC}{dQ} \times \frac{Q}{C} = \frac{dC}{dQ} \div \frac{C}{Q}$$

$$= \frac{MC}{AC} = \frac{\text{Margina cost}}{\text{Average cost}}$$

Thus, cost elasticity (K) is equal to the ratio of marginal cost (*d*C/*d*Q) to average cost (C/Q). It follows from this that

(*a*) If MC > AC, then K > 1

(*b*) If MC = AC, then K = 1 and

(*c*) If MC < AC, then K < 1.

Diagrammatically, when the MC curve is rising and is above the AC curve, K > 1, as shown by the area right to point E in figure 113. It is the case of **decreasing returns.** In the figure, it is the point E where **MC = AC.** It is case of **constant returns.** When MC < AC, K < 1. It is shown as the area to the left of point E in this figure, where the MC curve is falling and is below the AC curve. It is the case of **increasing returns.**

Elasticity of Average Cost

The elasticity of total cost is given by E(C) = $\frac{dC}{dQ}.\frac{Q}{C}$ and average cost is C/Q. Therefore, replacing C by C/Q. Thus

elasticity of average cost

$$E(C/Q) = \frac{d(C/Q)}{dQ}.\frac{Q}{C/Q}$$

$$= \frac{d(C/Q)}{dQ}.\frac{Q^2}{C} = \frac{Q^2}{C}\left(\frac{Q.\frac{dC}{dQ} - C}{Q^2}\right)$$

$$= \frac{Q^2}{C}.\frac{1}{Q^2}\left(Q.\frac{dC}{dQ} - C\right) = \frac{Q}{C}.\frac{dC}{dQ} - 1$$

$$= K - 1 \;(\because K = \text{elasticity of total cost})$$

The following results follows from this :

(*a*) if K(the elasticity of total cost) is greater than, equal to or less than unity, the elasticity of average cost is greater than, equal to or less than zero, and

(*b*) the elasticity of total cost exceeds the elasticity of average cost by unity, *i.e.,*

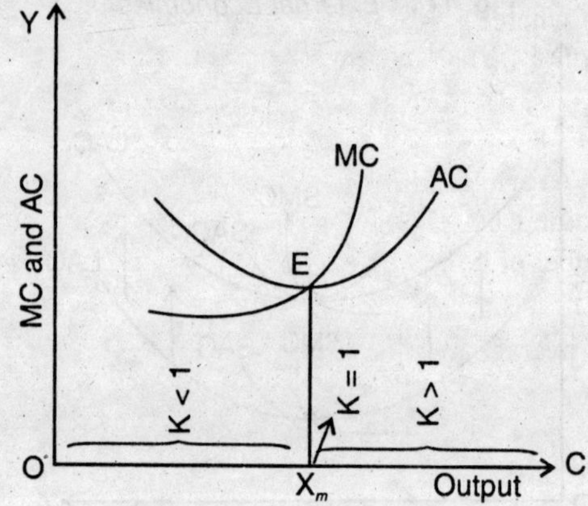

Fig. 113 : *Cost Elasticity*

$$E(C/Q) = K - 1$$

$$\text{or,}\quad K - E(C/Q) = 1$$

Elasticity of Marginal Cost

As we know, the elasticity of total cost is given by K = $\frac{dC}{dQ}.\frac{Q}{C}$. Therefore, the marginal cost is $\frac{dC}{dQ}$.

Thus

$$\text{elasticity of MC} = \frac{d(dC/dQ)}{dQ}.\frac{Q}{(dC/dQ)} \quad ...(1)$$

Since K is given by

$$K = \frac{Q}{C}.\frac{dC}{dQ} \quad \text{or} \quad \frac{K.C}{Q} = \frac{dC}{dQ} \quad ...(2)$$

Substituting the value of (2) in (1), we get,

$$E(MC) = \frac{d}{dQ}\left(\frac{C.K}{Q}\right).\frac{Q^2}{C.K}$$

THE CONCEPT OF REVENUE

The term 'revenue' refers to the receipts obtained by a firm from the sale of certain quantities of a commodity at various prices. The revenue concept relates to total revenue, average revenue and marginal revenue.

Total Revenue : Total revenue refers to the total amount of money that the firm receives from the sale of its products. Thus, the total revenue is obviously equal to the quantity sold multiplied by the selling price of the commodity, *i.e.*,

$$TR = P.Q.$$

where

TR = total revenue
P = price per unit
Q = quantity

Average Revenue : Average revenue can be obtained by dividing by the total revenue by the number of units sold. Thus,

$$\text{average revenue} = \frac{\text{total revenue}}{\text{total output sold}}$$

or, $$AR = \frac{TR}{Q} = \frac{P.Q}{Q} = P$$

Thus, average revenue is the price of commodity. It follows from this that the curve which relates average revenue to output is identical with the demand curve that relates price to output.

Marginal Revenue : Marginal revenue is the net revenue earned by selling on additional unit of the product. In other words, marginal revenue is the addition made to the total revenue by selling one more unit of the good. Putting it in algebraic expression marginal revenue is the addition made to total revenue by selling n units of a product instead of $(n-1)$ where n is any given number. Therefore,

Marginal Revenue = difference in total revenue in increasing sales from $(n-1)$ units to n units

$$MR_n = TR_n - TR_{n-1}$$

If TR stands for total revenue and Q stands for output, then marginal revenue (MR) can be expressed as follows :

$$MR = \frac{d(TR)}{dQ}$$

$\frac{d(TR)}{dQ}$ indicates the slope of the total revenue curve. Thus if the total revenue curve is given to us, we can find out marginal revenue at various levels of output by measuring the slopes at the corresponding points on the total revenue curve.

RELATION BETWEEN AR AND MR CURVES

The relation between average revenue and marginal revenue can be discussed under pure or parallel competition and imperfect competition.

1. Under Perfect Competition : The average revenue curve is a horizontal straight line parallel to the X-axis and the marginal revenue curve coincides with it. This is because under pure or perfect competition the number of firms selling an identical product is very large. The price is determined by the market forces of supply and demand so that only one price tends to prevail for the whole industry. It is OP as shown in figure 114. Each firm can sell as much as it wishes at the selling marker price OP. Thus, the demand for the firm's product becomes **infinitely elastic.** Since the demand curve is the firm's average revenue curve, the shape of the AR curve is horizontal to the X-axis at price OP and MR curve coincides with it.

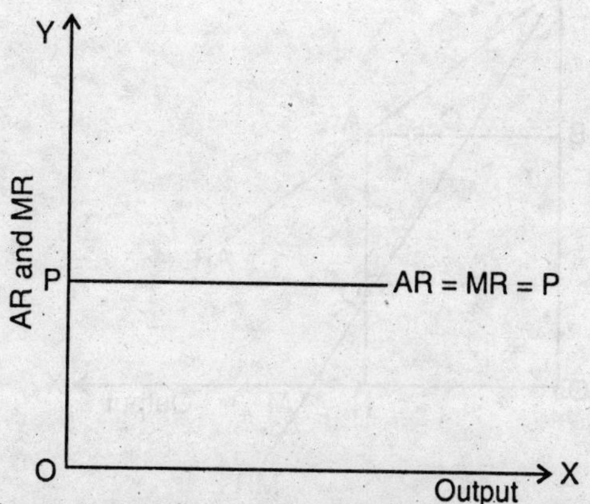

Fig. 114 : *Average and Marginal Revenue Curves Under perfect Competition*

Average revenue curve in this case (perfect competition) is a horizontal straight line. Horizontal straight line average revenue curve (AR) indicates that price or average remains the same at OP level when quantity sold is increased. Marginal revenue (MR) curve coincides with average revenue (AR) curve since marginal revenue is equal to average revenue.

2. Under Imperfect Competition : In all forms of imperfect competition, that is, monopolistic competition, oligopoly and monopoly, average revenue curve facing an individual firm slopes downward. This is because in imperfect competition when a firm lowers the price of its product, its quantity demanded and sales would increase and vice versa.

In figure 115 it will be observed that average revenue curve (AR) is falling downward and marginal revenue curve (MR) lies below it. The fact that MR curve is lying below AR curve indicates that marginal revenue declines more rapidly than average revenue. When OM units of the goods are sold, revenue is **zero.** If the quantity sold is increased beyond OM, marginal revenue will become **negative.**

When both AR and MR curves are straight lines, then if a perpendicular is drawn from a point on the AR curve to the Y-axis, MR curve will cut this perpendicular at its middle point.

Consider figure 115, where both AR and MR sources are straight lines. Point A is taken on the average revenue curve and a perpendicular AB is

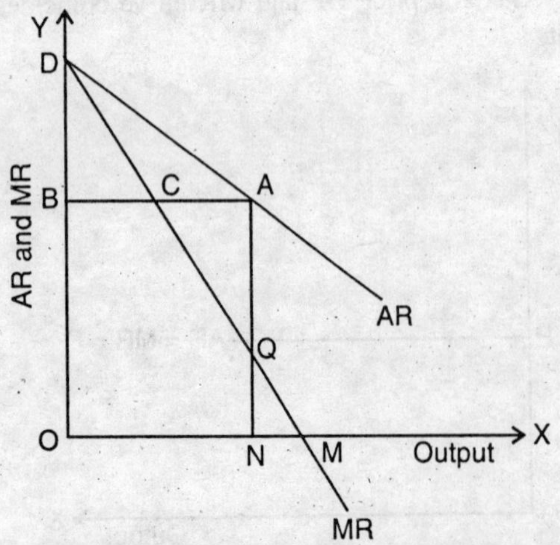

Fig. 115 : *Average and Marginal Revenue Curves under Imperfect Competition*

drawn on the Y-axis. MR curve cuts perpendicular AB at point C. Now if MR curve cuts halfway the distance between AR curve and Y-axis, then AC must be equal to BC. So in order to show that MR cuts halfway the distance between AR and Y-axis, we have to prove in figure that AC = BC.

Draw a vertical straight line from A so as to meet the X-axis at N. It means that when ON quantity of the good is sold, average revenue is equal to AN. Now there are two ways in which we can find out the total revenue earned by the sale of OM units of the good.

First, total revenue (TR)

= AR × quantity sold

= AN × ON

= Area ONAB ...(1)

Secondly, total revenue can also be obtained by taking a sum of marginal revenues of all the units of the good sold.

Thus, total revenue (TR)

= ΣMR

= Area ONQD ...(2)

Since total revenue for a given quantity of the good sold is to be the same which ever way it may be found, it follows that

ONAB = ONQD

But it will be noticed from the figure that

ONAB = ONQCB + ACQ

and also

ONQD = ONQCB + BDC

or ACQ = BDC

Thus triangles ACQ and BDC are equal in area.

Now, In Δs ACQ and BDC

$\angle$QAC = $\angle$DBC (right angles)

$\angle$ACQ = $\angle$BCD (vertically opposite angles)

$\angle$BDC = $\angle$AQC (alternate angles)

Therefore, ΔACQ and ΔBDC are similar.

We have proved above that triangles ACQ and BDC are equal in area as well as similar. Now when the two triangles are both equal and similar, then they are congruent (*i.e.,* equal in all respects).

Therefore Δs ACQ and BDC are congruent.

Hence,

AC = BC

It is thus proved that **given the straight-line average and marginal revenue curves, the marginal revenue curve will lie halfway from the average revenue curve.**

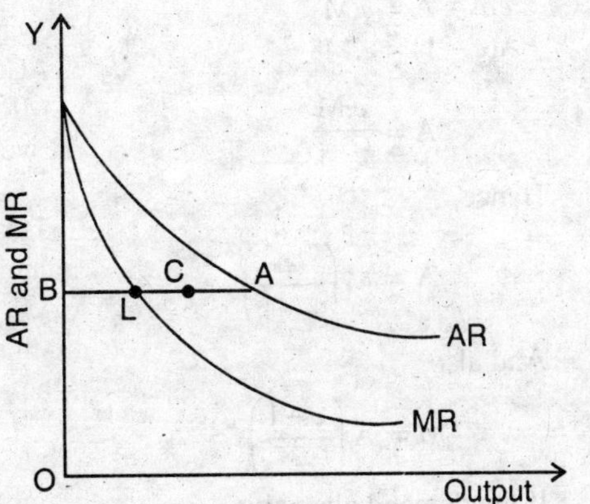

Fig. 116 : *AR and MR Curves : Convex to the Origin*

Marginal revenue curve corresponding to a convex or concave average revenue curve is not of straight-line shape but is either convex or concave to the origin. In either of these cases the marginal revenue curve will not lie halfway from the average revenue curve. If the average revenue curve is **convex** to the origin as in figure 116 the marginal revenue curve (MR) will also be convex to the origin and will cut any perpendicular drawn from AR curve to the Y-axis **more than halfway** as measured from the average revenue curve.

On the other hand, if the average revenue curve is **concave** to the origin as in fig. 117 the marginal revenue curve will also be concave and will cut any perpendicular line from the average revenue curve to the Y-axis **less than halfway** as measured from the average revenue curve.

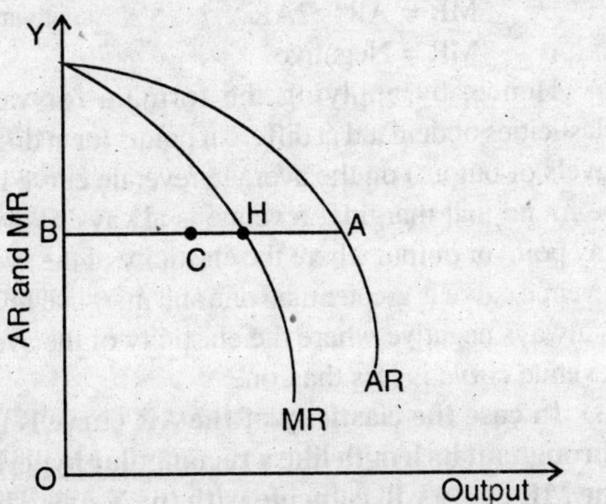

Fig. 117: *AR and MR Curves : Concave to the Origin*

In figure 116 and 117, C is the middle point on the perpendicular line AB.

AVERAGE REVENUE, MARGINAL REVENUE AND ELASTICITY OF DEMAND

There is a very useful relationship between elasticity of demand, average revenue and marginal revenue at any level of output. We have stressed above that the average revenue curve of a firm is really the same thing as the demand curve of consumer's for the firm's product. Therefore, elasticity of demand at any point on a consumer's demand curve is the same thing as the elasticity of demand on the given point on the firm's average revenue curve.

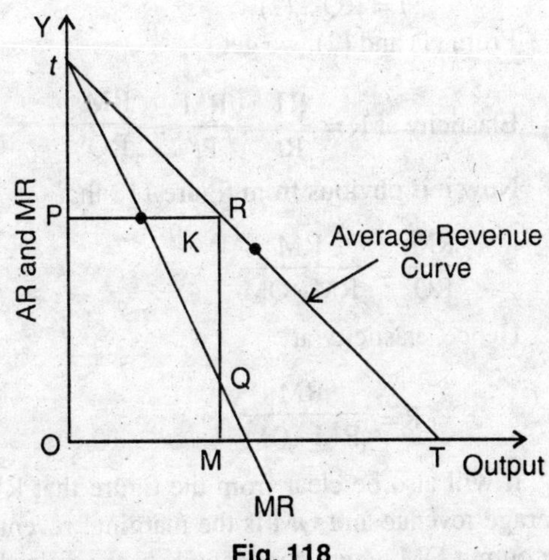

Fig. 118

We know that elasticity of demand at point R on the average revenue curve tT in figure 118 is $\frac{RT}{Rt}$.

With this measure of point elasticity of demand we can study the relationship between average revenue, marginal revenue and price elasticity at any level of output.

In figure 118, AR and MR are respectively average and marginal revenue curves. Elasticity of demand at point R on the average revenue curve :

$$= \frac{RT}{Tt}$$

Now in triangles PtR and MRT

$\angle t$PR = $\angle$ RMT (right angles)

$\angle t$RP = $\angle$ RTM (corresponding angles)

and $\angle$ PtR = $\angle$ MRT

Therefore, triangles PtR and MRT are equiangular.

$$\text{Hence, } \frac{RT}{Rt} = \frac{RM}{Pt} \quad ...(1)$$

In the triangles PtK and KRQ

PK = RK

$\angle$ PKt = $\angle$ RKQ (vertically opposite)

$\angle t$PK = $\angle$ KRQ (right angles)

Therefore, triangles PtK and KRQ are congruent (*i.e.*, equal in all respects).

Hence

Pt = RQ ...(2)

From (1) and (2), we get

$$\text{Elasticity at R} = \frac{RT}{Rt} = \frac{RM}{Pt} = \frac{RM}{RQ}$$

Now it is obvious from figure 118 that

$$\frac{RM}{RQ} = \frac{RM}{RM-QM}$$

Hence, elasticity at

$$R = \frac{RM}{RM-QM}$$

It will also be clear from the figure that RM is average revenue and QM is the marginal revenue at the output OM which corresponds to the point R on the average revenue curve. Therefore,

Elasticity at

$$R = \frac{\text{Average Revenue}}{\text{Average Revenue} - \text{Marginal Revenue}}$$

If, A stands for average revenue

M stands for marginal revenue

e stands for point elasticity on the average revenue curve.

then

$$e = \frac{A}{A-M}$$

It follows from this that

$e.A - e.M = A$

$e.A - A = e.M$

$A(e-1) = e.M$

$$A = \frac{e.M}{e-1}$$

Hence,

$$A = M\left(\frac{e}{e-1}\right)$$

And also,

$$M = A\left(\frac{e-1}{e}\right)$$

If the demand elasticity is equal to one then

$$MR = AR\left(\frac{e-1}{e}\right) = AR\left(\frac{1-1}{1}\right)$$

$$= AR \times 0 = 0$$

If $e > 1$, Say 2, then

$$MR = AR\left(\frac{2-1}{2}\right)$$

$$MR = \frac{1}{2}.AR$$

$$MR = AR - \frac{AR}{2}$$

MR = Positive

If $e < 1$, Say 1/2, then

$$MR = AR\left(\frac{1/2-1}{1/2}\right)$$

MR = AR − 2AR

MR = Negative

Hence, by applying the formula for various elasticities of demand at different points (or at different levels of output) on the average revenue curve it will be found that marginal revenue is always positive at any point or output where the elasticity of the average revenue curve is greater than one and marginal revenue is always negative where the elasticity of the average revenue curve is less than one.

In case the elasticity of the AR curve is unity throughout its length like a rectangular hyperbola, the MR curve will coincide with the X-axis, shown as a dotted line in figure 119.

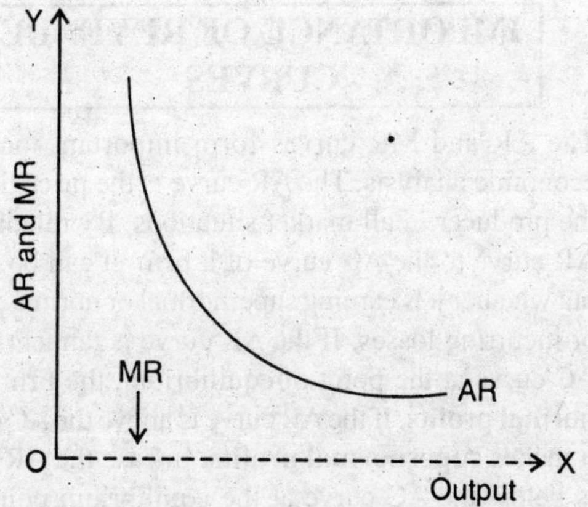

Fig. 119 : *Rectangular Hyperbola AR Curve*

Three Types of Revenue (AR, MR, TR) and Elasticity (*e*)

We are now in a position to describe the relationship between three types of revenue, namely, AR, MR and TR on the one side and elasticity on the other. From the formula

$$MR = AR\left(\frac{e-1}{e}\right)$$

We can know what would be the marginal revenue, if elasticity and AR are given to us. When the elasticity is equal to one, it follows from the above formula that marginal revenue will be equal to zero.

Thus,

$$MR = AR\left(\frac{e-1}{e}\right)$$

$$MR = AR\left(\frac{1-1}{1}\right)$$

$$MR = AR \times 0$$

$$MR = 0$$

Likewise, it can be proved that,

If $e > 1$, MR is positive, and

If $e < 1$, MR is negative.

In a straight-line demand curve we known that the elasticity at the middle point is equal to one. It follows that marginal revenue corresponding to the middle point of the demand curve (or AR curve) will be equal to zero. Consider figure 120. C is the middle point of the average revenue or demand curve AR. At point C elasticity is equal to one. Corresponding to C on the AR curve, marginal revenue will be zero. Thus

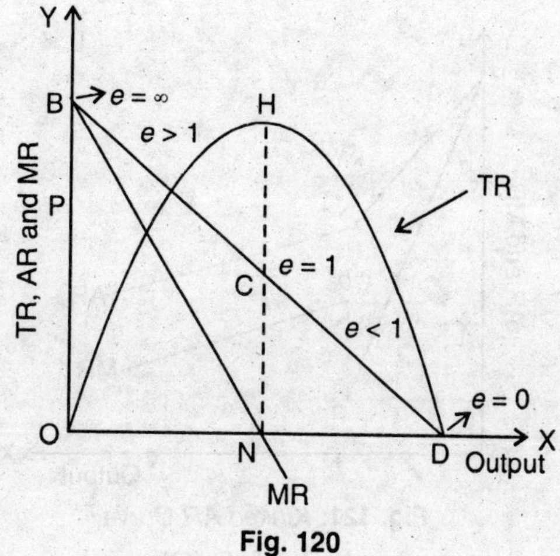

Fig. 120

MR curve is shown cutting the X-axis at point N which corresponds to point C on the AR curve. At a greater quantity than ON elasticity of the AR curve is less than one and the marginal revenue is negative. Marginal revenue being negative beyond ON means that total revenue will diminish if a quantity greater than ON is sold. Total revenue will be increasing upto ON output, since upto this marginal revenue remains positive. If follows therefore that **total revenue will be maximum where elasticity is equal to one.** This TR curve in this figure is shown to be at its highest level corresponding to the point C on AR curve or ON output where marginal revenue is zero and elasticity is equal to one.

Kinked Demand Curve and their Corresponding MR Curves

Under Oligopoly, the average and marginal revenue curves do not have a smooth downward slope. They possess Kinks. Since the number of sellers under Oligopoly is small, the effect of a price cut or price increase on the part of one seller will be followed by some changes in the behaviour of other firms. If a seller raises the price of his product, the other sellers will not follow him in order to earn larger profits at the old price. So the price-raising seller will experience a fall in the demand for his product. His average revenue curve in figure 121 becomes elastic after K and its corresponding MR curve rises discontinuously from *a* to *b* and then continues its course at the new higher level.

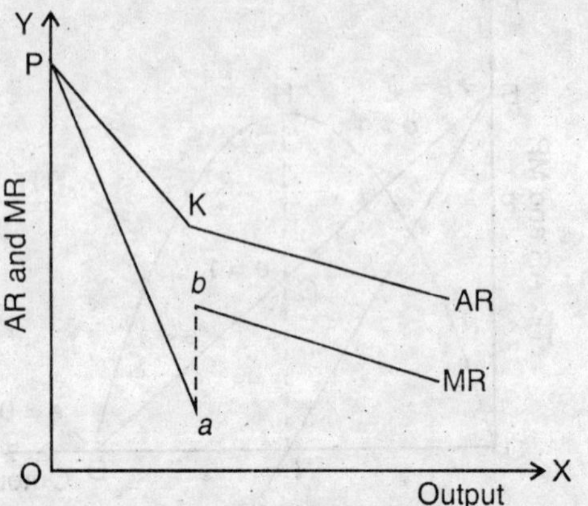

Fig. 121: *Kinked AR Curve*

On the other hand, if the Oligopolistic seller reduces the price of his product, his rivals also follow him in reducing the prices of their product so that he is not able to increase his sales. His AR curve becomes less elastic from K onwards as in figure 122. The corresponding MR curve falls vertically from *a* to *b* and then slopes at *a* lower level.

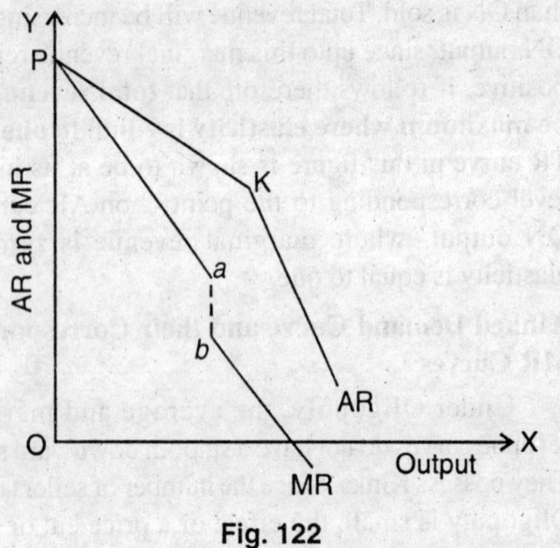

Fig. 122

IMPORTANCE OF REVENUE CURVES

The AR and MR curves form important tools for economic analysis. The AR curve is the price line for the producer in all market situations. By relating the AR curve to the AC curve of a firm, it can be found out whether it is earning supernormal or normal profits or incurring losses. If the AR curve is tangent to the AC curve at the point of equilibrium, the firm earns **normal profits.** If the AR curve is above the AC curve, it makes **supernormal profits.** In case the AR curve is below the AC curve at the equilibrium point, the firm incurs losses.

It can also be known from their relationship whether the firm is producing at its full capacity or under capacity. If the AR curve is tangent to the AC curve at its minimum point, (as under perfect competition) the firm produces at its **full capacity.** Where it is not so (as under imperfect competition), the firm possesses **idle capacity.**

The MR curve when intersected by the MC curve determined the equilibrium position of the firm under all market situations. Their point of intersection infact determines price, output, profit or loss of a firm.

Market Classification on the Basis of Cross Elasticity of Demand

Market Form	*Cross Elasticity of Demand*
1. Perfect Competition	Cross elasticity is infinite ($e_c = \infty$)
2. Monopolistic Competition	Cross elasticity is very high
3. Monopoly	Cross elasticity (e_c) is very low or zero

PERFECT COMPETITION

Perfect competition is a market structure characterised by a complete absence of rivalry among the individual firms. In other words, perfect competition implies no rivalry among firms.

Assumptions

The model of perfect competition is based on the following assumptions.

1. There are a large number of firms producing and selling a product.

2. The product of all firms is homogeneous.

The assumptions of large numbers of sellers and of product homogeneity imply that the individual firm in perfect competition is a **price-taker** : Its demand curve is infinitely elastic, indicating that the firm can sell any amount of output at the prevailing market price (figure 123). The demand curve of the individual firm is also its average revenue curve and its marginal revenue curve.

3. Both the sellers and buyers have perfect information about the prevailing price in the market.

4. Entry into and exit from the industry is free for the firms.

5. No government regulation.

6. Perfect mobility of factors of production.

Equilibrium of the Firm in the Short Run : By Curves of Total Revenue and Total Cost

The firm is in equilibrium when it maximises its profits (π), defined as the difference between the total cost and total revenue.

$$\pi = TR - TC$$

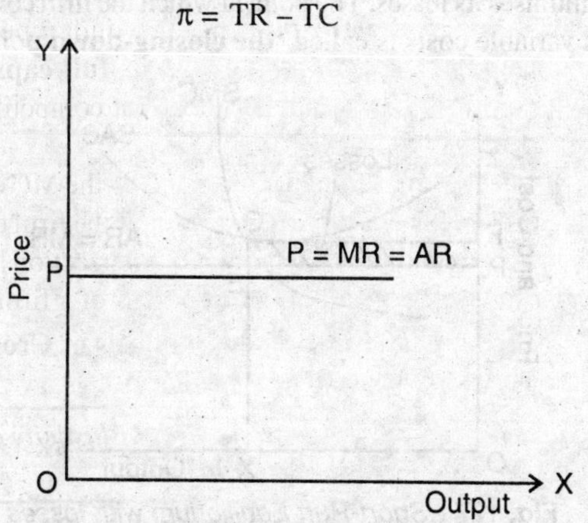

Fig. 123 : *Perfect Competition'*

Given that the normal rate of profit is included in the cost items of the firm, π is the profit above the normal rate of return on capital and the remuneration for the risk-bearing function of the entrepreneur. The firm is in equilibrium when it produces the output that maximises that difference between total receipt and total costs. The equilibrium of the firm may be shown graphically in two ways. Either by using the TR and TC curves, or the MR and MC curves.

In figure 124 we show the total revenue and total cost curves of a firm in a perfectly competitive market. The total revenue curve is a straight line through the origin, showing that the price is constant at all levels of output. The firm is a **price-taker** and can sell any amount of output at the going market price, with its TR increasing proportionately with its sales. The slope of the TR curve is the marginal revenue. It is constant and equal to the prevailing market price, since all units are sold at the same price. Thus in pure competition MR = AR = P.

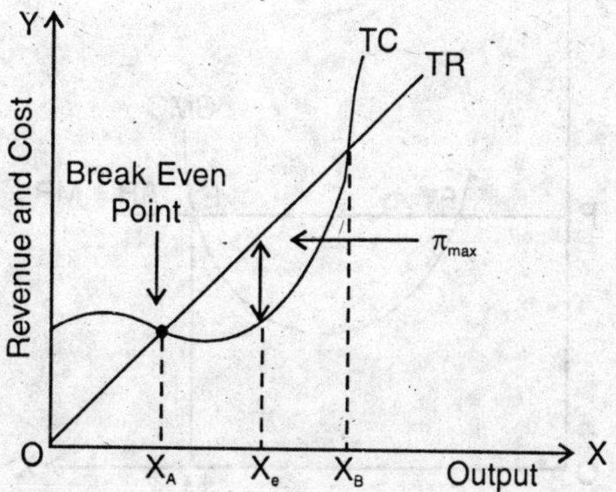

Fig. 124 : *Profit-Maximising Output : Equilibrium of the Firm*

The shape of the total-cost curve reflects the U shape of the average-cost curve, that is, the law of variable proportions. The firm maximises its profit at the output, X_e, where the distance between the TR and TC curves is the greatest. At lower and higher levels of output total profits is not maximised : at levels smaller than X_A and larger than X_B the firm has losses.

Equilibrium of the Firm : By Curves of Marginal Revenue and Marginal Cost (Identical Cost Conditions)

Identical cost conditions imply that all firms are facing same cost conditions, that is, their average and marginal cost curves are of the same level and shapes.

In figure 125 we show the average and marginal-cost curves of the firm together with its demand curve.

In order to decide about its equilibrium output, the firm will compare marginal cost with marginal revenue. It will be in equilibrium at the level of output at which marginal cost equals marginal revenue and marginal cost curve is curing marginal revenue curve from below. At this level it will be maximising its profits. Consider figure 125 in which price OP is prevailing in the market. PL would then be the demand curve or the average and marginal revenue curve of the firm. It will be seen from figure 125 that MC curve

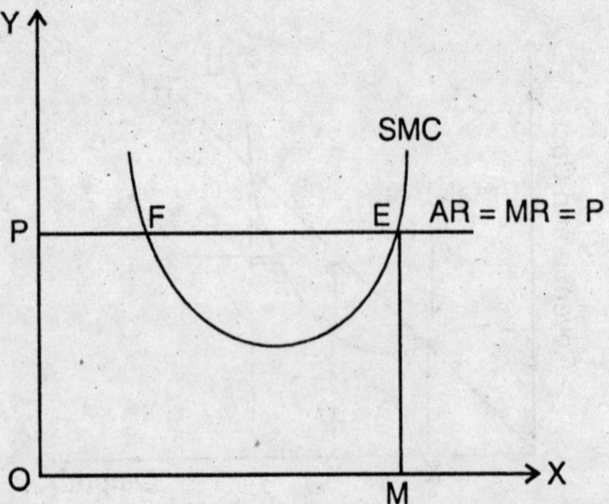

Fig. 125 : *Firm's Equilibrium Under Perfect Competition*

cuts average and marginal revenue curve at two different points, F and E. F can not be the position of equilibrium, since at F second order condition of firm's equilibrium, namely, that the marginal cost curve must cut marginal revenue curve from below at the point of equilibrium, is not satisfied. The firm will be increasing its profits by increasing production beyond F because marginal revenue is greater than marginal cost. The firm will be in equilibrium at point E or output OM since at E marginal cost equals marginal revenue as well as marginal cost curve is cutting marginal revenue curve from below. As under perfect competition MR curve is a horizontal straight line, the MC curve must be rising so as to cut the marginal revenue curve from below. Therefore, in case of perfect competition the **second order condition of firm's equilibrium** requires that MC curve must be

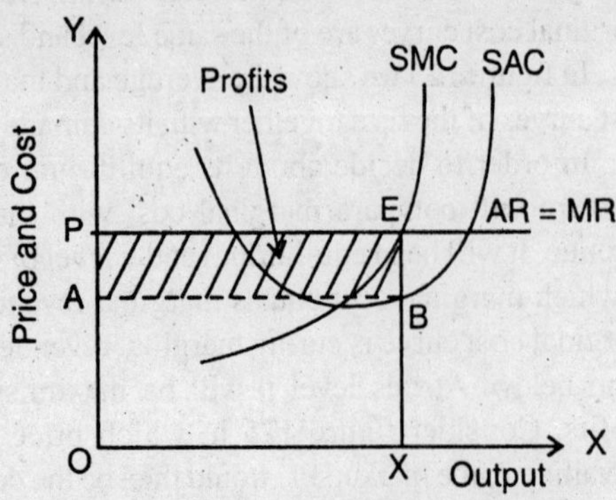

Fig. 126 : *Short-Run Equilibrium with Profit*

rising at the point of equilibrium. Hence the twin conditions of firms equilibrium under perfect competition are :

1. MC = MR = Price
2. (Slope of MC) > (Slope of MR)

But the fulfilment of the above two conditions does not guarantee that the profits will be earned by the firm. Whether the firm makes excess profits or losses depends on the level of the ATC at the short-run equilibrium. If the ATC is below the price at equilibrium (figure 126) the firm earns excess profits (equal to the area PABE). If, however, the ATC is above the price (figure 127) the firm makes a loss (equal to the area FPEC). In the latter case **the firm will continue to produce only if it covers its variable costs.** Otherwise, it will close down, since by discontinuing its operations the firm is better off : it minimises its losses. The point at which the firm covers its variable costs is called **'the closing-down point.'**

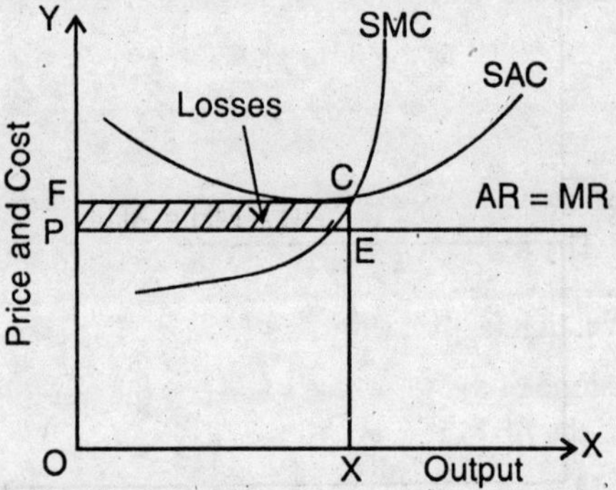

Fig. 127 : *Short-Run Equilibrium with losses*

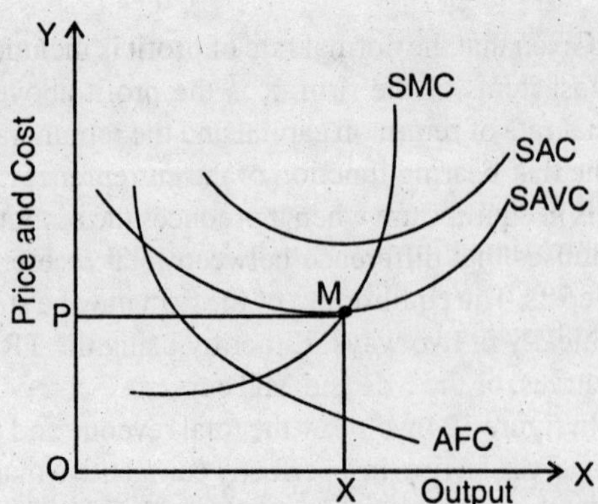

Fig. 128 : *Shut-Down Point for the Perfectly Competitive Firm*

In figure 128 the closing-down point of the firm is denoted by point M. If price falls below P the firm does not cover its **variable costs** and is better off its closes down.

MATHEMATICAL DERIVATION OF THE EQUILIBRIUM OF THE FIRM

The firm aims at the maximisation of its profits

$$\pi = R - C$$

Where

π = profit
R = total revenue
C = total cost

Clearly, $R = f_1(X)$ and $C = f_2(X)$, given the price P.

(a) The **first-order condition** for the maximisation of a function is that its first derivative (with respect to X in our case) be equal to zero. Differentially the total-profit function and equality to zero we obtain

$$\frac{d\pi}{dX} = \frac{dR}{dX} - \frac{dC}{dX} = 0$$

or

$$\frac{dR}{dX} = \frac{dC}{dX}$$

The term dR/dX is the slope of the total revenue curve, that is, the marginal revenue. The term $\frac{dC}{dX}$ is the slope of the total cost curve, or the marginal cost. Thus the first-order condition for profit maximisation is

$$MR = MC$$

Given that MC > 0, MR must also be positive at equilibrium. Since MR = P the first-order condition may be written as

$$MC = P$$

(b) The **Second-order condition** for a maximum requires that the second derivative of the function be negative (implying that after its highest point the curve turns downwards). The second derivative of the total-profit function is

$$\frac{d^2\pi}{dX^2} = \frac{d^2R}{dX^2} - \frac{d^2C}{dX^2}$$

This must be negative if the function has been maximised, that is

$$\frac{d^2R}{dX^2} - \frac{d^2C}{dX^2} < 0$$

which yields the condition

$$\frac{d^2R}{dX^2} < \frac{d^2C}{dX^2}$$

But $\frac{d^2R}{dX^2}$ is the slope of the MR curve and $\frac{d^2C}{dX^2}$ is the slope of the MC curve. Hence, the second-order condition may verbally be written as follows

(Slope of MR) > (Slope of MC)

Thus the MC must have a steeper slope than the MR curve or the MC must cut the MR curve from below. In perfect competition the slope of MR curve is zero, hence the second-order condition is simplified as follows

$$0 < \frac{d^2C}{dX^2}$$

Hence, the MC curve must have a positive slope or the MC must be rising.

LONG-RUNG EQUILIBRIUM OF THE FIRM (IDENTICAL COSTS)

It is assumed that all entrepreneurs are of equal efficiency. All factors are homogeneous and are available at constant and uniform prices, so that the cost curves of the firms are identical.

In the long run firms are in equilibrium when they have adjusted their plant so as to produce at the minimum point of their long-run AC curve, which is tangent (at this point) to the demand curve defined by the market price. In the long-run the firms will be earning just **normal profits,** which are included in the LAC. If they are making excess profits new firms will be attracted in the industry, this will lead to a fall in price and an upward shift of the cost curves due to increase of the prices of factors as the industry expands. These changes will continue until the LAC is tangent to the demand curve defined by the market price. If the firms male losses in the long run they will leave the industry, price will raise and costs may fall as the industry contracts, until the remaining firms in the industry cover their total costs inclusive of the normal rate of profit.

Figure 129 represents long-run equilibrium of firm under perfect competition. The firm cannot be in the long-run equilibrium at a price greater than OP in figure 129. Since if price is greater than OP, then the price line (demand curve) would lie somewhere above the minimum point of the average cost curve so that marginal cost and price will be equal where the firm is earning abnormal profits. Since there will be tendency for new firms to enter and compete away these abnormal profits the form cannot be in equilibrium at any price higher than OP. Likewise, the firm cannot be in long-run equilibrium at a price lower than OP in figure 129 under perfect competition.

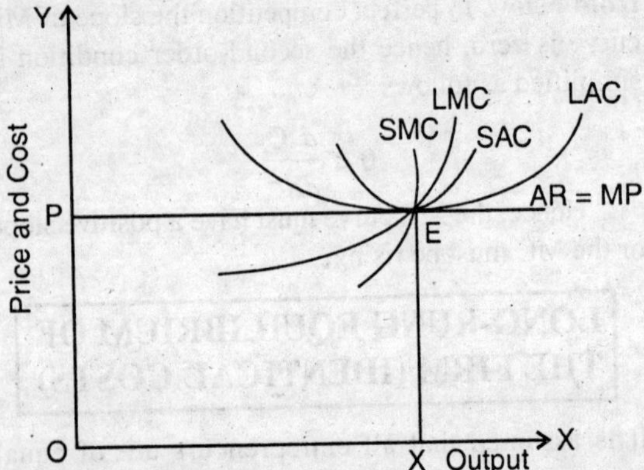

Fig. 129 : *Long-Run Equilibrium of the firm*

If price is lower than OP, the demand curve will lie below the average cost curve so that the marginal cost and price will be equal at the point where the firm is making losses. Therefore, there will be tendency for some of the firms in the industry to go out with the result that price will rise and the firms left in the field make normal profits. We therefore conclude that firm can be in long-run equilibrium under perfect competition only when price is at such a level that the horizontal demand curve is tangent to the AC curve, so the price equals average cost and firm makes only normal profits. Therefore, the condition for long-run equilibrium of firm can be written as :

SMC = SAC = LMC = LAC = MR = Price

It should be noted that a horizontal demand line can be tangent to a U-shaped average cost curve only at the latter's minimum point. Since at the minimum point of the average cost curve the marginal cost and average cost are equal, price in long-run equilibrium is equal to both MC and AC. In other words, double condition of long-run equilibrium is fulfilled at the minimum point of the average cost curve.

It is clear from above that **long-run equilibrium of the firm under perfect competition is established at the minimum point of the long-run average cost curve.** Operating at the minimum point of the long-run average cost curve signifies that the firm is of **optimum size,** that is, it is producing output at the **lowest possible cost.** The fact that the firm, working under conditions of perfect competition, tends to be of optimum size in the long run is beneficial from the social point of view in two ways. **Firstly,** working at optimum size implies that the resources of the society are being utilized in the most efficient way. **Secondly,** it signifies that the consumers are getting the goods at the lowest possible price.

SHORT-RUN EQUILIBRIUM OF THE FIRM : DIFFERENTIAL COST CONDITIONS

If entrepreneurs differ in efficiency the cost curves of the firms vary from each other. Firms with more efficient entrepreneurs will be able to produce at lower costs than the others. Thus different firms selling the same product at one price will be producing different quantities at different costs. More efficient firms employing better resources will have lower cost curves than others. For the sake of convenience we divide the firms having differential cost conditions into three categories A, B and C whose cost curves are shown in figure 130. Figure 130 represents differential cost conditions.

If price in market is OP, then the firm of every category will adjust output where price OP equals its marginal cost. Firm A will be in equilibrium at E and will be producing OM output, firm B will be in equilibrium at L and will be producing ON, form C will be in equilibrium at K and will be producing OT. While for all the firms, price equals their marginal cost at equilibrium output, but firm A in equilibrium is making super-normal profits, B is earning only normal profits and C is making losses. This is so because cost conditions are different for the three firms.

Thus, under conditions of different costs and in

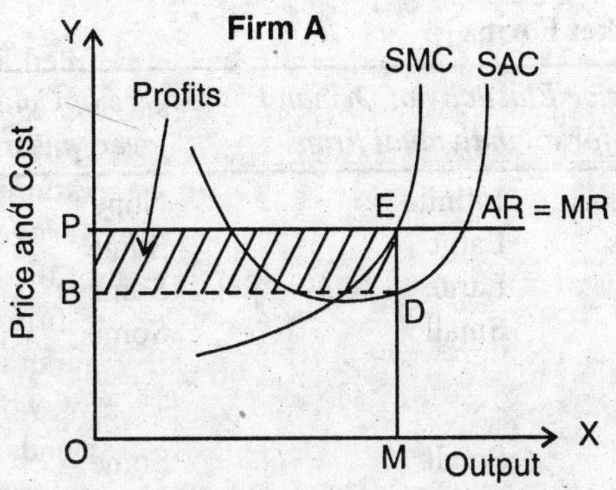

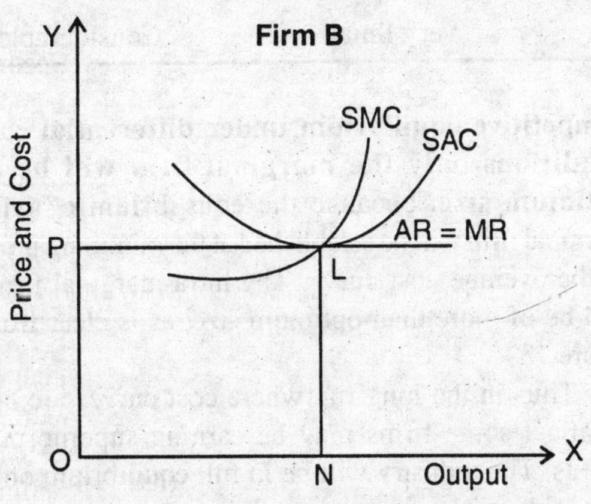

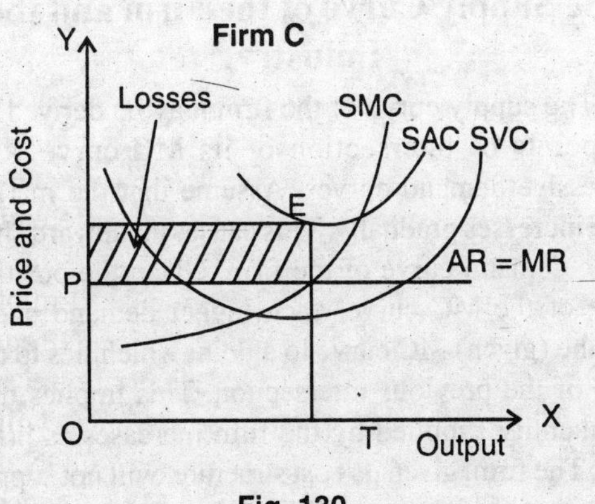

Fig. 130

short-run equilibrium, some firms in the industry may be earning super-normal profits. Some may be making only normal profits, and some others may be incurring losses. **In such a situation the industry cannot be in full equilibrium.**

LONG-RUN EQUILIBRIUM OF FIRMS : DIFFERENTIAL COST CONDITIONS

In case the entrepreneurs are of different efficiency, the cost curves of the firms will also differ. A firm with a superior entrepreneur than the others will be able to produce the same output at lower costs. Such a firm will be earning supernormal profits even in the long-run as compared to the other firms which may be earning only normal profits. The firm which earns supernormal profits is the **'intra-marginal firm'** as distinct from the 'marginal firm' which just earns normal profits. In other words, a marginal firm is one which will be the first to leave the industry if price falls. The marginal firm is the highest-cost firm which earns only normal profits. Since the marginal firm is the highest-cost firm making only normal profits, it will be first to quit the industry if the price falls as with the fall in price its profits sink below normal.

Figure 131 represents long-run equilibrium of firms, which are of three categories in respect of cost conditions. The price prevailing in the long-run is OP which equals marginal cost of firm A at output OQ and marginal cost of firm B at output OS. For firms of category B price is equal to average cost, therefore they make only normal profits. Thus, firms of category B are marginal firms which will go out of the industry if the price falls below the present price OP. But price OP is greater than average cost at equilibrium output of intra-marginal firm A and therefore this firm make super-normal profits. The price being equal to average cost of the marginal firm guarantees that the marginal firm will be making only normal profits and therefore there will be no tendency for new firms to enter or for some of the existing firms to leave the industry.

If price in the long run falls below OP in figure 131, the firms of category B will go out of the industry and some previous intra-marginal firms for which new price is equal to average cost firm will become marginal firms. We therefore conclude that in long-run competitive equilibrium under different cost conditions the output of individual firms and the number of firms in the industry is so adjusted that the following two conditions must be satisfied.

A Classification of Market Forms

Forms of Market Structure	*Number of Firms*	*Price Elasticity of Demand for an individual firms*	*Degree of Control over price*
(a) **Perfect Competition**	A large number of firms	Infinite	None
(b) **Imperfect Competition**	A large number of firms	Large	Some
(i) **Monopolistic Competition**	—	Large	Some
(ii) **Pure Oligopoly** (Oligopoly without Product Differentiation)	Few firms	Small	Some
(iii) **Differentiated Oligopoly** (Oligopoly with product differentiation)	Few firms	Small	Some
(c) **Monopoly**	One	Very Small	Considerable

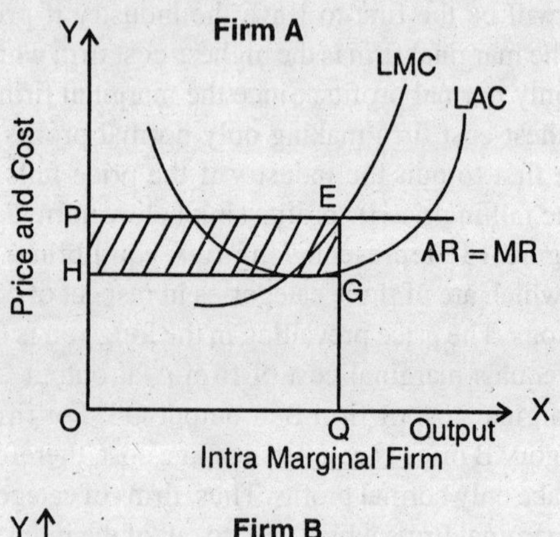

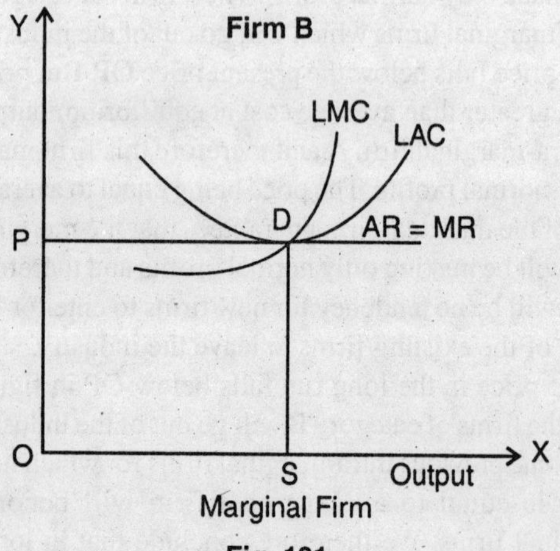

Fig. 131

1. Price = MC of all firms,

2. Price = AC of the marginal firm.

From above it follows that **in long-run competitive equilibrium under differential cost conditions only the marginal firm will be of optimum size,** because the equilibrium of only marginal firm will be established at the minimum point of the average cost curve. The intra-marginal firms will be of more than optimum size, as is clear from figure 131.

Thus in the long-run where cost curves are not identical some firms may be earning supernormal profits. The industry will be in full equilibrium only by accident.

The Supply Curve of the Firm and the Industry

The supply curve of the firm may be derived by the points of intersection of its MC curve with successive demand curves. Assume that the market price increases gradually. This causes an upward shift of the demand curve of the firm. Given the positive slope of the MC curve, each higher demand curve cuts the (given) MC curve to a point which lies to the right of the previous intersection. This implies that the quantity supplied by the firm increases as price rises. The firm, given its cost structure, will not supply any quantity if the price falls below P, because at a lower price the firm does not cover its variable cots (figure 132). If we plot the successive points of intersection of MC and the demand curves on a separate graph we observe that the supply curve of the individual firm is identical to its MC curve to the right of the closing-down point (above AVC) M.

Below P the quantity supplied by the firm is zero. As price rises above P the quantity supplied increases. The supply curve of the firm is shown in figure 133.

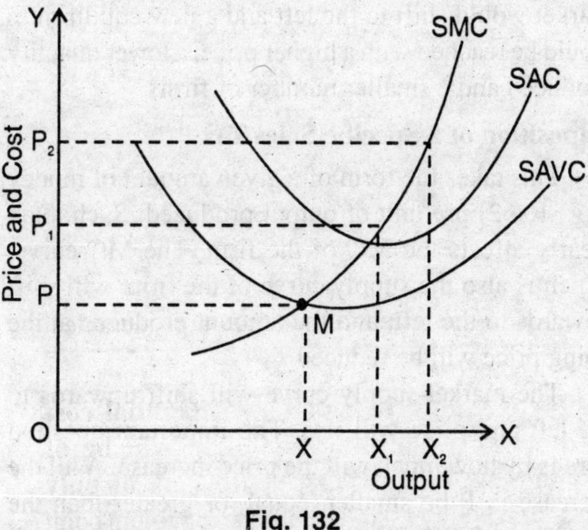

Fig. 132

The Industry-supply curve is the **horizontal summation** of the supply curves of the individual firms. It is assumed that the factor prices and the technology are given and that the number of firms is very large. Under these conditions the total quantity supplied in the market at each price is the sum of the quantities supplied by all firms at that price. In figure 134 we show the industry supply as a straight line with a positive slope. It should, however, be noted that the particular shape of the market-supply curve depends on the technology and on factors prices, as well as the size distribution of the firms in the industry. All firms are not usually of the same size. The particular size of each firm in perfect competition

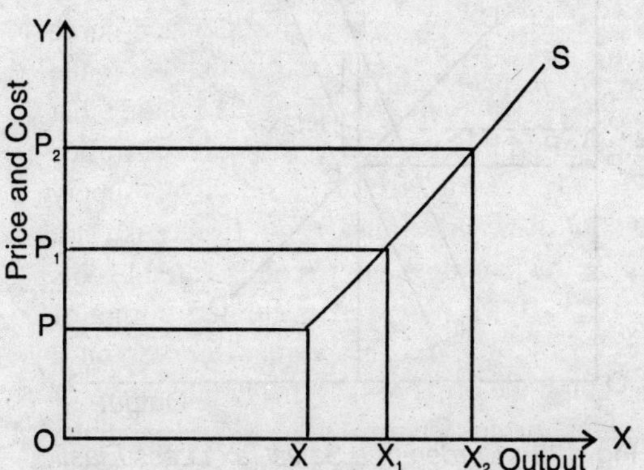

Fig. 133 : Short-Run Supply Curve of a Firm

depends on the entrepreneurial efficiency of the businessman, which is traditionally considered as a random attribute.

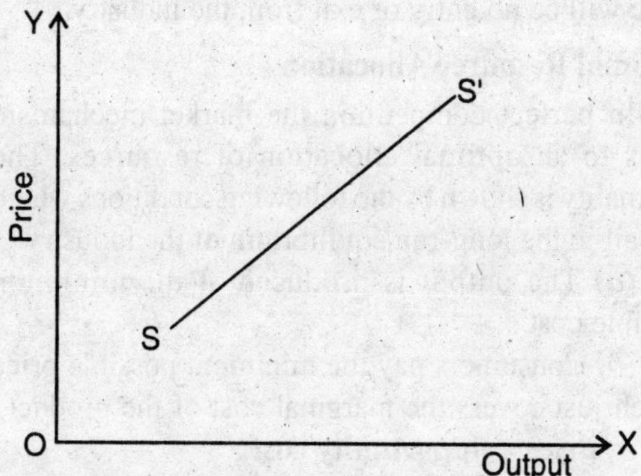

Fig. 134: ***Short-Run Industry Supply Curve***

SHORT-RUN EQUILIBRIUM OF THE INDUSTRY

Given the market demand and the market supply the industry is in equilibrium at that price at which the quantity demanded is equal to the quantity supplied. In figure 135 the industry is in equilibrium at price P, at which the quantity demanded and supplied is Q. However, this will be a short-run equilibrium, if at the prevailing price firms are making excess profits or losses.

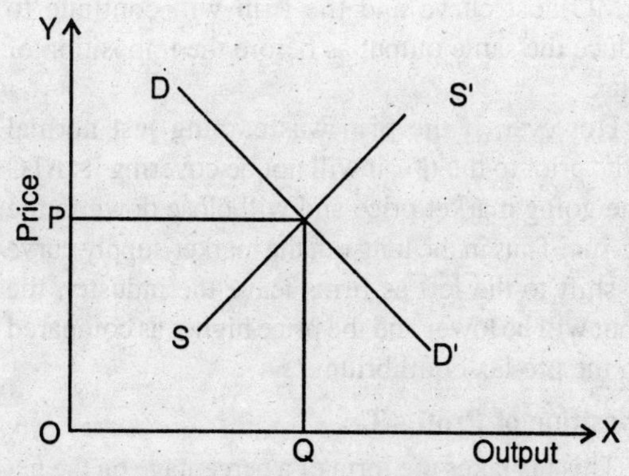

Fig. 135 : ***Short-Run Industry Equilibrium***

In the long-run, firms that make losses and cannot read just their plant will close down. Those that make excess profits will expand their capacity, while excess profits will also attract new firms into the industry. Entry exit and readjustment of the remaining firms in the industry will lead to a long run equilibrium in which forms will just be earning normal profits and there will be no entry or exit from the industry.

Optimal Resource Allocation

In perfect competition the market mechanism leads to an optimal allocation of resources. The optimality is shown by the following conditions which prevail in the long-run equilibrium of the industry :

(a) The output is produced at the minimum feasible cost.

(b) Consumers pay the minimum possible price which just covers the marginal cost of the product,, that is, **price = opportunity cost.**

(c) Plants are used at full capacity in the long run, so that there is no waste of resources.

(d) Firms only earn normal profits.

In the long run these conditions prevail in all markets, so that resources are optimally allocated in the economy as a whole.

Effect of Imposition of A Tax (Perfect Competition)

We will examine the effects of the imposition by the government of a lump-sum tax, a profits tax, and a specific tax, that is, a tax per unit of output.

Imposition of a Lump-Sum Tax (Per Period)

In the short run the **lump-sum tax** will not affect the MC cost curve and the firm will continue to produce the same output as before the imposition of the tax.

However, if the firm was earning just normal profits prior to the tax, it will not be covering its ATC at the going market price and will close down in the long-run. Thus in the long run the market-supply curve will shift to the left as firms leave the industry, the output will be lower and the price higher as compared with the pre-tax equilibrium.

Imposition of Profits Tax

This tax takes the form of a percentage on the net profit of the firm. The effects of a profits tax are the same with those of a lump-sum tax. The profits tax, while reducing the profits, will not affect its MC. Hence in the short-run the equilibrium of the firm and the industry will not change.

However, in the long-run, exit of firms will be inevitable if in the pre-tax period firms were earning just normal profits. In the long run the supply in the market would shift to the left and a new equilibrium would be reached with a higher price, a lower quantity produced and a smaller number of firms.

Imposition of a Specific Sales Tax

This takes the form of a given amount of money (*e.g.,* Rs. 2) pre unit of output produced. Such a tax clearly affects the MC of the firm. The MC curve, which is also the supply curve of the firm, will shift upwards to the left, and the amount produced at the going price will be reduced.

The market-supply curve will shift upwards to the left and price will rise. The important question here is by how much will the price increase : Will the increase in P be smaller, equal, or greater than the specific tax? This is an important question because it relates to who is going to bear the specific sales tax : the consumer-buyer, the firm, or both?

The answer to this question is that the burden of the specific tax that will be borne by the consumer (buyer) depends on the price elasticity of supply, given the market demand. In general, the most elastic the market supply the higher the proportion of the tax that the consumer will bear and the less the burden of the firm from the specific tax.

So long as the market supply has a positive slope the specific tax will be paid partly by the buyer and

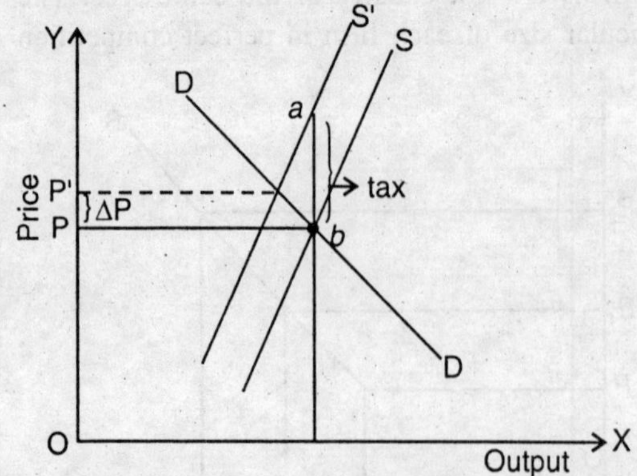

Fig. 136 : *Burden of a Sales Tax : Less Elastic Supply Curve*

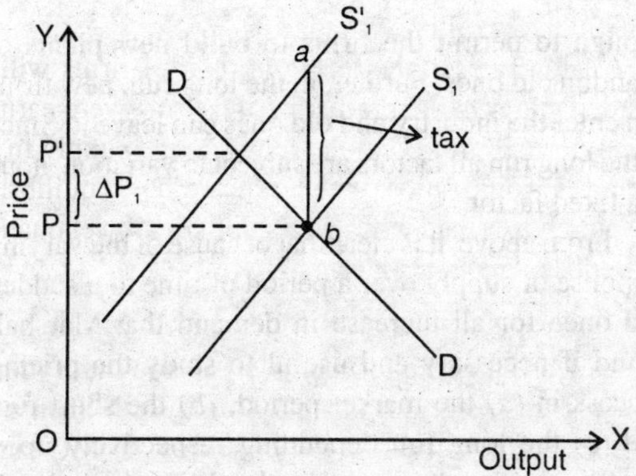

Fig. 137 : *Burden of a Sales Tax : More Elastic Supply Curve*

partly by the firm. The burden to the firm will be smaller the greater the elasticity of supply. In other words, the firm will be able to pass on to the consumer more of the specific tax, the more elastic the market supply. This is illustrated in figure 136 and 137. The demand curve is identical in both figures and the initial (pre-tax) price is the same, but the supply curve in figure 137 is more elastic. Imposition of a specific tax equal to *ab* raises the price by ΔP in figure 136 and by ΔP_1 in figure 137. Clearly $\Delta P_1 > \Delta P$, that is, the tax burden to the consumer is greater in the case of a more elastic supply curve (given the market demand).

In the limiting case of a market-supply curve with infinite elasticity the increase in price is equal to the specific tax and the whole tax burden is force by the consumer. In figure 138 the demand is the same as in

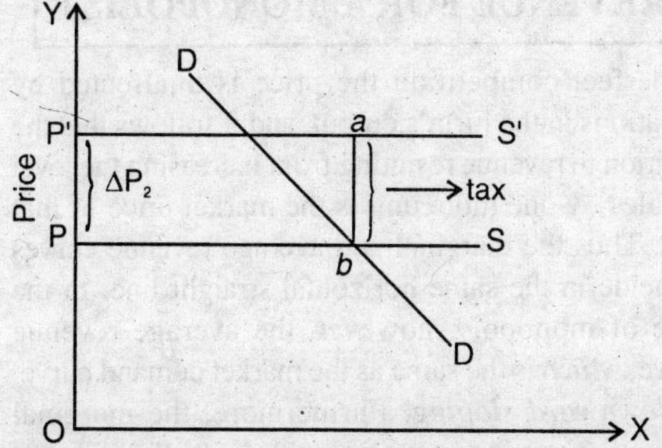

Fig. 138 : *Burden of a Sales Tax : Infinite Elastic Supply Curve*

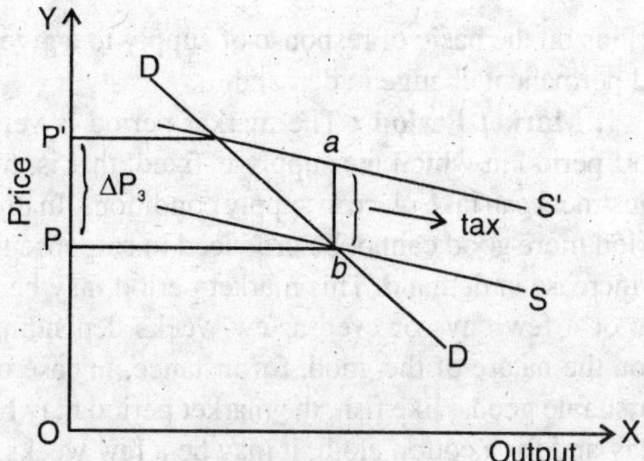

Fig. 139 : *Burden of a Sales Tax : Supply is Negatively Sloping*

figure 136 and 137, but the supply curve is parallel to the horizontal axis, showing infinite price elasticity, The imposition of a specific tax equal to *ab* leads to an equal increase in the price : $\Delta P_2 = ab$.

If the supply curve has a negative slope (figure 139) the imposition of a specific tax results in an increase in the price which is greater than the tax. In figure 139 the demand is identical as in the above-examined cases but the supply curve is negatively sloping (with its slope smaller than the slope of the DD curve). Under these conditions a specific tax of *ab* leads to an increase in the market price equal to ΔP_3, which is obviously larger than the unit tax.

Marshall's Time Analysis and Price

Marshall, who propounded the theory that price is determined by both demand and supply, also gave a great importance to the **time element** in the determination of price. Time element is of great relevance in the theory of value, since one of the two determinants of price, namely supply, depends on the time allowed to it for adjustment. It is worth mentioning that Marshall divided time into different periods from the view point of supply and not from the view point of demand. Time is short or long according to the extent to which supply can adjust itself. Marshall felt it necessary to divide time into different periods on the basis of response of supply because it always takes time for the supply to adjust fully to the changed conditions of demand.

Marshall divided time into following three

periods on the basic of response of supply to a given and permanent change in demand.

1. Market Period : The market period is very short period in which the supply is fixed, that is, no adjustment can take place in supply conditions. In this period more good cannot be produced in response to an increase in demand. This market period may be a day or a few days or even a few weeks depending upon the nature of the good, for instance, in case of perishable goods, like fish, the market period may be a day and for a cotton cloth, it may be a few weeks.

2. Short Run : Short run is a period in which supply can be adjusted to a limited extent. During the short period the firms can expand output with given equipment by changing the amounts of variable factors employed. Output can be expanded by making intensive use of given plant or capital equipment by varying the amount of variable factors.

3. Long Run : The long run is a period long enough to permit the firms to build new plants or abandon old ones. Further, in the long run, new firms can enter the industry and old ones can leave it. Since in the long run all factors are subject to variation, none is a fixed factor.

From above, it is clear that because of the varying response of supply over a period of time to a sudden and once for all increase in demand that Marshall found if necessary and useful to study the pricing process in *(a)* the market period, *(b)* the short run, and *(c)* the long run depending respectively upon whether the supply conditions have time to make *(i)* no adjustment *(ii)* some adjustment of labour and other variable factors, and *(iii)* adjustment of all factors and all costs. Therefore, Marshall explained how the equilibrium between demand and supply was established in three time periods which consequently determine market price, short-run price and long run price.

MONOPOLY

DEFINITION

Monopoly is a market structure in which there is a single seller, there are no close substitutes for the commodity it produces and there are barriers to entry. Two points are worth noting in this definition. *Firstly*, there must be a single producer or seller of a product if there is to be monopoly. A *second condition* which is essential for a firm to be called monopolist is that no *close substitutes* for the product of that firm should be available.

We can express the second condtion of monopoly in terms of *cross elasticity of demand* also. Cross elsticity of demand shows a change in the demand for a good as a result of change in the price of another good. Therefore, if there is to be monopoly *the cross elasticity of demand between the product of the monopolist and the product of any other producer must be very small.*

The above two conditions ensure that the monopolist can set the price of his product and can pursue an independent price policy. Power to influence price is very essence of monopoly. From this it must not be gathered that the monopolist is so powerful that he can dictate the price as wel as the amount sold. Monopolist can do one of these things only; either he can fix the price leaving the amount sold to the consumers, or he can fix the quantity he wants to produce and sell and leave the price to be determined by the demand of the consumers.

AVERAGE AND MARGINAL REVENUE FOR A MONOPOLIST

In perfect competition the price is unaffected by variations in the Firm's output, and if follows that the addition to revenue resulting from increasing the level of sales by one more unit is the market price of that unit. Thus the marginal and average revenue curves coincide in the same horizontal straight line. In the case of monopoly, however, the average revenue curve, which is the same as the market demand curve, is *downward sloping*. Furthermore, the marginal revenue curve does not coincide with the demand curve : since the side of an extra unit forces down the price at which all units already being sold can now be sold, the sale of an extra unit results in a net addition to revenue of an amount less that its own selling price.

It is easy to prove algebraically that, if the demand curve slopes downwards, marginal revenue is always less than price. Let subscripts n and $(n + 1)$ indicate the revenue associated with the sale of nth and the $(n + 1)$th unit. So that, e.g., TR_n is the total revenue associated with the sale of n units period.

$$MR_{n+1} = TR_{n+1} - TR_n$$
$$= (n + 1)\, P_{n+1} - n.P_n$$
$$= n.P_{n+1} + P_{n+1} - n.P_n$$
$$= n\,(P_{n+1} + P_n) + P_{n+1}.$$

Since the demand curve slopes downwards P_{n+1} (the price ruling when $n + 1$ units are sold) will be less than P_n (the price ruling when n units are sold). Thus the MR of the $(n + 1)$th unit is less than P_{n+1}.

Using Calculus, the proof is as follows :

$$P = f(Q)$$

and $\quad TR = Q.P = Q.f(Q)$

$$\therefore \quad MR = \frac{dTR}{dQ}$$
$$= Q.f'(Q) + f(Q)$$

But $f(Q)$ is the price and $f'(Q)$ is negative, since the demand curve slopes downard. Thus MR < P, and the difference is the marginal fall in price, $f'(Q)$, multiplied by the quantity already being sold, Q.

DEMAND AND REVENUE

Since there is a single Firm in the industry, the Firm's demand curve is the industry demand curve. The demand equation (linear demand function), *ceteris paribus*, is

$$X = b_0 - b_1.P$$

The clause cetris paribus implies that all the other factors (such as income, tastes, other prices which affect demand are assumed constant. Changes in these factors will shift the demand curve (Figure 140).

The slope of the demand curve (DD') is

$$\frac{dX}{dP} = \frac{d\,(b_0 - b_1.P)}{dX}$$
$$= -b_1$$

The price elasticity of demand is

$$e_P = \frac{dX}{dP}.\frac{P}{X}$$

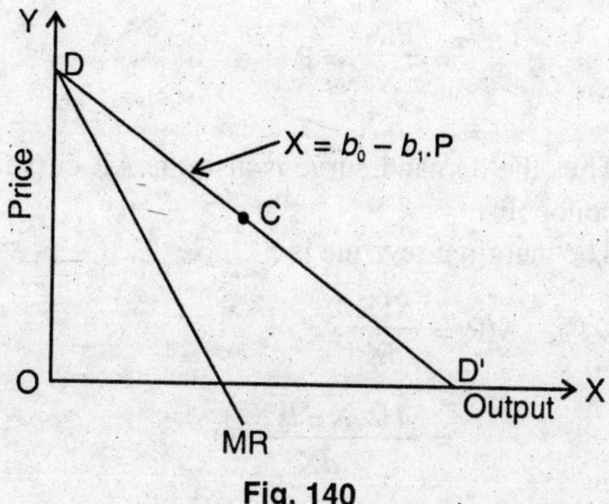

Fig. 140

$$= -b_1.\frac{P}{X}$$

That is, elasticity changes at any one point of the demand curve.

(a) At point D the elasticity approaches infinity.

$$e_P = -b_1.\frac{P}{X} \to \infty$$

(b) At point D' on the demand curve DD', the elasticity is zero.

$$e_P = -b_1.\frac{P}{X}$$
$$= -b_1.\frac{0}{X} = 0$$

(c) At the mid point C the price elasticity is unity.

$$e_P = -1$$

The total revenue of the monopolist is

$$TR = P.X$$

Solving the demand equation for P we find

$$P = \frac{b_0}{b_1} - \frac{1}{b_1}.X$$

Setting $\left(\frac{b_0}{b_1}\right) = a$ and $\left(\frac{1}{b_1}\right) = b$ we may rewrite the price equation as

$$P = a - b.X$$

Substituting into the revenue equation we find

$$TR = P.X$$
$$TR = (a - b.X)\,X$$
$$TR = a.X - b.X^2$$

The average revenue is equal to the price :

$$AR = \frac{TR}{X}$$

$$= \frac{P.X}{X} = P$$

$$= a - b.X$$

Thus the demand curve is also the AR curve of the monopolist.

The marginal revenue is :

$$MR = \frac{dTR}{dX}$$

$$= \frac{d(a.X - b.X^2)}{dX}$$

$$= a - 2b.X$$

That is, the MR is a straight line with the same intercept as the demand curve, but twice as steep.

The general relation between P and MR is found as follows. Given

$$TR = P.X$$

$$MR = \frac{dTR}{dX}$$

$$MR = \frac{d(P.X)}{dX}$$

$$MR = P.\frac{dX}{dX} + X.\frac{dP}{dX}$$

$$\therefore \quad MR = P + X.\frac{dP}{dX}$$

The marginal revenue is at all levels of output smaller than P, given that

$$P = MR - X.\frac{dP}{dX}$$

and the term $\left(X.\frac{dP}{dX}\right)$ is positive (sicne the slope of the demand curve, $\frac{dP}{dX} > 0$.

Hence P > MR

Costs

In the traditional theory of monopoly the shapes of the cost curves are the same as in the theory of perfect competition. The AVC, MC and ATC are U-shaped, while the AFC is a *rectangular hyperbola.* However, the particular shape of the cost curves does not make any difference to the determination of the equilibrium of the Firm, provided that the slope of the MC is greater than the slope of the MR curve.

One point should be stressed here. *The MC curve is not the supply curve of the monopolist, as is the case in perfect competition.* In monopoly there is no unique relationship betwen price and the quantity supplied.

Equilibrium of the Monopolist

A. Short-Run Equilibrium

The monopolist maximises his short-run profits if the following two conditions are fulfilled :

1. MC = MR
2. The slope of MC is greater than the slope of the MR at the point of the intersection.

In Figure 141 the equilibrium of the monopolist is defined by point E, at which the MC intersects the MR curve from below. Thus both condtions for equilibrium are fulfilled. Price is P and the quantity is X. The monopolist realises excess profits equal to the shaded area APCB. Note that the price is higher than the MR.

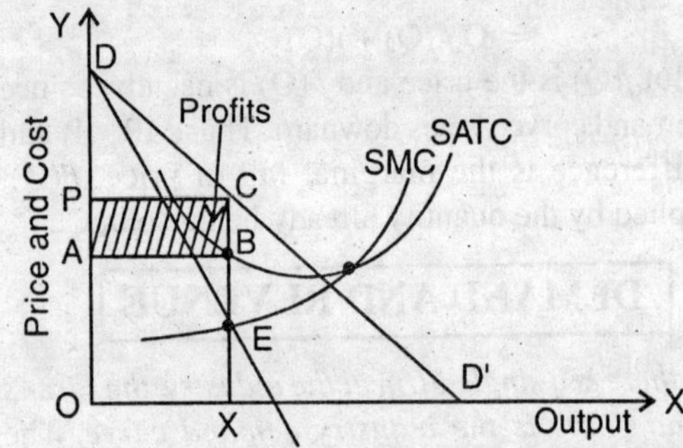

Fig. 141 : *Short-Run Equilibrium Under Monopoly*

It is generaly thought that monopolists always earn profits and therefore in layman's mind profits are generally associated with monopoly. But this is a wrong notion.

In the short-run, monopolist can make losses also. If demand is inadequate, the complete absence of competition is of little benefit to the seller. In the short-run, monopolist will continue working so long as price is above the average variable cost. If the price falls below average variable cost, the monopolist would shut down even in the short-run.

In perfect competition the Firm is a price-taker, so that its only decision is output determination. The monopolist is faced by two decisions : setting his price and his output. However, given the downward-sloping demand curve, the two decisions are interdependent. The monopolist will either set his price and sell the amount that the market will take at it, or he will produce the output defined by the intersection of MC and MR, which will be sold at the corresponding price, P. *The monopolist cannot decide independently both the quantity and the price at which he wants to sell it.* The crucial condition for the maximisation of the monopolist's profit is the equality of his MC and MR, provided that the MC cuts the MR from below.

Formal Derivation of the Equilibrium of the Monopolist

Given the demand function

$$X = g(P)$$

which may be solved for P

$$P = f_1(X)$$

and given the cost function

$$C = f_2(X)$$

The monopolist aims at the maximisation of his profit.

$$\pi = TR - C$$

(a) The first-order condition for maximum profit π is

$$\frac{d\pi}{dX} = 0$$

or, $$\frac{d\pi}{dX} = \frac{dTR}{dX} - \frac{dC}{dX} = 0$$

or, $$\frac{dTR}{dX} = \frac{dC}{dX}$$

that is **MR = MC**

(b) The second-order condition for maximum profit is

$$\frac{d^2\pi}{dX^2} < 0$$

or $$\frac{d^2\pi}{dX^2} = \frac{d^2TR}{dX^2} - \frac{d^2C}{dX^2} < 0$$

or $$\frac{d^2TR}{dX^2} < \frac{d^2C}{dX^2}$$

that is

$$\begin{bmatrix}\text{Slope} \\ \text{of MR}\end{bmatrix} < \begin{bmatrix}\text{Slope} \\ \text{of MC}\end{bmatrix}$$

A numerical example

Given the demand curve of the monopolist X = 50 – 0.5 P

Which may be solved for P

$$P = 100 - 2X$$

Given the cost function of the monopolist

$$C = 50 + 40X$$

The goal of the monopolist is to maximise profit

$$\pi = TR - C$$

(i) We first find the MR

$$TR = X.P$$
$$= X(100 - 2X)$$
$$= 100X - 2X^2$$

$$\therefore \quad MR = \frac{d(TR)}{dX}$$

$$= \frac{d(100X - 2X^2)}{dX}$$

$$= 100 - 4X$$

(ii) We next find the MC

$$C = 50 + 40X$$

$$\therefore \quad MC = \frac{dC}{dX}$$

$$= \frac{d(50 + 40X)}{dX} = 40$$

(iii) We equate MR and MC

$$MR = MC$$
$$100 - 4X = 40$$
$$X = 15$$

(iv) The monopolist's price is found by substituting X = 15 into the demand-price equation

$$P = 100 - 2X$$
$$= 70$$

(v) The profits is

$$\pi = TR - C$$
$$= 1050 - 650 = 400$$

This profit is the maximum possible, since the second-order condition is satisfied :

$$\because \quad \frac{dC}{dX} = 40$$

$$\therefore \quad \frac{d^2C}{dX^2} = 0$$

and $MR = \frac{dTR}{dX}$

$$MR = \frac{d(100 - 4X)}{dX}$$

$$\therefore \frac{d^2(TR)}{dX^2} = -4$$

Clearly $-4 < 0$.

NO UNIQUE SUPPLY CURVE FOR THE MONOPOLIST

There is no unique supply curve for the monopolist from his MC. Given his MC, the same quantity may be offered at different prices *depending on the price elasticity* of demand. Graphically this is shown in Figure 142. The X will be sold at price P_1 if demand is D_1, while the same quantity X will be sold at price P_2 if demand is D_2. Thus, there is no unique relationship between price and quantity.

Similary, given the MC of the monopolist, *various quantities may be supplied at any one price*, depending on the market demand and the corresponding MR curve. In Figure 143 we depict such a situation. The cost conditions are represented by the MC curve. Given the costs of the monopolist, he would supply OX_1, if the market demand is D_1, while at the same price P, he would supply only OX_2 if the market demand is D_2.

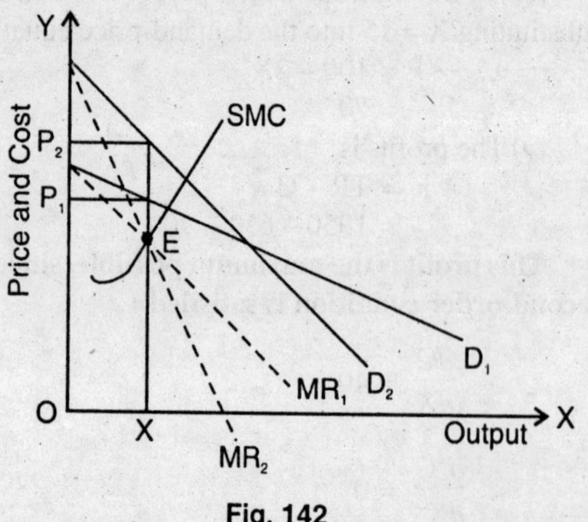

Fig. 142

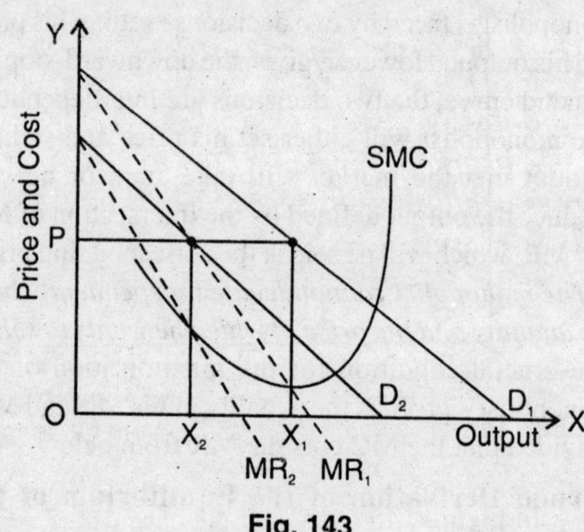

Fig. 143

B. Long-Run Equilibrium

In the long-run the monopolist has the time to expand his plant, or to use his existing plant at any level which will maximise his profit. With entry blocked, however, it is not necessary for the monopolist to reach an optimal scale (that is, to build up his plant until he reaches the minimum point of LAC). Neither is there any guarantee that he will use his existing plant at optimum capacity. What is certain is that the monopolist will not stay in business if he makes losses in the long run. He will most probably continue to earn supernormal profits even in the long-run, given that entry is barred. However, the size of his plant and the degree of utilisation of any given plant size depend entirely on the market demand. He may reach the optimal scale (minimum point of LAC) or remain at suboptimal scale (falling part of his LAC) or surpass the optimal scale (expand beyond the minimum LAC) depending on the market conditions. In Figure 144 we depict the case in which the market size does not permit the monopolist to expand to the minimum point of LAC. In this case not only is his plant of suboptimal size but also the existing plant is under utilized. This is because to the left of the minimum point of the LAC the SAC is tangent to the LAC at its falling part, and also because the short-run MC must be equal to the LMC. This occurs at E, while the minimum LAC is at *b* and the optimal use of the existing plant is at *a*. Since it is utilised at the level E', there is excess capacity.

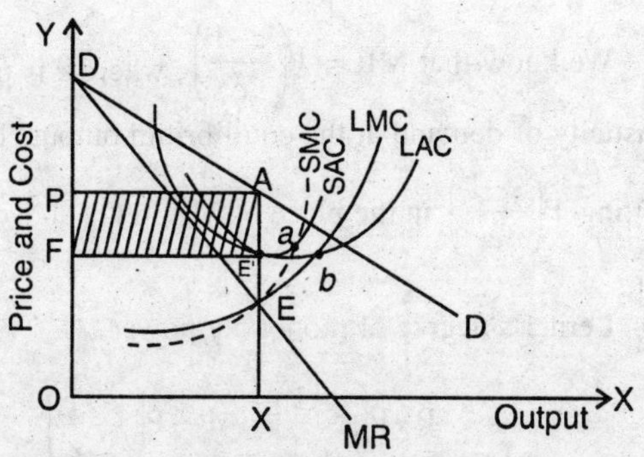

Fig. 144 : *Monopolist with Suboptimal Plant and Excess Capacity*

In Figure 145 we depict the case where the size of the market is so large that the monopolist, in order to maximise his output, must build a plant larger than the optimal and overutilise it. This is because to the right of the minimum point of the LAC the SAC and the LAC are tangent at a point of their positive slope, and also because the SMC must be equal to the LAC. Thus the plant that maximes the monopolist's profits leads to higher costs for two reasons : Firstly because it is larger than the optimal size, and secondly because it is overutilised.

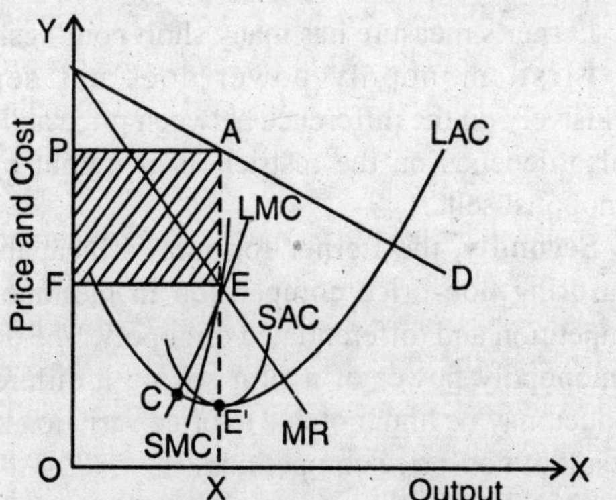

Fig. 145 : *Monopolist Operating in a Large Market : His Plant is Larger than the Optimal (C) and it is being overutilised.*

Finally in Figure 146 we show the case in which the market size is just large enough to permit the monopolist to build the optimal plant and use it at full capacity. It should be clear that which of the above situations will emerge in any particular case depends

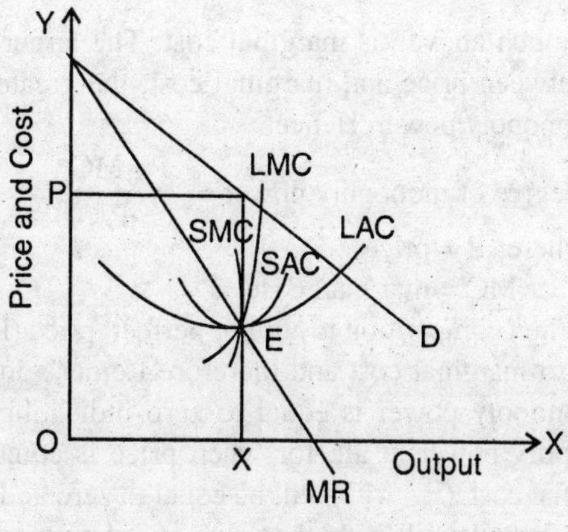

Fig. 146

on the size of the market (given the technology of the monopolist). There is no certainty that in the long-run the monopolist will reach the optimal scale, as is the case in a perfect competitive market. In monopoly there are no market forces similar to those in perfect competition which lead the firms to operate at optimum plant size in the long run.

Measurement of the Degree of Monopoly Power

Monopoly is a matter of degree. Monopoly power is not only enjoyed by the pure or ordinary monopolist but also by the producers and sellers of all those market categories in which monopoly element is present in a large or small measure. Thus producers or sellers in monopolistic competition and oligopoly enjoy monopoly power to a greater or lesser degree. By monopoly power we mean the amount of discretion which a producer or seller possesses in regard to the framing of his price and output policy.

Monopoly power indicates the degree of control which a producer of seller wields over the price and output to his product. Various measures of monopoly power have been suggested by different economists, we shall discuss some of them below.

Lerner's Measure

One of the earliest methods' to measure monopoly power is expressed by Prof. A.P. Lerner in terms of the bargaining strength. **The difference between price and marginal cost is the measure of the degree of monopoly power.** A seller's monopoly power depends upon his ability to sell his product at a price much above his marginal cost. The larger the gap between price and marginal cost, the greater is the monopoly power. Hence

$$\text{Degree of monopoly power} = \frac{P-MC}{P}$$

where P = price

MC = marginal cost

When competition is pure or perfect, price (P) is equal to marginal cost and therefore Lerner's index of monopoly power is equal to zero indicating no monopoly power at all, for when price is equal to marginal cost, (P – MC) will be equal to zero and the above formula will yield the value of index as zero.

Thus under pure or perfect competition, Lerner's index of monopoly power

$$\frac{(P-MC)}{P} = \frac{0}{P} = 0.$$

On the other hand, when the monopolised product entails no cost of production, that is, when the product is a free good whose supply is controlled by one person, the marginal cost will be equal to zero and Lerner's index of monopoly power $\left(\frac{P-MC}{P}\right)$ would be equal to one or unity. Thus when MC is equal to zero.

$$\text{Degree of monopoly} = \frac{P-MC}{P} = \frac{P-O}{P} = 1$$

It is thus clear that Lerner's index of **monopoly power can vary from zero to unity.** Within this range, the greater the value of the index $\left(\frac{P-MC}{P}\right)$, the greater the degree of monopoly power possessed by the seller.

Now it has been that **Lerner's index of monopoly power is nothing else but the inverse of the price elasticity of demand.** We can prove this as follows :

Lerner's degree of monopoly power

$$= \frac{P-MC}{P}$$

For profit maximisation, MC = MR, and this formula becomes

$$= \frac{P-MR}{P} \qquad ...(1)$$

We know that $MR = P\left(\frac{e-1}{e}\right)$, where e is price elasticity of demand at the equilibrium output. Thus putting $P\left(\frac{e-1}{e}\right)$ in the place of MR in (1) above we get,

Lerner's degree of monopoly power

$$= \frac{P-P\left(\frac{e-1}{e}\right)}{P} = \frac{P-P\left(1-\frac{1}{e}\right)}{P}$$

$$= \frac{P\left[1-\left(1-\frac{1}{e}\right)\right]}{P} = 1-1+\frac{1}{e} = \frac{1}{e}$$

= inverse of the elasticity of demand

It therefore follows that Lerner's index of monopoly power is equal to the inverse of price elasticity of demand. This degree of monopoly power can be judged by merely knowing the elasticity of demand at the equilibrium output. **The degree of monopoly varies inversely with the elasticity of the demand for the good.**

Its Limitation :

Lerner's measure has many short comings.

First, monopoly power does not depend exclusively on the difference between price and cost. It also depends on the restriction of output by the monopolist seller.

Secondly, the Lerner formula is incapable of measuring non-price competition in monopolistic competition and differentiated oligopoly. The degree of monopoly power of a firm selling a differential product may be high not due to price variation but as a result of non-price competition.

Thirdly, Lerner's measure is based upon only one aspect of monopoly, namely, its control over price which depends upon the availability and effectiveness of existing substitutes. It ignores the restrains on monopoly power put by the potential substitutes which would come to exist with the entry of new firms in the industry.

Lastly, the Lerner's measure is effected by changes over time in the ratio of capital to labour in an industry.

Despite these limitations, economists like **Dunlop** and **Kelecki** used this index to measure the degree of monopoly power. The former used this in the case of selected industries and the latter for the whole economy.

Triffin's Measure

Prof. Robert Triffin has improved upon Lerner's measure by suggesting **price cross-elasticity** instead of price elasticity of demand. The cross elasticity of demand points to the degree of dependence of a firm's product upon the prices of other firm's product. If demand for a firm's product does not depend upon the prices of other firm's products, then that firm will be completely independent of price and output policies of others and the cross elasticity of demand for its product will be zero. **The smaller the extent of cross-elasticity of demand for the product of a firm, the greater the degree of monopoly power enjoyed by the firm and vice versa.**

When the demand for the output of a firm or seller is not affected at all by the price of any other firm, the cross elasticity of demand for its product will be zero. Thus, when the cross elasticity of a firm's product with any product of another firm is zero, the firm will enjoy absolute monopoly power in pursuing his own price and output policy. Therefore, **Robert Triffin defined pure monopoly as one the cross elasticity of whose product is zero.**

The greater the cross elasticity of demand for a firm's product, the greater the degree of competition between the firms and the less the degree of monopoly power. In perfect competition, the products sold by various firms are completely homogeneous and therefore, perfect substitutes of each other.

According to Triffin, the cross elasticity of demand between the products of various firms under perfect competition is infinite and therefore **firms under perfect competition enjoy no monopoly power at all.**

Thus, pure monopoly having zero cross elasticity of demand enjoys absolute monopoly power and perfectly competitive firm having infinite cross elasticity of demand possesses zero monopoly power, But these are two limiting cases. Within these two limits, the less the coefficient of the cross elasticity of demand, the greater the monopoly power and vice versa.

Its Criticism

Like Lerner's measure, the Triffin measure is unsuitable for practical purposes. Pure monopoly like pure competition is unreal. **Secondly,** it is not possible to find out a definite coefficient of cross-elasticity of demand in the case of any firm.

Thirdly, according to some economists the cross-elasticity of demand of a firm under pure competition is also zero because its product has many perfect substitutes. So when one firm changes its price-output policy the other firms do not take any notice of it. Since the cross-elasticity of demand is also zero under pure competition, we can say that a competitive firm also possesses monopoly power.

Thus the method of measuring monopoly power in terms of cross-elasticity of demand is not correct because its coefficient is zero both under pure monopoly and pure competition. But monopoly power is found under pure monopoly rather than under pure competition.

Bain's Measure

Prof. J.S. Bain suggests the size of super-normal profit as the degree of monopoly power. **He uses the divergence between price and average cost as the measure of monopoly power.** Under perfect competition super-normal profits are competed away with entry of new firms in the industry. So the degree of monopoly power is zero when competition is pure. It is, therefore, under monopoly with no threat of entry of new firms that monopoly profits are the largest and the degree of monopoly power is absolute. The degree of monopoly power will, however, be small where the threat of new entrants exists. Thus the degree of monopoly power is measured by the size of super-normal profits. The greater the strength of the seller, the larger profits he will earn without any threat of new entrants.

The Bain measure is illustrated in figure 147 where the monopoly firm produces OM output and sells it at MP price. The difference between price and average cost (AC) is KM at OX per unit of output. It is equal to KABM, the excess profit which measures monopoly power.

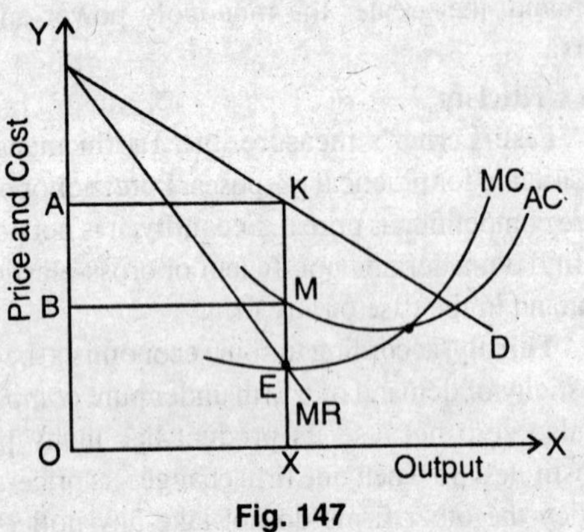

Fig. 147

But this measure is also not free from shortcomings. First, it is difficult to estimate the net income accruing to a firm. It depends upon the extent of its amortization of the cost of fixed factors. Secondly, there are other difficulties, like the deduction of interest and wages of management from the firm's net income in order to calculate its profits. Lastly, all profits accruing to a firm are not monopoly profit. Firms, whether competitive or monopolistic, often earn windfall profits when demand and cost condition change.

Rothschild's Measure

Rothschild's measures the degree of monopoly power as the ratio of the slope of a firm's demand curve to the slope of the industry demand curve. In figure 148, *dd* represents the demand curve of a firm which is elastic than DD the industry demand curve.

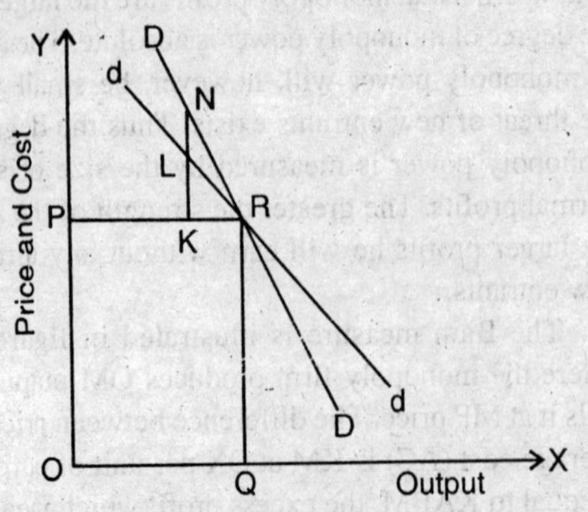

Fig. 148

Thus

$$\text{Degree of monopoly} = \frac{\text{Slope of } dd}{\text{Slope of DD}}$$

$$= \frac{KL/KR}{KN/KR} = \frac{KL}{KN}$$

Since under perfect competition the demand curve of a firm is horizontal, the Rothschild index equals zero. Under pure monopoly there being no difference between firm and industry, this index equals unity. Therefore the degree of monopoly power exists between zero and unity.

The Rothschild measure of the degree of monopoly power is more vague than the other measures. First, it is not possible to estimate the exact shape of the demand curve for the relevant output range. Second, this index requires that all competitions keep their prices constant or they readjust their prices so as to keep them identical with the price being charged by the monopolist. Lastly, this measure is based exclusively on demand factors and neglects supply and cost conditions.

Monopoly Equilibrium and Perfectly Competitive Equilibrium Compared

1. Under perfect competition, demand curve or the average revenue curve faced by an individual firm is perfectly elastic and is a horizontal straight line parallel to the X-axis. But under monopoly, demand curve or AR curve faced by the firm is falling downwards from left to right. Therefore, MR is less than AR at all levels of output and MR curve lies below the AR curve.

2. Both under perfect competition and monopoly, the firm is in equilibrium at that level of output where MC is equal to MR. But in perfect competition since MR is equal to AR or price, therefore, MC, when equal to MR in equilibrium condition, is also equal to price or AR. This is not true in case of a monopoly. Since under monopoly, MR is always less than AR or price, in equilibrium MC will, therefore, be equal to MR but it will be less than price.

Hence

Under perfect competition

MC = MR = AR = Price.

But under monopoly

MC = MR < AR = Price

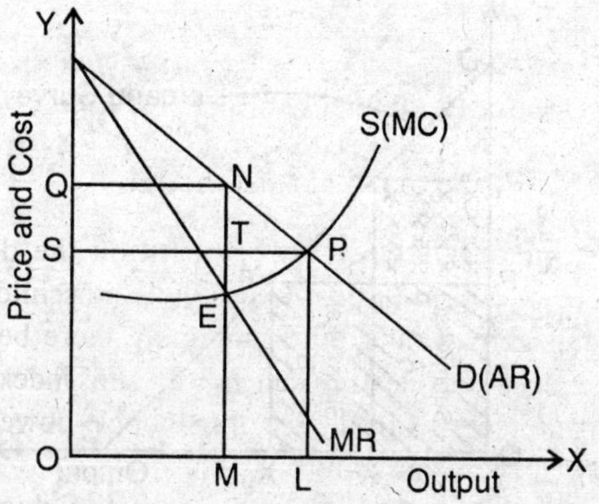

Fig. 149 : *Under Monopoly, price is higher and output smaller than under perfect competition*

3. Another significant difference between the two is that whereas a perfectly competitive firm is in long-run equilibrium at the minimum point of the long-run average cost curve, monopolistic firm is generally in equilibrium at the level of output where average cost is still declining and has yet not reached its minimum point.

4. Another important difference between monopoly equilibrium and perfectly competitive equilibrium is that under monopoly price is higher and output smaller than under perfect competition, assuming cost conditions in the two cases to be the same.

This can be explained with figure 149. In this figure, D is the demand curve. It is also the average revenue curve. S is the supply curve of the industry. It is in fact the lateral summation of the short-run summation of the short-run marginal cost curves of the various firms constituting the industry. Now under perfect competition, the price LP (= OS) will be determined at which demand curve D and supply curve S intersect each other. The equilibrium output determined is OL.

Now suppose that all the firms combine or merge to form a cartel, that is, become monopoly. Now a monopolist will be in equilibrium at that price-output level where MC equals MR. In this figure, MC equals MR at output OM and price fixed is MN. It is quite evident from the figure that when all the firms have merged together and become a monopoly, they have reduced the total output from OL to OM and raised the price from LP to MN.

5. Another difference between the two is that while under perfect competition, equilibrium is possible only when marginal cost is rising at the point of equilibrium, but monopoly equilibrium can be realised whether MC is rising, remaining constant or falling at the equilibrium output.

The equilibrium of the monopolist in these three cases is shown in figure 150, 151 and 152.

6. Another difference between monopoly and perfect competition may be noted. A monopolist can charge discriminatory prices for his goods but a firm operating under perfect competition cannot.

7. Another difference between the monopoly equilibrium and perfectly competitive equilibrium is that while under perfect competition in to long-run, a firm can earn only normal profits, but a monopolistic firm may be earning supernormal profits even in the long run.

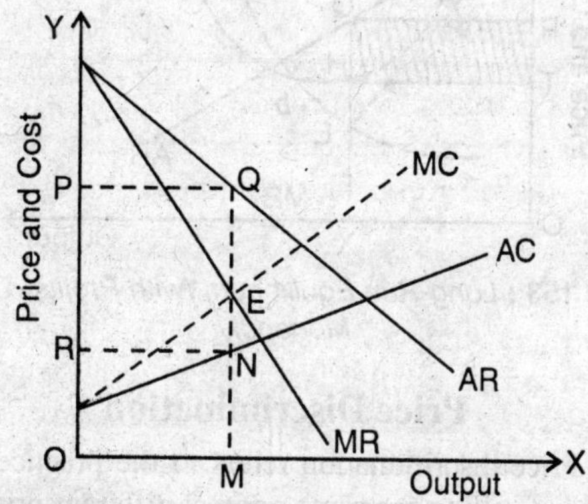

Fig. 150 : *Monopoly Equilibrium in case of Rising Costs*

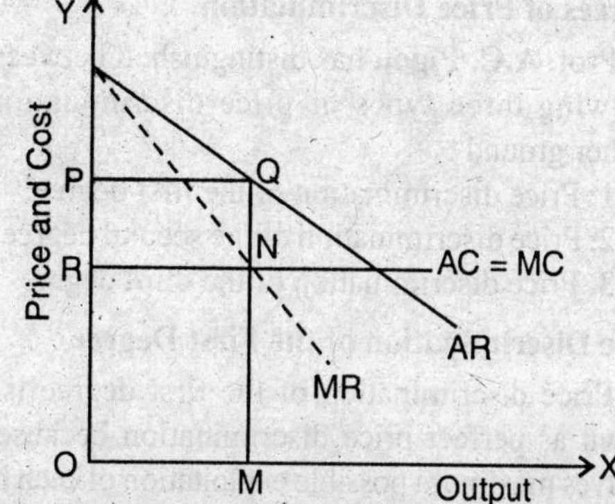

Fig. 151 : *Monopoly Equilibrium in Case of Constant Costs*

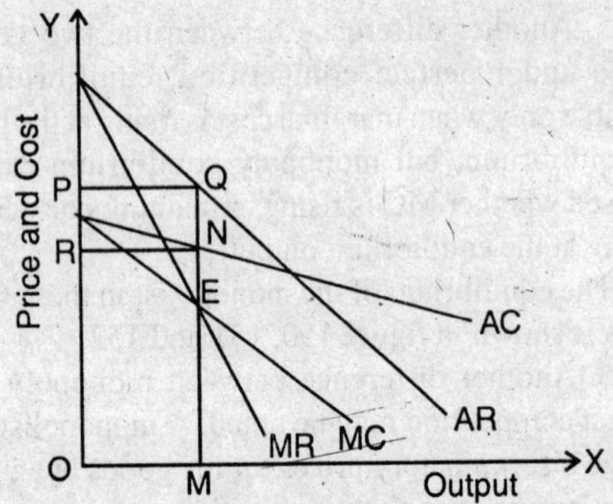

Fig. 152: *Monopoly Equilibrium in Case of Falling Cost*

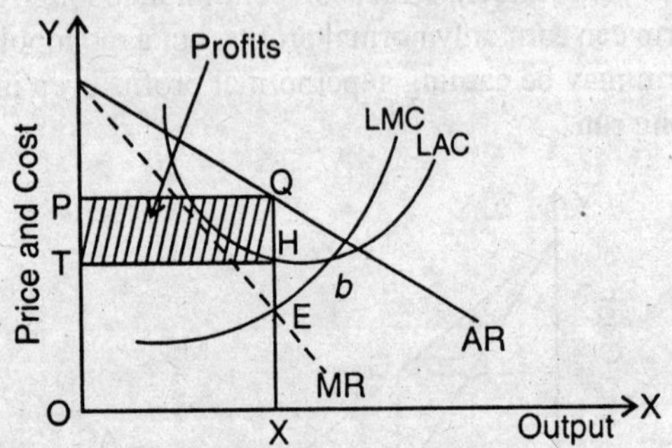

Fig. 153 : *Long-Run Equilibrium (with Profits) Under Monopoly*

Price Discrimination

Price discrimination refers to the practice of a seller of selling the same good at different prices to different buyers.

Degrees of Price Discrimination

Prof. **A.C. Pigou** has distinguished between the following three types of price discrimination on another ground :

1. Price discrimination of the first degree,
2. Price discrimination of the second degree, and
3. Price discrimination of the third degree.

Price Discrimination of the First Degree

Price discrimination of the first degree is also known as perfect price discrimination because this involves maximum possible exploitation of each buyer in the interest of a seller's profits. **Price discrimination of the first degree is said to occur when the monopolist is able to sell each separate unit of the output at a different price.**

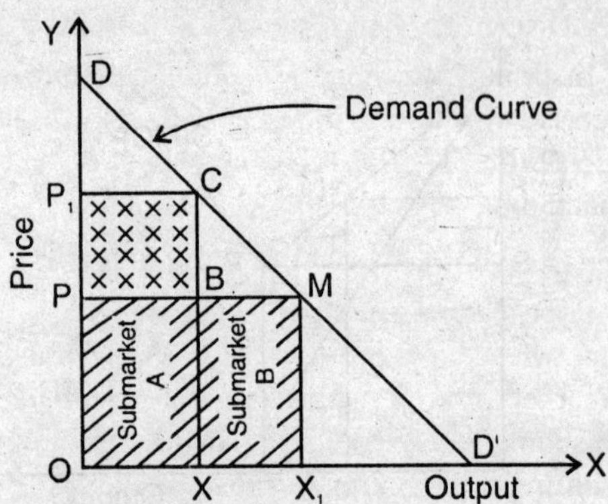

Fig. : *Third-degree Price Discrimination*

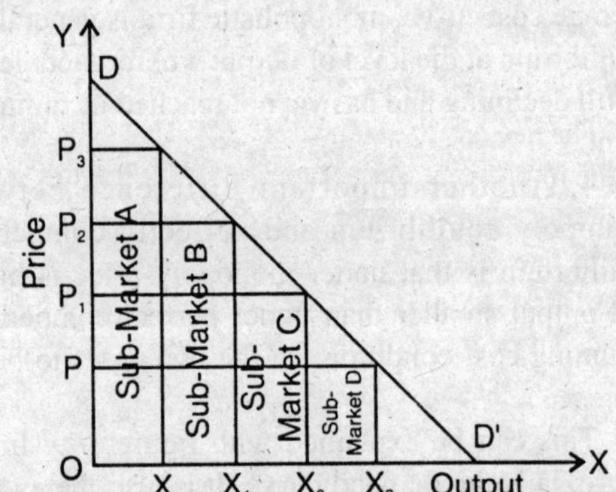

Fig. : *Different Groups under Price Discrimination of the Second Degree*

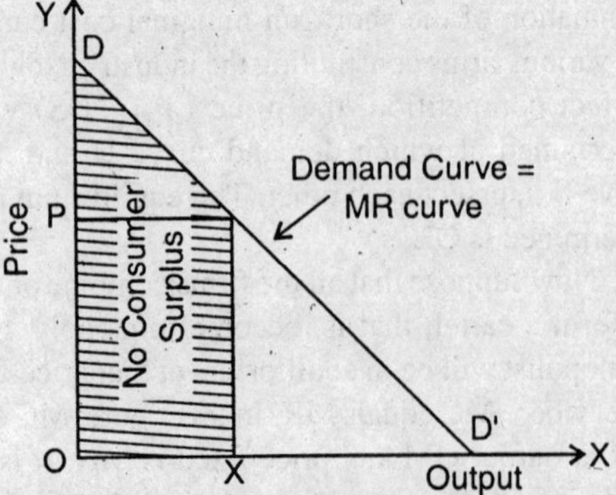

Fig. : *Price Discriminating Monopolist of the First Degrees Extracts all the Consumer's Surplus from the Buyers*

Price Discrimination of the Second Degree

In price discrimination of the second degree buyers are divided into different groups and from each group a different price is charged which is the lowest demand price of that group.

Price Discrimination of the Third Degree

Price discrimination of the third degree is said to occur when the seller divides his buyers into two submarkets or groups and charges a different price in each submarket. In this case monopolist will receive the entire consumer's surplus, First-degree price discrimination is also known as **'take-it-or-leave-it'** price discrimination, because in negotiating with each buyer the monopolist charges him the maximum price he is willing to pay under threat of denying the selling of any quantity to him : he offers each buyer a 'take-it-or-leave-it' choice. **In this case the demand curve also becomes the MR curve of the monopolist.**

When is Price Discrimination Possible ?

The necessary conditions, which must be fulfilled for the implementation of price discrimination are the following :

1. The market must be divided into sub-markets with different price elasticities.

2. There must be effective separation of the sub-markets, so that no reselling can take place from a low-price market to a high-price market.

Equilibrium Under Price Discrimination

The reason for a monopolist to apply price discrimination is to obtain an increase in his total revenue and his profits. By selling the quantity defined by the equalisation of his MC and his MR at different prices the monopolist realises a higher total revenue and hence higher profits as compared with the revenues he would receive by charging a uniform price. The monopolist can divide his total market into several sub-markets according as there are differences in demand elasticity, but for the sake of making our analysis simple we shall explain the case when the total market is divided into two sub-market.

In order to reach the equilibrium position, the discriminating monopolist has to take two decisions :

1. how much total output should be produce, and
2. how the total output should be shared between the two sub-markets and what prices he should charge in the two sub-markets.

It is assumed that the monopolist will sell his product in two sub-markets, each of them having a demand curve with different elasticity. In figure 154 the demand curve D_1 has a higher price elasticity than D_2 at any given price. The total-demand curve D is found by the **horizontal summation** of D_1 and D_2. The aggregate marginal revenue (MR) is the horizontal summation of the marginal-revenue curves MR_1 and MR_2. The marginal-cost curve is depicted by the curve MC.

The total quantity to be produced is defined by the point of intersection of the MC and the aggregate MR curves of the monopolist. In figure 154 the two curves intersect at point E, this defining a total output OX which must be produced. If the monopolist were to charge a uniform price this would be P, and his total revenue would be OXAP.

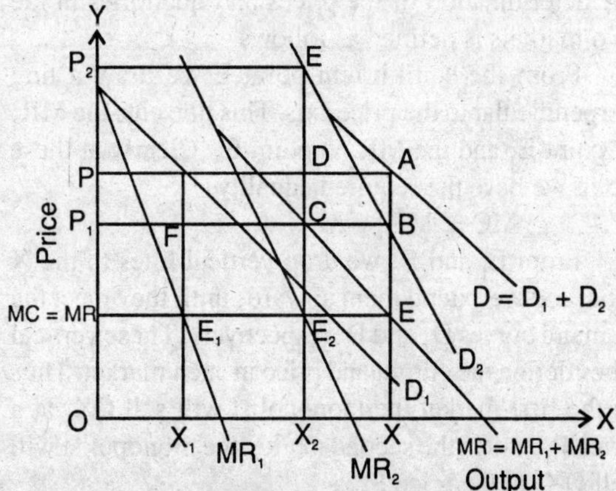

Fig. 154 : *Fixation of Total Output and different Prices in the two Sub-markets by the Discriminating Monopolist*

His profit would be the difference between this revenue and the cost for producing OX. However, the monopolist can achieve a higher profit by charging different prices in the two markets. The price and the quantity in each market is defined in such a way as to maximise profit in each market. Thus in each market he must equate the MR with the MC. However, the MC is the same for the whole quantity produced, irrespective of the market in which it is going to be sold. The MR in each market differs due to the difference in the elasticity of the two demand curves. The profit in each market is maximised by equating MC to the corresponding MR :

In the first market profit is maximised when

$MR_1 = MC$

In the second market profit is maximised when

$MR_2 = MC$

Clearly the total profit is maximised when the monopolist equates the common MC to the individual revenue

$$MC = MR_1 = MR_2$$

Hence, the following two conditions are required for the equilibrium of a discriminating monopolist :

1. Aggregate Marginal Revenue (AMR) = Marginal Cost (MC) of the total output.

2. $MR_1 = MR_2 = MC$.

If MR in one market were larger, the monopolist would sell more in that market and less in the other, until the above condition was fulfilled. Graphically the determination of the prices and quantities in the two markets is defined as follows.

From the equilibrium point E we draw a ling perpendicular to the price axis. This line cuts the MR_1 at point E_1 and the MR_2 at point E_2. Clearly at these point we have the required equality

$$MC = MR_1 = MR_2$$

From E_1 and E_2 we drop vertical lines to the X axis, and we extend them upwards until they meet the demand curves D_1 and D_2 respectively. These vertical lines define the output and price in each market. Thus in the first market the monopolist will sell OX_1 at a price P_1, and in the second market the monopolist will sell OX_2 at the price P_2.

Clearly,

$$OX_1 + OX_2 = OX.$$

From figure 154 it is obvious that the total revenue from price discrimination is larger than the revenue OXAP which would be received by charging a uniform price P. With price discrimination the total revenue is

$$P_1.OX_1 + P_2.OX_2 = OP_1FX_1 + OP_2EX_2$$

Comparing this revenue with the revenue from the unique price P we find the following :

Total revenue from price P :

$TR_1 = OXAP$

$TR_1 = OX_2DP + X_2XBC + CBAD$ ...(1)

Total revenue from P_1 and P_2 :

$TR_2 = OX_1FP_1 + OX_2EP_2$

But

$OX_1FP_1 = X_2XBC$

and

$OX_2EP_2 = OX_2DP + PDEP_2$

Therefore,

$TR_2 = X_2XBC + OX_2DP + PDEP_2$ ...(2)

Subtracting (1) from (2) we find

$$\begin{aligned} TR_2 - TR_1 = {} & [X_2XBC + OX_2DP + PDEP_2] - \\ & [OX_2DP + X_2XBC + CBAD] \\ = {} & PDEP_2 - CBAD \end{aligned}$$

Since $CBAD < PDEP_2$, it is obvious that

$$TR_2 > TR_1$$

Note that $PDEP_2$ is the additional revenue from selling OX_2 at price P_2 which is higher than P, while CBAD is the loss in revenue from selling OX_1 at price P_1 which is lower than P. The additional revenue from selling OX_2 at a higher price more than offsets the loss of revenue from selling OX_1 at a lower price, so that total revenue from discrimination is larger. Since the cost of producing OX is the same irrespective of the price at which it will be sold, the profits from price disenimination are larger as compared with those that would be obtained from selling all the output at the uniform price P.

The above case has been called third-degree price discrimination by the **British economist Pigou.** The increase in total revenue is achieved by taking away part of the consumer's surplus.

PRICE DISCRIMINATION AND THE PRICE ELASTICITY OF DEMAND

We know that

$$MR = P\left(1 - \frac{1}{e}\right)$$

In case of price discrimination we have

$$MR_1 = P_1\left(1 - \frac{1}{e_1}\right)$$

$$MR_2 = P_2\left(1 - \frac{1}{e_2}\right)$$

and $MR_1 = MR_2$

Therefore

$$P_1\left(1-\frac{1}{e_1}\right) = P_2\left(1-\frac{1}{e_2}\right)$$

or $$\frac{P_1}{P_2} = \frac{\left(1-\frac{1}{e_1}\right)}{\left(1-\frac{1}{e_2}\right)}$$

Where

e_1 = elasticity of D_1

e_2 = elasticity of D_2

If $e_1 = e_2$ the ration of prices is equal to unity:

$$\frac{P_1}{P_2} = 1$$

that is,

$$\mathbf{P_1 = P_2}$$

This means that **when elasticities are the same price discrimination is not profitable.** The monopolist will charge a uniform price for his product.

If price elasticities differ price will be higher in the market whose demand is less elastic.

This is obvious from the equality of MR's

$$P_1\left(1-\frac{1}{e_1}\right) = P_2\left(1-\frac{1}{e_2}\right)$$

if $|e_1| > |e_2|$ then

$$\left(1-\frac{1}{e_1}\right) > \left(1-\frac{1}{e_2}\right)$$

Thus for the equality of MR's to be fulfilled

$$P_1 < P_2$$

that is, the market with the higher elasticity will have the lower price.

MATHEMATICAL DERIVATION OF THE EQUILIBRIUM OF THE PRICE-DISCRIMINATING MONOPOLIST

Given the total of the monopolist

$$P = f(X)$$

Assume that the demand curves of the sub-markets are

$$P_1 = f_1(X_1)$$

and $$P_2 = f_2(X_2)$$

The cost of the firm is

$$C = f(X) = f(X_1 + X_2)$$

The firm aims at the maximisation of its profit

$$\pi = TR_1 + TR_2 - C$$

The first order condition for profit maximisation requires

$$\frac{d\pi}{dX_1} = 0 \text{ and } \frac{d\pi}{dX_2} = 0$$

(a) $$\frac{d\pi}{dX_1} = \frac{d(TR_1)}{dX_1} - \frac{dC}{dX_1} = 0$$

and $$\frac{d\pi}{dX_2} = \frac{d(TR_2)}{dX_2} - \frac{dC}{dX_2} = 0$$

(b) $$\frac{d(TR_1)}{dX_1} = \frac{dC}{dX_1}$$

or $$MR_1 = MC_1$$

and $$\frac{d(TR_2)}{dX_2} = \frac{dC}{dX_2}$$

or $$MR_2 = MC_2$$

But

$$MC_1 = MC_2 = MC = \frac{dC}{dX}$$

Therefore

$$MC = MR_1 = MR_2$$

The second-order condition for profit maximisation requires

$$\frac{d^2(TR_1)}{dX_1^2} < \frac{d^2C}{dX^2}$$

and $$\frac{d^2(TR_2)}{dX_2^2} < \frac{d^2C}{dX^2}$$

That is, the MR in each market must be increasing less rapidly than the MC for the output as a whole.

A numerical example

We use the same basic equations as in the example of the simple monopolist so as to be able to compare results.

Assume that the total demand is

$$X = 50 - 0.5P$$

or $$P = 100 - 2.X$$

Assume further that the demand function of two sub-markets are

$X_1 = 32 - 0.4P$ or $P_1 = 80 - 2.5X_1$

and $X_2 = 18 - 0.1P_2$ or $P_2 = 180 - 10.X_2$

(Clearly $X_1 + X_2 = X$)

Finally, assume that the cost function is

$$C = 50 + 40X$$
$$= 50 + 40(X_1 + X_2)$$

The firm aims at the maximisation of its profit

$$\pi = TR_1 + TR_2 - C$$

1. $TR_1 = X_1.P_1$

$$= X_1 (80 - 2.5X_1)$$
$$= 80X_1 - 2.5X_1^2$$
$$\therefore \quad MR_1 = \frac{d(TR_1)}{dX_1} = 80 - 5X_1$$

2. $TR_2 = X_2.P_2$

$$= X_2 (180 - 10X_2)$$
$$= 180\,X_2 - 10\,X_2^2$$
$$\therefore \quad MR_1 = \frac{d(TR_2)}{dX_2}$$
$$= 180 - 20X_2$$

3. $MC = \frac{dC}{dX_1} = \frac{dC}{dX_2} = \frac{dC}{dX} = 40$

Setting the MR in each market equal to the common MC we obtain

$$80 - 5X_1 = 40$$
$$180 - 20X_2 = 40$$
$$\therefore X_1 = 8 \text{ and } X_2 = 7$$
$$\because \quad X = X_1 + X_2$$
$$= 8 + 7 = 15$$

The prices are

$$P_1 = 80 - 2.5X_1$$
$$P_1 = 60$$
$$P_2 = 180 - 10X_2 = 110$$

The profit is

$$\pi = TR_1 + TR_2 - C$$
$$= 500$$

The elasticities re

$$e_1 = \frac{dX_1}{dP_1}.\frac{P_1}{X_1}$$
$$= (0.4).\frac{60}{8} = 3$$

$$e_2 = \frac{dX_2}{dP_2}.\frac{P_2}{X_2}$$
$$= (0.1).\frac{110}{7} = 1.57$$

Thus $e_1 > e_2$ and $P_1 < P_2$.

Comparing the above results with those for the example for the simple monopolist we observe that X (output) is the same in both cases but the π (profits) of the discriminating monopolist is larger.

Equilibrium Under Price Discrimination in the Dumping Case

A special case of Price discrimination is met when a producer is selling in two markets, one in which he faces perfect competition, while in the other the he has a monopoly. The demand curve for the product will be perfectly elastic for him in the market in which he faces perfect competition, while the demand curve will be sloping downwards in the market in which he enjoys monopoly position. Such situation might occur when a producer sells his product in his home country in which he has a monopoly and also in the world market which is perfectly competitive. Equilibrium in this situation is depicted in figure 155. In the home market in which the producer has a monopoly power, demand curve or the average revenue cure AR^H is sloping downward. So does the MR curve MR^H. In the world market in which he faces perfect competition the demand for his product is perfectly elastic. The AR curve AR^W of the producer in the world market is therefore a horizontal straight line and MR^W curve coincide with it. MC is the marginal cost curve of output. Aggregate marginal revenue curve in this case is the composite curve BFED which is the lateral summation of MR^H and MR^W. The MC curve intersects the aggregate marginal revenue curve BFED at point E and equilibrium output OM is determined. The total output OM is to be distributed between the home market and the world market in such a way that marginal revenue in each market is equal to each other and to the marginal cost ME. Thus, out of total output OM, amount OR will be sold in the home market. From the curve AR^H, it is clear that price OP^H will be charged in the home market. Rest of the amount RM will be sold in the world market at price OP^W.

Area CEFB represents the total profits earned by

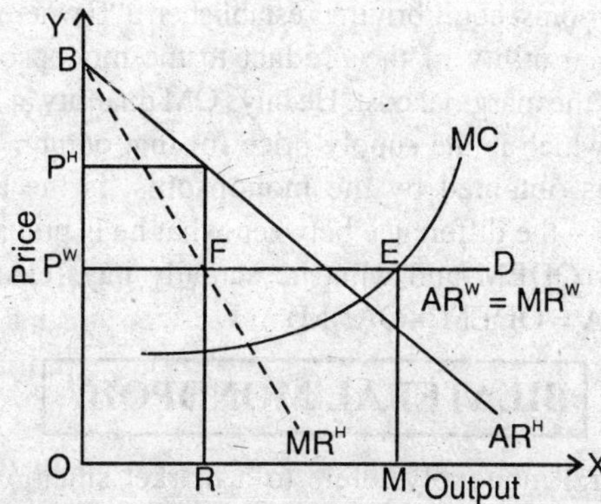

Fig. 155 : *Equilibrium of the Discriminating Monopolist When he has a monopoly in the home-market and faces perfect competition in the world market.*

the producer from both the markets. Price in the world market OP^W is lower than the price OP^H in the home market. **When a producer charges a lower price in the world market than in the home market, he is said to be dumping in the world market.**

Regulation of Monopoly

A monopolist is a suspect in the public eye. He generally exploits the consumers. All governments, therefore, consider it necessary to curb his profit making propensity in the interest of the consumers and the community at large.

The two common methods for regulation of monopoly are :

(a) Price Regulation

(b) Taxation

Price Regulation

It is usual for the Government to regulate prices charged by public utilities like gas and electric companies. The underlying object is to call forth the maximum output consistent with the monopolist's cost and consumer demand. This is shown in Fig. 156. In the absence of price fixation by the Government, the monopolist would produce OM output and charge OP (=MQ) price, because here MR = MC and Q is a point on the demand curve and shows what the consumers are prepared to pay. Now let us suppose the Government fixes a lower price OP^1 ($=ML^1$). At this price, the monopolist produces a larger output OM^1, since this price cuts the demand curve DD at L.

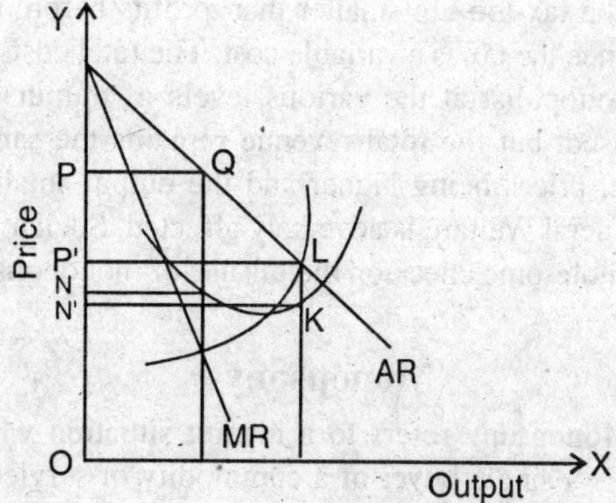

Fig. 156 : *Price Regulation*

Although the monopolist has been compelled to charge a lower price, yet the consuming public has taken a larger quantity. This compensates the monopolist. OM^1 is the new profit-maximising output and his profit will P^1N^1KL. The consumer are benefited by a large amount being made available to them at a lower price.

Taxation

Taxation is regarded as a very suitable device for regulating monopolies so that they are not able to exploit the consuming public by misusing their monopolistic power. Such taxes may be of two types: *(i)* Lumpsum tax irrespective of the quantity of the output and *(ii)* a fixed tax per unit of the output.

The lumpsum tax has to be borne entirely by the monopolist since it cannot be shifted to the consumers by way of the price rise. Already, the monopolist is supposed to have fixed a price which maximises his profit. If he could raise the price further he would have done so. If he could decrease the output to increase his profit, he would have done so. Since he has already fixed price and output which brings him maximum profit, he cannot now touch them. Hence, by imposing a lumpsum tax, the government can take away all or any proportion of his profit without adversely affecting the general welfare. This is, therefore, a very effective way of controlling the monopolist's behaviour.

As for the tax per unit of output, the monopolist will be induced to reduce output and raise the price in order to maximise his profit after paying the per unit tax. The price rise affects the consumer. The profits after the tax too are smaller than profits before the tax; since the tax is a variable cost. The total costs of the monopolist at the various levels of output are increased, but the total revenue remains the same. Hence, prices being higher and the output smaller, the general Welfare is adversely affected. Such a tax is a wholesome check on the misuse of monopolist's power.

Monopsony

Monopsony refers to a market situation when there is a single buyer of a commodity or service it applies to any situation in which there is a 'monopoly' element in buying.

The analysis of monopoly pricing is similar to that under monopoly pricing. Just as a monopolist is able to influence the price of the product by the amount he offers for sale, similarly the monopsonist is able to influence the supply price of his purchases by the amount he buys. Again, the monopolist aims at the maximisation of his surplus. The monopolist equates the marginal cost with his marginal revenue to maximise his profit. The monopsonist regulates his purchases in such a way that marginal cost equals marginal utility whereby his consumer's surplus is the maximum.

The determination of price under monopsony is explained in Fig. 157. The supply curve of the industry is the average cost curve of monopsonist. It is from the industry that the buys the product. This is represented by the curve AC/S in the Figure. MC is its corresponding marginal cost curve. MU is the marginal utility curve of the monopsonist. The monopsonist equilibrium is established at E where the marginal utility of the product to the monopsonist equals the marginal cost. He buys OM quantity at MB price which is the supply price for that output. The surplus obtained by the monopsonist is the area DEBA—the difference between what he is prepared to pay ODEM and what he actually pays OABM (DEBA = ODEM – OABM).

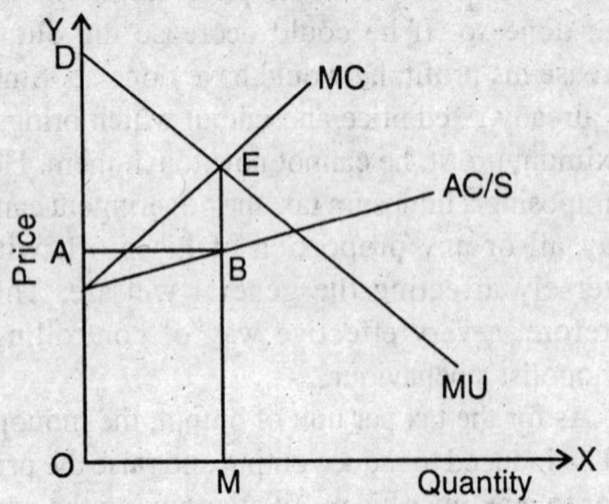

Fig. 157 : *Equilibrium Under Monopsony*

BILATERAL MONOPOLY

Bilateral monopoly refers to a market situation in which a single producer (monopolist) faces a single buyer (monopsonist). For example, if a single Firm produced all the copper in a country and if only one Firm used this metal, the copper market would be a bilateral monopoly market. The equilibrium in such a market cannot be determined by the traditional tools of demand and supply. Economic analysis can only define the range within which the price will eventually be settled. The precise level of the price (and output), however, will ultimately by defined by non-economic factors, such as the bargaining powers, skill and other strategies of the participant Firms. *Under conditions of bilateral monopoly economic analysis leads to indeterminancy which is finally resolved by exogenous factors.*

The following Fig. 158 illustrates the price-output determination in the case of bilateral monopoly. In this Figure DD is the demand curve, MC the marginal cost curve and ME represents the marginal cost of buying an additional unit.

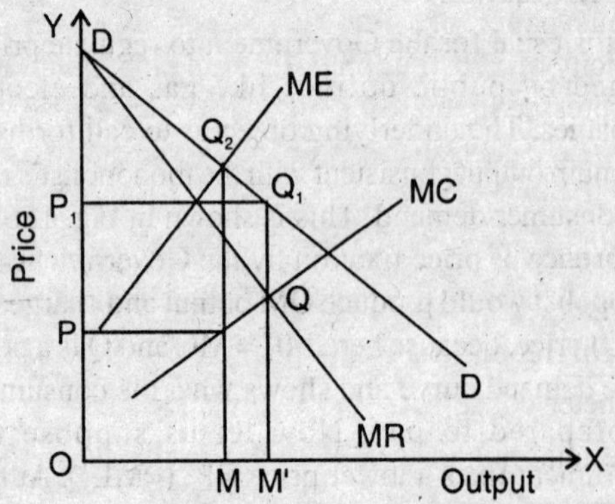

Fig. 158 : *Price-Output in Bilateral Monopoly*

In bilateral monopoly, each side wants to get the better of the other through bargaining skill. The monopolist will like the monopsonist to behave—as if he were one of the many buyers as in perfect competition, so that he (i.e., buyer) may accept the price fixed by him (the monopolist producer). Similarly, the monopsonist will like the monopolist to behave as if he were a perfect—competition producer unable to influence price, so that he (the monopsonist buyer) can purchase at his own price. Now nothing can be said as to who will succeed and how far. Most probably, there will be a compromise between he two extremes.

According to the analysis presented by this diagram, the monopolist will be maximising his profit (MC = MR) if he sold OM^1 output and charged OP_1 ($=M^1Q$) Price, since Q_1 is a point on the demand curve D showing what the purchaser will be willing to pay under perfect competition.

On the other hand, the monopsonist will like to buy OM at OP price, since Q_1, where DD and ME intersect, is a point where buyer's marginal valuation equals marginal cost of purchase. As we have said before, none can hope to achieve his objective completely and there will be a compromise between the positions that each would like to take. Hence, price will be some where between OP and OP_1 and the output between OM and OM^1 depending on the relative bargaining skill of the parties.

THE CES PRODUCTION FUNCTION

Arrow, Chenery, Minhas and **Solow** in their new famous paper of 1961 developed the Constant Elasticity of Substitution (CES) function which may be expressed in the form

$$TP = A\left[\alpha.C^{-\theta} + (1-\alpha)L^{-\theta}\right]^{-1/\theta}$$

Where TP is the total output, C is capital, L is labour. A is the efficiency parameter indicating the state of technology, α (alpha) is the distribution parameter concerned with the relative factor shares in the total output, and θ (theta) is the substitution parameter which determines the elasticity of substitution. And $A > 0$; $0 < \alpha < 1$; $\theta > -1$.

Its Properties

The CES production function possesses the following properties :

1. The CES function is homogeneous of degree one. If we increase the inputs C and L in the CES function by *n*-fold output TP will also increase by *n*-fold as

$$TP^1 = A\left[\alpha(nC)^{-\theta} + (1-\alpha)(nL)^{-\theta}\right]^{-1/\theta}$$

$$= A\left\{n^{-\theta}\left[\alpha C^{-\theta} + (1-\alpha)L^{-\theta}\right]\right\}^{-1/\theta}$$

$$= (n^{-\theta})^{-1/\theta}TP = n.TP$$

Thus like the Cobb-Douglas Production Function, the CES function displays constant returns to scale.

2. In the CES production function, the average and marginal products of the variables C and L are homogeneous of degree zero like all linearly homogeneous productions. For instance, the marginal productivities of inputs C and L are :

$$MP_C = \frac{dTP}{dC}$$

$$= \frac{\alpha}{A.\theta}.\left(\frac{TP}{C}\right)^{1+\theta}$$

$$\text{and } MP_L = \frac{dTP}{dL}$$

$$= \frac{1-\alpha}{A.\theta}.\left(\frac{TP}{L}\right)^{1+\theta}$$

3. From the above property, the slope of an isoquant, i.e., the Marginal Rate of Technical Substitution (MRTS) of capital for labour can be shown to be convex to the origin.

$$\text{MRTS of C for L} = \frac{-dC}{dL}$$

$$= -\frac{MP_L}{MP_C} = -\frac{(1-\alpha)}{\alpha}\left(\frac{C}{L}\right)^{1+\theta}$$

4. The parameter θ (theta) in the CES production function tedermines the elasticity of substitution. In this function, the elasticity of substitution.

$$\sigma = \frac{1}{1+\theta}$$

This shows that the elasticity of substitution is a constant whose magnitude depends on the value of the parameter θ. If $\theta = 0$, then $\sigma = 1$. This reveals that when $\sigma = 1$, the CES production function becomes the Cobb-Douglas production function.

Its Limitations

But the CES function has certain limitations. The CES production function considers only two inputs. It is, therefore, not possible to generalise this function to more than two inputs. Further, the parameter α of the CES function is not dimension less. Again, if data are fitted to the CES function, the value of the efficiency parameter A cannot be made independent of θ or of the units of P, C and L. Lastly, if the CES function is used to describe the production function of a Firm, it cannot be used to discribe the aggregate poduction function of all the Firms in the industry. Thus it involves the problem of aggregation of production functions of different firms in the industry.

Despite these limitations, the CES production function is useful in its application to prove Euler's theorem, to exhibit constant returns to scale, to show that average and marginal products of C and L are homogeneous of degree zero, and to determine the elasticity of substitution.

MONOPOLISTIC COMPETITION

The concept of monopolistic competition put forth by *Prof. Chamberlin* was a true revolutionary as well as more realistic than either pure competition or pure monopoly. Before Chamberlin, monopoly and competition were regarded as two mutually exclusive alternatives; one would be absent when the other exists. On the other hand, according to Chamberlin, in most of the real world economic situations, both monopoly and competitive elements are presents. Chamberlin's concept of monopolistic competition is thus a blending of competition and monopoly. The distinguishing feature of monopolistic competition which makes it as a blending of competition and monopoly is the *differentiation of the product*. This means that the products of various firms are not homogeneous but different though they are closely related to each other. Product differentiation does not mean that the products of various firms are altogether different. They are only slightly different so that they are quite similar and serve as close substitutes of each other.

Assumptions

The basic assumptions of Chamberlin's large-group model are the same as those of pure competition with the exception of the homogeneous product we may summarise them as follows :

1. There is a large number of sellers and buyers in the 'group'.

2. The products of the sellers are differentiated, yet they are close substitutes of one another.

3. There is free entry and exist of Firms in the group.

4. The goal of the Firm is profit maximisation, both in the short run and the long run.

5. The prices of Factors and technology are given.

6. The Firm is assumed to behave as if it knew its demand and cost curves with certainty.

7. The long run consists of a number of indentical short-run periods, which are assumed to be independent of one another in the sense that decisions in one period do not affect future periods and are not affected by past actions. The optimum decision for any one period is the optimum decision for any other period. Thus, by assumption, maximisation of short-run profits implies maximisation of long-run profits.

8. Finally Chamberlin makes the 'heroic' assumption that both demand and cost curves for all 'products' are uniform throughout the group. This requires that consumer's preferences be evenly distributed among the different sellers, and that differences between the products be such as not to give rise to differences in costs.

Cost Curves and Selling Cost

Chamberlin, in his model of monopolistic competition has assumed the traditional U-shaped cost-curves—AC, AVC and MC. In addition he has introduced a new cost, i.e. *Selling Cost*. "Selling Costs are defined as costs incurred in order to alter the

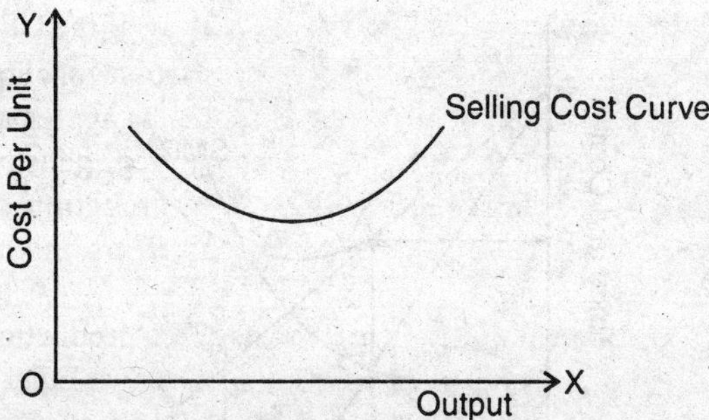

Fig. : *Selling Costs Curve*

position or the shape of the demand curve for a product." Selling costs include all the expenses that are intended to promote the sales, including cost of advertisement, salesman's salaries, expenses of sales department, margins granted to dealers, wholesalers and retailers, window displays and demonstration of new goods.

Chamberlin argues that the selling-costs curve is U-shaped, that is, there are economies and diseconomies of output will not required an equiproportional increase in selling costs, and this leads to a fall in the average selling expenditure. However, beyond a certain level of output the Firm will have to spend more per unit in order to attract customers from other Firms : as output expands the Firm has to attract customers which are well used to the product of other Firms. The U-shaped selling cost, added to the U-shaped production cost, yields a U-shaped ATC curve.

Product Differentiation and the Demand Curve

Product differentiation as the basis for establishing a downward-falling demand curve was first introduced in economic theory by *Sraffa*. Yet it was Chamberlin who elaborated the implication of product differentiation for the pricing and output decisions as well as for he selling strategy of the firm.

Under monopolistic competition no single firm controls more than a small portion of the total output of a product. No doubt there is an element of differentiation, nevertheless the products are close substitutes. As a result, a reduction in price will enable a Firm to increase its sales by attracting some customers of its competitors provided the latter do not reduce the price. Similarly, by raising its price it will be losing many of its customers to its rival Firms. A reduction in its price will no doubt increase the sales of the Firm but it will have little effect on the price-output conditions of other Firms, each will lose only a few of its customers. Likewise, an increase in its price will reduce its demand substantially but each of its rivals will attract only a few of its customers. Therefore, the demand curve (average revenue curve) of a Firm under monopolistic competition slopes downward to the right. It is highly elastic but not perfectly elastic within a relevant range of prices at which he can sell any amount. Since the other products are close substitutes he can neither sell above nor below the narrow range of prices as set by his rivals. This elasticity of an individual Firm's demand curve will, however, depend *Firstly*, upon the value of cross elasticity among the products of the rival sellers; and *Secondly*, on the number of sellers and the contribution of each of the total industry demand.

EQUILIBRIUM UNDER MONOPOLISTIC COMPETITION

The demand curve for the product of an individual Firm, as noted above, is downward sloping. Since the various Firms under monopolistic competition produce products which are close substitutes of each others, the position and elasticity of the demand curve for the product of any of them depend upon the availability of the competiting substitutes and their prices. Therefore, the equilibrium adjustment of an individual Firm cannot be defined in isolation to the general field of which it is a part. However, for sake of simplicity in analysis, conditions regarding the availability of substitute products produced by the rival Firms and prices charged for them are held constant while the equilibrium adjustment of an individual Firm is considered in isolation. Since close substitutes for his products are available in the market, the demand curve for the product of an individual Firm working under conditions of monopolistic competition is fairly elastic thus, although a Firm under monopolistic competition has a monopolistic control over his variety of the product but his control is tempered by the fact that there are close substitutes available in the market and that if he sets too high a price for his product, many of his customers will shift to the rival products.

A. Short-Run Equilibrium

The short-run analysis of the Firm under monopolistic competition is based on the following assumptions :

1. that the number of sellers is large and they act independently of each other. Each is a monopolist in his own spheres;
2. that the product of each seller is differentiated from the other products;
3. that the Firm has a determinate demand curve (AR) which is elastic;
4. that the factor-services are in perfectly elastic supply for the production of the product in question;
5. that the short-run cost curves of each Firm differ from each other; and
6. no new Firms enter the industry.

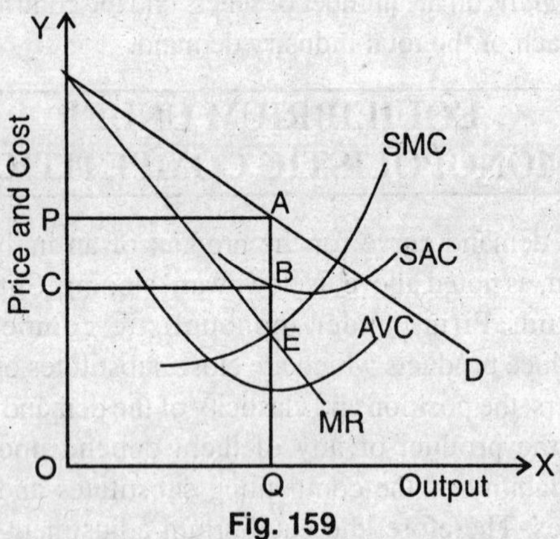

Fig. 159

Given these assumptions, each Firm fixes such price and output which maximises its profit. The equilibrium price and output is determined at a point where the short-run marginal cost equals marginal revenue.

Since costs differ in the short-run, Firm with lower units costs will be earning only normal profits.

In Figure 159 the short-run marginal cost curve (SMC) cuts the marginal revenue curve at E. This equilibrium point establishes the price QA (=OP) and output OQ. As a result the Firm earns *super normal profits* represented by the area PABC.

Figure 160 indicates the same equilibrium point, price and output. But in this case the Firm just covers

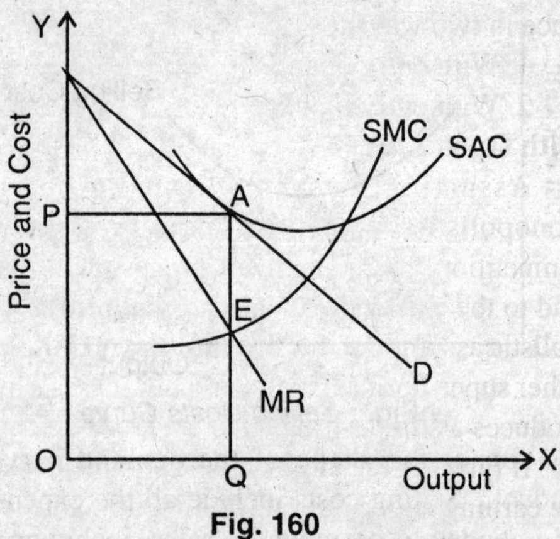

Fig. 160

the short-run average unit cost as represented by the tangency of demand curve (D) and the short-run average unit cost curve (SAC) at A. It earns just normal profits.

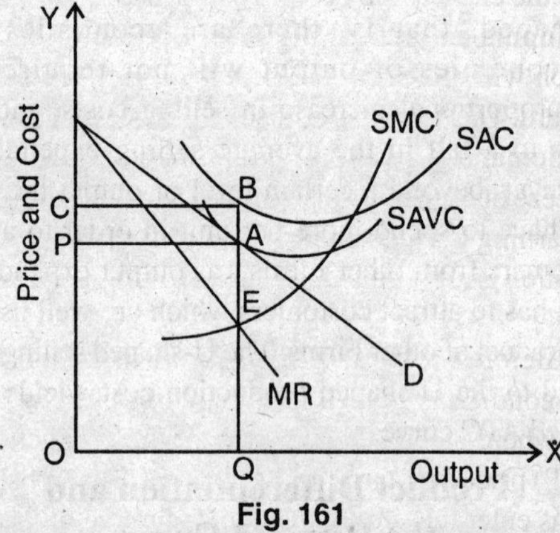

Fig. 161

Figure 161 shows a situation where the Firm is not able to cover its short-run average unit cost and therefore incurs losses. Price set by the equality of SMC and MR curve is QA which covers only the average Variable cost. The tangency of the demand curve (D) and the average variable cost curve (AVC) at A makes it a *shutdown point*. If the Firm lowers the price below QA, it will have to stop further production. However, at this price the Firm will incur losses equal to the area CBAP during the short-run in the hope of lowering its costs in the long-run.

B. Long-Run Equilibrium

In the Long-run the adjustment process may take

place in two ways :

1. With entry open
2. With entry blocked

With Open Entry

Assuming entry and exit of Forms in a monopolistic competitive industry as under pure competition, the adjustment process will ultimately lead to the existence of only normal profits. This is a realistic assumption for the long-run no Firm can earn either super-normal profits or incur losses, since each produces a similar product.

If Firms in the monopolistic competitive industry are earning super-normal profits, new Firms will be attracted into group. With the entry of new Firms, the existing market is divided among more sellers so that each Firm will sell less quantities of the product than before. As a result, the demand curves faced by individual Firms shift down to the left. At the same time the entry of new Firms will increase the demand for inputs and hence the prices of factor services which will shift the cost curves of individual Firms upward. This two-way adjustment process of lowering the demand curve and raising the cost curves will squeeze out super normal profits. Thus, each Firm will be earning only normal profits in the long-run. This situation is represented in Figure 163 vis-a-vis Figure. 162.

Before the entry of new Firms the demand and cost conditions of the Firm are represented in Figure 162 where it sells OQ quantity of the product at QA (=OP) price and earns PABC extra profits. When new Firms enter the group, the demand curve of the Firm shifts downward to D_1 and the long-run marginal and average cost curves shift upward as LMC_1 and LAC_1 as shown in Figure 163. As a result of these two opposite forces excess profits are squeezed out. The Firm earns only normal profits at the point of tangency (A_1) between the demand curve (D_1) and the long-run average cost curve (LAC_1). In this situation each Firm produced less than before (OQ) and also sells at a lower price (OP_1) with the result that further entry into the industry is stopped.

If firms cannot earn extra profits in monopolistic competition, they cannot incur losses either. In such a situation the losing Firms will leave the industry. Supply will be reduced and price will go up. On the other side, resources will become abundant with the exist of Firms, and they will become cheaper. Costs will fall. Ultimately, a rise in price and reduction in costs will eliminate losses. The final situation will be as shown in Figure 163 where each Firm and the industry as a whole will be in long-run equilibrium.

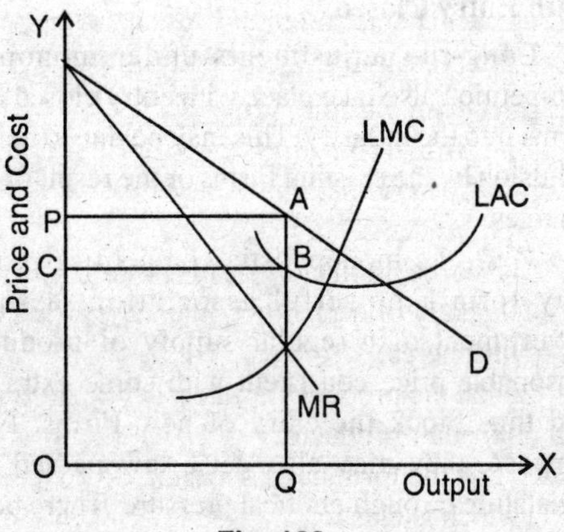

Fig. 162

This long-run equilibrium analysis under monopolistic competition reveals one important fact that each Firm and the entire industry will not produce optimum output. There will always be *excess capacity.* It is evident from Figure. 163 where the point of tangency between the demand curve D_1 and the LAC_1 curve is not at the lowest level L. Rather L is to the right of the point of tangency A_1. *This is because the demand curve D_1 is not horizontal but slopes downward to the right.* This each Firm under monopolistic competition has unutilized capacity even in the long-run.

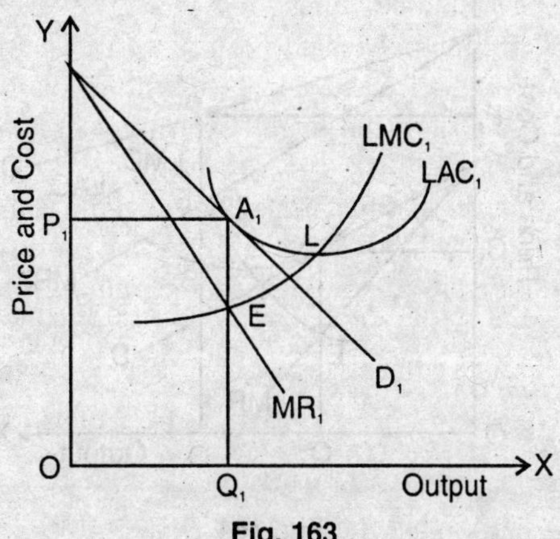

Fig. 163

With Entry Closed

Long-run adjustments under monopolistic competition also take place with entry closed for new Firms into the industry. This may be due to deliberate collusion by the existing Firms or the result of market changes.

First, the monopolistic competitive producers may form a powerful association, assure the government of a regular supply of product at a reasonable price consistent with some extra profits and thus block the entry of new Firms. For this purpose, they may also get a law passed by the legislature through political pressure. There being no threat of entry of new Firms, each Firms will have that price-output combination which brings in maximum profits. Such a profit-maximisation combination is brought about by the equality of long-run marginal cost curve and the marginal revenue curve. In Figure 162, the LMC curve cuts the MR curve at B. When OQ quantities of the product are sold at AQ price, the Firm earns PABC profits. If it tries to increase or decrease the output by changing the scale of production, the LMC would be higher or lower than MR and profits would shrink.

Secondly, if strong consumer preferences are developed for (differentiated) products of certain Firms their demand curves may shift upward. These Firms will thus be in a position to charge higher prices than other Firms and earn extra profits. But extra profits earned by such Firms will not attract new Firms into the industry. Strong consumer preferences for their products will acts as a barrier to the entrance of new Firms. Such a situation is illustrated in Figure 164.

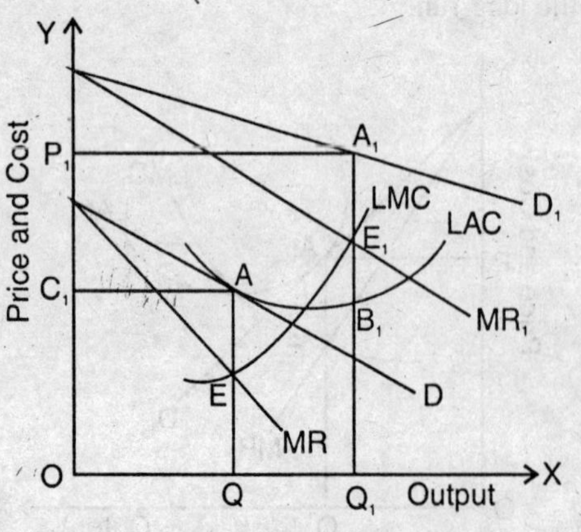

Fig. 164

The original demand curve and its corresponding marginal revenue curve faced by the Firm are D and MR respectively. With the increase in consumer preferences for the product, both the curves shift upward as D_1 and MR_1. The earlier output OQ and price QA were determined by the equality of the LMC curve and the MR curve at point E. This price output combination was realising only normal profits for the Firm. The change in consumer preferences towards the products brings about E_1 the new equilibrium level of OQ_1 output at a higher price Q_1A_1 which maximizes $P_1A_1B_1C_1$ profits. Strong consumer preferences for this product will deter new Firms from entering the industry.

Theory of Excess Capacity

The concept of excess capacity is not of recent origin rather it existed in the earlier works of Wicksell and Cairnes. Piero Sraffa and Mrs. Robinson also outlined it. But it was Chamberlin who expounded it in a most systematic manner followed by Kaldor, Kahn, Harrod and Cassels.

Theories of Chamberlin's monopolistic competition and Joan Robinson's imperfect competition have revealed that a Firm under monopolistic competition or imperfect competition in long-run equilibrium produces an output which is less than socially optimum or ideal output. This means that Firms operate at the point on the falling portion of long-run average cost curve, that is, they do not produce the level of output at which long-run average cost is minimum. Long-run equilibrium of a Firm under monopolistic competition is achieved when the demand curve (AR-curve) facing it becomes tangential to the long-run average cost curve so that it earns only normal profits. Under such circumstances Firms can reduce average cost (and hence price) by expanding output to the minimum level of long-run average cost, but it will not because its profits are maximised (equality of marginal revenue with marginal cost is attained) at the level of output smaller than that at which his long-run average cost is minimum.

Society's productive resources are fully utilised when they are used to produced the level of output which renders long-run average cost minimum.

This means a monopolistically competitive Firm produces less than the socially optimum or ideal output, that is, the output corresponding to the lowest point of average cost curve. This is in sharp contrast to the position of the Firm in long-run equilibrium under perfect competition, which operates at the minimum point of the long-run average cost curve. The amount by which the actual long-run output of the Firm under monopolistic competition falls short of the social ideal output is a measure of *excess capacity* which lie unutilised.

The existence of excess capacity under imperfect or monopolistic competition can be understood from Figures 165 and 166. Figure 166 depicts the long-run position of a perfectly competitive Firm which is in long-run equilibrium at the level of output ON corresponding to which long-run average cost is minimum. It is at output ON that the double condition of long-run equilibrium, namely, Price = MC = AC is fulfilled. It is thus clear that Firms under perfect competition produce socially ideal output. On the other hand, a Firm under monopolistic condition depicted in Figure 165 is in long-run equilibrium at output OM at which its MR is equal to MC and price is equal to average cost (Average revenue curve AR is tangential to average cost curve AC at point F corresponding to output OM). It will be noticed that at output OM average cost is still falling and goes on falling up to output ON.

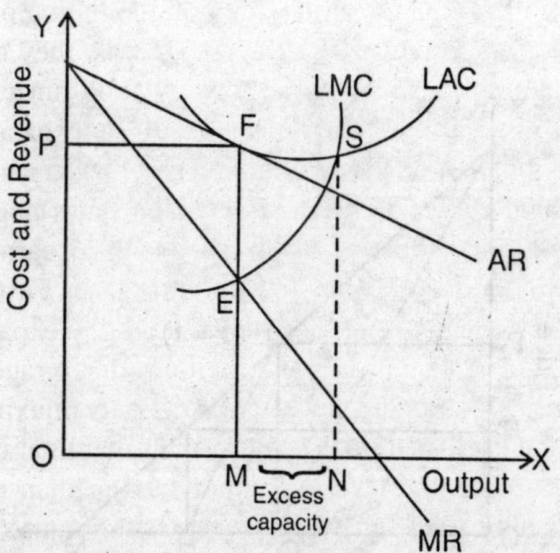

Fig. 165: *Production of Ideal Output (Socially Optimum) Under Imperfect Competition*

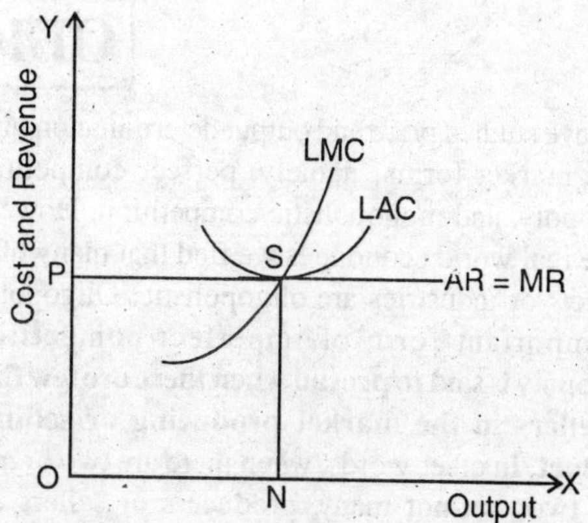

Fig. 166 : *Ideal or Socially Optimum Under Perfect Competition*

This means that the Firm can expand his production up to ON and reduce his long-run average cost to the minimum.

Ideal output is ON at which long-run average cost is minimum. Therefore, the Firm is producing MN less than the ideal output. This MN output represents the excess capacity which emerges under monopolistic competition.

It is worth noting that the concept of excess capacity refers only to the long-run. This is because in the short-run under any type of market structure (including perfect competition) there can be all sorts of departures from the ideal reflecting in complete adjustment to existing market conditions. *Another point worth noting is that excess capacity under monopolistic competition emerges because of the downward-sloping demand curve of the Firm.* A downward sloping curve can be tangent to a U-shaped average cost curve only at the latter's falling portion. It is only the horizontal demand curve or average revenue curve (as is actually found under perfect competition) which can be tangent to a U-shaped average cost curve at the latter's minimum point. From this, it also follows that the greater the elasticity of average revenue (or demand) curve confronting a monopolistically competitive firm, the less the excess capacity and vice versa. When the demand curve facing a Firm is perfectly elastic, there is no excess capacity, as is the case under perfect competition.

OLIGOPOLY

We have studied price and output determination under three market forms, namely, perfect competition, monopoly, and monopolistic competition. However, in the real world economies we find that many of the markets or industries are oligopolistic. Oligopoly is an important form of imperfect competition. **Oligopoly is said to prevail when there are few firms or sellers in the market producing or selling a product.** In other words, when there are two or more than two, but not many, producers or sellers of a product, oligopoly is said to exist. Oligopoly is also often referred to as "**Competition among the Few.**" The simplest case of oligopoly is duopoly which prevails when there are only two producers or sellers of a product.

When products of few sellers are homogeneous, we talk of **Oligopoly without Product Differentiation or Pure Oligopoly.** On the other hand, when products of the few sellers or firms instead of being homogeneous, are differentiated but close substitutes of each other, Oligopoly with Product Differentiation or Differentiated Oligopoly is said to prevail.

COURNOT'S DUOPOLY MODEL

The earliest duopoly model was developed in **1838** by the French economist **Augustin Cournot.**

Cournot assumed that there are two firms each owning a mineral well and operating with zero costs. They sell their output in a market with a straight line demand curve. **Each firm acts on the assumption that its competition will not change its output, and decides its own output so as to maximise profit.**

Cournot's duopoly model has been presented in figure 167. To begin the analysis, suppose that, initially, A is the only seller of mineral water in the market. In order to maximise his profits or revenue, he sells quantity OQ where his MC = O = MR, at price OP_2. His total profit is OP_2PQ.

Now let B enter the market. The market open to him is QM which is half of the total market. That is, he can sell his product in the remaining half of the market. He assumes that A will not change his price and output because he is making the maximum profit. That is, B assumes that A will continue to sell OQ at price OP_2.

Thus, the market available to him is QM and relevant demand curve is PM. When he draws his MR curve, PN, it bisects QM at point N where QN = NM. In order to maximise his revenue, B sells QN at price OP_1. His total revenue is maximum at QRP'N. Note that B supplies only $QN = \frac{1}{4}\left(\frac{1}{2}.\frac{1}{2}\right)$ of the market.

With the entry of B, Price falls to OP_1. Therefore, A's expected profit falls to OP_1, RQ. Faced with this situation, A attempts to adjust his output to the changed condition. He assumes that B will not change his output QN. Accordingly, A assumes that B will continue to supply ¼ of the market and he has ¾ $= \left(1-\frac{1}{4}\right)$ of the market available to him. To maximise his profit, A will therefore supply $\frac{1}{2}.\frac{3}{4}=\frac{3}{8}$ of the market. A's share has fallen from ½ to ¾.

Now B turns to react. Following Cournot's assumption B assumes that A will continue to supply only $\frac{3}{8}$ of the market and the market open to him $1-\frac{3}{8}=\frac{5}{8}$. To maximise his profit under the new

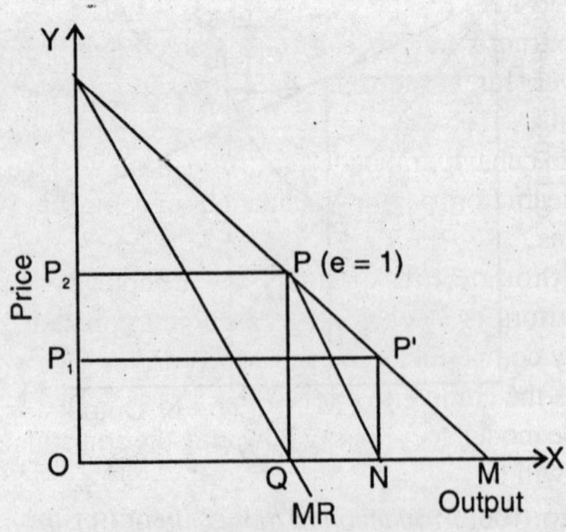

Fig. 167: *Cournot's Model*

conditions, B will supply $\frac{1}{2}.\frac{5}{8}=\frac{5}{16}$ of the market. It is new for A to reappraise the situation and adjust his price and output accordingly.

This process of action and reaction continues in successive periods. In the process A continues to loosen his market share and B continues to gain. Eventually a situation is reached when their market share becomes equal at $\frac{1}{3}$ each.

Thus the Cournot solution is stable. Each firm supplies $\frac{1}{3}$ of the market, at a common price which is lower than the monopoly price, but above the pure competitive price (which is zero in the Cournot example of costless production). It can be shown that if there are three firms in the industry, each will produce one-quarters of the market and all of them together will supply $\frac{3}{4}\left(=\frac{1}{4}.3\right)$ of the entire market OM. And, in general, if there are n firms in the industry each will provide $\frac{1}{(n+1)}$ of the market, and the industry output will be $\frac{n}{(n+1)}$. Clearly as more firms are assumed to exist in the industry, the higher the total quantity supplied and hence the lower the price. The larger the number of firms the closer is output and price to the competitive level.

Criticism

Cournot's model leads to a stable equilibrium. However, his model may be criticised on several accounts:

The behavioural pattern of firms is naive. Firms do not learn from past miscalculations of competitior's reactions.

Although the quantity produced by the competitors is at each stage assumed constant, a quantity competition emerges which drives P down, towards the competitive level.

The model does not say how long the adjustment period will be.

The assumption of costless production is unrealistic.

BERTRAND'S DUOPOLY MODEL

Bertrand developed his duopoly model in 1883. His model differs from Cournot's in that he assumes that each firm expects that the rival will keep its price Constant, irrespective of its own decision about pricing. Thus each firm is faced by the same **market demand,** and aims at the maximisation of its own profit on the assumption that the price of the competition will remain constant.

The model may be presented with the analytical tools of the reaction functions of the duopolists. In Bertrand's model the reaction curves are derived from **isoprofit maps** which are convex to the axes, on which we now measure the prices of the duopolists. Each isoprofit curve for firm A shows the same level of profit which would accrue to A from various levels of prices charged by this firm and its rival. The isoprofit curve for A is convex to its price axis (P_A). This shape shows the fact that firm A must lower its price up to a certain level (point e in figure 168) to meet the cutting of price of its competitior, in order to maintain the level of its profits at A_2. However, after that price level has been reached and if B continues to cut its price, firm A will be unable to retain its profits, even if it keeps its own price unchanged (at P_3). If , for example, firm B cuts its price at B, firm A will find itself at a lower isoprofit curve A_1 which shows lower profits. The reduction of profits of A is due to the fall in price, and the increase in output beyond the optimal level of utilisation of the plant with the consequent increase in costs. Clearly the lower the isoprofit curve, the lower the level of profits.

To Summarise : For any price charged by firm B there will be a unique price of firm A which maximises the latter's profit. This unique profit - maximising price is determined at the lowest point on the highest attainable isoprofit curve of A. The minimum points of the isoprofit curves lie to the right of each other, reflecting the fact that as firm A moves to a higher level of profit, it gains some of the customers of B when the latter increases its price, even if A also raises its price. If we join the lowest points of the successive isoprofit curves we obtain the reaction curve of firm A: this is the locus of points of maximum profits that A can attain by charging a certain price, given the

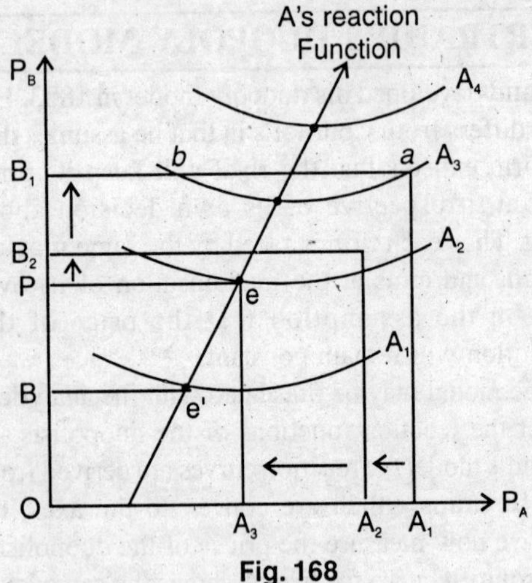

Fig. 168

price of its rival.

The reaction curve of firm B may be derived in a similar way, by joining the lowest points of its isoprofit curves (Figure 169).

Bertrand's model leads to a stable equilibrium, defined by the point of intersection of the two reaction curves.

Bertrand's model may be criticised on the same grounds as Cournot's model:

The behavioural pattern emerging from Bertrand's assumption is naive: firms never learn from past experience.

Each firm maximises its own profit, but the industry (Joint) profits are not maximised.

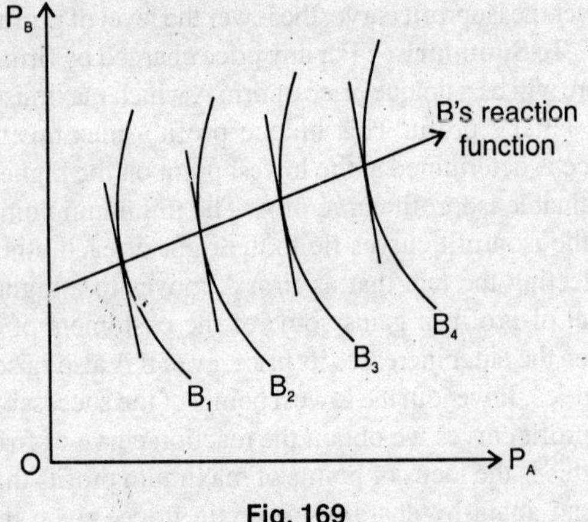

Fig. 169

The equilibrium price will be the competitive price. (In the example of costless mineral-water production, the price in Bertrand's model would fall to zero. If production is not costless, then price would fall to the level which would cover the costs of the duopolists inclusive of a normal profit.)

The model is 'closed'– does not allow entry.

STACKELBERG'S DUOPOLY MODEL

This model was developed by the German economist **Heinrich von stackelberg** and is an extension of Cournot's model. Stackelberg assumes that one of the duopolist (Say A) is sophisticated enough to play the role of a leader and the other (Say B) acts as a follower. The leading duopolist A recognises that his rival seller B has a definite reaction function which A uses into his own profit function and maximises his profits. In summary, if only one firm is sophisticated, it will emerge as the leader, and a stable equilibrium will emerge, since the naive firm will act as a follower.

However, if both firms are sophisticated, then both will want to act as leaders, because this action yields a greater profit to them. In this case the market situation becomes unstable. The situation is known as **Stackelberg's disequilibrium** and the effect will either be a price war until one of the firms surrenders and agrees to act as follower, or a collusion is reached, with both firms abandoning their naive reaction functions and moving to a point closer to (or on) the Edgeworth contract curve with both of them attaining higher profits. If the final equilibrium lies on the Edgeworth contract curve the industry profits (Joint profits) are maximised.

Stackelberg's model has interesting implications. It shows clearly that naive behaviour does not pay. The rivals should recognise their interdependence.

By recognising the other's reactions each duopolist can reach a higher level of profit for himself.

If both firms start recognising their mutual interdependence, each starts worrying about the rival's profits and the rival's reactions. If each ignores the other, a price war will be inevitable, as a result of which both will be worse off.

This model shows that a bargaining procedure and a collusive agreement becomes advantageous to both duopolists. With such a collusive agreement the duopolists may reach a point on the Edgeworth contract curve, thus attaining joint profit maximisation.

A Numerical Example of Stackelberg's Model

Assume that in a duopoly market the demand function is

$$P = 100 - 0.5\,(X_1 + X_2)$$

and the duopolist's costs are

$$C_1 = 5X_1$$

$$C_2 = 0.5\,X_2^2$$

The reaction functions are found by taking the partial derivatives of the duopolist's profit functions and equating them to zero:

$$\pi_1 = PX_1 - C_1$$

$$= 95\,X_1 - 0.5\,X_1^2 - 0.5\,X_1\,X_2$$

$$\pi_2 = PX_2 - C_2$$

$$= 100X_2 - X_2^2 - 0.5\,X_1\,X_2$$

The partial derivatives are

$$\frac{d\,\pi_1}{d\,X_1} = 95 - X_1 - 0.5\,X_2 = 0$$

$$\frac{d\,\pi_2}{d\,X_2} = 100 - 2X_2 - 0.5\,X_1 = 0$$

The reaction functions are

$$X_1 = 95 - 0.5\,X_2 \rightarrow \text{A's reaction curve}$$

$$X_2 = 50 - 0.25\,X_1 \rightarrow \text{B's reaction curve}$$

1. Stackelberg's solution with A being the sophisticated leader.

Firm A will substitute B's reaction function in its own profit equation, which it will then maximise as if it were a monopolist:

$$\pi_1 = PX_1 - C_1$$

$$= 95\,X_1 - 0.5\,X_1^2 - 0.5\,X_1\,X_2$$

Substitute

$$X_2 = 50 - 0.25\,X_1$$

Maximise

$$\pi_1 = 70\,X_1 - 0.375\,X_1^2$$

(a) First-order condition :

$$\frac{d\,\pi_1}{d\,X_1} = 70 - 0.75\,X_1 = 0$$

This yields output :

$$X_1 = 93\frac{1}{3}$$

and profit:

$$\pi_1 = 70\,X_1 - 0.375\,X_1$$

$$= 3267$$

(b) The second-order condition for profit maximisation is fulfilled.

Firm B would be the follower. It would assume that A would produce $93\frac{1}{3}$ units; thus B substitutes this amount in its reaction function.

$$X_2 = 50 - 0.25X_1$$

$$= 26\frac{2}{3}$$

and its profit would be

$$\pi_2 = 100X_2 - X_2^2 - 0.5\,X_1\,X_2$$

$$= 155.5$$

2. Stackelberg's solution if firm B is the sophisticated duopolist

Firm B will substitute A's reaction function in its own profit function, and it will proceed to maximise this profit as a monopolist.

$$\pi_2 = PX_2 - C_2$$

$$= 100X_2 - X_2^2 - 0.5\,X_1\,X_2$$

Substitute

$$X_1 = 95 - 0.5\,X_2$$

$$\pi_2 = 52.5X_2 - 0.75\,X_2^2$$

(a) The first-order condition for the maximisation of π_2 requires.

$$\frac{d\,\pi_2}{d\,X_2} = 52.5 - 1.5\,X_2 = 0$$

which yields output:

$$X_2 = 35$$

and profit :

$$\pi_2 = 52.5\,X_2 - 0.75\,X_2^2$$

$$= 918.75$$

(b) The second-order condition for the maximisation of π_2 is fulfilled.

The follower is now firm A which will act on the Cournot assumption; it will assume that the rival will keep his quantity at $X_2 = 35$, and will find its own output by substituting this quantity in its reaction function.

$X_1 = 95 - 0.5 X_2$
$= 77.5$

and its profit is

$\pi_1 = 95 X_1 - 0.5 X_1^2 - 0.5 X_1 X_2$
$= 3003$

3. Stackelberg's disequilibrium

If both entrepreneurs adopt Stackelberg's sophisticated pattern of behaviour, each will examine his profits if he acts as a leader and if he acts as a follower, and will adopt the action that will yield him the greatest profit.

Firm A Calculates its profits both as a leader and as a follower:

- If A is the leader his profits are 3267
- If A is the follower his profits are 3003

Clearly firm A will prefer to act as the leader.

Firm B similarly, calculates its profits as a leader and as a follower:

- If B is the leader his profits are 918.75
- If B acts as the follower his profits are 155.50

Thus firm B will also choose to act as the leader.

With both firms acting in the sophisticated way implied by Stackelberg's behavioural hypothesis both will want to act as leaders. As they attempt to do so they find that their expectations about the rival are not fulfilled and 'warfare' will start, unless they decide to come to a collusive agreement.

NON-COLLUSIVE MODELS OF OLIGOPOLY

The theory of non-collusive or uncoordinated oligopoly is one of the oldest theories of competition and monopoly or perhaps of all the theories of the behaviour of the individual firm. The non collusive models of oligopoly explain the price and output determination in a market structure in which oligopolists recognise their interdependence. A model of oligopoly was first of all put forth by **Cournot** in 1838. Cournot's model of oligopoly was subjected to criticism in 1883 by Joseph Bertrand, a French mathematician, whose criticism of Cournot provided a substitute model of oligopoly. In 1897, Edgeworth offered another model of oligopoly in an article published in an Italian Journal.

It should be noted that in Cournot's model, it is rival's output which is assumed by an oligopolist to remain fixed at the present level, while he contemplates a certain change in his own output. On the other hand, Bertand and Edgeworth in their models assume that the oligopolist believes that rival's price remains unchanged at the present level.

COLLUSIVE OLIGOPOLY

There are at least three major factor which bring collusion between the oligopolistic firms. Firsts collusion reduces the degree of competition between the firms and helps them act monopolistically in their effort of profit maximisation. Second, collusion reduces the oligopolistic uncertainty surrounding the market since cartel members, are not supposed to act independently and in the manner that is detrimental to the interest of other firms. Third, collusion forms a kind of barrier to the entry of new firms.

Collusion between oligopoly firms may take many forms depending on their relative strength, their objective and whether collusion is legal or illegal. There are however two main types of collusion:

(i) Cartels
(ii) Price leadership

CARTELS

A cartel is a formal organisation of the oligopoly firms in an industry. Cartels are the perfect form of collusion. A cartel is an organisation of independent firms within the same industry formed for the purpose of increasing the profits of the members of subjecting their competitive tendencies to some form of control. If follows common policies in relation to prices, outputs and sales territories. Cartels may be in the form of **open collusion** or secret collusion. Whether open or secret, cartel agreements are explicit and formal in the sense that agreements are enforceable on member firms willing to pursue an independent pricing policy. Cartels are therefore regarded as the perfect form of collusion.

A cartel performs a variety of services for its members. The two typical services of central importance are *(a)* fixing price for joint maximisation of industry profits; and *(b)* market sharing between its members. In this section, we will examine these two activities of cartels.

A. Cartels Aiming at Joint-Profit Maximisation

Cartels imply direct agreements among the competing oligopolist with the aim of reducing the uncertainty arising from their mutual interdependence. In this particular case the aim of the cartel is the maximisation of the industry profit. Let us suppose that a group of firms producing a homogeneous commodity form a cartel aiming at joint profit maximisation. The firms appoint a central management board with powers to decide *(a)* the total quantity to be produced; *(b)* the price at which it must be sold; and *(c)* share of each firm in the total output. The central management board is provided with cost figures of individual firms. Besides, it is supposed to obtain the necessary data required to formulate the market demand (AR) curve. The management board calculates the marginal cost (MC) and marginal revenue (MR) for the industry. Further, the management board holds the position of a multiplant monopoly. It determines the price and output for each firm in the manner a multiplant monopoly determines the price and output for each plant.

The model of price and output determination for each firm has been presented in figure 170. It is assumed for the sake of convenience that there are only two firms A and B, in the cartel. Their respective cost curves are given in the first two panels of the figure. In the third panel, the AR and MR curves represent the revenue conditions of the industry. The MC curve is the summation of MC curves of the individual firms. The MC and MR intersect at point C determining the industry output at OQ. The market price is determined at PQ. The industry output OQ is so allocated between firms A and B that their individual MC = MR. The share of each firm in the industry output OQ, can be obtained by drawing a line from point C and parallel to X-axis through MC_2 and MC_1. The points of intersection C_1 and C_2 determine the level of output for firms A and B respectively. Thus, the share of each of the two firms A and B, is determined at Oq_1 and Oq_2, where $Oq_1 + Oq_2 = OQ$.

Note that the firm with the lower costs produces a larger amount of output. However, this does not mean that A will also take the larger share of the attained joint profit. The total industry profit is the sum of the profits from the output of the two firms, denoted by the shaded areas of figures. The distribution of profits is decided by the central agency of the cartel.

B. Market-Sharing Cartels

This form of collusion is more common in practice because it is more popular. The firms agree to share the market, but keep a considerable degree of freedom concerning the style of their output, their selling activities and other decisions. There are two basic methods for sharing the market: non-price competition and determination of quotas.

Price Leadership

Another form of collusion is price leadership. In this form of co-ordinated behaviour of oligopolists one firm sets the price and the others follow it because

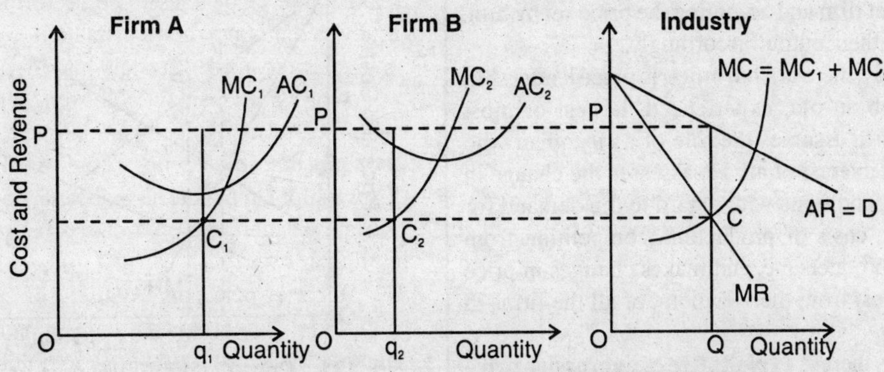

Fig. 170 : *Price and Output Determination Under Cartel*

it is advantageous to them or because they prefer to avoid uncertainty about their competitor's reactions even if this implies departure of the followers from their profit-maximising position. Price leadership is widespread in the business world. It may be practised either by explicit agreement or informally. In nearly all cases price leadership is tacit since open collusive agreements are illegal in most countries.

Price leadership is more widespread than cartels, because it allows the members complete freedom regarding their product and selling activities and thus is more acceptable to the followers than a complete cartel, which requires the surrendering of all freedom of action to the central agency.

If the product is homogeneous and the firms are highly concentrated in a location the price will be identical. However, if the product is differentiated prices will differ, but the direction of their change will be the same, while the same price differentials will broadly be kept.

Types of Price Leadership

Price leadership is of various types. Firstly, there is a price leadership of the dominant firm. Under this one of the few firms in the industry may be producing a very large proportion of the total production of the industry and may therefore dominate the market of the product. This dominant firm wields a great influence over the market of the product, while other firms are small and are incapable of making any impact on the market. As a result, the dominant firm estimates its own demand curve and fixes a price which maximises its own profits. The other firms which are small having no individual effects on the price, follow the dominant firm and accepting the price set by him, they adjust their output accordingly.

Secondly, there is a **barometric price leadership** under which an old, experienced, largest or most respected firm assumes the role of a custodian who protects the interest of all. He assesses the change in the market conditions with regard to the demand for the product, costs of production, competition from the related products etc. and makes changes in price which are best from the viewpoint of all the firms in the industry.

Thirdly, there is **exploitative** or **aggressive price** leadership under which a very large or dominant firm establishes its leadership by following aggressive price policies and thus compel the other firms in the industry to follow him in respect of price. Such a firm will often initiate a move threatening to compete the others out of the market if they do not follow him in setting their prices.

Price-Output Determination Under Price Leadership

Economists have developed various models concerning price-output determination under price leadership taking different assumptions about the behaviour of price leader and his followers. We shall confine ourselves to price-output determination under dominant price leadership and explain a simple case. We make the following assumptions:

1. There are two firms, A and B. The firm A has a lower cost of production than B.

2. The product produced by the two firms is homogeneous so that the consumers have no preference between them.

3. Each of the two firms has equal share in the market. In other words, demand curve facing each firm will be the same and will be half of the total market demand curve of the product.

Given the above assumptions, price and output determination under price leadership is illustrated in figure 171. Each firm is facing demand curve DD which is half of the total market demand curve for the product. MR is the marginal revenue curve of each firm. MC_a is the marginal cost curve of firm A and

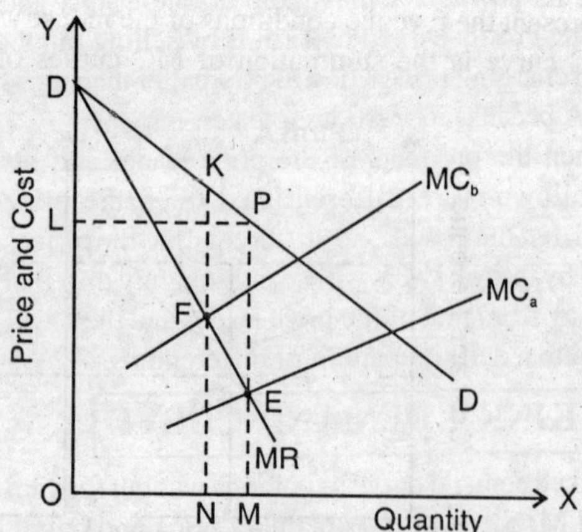

Fig. 171 : *Price-Output Equilibrium under Price Leadership*

MC_b is the marginal cost curve of firm B. MC_a lies below MC_b because we are assuming that firm A has a lower cost of production than firm B.

The firm A will be maximizing its profits by selling output OM and setting price MP, since at output OM, its marginal cost is equal to the marginal revenue. Firm B's profits will be maximum when it fixes price NK and sells output ON. It will be seen from the figure that profit maximizing price MP of firm A is lower than the profit-maximizing price NK of firm B. Since the two firms are producing a homogeneous product, they cannot charge two different prices. Because the profit-maximizing price MP of firm A is lower than the profit-maximizing price NK of firm B, firm A will dictate the price to the firm B or in other words, firm A will win if there is price war between the two and will emerge as a price leader and firm B will be compelled to follow. Thus firm A will be the price leader and firm B will be the price follower.

It should be noted that having been compelled to charge price MP, the firm B will produce and sell output OM. This is because at price MP, it can sell OM output like firm A because the demand curve facing each firm is the same. Thus both the firms will charge the same price (MP) and sell the same amount (OM). But there is an important difference between the two. While firm A, the price leader, will be maximizing its profits by selling output OM and charging price MP, the firm B will not be making maximum profits with this price output combination because its profits are maximum at output ON and price NK. Profits earned by firm B by selling output OM and charging price MP will be smaller than those of firm A because its costs are greater.

When the products of the price leader and his price-followers are differentiated, then the price charged by them will be different but the prices charged by the followers will be only slightly different either way from that of the price leader and they will conform to a definite pattern of differentials.

KINKY DEMAND CURVE

The Kinked demand curve hypothesis was put forward by **Paul M. Sweezy.** In explaining price and output especially under oligopoly with product differentiation economists often use the kinked

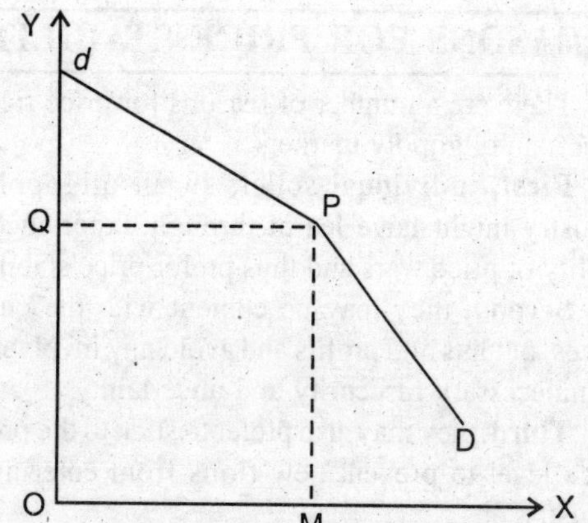

Fig. 172 : *Kinked Demand Curve Under Oligopoly.*

demand curve hypothesis. This is because when under oligopoly products are differentiated, it is unlikely that when a firm raises its price, all customers would leave it because some customers are intimately attached to it due to product differentiation. As a result, demand curve facing a firm under differentiated oligopoly is not perfectly elastic.

The demand curve facing an oligopolist, according to the kinked demand curve hypothesis, has a **'Kink'** at the level of the prevailing price. The kink is formed at the prevailing price level because the segment of the demand curve above the prevailing price level is highly elastic and the segment of the demand curve below the prevailing price level is inelastic. A kinked demand curve D with a kink at point P has been shown in figure 172. The prevailing price level is MP and the firm is producing and selling the output OM.

Now the upper segment *d*P of the demand curve dD is relatively elastic and the lower segment PD is relatively inelastic. This difference in elasticities is due to the particular competitive reaction pattern assumed by kinky oligopoly demand curve hypothesis.

The competitive reaction pattern assumed by the kinky oligopoly demand curve theory is as follows: **Each oligopolist believes that if he lowers the price below the prevailing level his competitors will follow him and will accordingly lower their prices, whereas if he raises the price above the prevailing level his competitors will not follow his increase in price.**

REASONS FOR PRICE STABILITY

There are a number of reasons for price rigidity in certain oligopoly markets.

First, individual sellers in an oligopolistic industry might have learnt through experience the futility of price wars and thus prefer price stability.

Second, they may be content with the current prices, outputs and profits and avoid any involvement in unnecessary insecurity and uncertainty.

Third, they may also prefer to stick to the present price level to prevent new firms from entering the industry.

Fourth, the sellers may intensify their sales promotion efforts at the current price instead of reducing it. They may view non-price competition better than price rivalry.

Fifth, after spending a lot of money on advertising his product, a seller may not like to raise its price to deprive himself of the fruits of his hard labour. Naturally, he would stick to the going price of the product.

Lastly, it is the kinked demand curve analysis which is responsible for price rigidity in oligopolistic markets.

In order to study the working of the kinked demand curve, let us analyse the effect of changes in cost and demand conditions on price stability in the oligopolistic market.

Decline in Costs

When the cost of production declines, the price is more likely to remain stable. When the cost of production falls, then the segment of the demand curve above the current price will become more elastic because with lower costs there is a greater certainty that the increase in price by an oligopolist will not be followed by his rivals and will thus cause greater in sales. On the other hand, with lower costs the segment of the demand curve below the current price will become more in elastic because with the decline in costs, there is then greater certainty that the reduction in price by an oligopolist will be followed by his rivals with the upper segment becoming more elastic and the lower segment more in elastic than before, the angle dPD will become less obtuse and hence the gap in the marginal revenue curve will increase As a result of the increase in the gap (that is, the length of discontinuity) in the MR-curve, the lower MC curve is likely to pass through this gap showing that the price and output remain the same as before.

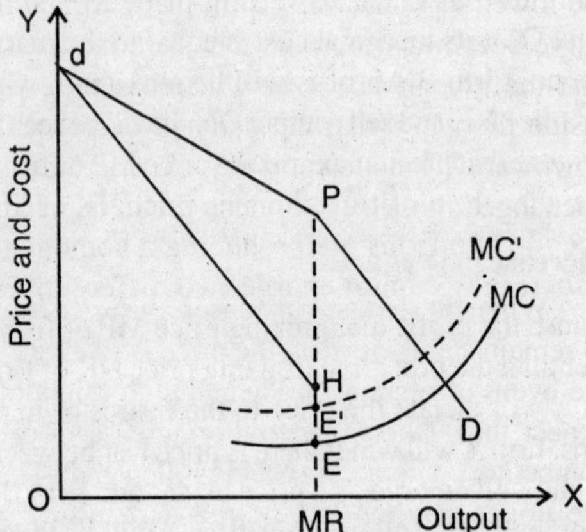

Fig. : *Changes in costs within limits do not affect the oligopoly price*

Rise in Cost

If there is a rise in the cost of the oligopolistic industry, the price is not likely to stay rigid. When there is a rise in cost of the industry an oligopolist can reasonably expect that his increase in price will be followed by the others in the industry. Consequently, the segment of the demand curve above the prevailing price will become less elastic and thereby make the angle dPD more obtuse and this will narrow down the gap in the MR-curve with the smaller gap in the MR-Curve, the higher MC curve is likely to cut it above the upper point H indicating that the equilibrium price will rise and the equilibrium output will fall. Thus it follows from the kinked demand curve theory that price is not likely to remain stable in the event of rise in cost.

Decrease in Demand

In case of decrease in demand, the price is very likely to remain inflexible and will not fall. When the demand decreases, it becomes more certain that if one oligopolist initiates the reduction in price, others will follows with the result that the lower segment of the demand curve will become more inelastic. On the other hand, in the case of a decline in demand it is very certain that the increase in price by one oligopolist will never be followed by others. As a result, the upper segment of the demand curve becomes more elastic, that is, it becomes more nearly horizontal. With the increase in the elasticity of the upper segment and the decrease in the elasticity of the lower segment, the gap in the marginal revenue curve becomes wider and therefore it is most likely that the given MC curve will cross the MR curve inside the gap when the demand curve dPD shifts downward. This indicates that the price will remain unchanged in the case of decrease in demand.

Increase in Demand

When the demand increases, the price is unlikely to remain stable, instead the price is likely to rise. In the event of increase in demand, an oligopolist can expect that if he initiates the increase in price, his competitors will most probably follow him. Therefore, the upper segment dP of the demand curve will become less elastic and the angle dPD will become more obtuse. As a result, the gap HR in the MR curve will decrease and if this gap decreases much, it is very likely that the marginal cost curve crosses the marginal revenue curve above the upper point H, that is, above the gap, indicating that the price will rise above MP.

From above, it is clear that the kinked demand curve analysis of oligopoly explains stability in price in the case of falling costs or declining demand, whereas, prices are likely to rise when the costs rise or demand increases.

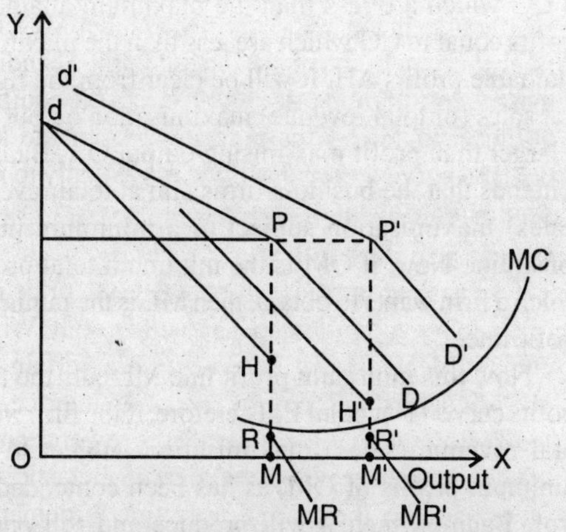

Fig. : *Changes in demand do not effect the oligopoly price.*

PROF. STIGLER'S EMPIRICAL STUDY REGARDING KINKY DEMAND CURVE

Prof. George J. Stigler has made an empirical study of the behaviour of the oligopolies in order to test the theory of Kinked demand curve. His empirical study suggests that there does not exist any 'Kink' in the demand curve confronting oligopolists. Prof. Stigler has therefore rejected the hypothesis of Kinked demand curve under oligopoly. It has been observed by him that in inflationary periods oligopolists do often follow one another's price rises, contrary to what is assumed in the kinky demand theory.

FULL-COST PRICING THEORY

After the marginalist revolution, profit maximisation by the firm is generally explained by the marginal analysis, that is, by the use of marginal revenue and marginal cost concepts. An important alternative approach to profit maximisation and marginal analysis based upon is the **full-cost pricing theory** which does not assume that rational firms seek to maximise profits. Full-cost pricing theory is also known as average-cost pricing theory, since in this theory price of a product is fixed on the basis of average cost.

In 1939, **Hall and Hitch** of the University of Oxford mounted a 'root-and-branch' attack on the notion of profit maximisation on the basis of answers to questionaires of 38 entrepreneurs, 33 of whom were manufacturers, 3 retailers and 2 builders. From this empirical study they found that firms for fixing prices do not maximise profits by equating marginal cost with marginal revenue. It is worth mentioning here that they argued not only against marginal analysis of pricing by the firms but also challenged the notion that in fixing prices firms maximise their profits. Profit maximisation, according to them, was a wrong way to approach the question of pricing by the business firms. Indeed they pointed out that business firms in the real world only tried to seek a satisfactory profits or, in other words, normal or conventional rate of profit. Thus, according to them, prices are fixed on the basis of full-cost, that is, average direct (variable) costs plus average overhead cost plus a margin for profit. Thus, a full-cost price includes *(i)* average variable cost (which Hall and Hitch call average direct cost), *(ii)* average overhead cost, and *(iii)* a normal or satisfactory margin of profit.

SALES MAXIMISATION MODEL OF OLIGOPOLY

Sales maximisation model of oligopoly is another important alternative to profit maximisation model. This has been propounded by **W.J. Baumol,** an American economist. Sales maximisation model represented one of the managerial theories of the firm because in it, the great importance had been given to the managerial role and to his pursuing self-interest in marking price output and advertising policies. Prof. Baumol thinks that managers are more interested in maximising sales than profits.

It should be noted that by sales maximisation Baumol does not mean the maximisation of the physical volume of sales but the maximisation of total revenue from sales, that is, the dollar value of the sales made. Therefore, his theory is also known as **revenue maximisation model.** Further Baumol does not ignore profit motive altogether. He argues that there is a minimum acceptable level of profits which must be earned by the management so as to finance future growth of the firm through retained profits and also to induce the potential share holders for subscribing to the share capital of the company. Thus, according to him, management of oligopolistic firms seeks to maximise sales or, in other words, total revenue subject to this minimum profit constraint

Sales Maximisation: Price-Output Determination

It is better to explain graphically price output determination in Prof. Baumol's sales or total revenue maximisation model. Consider figure 173 where the *y*-axis measures total revenue, total cost and total profits in terms of rupees and the *x*-axis measures the total output. TR and TC are respectively total revenue and total cost curves. Since total cost curve TC starts from the origin, it means the diagram refers to the long-run cost revenue situation. TP is the total profits curve which first rises and then after a point falls down ward. Since total profits are the difference between total revenue and total costs at various levels of

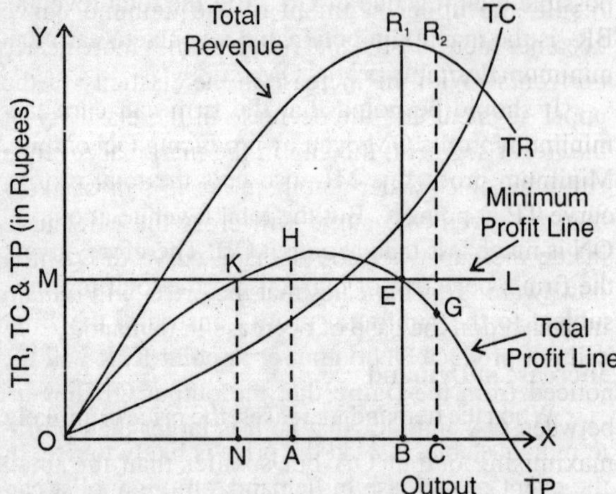

Fig. 173: *Baumol's Sales Maximisation Hypothesis*

output, therefore total profits curve measures the vertical difference between the TR and TC at various levels of output.

If the firm aims at maximising profits, it will produce OA output. This is because corresponding to OA output, the highest point of TP curve lies. But according to Prof. Baumol, the firm does not seek maximisation of profits. On the other hand, if the firm wants to maximise sales (or total revenue) it will fix output at OC level which is greater than OA. At output OC total revenue is CR_2 which is maximum in the diagram. At this total revenue (sales) maximising output level OC, the firm is making total profits equal to CG which are less than the maximum attainable profits equal to CG which are less than the maximum attainable profits AH. It will be clear from the figure that sales (or total revenue) maximisation output OC is larger than profit maximising output OA. Baumol contends that the business firms aim at total revenue (sales) maximisation subject to a minimum profit constraint. Now, if OM is the minimum total profits which a firm wants to obtain, then ML is the minimum profit line.

Now this minimum profit line ML cuts the total profits curve TP at point E. Therefore, if the firm wants total revenue (sales) maximisation subject to the minimum profits of OM, as has been contended by Prof. Baumol, then it will produce and sell output OB. At output OB, the firm will be having total revenue equal to BR_1 which is less than the maximum possible total revenue of CR_2. But the total revenue BR_2 is the maximum obtainable revenue to earn the minimum desirable profits OM.

It should be noted that the firm can earn the minimum profits OM even by producing ON output. Minimum profit line ML also cuts the total profits curve TP at point K. But the total revenue at output ON is much less than at output OB. Therefore, given the firm's objective of maximising the total revenue subject to the minimum profit constraint, the firm will not produce ON output or at point K. It will be noticed from the figure that the output OB lies in between OA and OC, that is, it is larger than profit maximising output OA but smaller than the total revenue maximising output OC. Thus, in Prof. Baumol's model, oligopolistic firm will be in equilibrium at output OB and will be earning profits BE (or OM). It should be carefully noted that the objective of total revenue (or sales) maximisation subject to the minimum profit constraint leads to a greater output and lower price than does profit maximisation.

The price charged at output OB will be equal to $\frac{\text{Total Revenue}}{\text{Output}}$ that is, $\frac{BR_1}{OB}$.

Note : The sales maximiser will produce a higher level of output as compared to a profit maximiser.

Proof.

A profit maximiser produces the output X_π defined by the equilibrium condition MR = MC or

$$\frac{dR}{dX} = \frac{dC}{dX}$$

Given that the marginal cost is always positive ($dc/dx > 0$) It is obvious that at the level X_π the marginal revenue is also positive $\left(\frac{dR}{dX} > 0\right)$. That is, TR is still increasing at X_π, since its slope is still positive. In other words, the maximum of the TR curve $\left(\text{where its slope is } \frac{dR}{dX} = 0\right)$ occurs to the right of the level of output at which profit is maximised. Hence $X_S > X_\pi$:

The sales maximiser sells at a price lower than the profit maximiser. The price at any level of output is the slope of the line through the origin to the relevant point of the total-revenue curve (corresponding to the particular level of output). In figure 174 the price of the profit maximiser is

$$P_{\pi m} = \begin{bmatrix}\text{slope} \\ \text{of OA}\end{bmatrix} = \frac{R_\pi}{T_\pi}$$

While the price of the sales maximiser is

$$P_{sm} = \begin{bmatrix}\text{Slope} \\ \text{of OB}\end{bmatrix} = \frac{R_s}{X_s}$$

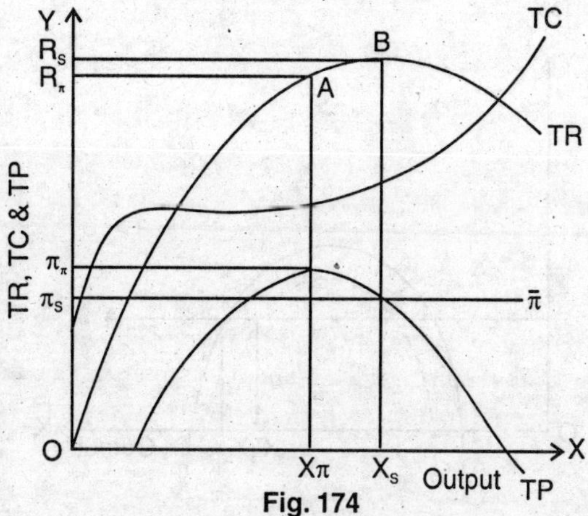

Fig. 174

It is obvious that (slope OA) > (slope OB), that is, the price of the profit maximiser is higher than the price of the sales maximiser.

The sales maximiser will earn lower profits than the profit maximiser. In figure 175 the profit of the sales maximiser is $O\pi_s$ which is lower than the profit $O\pi_n$ of the profit maximiser.

The sales maximiser will never choose a level of output at which price elasticity (e) is less than unity, because from the expression.

$$MR = P\left(1 - \frac{1}{e}\right)$$

We see that if $|e| < 1$, the MR < O, denoting that TR is declining. The maximum sales revenue will be where $|e| = 1$ (and hence MR = O) and will be earned only; if the profit constraint is not operative if the profit constraint is operative the price elasticity will be greater than unity.

An increase in the fixed costs will affect the equilibrium position of a sales maximiser: he will reduce his level of output and increase his price, since the increase in fixed costs shifts the total-profit curve downwards. Subject to the profit constraint, the sales maximiser will pass the increase in costs to the customers by charging a higher price. This is shown in figure 175. The increase in fixed costs shifts the total costs upwards and the total-profits curve downwards (π^1). Subject to the profit constraint π, the firm will reduce its output (to X's) and will increase its price.

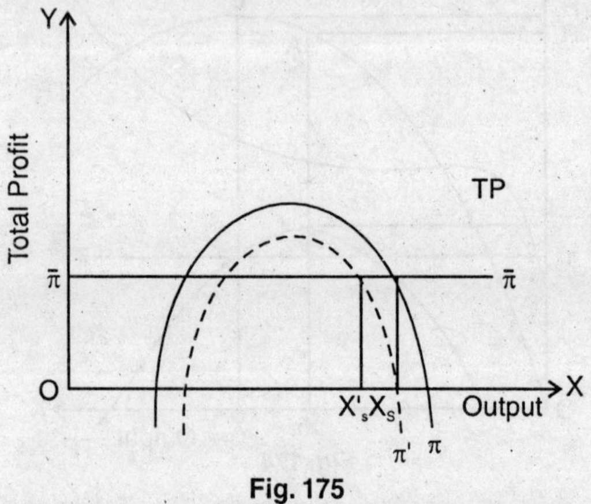

Fig. 175

This prediction is contrary to the traditional hypothesis of profit maximisation. A profit maximiser will not change his equilibrium position in the short run, since fixed costs do not enter into the determination of the equilibrium of the firm. So long as the fixed costs do not vary with the level of output the change in the TFC will not lead the profit maximiser to change his price and output in the short run.

The imposition of a lump-sum tax will have similar effects. If the firm is a profit maximiser the imposition of the lump-sum tax will not affect the price and output in the short-run: the profit maximiser will bear the whole burden of the lump-sum tax. If the firm is a sales maximiser, however, the lump-sum tax will shift the total profit curve downwards and, given the profit constraint, the firm will be led to cut its level of output and increase its price, thus passing on to the consumer the lump-sum tax. Baumol argues that firms do infact shift the tax on to the buyers, contrary to the accepted doctrine about the 'unshiftability' of the tax.

The imposition of a specific tax (per unit of output) will shift the profit curve downwards and to the left (figure 176). Given $\bar{\pi}$, the sales maximiser will reduce his output from X_s to X'_s and will raise his price, passing the tax to the buyers (at least partly). The profit maximiser will also reduce his output (from X_π to X'_π) and raise his price. However, the decrease in output will be larger than the decrease of the output of a profit maximiser.

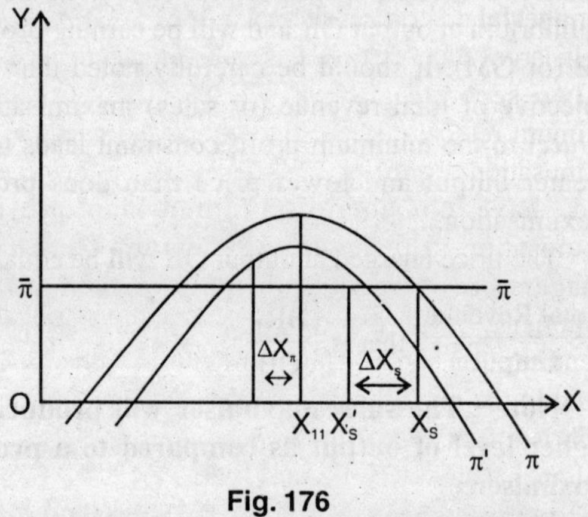

Fig. 176

A similar analysis holds for an increase in the variable cost. Both the sales maximiser and the profit maximiser will raise their price and reduce their output. The reduction in output, however, and the increase in price will be more accentuated for the sales maximiser, ceteris paribus.

A shift in demand will result in an increase in output and sales revenue but the effects on price are not certain in Baumol's model. Price will depend on the shift of the demand and the cost conditions of the firm.

SATISFACTION MAXIMISATION

Scitovsky favours maximisation of satisfaction in preference to the profit-maximisation objective of the firm. According to him, an entrepreneur would maximise profits only if his choice between more income and more leisure is independent of his income. In other words, the supply of entrepreneurship should have zero income elasticity. But an entrepreneur does not aim at profit maximisation. He wants to maximise satisfaction and keep his efforts and output below the level of maximum profits. This is because as his income (profit) increases, he prefers leisure to effort (output).

UTILITY MAXIMISATION

Williamson has developed the utility maximisation hypothesis as against profit maximisation. Like Baumol's sales maximisation theory, it is one of the managerial theories. It is also known as the **'managerial discretion theory.'**

In large modern firms, shareholders and managers are two separate groups. The former want the maximum return on their investment and hence the maximisation of profits. The managers, on the other hand, have consideration other than profit maximisation in their utility functions. Thus the managers are interested not only in their own emoluments but also in the size of their staff and expenditure on them. Thus Williamson's theory is related to the maximisation of the manager's utility which is a function of the expenditure on staff and emoluments and discretionary funds.

To pursue his goal of utility maximisation, the manager directs the firms's resources in three ways:

First, the manager desires to expand his staff and to increase their salaries. "More staff are valued because they lead to the manager getting more salary, more prestige and more security." **Second,** to maximise his utility, the manager indulges in "feather bedding" such as pretty secretaries, company cars, too many company phones, 'perks' for employees etc. Such expenditures are characterised as **'management slack'** by Williamson. **Third,** the manager likes to set up "discretionary funds" for making investments to advance or promote company projects that are close to his heart Discretionary funds (or profits or investments) are what remains with the manager after paying taxes, and dividends to shareholders in order to retain effective control of the firm.

Thus the manager's utility function is

$$U = f(S, M, ID)$$

Where U is the utility function, S is the staff expenditure, M is the management slack and ID is the discretionary investments. These decision variables (S, M, ID) yield positive utility and the firm will always choose their values subject to the constraint, $S \geq O$, $M \geq O$, $ID \geq O$. It implies that after-tax profits are big enough to pay satisfactory dividends and for economically necessary investment.

Further, Williamson regards price (P) as a function of output (X), expenditure on staff (S), and the state of environment which he calls 'a demand shift parameter' (E), So that $P = f(X, S, E)$.

The Williamson utility-maximisation model is explained diagrammatically in figure 177 where profits to the owner-stockholders are measured on the vertical axis and the staff or emoluments are measured along the horizontal axis. FC is the feasibility curve showing the combinations of profits and staff available to the manager. UU is the utility curve of the manager.

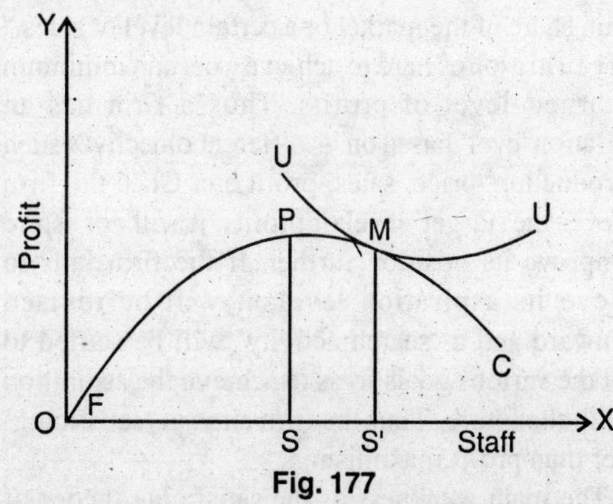

Fig. 177

To begin, as we move along the feasibility curve from point F upward, both profits and staff (or manager's emoluments) increase till point P. P is the profit maximisation point for the firm where SP is the maximum profit level by employing OS staff. But the manager chooses the tangency point M where his utility function UU and the feasibility curve FC touch each other. Here the manager's utility is maximised. The stockholders profits S'M are less than the profit-maximisation profits SP, but the staff or manager's emoluments are maximised. However, Williamson points out that factors like taxes, changes in business conditions, etc. by affecting the feasibility curve can shift the optimum tangency point. Similarly, factors like changes in staff, emoluments, profits of stockholders etc. by changing the shape of the utility function will shift the optimum position.

Williamson's utility-maximisation model is superior to Baumol's sales-maximisation model because it also explains the facts involved in Baumol's theory. Williamson does not treat sales maximisation as a single criterion like Baumol but as a means of the manager for increasing his staff and emoluments. This approach is rather more realistic.

SATISFICING THEORY

Herbert Simon was the first economist to propound the behavioural theory of the firm. According to him, the firm's principal objective is not maximising profits but satisficing. In Simon's words: "We must expect the firm's goals to be not maximising profits but attaining a certain level or rate of profit, holding a certain share of the market or a certain level of sales." Every firm aspires hard to achieve a certain minimum or 'target' level of profits. Thus a firm has an 'aspiration level' based on its different objectives such as production, price, sales, profit etc. Once the firm achieves the 'target' level of profits, it will not aspire to improve its position further. If the firm fails to achieve its aspiration level, it will be revised downward and a 'search activity' will be started to fulfil the various goals so as to achieve the aspiration level in the future. Thus the firm aims at 'satisficing' rather than profit maximising.

The main weakness of the satisficing theory of Simon is that he has not specified the 'target' level of profits which firm aspires to reach. Unless that is known it is not possible to point out the precise areas of conflict between the objectives of profit maximising and satisficing.

BEHAVIOURAL THEORY OF CYERT AND MARCH

Cyert and March have put forth a more systematic theory about the behaviour of the firm than the satisficing theory of Simon. They deal not only with the internal organisation of the firm but also with the problem of uncertainty.

Cyert and March regard the modern business firm as a complex organisation in which the decision making process should be analysed in variables that effect organisational goals, expectations and choice. It is difficult to visualise an organisation having goals. But they look at a firm as an 'organisational coalition' of managers, workers, share holders, suppliers, customers and so on. Looked at from this angle, the firm can be supposed to have different goals: Production, inventory, sales, market share and profit goals.

According to Cyert and March, all goals must be satisfied because they are relevant to price, output and sales strategy decisions of the organisation. These goals are regarded as the product of a 'bargaining learning process' in the organisational coalition. But it is not essential that the different goals may be resolved amicably. There may be conflict between these goals. The organisational coalition is thus a coalition of conflicting interests.

However, the conflicting interests can be reconciled by the distribution of 'side payments' to members of the coalition. Side payments may be in cash or kind, the latter being mostly in the form of 'policy side payments' i.e., the right to take part in the policy decisions of the organisation. But the actual amount of total side payments is not fixed for the coalition but depends upon the demand of the members and on the form of the coalition. However, if the side payments are in excess of what is required to maintain the organisation or the coalition, there appears what Cyert and March call **'organisational slack'**. The organisational slack is the difference between total resources and total necessary payments. Slack consists in payments to members of the coalition in excess of what is required to maintain the organisation. From time to time virtually every participant in an organisation obtains slack payments. Some participants ordinarily obtain a greater share of the slack than do others. In general, those members of the coalition who are full-time, tend to accumulate more slack than other members. The organisational slack helps the firm in maintaining itself under 'crisis' type situation. When there is a crisis type situation, the firm tries to dispose of over-stocked goods by reducing the retail price by one-third while on high-priced items a 40 percent mark-down is taken. In such a situation, side payments to members are likely to be reduced which are made up by organisation slack. This helps the coalition to continue as usual. In the mark-up model when prices are raised to meet increase in the cost of products during inflation, excess side payments are distributed among the members to satisfy their enhanced demand.

Besides side payments, the conflicting goals of the organisation are resolved by subjecting them to a constant review. This is because 'aspiration levels' of coalition members change with experience.

Hence the behavioural theory of Cyert and March is an important contribution to the theory of the firm which brings into focus 'multiple', changing and acceptable goals in managerial decision making and replaces maximising by satisficing.

THEORY OF GAMES

The theory of games is one of the most outstanding recent developments in economic theory. It was first presented by **Neumann** and **Morgenstern** in their classic work **Theory of Games and Economic Behaviour** published in 1944 which has been regarded as a "rare event" in the history of ideas.

Games theory grew as an attempt to find the solution to the problems of duopoly, oligopoly and bilateral monopoly. In all these market situations a **determinate solution** is difficult to arrive at due to the conflicting interests and strategies of the participants. The theory of games attempts to arrive at various equilibrium solutions based on the rational behaviour of the market participants under all conceivable situations.

The underlying idea behind game theory is that each participant in a game is confronted with a situation whose outcome depends not only upon his own strategies but also upon the strategies of his opponent. It is always so in chess or poker games, military battles and economic markets. We shall be concerned mainly with the various solutions of the duopoly problem. But before we start the analysis of the theory of games, it will be useful in digress on certain fundamentals of game theory.

A game has set rules and procedures which two or more participants follow. A participant is called a **player.** A strategy is a particular application of the rules leading to specific result. A move is made by one player leading to a situation having alternatives. A choice is the actual alternative chosen by a player. The various strategies followed by each player in relation to the other is called his **pay-off.** The **saddle point** in a game is the equilibrium point. There are two types of games: **constant-sum** and non-constant sum. In a **constant-sum game** what one player gains the other loses. The profits of the participants remain the same. Whereas in a non-constant-sum game, profits of each player differ and they may co-operate with each other to increase their profits.

The **pay off matrix** of a firm is a table showing the pay-offs accruing to this firm as a result of each possible combination of strategies adopted by it and by its rival. For example, assume that there are two firms in the industry. Firm I has to choose among five strategies (A_1, A_2 .....A_5) and firm II can react by adopting any one of six strategies open to it (B_1, B_2......B_6). Thus to each strategy of Firm I there are six possible counter strategies of Firm II, and similarly to each strategy of Firm II there are five counter strategies of the rival Firm I. Thus the pay off matrix of each firm will include $5 \times 6 = 30$ pay-offs, corresponding to the results of each possible combination of strategies selected by both rivals.

Let us denote each pay off Gij, where *i* refers to the strategy adopted by Firm I and J to the counter-strategy adopted by Firm II. Thus for the above example the pay off matrix for Firm I will be of the general form of table A. If Firm I adopts strategy A_1 and its rival reacts by adopting among the strategies open to it B_5, the pay off (gain) of Firm I will be G_{15}. If Firm I chooses strategy A_4 and its rival reacts with strategy B_6, the pay off of Firm I will be G_{46}, and so on.

Table A. Payoff matrix of Firm I

Firm I's strategies	Firm II's strategies B_1	B_2	B_3	B_4	B_5	B_6
A_1	G_{11}	G_{12}	G_{13}	G_{14}	G_{15}	G_{16}
A_2	G_{21}	G_{22}	G_{23}	G_{24}	G_{25}	G_{26}
A_3	G_{31}	G_{32}	G_{33}	G_{34}	G_{35}	G_{36}
A_4	G_{41}	G_{42}	G_{43}	G_{44}	G_{45}	G_{46}
A_5	G_{51}	G_{52}	G_{53}	G_{54}	G_{55}	G_{56}

In the theory of games the firms in oligopolistic markets are treated as players in a chess game: to each movement by one player the other may choose among several counter-movements. The counter-movements of rivals are probable but not certain.

Yet it is possible to choose a strategy which (under certain conditions) will maximise the firm's expected 'gain', after making due allowance for the effects of rival's probable reactions.

Two-Person Zero-Sum Game

A. Certainty Model

The simplest model is a duopoly market in which each duopolist attempts to maximise his market share. Given this goal, whatever a firm gains (by increasing its share of the market) the other firm loses (because of the decrease in its share). Thus any gain of one rival is offset by the loss of the other, and the net gain sums up to zero. Hence the name **'Zero-sum game'**.

The assumptions of the model are:

1. The firms have a given, well-defined goal. In our particular example the goal is maximisation of the market share.

2. Each firm knows the strategies open to it and to its rival, or concentrates on the most important of these strategies.

3. Each firm knows with certainty the pay-offs of all combinations of the strategies being considered. This implies that the firm knows its total revenues total costs and total profit from each combination of strategies.

4. The actions chosen by the duopolists do not affect the total size of the market.

5. Each firm chooses its strategy 'expecting the worst from its rival', that is, each firm acts in the most conservative way, expecting that the rival will choose the best possible counter-strategy open to him. This behaviour is defined as 'rational'.

6. In the zero-sum game there is no incentive for collusion, given assumption 4, since the goals of the firms are diametrically opposed.

In order to find the equilibrium solution we need information on the pay off matrix of the two firms. In our example the pay-offs will be shares of the market resulting from the adoption of any two strategies by the rivals. Assume that Firm I has four strategies open to it and Firm II has five strategies. The pay off matrices of the duopolists are shown in table B and table C.

Table B. Payoff matrix of Firm I

Firm I's strategies	Firm II's strategies B_1	B_2	B_3	B_4	B_5
A_1	(0.10)	0.20	0.15	0.30	0.25
A_2	0.40	(0.30)	0.50	0.55	0.45
A_3	0.35	0.25	(0.20)	0.40	0.50
A_4	0.25	(0.15)	0.35	0.60	0.20

Table C. Payoff matrix of Firm II

Firm I's strategies	Firm II's strategies B_1	B_2	B_3	B_4	B_5
A_1	0.90	0.80	0.85	0.70	0.75
A_2	[0.60]	[0.70]	[0.50]	0.45	0.55
A_3	0.65	0.75	0.80	0.60	[0.50]
A_4	0.75	0.85	0.65	[0.40]	0.80

Clearly the sum of the pay-offs in corresponding cells of the two payoff tables add up to unity, since the numbers in these cells are shares, and the total market is shared between the two firms. In general, in the two person zero-sum game we need not write both payoff matrices because of the nature of the game: the goals are opposing, and, in our example, the payoff table of Firm I contains indirectly information about the payoff of Firm II. Still we start by showing both tables, and then we show how the equilibrium solution can be found from only the first payoff matrix.

Choice of Strategy by Firm I

Firm I examines the outcomes of each strategy open to it. That is, Firm I examines each row of its pay off matrix and finds the most favourable outcome of the corresponding strategy, because the firm expects the rival to adopt the most advantageous action open to him. This is the behavioural rule implied by assumption 5 of this model.

Thus:

If Firm I adopts strategy A_1, the worst outcome that it may expect is a share of 0.10 (which will be realised if the rival Firm II adöpts its favourable strategy B_1).

If Firm I adopts strategy A_2, the worst outcome will be a share of 0.30 (If the rival adopts the best action for him, B_2).

If Firm I adopts strategy A_3, the worst outcome will be a share of 0.20 (if Firm II chooses the best open alternative, B_3).

If Firm I adopts strategy A_4, the worst outcome will be a share of 0.15 (which would be realised by action B_2 of Firm II).

Among all these **minima** (that is, among the above worst outcomes) Firm I chooses the **'maximum'**, the 'best of the worst'. This is called a **maximin strategy,** because the firm chooses the maximum among the minima. In our example the maximin strategy of Firm I is A_2, that is, the strategy which yields a share of 0.30.

Choice of Strategy by Firm II

Firm II behaves in exactly the same way. The only difference is that Firm II examines the columns of its pay off table, because these columns include the results-payoff of each of the strategies open to Firm II. For each strategy, that is, for each column, firm II finds the worst outcome (on the assumption that the rival will choose the best), and among these worst outcomes Firm II chooses the best. Thus, if Firm II uses its own payoff table, its behaviour is a maximin behaviour identical to the behaviour of Firm I.

However, as we said earlier, in the zero-sum game only one payoff matrix is adequate for the equilibrium solution. In our example the first payoff table will be used not only by Firm I but also by Firm II. Thus concentrating on the First payoff table we may restate the decision-making process of Firm II as follows. Firm II examines the columns of the (first) payoff matrix because these columns contain the information about the pay-offs of its strategies. For each column-strategy Firm II finds the maximum payoff (of Firm I) because this is the worst situation the firm (II) will face if it adopts the strategy corresponding to that column. Thus for strategy B_1 the worst outcome (for Firm II) is 0.40; for strategy B_2 the worst outcome is 0.30; for strategy B_3 the worst outcome is 0.50; for strategy B_4 the worst result is 0.60; for strategy B_5 the worst result is 0.50. Among these maxima of each column-strategy Firm II will choose the strategy with minimum value. Thus the strategy of Firm II is a **minimax** strategy, since it involves the choice of a minimum among the maxima pay-offs (Table D).

It should be stressed that although different terms are used for the choice of the two firms (maximin behaviour of Firm I, minimax behaviour of Firm II); the behavioural rule for both Firms is the same: each Firm expects the worst from its rival.

In our example the equilibrium solution is strategy A_2 for Firm I and B_2 for Firm II. This solution yields shares 0.30 for Firm I and 0.70 for Firm II. It is an equilibrium solution because it is the preferred one by both firms. This solution is called the **'saddle point'**, and the preferred strategies A_2 and B_2 are called **'dominant strategies'**.

Table D. Payoff Matrix

Firm I's strategies (maximum behaviour)	Firm II's strategies (minimum behaviour)				
	B_1	B_2	B_3	B_4	B_5
A_1	0.10	0.20	0.15	0.30	0.25
A_2	0.40	0.30	0.50	0.55	0.45
A_3	0.35	0.25	0.20	0.40	0.50
A_4	0.25	0.15	0.35	0.60	0.20

It should be clear that there exists no such equilibrium (saddle) solution if there is no payoff which is preferred by both firms simultaneously. Under certain mathematical conditions other solutions and strategy choices can be determined.

B. Uncertainty Model

The assumption that each firm knows with certainty the exact value of the payoff of each strategy is unrealistic. The most probable situation in the real business world is that the firm, by adopting a certain strategy, may expect a range of results for each counter-strategy of the rival, each result with an associated probability. Thus the payoff matrix is constructed so as to include the expected value of each payoff. The expected value is the sum of the products of the possible outcomes of a pair of strategies (adopted by the two firms) each multiplied by its probability:

$$E(G_{ij}) = g_{1i}P_1 + g_{2i}P_2 + \ldots\ldots + g_{ni}P_n$$

$$\sum_{S=1}^{n} g_{Si}\, P_S$$

where

g_{Si} = the Sth of the n possible outcomes of strategy *i* of Firm I (given that Firm II has chosen strategy J)

P_S = the probability of the Sth outcome of strategy *i*

For example, assume that Firm I chooses strategy A_1 and Firm II reacts with strategy B_1. This pair of simultaneous strategies may yield the shares for Firm I each with a certain probability, shown in the second column of table D. Thus expected payoff of the pair of strategies A_1 and B_1 is

$$E(G_{11}) = (0.00)(0.00) + (0.05)(0.05) + (0.15)(0.05) + \ldots + (0.95)(0.02) + (1)(0) = 0.458$$

In a similar way we find the expected payoff of all combinations of strategies. Given the matrix of expected pay-offs, the behavioural pattern of the firms is the same as in the certainty model.

That is:

Firm I adopts the **maximin strategy.** It finds for each row the minimum expected payoff, and among these minima the firm chooses the one with the highest value (the maximum among the minima).

Firm II adopts the **minimax strategy.** It finds for each column the maximum expected payoff, and among these maxima Firm II chooses the one with the smallest value (the minimum among the maxima).

Table D

Possible shares of Firm I for the pair of strategies A_1, B_1	*Probability of each share*
0.00	0.00
0.05	0.05
0.15	0.05
0.25	0.10
0.35	0.15
0.45	0.25
0.55	0.20
0.65	0.10
0.75	0.05
0.85	0.03
0.95	0.02
1.00	0.00
	$\sum Pi = 1$

Although the uncertainty zero-sum game seems simple, its assumptions are quite stringent:

1. The firms maximise their expected pay-offs.

2. The zero-sum game assumes that both firms assign the same probability to each pair of pay-offs; they make the same judgement. This implies that the firms must have the same information and the same objective criteria with which to evaluate the probabilities of the different pay-offs. Otherwise the probability distribution of the pay-offs will not be objective.

3. The firms maximise their total utility, and the utility of each payoff is proportional to the value assumed by the payoff.

The above assumptions are clearly strong and unrealistic. Further more, the basic condition of the zero-sum game, that the 'gain' of one firm is equal to the 'loss' of the other, is rarely met in the real business world. Usually the 'gains' are not 'offset' by equal 'losses'. Only in the case of a share goal, and in the rare case of extinction tactics, we have a zero-sum game. In most cases we have a non-zero-sum game.

FACTOR PRICING ANALYSIS

Theory of factor pricing or the theory of distribution is concerned with analysis of how and in what manner the factors of production get remuneration for their contribution to the production process as the production of goods and services in an economy is the result of the joint efforts of factors of production.

Though like the pricing of goods, the factor pricing is also based on market demand and supply, the essential difference between these two lies in the force operating behind demand and supply of these factors. How much will be the demand for a factor depend upon the quantity of goods that it helps to produce and the extent of demand for these goods in the market. Thus, the demand for a factor of production depends upon the demand for its products in the market. This type of demand is known as derived demand.

CONCEPTS OF PRODUCTIVITY

Average Physical Productivity is the total production divided by the number of units of a factor employed.

Average Productivity of a factor

$$= \frac{\text{Total Output}}{\text{Total Number of units of a factor}}$$

Marginal physical productivity of a factor is the increase in total output caused by employing an additional unit of the factor, quantity of other factors remaining fixed.

$$MP_L = \frac{dX}{dL} \text{ and } MP_K = \frac{dX}{dK}$$

Where

MP_L = marginal productivity of labour

MP_K = marginal productivity of capital

dX = change in output

dL = change in labour

dK = change in capital.

Marginal Revenue Product (MRP)

Marginal Revenue Product is the increment in the total value product caused by employing an additional unit of a factor, the expenditure on other factors remaining unchanged. In other words, marginal revenue product is the marginal physical product of the factor multiplied by the marginal revenue.

$$MRP = MPP \times MR$$

Value of Marginal Product (VMP)

It means the marginal physical product of the factor multiplied by the price of the product (i.e. average revenue).

$$VMP = MPP \times \text{Price (or AR)}$$

Since under perfect competition the demand curve of the product facing an individual firm is perfectly elastic and therefore price and marginal revenue are equal, the value of marginal product and marginal revenue product are equal to each other as is shown in Figure 178. But since in monopoly or imperfect competition average revenue (or demand curve) is falling downward and MR curve lies below the average revenue curve, price is not equal to marginal revenue. Therefore, in monopoly or in others forms of imperfect competition, MRP will not be equal to the value of marginal product (VMP). Since price is higher than marginal revenue under monopoly or monopolistic competition in the product market, the value of marginal product (VMP) will be larger than the marginal revenue product (MRP) and the marginal revenue product (MRP) curve will lie below the value of marginal product (VMP) curve as is shown in figure

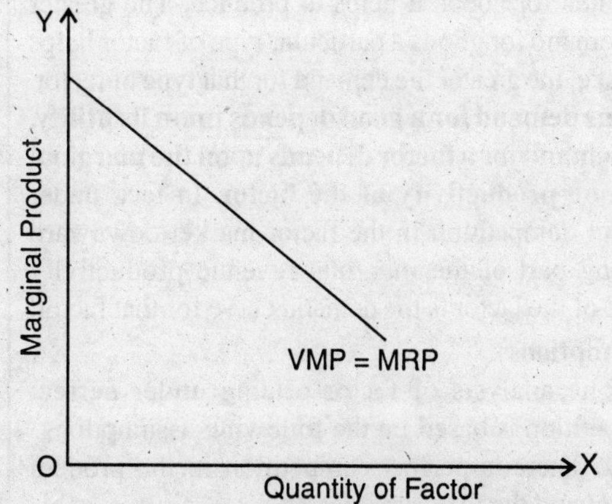

Fig. 178: *VMP and MRP under perfect competition in the Product Market*

179. Thus, **in perfect competition MRP and VMP have identical meanings but in imperfect competition they diverge.**

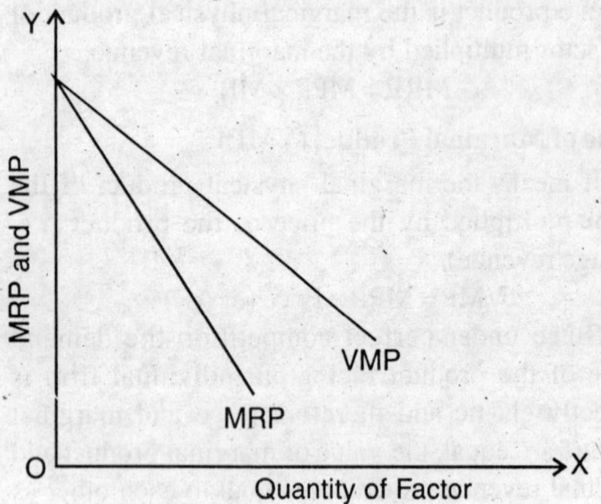

Fig. 179: *VMP and MRP under Imperfect Competition in the Product Market*

FACTOR PRICES UNDER PERFECT COMPETITION

According to the modern theory of pricing of factors of production, under condition of perfect competition it is the forces of demand for and supply of factors which determine their prices. The demand for a factor service is **derived demand** which is derived from the demand for the product that it helps to produce. Thus the demand for a factor ultimately depends upon the demands for goods it helps to produce. The greater the demand for goods a particular type of factor helps to make, the greater the demand for that type of factor. **Just as demand for a good depends upon its utility, the demand for a factor depends upon the marginal revenue productivity of the factor.** In fact, under perfect competition in the factor market downward sloping part of the marginal revenue productivity curve of the factor is the demand curve for that factor.

Assumptions

The analysis of factor pricing under perfect competition is based on the following assumptions.

1. There is perfect competition in the product market and the factor market.

2. The number of buyers and sellers of factor services is large.

3. All units of a factor are homogeneous.

4. Factors of production are perfectly mobile.

5. There is perfect substitutability between factors and their units.

6. All factor-units are divisible.

7. Buyers and sellers of factor services have complete knowledge about market conditions.

8. Buyers and sellers of factor services have complete freedom to enter and leave the market.

The supply of a factor service means the number of units which a resource owner sells at a particular price. There is a direct relationship between price and the supply of a factor service. This is in the short-run when the supply of productive service is not perfectly elastic. More of it will be supplied at a higher price and less at a lower price. Thus the shape of the supply curve of a factor service is upward sloping from left to right, i.e. it has a positive slope.

Under a perfectly competitive factor market there are many buyers of a productive service so that a single firm purchases only a small portion of the total factor service and in no way influences its market price. It takes the price of the factor service as given and employs as many units as it needs at that price. Thus the supply of a factor service to the firm is **perfectly elastic** in the long-run at the given market price. As a result, for a firm working under perfect competition in the factor market, the extra cost of hiring an extra unit of the factor will be equal to the price of the factor which remains unchanged. Thus, marginal factor cost under perfect competition in the factor market is equal to the price of the factor (P_f = MFC). This is shown in figure 180. In this figure, ruling price of the factor in the market is OP, which the firm has to accept as given and constant. Supply curve of the factor (or AFC curve) is horizontal straight line and MFC curve coincides with it.

Determination of Factor Price

Given the demand and supply conditions of the factor service as enumerated above the firm will continue to employ more units of a particular factor service so long as the additional revenue obtained from an additional unit of the factor service (MRP) exceeds the extra cost of employing it (MFC). It will be earning maximum profits at the point at which the MRP equals the MFC. If the firm employs less than this, MRP would be higher than MFC and it would be to its advantage to hire more units of the factor service because they would add to revenue more than costs. In case the firm decides to hire beyond the point of equality of MRP and MFC, it would be a loser because costs would rise more than revenue. Thus in a perfectly competitive factor market the firm will be in equilibrium when MRP ≥ MFC which implies two conditions.

1. MRP must equal MFC

2. The MRP curve must cut the MFC curve from above at the equilibrium point.

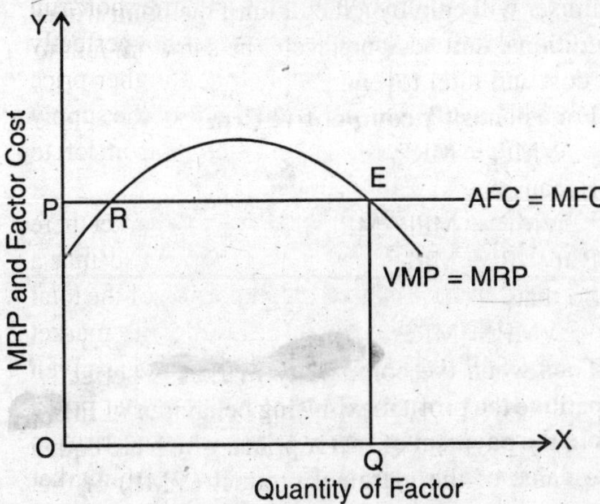

Fig. 180 : *Employment of a factor by a Firm Under Conditions of Perfect Competition.*

The pricing of a factor service as stated above can be explained diagrammatically. In Figure 180, VMP = MRP is the demand curve and AFC = MFC is the supply curve of the factor service. Since the price of the factor service is given and constant at OP for the firm, the MRP curve cuts the MFC curve at E from above. This is the equilibrium point for the firm at which it employees OQ units of the factor service. The MRP curve also cuts the MFC curve at R. But this cannot be the equilibrium point because MRP cuts MFC from below. It is not the point of maximum profit for the firm because MRP is higher than MFC beyond this point R. Thus E is the point of equilibrium in a perfectly competitive factor market when

MRP = VMP = MFC = AFC = Price

Under perfect competition in both factor and product markets, a firm may be at a profit or at a loss in the short-run. But in the long-run it must earn normal profits.

FORMAL DERIVATION OF THE EQUILIBRIUM OF THE FIRM IN PERFECTLY COMPETITIVE MARKETS

The production function is

$$X = f(L)_{\bar{k}}$$

The total cost consists of the variable cost $\bar{w}.L$ and the fixed cost F

$$C = \bar{w}.L + F$$

Where $\bar{w}$ = wage rate

L = quantity of labour

The revenue of the firm is

$$R = \bar{P}x.X$$

$$= \bar{P}x.\,[f\,(L)]$$

The firm wants to maximise its profit

$$\pi = R - C$$

$$\pi = \bar{P}x.\,[f\,(L)] - (\bar{w}.L + F)$$

Setting the first derivative of the profit function with respect to labour equal to zero we obtain

$$\frac{d\pi}{dL} = \bar{P}x.\left(\frac{dX}{dL}\right) - \bar{w} = O$$

Rearranging

$$\bar{P}x.(MPP_L) = \bar{w}$$

$$\left(\text{give } \frac{dX}{dL} = MPP_L\right)$$

or $\quad VMP_L = \bar{w}$

FACTOR PRICING UNDER IMPERFECT COMPETITION

Factor pricing under imperfect competition or monopoly is studied under three categories:

(a) When the factor market is perfectly competitive and the product market is imperfectly competitive or monopolistic.

(b) When there is monopsony in the factor market and perfect competition in the product market.

(c) When there is monopsony in the factor market and monopoly in the product market.

We discuss these variants of factor pricing under imperfect competition.

A. Factor Market Perfectly Competitive and Product Market Imperfectly Competitive or Monopolistic

In a perfectly competitive factor market, the price of the factor service is given for the firm and does not affect the volume of its purchases. The supply curve or the cost curve is horizontal to the X – axis (AFC = MFC). But because there is imperfect or monopoly in the product market, the MRP curve will lie below the VMP curve. Since we know that under imperfect competition or monopoly in the product market marginal revenue is less than the price (AR) of the product, therefore the MRP will be less than the value of marginal product (VMP). Symbolically,

$$MRP < VMP$$

$\because$ MR < P (Under imperfect competition both AR and MR curves slope downward)

The firm will be in equilibrium where MRP equals MFC, the price of the factor under perfect competition. This is shown in figure 181 by point E where the firms employs OQ units of factor service at OP price. Hence the MRP of employing OQ units is QE which is less than QA the value of its marginal product. Thus the factor service gets less than the value of its marginal product by EA amount. This means that when the firms have monopolistic power the factor is paid its MRP which is smaller than the VMP. This effect has been called **monopolistic exploitation** by **Joan Robinson.**

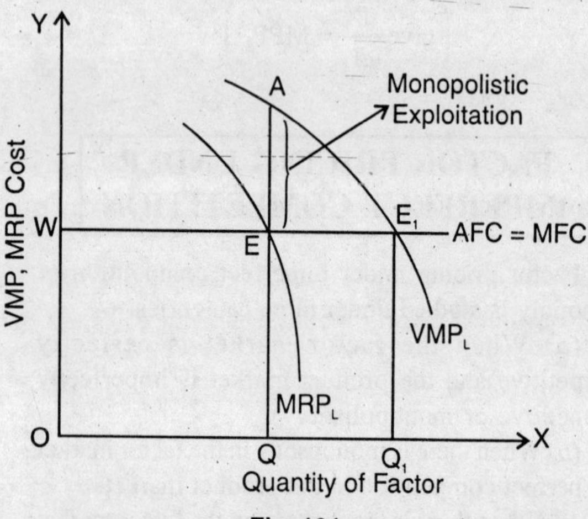

Fig. 181

When the firm equates MRP with MFC it employs less units of the factor service because of imperfect competition in the product market than what is would have had there been perfect competition. Thus it employs OQ units of the factor, as compared with OQ_1 units (where VMP = MFC) that a competitive product seller would employ consequently. Under imperfectly competitive product market, the demand for the factor will be less by Q_1Q.

According to Joan Robinson a productive factor is exploited if it is paid a price less than the value of its marginal product (VMP). We saw that a profit maximiser will employ a factor until the point where an additional unit adds precisely the same amount to total cost and total revenue.

For a **perfectly competitive firm**

$$VMP_L = MRP_L$$

Because:

$$VMP_L = MPP_L.MR_X$$

But $P_X = MR_X$

So that

$$VMP_L = MRP_L$$

Thus when the commodity market is perfectly competitive the profit maximising behaviour of firms leads to the payment of factor prices which are equal to the value of the marginal product (VMP) of the factors.

However, the condition of equilibrium of a monopolistic firm is

$$MRP_L = MPP_L.MR_X = w$$

and $MR_x < Px$, so that factors are paid less than the value of their marginal product. The difference AE in figure 181 shows that profit maximising behaviour of imperfectly competitive firms causes the factor price to be less than the value of its marginal product.

B. Monopsony in the Factor Market and Perfect Competition in the Product Market

A monopsonist firm is a single buyer of a particular factor in the market. Since the firm is the market for the factor in this case, the supply of factor service to the monopsonist is identical to its supply to the market. Thus the supply curve to the firm (AFC) is positively sloping from left to right upward. The firm can employ more units of the factor service by offering a higher price per unit. The MFC curve to this AFC curve will also be sloping upward and will be above the AFC curve throughout its length.

Since we are assuming perfect competition in the product market, the value of the marginal product will be equal to the marginal revenue product (VMP = MRP). The firm can sell any amount without affecting the price of the product and the value of the marginal product (VMP) therefore coincides with the marginal revenue product (MRP), as shown in figure 182.

The firm is in equilibrium at point E in figure 182 where the MRP curve cuts the MFC curve from above and equals it at that point. The firm employs OQ units of the factor service by paying OP (= QA) price for them. In this case, there is **monopsonistic exploitation** of the factor because the factor service is being paid less than its marginal revenue product. For OQ units the factor is being paid QA (= OP) price whereas its marginal revenue product is QE. The difference between the MRP and the price paid to the factor is AE (QE – QA) which measures monopsonistic exploitation per unit of the factor employed.

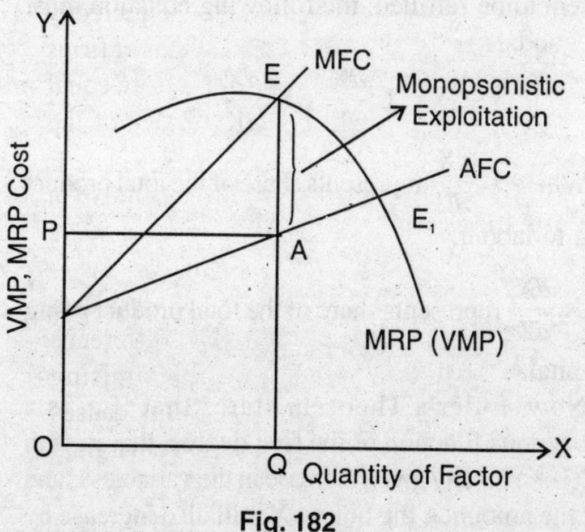

Fig. 182

C. Monopsony in the Factor Market and Monopoly in the Product Market

When there is monopsony in the factor market and monopoly in the product market, MRP < VMP and the MFC > AFC. This implies that the MRP curve will lie below the VMP curve and MFC curve will lie above the AFC curve, as shown in figure 183.

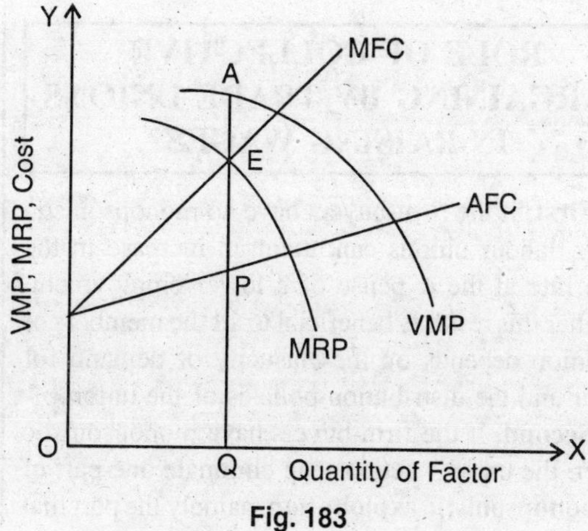

Fig. 183

As usual, the firm is in equilibrium at point E where the MRP curve cuts the MFC curve from above and equals it. The firm employs OQ units of the factors service at QP price which is less than QE the marginal revenue product of the factor. Thus due to its monopsonistic position in the factor market, the firm exploits the factor units used to the extent of PE (QE – QP). On the other hand, due to its monopolistic position in the product market, the MRP of the factor is less than its VMP and the firm exploits the factor units employed further to the extent of EA amount. We may conclude that in the case of monopsony in the factor market and monopoly in the product market, the factor used in production by the firm is doubly exploited: **first,** due to the excess of MRP over the price of the factor, and **second,** due to the excess of the VMP over the marginal revenue product of the factor.

IN SUMMARY

(a) In perfectly competitive markets the factor is paid its VMP.

(b) If the firm has monopolistic power in the product market but no power in the input market, the factor is paid its MRP < VMP.

(c) If the firm has both monopolistic power in the product market and monopsonistic power in put market the factor is paid a price which is even lower than its MRP. This is the basic characteristic of monopsonistic exploitation.

ROLE OF COLLECTIVE BARGAINING BY TRADE UNIONS IN RAISING WAGES

First. If the firm-buyers have no monopsonistic power, labour unions can attain an increase in the wage rate at the expense of a lower employment. Whether this result is beneficial to all the members of the union depends on the elasticity of demand for labour and the distribution policies of the union.

Second. If the firm-buyers have monopsonistic power, the union's actions can eliminate one part of the **monopsonistic exploitation**, namely the part that is solely attributable to the monopsonistic power of the firms. However, the other portion of the monopsonistic exploitation, that which is due to the monopoly power of firms in the product market, cannot be eliminated by trade union action.

Third. If the firm-buyers have monopsonistic power, trade unions can increase the total wage bill in cases, by either increasing employment, or the wage rate, or both. Only if the demand for labour is elastic can the union harm its members, if it sets the wage rate above the maximum level for the initial (pre-union) level of employment.

THE 'ADDING-UP' PROBLEM: 'PRODUCT EXHAUSTION' THEOREMS

As soon as it was propounded that the factors of production are paid equal to their marginal products, a perplexing problem cropped up over which there was a serious debate among the famous economists at that time. The perplexing problem which was posed was that if all factors were paid rewards equal to their marginal products, would the total product be just exactly exhausted? In other words, If each factor is rewarded equal to its marginal product, the total product should be disposed of without any surplus or deficit. The problem of proving that the total product will be just exhausted if all factors are paid rewards equal to their marginal products has been called **"Adding-up-Problem"** or **Product Exhaustion Problem**.

Wicksteed's Solution of Product Exhaustion Problem

Philip Wicksteed was one of the first economists who posed this problem and provided a solution for it. Wicksteed applied a mathematical proposition called **Euler's Theorem** to prove that the total product will be just exhausted if all the factors are paid equal to their marginal products. Let X stand for the total output of the product, L stand for the labour and K stand for the capital. Then, the adding-up problem implies that,

$$X = MP_L.L + MP_K.K$$

That is, the marginal product of labour (MP_L) multiplied by the amount of labour (L) plus the marginal product of capital (MP_K) multiplied by the amount of capital (K) equals the total product of the firm. Marginal products of various factors can be expressed as partial derivatives. Thus, the marginal product of labour can be expressed as $\frac{dX}{dL}$, and the marginal of capital as $\frac{dX}{dK}$, then for the adding-up problem to be fulfilled, the following equation must hold good:

$$X = L.\frac{dX}{dL} + K.\frac{dX}{dK}$$

Where $L.\frac{dX}{dL}$ represents share of the total product going to labour.

$K.\frac{dX}{dK}$ represents share of the total product going to capital.

Now, Euler's Theorem states that if X is a homogenous function of the first degree, that is, if in $X = f(L,K)$ for any given increase in the variables L and K by the amount n the output X will also increase by n. Thus homogeneous function of the first degree or linearly homogeneous function is of the following form:

$$nX = f(n.L, n.K)$$

Now according to Euler's theorem for this linearly homogeneous function:

$$X = L.\frac{dX}{dL} + K.\frac{dX}{dK}$$

Thus if production function is homogeneous of

the first degree, then according to Euler's Theorem the total product.

$$X = L.\frac{dX}{dL} + K.\frac{dX}{dK}$$

Where $\frac{dX}{dL}, \frac{dX}{dK}$ are partial derivatives of the production function and therefore represent the marginal products of labour and capital respectively. It follows therefore that if production function is homogeneous of the first degree **(that is, where there are constant returns to scale),** then, according to Euler's Theorem, if the various factors, L and K are paid rewards equal to their marginal products, the total products will be just exhausted, with no surplus or deficit.

In the above way, Wicksteed assuming constant returns to scale and applying Euler's Theorem, proved the adding-up problem, that is, demonstrated that if all factors are paid equal to their marginal products, the total product will be just exactly exhausted.

Wicksteed's solution was criticized by Walras, Barone Edgeworth and Pareto. It has been asserted by these writers that production function is not homogeneous of the first degree, that is, returns to scale are not constant in the actual world. Critics pointed out that production function is such that it yields a U-shaped long run average cost curve. The U-shape of the long-run average cost curve implies that up to a point increasing returns to scale occur and after it diminishing returns to scale are found. In case a firm is still working under increasing returns to scale, then if all factors are paid equal to their marginal products, the total factor rewards would exceed the total product. On the other hand, if a firm is working under diminishing returns to scale, and all factors are paid equal to their marginal products the total factor rewards would not fully exhaust the total product and will therefore leave a surplus. It follows that Euler's Theorem does not apply and therefore the adding-up problem does not hold good when either there are increasing returns to scale or decreasing returns to scale.

Another drawback pointed out in Wicksteed's solution is that when there is constant returns to scale, the long run average cost curve of the firm is a horizontal straight line which is incompatible with perfect competition. (Under horizontal long-run average cost curve, the firm cannot have a determinate equilibrium position). But competition was essential to the marginal productivity theory and therefore to Wicksteed's solution. Thus Wicksteed solution leads us to two contradictory things.

Wicksell, Walras and Barone's Solution of Production Exhaustion Problem

After Wicksteed, Wicksell, Walras, Barone, each independently, advanced more satisfactory solution to the problem that marginally determined factor rewards would just exhaust the total product. These authors assumed that the typical production function was not homogeneous of the first degree, but was such that yielded U-shape long-run average cost curve. They pointed out that in the long-run under perfect competition, the firm was in equilibrium at the minimum point of the long-run average cost curve. At the minimum point of the LAC-Curve, the returns to scale are momentarily constant, that is, returns to scale are constant within the range of small variations of output. Thus the condition required for the marginally determined rewards to exhaust the total product, that is, the operation of constant returns to scale, was fulfilled at the minimum point of the long-run average cost curve, where a perfectly competitive firm is in long-run equilibrium. Thus in the case of perfectly long-run equilibrium if the factors are paid rewards equal to their marginal products, the total product would be just exactly exhausted.

THE THEORY OF RENT

Rent as an economic surplus, as used by modern economists means the earning of a factor of production in excess of the minimum amount necessary to keep it in its present use. It is not a differential surplus, the difference between the superior and the inferior grades of lands as **Ricardo** meant by rent. Moreover, it accrues not to land alone, but to all other factor services.

RICARDIAN THEORY OF RENT

David Ricardo was a brilliant 19th century economist of England who propounded a systematic theory of rent which is in many ways the basis of the modern concept of rent.

Ricardo defined rent as follows: **"Rent is that portion of the produce of earth which is paid to the land lord for the use of the original and indestructible powers of the soil."** It should be noticed that land rent, according to Ricardian definition, is a payment for the use of only land and is different from contractual rent which includes.

- According to Ricardo, marginal land earns no rent.
- In Ricardian Theory, rent is not price determining. In fact, in this theory rent is price determined, that is, it is price which determines rent. To quote Ricardo, **"Corn is not high because a rent is paid, but a rent is paid because corn is high."**

MODERN THEORY OF RENT

Modern theory of rent does not confine itself to the determination of the reward of only land as a factor of production. Rent according to the modern sense can arise in respect of any factor of product ion. It is a surplus payment in excess of transfer earnings of that factor. **Transfer earnings means the amount of money which any particular unit of a factor could earn in its next best alternative use.** In other words, economic rent in such a case is the difference between the present earnings and transfer earnings. **In Joan Robinson's words,** "The essence of the conception of rent is the conception of a surplus earned by a particular part of a factor of production over and above the minimum earnings necessary to induce it to its work."

HOW ECONOMIC RENT ARISES

Now the question is how economic rent arises. Economic rent in the sense of surplus over transfer earnings will arise when the supply of the factor units is less **than perfectly elastic or not perfectly elastic.** From the point of view of elasticity of supply, there are three possibilities:

(a) When the supply is perfectly elastic
(b) When it is less than perfectly elastic, and
(c) When it is inelastic.

(a) When the supply of factor units is perfectly elastic

In this case, there will be no surplus or economic rent and the actual earnings and transfer earnings will be equal. When the supply of a factor is perfectly elastic, it means that at a given price, or remuneration, the entrepreneur can engage or employ any number of the factor units. It is obvious that, when the factor units are available at a minimum price or transfer earnings, their equilibrium price will be equal to that minimum price at which the present earnings are equal to the transfer earnings. Thus, no factor unit in such a situation will be able to earn more than its transfer earnings. That is, there will be no rent or surplus earnings.

This is shown in figure 184 given below. In this figure, the supply curve of the factor of production SS is perfectly elastic and is, therefore, shown as a horizontal straight line. This means that all factor units are available at the given price OS or in other words, the transfer earnings of each factor unit are also equal to OS. DD is the demand curve. The two curves intersect at P. OM is the quantity of the factor used. The price determined is OS. The total earnings are OSPM. But since transfer earnings are equal to the actual earnings, they are also equal to OSPM. There is no surplus and hence no rent.

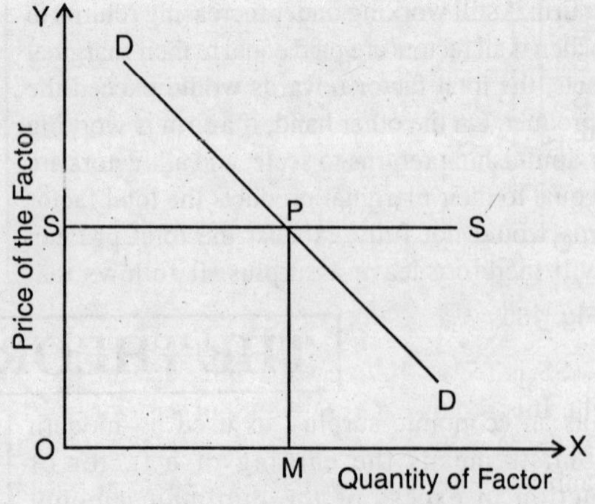

Fig. 184 : *Perfectly Elastic Supply*

If this firm does not pay the price OS, the factor units will be shifted to some other use and earn there as much, because present earnings are equal to transfer earnings.

Thus, it is clear that if the supply of factor units is perfectly elastic for a particular use or industry, then no factor unit can earn surplus or economic rent.

(b) Less than Perfectly Elastic Supply

Now let us take a case when the supply is less than perfectly elastic, i.e., it is some what elastic. This means that the transfer earnings of all the factor units are not equal. As, in some industry or use, the price of the factor increases, more and more of the factor units will offer their services to this industry in use. Suppose that in a particular industry or use, a factor unit can earn Rs. 200 p.m. It is obvious that only such units of the factor will offer their services to this industry whose price in other alternative occupations is less than Rs. 200 or in other words the transfer earnings are less than the present earnings. In this manner, as the price paid for a factor in a particular industry or occupation increases, the supply of the factor will increase if the transfer earnings are less. It is clear that the supply of a factor of production depends on its transfer earnings. This is shown in the figure 185.

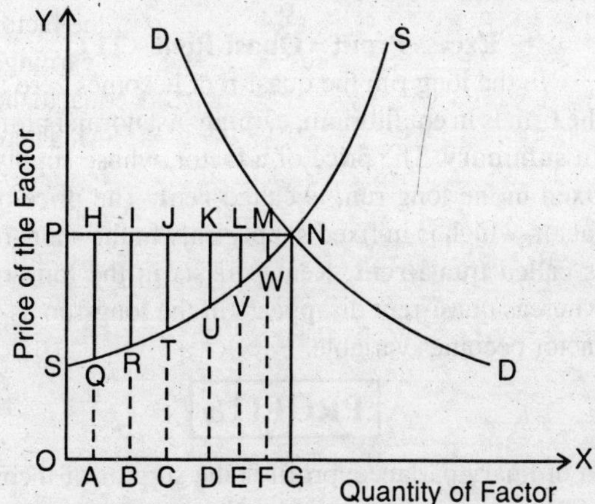

Fig. 185 : *Elastic But not perfectly Elastic Supply*

SS is the supply curve sloping upwards to the right. It is somewhat elastic but not perfectly elastic as in the case (a). The supply curve SS indicates what quantity of the factor will be available at various prices. In other words, it shows the transfer earnings of different factor units. Thus, the transfer earnings of A unit of the factor, is AQ whereas the price is OP. Therefore, surplus or rent, is HQ. In the same manner, the other units earn surplus or rent. It is assumed that all factor units are equally useful for this industry. Hence, the price of all factor units in the industry will be the same. The supply curve cuts DD demand curve at N. In this case, OG is the quantity of the factor used. The rent or price per unit is OP (= GN). But the transfer earnings of each factor unit are less than the price OP. All units except the last G unit are earning more than their transfer earnings. That is they are earning economic rent. Economic rent or surplus will be different for different units because the transfer earnings are different, although the price is the same.

The total earnings are OGNP. But the transfer earnings are OGNS. Hence

Economic Rent = OGNP – OGNS = PNS

(c) Absolutely Inelastic Supply

Now we come to a case when the supply of a factor is absolutely inelastic. The obvious example of this case is the supply of land for the community as a whole. We know that land for the community is fixed and it cannot be increased or decreased whatever the price offered. High price will not increase it or low price will not decrease it. That is why it is said that land has no supply price.

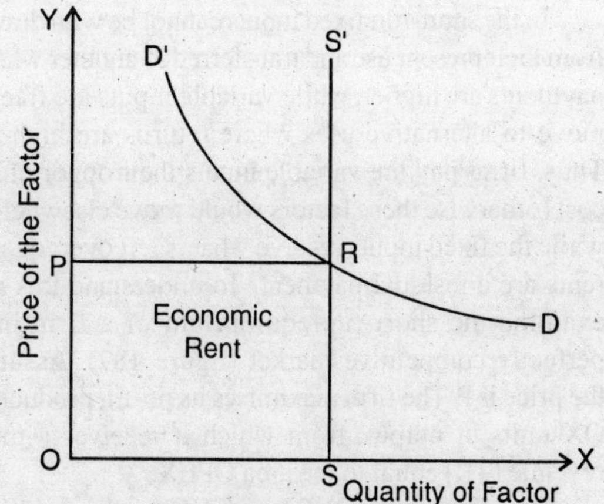

Fig. 186 : *Absolutely Inelastic Supply*

In the figure 186, the supply curve SS shows an absolutely inelastic supply which represents the supply of land for the community as a whole. Since the supply is fixed, the supply curve SS' is a vertical straight line. This means that from the point of view of the community as a whole, the transfer earnings are zero, since the land cannot be transferred to any other place.

In this figure DD' is the demand curve for the whole land. The supply curve SS' and the demand curve DD' intersect at R. In equilibrium the price of land or rent is determined at OP and the total earnings of land are equal to OPRS area. Since in this situation the transfer earnings of land are zero, the entire earnings of land, i.e., OPRS is rent.

Thus, it is clear that is case the supply of a factor is absolutely inelastic, its earnings are rent.

Conclusion. We may conclude that rent arises when the supply of a factor is less than perfectly elastic.

QUASI-RENT

The doctrine of quasi-rent was introduced in to economic literature by **Marshall** who extended Ricardo's theory of land-rent to other factors fixed in supply during the short-run.

In short run some factors are fixed, while in the long-run they become variable. The payment to an input which is in fixed supply in the short run is called **quasi-rent,** because it disappears in the long-run (as the factor becomes variable), unlike rents which persist in the long-run.

In the short-run fixed inputs cannot be with drawn from their present use and transferred to another where payments are higher, while variable inputs are free to move to alternative uses where returns are highest. Thus, firms pay the variable inputs their opportunity cost (otherwise these factors would move elsewhere), while the fixed inputs receive what is left over; quasi-rents are a residual payment. To understand this we examine the short-run equilibrium of a firm in a perfectly competitive market (figure 187). Assume the price is P. The firm maximises its profit, producing OX units of output, from which it receives a total revenue (TR) equal to the area OPEX.

The firm pays OXBA = TVC to the variable factors. (it cannot pay less and keep them in its employment). The fixed factors earn the residual ABEP, which is the quasi-rent. Thus

Quasi-Rent = TR – TVC

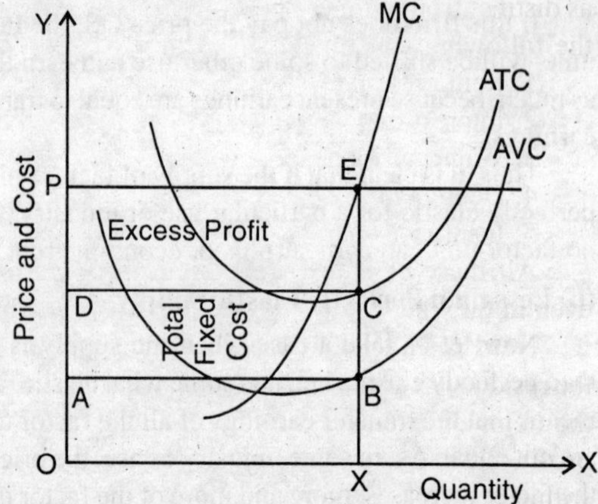

Fig. 187 : *Quasi Rent*

The quasi-rent can be divided into two parts, the total fixed cost (area ABCD in figure 187) and excess (or pure) profit (DCEP). The TFC is the opportunity cost of the fixed factors, that is, the return that would have been earned if the fixed factors were utilised in their best alternative employment (e.g. by another firm in the same industry which pays higher returns on the fixed factors). The excess profit is the difference between the quasi-rent and the TFC:

Quasi-Rent = TFC + Excess Profit

or

Excess Profit = Quasi-Rent – TFC

In the long run the quasi-rent becomes zero and the firm is in equilibrium, earning just normal profits. **In summary.** The price of a factor, whose supply is fixed in the long-run, is called **rent.** The price of a factor, which is in fixed supply only in the short-run, is called **quasi-rent**. Rent persists in the long-run, whereas quasi-rent disappears in the long-run as the factor becomes variable.

PROFITS

In ordinary parlance, profit is the surplus of income over expenses of production according to a businessman. It is the amount left with him after he has made payments for all factor services used by him in the process of production. But he may not have been careful in calculating all such expenses of production in the economic sense. Therefore, economists regard businessman's profit as gross profit as distinct from pure or net profit because it includes the following constituents.

1. Rent on Land
2. Interest on Capital
3. Wages of Management
4. Depreciation changes
5. Insurance charges

All these elements are present in **gross profit** even in the long-run as they are relatively stable.

Net Profit : Net, true, economic or pure profit is the residue left to the entrepreneur after deducting all the items enumerated above from gross profit. Net profit, however, includes the following elements within it.

1. Reward for Uncertainty Bearing
2. Reward for coordination
3. Rent of Ability
4. Reward of Innovation
5. Monopoly Gains
6. Windfalls

We may conclude that an economist's profit is quite distinct from a businessman's profit. The former is concerned with net profit which is arrived at by deducting from the businessman's gross profit, the remuneration for the latter's own land, labour and capital.

SOME IMPORTANT POINTS

- **Prof. J.B. Clark** propounded his dynamic theory of profit in 1900. According to him profits are a dynamic surplus.
- The Rent Theory of Profit was propounded by the American economist, **F.A. Walker.**
- The risk theory of profit is associated with H.B. Hawley who regards risk-taking as the main function of the entrepreneur. Profit is the residual income which the entrepreneur receives because he assumes risks.
- **Prof. Frank H. Knight** regards profit as the reward of bearing non-insurable uncertainties.
- The Innovation Theory of Profit is associated with **Joseph A. Schumpeter.** According to Schumpeter, the principal function of the entrepreneur is to make innovations and profits are a reward for performing this important function.

WELFARE ECONOMICS

The literature on welfare economics has grown rapidly in recent years. Vilfredo Pareto considered the question of maximising social welfare on the basis of general optimum conditions. Marshall and Pigou, the neo-classical economists, concentrated on particular sectors of the economic system in their postulates of welfare economics. It was **Prof. Robbin's** ethical neutrality view about economics that led to the development of welfare economics as an important field of economic studies. **Kaldor**, **Hicks** and **Scitovsky** have laid the foundations of the **New Welfare Economics** with the help of the **'compensation principle'** avoiding all value judgements. On the other hand, **Bargson, Samuelson** and others have developed the concept of the **Social Welfare Function** without sacrificing value judgements.

Welfare economics has been defined by **Scitovsky** as "welfare economics is that branch of economic analysis which is concerned primarily with establishment of criteria that can provide a positive basis for adopting policies which are likely to maximise social welfare." In short, welfare economics is to prescribe criteria or norms with which to judge the desirability of certain economic re-organisations and prescribe policies on that basis.

POSITIVE ECONOMICS AND WELFARE ECONOMICS

Welfare economics is a normative study. Hence it is important to know the difference between **positive economics** and **normative economics**. Positive economics is concerned with explaining what is, that is, it describes theories and laws to explain observed economic phenomena, whereas normative economics is concerned with what should be or what ought to be the things.

In positive macro-economics, we are broadly concerned with explaining the determination of relative prices and the allocation of resources between different commodities. In positive macro-economics we are broadly concerned with how the level of national income and employment, aggregate consumption and investment and the general level of prices are determined. In these parts of positive economics, what should be the prices, what should be the saving rate, what should be the allocation of resources, and what should be the distribution of income are not discussed. These questions of, what should be and what ought to be, fall within the purview of normative economics. Thus, given the profit maximisation assumption, positive economics states that monopolist will fix a price which will equate marginal cost with marginal revenue. The question what price should or ought to be fixed so that maximum social welfare is achieved lies outside the purview of positive economics. Similarly, given the monopsony in the labour market, positive economics explains what actual wage rate is determined. It does not go into the question how wage rate should be paid to the labourer so that they should not be exploited. Likewise, how national income between different individuals is distributed falls within the domain of positive economics. But positive economics is not concerned with the question of how income should be distributed. On the other hand, normative economics is concerned with describing what should be the things. It is therefore, also called **prescriptive economics.** What price for a product should be fixed, what wage rate should be paid, how income should be distributed, etc., fall within the purview of normative economics.

It should be noted that normative economics involves **value judgements** or what are simply known as values. By value judgements or values, is meant the conceptions of the people about what is good or bad. These conceptions regarding values of the people are based on the ethical, political, philosophical and religious beliefs of the people and are not based upon any scientific logic or law. Because normative economics involves value judgements, eminent economist Prof. Robbins contended that economics should not become normative in character.

Value judgements of various individuals differ and their rightness or wrongness cannot be decided on the basis of scientific logic or laws. Therefore, in our view, positive economics should be kept separate and distinct from normative economics. However, because normative economics involves value judgements, it does not mean that it should be considered as useless or not meaningful and should not be the concern of economics. As a matter of fact, many vital issues concerning economic welfare of the society necessarily involve some value judgements.

From the above it seems that difference between positive and welfare economics is quite clear; in one case what a man does without considering the favourable or unfavourable effects on others while in the other it is what he should do and must consider the favourable or unfavourable effects on others.

NEO-CLASSICAL WELFARE ECONOMICS

Neo-Classical economists **Marshall, Pigou, Cannon** and his followers considered economics as a normative science. Marshall formulated the concepts of **'Consumer's Surplus'** and **'National Dividend'** in his **'Principles of Economics'** published in 1890. These concepts became the basis of old welfare economics.

Pigovian Welfare Economics

A.C. Pigou is another important neo-classical economist who laid the scientific foundation of welfare economics through the publication of **'Economics of Welfare'** in 1932. Welfare is a mental phenomenon and 'the elements of welfare are the states of consciousness' which is made of utilities or satisfaction of human wants. Pigou also differentiated economic welfare from general (social) welfare. The former is a part of the latter. General welfare depends on a large number of economic and non-economic variables. Economic welfare alone is the subject matter of economics. Pigou limited the scope of welfare economics to economic welfare because general (or social) welfare is a very wide and complex term.

Pigovian welfare economics is related to the

satisfaction derived from the use of exchangeable goods and services. Pigovian welfare economics is based on the following assumptions:

A. Every individual attempts to maximise his satisfaction from the use of limited monetary resources.

B. Satisfaction derived from the consumption of goods and services can be compared interpersonally and intrapersonally.

C. Marginal utility of money income decreases with every increase in it which implies that the marginal utility of a unit of money to the poor is greater than that of the rich.

Pigou's Dual Criterion of Welfare

Pigou formulated dual criterian to maximise welfare on the basis of the above assumptions. They are:

1. An increase in national income brought about either by increasing some goods without reducing the others or by transferring factors from less productive to more productive activities increases economic welfare.

2. Any reorganisation of the economy, which increases the purchasing power of the poor without reducing the national income, increases social welfare.

In this way Pigou explicitly brought the conditions of maximisation of welfare. The **first condition** states that given the tastes and income distribution, the level of social welfare increases with any increase in national income. **Second** condition states that given the constant level of national income, the transfer of purchasing power from the rich to the poor will also increase economic welfare.

A Critique of Neo-Classical Welfare Economics

Neo-classical economists particularly Marshall and Pigou made significant contribution to the development of welfare economics by giving the concept of consumer's surplus and economic surplus. Pigou also discussed the various types of externalities, which are great obstacles in the achievement of maximum welfare, in his **'Economics of Welfare'.** But neo-classical welfare economics is based on the unrealistic assumption of cardinal utilities which can be compared interpersonally and intrapersonally. Secondly, national income is not an appropriate measure of social welfare because it is the product of real outputs and their prices. Therefore, it is possible, that national income increases only due to rise in price level without any increase in the quantity and quality of goods and services. Thirdly, Dr. Graff is of the opinion that money is not an appropriate and satisfactory measure of economic welfare because the value of money changes with variation in price level and welfare does not depend only on exchangeable goods and services. Fourthly, Pigou's 'man's equal capacity for satisfaction' assumption is based on an ethical rather than an scientific principle.

ANALYSIS OF EXTERNALITIES OR DIVERGENCES BETWEEN PRIVATE AND SOCIAL COSTS AND RETURNS

Divergences between private and social costs and returns (benefits) are known as **externalities.** Externalities are, in fact, **market imperfections** where the market offers no price for service or disservice. These externalities lead to misallocation of resources and cause production or consumption to fall short of an optimum level. Thus they do not lead to maximum social welfare, Pigou's major contribution lies in studying the main causes leading to divergences between private and social costs and returns and in suggesting measures for removing these divergences.

External Economies of Production

When some firm renders a benefit or cost of a service to other firms without appropriating to itself all the benefit or cost of the service, it is an external economy External economies (or diseconomies) therefore reflect non-market interdependence. The act of producing a good on the part of one firm may either benefit or impose costs on other firms without passing through the market process. In other words, the benefit or cost is not market process. Hence external economies involve non-market interdependence.

External economies of production may also arise when the expansion of a firm makes it possible for other firms in the industry to obtain their inputs at low cost. In all such cases, social marginal benefits exceed the private marginal benefits and the private costs exceed the social costs. For the expanding firm does not receive any remuneration for the costs incurred by it and the benefits which it has conferred on others.

External Diseconomies of Production

External diseconomies of production also lead to divergence between private and social costs and returns when the production of a commodity or service by a firm affects adversely other firms in the industry. Professor Pigou's example of air pollution explains these divergences. Suppose a factory is situated in a residential or populated area and it emits smoke. The smoke from the factory soils clothes, household articles, buildings and damages the health of the inhabitants of the area. As a result, the maintenance costs of the inhabitants increase in the form of increased expenses on washing clothes, cleaning of household articles and rooms, and cleaning and painting of buildings and enhanced medical expenses. These are social costs for which the factory does not compensate the inhabitants of the area and in a sense benefits itself. The private costs are thus less than the social costs, and the private benefits to the factory are higher than the social benefits because the factory-owner escapes costs incurred by the inhabitants of the area and thereby gets private benefits.

External Economies of Consumption

External economies of consumption arise from non-market interdependences of the satisfactions enjoyed by different consumers. An increase in the consumption of a good or service which affects favourably the consumption patterns and desires of other consumers is an external economy of consumption. When an individual installs a TV set, the satisfaction of his neighbours increases when they and their children view the various programmes. This is a case of external economy in consumption in which social benefit is larger and social cost is lower than private benefit and cost, because the TV-owners does not receive any money in return as the neighbours are not asked to pay anything for seeing TV programmes.

External Diseconomies of Consumption

When the consumption of a good or service by one consumer confers a **disadvantage** or effects adversely the consumption patterns and desires of other consumers, it is an external diseconomy of consumption. Diseconomies of consumption especially arise in the case of dress fashions and articles of conspicuous consumption. When a rich lady in a particular locality adopts a new style of dress, it leads to the discarding of clothes already in use not only by her but by other women who emulate her. This results in higher social costs and lower social benefits than private costs and benefits. Individuals who are not in a position to emulate the consumption patterns of their rich neighbours feel dissatisfied and jealous. As a result, their productive efficiency falls and serious divergences emerge between social and private costs and returns. Other instances are of noise nuisance from loud-speakers.

Conclusion. We may conclude the discussion in the words of **Prof. Baumol,** "External economies and diseconomies can lead to a misallocation of resources even in the world of perfect competition. Too much may be produced by industries in which external diseconomies prevail, while there may be a less than optimal output of commodities whose production involves external economies. In principle it is even possible that, where there are external diseconomies, the presence of monopolies can lead to output smaller and therefore more nearly optimal than those which would result from competition."

THE CASE OF PUBLIC GOODS

Another cause of divergences between private and social costs, and private and social benefits is the case of public goods which Pigou completely ignored. According to Samuelson, 'each individual's consumption of such a good (public good) leads to no subtractions from any other individual's consumption of that good, every individual benefits from public goods. But divergences arise when one individual arranges for a public good he confers a benefit on some other individuals and thereby creates a social benefit that is higher than his own private benefit. When a person manages a municipal street light in from of his house through his personal efforts all the residents of the locality benefit from it. The social benefit far exceeds his own benefit.

Remedial Measures

To bring about the equality of private and social costs and benefits, Pigou favoured state interference rather than self-interest. He, therefore, suggested the use of taxes, subsidies and other social control measures to close the gap between private and social costs and benefits arising from externalities in production and consumption.

CONDITIONS OF PARETO OPTIMALITY

Neo-classicals and earlier economists defined social welfare as a sum total of cardinally measurable utilities of different members of the society. An optimum allocation of resources was one which maximised the social welfare in this sense. **Pareto** was the first to part with this traditional approach to social welfare in two important respects. First, he rejected the notion of cardinal utility and its additive nature and, second, he detached welfare economies from the interpersonal comparisons of utilities. **Pareto's concept of maximum social welfare which is based upon ordinal utility and is also free from value judgements occupies a significant place in modern welfare economists. Pareto optimum may not be sufficient condition for attaining maximum social welfare but it is a necessary condition for it.** Pareto optimum (often called Economic Efficiency) is a position from which it is impossible to make anyone better off without making someone worse off by any reallocation of resources of inputs and outputs. Thus in the Pareto optimum position the welfare of an individual of the society cannot be increased without decreasing the welfare of another member.

Pareto Criterion

This criterion refers to economic efficiency which can be objectively measured. It is called pareto criterion after the famous Italian economist **Vilfredo Pareto.** According to this criterion any change that makes at least one individual better-off and no one worse-off is an improvement in social welfare. Conversely, a change that makes no one better-off and at least one worse-off is a decrease in social welfare.

The criterion can be stated in a some what different way: a situation in which it is impossible to make anyone better-off without making someone worse-off is said to be Pareto-optimal or Pareto efficient.

Pareto criterion can be explained with the help of **Samuelson's utility possibility** curve. **Utility possibility curve is the locus of the various combinations of utilities obtained by two persons from the consumption of a particular bundle of goods.**

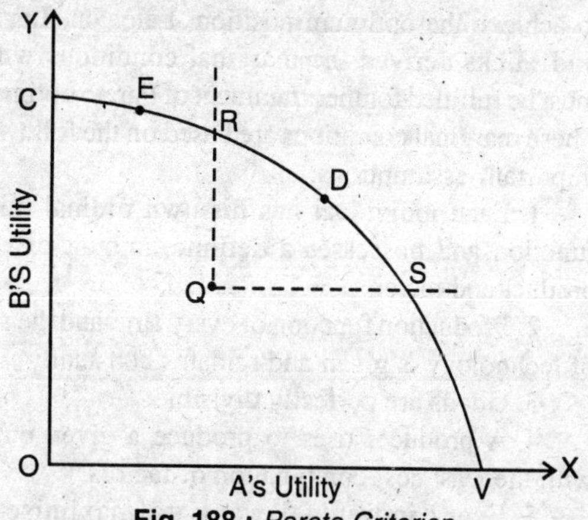

Fig. 188 : *Pareto Criterion*

In figure 188, CV is a utility possibility curve which shows the various levels of utilities obtained by two individuals A and B of the society resulting from the redistribution of a fixed bundle of goods and its consumption by them. According to Pareto criterion, a movement from Q to R, or Q to D, or Q to S represents the increase in social welfare because in such movements the utility of either A or B or both increases. A movement from Q to R implies that the utility or welfare of B increases, while that of A remains the same. On the other hand, a movement from Q to S implies that while A has becomes better off, B is no worse off. And a movement from Q to D or any other point on the segment between R and S will mean increase in welfare or utility of both the individuals. Thus points R, D and S are preferable to Q from point of view of social welfare. But unfortunately Pareto criterion does not help us in evaluating the changes in welfare if the movement as a result of redistribution is from the point Q to a point outside the segment RS, such as point E on the utility possibility curve CV. As a result of the movement from point Q to E, the utility of A decreases while that of B increases. In such circumstances, Pareto criterion can not tell us as to whether social welfare increases or decreases.

Marginal Conditions of Pareto Optimum

Pareto concluded from his criterion that competition leads the society to an optimum position but he had not given any mathematical Proof. of it, nor he derived the marginal conditions to be fulfilled to achieve the optimum position. Later on, **Lerner and Hicks** derived the marginal conditions which must be fulfilled for the attainment of Pareto optimum. These marginal conditions are based on the following important assumptions:

1. Each individual has his own ordinal utility function and possesses a definite amount of each product and factor.
2. Production function of every firm and the state of technology is given and remains constant.
3. Goods are perfectly divisible.
4. A producer tries to produce a given output with the least cost combination of factors.
5. Every individual wants to maximise his satisfaction.
6. Every individual purchases some quantity of all goods.
7. All factors of production are perfectly mobile.

Given the above assumptions various marginal conditions (first order conditions) required for the achievement of Pareto optimum or maximum social welfare are explained below:

1. The Optimum Distribution of Products among the Consumers: Efficiency in Exchange.

The first condition relates to the optimum distribution of the goods among the different consumers composing a society at a particular point of time. The condition says: **"The marginal rate of substitution between any two goods must be the same for every individual who consumes them both."**

Thus,

$$MRS^{A}_{x,y} = MRS^{B}_{x,y}$$

2. The Optimum Allocation of Factors

The second condition for Pareto optimum requires that the available factors of production should be utilized in the production of different goods in such manner that it is impossible to increase the output of one good without a decrease in the output of another or to increase the output of both the goods by any reallocation of factors of production. This situation would be achieved if **"The marginal technical rate of substitution (MRTS) between any pair of factors must be the same for any two firms using both to produce the same product."** Thus

$$MRTS^{x}_{L,K} = MRTS^{y}_{L,K}$$

3. The Optimum Direction of Production.

The third condition relates to the technical conditions of production and the state of consumer's preferences. The fulfilment of this condition determines the optimum quantities of different commodities to be produced with given factor endowments. This condition states that **"the marginal rate of substitution between any pair of products for any person consuming both must be the same as the marginal rate of transformation (for the community) between them."**

Thus

$$MRPT_{x,y} = MRS^{A}_{x,y} = MRS^{B}_{x,y}$$

According to this condition, for the attainment of maximum social welfare goods should be produced in accordance with consumer's preferences.

In summary. A Pareto-optimal state in the economy can be attained if the following three marginal conditions are fulfilled:

1. The $MRS_{x,y}$ between any two goods be equal for all consumers.
2. The $MRTS_{L,K}$ between any two inputs be equal in the production of all commodities.
3. The $MRPT_{x,y}$ be equal to the $MRS_{x,y}$ for any two goods.

A situation may be Pareto-optimal without maximising social welfare. However, welfare maximisation is attained only at a situation that is Pareto-optimal. In other words, Pareto optimality is a necessary but not sufficient condition for welfare maximisation. **All points on the PPC are Pareto-optimal.**

The Second-Order and Total Conditions

The marginal or the first order conditions explained above are 'necessary' but not sufficient for the attainment of maximum social welfare because the marginal conditions by themselves do not guarantee maximum welfare, for the marginal conditions can be fulfilled even at the level of minimum welfare. To attain the maximum welfare position second-order conditions together with the marginal conditions must be satisfied. The second order conditions require that all indifference curves are convex to the origin and all transformation curves concave to it in the neighbourhood of any portion where marginal conditions are satisfied.

But even the satisfaction of both (first and second order conditions) does not ensure the largest maximum welfare because even marginal conditions are fulfilled, it may still be possible to move to a position where social welfare is greater. To attain the maximum social welfare, another set of conditions which are called by **Hicks** as the **'total conditions'** must also be satisfied. The total conditions state, **"that if welfare is to be a maximum, it must be impossible to increase welfare by producing product not otherwise produced or by using a factor not otherwise used."** If it is possible to increase welfare by such activities the optimum position is not determined by marginal conditions alone.

Therefore, welfare will be really maximum if the marginal as well as total conditions are satisfied. But such a social optimum too is not a unique one. It is one of a large number of optima. The whole analysis of conditions of Pareto optimality assumes a given distribution of income. With a change in the distribution of income Pareto optimality will be achieved with different output-mix of various products and different allocation of various factors among products. Thus, a new optimum will emerge due to redistribution of income and there are no criteria to judge whether the new optimum is better or worse than the previous social optimum. For this can be known with the help of some value Judgements regarding income distribution which has been ruled out by the Pareto criterian.

Its Criticism

Pareto Criterion and the concept of Pareto optimality or maximum social welfare based on it occupies a significant place in welfare economics. To Judge the efficiency of an economic system, the notion of Pareto optimality has been used to bring out the gains of trading or exchange of goods between individuals. But even Pareto criterion which rules out comparing those changes in policies which make some worse off has been a subject of controversy and has been criticised on several grounds.

1. There can be an infinite number of Paretian optima, each with a different level of welfare.

2. The Pareto criterion is not completely free from value Judgements.

3. An important limitation of Pareto criterion is that it cannot be applied to Judge the social desirability of those policy proposals which benefit some and harm others.

4. A chief drawback of Pareto-optimality analysis is that it accepts the prevailing income distribution and no attempt is made to find an optimal distribution of income, since it is thought that there does not exist any objective, value-free and scientific way of finding optimal distribution of income. Thus Pareto optimality analysis remains either silent or biased in favour of status quo on the issue of income distribution.

Perfect Competition And Pareto Optimality

All the marginal conditions of attaining Pareto optimality are fully satisfied under perfect competition. Now we shall show how perfect competition satisfies all the marginal conditions required for the achievement of Pareto optimum.

Perfect Competition And Optimal Distribution of Goods or Efficiency in Exchange

The condition for Pareto optimality with regard to the distribution of goods among consumers requires that the marginal rate of substitution (MRS) between any two goods, say X and Y, must be the same for any pair of consumers. Let A and B be the two consumers between whom two goods X and Y are to be distributed. Under perfect competition prices of all goods are given and same for every consumer. It is also assumed that consumers try to maximize their satisfaction subject to their budget constraint. Now, given the price of two goods, consumer A will maximize his satisfaction when he is buying the two goods X and Y in such amounts that:

$$MRS^{A}_{x,y} = \frac{P_x}{P_y} ......(i)$$

Likewise, the consumer B will also be in equilibrium when is he is purchasing and consuming the two goods X and Y in such amounts that:

$$MRS^{B}_{x,y} = \frac{P_x}{P_y} ......(ii)$$

Since this is essential condition of perfect competition that prices of goods are the same or uniform for all consumers, the price ratio of the two goods $\left(\frac{P_x}{P_y}\right)$ in equations *(i)* and *(ii)* above will be the same for consumers A and B. Thus under perfect competition.

$$MRS^{A}_{x,y} = MRS^{B}_{x,y}$$

Perfect Competition and Optimal Allocation of Factors

The second marginal condition for Pareto optimality relates to the optimal allocation of factors in the production of various goods. This condition requires that for the optimal allocation of factors marginal rate of technical substitution (MRTS) between any two factors must be the same for all producers. This condition is also satisfied by perfect competition. For a producer working under perfect competition prices of factors he employs are given and constant and he is in equilibrium at the combination of factors where the given isoquant is tangent to an iso-cost line. As is well known, the slope of the isoquant represents marginal rate of technical substitution between the two factors and the slope of the iso-cost line measures the ratio of the prices of two factors. Thus, under perfect competition, a cost minimizing producer A will equate MRTS between labour and capital with the price ratio of these two factors. Thus under perfect competition:

$$MRTS^{A}_{L,K} = \frac{P_L}{P_K} ......(i)$$

Where P_L and P_K are the prices of labour and capital respectively and $MRTS^{A}_{L,K}$ is the marginal rate of technical substitution between labour and capital of producer A. Similarly, producer B working under perfect competition will also equate his marginal rate of technical substitution between the two factors with their price ratios. Thus

$$MRTS^{B}_{L,K} = \frac{P_L}{P_K} ....(ii)$$

Since under perfect competition $\frac{P_L}{P_K}$ will be the same for all the producers. Therefore

$$MRTS^{A}_{L,K} = MRTS^{B}_{L,K}$$

Perfect Competition and Optimum Direction (i.e. Composition) of Production: General Economic Efficiency

This condition states that marginal rate of substitution between any two commodities for any consumer should be the same as the marginal rate of transformation for the community between these two commodities.

Under conditions of perfect competition, each firm to be in equilibrium produces so much output of a commodity that its marginal cost is equal to the price of the commodity. Thus, for firms in perfect competition,

$$MC_x = P_x \text{ and } MC_y = P_y$$

Where MC_x and MC_y are marginal costs of productions of commodities X and Y respectively and P_x and P_y are prices of commodities X and Y. Therefore, it follows that firms in perfect competition will be in equilibrium when they are producing commodities in such quantities that

$$\frac{MC_x}{MCy} = \frac{P_x}{P_y}$$

The ration of marginal costs of two commodities represents the marginal rate of transformation between them. Therefore, for each producing firm in perfect competition:

$$MRT_{xy} = \frac{MC_x}{MCy} = \frac{P_x}{P_y} ......(i)$$

When there prevails perfect competition on the buying side, each consumer maximises his satisfaction and is in equilibrium at the point where the given price line is tangent to his indifference curve. In other words, each consumer is in equilibrium when:

$$MRS_{xy} = \frac{P_x}{P_y} \quad ...(ii)$$

Since, under perfect competition, the ratio of prices of two commodities $\left(\frac{P_x}{P_y}\right)$ is the same for a consumer and a producer it follows from *(i)* and *(ii)* above that

$$MRS_{xy} = MRT_{xy}$$

We thus see that all first order marginal conditions required for the attainment of Pareto-optimality or maximum social welfare are fulfilled under perfect competition. It is in this sense that perfect competition represents economic optimum from the viewpoint of social welfare.

Perfect Competition does not always ensure Pareto Optimality

Perfect competition does not guarantee that second order conditions required for the achievement of Pareto optimality will also be fulfilled. Besides, when externalities, that is, external economies and diseconomies in production and consumption are present, perfect competition will not lead to Pareto optimality.

Further, even if the above two factors, namely, non-fulfilment of the second order conditions and the existence of externalities are not actually found, the perfect competition will not lead to economic efficiency or Pareto optimality if the given distribution of income is not optimal from the viewpoint of social welfare.

Finally, there is another factor which prevents the achievement of Pareto-optimality or maximum social welfare even when perfect competition prevails in the economy. This factor relates to the employment or utilisation of available resources. Pareto optimality will not be attained if the available resources are not fully employed or utilised.

It follows from above that perfect competition though a necessary condition is not a sufficient condition for Pareto-optimality. Therefore, that a free enterprise economy characterised by perfect competition ensures efficient allocation of resources or maximum social welfare cannot be accepted without some qualifications. And these qualifications are:

1. the second order conditions are satisfied,
2. the externalities in production and consumption are absent,
3. prevailing distribution of income is optimal from the social point of view, and
4. available resources are fully employed.

Obstacles to the Attainment of Pareto Optimality or Maximum Social Welfare

We have explained above the conditions for the attainment of Pareto optimality or maximum social welfare. We have also briefly discussed above that with some qualifications perfect competition ensures the achievement of Pareto optimality or maximum social welfare. Now the pertinent question is what are the factors which hinder the attainment of Pareto-optimality and maximum social welfare. The main obstacles are:

1. the existence of monopoly or imperfect competition,
2. the presence of externalities, i.e. external economies and diseconomies in production and consumption:
3. the consumption of Public Goods, and
4. the lack of perfect knowledge.

THE THEORY OF SECOND BEST

If all the Pareto optimality conditions are met, it represents the **first best solution.** But, as we have discussed above, there are certain obstacles like monopoly, externalities and indivisibilities that lead to Pareto non optimality. In searching for the **second best** solution, **Lipsey and Lancaster** showed that the second best solution does not involve competitive behaviour in the rest of the economy. **"The theory of the second best states that if one or more of the first-order conditions for Pareto optimality cannot be satisfied because of institutional constraints, in general it is neither necessary nor desirable to satisfy the remaining Pareto conditions."**

The theory of the second best is explained diagrammatically in figure 189 where PP_1 is the production possibility frontier of the society for two goods X and Y. I_1, I_2 and I_3 are the community indifference curves. The Pareto-optimality point is E. But there is some constraint (say, in the form of externalities or indivisibilities) which makes this optimal point unattainable. Such a constraint is represented by the line MN. Given this constraint, the optimal point need not be on the product possibility frontier PP_1 such as B because it is on a lower community indifference curve I_1.

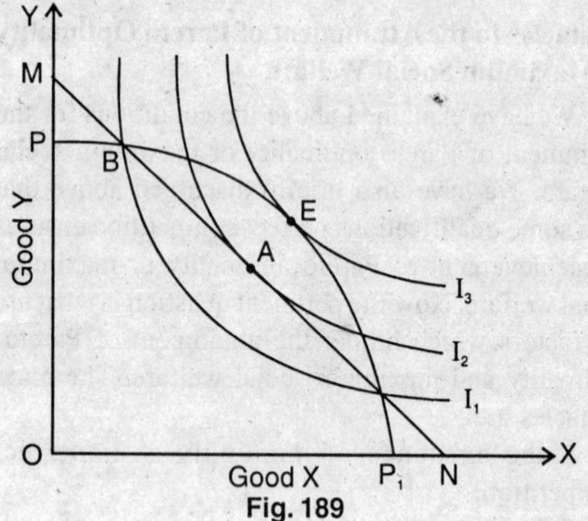

Fig. 189

But point A is definitely preferable to point B even if it not on the PP_1 frontier. This is because point A is on a higher indifference curve I_2. Thus the attainment of the second best optimum position at point A does not require the usual first best Pareto optimality condition as at point E.

There is, however, no general theory of the second best. "This theory has been used to question the desirability of policies to obtain the Pareto conditions on a piecemeal basis."

THE COMPENSATION CRITERIA OR NEW WELFARE ECONOMICS

The compensation criteria also known as the New Welfare Economics, have been formulated by Hicks, Kaldor and Scitovsky. Accepting Pareto's ordinal measurement of utility and the impossibility of its interpersonal comparisons, they tried to show that social welfare could be increased without making **value judgements.**

Assumptions. The various compensation criteria are based on the following assumptions:

(a) Each individual's satisfactions are independent from the others so that he is the best Judge of his welfare.

(b) There is the absence of external effects in production and consumption.

(c) The tastes of the individuals remain constant.

(d) The problems of production and exchange can be separated from the problems of distribution. Compensation principle accepts the level of social welfare to be a function of the level of production. Thus it ignores the effects of a change in distribution on social welfare.

(e) Utility can be measured ordinally and interpersonal comparisons of utilities are not possible.

Kaldor-Hicks Welfare Criterian

Nicholas Kaldor was the first economist to give a welfare criterion based on compensating payments. Kaldor's criterion helps us to measure the welfare implications of a movement in either direction on the contract curve in terms of Edgeworth box diagram. **According to Kaldor's welfare criterion, if a certain change in economic organisation or policy makes some people better off and other worse off, then that change will increase social welfare if those who gain could compensate the losers and still be better off than before.** Thus, if any policy change benefits any one section of the society to such an extent that he is better off even after the payment of compensation to the other section of the society out of the benefits received, then that change leads to increase in social welfare. **Prof. J.R. Hicks** supported Kaldor for employing compensation principle to evaluate the change in social welfare resulting from any economic reorganisation that benefits some people and harms the others. This criterion states that, "if A is made so much better by the change that he could compensate B for his loss and still have something left over, than the reorganisation is unequivocal improvement." In other words, a change is an improvement if the losers in the changed situation cannot profitably bribe the gainers not to change from the original situation.

Hicks has given his criterion from the loser's point of view, while **Kaldor** had formulated his criterion from gainer's point of view. Thus the two criteria are really the same though they are clothed in different words.

Kaldor-Hicks criterion can be explained with the help of the utility possibility curve. In figure 190 ordinal utility of two individuals A and B is shown on X and Y axes respectively. DE is the utility possibility curve which represents the various combinations of utilities obtained by individuals A and B.

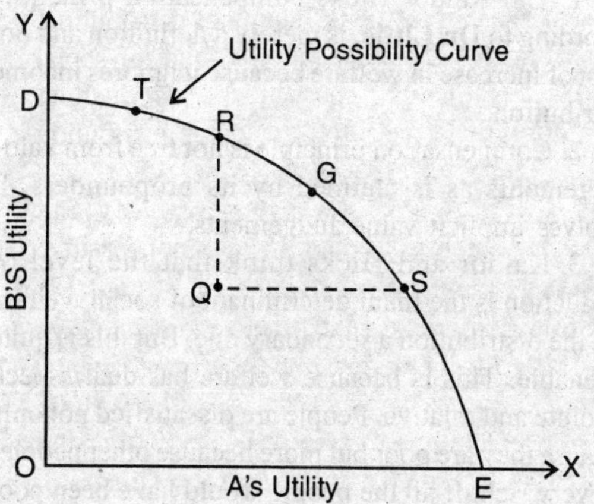

Fig. 190 : *Kaldor-Hicks criterion Explained with Utility Possibility Curve*

As we move downward on the curve DE, utility of A in creases while that of B falls. On the other hand, if we move up on the utility curve ED, utility of B increases while that of A falls.

Suppose the utilities obtained by A and B from the distribution of income or output between than are represented by point Q inside the utility possibility curve DE. Let us assume that as a result of some change in economic policy, the two individuals move from point Q to point T on the utility possibility curve DE. As a result of this movement, utility of individual B has increased while the utility of A has declined, that is, B has become better off and A has become worse off than before. Therefore, this movement from point Q to point T cannot be evaluated by means of Pareto criterion of course points such as R, G, S or any other point on the segment RS of the utility possibility curve DE are socially preferable to point Q on the basis of Pareto criterion. But since the movement from Q to T involves interpersonal comparison of utility it cannot be said whether or not social welfare increases on the basis of Pareto criterion. However, the compensation principle propounded by Kaldor-Hicks enables us to say whether or not social welfare has increased as a result of movement from Q to T. According to Kaldor-Hicks criterion, we have to see whether the individual A who gains with the movement from position Q to position T could compensate the individual A who is loser and still be better off than before. Now, it will be seen from figure 190 that utility possibility curve DE passes through points R, G and S. This means that by mere redistribution of income between the two individuals, that is, if individual B gives some compensation to individual A for the loss suffered, they can move to the position R. It is evident from the figure that at position R individual A is as well off as compared to position Q. It means due to a policy change and consequent movement from position Q to position R gainer (individual B) could compensate the loser (individual A) and still is better off than at Q. Therefore, according to Kaldor-Hicks criterion, social welfare increases with the movement from position Q to position T, for from T they could move to the position R through mere redistribution of income.

SCITOVSKY PARADOX

Scitovsky pointed out an important limitation of Kaldor-Hicks criterion that it might lead to contradictory results. He showed that if in some situation position A on Kaldor-Hicks criterion, it may be possible that position A is also shown to be an improvement over B on the basis of some criterion. For getting consistent results when position B has been revealed to be preferred to position A on the basis of a welfare criterion, then position A must not be preferred to position B on the same criterion. **According to Scitovsky,** Kaldor-Hicks criterion involves such contradictory and inconsistent results. Since Scitovsky was the first to point out this paradoxical result in Kaldor-Hicks criterion, it is known as **'Scitovsky-Paradox'**. How kaldor-Hicks criterion may lead to contradictory results in some situations is depicted in figure 191. In this figure JK and JH are the two utility possibility curves which intersect each other. Now suppose that the initial position is at point C on JK. Further suppose that due to a certain policy change, utility possibility curve changes and takes the position GH and the two individuals find themselves at position D. Position C is superior to position D on Kaldor-Hicks criterion because from position D movement can be made through mere redistribution to position F at which both individuals are better off as compared to the original position C. Thus movement from position C to position D satisfies kaldor-Hicks criterion. But, as has been pointed out by Scitovsky, reverse movement from position D on the new utility possibility curve GH to the position C on the old utility possibility curve JK also represents an improvement on Kaldor-Hicks criterion, that is, C is socially better than D on Kaldor-Hicks criterion. This is because from position C movement can be made by mere redistribution of income to position E as the utility possibility curve JK on which position C lies also passes through the position E.

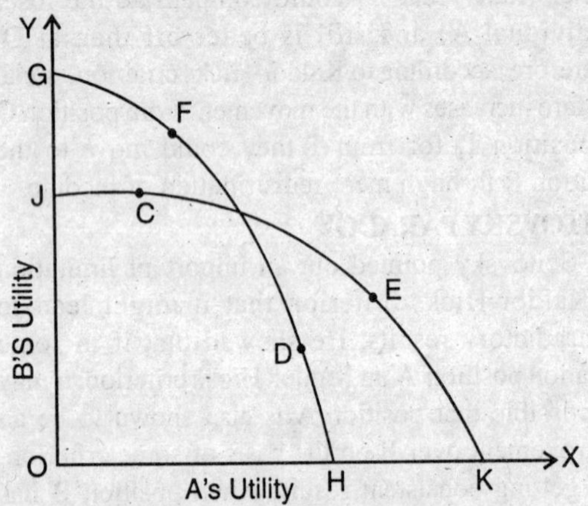

Fig. 191 : *Scitovsky Paradox*

And, as will be observed from figure 191, at position E both the individuals are better off than at D. We thus see that the movement from position C to the position D due to a policy change is passed by the Kaldor-Hicks criterion and also the movement back from position D to position C is also passed by the Kaldor-Hicks criterion. This implies that D is socially better than C on this criterion and C is also socially better than D on the same criterion. So Kaldor-Hicks criterion leads us to contradictory and inconsistent results. It is mention worthy that these contradictory results are obtained by Kaldor-Hicks criterion when following a policy change new utility possibility curve intersects the former utility possibility curve. After bringing out the possibility of contradictory results in Kaldor-Hicks criterion which is generally known as **Scitovsky's Double Criterion.**

Its Criticism

The compensation principle has been bitterly criticised by the various welfare economists.

1. The Kaldor-Hicks compensation principle, according to **Dr. Little,** is merely a definition and not a test of increase in welfare because it ignores income distribution.

2. Compensation principle is not free from value Judgements as is claimed by its propounders. It involves implicit value Judgements.

3. Kaldor and Hicks think that the level of production is the main determinant of social welfare and the distribution a secondary one. But this is quite untenable. This is because welfare has dual aspect: absolute and relative. People are dissatisfied not only because they are poor but more because other peoples are very rich. If all the people would have been poor they would not have been dissatisfied very much. Thus a lower total output equitably distributed is preferred to larger output, inequitably distributed, from the point of view of social welfare.

4. This criterion does not take into consideration the payment of actual compensation. It recognises only potential compensation with which actual increase in welfare cannot be measured.

5. Compensation principle does not take into account the external effects on consumption and production. The exponents of compensation principle are of the opinion that an individual's welfare depends solely upon his own level of production and consumption and is not effected by the production and consumption activities of the others. But this is not a realistic assumption because a person's level of satisfaction (or dissatisfaction) depends to a large extent upon the consumption of goods and services by other persons.

The Social Welfare Function

The concept of social welfare function was first introduced by **Prof. Bergson** and latter on developed by **Samuelson, Tintner** and **Arrow**. They are of the view that no meaningful propositions can be made in welfare economics without introducing value Judgements. The concept of social welfare is an attempt at providing a scientifically normative study of welfare economics.

A social welfare function shows the factors on which the welfare of a society is supposed to depend.

Bergson defines it "as a function either of the welfare of each member of the community or of the quantities of products consumed and services rendered by each member of the community." In its original form the Bergson social welfare function is formulated in a completely general manner. It is a function which establishes a relation between social welfare and all possible variables which effect each individual's welfare, such as a services and consumption of each individual. It can be regarded as a function of each individual's welfare, which in turn depends both on his personal well being and on his appraisal of the distribution of welfare among all members of the community. Thus the social welfare function is an ordinal index of society's welfare and is a function of individual utilities. It is expressed as

$$W = F(U_1 U_2 .... U_n)$$

Where W is the social economic welfare, F is for function, and U_1, U_2,........U_n are the levels of utilities of 1, 2,........*n*, individuals. W is an increasing function of these utilities.

Assumptions

The Bergson social welfare function is based on certain assumptions:

(a) It assumes that social welfare depends on each individual's wealth and income and each individual's welfare depends in turn on his wealth and income and on the distribution of welfare among the members of the society.

(b) It assumes the presence of external economies and diseconomies with their consequent effects.

(c) Interpersonal comparisons of utility involving value Judgements are freely permissible.

We can explain the social welfare function with the help of social indifference curves or welfare frontiers. Let us assume a society of two persons. In such a case social welfare function can be represented with the help of social indifference curves.

In figure 192 the utility of individuals A and B has been represented on the horizontal and vertical axes respectively. W_1, W_2 and W_3 are the social indifference curves representing successively higher levels of social welfare. **A social indifference curve is a locus of the various combinations of utilities of A and B which results in an equal level of social welfare.**

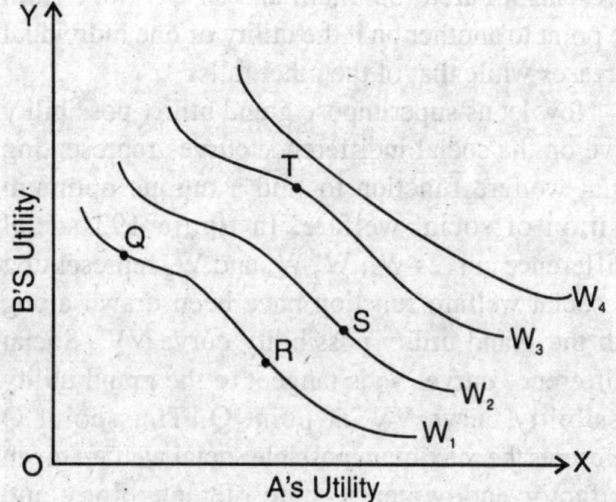

Fig. 192 : *Social Indifference Curves depicting Social Welfare Function*

The properties of social indifference curve are just like that of individual consumer's indifference curves. Given a family of social indifference curves, the effects of a proposed change in policy on social welfare can be evaluated. In terms of figure 192 any policy change that moves the economy from Q to T is an improvement. Similarly, a movement from Q to S or from R to S also represents an improvement in social welfare and a movement from T to Q or T to S represents a decrease in social welfare. A movement along the same social indifference curve represents no change in the level of social welfare. The significance of social welfare function is that it enables us to obtain a unique optimum position regarding social welfare. This unique optimum position is best of all the Pareto optima and therefore ensures the maximum social welfare. Now let us include the concept of **grand utility possibility frontier** in our attempt to obtain a unique optimum position with the aid of social welfare function.

Grand utility possibility frontier is a locus of the various physically attainable utility combinations of two persons when the factor endowment, state of technology and preference orders of the individuals are given. In other words, every point on the grand utility possibility curve represents the optimum position with regard to the allocation of the products among the consumers, allocation of factors among different products and the direction of production. Thus every point on the grand utility possibility curve represents a Pareto optimum and as we move from one point to another on it the utility of one individual increases while that of the other falls.

Now let us superimpose grand utility possibility curve on the social indifference curves representing social welfare function to find a unique optimum position of social welfare. In figure 193 social indifference curves W_1, W_2 W_3 and W_4 representing the social welfare function have been drawn along with the grand utility possibility curve VV'. Social indifference curve W_3 is tangent to the grand utility possibility curve VV' at point Q. Thus point Q represents the maximum possible social welfare given the factor endowments, state of technology and preference scales of the individuals. Point Q is known as the point of **constrained bliss** since, given the constraints regarding factor endowments and the current technology, Q is the highest possible state of social welfare which the society can attain.

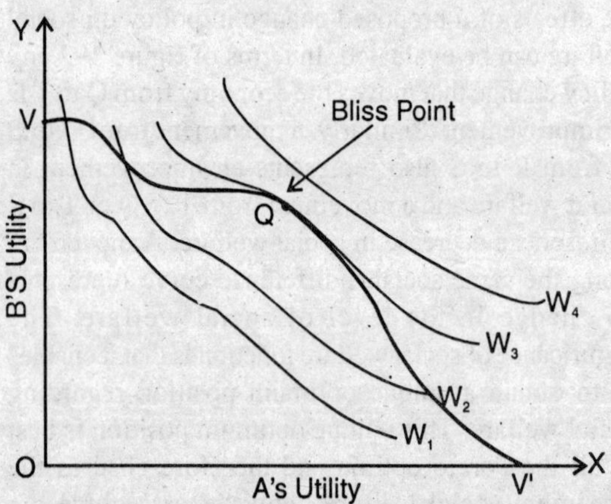

Fig.193 : *Maximisation of Social Welfare*

Social welfare represented by the social indifference curve W_4 is higher than at Q but it is not possible to attain it, given the technology and factor endowment. Thus, from among a large number of Pareto optimum points on the grand utility possibility curve, we have a unique optimum point Q at which the social welfare is the maximum. The point of constrained bliss represents the unique pattern of production of goods, unique distribution of goods between the individuals and the unique combination of factors employed to produce the goods.

Arrow's Social Choice and Individual Values

Bergson and Samuelson made significant contribution to welfare economics by introducing explicit value Judgements in the form of social welfare function. However, Bergson and Samuelson did not deal with the question as to how to get these value Judgements or what these value Judgements could be for constructing a social welfare function. It was this problem left untouched by Samuelson and Bergson, which was explored by **Arrow** in his path breaking work **"Social Choice and Individual Values"**. K.J. Arrow in his social choice and Individual values has demonstrated the impossibility of obtaining the social welfare function even if individual preferences are consistent. He suggests five minimum conditions or criteria which social choices must satisfy in order to reflect preferences of individuals. They are as follows:

1. Collective Rationality
2. Responsiveness to Individual Preferences
3. Non-imposition
4. Non dictatorship
5. Independence of Irrelevant Alternatives

Arrow demonstrates that it is not possible to satisfy all these five conditions and obtain a transitive social choice for each set of individual preferences without violating at least one condition. In other words, social choice is inconsistent or undemocratic because no voting system allows these five conditions to satisfied. This has come to be known as the **Arrow Impossibility Theorem.**

Its Criticism

Arrow's general impossibility theorem has been criticised by Samuelson, Little and other welfare economists.

According to Little, Arrow's negative conclusions have no relevance in welfare economics. His impossibility theorem relates to a decision making process and not to a social welfare function.

Baumol shows that "Arrow's requirements are more strict than they seem at first view and that inconsistent or "undemocratic" social choice making is not really the only alternative.

Moreover, the Arrow theorem is based on the

assumption of a majority voting pattern which does not take into consideration the possibility of a voting system that requires unanimity and permits buying and selling of votes.

Types of Equilibrium

The main types of equilibrium are as follows:

Stable, Neutral and Unstable Equilibrium

A system is in **stable equilibrium** if, when any small disturbance takes place, forces come into play to re-establish the initial position; It is in **neutral equilibrium** if, when such a disturbance takes place, no reestablishing forces and no further disturbing forces are evoked, so that the system remains at rest in the position to which it has moved; it is in unstable equilibrium if the small disturbance calls forth further disturbing forces which act in a cumulative manner to drive the system from its initial position.

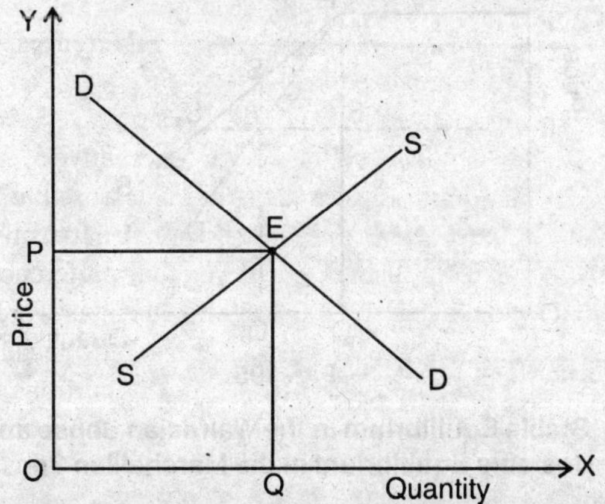

Fig. : *Stable Equilibrium: Downward sloping demand curve and upward sloping supply curve*

Stability Conditions of Equilibrium-Walras Vs. Marshall

There are two different approaches of stability conditions of equilibrium one by **Marshall** and the other by **Walras.** Marshall's approach is the **price-dependent approach** which depends on **quantity movements;** while **Walra's** approach is **quantity dependent approach** which depends on **price movements** to reach equilibrium level. The Marshallian stability condition is based on the assumption that when the excess demand price is positive, producers will increase the supply of the

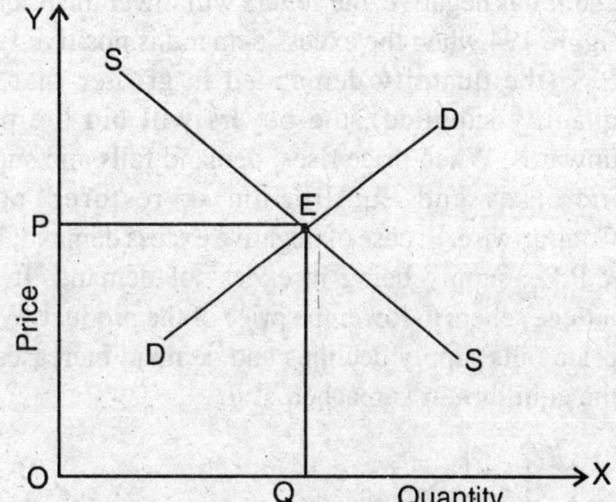

Fig. : *Unstable Equilibrium: Upward sloping demand curve and downward sloping supply curve*

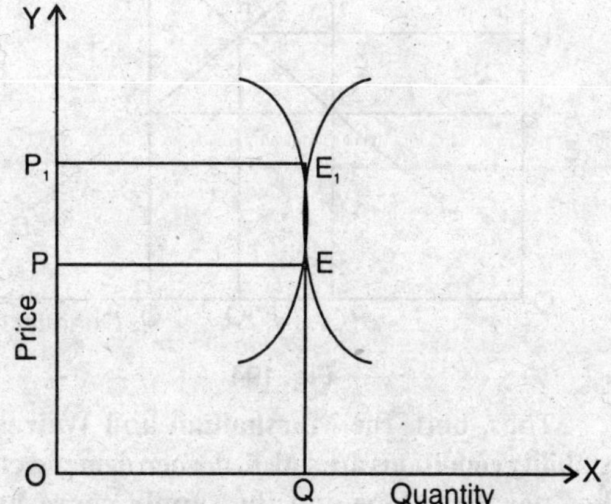

Fig. : *Neutral Equilibrium over a given range*

product, and reduce it when it is negative. In figure 194 at OQ_1 level, when the excess demand price is positive, $d_1Q_1 > SQ_1$, (the demand prices is greater than the supply price) it means that the consumers are offering a higher price than S being charged by the producers who will increase the supply. When supply increases, price falls which will increase demand and equilibrium will be restored at OQ level. Similar reasoning holds for the converse case when at OQ_2 the excess demand price is negative, $dQ_2 < S_1Q_2$. It will induce producers to reduce the quantity supplied. When supply falls, price increases which will reduce the demand and equilibrium will be restored at OQ.

On the other hand, the Walrasian stability condition is based on the assumption that when excess demand is positive, buyers will raise the price and if it is negative, the sellers will lower the price. In figure 194 when the excess demand is positive $P_2d > P_2S$ (the quantity demanded is greater than the quantity supplied), the buyers will bid the price upwards. When price rises, demand falls and supply increases and equilibrium is restored at E. Contrariwise, in case of negative excess demand, $P_1d_1 < P_1S_1$, supply being in excess of demand, It will induce sellers to lower the price of the product. When price falls supply declines and demand increases till the equilibrium is reached at E.

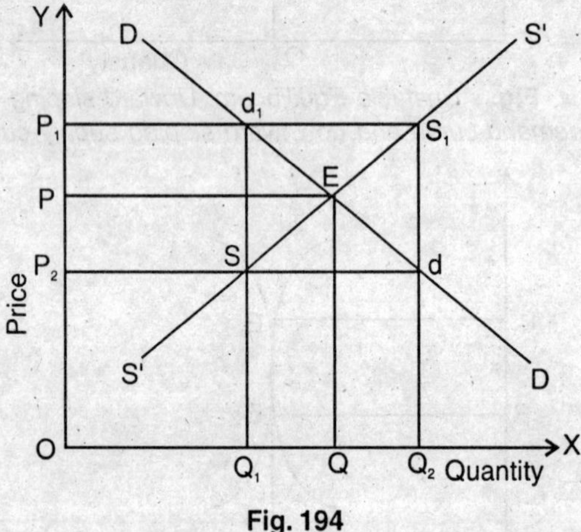

Fig. 194

Thus, **both the Marshallian and Walrasian stability conditions are satisfied when demand curve has negative slope and the supply curve has a positive slope** (in figure 194).

If however, the supply curve has a negative slope, the Marshallian and Walrasian conditions cannot be fulfilled simultaneously. Both the conditions will hold in opposite directions. When equilibrium is stable in the Marshallian sense, it will be unstable in the Walrasian sense, and vice versa. Let us first study these stability conditions with the help of straight line curves.

Figure 195 illustrates stable equilibrium in the Marshallian sense and unstable in the Walrasian sense. At the price OP_1 the excess demand price S_2d is negative, $dQ_1 < S_2Q_1$ the demand price being less than the supply price, it will induce producers to reduce their supply from Q_1 to Q. Price will rise, demand will fall and equilibrium will be restored at E. However, in the other case price OP_1 the excess demand dS_1 being negative $P_1d < P_1S_1$, it will induce sellers to reduce the price of their product still further. Price and quantity will move farther away from the equilibrium point E. Equilibrium is unstable.

Figure 196 illustrates Marshall's unstable and Walras's stable equilibrium. At the price OP_1 the excess demand price dS_1 is positive, $dQ_1 > S_1Q_1$. Since the consumer's are prepared to pay more than the actual price, producer will tend to increase the supply but the excess demand price also increases. Thus, both price and quantity continue to move farther away

Stable Equilibrium in the Marshallian Sense and Unstable in the Walrasian Sense.

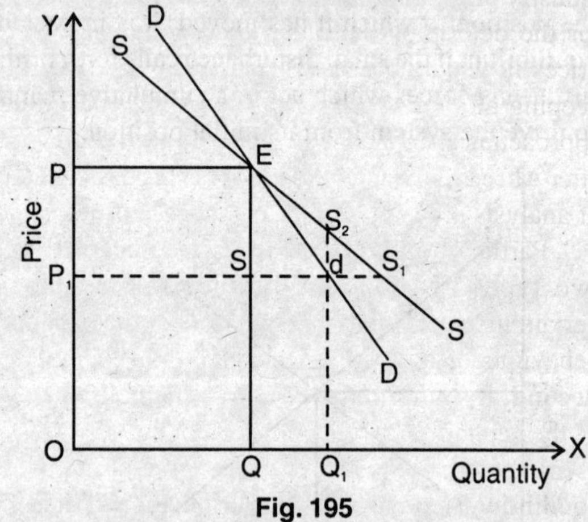

Fig. 195

Stable Equilibrium in the Walrasian Sense and Unstable Equilibrium in the Marshallian Sense.

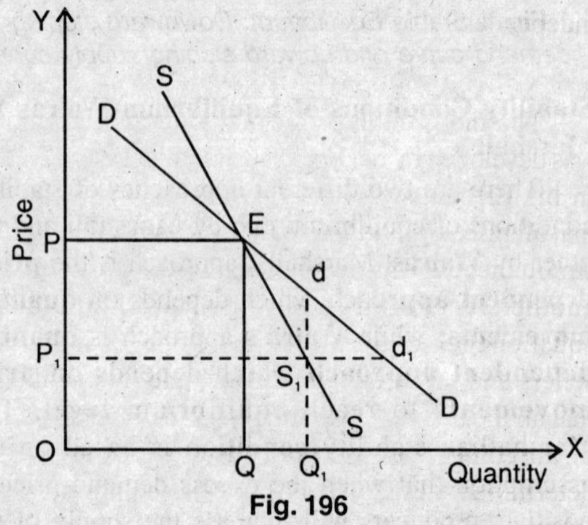

Fig. 196

from the equilibrium level. In the Walrasian sense, at the price OP_1, the excess demand S_1d_1 is positive, $P_1d_1 > P_1S$. Demand being more than the supply, competition among buyers will raise the price to the equilibrium level OP. Equilibrium is stable.

It follows from the above discussion that geometrically equilibrium is stable in the Marshallian sense if the demand curve is steeper than the supply curve and unstable if it is less than the letter. The same reasoning holds for the converse Walrasian case.

Partial Equilibrium

Partial equilibrium analysis is the study of the equilibrium position of an individual, a firm, an industry or group of industries. It is a market process for the determination of product prices and factor prices in which one or two variables are discussed, keeping all others constant. The partial equilibrium approach is also known as **'Marshallian approach'** after Alfred Marshall, who used it as his basic method of analysis in his Principles of Economics.

Partial equilibrium analysis is concerned with two types of economic problems. **First,** those pertaining to only particular aspects of the economic behaviour of a certain individual, firm or industry. **Second,** it studies only the first-order consequences of the economic events.

In summary, the basic characteristic of a partial equilibrium approach is the determination of the price and quantity in each market by demand and supply curves drawn on the ceteris paribus clause. Each market in the Marshallian methodology is regarded independently of the others.

General Equilibrium

The most ambitious general equilibrium model was developed by the French economist **Leon Walras.** In his Elements of Pure Economics Walras argued that all prices quantities in all markets are determined simultaneously through their interaction with one another. Walras used a system of simultaneous equations to describe the interaction of individual sellers and buyers in all markets, and he maintained that all the relevant magnitudes (prices and quantities of all commodities and all factor services) can be determined simultaneously by the solution of this system.

General equilibrium analysis is an extensive study of a number of economic variables, their interrelations and interdependences, for understanding the working of the economic system as a whole. It brings together the cause and effect sequences of changes in the prices and quantities of commodities and services in relation to the entire economy. An economy can be in general equilibrium only if all consumers, all firms, all industries and all factor-services are in equilibrium simultaneously and they are interlinked through commodity and factor prices.

The Cobweb Theorem

Prices and outputs of many commodities show pronounced cyclical movements over long periods of time. Their prices rise and fall in a continued wavelike pattern over a period of time while their production moves up and down in counterwaves. Thus the price and quantity movements of these commodities trace a cobweb like pattern. Such examples are frequently found in agriculture where supply coming on to the market at any one time is the result of decisions taken in the past, while decisions taken about production in the present will have their effect on the actual supply coming forward to the market only at some time in future. Thus supply reacts to price changes with at time lag. The simplest possible time lag in one year and it is this period that we consider in our example below.

Let us suppose that our commodity is produced in an annual crop, say wheat. Once the crop is planted, the supply may be taken as more or less fixed for the year, if we neglect the effects of the weather and other uncertain factors. A change in price will, accordingly, have no effect on the magnitude of this year's total supply. It will, however, effect next year's supply since a low price may induce farmers to plant less for the next year as they would expect low price to continue in the next year as well. On the other hand, a high price this year will induce farmers to produce more next year as they would expect high price to continue in the next year as well. Thus output in year 2 is a response to price in year 1, output in year 3 is a response to price in year 2, and so on. Thus supply in period t would be in response to price in year $(t-1)$.

This gives the supply function as

$$S_t = f(P_{t-1})$$

As against this, the demand function is $D_t = f(P_t)$ indicating that demand in period t depends on the price in the same period.

There are three possibilities in the Cobweb model—

(a) Perpetual Oscillation
(b) Damped Oscillation
(c) Explosive Oscillation

Perpetual Oscillation

Figure 197 gives the case of perpetual oscillation. $D_t = f(P_t)$ is the demand curve for wheat in period t while $S_t = f(P_{t-1})$ is the supply curve of wheat in period t.

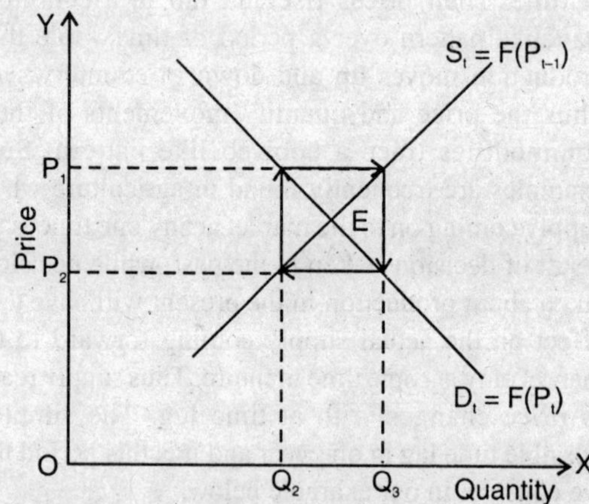

Fig. 197 : *Cobweb Model-Perpetual Oscillation*

Let us suppose that price in 1 period OP_1. In response to this price the farmers produce an output of OQ_2 in period 2. But according to the demand curve, output OQ_2 can be sold only at a low price OP_2. Thus the price in period 2 becomes OP_2. In response to this low price, farmers bring forth a lower supply of wheat in period 3 equal to OQ_3. This small quantity in period 3 will fetch a higher price OP_1. Hence the price in period 3 is the same as the price in year 1. Thus the price and quantity perpetually oscillate round and round as the arrows in the figure indicate. In this example, the odd-numbered years have high prices and low outputs while the even numbered years have low prices and high outputs. **Perpetual oscillation takes place when the slopes of the demand curve and the supply curve are equal.**

Damped Oscillation

Let us now consider the case of damped oscillation. Consider figure 198. In this figure the demand curve is D_t and the 'lagged' supply curve of wheat is S_t.

The price in period 1 is OP_1. In response to this price, the farmers produce an output of OQ_2 in period 2. However, this output in period 2 can be sold at a price OP_2. Due to this low price, the farmers will plant less crop resulting in a low supply of OQ_3 of wheat in period 3. According to the demand curve, this low output will fetch a high price of OP_3 in period 3. As a result, the supply of wheat will expand to OQ_4 in period 4. This will fetch a price of OP_4 in period 4. And so on. Thus the path of the annual price quantity positions is traced by the thick cobweb like line connecting them.

Since oscillations around the equilibrium price-quantity become smaller and smaller, this is a case of damped oscillations.

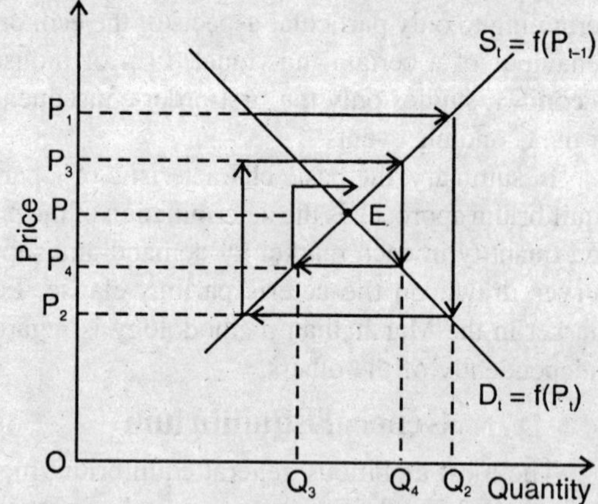

Fig. 198: *Cobweb Model: Damped Oscillation*

In this case equilibrium at point E is stable. **This always happens in the case where the slope of the supply curve is greater than that of the demand curve.**

Explosive Oscillation

If the slope of demand of the demand curve is greater than that of the supply curve, the cobweb line keeps moving further and further away from the point

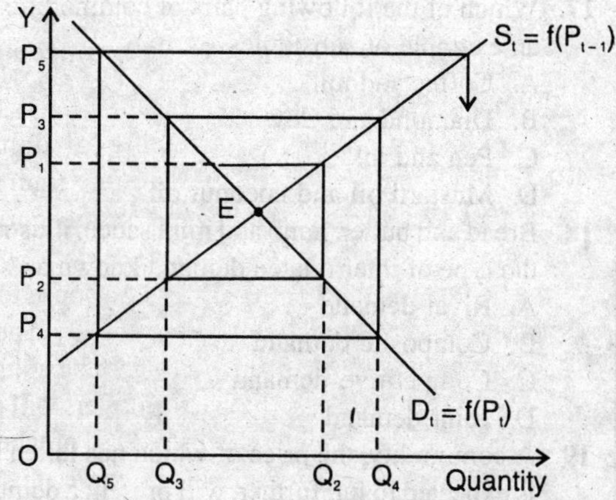

Fig. 199 : *Cobweb Model: Explosive Oscillation*

of equilibrium. Thus the oscillations are explosive and equilibrium unstable. To illustrate this case consider figure 199 where, once again, the demand curve is $D_t = f(P_t)$ and supply curve is $S_t = f(P_{t-1})$.

As earlier, the price the period 1 is OP_1. In response to this price, the farmers produce an output of OQ_2 in period 2. However, this output in period 2 can be sold only at a price OP_2. Due to this low price, the farmers will plant less crop resulting in a low supply of OQ_3 of wheat in period 3. This low output will fetch a high price of OP_3 in period 3. As a result, the supply of wheat will expand to OQ_4 in period 4. This will fetch a price of OP_4 in period 4. And so on. As can be seen, the cobweb line keeps moving further and further away from the point of equilibrium E.

EXERCISE

1. The law of Demand refers to
A. Price-supply relationship
B. Price-cost relationship
C. Price-demand relationship
D. Price-income relationship

2. In a typical demand schedule, quantity demanded
A. Varies directly with price
B. Varies proportionately with price
C. Varies inversely with price
D. Is independent of price

3. Normally when price per unit of a good falls, its
A. Quantity demanded increases
B. Quantity demanded decreases
C. Quantity demanded remains constant
D. None of these happens

4. A fall in the price of a commodity leads to
A. A shift in demand
B. A fall in demand
C. A rise in consumers real income
D. A fall in the consumers real income

5. Demand schedule is shown as
A. A result of increase in the size of the family
B. A result of change in state
C. A function of price alone
D. None of these

6. Market demand for any good is a function of the
A. Price per unit of the good
B. Price per unit of other goods
C. Income of consumers
D. Tastes of consumers
E. All of the above

7. The demand curve for a commodity is generally drawn on the assumption that
A. The commodity has no substitutes
B. Tastes, income and all other prices remain constant
C. The average house hold consists of two persons
D. Purchases of the commodity are made by a free market.

8. A typical demand curve cannot be
A. Convex to the origin
B. A straight line parallel to y-axis
C. A straight line parallel to x-axis
D. Rising upwards to the right

9. When the law of demand operates the demand curve
A. Slopes downward from left to right
B. Slopes upward from left to right
C. Slopes upward from right to left
D. Parallel to horizontal axis

10. For most consumers apples and oranges are substitutes goods. Therefore we would expect a rise in the price of apples to lead to

A. A right ward shift in the demand curve of oranges

B. A left ward shift in the supply curve of apples

C. A downward change in the demand curve of oranges

D. A fall in the price of oranges

11. 'Ceteris paribus' clause in the Law of Demand does not mean

A. The price of the commodity does not change

B. The price of its substitutes does not change

C. The income of the consumer does not change

D. The price of complementary goods does not change

12. Which of the following could provide an example of exceptional demand curves?

I. Demand for "Giffen goods'

II. Demand based on fears of a future rise in prices

III. Demand for second-hand clothes

IV. Demand for daily newspapers

A. I only B. I and II

C. II and III D. I, II, III and IV

13. Which one of the following is true increase of normal goods?

A. When Price increases, demand decreases

B. When Price increases, demand also increases

C. When Price remains constant, demand falls down

D. When Price falls down, demand remains constant

14. An exceptional demand curve is one that slopes:

A. Upwards to the right

B. Down wards to the right

C. Upwards to the left

D. Horizontally

15. When there is decrease in demand the demand curve–

A. Moves downwards towards the axis

B. Moves upwards away from the axis

C. Remains unchanged

D. None of the above

16. Two goods have to be consumed simultaneously are

A. Identical B. Complementary

C. Substitutes D. None of these

17. Which of the following pairs of commodities is an example of substitutes

A. Coffee and milk

B. Diamond and Cow

C. Pen and ink

D. Mustard oil and coconut oil

18. Bread and butter, lamb and mint sauce, illustrate the type of inter related demand known as

A. Rival demand

B. Composite demand

C. Competitive demand

D. Joint demand

19. A commodity, the price of which has fallen but is expected to fall further, will present a demand curve

A. Regressive at the lower end

B. Regressive at the upper end

C. Kinked in the middle

D. Downward sloping to right

20. When an individual's income falls (while everything else remains the same), his demand for an inferior goods:

A. Increases

B. Decreases

C. Remains unchanged

D. We cannot say without additional information

21. If two goods are complements, this means that a rise in the price of one commodity will induce

A. An upward shift in demand for the other commodity

B. A rise in the price of the other commodity

C. A downward shift in demand for the other commodity

D. No shift in demand for the other commodity

22. An income-demand curve for a "Luxury commodity" slopes:

A. Upwards to the right from the origin

B. Vertically

C. Upwards from left to right only beyond a certain level of consumer's income

D. Horizontally

23. An income demand curve for inferior commodity always slopes

A. Upwards to the right

B. Backwards to the left

C. Downwards to the right
D. Horizontally

24. 'Change in quantity demanded' refers to
A. Upward shift of the demand curve
B. Downward shift of the demand curve
C. Movement on the same demand curve
D. None of these

25. When the price of a substitute of commodity X falls, the demand for X—
A. Rises
B. Falls
C. Remains unchanged
D. Any of the above

26. An increase in demand can result from
A. A decline in market price
B. An increase in income
C. A reduction in the price of substitutes
D. An increase in the price of complements
E. All of the above

27. If the price of coffee suddenly shoots up, ceteris paribus, the demand for Tea is expected to—
A. Move rightward along the original demand curve
B. Increase
C. Remain unaffected
D. Decrease

28. In the case of Giffen good like bajra, a fall in its price tends to—
A. Make the demand remain constant
B. Reduce the demand
C. Increase the demand
D. Change demand in an abnormal way

29. Cross demand is the change in the quantity demanded to a given commodity in response to the
A. Change in the utility of another commodity
B. Change in the price of another commodity
C. Change in the nature of another commodity
D. Change in the size of another commodity

30. To calculate the elasticity of demand which of the following formula is used
A. $\dfrac{\text{Percentage change in demand}}{\text{Original demand}}$
B. $\dfrac{\text{Proportionate change in demand}}{\text{Proportionate change in price}}$
C. $\dfrac{\text{Change in demand}}{\text{Change in price}} \div \dfrac{\text{original demand}}{\text{original price}}$
D. $\dfrac{\text{Change in demand}}{\text{Change in price}}$

31. When the demand curve is a rectangular hyperbola, it represents
A. Unitary elastic demand
B. Perfectly elastic demand
C. Perfectly inelastic demand
D. Relatively elastic demand

32. If total consumer expenditure on a good falls as its price falls this indicates that
A. $e_P < 1$ B. $e_P > 1$
C. $e_P = 1$ D. $e_P = \infty$

33. Market demand is
A. The sum of all individual demands
B. Demand at prevailing average prices
C. Ability to pay the price asked
D. Demand in a perfectly free market

34. Extension and contraction of demand are results of
A. Change in consumer's income
B. Change in consumer's tastes
C. Change in price
D. None of these

35. 'Extension of demand' means
A. More quantity demanded at a lower price
B. More quantity demanded at a higher price
C. More quantity demanded at the same price
D. None of these

36. A negative income elasticity of demand for a commodity indicates that as income falls the amount of the commodity purchased
A. Rises
B. Falls
C. Remains unchanged
D. Any of the above

37. Giffen goods are those goods—
A. For which demand increases as price increases
B. Which have a high income elasticity of demand
C. Which are in very short supply
D. None of these

38. In measuring price-elasticity
   A. Price is a dependent variable and quantity is an independent variable
   B. Price is a independent variable and quantity is a dependent variable
   C. Price and quantity both are independent variables
   D. Price and quantity both are dependent variables

39. The demand for pepper is likely to have a low price elasticity because it—
   1. Involves only a small proportion of consumers expenditure
   2. It is single-use goods
   3. Has no close substitutes
   4. Can readily be foregone
   A. 1 and 2 only B. 1 and 3 only
   C. 2 and 3 only D. 2 and 4 only
   E. 2,3 and 4 only

40. Consider a demand curve which takes the form of a straight line cutting both axis. Elasticity at the mid point of the line would be
   A. 0 B. 1.0
   C. 1.5 D. 2.0

41. When with a change in price the total outlay on a commodity remains constant, it is a case of
   A. Perfect elasticity B. Perfect inelasticity
   C. Unit elasticity D. Zero elasticity

42. Income-Elasticity of demand will be zero when a given change in income brings about
   A. A less than proportionate change in quantity demanded
   B. A more than proportionate change in quantity demanded
   C. The same proportionate change in demand
   D. No change in demand

43. Cross elasticity of complementary goods is
   A. Negative B. Zero
   C. High D. Infinite

44. One common definition of luxury goods is goods with an income elasticity
   A. Greater than one
   B. Equal to one
   C. Less than one but more than zero
   D. None of these

45. Match the following:
   1. For a given 10 percent change in price, demand changes by zero percent — *(i)* $e > 1$
   2. For a given 10 percent change in price, demand changes by 5 percent — *(ii)* $e = 1$
   3. For a given 10 percent change in price, demand changes by 10 percent — *(iii)* $e < 1$
   4. For a given 10 percent change in price, demand changes by 20 percent — *(iv)* $e = 0$

	1	2	3	4
A.	*iii*	*i*	*ii*	*iv*
B.	*iv*	*iii*	*ii*	*i*
C.	*i*	*ii*	*iii*	*iv*
D.	*ii*	*iii*	*i*	*iv*

46. A straight line, downward-sloping demand curve implies that, as price falls, the elasticity of demand
   A. Increases
   B. Decreases
   C. Remains the same
   D. is zero

47. In the longer period permitting adjustment, demand is likely to be
   A. Inelastic B. Elastic
   C. Unit elastic D. Cannot be known

48. Elasticity of demand is equal to unity while marginal revenue is
   A. Positive B. Zero
   C. Negative D. Indeterminate

49. A demand curve which takes the form of a horizontal line parallel to the quantity axis illustrates elasticity which is
   A. Zero B. Infinite
   C. > 1 D. < 1

50. Which of the following does not have a uniform elasticity of demand at all points—
   A. A downward sloping demand curve
   B. A vertical demand curve
   C. A rectangular hyperbola demand curve
   D. A horizontal demand curve

51. If the percentage increase in the quantity of a commodity demanded is smaller than the

percentage fall in its price, the coefficient of price elasticity of demand is—

A. Greater than 1 B. Equal to 1
C. Less than 1 D. Zero

52. Match the following

1. Responsiveness of demand to change in price — *(i)* Income elasticity of demand
2. Responsiveness of demand to change in tastes — *(ii)* Price elasticity of demand
3. Responsiveness of demand to change in income — *(iii)* Cross elasticity of demand
4. Responsiveness of demand to change in price of related goods. — *(iv)* Taste elasticity of demand

	1	2	3	4
A.	*i*	*ii*	*iii*	*iv*
B.	*iv*	*iii*	*i*	*ii*
C.	*iii*	*iv*	*ii*	*i*
D.	*ii*	*iv*	*i*	*iii*

53. A monopolist charging high price operates on

A. The elastic part of a demand curve
B. The inelastic part of a demand curve
C. The constant elastic part of a demand curve
D. Ignores elasticity of demand altogether

54. Elasticity of demand in the following figure at point Q_1 is

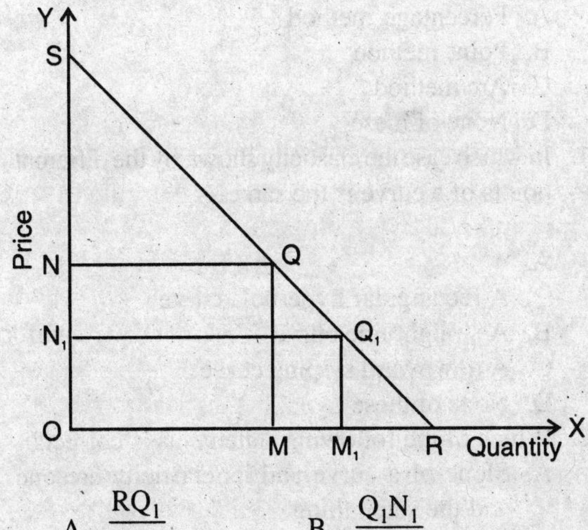

A. $\frac{RQ_1}{SQ_1}$ B. $\frac{Q_1N_1}{OS}$

C. $\frac{Q_1F}{RQ_1}$ D. $\frac{RQ}{RQ_1}$

55. Arc elasticity gives a better measure of point elasticity of a curvilinear demand curve as

A. The size of the arc becomes smaller
B. The curvature of the demand curve over the arc becomes less
C. Both of the above
D. Neither of the above

56. Ceteris paribus, a change in the price of a commodity causes the quantity purchased of its complements to move

A. In the same direction
B. In the opposite direction
C. In an insignificant manner
D. Cannot be known

57. If there were no changes in the quantity of food sold, even when its price falls, we would know that—

A. Demand was entirely inelastic
B. Demand was entirely elastic
C. Demand was more elastic than one
D. Demand was unit elastic

58. When the income elasticity of demand is greater than unity, the commodity is

A. A necessity
B. A luxury
C. An inferior good
D. A non-related good

59. Which of the following statement is correct—

A. When the slope of the demand curve is zero, demand is infinitely elastic and when the slope is infinite, elasticity is zero
B. When the slope of the demand curve is zero, elasticity is also zero and when the slope is infinite, elasticity is also infinite
C. When the slope of the demand curve is zero, elasticity is unity and also when the slope is infinite, elasticity is unity
D. None of these

60. If two commodities are substitutes a change in the price of one, ceteris paribus, causes a change in the quantity purchased of the other

A. In the same direction
B. In the opposite direction

C. In an insignificant manner

D. Cannot be known

61. Income elasticity of demand is expressed as

A. $\frac{\text{Percentage change in quantity demanded}}{\text{Percentage change in income}}$

B. $\frac{\text{Percentage change in income}}{\text{Change in quantity demanded}}$

C. Change in quantity demanded $\times \frac{\text{Change in marginal income}}{100}$

D. $\frac{\text{Change in income}}{100 \times \text{change in quantity demanded}}$

62. In the case of an inferior commodity, the income elasticity of demand is

A. Positive B. Unitary

C. Negative D. Infinity

63. Income elasticity of demand will be zero when a given change in income brings about—

A. A less than proportionate change in quantity demanded

B. A more than proportionate change in quantity demanded

C. The same proportionate change in demand

D. No change in demand

64. The degree of price elasticity of demand used for goods is influenced by whether

1. It has close substitutes
2. Its output is easily altered
3. It account for a small input
4. It is a durable use or single use goods

A. 1, 3 and 4 only B. 1 and 2 only

C. 2 and 3 only D. 2, 3 and 4 only

65. Pick out the correct formula for arc elasticity

A. $\frac{\Delta q}{\Delta P} \cdot \frac{P_1 + P_2}{q_1 + q_2}$ B. $\frac{\Delta P}{\Delta q} \cdot \frac{P_1 + P_2}{q_1 + q_2}$

C. $\frac{\Delta P}{\Delta q} \cdot \frac{100}{q_1 + P_1}$ D. $\frac{\Delta q \times 100}{P}$

66. A country is advised to devalue (reduce external value of) its currency only when its exports face

A. Inelastic demand in foreign markets

B. Elastic demand in foreign markets

C. Unit elastic demand in foreign markets

D. None of these

67. Consider the following demand schedule

Price per unit (Rs.)	*Quantity demanded* (000)
6	3
5	9
4	15
3	20

When price falls from Rs. 5 to Rs. 4, elasticity of demand can be expressed numerically as

A. 1.0 B. 2.5

C. 3.3 D. 3.75

68. Two commodities are considered to be perfect substitutes for each other if the elasticity of substitution is

A. Positive B. Negative

C. Zero D. Infinite

69. If a straight line demand curve is tangent to a curvilinear demand curve, the elasticity of the two demand curves at the points of tangency is—

A. The same

B. Different

C. Can be the same or different

D. Depends on the location of the point of tangency

70. Which of the following is the method of measuring elasticity of demand when changes in price of a commodity is substantial—

A. Percentage method

B. Point method

C. Arc method

D. None of these

71. In which case the elasticity shown by the different points of a curve is the same—

A. A rectangular hyperbola curve

B. A straight line curve

C. A downward sloping curve

D. None of these

72. Which of the following statements is correct?

A. Slope of a curve and its elasticity are one and the same thing

B. Slope of a curve may remain constant; elasticity still can and does change

D. Two parallel demand curves, each cutting the two axis, have the same elasticity at a point corresponding to the same price

73. A demand curve is a boundary concept because it shows
A. The maximum price and minimum quantity
B. The minimum price and minimum quantity
C. The maximum quantity and the minimum price
D. Both price and quantity is maximum

74. In case the two commodities are good substitutes, cross-elasticity will be
A. Positive B. Unitary
C. Negative D. Infinite

75. In case the two commodities are complements, cross elasticity will be
A. Positive B. Unitary
C. Negative D. Infinite

76. If cross-elasticity of one commodity for another turns out to be zero, it means they are
A. Close substitutes
B. Good complements
C. Completely unrelated
D. None of these

77. A high value of cross-elasticity indicates that the two commodities are
A. Very good substitutes
B. Poor substitutes
C. Good complements
D. Poor complements

78. The vertical demand curve for a commodity shows that its demand is
A. Highly elastic B. Perfectly elastic
C. Fairly elastic D. Moderately elastic

79. If more is demanded at the same price or the same quantity is demanded at a higher price, this is known as
A. Extension of demand
B. Contraction of demand
C. Increase in demand
D. Decrease in demand

80. Utility may be defined as
A. The power of a commodity to satisfy wants
B. The usefulness of a commodity
C. The level of satisfaction given by a commodity
D. The desire for a commodity

81. The economic analysis expects the consumer to behave in a manner which is
A. Rational B. Irrational
C. Emotional D. Indifferent

82. The economically relevant range of the total utility curve is the portion over which
A. The total utility is rising at a declining rate
B. The total utility is rising at an increasing rate
C. The total utility is maximum and constant
D. The total utility is declining

83. After reaching the saturation point, consumption of additional units of the commodity cause
A. Total utility to fall and marginal utility to increase
B. Total utility and marginal utility both to increase
C. Total utility to fall and marginal utility to become negative
D. Total utility to become negative and marginal utility to fall

84. Which of the following concepts are most closely associated with Alfred Marshall?
A. Marginal utility theory
B. Price mechanism under monopoly
C. Modern theory of wage
D. Interest theory

85. The law of Equi-Marginal utility states
A. $MU_x.P_x = MU_y.P_y = MU_z.P_z$
B. $\frac{MU_x}{P_x} = \frac{MU_y}{P_y} = \frac{MU_z}{P_z} = MU_m$
C. $\frac{MU_x}{P_x} > \frac{MU_y}{P_y} > \frac{MU_z}{P_z} > MU_m$
D. $\frac{MU_x}{P_x} < \frac{MU_y}{P_y} < \frac{MU_z}{P_z} < MU_m$

86. Law of diminishing Marginal utility states
A. Total utility diminishes with the consumption of every additional unit
B. Utility always diminishes whether something is consumed or not
C. Utility first increases and after that

diminishes at every point

D. The additional benefit which a person derives from a given increase of his stock of a thing diminishes with every increase in stock that he already has

87. Marginal utility (MU) curve is always
A. Rising
B. Falling
C. Parallel to x-axis
D. Parallel to y-axis

88. The total utility is maximum when
A. M.U. is zero
B. A.U. is the highest
C. M.U. is the highest
D. M.U. is equal to A.U.

89. The falling part of a TU curve show
A. Increasing marginal utility
B. Decreasing marginal utility
C. Zero marginal utility
D. Negative marginal utility

90. MU of nth unit is found by the following formula
A. $\frac{TU}{n}$ B. TU.n
C. $TU_n - TU_{(n-1)}$ D. TU + n

91. Total utility curve is
A. Concave to x-axis
B. Convex to x-axis
C. Concave or convex depending on situations
D. Concave to y-axis

92. "Utils" is a term used
A. By Marshall in Demand theory
B. By Walras to measure cardinal utility
C. To mean Marginal utility
D. None of the above

93. Given below is the MU schedule for commodities x and y
MU_x 11 10 9 8 7 6
MU_y 19 17 15 13 12 10
If price is Rs. 1 permit in each case the consumer will spend his 10th rupee on
A. Commodity *x*
B. Commodity *y*
C. Commodity *x* and *y*
D. Save from both

94. A consumer's demand curve can be obtained from
A. Income-consumption curve
B. Engel's curve
C. Price-consumption curve
D. None of these

95. A consumer will be in equilibrium if he consumes three commodities when
A. $\frac{\text{Price of } x}{\text{Price of } y} = \frac{\text{Price of } y}{\text{Price of } z} = \frac{\text{Price of } y}{\text{Price of } x} = K$
B. $\frac{MU_x}{P_x} = \frac{MU_y}{P_y} = \frac{MU_z}{P_z} = K$
C. $P_x = P_y = P_z = Z$
D. $MU_z = MU_x = MU_y$

96. 'Marginal utility approach' was finalised by
A. J.R. Hicks B. Alfred Marshall
C. J.S. Mill D. A.C. Pigou

97. A consumer will be maximizing his utility if he allocated his money income so that—
A. The marginal utility of the last unit of each product consumed is equal
B. The marginal utility from he last rupee spent on each purchased product is the same
C. Elasticity of demand is the same for all purchased products
D. Total utility gained from each product consumed is the same

98. Adam Smith spoke about the famous diamond water paradox to show that
A. Utility is related to supply
B. Utility is related to demand
C. Utility could be the cause of value
D. Utility could not be the cause of value

99. The area which lies under the demand curve for a given good measures
A. Marginal utility
B. Total utility
C. Disutility
D. Marginal cost of production

100. Which of the following creates time utility?
A. Farmer B. Carpenter
C. Trader D. Driver

101. Total utility of a commodity can be found by
A. Multiplying the number of units by its marginal utility

B. Adding up the marginal utility of all units
C. Multiplying price by number of units
D. None of these

102. "The concept marginal utility is useful for explaining diamond-water paradox" this statement is
A. Absolutely correct
B. Partially correct
C. Absolutely wrong
D. None of these

103. MU curve will be below x-axis when
A. MU is positive B. MU is negative
C. MU is zero D. MU is constant

104. As a consumer increases his consumption of a commodity, the total utility he derives from its consumption increases, but at a diminishing rate. This is—
A. A statement of fact
B. An economic law
C. A hypothesis
D. None of the above

105. A consumer reaches equilibrium at the point where
A. MU = P B. MU < P
C. MU > P D. TU = P

106. At the saturation point of commodity y the MU is
A. Positive B. Zero
C. Negative D. None of the above

107. The term optimum allocation on consumer's expenditure on various goods and services is used in
A. Law of demand
B. Giffen paradox
C. Law of equi-marginal utility
D. Law of diminishing marginal utility

108. A falling MU curve illustrates
A. The principle of diminishing marginal utility
B. The principle of diminishing marginal rate of substitution
C. The principle of equi-marginal utility
D. None of these

109. Which of the following is most closely connected with Paul A. Samuelson?
A. Indifference curve analysis
B. Marginal utility analysis
C. Revealed preference theory
D. Liquidity preference theory

110. The Law of Equi-Marginal utility tells that if price of commodity falls
A. More units of it will be bought
B. Less units of it will be bought
C. Same units of it will be bought
D. Nothing of it will be bought

111. Which of the following is called as the Gossen's First Law?
A. Law of substitution
B. The Law of equi-marginal utility
C. The Law of diminishing utility
D. The Law of indifference

112. After reaching the saturation point additional unit of the commodity causes
A. Total utility to fall and marginal utility to become negative
B. Total utility and marginal utility both to increase
C. Total utility and marginal utility both to decrease
D. Total utility become negative and marginal utility to fall

113. A stable equilibrium position is one in which
A. There are never any departures from the equilibrium position
B. There are only two forces influencing equilibrium
C. Any departure from the equilibrium position calls into play forces which end to restore that position
D. There are endless oscillations

114. Marginal utility has no place in a ordinal theory because it is
A. Introspective B. Subjective
C. Not observable D. Additive

115. At the point of inflexion, the marginal utility is
A. Increasing B. Decreasing
C. Maximum D. Negative

116. Ordinal approach is based on
A. Law of maximum satisfaction
B. Utility could not be measured in cardinal numbers
C. Utility could not be measured in ordinal

numbers

D. Utility can be measured

117. Put into chronological order on the basis of development

(i) Law of demand

(ii) Law of indifference

(iii) Law of diminishing marginal utility

(iv) Revealed preference curve

(v) Indifference curve

A.	*i*	*ii*	*iii*	*iv*	*v*
B.	*i*	*v*	*iii*	*iv*	*ii*
C.	*i*	*iii*	*ii*	*v*	*iv*
D.	*i*	*iii*	*iv*	*ii*	*v*

118. Match the following:

1. Principles of Economics (i) Gunnar Myrdal
2. Diamond water paradox (ii) J.K. Galbraith
3. Value and Capital (iii) Alfred Marshall
4. Asian Drama (iv) J. R. Hicks
5. Language of Economics (v) Adam Smith

	1	2	3	4	5
A.	*i*	*ii*	*iii*	*v*	*iv*
B.	*ii*	*iv*	*iii*	*v*	*i*
C.	*v*	*ii*	*iii*	*i*	*iv*
D.	*iii*	*v*	*iv*	*i*	*ii*
E.	*iv*	*v*	*iii*	*ii*	*i*

119. The price which a consumer would be willing to pay for a commodity equals to his

A. Total utility

B. Marginal utility

C. Average utility

D. Does not have any relation to any one of these

120. Gossen's second law states that—

A. When the income increases the money value or real income will decrease

B. The consumers consume only when $\frac{P_x}{P_y} = MU_m$

C. Once a person has spent his entire income he would have maximised his total pleasure from it only if the satisfaction gained from the last item of each commodity bought was the same

D. None of these

121. The concept of indifference curves analysis was given scientific touch by—

A. Irving Fisher in 1982

B. F.Y. Edgeworth in 1881

C. Slutsky in 1915

D. Alfred Marshall in 1921

122. Economists associated with the development of indifference curve analysis are

A. Hicks and Allen

B. Hicks and Robbins

C. Marshall and Hicks

D. Hicks and Walras

123. The indifference curve technique

A. Has replaced utility technique altogether

B. is used as alternative to the utility technique

C. is used along with the utility approach

D. Has become a part of the utility approach

124. Which of the following is one of the assumptions of the indifference curve analysis—

A. Cardinal utility

B. Ordinal utility

C. Independent utility

D. Constant marginal utility of money

125. Other things remaining the same, when a consumer's income increases, his equilibrium point moves to

A. A higher indifference curve

B. A lower indifference curve

C. Remains unchanged on the same indifference curve

D. Moves to the left-hand side on the same indifference curve

126. The general equation of the budget constraint line is

A. $P_x \cdot Q_x + P_y \cdot Q_y = M$

B. $\frac{P_x}{M} = Qx$

C. $Q_x \cdot P_x = M + P_y$

D. $P_x + P_y = O$

127. An indifference curve is always

A. Concave to the origin

B. Convex to the origin

C. A vertical straight line

D. A horizontal straight line

128. When the consumer's income increases, the

budget line on an indifference map moves to

A. A parallel position to the right
B. A parallel position to the left
C. A parallel position to the origin
D. None of the above

129. Goods X and Y are perfect substitutes. A consumers's indifference curve for these commodities is represented by a

A. Upward sloping straight line
B. Upward sloping curve which is convex from below
C. Downward sloping straight line
D. Downward sloping curve which is convex to origin

130. The indifference curve which is 'L' shape represents

A. Perfect complementarity
B. Perfect substitutability
C. No substitutability
D. Non Complementarity

131. "We are much better off when drawing purely imaginary indifference curves than we are when speaking of purely imaginary utility functions." This is remarked by—

A. J. R. Hicks B. Allen
C. Schumpeter D. Paul A. Samuelson

132. Indifference curve is downward sloping from left to right since more *x* and less *y* give

A. Less satisfaction
B. More satisfaction
C. Equal satisfaction
D. Maximum satisfaction

133. When the price of one commodity in a combination of commodities falls in such a way that the consumer's real income changes but he remains on the same level of satisfaction as before, It is known as

A. Income effect
B. Variation effect
C. Price effect
D. Compensating variation in income

134. If two goods are perfect substitutes for each other, it necessarily follows that

A. An indifference curve relating the two goods will be curvilinear
B. An indifference curve relating the two goods will be linear
C. An indifference curve relating the two goods will be divided into two segments which meet at a right angle
D. An indifference curve relating the two goods will be convex to the origin

135. MRS_{xy} and MRS_{yx} both will be zero where the commodity *x* and *y* are

A. Complement to each other
B. Substitutes to each other
C. Perfect complementarity
D. Imperfect complementarity

136. The amount of a commodity that the consumer would purchase per unit of time at various levels of his income is shown by

A. Contract curve
B. Lorenz curve
C. Engel curve
D. Indifference curve

137. All the points on a budget line represent

A. Increasing total expenditure
B. Decreasing total expenditure
C. The same total expenditure
D. None of the above

138. If the $\frac{MU_x}{MU_y}$ for individual A is greater than the $\frac{MU_x}{MU_y}$ for individual B it is possible for individual A to gain by giving up

A. Y in exchange for more X from B
B. Y in exchange for more X from A itself
C. Y in exchange for less X from B
D. X in exchange for less Y from A

139. If indifference curve has a positive slope, it means

A. Consumer preferences unpredictable
B. Consumer preferences are irrational
C. *x*-is a discommodity
D. *y*-is a discommodity

140. For perfect substitutability between *x* and *y*—

A. MRS_{xy} will be constant
B. MRS_{xy} will be decreasing
C. MRS_{xy} will be increasing
D. None of the above

141. Match the following—

1. Various combinations of two commodities that a consumer can purchase	*(i)* Indifference map
2. Various combinations of two Commodities that give consumer equal satisfaction	*(ii)* Indifference curve
3. A set of indifference curves	*(iii)* Budget line
4. Point of tangency of a budget line and an indifference curve	*(iv)* Consumer's equilibrium

	1	2	3	4
A.	*i*	*ii*	*iv*	*iii*
B.	*iv*	*iii*	*i*	*ii*
C.	*ii*	*iii*	*iv*	*i*
D.	*iii*	*ii*	*i*	*iv*

142. On an indifference map higher indifference curves show

A. The same lower level of satisfaction
B. The optimum level of satisfaction
C. The higher level of satisfaction
D. Levels of satisfaction among which the consumer is indifferent

143. Match the following:

1. Cardinal approach	*(i)* Marginal utility
2. Ordinal approach	*(ii)* Alfred Marshall
3. Hicks-Allen approach	*(iii)* J.R. Hicks
4. Consumer's surplus	*(iv)* Indifference curve
	(v) Revealed preference theory

	1	2	3	4
A.	*i*	*ii*	*iii*	*iv*
B.	*i*	*v*	*iv*	*ii*
C.	*i*	*iii*	*iv*	*ii*
D.	*i*	*iii*	*ii*	*iv*

144. On an indifference map, if the income consumption curve slopes downwards to the right it shows that

A. X is an inferior good
B. Y is an inferior good
C. Both X and Y are superior goods
D. Both X and Y are inferior goods

145. Price effect in indifference curve analysis arises—

A. when the consumer becomes either better off or worse off because price change is not compensated income change
B. When income and price change
C. When the consumer is better off due to a change in income and price
D. None of the above

Question 146 to 147 are based on he following figure—

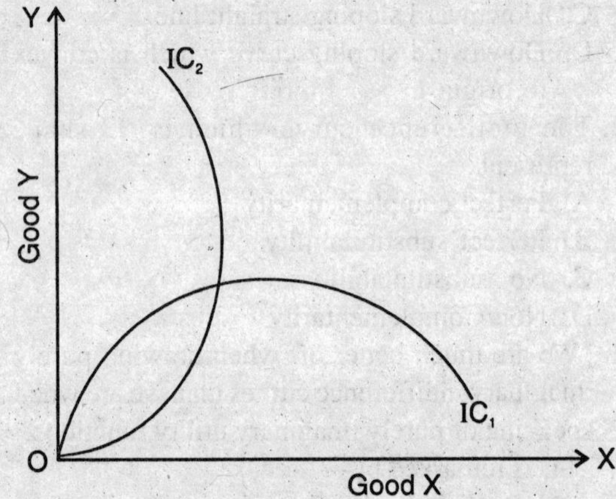

146. If curve IC_2 represents the income consumption curve, then we can conclude that—

A. X only is an inferior good
B. Y only is an inferior good
C. Both X and Y are inferior good
D. X only is a superior good

147. If we assume that curve IC_1 is the income consumption curve, it can be concluded that—

A. Only *y* is an inferior good
B. Neither *y* nor *x* is an inferior good
C. Only *x* is an inferior good
D. *x* is inferior but *y* is a superior good

148. In the case of an inferior good, the income effect

A. Partially offsets the substitution effect
B. Reinforces the substitution effect
C. Is equal to the substitution effect
D. More than offsets the substitution effect

149. The substitution effect works to encourage a consumer to purchase more of a product when the price of that goods is falling because

A. The consumer's real income has increased

B. The consumer's real income has decreased
C. The product is now relatively less expensive the before
D. Other products are now less expensive than before

150. The total effect of a price change of a commodity is
A. Substitution effect + Price effect
B. Substitution effect + Income effect
C. Substitution effect + Demonstration effect
D. Substitution effect – Income effect

151. The Engel curve passes through the tangency point of
A. Budget line and indifference curve
B. Price line and iso cost line
C. Iso-quant and budget line
D. None of these

152. In the case of a normal good, the income effect
A. Is always equal to the substitution effect
B. Completely offsets the substitution effect
C. Partially offset the substitution effect
D. Reinforces the substitution effect

153. The Doctrine of consumer's surplus is based on
A. Indifference curve analysis
B. Revealed preference theory
C. Law of substitution
D. The law of diminishing marginal utility

154. The Revealed Preference Theory was formulated by
A. Lionel Robbins B. Paul Samuelson
C. Joan Robinson D. Alfred Marshall

155. Consider the diagram below which shows a demand curve (d)

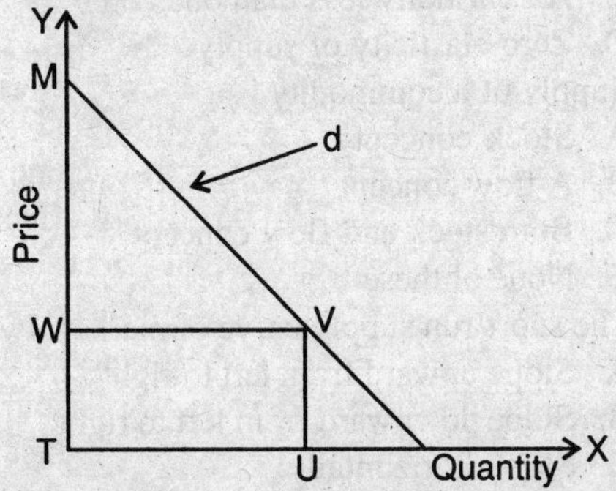

Total expenditure on a commodity is represented by the area TUVW. Consumer's surplus is represented by
A. The area MWV B. The area XTWV
C. $\frac{XW}{XT}$ D. $\frac{TU}{UV}$

156. Consumer's surplus is the highest in the case of
A. Necessities
B. Comforts
C. Luxuries
D. Conventional necessities

157. The case of a right angled indifference curve occurs when
A. The two goods are perfect complement
B. The two goods are perfectly substitutes
C. The two goods are inferior
D. The two goods are normal

158. While analysing Marshall's measure of Consumer's surplus one assumes
A. Imperfect competition
B. Perfect competition
C. Monopoly
D. Monopsony

159. The revealed preference theory assumes
A. Strong ordering B. Weak ordering
C. Introspection D. None of these

160. Slutsky's theory in consumption theory relates to
A. Income effect
B. Substitution effect
C. Complementarity of goods
D. Both (A) and (B)

161. A consumer's demand curve can be obtained from
A. Income consumption curve
B. Engel's curve
C. Lorenz curve
D. Price consumption curve

162. Who demonstrated the abnormal shape of demand curve for diamonds through the doctrine of conspicuous consumption?
A. Thorstein Veblen B. Robert Giffen
C. David Ricardo D. Alfred Marshall

163. We can separate the income effect from the substitution effect of the price fall of reducing the consumers—
A. Money income sufficiently to keep his real

income constant

B. Money income to make his real income higher

C. Money income to make his real income lower

D. None of these

164. What was Robert Giffen's observation in relating to price and quantity demanded.

A. A commodity whose price and quantity demanded vary in different direction

B. A commodity whose price and quantity demanded vary in same direction

C. A commodity whose price and quantity demanded is always constant

D. Both (A) and (B) are correct

165. The Revealed Preference Theory is based on

A. The assumption of indifference

B. Utility and demand

C. Introspection

D. Observed consumer behaviour

166. A rightwards shifte in supply curve indicates

A. A decrease in supply

B. An increase in quantity supplied

C. An increase in supply

D. None of the above

167. Other things being equal a decrease in the quantity supplied to the market at given prices leads to—

A. A higher price and a contraction of demand

B. A lower price and an expansion of demand

C. A higher price and an expansion of demand

D. A lower price and a contraction of demand

168. Other things being eqùal an increase in supply can be caused by

A. A rise in the price of the commodity

B. An improvement in the techniques of production

C. A rise in the income of the consumer

D. An increase in the income of the seller

169. When the market supply curve for a commodity is negatively sloped, we have a case of—

A. The general equilibrium

B. Partial equilibrium

C. The stable equilibrium

D. None of the above, unless additional information is given

170. If the supply curve of a commodity is positively sloped, a rise in the price of the commodity ceteris paribus, results in and is referred to as

A. A decrease in demand

B. A decrease in quantity supplied

C. A decrease in supply

D. A decrease in both demand and supply

171. The market period supply curve for perishable commodities is—

A. Relatively inelastic

B. Perfectly inelastic

C. Relatively elastic

D. Perfectly elastic

172. Any supply curve which is a straight line passing through the origin whatever its slopes will possess—

A. Unitary elasticity of supply

B. An elasticity which is greater than one

C. An elasticity which is less than one

D. An elasticity which is greater than zero

173. External economies are witnessed in

A. A rising supply curve

B. A rising demand curve

C. A falling supply curve

D. A falling demand curve

174. For a positively sloped straight line supply curve that intersects the price axis is—

A. Equal to zero B. Equal to one

C. Greater than one D. Constant

175. Any straight line supply curve which cuts the x-axis will have

A. An elasticity greater than one

B. Unitary elasticity of supply

C. An elasticity less than one

D. Zero elasticity of supply

176. Supply of a commodity is a

A. Stock concept

B. A flow concept

C. Both stock and flow concept

D. None of these

177. The short-run supply curve of market always

A. Slope upward from left to right

B. Slope downward from left to right

C. Slope horizontally

D. None of the above

178. The concept of supply curve as it is used in

economic theory is relevant only for the case of—
A. Monopoly
B. Perfect or pure competition
C. Monopolistic competition
D. Oligopoly competition

179. "Production" may be defined as an act of—
A. Creating utility
B. Earning profit
C. Destroying utility
D. Providing services

180. In general, most of the production functions measure
A. The productivity of factors of production
B. The relation between the factors of production
C. The economies of scale
D. The relations between change in physical inputs and physical output

181. In the long-run
A. All factors can be used in different proportions
B. Management can be re-organised
C. A firm can experience returns to scale
D. All of these

182. A set of all possible production combinations while producing two commodities is
A. Isoquant map
B. Iso cost line
C. Production possibility curve
D. Production functions

183. Economies of scale means—
A. Reductions in unit cost of production
B. Reductions in unit cost of distribution
C. Addition to the unit cost of production
D. Reduction in the total cost of production

184. Marginal product is
A. What is produced when all factors of production are employed at optimum efficiency
B. The extra output obtained from employing an additional unit of a factor
C. What is left to the entrepreneur after he has paid all his expenses
D. Annual output of the most efficient firm in the industry

185. Marginal product becomes negative—
A. In no circumstances
B. When total output turns down
C. When total output grows swiftly
D. When total output ceases to grow swiftly

186. When the average product is at its maximum the equality can be reached between
A. The marginal product and total product
B. The marginal product and average product
C. The marginal product and primary product
D. The marginal product and final product

187. When average product increases, the marginal product is
A. Less than the average product
B. More than the average product
C. Equal to the average product
D. None of the above

188. In short run the law of variable proportions is also known as the
A. Law of increasing returns
B. Law of diminishing returns
C. Law of constant returns
D. Law of return to scale

189. Increasing returns to scale can be explained in terms of
A. Fixed scale of plant
B. Optimum factor proportions
C. External and internal economics
D. Labour productivity

190. Imagine a graph showing production possibilities. What does an outward shift of the production possibilities curve indicate—
A. Inflation
B. Over production
C. Economic growth
D. Over full employment

191. The expansion path of production theory is analogous in consumption theory to the—
A. Price consumption line
B. Engel curve
C. Income consumption line
D. Budget constraint line

192. The Law of variable proportions comes into being when
A. There are only two variable factors

B. There is a fixed factor and a variable factor
C. All factors are variable
D. Variable factors yield less

193. Which of the stages is relevant for a firm which aims at maximum economic efficiency in the following diagram—

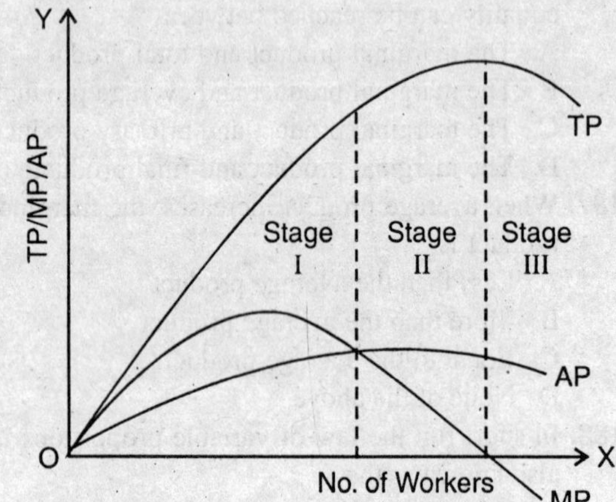

A. Stage I B. Stage II
C. Stage III D. Stage IV

194. From the above figure in stage III the MP curve becomes negative because of—
A. Fixed factor quantity exceed variable factor
B. Variable factor quantity exceed fixed factor
C. Both the factors are used at the highest proportion
D. None of the above

195. Increasing returns imply
A. Constant average cost
B. Diminishing cost per unit of output
C. Optimum use of capital and factor
D. External economies

196. Law of Diminishing Returns to factors is relevant to
A. Short period
B. Long period
C. Secular period
D. Both short and long periods

197. A long run Analysis of production is called—
A. Economies of scale
B. Law of variable proportion
C. Law of increasing returns
D. Law of Returns to scale

198. The elasticity of substitution between two inputs in CES production function—
A. Decrease continuously
B. Increase continuously
C. Remains constant
D. None of these

199. The Law of Diminishing Return depends on the assumption that
A. Total output is constant
B. The state of technical knowledge is unchanged
C. Land is the factor kept constant
D. Average output declines faster than marginal output

200. Increasing returns is not caused by
A. Technological advance
B. Specialisation of labour
C. Marketing economies
D. Varying factor proportions

201. "The increasing returns to scale occurs because larger scale provides greater specialisation to various factors." According to
A. Joan Robinson B. Alfred Marshall
C. Chamberlin D. Paul. A. Samuelson

202. Isoquant refers to
A. Another name of indifference curve
B. The production Indifference curve
C. An equal quantity curve of a consumer
D. An equal cost curve of a producer

203. The law of increasing returns is only applicable to agriculture; According to
A. Classical school B. Neo-classical school
C. Modern school D. J.M. Keynes

204. If, by increasing the quantity of labour used by one unit, the firm can give up 2 units of capital and still produce the same output, then the $MRTS_{LK}$ is:
A. $\frac{1}{2}$ B. 2
C. 1 D. 4

Directions: *Q.No. 205 to 211 are based on Cobb-Douglas Production Function*
$Q = A.L^{\alpha}.K^{\beta}$

205. The elasticity substitution between the two inputs is—
A. Zero B. $\frac{\alpha}{\beta}$

C. Infinite D. Unity

206. The returns to scale are measure by

A. $\alpha+\beta$ B. $\alpha-\beta$

C. $\alpha.\beta$ D. $\frac{\alpha}{\beta}$

207. The efficiency parameter indicating the state of technology is given by—

A. A B. K

C. L D. α

208. The MRTS of capital for labour is given by—

A. $\frac{\alpha}{\beta}$ B. $\frac{\alpha+\beta}{K+L}$

C. $\frac{\alpha}{\beta}.\frac{L}{K}$ D. $\frac{K}{L}$

209. The efficiency of production is measured by—

A. $A(\alpha+\beta)$ B. A

C. $\alpha.\beta$ D. $\frac{A}{\alpha+\beta}$

210. The output elasticity with respect to labour input is measured by—

A. β B. A

C. α D. βA

211. The factor intensity is measured by—

A. $\frac{\alpha}{A}$ B. $\frac{\alpha}{\beta}$

C. A+B D. $\alpha+\beta$

212. The marginal product curve is above the average product curve when the average product is—

A. Decreasing

B. Increasing

C. Becomes constant

D. None of the above

213. Written in this form, the CES constant Elasticity of substitution production function exhibits—

A. Increasing returns to scale

B. Constant returns to scale

C. Decreasing returns to scale

D. None of the above

214. Increasing returns to scale can be explained in terms of—

A. External diseconomies and internal economies

B. External and internal economies

C. External and internal diseconomies

D. Optimum factor combination

215. Which of the following is the correct statement—

1. The slope of the Isoquants represents the MRTS
2. The MRTS of the inputs x and y = $\frac{MP_x}{MP_y}$
3. The elasticity of substitution between two inputs *x* and *y* is proportionate change in the ratio two inputs divided by proportionate change in the MRTS
4. if degree of homogeneity is greater than one, the production function is increasing returns to fixed factor

A. 1, 2, 3 and 4 B. 1, 3 and 4

C. 2, 3 and 4 D. 1, 2 and 3

216. When the AP_L is positive but declining, the MP_L could be —

A. Declining B. Zero

C. Negative D. Any of the above

217. The point which shows the maximum marginal product in the total product curve represents

A. Least cost combination

B. Producer's equilibrium

C. Expansion path

D. Point of inflexion

218. If the $MRTS_{LK}$ equals 2, then the MP_K/MP_L is---

A. 2 B. 1

C. ½ D. 4

219. The isoquants are convex to origin because of—

A. Diminishing MRTS

B. Increasing MRTS

C. Increasing returns to scale

D. Decreasing returns to scale

220. In the short run Analysis, MP = O at the level in which—

A. Marginal product is maximum

B. Average product is maximum

C. Total product is maximum

D. Total profit is maximum

221. The law of Diminishing Returns is applied to all fields of production was stated by

A. Walras B. A.C. Pigou

C. Alfred Marshall D. David Ricardo

222. A right angled isoquants map represents—

A. A fixed proportion production function

B. A variable proportion production function
C. A homogenous production function
D. None of the above

223. At the point of producers equilibrium—
A. The isoquant is tangent to the iso cost
B. The $MRTS_{LK}$ equals $\frac{P_L}{P_K}$
C. $\frac{MP_L}{P_L} = \frac{MP_K}{P_K}$
D. All of the above

224. Which of the following is incorrect in connection with Ridge line—
1. Two ridge lines can be drawn on a particular isoquant map
2. The production techniques are technically efficient between the two ridge lines
3. The upper ridge line is the locus points on isoquants where the MRTS of input is taken on *x*-axis for input taken on y axis is infinite.
4. The upper ridge line is the locus of points on isoquants where the marginal product of input taken on y axis is zero
5. The lower ridge line is the locus of points on isoquants where the marginal product of input taken on *x*-axis is negative

A. 5 only B. 1, 2, 3, 4, 5
C. 1, 2, 3 and 5 D. 4 only

225. The elasticity of technical substitution is measured by
A. The slope of the isoquant
B. The change in the slope of the isoquant
C. The ratio of factor inputs
D. None of the above

226. The following Table shows the various combinations of labour (L) and capital (K) and the resulting outputs—

Combination	*Output (Units)*
1L + 1K	200
2L + 2K	400
3L + 3K	600
4L + 4K	800
5L + 5K	1000

This Table shows the
A. Constant returns to scale
B. Diminishing returns to scale
C. Increasing returns to scale
D. None of the above

227. The production function underlying the data in the above Table is
A. Linear Homogeneous Production Function
B. Non-Linear Production Function
C. Cobb-Douglas Production Functions
D. None of these

228. Iso-quants are also known as
A. Equal revenue curves
B. Equal cost curves
C. Equal product curves
D. Indifference curves

229. The slope of the iso-cost line is determined by
A. Prices of the two factors
B. Productivity of the two factors
C. Degree of substitutability of two factors
D. None of these

230. All money costs can be regarded as:
A. Social costs B. Opportunity costs
C. Explicit costs D. Real costs

231. The cost assigned to factors of productions that the firm neither hires nor purchases is called—
A. Social cost B. Opportunity cost
C. Economic cost D. Imputed cost

232. Of the followings which one correspond to fixed cost—
A. Labour costs
B. Payments for raw material
C. Transportation charges
D. Insurance premium on property

233. If the supply curve is not a straight line but curvilinear, the elasticity on all points of the supply curve is
A. Equal B. Different
C. Zero D. Infinity

234. The average profit is equal to the difference between
A. AC and TC B. AC and VC
C. AC and AR D. AC and TR

235. Average fixed costs—
A. Remain the same whatever the level of output
B. Increase as output increases
C. Diminish as output increases
D. Do not show any uniform pattern

236. When the production increases, the average fixed cost will decrease in—

A. Long period B. Short period
C. Always D. None of the above

237. The firm producing at the minimum point of the AC curve is said to be

A. Operating under diminishing cost
B. Making Optimum use of plant capacity
C. Operating at excess capacity
D. Operating under increasing costs

238. Rectangular hyperbola is the shape of

A. TFC B. AFC
C. FC D. MC

239. Which is the best definition of the marginal firm—

A. The firm with the largest profit
B. The firm with lowest costs
C. The firm which makes only normal profit
D. The firm which equates its marginal costs with marginal revenue

240. In short-run, a firm would remain in business as long as which one of the following of costs is covered?

A. Total costs B. Fixed costs
C. Variable costs D. Constant costs

241. The vertical distance between TVC and TC is equal to

A. MC B. AVC
C. TFC D. None of these

242. Each short-run average cost curves coincides with long run cost curves—

A. At upper point
B. At lower point
C. At middle point
D. No permanent position

243. The MC curve cuts the AVC and ATC curves

A. At the falling parts of each
B. At different points
C. At their respective minimas
D. At the rising parts of each

244. The normal long run average cost curve is influenced by the

A. Principle of constant returns to scale
B. Economies and diseconomies of large scale production
C. Principle of diminishing returns
D. All of the above

245. Marginal cost curve always cuts the average cost curve

A. From below on the falling portion of the AC curve
B. From below on the rising portion of the AC curve
C. From below at the minimum point of the AC curve
D. From below at any point on the AC curve

246. The economies and diseconomies of large scale production is determined by—

A. The long run MC curve
B. The long run AC curve
C. The normal long run AC curve
D. The normal long run TC curve

247. Which is an inverted 'U' shaped curve?

A. AC B. MP
C. TC D. FC

248. An entrepreneur will stay in business in the long run as long as he meets

A. His domestic expenditure
B. All costs of production
C. Fixed costs of production
D. Variable costs of production

249. Which of the following is an implicit cost of production?

A. Wages of the labour
B. Charges for electricity
C. Interest on owned money capital
D. Payment for raw materials

250. Average fixed cost

A. Increases as output increases
B. Remains the same whatever the level of output
C. Diminishes as output increases
D. All the three are possible

251. If the total cost curve is plotted, marginal cost can be illustrated by—

A. A U-shaped curve cutting the total cost curve at its lowest point
B. The slope of a tangent to the curve at any given output
C. A straight line from the origin to the mid-point of the curve
D. A straight line cutting the curve at its lowest point

252. 'The price which is necessary to retain a given unit of a factor in a certain industry may be called its transfer earnings or transfer price.' Defined by

A. Prof. Lipsey B. Alfred Marshall
C. Robertson D. Joan Robinson

253. "The opportunity cost of using any factor is what is currently forgone by using it." This definition of opportunity cost is given by—

A. Joan Robinson B. Prof. Lipsey
C. Marshall D. Paul A. Samuelson

254. A loss bearing firm will continue to produce in the short run so long as the price at least covers

A. Average variable costs
B. Average fixed costs
C. AVC + AFC
D. Marginal costs

255. Marginal cost curve

A. Has the shape of a rectangular hyperbola
B. Has the shape of the alphabet U
C. Has the shape of the inverted U
D. All of these

256. "Steps downwards at first and then upwards" it is the movement of

A. AVC curve B. TFC curve
C. TVC curve D. TC curve

257. The optimum output is the one which is produced

A. By the optimum firm
B. At the maximum average cost
C. At the minimum average cost
D. At zero marginal cost

258. A concept which has importance in the equilibrium analysis and thus economic analysis is

A. AFC B. TFC
C. Opportunity Cost D. MC

259. To maximise profits during short run, a firm should produce the output that will

A. Minimize marginal cost
B. Yield maximum total revenue
C. Maximize marginal revenue
D. Equate marginal revenue with marginal cost

260. The prime cost may be considered as

A. Variable cost B. Direct cost
C. Sunk cost D. Fixed cost

261. Why the average fixed cost curve does not touch the output axis—

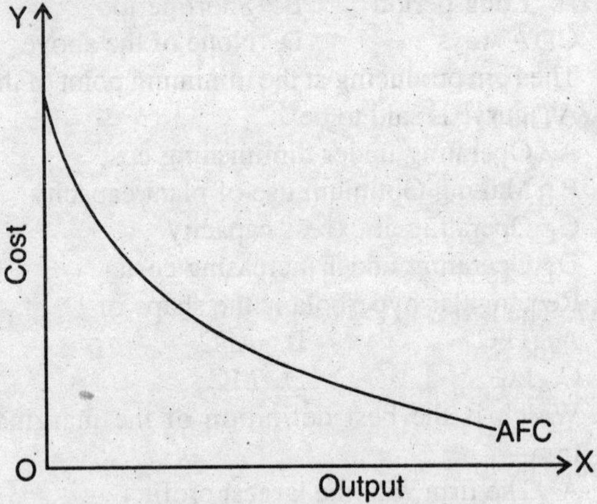

A. Because AFC cannot be negative
B. Because AFC cannot be zero
C. Because AFC cannot be less than one
D. None of these

262. An Iso-cost line represents—

A. Combinations of two inputs which yield the same amount of output
B. Combinations of two inputs which cost the same amount to a firm
C. Combinations of two inputs which yields varying amounts of output
D. Combinations of two inputs which cost different amounts of outlay to a firm

263. A firm may be considered to be of optimum size when—

A. Its fixed and average costs are equal
B. Its average cost is at a minimum
C. Its total cost and total revenue curve coincide
D. It is faced with a horizontal demand curve

264. Which of the following market situations explains marginal cost equal to price for attaining equilibrium—

A. Perfect competition
B. Monopoly and imperfect competition
C. Oligopoly
D. Monopoly only

265. Minimum marginal cost occurs at the output where—

A. The total product is at a maximum
B. The marginal product of the variable factors

is at a maximum

C. The factors are combined in their best possible proportion

D. The average product of the variable factors is at a maximum

266. The MP of a factor—

A. Is always positive

B. Is always either positive or zero

C. Can be positive, negative or zero

D. Is always negative

267. The LAC curve is tangent to the lowest point on the SAC curves when the LAC curve is

A. Falling B. Rising

C. At its minimum D. None of the above

268. The lowest point of the TC curve is

A. The left of the lowest point of the AVC curve

B. The right of the lowest point of the AVC curve

C. The same as the lowest point of AVC curve

D. None of these

269. Short-run cost curve are influenced by

A. Principle of returns to scale

B. Law of variable proportions

C. External and internal economies and diseconomies

D. None of these

270. If ATC curve is a rising straight lines, then as output expands, MC curve will

A. Lie below the ATC

B. Both will be the same

C. Lie above the ATC curve

D. Any of the above

271. The supply curve for the short-run competitive firm is the same as

A. Marginal cost curve

B. Average variable cost curve

C. That part of the MC curve which equals or is greater than AVC

D. Average total cost curve

272. Average fixed cost can be obtained through

A. $AFC = \frac{TFC}{TC}$

B. $AFC = \frac{TFC}{MC}$

C. $AFC = TC + TVC$

D. $AFC = MC + TVC$

273. When the law of diminishing returns begins to operate the TVC curve begins to—

A. Fall at an increasing rate

B. Rise at a decreasing rate

C. Fall at a decreasing rate

D. Rise at an increasing rate

274. The advertisement cost is included in—

A. Fixed cost

B. Some times in fixed cost sometimes in variable cost

C. Always in variable cost

D. Never included in variable cost

275. Where the leading firms in an industry combine to pursue a common policy in their interests, but retain their separate identities, such a combination is generally known as—

A. Trust

B. Cartel

C. Joint-stock company

D. Holding company

276. MC is given by—

A. The slope of the TFC curve

B. The slope of the TVC curve but not by the slope of the TC curve

C. The slope of the TC curve but not by the slope of TVC curve

D. Either the slope of the TVC curve or the slope of the TC curve

277. All of the following curves are U-shaped except—

A. The AVC curve B. The AFC curve

C. The AC curve D. The MC curve

278. In all forms of imperfect competition the average revenue curve facing the individual firm slopes—

A. Upward B. Downward

C. Horizontally D. Vertically

279. If marginal cost is above average variable cost at a time when output is rising, then—

A. Average total cost is falling

B. Average variable cost is rising

C. Average variable cost is falling

D. Average total revenue is rising

280. Normal profits are considered as

A. Explicit costs B. Implicit costs

C. Social costs D. Private costs

281. Opportunity costs are also known as—
A. Spill-over costs B. Money costs
C. Alternative costs D. External costs

282. At the point where a straight line from the origin is tangent to the TC curve, AC
A. is minimum
B. Equals MC
C. Equals AVC plus AFC
D. is all of the above

283. The slope of the TVC or total cost curve indicates the
A. Marginal revenue B. Average cost
C. Marginal cost D. Variable cost

284. The general average curve is also known as—
A. Total unit cost curve
B. Average total unit cost curve
C. Total marginal unit cost curve
D. Total variable unit cost curve

285. Even if costs increase, the MC remains unaffected, the cost is
A. Variable cost B. Fixed cost
C. Total fixed cost D. Average cost

286. The law of diminishing returns or increasing cost will operate at an earlier level in agriculture than in industry because—
A. Agriculture is an industry where land is used extensively
B. More labour is used in agriculture
C. Less mechanisation is applicable to agriculture
D. None of the above

287. Generally the profits are maximised in the short-run at the point at which—
A. Marginal cost of production is equal to the marginal return
B. Marginal return is negative
C. Marginal return is zero
D. Marginal cost is zero

288. With the expansion of output, the short-run average cost curve, beyond a point, starts rising because
A. Average fixed cost increases sharply
B. More production yields lower per unit price
C. The law of variable proportions applies to short-run production
D. Sales expenses become much larger

289. The cost, 'what has to be paid to retain it in its present use' is called—
A. Normal cost
B. Social cost of a factors of production
C. Opportunity cost of a factors
D. Economic cost of a factors of production

290. Minimum marginal cost occurs at the output where—
A. The total product is at a maximum
B. The marginal product of the variable factor is at a maximum
C. The factors are combined in their best possible proportions
D. The average product of the variable factors is at a maximum

291. Empirical evidence has shown, that due to technological change and people fear by doing' trends—
A. Changed the shape of LAC curve to be 'U' shaped rather than 'L'
B. Changed the shapes of LAC curve to be 'L' shaped rather than 'U'
C. Changed the shape of SAC curve to 'U' shaped rather than 'L'
D. None of these

292. If the long run average cost curves are 'L' shaped rather than 'U' shaped.. Due to technological change take place and, people by doing so the long run curve will flatter in
A. Heavy industries only
B. Both Heavy and agricultural industries
C. Agricultural industries only
D. Iron and steel industry only

293. The point on which the average cost is minimum in a firm short-run average cost curve will also be the minimum cost point on the firm's long run average cost curve. This is true
A. Always
B. Never
C. When LAC is falling
D. Only at that level of output when LAC is at its minimum

294. Marginal revenue will be zero if the elasticity of demand is—
A. Less than one B. Greater than one

C. Equal to one D. Equal to Zero

295. $MR_n = TR_n - TR_{n-1}$ is the algebraic expression of—

A. The addition to TR earned by selling n units of product instead of (n – 1) units

B. Marginal Revenue, the addition to TR earned by selling n units of product instead of (n – 1) units

C. Information is insufficient

D. None of the above

296. In general, if the average revenue curve is a straight line, the marginal revenue curve will be—

A. U-shaped B. A straight line

C. C-shaped D. Bell-shaped

297. When AR is falling, MR will be

A. Equal to AR

B. Less than AR

C. More than AR

D. Either more or equal to AR

298. When the units of factor increases marginal revenue productivity of a factor—

A. Will fall or diminish

B. Will rise or increase

C. Will have no change

D. None of the above

299. Assume that a firm's total revenue curve takes the form of a straight line which passes through the origin. We may deduce that—

A. Price exceeds marginal revenue

B. Price and marginal revenue equal

C. Total costs and total revenue are equal

D. Elasticity of demand for the product is unity

300. Which of the following formula explain the term average revenue?

A. $AR = \dfrac{\text{Total units produced}}{\text{Total Revenue}}$

B. $AR = \dfrac{\text{Total Revenue}}{\text{Number of units produced}}$

C. AR = MR × No. of units produced

D. AR = TR – MR

301. Marginal revenue will be positive if elasticity of demand is

A. Less than one B. More than one

C. Equal to one D. Equal to zero

302. The relationship between elasticity of demand (e), Average Revenue (AR) and Marginal Revenue (MR) is shown by the following formula

A. $e = \dfrac{AR}{AR - MR}$ B. $e = \dfrac{MR}{AR - MR}$

C. $e = \dfrac{TR}{AR - MR}$ D. $e = \dfrac{AR}{MR}$

303. Using Total Revenue and total cost curves, the level of output that gives maximum profits will be one where

A. TR and TC curves intersect

B. Where the gap between TR and TC is maximum and TR curve lies below TC curve

C. Where the gap between TR and TC is maximum and TR curve lies above TC curve

D. Where TR = TC curve

304. Marginal Revenue will be negative if the demand is

A. Relatively elastic

B. Unitary elastic

C. Relatively inelastic

D. Perfectly elastic

305. When AR is constant, MR is

A. Equal to AR B. More than AR

C. Less than AR D. Equal to zero

306. On a less than perfectly elastic demand curve, the MR for a given price and output is equal to price multiplied by

A. $\left(1 - \dfrac{1}{e}\right)$ B. $\left(e - \dfrac{1}{e}\right)$

C. $\left(\dfrac{1}{e} - 1\right)$ D. $\left(\dfrac{1}{e} - e\right)$

307. If a demand curve exhibits unit elasticity for all prices the MR curve—

A. is identical with it

B. Lies below the demand curve

C. is identical with the *x*-axis

D. is identical with the *y*-axis

308. The following figure gives the cost of a firm

1.	No. of units produced	10
2.	Total variable cost	200
3.	Total average cost	30

The average fixed cost is

A. 30 B. 10

C. 20 D. Data is not sufficient

309. If AR curve is a falling straight line, MR curve will lie below it in such a way that any line drawn from a point from *y*-axis parallel to *x*-axis to meet the AR curve is intersected by the MR curve

A. Mid-way

B. More than half-way

C. Less than half-way

D. Any where

310. In general, profit will be at a maximum where

A. MC = MR B. MC > MR

C. MC < MR D. MC = MR = 1

311. Which of the following persons is engaged in "secondary production"?

1. A bricklayer
2. An automobile assembly-line worker
3. An accountant
4. A cinema projectionist

A. 1 only B. 1 and 2 only

C. 2 and 3 only D. 1, 2, 3 and 4

312. An increase in a firm's fixed costs will—

A. Change marginal costs but not total costs

B. Change both marginal and total costs

C. Change variable costs but not marginal costs

D. Change total costs but not marginal costs

313. The time period and elasticity of time are related—

A. Indirectly

B. Directly

C. In direct proportion

D. None of the above

314. The LAC curve—

A. Falls when the LMC curve falls

B. Rises when the LMC curve rises

C. Goes through the lowest point of the LMC curve

D. Falls when LMC < LAC and rises when LMC > LAC

315. Which of the following occupations should be included under the heading of "Primary production"?

1. Quarrying 2. Fishing
3. Farming 4. Coal mining

A. 1 only B. 1 and 2

C. 1 and 3 D. 1, 2, 3 and 4

316. Thomas Malthus believed—

A. The population of a country will always increase

B. Production cannot keep on increasing

C. Food supplies place a limit to the growth of population

D. Population increase leads to a fall in output

317. Which of the following statements is correct or more nearly correct—

A. An increase in the price of commodity represent a fall in its value

B. Value has nothing to do with price

C. If the price of a commodity falls, its value relative to other goods does not change

D. The price of a good is its value measured in terms of money

318. The real aim of production is

A. To create material goods

B. To eliminate poverty

C. To satisfy peoples wants

D. To provide basic necessities

319. The MC curve reaches its minimum point before the AVC curve and the AC curve. In addition the MC curve intersects the AVC curve and the AC curve at their lowest point. The above statement are both true—

A. Always B. Never

C. Often D. Sometimes

320. A rise in the price of a commodity will generally call forth a bigger supply and this will be brought about partly by existing firms expanding their output and partly by

A. The general expansion of the market

B. New firms being attracted into the industry

C. The discovery of new sources of raw materials

D. Changes in the general level of consumer's incomes.

321. Competition

A. Is inevitable but has desirable forms that can be selected on an economic basis

B. Is 'Fair' if everybody has an equal chance of being selected

C. Is discriminatory

D. Is desirable

322. Under perfect competition a firm will be in equilibrium if
A. MC = MR
B. MC cuts the MR from below
C. MC rises when it cuts the MR
D. All the above three conditions are fulfilled

323. If the demand curve confronting an individual firm is perfectly elastic then—
A. The firm is a price taker
B. The firm cannot influence the price
C. The amount the firm places on the market is small relative to the total supply
D. All of the above

324. Efficient allocation of resources is likely to be achieved under
A. Monopoly
B. Monopolistic competition
C. Perfect competition
D. Any market form

325. When the perfectly competitive firm and industry are both in long run equilibrium—
A. P = MR = SAC = LAC
B. D = MR = SMC = LMC
C. P = MR = Lowest point on the LAC curve
D. All of the above

326. In the following diagram of a competitive firm T point include

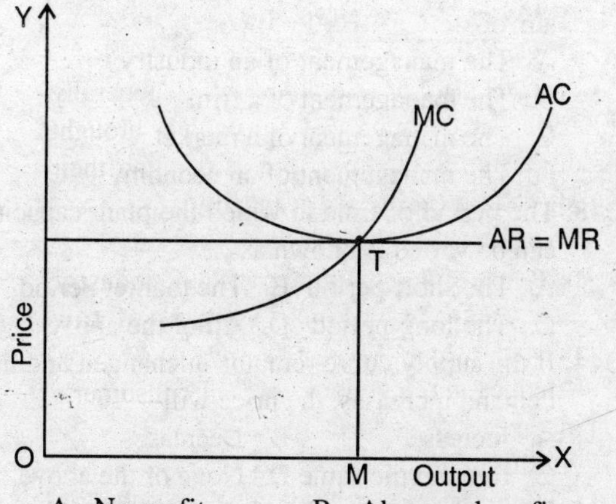

A. No profit B. Abnormal profit
C. Normal profit D. Heavy loss

327. By "normal profits" is meant
A. The profit made by the marginal entrepreneur in a normal year
B. The payment made to the marginal entrepreneur for his abilities
C. The surplus profit made by the least efficient firms
D. The payment needed to keep an entrepreneur in an industry

328. The change in TR resulting from the sale of the one unit more of output, means—
A. MR from a given input
B. MR from a given output
C. AR from a given output
D. MR from MC

329. Under the perfect competition the transportation cost
A. is considered to be negligible and thus, ignored
B. is considered to be vital for the calculation of total cost
C. is charged along with the price of the commodity
D. Excluded from the prime cost

330. In perfect competition, there is a process of
A. Free entry but restricted exit of the firms
B. Free entry and free exit of the firms
C. Restricted entry and exit of the firms
D. Semi-free exit but absolute free entry

331. In perfectly competitive market
A. Firm is the price-giver and the industry the price-taker
B. Firm is the price-taker and industry the price giver
C. Both are the price-takers
D. None of these

332. Match the following

1. Increasing cost industry	*i.* Horizontal long run supply Curve
2. Decreasing cost industry	*ii.* Positively sloped long run supply curve
3. Constant cost industry	*iii.* Negatively sloped long run supply curve

	1	2	3
A.	*i*	*ii*	*iii*
B.	*iii*	*ii*	*i*
C.	*ii*	*iii*	*i*
D.	*ii*	*i*	*iii*

333. Price taker firms

A. Advertise to increase the demand for their product

B. Do not advertise, because most advertising is wasteful

C. Do not advertise because they can sell as much as they want at the current price

D. Who advertise will get more profits than those who do not

334. If factor prices and factor quantities move in the same direction we have—

A. A constant cost industry

B. A decreasing cost industry

C. An increasing cost industry

D. Inadequate data to tell precisely what will happen

335. In conditions of pure competition, in which the demand for a firm's product is infinitely elastic, the firm's average revenue curve will be—

A. A vertical straight line

B. A horizontal straight line

C. A U-shaped

D. A straight line at 45° to the horizontal axis

336. "The more nearly perfect a market is, the stronger is the tendency for the same price to be paid for the same thing at the same in all parts of the market," is the definition of perfect competition by—

A. Prof. Benham B. J.S. Mill

C. Jevons D. Prof. Marshall

337. With increasing returns to scale, the equilibrium in a market is incomplete. This is

A. Only in the case of perfectly competitive market

B. Only in the case of imperfectly competitive market

C. Only in the case of monopolistic market situations

D. None of the above

338. In finding equilibrium position of a profit maximising firm, which technique is most convenient—

A. Total revenue and total cost technique

B. Marginal revenue and marginal cost technique

C. Demand and supply technique

D. None of these

339. In the case of consumer's demand curve, determined the price but in the case of producer—

1. AR curve determined the price
2. AR curve determined the price and income
3. MR curve determined the price
4. MR curve and AR curve are determined the price

A. 1 only B. 2 only

C. 3 only D. 4 only

340. Under competitive conditions the industry will be in equilibrium

A. When each firm is in equilibrium equating MC with MR

B. When all the firms are earning only normal profits

C. When firms outside have no tendency to enter the industry and those within, have no tendency to leave the industry

D. When all the three conditions are fulfilled

341. In the long run competitive equilibrium the theory predicts that

A. TC = TR and MC = MR

B. Firms operate at a minimum average total cost

C. There is no incentive for entry or exit of firms

D. All these conditions exist

342. 'Maximisation of total profit' is the fundamental aim of—

A. The management of an industry

B. The management of a firm

C. The management of a market

D. The management of an economy

343. The period of time in which the plant capacity can be varied is known as

A. The short period B. The market period

C. The long period D. All of the above

344. If the supply curve remains unchanged and the demand increases, the price will—

A. Increase B. Decrease

C. Remain the same D. None of the above

345. When the greater the elasticity of supply the change in the new equilibrium price will

A. Be higher

B. Be higher than previous price

C. Be lower

D. Be lower than previous price

346. One would expect a firm to close down rather than continue producing in the short-period if—

A. Total revenue were more than total variable cost

B. Total revenue were less than total variable cost

C. Variable costs were to fall below fixed costs

D. Variable costs were to rise above fixed costs

347. Under perfect competition, a firm will be in equilibrium when its AC is

A. At a maximum

B. At a minimum

C. Covering only prime costs of production

D. Covering wages and salaries only

348. Expanding output till the rising marginal cost is less than price, is the nature of—

A. Imperfectly competitive market

B. Perfectly competitive market

C. Perfectly competitive firm

D. Perfectly competitive industry

349. At the shut-down point

A. P = AVC

B. TR = TVC

C. The total losses of the firm equal TFC

D. All of the above

350. Which of the following statement is correct in connection with the below diagram—

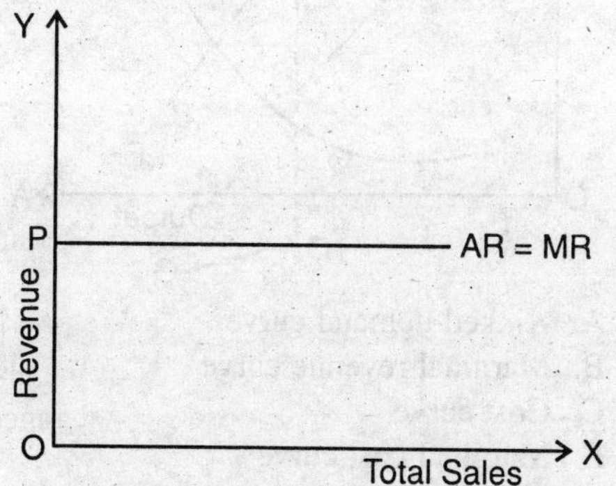

1. The firm is styled as price taker as constrasted to price maker industry
2. The firm is styled as price maker as contrasted to price taker industry
3. The firm is styled as price taker as same in price maker industry

A. 1 only B. 1 and 2 only

C. 3 only D. 2 only

351. When at a given price, the quantity demanded of a commodity is more than the quantity supplied, there will be

A. An upward pressure on price

B. A downward pressure on price

C. Price will remain unaffected

D. All of these

352. The competitive equilibrium leads to

A. The firms producing with excess capacity

B. The firms producing at their minimum costs

C. Firms producing at a cost higher than the minimum

D. Some firms producing under decreasing costs and others under increasing costs

353. If more firms enter a competitive industry the theory predicts that

A. Both marginal and average cost curves rises

B. The industry short-run supply curves shifts upwards to the right

C. Output of every firm increases

D. The price of the product rises

354. Using TR and TC, a profit maximising firm will be in equilibrium at a point—

A. Where the gap between the two is the smallest

B. Where the gap between the two is the greatest

C. Where the two become equal

D. None of these

355. An entrepreneur will stay in business in the long run as long as he meets

A. All costs of production

B. Fixed costs of production

C. Variable costs of production

D. None of these

356. When the TR curve and TC curve are parallel and TR exceeds TC:

A. Normal profit is maximized

B. Normal profit is minimised

C. Total profit is maximised

D. Total profit is minimised

357. A perfectly competitive firm will always expand output as long as—

A. Rising marginal cost is less than price

B. Rising marginal cost is less than the marginal

revenue

C. Rising marginal cost is less than the average cost

D. None of the above

358. In long run competitive equilibrium

A. Every firm will earn economic profit

B. Every firm will incur losses

C. Every firm will earn only normal profit

D. The marginal firm will earn no profit

359. A firm under perfect competition faces for its product

A. A horizontal demand curve

B. A downward sloping demand curve

C. An upward rising demand curve

D. A vertical demand curve

360. Long run equilibrium price of a perfect competitive firm is always

A. Above the LAC B. Below the LAC

C. Equal to AFC D. Equal to LAC

361. If the firms under perfect competition have different costs, abnormal profits will be earned in the long run only by—

A. Marginal firm

B. All the firms

C. Intra marginal firms

D. None of the firms

362. A perfectly competitive industry becomes a monopoly. With the same cost conditions, it will now sell

A. An unchanged output at a higher price

B. A larger output at the old price

C. A larger output at a higher price

D. A reduced output at a higher price

363. Under price discrimination price will be higher in the market where demand is—

A. Unitary elastic B. Highly elastic

C. Less elastic D. None of the above

364. From the resource allocation view point, perfect competition is preferable because

A. The firms operate at excess capacity levels

B. There is a whole variety of output produced

C. There is no restriction on entry and exit of firms

D. There is no idle capacity

365. 'The competition among buyers, each trying to get enough of the product to satisfy his wants' tends to move

A. The consumer's price

B. The market price

C. The equilibrium price

D. All of the above

366. The supply function, would shot downward and to the right if the MC of all of the firms in a perfectly competitive industry were to

A. Decrease B. Increase

C. No change D. None of these

367. Excess capacity is not found under

A. Monopoly

B. Monopolistic competition

C. Perfect competition

D. Oligopoly

368. Consumers are likely to get a variety of goods under

A. Perfect competition

B. Monopoly

C. Imperfect competition

D. Oligopoly

369. The line ACDG represents

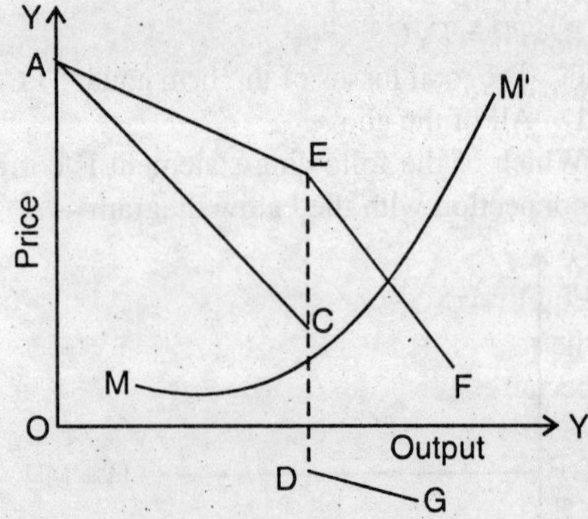

A. Kinked-demand curve

B. Marginal revenue curve

C. Cost curve

D. Marginal cost curve

370. Under perfect competition a firm can produce with

A. An optimum plant

B. An optimum output

C. Maximum profit

D. Identical products at low cost

371. Under perfect market and in case of decreasing

marginal cost the firm's equilibrium with respect to level of production—

A. Cannot be achieved
B. Can be achieved after a small level of output
C. Can be achieved after a high level of output
D. Will result in run-away inflation

372. A monopoly producer has

A. Control over production but not price
B. Control over production as well as price
C. Control neither on production nor on price
D. Control over production, price and consumers

373. A profit-maximising monopolist in two separate markets will—

A. Charge the same price in both markets
B. Always charge a higher price in the market where he sells more
C. Always charge a higher price in the market where he sells less
D. Adjust his sales in the two markets so that his MR in each market just equals his aggregate marginal cost

374. A circumstance in which it might pay a monopolist to cut the price of his product is where

A. MC is falling
B. MR is greater than MC
C. His advertising costs are increasing
D. Average costs seem about to fall

375. Equilibrium of monopolist will never lie below the middle point of the average revenue curve because below the middle point—

A. Elasticity of demand is less than one
B. MR is negative
C. Both (A) and (B)
D. Market laws cease to be operate

376. In a monopoly market an upward shift in the market demand results in a new equilibrium with

A. A higher quantity and the same price
B. A higher quantity and a lower price
C. A higher quantity and higher price
D. All the above

377. A centralised cartel

A. Leads to the monopoly solution
B. Behaves as the multiplant monopolist if it wants to minimise the total cost of production
C. Is illegal in the U.S.
D. All of the above

378. Price discrimination is possible

A. When elasticities of demand in different markets are the same at the ruling price
B. When elasticities of demand are different in different markets at the ruling price
C. When elasticities cannot be known
D. None of these

379. The imposition of a per unit tax causes the monopolist's—

A. Average cost curve to shift up
B. Average cost and marginal cost curves to shift up, because the per unit tax is like a fixed cost
C. Average cost and marginal cost curves to shift up, because the per unit tax is like a variable cost
D. All of the above

380. One way the government can induce a monopolist to expand his output is by imposing

A. A specific tax on the monopolist's output
B. A price ceiling that make the monopolist lower his price
C. A price floor that make the monopolist raise his price
D. A heavy tax on the monopolist's profits

381. When a monopolist is in

A. Short-run equilibrium, he will also be in long-run equilibrium
B. Long-run equilibrium, he will also be in short-run equilibrium
C. Long-run equilibrium, he may or may not be in short-run equilibrium
D. None of the above

382. OPEC is an example of the type of producer's organization known as a

A. Marketing board
B. Producer's cooperative
C. Trust
D. Cartel

383. In monopoly, the relationship between average revenue and marginal revenue curves is as follows—

A. Average revenue curve lies above the MR

curve

B. AR curve coincides with the MR-curve

C. AR curve lies below the MR-curve

D. AR curve is parallel to the MR-curve

384. A firm practising price discrimination will be—

A. Charging different prices for different qualities of a product

B. Buying in the cheapest and selling in he dearest markets

C. Charging different prices in different markets for a product

D. Buying only from firms selling in bulk at a distance

385. Equilibrium of a discriminating monopolist requires the fulfilment of which one of the following conditions—

A. It must be profitable for him to sell output in more than one market

B. MR in both markets must be the same

C. MR in both markets must also be equal to the marginal cost of producing the monopolist's aggregate output

D. All the above

Questions 386 and 387 are based on the following diagram showing a firm's cost and revenue curves

MC = Marginal cost

MR = Marginal Revenue

AC = Average cost

AR = Average Revenue

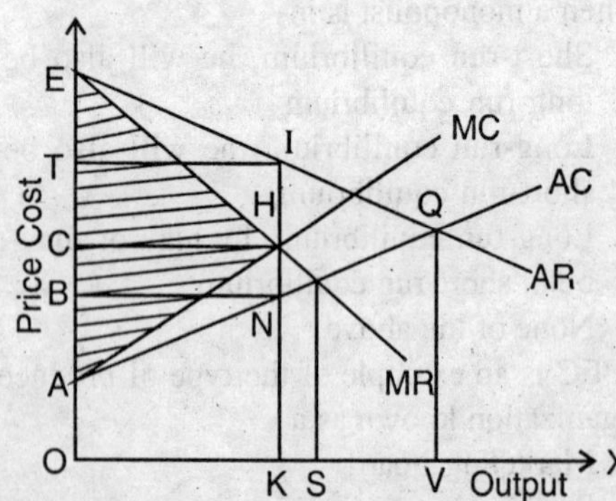

386. The most profitable output for the firm to produce is

A. OS B. OV

C. OK D. OA

387. The amount of profits will be shown by

A. INQ B. TICH

C. ACH D. Either AEH or BTIN

388. The difference between monopoly equilibrium and competitive equilibrium is

A. The MC should rise at the point of equilibrium under perfect competition whereas under monopoly it can rise, fall or remain constant

B. There is no difference at all

C. Under perfect competition the MC = MR whereas under monopolistic conditions this need not be the case

D. None of the above

389. If a monopolist is producing under decreasing cost conditions, increase in demand is beneficial to the society because

A. Consumers get better quality goods

B. Cost of production falls and hence price will follow

C. Goods will be sold in many markets

D. None of the above answers is correct

390. The hypothesis that the firms seek to maximise their sales revenue own its origin to

A. W.J. Baumol B. J.S. Baumol

C. W.J. Hicks D. J.W. Baumol

391. If the individual firm's demand curve is coincident with the market demand curve then

A. The firm is price-taker

B. The firm is a monopolist

C. The firm can set any price it wants without limitation

D. Marginal revenue is equal to average revenue

E. None of above

392. Even in the long run equilibrium, the pure monopolist (as opposed to the perfectly competitive firm) can make abnormal profits because of

A. Blocked entry B. High price he charges

C. His low LAC D. Advertising

393. In the short run, the monopolist

A. Incurs a loss B. Breaks down

C. Makes a profit D. Any of the above

394. Price discrimination is possible

A. Only under monopoly situation

B. Under any market form

C. Only under monopolistic competition

D. Only under perfect competition

395. The imposition of a ceiling on a monopolist's price will effect his
A. Profits only
B. Average revenue in the short-run only
C. Equilibrium output only
D. Equilibrium output and profits

396. Which one of the following is identical with multiplant monopolist?
A. Cartel aiming at joint profit maximisation
B. Oligopoly with low-cost firm as leader
C. Market sharing cartels
D. Oligopoly with dominant firm as leader

397. Price control is one of the monopoly regulations which is most advantageous for—
A. The producer B. The consumer
C. The government D. The seller

398. Pure Monopoly exists
A. When there is a single producer
B. When there is a single producer without any close substitutes
C. When there is a single producer with close substitutes
D. When a few producers control the industry

399. Under monopoly the supply curve is absent because
A. The monopolist always makes profit
B. There is no entry for others
C. Equilibrium involves MC = MR and MR < P
D. The monopolist controls the supply

400. If a single monopolist enjoying internal economies of scale is replaced by a large number of producers operating under perfect competition, it may be said that—
A. Price will increase and output will fall
B. Both price and output will rise
C. Price will increase but the effect on output will be indeterminate
D. Output will fall but the effect on price will be indeterminate

401. The degree of monopoly power can be measured by the formula

A. $\frac{P - MC}{P}$ B. $\frac{AR}{AR - MR}$

C. $\frac{MR}{AR - MR}$ D. $\frac{AR - MR}{MR}$

402. Bilateral monopoly means
A. Two rival sellers only
B. Two rival buyers only
C. A monopoly seller buying his input from many suppliers
D. A monopolist facing a monopsonist

403. A monopolist who is selling in two markets in which demand is not identical will be unable to maximise his profits unless he
A. Sells below costs of production in both markets
B. Practices price discrimination
C. Equates the volume of sales in both markets
D. Equates marginal costs with marginal revenue in one market only

404. A firm enjoys maximum control over the price of its product under
A. Monopoly
B. Perfect competition
C. Oligopoly
D. Imperfect competition

405. Under bilateral monopoly the price is higher if—
A. The monopolist has his way
B. The monopolist acts as a competitor
C. The monopsonist has his way
D. The monopsonist sells his own product in a monopoly market

406. One equates price and MC to maximise profit, the other one equates MC and MR for the same purpose they are
A. Monopolist and perfect competitor
B. Monopsonist and perfect competitor
C. Oligopolist and monopolist
D. Perfect competitor and duopolist

407. The equilibrium level of output for the pure monopolist is where
A. MR = MC B. MR > MC
C. MR < MC D. P<AC

408. If the price is statutorily fixed and equal to MC, monopoly profits will be
A. Increased B. Decreased
C. Eliminated D. At same level

409. Given the cost conditions
A. Monopoly output and price will be higher than under pure competition

B. Monopoly output will be lower and price higher than under pure competition
C. Monopoly output will be higher and prices lower than under pure competition
D. Monopoly output and price will be lower than under pure competition

410. A monopolist will fix the equilibrium output of his product where the elasticity of his AR curve is
A. Greater than or equal to one
B. Equal to or less than one
C. Less than one but more than zero
D. Zero

411. The monopolists shifts up the SAC and SMC curve, because of the imposition of
A. A per unit tax
B. A per unit price
C. A per unit tax like a variable cost
D. A per unit excise duty

412. If a commodity sold under monopoly is got free of cost, MC curve will be—
A. Identical with the x-axis
B. Identical with the MR
C. A horizontal straight line above x-axis
D. Identical with y-axis

413. A monopolist has control over the price he charges for his product. He will be able to maximise his profit by
A. Lowering the price, if the demand curve is elastic
B. Lowering the price, if the demand curve is inelastic
C. Raising the price, if the demand curve is elastic
D. None of the above is applicable

414. A monopoly producer usually earns
A. Abnormal profits
B. Only normal profits
C. Neither profits nor losses
D. Profits and losses which are uncertain

415. Clark-Wicksteed product exhaustion theorem says that—
A. Given a linearly homogenous production function, the product is exhausted
B. Total product is exhausted only under conditions of monopoly
C. In long-run competitive equilibrium, the total product will be exhausted in rewarding the factors
D. Total product is exhausted only under laissez-faire

416. Under monopoly and imperfect competition MC is
A. More than the price
B. Less than the price
C. Equal to the price
D. Any one of the above

417. The limit to the long-run growth of a firm under imperfectly competitive conditions is set by—
A. Fear of falling demand
B. Fear of prices falling more than costs
C. Fear of rising costs
D. Fear of external diseconomies

418. The AR curve and industry demand curve are same
A. In case of monopoly
B. In case of oligopoly
C. In case of perfect competition
D. None of the above

419. Which form of monopoly regulation is most advantageous for the consumer?
A. Price control
B. Per unit tax
C. Lump sum tax
D. All of the above three form are equally advantageous

420. In the long-run, due to blocked entry pure profits can be made by
A. Pure oligopolist B. Pure monopolist
C. Pure duopolist D. None of the above

421. If 'e' is the elasticity of demand for the product of a monopolist than $\frac{e}{e-1}$ is the—
A. Ratio $\frac{P}{MR}$ B. Ratio $\frac{P}{AR}$
C. Ratio $\frac{Q}{MR}$ D. Ratio $\frac{Q}{AR}$

422. It does not exceed super normal profit, will reduce excess profit of a monopolist; i.e.
A. The imposition of income tax
B. The imposition of price control

C. The imposition of lump sum tax price period
D. The imposition of lump sum tax once in a year

423. With which of the following economists would you associate 'the model of Managerial enterprise'?
A. R.A. Gordan B. R. Marris
C. Baumol D. Scitovsky

424. The imposition of a maximum price at the point where the monopolist's MC curve intersects his AR curve cause the monopolist to
A. Break even B. Incur losses
C. Make profits D. Any of the above

425. The firms are under severe pressure to keep their costs low, a situation characterised by—
A. Strong competition with perfect competition
B. Strong competition
C. Oligopolist competition
D. Monopolist competition

426. Dumping means selling at
A. A higher price in home market and a lower price in foreign market
B. A lower price in the home market and a higher price in foreign market
C. The same price in the home and the foreign market
D. None of the above

427. Consideration of the external effect of a fall in the factor price will make the market demand curve of the factor
A. Less elastic than otherwise
B. More elastic than otherwise
C. Vertical
D. Will have no effect on the elasticity of the market demand curve for the factor

428. Which one of the following statements is not true with respect to a firm in circumstances of imperfect competition?
A. Advertising will improve its profit
B. There is no perfect substitute for the product it sells
C. MR is equal to price at all output levels
D. its demand curve is inelastic at some point within its entire range

429. Which of the following economists said that the problem of bilateral monopoly has a solution if the Monopsony buyer of the factor sells his own product in a monopoly?
A. Hicks B. Cournot
C. Marshall D. Kaldor

430. Monopsonistic exploitation occurs when—
A. The factor market is monopsonistic
B. The factor market is competitive
C. The product market is competitive
D. The product market is monopolistic

431. Which of the following represents the AR curve of a firm?
A. The curve representing the cost per unit of output
B. The demand curve of consumers for the firm's product
C. Total receipts realized by the firm
D. All of the above

432. The least cost criterion for the monopsonist is expressed as

A. $\frac{MP_L}{MP_K} = \frac{P_L}{P_K}$ B. $\frac{MP_L}{MC_L} = \frac{MP_K}{MC_K}$

C. $\frac{MP_L}{P_K} = \frac{P_L}{MP_K}$ D. $\frac{MC_L}{MP_K} = \frac{MP_L}{MC_K}$

433. The figure below explains price and employment determination under—

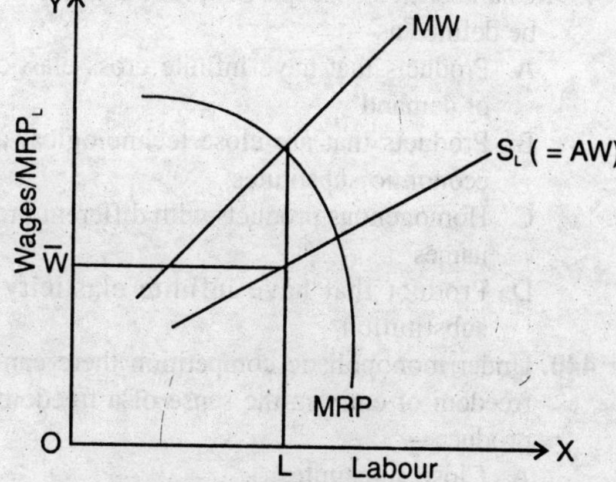

A. Pure Monopoly Market
B. Monopolistic Market
C. Monopsony Market
D. Oligopoly Market

434. Price discrimination is undertaken with the aim of
A. Increasing sales and maximising profits

B. Reducing sales and raising prices
C. Minimising cost and maximising revenue
D. Serving the markets without earning profits

435. Modern theories of imperfect competition were inspired by
A. Joan Robinson B. Sraffa
C. Cournot D. Chamberlin

436. The strength of a monopolist may be assessed by—
A. The size of his total revenue
B. The gap between AR and MR
C. The size of consumer's surplus accruing to him
D. The long-term price of his product

437. The theory of monopolistic competitions is developed by—
A. E.H. Chamberlin
B. H.E. Chamberlin
C. Mrs. John Robinson
D. Joan Robinson

438. Which of the following conditions are met in the long-run equilibrium in monopolistic competition where the firm is earning only normal profits
A. MC = AC B. P = ATC
C. P = MR D. P = MC

439. Chamberlin's concepts of 'product group' may be defined as—
A. Products that have infinite cross elasticity of demand
B. Products that are close technological and economic substitutes
C. Homogenous products with different brand names
D. Product that have infinite elasticity of substitution

440. Under monopolistic competition there can be freedom of entry in the sense of a freedom to produce—
A. Close substitutes
B. Perfect substitutes
C. Complementary goods
D. Perfect complementary goods

441. In the case of monopolistic competition
A. The long-run supply curve can be defined
B. The long-run supply curve cannot be defined
C. The short-run supply curve cannot be defined
D. The short run supply curve can be defined

442. The sale of 'branded' articles is common in a situation of
A. Excess capacity
B. Monopolistic competition
C. Monopoly
D. Pure competition

443. 'Negative sloped with higher elasticity demand curve' is related to—
A. High price level
B. Monopolistic competitor
C. Oligopolistic competitor
D. Low price level

444. Monopolistic competition takes account of all the following except—
A. Selling cost
B. Product differentiation
C. Price competition
D. Reaction function

445. If there is effective price competition in the market, the monopolistic competition does not create excess capacity. According to
A. Joan Robbinson
B. Robertson
C. Paul A. Samuelson
D. Chamberlin

446. Competitors in monopolistic competition have full control over
A. The price of their product
B. Product quality
C. The shape of the market demand curve
D. The elasticity of product substitutions

447. When the product market is monopolistic and the labour market monopsonistic, collective bargaining will
A. Raise employment
B. Raise the wage
C. Raise wage and lower employment
D. Raise both wage and employment

448. Chamberlin's measure of excess capacity is
A. More than what is normally understood an excess capacity
B. The same as what is normally understood an excess capacity

C. Less than what is normally understood an excess capacity
D. Zero

449. Monopolistic can fix
A. Both price and output
B. Either price or output
C. Neither price nor output
D. None

450. Selling costs are incurred under monopolistic competition to
A. Attract more customers
B. Prevent its customers from going to others
C. Establish superiority of its product vis-a-vis the others
D. All of the above

451. A firm in long run equilibrium under monopolistic competition makes only—
A. Normal profits
B. Monopoly profits
C. Super normal profits
D. Losses

452. The term 'group equilibrium' is related to—
A. Analysis of Monopolistic competition
B. Analysis of Chamberlin
C. Analysis of Monopolistic competition by E.H. Chamberlin
D. Analysis of Monopolistic competition by Robinson

453. Monopolistic competition differs from perfect competition due to
A. Large number of firms and heterogeneous product
B. Large number of firms and homogeneous product
C. Small number of firms and differentiated products
D. Only a few firms and similar products

454. Selling cotton at higher price in Delhi and lower price in London: means
A. Slumping
B. Dumping
C. Dumping of cotton market
D. Dumping refers to selling of cotton

455. If an oligopolist incurs losses in the short-run, then in the long-run
A. He will go out of business
B. He will stay in business
C. He will break even
D. Any of the above is possible

456. In an oligopoly, a firm while deciding about its own price and output policy has
A. To take account of the likely reactions of the other firms
B. Has not to bother about other firms
C. Assume that others will not react
D. To act independently of the others

457. A firm with the highest cost of production is not plausible in the case of
A. Price leadership under oligopoly
B. Price leadership under monopoly
C. Price leadership under bilateral monopoly
D. Price leadership under monopolistic competition

458. The dominant firm price leader's market share
A. is lower, the higher the follower's costs
B. is higher, the lower the follower's costs
C. is lower, the lower the follower's costs
D. is invariant with the follower's costs

459. In the case of price leadership by the dominant firm, when all the firms in the purely oligopolistic industry will produce their best level of output?
A. Always B. Often
C. Never D. None of these

460. Joint profits are maximised in the model cartel, which is a model of—
A. Duopoly B. Duopsony
C. Oligospony D. Oligopoly

461. In collusive oligopoly for joint profit maximisation
A. The highest cost firm makes the highest profit
B. The lowest cost firm makes the highest profit
C. The lowest cost firm produces the largest output
D. None of the above is true

462. MC-curve should be kinked in
A. Duopoly
B. Monopsony
C. Collusive oligopoly
D. Oligopolistic competitions

463. A kinked demand curve is most consistent with

which one of the following market situations?
A. Pure competition
B. Pure monopoly
C. Oligopoly
D. Monopolistic competition

464. A kinked demand curve has
A. A lower elasticity above the point of kink and a higher elasticity below it
B. A higher elasticity above the point of kink and a lower elasticity below it
C. A uniform elasticity both above and below the point of kink
D. None of the above

465. The kinked demand model explained—
A. Price flexibility
B. Price rigidity
C. Demand flexibility
D. Demand rigidity

466. 'If an oligopolist decreases his price the rivals will follow'. This is the basic assumption of—
A. The kinked supply curve
B. The oligopolistic demand curve
C. The kinked demand curve
D. The demand curve

467. Each seller determines his price on the assumption that his rival will keep his price constant, under—
A. Bertrand's Model
B. Samuelson's Model
C. Edge worth Model
D. Price leadership

468. Duopoly is a market situation when
A. There is only one producer of a given product
B. There are two producers of a given product
C. There are more than two producers
D. There are a few producers

469. The earliest duopoly model was developed by
A. Bertand B. Cournot
C. Ricardo D. Edgeworth

470. 'The equilibrium prices of duopoly model are obtained at the intersections of their reaction curves'. It is correct in the case of—
A. Edgeworth Model
B. Bertrand's Model
C. Bertrand's Duopoly Model
D. None of the above

471. Which of the following used the kinked demand curve only to explain why oligopoly prices are 'sticky'?
A. P.M. Sweezy B. Chamberlin
C. Hall and Hitch D. Stigler

472. In the Stackelberg model of duopoly the cournot behaviour assumption is applied to
A. Leader B. The follower
C. Both (A) and (B) D. Neither (A) and (B)

473. With reference to the Cournot's model, determine which of the following statements is false
A. The solution is stable
B. Each duopolist assumes the others will keep its price constant
C. The duopolists do not recognise their interdependence
D. Each duopolist assumes the other will keep its quantity constant

474. With reference to the Edgeworth Model, determine which of the following statements are correct?
A. It explains price rigidity
B. The duopolists recognised their interdependence
C. Each duopolist assumes the other keeps its price constant
D. Each duopolist assumes the other keeps its quantity constant

475. Each seller ultimately supplies one third of the market and charges the same prices. This is the conclusion of—
A. Bertrand's duopoly model
B. Edgeworth's duopoly model
C. Cournot's duopoly model
D. Collusive duopoly model

476. The equilibrium is unstable and indeterminate under—
A. Edgeworth duopoly model
B. Edgeworth oligopoly model
C. Edgeworth model
D. Edgeworth and Pareto model

477. The kinked-demand curve is appropriate when
A. Inter-firm knowledge is low
B. There is a general depression
C. Inter-firm knowledge is high
D. There is a general prosperity

478. The lower portion of the kinked-demand curve, is noted for bringing in just a few new consumers. So it is—

A. Relatively elastic
B. Relatively in elastic
C. Relatively no response
D. None of the above

479. In the following diagram the total consumer's surplus is measured by—

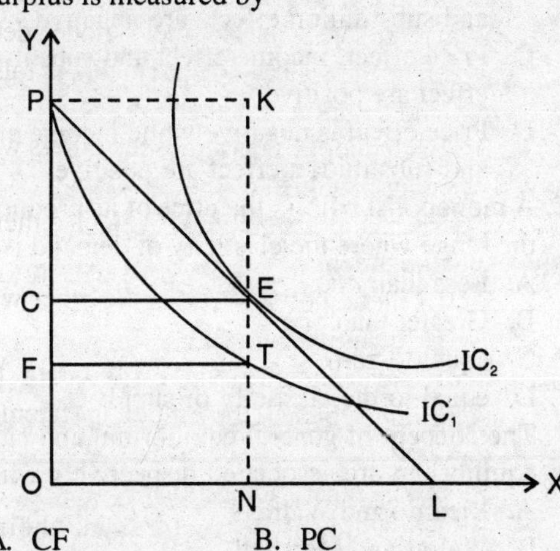

A. CF B. PC
C. CFTE D. PKE

480. A monopolist can fix—

A. Only price not output
B. Both price and output
C. Either price or output
D. Neither price nor output

481. Each seller assumes his rival's output as constant in the model of—

A. Cournot B. Edgeworth
C. Bertrand D. Price-leadership

482. Substitution effect is always—

A. Negative
B. Positive
C. Positive and negative both
D. Equal to income effect

483. Which of the following statements are true regarding the Cobb-Douglas production function—

1. It is long period production function
2. It is short period production function
3. It assumes increasing returns to scale
4. Out-put elasticities with respect to factors are constant

Choose the correct answer from the code given below

A. 1 and 3 B. 1 and 4
C. 2 and 3 D. 3 and 4

484. Vertical supply curve is the characteristic of—

A. Short-period market
B. Long-period market
C. Very long-period market
D. Very short-period market

485. Which type of equilibrium is shown in the following function for a commodity, where S is supply, D is demand, P is price and t refers to time—

$S_t = f(P_t)$
$D_t = f(P_t)$
$S_t = D_t$

A. Partial equilibrium
B. Static equilibrium
C. Partial and static equilibrium
D. Dynamic equilibrium

486. In bilateral monopoly there:

A. is a single buyer and large number of sellers
B. is a single seller and large number of buyers
C. is a single seller and a single buyer
D. are a large number of buyers and a large number of sellers

487. Where two factors of production are perfectly complementary, the shape of the equal product curve is—

A. Convex to the origin
B. Concave to the origin
C. Right angled
D. None of the above

488. In case of monopoly, which of the following relations is true—

A. $MR = AR\left(1-\frac{1}{e}\right)$

B. $MR = AR\left(1+\frac{1}{e}\right)$

C. $AR = MR\left(1-\frac{1}{e}\right)$

D. $AR = MR\left(1+\frac{1}{e}\right)$

Where MR = marginal revenue

AR = average revenue
e = elasticity of demand

489. Lerner's index of monopoly power is indicated by—

A. $\frac{P-MC}{P}$ B. $\frac{P-MC}{MC}$

C. $\frac{P-AC}{AC}$ D. $\frac{P-MR}{P}$

490. In Edgeworth's box diagram, the curve showing the equilibrium of two consumers is known as—

A. Income-consumption curve
B. Ridge lines
C. Expansion path
D. Contract curve

491. As a result of increase in the price of tea from Rs. 40 to Rs. 50 per pound, the demand for coffee increases from 600 pound to 720 pounds. The cross elasticity of demand is—

A. $\frac{1}{2}$ B. $\frac{2}{3}$

C. $\frac{3}{4}$ D. $\frac{4}{5}$

492. Taking capital as constant, if we go on increasing the quantity of labour average product of labour will be maximum in—

A. The middle of the second stage
B. The end of the 1st stage
C. The end of the second stage
D. The end of third stage

493. Who among the following Economists propounded the innovation theory of profit—

A. Karl Marx B. F.H. Kinght
C. J. Schumpeter D. A. Marshall

494. The validity of kinked demand curve was empirically tested and questioned by—

A. D.S. Watson B. Hall and Hitch
C. G.J. Stigler D. F. Maeklap

495. In cobb-Douglas production function, $Q = Ak^{\alpha}L^{\beta}$, α and β measure—

A. Elasticity of substitution
B. Input shares
C. Output elasticities of inputs
D. Technological condition

496. The product transformation curve is derived from—

A. The contract curve related to consumption
B. The utility possibility curve
C. The social welfare function
D. The production contract curve

497. In case of Giffen goods—

A. Price effect and income effect are positive, substitution effect is negative
B. Price effect is positive while income effect and substitution effects are negative
C. Price effect, income effect and substitution effect are positive
D. Price effect is negative while income effect and substitution effect are positive

498. A monopolist will fix the price of its product, in the range where the elasticity of demand is—

A. Less than one
B. Greater than one
C. equal to zero
D. equal to the elasticity of supply

499. The concept of general equilibrium and partial equilibrium are associated respectively with—

A. Ricardo and Walras
B. Walras and Marshall
C. Arrow and Devreau
D. Keynes and Hansen

500. In the case of complementary goods, the indifference curve is—

A. Downward sloping to the right
B. Horizontal line parallel to x-axis
C. Concave to origin
D. Upward rising line from left to right

501. Classical writers could not resolve the 'water-diamond' paradox because they could not distinguish between

A. AU and MU B. MU and TU
C. AU and TU D. MU and MC

Where AU = average utility
MU = marginal utility
TU = total utility
MC = marginal cost

502. Which one of the following statements is an apt reflection of J. R. Hick's Indifference curve Analysis of demand?

A. Pareto's theory with Marshall's method
B. Pareto's theory with Marshall's method

C. Marshall's theory with Pareto's method
D. Marshall's theory with Marshall's method

503. The revealed preference approach can be described by—
A. Strong ordering and lexicographic preference pattern
B. Rationality, Consistency and Transitivity
C. Rationality and Weak ordering
D. Transitivity and Weak ordering

504. Expansion path in the theory of production corresponds to
A. Engel's curve
B. Price consumption curve
C. Income consumption curve
D. Budget constraint

505. If capital 'K' is plotted on the vertical axis and labour 'L' on the horizontal axis, then the slope of the straight line iso-cost curve will be—

A. $\frac{P_K}{P_L}$ B. $\frac{P_L}{P_K}$

C. $-\frac{P_L}{P_K}$ D. $-\frac{P_K}{P_L}$

506. Quasi rent is
A. Equal to the firm's total profits
B. Greater than firm's total profits
C. Smaller than firm's total profits
D. Not related to firm's profits

507. The backward-bending supply curve for labour exists—
A. Only in inflationary conditions
B. Wherever income effect overcomes substitution effect
C. Only in labour intensive industry
D. Only in a high cost industry

508. An ethical or value Judgement must be made in order to derive the
A. Transformation curve
B. Grand utility possibility
C. Consumption contract curve
D. Social welfare function

509. According to the Kaldor-Hicks compensation criterion, a change in economic policy leads to an improvement in social welfare, if
A. The gainers can just compensate the losers
B. The losers can profitably bribe the gainers to induce them to stay in the old position
C. The gainers can compensate the losers for their loss and still remain better-off themselves than before
D. The losers do not oppose the change

510. Match List I with List II and select the correct answer using the codes given below the lists—

	List I *(Curves)*		*List II* *(Ideas)*
a.	Offer curve	1.	Market segmentation
b.	Laffer curve	2.	Sticky price
c.	Lorenz curve	3.	Reciprocal demand
d.	Kinked curve	4.	Inequalities
		5.	Public revenue

Codes:	*a*	*b*	*c*	*d*
A.	1	4	5	3
B.	3	5	4	2
C.	1	5	3	2
D.	4	2	3	1

511. The situation in which total revenues equal total cost, is known as
A. Monopolistic competition
B. Equilibrium level of output
C. Break-even point
D. Perfect competition

512. The relationship between price of a commodity and the demand for it—
A. is a positive relationship
B. is an inverse relationship
C. They are independent of each other
D. They do not have any relationship

513. Total utility is maximum at a point, then marginal utility is
A. Positive
B. Zero
C. Negative
D. Positive but decreasing

514. In the compensating variation method of measuring the substitution effect of a rise in price, the consumer is
A. Under-compensated
B. Over-Compensated
C. Just compensated
D. Unaffected

515. When both the demand and the supply curves slope downwards and the demand curve is steeper than the supply curve, the equilibrium is—

A. Stable in both Marshallian and Walrasian sense

B. Unstable in both Marshallian and Walrasian sense

C. Stable in the Marshallian sense but unstable in the Walrasian sense

D. Unstable in the Marshallian sense but stable in the Walrasian sense

516. Consider the following combinations of inputs and outputs—

Labour	*Capital*	*Output*
5	10	1
6	12	2
7	14	3
8	16	4
9	18	5
10	20	6

This production technology satisfies

A. Increasing returns to scale

B. Diminishing returns to scale

C. Constant returns to scale

D. Increasing returns initially, followed by decreasing returns to scale

517. On the expansion path of the firm operating with homogeneous production function, which among the following remain constant?

1. Input ratio
2. Price ratio of inputs
3. Marginal rate of technical substitution between the factors
4. Elasticity of substitution

Select the correct answer using the codes given below—

A. 1 and 4 B. 2 and 1

C. 2, 3 and 4 D. 1, 2, 3 and 4

518. The kinked demand curve is reflected in a discontinuity in the—

A. Total revenue curve

B. Marginal cost curve

C. Average revenue curve

D. Marginal revenue curve

519. Rent earned by factor of production equals

A. What this factor earn in its next best use

B. The sum of what this factor earns in its current use and what it can earn in its next best use

C. Its transfer earnings

D. The difference between what this factor is currently earning and what it can earn in its next best use

520. In the context of cost minimisation by a competitive producer, which one of the following is not correct?

A. Marginal rate of technical substitution of the factors equals relative factor price ratio

B. Ratio of marginal physical productivities of the factors equals the ratio of factor prices

C. Slope of the isoquent in question equals slope of the budget line

D. Marginal rate of technical substitution of factors of production divided by relative factor price ration is zero

521. In the short-run, the supply curve of a competitive firm is

A. The rising portion of the marginal cost curve lying above the minimum point of the average variable cost curve

B. The falling portion of the MC-curve lying before the minimum point of the average variable cost curve

C. The rising portion of the MC-curve after the highest point of total cost curve

D. None of the above

522. Suppose, there is a situation where two individuals are engaged in exchange and if individual 1 is a price-maker and individual 2 is a price-taker, equilibrium—

A. takes place on the offer curve of individual 1

B. takes place on the offer curve of individuals 2

C. takes place at the intersection point of the two offer curves

D. is indeterminate

523. In the long run, the market price of a commodity is equal to its minimum average cost of production, if there is

A. Perfect competition

B. Monopoly

C. Oligopoly

D. Monopolistic competition

524. In the linearly homogeneous Cobb-Douglas

production function with two inputs, the elasticity of substitution between the inputs is

A. Zero B. Greater than one

C. One D. Less than one

525. Suppose that there are two goods, *x* and *y*, facing a consumer. The price are P_x = Rs. 4 and P_y = Rs. 5. He has Rs. 110 to spend on these goods. Suppose, he is currently buying 15 units of good *x* (with marginal utility equal to 40) and 10 units of good *y* (with marginal utility equal to 45). In the above context, which one of the following statements is correct?

A. His total utility will increase if he reallocates his spending towards more of good *x* and less of good *y*

B. His total utility will increase if he spends more on good *y* and less on good *x*

C. His total utility will increase if he spends less on both the goods

D. His total utility is being maximized subject to the budget constraint he is facing

526. If an individual is observed to work less in response to an increase in the wage rate for his services, this implies that—

A. For this individual, leisure is a normal good

B. For this individual, leisure is an inferior good

C. The individual is irrational

D. Leisure could be a Giffen good

527. Consider the demand curve depicted in the following diagram—

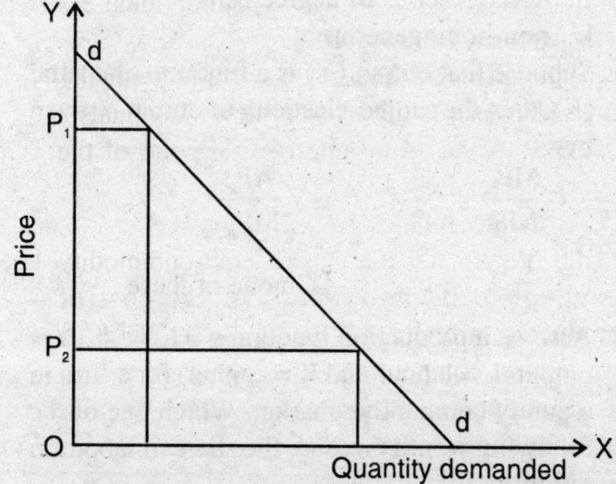

The elasticities of demand at prices P_1 and P_2 are different because, at these prices

A. Slopes are different

B. Prices are different

C. Quantities are different

D. Price-quantity ratios are different

528. Given the demand function $Q = \frac{20}{P}$, where P = Price of product and Q = quantity of product, the elasticity of demand at P = 10 would be

A. 0 B. –1

C. –2 D. ∞

529. Match List-I (MRS_{xy}) with List-II (The shape of Indifference Curve IC) and select the correct answer using the codes given below the lists:

List-I	*List-I*
a. MRS_{xy} = Zero	1. Right - angled
b. MRS_{xy} = Constant but non-zero	2. Straight line with negative slope
c. Decreasing MRS_{xy}	3. IC is concave to the origin
d. Increasing MRS_{xy}	4. IC is convex to the origin

Codes:	*a*	*b*	*c*	*d*
A.	1	2	4	3
B.	3	4	2	1
C.	1	4	2	3
D.	3	2	4	1

530. Which one of the following assumptions is not correct for the revealed preference analysis?

A. Consistency B. Transitivity

C. Rationality D. Weak-ordering

531. A consumer spends all his income of Rs. 500 equally on two goods *x* and *y* by purchasing 50 units of *x* at Rs. 5 per unit and 25 units of *y* at Rs 10 per unit. Because of recession, prices of *x* and *y* fall by 50% and his employer reduces his salary from Rs. 500 to Rs. 250. In this situation he is expected to

A. increase the purchase of both *x* an *y* as they are now cheaper

B. decrease the purchase of both *x* and y as his income goes down

C. leave the purchase basket unaltered at 50 of *x* and 25 of *y*

D. alter his purchase in an uncertain way

532. Assertion (A) : If the monopolist faces identical

demand curves for his commodity in two separate markets, by practising third degree price discrimination, he cannot increase his TR and total profits

Reason (R) : As the marginal revenue curves are identical when the demand curves in the two markets are the same, the monopolist will not charge different prices in each market to maximise profits.

A. Both Assertion and Reason are true and Reason is the correct explanation of Assertion
B. Both Assertion and Reason are true but Reason is Not a correct explanation of A
C. Assertion is true but Reason is false
D. Assertion is false but Reason is true

533. Assertion : Consumer's surplus is the difference between the potential price and the actual price

Reason : There exists an inverse relationship between the price and the consumer's surplus.

A. Both Assertion and Reason are true and Reason is the correct explanation of Assertion
B. Both Assertion and Reason are true and Reason is not a correct explanation of Assertion
C. Assertion is true but Reason is false
D. Assertion is false but Reason is true

534. Assertion : The long-run cost curve is L-shaped rather than U-shaped.

Reason : The new techniques of production of large plants reduce the total costs per unit of output.

A. Both Assertion and Reason are true and Reason is the correct explanation of Assertion
B. Both Assertion and Reason are true and Reason is not a correct explanation of Assertion
C. Assertion is true but Reason is false
D. Assertion is false but Reason is true

535. Assertion : The imposition of a per unit tax causes the monopolists average cost and marginal cost curves to shift up.

Reason : The per unit tax is like a variable cost.

A. Both Assertion and Reason are true and Reason is the correct explanation of Assertion
B. Both Assertion and Reason are true but Reason is not a correct explanation of Assertion
C. Assertion is true but Reason is false
D. Assertion is false but Reason is true

536. When the price-elasticity of demand is unity, the marginal revenue would be

A. Less than zero B. Equal to zero
C. Equal to one D. Greater than one

537. The total area under the demand curve of a good, measures—

A. Marginal utility
B. Total utility
C. Consumer's surplus
D. Producer's surplus

538. If the price-consumption curve is horizontal, the price-elasticity of demand for *x* [the price of which falls] would be

A. Zero B. One
C. Greater than one D. Less than one

539. If two demand curves intersect, then at the point of intersection—

A. they are equally elastic
B. the steeper curve is more elastic
C. the flatter curve is more elastic
D. their elasticity cannot be compared

540. The production function $y = LK$ is

A. homogeneous of degree 2
B. homogeneous of degree 1
C. homogeneous of degree zero
D. non-homogeneous

541. Suppose that output (Y) is a function of capital (K); then the capital-elasticity of output is given by—

A. $\frac{MP_k}{AP_K}$ B. $\frac{AP_k}{MP_K}$
C. $\frac{Y}{K}$ D. none of these

542. Assume a production function $y = L^{\alpha}K^{1-\alpha}$ (Y = output, L = labour and K = capital) for a firm in a purely competitive market. Which one of the following would measure the share of labour in output?

A. α B. $L(\alpha)$

C. L^{α} D. $\frac{\alpha}{L}$

543. A supply curve will have a price-elasticity equal to 1 only when it is

A. a straight line with a positive intercept
B. a straight line with a negative intercept
C. a straight line passing through the origin
D. Horizontal

544. Under perfect competition (when input prices are fixed and there are no external economies or diseconomies), the industry supply curve is derived by

A. vertically adding the average cost curves
B. horizontally adding the average cost curves
C. vertically adding the marginal cost curves
D. horizontally adding the marginal cost curves

545. Starting from a monopoly equilibrium without any policy intervention, market efficiency can be improved by imposing a

A. per-unit production tax
B. per-unit sales tax
C. profit tax
D. price ceiling below the existing equilibrium price

546. Application of the 'Marginal-cost pricing' principle in a decreasing cost industry would lead to—

A. Surpluses
B. Losses needing subsidies
C. Neither surpluses nor losses
D. A decline in output

547. In monopolistic competition, a firm is in long-run equilibrium

A. at the minimum point of the long-run average cost curve
B. in the declining segment of the long-run average cost curve
C. in the rising segment of the long-run average cost curve
D. When the price is equal to marginal cost

548. Income inequalities in a country can be measured by—

A. Lorenz curve
B. Gini coefficient
C. Proportion of income received by different size groups
D. All of the above

549. The **Adding Up Theorem** under constant returns to scale holds when the factors of production are paid according to their

A. Marginal productivities
B. Average productivities
C. Total productivities
D. Ration of marginal productivities to average productivities

550. Rent earned by a factor of production equals

A. What this factor can earn in its next best use
B. the sum of what this factor earns in its current use and what is can earn in its next best use
C. its current earnings
D. the difference between what this factor is currently earning and what it can earn in its next best use

551. If in a purely competitive market with downward-sloping demand and upward-sloping supply curves, a specific excise tax per unit of output is imposed, then

A. price rises by the amount of the tax
B. the price-rise is less than the amount of the tax
C. the price-rise is greater than the amount of the tax
D. the price remains the same

552. Market failure may NOT arise in the case of—

A. increasing returns to scale
B. public goods
C. the consumption externalities
D. income inequalities

553. A given economic state is Pareto-optimum if a policy-change can

A. make everyone better off
B. make someone better off and some one worse off
C. make someone better off and all others worse off
D. not make anyone better off without making someone worse off

554. The theory of Distribution analysis the principles which explain

A. The distribution of goods among consumers
B. The allocation of resources in different sectors of the economy
C. The distribution of income amount factors

of production

D. The distribution of profits among share holders

555. While analysing the marginal productivity theory of distribution, Clark gave more emphasis to

A. Demand for labour

B. Supply of labour

C. Both demand as well as supply of labour

D. Profit maximisation

556. We say of the demand for a factor that it is a "derived demand", because

A. It is derived from the entrepreneur's need for profit

B. It stems from government policy relating to labour

C. It emerges from the demand for the final product

D. It is derived from long period expectations

557. "The allocation of resources among industries and firms" are analysed by the

A. Theory of pricing

B. Theory of distribution

C. Theory of production

D. Theory of consumption

558. The concept of the 'reserve army of labour' is due to—

A. Karl Marx B. David Ricardo

C. Adam Smith D. J.S. Mill

559. Who suggested that the price of a factor or production is determined by the demand and supply forces?

A. Marshall and Hicks

B. Clark and Allen

C. Lipsey and Samuelson

D. Jevons and Walras

560. In classical economics primary factors of production refers to

A. Land and capital

B. Labour and land

C. Labour and capital

D. Labour and enterprise

561. In practice the reward paid to a factor depends upon—

A. Its productivity and the price of the product it makes

B. Value of its output minus profit tax

C. General directives of the government

D. Its cost and the price of the product it makes

562. The increase in output as a result of one unit increase in factor is known as

A. Marginal revenue product

B. Marginal physical product

C. Marginal revenue

D. None of these

563. Marginal physical product and marginal revenue product change exactly similarly only when—

A. The price of the product remains constant

B. The product remains unchanged

C. The price of the product falls regularly

D. None of the above

564. The price elasticity of demand in demand function $q = ap^b$ is

A. a B. 1

C. b D. ab

565. A fall in the price of fish will have comparatively little effect on demand for meat, whereas a fall in the price of chicken will have a far greater effect on the demand for mutton, because

A. Chicken is a much better substitute for mutton than fish for meat

B. Chicken and fish are complementary goods

C. meat and fish are substitutes

D. meat is a better substitute to fish than to chicken

566. If the price elasticity of demand is 0.5, a 10 percent increase in price leads to—

A. 5% increase in demand

B. 5% decrease in demand

C. 0.5 units decrease in demand

D. 0.5 units increase in demand

567. An upward sloping supply curve implies that

A. the producer will cut back on production when price rises because he can sell a smaller amount and obtain the same total profit

B. the producer will increase output when price rises in an attempt to increase profits even more

C. the producer is not responsive to the true needs of consumers

D. Consumers will buy more of the product when its price rises

568. Diminishing returns refers to an eventual fall in

A. the average product of he variable factor

B. the marginal product of the fixed factor
C. the total product
D. the marginal product of the variable factor

569. Which one of the following is true?
A. Total product is at a maximum when marginal product has fallen to zero
B. Total product is at a maximum when marginal product is falling
C. Total product is at a minimum when marginal product is zero
D. Total product increases when marginal product is zero

570. For a competitive firm, the demand curve is also—
A. the total revenue curve
B. the average revenue curve
C. the marginal revenue curve
D. both (B) and (C)

571. The slope of the iso-cost line measures
A. the marginal rate of technical substitution
B. the marginal rate of substitution
C. the ratio of input prices
D. Optimal combination inputs

572. Monopolistic competition and oligopoly are alike in terms of
A. non-price competition
B. strong mutual interdependence among firms
C. kinked demand analysis
D. the number of firms

573. In a general competitive equilibrium, the slope of the production possibility frontier equals
A. the slope of the iso cost line of a firm
B. the slope of a consumer's budget line
C. the input price ratio
D. the ratio of marginal products

574. Efficiency in the distribution of products among consumers occurs when
A. Marginal rate of technical substitution are equal
B. Consumer's marginal rate of substitution are equal
C. P = MC
D. $P_x = MU_x$

575. In order to get a Pareto-optimal distribution the goods must be distributed in a fashion such that—
A. MRS between any two goods is different for different individuals
B. MRS between any two goods of individual is greater than those of others
C. MRS between any two goods is the same for all individuals
D. MRS between any two goods of one individual is less than those of others

576. Profit can be considered in economic terms as—
A. A residual award but not a cost
B. Both a cost and residual reward
C. A cost but not a residual reward
D. A reward accruing only to the marginal entrepreneur

577. Frank H. Kinght regards profits as—
A. Payments received by an entrepreneur who is seeking to maximise his profits and faces a downward sloping demand curve for the produce which he is selling
B. A chance of distribution of income among entrepreneurs
C. The payments received by entrepreneurs who take highly risky projects involving bold innovations
D. The payments received by an entrepreneur for his risk-taking and activities in which some elements of uncertainty are involved

578. In Schumpeter's view an entrepreneur is—
A. An individual participating in activities in which any risk uncertainty or speculation exists
B. The individual who furnishes the money capital to finance any enterprise and thus bears the risk
C. An innovator of new products and processes
D. The person responsible for decisions concerning operations of an enterprise

579. 'Interest is a reward for parting with liquidity', according to
A. J.M. Keynes B. Alfred Marshall
C. G. Von Haberler D. Bertil Ohlin

580. The advocate of the Loanable Fund Theory of Interest is
A. Keynes B. Lionel Robbins
C. Robertson D. Paul Samuelson

581. The Loanable funds theory lays emphasis on the interplay of
A. Monetary factors

B. Real factors
C. Both monetary as well as real factors
D. Liquidity preference

582. Which theory is called as the Neo-classical theory of Rate of interest?
A. The Keynesian Theory
B. Liquidity Preference Theory
C. The Time Preference Theory
D. Loanable Funds Theory

583. The classical theory of interest lays more emphasis on
A. Real factors B. Monetary factors
C. Liquidity preference D. All of these

584. In the classical theory, the rate of interest is determined by the
A. Supply of saving curve
B. Investment demand curve
C. Intersection between these two curves
D. None of these

585. Interest is "Price paid for the use of capital in any market." This view of interest has been expressed by—
A. S.E. Harris B. Lipsey
C. Fisher D. Marshall

586. The Ricardian Theory and the Modern Theory of rent are
A. Similar B. Same
C. Altogether different D. Slightly different

587. If the supply of a factor cannot be increased in the short period and demand for it increases it will:
A. Earn an economic rent
B. Earn a quasi-rent
C. Earn a windfall profit
D. Increase its transfer earnings

588. According to the Modern Theory, rent arises on
A. Labour only B. Land only
C. Capital only D. All factors

589. According to the Modern theory, rent is the difference between
A. Actual earning and transfer earning
B. A land's produce and B land's produce
C. Reward of marginal and sub marginal units of a factor
D. All of these

590. First of all the term 'Quasi-rent' was used by—
A. Marshall B. Adam Smith
C. John Robinson D. None of these

591. Quasi-rent is a
A. Short-period phenomenon
B. Long-period phenomenon
C. Time phenomenon
D. None of the above

592. Quasi-rent is
A. Price-AVC B. Price-AFC
C. Price -ATC D. Price-MC

593. The Modern Theory of Rent has been developed by—
A. J.M. Kynes B. Alfred Marshall
C. Joan Robinson D. D.H. Robertson

594. A factor will not earn rent if
A. Its supply is elastic
B. Its supply is inelastic
C. Its supply cannot be varied
D. Its supply is perfectly elastic for all amount

595. 'In a sense all rents are scarcity rents, and all rents are differential rents' are words of
A. Ricardo B. Adam Smith
C. K.F. Boulding D. Marshall

596. That the rent of land is a return for the use of the "original and indestructible powers of the soil" was the essence of the theory proposed by
A. Adam Smith B. Ricardo
C. John Stuart Mill D. Alfred Marshall

597. In the Ricardian theory of economic rent, transfer earnings of land are presumed to be
A. Equal to rent B. Negative
C. Positive D. Zero

598. Transfer earnings are
A. The maximum payment necessary to retain the factor in its employment
B. The level of earnings required to tempt factors to take up less remunerative employment
C. That part of a factor's earnings classed as Economic Rent
D. Payments made to labour during periods of retraining

599. The relation between rent and price is as follows—
A. Rent is price determined, not price determining
B. Rent has nothing to do with price and is determined independently

C. Rent determines price
D. All of these

600. The Ricardian Theory considered rent as—
A. A gross surplus
B. A net surplus
C. A differential surplus
D. None of these

601. Economic rent is earned by a factor when its
A. Supply is perfectly elastic
B. Supply is inelastic
C. Supply is more than its demand
D. Demand is less than its supply

602. Economic rent earned by any factor will be highest if its elasticity of supply is
A. Zero B. Between Zero and one
C. Equal to one D. Infinity

603. According to the Ricardian Theory, rent is
A. Difference of product of superior land and interior land
B. Difference of income between smaller formers and bigger farmers
C. Surplus of product of all categories of land above the marginal land
D. None of these

604. Under conditions of monopsony in the labour market, the trade unions can succeed in achieving higher wage rates
A. Without decreasing employment
B. With increasing employment
C. With unemployment
D. All the above

605. Which of the following statements is not true? A trade union is likely to be successful in obtaining a wage increase when
A. The demand for the product made by the labour is inelastic
B. There is full employment
C. The supply of labour saving equipment is elastic
D. Labour costs form a small proportion of total costs

606. Where there is perfect competition in the labour market as well as the product market, labour will be subjected to
A. Monopolistic exploitation
B. Non exploitation
C. Monopsonistic exploitation
D. Both (A) and (B)

607. With perfect competition in the labour market and monopoly in the product market the monopolistic exploitation of labour is equal to the difference between
A. MU and AW B. MRP and AW
C. VMP and MRP D. MRP and ARP

608. When there is monopsony in the labour market and monopoly in the product market, total of monopsonistic and monopolistic exploitation is the difference between
A. VMP and AW B. VMP and MW
C. MRP and MW D. ARP and AW

609. A trade-union entering a perfectly competitive labour market can raise the wage above the free market level
A. Along with an increase in employment
B. Keeping the employment at the existing level
C. Only at the cost of lowering the amount of employment
D. Either (A) or (C) depending upon the relative elasticities of demand and supply curves of the commodity being produced

610. A negatively sloped supply curve of labour of an individual indicates that the substitution effect of an increase in the wage rate is
A. Equal to income effect
B. Weaker than income effect
C. Stronger than income effect
D. Either (*b*) or (*c*) depending upon his income level

611. Under condition of Monopsony in the labour market, the trade unions can succeed in achieving higher wage rates
A. Without decreasing employment
B. With increasing employment
C. Without unemployment
D. All the above

612. Income effect results in
A. Upward sloping supply curve of labour
B. Downwards sloping supply curve of labour
C. Backward sloping supply curve of labour
D. Zero slope of supply curve of labour

613. Which of the following statements is not true? A trade union is likely to be successful in

obtaining a wage increase when—
A. The demand for the product made by the labour is inelastic
B. There is full employment
C. The supply of labour saving equipment is elastic
D. Labour costs form a small proportion of total cost

614. When there is monopsony in labour market and perfect competition in product market, the monopsonistic exploitation in the equilibrium situation is the difference between
A. VMP and MRP B. ARP and MRP
C. MW and AW D. MW and MRP

615. The demand curve for labour is also its
A. Average revenue productivity curve
B. Marginal revenue productivity curve
C. Total revenue productivity curve
D. Total utility curve

616. Wage-offer curve shows the relationship between
A. Wage offered by two competing firms
B. Wage rate and general price level
C. Money income and real income
D. Money income of an individual and the work effort that he is ready to put in

617. The backward-bending supply curve for labour exists
A. Only in inflationary conditions
B. Wherever income effect overcomes substitution effect
C. Only in labour intensive industry
D. Only in a high cost industry

618. According to the subsistence theory of wages, the long run supply curve of labour is—
A. Perfectly elastic
B. Perfectly inelastic
C. A straight line sloping up towards right passing through the origin
D. A straight line sloping up towards right cutting and intercept on y-axis

619. The subsistence wage theory is due to—
A. T. R. Malthus B. David Ricardo
C. Adam Smith D. J. S. Mill

620. Which one of the following is not true in the wage fund theory?
A. Wages depend upon the wage-fund set aside for the purchase of labour
B. Wages depend upon the number of workers seeking employment
C. Wage could rise only by a reduction in the number of workers
D. Trade unions and collective bargaining can raise the wages for labour class as a whole

621. Collective bargaining refers to—
A. Inter-union discussions aimed at resolving an industrial dispute
B. Negotiation between employer's associations and worker's unions
C. The determination of factor prices in a collective economy
D. Government trade union decisions on industrial legislation

622. Wages Fund Theory was formulated by
A. Physiocrats B. J. S. Mill
C. Walker D. Marshall

623. For the equilibrium level of employment of a factor of production the necessary condition is
A. MRP = ARP B. ARP = AFC
C. MRP = MFC D. MRP = VMP

624. When there is monopsony in labour market and monopoly in product market, the total exploitation in the equilibrium situation is the difference between
A. VMP and MRP B. VMP and AW
C. MRP and MW D. MRP and AW

625. An employer will continue to hire units of a variable factor until MRP
A. Equals its AW B. More than AW
C. Less than MW D. Equals its MW

626. Assertion (A): Long run equilibrium of the industry in a perfectly competitive market occurs at the point where price equals minimum long run average cost.
Reason (R): In this position of zero economic profit, there is no tendency on the part of any existing firm to stage on exit, and no potential entrant wants to enter the industry.
A. Both A and R are individually true and R is the correct explanation of A
B. Both A and R are individually true but R is not the correct explanation of A
C. A is true but R is false
D. A is false but R is true

627. Assertion (A): In perfect competition a firm is

price-taker and the industry is price-maker.

Reason (R): No individual firm can influence the price.

A. Both A and R are individually true and R is the correct explanation of A

B. Both A and R are individually true but R is not the correct explanation of A

C. A is true but R is false

D. A is false but R is true

628. Assertion (A): Monopolistic competition is a market situation where there is product differentiation.

Reason (R): Product differentiation is also a characteristic of monopoly market.

A. Both A and R are individually true and R is the correct explanation of A

B. Both A and R are individually true but R is not the correct explanation of A

C. A is true but R is false

D. A is false but R is rue

629. Assertion (A): The average fixe cost cuve is rectangular hyperbola.

Reason (R): The rate of increase in average variable cost is higher than the rate of decrease in the average fixed cost.

A. Both A and R are individually true and R is the correct explanation of A

B. Both A and R are individually true but R is not the correct explanation of A

C. A is true but R is false

D. A is false but R is true

630. Assertion (A): For inferior goods, the income elasticity of demand is negative.

Reason (R): As income rises, goods on which spending grows relatively faster than income will occupy a rising share of income.

A. Both A and R are individually rue and R is the correct explanation of A

B. Both A and R are individually true but R is not the correct explanation of A

C. A is true but R is false

D. A is false but R is true

ANSWERS

1	**2**	**3**	**4**	**5**	**6**	**7**	**8**	**9**	**10**
C	C	A	B	C	E	B	D	A	A
11	**12**	**13**	**14**	**15**	**16**	**17**	**18**	**19**	**20**
A	B	A	A	A	B	D	D	A	A
21	**22**	**23**	**24**	**25**	**26**	**27**	**28**	**29**	**30**
A	C	B	C	B	B	B	B	B	B
31	**32**	**33**	**34**	**35**	**36**	**37**	**38**	**39**	**40**
A	A	A	C	A	A	B	B	C	B
41	**42**	**43**	**44**	**45**	**46**	**47**	**48**	**49**	**50**
C	D	A	A	B	B	B	B	B	C
51	**52**	**53**	**54**	**55**	**56**	**57**	**58**	**59**	**60**
C	D	B	A	C	B	A	B	A	A
61	**62**	**63**	**64**	**65**	**66**	**67**	**68**	**69**	**70**
A	C	D	A	A	B	C	D	A	C
71	**72**	**73**	**74**	**75**	**76**	**77**	**78**	**79**	**80**
A	C	D	A	C	C	A	B	C	A
81	**82**	**83**	**84**	**85**	**86**	**87**	**88**	**89**	**90**
A	A	C	A	B	D	B	A	D	C
91	**92**	**93**	**94**	**95**	**96**	**97**	**98**	**99**	**100**
A	B	A	C	B	B	B	B	B	C
101	**102**	**103**	**104**	**105**	**106**	**107**	**108**	**109**	**110**
B	A	B	C	A	B	C	A	C	A
111	**112**	**113**	**114**	**115**	**116**	**117**	**118**	**119**	**120**
C	A	C	D	C	B	C	D	D	C
121	**122**	**123**	**124**	**125**	**126**	**127**	**128**	**129**	**130**
B	C	B	B	A	A	B	A	C	A

131	132	133	134	135	136	137	138	139	140
C	C	D	B	C	C	C	B	C	A
141	142	143	144	145	146	147	148	149	150
D	C	B	B	A	A	A	A	C	B
151	152	153	154	155	156	157	158	159	160
A	D	D	B	A	A	A	B	B	B
161	162	163	164	165	166	167	168	169	170
C	A	A	B	D	C	A	B	D	C
171	172	173	174	175	176	177	178	179	180
B	D	C	C	D	B	A	B	A	D
181	182	183	184	185	186	187	188	189	190
D	C	A	B	B	B	B	B	C	C
191	192	193	194	195	196	197	198	199	200
C	B	B	B	B	A	D	C	B	D
201	202	203	204	205	206	207	208	209	210
C	B	A	B	D	A	A	C	C	C
211	212	213	214	215	216	217	218	219	220
B	B	B	B	D	D	D	C	A	C
221	222	223	224	225	226	227	228	229	230
C	A	D	A	D	A	A	C	A	C
231	232	233	234	235	236	237	238	239	240
D	D	B	C	C	B	B	B	C	C
241	242	243	244	245	246	247	248	249	250
C	B	C	B	C	C	B	B	C	C
251	252	253	254	255	256	257	258	259	260
B	B	B	A	B	C	C	D	D	D
261	262	263	264	265	266	267	268	269	270
B	B	B	A	B	C	C	B	B	C
271	272	273	274	275	276	277	278	279	280
C	A	D	D	B	D	B	B	B	B
281	282	283	284	285	286	287	288	289	290
C	D	C	B	B	A	A	C	C	A
291	292	293	294	295	296	297	298	299	300
B	B	D	C	B	B	B	A	B	B
301	302	303	304	305	306	307	308	309	310
B	A	C	C	A	A	C	B	A	A
311	312	313	314	315	316	317	318	319	320
B	B	C	D	D	C	D	C	A	B
321	322	323	324	325	326	327	328	329	330
B	D	D	C	C	C	D	B	A	B
331	332	333	334	335	336	337	338	339	340
B	C	C	C	B	D	A	B	A	D
341	342	343	344	345	346	347	348	349	350
D	B	C	A	C	B	B	C	D	A
351	352	353	354	355	356	357	358	359	360
A	B	B	B	C	C	D	C	A	D
361	362	363	364	365	366	367	368	369	370
C	D	C	D	D	B	C	C	B	A
371	372	373	374	375	376	377	378	379	380
A	A	D	B	C	D	D	B	C	B
381	382	383	384	385	386	387	388	389	390
B	D	A	C	D	C	D	A	B	A

391	392	393	394	395	396	397	398	399	400
B	A	D	A	D	A	B	B	C	C
401	402	403	404	405	406	407	408	409	410
A	D	B	A	A	A	A	C	B	C
411	412	413	414	415	416	417	418	419	420
A	A	A	A	A	B	B	A	A	B
421	422	423	424	425	426	427	428	429	430
A	C	B	D	B	A	B	C	B	A
431	432	433	434	435	436	437	438	439	440
B	B	C	A	B	B	A	B	B	A
441	442	443	444	445	446	447	448	449	450
C	B	B	D	D	B	D	A	B	D
451	452	453	454	455	456	457	458	459	460
A	C	C	D	D	A	A	C	A	D
461	462	463	464	465	466	467	468	469	470
C	C	C	B	B	C	A	B	B	C
471	472	473	474	475	476	477	478	479	480
C	B	B	C	C	A	A	B	A	C
481	482	483	484	485	486	487	488	489	490
A	B	B	D	C	C	C	A	A	D
491	492	493	494	495	496	497	498	499	500
D	B	C	C	C	D	B	B	B	B
501	502	503	504	505	506	507	508	509	510
B	C	B	B	B	A	B	D	C	B
511	512	513	514	515	516	517	518	519	520
C	B	B	C	C	C	A	D	D	D
521	522	523	524	525	526	527	528	529	530
A	A	A	C	D	A	D	B	A	D
531	532	533	534	535	536	537	538	539	540
C	A	A	A	A	B	B	B	C	B
541	542	543	544	545	546	547	548	549	550
A	A	C	D	A	A	B	D	A	D
551	552	553	554	555	556	557	558	559	560
B	C	D	C	A	C	B	A	A	B
561	562	563	564	565	566	567	568	569	570
A	B	A	C	A	B	B	D	A	D
571	572	573	574	575	576	577	578	579	580
C	B	B	B	C	B	D	C	A	C
581	582	583	584	585	586	587	588	589	590
C	D	A	C	D	C	B	D	A	A
591	592	593	594	595	596	597	598	599	600
A	A	C	D	D	B	D	A	A	C
601	602	603	604	605	606	607	608	609	610
B	A	C	D	C	B	C	A	C	B
611	612	613	614	615	616	617	618	619	620
D	C	C	C	B	D	B	A	A	D
621	622	623	624	625	626	627	628	629	630
B	B	C	B	D	A	A	C	B	C

UNIT II : MACRO ECONOMIC ANALYSIS

DETERMINATION OF OUTPUT AND EMPLOYMENT

CLASSICAL THEORY OF EMPLOYMENT

The classical theory assumes the existence of full employment without inflation. Given wage-price flexibility, there are automatic forces in the economic system that tend to maintain full employment, and produce output at that level. Thus full employment is ragarded as a normal situation and any deviation from this level is something abnormal which automatically tends towards full employment. The classical theory of output and employment is based on the following assumptions:

1. There is the existence of full employment without inflation.

2. There is perfect competition in labour and product markets.

3. There is a closed *laissez faire* capitalist economy without foreign trade.

4. Labour is homogenous.

5. Total output of the economy is divided between consumption and investment expenditures.

6. The quantity of money is given.

7. Wages and prices are flexible.

8. Money wages and real wages are directly related and proportional.

9. Capital stock and technological knowledge are given in the short run.

Say's Law and Classical Theory

According to the classical theory propounded by Ricardo and Adam Smith, levels of income and employment are governed by fixed capital stock on the one hand and wage-goods fund on the other. In fact, the wage goods surpluses are also called by them as capital and have been given the name of circulating capital or liquid capital in contrast to the fixed capital consisting of machines, plants, factory buildings, irrigation works, etc. It may be noted in the begining that the classical theory believes in full employment or near full employment prevailing in the economy. This belief of classical theory regarding the existence of full employment in the economy is based on **Say's Law** put forward by a Frenchy economist **J. B. Say**. According to J. B. Say's law, **"Supply creates its own demand"**. This implies that every increase in production made possible by the increase in the productive capacity or the stock of fixed capital will be sold in the market and there will be no problem of lack of demand.

Thus, classical economists rule out the possibility of overproduction; there being no problem in selling the output produced. Thus, deficiency in demand being no problem, the process of capital accumulation and expansion of productive capacity will continue till all people are employed and there is no reason why the productive capacity created remains unutilized or underutilized.

According to this theory, the income which is not spent on consumer goods and thus saved will be automatically invested. Indeed, in classical theory, saving and investment are two factors of the same phenomenon *i.e.*, an act of saving is an act of investment itself. Thus, the leakage caused by the saving in the income flow is made up by the investment expenditure. In this way, a given productive capacity continue to be fully utilized and no problem of deficiency of demand arises.

Classical economists thought that if price mechanism in a capitalist economy is allowed to work freely without any interference by the Government, then there is always a tendency to full employment in it. Of course, they admitted that in an advanced capitalist economy often certain circumstances arise due to which economy is not in a full-employment equilibrium. But they firmly believed that there was always a tendency to full employment in the economy and certain economic forces automatically operate so as to move the economy towards full employment. Therefore, according to the classical economists when ever there are lapses from full employment level, then these are removed automatically by the working of **free price mechanism.**

Price Flexibility and Employment

In the classical model of employment, changes in money wages and real wages are directly related and are propoportional. When there is a cut in the money wage, the real wage is also reduced to the some extent which reduces unemployment and ultimately brings full employment in the economy. This relationship is based on the assumption that prices are proportional to the quantity of money. It is argued that in a competitive economy a reaction in the money wage reduces the cost of production and prices of products thereby raising their demand. In order to meet the increased demand for the products, more workers are employed to produce them.

As employment increases, total output also increases till full employment is reached. But when the economy is at the full employment level, total output becomes stable. Thus, given the stocks of capital, technological knowledge and resources, a precise relation exists between total output and the amount of employment. Total output is an increasing funciton of the number of workers.

$$Q = f(K, T, N)$$

Where Q = total output

K = capital stock

T = technological knowledge

N = number of workers

This production function shows that in the short run the total output is an increasing function of the number of workers given the capital stock and technological knowledge.

Keynes's Criticism of Classical Theory

Keynes in his renowned book **"General Theory"** severely criticised the classical theory of employment. Keynes attacked the classical theory on the following counts.

1. Keynes rejected the fundamental classical assumption of full employment equilibrium in he economy. He considered it as unrealistic. He regarded full employment as a special situation. The general situation in a capitalist economy is one of underemployment.

2. Keynes refuted Say's law of markets that supply always created its own demand. He maintained that all income earned by the factor owners would not be spent in buying products which they helped to produce. A part of the income is saved and is not automatically invested because saving and investment are distinct functions. so when all earned income is not spent on consumption goods and a portion of it is saved, there results a deficiency of aggregate demand. This leads to general over production because all that is produced is not sold. This, in turn, leads to general unemployment.

3. The classicists believed that saving and investment were equal at the full employment level and in case of any divergence the equality was brought about by the mechanism of rate of interest. Keynes held that the level of saving depended upon the level of income and not on the rate of interest. Similarly investment is determined not only by rate of interest but by the marginal efficiency of capital. A low rate of interest cannot increase investment if business expectations are low.

4. Keynes did not agree with the classical view that the **laissez-faire** policy was essential for an automatic and self-adjusting process of full employment equilibrium. He pointed out that the capitalist system was not automatic and self-adjusting because of the non-egalitarian structure of its society. Keynes, therefore, advocated state intervention for adjusting supply and demand within the economy through fiscal and monetary measures.

5. The classical economists regarded money as neutral. Therefore they excluded the theory of output, employment and interest rate from the monetary theory. According to them, the level of output and employment, and the equilibrium rate of interest were determined by real forces. Keynes criticised the classical view that the monetary theory was separate from the value theory. He integrated monetary theory with value theory, and brought the theory of interest in the domain of monetary theory.

6. Kenes refuted the Pigovian formulation that a cut in money wage could achieve full employment in the economy. The greatest fallacy in Pigou's analysis was that he extended the argument to the economy which was applicable to a particular industry.

Keynes also did not accept the classical view that there was a direct proportionate relationship between money wages and real wages. According to him, there is an inverse relation between the two. When money wages fall, real wages rise and vice versa.

7. The classicists believed in the long-run full employment equilibrium through a self-adjusting process. Keynes had no patience to wait for the long period for he believed that "In the long-run we are all dead."

Conclusion

We have discussed above classical theory of employment. In brief this law states that supply creates its own demand. From this, it has been concluded that in a free enterprise capitalist economy, there is always a tendency towards full employment. If at sometimes unemployment appears in the economy, then wages would decline, the rate of interest and price would also fall and as a result of this employment of labour would increase and unemployement will be automatically removed, provided the economy is allowed to work freely without any interference by Government and trade unions. Hence a state of full employement will be established. In this way due to the flexibility of wages, prices and interest rate, there can neither be general over production, nor unemployment in the economy for a long time. Therefore, classical and neo-classical economists thought that there is always a tendency towards full-employment provided no restrictions are placed in the working of free and perfect competition. But keynes proved this as invalid not only theoretically but also practically. Keynes put forward a new theory of income and employment which is the correct explanation of the phenomenon in a developed capitalist economy. For this purpose, keynes invented new concepts such as propensity to consume, marginal efficiency of capital, liquidity preference which effect the level of income and employment in the economy. Keynes also proved that a cut in wages will not cure depression and unemployment but will worsen them. Following Keynesian revolution in econimic theory and the recognition of the fact that economic fluctuations or lapses from full-employment will not be automatically corrected, it is now almost universally believed that Government should play an active and important role to promote economic stability at the level of full employment by taking appropriate fiscal and monetary measures. Laissez faire policy cannot, therefore, be followed by the Government in the modern world.

KEYNES'S THEORY OF EMPLOYMENT

Concept of Effective Demand

The priciple of 'effective demand' is basic to Keynes analysis of income, output and employment. Prior to Keynes no satisfactory explanation was given of the factors determining the level of employment in the economy. The economists mostly assumed the prevalence of the state of full employment believing in Say's Law of Markets. **T. R. Malthus** tried hard to convince Ricardo that demand in general might fall short of supply in general and the deficiency of aggregate demand might cause general over production and hence general unemployment. But Malthus failed to explain how effective demand could be deficient or excessive. It was Keynes, who for the first time, put forward a systematic and convincing theory of employment based on the **"Principle of Effective Demand."**

Meaning of Effective Demand

Effective demand represents the money actually spent by people on the products of industry. Keynes used the term 'effective demand' to denote the total demand for goods and services at various levels of employment. Different levels of employment represent different levels of aggregate demand. But there can be a level of employment where aggregate demand equals aggregate supply. This is the point of effective demand.

Determinants of Effective Demands

Fro an understanding of Keynes theory of employment and how an equilibrium level of employment is established in the economy, we must know the determinants of effective demand—the aggregate demand function and the aggregate supply function and their interrelationship.

Aggregate Supply

When entrepreneurs employ some people they incur some cost of production. If the proceeds obtained from the sale of output produced by a certain number of people employed is greater than the cost of production incurred, then it will be worthwhile to employ them. This cost of production incurred on the employment of a certain number of labourers must be received by the entrepreneur, otherwise they will not produce and provide employment to labour. At any given level of employment of labour, **aggregate supply price is the total amount of money which all the entrepreneurs in the economy taken together must expect to receive from the sale of** the output produced by the given number of labourers employed. In other words, the aggregate supply price is the total cost of production incurred by employing a certain given number of labourers. It is obvious that if the cost of production incurred by the entrepreneur in employing a certain number of labourers is not covered, they will reduce the amount of employment offered. As the amount of employment of labour increases, the total cost of production will also increase. Therefore, aggregate supply price will rise as more labour is employed to produce goods and serices. Thus we can construct a schedule and curve of aggregate supply showing aggregate supply price at different levels of employment. The curve of aggregate supply price is represented by AS in figure 1.1. This curve of aggregate supply price starts from the point of origin and slopes upward to the right. In the beginning aggregate supply price curve AS rises slowly, afterwards it rises rapidly. This curve As shows that as the number of men employed is increased. the aggregate supply price rises slowly in the begining and rapidly afterwards. This is because cost of production rises as more people are employed and further due to the operations of law of diminishing returns total cost of production increases at an increasing rate. Once all the men willing to get employment are employed, then we have a state of full employment. When the state of full employment is reached further inreases in aggregate demand or monetary expenditure will be unable to increase employment further since output of goods and services cannot be increased further as no more labour is available for production after full employment level is reached. Therefore, aggregate supply curve assumes a vertical shape after full employment is reached. In figure 1.1., ON_F is the level of full employment at which aggregate supply price assumes a vertical shape.

Aggregate Demand

It is the aggregate demand which plays a more important role in the detemination of employment. Aggregate demand price at any level of employment is the amount of total money or price (proceeds) which all the firms or entrepreneurs in the economy **actually expect** to receive from the sale of output produced by a given number of men employed. In other words, aggregate demand price represents the amount of expenditure expected by the entrepreneurs when a given number of men are employed to produce goods and services. Like the aggregate supply price, aggregate demand price also varies at different levels of employment. This is because at different levels of

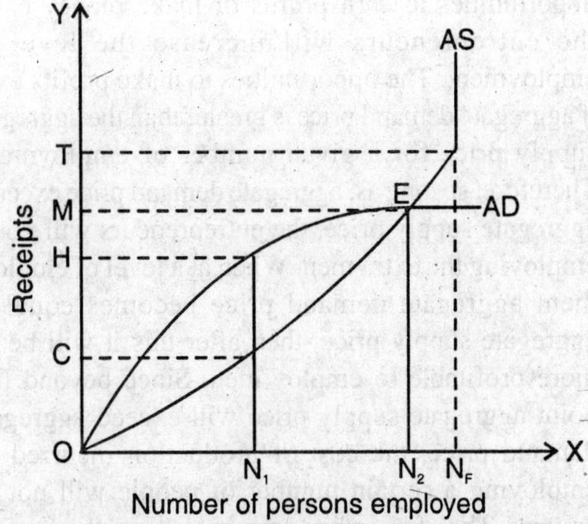

Fig. 1.1 : *Determination of Employment: Keynesian Theory*

employment different income levels would be generated and at different income levels, consumption demand would be different. Therefore, we can construct a schedule or curve of aggregate demand price showing different aggregate demand price at different levels of employment. The curve of aggregate demand is shown by the curve AD in figure 1.1. The aggregate demand price curve also rises from left to right. It will be seen in figure 1.1 that when ON_1 number of men are employed, the aggregate demand price is OH and when ON_2 men are employed, agregate demand price is OM.

Determination of the Equilibrium Level of Employment by Effective Demand

In figure 1.1. we have shown together aggregate suply curve and aggregate demand curve. The amount of employment is measured along the *x*-axis and the receipts or proceeds obtained at various levels of employment are measured along the *y*-axis. As said above, aggregate supply curve shows the revenue or receipts which **must be received** by the entrepreneurs so as to provide employment to a given number of men. Whereas aggregate demand curve shows proceeds or receipts which entrepreneurs actually expect to receive at different levels of employment and production. These aggregate demand and the aggregate supply curves determine the level of employment in the economy. Given that the perfect competition prevails in the economy, then so long as opportunities to earn profits or make money exist, the entrepreneurs will increase the level of employment. The opportunities to make profits exist if aggregate demand price is greater than the aggregate supply price for a given number of employment. Therefore, so long as, aggregate demand price exceeds aggregate supply price, the entrepreneurs will go on employing the extra men. When at a level of employment aggregate demand price becomes equal to aggregate supply price, then after this it will be no more profitable to employ men. Since beyond this point aggregate supply price will exceed aggregate demand price, the cost of production incurred on employing a certain number of people will not be covered. Therefore, when aggregate demand price falls short of aggregate supply price, employment of labour will fall. Equilibrium level of employment is determined by the intersection of aggregate demand curve and the aggregate supply curve, where the amount of money which the entrepreneurs actually expect to receive from employing a certain number of men is equal to the amount of money which they must receive. In other worlds, the employment of labour will be in equilibrium at the level at which aggregate demand price equals aggregate supply price. It will be seen in figure 1.1 that aggregate supply curve and aggregate demand curve intersect at point E and therefore ON_2 level of employment is determined.

However, it will be seen from figure 1.1 that in the situation of equilibrium at the employment level ON_2, N_2 N_F persons remain unemployed. Thus equilibrium at E represent an **under-employment equilibrium.** It is important to note that N_2 F_2, persons are **involuntarily unemployed**: they are willing to work at the existing wages but are unable to find jobs. It is important to remember that, according to Keynes, this unemployment is due to **deficiency of aggregate demand.**

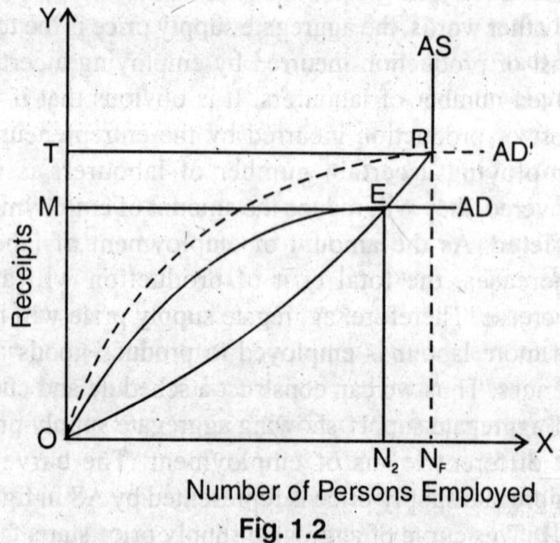

Fig. 1.2

This unemployment will be removed and full employment equilibrium will be reached if through increase in investment demand or increase in consumption, or increase in both aggregate demand curve shifts upward so that it intersects the aggregate supply curve at point R as depicted in figure 1.2. It will be seen that with the intersection of aggregate demand and aggregate supply curves at point R, equilibrium is established at full employment level ON_F.

It is thus clear that employment in the economy in the **short-run** is determined by effective demand. The higher the level of effective demand, the greater is the volume of employment and vice versa. Unemployment is due to the deficiency of effective demand and the basic remedy to remove this unemployment is to raise the level of effective demand. The classical economists believed that effective demand was always large enough to ensure full employment. But Keynes proved that it was not so and that is why the phenomenon of unemployment is common in free market capitalist economies.

Equilibrium Not Necessarily At Full Eemployment

It is not necessary that the equilibrium levels of employment is always at full employment. Equality between aggregate demand and aggregate supply does not necessarily indicate the full employment level. The economy can be in equilibrium at less than full employment or, in other words, an under employment equilibrium can exist. The classical economists denied that there could be an equilibrium at less then full employment, because they believed that supply would always create its own demand and therefore no problem of deficiency of aggregate effective demand would be experienced. Keynes demolished the classical thesis of full employment both on theoretical grounds and by illustrations from real life.

According to Keynes, aggregate demand and aggregate supply will be equal at full employment only if investment demand is sufficient to cover the gap between the aggregate supply price corresponding to full employment and the consumption expenditure out of income at the full employment level. The view of Keynes is that investment demand generally falls short of this gap between full-employment income and consumption. According to him, when inducement to invest in capitalist countries declines due to the fall in marginal efficiency of capital, aggregate demand falls so that equilibrium is established at less than full employment level. As a result, output and income of the community also fall.

DETERMINATION OF NATIONAL INCOME : KEYNESIAN THEORY

We explained earlier the Keynesian theory with special reference to the determination of employment. It is worth noting here that the Keynesian theory is relevant in the context of the **short run** only since the stock of capital, techniques of production, efficiency of labour, the size of population, forms of business organisation have been assumed to remain constant in this theory. Therefore, in the Keynesian theory which deals with the short run, the level of income of the country will change as a result of changes in the level of labour employment. Thus, in an advanced capitalist economy in the short-run, income is a function of employment. Infact, both income and employment go together. The higher the level of employment; the higher the level of income. As level of employment is determined by aggregate demand and aggregate supply, the level of income is also determined by aggregate demand and aggregate supply.

Aggregate Supply

Equilibrium level of national income in the short run depends upon aggregate demand and aggregate supply. The aggregate supply depends on physical or technical conditions of production which do not change in the short-run. Since Keynes assumes the aggregate supply to be stable, he concentrates his entire attention upon the aggregate demand to fight depression and unemployment.

Aggregate Demand

Aggregate demand is determined by consumption demand and investment demand. Therefore,

Aggregate Demand = Consumption Demand + Investment Demand

$$AD = C + I$$

Where AD = aggregate demand
C = consumption demand
I = investment demand

Consumption Demand : As for consumption demand, it depends upon the propensity to consume of the community and the level of national income. Given the propensity to consume, as income will increase consumption demand will also increase. In other words, given the propensity to consume, consumption demand is a function of income. Consider figure 1.3 in which income is measured along the *x*-axis and consumption demand (C) and investment (I) are shown on the *y*-axis. In this figure, a straight line OZ which makes 45° angle with the *x*-axis has been drawn. This straight line OZ with 45° angle with the *x*-axis represents the aggregate supply curve of the economy. This is also often called income line. In this figure a curve C has also been drawn which shows the propensity to consume slopes upward from left to right, which shows that as income increases the amount of consumption demand also increases. The gap between propensity to consume curve C and the income line OZ represents the saving of the community. The reason for this is that a part of the income is consumed and a part is saved, i.e.

National Income = Consumption + Saving

or Y = C + S

where Y = income

C = consumption

S = saving

It will be seen fro the figure that the gap betwene the propensity to consume curve C and the income line OZ goes on increasing as income increases. In other words, the amount of saving or saving gap increases as income increases. It is worth mentioning that in the short run propensity to consume does not change. This is because the propensity to consume, that is, the whole propensity to consume curve C depends upon the tastes, preferences, the income distribution in the society, the population level, etc. which do not undergo any change in the short-run.

Investment Demand

The other constituent of the aggregate demand is investment which is a crucial factor in the determination of equilibrium level of national income. Investment demand depends upon two factors:

1. Marginal efficiency of capital
2. Rate of interest

Of these two factors, rate of interest is comparatively stable and does not frequently change in the short-run. Therefore, the fluctuations in the level of investment demand chiefly depend upon the changes in the marginal efficiency of capital. The MEC means the expected rate of profit which the business community hopesto get from the investment in capital assets. MEC depends upon the replacement cost of the capital goods on the one hand and profit expectations of entrepreneur on the other.

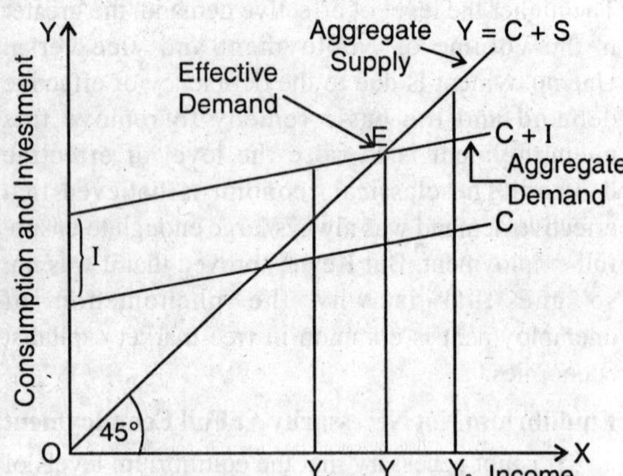

Fig. 1.3: *Equilibrium Level of National Income*

In Keynesian theory of income determination, investment is not taken to be function of income. In actual practice when the level of icome rises, the demand for goods will also rise and this will favourably effect the expectations of the entrepreneurs regarding making of profits. Rise in the profit expectations will raise the MEC which in turn will increase the level of investment. But it is quite clear that investment demand does not directly depend upon income; It is only effected indirectly by changes in income.

Therefore, in our figure we have taken a given level of investment demand independent of the level of income. The distance between the C curve and the C + I curve is parallel to the C - curve throughout which indicates that the level of investment is constant and does not change with the change in income.

Equilibrium Level of Income : Equality of Aggregate Demand and Aggregate Supply

The equilibrium level of national income is determined at a point where the aggregate demand function intersects the aggregate supply function. The aggregate demand function is represented by C + I in the figure 1.3. It is drawn by adding to the consumption function C and the investment demand I. The 45° line represents the aggregate supply function (Y = C + S).

The aggregate demand function C + I intersects the aggregate supply function Y = C + S at point E and the equilibrium level of income OY is determined.

Therefore, E is the equilibrium point and OY represents the equilibrium level of national income. Now, income cannot be in equilibrium at levels smaller than OY.

This is because at any level of income smaller than OY, aggregate demand exceeds aggregate supply of output since C + I curve lie above 45° line which depicts aggregate supply of output. This excess demand will lead to the decline in inventories of goods below the desired levels. This unintended fall in inventories will induce the firms to expand their output of goods and services to meet the extra demand for them and keep their inventories of goods at the desired level. Thus when at a given level of national income, aggregate expenditure (i.e. aggregate demand) exceeds aggregate supply of output, national income will increase. With this increase in national income or output, employment of labour will also rise to produce the increment in output. This process of expansion in output under the pressure of excess demand will continue till national income OY is reached.

On the contrary, the level of national income cannot be greater than OY because at any level greater than OY, aggregate expenditure or demand (C + I) falls short of aggregate supply of output. This will cause the increase in inventories of goods with the firms beyond the desired levels. To this situation of the unintended increase in inventories of goods, the firms will respond by cutting down production to keep their inventories at the desired levels. Thus, deficiency in aggregate demand relative to the aggregate supply of output will lead to the fall in national income and output until the level OY is reached where aggregate demand (C + I) is equal to the value of aggregate supply. Thus OY is the equilibrium level of national income.

Criticism of Keynesian Theory

1. Closed Economy : The Keynesian theory is based on the assumption of a **closed economy** which excludes the impact of foreign trade on the level of

The Keynesian theory may also be presented in a tabular form as under:

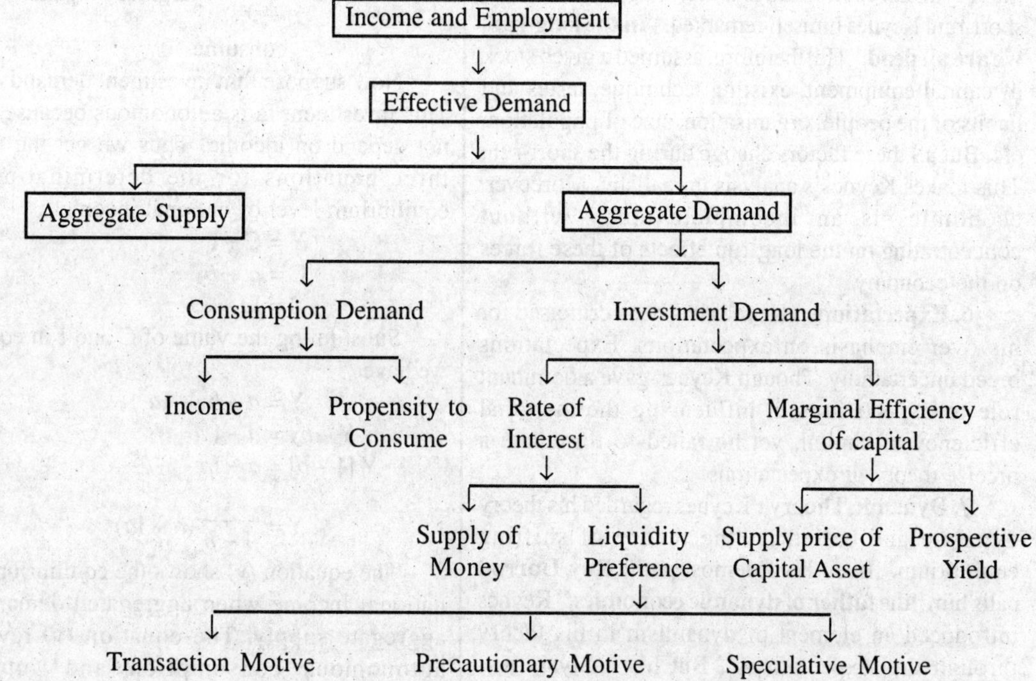

employment and income. This makes Keyne's analysis unrealistic because all economies are open economies, and foreign trade has an important impact on their level of employment. Thus, Keyne's neglect of the repercussions of foreign trade on the volume of employment is a serious defect in his theory.

2. Perfect Competition : Another weakness of the Keynesian theory is that it is based on the unrealistic assumption of perfect competition. This makes his theory inapplicable to socialist or communist societies where the entire economy is regulated by the state.

3. General Theory : Keynes considered his theory as a "general theory." But as is clear from the above points, it is not a general theory but a special theory which is applicable only under static conditions in a perfectly competitive closed economy. Moreover, it fails to solve the problems of underdeveloped countries.

4. Problem of Unemployment : Keynes has been criticised for tackling only **cyclical unemployment**, and neglecting other types of unemployment to be found in capitalist economies.

5. Short-run Economics : Another criticism of the Keynisian economics is that it is applicable to the short-run. Keynes himself remarked, **"In the long-run, we are all dead."** He, therefore, assumed a given stock of capital equipment, existing technique, tastes and habits of the people, organisation, size of population, etc. But all these factors change during the short-run. This makes Keynes's analysis unrealistic. Moreover, economics is an incomplete study without concentrating on the long-run effects of these forces on the economy.

6. Expectations : Keynes has been criticised for his over emphasis on expectations. Expectations breed uncertaintuy. Though Keynes gave a dominant role to expectations in influencing the marginal efficiency of capital, yet he failed tó formulate a precise theory of expectations.

7. Dynamic Theory : Keynes regarded his theory dynamic and called it "the theory of shifting equilibrium." Even his foremost pupil **Roy Harrod** calls him **"the father of dynamic economics."** Keynes introduced an element of dynamism in his theory through the 'expectations'. But his analysis was concerned with the level of employment at any time. It is a log less analysis.

Determination of Equilibrium Level of National Income : Algebraic Analysis

A study of how the level of national income is determined will become more clear by using simple mathematics. As has been explained above, the level of national income is in equilibrium at which aggregate demand equals aggregate supply of output. In a simple model of income determination in which we do not consider the impact of Government expenditure and taxation and also exports and imports, the national income is the sum of consumption demand (C) and investment demand (I), that is,

$$Y = C + I$$

Suppose the consumption function is of the following form—

$$C = a + by$$

Where c = consumption

a = autonomous consumption expenditure

$b = \frac{\Delta c}{\Delta y}$ = marginal propensity to consume

Now suppose that investment demand equals Ia. This investment Ia is autonomous because this does not depend on income. Thus we get the following three equations for the determination of the equilibrium level of national income

$$Y = C + I \qquad \text{.....}(i)$$

$$C = a + by \qquad \text{.....}(ii)$$

$$I = Ia \qquad \text{.....}(iii)$$

Substituting the value of C and I in equation *(i)* we have

$$Y = a + by + Ia \qquad \text{.....}(iv)$$

$$Y - by = a + I a$$

$$Y[1 - b] = a + Ia$$

$$Y = \frac{1}{1-b}(a + Ia) \qquad \text{.....}(v)$$

The equation *(v)* shows the equilibrium level of national income when aggregated demand equals aggregate supply. The equation *(v)* reveals that autonomous consumption and autonomous investment (a + Ia) generates so much expenditure or demand that becomes equal to the income generated by the production of goods and services. From the equation (v) it also follows that the equilibrium level of national income can be known from multiplying the elements of autonomous expenditure (that is, a + Ia) by the term $\frac{1}{1-b}$ which is equal to the value of multiplier.

Equilibrium Level of National Income when there is no Autonomous Element (a) in the Consumption Function and Autonomous Investment Equals Ia

When there is no autonomous element(that is, the intercept term) in the consumption function, the consumption function takes the following form:

$$c = bY$$

As matter of fact, empirical studies reveal that the long-run consumption function actually takes the form $c = by$ in which there is no constant element in consumption function. Thus, when autonomous consumption is zero and autonomous investment equals Ia the equilibrium level of income can be obtained as under—

$$Y = C + I$$

$$Y = by + Ia$$

$$Y - by = Ia$$

$$Y[1-b] = Ia$$

$$Y = \left(\frac{1}{1-b}\right) Ia$$

Thus we find that in this situation the equilibrium level of national income is equal to autonomous investment (Ia) multiplied by the value of multiplier $\left(\frac{1}{1-b}\right)$ where b stands for marginal propensity to consume.

Illustration of Equilibrium Level of Income with a Numerical Example

Let us take an example. Suppose in an economy, autonomous investment (Ia) equals Rs. 600 crores and the following consumption function is given—

$$C = 200 + 0.8\,Y$$

Given the above we are required to find the equilibrium level of income.

Solution :

$$Y = C + Ia$$

$$C = 200 + 0.8\,Y$$

$$Ia = 600$$

The equilibrium level of income is

$$Y = \frac{1}{1-b}(a + Ia)$$

$$\because \text{MPC } (b) = 0.8 = \frac{4}{5}$$

and autonomous investment (a) = Rs. 200

$$\therefore \quad Y = \frac{1}{1-4/5} \times (200 + 600)$$

$$= \left(\frac{1}{1/5}\right) \times (800)$$

$$= 5 \times 800 = 4000$$

GOVERNMENT EXPENDITURE AND NATIONAL INCOME

In our above analysis we have not taken into account the rate of Government expenditure in the determination of national income. However, in all economies today including the free market capitalist economies the Government expenditure on goods and services plays an important role in the determination of national income and therefore it should also be included in the analysis of income determination. We assume that Government spends on goods and services keeping taxes unchanged. We denote Government expenditure by G. Thus when we take into account the income generating effects of Government expenditure, we get the following equation for the equilibrium level of National Income.

$$Y = C + I + G$$

Where Y is national income or output and C + I + G represents the level of aggregate demand including Government expenditure, G. Since consumption function is

$$C = a + bY$$

Where b = mpc

a = autonomous consumption expenditure

We can rewrite the equilibrium level of national income as under:

$$Y = a + by + Ia + G$$

$$Y - by = a + Ia + G$$
$$Y [1 - b] = a + Ia + G$$
$$Y = \frac{1}{1-b}(a + Ia + G)$$

Thus it is clear that the equilibrium level of income (when impact of Government expenditure is also considered) is equal to the sum of three types of fixed autonomous expentiture, namely, autonomous consumption, autonomous investment and Government expenditure $(a + I + G)$ multiplied by the value of the multiplier $\left(\frac{1}{1-b}\right)$.

TAXES AND EQUILIBRIUM INCOME

In our above analysis of impact of Government expenditure on national income we have ignored the effect of taxes. We assumed that increase in Government expenditure was financed by borowing by the Government. The equilibrium level of income is

$$Y = C + Ia + G$$
$$\because \quad C = a + bY_d$$

where Ya = disposable income

Since disposable personal income is less than net national income (product) by the amount of taxes. Therefore

$$Y_d = Y - T$$

The consumption function becomes

$$C = a + b(Y - T) \text{ [where T = tax]}$$

With this consumption function, with investment assumed to be entirely autonomous (Ia) and with fixed amounts of government purchases and tax receipts assumed per time period, the equilibrium level of income is given by

$$Y = a + b(Y - T) + Ia + G$$
$$Y - b.Y = a - b.T + Ia + G$$
$$Y[1 - b] = a - b.T + Ia + G$$
$$Y = \frac{1}{1-b}(a - b.T + Ia + G)$$

In this form, it may be seen that a change in any single value within the parentheses will produce a change in income equal to the change in that value times the ordinary multiplier, $\left(\frac{1}{1-b}\right)$.

If now, for example, we assume a change in G, the other values remaining unchanged, the new equilibrium level of Y is equal to the original level of Y plus the change in Y:

$$Y + \Delta y = \frac{1}{1-b}(a - b.T + Ia + G) + \quad \frac{1}{1-b}\Delta G$$

subtracting Y from both sides, there remains

$$\Delta y = \frac{1}{1-b}\Delta G \text{ or, } \frac{\Delta y}{\Delta G} = \frac{1}{1-b} = \textbf{Government}$$

Expenditure Multiplier

where b = marginal propensity to consume

In the same, we will find that

$$\Delta Y = \frac{-b}{1-b}.\Delta T$$

$$\frac{\Delta Y}{\Delta T} = \frac{-b}{1-b} = \textbf{Tax Multiplier}$$

It is clear from above that a change in T of the same size as the change in G will produce a smaller change in Y and the change will be in the opposite direction.

FOREIGN TRADE AND NATIONAL INCOME

Foreign trade, that is, volume of exports and imports of a country also effects the level of national income of the country. We now extend the Keynesian model of determination of national income by including the effect of exports and imports of a country on the generation of income. For example, the exports of India represent the foreign demand and generates income for the Indian people. On the other hand, imports represent the demand for foreign goods by the Indians and generate incomes for the people of other countries therefore, imports tend to reduce the aggregate expenditure. It therefore follows that national income will depend on the net exports, that is, exports minus imports (X – M, where X-stands for exports and M for imports). The exports and imports of a country depend to a great edtent on the level of economic activity. Thus, when the growth of industrial output in India is rapid, it will generate greater demand for imported materials. On the other hand, the higher industrial growth would also cause our exports to rise provided there is demand for our goods abroad. However, in the Keynesian model of income determination, exports and imports are considered as autonomous, that is, independent of income, being determined outside the model. Further, as mentioned above, the increase or decrease in aggregate expenditure or demand due to exports and imports depends on the net exports, that is, (X – M). If net exports are positive, there will be addition to the aggregate demand or expenditure of a country. On the other hand, if the net exports are negatives there will be decrease in aggregate expenditure.

When we include net exports in our analysis we get the following equation for the equilibrium level of income

$$Y = C + I + G + (X - M)$$

Since $C = a + b.Y$

$$Y = a + b.Y + I + G + (X - M)$$

or $Y - b.Y = a + I + G + (X - M)$

$$Y[1 - b] = a + I + G + (X - M)$$

$$Y = \frac{1}{1-b}[a + I + G + (X - M)]$$

Thus, the equilibrium level of income is the sum of all fixed autonomous expenditures [*i.e.* $a + I + G + (X - M)$] times the value of multiplier $\left(\frac{1}{1-b}\right)$.

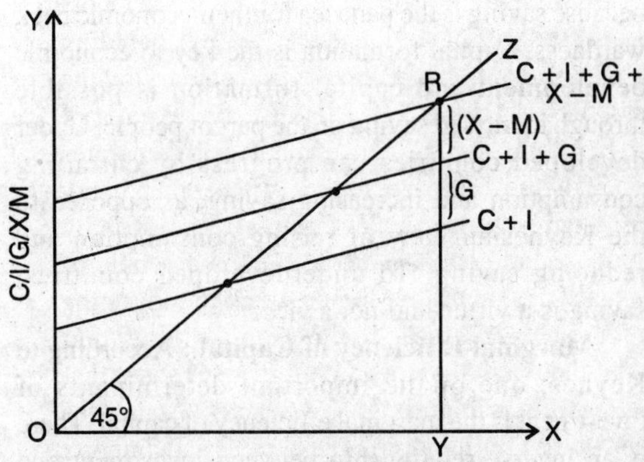

Fig. 1.4 : *Determination of National Income with Foreign Trade*

Graphic Illustration

In figure 1.4 we have depicted the determination of national income when there are positive net exports (*i.e.* (X – M) > O). To obtain the aggregate demand curve incorporating the positive net exports we add the amounts of net exports to (C + I + G) to get the higher aggregate demand curve [C + I + G + (X – M)] which intersects the 45° line at point R and determines a higher level of income OY. If the net exports (X – M) were negative, that is, imports exceed exports, (X – M) < O, the aggregate demand curve incorporating net exports would lie at a lower level than C + I + G + X – M curve and determine a lower level of income than OY.

Applicability of Keynes's Theory to Under Developed Countries

The Keynesian theory is not applicable to every socio-economic set up. It only applies to advanced democratic capitalist economies. Before we study the applicability of Keynesian economies to under developed countries, it is essential to analyse the assumptions of Keynesian economics vis-a-vis the conditions prevailing in under-developed economies.

Keynesian Assumptions and Underdeveloped Countries

The Keynesian economics is based on the following assumptions which limit its applicability to underdeveloped countries.

1. The Keynesian theory is based on the existence of cyclical unemployment which occurs during a depression. It is caused by deficiency in effective demand. Unemployment can be removed by an increase in the level of effective demand. But the nature of unemployment in an underdeveloped country is quite different from that in a developed economy. In such economies unemployment is chronic rather than cyclical. It is not due to lack of effective demand but is the result of deficiency in capital resources. Apart from chronic unemployment, under developed countries suffer from disguised unemployment. Thus the Keynesian assumptions of cyclical unemployment and economic instability hardly tenable in an underdeveloped economy.

2. The Keynesian economics is a short period

analysis in which Keynes takes "as given the existing skill and quantity of available equipment, the existing technique, the degree of competition, the tastes and habits of the consumer." The development economics, however, is a long period analysis in which all the basic factors assumed by Keynes as given change over time.

3. The Keynesian theory is based on the assumption of a closed economy. But underdeveloped countries are not closed economies. They are open economies in which foreign trade plays a dominant role in developing them. Thus the Keynesian economics has little relevance to underdeveloped countries in this respect.

4. According to Keynesian analysis labour and capital are unemployed simultaneously. When labour is unemployed, capital and equipment are also not fully utilised or there is excess capacity in them. But this is not so in underdeveloped countries. When labour is unemployed, there is no question of capital being unutilized because there is acute shortage of capital and equipment.

The Keynesian Tools and Underdeveloped Countries

Thus the assumption on which the Keynesian theory is based are not applicable to the conditions prevailing in underdeveloped countries. We now study the principal tools of the Keynesian theory to test their validity to underdeveloped countries.

Effective Demand : Unemployment is caused by the deficiency effective demand, and to get over it, Keynes suggested the stepping up of consumption and non-consumption expenditures. In an underdeveloped country, however, there is no involuntary unemployment but disguised unemployment. Unemployment is caused not by lack of complementary resources. The concept of effective demand is applicable to those economies where unemployment is due to excess savings; and in such a situation the remedy lies in stepping up the levels of consumption and investment through various monetary and fiscal measures. But in an underdeveloped economy income levels are extremely low, the propensity to consume is very high and savings are almost nil. All efforts to increase money incomes through monetary and fiscal measures will, in the absence of complementary resouces, lead to price inflation. Here the problem is not one of raising the effective demand but one of raising the levels of employment and per capita income in the context of economic development.

Propensity to Consume : One of the important tools of Keynesian economics is the propensity to consume which highlights the relationship between consumption and income. When income increases, consumption also increases but by less than the increment in income. This behaviour of consumption further explains the rise in saving as income increases.

In underdeveloped countries these relationships between income, consumption and saving do not hold. People are very poor and when their income increases, they spend more on consumption goods because their tendency is to meet their unfulfilled wants. The MPC is very high in such countries, whereas the MPS is very low. Keynesian economics tells us that when the MPC is high consumer demand, output and employment, increase at a faster rate with the increase in income. But in an underdeveloped country it is not possible to increase the production of consumer goods due to the scarcity of co-operant factors, when consumption increases with the rise in income. As a result, prices rise instead of a rise in the level of employment.

Saving : On the saving side, Keynes regarded saving as a social vice for it is excess of saving that leads to a decline in aggregate demand. Again, this idea is not applicable to underdeveloped countries because saving is the panacea for their economic back wardness. Capital formation is the key to economic development and capital formation is possible through increased saving on the part of people. Under developed countries can progress by curtailing consumption and increasing saving, as opposed to the Keynesian view of raising consumption and reducing saving. To underdeveloped countries, saving is a virtue and not a vice.

Marginal Efficiency of Capital : According to Keynes, one of the important determinants of investment is the marginal efficiency of capital. There is an inverse relationship between investment and MEC. When investment increases, the MEC falls, and when investment declines, the MEC rises. This relationship is, however, not applicable to underdeveloped countries. In such economies, investment is at a low level and the MEC is also low. This paradox is due to the lack of capital and other resources small size of the market, low demand, high costs, underdeveloped capital and money markets, uncertainties, etc. All these factors keep the MEC and investment at a low level.

The Multiplier : The Keynesian concept of multiplier is based on the following four assumptions.

a. Involuntary unemployment

b. An industrialized economy where the supply curve of output slopes upward to the right

c. Excess capacity in the consumption goods industries

d. Comparatively elastic supply of the working capital required for increased output.

But the assumptions on which the multiplier theory is based do not hold valid in the case of an underdeveloped country. Thus, the Keynesian principle of multiplier does not operate in an underdeveloped country like India mainly due to these reasons.

Firstly, involuntary unemployment of the Keynesian type is not to be found, **secondly,** the supply of agricultural and non-agricultural output is inelastic due to the working of certain factors peculiar to such economies, and **thirdly,** absence of excess capacity in consumption goods industries.

CONSUMPTION FUNCTION

Consumption function can be defined as the schedule detailing the relationship between aggragate consumption expenditures and income, Therefore

$$C = f(Y)$$

Where C is consumption, Y is income, and f is the functional relationship. Thus the consumption function indicates a functional relatinship between C and Y, where C is the dependent and Y is the independent variable. This relationship is based on the ceteris paribus (other things being equal) assumption, as such only income-consumption relationship is considered and all possible influences on consumption are held constant.

The consumption function has two technical attributes or properties:

1. The average propensity to consume
2. The marginal propensity to consume

The Average Propensity to Consume

Average propensity to consume is the ratio of the amount of consumption to total income. Therefore, average propensity to consume is calculated by dividing the amount of consumption by the total income. Thus,

$$APC = \frac{C}{Y}$$

Where

APC = average propensityh to consume

C = amount of consumption

Y = level of income

Diagrammatically, the average propensity to consume is any one point on the consumption curve. In figure 1.5, point R measures the APC of the CC curve which is OC'/OY'.

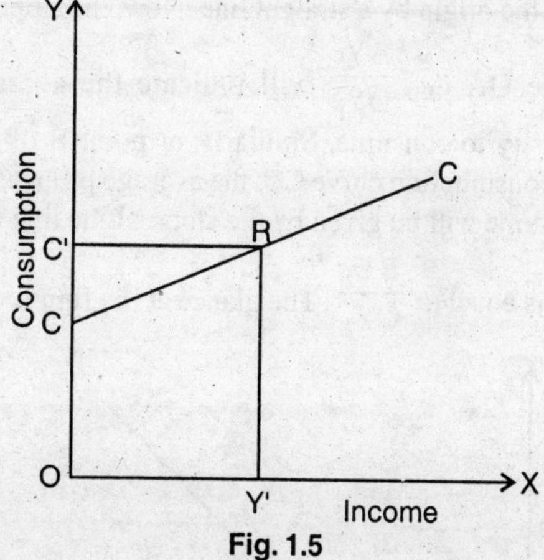

Fig. 1.5

If with the increase in income, average propensity to consume remains constant, the consumption function curve or propensity to consume curve will be **linear** or straight line as is shown by the curve CC in figure 1.6.

When wit' the increase in income, average propensity to consume declines, then the curve of consumption function is not a straight line passing through the origin and has a shape as shown in figure 1.7. From any point on the propensity to consume curve CC we can find out average propensity to

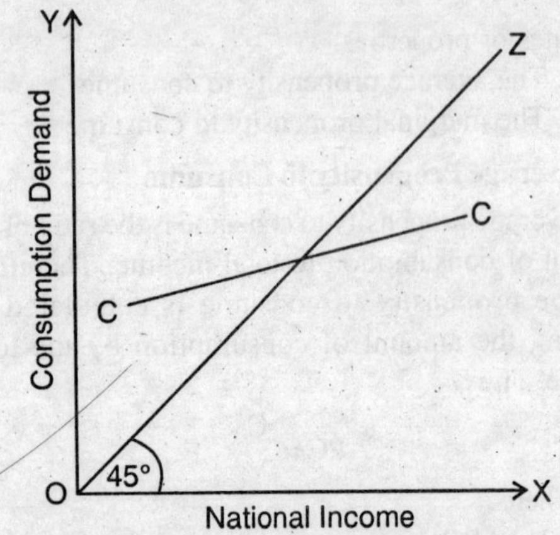

Fig. 1.6 : *Linear Consumption Function*

consume by joining that point with the point of origin by a straight line whose slope will measure the average propensity to consume. In figure 1.7, if we have to find out average propensity to consume at point A on the propensity to consume curve CC, we connect point A with the origin by a straight line. Now, the slope of the line OA *i.e.,* $\frac{AY_1}{OY_1}$ will indicate the average propensity to consume. Similarly, at point B of the given consumption curve CC, the average propensity to consume will be given by the slope of the line OB which is equal to $\frac{BY_2}{OY_2}$. The glance at the figure will

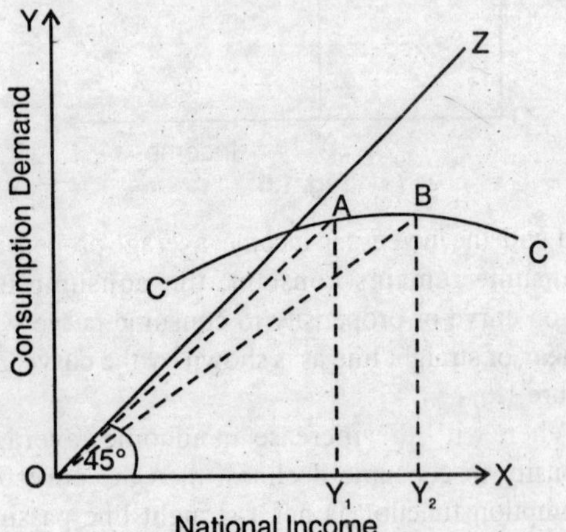

Fig. 1.7 : *Non-Linear Consumption Function : Average Propensity to Consume*

show that the slope of the line OB is smaller than the slope of the line OA. Therefore, average propensity to consume at point B or at income level OY_2 is less than that at point A or the income level OY_1.

Marginal Propensity to Consume

The marginal propensity to consume (MPC) measures the change in consumption resulting from a change in income. In other words, marginal propensity to consume may be defined as the ratio of the change in consumption to the change in income or as the rate of change in the average propensity to consume as income changes. Thus,

$$MPC = \frac{\Delta C}{\Delta Y}$$

Where

MPC = marginal propensity to consume

ΔC = change in consumption

ΔY = change in income

Significance of MPC

Marginal propensity to consume needs to be carefully distinguished from average propensity to consume. Whereas average propensity to consume is the ratio of total consumption to total income, *i.e.* $\frac{C}{Y}$, the marginal propensity to consume is the ratio of change in consumption to the change in income, *i.e.* $\frac{\Delta C}{\Delta Y}$.

When income increase, the MPC falls but more than the APC. Contrariwise, when income falls, the MPC rises and the APC also rises but at a slower rate than former. Such changes are only possible during cyclical fluctuations whereas in the short-run there is no change in the MPC and MPC < APC. In the long-run MPC = APC.

It is worth noting that when average propensity to consume remains constant, marginal propensity to consume is equal to it. Marginal propensity to consume can be estimated by drawing the tangent at a point on the consumption function.

When marginal propensity to consume declines with the increase in income, consumption curve is non-linear whose slope declines as income rises. But if consumption curve is a straight line *i.e.,* the slope of the consumption curve remains constant then MPC which is given by the slope of the propensity to consume curve (consumption curve) remains constant.

It is worth noting that marginal propensity to consume is neither zero nor equal to one. It has been found by empirical studies that marginal propensity to consume varies between zero and unity. If the MPC was zero, then the whole of the increment in income would have been saved and the consumption curve would have a horizontal shape. On the other hand, if the MPC was equal to unity, then the whole of the increment in income would be consumed and in that case consumption curve would have coincided with 45° line.

PROPENSITY TO SAVE

We will now explain what happens to saving when income increases. Saving is defined as that part of income which is not consumed because disposable income is either consumed or saved. Thus,

$$Y_d = C + S \text{ or } S = Y_d - C$$

where

Y_d = disposable income

C = consumption

S = saving

Average Propensity to Save (APS)

An important relationship between income and saving is described by the concept of average propensity to save (APS). Average propensity to save is the proportion of disposable income that is saved. Thus,

$$APS = \frac{\text{Saving}}{\text{Income}} = \frac{S}{Y}$$

Like the average propensity to consume (APC) average propensity to save also varies as income increases. As seen above, average propensity to consume falls as income increases. This implies that average propensity to save will increase as income rises.

Let us derive an important relation ship between average propensity to consume and average propensity to save. Restating below the relation that income is either consumed or saved:

$$C + S = Y$$

Dividing both sides by disposable income Y we have

$$\frac{C}{Y} + \frac{S}{Y} = \frac{Y}{Y} \text{ or } \frac{C}{Y} + \frac{S}{Y} = 1$$

Since $\frac{C}{Y}$ is average propensity to consume and $\frac{S}{Y}$ is average propensity to save, we have

$$APC + APS = 1 \text{ or } APS = 1 - APC$$

Marginal Propensity to Save (MPS)

Whereas average propensity to save indicates the proportion of income that is saved, marginal propensity to save represents how much of the additional disposable income is devoted to saving. The marginal propensity to save is therefore change in savings induced by a change in the disposable income. Thus,

$$MPS = \frac{\Delta S}{\Delta Y}$$

Since the additional income is either consumed or saved, the sum of marginal propensity to consume and marginal propensity to save is equal to one.

$$MPC + MPS = 1$$

This can be mathematically proved as under.

From C+ S = Y, it follows that any change in income (ΔY) must induce either change in consumption (ΔC) or change in saving (ΔS). Thus

$$\Delta C + \Delta S = \Delta Y$$

Dividing both sides by ΔY we have

$$\frac{\Delta C}{\Delta Y} + \frac{\Delta S}{\Delta Y} = \frac{\Delta Y}{\Delta Y}$$

$$MPC + MPS = 1$$

Keynes's Psychological Law of consumption

Keynes propounded a basic law about the consumption function. This has been described as **psychological law** of consumption by **Prof. Kurihara.** According to this law of consumption, when the aggregate income increases, consumption expenditure will increase but by a some what smaller amount. It means that out of the increment in income, a part is saved and not consumed. In other words, marginal propensity to consume is less than one.

Keynes's psychological law of consumption is based upon three assumptions—

1. The marginal propensity to consume will be less than one provided the psychological and institutional complex of the society remains constant.

2. The second assumption on which the Keynes's law of consumption is based is that the normal conditions should continue to prevail in the economy, that is, neither any war should break out nor should occur any revolution, hyper-inflation, or any other extraordinary event.

3. The third assumption underlying, the Keynesian law is that it applies to an advanced capitalist country in which the Government does not interfere in the working of free private enterprise. In other words, it applies where the Government follows a **laissez faire** policy.

THEORIES OF CONSUMPTION

The Absolute Income Hypothesis

Keynes's Consumption income relationship is known as the absolute income of the current period increases consumption also increases but by less than the increase in income, and vice versa. This means that the consumption income relationship is **non-proportional. James Tobin** and **Arthur Simithies** tested this hypothesis in separate studies and came to the conclusion that the short-run relationship between consumption and income is non-proportional but the time-series data show the long-run relationship to be proportional. The latter consumption income behaviour results through an upward shift in the short-run non-proportional consumption function due to factors other than income.

Relative Income Theory of Consumption

An American economist **J. S. Duesenberry** put forward the theory of consumber behaviour which lays stress on **relative income** of an individual rather than his absolute income as a determinant of his consumption. Another important departure made by Duesenberry from Keynes's consumption theory is that, according to him, the consumption of a person does not depend on his current income but on a certain previously reached income level.

As viewed by Duesenberry, consumption and saving decision are greatly influenced by the social environment in which one lives. Thus, an individual with a given income consumes more if he lives in an affluent neighborhood than if he lives in a poorer one. In addition, his consuming behaviour within a neighborhood is relative to the consuming patterns of his neighbors (i.e. he spends in order to maintain a certain economic status within the neighborhood). If the distribution of income is relatively constant, it is highly probable that an individual's average propensity to consume is constant since his consumption is related to his relative income within a community and is not related to his absolute level of income. Thus, this conclusion of the relative income hypothesis differs from the Keynesian theory of consumption according to which, as seen above as absolute income of a community increases, it will devote a smaller proportion of its income to consumption expenditure, that is , its APC will decline.

It is important to note that relative income theory implies that with the increase in income of a community, the relative distribution of income remaining the same, it does not move along the same aggregate consumption function, but its consumption function shifts upward. This is illustrated in figure 1.8. Suppose a family A has Y_1 level of income and is spending Y_1A on consumption. Suppose its income level rises to Y_2. Now, its consumption could not rise only to Y_2B (*i.e.* the consumption of the family B at Y_2 income level) but to Y_2A' where A' lies on the same ray from the origin as the previous point A of consumption. This implies that the consumption expenditure of family A has risen in the same proportion as its income with the result that its average propensity to consume remains constant.

Likewise, if income of family B which is having consumption expenditure Y_2B at income level Y_2, rises to Y_3, its consumption expenditure will increase to Y_3B' where B' lies on same ray from the origin as B. This again means that the proportion of income devoted to consumption by family B (*i.e.* its APC) remains constant as there is increase in its absolute income. Thus if the proportion of income devoted to consumption of the average family at each income level remains the same as its income increases, the aggregate consumption of the community as proportion of its income also remains constant though its absolute consumption and absolute savings increase with the absolute increase in income.

In figure 1.8, it will be seen that if points like A' and B' are joined together we get a new consumption function curve C'.

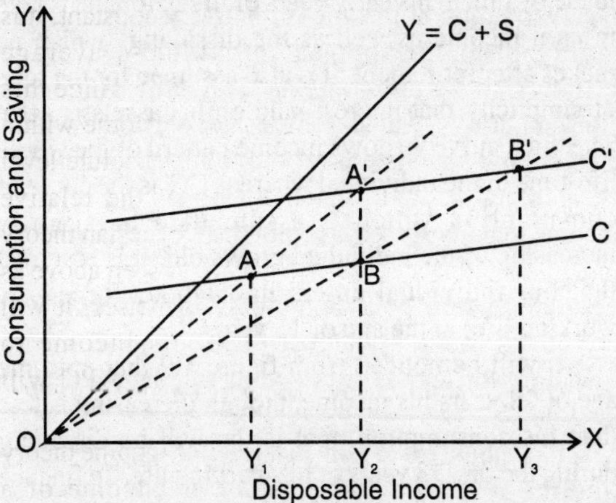

Fig. 1.8 : *Duesenberry's Relative Income Theory of Consumption*

The relative income theory suggests the following relation ships for the average propensity to consume and the marginal propensity to consume:

1. There is constant growth in the level of income. The APC is constant. The MPC equals the APC.

2. Current income is falling and is below the previous income level. The APC is rising. The MPC is less than the APC.

3. Income is rising but is below the previous income level. The APC is falling. The MPC is increasing. The MPC is less than the APC.

4. Income is rising and is above a previous income level. The APC is constant. The MPC equals the APC.

Demonstration Effect

By emphasizing relative income as determinant of consumption, the relative income hypothesis suggest, that individuals or households try to imitate or copy the consumption levels of their neighbours or other families in a particular community. This is called **demonstration effect** or **Duesenberry effect.** Two things follow from this. **First,** the average propensity to consume does not fall. This is because if incomes of all families increase in the same proportion, distribution of relative incomes would remain unchanged and therefore the proportion of consumption expenditure to income which depends on relative income will remain constant.

Secondly, a family with a given income would devote more of his income to consumption if it is living in a community in which that income is regarded as relatively low because of the working of demonstration effect. On the other hand, a family will spend a lower proportion of its income if it is living in a community in which that income is considered as relatively high because demonstration effect will not be present in this case.

For example, the recent studies of household expenditure made in India reveal that the families with a given income, say Rs. 3000 per month spend a larger proportion of their income on consumption if they live in urban areas as compared to their counterparts in rural areas. The higher propensity to consume of families living in urban area is due to the working of demonstration effect where families with relatively higher income reside whose higher consumption standards tempt others in lower income brackets to consume more.

Ratchet Effect

The other significant part of Duesenberry's relative income hypothesis is that it suggests that when income of individuals or households falls, their consumption expenditure does not fall much. This is often called a **ratchet effect**. This is because, according to Duesenberry, the people try to maintain their consumption at the highest level attained earlier. This is partly due to the demonstration effect explained above. People do not want to show their neighbours that they no longer afford to maintain their high standard of living. Further, this is also partly due to the fact that they become accustomed to their previous higher level of consumption and it is quite hard and difficult to reduce their consumption expenditure when their income has fallen. They are able to maintain their consumption level by reducing their savings. Therefore, the fall in their income, as during the period of recession or depression, does not result in decrease in consumption expenditure very much as one would conclude from family budget studies.

Life Cycle Theory of Consumption

An important Post-Keynesian theory of consumption has been put forward by **Modigliani and Ando** which is known as **Life Cycle Theory.** According to Life Cycle Theory, **the consumption is any period is not the function of current income of that period but of the whole life-time expected income.**

Thus, in life cycle hypothesis the individual is assumed to plan a pattern of consumption expenditure based on expected income in their entire life-time. It is further assumed that individual maintains a more or less constant or slightly increasing level of consumption. However, this level of consumption is limited by his expectations of life-time income. A typical individual in this theory in his early years of life spends on consumption either by borrowing from others or spending the assets bequeathed from his parents. It is in his main working years of his life-time that he consumes less than the income he earns and therefore makes net positive savings. He invests these savings in assets, that is accumulated wealth which he consumes in the future years. In his life time after retirement he dissaves, that is, consumes more than his income in these later years of his life but is able to maintain or even slightly increase his consumption in the life-time after retirement. Life cycle hypothesis

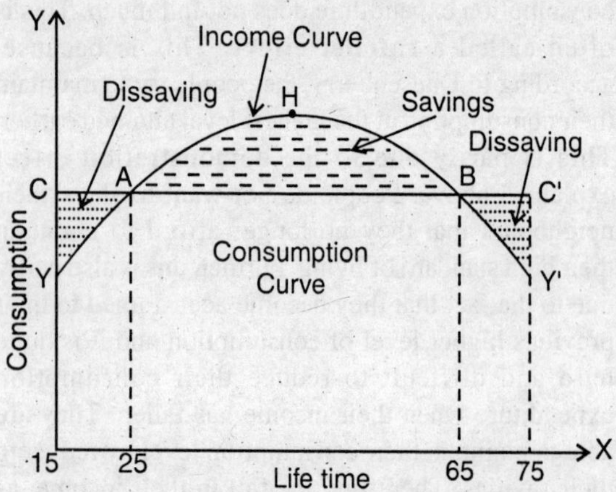

Fig. 1.9 : *Life Cycle Theory of Consumption*

has been depicted in figure 1.9. It is assumed that a typical individual knows exactly at what age he will die. In figure 1.9 it is taken that the individual would die at the age of 75 years. That is, year 75 is his expected life time. It is further assumed in the life cycle theory that net savings in the entire life-time is zero, that is, the savings done by the individual in his working years of his life is equal to the dissavings made by him in his early years of life before he is able to earn income as well as the dissavings which he makes after retirement. It is also assumed for the sake of simplicity that interest paid on his assets is zero. The thick curve *y*-shows income pattern of the whole life-time of the individual whereas CC' is the curve of consumption which is assumed to be slightly increasing as the individual grows old. It is assumed that our individual enters into labour force (*i.e.* working life) at the age of 15 years.

It will be noticed from figure 1.9 that upto the age of 28 years his income, though increasing is less than his consumption, that is, he will be dissaving during the first 13 years of his working life. To finance his excess consumption over his income, he may be borrowing from others. Beyond the age of 25 or point A on the income and consumption curves and upto the age of 65 years his income exceeds his consumption, that is, he will be saving during this period of his working life. With these savings he will build up assets or wealth. He may use these savings or wealth to pay off his debt incurred by him in the early stage of his working life. Another important motive of his savings and buildings up assets or wealth is to provide for his consumption after retirement when his income drops below his level of consumption. It will be observed from the figure 1.9 that beyond point B his current from the figure 1.9 that beyond point B his current income falls shorts of his consumption and therefore he once again dissaves. He would be using his accumulated assets or wealth from his earlier working years to meet the dissavings after retirement at the age of 65. It is important to note that we assume that he does not intend to leave any assets for his children. Given this assumption, his net savings over his life time will be zero. Therefore, in figure 1.9 his savings during the period when he earns more than his consumption expenditure, that is, the shaded area

AHB will be equal to the two areas of dissavings, CYA + BC'Y'. Thus he dies leaving behind no assets or wealth. He has planned his consumption expenditure over the years that his net savings at the time of death are zero.

Some important conclusions follow from the life cycle theory of consumption. The fundamental idea of the life-cycle hypothesis is that people make their consumption plans for their entire life time and further that they make their life time consumption plans on the basis of their expectations of life time income. Thus in the life cycle model consumption is not a mere function of current income but a function of the expected life time income.

Its Criticism

The life cycle hypothesis is not free from certain limitations.

1. The contention of Ando and Modigliani that a consumer plans his consumption over his life time is unrealistic because a consumer concentrates more on the present rather than on the future which is uncertain.

2. The life cycle hypothesis pre-supposes that consumption is directly related to the assets of an individual. As assets increase his consumption increases and vice versa. This is also unwarranted because an individual may reduce his consumption to have larger assets.

3. Consumption depends upon one's attitude towards life. Given the same income and assets, one person may consume more than the other.

Despite these, the life cycle hypothesis is superior to the other hypotheses discussed above because it includes not only assets as variable in the consumption function but also explains why MPC < APC in the short-run and the APC is constant in the long-run.

Permanent Income Theory of Consumption

Permanent income theory of consumer behaviour has been put forward by a well-known American economist, **Milton Freidman.** Though Friedman's permanent income hypothesis differs from life cycle consumption theory in details, it has important common features with the latter. Like the life cycle approach, according to Friedman, consumption is determined by long-term expected income rather than current level of income. It is this long-term expected income which is called by Friedman as permanent income on the basis of which people make their consumption plans.

Relationship between Consumption and Permanent Income. According to permanent income hypothesis, Friedman thinks that consumption is proportional to permanent income.

$$C_P = K.Y_P$$

Where

Y_P = permanent income

C_P = permanent consumption

K = proportion of permanent income that is consumed

The proportion or fraction K of permanent income that is consumed depends upon the following factors:

1. Rate of interest (*r*) : The higher the rate of interest the people would tend to save more and thus consumption expenditure will decrease. The lowering of rate of interest will have opposite effect on the consumption.

2. The relative amounts of income from physical assets (*i.e.* non-human wealth) and income from labour (*i.e.* human wealth) also effects consumption expenditure. This is denoted by the term w in the permanent consumption function and is measured by the ratio of non-human wealth to income. In his permanent income hypothesis Friedman suggests that consumption expenditure depends a good deal on the wealth or assets possessed by the people. The greater the amount of wealth or assets held by an individual the greater would be its propensity to consume and vice-versa.

3. Lastly, household's preference for immediate consumption as against the desire to add to the stock of wealth or assets also determines the proportion of permanent income to be devoted to consumption. The desire to add to one's wealth rather than to fulfil one's wants of immediate consumption is denoted by u.

Thus rewriting the consumption function based on Friedman's permanent income hypothesis we have

$$C_P = K(r, w, u)Y_P$$

This equation tells that over the long period consumption increases in proportion to the change in Y_P. This is attributable to a constant K (= C_P / Y_P)

which is independent of the size of income. Thus K is the permanent average propensity to consume. The propensity to consume has been influenced by three factors. First, there has been a sharp decline in the farm population which has tended to increase consumption with urbanisation. This has tended to increase K. Second, there has been a sharp decline in the size of families. It has led to increase in saving and reduction in consumption thereby reducing the value of K. Third, larger provision by state for social security. This has reduced the need for keeping more in savings. It has increased the tendency to consume more resulting in the rise in the value of K. The overall effect of these offsetting forces is to raise consumption in proportion to the change in the permanent income component.

Permanent and Transitory Income. In addition to permanent income, the individual's income may contain a transitory component that Friedman calls as a **transitory income.** A transitory income is a temporary income that is not going to persist in future periods. According to Friedman, transitory income is not likely to have much effect on consumption. Thus, income of an individual consists of two parts, permanent and transitory, which we may write as under:

$$Y_m = Y_P + Y_t$$

Where Y_m is measured income in a period, Y_P is the permanent income and Y_t is transitory income.

Transitory income may rise or fall with wind fall gains or losses and cyclical variations. If the transitory income is positive due to a wind fall gain, the measured income will rise above the permanent income. If the transitory income is negative due to theft, the measured income falls below the permanent income. The transitory income can also be zero in which case measured income equals permanent income.

Assumptions : Freidman gives a series of assumptions concerning the relationships between permanent and transitory components of income and consumption.

1. There is no correlation between transitory and permanent incomes.

2. There is no correlation between permanent and transitory consumption.

3. There is no correlation between transitory consumption and transitory income.

4. Only differences in permanent income effect consumption systematically.

These assumptions give the explanation of the cross-section result (short-run) that MPC < APC. The cross-sectional results of Friedman's theory give a linear and proportional consumption function because if persons are classified in terms of their measured (or current) income, they also tend to be classified on the basis of their short-run income experience. Thus persons with the highest incomes will also tend to be those who have temporary increases in their incomes. Conversely, those with the lowest incomes will also tend to be the ones with temporary decreases in their incomes. Therefore, the ratio of consumption to measured income will tend to be higher for those at the bottom of the income range than those at the top on a short-run consumption function. Thus, according to this hypothesis, persons whose measured income is higher than their permanent income will be consuming smaller fractions of measured income than those persons whose measured income is less than their permanent income. We, therefore, get a measured short-run consumption function in the form $C = a + b.Y$, where $b.Y$ measures the differences in income. The value of $b.Y$ in the hypothesis is taken as $b.Y = K.PY$, where PY is the proportion of difference in measured income attributable to a difference in permanent income; and K is the ratio of permanent

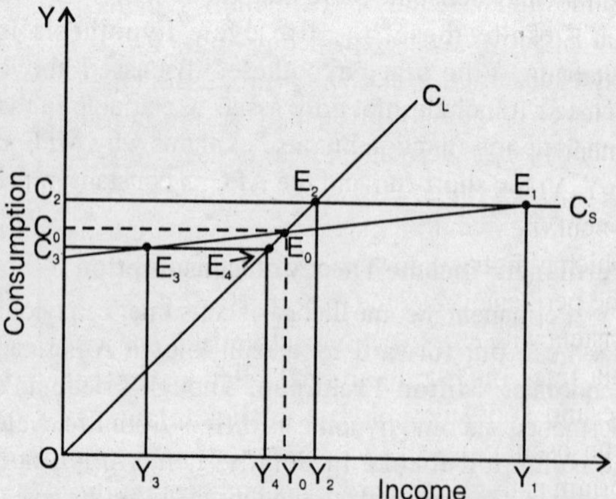

Fig. 1.10 : *Permanent Income Hypothesis: Long-Run and Short-Run Consumption Function*

consumption to permanent income which is a constant, APC = MPC. This gives us the proportional long-run consumption function, $b.Y = K. PY$.

Figure 1.10 explains the permanent income hypothesis where C_L is the long-run consumption function which represents the long-run proportional relationship between consumption and income of an individual. Over the long-run, transitory components of both variables cancel out and there is proportional relation between the permanent components. C_S is the non-proportional short-run consumption function where measured income includes both permanent and transitory components.

At OY_0, income level where the C_S and C_L lines coincide at E_O, changes in permanent income and measured income are identical, and so are permanent and measured consumption as shown by OC_0. Here transitory factors are non-existence and $P_Y = 1$. If we move to the left of point E_O on the C_S curve at E_3, the measured income declines to OY_3, due in part to the negative transitory income component (*i.e.* windfall losses). Since the permanent consumption will remain at OC_3 (= Y_4 E_4) and equal measured consumption ($Y_4 E_4 = Y_3E_3$). Thus when PY < 1, It is possible for measured consumption (Y_3E_3) to be higher than measured income (OY_3) because of the relative stability of the permanent income factor which does not allow measured consumption to decline in the same proportion and keeps it generally stable due to unchanging wealth position of the family. On the other hand, a movement to the right of point E_O on the C_S curve at E_1 shows measured income to be OY_1 and measured consumption as OC_2 (= Y_1E_2). But OC_2 (= E_2Y_2) level of consumption can be maintained permanently at the permanent income level of OY_2. Thus, Y_1Y_2 is the positive transitory income component (*i.e.* windfall gains) in measured income OY_1 which is higher than the permanent income OY_2.

The permanent income hypothesis of Friedman is consistent with cross-section budget data. The long run data trace out a proportional relation between income and consumption. But studies relating to short-run oscillations of income around a long-run equilibrium path generally reveal a non-proportional relationship between measured income and measured consumption.

Its Criticism

This hypothesis is not free from certain weaknesses.

1. Friedman's assumption that there is no correlation between transitory components of consumption and income is unrealistic.

2. Friedman's hypothesis states that the APC of all families, whether rich or poor, is the same in the long-run. But this is against the ordinary observed behaviour of households.

3. Friedman's use of the terms "Permanent," "transitory," and "measured" have tended to confuse the theory. The concept of measured income improperly mixes together permanent and transitory income on the one hand, and permanent and transitory consumption on the other.

4. Another weakness of the permanent income hypothesis is that Friedman does not make any distinction between human and non-human wealth and includes income from both in a single term in the empirical analysis of this theory.

THE CONCEPT OF MULTIPLIER

The concept of multiplier was first developed by **Richard F. Kahn** in 1931. Kahn's multiplier was the 'employment multiplier.' Keynes took the idea from Kahn and developed the **Investment Multiplier.** The concept of Investment Multiplier constitutes an important pillar in the whole edifice of the Keynesian theory of income and employment. The concept of multiplier is closely connected with the MPS.

The multiplier expresses a relationship between an initial investment and the final increment in aggregate income. To be more accurate, the multiplier is the ratio of the change in income to the change in investment. It shows by how many times the effect of an initial change in investment is multiplied by causing changes in consumption and finally in the aggregate income. According to Keynes, the multiplier establishes "a precise relationship between aggregate employment, income and the rate of investment given the propensity to consume. Whenever an investment is made in the economy, the effect is to increase aggregate income not only by the amount of original investment, but by something much more than that.

There is, thus, a precise relationship between the initial investment and the ultimate increase in income. This relationship Keynes designates as 'K'.

In the words of Alvin H. Hansen, Keynes's investment multiplier is the coefficient relating an increment of investment to an increment in income. The multiplier is the number by which an initial change in aggregate monetary demand must be multiplied to find out the eventual change in income. It is the ratio of the change in one of the components of aggregate demand, viz. Planned investment, consumption expenditure, export receipts or governmental expenditure, to the total change in national income. The general form of the multiplier is $\frac{1}{1-MPC}$. In the multiplier theory, the important element is the multiplier coefficient 'K', which refers to the power by which an initial investment expenditure is multiplied to obtain a final increase in income. The value of the multiplier is determined by the MPS. The higher the MPC, the higher the value of the multiplier and vice versa.

Assumptions of Multiplier

The Keynesian theory of Multiplier requires specific conditions under which it operates. Some assumptions are necessary for its smooth movement. They are as follows—

1. There is a change in investment.
2. Marginal propensity to consume is constant.
3. Consumption is a function of current income.
4. There are no time lags in the multiplier process. An increase (decrease) in investment instantaneously leads to a multiple increase (decrease) in income.
5. The new level of investment is maintained steadily for the completion of the multiplier process.
6. There is net increase in investment.
7. Consumer goods are available in response to effective demand for them.
8. There is a surplus capacity in consumer goods industries to meet the increased demand for consumer goods in response to a rise in income following increased investment.
9. Other resources of production are also easily available within the economy.
10. There is an industrialised economy in which the multiplier process operates.
11. There is a closed economy unaffected by foreign influences.
12. There are no changes in prices.
13. The accelerator effect of consumption on investment is ignored.
14. There is less than full employment level in the economy.

Derivation of the Multiplier

The size of the multiplier depends upon the size of the MPC. The two are closely related. Given the MPC, the multiplier can be easily derived. Keynes has expressed it by the symbol K. 'K' can be found out from the formula

$$K = \frac{1}{1-MPC} \text{ or } K = \frac{1}{MPC}$$

The multiplier is derived as follows:

$$\Delta Y = K.\Delta I$$

$$K = \frac{\Delta Y}{\Delta I}$$

ΔI is increased investment and ΔY is increased income. Aggregate saving S is equal to aggregate investment I. By the same argument increased saving ΔS must be equal to increased investment ΔI.

Saving is the difference between income (Y) and consumption (C) so that

$$S = Y - C.$$

By the same reasoning

$$\Delta S = \Delta Y - \Delta C$$

Since $\Delta S = \Delta I$, we can substitute $\Delta Y - \Delta C$ for ΔI.

Substituting $\Delta Y - \Delta C$ for ΔI we have

$$K = \frac{\Delta Y}{\Delta Y - \Delta C}$$

Dividing both the numerator and the denominator by ΔY we get,

$$K = \frac{\frac{\Delta Y}{\Delta Y}}{\frac{\Delta Y}{\Delta Y} - \frac{\Delta C}{\Delta Y}} \text{ or } K = \frac{1}{1 - \frac{\Delta C}{\Delta Y}}$$

The denominator $\left(1 - \frac{\Delta C}{\Delta Y}\right)$ is $1 - MPC$ which is the MPS. So, multiplier K is the reciprocal of the fraction saved, that is, $\frac{1}{MPS}$.

If MPC = $\frac{\Delta C}{\Delta Y}$ is deducted from 1 we get the MPC. So that MPS = 1 – MPC.

$$\therefore K = \frac{1}{MPS}$$

MPC and Multiplier

Multiplier varies directly with the MPC and inversely with the MPS. Since the MPC is always greater than zero and less than one (*i.e.* $0 < MPC < 1$), the multiplier is always between one and infinity (*i.e.* $1 < K < \infty$).

1. The MPC is very rarely zero. If it is zero, the multiplier is 1. What this means is that nothing is spent by consumers out of increased income. The whole increased income is saved, with the result that the multiplier is one. Suppose there is a new investment of Rs. 10 crore in public works and the MPC is zero. It means that the whole of Rs. 10 crore is saved. The multiplier is one. The aggregate income increase by Rs. 10 crore.

2. The other limiting case is when MPC is 1.

What this implies is that the consumers spend the whole of the increment of their incomes on consumption and nothing is saved; and the MPS is zero. The result in such a case is highly "explosive." Suppose Rs. 10 crore is invested in public works. The workers who receive Rs. 10 crore shall spend the whole of it on consumption. Others who receive increased incomes shall also spend the whole of them. In this way, Rs. 10 crore shall emerge and re-emerge and result in an infinite increase in income. It will soon lead to full employment in the economy and then create a limitless inflationary spiral.

Both these cases are rare. Actually the multiplier can never be 1 or infinity It generally varies between 1 and infinity.

Leakages of Multiplier

Leakages are the potential diversions from the income stream which tend to weaken the multiplier effect of new investment. Given the marginal propensity to consume, the increase in income in each round declines due to leakages in the income stream and ultimately the process of income propagation "peters out." The following are the important leakages:

1. Saving
2. Strong Liquidity Preference
3. Purchase of old stocks and securities
4. Debt cancellation
5. Price Inflation
6. Net Imports
7. Undistributed Profits
8. Taxation
9. Excess Stocks of Consumption Goods.

THE PARADOX OF THRIFT

An interesting paradox arises when all people in a society try to save more but in fact they are unable to do so. According to this paradox of thrift, the attempt by the people as a whole to save more for hard times such as impending period of recession or unemployment may not materialise and in their bid to save more the society in fact may not only end up with the same savings (or, even lower savings) but also in the process cause their consumption or standard of living to decline. According to classical economists, savings determine investment which plays a crucial role in accelerating the rate of economic growth. However, the paradox of thrift shows that the efforts to save more, especially at times of depression, may actually deepen the economic crisis and cause output to fall and unemployment to increase. It goes to the credit of Keynes that with his multiplier theory he has been able to resolve the paradox of thrift.

According to the Keynesian theory, the saying "penny saved is penny earned" is quite inappropriate for the economy as a whole when it is working at under-employment equilibrium, that is, when there prevails recession or depression. Keynes has showed that if all people in a society decide to save more, they may actually fail to do so but nevertheless reduce their consumption. This is because according to Keynes, the effort to save more by all in a society will lower the aggregate demand for goods and services resulting in a drop in the level of national income. At the lower level of national income the savings fall to original level but consumption will be less than before which implies that the people would become worse off.

DYNAMIC OR PERIOD MULTIPLIER

Keynes's logical theory of the multiplier is an instantaneous process without time lag. It is a timeless **static equilibrium analysis** in which the total effect of a change in investment on income is instantaneous so that consumption goods are produced simultaneously and consumption expenditure is also incurred instantaneously. But this is not borne out by facts because a time lag is always involved between the receipt of income and its expenditure on consumption goods and also in producing consumption goods. Thus "the timeless multiplier analysis disregards the transition and deals only with the new equilibrium income level" and is, therefore, unrealistic.

The dynamic multiplier relates to the time lags in the process of income generation. The series of adjustments in income and consumption may take months or even years for the multiplier process to complete, depending upon the assumption made about the period involved. This is explained in Table where if each round is of one month and it takes seventeen rounds for an initial investment of Rs. 100 crores to generate an income of Rs. 200 crores, given the value of MPC to be 0.5, then the multiplier process will take 17 months to complete.

Table: Dynamic Multiplier

(Rs. Crores)

Period in Months	*ΔI (Increment in) Investment)*	*ΔC = 0.5 ΔY (Increment in consumption)*	*ΔY (Increment in Income)*
0	0	0	0
t + 1	100	0	100
t + 2	100	50	100 + 50
t + 3	100	25	150 + 25
–	–	–	–
–	–	–	–
t + n	100	100	200

The Table shows that if the MPC remains constant at 0.5 throughout, an initial increase of Rs 100 crores of investment will first raise income by 100 crores in the first month. Out of this Rs. 50 crores will be spent on consumption. This will raise income in the second month to Rs. 50 crores, and out of this Rs. 25 crores will be spent on consumption. This will go to increase income in the third month by Rs. 25 crores, and successive increments in income get smaller and smaller in each period till in the sevententh month the income increases by Rs. 0.001 crore. This can also be explained algebraically as:

$$\Delta Y = \Delta I + \Delta I.C + \Delta I.C^2 + ...\Delta I\, C^{n-1} \quad [\text{C is MPC}]$$

$$\Delta Y = 100 + 100\,(0.5) + 100\,(0.5)^2 + ...+ 100\,(0.5)^{n-1}$$

$$\Delta Y = \frac{100}{1-0.5} = 200 \text{ crores}$$

It is now easy to generalise. Let the MPC be denoted by the symbol C and let the upward shift in the investment function be denoted as ΔI. On the first day income rises by ΔI; on the second day by and additional $C\Delta I$; on the third day by yet another $C^2\Delta I$ and on any arbitrary day n by the additional $C^{n-1}\Delta I$. Therefore, by day n the increase in income over its initial level will be given by the geometric series

$$\Delta Y = \Delta I + C.\Delta I + C^2.\Delta I + C^3.\Delta I + ...+ C^{n-1}.\Delta I \quad .....(1)$$

which can be written as

$$\Delta Y = \Delta I\,(1 + C + C^2 + C^3 + ...+ C^{n-1}) \quad ....(2)$$

There is an easy way for simplifying a geometric series. Multiply both sides of equation (2) by the term C. Both sides of any equation can always be multiplied by some constant. If we do this, we get

$$C.\Delta Y = \Delta I\,(C + C^2 + C^3 + C^4 + ...+ C^{n-1} + C^n) \quad ....(3)$$

If we subtract equation (3) from equation (2) we are left with

$$\Delta Y - C.\Delta Y = \Delta I\,(1 - C^n)$$

Solving for ΔY we get

$$\Delta Y = \frac{\Delta I\,(1 - C^n)}{1 - C} \quad ...(4)$$

If the multiplier process is permitted to go on long enough we can let *n* become as large as we like. Since C is a fraction, the term C^n will approach zero as *n* tends to infinity, and when that happens equation (4) reduces to

$$\Delta Y = \frac{\Delta I}{1 - C}$$

This expression predicts the change in the equilibrium level of income. If we divide both sides of the expression by ΔI, we get the multiplier

$$\frac{\Delta Y}{\Delta I} = \frac{1}{1 - C} = \frac{1}{1 - MPC}$$

which equals the reciprocal of MPS.

This process of dynamic income propagation assumes that there is a consumption lag and no investment lag so that consumption is a function of the income of the preceding period *i.e.*, $C_t = f(Y_{t-1})$ and investment is a function of time (t) and of constant autonomous investment ΔI, *i.e.* $I_t = f(\Delta I)$. In figure 1.11, C + I is the aggregate demand function and the 45° line is the aggregate supply function. If we begin in period to where with an equilibrium level of OY_O income, investment is increased by ΔI, then in period t income rises by the amount of the increased investment (from t_0 to t). The increased investment is shown by the new aggregate demand function $C + I + \Delta I$. But in period t_0 consumption lags behind, and is still equal to the original income E_0. But at Y_0 level total demand rises from Y_0t_0 to $Y_0\,t$. There is now an excess of demand over supply equal to $t_0\,t$. In period t consumption rises due to the rise in demand to Y_0t. Now investment increases income still higher to OY_1 in period $t + 1$ and to increase in consumption from t to E_1. But at this level total demand is Y_1E_1 which exceeds total supply by AE_1. This will further tend to

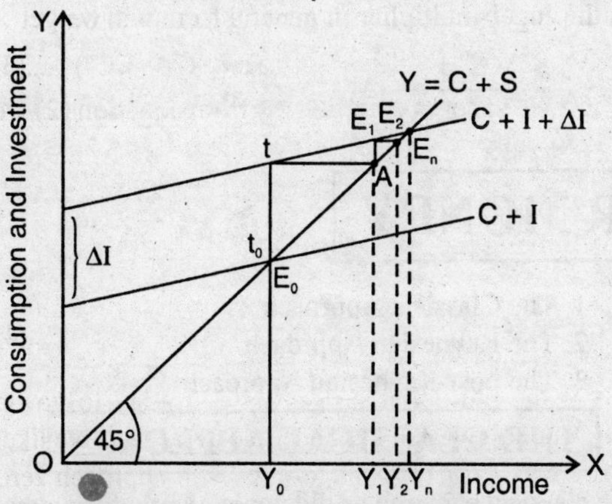

Fig. 1.11: *Dynamic Multiplier*

raise income to OY_2 in period $t + 2$ and to increase in consumption to $E_1\,E_2$. This leads to a rise in demand to Y_2E_2, leading to an excess of total demand over total supply by BE_2. This process of income generation will continue till the aggregate demand function $C + I + \Delta I$ equals the aggregate supply function 45° line at E_n in the nth period, and the new equilibrium level of income is determined at OY_n. The curved steps E_O to E_n is the path of income propagation showing the dynamic process of multiplier.

THE PRINCIPLE OF ACCELERATION

The term "**acceleration principle**" was first introduced into economics by **J.M. Clark** in 1917. It was further developed by Hicks, Samuelson, and Harrod in relation to the business cycles.

The principle of acceleration is based on the fact that the demand for capital goods is derived from the demand for consumer goods which the former help to produce. The acceleration principle explains the process by which an increase (or decrease) in the demand for consumption goods leads to an increase (or decrease) in investment on capital goods.

Symbolically,

$$\beta = \frac{\Delta I}{\Delta C} \text{ or } \Delta I = \beta\,\Delta C$$

where

β = accelerator coefficient

ΔI = net change in investment

ΔC = net change in consumption expenditure

This version of the acceleration principle has been more broadly interpreted by Hicks as the ratio of induced investment to changes in output it calls forth. Thus,

$$\Delta I = \gamma\,\Delta Y$$

where

γ = accelerator

It shows that the demand for capital goods is not derived from consumer goods alone but from any direct demand of national output.

There is little difference between $\Delta I = \gamma\,\Delta Y$, as defined by **Hicks** and $\Delta I = \beta\,\Delta C$, as defined by

Samuelson and others. The accelerator γ and β are the same. Hicks takes the increase in final output (ΔY) while Samuelson takes the increase in the demand for consumer goods (ΔC). In Hicks's model net investment equals $I_{nt} = \gamma\ (Y_t - Y_{t-1})$ while in Samuelson's model $I_{nt} = \beta\ (C_t - C_{t-1})$.

Assumptions

The acceleration principle is based upon the following assumptions.

1. The acceleration principle assumes a constant capital-output ratio.
2. It assumes that resources are easily available.
3. The acceleration principle assumes that there is no excess or idle capacity in plants.
4. It is assumed that the increased demand is permanent.
5. The acceleration principle also assumes that there is elastic supply of credit and capital.
6. It further assumes that an increase in output immediately leads to a rise in net investment.

SUPER MULTIPLIER

In order to measure the total effect of initial investment on income, **Hicks** has combined the multiplier and the accelerator mathematically and given it the name of the **super-multiplier**. The combined effect of the multiplier and the accelerator is also called the **leverage effect** which may lead the economy to very high or low level of income propagation.

The super-multiplier is worked out by combining both induced consumption (C.Y) and induced investment $(\gamma.Y)$. Hicks divides the investment component into autonomous investment and induced investment so that investment $I = I_a + \gamma.Y$,

where

I_a = autonomous investment

$\gamma.Y$ = induced investment

Since

$$Y = C + I$$

Therefore

$$\Delta Y = C.\Delta Y + \Delta I_a + \gamma.\Delta Y$$

$$\Delta Y - C.\Delta Y - \gamma.\Delta Y = \Delta I_a$$

$$\Delta Y[1 - C - \gamma] = \Delta I_a$$

$$\frac{\Delta Y}{\Delta I_a} = \frac{1}{1 - C - \gamma}$$

$$\frac{\Delta Y}{\Delta I_a} = \frac{1}{S - \gamma}$$

or

$$K_S = \frac{1}{1 - C - \gamma} = \frac{1}{S - \gamma}$$

where

K_S = super multiplier

C = marginal propensity to consume

γ = marginal propensity to invest

S = marginal propensity to save

The super-multiplier tells us that if there is an initial increase in autonomous investment, income will increase by K_S times the autonomous investment. So the super-multiplier in general form will be

$$\Delta Y = \frac{1}{1 - C - \gamma}.\Delta I_a = K_S.\Delta I_a$$

DEMAND FOR MONEY

The demand for money arises from two important functions of money. The first is that money act as a medium of exchange and the second is that it is a store of value. This individuals and businesses wish to hold money partly in cash and partly in the form of assets. There are three approaches to the demand for money:

1. The Classical Approach
2. The Keynesian Approach
3. The post-Keynesian Approach

THE CLASSICAL APPROACH

The classical economists did not explicitly formulate demand for money theory but their views are inherent in the quantity theory of money. They emphasized the transactions demand for money in terms of the velocity of circulation of money. This is because money acts as a medium of exchange and facilitates the exchange of goods and services. In Fisher's "Equation of Exchange",

$$MV = PT$$

where

M = total quantity of money
V = circulation velocity of money
P = price level
T = total amount of goods and services exchanged form money

The right hand side of this equation PT represents the demand for money which, in fact, "depends upon the value of the transaction to be undertaken in the economy, and is equal to a constant fraction of those transaction." MV represents the supply of money which is given and in equilibrium equals the demand for money. Thus the equations becomes

$$M_d = PT$$

This transactions demand for money, in turn, is determined by the level of full employment income. This is because the classicists believed in Say's Law whereby supply created its own demand, assuming the full employment level of income. Thus the demand for money in Fisher's approach is a constant proportion of the level of transactions, which in turn, bears a constant relationship to the level of national income.

THE NEOCLASSICAL THEORY

The neoclassical theory of the demand for money was put forward by the *Cambridge economists* **Marshall** and **Pigou**. The Cambridge demand equation for money is

$$M_d = K.Y \qquad ...(1)$$

Where

M_d = amount of money demanded
Y = money value of national income
K = Constant

Since, by definition, Y = P.*y*, where P is the general price level and *y* real national income, equation (1) can be written alternatively in its equivalent form as

$$M_d = K.Py \qquad ...(2)$$

K is the fraction of the real money income (P*y*) which people wish to hold in cash and demand deposits.

We may illustrate equation (1) diagrammatically as in Figure 1.12. M_d is shown to be a linear function of Y. It goes through the origin. The tangent of the angle which it makes with the horizontal axis = $M_d/Y = K$

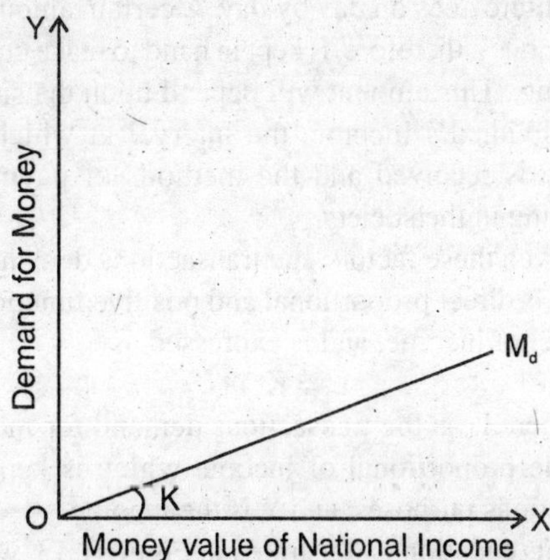

Fig. 1.12 : *The Cambridge Demand for Money Function*

The Key Feature of the Cambridge equation is that it makes the demand for money a function of money income, and only of it.

Cambridge equation is the simplest demand function for money. It has played a very important role.

THE KEYNESIAN APPROACH : LIQUIDITY PREFERENCE

What is known as the Keynesian theory of the demand for money was first formulated by **Keynes** in his well-known book, *The General Theory of Employment, Interest and Money (1936)*. It has been developed further by other economists of Keynesian persuasion. Keynes suggested three motives which led to the demand for money in an economy :

1. The Transactions Demand
2. The Precautionary Demand
3. The Speculative Demand

The Transactions Demand for Money

The transactions demand for money arises from

the medium of exchange function of money in making regular payments for goods and services. According to Keynes, it relates to "the need of cash for the current transactions of personal and business exchange." In other words people hold money or cash balances for transactions purposes, because receipt of money and payments do no coincide. Most of the people receive their incomes weekly or monthly while the expenditure goes on day by day. A certain amount of ready money, therefore, is kept in hand to make current payments. This amount will depend upon the size of the individual's income, the interval at which the income is received and the methods of payments prevailing in the society.

Given these factors, the transactions demand for money is direct proportional and positive function of the level of income, and is expressed as

$$L_t = K.Y$$

where L_t is the transactions demand for money, K is the proportional of income which is kept for transactions purposes, and Y is the income.

This equation is illustrated in Figure 1.13, where the line KY represents a linear and proportional relation between transactions demand and the level of income.

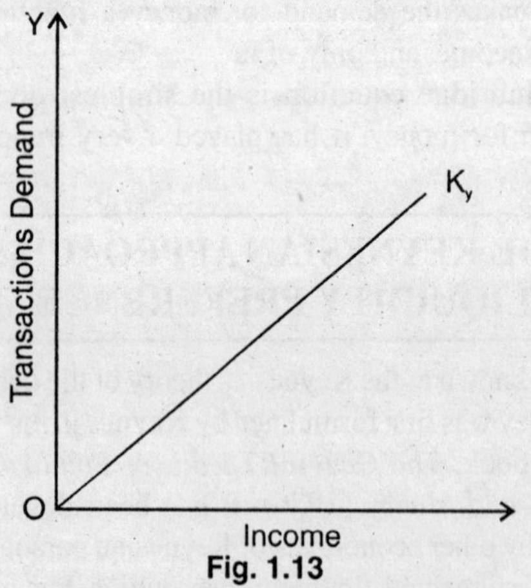

Fig. 1.13

Interest Rate and Transactions Demand

Regarding the rate of interest as the determinant of the transactions demand for money, Keynes made the L_t function interest inelastic. But he pointed out that the "demand for money in the active circulation is also to some extent a function of the rate of interest, since a higher rate of interest may lead to a more economical use of active balances. In recent years, two post-Keynesian economists **W.J. Baumol** and **James Tobin** have shown that the rate of interest is an important determinant to transactions demand for money. They have also pointed out that the relationship between transactions demand for money and income is not linear and proportional. Rather changes in income lead to proportionately smaller changes in transactions demand.

The modern view is that the transactions demand for money is a function of both income and interest rates which can be expressed as

$$L_t = f(Y, r)$$

Precautionary Demand for Money

Precautionary motive for holding money refers to the desire of the people to hold cash balances for unforeseen contingencies. People hold a certain amount of money to provide for the danger of unemployment, sickness, accidents, and the other uncertain perils. The amount of money demanded for this motive will depend on the psychology of the individual and the conditions in which he lives.

Keynes held that the precautionary demand for the money, like transactions demand, was a function of the level of income. But the post-Keynesian economists believe that like transactions demand, it is inversely related to high interest rates.

Speculative Demand For Money

The speculative motive of the people relates to the desire to hold one's resources in liquid form in order to take advantage of market movements regarding the future changes in the rate of interest (or bond prices). The truly novel and revolutionary element of Keynes's theory of the demand for money is the component of *the speculative demand for money.*

Money held under the speculative motive serves as a store of value as money held under the precautionary motive does. But it is a store of money meant for a different purpose. The cash held under this motive is used to make speculative gains by dealing in bonds whose prices fluctuate. If bond prices are expected to rise which, in other words, means that the rate of interest is expected to fall, businessmen will buy bonds to sell when their prices actually rise.

If, however, bond prices are expected to fall, i.e., the rate of interest is expected to rise, businessmen will sell bonds to avoid capital losses. Nothing being certain in the dynamic world, where guesses about the future course of events are made on precarious basis, businessmen keep cash to speculative on the probable future changes in bond prices (or the rate of interest) with a view to making profits.

Given the expectations about the changes in the rate of interest in future, less money will be held under the speculative motive at a higher current rate of interest and more money will be held under this motive at a lower current rate of interest. The reason for this inverse correlation between money held for speculative motive and the prevailing rate of interest is that at a lower rate of interest less is lost by not lending money or investing it, that is, by holding on to money, while at a higher current rate of interest holders of cash balances would lose more by not lending or investing.

Thus the demand for money under speculative motive is a function of the current rate of interests increasing as the interest rate falls and decreasing as the interest rate rises. Thus, *demand for money under this motive is a decreasing function of the rate of interest.* This is shown in Figure 1.14. Along OX is represented the speculative demand for money and along OY the current rate of interest. The liquidity preference curve LP is a downward sloping towards the right signifying the higher the rate of interest, the

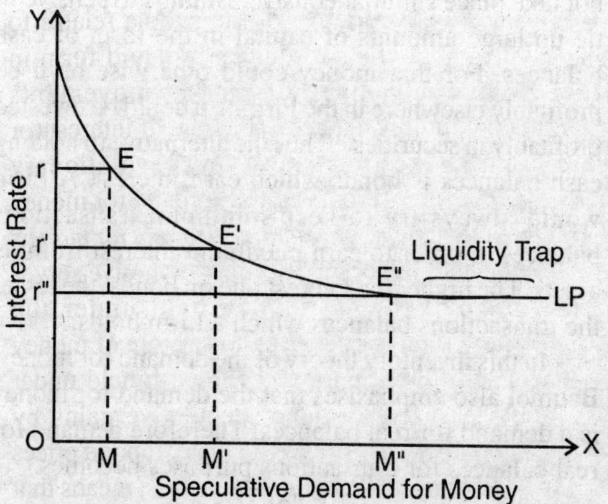

Fig. 1.14 : *Demand for Money for Speculative Motive*

lower the demand for money for speculative motive, and vice versa.

Thus at the high current rate of interest O*r*, a very small amount OM is held for speculative motive. This is because at a high current rate of interest much money would have been lent out or used for buying bonds and therefore less money would be kept as inactive balances. If the rate of interest falls to O*r*', then a greater amount OM' is held under speculative motive. With the further fall in the rate of interest to O*r*". Money held under speculative motive increases to OM".

Liquidity Trap

At very low rate of interest, such as *r*" in Figure 1.14, the LP curve becomes *perfectly elastic* and the speculative demand for money is infinitely elastic. This perfectly elastic portion of liquidity preference curve indicates the position of *absolute liquidity preference* of the people. That is, at a very low rate of interest people will hold with them as inactive balances any amount of money they come to have. This portion of liquidity preference curve with absolute liquidity preference is called *liquidity trap* by the economists because expansion in money supply gets trapped in the sphere of liquidity trap and therefore cannot affect rate of interest and therefore the level of investment. According to Keynes, it is because of the existence of liquidity trap that monetary policy becomes ineffective to tide over economic depression.

The phenomenon of liquidity trap possesses certain important implications.

First, the monetary authority cannot influence the rate of interest even by following a cheap money policy. An increase in the quantity of money cannot lead to a further decline in the rate of interest in a liquidity-trap situation.

Second, the rate of interest cannot fall to zero.

Third, the policy of a general wage cut cannot be efficacious in the face of a perfectly elastic liquidity preference curves, such as LP in Figure 1.14.

Thus the speculative demand for money is a decreasing function of the rate of interest. The higher the rate of interest, the lower the speculative demand for money, and the lower the rate of interest, the higher the speculative demand for money. It can be expressed algebraically as

$$L_S = f(r)$$

where L_s is the speculative demand for money and r is the rate of interest.

The Total Demand for Money

According to Keynes, money held for transactions and precautionary purposes is primarily a function of the level of income, $L_T = f(Y)$, and the speculative demand for money is a function of the rate of interest, $L_S = f(r)$. Thus the total demand for money is a function of both income and the interest rate :

$$L_T + L_S = f(Y) + f(r)$$

or, $$L = f(Y) + f(r)$$

or, $$L = f(Y, r)$$

where L represents the total demand for money.

Thus the total demand for money curve can be derived by the *lateral summation* of the demand function for transactions and precautionary purposes and the demand function for speculative purposes as illustrated in Figure 1.15.

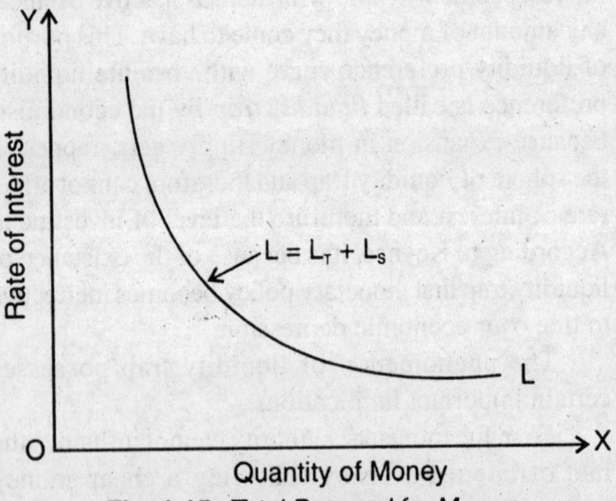

Fig. 1.15: *Total Demand for Money*

THE POST-KEYNESIAN APPROACHES

Keynes believed that the transactions demand for money was primarily interest inelastic. **Prof. Baumol** has analysed the interest elasticity of the transactions demand for money on the basis of his inventory theoretical approach. Further, in the Keynesian analysis the speculative demand for money is analysed in relation to uncertainty in the market. Prof. Tobin has given an alternative theory which explains liquidity preference as behaviour towards rist. The third important post-Keynesian development has been Friedman's formulation that the demand for money is not merely a function of income and the rate of interest, but also of the total wealth.

Baumol's Inventory Theoretic Approach

The inventory theoretic approach to the demand for money is associated with the name of **W. Baumol**. The most famous result of Baumol is the **Square-root-law** of the demand for money. William Baumol has made an important addition to the Keynesian transactions demand for money. Keynes regarded transactions demand for money as a function of the level of income, and the relationship between transactions demand and income as linear and proportional. Baumol shows that the relation between transactions demand and income is neither linear nor proportional. Rather, changes in income lead to less than proportionate changes in the transactions demand for money. Further, Keynes considered transactions demand as primarily interest inelastic. But Baumol analyses the interest elasticity of the transactions demand for money.

Baumol's analysis is based on the holding of an optimum inventory of money for transactions purposes by a firm or an individual. He writes : "A Firm's cash balance can usually be interpreted as an inventory of money which its holder stands ready to exchange against purchases of labour, raw materials, etc." Cash balances are held because income and expenditure do not take place simultaneously. "But it is expensive to tie up large amounts of capital in the form of cash balances. For that money could otherwise be used profitably elsewhere in the Firm.... it could be invested profitably in securities." Thus the alternative to holding cash balances is bonds which earn interest. A Firm would always try to keep minimum transactions balances in order to earn maximum interest from its assets. The higher the interest rate on bonds, the lesser the transactions balances which a Firm holds.

In this inventory theory of the demand for money, Baumol also emphasises that the demand for money is a demand for real balances. Therefore demand for real balances for transactions purposes becomes.

$$M_d = \frac{1}{2}\sqrt{\frac{2b.Y}{r}} \times P$$

Where

M_d = demand for money

P = price level

This equation shows that the demand for real transactions balances "is proportional to the square root of the volume of transactions and inversely proportional to the square root of the rate of interest." It means that the relationship between changes in the price level and the transactions demand for money is direct and proportional.

Its Superiority Over the Classical and Keynesian Approaches

Baumol's inventory theoretic approach to the transactions demand for money is an improvement over the classical and Keynesian approaches.

The cash balance quantity theory of money assumed the relationship between the transactions demand and the level of income as linear and proportional. Baumol has shown that this relationship is not accurate. No doubt it is true the transactions demand increases with in income but it increases less than proportionately because of the economies of scale in cash management.

Baumol's theory also has the merit of demonstrating the interest elasticity of the transactions demand for money as against the Keynesian view that it is interest inelastic.

Further, Baumol analyses the transactions demand for real balances thereby emphasising the absence of money illusion.

Again, Baumol's inventory theoretic approach is superior to both the classical and Keynesian approaches because it integrates the transactions demand for money with the capital-theory approach by taking assets and their interest and non-interest costs into account.

Tobin's Portfolio Selection Model : The Risk Aversion Theory of Liquidity Preference

James Tobin in his famous article "*Liquidity Preference as Behaviour Towards Risk*" Formulated the risk aversion theory of liquidity preference based on portfolio selection. This theory removes two major defects of the Keynesian theory of liquidity preference. One, Keynes's liquidity preference function depends on the inelasticity of expectations of future interest rates; and two, individuals hold either money or bonds. Tobin has removed both the defects. His theory does not depend on the elasticity of expectations of future interest rates but proceeds on the assumption that the expected value of capital gain or loss from holding interest -bearing assets is always zero.

Moreover, it explains that an individual's portfolio holds both money and bonds rather than only one at a time.

Its Superiority Over Keynesian Theory

Tobin's risk aversion theory of portfolio selection is superior to the Keynesian liquidity preference theory of speculative demand for money. First, Tobin's theory does not depend on inelasticity of expectations of future interest rates, but proceeds from the assumption that the expected value of capital gain or loss from holding interest bearing assets is always zero. In this respect, Tobin regards his theory as a logically more satisfactory foundation for liquidity preference than the Keynesian theory.

Second, this theory is superior to Keynes's theory in that it explains that individuals hold diversified portfolios of bonds and money rather than either bonds or money.

Third, like Keynes, Tobin regards the demand for money as closely dependent on interest rates and inversely related to interest rates. But he is more realistic than Keynes in not discussing the perfect elasticity of demand for money (the liquidity trap) at very low rates of interest.

Fourth, the real importance of the portfolio theory lies in "not what it tells directly about the aggregate economy, but rather it represents an interesting approach to the existence of uncertainty, and approach that probably has scope for considerable development in the future."

FRIEDMAN'S THEORY

Friedman, in his essay "*The Quantity Theory of Money—A Restatement*" published in 1956, set down a particular model of quantity theory of money.

In his reformulation of the quantity theory, Friedman asserts that "money does matter." *He points out that his quantity theory is a theory of the demand for money*. It is not a theory of output, money incomes or prices.

Friedman's theory of the demand for money is partly Keynesian and partly non-Keynesian. Instead, for identifying the key determinants of the demand for money, he classifies the holders of money as between *(a)* ultimately wealth-holders and *(b)* business enterprises. All the essentials of his theory have been set out in respect of the former, and comparatively much less about the latter. He emphasises the role of money as an asset and in this he generalises Keynes's analysis of the speculative demand for money by treating the total demand for money as part of capital or wealth theory, concerned with the composition of the balance sheet or portfolio of assets.

According to Friedman, the analysis of the demand for money on the part of the ultimate wealth owning units is formally identical with that of the demand for any durable consumer good. The demand for money depends upon three major sets of factors :

(a) the total wealth to be held in various forms

(b) the price and return on this form of wealth and alternate forms

(c) the tastes and preferences of the wealth-owing units.

He, therefore, regards the amount of real cash balances (M/P) as a commodity which is demanded because it yields services to the person who holds it. Thus money is an asset or capital good. Hence the demand for money forms part of capital or wealth theory.

Friedman's theory of the demand function for money for an individual wealth-holder is summed up symbolically below :

$$M_d = f(Y, P, r_b, r_e, p^e, w, u) \quad ...(1)$$

where

M_d = total stock of money demanded

Y = total permanent income

P = price level

r_b = yield on bonds

r_e = yield of equities

p^e = expected rate of change of prices of goods and hence the expected rate of return on real assets

w = ratio of non-human to human wealth

u = tastes and preferences and all other relevant variables.

The aggregate demand function for money is the summation of individual demand functions. So equation (1) being the demand function of an individual wealth holder also represents the aggregate demand function of all wealth holders in the community.

THE QUANTITY THEORY OF MONEY

For generations economists have been engaged in answering the question : What causes changes in the price level or the value of money? Right from **Davanzatti** and **Jean Bodin** in the 16 century to David Hume (1752) in the 18th century, to Simon Newcomb (1886), and Knut Wicksell (1898) in the 19th century to Irving Fisher (1911), Alfred Marshall (1923), A.C. Pigou (1917), Keynes (1930 and 1936), Patinkin (1948) and Friedman (1957) in the 20th Century, economists believed that the quantity theory of money explains the causes of changes in the price level or the value of money. Before we study the views of some of the economists on the relationship between money and prices it is essential to know the relation between the price level and the value of money.

By value of money is meant the purchasing power of money over goods and services within a country. The relation between value of money and the price level is an inverse one. When the price level rises, the value of money falls, and vice versa. The various versions of the quantity theory of money are attempts at explaining the causes of changes in the value of money.

Fisher's Cash Transactions Approach

In the words of **Fisher,** "Other things remaining unchanged, as the quantity of money in circulation increases, the price level also increases in direct proportional and the value of money decreases and vice versa." If the quantity of money is doubled, the price level will also double and the value of money will be one half. On the other hand, if the quantity of money is reduced by one half, the price level will also be reduced by one half and the value of money will be twice.

Fisher has explained his theory in terms of his equation of exchange :

$$PT = MV + M'V'$$

where

P = price level of 1/P = the value of money;

M = the total quantity of legal tender money;

V = the velocity of circulation of M;

M' = the total quantity of credit money;

V' = the velocity of circulation of M;

T = the total amount of goods and services exchanged for money or transactions performed by money.

This equation equates the demand for money (PT) to the supply of money (MV + M'V'). In order to find out the effect to the quantity of money on the price level or the value of money, we write the equation as

$$P = \frac{MV + M'V'}{T}$$

Fisher points out that the price level (P) varies directly as the quantity of money (M + M'). Provided the volume of trade (T) and velocity of circulation (V, V') remain unchanged.

Assumptions of the Theory

Fisher's theory is based on the following assumptions :

1. V and V' are assumed to be constant and are independent of changes in M and M'.

2. The proportion of M' to M remains constant.

3. T also remains constant and is independent of other factors such as M, M', V and V'.

4. P is a passive factor in the equation of exchange which is affected by the other factors.

5. It is assumed that the demand for money is proportional to the value of transactions.

6. The supply of money is assumed as an exogenously determined constant.

7. The theory is applicable in the long run.

8. It is based on the assumption of existence of full employment in the economy.

Fisher's quantity theory of money is explained with the help of a numerical example. Suppose the quantity of money is Rs. 5,00,000 in an economy, the velocity of circulation of money (V) is 5; and the total output to be transacted (T) is 2,50,000 units, the price level (P) will be :

$$P = \frac{MV}{T}$$

$$= \frac{500000 \times 5}{250000} = \text{Rs. 10 per unit}$$

If now, other things remaining the same, the quantity of money is doubled, i.e., increased to Rs. 1000000 then :

$$P = \frac{10000 \times 5}{250000} = \text{Rs. 20 per unit}$$

We thus see that according to the Fisher's quantity theory of money, price level varies in direct proportion to the quantity of money.

The Cambridge Cash Balances Approach

As an alternative to Fisher's quantity theory of money, *Cambridge economists* Marshall, Pigou, Robertson and Keynes theory, they regarded the determination of value of money in terms of supply and demand.

The supply of money is exogenously determined at a point of time by the banking system. Therefore, the concept of velocity of circulation is altogether discarded in the cash balances approach because it 'obscures the motives and decisions of people behind it.' On the other hand, the concept of demand for money plays the major role in determining the value of money. The demand for money is the demand to hold cash balances for transactions and precautionary motives.

Thus the cash balances approach considers the demand for money not as a medium of exchange but as a store of value. The Cambridge equations show that given the supply of money at a point of time, the value of money is determined by the demand for cash balances. When the demand for money increases, people will reduce their expenditure on goods and services in order to have larger cash holdings. Reduced demand for goods and services will bring down the price level and raise the value of money. On the contrary, fall in the demand for money will raise the price level and lower the value of money.

The Cambridge cash balances equations of Marshall, Pigou, Robertson and Keynes are discussed below.

Marshall's Equation

Marshall's equation can be stated as :

$$M = K.PY$$

where

M = the exogenously determined supply of money;

K = the fraction of the real money income (PY) which people wish to hold in cash and demand deposits;

P = the price level;

Y = the aggregate real income of the community.

Thus, the price level $P = \frac{M}{K.Y}$ or the value of money (the reciprocal of price level) is $P = \frac{K.Y}{M}$.

Pigou's Equation

Pigou was the first Cambridge economist to express the cash balances approach in the form of an equation :

$$P = \frac{KR}{M}$$

where

P = the purchasing power of money or the value of money;

K = the proportion of total real resources or income (R) which people wish to hold in the form of titles to legal tender;

R = the total resources or real income;

M = the number of actual units of legal tender money

The demand for money, according to Pigou, consists not only of legal money or cash but also bank notes and bank balances. In order to include bank notes and bank balances in the demand for money, Pigou modifies his equation as

$$P = \frac{KR}{M}[c + h(1-c)]$$

where

c = the proportion of total real income actually held by people in legal tender including token coins;

$(1 - c)$ = the proportion kept in bank notes and bank balances;

h = the proportion of actual legal tender that bankers keep against the notes and balances held by their customers.

Pigou points out that when K, R, C and h are taken as constants then the two equations give the demand curve for legal tender as a *rectangular hyperbola*. This implies that the demand curve for money has a *uniform unitary elasticity*. This is shown in Figure 1.16 where DD_1 is the demand curve for money and Q_1M_1, Q_2M_2 and Q_3M_3 are the supply curves of money drawn on the assumption that the supply of money is fixed at a point of time. The value of money or Pigou's purchasing power of money P is taken on the vertical axis. The Figure shows that when the supply of money increases from OM_1 to OM_2 the value of money is, reduced from OP_1 to OP_2. The fall in the value of money by P_1P_2 exactly equals the increase in the supply of money by M_1M_2. If the supply of money increases three times from OM_1 to OM_3, the value of money is reduced by exactly one-third from OP_1 to OP_3. Thus the demand curve for money DD_1 is a rectangular hyperbola because it shows changes in the value of money exactly in reverse proportion to the supply of money.

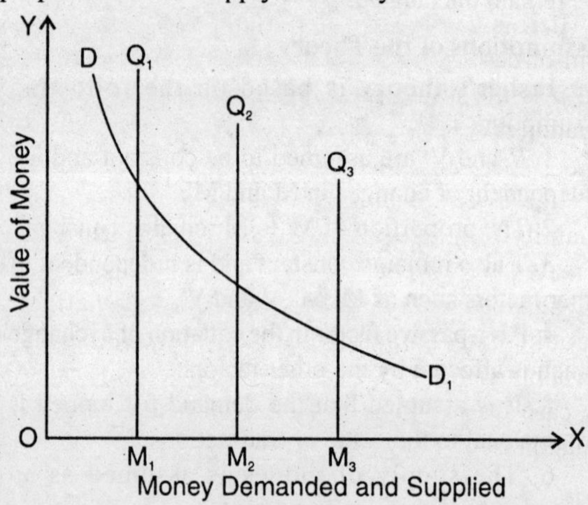

Fig. 1.16

Robertson's Equation

To determine the value of money or its reciprocal the price level, Robertson formulated an equation similar to that of Pigou. The only difference between the two being that instead of Pigou's total real resources R, Robertson gave the volume of total transactions T. The Robertsonian equation is

$$M = PKT \quad \text{or} \quad P = \frac{M}{KT}$$

where

P = the price level;

M = the total quantity of money;

K = the proportion of the total amount of goods and services (T) which people wish to hold in the form of cash balances;

T = the total volume of goods and services purchased during a year by the community.

Keynes's Equation

Keynes in his *A Tract on Monetary Reforms (1923)* gave his Real Balances Quantity Equation as an improvement over the other Cambridge equations. According to him, people always want to have some purchasing power to finance their day to day transactions. The amount of purchasing power (or demand for money) depends partly on their tastes and habits, and partly on their wealth. Given the tastes, habits and wealth of the people, their desire to hold money is given. This demand for money is measured by consumption units. A consumption unit is expressed as a basket of standard articles of consumption or other objects of expenditure.

If K is the number of consumption units in the form of cash, n is the total currency in circulation, and p is the price for consumption units then the equation is

$$n = pk$$

If K is constant, a proportionate increase in n (quantity of money) will lead to a proportionate increase in p (price level.)

This equation can be expanded by taking into account bank deposits. Let K' the number of consumption units in the form of bank deposits, and r the cash reserve ratio of banks, then the expanded equation is

$$n = p\,(K + rK')$$

Again, if K, K' and r are constant, p will change in exact proportion to the change in n.

Keynes regarded his equation superior to other cash balances equations. The other equation fail to point how the price level (p) can be regulated. Since the cash balances (K) held by the people are outside the control of the monetary authority, p can be regulated by controlling n and r. It is also possible to regulated bank deposits K' by appropriate changes in the bank rate. So p can be controlled by making appropriate changes in n, r and K' so as offset changes in K.

CASH BALANCES APPROACH VERSUS TRANSACTIONS APPROACH

The Cambridge cash balances approach to the quantity theory of money is superior to Fisher's transactions approach in many respects. They are discussed as under.

The cash balances approach emphasises the importance of holding cash balances rather than the supply to money which is given at a point to time. It thus led Keynes to propound his theory of liquidity preference and of the rate of interest, and to the integration of monetary theory with the theory of value and output.

The cash balances version of quantity theory is superior to the transactions version because the former determines the value of money. But in the transactions approach, the determination of value of money is artificially divorced from the theory of value.

The cash balances approach is superior to the transactions approach because it altogether discards the concepts of velocity of circulation of money which 'Obscures the motives and decisions of people behind it.'

Again the cash balances version is more realistic than the transactions version of the quantity theory, because it is related to the short period while the latter is related to the long period.

In the cash balances equation, transactions relating to final goods only are included where P refers to the price level of final goods. On the other hand, in the transactions equation P includes all types of transactions. This creates difficulties in determining the true price level. Thus the former equation is simpler and realistic than the latter.

RELATIONSHIP BETWEEN MONEY AND PRICES : FRIEDMAN AND OTHER MONETARIST'S VIEW

The relation between money and prices put forward by crude quantity theory of money was based on two assumptions, namely, (1) the velocity of money (V) is constant, and (2) the real national product (Y) remains fixed at the full-employment level. But both these assumptions are questionable. Monetarists led by Milton Friedman have restated and modified the quantity theory of money and have presented a more sophisticated version of it. These monetarists continue to assume that velocity of money (V) remains constant but they recognise that in the short-run the economy is often at less than full employment level and as a result the real national output (Y) may change considerably. They restate their quantity theory of money in the following way :

$$MV = PT$$

where

M = Money supply

V = Velocity of circulation of money

PY = Nominal national product or national income in money form; P is the price level and Y is the real national product.

It follows from the above equation that given the constant velocity of money (V), the nominal national product (PY) would be proportional to the money supply. The increase in money supply will lead to increase in expenditure on purchase of final goods and services. That is, increase in money supply directly causes increase in aggregate demand for final goods and services. To the extent the real national product (Y) which consists of final goods and services increases, the effect on price level (P) is less. Thus, when their is slack in the economy, that is, there exist a lot of idle productive capacity or capital stock and a large magnitude of unemployment of labour, as it happens during period of recession, the real aggregate output will increase considerably with relatively little effect on the price level. But when the economy is at full employment level of output, the expansion of money supply will have its full effect on raising the rice level, the real national Product (Y) remaining constant.

KEYNES'S REFORMULATED QUANTITY THEORY OF MONEY

The Keynesian reformulated quantity theory of money is based on the following assumptions :

1. All factors of production are in perfectly elastic supply so long as there is any unemployment.

2. All unemployed factors are homogeneous, perfectly divisible and inter changeable.

3. There are constant returns to scale so that prices do not rise or fall as output increases.

4. Effective demand and quantity of money change in the same proportion so long as there are any unemployed resources.

Given these assumptions, the Keynesian chain of causation between changes in the quantity of money and in prices is an indirect one through the rate of interest. How the increase in money supply can lead to the rise in aggregate expenditure and price level can be represented by the following scheme:—

$$Ms\uparrow \rightarrow r\downarrow \rightarrow I\uparrow \rightarrow AD\uparrow \rightarrow Y\uparrow$$

Where M_s stands for supply of money, *r*, I, AD, andY stand for rate of interset,investment, aggregate demand and income respectively.

According to this, when the quantity of money is increased, its first impact is on the rate of interest which tends to fall. Given the marginal efficieny of capital, a fall in the rate of interest will increase the volume of investment. The increased investment will raise effective demand through the multiplier effect there by increasing income, output and employment. Since the supply curve of factors of production is perfectly elastic in a situation of unemployment, wage and non wage factors are available at constant rate of remuneration. There being constant returns to scale, prices do not rise with the increase in output so long as there is any unemployment.

Under these circumstances, output and employment will increase in the same proportion as effective demand, and the effective demand will increase in the same proportion as the quantity of money. But "Once full employment is reached, output ceases to respond at all to chages in the supply of money and so in effective demand". The elasticity of supply of output in response to changes in the suppy, which was infinite as long as there was unemployment falls to zero. The entire effect changes in the supply of money is exerted on prices, which rise in exact proportion with the increase in effective demand.

Thus so long as there is unemployment, output

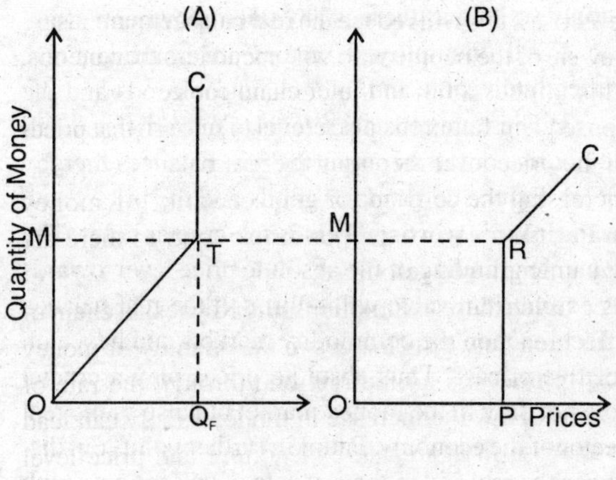

Fig. 1.17

will change in the same proportion as the quantity of money, and there will be no change in prices; and when there is full employment, prices will change in the same proportion as the quantity of money. **Therefore, the reformulated quantity theory of money stresses the point that with increase in the quantity of money prices rise only when the level of full employment is reached, and not before this.**

The reformulated quantity theory of money is illustrated in figure 1.17 (A) and (B) where OTC is the PRC is the price curve relating to the quantity of money. Panel A of the figure shows that as the quantity of money increases from O to M, the level of output also rises along the OT portion of the OTC curve. As the quantity of money reaches OM level, full employment output OQ_f is being produced. But after point cannot raise output beyond the full employment level OQ_f.

Panel B of the figure shows the relationship between quantity of money and prices. So long as there is unemployment, prices remain constant whatever the increase in the quntity of money. Prices start rising only after the full employment level is reached. In the figure, the price level OP remains constant at the OM quantity of money corresponding to the full employment level of output OQ_f But an increase in the quantity of money above OM raise prices in the same proportion as the quantity of money. This is shown by the RC portion of the price cutve PRC.

SUPERIORITY OF THE KEYNESIAN THEORY OVER THE TRADITIONAL QUANTITY THEORY OF MONEY

The Keynesian theory of moeny and prices is superior to the traditional quantity theory of money for the following reasons.

1. Keynes's reformulated quantity theory of money is superior to the traditional approach in that he discards the old view that the relationship between the quantity of money and prices is direct and proportion. Instead, he establishes an indirect and non-proportional relationship between quantity of money and prices.

2. In establishing such a relationship, Keynes brought about a transition from a pure monetary theory of prices to a monetary theory of output and employment. In so doing, he integrates monetary theory with value theory. He integtates monetary theory of output and employment through the rate of interest. The Keynesian theory is, therefore, superior to the traditional quantity theory of money because it does not keep the real and compartments with 'no doors or windows between the theory of value and theory of money and prices.

3. The traditional quantity theory is based on the unrealistic assumption of full employment of resources. Under this assumption, a given increases in the quantity of money always leads to a proportionate increase in the price level. **Keynes,** or the other hand, believes that full employment is an exception.

4. Further, the Keynesian theory is superior to the traditional quantity theory of moeny in that it emphasises important policy umplications. The traditional theory believes that every increases in the quantity of money leads to inflation. Keynes,on the other hand, establishes that so long as there is unemployment, the rise in prices is gradual and there is no danger of inflation.

PATINKIN'S INTERGATION OF MONETARY AND VALUE THEORY: THE REAL BALANCE EFFECT

Don Patinkin in his monumental work Money, Interest and Prices criticised the cambridg economists for the homogeneity postulate and the dichotomisation of goods and money markets and reconciles the two markets through the **real balance effect.**

The homogeneity postulate states that the demand and supply of goods are affected only by relative prices. It means that a doubling of money prices will have no effect on the demand and supply of goods. Mathematically, the demand and supply fuctions for goods are homogenous of degree zero in prices alone. Thus, this homogenetity postulate precludes the price level from market. **Patinkin** criticises this postulate for its failure to have any determinate theory of money and prices.

Another closely related assumption which Patinkin criticises is the dichotomisation of the goods and many markets in the neo-classical analysis. This dichomisation means that the relative price level is determined by the demand and supply of goods, and the absolute price level is determined by the demand and supply of money. Like the homogenetiy postulate, this assumption also implies that the price level has absolutely no effect on the monetary sector of the economy, and the level of monetary prices, in turn, has no effect on the real sector of the economy.

After condemning the neo-classical assumptions outlined above, **Patinkin** integrates the money market and the goods market of the economy which depend not only on relative prices the real pucchasing power of the stock of cash holding of the people.

When the price level changes, it affects the purchasing power of people's cash holdings which in turn, affects the demand and supply of goods. This is the **real balance effect.** Patinkin denies the existences of the homogeneity postulate and the dichotomistion assumption through this effect. For this, Patinkin introduces the stock of real balance (M/P) held by community as an influence on their demand for goods.

Thus the demand for a commodity depends upon real balance as well as relative prices. Now if the price level rises, this will reduce the real balance (purchasing power) of the people who will spend less than before. This implies a fall in the demand for goods and the consequent fall in the price level. Contrariwise, a fall in the price level increases the real balances thereby increasing the demand for goods and the price level. In **Patinkin's words:** "This is the crucial point. The dynamic grouping of the absolute price level towards its equilibrium value will—through the real balance effect reaction the commodity markets and hence on relative prices." Thus absolute prices play a crucial role not only in the money market but also in the real sector of the economy. Patinkin further points out that "once the real and monetary data of an economy with outside money are specified, the equilibrium values of relative prices, the rate of interest, and the absolute price level are simultaneously determined by all the markets of the economy." In this way Patinkin also introduces the real balance effect in the general equilibrium analysis.

Besides removing the classical dichotomy and the homogeneity postulate and integrating the monetary and value theory through the real balance effect, Patinkin also validates the quantity theory conclusion. According to Patinkin, the real balance implies that people do not suffer from **"money illusion."** They are interested only in the real value of their cash holdings. In other words, they hold money for **'what it will buy.'** This means that a doubling of the quantity of money will lead to a doubling of the price level, but relative prices and the real balances will remain constant and the equilibrium of the economy will not be changed.

The Patinkin analysis is illustrated diagrammatically in figure 1.18 by using the IS and LM curves because the IS curve represents the goods sectorand the LM cutve represents the monetary sector of the economy. To begin with we take a situation when the economy is in equilibrium at OY_f level of income when the IS and LM curves intersect at point A and the rate of intersect is OR. Thus OY_f is the full employment level of income. Suppose at this level the quantity of money is increased, given the same rate of interest OR. The increased money supply, shown by LM_1 curve, leads to increased demand and the consequent rise in the price level. Further, this increased money supply raises the demand for bonds thereby lowering the rate of interest to OR_1. The fall in the rate of interest encourages investment and income which further increase the price level in goods market. The rise in the price level is implicit in the increase in income from OY_f to OY_1, at the new equilibrium point B.

At this stage, Patinkin's real balance effect starts operating to restore the full employment equilibrium level OY_f. With the rise in the price level, the real balance of the people are reduced who accordingly start spending less than before. This leads to a fall in the demand for goods and consequent fall in the prices level. On the other hand, to maintain the same real balances, people increase the demands for money and consequently the rate of interest rises. These are shown by the upward shifting of the LM_1 curve to its original position as th LM curve and of the rate of interest to OR from OR_1 respectively. Thus the full employment equilibrium is reestablished at OY_f level through the real balance effect.

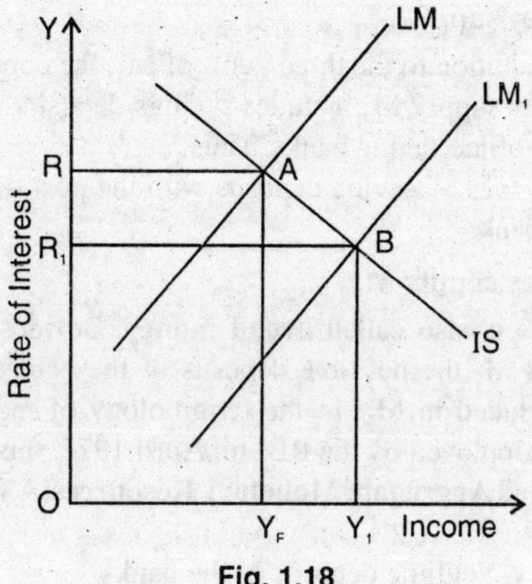

Fig. 1.18

SUPPLY OF MONEY

By money supply we mean the total volume of monetary media of exchange available to the community for use in connection with the economic activity of the country. There are three alternative views regarding the definition of money supply. The most common view is associated with the traditional and Keynesian thinking which stresses the medium of exchange function of money. According to this view, money supply is defined as currency with the public and demand deposits with commercial banks (M_1).

The second definition is broader and is associated with the modern quantity theorists headed by **Friedman.** Prof. Friedman defines the money supply at any moment of times as "literally the number of dollors people are carrying around in their pockets, the number of dollars they have to their credit at banks in the forms of demand deposits, and also commercial bank time deposits. Thus this definition includes M_1 plus time deposits of commercial banks in the supply of money. It stresses the store of value function of money or what Friedman says, a temporary abode of purchasing power.'

The third definition is the broadest and is associated with **Gurley and show.** According to them—

Money Supply = Demand Deposits + Currency with the public + Time Deposits + Deposits of saving banks

FOUR CONCEPT OF MONEY SUPPLY

From April 1977, the Reserve Bank has adopted four concepts of money supply in its analysis of the quantum of and variations in money supply. These four concepts of measures of money supply are explained below.

1. Money supply M_1 or Narrow Money

This is the narrow measure of money supply as defined above and is compose of the following items:

$$M_1 = C + DD + OD$$

where

C = Currency with the public

DD = Demand deposits of banks,

OD = Other deposits of the RBI.

2. Money supply M_2

In addition to the three items of M_1, the concept of money supply M_2 includes savings deposits with the post office saving banks. Thus,

$M_2 = M_1$ + saving deposits with the post office saving bank.

3. Money supply M_3

This is also called **broad money.** Besides the items of M_1 the net time deposits of the banks are also included in M_3. In the terminology of money supply employed by the RBI till April 1977, this M_3 was called **Aggregate Monetary Resources**(AMR). Thus

M_3 + Net time deposits of the banks.

4. Money Supply M_4

The measure M_4 of money supply includes not only all the items of M_3 described above but also the total deposits with the post office savings organisation. However, this excludes contribution's made by the public to the national saving certificates. Thus,

$M_4 = M_3$ + Total Deposits of post office saving organistion.

HIGH POWERED MONEY

High powered money or what is also called **reserve money** or **monetary base** consists of currency issued both by Government and Reserve Bank of India. It is important to note that a part of currency issued is held by the public and a part is held by Banks as reserves. Accordingly, the high powered money can be obtained as sum of currency held by the public and the part held by the banks as reserves.Thus

$$H = C + R$$

Where

H = The amount of high powered money,

C = Currency held by the public,

R = Cash reserves of currency with the banks.

THE THEORY OF MONEY SUPPLY

The theory of money supply explains what determines the stock or suply of money in the economy. The theory of money supply is based on the supply of and demand for high powered money. Some economists call it **'The H Theory of Money Supply'**. However it is more popularly called **'Money multiplier Theory of Money Supply'** because it explains the determination of money supply as a certain multiple of the high powered money. How the high powered money (H) is related to the total money supply is graphically depicted in figure 1.19. The base of this figure shows the supply of high powered money (H), while the top of the figure shows the total stock of money supply. It will be seen that the total stock of money supply (that is, the top) is determined by a multiple of the high powered money (H). It will be further seen that whereas currency held by the publlic uses the same amount of high powered money, that is, there is one to one relationship between the currency held by the public and the use of high powered money. In sharp contrast to this, bank deposits are a multiple of the cash reserves which are part of the supply of high powered money. That is, one rupee of high powered money kept as bank reserves gives rise to much more amount of deposits. Thus, the relationship between money supply and the high powered money is determined by the money multiplier. The money multiplier which we denote by m is the ratio of total money supply (M_s) to the stock of high powered money, That is,

$$m = \frac{M_s}{H}$$

The value of multiplier depends on the preference

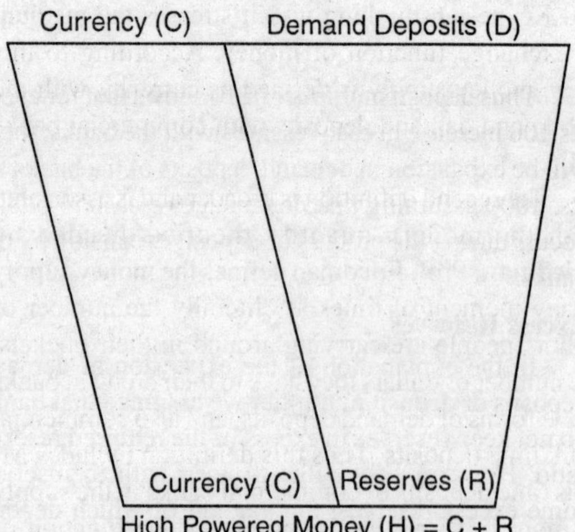

Fig. 1.19 : *The High Powered Money and the Stock of Total Money-Supply*

of the public to hold currency relative to deposits, (that is, ratio of currency to deposits which we denote by K) and bank's desired ratio of reserves to deposits.

Determinants of the Money Supply

There are two theories of the determination of the money supply. According to the first view, the money sypply is determined exogenously by the central bank. The second view holds that the money supply is detemined endogenously by changes in the economic activity which affect people's desire to hold currency relative to deposits, the rate of interest, etc.

Thus the determinants of money supply are both exogenous and endogenous which can be described broadly as: the minimum cash reserve ratio, the level of bank reserves, and the desire of the people to hold currency relative to deposits. The last two determinants together are called the monetary base or the high powered money.

The Deposit Multiplier

The ratio of change in total deposits to a change in reserves is called the **deposit multiplier** which depends on cash reserve ratio. The value of deposit multiplier is the reciprocal of cash reserve ratio. Thus

$$d_m = \frac{1}{r}$$

where d_m = deposit multiplier
r = cash reserve ratio

If cash reserves ratio is 10 per cent of deposits, then

$$d_m = \frac{1}{0.10} = 10$$

Thus deposit multiplier of 10 shows that for every Rs.100 increase in cash reserves with the banks, there will be expansion in demand deposits of the banks by Rs. 1000 assuming that no leakage of cash to public occurs during the process of deposit expansion by the banks.

Excess Reserves

In the explanation of the expansion of demand deposits or deposit multiplier we assumed that banks do not keep reserves in excess of the required reserve ratio. However banks like to keep with themselves some excess reserves, the amount of which depend on the extent of liquidity (i.e. availability of cash with them) and profitability of making investment and rate of interest on loans advanced to busiess firms. Therefore, the desired reserve ratio is greater than the statutory minimum required reserve ratio. Obviously, the holding of excess reserves by the banks also reduce the value of deposit multiplier.

MONEY MULTIPLIER

Theory of money supply explains how a given supply of high powered money (wich is also called monetary base or reserve money), leads to multiple expansion in money supply through the working of money multiplier. We have seen above how a small increase in reserves of currency with the banks leads to a multiple expansion in demand deposits by the banks through the process of deposit multiplier and thus causes growth of money supply in the economy. Deposit multiplier measures how much increase in demand deposits (or money supply) occur as a result of a given increase in cash reserves with the banks depending on the required reserve ratio *(r)* if there are no cash drainage from the banking system. But in the real world drainage of currency do take place which reduce the extent of expansion of money supply following the increase in cash reserves with the banks. Therefore, the deposit multiplier exaggerates the actual increase in money supply from a given increase in cash reserves with the banks. In contrast, money multiplier which takes into account these leakages of currency from the banking system and therefore measures actual increase in money supply when the cash reserves with the banks increases. The money multiplier can be defined as increase in cash reserves (or high power money), drainage of currency having been taken into account. Therefore, money multiplier is less than the deposit multiplier. Let M stand for total money supply, H for high powered money, the money multiplier *(m)* is then given by

$$m = \frac{M}{M}$$

Derivation of Money Multiplier

We can derive the equilibrium stock of money supply and the value of money multipilier by considering the supply of and demand for (1) high powered money, and (2) the total money stock. The

Central Bank of a country can control and fix the supply of high powered money which we denote by H. On the other hand, demand for high powered money comes from (1) the public who want to use it as currency for making payments for goods and services and for other motives, and for other motives and (2) the banks who require it for keeping reserves. As mentioned above, the public wishes to have a certain ratio of currency to deposits, which we denote by K and the banks desire to have a certain ratio of reserves to deposits, which we call *r*. The desired amount of currency by the public which we denote by C will be equal to the currency deposits ratio (k) multuplied by total deposits which we all as D. Thus

$$C = KD$$

Let R represent the total reserves desired by the banks which will be equal to the desired reserve deposit ratio *(r)* times the deposits, that is, $R = rD$. Thus, the total demand for high powered money will be equal to

$$= C + R$$
$$= KD + rD$$
$$= (K + r)\,D$$

The monetary equilibrium between the supply of and demand for high powered money is given by:

$$H = (K + r)\,D \qquad ...(1)$$

where

H = The supply of high powered money.

We now consider the supply of and demand for total money stock. Let M stand for the total money supply. Demand for total money supply or stock depends upon demand of public for currency and bank deposits. Public's demand for currency will be equal to KD where K represents the desired currency deposit ratio and D stands for bank deposits. Since in the state of monetary equilibrium the supply of and demand for money will be equal. we have

$$M = C + D$$
$$M = KD + D$$
$$= (1 + K)\,D \qquad ...(2)$$

The equation (1) describes the monetary equilibrum regarding high powered money and the equation (2) describes the monetary equilibrium with regard to the total money supply. Now, the money multiplier which we denote by *m* is the ratio of total money supply (M) to the quantity of high powered money (H). This, dividing equation (2) by equation (1) we get the expression for money multiplier as under:

$$m = \frac{M}{H}$$

$$m = \frac{(1+K)\,D}{(r+K)\,D}$$

$$m = \frac{1+K}{r+K} \qquad ...(3)$$

This money multiplier is equal to $\frac{1+K}{r+K}$ whose value depends on currency deposit ratio (K) and reserve deposit ratio *(r)*. It is worth mentioning that K and *r* are behavioural ratios depending on the behavior of the public and banks and are not therefore determined by the policy of Reserve Bank.

We can obtain the value of money multiplier if we know the values of desired currency deposits ratio (K) of the public and desired reserves ratio *(r)* of the banks. Suppose $K = 0.4$ and $r = 0.2$. We can then obtain the value of multiplier:

$$m = \frac{1+K}{r+K}$$

$$= \frac{1+0.4}{0.2+0.4} = \frac{1.4}{0.6} = 2.33$$

MONEY SUPPLY AND ITS DETERMINANTS

Rearranging money multiplier equation (3), we can know the determinants of money supply in the economy. Thus

$$\frac{M}{H} = \frac{1+K}{r+K}$$

$$M = H\left(\frac{1+K}{r+K}\right)$$

or, $$M = H.m \qquad ...(4)$$

It follows from (4) that money supply in an economy is determined by–

(a) Supply of high – powered money (H)

(b) The value of money multiplier (*m*)

While the Central Bank of a country can control the supply the supply of high powered money, the value of multiplier is determined by two behaviour ratios, currency deposit ratio (K) of the public and desired reserve deposit ratio (r) of banks.

From the equation (4) expressing the determinants of money, it follows that money supply will increase:

1. When the supply high powered money H increases;

2. When the currrency– deposit ratio decreases;

3. When the reserve–deposit ratio falls.

The relation between the money supply and high–powered money is illustrated in figure 1.20. The horizontal curve H_s shows the given supply of high powered money. The curve H_d shows the demand for high–powered money. The slope of the H_d curve is equal to the term $\left(\frac{r+K}{1+K}\right)$. Given r, k and H_s, the equilibrium money supply is OM. If the money supply is larger than this, say OM_1, there will be excess demand of high–powered money. On the contrary, a less than OM money supply will mean less demand for high–powered money.

If there is an increase in any one of the ratios r and k, there would be an increase in the demand for high–powered money. This is shown by the H'_d curve in figure 1.20 where the increase in the demand for high–powered money leads to decline in the money

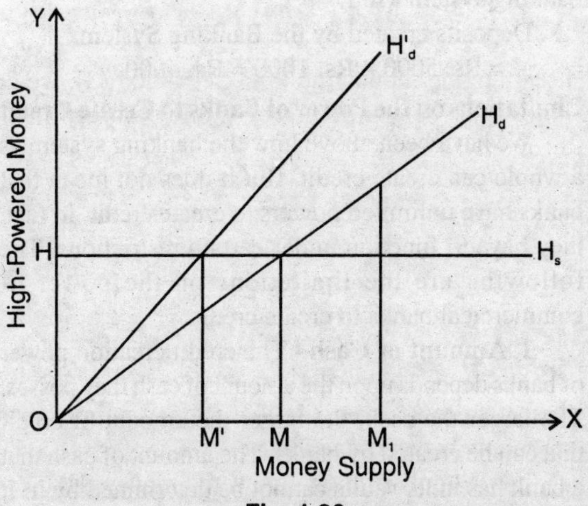

Fig. 1.20

supply to OM:

The supply of money varies directly with changes in the high–powered money. This is shown in figure 1.21. An increase in the supply of high–powered money by ΔH shifts the H_s curve upward to H_s. At E, the demand and supply of high–powered money is in equilibrium and money supply is OM. With the increase in the supply of high–powered money to H_s, the supply of money also increases to OM_1 at the new equilibrium point E_1. Further 1.21 reveals the operation of the money multiplier. With the increase in the high–powered money by ΔH, the money supply increases by $m.\Delta H = \Delta M$ Where m is the money multiplier.

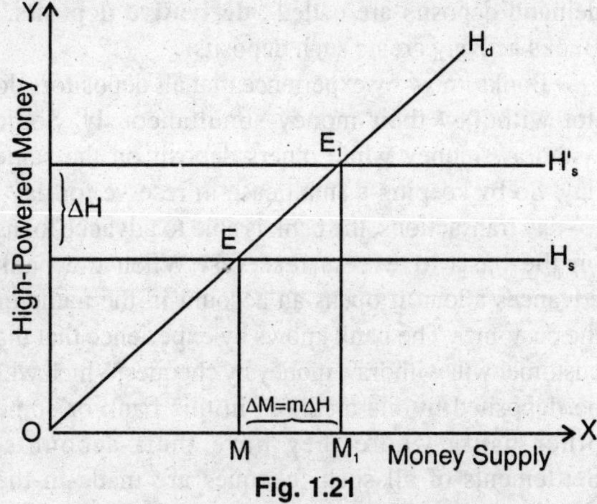

Fig. 1.21

Factors Determining Money Supply in India

Reserve Bank of India classifies factors determining money supply into the four following categories–

A.Government borrowing from the banking system;

B. Borrowing of the private or commercial sector from the banking suystem;

C. Changes in net foreign assets held by the Reserve Bank of India caused by changes in balance of payments position; and

D. Government's currency liabilities to the public.

THE CREATION OF CREDIT

The creation of credit or deposits is one of the most important functions of commercial banks. Like other corportions, banks aim at earning profits. For this purpose, they accept cash in demand deposits and advance a loan on credit to customers. When a bank advances a loan, it does not pay the amount in cash. But it opens a current account in his name and allows him to withdraw the required sum by cheques. In this way, the bank creates credit or deposits.

Demand deposits arise in two ways: **One**, when customers deposits currency with commercial banks, and **two**, when banks advance loans, discount bills, provide overdraft facilities, and make investments through bonds and securities. The first type of demand deposits are called **"Primary deposits."** Banks of demand deposits are called **"derivative deposits."** Banks actively create such deposits.

Banks know by experience that all depositors do not withdraw their money simultaneously. Some withdraw money while others deposit on the same day. So by keeping a small cash in reserve for day–to–day transactions, the bank is able to advance loans on the basis of excess reserves. When the bank advances a loan it opens an account in the name of the customer. The bank knows by experience that the customer will withdraw money by cheques Which will be deposited by his creditors in this bank or some other bank, where they have their accounts. Settlements of all such cheques are made in the clearing house. The same procedure is followed in other banks. Thus banks are able to create credit or deposits by keeping a small cash in reserves and lending the remaining amount.

The bank provides overdraft facility to a customer on the basis of some security. It enters the amount of the overdraft in the existing account of the customer and allows him to draw cheques for the overdraft amount agreed upon. It thus creates a deposit.

The Process of Credit Creation

Let us explain the acutal process of credit creation. We have seen above that the ability of banks to create credit depends on the fact that banks need only a small percentage of cash to deposits. If banks kept 100 per cent cash against deposits, there would be no credit creation. Modern banks do not keep 100 per cent cash reserves. They are legally required to keep a fixed percentage of their deposits in cash say 10, 15, or 20 per cent. They lend and/or invest the remaning amount. Thus it is the required cash reserve ratio that becomes the basis of credit creation. The smaller the required cash reserve ratio the larger the expansion of deposits or credit. Thus total deposits created by banking system is

$$= \frac{1}{r} \cdot D$$

where

D = Deposits of the bank

r = required cash reserve ratio

In the above equation, $\frac{1}{r}$ is called the **deposit multiplier** with determines the limits to deposit expansion by a bank. If a bank has Rs. 1000 in deposits and its legal minimum ratio or the required cash reserves ratio (r) is 20 per cent; it can create credit to the extent of Rs. 5000.

$$= \frac{1}{r} \cdot D = \frac{1}{0.20} \cdot 1000$$

$$= 5000$$

The bank is "loaned up" to the limit of Rs. 5000 and it cannot create more deposits till its reserves increase further.

We are now a position to state how much depsits have been created by the banking system out of the currency deposits of Rs. 1000.

Total Deposits =Rs. 5000

Out of the total deposits of Rs. 5000, the deposits of Rs. 1000 in cash was made in the bank system. The remaining deposits have been created by the banking system itself.

Deposits created by the Banking System

= Rs. 5000 – Rs. 1000 = Rs. 4000

Limitations on the Power of Banks to Create Credit

We have been above how the banking system as a whole can create credit. But it does not mean that banks have unlimited powers to create credit. In fact, they have to function under certain restrictions. The following are the limitations on the power of commercical banks to create credit.

1. Amount of Cash– The credit creation power of banks depends upon the amount of cash they posses. The larger the cash, the larger the amount of credit that can be created by banks. The amount of cash that a bank has in its vaults cannot be determined by it. It depends upon the primary deposits with the bank.

2. Proper Securities– An important factor that limits the power of bank to create credit is the availability of adequate securities. Of proper securities are not available with the public, a bank cannot create credit.

3. Banking Habits of the People– The banking habits of the people also govern the power of credit creation on the part of banks. If people are not in the habit of using cheques, the grant of loans will lead to the withdrawl of cash from the credit creation stream of the banking system. This reduces the power of banks to create credit to the desired level.

4. Minimum Legal Reserve Ratio– The minimum legal reserve ration of cash to deposists fixed by the central bank is an important factor which determines the power of banks to create credit. The higher this ratio (r), the lower the power of banks to create credit; and the lower the ratio, the higher the power of banks to create credit.

5. Behaviour of Other Banks– The power of credit creation is further limited by the behaviour of other banks.If some of the banks do not advance loans to the extent required of the banking system, the chain of credit expansion will be broken.

6. Economic Climate– Banks cannot continue to create credit limitlessly. Their power to create credit depends upon the economic climate in the country.

7. Credit Control Policy of the Central Bank– The power of commercial banks of create credit is also limited by the credit control policy of the central bank. The central bank incfluences the amount of cash reserves with banks by open market operations, discount rate policy and varying margin requirements. Accordingly, it affects the credit expansion or contraction by commercial banks.

FUCTIONS OF MONEY

Money is a matter of functions four, A medium, a measure, a standard, a store.

Money in a modern economy performs important functions which have been classified by Kinley as follow:

Primary Functions

(*a*) Medium of Exchange
(*b*) Measure of Value

Secondary Functions

(*a*) Standard of Deferred Payment
(*b*) Store of Value
(*c*) Transfer of value

Contingent Functions

(*a*) Distribution of National Income
(*b*) Equating of Marginal Utilities
(*c*) Basis of Credit
(*d*) Liquidity to Wealth

> If number of goods is n, the number of exchange ratios under barter economy will be $\frac{n(n-1)}{2}$. But with money, there will be only n money prices.

INFLATION AND DEFLATION

By inflation, in ordinary language, we mean a general rise in prices. However, when discussing inflation, we are thinking of a persistent rise in prices rather than a once–for–all rise in prices (which may be, for example, brought about by a bad weather leading to destruction of crops).

INFLATIONARY GAP

Inflationary gap arises when consumption and investment spending together is greater than the full employment GNP level. This means that people are demanding more goods and services than can be produced. In other wores, the amount by which the actual aggregate demand exceeds the level of national income corresponding to full employment is known as **inflationary gap** because this excess in aggregate demand causes inflation or rise in prices in the country.

Diagramatically, the inflationary gap EE' is shown in figure 1.22. Y_f is the full employment level of income which is arrived at by the equality of aggregate consumption and investment expenditure line C + I + G and the 45° line representing aggregate supply of goods at point E. At the full employment level, there is excess demand because consumers, firms and government expenditure more than the available output at current prices by EE' amount. This increased demand or expenditure shifts the C + I + G curve upward to C + I + G′ position. This intersects the 45° line at E_1 so that the total expenditure is $E_1 Y_1$ while the available output is EY_f. Thus E_1A = EE' is the inflationary gap.

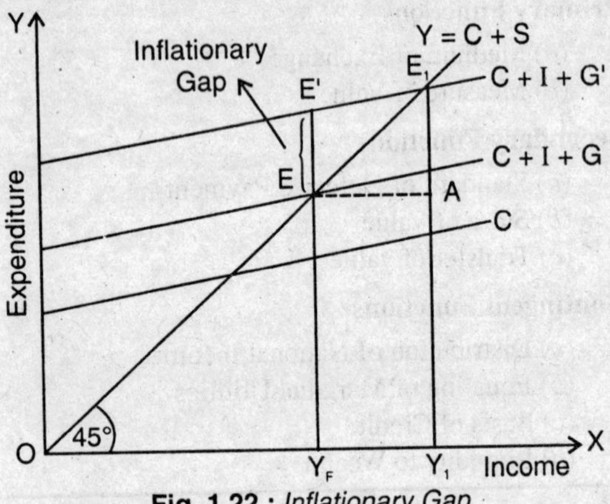

Fig. 1.22 : *Inflationary Gap*

The inflationary gap can be wiped out by increase in saving so that aggregate demand is reduced. Another soluation is to raise the value of available output to match the disposable income. But output cannot be increased during the short run. Private investment cannot be reduced while the government expenditure is autonomous. So both cannot be reduced during the short run. Thus the only alternatives left to the government are to increase taxation and induce saving.

DEFLATIONARY GAP

Deflationary gap represents the difference between the acutal aggregate demand and the aggregate demand which is required to establish the equilibrium at full employment level of income.

The concept of deflationary gap is illustrated in figure 1.23 in which along the x–axis national income is measured and long the y–axis expenditure is measured. Suppose national income at the equilibrium level of full employment is equal to OY_f. Now the equilibrium level of income and employment would be established at OY_f when aggregate demand (C + I +G) is equal to Y_fE (which is equal to national income OY_f). But in the real world if aggregate demand is less than the full employment level of income OY_f or it is less than Y_FE then the problem of deficiency of aggregate demand will arise. Therefore, EH in figure 1.23 represents deflationary gap.

It should be carefully understood that due to deflationary gap E, the level of national income and employment will decline. The decline in national income and employment will not only be equal to the deflationary gap EH but it will be much greater than this. The decline in national income is determined by the value of the multiplier. In figure 1.23 when aggregate demand is Y_FH i.e, deflationary gap is equal to EH, then the aggregate demand curve is C + I + G' which cuts the 45° line at point Q as a result of which equilibrium is established at OY_1 level of national income. It will be seen from figure 1.23 that OY_1 is less than full employment level of income OY_f

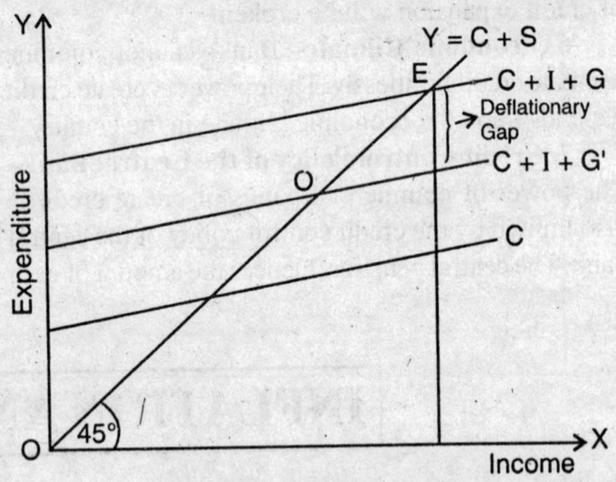

Fig. 1.23 : *Deflationary Gap*

DEMAND–PUSH INFLATION

Basically, inflation represents a stuation where by the pressure of aggregate demand for goods and services exceeds the available supply of output. In such a situation, the rise in price level is the natural consequence. Now this excess of aggregate demand over supply may be the result of more than one force at work. As we know, aggregate demand is the sum of consumer's spending on goods and services, government spending on goods and services and net investment being contemplated by the entrepreneurs. Inflation is thus caused when aggregate demand for all purposes–consumption, investment and government expenditure, exceeds the supply of goods at current prices. Thus is demand pull inflation.

Demand–pull inflation can be illustrated with aggregate demand and aggregate supply curves. Consider figure 1.24 in which aggregate demand and suply are measured along the x–axis and general price level along the Y–axis. Curve AS represents the aggregate supply which rises upward in the beginning but when at full employment level aggregate supply OY_f is reached, aggregate supply curve AS takes a vetical shape. This is because after the level of full employment, supply of output cannot be increase. When aggregate demand curve is AD_1, the equilibrium is at thc full cmployment level where price level OP_1 is determined.

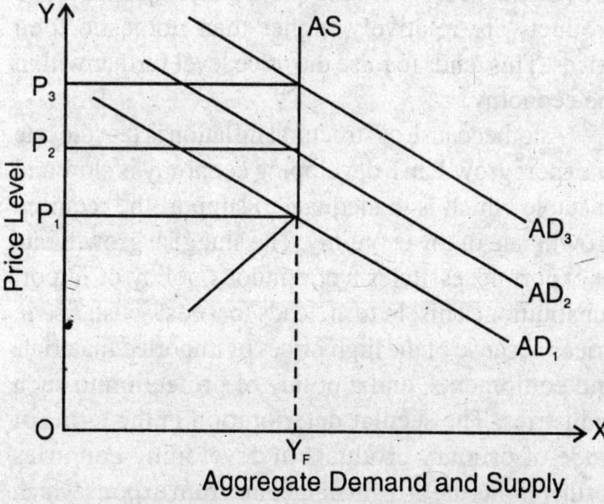

Fig. 1.24 : *Demand-Pull Inflation*

Now, if the aggregate demand increases to AD_2 and aggregate supply cannot be raised, the price level will rise to OP_2 due to the excess of demand. If the aggregate demand further increases to AD_3, the price level rises to OP_3 under the pressure of more demand.

COST–PUSH INFLATION

We can visualise a situtation where, even though there is no increase in aggregate demands, prices may still rise. This may happen if costs, particularly the wage costs, go on rising. Now as the level of employment rises, the demand for workers also rises so that the bargaining position of the workers becomes stronger. To exploit this situation, they may ask for an increase in wage rates which are not justifiable on grounds either of a prior rise of productivity or of cost of living.

The employers in a situation of high demand and employment are more agreeable to concede these wage claims, because they hope to pass on these rises in costs to the consumers in the shape of rise in prices. If this happens, we have another inflationary factor at work and the inflation thus caused is called the **wage–induced** or **cost–push inflation.**

Besides the increase in wages of lablur without any increase in its productivity, there is another factor responsible for cost–push inflation. This is the increase in the profit margin by the firms, working under monopolistic or oligopolistic conditions and as a result charging higher prices from the consumers. In the former case when the cause of cost–push–inflation is the rise in wages, it is called **wage–push inflation** and in the latter case when the cause of cost–push inflation is the rise in profit margins, it is called **profit–push–inflation.**

The cost–push–inflation can also be illustrated with the aggregate demand and supply curves. Consider figure 1.25 where aggregate supply and demand are measured along the x–axis and price level along the Y–axis. AD is the aggregate demand curve and AS_1 and AS_3 curves are aggregate supply curves.

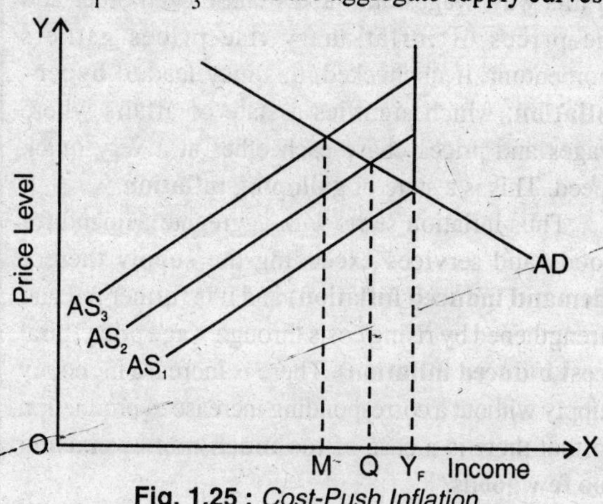

Fig. 1.25 : *Cost-Push Inflation*

Since aggregate supply curves become vertical at full emloyment level their vertical portions coincide.

Now, when wages increase, and as a result cost of production increases, the aggregate supply curve would shift upward. As will be seen in figure 1.25, when there is an upward shift in the aggregate supply curve form AS_1, to AS_2 due to the rise in wages, price level rises from OP_1 to OP_2. It should be noted that price level OP_1 corresponds to the full employment, since aggregate demand curve AD intersects original aggregate supply curve AS at full employment level OY_f. If the wages further rise and the aggregate supply curve shifts upwards to AS_3, the equilibrium price level rises to OP_3.

We have thus seen above that cause of inflation may be that aggregate demand has become excessive in relation to supply of output (demand–pull–inflation) or it may be that costs have risen because of the increase in wages of labour or profit margins of the producers (cost–pust–inflation).

WAGE-PRICE SPIRAL

A rise in prices reduces the real consumption of wage earners. They will, therefore, press for higher money wages to compensate themselves for the higher cost of living. Now an increase in wages, if granted, will raise the cost of production, and therefore, entrepreneurs will be tempted to raise the cost of living still further and the workers ask for still higher wages. In this way, wages and prices chase each other and the prices of inflationary rise prices gathers momentum. If unchecked, this may lead to **hyper–inflation**, which signifies a state of affairs where wages and prices chase each other at a very quick speed. This is a state of **galloping inflation**.

Thus inflation starts with aggregate demand for goods and services exceeding the supply thereof (**demand induced inflation**) and it is further fed and strengthened by rising costs through wage price spiral (**cost induced inflation**). There is increase in money supply without a corresponding increase in production so that there is a case of **too much money chasing too few goods.**

STRUCTURAL INFLATION

The structuralist school of South America stresses structural rigidities as the principal cause of inflation in developing countries.

The structuralists hold the view that inflation is necessary with growth. According to this view, as the economy develops rigidities arise which lead to structural inflation. In the initial phase of economic development, there are increases in non–agricultural incomes accompanied by high growth rate of population that tend to increase the demand for good. But its domestic supply is inelastic, thereby raising the prices of food products. The output of food does not increase when prices rise because their production is inelastic due to a defective system of land tenure and other rigidities in the form of lack of irrigation, finance, markting etc. and bad harvests. To prevent the continuous rise in the prices of food products, food can be imported. But it is not possible to import food in large quantities due to a foreign exchange constraint. Moreover, the prices of imported food products are relatively higher than domestic food prices. This tends to raise the price level further within the economy.

Another cause of structural inflation is that the rate of export growth in a developing economy is slow and unstable which is inadequate to support the required growth rate of the economy. The sluggish growth rate of export necessitates a continuous policy of import substitution. This, in turn, leads to a cost–push rise in prices because of the high prices of imported materials and equipments, and a policy of protection to such industries. The secular deterioration in the terms of trade of primary products in developing conntries further limits the growth of income from exports which often leads to exchange rate devaluation.

So far as the money supply is concerned, it automatically expands when prices rise in a developing country. As prices rise, firms need larger funds from banks. And the government needs more money to finance large deficits, in order to meet its expanding expenditure, and wages of its employees. For this, it borrows from the Central Bank which leads to monetary expansion and to a further rise in the rate of inflation.

Thus, structural inflation may result from supply inelasticities, downward inflexibility of prices and income increases in a developing country. Increase in money supply is essential but it plays a permissive and supplimentary role in the inflationary process.

STAGFLATION

The word "Stagflation" is the combination of stag plus flation, taking 'stag' from stagnation and 'flation' from inflation. Thus it is a paradoxical situation where the economy experiences stagnation or unemployment alongwith a high rate of inflation. It is, therefore, also called **inflationary recession**. In other words, the stagflation refers to a situation when a high rate of inflation occurs simultancously with a high rate of unemployment.

One of the principal causes of stagflation has been restriction in the aggregate supply. When aggregate supply is reduced, there is a fall in output and employment, and the price level rises. A reduction in aggregate supply may be due to a restriction in labour supply. The restriction in labour supply, in turn, may be caused by a rise in money wages on account of strong unions or by a rise in the legal minimum wage rate, or by increased tax rates which reduce workeffort on the part of workers.

When wages rise, firms are forced to reduce production and employment. Consequently, there is a fall in real income and consumer expenditure. Since the decline in consumption will be less than the fall in real income, there will be excess demand in the commodity market which will push up the price level.

The rise in the price level, in turn, reduces output and employment in the following three ways:

(*a*) It reduces the real quantity of money, raises interest rates and brings a fall in investment expenditure.

(*b*) The rise in the price level reduces the real value of cash balances with the government and the private sector via the pigou effect which reduces their consumption expenditure.

(*c*) The rise in prices of domestic goods makes exports dearer to foreighers and makes exports goods relatively more attractive to domestic output and employment.

Restriction on aggregate supply may also be caused by external factors such as rise in the world prices of foods grains and crude aid prices. In all these cases, the domestic price level is raised by outside forces. When international prices of food grains and crude oil rise, they lead to the outflow of purchasing power away from domestic consumers. They accentuate inflation, raise wages and prices. As a result, the real quantity of money declines, interest rates rise and investment declines, via the pigou effect, and making exports dearer and imports attractive, domestic output and employment decline. They lead to **Stagflation**.

The phenomenon of stagflation is illustrated in figure 1.26, where employment is measured on the horizontal axis and the price level on the vertical axis.

The initial equilibrium is at E where aggregate demand curve AD intersects the aggregate supply curve AS and the price level is OP and the employment level is ON. When the aggregate supply is reduced due to any of the factors mentioned above, the aggregate supply curve S shifts to the left at AS_1. The new equilibrium is at E_1 where AS_1 intersects the AD curve. Now the price level rises from OP to OP_1 and the level of employment declines from ON to ON_1.

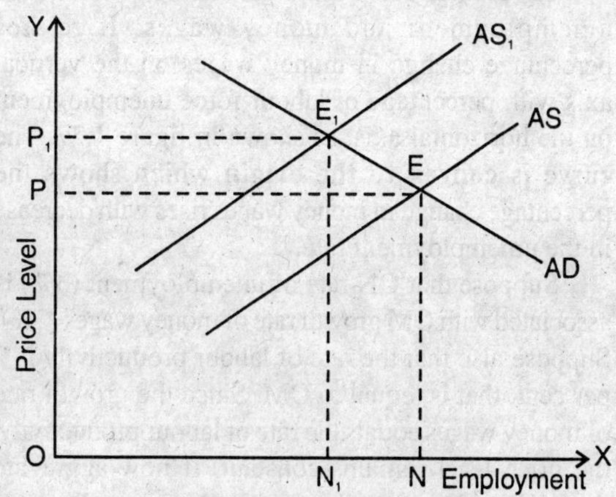

Fig. 1.26 : *Stagflation*

PHILLIPS CURVE

Professor Phillips urged there was a close link between the level of unemployment and the rate of wage increase. Phillips curve expresses an inverse

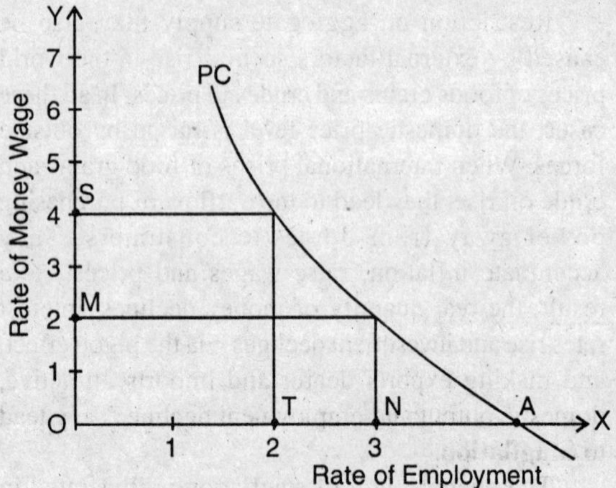

Fig. 1.27 : *Phillips Curve*

relationship between the rate of unemployment and the rate of increase in money wages.

Prof. Phillips studied the relationship between unemployment and changes in money wages in the U.K. over the period 1862–1957. As a result of this study, he seems to have discovered a stable and inverse relationship over the whole period between the rate of wage increase and the per cent of unemployment.

The Phillips curve depicts the **trade off** betweeen umemployment and money wages. It relates percentage change in money wages on the vertical axis with percentage of labour force unemployment on the horizontal axis, as shown in figure 1.27. The curve is **convex to the origin** which shows the percentage change in money wages rises with decrease in the umemployment rate.

Suppose that ON rate of unemployment (3%) is associated with OM growth rate of money wages (2%). Suppose also that the rate of labour productivity is 2 per cent, that is, equal to OM. Since the growth rate of money wages equals the rate of labour productivity, the price level remains constant. If now aggregate demand is increased, this lowers the unemployment rate to OT (2%) and raises the wages rate to OS (4%) per year. If lower productivity continues to grow at 2% per annum, the price level will also rise at the rate of 2 per cent per annum at OS in the figure.

Thus a money wage rate increase which in excess of labour productivity leads to inflation. To keep wage increase to the level of labour productivity (OM) in order to avoid inflation, ON rate of unemployment will have to be tolerated.

Samuelson and Solow extended the Phillip's analysis to the **trade off** between the level of unemployment and the rate of change in the level of prices. Thus, **the Phillips curve suggests that unemployment can always be reduced by having more inflation and that the inflation rate can also be reduced by having more unemployment.**

Its Criticism

Economists have criticised the phillips curve. They argue that the phillips curve relates to the short run and it does not remain stable. It shifts with changes in expectations of inflation. *In the long run, there is no trade off between inflation and employment.* These views have been expounded by *friedman and phelps* in what has come to be known as the "accelerationist" hypothesis.

According to friedman, the long run phillips curve is vertical.

Tobin's View : James Tobin in his presidential address before the American Economic Association in 1971 proposed a compromise between the negatively sloping and vertical phillips curve. Tobin believes that them is a phillips curve within limits, but as the economy expands and employment grows, the curve becomes even more fragile and vanishes until it becomes vertical at some critically low rate of unemployment. Thus Tobin's Phillips curve is kinked-shaped, a part like a normal phillips curve and the rest vertical, as shown in figure 1.28. In the figure Uc is the critical rate of unemployment at which the

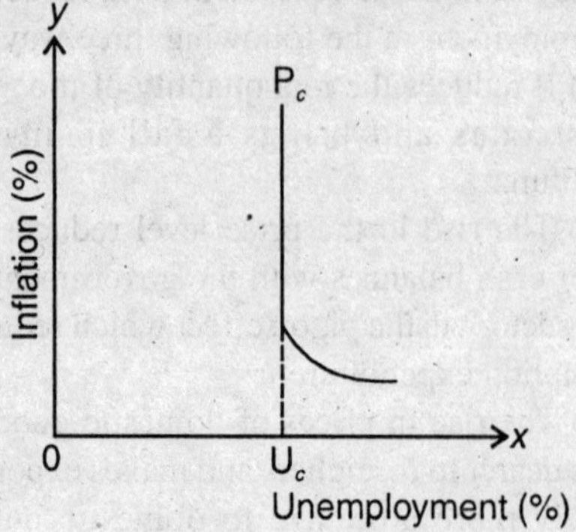

Fig. 1.28

phillips curve becomes vertical where there is no trade off between unemployment and in flation. According to Tobin, the vertical portion of the curve is not due to increase in the demand for more wages but emerges from imperfections of the labour market. At the Uc level, it is not possible to provide more employment because the job seekers have wrong skills or wrong age or sex or are in the wrong place.

Regarding the normal portion of the phillips curve which is negatively sloping, wages are sticky downward because labourers resist decline in their relative wages.

Solow's View : Like Tobin *Robert Solow* does not believe that the phillips curve is vertical at all rate of inflation. According to him, the curve is vertical at positive rates of inflation and is horizontal at negative rates of inflation as shown in figure 1.29.

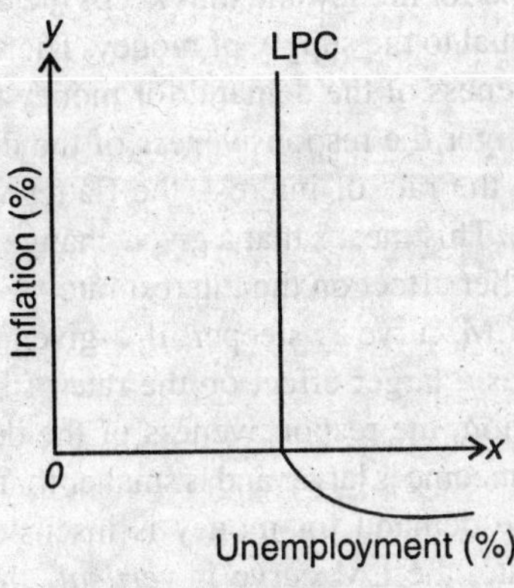

Fig. 1.29

Policy Implications of the phillips curve

The phillips curve has important policy implications. It suggests the extent to which monetary and fiscal policies can be used to control inflation without high levels of unemployment. In other words, it provides a guide line to the authorities about the rate of inflation which can be tolerated with a given level of unemployment. For this purpose, it is important to know the exact position of the phillips curve. If the curve is PC_1 as in figure 1.30, where there labour productivity and the wage rate are equal at point E, both full employment and price stability would be possible. Again a curve to the left of point E suggests full employment and price stability as consistent policy objectives. It implies that a lower level of inflation can be traded-off for a low level of unemployment. If, on the other hand, the phillips curve is PC as in the figure. It suggests that the authorities will have to choose between price stability and more unemployment. Thus by observing the position of the phillips curve the authorities can decide about the nature of monetary and fiscal policies to be adopted. For instance if the authorities find that the inflation rate P_2 is in compatible with the unemployment rate U_1 of figure 1.30, they would adopt such monetary and fiscal policies as to shift the phillips curve PC to the left in the position of PC_1 curve. This will give a better trade-off between a lower inflation rate P_1 with the same level of unemployment U_1.

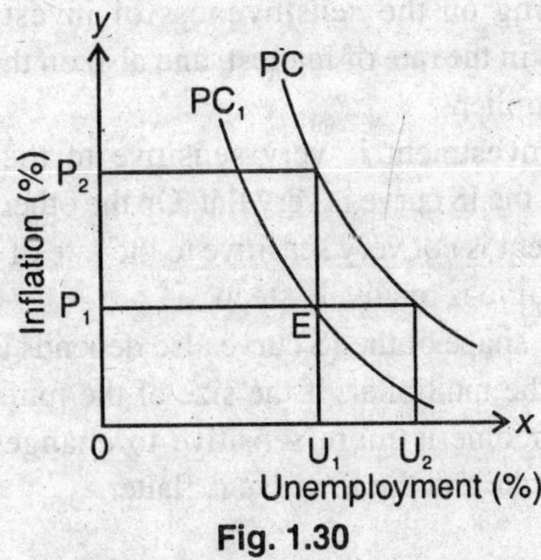

Fig. 1.30

IS AND LM FUNCTIONS : GENERAL EQUILIBRIUM OF PRODUCT AND MONEY MARKETS

The term IS is the shorthand expression of the equality of investment and saving which represents the product market equilibrium. On the other hand, the term LM is the shorthand expression of the equality of money demand and money supply and representy the money market equilibrium.

The Product Market

The product market is in equilibrium when saving and investment are equal. Saving is a direct function of the level of income,

$$S = f(y) \quad \text{....(1)}$$

Investment is a decreasing function of the interest

rate,

$$I = f(r) \quad ....(2)$$

In case of equilibrium, S = I

The IS Schedule reflects the equilibrium of the product market. It shows the combinations of interest rates and income levels where saving-investment equality takes place so that the product market of the economy is in equilibrium. It is also known as "real" equilibrium.

The slope of the IS curve

Figure 1.31 shows that the IS curve slopes downward from left to right. This negative slope reflects the increase in investment and income as the rate of interest falls. The IS curve may be Flat or steep depending on the sensitiveness of investment to changes in the rate of interest, and also on the size of the multiplier.

If investment is very sensitive to the rate of interest, the IS curve is very flat. On the other hand, if investment is not very sensitive to the rate of interest, the IS curve is relatively steep.

The shape of the IS curve also depends upon the size of the multiplier. If the size of the multiplier is large, income is more sensitive to changes in the interest rate and the IS curve is flatter.

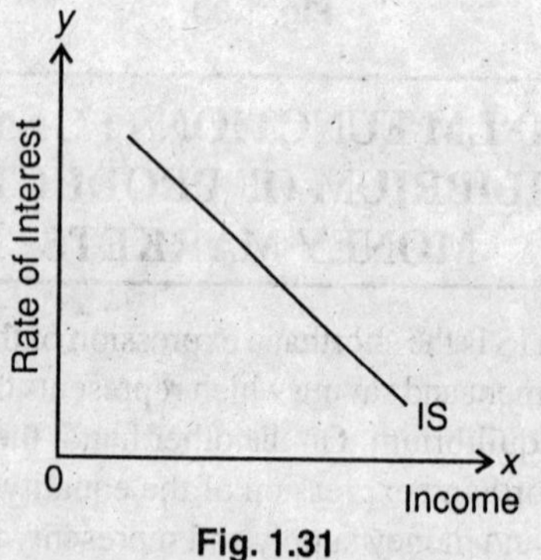

Fig. 1.31

A few more properties of the IS curve may be noted. *First,* the IS curve shifts to the right or left as a result of an increase or decrease in autonomous or government investment. *Second,* any point to the right of a given IS curve shows excess supply in the product market and any point to the left of an IS curve shows excess demand in the product market.

The Money Market

The money market is in equilibrium when the demand and supply of money are equal. Denoting L for money demand and M for money supply, in equilibrium L= M. The demand for money $L = L_t + L_s$, where L_t is the transactions demand for money which is a direct function of the level of income, $L_t = f(y)$. L_s is the speculative demand for money which is a decreasing function of the rate of interest, $L_s = f(r)$. Thus in money market equilibrium,

$$M = L_t(y) + L_s(r)$$

The Slope of the LM curve

The LM curve slopes upward from left to right because given the supply of money, an increase in the level of income increases the demand for money which leads to higher rate of interest. This, in turn, reduces the demand for money and thus keeps the demand for money equal to the supply of money. The smaller the responsiveness of the demand for money to income, and the larger the responsiveness of the demand for money to the rate of interest, the flatter will be the LM curve. This means that a given change in income has a smaller effect on the interest rate.

The LM curve is steeper, if a given change in income has a larger effect on the rate of interest. In this situation, the responsiveness of the demand for money to income is larger and is smaller for the interest rate. If the demand for money is insensitive to the interest rate, the LM curve is *vertical* that is, it is *perfectly inelastic.* This is shown in figure 1.32 as the portion from T above on the LM curve. In this case, a large change in the interest rate is accompanied by almost no change in the level of income to maintain

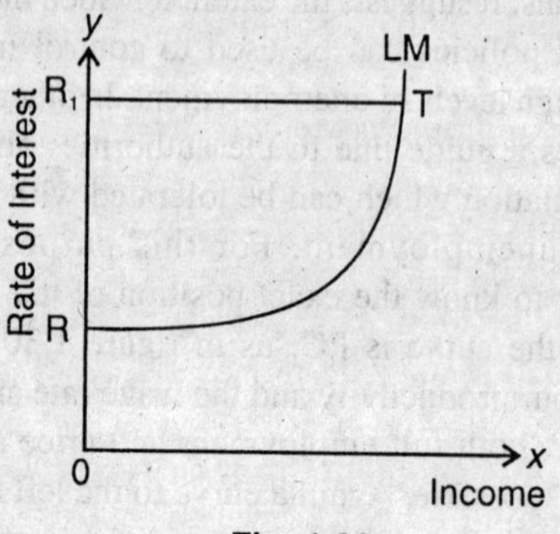

Fig. 1.32

money market equilibrium. If the demand for money is very sensitive to the rate of interest, the LM curve is *horizontal* that is, It is a *perfectly elastic.* In this case, a small change in the interest rate is accompanied by a large change in the level of income to maintain the money market equilibrium.

Shifts in the LM curve

The LM curve shifts downward to the right when the stock of money supply is increased and it shifts upward to the left if the stock of money supply is reduced.

The LM curve shifts upward to the left if there is an increase in the money demand function which raises the quantity of money demanded at the given interest rate and income level. On the other hand, the LM curve shifts downward to the left if there is a decrease in the money demand function which lowers the amount of money demanded at given levels of interest rate and income.

Another important property of the LM curve is that on any point to the right of the LM curve, there is excess demand for money in the money market, and on any point to the left of the LM curve, there is excess supply of money in the money market.

General Equilibrium of Product and Money Market

Now we study how these markets are brought into simultasneous equilibrium. It is only when the equilibrium pairs of in terest rate and income of the Is curve equal the equilibrium pairs of interest rate and income of the LM curve that the general equilibrium is established. In other words, when there is a single pair of interest rate and income level in the product and money markets that the two markets are in equilibrium.

Such an equilibrium position is shown in figure 1.33 where the IS and LM curves intersect each other at point E relating Y level of income to R interest rate. This pair of income level and interest rate leads to simultaneous equilibrium in the real or goods (saving investment) market and the money (demand and supply of money) market.

This general equilibrium position persists at a point of time, given the price level. If there is any deviation from this equilibrium position, certain forces

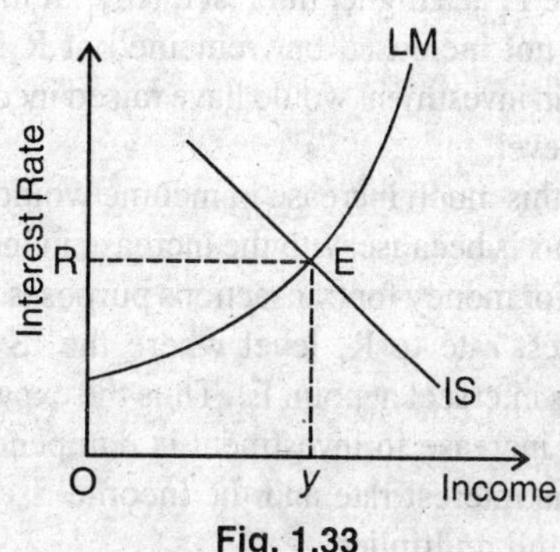

Fig. 1.33

will act and react in such a manner that the equilibrium will be restored.

Shifts in the IS and LM Functions : Changes in General Equilibrium

The general equilibrium combination of Y income level and R rate of interest may change either due to a shift in the IS function or the LM function, or by both thc funtions shifting simultaneously. The IS function may sihft due to changes in the saving function or the investment function and the shifts in the LM function may be caused by changes in the money supply or liquidity preterence.

Shifts in the IS Function. The IS function shifts to the right with a reduction in saving. The IS function also shifts to the right by an autonomous increase in investment.

The shifting of the IS curve to the right and the consequent equilibrium with the given LM curve is illustrated in figure 1.34. With the increase in the outonomous investment (or reduction in saving), the IS curve moves from IS to IS_1 and the new equilibrium is established at point E_1 which indicates a higher level

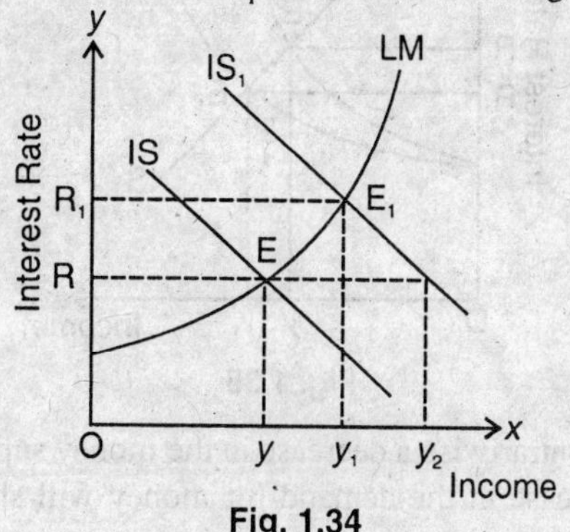

Fig. 1.34

of income Y_1 at a higher interest rate R_1. If the interest rate had not increased but remained at R level, the increase in investment would have raised income from Y to Y_2 level.

But this much increase in income would not take place. This is because with the increase in income the demand for money for transactions purposes will raise the interest rate to R_1 level where the IS and LM functions intersect at point E_1. Thus the expansionary affect of increase in investment is dampened by the rise in the interest rate and the income rises by less than the full multiplier.

In the opposite case when investment falls or saving increases, the IS function will shift to the left and the equilibrium will be established at a lower level of income and interest rate.

Shifts in the LM Function. The LM function shifts to the right with the increase in the money supply, given the demand for money or due to the decrease in the demand for money, given the supply of money.

This is depicted in figure 1.35. With the increase in the money supply the LM curve shifts to the right as LM_1 which moves the economy to a new equilibrium point E_1 where the IS curve intersects the LM_1 curve. The increase in the money supply bring down the interest rate to R_1 in the money market. This, in turn, increases investment there by raising the level of income to Y_1. Thus the effect of the increase in money supply is to shift the LM function to the right and a new equilibrium is established at a lower interest rate and higher income level.

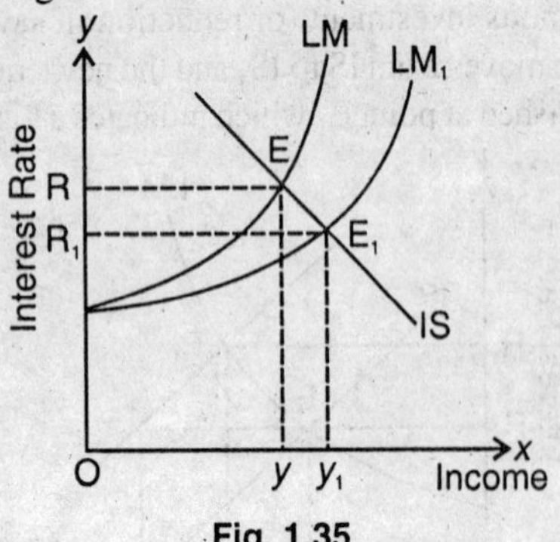

Fig. 1.35

Contrariwise a decrease in the money supply, or an increase in the demand for money will shift the LM function to the left such that a new equilibrium is established at a higher interest rate and lower income level.

Effectiveness of Monetary and Fiscal Policies

The relative effectiveness of monetary and fiscal policy has been the subject of controversy among economists. The monetarists regard monetary policy more effective than fiscal policy for economic stabilisation. On the other hand, the keynesians hold the opposite view. In between there two extreme views, there are the synthesists who advocate the middle path. Modern economists explain these three views in terms of the elasticities of the IS-LM curves. The IS curve represents fiscal policy and the LM curve represents monetary policy.

The IS-LM technique explains the effectiveness of monetary and fiscal policies in relation to the keynesian, monetarist and synthesist views in terms of the elasticities of the IS-LM curve. The LM curve slopes upward to the right and has three segments, as shown in figure 1.36. Starting from the left it is *perfectly elastic*. This segment is known as "*the keynesian range*". AT the other extreme to the right, the LM curve is *perfectly inelastic*. This segment of the curve is known as "the classical range." In between these two segments of the curve is "*the intermediate range.*" The keynesian range represents the fiscalist or Keynesian view, the classical range the monetarist view, and the intermediate range the synthesist view.

Monetary Policy

Monetary policy is explained in figure 1.36 where the three-range LM curves LM_1 and L_2 are shown with three IS curves. The LM_2 curve emerges after an increase in the money supply.

First consider the *Keynesian range* where the LM curve is perfectly elastic. This is the Keynesian liquidity trap situation in which the LM curve is horizontal, and the interest rate connot full below OR_1. An increase in the money supply shifts the LM curve from LM_1 to LM_2. This shift in the curve has no effect on the rate of interest. Consequently, investment is not affected at all so that the level of income remains unchanged at OY_1. Thus under the Keynesian assumption of the liquidity trap, the horizontal portion of the LM curve is not affected by an increase in the

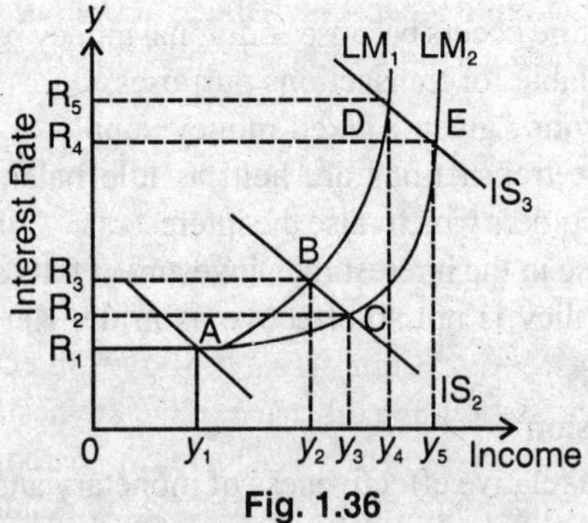

Fig. 1.36

money supply. This IS curve intersects the LM curve in the flat rangeat A with little effect on the interest rate, and consequently on investment and income. *Monetary policy is therefore, totally ineffective in the Keynesian range.*

In the classical range, the sytem is in equilibnrium at D where the IS_3 curve intersects the LM_1 curve and the interest rate is OR_5 and income level OY_4. An increase in money supply shifts the LM_1 curve to the right to LM_2 position. As a result, the income level increases from OY_4 to OY_5, and the interest rate falls from OR_5 to OR_4 when the IS_3 curve crosses the LM_2 curve at E. The increase in the income level and fall in the interest rate as a result of the increase in the money supply is based on the classical assumption that money is primarily a medium of exchange. Thus the monetany policy is highly effective in the classical range when the economy is at high levels of income and interest rate and utilises the entive increase in the money supply for transactions purposes the rely raising national income by the full increase in the money supply.

Now consider the intermediate range when the initial equilibrium is at B where the IS_2 curve interesects the LM_1 curve, and the income level is OY_2 and the interest rate is OR_3. The increse in the money supply shifts the LM_1 curve to LM_2 position. As a result, the new equilibrium is established at point C where the IS_2 curve crosses the LM_2 curve. It shows that with the increse in the money supply the rate of interest falls from OR_3 to OR_2 and the income level rises from OY_2 to OY_3. In the intermediate range the increase in income by Y_2Y_3 is less than that in the classical range Y_4Y_5. This is because in classical case the entire increase in the money supply is obsorbed for transactions purposes. But in the intermediate case, the increase money supply is partly absorbed for speculative purposes and partly for transactions purposes. That which is held for speculative purposes is not invested by wealth holders and remains with them in the turn of idle balances. This has the effect of raising the income level by less than the increase in the money supply. Thus in the intermediate range monetary policy is less effective than in the classical range.

Fiscal Policy

Fiscal policy is explained in terms of figure 1.37 in which the three range LM Curve is taken along with six IS curves that nise after increase in government expenditure in the case of the Keynesian, intermediate and classical ranges.

Consider first the keynesian range when the initial equilibrium is at A where the IS_1 curve intersects the LM curve. Suppose the government expenditure is increased. This brings about new equilibrium at B where the IS_2 curve cuts the LM curve . Consequently the income level rises from OY_1 to OY_2 with the interest rate unchanged at OR. The increase in income in the keynesian case is equal to the full multiplier times the increase in government expenditure. This *in the Keynessian range, the fiscal policy is very ettective.*

In the classical range, the LM curve is perfectly inelastic and the IS_5 curve intersects it at E so that the interest rate is OR_3 and the income level is OY_5. When the government expenditure increases for an expansionary fiscal policy, the IS_5 curve shifts upward to IS_6. As a result, the IS_6 curve crosses the LM curve at F and the interest rate rises to OR_4 with income remaining unchanged at OY_5. This is became the classical case relates to a fully employed economy where the increase in government expenditure has the effect of raising the interest rate which reduces private investment. Since the increase in government expenditure exactly equals the reduction in the private investment, there is no effect on the level of income which remaining constant at OY_5. Thus *fiscal policy is not at all effective in the classical range.*

In the *intermediate range,* the initial equilibrium

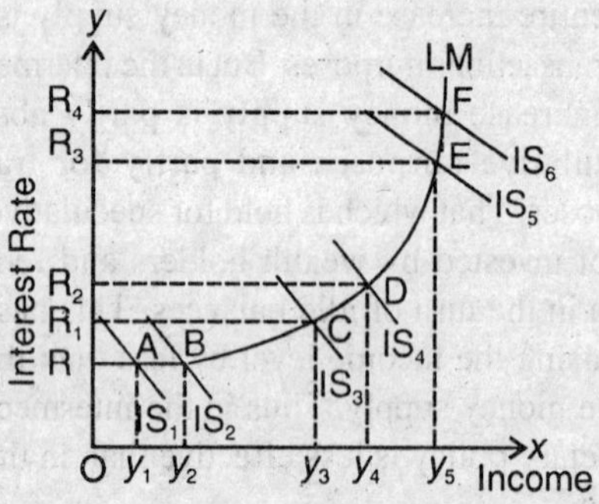

Fig. 1.37

is at C where the IS_3 curve intersects the LM curve. Here OR_1 is the interest rate with OY_3 the level of income with the increase in the government expenditure, the IS_3 curve shifts upword to the right from IS_3 to IS_4 and the new equilibrium is established at point D. As a result, the increase in government expenditure raises the income level from OY_3 to OY_4 and the interest rate from OR_1 to OR_2. The increase in both the income level and the interest rate in the intermediate range is due to two reasons. First, the increase in income resulting from a rise in government expenditure occurs because additional money balances are available for transactions purposes.

Second, given a fixed money supply, a part of available transactions are held as idle balances by wealth holders which raise the interest rate. As a result of the rise in the interest rate, investment falls and the fiscal policy is not so effective as in the Keynesian range.

Conclusion

The relative effectiveness of monetary and fiscal policy depends upon the shape of the IS and LM curves and the economy's initial position. If the economy is in the Keynesian range, monetary policy is in effective and fiscal policy is highly effective. On the other hand, in the classical range, monetary policy is effective and fiscal policy is ineffective. But in the intermediate range both monetary and fiscal policies are effective. In fact, in the intermediate range, the effectiveness of monetary and fiscal policies depends largely on the elasticities of the IS curve. If the IS curve is inelastic, fiscal policy is more effective than monetary policy. On the other hand, if the IS curve is elastic, monetary policy is more effective than fiscal policy.

EXERCISE

1. In the IS-LM model of income determination, an increase in the propensity to save leads to a—
   A. right ward shift of the LM curve
   B. right ward shift of the IS curve
   C. left ward shift of the LM curve
   D. left ward shift of the IS curve
2. Under the Keynesian system, a full in money wage rate will lead to a/am—
   A. increase in employment
   B. fall in the price level
   C. fall in the interest rate
   D. fall in the quantity of money
3. If there is to be large oscillation in the path of income through the intraction of multiplier and accelerator then the—
   A. value of marginal propensity to save must be less than the value of accelerator
   B. value of marginal propensity to save must be greater than the value of accelerator
   C. value of accelerator must be greater than one
   D. Sum of the value of marginal propensity to save and accelerator must be greater than one
4. Match List-I with List-II and select the correct answer using the codes given below the lists—

List-I	List-II
(a) $C = 4 + 0.6Y$	1. LM function
(b) $I = 80 - 5i$	2. IS function
(c) $0.3y - 20i - 150 = 0$	3. Consumption function
(d) $0.3y + 20i - 150 = 0$	4. Investment function

Codes :	*(a)*	*(b)*	*(c)*	*(d)*
A.	3	4	1	2
B.	4	3	1	2
C.	3	4	2	1
D.	4	1	2	3

5. Neutrality of money implies that a given increase in the money supply will—

A. increase all prices in the same proportion
B. increase all prices in different proportions
C. decrease all prices in the same proportion
D. not change prices at all.

6. The theory that the transactions demand for money also depends on the rate of interests, was put forward by—

A. Keynes and Pigou
B. Bumal and Tobin
C. Hicks and Solow
D. Samuelson and Meada

7. Where M is money-supply, *i* is rate of interest and I is investment, the correct likely sequence would be—

A. M decreases, *i* goes down, I goes down, GNP goes down
B. M decreases, *i* goes up, I goes down, GNP goes down
C. M decreases, *i* goes up, I goes up, GNP goes up
D. M goes up, *i* goes up, I goes up, GNP goes up

8. The quantity theory of money implies that an increase in the price level will be associated with—

A. an increase in out put
B. an increase in money supply
C. a decrease in money supply
D. both (A) and (B)

9. High powered money is—

A. Bank's reserves at the Central Bank
B. all loans and advances of banks
C. money held by banks
D. currency held by public and reserves with the Central Bank

10. Which one of the following pair is NOT correctly matched ?

A. Inflationary Gap : Keynes
B. Cash Balance Approach : Pigou
C. Accelerator-Multiplier : Hicks Analysis
D. Equation of Exchange : Marshall

11. Given the total investment expenditure, an increase in the propensity to save will lead to a—

A. rise in income
B. rise in the rate of interest
C. fall in savings
D. fall in income

12. If the investment multiplier is 4, the relevant consumption function is given by—

A. $c = 28 + 0.75y$ B. $c = -28 + 0.78y$
C. $c = 28 + 0.70y$ D. $c = 28 + 0.40y$

13. Which of the following is consistent with the cross-sectional consumption function ?

A. APC = MPC B. MPC = O
C. APC > MPC D. APC = O

14. The speculative demand for money depends on—

A. interest rate B. income
C. profit D. out put

15. Consider the following statements—

Classical economists believed that unemployment in an economy would persist because of

1. labour-saving technical progress.
2. deficiency in demand for goods.
3. Government in tervention in the free working of the economy.

Which of the above statements is/are correct?

A. 1, 2 and 3 B. 1 and 2
C. 2 and 3 D. 3 alone

16. Liquidity preference curve slopes down ward to right because—

A. as rate of interest rises, the opportunity cost of holding money falls.
B. as rate of interest rises, the opportunity cost of holding money rises.
C. as rate of interest falls, the opportunity cost of holding money does not change.
D. when the rate of interest is low, the central banks reduces the supply of money.

17. Quantity theory of money should be regarded as a theory of demand for money. This view has been given by—

A. D.H. Robertson B. J.M. Keynes
C. A.C. Pigou D. M. Friedman

18. Inflation is unjust and deflation is inexpedient. of the two, deflation is worse. Who made this statement—

A. J.M. Keynes B. G. Crowther
C. A. Marshall D. A.H. Hansen

19. The quantity theory of money was first propounded by—
A. D. Ricardo B. Davanzatti
C. D. Hume D. J. Mill

20. Money is an asset. Its demand is determined along with the demand for all the other assets. This view has been held by—
A. A. Marshal B. J. Tobin
C. M. Friedman D. H. Johnson

21. Who among the following Economists, was the first to mention effective demand as a determinant of the level of economic activity—
A. D. Ricardo B. T.R. Malthus
C. A. Marshall D. J.M. Keynes

22. In classical theory of employment what ensures the perfect clearing of the labour market—
A. flexibility of interest rate
B. flexibility of wage rate
C. flexibility of prices of the commodity
D. classical assumptim of perfect competition in the product market

23. When a linear consumption function undergoes a parallel shift down wards, the investment multiplier—
A. falls B. rises
C. doubles D. does not change

24. A direct increase in initial employment leads to a multiple increase in total employment. This relationship was propounded by—
A. J.M. Keynes B. R.F. Kahn
C. A.C. Pigou D. J. Robertson

25. Who among the following Economists introduced the concept of permanent income as a determination of consumption function—
A. M. Friedman
B. J.M. Keynes
C. J.S. Duesenberry
D. N. Kaldor

26. An increase in money supply leads to—
A. rightward shift of IS curve
B. leftward shift of IS curve
C. leftward shift of LM curve
D. rightward shift of LM curve

27. Consider the following statements in relation to Accelerator and choose the correct answer from the code given below—
1. It depends on the rate of growth of demand.
2. It works when there is no idle capacity in the economy.
3: It increases with increase in the rate of depreciation.
4. It depends on the level of demand.

Code :
A. 1 and 2 are correct.
B. 2 and 3 are correct.
C. 3 and 4 are correct.
D. 2, 3 and 4 are corect.

28. According to the IS-LM model, given by Hicks-Hansen there is simultaneous equilibrium between—
A. income level and rate of interest
B. income level and consumption
C. inflation and unemployment
D. demand and supply of money

29. Okun's law postulates a—
A. positive relationship between unemployment and real gross domestic product.
B. negative relationship between enemployment and real gross domestic product.
C positive relationship between money supply and price level.
D. negative relationship between money supply and rate of interest.

30. Which of the curves shown in the diagram below truly represent Keynes saving function—

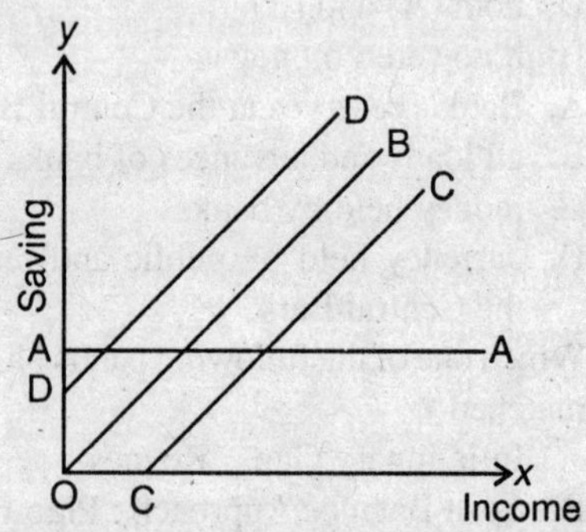

A. AA B. OB
C. DD D. CC

31. Before full employment, if price level falls, aggregate demand will increase which will lead to rise in employment and income. This relationship between price level and aggregate

demand has been called—
A. real balance effect
B. income effect
C. price effect
D. employment effect

32. In which of the following situations will an increase in money supply have no effect on equilibrium effect—
A. LM is steeply sloped and IS is relatively flat.
B. LM is vertical and IS is steeply sloped.
C. LM is steeply sloped and IS is vertical.
D. LM is relatively flat as is IS.

33. **Assertion (A) :** Keynes pointed out that during depression private investment is not induced.
Reason (R) : The marginal productivity of capital is high in depression.
Choose the correct answer from the code given below—
A. Both A and R are true and R is the correct explanation of A.
B. Both A and R are true and R is *not* the correct explanation of A.
C. A is true but R is false.
D. A is false but R is true.

34. Keynes was most concerned with—
A. demand-pull inflation
B. cost-push inflation
C. structural inflation
D. stagflation

35. The speculative demand for money depends only on the expected prices of bonds. This view has been held by—
A. J.M. Keynes B. K. Wickscell
C. D.H. Robertson D. M. Friedman

36. Money multiplier is the ratio between—
A. quantity of total money and money national income
B. quantity of primany money and quantity of secondary money
C. quanity of primary money and quantity of total money
D. quantity of money and aggregate investment

37. According to the quantity theory of money, the price level rises if—
A. there is a decrease in money supply
B. the velocity of circulation of money rises
C. the aggregate volume of transactions increases
D. the real demand for money rises

38. Let $I = 5 + 0.2y$; $S = -15 + 0.3y$ and $\overline{G} = 5$ (where I = Investment, y = National Income, S = Saving and $\overline{G}$ = Government spending). What is the equilibrium level of y?
A. 200 B. 100
C. 250 D. 300

39. Consider the following statements—
1. Absolute Income Hypothesis is associated with Keynes
2. $S = -20 + 0.4y$ and $C = 20 + 0.6y$ yield the same investment multiplier
3. Investment multiplier rises when ever income tax is introduced in the system
4. Bond price and interest rates are directly related which of the above statements is/are correct ?

A. 1 alone B. 2 and 3
C. 3 and 4 D. 1 and 2

40. Consider the following statements relating to classical theory of employment—
1. Classical theory is based on the assumption of full employment
2. Classical version of full employment is a situation where involuntary unemployment is present
3. Classical version of full employment is consistent with seasonal unemployment and frictional unemployment
4. Classical economists advocated wage cuts to reduce the unemployment level

Which of the above statements are correct?
A. 1, 2 and 3 B. 2, 3 and 4
C. 1, 3 and 4 D. 1 and 2

41. Which one of the following saving functions corresponds to the investment multiplier of 5 ?
A. $S = -28 + 0.25y$ B. $S = -40 + 0.75y$
C. $S = -60 + 0.20y$ D. $S = -75 + 0.60y$

42. When investment is negatively related to the rate of interest, the equilibrium output in the goods market is—
A. unrelated to the rate of interest
B. inversely related to the rate of interest
C. positively related to the rate of interest

D. indeterminate

43. Consider the following statements denoting the relationship between marginal propensity to consume and value of multiplier—
 1. Higher the marginal propensity to consume, higher is the multiplier
 2. Higher the marginal propensity to consume lower is the multiplier
 3. When the marginal propensity to consume is one, multiplier takes the value of infinity

Which of the above statements is/are correct?
A. 1 alone B. 2 and 3
C. 1, 2 and 3 D. 1 and 3

44. An increase in fiscal spending leads to—
A. a shift of the Phillips curve to the right
B. a shift of the Phillips curve to the left
C. movement along the Phillips curve such that unemployment rises and inflation falls
D. movement along the Phillips curve such that unemployment falls and inflation rises

45. Consider the following statements—
 1. According to the accelerator modeles, investment demand is proportional to the change in GNP
 2. The real rate of interest is the nominal rate of interest plus the inflation rate
 3. The higher the real interest rate, the higher is the rental cost of capital
 4. Investment is a stock concept

Which of the above statements are correct?
A. 2 and 3 B. 1 and 2
C. 1 and 3 D. 1, 2, 3 and 4

46. 'The propensity to consume of an individual with respect to his disposable income and wealth depends on his age.' The statement refers to the
A. relative income hypothesis
B. permanent income hypothesis
C. life-cycle hypothesis
D. absolute income hypothesis

47. When income falls, what happens to the liquidity preference curve?
A. It does not shift
B. It shifts to the left
C. It shifts to the right
D. It becomes parallel to the vertical axis

48. Consider the following statements—
 1. If Government expenditure increases the IS curve shifts to the right
 2. If the taxes increase the IS curve shifts to the right
 3. If the price level increases the LM curve shifts to the left
 4.. The more interest elastic the investment function, the more interest elastic will be the IS curve

Which of the above statements is/are correct ?
A. 2, 3 and 4 B. 1, 3 and 4
C. 1 and 2 D. 2 alone

49. Stagflation refers to situation which is characterised by—
A. deflation and rising unemployment
B. inflation and rising employment
C. inflation and rising unemployment
D. stagnant employment and deflation

50. The elasticity in respect of speculative demand for money under the liquidity trap condition is
A. zero B. one
C. greater than one D. infinite

51. When the intrinsic value of money and its face value are equal, it is called
A. token money B. full-bodied money
C. quasi-money D. fiat money

52. Which one of the following according to Miltan Friedman is NOT a key deteminant of the demand for money ?
A. Aggregate wealth
B. Precautionary motive
C. Relative rates of return obtainable on different forms of assests
D. Physical non-human capital goods and human capital

53. Which one of the following factors affects velocity of circulation ?
A. Time unit of income receipts
B. Frequency of transaction
C. Liquidity preference
D. All of the above

54. Which one of the following statements is correct is respect of equation of exchange MV = PT ?
A. If M is doubled, leaving V and T unaffected, then P must double
B. If M is doubled, leaving V unaffected, then

P will be halved

C. If M and T are doubled, leaving V unaffected, then P will be halved

D. If M is doubled, V is halved, leaving T unaffected, then P gets multiplied 3 times

55. Match List-I (Name of the Economist) with List-II (Concept /Theory) and select the correct answer using the codes given below the Lists;

List-I	List-II
(a) A.W. Phillips	1. Central Bank
(b) Findlay Shirras	2. Trade-off between wage and unemployment rate
(c) J.M. Keynes	3. Theory of profit
(d) R.S. Sayers	4. Taxable capacity
	5. Liquidity trap

Codes :	*(a)*	*(b)*	*(c)*	*(d)*
A.	5	4	1	2
B.	2	3	5	1
C.	5	3	1	2
D.	2	4	5	1

56. To which one of the following, does the liquidity trap correspond?

A. Consumption function

B. Production function

C. Money demand function

D. Labour demand function

57. The speculative demand for money, according to Keynes, is a function of—

A. Rate of interest B. Level of income

C. Level of savings D. Level of output

58. Anticipation of an increase in the rate of inflation will—

A. cause the short run Phillips curve to shift upward to the right

B. cause an increase in the real rate of interest

C. reduce the normal rate of unemployment in the long run

D. cause the rate of inflation to slow down, other things remaining constant

59. Fisher's quantity theory of money has mainly been criticised because—

A. it does not tell us as to how the change in the quantity of money influence the price level

B. it over emphasises the demand for money by assuming supply of money as being constant

C. it analyses short term variations in the value of money

D. it emphasises too much on the price level

60. Gresham's law explains that—

A. two grams of silver is equal to half gram gold for conversion

B. good money chases bad money out

C. velocity of circulation of money fluctuates rapidly

D. bad money drives good money out of circulation

61. Match List-I (Economists) with List-II (Concepts) and select the correct answer using the codes given below the lists—

List-I	List-II
(a) Keynes	1. Money illusion
(b) Modigliani	2. IS-curve
(c) Hicks	3. Life cycle hypothesis
(d) Pigou	4. Liquidity trap

Codes :	*(a)*	*(b)*	*(c)*	*(d)*
A.	4	1	2	3
B.	2	3	4	1
C.	4	3	2	1
D.	2	1	4	3

62.

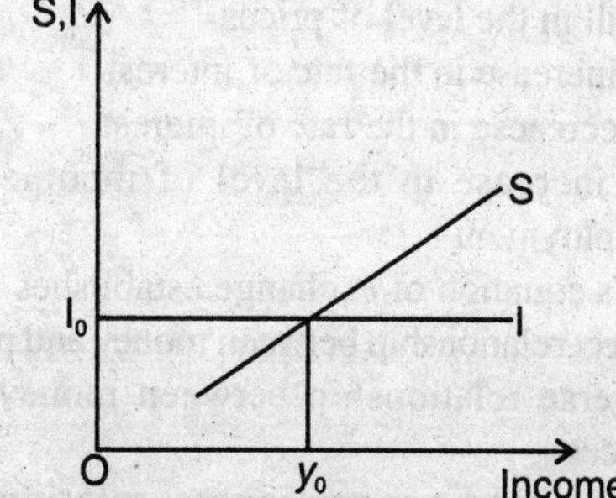

In respect of the diagram given above, consider the following statements—

1. Saving (S) is autonomous.
2. Investment (I) is autonomous.
3. Saving is determined by income (Y).
4. Investment (I) is not autonomous.

Which of these statements are correct ?

A. 2 and 3 B. 3 and 4

C. 1 and 4 D. 1 and 2

63. Assume consumption function of an economy to be C = Rs. 30 Crore + 0.8 Y. Investment is Rs.

40 Crore. Then, the equilibrium level of income is

A. Rs. 700 crore B. Rs. 350 crore
C. Rs. 560 crore D. Rs. 140 crore

64. M_2, money supply measure in india, constitutes
A. M_1 + all post-office deposits
B. M_1 + time deposits of cummercial banks
C. M_1 + post-office saving deposits
D. M_3 + all post-office deposits

65. Consider the following items—
1. Currency with the public
2. Cash with banks
3. Post-office saving bank deposits
4. Time deposits with the banks

Reserve money includes
A. 1, 2 and 3 B. 2, 3 and 4
C. 1 and 2 D. 1, 2, 3 and 4

66. According to Keynes, transaction demand for money L can be stated as (symbols have the usual meaning)
A. $L = K(y)$ B. $L = I(r)$
C. $L = K(y) + I(r)$ D. $L = Y - I$

67. Supply of money remaining the same, when there is an increase in demand for money, there will be
A. a fall in the level of prices
B. an increase in the rate of interest
C. a decreacse in the rate of interest
D. an increase in the level of income and employment

68. Fisher's equation of exchange establishes
A. direct relationship between money and prices
B. inverse relationship between money and prices
C. direct and proportionate relationship between money and prices
D. inverse and porportinate relationship between money and prices

69. Consider the following statements—
A rise in the general level of prices may be caused by
1. an increase in the money supply
2. a decrease in the aggregate level of output
3. an increase in the effective demand.

Of these statements
A. 1 alone is correct
B. 1 and 2 are correct
C. 2 and 3 are correct
D. 1, 2 and 3 are correct

70. Match List-I with List-II and select the correct answer using the codes given below the lists—

List-I	List-II
(a) A continuous increase in general price level	1. Hyper inflation
(b) Raising prices deliberately to relieve depression	2. Disinflation
(c) Fall in prices without a decline in the existing level of employment, out put and income	3. Stagflation
	4. Reflation
(d) Recession accumpanied by inflation	5. Inflation

Codes :	*(a)*	*(b)*	*(c)*	*(d)*
A.	5	1	2	4
B.	1	3	2	5
C.	1	4	5	3
D.	5	4	2	3

71. Consider the following types of assets held by a commercial bank—
1. Money at call and short notice
2. Government securites
3. Advances
4. Cash

The correct DECREASING order (highest to lowest) of liquidity of the given assents is—
A. 4, 1, 3, 2 B. 1, 4, 3, 2
C. 1, 4, 2, 3 D. 4, 1, 2, 3

72. In the given diagram, LK represents—

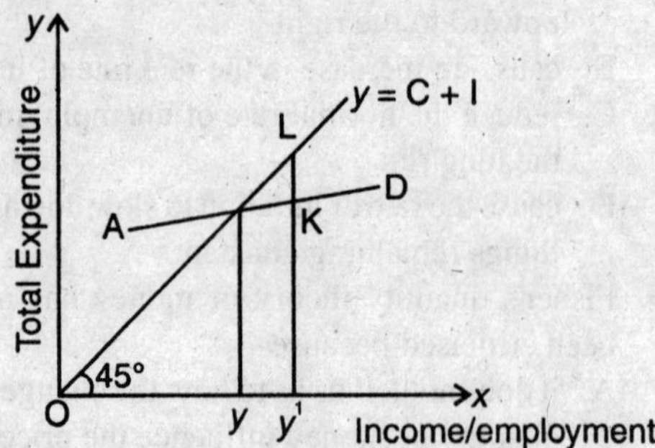

A. deficiency of demand
B. excess demand

C. deficiency of supply
D. excess supply

73. Assuming that: change in investment $\Delta I = 25$
marginal propensity to save (MPS) = 0.5
marginal propensity to investment (MPI) = 0
the change in income Δy will equal to—

A. 25 B. 50
C. 200 D. 100

74. Given the total investment expenditure an increase in the propensity to save will lead to a—

A. fall in the rate of interest
B. fall in income
C. rise in the rate of interest
D. rise in income

75. Investment multiplier can be obtained from (symbols have the usual meaning)

A. $\frac{1}{1-\frac{\Delta c}{\Delta s}}$ B. $\frac{1}{1-\frac{\Delta c}{\Delta y}}$

C. $\frac{1}{1+\frac{\Delta c}{\Delta s}}$ D. $\frac{1}{1+\frac{\Delta c}{\Delta y}}$

76. If there is an expectation of a rise in the price level, investment will be encouraged because

A. there will be an increase in the production of capital goods
B. there will be a rise in the prospective return from captial
C. people will save more and the interest rate will fall
D. the cost of prduction of capital goods will fall

77. The aggregate demand curves slopes downwards because an increase in price level leads to

A. reduction in real balances and increase in interest rate
B. increase in the interest rate and reduction in aggregate spending
C. reduction in real balances alone
D. reduction in real balances, increase in interest rate and reduction in aggregate spending

78. According to permanent income hypothesis, the

A. long-run aggregate Average propensity to consume (APC) equals long-run aggregate Marginal Propensity to consume (MPC)
B. long-run aggregate APC is greater than the long run aggregate MPC
C. long -run aggregate APC is less than the long-run aggregate MPC
D. APC of every individual is equal irrespective of different levels of income of families

79. Match List-I with List-II and select the correct answer using the codes given below the lists—

List-I	List-II
(a) Supply creates its own demand	1. J.B. Say
(b) Chioce reveals preference	2. Adam Smith
(c) Division of labour is limited by the extent of the market	3. Ricardo
(d) Corn in high not because rent is paid, but rent is paid because corn is high	4. Samuelson

Codes :	*(a)*	*(b)*	*(c)*	*(d)*
A.	1	4	2	3
B.	1	4	3	2
C.	4	1	3	2
D.	4	1	2	3

80. In the given diagram, speculative demand for money curve $l(r)$ has four regions R_1, R_2, R_3, and R_4. Liquidity trap is indicated by the regions.

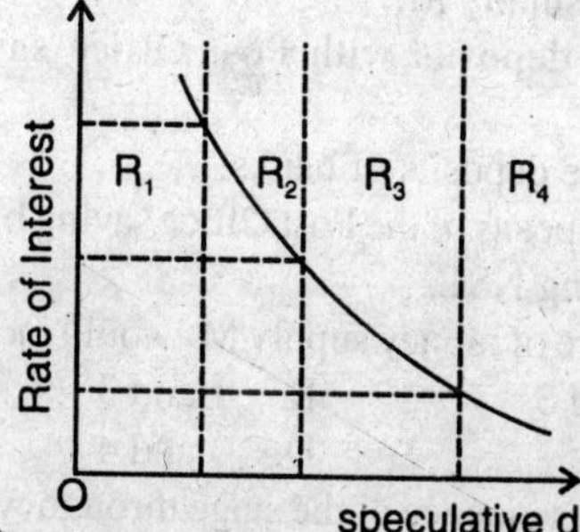

A. R_1 alone B. R_1 and R_4
C. R_3 and R_4 D. R_4 alone

81. According to Keynes, marginal propensity to consume

A. can never exceed unity
B. may exceed unity when dissaving occurs
C. can never exceed the average propensity to consume
D. is the reciprocal of the marginal propensity to save

82. Super multiplier refers to
A. interaction of the Multiplier and the Accelerator
B. reciprocal of the marginal propensity to consume
C. capital output ratio
D. budget maltiplier

83. A Production Possibility Frontier (PPF) is shown in the given diagram. A Less Developed Country (LDC) will be

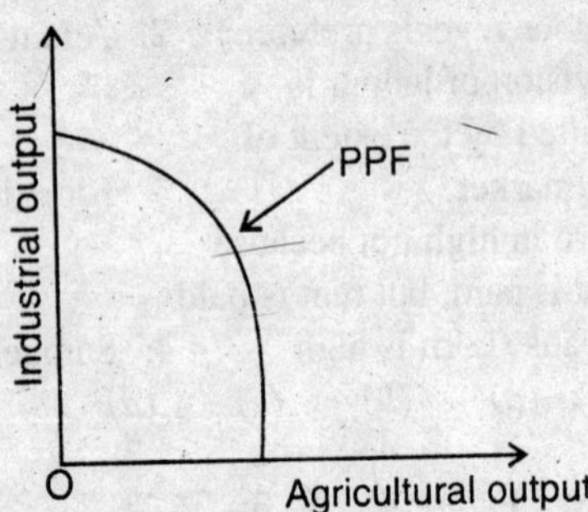

A. inside the PPF
B. on the PPF
C. above the PPF
D. at a point which coincides with the origin

84. Consider the following :
1. Money supply M_1.
2. Saving deposits with Post Office saving banks.
3. Net time deposits of banks.
4. Total deposits of the Post Office saving banks excluding NSC.

The measure of money supply M_3 would include
A. 1, 2 and 3 B. 1 and 3
C. 1 and 4 D. 3 and 4

85. The correct sequence of the stage through which a trade cycle in an economy passes is
A. Depression, Inflation, Reflation, Disinflation
B. Reflation, Disinflation, Inflation, Depression
C. Depression, Reflation, Inflation, Disinflation
D. Inflation, Depression, Disinflation, Reflation

86. The credit multiplier is based on which of the following assumptions?
1. The cash reserve ratio remains constant.
2. The banks maintain a fixed relationship between deposit liabilities and cash reserves.
3. People prefer higher cash holding.
4. People have well developed banking habits.

Select the correct answer using the codes given below—

Codes :
A. 1, 2 and 3 B. 2, 3 and 4
C. 1, 3 and 4 D. 1, 2 and 4

87. If cash reserve ratio is 40% and the commercial banks get a fresh cash of Rs. 15 crores as a result of government spending then the increase in loans advanced by the commercial banks will be
A. Rs. 37.5 crores B. Rs. 40 crores
C. Rs. 60 crores D. Rs. 30.5 crores

88. Liquidity preference refers to—
A. the extent to which investors prefer to keep their assets in money
B. RBI's share holdings in other financial institutions
C. community's preference for gold
D. community's effective demand for capital goods

89. Consider the following statements :
Intersection of the IS and LM curves corresponds to—
1. equilibrium in the real sector.
2. equilibrium in the monetary sector.
3. liquidity trap necessarily.
4. walrasian general equilibrium.

of these statements
A. 1 and 3 are correct
B. 1 and 2 are correct
C. 2, 3 and 4 are correct
D. 1, 2, 3 and 4 are correct

90. Match List-I with List-II and select the correct answer using the codes given below the lists—

List-I	List-II
(a) $c = 9 + 0.1y$	1. IS realation
(b) $0.25y - 20i - 193 = 0$	2. Consumption relation
(c) $0.06y + 29i - 500 = 0$	3. Investment relation
(d) $I = 50 - 10\,i$	4. LM relation

Codes :	(a)	(b)	(c)	(d)
A.	4	3	2	1
B.	4	3	1	2
C.	2	4	3	1
D.	2	4	1	3

91. Excess of ex-ante savings over ex-ante investment means that—
A. income will fall
B. income will rise
C. income will remain the same
D. price will rise and inventories will accumulate

92. Which one of the following consumption functions corresponds to the income multiplier, R = 4?
A. $c = 24 + 0.5y$ B. $c = 240 + 0.25y$
C. $c = 24 + 0.55y$ D. $c = 240 + 0.75y$

93. Consider the following statements—
1. Points to the left of the IS curve indicate excess supply of goods.
2. Points to the right of the LM curve indicate excess demand for money.
3. Points to the right of the IS curve indicate excess supply of money.
4. Points to the right of the IS curve indicate excess supply of goods.

of these statements
A. 2 and 4 are correct
B. 1 and 3 are correct
C. 2 and 3 are correct
D. 1, 2 and 3 are correct

94. Suppose, MPC falls. The IS curve shifts to the left. Then what happens ceteris paribus?
A. The level of equilibrium becomes lower
B. The level of equilibrium becomes higher
C. There is no change in equilibrium
D. Only the rate of interest becomes lower

95. Match List-I with List-II and select the correct answer using then codes given below the Lists—

List-I	List-II
(a) Life Cycle Hypothesis	1. Keynes
(b) Permanent Income Hypothesis	2. Duesen berry
(c) Absolute Income Hypothesis	3. Friedman
(d) Relative income Hypothesis	4. Ando-Modigliani

Codes :	*(a)*	*(b)*	*(c)*	*(d)*
A.	4	3	1	2
B.	4	3	2	1
C.	3	2	1	4
D.	3	2	4	1

96. The author of employment multiplier is—
A. Lord Beveridge B. Keynes
C. R.F. Kahn D. J.R. Hicks

97. In a two sector econmy, the saving and investment functions are as follows—
$S = -10 + 0.2Y$
$I = -3 + 0.1Y$
what will be the equilibrium level of income?
A. 70 B. 80
C. 90 D. 100

98. The IS-LM model has been formulated by—
A. J.R. Hicks B. F. Modigliane
C. P.A. Samuelson D. J.M. Keynes

99. The speculative demand for money is—
A. interest determining
B. interest determined
C. income determing
D. income determined

100. Which one of the following is represented by M_3?
A. M_1 + post office savings bank deposits
B. Currency with the public + demand deposits
C. M_1 + time deposits with bank
D. None of these

101. In an economywhere people always consume half of any additional income and save the other half, an additional Govt. expenditure of Rs. 20,000 can create an additional income of—
A. Rs. 10,000 B. Rs. 40,000
C. Zero D. Rs. 20,000

102. When a linear consumption function undergoes a parallel shift down wards, the investment multiplier will—
A. fall B. rise marginally
C. remain as before D. become double

103. If the consumption function passes through the origin, then APC = MPC it must be—
A. linear without any intercept
B. non-linear without any intercept
C. linear with a negative intercept on the income axis
D. linear with a positive intercept on the consumption axis

104. Given the comsumption function
$c = 205 + 0.9y$
what is the multiplier?
A. 0.09 B. 10.0

C. 0.9 D. 9.00

105. Suppose that the money supply in an economy is constant and the demand for money is a function of income and interest rate, then if the level of income increases, there will be—

A. a decrease in the quantity of money demanded and an increase in the rate of interest

B. an increase in the quantity of money demanded and an increase in the rate of interest

C. a decrease in the quantity of money demanded and a decrease in the rate of interest

D. an increase in the quantity of money demanded and a decrease in the rate of interest

106. Portfolio theory of the demand for money assumes that the individual—

A. disregards risk B. is risk neutral

C. is risk lover D. is risk averse

107. If the rate of interest increases, people holdig bonds will—

A. experience a capital gain on the bonds

B. experience a capital loss on the bonds

C. not be able to find a buyer should they decide to sale

D. experience neither capital gains nor a capital loss

108. When the demand for money is infinitely interest elastic, the effectiveness of an expansionary monetary policy is—

A. the highest B. mode rate

C. very low D. nil

109. Assertion (A): Real rate of interest is better indicator of returns on savings than nominal rate of interest.

Reason (R): The real rate of interest is estimated after removing the effect of the expected rate of inflation.

A. Both A and R are true and R is the correct explanation of A

B. Both A and R are true but R is not a correct explanation of A

C. A is true but R is false

D. A is false but R is true

110. Assertion (A): If the government expenditure and taxation are increased by an equal amount, the equilibrium income of the economy will remain the same, ceteris paribus.

Reason (R): A given change in the government expenditure affects aggregate spending more than an equal amount of tax.

A. Both A and R are true and R is the correct explanation of A

B. Both A and R are true but R is not a correct explanation of A

C. A is true but R is false

D. A is false but R is true

111. Assertion (A): In India, monetary policy alone cannot eliminate inflation.

Reason (R): There are structure factors which make prices rigid in the downward direction but flexible in the upward direction.

A. Both A and R are true and R is the correct explanation of A

B. Both A and R are true but R is not a correct explanation of A

C. A is true but R is false

D. A is false but R is true

112. Assertion (A): Keynes pointed out that during depression, pivate investment is not induced.

Reason (R): The marginal productivity of capital is high in depression.

Choose the correct answer from the code given below:

A. Both A and R are true and R is the correct explanation of A.

B. Both A and R are true and R is not the correct explanation of A

C. A is true but R is false

D. A is false but R is true

113. Assertion (A): Money is a link between the present and the future.

Reason (R): Money is a store of value.

A. Both A and R are true and R is the correct explanation of A

B. Both A and R are true but R is not a correct explanation of A

C. A is true but R is false

D. A is false but R is true

114. Assertion (A): According to Baumol, the

transactions demand for cash varies with respect to the square-root of the volume of transactions.

Reason (R): Transaction demand for money is a function of income.

A. Both A and R are true and R is the correct explanation of A
B. Both A and R are true but R is not a correct explanation of A
C. A is true but R is false
D. A is false but is true

115. Assertion (A): There would be no trade-off between inflation and unemployment even in the short run if people's expectations are rational.

Reason (R): Rational expectations imply forecasting the future correctly.

A. Both A and R are true and R is the correct explanation of A
B. Both A and R are true but R is not a correct explanation of A
C. A is true but R is false
D. A is false but R is true

116. Assertion (A): The major distinguishing feature of a commercial bank is its ability to create money.

Reason (R): It has a legal power to do so.

A. Both A and R are true and R is the correct explanation of A
B. Both A and R are true but R is not a correct explanation of A
C. A is true but R is false
D. A is false but R is true

ANSWERS

1	2	3	4	5	6	7	8	9	10
D	C	A	A	D	B	B	B	D	D
11	12	13	14	15	16	17	18	19	20
D	A	A	A	D	B	D	A	B	C
21	22	23	24	25	26	27	28	29	30
B	B	D	B	A	D	D	A	B	D
31	32	33	34	35	36	37	38	39	40
A	D	C	A	A	B	B	A	D	C
41	42	43	44	45	46	47	48	49	50
C	B	D	D	C	C	B	B	C	D
51	52	53	54	55	56	57	58	59	60
B	B	D	A	D	C	A	B	A	D
61	62	63	64	65	66	67	68	69	70
C	A	B	C	A	A	B	C	D	D
71	72	73	74	75	76	77	78	79	80
D	B	B	B	B	B	D	A	A	D
81	82	83	84	85	86	87	88	89	90
A	A	A	B	C	D	A	A	B	D
91	92	93	94	95	96	97	98	99	100
A	D	A	A	A	C	A	A	B	C
101	102	103	104	105	106	107	108	109	110
B	C	A	B	B	C	B	D	A	D
111	112	113	114	115	116				
A	C	A	B	A	C				

UNIT III : NATIONAL INCOME ACCOUNTING

CONCEPT AND MEASUREMENT

INTRODUCTION

Economic well-being of society is obviously influenced by the volume of total output as well as by composition of the output and relative size of the shares received by various groups. The portion of economic theory which deals with the determination of total output is known as *National Income Analysis* or the process of National Income Accounting.

National income is an uncertain term which is used interchangeably with national dividend, national output and national expenditure. On this basis, national income has been defined in a number of ways. In common parfance, national income means the total value of goods and services produced annually in a country. In other words, the total amount of income accruing to a country from economic activities in a year's time, is known as national income. It includes payments made to all resources in the form of wages, interest, rent and profits.

DEFINITIONS OF NATIONAL INCOME

The definitions of national income can be grouped into two classes. One, the *traditional definitions* advanced by Marshall, Pigou and Fisher; and two, modern definitions. According to Marshall, "*The labour and capital of a country acting on its natural resources produce annually a certain net aggregate of commodities, material and immaterial imcluding services of all kinds. This is the true net annual income or revenue of the country or national dividend.*" In this definition, the word 'net' refers to deductions from the gross national income in respect of depreciation and weaving out of machines. And to this must be added income from abroad.

National income, according to *Pigou, "is that part of the objective income of the community including, of course, income derived from abroad, which can be measured in money."*

Fisher odopted *'Consumption'* as the criterion of national income whereas Marshall and Pigou regarded it to be production. According to Fisher, "The national dividend or income consists solely of services as received by ultimate comsumers, whether from their material or human environments. Thus, a piano, or an overcoat made for me this year is not a part of this year's income, but an addition to the capital. Only the services rendered to me during this year by these things are income." fisher's definition is considered to be better them that of Marshall or Pigou, because Fisher's definition provides an adequate concept of economic welfare which is dependent on consumption and consumption represents our standard of living.

From the modern point of view, *Simon Kuznets* has defined national income as "the net output of cmmodities and services flowing during the year from the country's productive system in the hands of the ultimate consumers."

CONCEPTS OF NATIONAL INCOME

There are various concepts of national income which we shall study one by one.

1. Gross National product (GNP)

Gross National product is defined as the total market value of all final goods and services produced in a year. Two things must be noted in regard to gross national product. *First,* it measures the market value of annual output. In other words, GNP is a *monetary measure.*

Secondly, for calculating gross national product accurately, all goods and services produced in any given year must be counted once, and not more than once. Most of the goods go through a series of production stages before reaching a market. As a result, parts or components of mony goods are bought and sold many times. Hence to avoid counting several times the parts of goods that are sold and resold, gross national product only includes the market value of final goods and ignores transactions involving intermediate goods.

The "gross national product at market prices" may be obtained by adding up :

A. What private persons spend on consumption, or what is called *personal consumption* expenditure.

B. What private businessmen spend on replacement, renewal and new investment. This is called *gross domestic private investment.*

C. What the rest of the world spends on the output of the national economy over and above what this economy spends on the output of the rest of the world, *i.e.*, export-import or net foreign investment; and

D. What the government spends on the purchase of goods and services, *i.e.*, *government purchases.*

2. GNP at Factor Cost

GNP at factor cost is the sum of the money value of the income produced by and accruing to the various factors of production in one year in a country.

GNP at market prices, always includes indirect taxes levied by the government on goods which raise their prices. But GNP at factor cost is the income which the factors of production receive in return for their services alone. It is the cost of production. Thus GNP at market prices is always higher than GNP at factor cost. Therefore, in order to arrive at GNP at factor cost, we deduct indirect taxes from GNP at market prices. Again, it of ten happens that the cost of production of a commadity to the producer is higher than the price of a similar commodity in the market. In order to protect such producers, the government helps them by granting monetary help in the form of subsidy equal to the difference between the market price and the cost of production of the commodity. Thus in order to arrive at GNP at factor cost, subsidies are added to GNP at market prices.

GNP at Factor Cost = GNP at Market Prices – Indirect Taxes + Subsidies.

3. Gross Domestic Product (GDP)

GDP = GNP – Net Foreign Investment

Net Foreign Investment = Export – Import
(X – M)

∴ GDP = GNP – (X – M)

4. Net National Product (NNP)

GNP includes the value of total output of consumption goods and investment goods. But the process of production uses up a certain amount of fixed capital. Some fixed equipment wears out, its other components are damaged or destroyed, and still other some rendered obsolete through technological changes. All this process is termed depreciation or capital consumption allowance. In order to arrive at NNP, we deduct depreciation from GNP. The word 'net' refers to the exclusion of that part of total output which represents depreciation.

NNP = GNP – Depreciation

5. NNP at Market Prices

Net National Product at Market prices is the net value of final goods and services evaluated at market prices in the course of one year in a country. If we deduct depreciation from GNP at market prices, we get NNP at market prices. Thus NNP at Market Prices = GNP at Market Prices – Depreciation.

6. NNP at Factor Cost

Net National Product at factor cost is the net output evaluated at factor prices. It includes income earned by factors of production through participation in the production process such as wages and salaries, rates, profits, etc. It is also called *National Income.* This measure differs from NNP at market prices in that indirect taxes are deducted and subsidies are added to NNP at market prices in order to arrive at NNP at factor cost. Thus

NNP ar factor cost = NNP at Market Prices – Indirect Taxes + Subsidies.

= GNP at Market Prices – Depreciation – Indirect Taxes + Subsidies.

= National Income

7. NDP at Factor Cost

Net Domestic Product at factor cost is arrived by making adjustments for net indirect taxes *i.e.* indirect taxes and subsidies in the Net Domestic Product at market prices. The market prices contain an element of indirect taxes which though paid out by the buyers in the form of Product Prices, do not accrue to the production units.

Hence to find out factor incomes, we deduct the indirect taxes from the Net Domestic Product at market prices. Like wise, we add subsidies to the Net Domestic Product at market prices because these subsidies form the factor incomes though they are not a part of the market prices. Thus,

Net Domestic Product at Factor Cost = Net Domestic Product at Market Prices – Indirect Taxes + Subsidies.

8. Private Income

Private income is income obtained by private individuals from any source, productive or other wise, and the retained income of corporations. It can be arrived at from NNP at factor cost by marking certain additions and deductions. The additions include transfer payments such as pensions, unemployment allowances, sickness and other social security benefits, gifts and remittances from abroad, windfall gains and from lotteries or from horse racing , and interest on public debt. The deductions include income from government departments as well as surpluses from public under takings and employee's contribution to social security schemes like provident funds, life insurance, etc. Thus,

Private Income = National Income + Transfer payments + Interest on Public Debt – Social Security. Profits and Surpluses of Public under takings.

9. Personal Income

Personal income is the total income received by the individuals of a country from all sources before direct taxes in one year. Personal income is never equal to the national income, because the former includes the transfer payments where as they are not included in national income. Personal income is derived from national income by deducting undistributed corporate profits, profit taxes, and employee's contributions to social security schemes. But business and government transfer payments, and transfer payments from abroad in the form of gifts and remittances, wind fall gains and interest on public dept which are a source of income for in dividuals are added to national income. Thus,

Personal Income = National income – Undistributed Corporate profits – Profit Taxes – Social Security Contributions + Transfer Payments + Interest on Public Debt.

Personal income differs from private income in that it is less than the latter because it excludes undistributed corporate profits. Thus,

Personal Income = Private Income – Undistributed Corporate Profits – Profit Taxes

10. Disposable Income

The concept of disposable income tells us the amount of money available to individuals and house holds in a year for the purposes of spending. After a good part of personal income is paid to government in the form of personal taxes like income tax, personal property tax etc, what remains of personal income is called disposable income. Thus,

Disposable Income = Personal Income – Direct Taxes. Disposable Income can either be consumed or saved. Therefore,

Disposable Income = Consumption + Saving.

11. Real Income

Real income is national income expressed in terms of a general level of prices of a particular year taken as base. National income is the value of goods and services prduced as expressed in terms of money at current prices. But it does not indicate the real state of the economy. It is possible that the net national product of goods and services this year might have been less than that of last year, but owing to an increase in prices, the NNP might be higher this year. On the contrary, it is also possible that NNP might have increased but the price level might have fallen, as a result of which national income would appear to be less than that of the last year. In both the situations, the national income does not depict the real state of the country. To rectify such a mistake, the concept of real income has been propounded.

In order to find out the real income of a country, a particular year is taken as base year when the general price level is neither too high nor too low and the price level for that year is assumed to be 100. New the general level of the prices of the given year for which the national income (real) is to be determined is assessed in accordance with the prices of the base year. For this purpose the following formula is employed

Real National Income = National Income for the current year × $\frac{100}{\text{Current year Index}}$

Suppose 1970 is the base year and the national income for 1980 is Rs. 20000 crores and the index number for this year is 250. Hence,

Real National Income for 1966 = 20000 × $\frac{100}{250}$

= Rs. 80000 crores.

This is also known as National Income at constant prices.

12. Per Capita Income

The average income of the people of a country in a particular year is called Per Capital Income for that year. This concept also refers to the measurement of income at current prices and at constant prices. For instance, in order to find out the per capital income for 2001, at current prices, the national income of a country is divided by the population of the country in that year

Per Capita Income for 2001

$$= \frac{\text{National income for 2001}}{\text{population in 2001}}$$

Similarly, for the purpose of arriving at the Real Per Capita Income, the following formula is employed.

Real Per Capita Income for 2001

$$= \frac{\text{Real National Income for 2001}}{\text{Population in 2001}}$$

This concept enables us to know the average income and the standard of living of the people. But it is not very reliable, because in every country due to unequal distribution of national income a major portion of it goes to the richer sections of the society and thus income received by the common man is lower than the per capita income.

METHODS OF MEASURING NATIONAL INCOME

There are four methods of measuring national income. which method is to be employed depends on the availability of data in country and the purpose in hand.

1. Product Method

Accordig to this method, the total value of final goods and services produced in a country during a year is calculated at market prices. To final out the GNP, the data of all productive activities, such as agricultural products, wood received from forests, mineral received from mines, commodities produced by industries, the contributions to production made by transport, communications, insurance companies, lawyers, doctors, teachers etc. are collected and assessed at market prices. Only the final goods and services are included and the intermediary goods and services are left out.

2. Income Method

According to this method, the net income payments received by all citizens of a country in a particular year are added up, *i.e.* net incomes that accrue to all factors of production by way of net rents, net wages, net interest and net profits are all added together but incomes received in the form of transfer paymets are not included in it. The data pertaining to income are obtained from different sources, for instance, from income tax department in respect of high income groups and in case of workers from their wages will.

3. Expenditure Method

According to this method, the total expenditure incurred by the society in a particular year is added together and includes personal consumption expenditure, net domestic investment, government expenditure on goods and services and net foreign investment. This concept is based on the assumption that national income equals national expenditure.

4. Value Added Method

Another method of measuring national income is the value added by industries. The difference between the value of material outputs and inputs at each stage of production is the value added. If all such differences are added up for all industries in the economy, we arrive at the gross domestic product.

SIGNIFICANCE OF NATIONAL INCOME ESTIMATES

There are several important uses of the estimates of national income and, therefore, there is a great need for their regular preparation. The following are some of the important uses of National Income estimates

First, national income estimate reveals the over - all production performance of the economy as it seeks to measure the level of production in a year. Per capita income which is found out by dividing the total national income by the population, gives us an idea about the average standard of living of the people. Thus, the figures of national income and percapita income will indicate the level of economic welfare of the people of a country.

Secondly, by comparing national income estimates over a period of time, we can know whether the economy is growing or stagnant or declining.

Thirdly, the national income estimates show the contributions made by the the various sectors of the economy such as agriculture, manufacturing industry, trade, etc., to the national income.

In the fourth place, national income estimates throw light on the distribution of national income among different categories of income such as wages, profits, rent and interest. The distribution of national income between wages on the one hand and profits, interest and rent on the other is of special significance since the inequality in the personal distribution of income depends to a great extent on the share of working classes (i.e., wages) and the share property owners (*i.e.,*rent, profits and interest).

Fifthly, with the help of national income estimates of various countries of the world we can compare the standards of living and the levels of economic welfare of the people living in those countries.

DIFFICULTIES IN THE MEASUREMENT OF NATIONAL INCOME

To calculate the national income of a country is a complicated problem and is beset with the following difficulties :

1. National income is always measured in money, but there are a number of goods and services which are difficult to be assessed in terms of money, *e.g.,*painting as a hobby by an individual, the bringing up of children by the mother. Similarly, when the owner of a firm gets married to his lady secretary, her services, though a part of national income are not included in it. By excluding all such services from it, the national income will work out to be less than what it actually is.

2. The greatest difficulty in calculating the national income is of double counting, which arises from the failure to distinguish properly between a final and an intermediate product. There always exists the fear of goods or a service being included more than once. If it so happens, the national income would work out to be many time the actual. Flour used by a bakery is an intermediate product and that by a house hold the final product. To solve this difficulty, only the final goods and services are taken in to account and that is not so easy a task.

3. Income earned through illegal activities such as gembling or illicit extraction of wine etc. is not included in national income. Such goods and services do have value and meet the needs of the consumers. But by leaving them out the national income works out to less than the actual.

4. Then there arises the difficulty of including transfer payments in the national income. Individuals get pension, unemployment allowance and interest on public loans, but whether these should be included in national income is a difficult problem. On the one hand, these earnings are a part of individual income and on the other they are government expenditure. To avoid this difficulty these are deducted from national income.

5. The question of calculation of depreciation on capital consumption presents another formidable difficulty. If there were no changes in the form or quality of capital, there would not be much of a problem; but in fact both the amount and the composition of our capital are changing all the time. There are not accepted standard rates of depreciation applicable to the various categories of macines. Unless from the gross national income correct deductions are made for depreciation, the estimate of net national income is bound to go wrong.

6. All inventory changes whether negative or positive are included in the GNP. The procedure is to take positive or negative changes in physical units of inventories and multiply than by current prices. Then this figure is added to total current production of the firm. But the problem is that firms record inventories at their original costs rather than at replacement costs, When prices rise there are gains in the book value of inventories. Contrariwise, there are losses when prices fall. So the book value of inventories overstates or understates the actual inventories. Thus for correct imputation of GNP, inventory evaluation is required. But inventory valuation is a very difficult and cumbersome procedure.

7. In calculating national income, a good number of public services are also taken which cannot be estimated correctly. How should the police and military services be estimated ? In the days of war, the forces are active, but during peace they rest in cantonments. Similarly, to estimate the contribution made to national income by profits earned on irrigation and power projects in terms of money is also a difficult problem.

8. Another major problem arises with regard to the treatment of income arising out of activities of the foreign firms in a country. Should their income firm a part of the national income of the country in which they are located or should it belong to the national income of the country owning the firm? On this point, the IMF viewpoint is that production and income arising from an enterprise should be ascribed to the territory in which production takes place. However, profits earned by foreign branches and subsidiaries are credited to the parent country.

PROBLEMS OF MEASUREMENT IN A DEVELOPING ECONOMY

In a developing economy, complete and reliable information relating to the various methods of estimating nationl income are not available due to the following problems :

1. Non-monetised sector
2. Lack of occuptional specialisation
3. Non-market Transactions
4. Illiteracy
5. Non availability of Data

SOCIAL ACCOUNTING

The term 'social accounting' was first introduced into economics by *J.R. Hicks* in 1942. In his words, it means 'nothing else but the accounting of the whole community or nation, just as private accounting is the accounting of the individual firm'. Social accounting, also known as national income accounting, is a method to present statistically the interrelationships between the different sectors of the economy for a thorough understanding of the economic conditions of the entire economy. It is a technique of presenting information about the nature of the economy of a society with a view not merely to get an idea of its prosperity, past or present, but also to get guidelines for collective (or state) policy to influence (or regulate) the economy. In other words, social accounting describes statistically the economic activities of the different sectors of the entire economy, indicates their mutual relationship and provides a frame work for analysis.

The principal forms of economic activity are production, consuption, capital accumulation, government transactions and transactions with the rest of the world.These are the components of social accounting. If the incomings and outgoings of a country relating to these five activities are shown in the form of accounts, they show a closed network of flows representing the basic structure of the economy. These flows are always expressed in money terms. We classify these flows as follows :

1. Production Account
2. Consumption Account
3. Government Account
4. Capital Account
5. Foreign Account

INPUT-OUTPUT ACCOUNTING

The input-output analysis was first developed by W.W. Leontief in his 'The structure of the American Economy.' The input-output analysis tells us that there are industrial inter-relationships and inter-dependencies in the economic system as a whole. The inputs of one industry are the outputs of another industry and *vice versa*, so that ultimately their mutual relationships lead to equilibrium between supply and demand in the economy as a whole. Coal is an input for steel industry and steel is an input for coal industry, though both are the outputs of their respective industries. A major part of economic activity consits in producing intermediate goods (inputs) for further use in producing final goods (outputs). There are flows of goods in "whirlpools and cross currents" between different industries. The supply side consits of inter-industry flows of intermediate products and the demand side of the final goods. In essence, the input-output analysis implies that in equilibrium the money value of aggregate output of the whole economy must equal the sum of the money values of inter-industry inputs plus the sum of money values of inter-industry outputs.

The national income accounts are related to an economy's final product. They do not explicitly show the inter-industry flows of outputs and their relationships with the goods and services demanded. The input-output analysis analyses these relationships. It is, thus, an improvement over the national income accounting method.

FLOW OF FUNDS ACCOUNTS

National income accounts do not tell anything about monetany or financial transactions where by one sector places its saving at the disposal of the other sectors of the economy by means of loans, capital transfers, etc. The flow of funds accounts were developed by *Professor Morris Copeland* in 1952 to overcome this weakness of national income accounting.

The flow of funds accounts show the financial transactions among different sectors of the economy and the link between saving and investment aggregates with lending and borrowing by them. This system of accounts is concerned with the sources and uses of funds by the various sectors of the economy. "The account for each sector reveals all the sources of funds (whether from income or borrowing) and all the uses to which the funds are put (whether for spending or lending), this way of looking at transactions in their entirely has come to be known as the flow of funds as the flow of funds approach or sources and uses of funds."

The flow of funds accounting system is presented in the form of a matrix which is divided into a number of sectors, such as households, corporate business, non-corporate business, farm business, non-farm business, commercial banks, saving institutions, insurance companies, other investors, local, state and central governments, and the rest of the world sector which includes foreign individuals, firms and government. The columns of the matrix are used for institutional sector classification and the rows for various types of transactions.

BALANCE OF PAYMENTS ACCOUNTS

The balance of payments account of a country is a systematic record of all its economic transactions with the outside world in a given year. It is a statistical record of the character and dimensions of the country's economic relationships with the rest of the world. It shows the country's trading position, changes in its net position as foreign lender or borrower and changes in its official reserve holdings.

EXERCISE

1. Which of the following is not, by definition, equal to National Income ?
   A. National output B. National expenditure
   C. National product D. National wealth

2 If GNP is 16% higher than the last year's and the rate of inflation is 9%, production in the economy has grown by
   A. 4% B. 5%
   C. 6% D. 7%

3. Which of the following is a transfer payment ?
   A. Payment made to housewife
   B. Pocket allowance to children

C. Maintenance allowance to old parents
D. All of the above

4. The difference between gross domestic product and net domestic product equals
A. Transfer payments
B. Depreciation cost
C. Indirect taxes
D. Subsidies

5. The best method of computing national income is
A. Product Method
B. Income Method
C. Expenditure Method
D. Combination of income and production method

6. Which of the following will directly increase the GNP?
A. A rise in the market price
B. A surplus in budget
C. An increase in investment
D. A deficit in budget

7. "National dividend is that part of objective income of the community, including of course the income derived from abroad which can be measured in money"
This is the remark of
A. Marshall B. J.R. Hicks
C. David Ricardo D. A.C. Pigou

8. While calculating personal income, we have to deduct the following from private income :
A. Saving of private corporate sector and corporation tax
B. Consumption of fixed capital
C. Direct taxes paid by households
D. All of the above

9. The National income is equal to
A. GNP – Subsides – Taxes
B. NNP – Indirect Taxes + Subsidies
C. NNP – Direct Taxes + Subsides
D. GNP – Subsidies + Taxes

10. "National income as the aggregate net product of, and the sole source of, payment for all the agents of production" has been defined by
A. A.C. Pigou B. Alfred Marshall
C. Robbins D. Dusenbery

11. "The labour and capital of a country acting upon its natural resources produce annually a certain net aggregate of commodities, material and immaterial including services of all kinds." This definition of National Income is given by
A. Adam Smith B. Lionel Robbins
C. John Stuart Mill D. Alfred Marshall

12 The total income earned in any given year by the owners of productive resources is measured by
A. Personal income
B. Disposable Income
C. Gross national product
D. National income

13. In calculating a country's GNP at market prices one of the following is not included
A. Wages and salaries before tax
B. Indirect taxes
C. Bonds to the employes
D. Depreciation allowances

14. An example of double counting in national income would be
A. Wages of bus and train drivers
B. Cotton output and cotton cloth output
C. Electricity output and water output
D. Tax receipts and earnings of inland revenue officials

15. Double counting must be avoided when calculating national income. This means that there must be a deduction of the value of
A. Food subsidies
B. Personal consumption of alcoholic drinks
C. Transfer payments
D. Net interest from abroad

16. Which of the following is counted in determining GNP ?
A. A do it yourself roof repair job
B. A housewife's work at home
C. An operation performed in a hospital
D. Vegetables grown by a farmer for his own use

17. Among these statements which one clearly explains the meaning of "Subsidies"
A. Payment by Government for purchase of goods and services
B. Payment by business enterprises to factors of production
C. Payment by companies to shareholders

D. Payment by Government to business enterprises without buying any goods and services

18. The difference between Gross National Product and Gross Domestic Product is equal to

A. Gross Domestic investment
B. Net Foreign Investment
C. Net imports
D. Net factor income from abroad

19. Net domestic product at factor cost equals net domestic product at market prices

A. Plus subsidies – indirect taxes
B. Minus subsidies + indirect taxes
C. Minus subsidies
D. Plus indirect taxes

20. When gross investment is positive, net investment

A. is the highest
B. is zero
C. is positive
D. can be either positive or negative

21. National product is not affected by which of the following?

A. Sale of a second hand automobile by A to B
B. Sale of a new car by an automobile dealer
C. Sale of a new car by an automobile company
D. Sale of a new car on hire purchase

22 Net foreign investment is equal to

A. Total amount of foreign investment in a country
B. Investment by foreigners during a particular year
C. Investment by local resident in a foreign country
D. Investment by the foreigners in this country minus investment by resindents of this country in foreign countries during a given time period

23. "Disposable income" does not include

A. Business transfer payments
B. Social security benefits
C. Corporate dividends
D. Personal income taxes

24. Circular flow of income in a two sector sector model implies

A. Payments from households to firms and back again
B. Payments from firms to firms
C. Payments from households to households
D. Payments from households to firms

25. Which one of the following is not a Transfer Payment in National Income accounting ?

A. Interest on government bonds held by indians
B. Drought relief payments
C. Unemployment benefits
D. Salaries of supreme court judges

26. Which one of the following is a transfer income?

A. The salary of an M.P.
B. Company dividends to share holders
C. Rents from house property
D. Unemployment allowance

27. The smallest national income accounting aggregte is usually

A. PI B. GNP
C. DPI D. NI

28. Which one of the following is not induded in calculating gross naitonal product of an economy?

A. Wages and salaries before tax
B. Depreciation allowances
C. Indirect taxes
D. Subsidies

29. For the study of the long term growth of the economy we use

A. Real GNP
B. Transfer payments
C. Per capita income
D. Disposable income

30. Interest on the national debt is included in

A. NNP B. GNP
C. Personal income D. National income

31. Double counting has the effect of

A. Underestimating national product
B. Overestimating national product
C. Distorting national product
D. Misleadig conclusions about national income

32 The Government sector's contribution to GNP is measured by

A. Government purchases of goods and services
B. Wages and salaries paid by the government

C. Inter-governmental surplus
D. The size of the government surplus

33. A certain part of corporate business income gets into the calculation of personal income.Which is that?
A. Government transfer payments
B. Social security payment made by firms
C. Dividends
D. None of the above

34. Depreciation means
A. Destruction of a plant in a fire accident
B. loss of equipment over time due to wear and tear
C. Closure of the plant due to raw material problem
D. Closure of the plant due to lockout

35. Which of the following is not a method of estimating GNP?
A. The value added approach
B. Product approach
C. Income approach
D. The financial approach

36. Depreciation is the loss of value of
A. Capital assets
B. Stocks
C. Intermediate goods
D. Final goods

37. If value added at different stages are added, the total will
A. Equal the value of the final product
B. Underestimate the value of the final product
C. Overestimate the value of the final product
D. Misrepresent the value of the final product

38. GNP is Rs. 600 crores and NNP is Rs. 475 crores: therefore depreciation is
A. Rs. 100 B. Rs.175
C. Rs. 50 D. Rs. 125

39. Which of the following is not true?
A. GNP – Depreciation = NNP
B. GNP = GDP + Net income from abroad
C. $NNP_{FC} = NNP_{MP}$ + Subsidies – Indirect taxes
D. GNP = NNP – Depreciation

40. NNP at market prices and NNP at factor costs will be equal when there is
A. No direct tax
B. No indirect tax
C. No subsidy
D. No indirect tax and no subsidy

41. Gross domestic product at factor cost plus net income from abroad minus capital consumption is equal to
A. Gross domestic product at market prices
B. Gross national product at factor cost
C. Net national product at market prices
D. Net natonal product at factor cost

42 In a closed economy model one of the sectors below is not to be considered which?
A. Households B. Firms
C. Government D. Foreign trade

43. National product at market prices is higher then national product at factor cost by the amount of
A. Subsidies
B. Indirect taxes
C. Indirect taxes plus subsides
D. Indirect taxes minus subsidies

44. Net exports are negative when
A. Net investment is positive
B. Exports are exceeded by imports
C. Exports exceed private transfer to foreignous
D. Imports are exceeded by exports

45. The importants leakages in the circular flow of income are as follows except onewhich?
A. Saving
B. Imports
C. Government expenditure
D. Taxes

46. Which of the following formula could be used for calculating the per capita income of a country
A. $\frac{\text{Total family income}}{\text{Number of family members}}$
B. $\frac{\text{National Income}}{\text{Total Population}}$
C. $\frac{\text{Total income of various industries}}{\text{Total number of industrial workers}}$
D. $\frac{\text{Total government revenue}}{\text{Total population}}$

47. Per capita income increases when
A. GNP increases at the same rate as population
B. GNP increases slower than population
C. GNP increases faster than population

D. GNP does not increase and population increases slowly.

48. This year, if national product at factor cost is Rs, 600 crores, indirect taxes Rs. 200 crores and subsidies Rs. 75 crores, national product at market prices is :

A. Rs. 750 crores B. Rs. 725 crores
C. Rs. 500 crores D. Rs. 250 crores

49. Which one of the following measures does not imclude final goods and services

A. GNP
B. NNP
C. Disposable income
D. National income

50. Imports into a country generate income for

A. Domestic manufacturers
B. Government
C. Trader
D. Foreign products

51. A household in a two sector model is essentilally a unit of

A. Consumption B. Productioin
C. Investment D. None of the above

52 When less output is consumed than produced during a given income period, national wealth

A. Increases
B. Remains unchanged as there is no relationship
C. Decreases
D. May increase or decrease

53. National product at current prices is higher than national product at constanst prices during a period of

A. Rising prices B. Falling prices
C. Stable prices D. Changing costs

54. Which of the following items are not included in estimating National income or $NNP_{FC?}$

A. Salary income of artists, dancers and singers
B. Income of smugglers
C. Payments to form workers in food grains
D. Payments of bank interest for capital borrowed

55. The purchase of a new home is included in the GNP as a part of

A. Capital consumption allowance
B. Personal comsumption expenditures
C. Investment
D. Personal saving

56. Expenditure on defence is an item of

A. Private investment
B. public investment
C. Private consumption
D. Public consumption

57. GNP at market prices is Rs, 200 : net property income form from abroad is Rs. 20 and indirect tanes are Rs. 20 and subsidies are Rs. 10; GDP factor cost is—

A. Rs. 160 B. Rs. 180
C. Rs. 200 D. Rs. 250

58. National income at cosstant prices can be found out by

A. $\frac{\text{Price index number}}{\text{N.I. at current prices}} \times 100$

B. $\frac{\text{N.I. at current prices}}{\text{Price index number}} \times 100$

C. $\frac{\text{N.I. at market prices}}{\text{Price index number}} \times 100$

D. $\frac{\text{N.I. at factor cost}}{\text{Price index number}} \times 100$

59. A " refigerater " operating in a chemist's shop is an example of

A. Intermediate good B. Final good
C. Producer's good D. Consumer's good

60. The workers were classified as "Productive and unproductive" on the productivity context by

A. David Ricardo B. J.S. Mill
C. Adam Smith D. Karl Marx

61. Consider the following satements—

The study of national income accounts is of great importance because it

1. reveals the change in the size and composition of the national product.
2. provides us with information about the distribution of national income in the society among various groups.
3. reveals the manner in which national expenditure is divided between consumption and investment.

A. 1 and 2 are correct
B. 2 and 3 are correct

C. 1 and 3 are correct
D. 1, 2 and 3 are correct

62 Consider the following types of income :
1. Personal income
2. Private income
3. Disposable income
4. National income

The correct sequence in *descending* order of their magnitude is
A. 4, 2, 1, 3 B. 4, 2, 3, 1
C. 2, 4, 3, 1 D. 2, 4, 1, 3

63. The national income of a country for a given period is equal to the
A. total value of goods and services produced by the nationals
B. sum of total consumption and investment expenditure
C. sum of personal income of all individuals
D. money value of final goods and services produced

64. Gross National savings measure the
A. amount of GNP not consumed
B. excess of income over consumption plus the net taxes
C. sum of retained earnings and depreciation amounts
D. excess of disposable income over consumption

65. Social accounting system in India is classified into which one of the following sets of sectors?
A. Enterprise, households and government
B. Assets, liabilities and debt position
C. Public sector, private sector and joint sector
D. Income, production and expenditure

66. For a closed economy having no foreign trade which one of the following is correct?
A. GDP = GNP B. GDP > GNP
C. GDP < GNP D. GDP $\gtrless$ GNP

67. Which of the following statements explain the difference between NNP(Net National Product) and NMP (Net Material Product)?
1. NNP includes services.
2. NNP excludes services.
3. NMP includes services.
4. NMP excludes services.

Select the correct answer using the codes given below.

Codes :
A. 1 and 4 B. 2 and 4
C. 1 and 3 D. 2 and 3

68. **A :** Y = C + I (where Y = National Income, C = Consumption, I = Investment)
R : C and I are important determinants of national income
A. Both A and R are true and R is not correct explanation of A.
B. Both A and R are true but R is not correct explanation of A.
C. A is true but R is false.
D. A is false but R is true.

69. The GNP gap is the gap between
A. GNP and NNP
B. GNP and depreciation
C. GNP and GDP
D. Potential and actual GNP

70. Which one of the following is the most important limitation of the per capita GNP as the Measure of welfare?
A. The increase in the per capita GNP may not always raise the real standard of living of the masses
B. This measure does not take into account the increase in the population
C. This measure does not take into account the employment aspect
D. This measure does not take into consideration government expenditure

71. The 'Hindu rate of growth'
A. refers to growth of Hindu population
B. is the term used by Raj Krishna to represent the nature of the growth of the Indian economy at around 3.5 percent per year
C. is the term used by Amartya sen to represent the nature of the growth of the Indian economy at around 3.5 percent per year
D. is the term used by V.K.R.V. Rao to decide the nature of the growth of the Indian economy at around 4 Percent

72 Value added means value of
A. output at market prices
B. goods and services less depreciation
C. goods and services less cost of intermediate

goods and services

D. output at factor cost

73. Which one of the following statements is correct?

A. Gross national product includes depreciation

B. Value added includes transfer payments

C. Personal income includes undistributed profits

D. Disposable income includes personal taxes

74. The GNP at market prices for 1983-84 was Rs. 192866 crores and the GNP at factor cost was Rs. 171201 crores. The government paid at Rs. 5107 crores as subsidies during the year. The amount of indirect taxes in crores for the year should work out to

A. Rs. 31879 B. Rs. 26772

C. Rs. 21665 D. Rs. 16558

75. GNP exceeds NNP by

A. the amount of total taxes

B. government expenditure

C. transfer payments

D. the difference between gross investment and net investment

76. National Income total reveals :

1. Production side of the economy
2. Distribution side of the economy
3. Expenditure side of the economy

Choose your answer from

A. 1 only B. 2 only

C. 1, 2 and 3 D. 3 only

77. National Income is the—

A. Net National Product at market price

B. Net National Product at factor cost

C. Net Domestic Product at market price

D. Net Domestic Product at factor cost

78. Improvement in the standard of living in a country are best reflected be increase in—

A. GNP at constant prices

B. Per capita income at constant prices

C. Per capita income at current prices

D. GNP at current prices

79. Which one of the following statements is not correct?

A. Compensation of employees *plus* operating surplus plus mixed income of self employed *plus* consumption of fixed capital equals GDP at factor cost

B. GDP at factor cost *plus* indirect taxes *minus* subsidies equals GDP at market prices

C. GDP at factor cost *minus* depreciation equals net domestic porduct at factor cost

D. GDP at market prices *minus* net receipts from abroad *plus* indirect taxes *minus* subsidies equals net national product

80. Which one of the following constitutes governmet consumption expenditure?

A. Compensation to employees *plus* net purchases from business enterprises

B. Wages and salaries of government employees

C. Government expinditure on defence

D. Transfer payments to individuals and state governmets

81. Which one of the following denotes net state domestic product?

A. Money value of final goods and services produced within the boundary of a state *plus* net inflow of income from outside the state

B. Money value of final goods and services produced within the boundary of a state minus depreciation *plus* indirect taxes of fixed assets

C. Money value of final goods and service produced with the boundary of a state *minus* depreciation *plus* indirect taxes

D. Money value of goods and services consumed within the boundary of a state *pluls* net income from outside the state

82 Which one of the following equals the value of output of a factory?

A. Total value added by factors

B. Value of all non-factor inputs *plus* indirct taxes

C. Payments for factor inputs and non factor inputs

D. Payments for non-factor inputs *plus* wages

83. Which one of the following items is excluded in calculating national income?

A. Service of a rental TV set

B. Rs. 10,000/- won in a lottery

C. Rented residences

D. Paid house work

84. In which of the following sectors, is product method used in conputing national income in India?
1. Agri culture and allied activities
2. Mining and quarrying
3. Registered manufacuring
4. Unregistered manufacturing

Select the correct answer using the codes given below :

Codes :

A. 2, 3 and 4 B. 1, 2 and 3
C. 1 and 3 D. 1, 3 and 4

85. Consider the following statements regarding saving different sectors of an economy :
1. Savings of private corporate sector constitute undistributed profits
2. Saving of private corporate sector constitute excess of income over expenditure
3. Saving of government sector constitute excess of revenue receipts over revenue expenditure
4. Saving of government sector constitute excess of total revenue over total expenditure

Of the above statements

A. 2 and 3 are correct
B. 3 and 4 are correct
C. 1 and 3 are correct
D. 2 and 4 are correct

86. The implicit national income deflator represents a price index number of the type known as

A. Laspeyre's index number
B. Fisher's index number
C. Paasche's index number
D. Marshall-Edgeworth's index number

87. Human Development Index (HDI) is a composite index of

A. Health, literacy and employment
B. National income, size of population and the general price level
C. National income, per capita income and per capita consumption
D. Physical resources, monetary resources and populatoin size

88. Which one of the following agencies in india is responsible for computation of national income?

A. NCAER B. C.S.O.
C. N.S.S D. R.B.I

89. Which one of the following represents the saving in the privte corporate sector?

A. Total profits of a company
B. Undistributed profits
C. Excess of income over expenditure
D. Dividends paid to share holders

90. An economy's Net National Income is \$ 20,000 million, indirect taxes are \$ 2000 million, subsidies are \$ 1000 million and its population 150 million. What will be the National Income at factor cost?

A. \$ 21000 million B. \$ 19000 million
C. \$ 23000 million D. \$ 22000 million

91. Given are the following informations about an economy :

Consumption = Rs. 5000
Gross Investment = Rs. 1000
Govt. Purchases = Rs. 800
Exports = Rs. 600
Imports – Rs. 800
Depreciation = Rs. 250

What is the GNP at market prices?

A. Rs. 7100 B. Rs. 6850
C. Rs. 6600 D. Rs. 6350

92 Consider the following statements :
1. In an economy where productive capacities are increaing, gross private domestic investment exceed depreciation
2. Interest on the public debt is not a part of national income but is included in personal income
3. Disinvestment occurs when inventories expand
4. The purchase of new home is included in the GNP as a part of investment

Which of the above statements are correct?

A. 1 and 2 B. 3 and 4
C. 1, 2 and 4 D. 1, 3 and 4

93. Assertion (A) : Per capita income figures are poor tools of ordinal ranking of countries with respect to the real well being.

Reason (R) : A good portion of the national income in poor countries is unreported.

Codes :

A. Both A and R are true and R is the correct

explanation of A

B. Both A and R are true but R is *Not* a correct explanation of A

C. A is true but R is false

D. A is false but R is true

94. Estimate gross national product from the data given below :

Value of consumer goods and services	Rs. 20000 crore
Value of capital goods and services	Rs. 10000 crore
Value of exports	Rs. 4000 crore
Value of Imports	Rs. 2600 crore
Total depreciation	Rs. 1600 crore

Which one of the following is correct—

A. Rs. 31400 crore B. Rs. 38600 crore

C. Rs. 29800 crore D. Rs. 29200 crore

95. National income at market price is equal to

A. the sum of wages, interest, rent and profits earned

B. national income at factor cost *plus* indirect taxes minus subsidies

C. the sum of earnings of all the factors *plus* direct tax *minus* subsidies

D. total quantity of goods and services produced

96. Which of the following prevents national income from falling to zero when gross investment falls to zero—

A. consumption B. multiplier

C. accelerator D. none of the above

97. In India, the main source of national income is

A. Primary sector B. Secondary sector

C. Tertiary sector D. Foreign sector

98. The GNP of an economy at market prices is Rs.1000. Net factor income from abroad is Rs. 1000, indirect taxes Rs. 800, subsidies Rs. 500 and depreciation Rs.1000. What is the GDP at market prices?

A. Rs. 9000 B. Rs. 7700

C. Rs. 11000 D. Rs. 13300

99. Consider the following statemets—

1. At the time of rising prices, NNP at current prices is less than NNP at constant prices.
2. At the time of rising prices, NNP at current prices is higher than NNP at constant prices.
3. NNP at current prices and NNP at constant prices are always same irrespective of changes in prices.
4. NNP at current prices is equal to NNP at constant prices at the time of stable prices.

Which of these statements are correct?

A. 1and 2 B. 1 and 3

C. 2 and 3 D. 2 and 4

100. Match List-I with List-II and select the correct answer using the codes given below the lists :

List-I	List-II
(a) Capital consumption allowances	1. Are included in estimating National Income at factor cost
(b) Subsidies	2. Are excluded while calculating disposable income
(c) Personal taxes	3. Are exclluded in calculating personal outlays
(d) Personal savings	4. Are excluded in estimating Net National Product

Codes :	*(a)*	*(b)*	*(c)*	*(d)*
A	3	1	2	4
B.	4	1	2	3
C.	3	2	1	4
D.	4	2	1	3

101. Assume that between 1985 and 1995, GNP increased from Rs. 1000 crore to Rs. 1500 crore and the index of prices increased from 100 to 200. Which one of the following expresses GNP for 1995 in terms of 1985 prices?

A. Rs. 1000 crore B. Rs. 750 crore

C. Rs. 1500 crore D. Rs. 500 crore

102. Which one of the following statements relating to transfer payments, capital gains and illegal activities is correct?

A. Market trasactions such as transfer payments, capital gains are includded and illigal activities are omitted in national product

B. Market transactions such as transfer payments, capital gains and illegal activities are omited in national product

C. Market transactions such as transfer payments are included but capital gains and illegal activities are omitted in national product

D. All the three market transactions should be included in national product

103. National income will be higher than net national product because

A. there being no depreciation
B. inclusion of services
C. inclusion of profits
D. net inflow of umilateral transfers from abroad

104. Social accunting of national income addresses to the issue of

A. public expenditure on social in frastructure
B. revenue receipts from and public expenditure on social services
C. estimating what is being produced, where, how much and how and who consumes what and how much
D. share of national income going to the socially back ward groups

105. Gross Domestic Product is the monetary value of

A. stock of goods and services
B. all final goods and services produced in a year
C. goods produced for the market only
D. goods produced for the market and for self comsumption

106. As the country develops, we should find that the—

A. relative percentage share of the primary sector in the national income goes down
B. absolute share of the agriclutural sector in the national income goes down
C. better redistribution of national income is ensured by the market only
D. absolute share of the primary sector in the national income goes down

107. National income at market price rises due to—

A. taxes
B. additional supply of goods from imports
C. subsidies
D. savings on account of keeping many government posts vacant

108. If consumer price index in city A is 200 and in city B is 250, per capita income of Rs 4000 in both cities is in fact equal to

A. Rs. 5000 for A and Rs. 4000 for B
B. Rs. 3200 for A and Rs. 4000 for B
C. Rs. 4000 for A and Rs. 3000 for B
D. nothing can be said on this basis

109. In the acconting of the state domestic products

A. transfer payments like pension, scholarships etc. are included
B. indirect taxes are not included but direct taxes are
C. direct taxes are not included but indirect taxes are
D. supra-regional imcomes, as allocated by the CSO are included.

110. For a study of the long term growth of the economy we use

A. Real GNP
B. Money GNP
C. Per capita income
D. Property of the individual

111. Assertion (A): Transfer earnings are not to be included in the national income estimation.

Reason (R): Transfer earnings are not payments for factor services.

A. Both A and R are true but R is the correct explanation of A
B. Both A and R are true but R is not a correct explanation of A
C. A is true but R is false
D. A is false but R is true

112 Assertion (A): Continuous increase in Real National Income is an indication of economic growth.

Reason (R): Increase in National Income does not necessarily reflect increase in per capita income.

A. Both A and R are true and R is the correct explanation of A
B. Both A and R are true but R is not a correct explanation of A
C. A is true but R is false
D. A is false but R is true

113. Assertion (A): The GNP is the value of all goods and services produced annually in the nation.

Reason (R): The most comprehensive measure of national output is the GNP.

A. Both A and R are individually true and R is

the correct explanation of A
B. Both A and R are individually true but R is not the correct explanation of A
C. A is true but R is false
D. A is false but R is true

114. Assertion (A): Banking sector's contribution to national income is zero.

Reason (R): By the usual methods of calculation, the net factor payments in the banking sector amounts to zero.

A. Both A and R are individually true and R is the correct explanation of A
B. Both A and R are individually true but R is not the correct explanation of A
C. A is true but R is false
D. A is false but R is true

ANSWERS

1	2	3	4	5	6	7	8	9	10
D	D	D	B	D	C	D	A	B	B
11	12	13	14	15	16	17	18	19	20
D	D	D	B	C	C	D	D	A	D
21	22	23	24	25	26	27	28	29	30
A	D	D	A	D	D	C	B	A	C
31	32	33	34	35	36	37	38	39	40
B	A	C	B	D	A	A	D	D	D
41	42	43	44	45	46	47	48	49	50
D	D	D	D	C	B	C	B	C	D
51	52	53	54	55	56	57	58	59	60
A	A	A	B	C	D	B	B	C	C
61	62	63	64	65	66	67	68	69	70
D	A	D	C	D	A	A	A	D	A
71	72	73	74	75	76	77	78	79	80
B	C	A	D	D	C	B	B	A	A
81	82	83	84	85	86	87	88	89	90
C	C	B	B	D	A	A	B	B	B
91	92	93	94	95	96	97	98	99	100
C	A	A	A	B	A	C	A	D	B
101	102	103	104	105	106	107	108	109	110
B	B	B	C	B	A	A	A	C	A
111	112	113	114						
A	B	C	D						

UNIT IV : DEVELOPMENT AND PLANNING

GROWTH AND DEVELOPMENT—CONCEPTS

The term 'economy growth' refers to increases over time in a country's real output of goods and services—or more appropriately product per capita. The term 'economic development', in contrast, is more comprehensive. It implies progressive changes in the socio-economic structure of a country. Viewed in this way, economic development involves a steady decline in agriculture's share in GNP and a corresponding increase in the share of industries, trade, banking, construction and services. This transformation in economic structure is invariably accompanied by a shift in the occupational structure of the labour force and an improvement in its skill and productivity.

In fact, the terms 'development' and 'growth' have nothing to do with the type of economy. The distinction between the two relates to the nature and causes of change. *Schumpeter* makes the distinction clearer when defines development as a discontinuous and spon taneous change in the stationary state which forever alters and displaces the equilibrium state previously existing; while growth is a gradual and steady change in the long run which comes about by a gradual increase in the rate of savings and population. This view of schumpeter has been widely accepted and elaborataed by the majority of econmists. According to Kindleberger, "Economic growth means more output, while econmic development implies both more output and changes in the technical and institutional arrangements by which it is produced and distributed. Growth may well invole not only more output derived from greater amounts of inputs but also greater efficiency, *i.e.*, an increase in output per unit of input. Development goes beyond this to imply changes in the composition of output and in the allocation of inputs by sectors."

Friedman defines growth as an expansion of the system in one or more dimensions without a change in its structure, and development as an innovative process leading to the structural transformation of social systems.

Thus *economic growth* is related to a quantitative sustained increase in the country's per capita output or income accompanied by expansion in its labour force, consumption, capital and valume of trade. On the other hand, economic development is a wider term. It is related to qualitative change in economic wants, goods incentives and institutions.

CHARACTERISTICS OF AN UNDER DEVELOPED COUNTRY

1. General Poverty
2. Agriculture, the Main Occupation
3. A Dualistic Economy
4. Underdeveloped Natural Resources
5. Demographic Features
6. Unemployment and Disguised Unemployment
7. Economic Backwardness
8. Lack of Enterprise and Initiative
9. Insufficient capital Equipment
10. Technological Backwardness
11. Foreign Trade orientation

VICIOUS CIRCLES OF POVERTY

There are circular relationships known as the 'vicious circles of poverty' that tend to perpetuate the low level of development in LDCs. *Nurkse* explains the idea in these words : "It implies a circular constellation of forces tending to act and react upon one another in such a way as to keep a poor country in a state of poverty. For example, a poor man may not have enough to eat; being under fed, his health may be weak; being Physically weak, his working capacity is low, which means that he is poor, which in turn means that he will not have enough to eat; and so on. A situation of this sort relating to a country as a whole, can be summed up in the trite proposition . "A country is poor because it is poor."

The basic vicious circle stems from the fact that in LDCs total productivity is low due to deficiency of capital, market in perfections, economic backwardness and under development. However, the vicious circles operate both on the demand side and the supply side, The *demand side* of the vicious circles is that the low level of real income leads to a low level of demand which, in turn, leads to a low rate of investment and hence back to deficienity of capital, low productivi by and low income. This is shown in figure 1.1. Low productivity is reflected in low real income. The low level of real income means low saving. The low level of saving leads to a low investment and to deficiency of capital. The deficiency of capital, in turn, leads to a low level of productivity and back to low income. Thus the vicious circle is complete from the supply side. It is depicted in figure 1.2. The low level of real income, reflecting low investment and capital deficiency is a common feature of both the vicious circles.

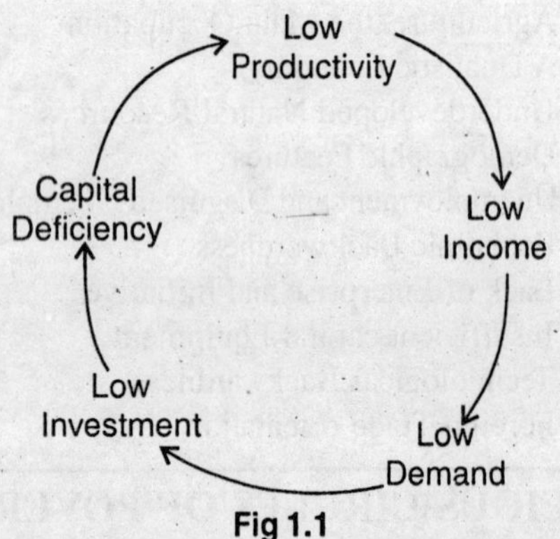

Fig 1.1

A third vicious circle envelops underdeveloped human and natural resources. Development of natural resources is dependent upon the productive capacity of the people in the country. If the people are backward and illiterate, lack in technical skill, knowledge and entrepreneurial activity, the natural resources will tend to remain unutilized, underutilized or even misutilized. On the other hand, people are economically backward in a country due to under developed natural resources. Underdeveloped natural resources are, therefore, both a consequence and cause of the backward people.

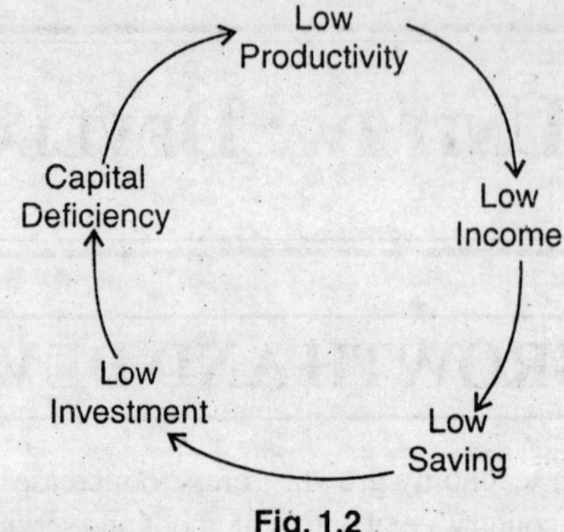

Fig. 1.2

MODERN ECONOMIC GROWTH

Professor Simon Kuznets defined modern economic growth "as a long-term rise in capacity to supply increasingly diverse economic goods to its population, this growing capacity based on advancing technology and the institutional and ideological adjustments that it demands." This definition has three components :

First, the economic growth of a nation is identified by the sustained increase in the supply of goods.

Second, advancing technology is the permissive factor in economic growth which determines the growth of capacity in supplying diverse goods to the population.

Third, for an efficient and wide use of technology and its development, institutional and ideological adjustments must be made to effect the proper use of innovations generated by advancing stock of human knowledge. For example, modern technology is incompatible with the rural mode of life, the large and extended family pattern, family enterprise and illiteracy.

Characteristics

Professor Simon Kuznets has pointed out six characteristics of modern economic growth that have emerged in the analysis based on national product and its components, population, labour force and the like.

1. High Rates of Growth of per capita Product and Population: Modern economic growth, as revealed by the experience of the developed countries since the late eighteenth or early nineteenth century, is characterised by the high rates of increase in per capita product accompanied by substantial rates of population growth. The extremely high rate of increase are at least five times as high for population and at least ten times as high for production as observed in the post. Professor Kuznets has shown that the rataes of population growth of thirteen countries, excluding france, have been high in modern times than in pre-modern times. Leaving france with a population increae of 2.5 percent per decade, the rates of population growth range from 6-7 percent for UK, Sweden, Italy and the former USSR, to 8 percent for switzerland and Norway.to 10-14 percent for Denmark, Germany, Japan and the Netherlands and to 19-20 percent for Canada, the United States and Australia"

The decade rates of growth in per capita product of all these developed countries, except Australia with 8 percent decade rate, are above 13 percent . They range from 13.5-14.1 percent for the Netherlands and the UK, to 16-15 percent for Switzerland, the united states, France, Germany, Canada, Italy, Nor way and Denmark and to above 26 percent for Japan, 28.3 percen for Sweden and 43.9 percent for the former USSR.

2. The Rise in productivity : Modern economic growth is characterised by a rise in the rate of per capita product due to improvements in the quality of inputs which led to greater efficiency or rise in productivity per unit of input. This is traceable either to an increase in input of resources of labour and capital or to an increase in efficiency or to both. Increase in efficiency implies greater output per unit of input.

The growth of national product has been due to the enormous addition to population which led to a large increase in labour force. The increase in national product in trun led to a considerable increase in capital accumulation and hence in reproducible capital. The proportions of labour force to total population showed an upward trend for all developed countries except Switzerland, Italy and Australia.

Economic growth of developed nations has been accompanied by the long-term decline in number of man-hours per capita. This tendency reflects increase in efficiency or productivity. Leaving the exceptional case of Italy where man-hours per capita declined by 7.5 percent per decade, the overall decline in man-hours per capita per decade for all other developed countries ranged between 4.1 percent for Great Britain, 2 to 2.4 percent for Belgium. Germany, Denmark, Sweden, Nor way and the united States, 2.8 to 3.5 percent for Canada, France and Australia and 4.1 percent for Switzerland and 4.5 percent for Netherlands.

3. High Rate of Structural Transformation: Structural transformations in modern economic growth include the shift away from agriculture to non-agricultural activities and from industry to services, a change in the scale of productive unit and a related shift from personal enterprises to impersonal organization of economic firms, with a corresponding change in the occupational status of labour.

4. Urbanisation: Modern economic growth has been characterised by the movement of an increasing proportion of the population in developed countries from rural areas to urban areas. This is urbanisation. Urbanisation is largely a product of in dustrialisation. The economies of scale arising from non-agricultural pursuits as a result of technological changes led to the movement of a large proportion of labour and population from the rural to the urban area. As the technical means of transportation, communication and organisation grew more effective, there was the spread of increasing optimum scale units. All these processes affected the grouping of population by social and economic status and transformed the basic pattern of life. The effects of urbanisation on modern economic growth of developed nations led to the decline in birth-rate and the shift toward the small family. It brought people together from different rural areas who initiated and learnt from each other and from those already living in towns. It facilitated the developmemt of impersonal relations of modern life and also taught cooperation. Above all, it created conditions for the intense intellectual activity associated with modern civilisation and there by created favourable conditions for the increase in knowledge.

THEORIES OF ECONOMIC DEVELOPMENT

A. THE CLASSICAL THEORY OF ECONOMIC DEVELOPMENT

The main features of classical economic theory are:

1. Laissez-Faire Policy: The classical economists believe in the existence of and automatic free market and perfectly competitive economy which is free from any government interference. It is the "invisible hand" which maximises the national income.

2. Capital Accumulation, the Key to Progress: All classicists regard capital accumulation as the key to economic progress. They, therfore, lay emphasis on larger savings. Only capitalists and landlords are capable of saving, according to them. The working class is incapable of saving because it gets wages equal to the subsistence level.

3. Profits, the Incentive to Investment: According to the classicists, profits induce investment. The larger the profits, the greater the capital accumulation and investment.

4. Tendency of Profits to Declin: Profits do not increase continuously. They tend to decline when competition increases for langer capital accumulation among capitalists. The reason, according to Smith, is increase in wages due to competition among capitalists whereas, according to Ricardo, when wages and rent rise with the increase in the price of corn, profits decline.

5. Stationary State: All classical economists visualize the stationary state as the end of the process of capital accumulation. When once profits start declining, this process continues till profits become zero, population and capital accumulation stop increasing and the wage rate reaches the subsistence level. According to Smith, it is the scarcity of natural resources that finally stops growth and leads the economy to the stationany state.

In broad outline, the classical theory of economic development may be stated thus: Suppose an expected increase in profits brings about an increase in investment which adds to the existing stock of capital and to the steady flow of improved techniques. This increase in capital accumulation raises the wage fund. As a result wages rise. Higher wages induce an accelerated population growth which causes the demand for food to rise. Food production is raised by employing additional labour and capital. But diminishing returns to land bring about a rise in labour cost. Consequently, the price of corn goes up and in turn rents increase, wages rise, there by reducing profits. Reduction in profits implies reduction in investment, retarded technological progress, diminution of wages fund and slowing down of population growth and capital accumulation. When this happens, capital accumulation ceases, population becomes constant and the stationary state sets in.

Criticisms

The classical theory of development has been criticised due to following reasons :

1. Ignores Middle Class
2. Neglects Public Sector
3. Less Importance to Technology
4. Wrong Notions about Wages and Profits
5. Unrealistic Growth Process

B. THE MARXIAN THEORY OF ECONOMIC DEVELOPMENT

Marx contributed to the theory of economic development in three respects, namely, in broad respect of providing an economic interpretation of history, in the narrower respect of specifying the motivaing forces of capitalist development, and in the final respect of suggesting an alternative path of planned economic development.

Marx uses his theory of *surplus value* as the economic basis of the 'class struggle' under capitalism and it is on the basis of his theory of surplus value that he builds the superstructure of his analysis of economic development. The surplus value. believes Marx, arises because labour, which is the abslolute and ultimate source of all economic or exchange value, produces more economic value than the cost of labour itself as measured by the supply price of labour or, the subsistence wage that barely maintains the labour force intact. Exploitation does exist since workers fail to receive the whole of the value of the output. The difference between the value of total output and the supply price of labour represents the surplus value which is exporpriated by the capitalists, who are the owners of non-human instruments of production, capital equipment and land. It is the ownership to these instruments of production that enables the capitalists to extract surplus value from labour by forcing them to work longer hours and receive subsistence wage and thus grab a disproportionately large slice of the national cake for them selves. The theory of surplus value thus, implies that there is an antagonism between the share of wages and profits. More profits are clearly at the expense of workers since their magnitude is determined directly by the magnitude is determined directly by the magnitude of surplus value that capitalists extract from labour. *In the Words of Peterson :*

"The notion of surplus value is crucial to the Marxian therory of ecnomic development; surplus value is the source of all profit and thus the amount of surplus value that can expropriated by the capitalistic class will determine the relative share of profit in the income total"

According to Marx, it is surplus value that leads to capital accumulation.The capitalist's main motive is to increase the surplus value whlich goes to swell his profits.

To explain the origin of profit and to analyse the relation between wages and profits, Marx separates capital into *Constant capital* and *Variable capital.* Capital invested in stocks or raw materials or equipment which directly assists the productivity of labour, Marx calls *constant capital* (C). Capital devoted to the purchase of labour power in the form of wages or direct subsistence, he terms *variable capital* (V). The Surplus value is denoted by (S). So the total value of product = $c+v+s$

In order to analyse the nature of cpitalist accumulation, Marx establishes certain relationships between c, v and s. The ratio of constant capital to total capital $\left(\frac{c}{c+v}\right)$ is termed as the *orgenic composition of capital.* The ratio of surplus value (S) to the variable capital (V) has been termed the rate of exploitation by Marx.

$$\text{Rate of Exploitation} = \frac{S}{V}$$

According to Marx the rate of profit is not dependent solely on the rate of exploitation. The rate of profit can change even though the rate of exploitation remains constant, if a change occurs in the organic composition of capital. The influence of technical progress is to alter the organic composition of capital, generally in the direction of raising the ratio of constant to total capital. Hence the tendency of industrial progress is to lower the rate of profit- even though there is no decrease in the rate of exploitation.

One of the consequences of capital accumulation is the concentration of capital in gigantic enterprised. Competition among capitalists forces them to cheapen their products. This can be done by introducing labour saving machines which increase labour productivity. Those capitalists who are unable to replace labour by machines are 'squeezed out' and their enterprises are taken over by big capitalists. Capital accumulation and concentration involve increase in constant capital and decline in variable capital. The rapid growth of constant capital as compared with variable capital leads to a relative decrease in the demand for labour. This process of supplanting labour by machines creates an *industrial reserve army* which increase as capitalism develops. The larger the industrial reserve army, the worse are the conditions of the employed workers, since the capitalist can dismiss dissatisfied and troublesome workers, being able to replace them from the ranks of the reserve army. Capitalists are also able to cut down wages to a semi-starvation level and appropriate more and more surplus value. This is the law of the increasing misery of the masses under capitalism. This is shown in Figure 1.3 where the labour force is taken on the horizontal axis and the wage rate on the vertical axis. D is the demand curve for labour and S is the supply curve of labour.

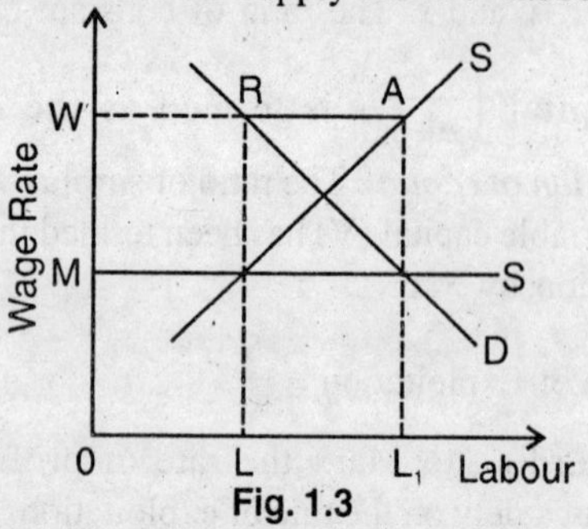

Fig. 1.3

At the wage rate W, there is an increase in the industrial reserve army equal to RA (LL_1). As the industrial reserve army expands, capitalists start adopting labour-saving machines and reduce the wage rate to minimum subsistence level OM in order to have more surplus value.

But when the capitalist is replacing the workers by machines, he is killing the goose that laid the golden eggs. There is a continual reduction of the surplus value. Marx believes that technological progress tends to increase the organic composition of capial. Since the rate of profit is inversely related to the organic composition of capital the former tends to decline with accumulation. Marx explained this tendency of falling rate of profit in terms of the following equation :

The rate of profit is equal to the ratio of total surplus value (S) to the total capital (C+V).

Thus $P = \frac{S}{C+V}$

where P stands for the rate of profit

Now $$P = \frac{S}{C+V} \quad ...(i)$$

Multiplying both the numerator and the denominator by V we get

$$P = \frac{S \times V}{V(C+V)}$$

$$= \frac{S}{V} \times \frac{V}{(C+V)} \quad ...(ii)$$

Here $\frac{S}{V}$ is the rate of exploitation and $\frac{V}{C+V}$ is the ratio of variable capital to total capital $\frac{V}{C+V}$ can also be expressed as :

$$\frac{V}{C+V} = \left(1 - \frac{C}{C+V}\right) \quad ...(iii)$$

substituting (*iii*) in (*ii*)

$$P = \frac{S}{V}\left(1 - \frac{C}{C+V}\right)$$

Now given the rate of exploitation $\left(\frac{S}{V}\right)$, the rate of profit is related inversely with the organic composition of capital $\left(\frac{C}{C+V}\right)$.

The greater the $\frac{C}{C+V}$, the lesser will be the rate of profit and *vice versa*. As greater accumulation and technology results in a more capital-intensive productive process or as there is an increase in the capital-output ratio, the rate of profit tends to decline. From this follows the Marxian conslusion about the inevitable eventual, collapse of the capitalist economic superstructure. Summing up the Marxian views about the collapse of capitalism, *W.C. Peterson* remarks,"The process of capital accumulation and growth leads inevitably to a severe economic crisis. This crisis is the result of both the "falling rate of profit", which must sooner or later adversely affect capital accumulation it self and second, over-production because of an insufficiency of aggregate demand. The latter stems from the progressive decline in the relative share of wage income in the output total. Marx thought the capitalist system would be increasingly wrecked by crises of greater and greater severity until finally it would collapse amidst an uprising of the working class that would usher in the era of communism."

Criticisms

Marx's theory of capitalist development has been accepted by his followers as a gospel truth while it has been severely criticised by his opponents for the following reasons :

1. Surplus Value Unrealistic
2. Technological Progress Helpful in Increasing Employment.
3. Falling Tendency of Profits not Correct

4. Marx could not Undrestand Flexibility in capitalism

5. Static Analysis

Conclusion

Despite these weaknesses, some to the Marxian tools pertaining to his theory of economic development have ever since become part and parcel of the theory of economic growth. Technological progress and innovations are the main stay of any theory of economic development. Similary capital accumulation is the fundamental idea behind economic growth. Profits are still regarded as both the hallmark of capitalist development and its Achilles'heal. Marx showed that economic development does not follow a smooth course but comes about in "fit and starts." Business cycles are inevitable. He pointed output that a state of under-consumption was the main cause of depression and that for stable growth a proper balance between investment and consumption was essential. He also indicated that too low or too high wages in relation to total output can adversely affect investment and thus stifle economic growth.

C. THE SCHUMPETERIAN THEORY

Schumpeter assumes a perfectly competitive economay which is in stationary equilibrium. In such a stationary state, there is perfect competitive equilibrium : no profits, no interest rates, no savings, no investments and no involuntary unemployment. This equilibrium is characterised by what Schumpeter terms the "*circular flow*" which continues to repeat it self in the same manner year after year, similar to the circulation of the blood in an animal organism. In the circular flow, the same products are produced every in the same manner.

According to *Schumpeter*, "development is spontaneous and discontinuous change in the channels of the *circular flow*, disturbance of equilibrium, which for ever alters and displaces the equilibrium state previously existing". These 'spontaneous and discontinuous' changes in economic life are not forced upon it from without but arise by its own initiative from within the economy and appear in the sphere of industrial and commercial life. Development consits in the carrying out of new combinations for which possibilities exist in the stationary state. New combinations come about in the form of innovations. An innovation may consist of :

1. the introduction of a new product;
2. the intrduction of a new method of production;
3. the opening up of a new market;
4. the conquest of a new source of supply of raw materials or semi-manufactured goods; and
5. the carrying out of the new organisation of any industry like the creation of a monopoly.

According to Schumpeter, it is the introduction of a new product and the continual improvements in the existing ones that lead to development. Schumpeter assigns the role of an innovator not to the capitalist but to the *entrepreneur*. The entrepreneur is not a man of ordinary managerial ability, but one who introduces something entirely new. He does not provide funds but directs their use. To perform his economic function, the entrepreneur requires two things: *First,* the existences of technical knowledge in order to produce new products, second, the power of disposal over the factors of production in the form of credit. According to Schumpeter, reservoir of untapped technical knowledge exists which he can make use of. Therefore, credit is essential for development to start.

Schumpeter's model starts with the breaking up the circular flow with an innovation in the form of a new product by an entrepreneur for the purpose of earning profits. In order to break the circular flow, the innovating entrepreneurs are financed by *bank-credit* expansion. Since investmet in innovations is risky, they must pay interest on it. Once the new innovation becomes successful and profitable, other entrepreneurs follow it in "Swarm-like clusters". Innovations in one field may induce other innovations in related fields. The emergence of a motor car industry may, in turn stimulate a wave of new investments in the construction of highways, rubber tyres and petroleum products, etc. But the spread of an innovation is never cent percent. Since investment is assumed to be financed by creation of bank-credit, it increases money incomes and prices and helps to create a cumulative expansion throughout the economy. With the increase in the purchasing power of the consumers, the demand for the products of the old industries increases in relation to supply. Prices rise, profits increase and old industries expand by borrowing from the banks it induces a secondary wave of credit inflation which is super-imposed on the primary wave of innovation. Over-optimism and speculation add further to the boom. After a period of gestation the new products start appearing in the market displacing the old products and enforcing a process of liquidation, re-adjustment and absorption. The demand for the old products is decreased. Their prices fall. The old firms contract output and some are even forced to run into liquidation. As the innovators start repaying bank loans out of profits, the quantity of money is decreased and prices tend to fall. Profits decline Uncertainty and risks increase, the in pulse for innovatoin is reduced and eventually comes to an end. Depression ensues.

Schumpeter believes in the existence of the Kondratief long-wave of upswings and downswings in economic activity. Each long-wave upswing is brought about by an innovation in the form of a new product which leads to further innovations in the methods of production, new forms of business organisation, new sources of supply of raw materials and intermediate products and new markets. Thus there is abundance of goods available for the masses. Once the upswing ends, the long-wave downswing begins and the painful process of readjustment to the "point of previous neighbourhood of equilibrium" starts. Ultimately the natural forces of recovery bring about a revival. Once again equilibrium is restored. Then some enterprising entrepreneurs begin with a new set of innovations, others follow and a new boom begins. Schumpeter describes this process of capitalist development as one of "creative destruction", where in the old economic structures of society are being continually destroyed and the new structures are being continually created in their place. Schumpeter's cyclical process of economic development is illustrated in figure 1.4 where the secondary wave is super imposed on the primary wave of innovation with over-optimism and speculation, development proceeds more rapidly in the prosperity phase. When recession starts, the cycle continues downward below the equilibrium level to the depression phase. Ultimately; another innovation brings about revival.

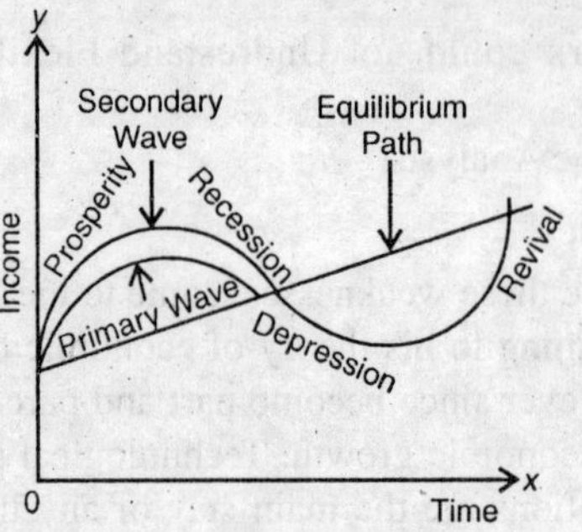

Fig. 1.4

Thus, entrepreneurs are the key figures in the schumpeterian analysis. They bring about economic development in spontaneous and discontinuous manner. "Can capitalism survive? No, I do not think it can", wrote schumpeter, as his final appraisal of the future of capitalism. To him, the very success of capitalism "undermines the social institutions which protect it, and "inevitably"creates conditions in which it will not be able to live and which strongly point to socialism as the heir-apparent".

According to schumpeter, capitalism can maintain itself only so long as entrepreneurs behave like knights and pioneers. But such daring innovators are being destroyed by the cpitalilst system itself which rests on a a rational attitude. This enquiring, sceptical and rational attitude permeates the entire capitalist society. As a result, three forces are discernible, that are the beginning of the creeping death of capitalism. They are :

1. the decadence of the entrepreneurial function;
2. the disintegration of the bourgeois family;
3. the destruction of institutional framework of the cappitalist society.

Criticisms of the Theory

Schumpeter's theory has certain weaknesses.

1. Schumpeter's analysis of the process of transition from capitalism to socialism is not correct.

2. Schumpeter gives too much importance to bank-credit in his theory.

3. The downswings and the upswings are not essehtial for economic development.

4. Economic development not only depends on innovations but also on many economic and social changes.

5. Schumpeter's contention that cyclical changes are due to innovations is also not correct.

To conclude with *Meier and Baldwin*, "Schumpeter's broad socio-economic analysis of capitalist process is generally admired. Yet few seem prepared to accept its conclusions. His arguments are stimulating but not completely convincing..... Although Schumpeter's analysis is provocative, it seems one-sided and over-emphasized".

SCHUMPETER'S ANALYSIS AND UNDERDEVELOPED COUNTRIES

The applicability of Schumpeter's theory to underdeveloped countries is limited for the following reasons :

1. Different Socio-Economic Order
2. Lack of Entrepreneurship
3. Not Applicable to Socialist Countries
4. Not Applicable to Mixed Economies
5. Neglects Populaion Growth
6. Neglects External Effects
7. Neglects Savings
8. Neglects Consumption
9. Unsatisfactory Explanation of Inflationary Forces.

Conclusion

All the same, Schumpeter's theory underlines the importance of inflationary financing and innovations as the main factors in economic development. Infalationary financing is one of the potent methods which every underdeveloped country tries to use at one time or another. His analysis is relevant to underdeveloped countries from the standpoint of long range increase in productivity and absorption of surplus labour in gainful employment as a result of innovations. Though it purports to analyee the problems of western capitalism, "it can certainly give clues to problems that may arise in underdeveloped countries, once the process of industrialisation begins, as well as provide a lesson for avoiding waste and extra hardships that attend an un planned uncoordinated development."

THEORY OF GROWTH

A. HARROD-DOMAR MODEL

R.F. Harrod and E. Domar have made a distinct contribution in evolving dynamic models to suit the changing conditions of an economy. Both these models are very similar, and to answer the questions posed by the post—Keynesians. In fact, one can say that Domar's model is the American version of Harrod's model, or alternatively Harrod's model is the English Version of Domar's model. Both these models stress on the conditions which are very essential for achieving and maintaining steady growth.

Like classical economists, Harrod and Domar assign a crucial role to capital accumulation and investment in the process of growth. Investment plays a double role. On the one hand, investment (through the operation of multiplier) generates income and, on the other hand, it increases the productive capacity, by enlarging the capital stock. In other words, investment affects the level of income as well as production. The effect of investment on income is known as '*Multiplier Effect*' and that on production is known as '*Productivity Effect*' or '*Sigma Effect*'. In mathematics sigma is denoted by. Multiplier effect is the Keynesian tool and productivity effect is the classical tool. *Harrod-Domar* analysis takes into consideration both the tool. In short, Harrod-Domar model strikes a synthesis between the multiplier effect and productivity effect. The simultaneous operation of these two effects is an essential condition for dynamic equilibrium.

Assumptions : The main assumptions of Harrod-Domar model are as follow:

1. An inital full-employment level of income has already been achieved.

2. There is no government interference in the functioning of the economy, *i.e.*, the policy of *laissez-faire* prevails.

3. The model is based on the principle of "closed economy", there are no exogenous factors or forces

influencing the growth variables of the economy. In short, government restrictions on trade and the complications caused by international trade are ruled out.

4. There are no lags in adjustment, *i.e.*, the Economic Variables, such as saving, investment, income and expenditure adjust them-selves in the same period of time. To make it cleaver, it can be stated that any change in saving brings about corresponding changes in the level of investment in the same period of time. All these variables relate to the same period of time.

5. The average propensity to save (APS) and the marginal propensity to save (MPS) are equal to each other. In other words, APS = MPS or $\frac{S}{Y} = \frac{\Delta S}{\Delta Y}$; *i.e.*, the absolute change in saving is equal to the relative change in saving.

6. Propensity to save and "Capital Coefficient" (*i.e.*, capital-output ratio) are constant. The law of constant returns operates in the economy because the capital-output ratio is assumed constant.

7. Income, investment and saving are all defined in the net sense, *i.e.*, they are over and above dipreciation. In other words, depreciation charges are not included in these variables.

8. Saving and investment are equal in ex-ante as well as in ex-post sense, *i.e.*, there is accounting as well as functional equality between saving and investment. The equality can be expressed as

So = Io (accounting equality)

Sc = Ic (functional equality)

So and Io are observed saving and observed investments respectively.

So and Ic are expected saving and expected investments respectively.

DOMAR'S MODEL

Domar's analysis shows, that he is very emphatic about the necessity of viewing growth from the demand as well as the supply side. He is of the opinion that pre-Keynessian analysis emphasised the capacity (supply side) of the problem and the Keynesian approach concentrated on the demand side alone. But his emphasis on the dual character of the investment process makes the approach to the equilibrium rate of growth from investment (capital) point of view more promising. Investment increases the productive capacity and also generate income, thus providing us both sides of the equation, the solution of which yields the required rate of growth.

The following symbols are used in Domar's model:

Y_α = level of net national income or level of effective demand at full-employment (demand side)

Y_s = level of productive capacity or supply at full-employment level (supply side)

K = real capital

I = net investment, which results in the increase of real capital *i.e.*, Δk

α = marginal propensity to save, which is the reciprocal of multiplier *i.e.*, $\frac{1}{\text{multiplier}}$

σ = sigma or productivity of capital or of net investment

It would be interesting to explain Domar's model with the help of equations used by K.K. Kurihara and the above notations are used in the equations, given below:

$$Y\alpha = \frac{I}{\alpha} \qquad ...(1)$$

This equation explains (*a*) that the level of effective demand ($y\alpha$) is directly related to the level of investment (I). Any increase in the level of investment will directly increase the level of effective demand and *vice versa*. (b) The effective demand is inversely related to the MPS(α). Any increase in MPS(α) will decrease the level of effective demand and *vice versa*. This is the demand side.

$$Ys = \sigma K \qquad ...(2)$$

This equation explains that the supply of output (Ys) at full employment depends upon two factors, *i.e.*, productive capacity of the capital (σ) and the amount of the capital (K). Any increase or decrease in any of these two factors will raise or reduce the supply of output. If the productivity of capital (σ) increase, that will favourably affect the supply. Similar will be the effect of real capital on supply of output. This is the supply side.

For equilibrium, the demand and supply should be equal. Therefore,

$$Y\alpha = Ys$$

$$\frac{I}{\alpha} = \sigma K$$

or $$I = \alpha\sigma K \quad ...(3)$$

This is the condition for "*achieving the steady growth*". Now we proceed further to explain the condition for maintaining the steady growth. For that we have to add increments to the demand as well as to the supply equations discussed above. The demand and supply equations in the incremental form can be written as follows :

$$\Delta Y\alpha = \frac{\Delta I}{\alpha} \quad ...(4)$$

Increments have been shown in the level of effective demand and investment, because they are variables, but increment has not been shown in 'α' because it remains constant on the basis of the assumptions employed.

$$\Delta Ys = \sigma\Delta k \quad ...(5)$$

Change in the supply of output (ΔYs) can take place because of change in real capital (ΔK), as the productivity of capital (σ) remains constant. Moreover the change in real capital is equal to net investment. Therefore

$$\Delta K = I$$

substituting the value of ΔK in (S) we get

$$\Delta Ys = \sigma I \quad ...(6)$$

The equality between (4) and (6) will provide us the conditions for the maintenance of steady growth. Equating these two equations (4) and (6) we get,

$$\Delta Y\sigma = \Delta y_s \text{ or } \frac{\Delta I}{\alpha} = \sigma I \text{ or } \frac{\Delta I}{I} = \sigma\alpha$$

This shows that the rate of growth of net investment $\left(\frac{\Delta I}{I}\right)$ should be equal to the product of marginal propensity to save (α) and the productivity of capital (σ). This equality must be ensured to maintain the stable and steady growth of the economy. In Kurihara's words, "It is an increase in productive capacity (ΔYs) due to increment of real capital (ΔK), which must be matched by an equal increase in effective demand ($\Delta Y\alpha$) due to an increment of investment (ΔI), if a growing economy with an expanding stock of capital is to maintain continuous full employment." So, the essential and sufficient condition for maintaining the steady growth of an expanding economy is

$$\frac{\Delta I}{I} = \sigma\alpha$$

or $$\frac{\Delta Y}{Y} = \sigma\alpha \quad (\because \frac{\Delta Y}{Y} \text{ is also equal to } \frac{\Delta I}{I})$$

In the words of Meier and Baldwin, "The answer to the problem of what rate of growth is necessary to maintain a continuous state of full employment is that, investment and real income must grow at a constant annual percentage rate (or compound interest rate) equal to the product of the propensity to save and the average productivity of investment (the inverse of capital coefficient or accelerator)."

Domar's equation of steady growth rate can be explained with the help of a numerical example. Suppose the productivity of capital (σ) is 25% and the marginal propensity to save 'α' is 12% then, the growth rate of investment $\left(\frac{\Delta I}{I}\right)$ would be equal to $\sigma\alpha$

i.e.,

$$\frac{25}{100} \times \frac{12}{100} = \frac{3}{100} = 3\%$$

Thus income or investment must grow at the annual rate of 3% if full employment growth rate or steady growth rate is to be maintained. In brief, "Full employment requires that investment and income grow at a constant annual relative rate equal to the product of propensity to save and the average productivity of investment".

Path of Disequilibrium : If the investment grows at a constant percentage rate $\sigma\alpha$, the productive capacity, although continually growing, will be fully used. On the other hand, if investment grows at a greater or lesser rate than the $\sigma\alpha$, then the following two types of situations will arise:

(*i*) when $\frac{\Delta I}{I}$ or $\frac{\Delta Y}{Y} > \sigma\alpha$

(*ii*) when $\frac{\Delta I}{I}$ or $\frac{\Delta Y}{Y} < \sigma\alpha$

Under the first situation, inflation will appear in economy because as higher rate of income it will provide greater purchasing power to the people. This will result in the expansion of demand, leading to the emergence of inflation as the productive capacity ($\sigma\alpha$) will not cope with the increased level of income or investment. *The first situation will, therefore, create inflation in economy.*

The second situation, under which growth rate of income or investment $\left(\frac{\Delta Y}{Y} \text{ or } \frac{\Delta I}{I}\right)$, is lagging behind the productive capacity, will result in over-production. The lesser growth rate of income will put a constraint on the purchasing power of the people, thus reducing the level of demand and resulting in the overproduction of goods,

So, under these situations, the maintenance of stable and steady growth is impossible and economy will be under the constant strain of either inflation or overproduction and unemployment.

Harrod's Model

So far, we have discussed Domar's model, which explains the conditions for achieving and maintaining the dunamic equilibrium Harrod's growth model also concentrates on these issues. Broadly speaking *R.F. Harrod*, has raised three sets of issues:

1. How can steady growth rate be achieved in the model with a fixed capital-output ratio (capital-coefficient) and the fixed saving income ratio (propensity to save)?
2. How can the steady growth rate be maintained? or what are the conditions for maintaining the stable growth?
3. How do natural factors put a ceiling on the growth rate of the economy?

In order to discuss these three sets of issues, Harrod has explained three growth rates. The growth rates are:

(a) Actual growth rate

(b) Warranted growth rate

(c) Natural growth rate

Now we discuss these growth rates sepaprately.

***(a)* Actual Growth Rate:** It is the growth rate, which is determined by the actual amount of saving and investment in the country. In other words, it can be defined as the ratio of change in income (ΔY) to the total income (Y) in the given period. If actual growth rate is denoted by G, then $G = \frac{\Delta Y}{Y}$.

According to Harrod, actual growth rate G is determined by two factors, saving-income ratio and capital-output ratio, which remain fixed in a given period. The relationship between the actual growth rate and its determinants, can be expressed in the form of an equation given below:

$$GC = S \qquad ...(1)$$

Where G is the actual rate of growth, C represents the capital output ratio or $\frac{\Delta K}{\Delta Y}$, S refers to the saving-income ratio (S/Y). This equation explains the simple truism that saving and investment (in the ex-post sense) are equal to each other. This simple truism is explained below:

$$\text{Since} \qquad G = \frac{\Delta Y}{Y} \text{ and } C = \frac{\Delta K}{\Delta Y}$$

$$\text{or } C = \frac{I}{\Delta Y} \; [\because \Delta K = I] \text{ and } S = \frac{S}{Y}$$

Substituting the values of G, C and s in equation (1), we get

$$\frac{\Delta Y}{Y} \times \frac{I}{\Delta Y} = \frac{S}{Y}$$

$$\frac{I}{Y} = \frac{S}{Y} \text{ or } I = S.$$

Thus, equation (1) explains that the condition for achieving the steady growth rate or dynamic equilibrium is that ex-post saving must be equal to ex-post investment. In cther words, there should be accounting equality between saving and investment, if dynamic equilibrium is to be achieved.

***(b)* Warranted Growth Rate:** Warranted growth rate refers to that growth rate of the economy, when it is working at full capacity by making full and optimum use of machine and manpower. It is also known as "*Full capacity growth rate*" *or* "*Full-employment growth rate*" or "*Potential growth rate*". This growth rate is denoted by G*w* and has been defined by *Meier and Baldwin* in these words, "G*w* is interpreted as the rate of income growth required for the full *utilisation* of a growing stock of capital, so that entrepreneurs will be satisfied with the amount of investment actually made".

Warranted growth rate (G*w*) is determined by two factors-

(*i*) capital-output ratio

(*ii*) saving-income ratio

The relationship between the warranted growth rate and its determinants can be expressed in the form of an equation G*w* C*r* =S

Where G*w* refers to warranted growth rate, C*r* denotes the amount of capital required to maintain the warranted growth rate or the growth rate of output. S is the saving-income ratio.

Having discussed the two rates of growth (*i.e.*, actual and warranted), we now discuss the issue, as how to achieve the steady growth. According to Harrod, the economy can achieve stable growth if G = G*w* and C = C*r i.e.* actual growth rate must be equal to the warranted growth rate. In other words, growth rate of income must be equal to the growth rate of output. Secondly, the capital-output ratio needed to achieve G, must be equal to the required capital-output to maintain G*w*, given the saving coefficient (S). This amounts to saying that actual investment (ex-post investment) must be equal to the expected investment (ex-ante investment), if an economy were to achieve the objectives of stable growth.

Instability of Growth: We have just discussed that the stable growth of economy requires an equality between G and G*w* on the one hand, and C and C*r* on the other. But the reader should bear in mind that this type of equality is rarely found in the economy, however planned and regulated it may be. Harrod analyses this situation, when these conditions are not satisfied.

(*i*) when G > G*w* then C < C*r*

(*ii*) when G < G*w* then C > C*r*

Proof : G C = S and G*w* C*r* = S

or $$GC = \frac{s}{c} \text{ or } Gw = \frac{s}{Cr}$$

if G > G*w*

$$\frac{s}{c} > \frac{s}{Cr} \quad \text{or} \quad \frac{1}{C} > \frac{1}{Cr}$$

cross multiplying

$$Cr > C \quad \text{or} \quad C < Cr$$

Similarly it can be proved

When G*w* < G then C > C*r*

We take up the discussion of the first situation when G is greater than G*w*. Under this situation the growth rate of income being greater than the growth rate of output, the demand for output (because of higher level of income) will exceed the supply of output (because of lower level of output) and the economy will experience a chronic inflation. It can be explained in another way too when C < C*r*. Under this situation the actual amount of capital falls short of the required amount of capital. This will lead to deficiency of capital, which in turn would adversely affect the volume of goods to be produced. Fall in the level of output will result in the scarcity of goods and hence inflation and the growth of economy under inflation can never be stable.

If, on the other hand, G is less than G*w*, then the growth rate of income will be less than the growth rate of output. Under this situation there would be more goods for sale, but the income would not be sufficient to purchase those goods. In Keynesian terminology we can say,that there would be deficiency of demand and the economy will face the problem of chronic deflation. This situation can also be explained when C is greater than C*r*. Under this situation, the actual amount of capital is more than the required amount of capital for investment. when the capital amount available is more, it would dampen the marginal efficiency of capital and lead to *chronic depression* and unemployment. Thus growth of the economy under the situation of chronic depression can never be stable.

On the basis of the above discussion, we can conclude that stable growth or steady-state growth can occur only when G = G*w*. Any deviation of G from G*w* will result in cumulative departure from the path of steady growth. In other words, the economy will be in a state of instability when G and G*w* are not equal to each other. The equilibrium between G and G*w* is called *steady-state equilibrium* or *knife-edge equilibrium.*

Harrod also states that deviations of G from G*w* are unstable. If G departs from G*w* then it will depart farther and farther from it, as departure from the path of steady growth is self-sustaining. It feeds on itself.

In contrast, if G is less than G*w*, then desired saving would exceed desired investment, the entreprenuers will be pessimistic about the future and they will keep the level of output below G*w*, and this would further retard the growth.

***(c)* Natural Growth Rate:** If it is assumed that propensity to save or capital-output ratio does not change,what will stop income from shooting up or down without limit? Harrod points out that generally there is an upper limit to the expansion of output, which is determined by natural conditions such as size of the labour force, natural resources, capital equipment and state of technical knowledge. This limit is called *"full employment ceiling"*. This upper limit may change as the factors of production grow, and technological progress takes place. Harrod calls the growth in this upper full employment ceiling the natural growth rate. In other words, it is the maximum growth rate, which an economy can achieve with its available natural resources. Natural growth rate is denoted by G*n*.

Interactions of G, G*w*, G*n*: While discussing the interaction of three rates if growth, Harrod points out that in the years after recession G may be higher than G*n* for a considerable period of time, but it will not continue to rise indefinitely. In other words, the process of expansion cannot go on indefinitely, as it is limited by the availability of natural factors. The ceiling fixed by labour and natural resources prevent further rise. This has been, shown in figure 1.5. The economy cannot remain at the ceiling level; it has either to rise or fall.

When G touches G*n*,G*w* cannot lag behind, but will tend to catch up with it. Since the rate of rise of G

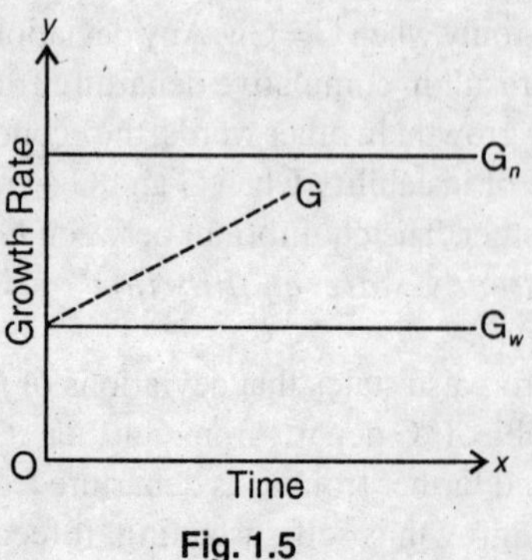

Fig. 1.5

cannot be maintained, G*n* will exceed G and then the downtrend starts. The downtrend will result in over-production, which in turn will lead to a cumulative downswing. The economy will face the problem of secular stagnation and chronic unemployment. This has been shown in the diagram. But this down trend cannot continue undefinitely. The reason is that the lower limit of depression is set by the minimum consumption level. As the consumption level cannot fall below a minimum level, so the fixed capital too cannot fall though working capital may be reduced. In this way gross investment cannot be negative. This position, combined with the investor's expectation for the bright future generated by the actual resources position, will gradually set the wheels of recovery in motion. The economy will once again be in the upward phase. This has been shown in figure 1.6

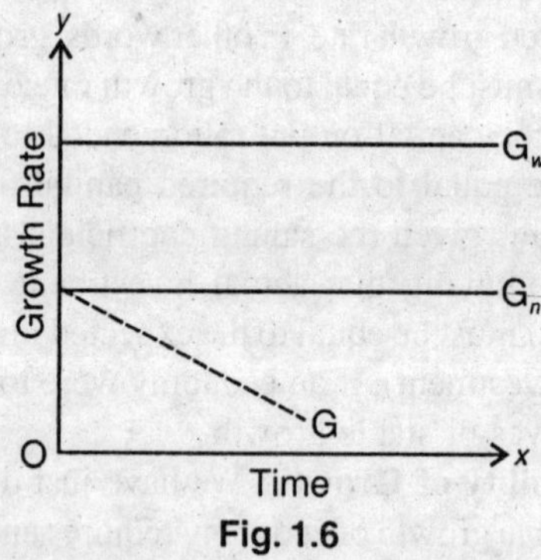

Fig. 1.6

Analysis of Business Cycle: From the study of this model, it is quite evident, that the process of growth of a capitalist economy is never steady because of its in herent characteristics. There cannot be a steady growth of income and output in such an economy. There will always be ups and downs in a capitalist economy. Therefore cyclical fluctuations are implicit in the phenomena of growth in such an economy.

Business cycles are not free to vary without limit. In upward direction G*n* provides a limit in the form of a "full employment ceiling" beyond which real income cannot expand in short period because of the shortage of labour and capital. In the downward direction there is also a limit set by a floor of autonomous investment, because gross investments cannot be negative.

Main Point: The main points of the Harrod-Domar analysis can be summarised as below:

1. Investment is the centre of the problem of steady and stable growth, because investment plays a double role; on the one hand, it generates income and on the other, it increases the productive capacity of the economy.

2. The increased capacity can result in greater output or greater unemployment depending on the behaviour of income.

3. Conditions can be stated for the behaviour of income, that will allow full employment to be maintained over time. These conditions specify the growth rates,which can ensure full employment of labour and full utilisation of capital stock.

4. These conditions, however, designate only a steady line of growth for the economy. The actual growth rate may differ from the warranted rate of growth. If the actual growth rate is greater than the warranted rate of growth, the economy will experience chronic inflation. If the actual growth rate is less than the warranted growth rate, the economy will slide towards chronic deflation.

5. The business cycles are viewed as the deviation from the path of steady growth. These deviations become self-aggravating and self-cumulating, but are limited in the upward trend by the "full employment ceiling" and in the downward direction by the floor of autonomous investment and consumption.

COMPARISON OF HARROD AND DOMAR MODELS

Now we discuss in what sense these models are similar and in what sense they are different.

Similarities

(i) Both the models are based on similar assumptions. It is for this reason that the names of Harrod and Domar are bracketed together in the context of growth models.

(ii) Both the models employ the Keynesian saving-investment equality as the equilibrium condition for the steady growth of economy.

(iii) Harrod's warranted growth rate G*w* signifies the same thing as the product of marginal propensity to save (α) and the productivity of capital (σ) in Domar's model. In other words $Gw = \alpha\sigma$. Both these models stress that knife edge equilibrium path for an economy is highly unstable. It is due to the inherent characteristic of a capitalist economy.

(iv) Both the models have been discussed in the context of advanced economies, where capital is fund in abundance. So, these models solve the problems of advanced economies rather than these of backward and poor economies.

Differences

No doubt both the models have been evolved in a similar set of circumstances, yet slight differences between the two models are explained below.

(i) Harrod and Domar have used marginal propensity to save in their models, but this is represented by the different notations. In Domar's model the marginal propensity to save is denoted by α (Alpha) and in Harrod's model it is denoted by S. Both α and s are the propensities to save expressed as ratios.

(ii) In Domar's model, the productivity of capital is represented by σ (Sigma), which means that,it is the inverse of capital-output ratio. In Harrod's model capital-output ratio is represented by C, which is less than one. So Domar's σ is equal to $\frac{1}{C}$ (reciprocal of C) in Harrod's model. The only numerical difference between Domar's co-efficient is that the one is the inverse of the other. This co-efficient belongs to the supply side and is known as the acceleration coefficient. When investors invest an additional amout in production, it accelerates the increase of income.

(iii) Though Harrod and Domar have employed the same acceleration coefficient with only different symbols in their models, yet there is a hidden difference between c and σ. Harrod's acceleration coefficient may be called psychological and Domar's technological. Harrod is of the opinion that producers invest C times the increment of the income. It means that, when income increases, the producer's psyshology is to make net investment C time of that increase. It is true that there are technical considerations behind the operation, but immediately it is the producer's psychology that determines how much to invest. Hence the acceleration coefficient is

psychological.

Domar's acceleration coefficient is technological. Domar has used productivity of capital (σ) in his model and it explains the relationship between investment and output. Investment is the independent variable and output or income is the dependent variable. Since output is determined by the nature of technology it is technological. It is the technology that determines the amount of income or output to be obtained by given rise of investment.

Limitations of these Models: Some of the assumptions made by these models make it quite unrealistic.

1. The constancy of the propensity to save and the capital-output ratio are unrealistic as they tend to change in the long-run.

2. The assumption that labour and capital are used in fixed proportions is untenable. In normal practice, labour and capital enjoy a certain degree of substitutability.

3. Both the models overlook changes in price levels. In the words of **Meier and Baldwin,**"If allowance is made for price changes and variable proportions in production, then the system may have much stronger stability than the Harrod model suggests".

4. The assumption regarding constancy of interest rates is irrelevant to the analysis. A reduction in interest rates during periods of over-production can make capital intensive processes more profitable by in creasing the demand for capital and there by reduce excess supply of goods.

5. The model ignores developmental programmes under taken by the government which help to speed up the process of development.

6. The model has not dealt with the distinguishing factors between capital and consumer goods.

Despite their limitations, these models form an important aspect in the field of economic growth because "they represent a stimulating attempt to dynamise and secularise keynes' static short-run saving and investment theory".

B. THE SOLOW MODEL (LONG-RUN GROWTH MODEL)

Prof R.M. Solow builds his model as an alternative to the Harrod-Domar model. The latter model is at best a knife-edge balance built on three key parameters *viz*, the saving ratio, the capital-output ratio and the rate of increase of the labour force. If the magnitudes of these parameters change the consequence would be gloomy, perpetuating growing unemployment or chronic inflation. The balance itself is poised on the equality between G*w* and G*n* which is very delicate. If once the fixed proportions assumtion of the Harrod-Domar model is abandoned, the knife-edge balance also disappears with it.

Assumptions: Solow builds his model around the following assumptions:

(a) One composite commodity is produced.

(b) Output is measured in net terms.

(c) Constant returns to scale.

(d) There are only two factors-labour and capital. They are paid according to their marginal physical productivites. They are substitutable for each other.

(e) Prices and wages are flexible.

(f) There is not only perpetual full employment of labour but also full employment of the available stock of capital.

(g) There is neutral technical progress.

On the basis of these assumptions Solow's model shows that there would be a tendency for capital-labour ratio to adjust itself through time in the direction of equilibrium ratio. If the initial ratio of capital to labour is more, capital and output would grow more slowly than labour force and *vice versa.*

Solow takes output as a whole, the only commodity, in the economy. Its annual rate of production is designated as Y_t which represents the real income of the community, part of it is consumed and the rest is saved and invested. That which is saved is a constant S, and the rate of saving is $S.Y_t$. K_t is the stock of capital. Thus net investment is the rate of increase of this stock of capital *i.e.,* $\frac{dk}{dt}$ or K. So the basic identity is K = S.Y ...(1)

Since output is produced with capital and labour, technological possibilities are represented by the production function

$$Y = F(K, L) \qquad ...(2)$$

That shows constant returns to scale. Inserting equation (2) in (1) we have

$$K = S\,F(K, L) \qquad ...(3)$$

In equation (3), L represents total employment. Since population is growing exogenously, the labour force increases at a constant relative rate n. Thus

$$Lt = Loe^{et} \quad ...(4)$$

N = Harrod's natural rate of growth in the absence of technological change.

Lt = the available supply of labour at time (t) the right hand side of equation (4) shows the compound rate of the growth of labour force from period O to period T. Equation (4) can be regarded as a supply curve of labour. By inserting equation (4) in (3), Solow gives the basic equation

$$K = SF(K, Loe^{nt}) \quad ...(5)$$

Solow regards this basic equation as determining the time path of capital accumulation, K, that maust be followed if all available labour is to be fully employed. It also provides the time profile for capital stock. Once the time paths of capial stock and of the labour force are known, the corresponding time path of real output can be computed from the production function.

Posisble Grath Patterns. In order to find out if there is always a capital accumulation path consistent with any rate of growth of the labour force towards steady state, Solow introduced his fundamental equation.

$$R = SF(r, 1) - nr \quad ...(6)$$

In this equation r is the ratio of capital to labour (K/L), n is the relative rate of change of the labour force (L/L). The function SF (r, 1) represents output per worker as a function of capital per worker. In other words, it is the total product curve as varying amounts r of capital are employed with are unit of labour. Equation (6) states that the rate of change of capital-output ratio ($\bar{r}$) is the difference of two terms, one representing the increment of capital SF (r, 1) and the other increment of labour (nr).

The possible growth patterns based on his fundamental equation (6) are illustrated in the following figure 1.7.

The straight line passing through the origin is the function nr. The other curve represents the function SF (r, 1). It is so drawn as to show diminishing marginal productivity of capital. At the point of intersection of the two curves nr = SF (r, 1) and $\bar{r}$ = o, then $r = \bar{r}$. When $\bar{r} = 0$ the capital-labour ratio is a constant and the capital stock must expand at the same rate as

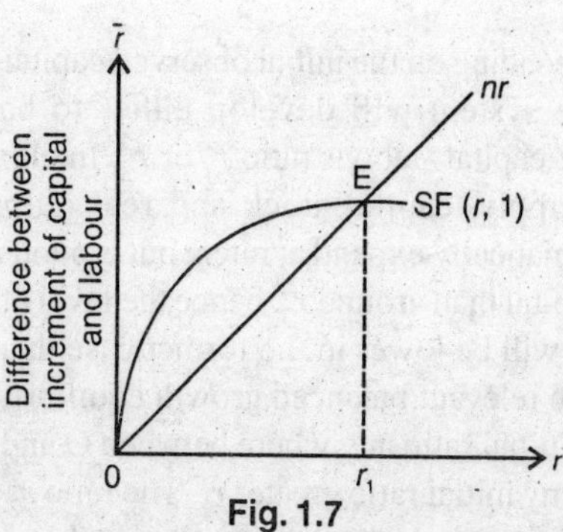

Fig. 1.7

the b labour force, *i.e., n.* Once the capital-labour ratio $\bar{r}$ is established. It will be maintained, and capital and labour will grow in proportion. Assuming constant returns to scale real output will also grow at the some relative and output per hand of labour force will be constant. At r' then will be the balanced growth equilibrium.

What will be the behaviour of the capital-labour ratio if then is a divergence between $\bar{r}$ and R. If r lies to the right of $\bar{r}$ or $r > \bar{r}$, $nr <$ SF (r, 1), and R will decrease toward $\bar{r}$. On the contrary, if r lies to the left of $\bar{r}$ or $r < \bar{r}$, $nr <$ sF (r, 1), and r will increase toward $\bar{r}$. Thus the equilibrium value $\bar{r}$ is stable.

But the strong stability shown in the above figure is not inevitable. It depends on the shope of the productivity curve SF (r, 1). In figure 1.8 the productivity curve SF (r, 1) intersects the curve nr at three points r_1, r_2, r_3. But r_1 and r_3 are stable equilibrium positions because the total productivity curve SF (r, 1) is above nr but at r_2 it is below nr. Therefore, r_2 is an unstable equilibrium position.

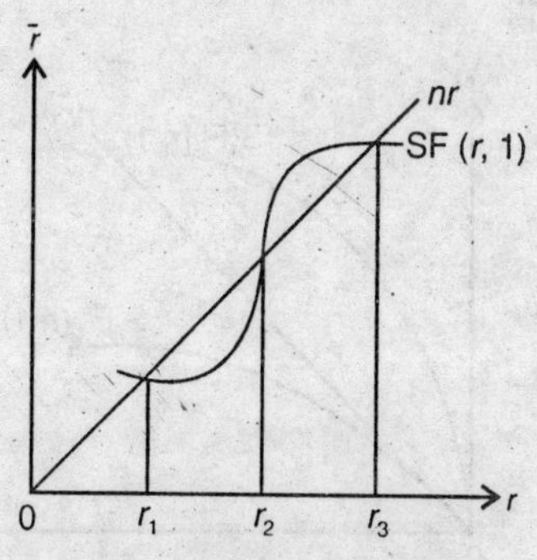

Fig. 1.8

"Depending on the initial observed capital-labour ratio, the system will develop either to balanced growth at capital -labour ratio r_1 or r_3. In either case labour supply, capital stock and real output will asymptomatically expand at raten, but around r_1 there is less capital than around r_3, hence the level of output per head will be lower in the former case than in the latter. The relevant balanced growth equilibrium is at r_1 for an initial ratio any where between O and r_2, it is ar r_3 for any initial ratio greater r_2. The ratio r_2 is itself an equilibrium growth ratio, but an unstable one, any accidental disturbance will be magnified over time. Figure 1.8 has been drawn so that production is possible without capital; hence the origin is not an equilibrium 'growth' configuration."

Solow points out that figure 1.8 does not exhaust all possibilities, the shows two more possibilities, as shown in figure 1.9. The curve NR depicts the equilibrium growth path where the warranted and natural rates of growth are equal. The curve $S_1F^1(r, 1)$ which is above *nr* represents a highly productive system in which capital and income increase more rapidly than the labour supply. In this system, which is of perpectual full employment, income and saving increase so much that the capital-labour ratio increases limitlessly. On the other hand, the curve $S_2F''(r, 1)$ depicts a highly unproductive system in which the full employment path leads to ever diminishing per capita income.

However, aggregate income rises in this system because net investment is always positive and the labour supply is increasing. It is to be noted that both the systems have diminishing marginel productivity throughout.

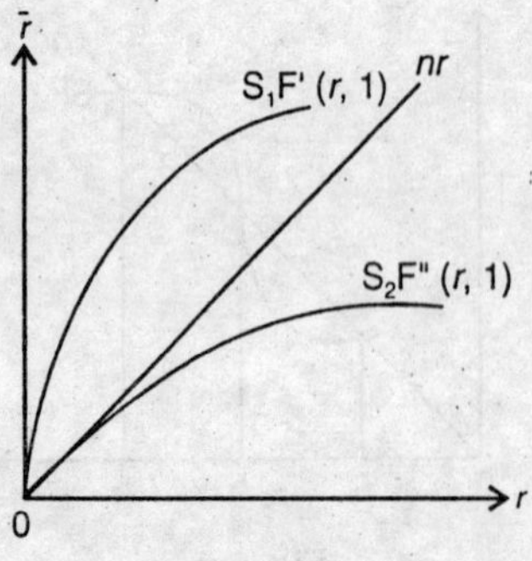

Fig. 1.9

Professor Solow concludes his model thus: "When production takes place under the usual neo-classical conditions of variable proportions and constant returns to scale, no simple opposition between natural and warranted rates of growth is possible. There may not be ...... any knife ...... edge. The system can adjust to any given rate of growth of the labour force, and eventually approach a state of steady proportional expansion".*i.e.,*

$$\frac{\Delta K}{K} = \frac{\Delta L}{L} = \frac{\Delta Y}{Y}$$

Critical Appraisal

Solow is a pioneer in constructing a neo-classical model. The solow model is a major improvement over the Harrod-Domar model. The takes a continuous production function which has come to be known as the new-classical production in analysing the process of growth. The assumption of substitutability between labour and capital gives the growth process an adjustability and provides a touch of realism.

The aim of the Solow model "was to examine what might be called the fight-rope view of economic growth and to see where more flexible assumptions about production would lead to a simple model". Still the solow model is weak is weak in many respects.

1. The model takes up only the problem of balance between Harrod's G*w* and G*n* and leaves out the problem of balance between G and G*w*.

2. There is the absence of an investment function in this model. If the investment function is introduced than the model would present all instabilities noticeable in the Harrodian model. *Prof. A. Sen* mentions in this connection that the assumption of substitutability between labour and capital does not seem to be a key difference between neo-classical and neo-Keynesian studies of growth and the main difference seems to lie in the investment function and the consequent failure to assign a major role to entrepreneurial expectations about the future.

3. The labour-augmenting technical progress on which the theory is based is a special case of Harrod-Domar neutral technical progress of the Cobb-Douglas production function which does not posses any empirical justification.

4. Flexibility of factor prices assumption of solow

may bring difficulties in the path towards steady growth.

5. The model is based on the unrealistic assumption of homogeneous and malleable capital. Capital goods are of aggragation.

6. The model leaves out the causative process of technical progress and treats the latter as an exgeneous factor in the growth process. Solow ignores the problem of inducing technical progress through learning, investment research and capital accumulation.

C. LEWIS' THEORY OF UNLIMITED SUPPLIES OF LABOUR

Professor W. Arthur Lewis has developed a very systematic theory of Economic Development with Unlimited supplies of labour. Like the classical economists, he believes that in many underdeveloped countries an unlimited supply of labour is available at a subsistence wage. Economic development takes place when capital accumulates as a result of the withdrawal of surplus labour from the "subsistence" sector to the "capitalist" sector. Since the supply of labour is unlimited, new industries can be established or existing industries expanded without limit at the current wage by drawing upon labour from the subsistence sector. The main sources from which workers would be coming for employment at the subsistence wage as economic development proceeds are "the farmers, the casuals, the petty traders, women, in the household and population growth". But the capitalist sector also needs skilled workers. Lewis argues that skilled labour is only a "*quasi bottleneck*" a temporary bottleneck-which can be removed by providing training facilities to unskilled workers.

Capitalists aim at profit maximisation. It is they who save and automatically invest what they save. Since the marginal productivity of labour in the capitalist sector is higher than the capitalist wage, this results in capitalist surplus. This surplus is reinvested in new capital assets. Capital formation takes place and more people are employed from the subsistence sector. This process continues till the capital-labour ratio rises and the supply of labour becomes in elastic and the surplus labour disappears. Thus capital formation depends on the capitalist surplus. The lewis theory can be explained with the help of the figure 1.10. The horizontal axis measures the quantity of labour employed and the vertical axis, its wage and marginal product. OS represents average subsistence wage in the subsistence sector, and OW the capitalist wage. At OW wage in the capitalist sector, the supply of labour is unlimited, as shown by the horizontal supply curve of labour WW. In the beginning, when ON_1 labour is employed in the capitalist sector, its marginal productivity curve is $P_1 L_1$ and the total output of this sector is $OP_1 Q_1 N_1$. Out of this, workers are paid wages equal to the area $OW Q_1 N_1$. The remaining area $WP_1 Q_1$ shows surplus output. This is the capitalist surplus or total profit earned by the capitalist sector. When this surplus is reinvested, the curve of marginal productivity shifts upwards to P_2L_2. The capitalist surplus and employment are now larger than before being $WP_2 Q_2$ and ON_2 respectively. Further reinvestments raise the marginal productivity curve and the level of employment to $P_3 L_3$ and ON_3 and so on, till the entire surplus labour is absorbed in the capitalist sector. After this, the supply curve WW will slope from left to right upwards like an ordinary supply curve, and wages and employment will continue to rise with development.

Thus, capital is formed out of profits earned by the capitalists. According to Lewis, if technical progress is capital-saving, it may be considered as an increment in capital, and if it is labour saving, it may be considered as an increment in the marginal productivity of labour. As such, he does not make any distinction between the growth of technical knowledge and the growth of productive capital and

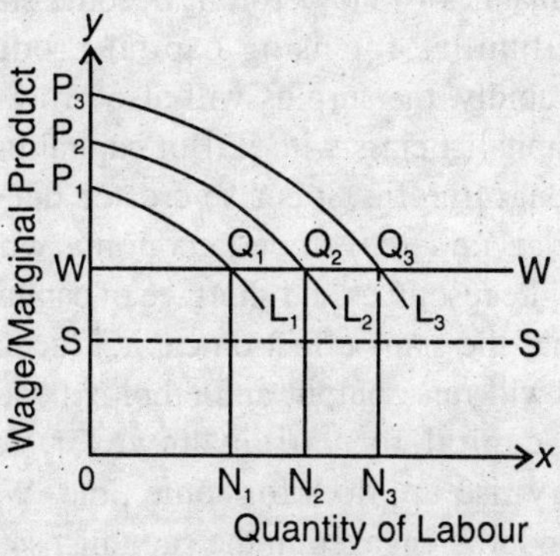

Fig. 1.10

treats them as a "single phenomenon" with the result that technical progress tends to raise profits and increase employment in the capitalist sector.

"The central problem in the theory of economic development", according to Lewis, "is to understand the process by which a community which was previously saving and investing 4 or 5 percent of its national income or less converts itself into an economy where valountary saving is running at about 12 to 15 percent of national income or more. This is the central problem because the central fact of economic development is rapid capital accumulation (including knowledge and skills with capital)". In underdeveloped countries with surplus labour, only 10 percent of the people with the largest income save who receive about 40 percent of the national income. The wage and salary classes hardly save 3 per cent of the national income. But the dominant classes consisting of landlords, traders, moneylenders, priests, princes are engaged in prodigal consumption rather than in productive investment. It is, therefore the state capitalist and indigenous private capitalist who create capital out of profits earned. "The indigenous private capitalist is bound up with the emergence of new opportunities, especially some thing that widens the market, associated with some new technique which greately increases the productivity of labour, and hence the capitalist surplus. The state capitalist, on the other hand, can accumulate capital even faster than the private capitalists, since he can use for this purpose not only the profits of the capitalist sector, but also what he can force or tax out of the subsistence sector". Thus, once a capitalist sector has emerged it is only a matter of time before it become sizable. If the opportunities for using capital productivity increase rapidly, the surplus will also grow rapidly, and the capitalist class with it. But capital is creates not only out of profits, it is also created out of *bank credit.* in an underdeveloped economy which has abundant idle resources and shortage of capital, credit creation has the same effect on capital formation as profits. It will raise output and employment. Credit financed capital formation, however, leads to inflationary rise in prices for some time. When the surplus labour is engaged in the capitalist sector and paid out of created money, prices rise because income increases while consumer-goods output remains constant. This is only a temporary phenomenon, for as soon as capital goods start producing consumption goods, prices start falling. In the words of Lewis, "Inflation for the purpose of capital formation is very different kettle of fish. It is self destructive. Prices begin to rise but are sooner or later overtaken by rising output, and may, in the last stage, end up lower than they were at the beginning".

The theory shows that "if unlimited supplies of labour are available at a constant real wage, and if any part of profits is reinvested in productive capacity, profits will grow continuously relatively to the national income". But the process of growth cannot go on indifinitely, if as a result of capital accumulation no surplus labour is left. It may also stop if, despite the existence of surplus labour, real wages rise so high as to reduce the capitalist profits to the level where they are all consumed and nothing is left for net investment.

A Critical Appraisal

The Lewis theory is applicable to overpopulated underdeveloped countries under certain set conditions. Its applicability is, therefore, circumscribed by its assumptions which are the bases of criticisms discussed below:

1. Wage Rate not constant in the capitalist sector
2. Not Applicable if Capital Accumulation is Labour Saving
3. Skilled Labour not a Temporary Bottleneck
4. Multiplier Process does not Operate in LDC
5. This is a one-sided theory because Lewis does not consider the possibility of progress in the agricultural sector.
6. Mobility of Labour not so Easy
7. *Schultz* does not agree that the marginal productivity of labour in overpopulated under-developed countries is zero or negligible. If it were so, the subsistence wage would also be zero.
8. Lewis assumes that when the surplus labour is withdrawn from the subsistence sector to the capitalist sector, the agricultural production remains unaffected in the subsistence sector. But the fact is that withdrawal of workers from the farms will reduce output.
9. It is not correct to say that only 10 per cent of the people with the largest income save. Infact, people

with low incomes also save due to social reasons and even small farmers save for capital accumulation in underdeveloped countries.

10. Inflation not Self-Destructive.

Conclusion

Despite these limitations, the Lewis theory has the merit of explaining in a very clear cut way the process of development. This two sector theory has great analytical value. It explains how low capital formation takes place in underdeveloped countries which have plethora of labour and scarcity of capital. His study of the problems of credit inflation, population growth, technological progress, and international trade gives the theory a touch of realism.

D. FEI-RANIS THEORY OF DEVELOPMENT

John Fei and **Gustav Ranis** in an article entitled "A Theory of Economic Development" analyse "the transition process through which an underdeveloped economy hopes to move from a condition of stagnation to one of self-sustained growth", Their theory is an improvement over Lewis's theory of Unlimites Supplies of Labour because Lewis failed to present a satis factory analysis of the growth of the agricultural sector.

Fei-Ranis theory relates to an underdeveloped labour-surplus and resource-poor economy in which the vast majority of the population is engaged in agriculture amidst widespread unemployment and high rates of population growth. The agrarian economy is stagnant. People are engaged in traditional agricultural pursuits. Non-agricultural pursuits exist but they are characterised by a modest use of capital. There is also an active and dynamic industrial sector. Development consists of the re-allocation of surplus agricultural workers, whose contribution to output is zero or negligible, to the industrial sector where they become productive at a wage equal to the institutional wage equal to the institutional wage in agriculture.

Assumptions

In presenting their theory of economy development, Fei and Ranis make the following assumptions :

1. There is a dual economy divided into a traditional and stagnant agricultural sectoı and an active industrial sector.

2. The output of the agricultural sector is a function of land and labour alone.

3. There is no accumulation of capital in agriculture except in the form of land reclamation.

4. Land is fixed in supply.

5. Agricultural activity is characterised by constant returns to scale with labour as a variable factor.

6. It is assumed that the marginal productivity of labour becomes zero at some point. If population exceeds the quantity at which the marginal productivity of labour becomes zero, labour can be transferred to the industrial sector without loss in agricultural output.

7. The output of the industrial sector is a function of capital and labour alone. Land has no role as a factor of production.

8. Population growth is taken as an exogenous phenomenon.

9. The real wage in the industrial sector remains fixed and is equal to the initial level of real income in the agricultural sector. They call it the institutional wage.

10. Workers in either sector consume only agricultural products.

Given these assumptions,Fei and Ranis analyse the development of a labour-surplus economy into three phases.

In the first phase, the disguised unemployed workers, who are not adding to agricultural output, are transferred to the industrial sector at the constant institutional wage.

In the second phase, agricultural workers add to agricultural output but produce less than the institutional wage they get. Such workers are also shifted to the industrial sector. If the migration of workers to the industrial sector continues, a point is eventually reached when farm workers produce output equal to the institutional wage. This begins the third phase which marks the end to the take-off and the beginning of the self-sustained growth when farm workers produce more than the institutional wage they get. In this phase, the surplus labour is exhausted and the agricultural sector becomes commercialised.

Thus, Fei-Ranis model is an improvement over the Lewis model. The Lewis model ignores the development of the agricultural sector and concentrates exclusively on the industrial sector. The Fei-Ranis model shows the interaction between the two sectors in initiativg and accelerating development. Moreover, its explanation of the Lewis turning point is more realistic. But the major merit of the theory is that it shows the importance of agricultural products in capital accumulation in underdeveloped countries.

Despite these merits, the model is not free from criticisms which are discussed below.

1. Fei and Ranis begin with the assumption that the supply of land is fixed during the development process. But in the long run, the amount of land is not fixed.

2. The model is based on the assumption of a constant institutional wage which is above the MPP during phases I and II of the development process. But there is no empirical evidence to support this assumption. In fact, in labour surplus underdeveloped countries, wages paid to the agricultural workers are much below their MPP.

3. The theory assumes that the institutional wage remains constsant in the first two phases even when agricultural productivity increases.This is highly unrealistic because with a general rise in agricultural productivity, farm wages also tend to rise.

4. This model is based on the assumption of a closed economy where foreign trade does not exist. But this assumption is unrealistic because underdeveloped countries are not close but open economies which import agricultural commodities when shortages arise.

Conclusion

However, these limitations do not undermine the improtance of the Fei-Ranis model for the economic development of labour surplus countries. It systematically analyses the development process from the take-off to self-sustained growth through the interaction of the agricultural and industrial sectors of an under developed economy.

E. MEADE'S GROWTH MODEL

Prof. J.E. Meade has presented a growth model which analysis the relationship between income growth and population growth in an economy. This model draws attention to the role of population growth, capital increase and technology in determining the increase of income per head. It also analyses the conditions necessary for stable growth of income per head, when population changes along with other determinants.

Assumptions

Meade constructs his model around the following assumptions :

1. There is a laissez-faire closed economy where there is perfect competition.

2. There are constant rerurns to scale.

3. Two commodities-consumption goods and capital goods-are produced in the economy.

4. Machines are the only form of capital in the economy.

5. All machines are assumed to be alike.

6. It is assumed that there is a constant money price of consumption goods.

7. There is full use of land and labour.

8. The ratio of labour to machinery can be changed both in the short and the long run. Meade calls this the assumption of perfect malleability of machinery.

9. It is further assumed that there is perfect substitutability in production between capital goods and consumption goods.

According to this model, net output produced in an economy depenes upon four things :

i. net stock of capital in the form of instruments of production (machines),

ii. the labour force,

iii. land and natural resources,

iv. the state of technical knowledge,

These four factors may be expressed in the form of a production function as given below :

$$Y = F(K, L, N, T)$$

where Y = net national income or output
K = existing stock of machines
L = existing labour force
N = natural resources
T = state of technical knowledge

Assuming the amount of land or natural resources to be fixed, net output can increase in any one year with the growth in K,L and T. This relationship is shown as

$$\Delta Y = V\Delta K + W\Delta L + \Delta Y'$$

where Δ in each case represents an increase, V is the marginal product of capital, W is the marginal product of labour and Y' is used in place of t. Thus "the increase over the year in the rate of annual net output (ΔY) is equal to the increase in the stock of machinery (ΔK) multiplied by its marginal products (V) plus the increase in the amount of labour (ΔL) multiplied by its marginal product (w) plus the increase in the rate of annual output due to technical progress (ΔY')". The annual proportionate growth rate of output is

$$\frac{\Delta Y}{Y} = \frac{VK}{Y} \cdot \frac{\Delta K}{K} + \frac{WL}{Y} \cdot \frac{\Delta L}{L} + \frac{\Delta Y'}{Y}$$

where

$\frac{\Delta Y}{Y}$ = annual proportionate rate of growth of output

$\frac{\Delta K}{K}$ = annual proportionate rate of growth of capital

$\frac{\Delta L}{L}$ = annual proportionate rate of growth of labour

$\frac{\Delta Y'}{Y}$ = annual proportionate rate of growth due to technological improvement

Let these proportionate growth rates be expressed as *y, k, l and r* respectively, the proportional marginal product of capital $\frac{VK}{Y}$ as U and the proportional marginal product of labour WL/Y as Q. Now the basic relationship is $y = Uk + Ql + r$

This shows that the growth rate of output (y) is the weighted sum of three other growth rates, first the sum of the growth rate in the stock of capital (K) weighted by the proportional marginal product of capital (U) plus the growth rate of population (l) weighted by the marginal produced of labour (Q) plus the growth rate of technology (r).

The growth of the economy is shown by the rise in the *per capita real income.* The per capita real income is indicated symbolically *y-l*. Thus, if *y* or total income increase by 15% per annum and *l* or labour force grows by 10% per annum, income per head will increase by 5% per annum. The growth rate of real income per head can, therefore, be expressed as follows :

$$\begin{aligned} y - r &= Uk + Ql + r - l \\ &= Uk - l + Ql + r \\ &= Uk - (1 - Q)\,l + r \end{aligned}$$

In the above equation, $(y - l)$ represents the different between the growth rate of total output or income and the growth rate of real income per head. According to the above equation this growth rate in real income per head $(y - l)$ is the result of three factors.

i. It is raised by an increase in real capital (K) weighted by its proportional marginal product (U) ;

ii. It is depressed by the growth rate in the labour force (l) weighted by minus the proportional marginal product of labour (1 – Q) ;

iii. It is raised by technical progress.

The middle term on the right-hand side of this equation, *i.e.,* $[-(1 - Q)l)]$ indicates the tendency for diminishing returns to labour as the supply of labour is increased.

One of the important factors contributing to the growth rate of output is the annual rate of capital accumulation in the economy. This fact is implied in the element UK. $U = \frac{VK}{Y}$ and $K = \frac{\Delta K}{K}$, but ΔK, the addition to the stock of capital is equal to the saving out of the net national income. Therefore ΔK = SY and $K = \frac{\Delta K}{K} = \frac{SY}{K}$ where SY represents the amount annually added to the stock of capital through savings.

Hence $UK = \frac{VK}{Y} \times \frac{SY}{K} = VS$, and the basic growth relationship can be expressed as

$$y - l = VS - (1 - Q)\,l + r$$

If the growth of labour force (l) and the development of technology (t) are assumed to be constant, then the change in income (output) per head would depend on the changes in the values of V, S and Q over time.

If l and t remain unchanged and S increases, then capital per head would increase and the marginal product of capital would decline. But this decline in the marginal product of capital could be slowed down if there a possibility of substituting capital for other factors. Similarly, if we could allow an increase in *r*, or improvement in technology, the decline in the marginal product of capital would be offset. In other words, if the labour force is assumed to be constant, then an increase in income will depend on three factors-the size of savings, the productivity of capital and the state of technology. Symbolically, $y = \text{VS} + r$

After this, *Meade* analyses the conditions of a state of *Steady economic growth.* It is a state in which the growth rate in total output (income) is constant and so is the growth rate in income per head. It is assumed that population is growing at a constant proportionate rate (l) and the rate of technical progress does not change.

The state of steady economic growth requires the existence of the following three conditions to ensure a constant growth rate in total income :

(a) All clasticities of substitution between the various factors are equal to unity.

(b) Technical progress is neutral towards all factors.

(c) The proportions of profits saved, of wages saved and of rent saved are all constant.

Conditions (a) and (b) mean that the proportions of the national income going to profits (U), wages (Q) and rents (Z) remain constant. So do the proportions of national income saved out of these remunerations of factors remain constant as per condition (c). Let these savings out of profits (U), wages (Q) and rents (Z) be represented by Sv, Sw and Sg respectively, so that total savings

$$\text{S} = \text{S}v\text{U} + \text{S}w\text{Q} + \text{S}g\,\text{Z}$$

since all the elements in this equation are constant vide conditions, (a), (b) and (c), it follows that the ratio of total savings to total national income (s) will also be constant.

The growth rate of income is represented by the basic relationship $y = \text{U}k + \text{Q}l + r$ where in U, Q, l and r are assumed to be constant. Therefore, for y to be constant (as required by the state of steady economic growth), K should be constant. We know that K = $\frac{\text{SY}}{\text{K}}$ but S is constant as seen in the preceding para. So K will be constant if $\frac{\text{Y}}{\text{k}}$ is constat $\frac{\text{Y}}{\text{k}}$ will be constant if the rate of growth of Y and K is the same which implies the equality of y and k itself, *i.e.,* $y = k$. The obvious conclusion follows that the growth rate of income will be constant if the growth rate of capital stock (k) is equal to the growth rate of naional income (y).

Criticisms

Professor Meade's neo-classical model has been subject to severve criticisms by a number of economists, who felt that many of its assumptions were unrealistic. The assumption of an economy that operated on the wheels of perfect compitition was very diverse from reality. Further it was wrong to assume that production units were independent of one another.

The assumption of the neoclassical theory that these are only constant returns to scale was also considered defective. In reality, increasing returns to scale (rather than constant) were in consonance with the growth process.

The model, it was felt, suffered from another major defect, *i.e.,* it assumed that all kinds of machinery were perfectly malleable. It assumed that the labour-machinery ratio could be altered both in the long and short-run. Alteration in the short-run was definitely not possible.

The fact that the model gave no place or scope for uncertainties was felt inadequate. The interrelaties of all variables were regarded as being certain. Thus the practicability of the model was lost. This issue was raised by Butterick.

Like the Harrod-Domar and the Joan Rabinson models, Meade's model took in to its reckoning a *laissez faire* economy free of foreign trade which was divergent from reality.

The roles ployed by institutions were totally ignored from the point of view of economic growth.

Despite these defects, the Meade model has the chief merit of demonstrating the influences of population growth, capital accumulation and technical progress on the growth rate of national income and per capita real income over time. Further, the state of steady growth is indeed Mrs Robinson's

Golden Age explained in a more realistic manner by studying the behaviour of those variables which she assumes as constants.

F. LEIBENSTEIN'S CRITICAL MINIMUM EFFORT THESIS

The Critical Minimum Effort Thesis was develped by *Harvey Leibenstein* in his book "Economic Backwardness and Economic Growth," 1957. This thesis supported the Theory of Balanced Growth and the Theory of 'Big Push'.

Prof. Harvey Leienstein has porpounded his thesis of critical minimum effort, as an attempt to provide a lasting solution to the problems of development, faced by underdeveloped countries. The most pressing problem of underdeveloped countries is the vicious circle of poverty. Which an atmosphere of inertia in the economy. Because of such an atmosphere, the development variables (income, employment, Saving, investment, etc,) move in the backward direction and thus reverse the process of development. Hence, a minimum effort is needed to overcome the original inertia of the underdeveloped economics. In other words, critical minimum effort is necessary to achieve a steady, secular growth, raising per capita income in the long period. Leibenstein has expressed the idea in these words. "In order to achieve the transition from the state of backwardness to the more developed state, where, we can expect steady secular growth, it is necessary, though not always a sufficient condition, that at the same point or during the same period, the economy should receive a stimulus to growth that is greater than a certain minimum size." Thus, critical minimum effort is the only way to break the vicious circle of poverty and to release the force of growth.

Explanation of the Theory : Every economy is under the influence of two forces-"stocks" and "stimulants" stocks dampen and depress the developmental forces. They are also referred to as "income-depressing forces", which reverse the wheels of development stimulants impress and encourage the developmental forces. They are "income generating forces", which lubricate the wheels of development. Income despressing forces are evil forces and the income-generating forces are known as good factors. These two not only co-exist but interact with each other. It usually happens that evil forces triumph in the initial stages, but ultimately the good forces come out victorious; the bad forces nip the developments in the initial stages, but in the long-run the income-generating forces over-power the bad forces and the process of development starts. The question is to what extent is the minimum effort needed? Here, Leibenstein stresses a 'particular level' of investment which can ensure the steady, secular growth or which can break the vicious circle of poverty. "If the level of investment is less than a particular level then the derived goal of steady growth cannot be realised. The level of investment should be higher than a particular level."

The particular level is what Leibenstein calls the critical minimum. Hence,the crux of the theory is that any level of investment lower than the critical minimum cannot ensure the sustained growth. The term'critical' is the indicator of the fact that the level of investment should at least be of such an order which could raise per capita income for achieving sustained growth.

According to this thesis, "a development programme must be at least of a certain size, or of a critical Minimum to reduce the indivisibilities and discontinuites in the economies, overcome the economies of scale, have an impact on values and offset certain other factors that arise to depress development."

The underdeveloped country is caught in a vicious circle as it has a low per capita income sustained growth is possible only when a certain minimum critical effort is made to raise the percapia income. In other words, the underdeveloped economy should receive the necessary stimulus to growth. According to Leibenstein, every economy is under the impact of shocks and stimuli. A shock has an adverse impact on the per capita income and a stimulus has the effect of raising it. In underdeveloped countries, the impact of shocks is greater than that of the stimuli.

According to Leibenstein, there are income-depressing factors like population growth and also income-stimulating factors in underdeveloped countries. There is a biologically determined maximum rate of population growth between 3 and 4%. The rate of population growth is relevant to the level of per capita income. It is related to the various stages of economic development. The rate of population growth is an increasing function of income up to a certain level of income and beyond that it is the decreasing function of income.

To begin with, at the subsistence equilibrium level of income, fertility and mortality rates are high. If the per capita income is to be pushed above the subsistence equilibrium level, the mortality rate follows it without any decline in the fertility rate. Consequently, there is a higher rate of growth of population. But this trend will continue only to a certain point. Beyond the point, increase in per capita income has the effect of reducing the fertility rate. As development is accelerated, the rate of population growth declines. Increased specialisation and social and economic mobility created by the sources of development lead to a constant rate of growth of population. As the economic tends to move along the path of sustained growth, the rate of growth of population declines. Therefore, Leibenstein argues that a critical minimum effort is necessary to overcome the Malthusian underemployment equilibrium.

The Critical Minimum Effort Thesis assumes the existence of certain favourable conditions, *i.e.* income-stimulating factors expand at a higher rate than the income-depressing factors. The favourable conditions are created in the path of development by what are called "the Growth Agents." These represent the quantum of capacities residing in the members of the population to carry out growth contributing activites. These agents may be the entrepreneurs, the investors, the savers and the innovators.

According to Leibenstein, "whether or not the growth agents expand will depend on the anticipated outcome of such activites, the actual result, and on the incentives for further expansion or contraction generated by the interaction of the anticipation, the activities and the results." They are :

1. The positive incentives which secure growth and national income.

2. Zero-sum incentives which do not raise national income but have only a distributive effort. The zero-sum activities are not real income creating activities, but simple transfers of liquidity from some holders to others.

According to Leibenstein, the Critical Minimum Effort will create a series of the following effects :

A. An expansion of growth agents ;

B. An increase in their contribution, per unit of capital due to a decline in the capital-output ratio ;

C. An ultimate decline in the effectiveness of factors inhibiting growth ;

D. The creation of social and environmental conditions that promote social and economic mobility;

E. Increased specialisation and expansion of secondary and tertiary sectors ; and

F. "The development of an atmosphere that leads to changes more conducive to economic and social changes and especially an environment that leads to eventual fertility decline and an eventual decline in the rate of population growth."

Criticisms: Leibenstein's Thesis is a logical and realistic analysis of the factors containing development process. It stresses the need for sustainded development in an underdeveloped country. The thesis suffers from certain inadequacies.

1. Critrics do not accept the relationship between per capita income and population growth, formulated by Leibenstein.

2. Secondly, the thesis does not take into consideration the influence of external factors, including foreign capital.

3. Thirdly, Leibenstein's thesis does not take into account the role of government in bringing down the fertility rate.

4. Finally, critics feel that the functional relationship between the level of per capita income and the rate of growth of total income is a complex process. They think that Leibenstein's approach is over-simplified.

G. NELSON'S LOW-LEVEL EQUILIBRIUM TRAP

R.P. Nelson developed the theory of Low-Level Equilibrium Trap for underdeveloped countries. Like Leibenstein's Critical Minimum Effort Thesis, Nelson's theory is also based on the Malthusian hypothesis that with the increase in the per capita income of a country above the 'minimum subsistsence level', population tends to increase. Initially population grows rapidly with an increse in per capita income. But when the growth rate of population reaches "an upper physical limit," it starts declining with further increase in per capita income.

According to Nelson, "The malady of underdeveloped economic can be diagnosed as a stable equilibrium level of per capita income at or close to subsistence requirements." At a stable equilibrium level of per capita income, the rate of saving and consequently the rate of net investment are at a low level. Efforts made to raise the rate of saving and investment through an increase in the rate of growth of total national income are accompanied by a high rate of population growth which pushes back the per capita income to its stable equilibrium level. Thus, underdeveloped economies are caught in a low-level equilibrium trap.

Nelson mentions four slocial and technological conditions which are conducive to trapping. They are :

(a) A high correlation between the level of per capita income and the rate of population growth.

(b) A low propensity to direct additional per capita income income to increasing per capita investment.

(c) Scarcity of uncultivable arable land.

(d) Inefficient methods of production.

A study of the economic development of underdeveloped countries reveals that most of them are caught in the low-level equilibrium trap due to the presence of the above noted conditions.

Nelson uses three sets of relationships to show the trapping of an economy at a low level of income. *First,* income is a function of the capital stock, the level of technology and the size of the population. *Second,* net invstment consists of capital created out of savings in the form of additions to the stock of tools and equipment in the industrial sector plus additions of new land to the amount of land under under cultivaltion. Third, "with low per capita incomes, short run changes in the rate of population growth are causes by changes in the death rate, and change in the death rate are caused by changes in the level of per capita income. Yet once per capital income reaches a level well above subsistence requirements, further increases in per capita income have a negligible effect on the death rate."

Nelson point towards a number of factors to escape the low-level equilibrium trap. *First,* there should be a favourable socio-political environment in the country. *Second,* the social structure should be changed by laying greater emphasis on thrift and entre-preneurship. Greater incentives shoould be provided to produce more. A and incentives should also be provided to limit the size of the family. *Third,* measures should be adopted to change the distribution of incomes at the same time enabling accumulation of wealth by investors. *Fourth,* there should be an all-pervading government investment programme. *Fifth,* income and capital should be increased by obtaining funds from abroad. *Sixth,* improved production techniques should be used to utilise existing resources more fully so that income is increased from given inputs.

To escape the low-level equilibrium trap in underdeveloped countries requires the simultaneous adoption of all these measures so that the growth rate of income is increased more than the growth rate of population. Once this is a achieved above a certain minimum per capita income level, sustained growth will take place without further government action until a high level of per capita income is reached.

H. THE "BIG PUSH" THEORY

The theory of the "big push" is associated with the name of *Professor Paul N. Rosenstein-Rodan.* The thesis is that a "big push" or a large comprehensive programme is needed in the form of a high minimum amount of investment to over-come the obstacles to development in an underdeveloped economy and to launch it on the path to progress.

The theory states that proceeding "bit by bit" will not launch the economy success fully on the development path; rather a minimum amount of investment is a necessary condition for this. It necessitates the obtaining of external economies that arise from the simultaneous establishment of technically interdependent industries. Thus, indivisibilities and external economies flowing from a minimum quantum of investment are a prerequisite for launching economic development successfully.

Rosenstein-Rodan distinguishes between three different kinds of indivisibilities and external economies.

1. indivisibilities in the production function, especially the indivisibility of the supply of social overhead capital;
2. indivisibilities of demand;
3. indivisibilities in the supply of savings.

Given these three indivisibilities and the external economies to which they give rise, a "big push" or a minimum quantum of investment is required to overcome the obstacles to development in underdeveloped countries. "There may be finally a phenomenon of indivisibility in the vigour and drive required for a successful development policy," writes Rodan. But proceeding bit by bit in an isolated and small way does not lead to a sufficient impact on growth. A climate for development is only created when investment of a minimum speed or size is made with in an underdeveloped economy.

I. THE DOCTRINE OF BALANCED GROWTH

The theory of balanced growth implies that there should be simultaneous investment in a variety of enterprises and there should be harmonious growth of the different parts of the economy. It implies balance between defferent consumer goods industries and capital goods industries. It also implies balance between agriculture and industry, between domestic and export sectors, between economic and social over heads and between vertical and horizontal external economies. The theory of balanced growth implies that the state must ensure simultaneous investments. It also implies controlled planning.

The theory of balanced growth has been developed by Rosenstein Rodan, Ragnar Nurkse, Arthur Lewis, Scitovsky and Harvey Leibenstein.

Main Versions of the Theory of Balanced Growth

Rosenstein Rodan's Version : *Rosenstein-Rodan* was the first ecnomist who propounded the theory of balanced growth without using these words in his 1943 article. He realised the importance of pecuniary external economic. In underdeveloped economies, lack of market is a serious obstacle. No investor anticipates a market large enough to justify an investment, even though investment project is profitably based upon the availability of pecuniary external economies.

In addition to the lack of demand, Rodan mentions two difficulties on the supply side. Lack of infrastructure makes other investments uneconomic and huge capital required to build these infrastructures is not available. In addition, the absence of ability to save is another limitation.

To tackle these problems on the demand and supply sides, Rodan favours a comprehensive investment programme. This will cause an overall rise in demand which will make all projects profitable. At the same time, infrastructural facilities will be made available for the use of industries. This investment programme must of course be carried out by a central planning agency or a central authority.

Ragnar Nurkse's Version : Nurkse's Version given in his book "Problems of capital Formation in Underdeveloped Countries" broadly follows the approach of Radan. According to Nurkse "low real income is a reflection of low productivity, which in turn is due largely to lack of capital. The lack of capital is the result of the small capacity to save and so the circle is complete." On the other hand, inducement to invest is limited by the size of the market. This creates another vicious circle on the demand side.

To break the vicious circle, Naurkse favours a more or less synchronised application of capital to a wide range of different industries. This will lead to an over-all enlargenmet of the market. Most of the industries producing mass consumption goods are complementary.

Nurkse's Version depends on the principle of complimentarity in various directions between wants, between factors of production and between products at various stages of production. This kind of complementarity leads to the emergence of several external economies. Here, external economies refer to the economies which raise out of the establishment of a new industry, or from the expansion of an existing industry and those available to other industries. The scarcity of factor supply ensures that the relationship is mostly competitive. The supplies of skilled labour, capital and entrepreneur are comparatively in elastic.

J. THE CONCEPT OF UNBALANCED GROWTH

The theory of unbalanced growth is the opposite of the doctrine of balanced growth. According to this concept, investment should be made in selected sectors rather than simultaneously in all economy. No underdeveloped country possesses capital and other resources in such quantities as to invest simultaneously in all sectors. Therefore, investment should be made in a few selected sectors or industries for their rapid development and the economies accruing from them can be utilized for the development of other sectors. Thus the economy gradually moves from the path of unbalanced growth to that of balanced growth. Economists like *Singer, Kindleberger, Streeten,* etc, have expressed their view in favour of the unbnalanced growth doctrine which are in fact the criticisms of the theory of balanced growth. It is , however, *Hirschman* who has propounded the doctrine of unbalanced growth in a systematic manner.

Hirschman's View : The concept of 'unbalanced growth ' has been popularized by Hirschman. It is his contention that deliberate unbalancing the economy, according to a predesigned strategy, is the best way to achieve economic growth in an underdeveoped country. According to *Hirschman,* investments in strategically selected industries or sectors of the economy will lead to new investment opportunities and so pave the way to further economic development. He maintains that "development has of course proceeded in this way, with growth being communicated from the leading sectors of the economy to the followers, from one industry to another, from one firm to another." He regards development as a "*chain of disequilibria*" that must keep alive rather than eliminate the disequilibria, of which profits and losses are symptoms in a competitive economy. If the economy is to be kept moving ahead, the task of development policy is to maintain tensions, disproportions and disequilibria. This "seesaw advance" is induced by one disequili-brium that in turn leads to a new disequilibrium and so on *ad infinitum.*

According to Hirschman, history show,only unbalanced growth in many countries. Balanced growth was the result of the flow of innovations and changing factor combinations. It was not created by the simultaneous expansion of mutually supporting sectors as assumed by the authors of balanced growth. Hirschman considered that balanced growth was not a process but a goal to be achieved through a series of imbalances over a period of time.

Hirschman stresses three aspects of unbalanced growth :

A. A Chain of unbalanced growth sequences initiated by private entrepreneurs and the state.
B. Unbalance in the direction of shortage of social overheads.
C. Development to be initiated in those sectors which are linked to the maximum extent with other sectors.

Development can only take place by unbalancing the economy. This is possible by investing either in Social Overhead Capital (SOC) or in Directly Productive Activites (DPA). The former creates external economies while the latter appropriates external economies.

Unbalancing the Economy with Social Overhead Capital (SOC) : SOC has been defined as "comprising those basic services without which primary, secondary and tertiary productive activities cannot function." A large investment in SOC will encourage private investment later in direct productive activites (DPA). For example cheaper supply of electric power may encourage the establishment of small industries. Unless SOC investment provide cheap or improved services, private investments in DPA will not be encouraged. Thus, the SOC approach to economic development is to 'unbalance' the economy so that subsequently investment in DPA are stimulated. As Hlirschman puts it, "Investment in SOC is advocated not because of its permits and in fact invites DPA to come in. Some SOC investment is required as a prerequistite of DPA investment."

Unbalancing theEconomy with DPA : An inbalance can also be created vice DPA. A government might directly or indirectly invest in DPA instead of investing in SOC. If DPA investment is undertaken first,the shortage of soc facilities is likely to raise production costs substantially. In course of time, political pressures might stimulate investment in SOC also. Investment sequences are generated by profit expectations and political pressures. Profit expectations generate the sequence from SOC to DPA and political pressures from DPA to SOC.

Hirschman refers to two routes in the path of development. The first sequence is by expanding SOC. It is called by him the process of "development" vice excess capacity of SOC." The second sequence is by expanding DPA. It is called by him the process to "development via shortage of SOC." According to Hirschman, "development via shortage is an instance of disorderly, compulsive sequence, while via excess SOC capacity is essentially permissive." It is pointed out that development via excess capacity is more continuous and smoother and Hirschman calls this self-propelling. But the process of development via shortage of SOC capacity is not so.

Linkage : Hirschmang also analyses the problem of finding out what kind of imbalance is likely to be more effective. Any particular investment can have both effects called the '*forward linkage*' and 'backward linkage'. The former will encourage investment in subsequent stages of production, while the latter will encourage investment in earlier stages of production. The problem is to choose projects which will have these greatest "total" linkage. The projects with greatest linkage vary from country to country and they can be found out only through empirical studies of input-output tables. Hirschman says, "*The industry with the highest combined linkage score is iron and steel.*

Hirschman points out that operations some where in the middle of the production process may have higher total linkage effectes than operations at the beginning or end of the production process. This is because in underdeveloped countries the inter-dependence and linkage effects are weak. Primary production in underdeveloped countries has weak backward and forward linkage. According to Hirschman, a meaningful concept of linkage would be investment decisions up or down the line, which are prompted by creation of a particular industry.

In the case of underdeveloped countries, backward linkage is more reliable than forward linkage. In this connection, Hirschman is not in favour of too early encouragement of import-replacing industries. He regards forward linkage as "an important, powerful reinforcement to backward linkage" rather than as 'an independent inducement mechanism.'

K. KALDOR'S MODEL OF GROWTH

Professor Kaldor in his A Model of Economic Growth Follows the Harrodian dynamic approach and the keynesian techniques of analysis. The othe neo-classical models treat the causation of technical progress as complectely exogenous, but kaldor attempts "to provide a framwork for relating the genesis of techical progress to capital accumulation."

Assumptions : The basic properties or assumptions of Kaldor's model are as follows—

1. It is based on the Keynesian full employment assumption in which the short-period supply of aggregate goods and services is inelasric and irresponsive to any increase in monetary demand.

2. It assumes that technical progress depends on the rate of capital accumulation. For this, kaldor postulates "the technical progress function" which is a joint product of two tendencies : growth of capital and growth of productivity. The capital-output ratio will depend upon the relation between the two.

3. Income consists of wages and profits where wages comprise salaries and earning of manual labour, and profits comprise incomes of entrepreneurs as well as property owners.

4. Total savings consist of savings out of wges and savings out of profits.

5. It is assumed that the share of profits in total income is a function of investments, given the propensity to save out of profits.

6. All macro-economic concepts of income, wages, profits, capital, saving and investment used in the model are expressed at constant prices.

7. Monetary policy plays a passive role in the model in that money wages may be rising faster than productivity or pari passes with productivity, or money wages may be constant

8. It is assumed that there are no effects of a change in the share of profits and wages, and of a change in interest rates on the choice of techinques adopted.

9. The choice of techniques is assumed to alter

with the accumulation of capital and the progress of techniquess in the capital goods making industries.

Given these assumptions, the model operates under two stages :

A. Constant Working Population

B. Expanding Population

In the first case, the proportionate growth rate of total real income will be the same as the proportionate growth rate of output per head. In the second case, the proportionate change in total real income is the sum of the proportionate change in output per head and the proportionate change in the total working population. We discuss these two versions of the model below.

A. Constant Working Population : For the operation of the model, kaldor postulates three functions :

(i) the saving function

(ii) the investment function, and

(iii) the technical progress function

The three functions are explained in terms of linear equations as under :

(i) Saving function

$$S_t = \alpha P_t + \beta(Y_t - P_t) \qquad ...(1)$$

where $1 > \alpha > \beta > 0$

In equation (1), savings (S_t) consist of savings (α) out of profits (P_t) and savings (β) out of wages ($Y_t - P_t$) in period *t*. The inequalities $1 > \alpha > \beta > 0$ show that α and β lie between O and 1, that α is greater than β.

(ii) Investment function

$$Kt = \alpha\, Yt{-}1 + \beta\left(\frac{Pt-1}{kt-1}\right) Yt{-}1 \qquad ...(2)$$

$$It = Kt{+}1{-}Kt \qquad ...(2.1)$$

where $\alpha' > 0$ and $\beta' > 0$

Equation (2) shows that the stock of capital (Kt) at time *t* is a coefficient α' of the output of the previous period(Yt-1) and coefficient β' of the rate of profit on capital of the period $\left(\frac{P_{t-1}}{K_{t-1}}\right)$ multiplied by the output of the previous period (Y_{t-1}). Equation 2.1 shows the investment function where investment in period *t* equals the stock of capital in the next period (K_{t+1}) minus the stock of captial in the current period (K_t). The inequalities $\alpha' > 0$, and $\beta' > 0$ reveal that the value of the coefficient α' and β' are greater than zero.

(iii) Technical Progress function

$$\frac{Y_{t-1} - Yt}{Yt} = a'' + b''.\frac{I_t}{K_t} \qquad ...(3)$$

where

$$\alpha'' > 0 \text{ and } 1 > \beta'' > 0$$

Equation**(3)** shows that the rate of growth of income is an increasing function of the rate of net investment expressed as the proportion of the stock of capital $\frac{I_t}{K_t}$ in period *t* multiplied by the capital per head β'' plus the coefficient of technical progress α'' there the value of the coefficient of technical progress is greater than zero but of capital per head lies between 0 and 1.

Given these functions, if we start from a point of time, *t* = 1, the existing stock of capital K_1 can be regarded as a datum, inherited from the past. Taking Y_0 and K_0 as the income and capital of the previous period, Y_1 can be taken as the given income which the fully employed labour force (constant population) produces with the help of the capital stock K_1.

The technical progress function as given by equilibrium **(3)** shows the the growth of income and capital from period *t*+1 onwards where by the economy gradually moves from a short-period equilibrium to a long-period equilibrium of steady growth. Taking the identity S_t=I_t, it is the level of profits which brings about the equality of saving and investment : For a state equilibrium path,the following condition should be fulfiled.

$$\alpha - \beta > \beta' \frac{Y_t}{K_t} \qquad ...(4)$$

This implies that the growth rate of savings should be greater than that of investment for the stable equilibrium. But this is only a necesssary conditions. The sufficient conditions for the stable equilibrium path should be

$$P_t \leq (Y_t - w) \qquad ...(5)$$

$$\frac{P_t}{Y_t} \geq m \qquad ...(6)$$

In fact, equation **(5)** and **(6)** are inequalities which act as constraints on the stability of the equilibrium path. Equation **(5)** indicates that the level of profits (P_t) should not exceed income minimum wages (Y_t – w). While equation **(6)** indicates that the rate of profit (P_t/Y_t) should be greater than the minimum margin of profits (m) so that the entrepreneurs should continue to make further investments. Equation **(4)**, **(5)** and **(6)**, imply that the equilibrium brought about by the equality of saving and investment through the mechanism of profits would not be a stable one. However, the steady growth path would depand on the 'technical dynamism' of the economy, *i.e.,*on the technical progress function, as given by the following condition.

$$G = \frac{\alpha''}{1-\beta''} \qquad ...(7)$$

Where G is the growth rate of output which is determined by the technical progress function, as given on the right of the equation.

This is illustrated in figure 1.11 where the proportionate growth of capital $\left(\frac{K_{t+1}-K_t}{K_t}\right)$ is measured horizontally and the proportionate growth of income $\left(\frac{Y_{t+1}-Y_t}{Y_t}\right)$ vertically. Poiny G as determined by the technical progress function TT′and the 45°line is one of steady growth where the proportionate growth of income equals the proportionate growth of capital.

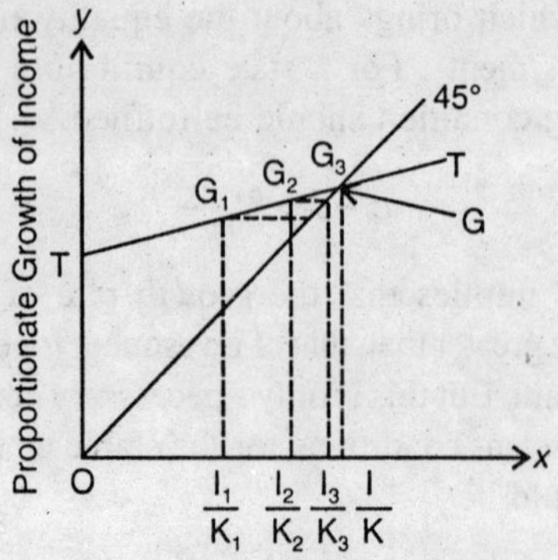

Fig. 1.11

Starting from period t_1 where the growth of output G_1 is greater than the growth of capital $\left(\frac{I_1}{K_1}\right)$, the rate of investment will increase in the subsequent period so as to make I_2/K_2 equal G_1 at A. This will, in turn, raise the growth of output in period t_2 to G_2. The rate of investment will increase further to $\frac{I_3}{K_3}$ in period t_3, so as to make $\frac{I_3}{K_3}$ equal G_2 at B. Similarly, the growth of output in subsequent periods will rise till point G is reached. This process will be reinforced by changes in the rate of profit on capital (P_t/K_t). An associated change in $\frac{P_t}{K_t}$ will make the increase in $\frac{I_t}{K_t}$ even greater.

B. Expanding Population : Leaving the assumption of constant working population, Kaldor studies the relation between growth in population and growth in income. Starting from the Malthusian contention that the growth rate of population is a function of the rate of increase of the means of subsistence, he assumes that : *(a)* "For any given fertility rate........ the percentage rate of growth in population cannot exceed a certain minimum however real income is rising," and *(b)* "the rate of population growth will rise moderately as a function of the rate of growth of income over some interval of the latter before that maximum is reached."

Given these assumptions,the relation of population growth with the growth in income is expressed by Kaldor algebraically as under :

$$I_t = g_t\,(g_t \geq \lambda) \text{ and } I_t = \lambda$$

Where it is the percentage rate of growth of population, g_t is the percentage rate of growth of income, and λ is the maximum rate of population growth. If $g_t < \lambda$ and so is $I_t > \lambda$, the rate of growth of income and population will continue to rise till the growth rate of population equals λ.

This relation between population growth and income growth is represented in figure 1.12, where the proportionate rate of growth of population $\left(\frac{1}{L}.\frac{dt}{dt}\right)$ is measured vertically and proportionate rate of growth of income $\left(\frac{1}{Y}.\frac{dy}{dt}\right)$ is measured horizontally. OY is the growth path of income PL λ is the curve of the growth rate of population. As the growth rate of income increase, the growth rate of population also rises till the λ curve becomes horizontal as a level where the rate of growth of income (OY) exceeds the former, as at point E. In the long run, population would grow at its maximum rate indicated by $\angle\lambda$ portion of the dotted population-growth rate curve. This assumes that the shape and position of the technical progress function , as given by the coefficients α'' and β'' in equation **(3)** are not affected by the changes in population. The implies that there are constant returns to scale, that is ,"an increase in numbers,given the amount of capital per head, leaves output per head unaffected."

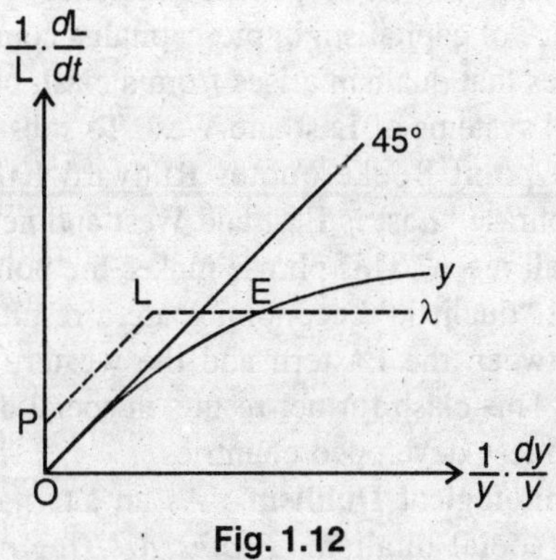

Fig. 1.12

But in an underdeveloped economy with a low capacity to absorb technical changes due to the scarcity of land and capital, the technical progress function will be lowered with the increase in the growth rate of population. In this situation, the technical progress function will cut the capital axis positively as at A in figure 1.13. This implies that in order to maintain output per head at a constant level,a certain percentage growth in capital per head will be required. We have therefore, two points of intersection P′ and P of the technical progress function. Point P' is of unstable equilibrium and point P of stable long-run equilibrium. If the rates of growth of income and capital continue to diminish in the economy, both the output per head and capital per head may cease to grow.

This may happen if the economy is to the left of point P′. If this situation persits, the technical progress

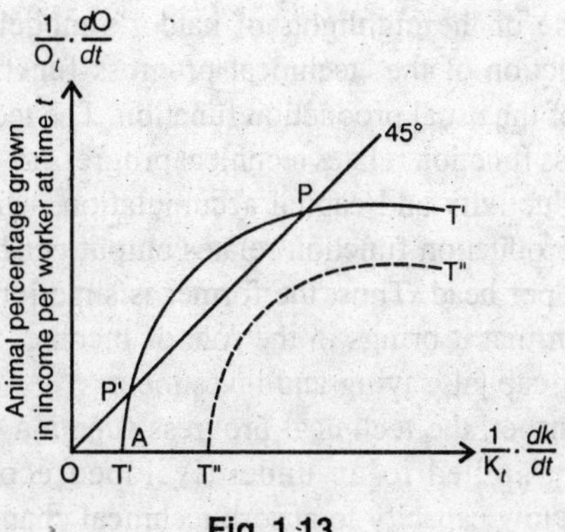

Fig. 1.13

function TT′ may slip down as the dotted curve T″T″ in figure 1.13. In this situation, there will not be any long-run equilibrium. Rather, there may be stagnation in the economy.

The conclusion emerges from the above analysis that growth in population will lead to long-run equilibrium growth in income depending upon the relative strength of the following two factors.' "*(i)* the maximum rate of population increase λ and *(ii)* the rate of technical progress which causes a certain percent age increase in productivity, α'' in equation **(3)** above, when both population and capital per head are held constant."

A Critical Appraisal

Kaldor's model is based on the Keynesian tools of analysis and follows Harrod's dynamic approach in regarding the rates of change in income and capital as the dependent variables of the system. But his model is quite different from the Harrodian and other models. Moreover, the model explains not only the steady growth path of the economy but also certain features of the growth process which are not explicitly dealt with by the other neo-classical model builders.

Again, the division of the model in to two stages-constant population and expanding population-is an attempt to reconcile the Harrodian warranted and natural rates of growth by demonstrating the long-run tendency for the two to coverage by mutual interaction. The expanding population version of the model is particularly useful in demonstrating the effect of population growth on the growth of income in underdevelped countries.

One of the highlights of kaldor's model is the introduction of the 'technical progress function' in place of the usual production function. The technical progress function relates technical progress to growth of productivity and capital accumulation, while the usual production function relates output per head to capital per head. Thus, the former is superior to the latter in that it brings in the role of income, wages, profits, capital, saving and investment.

Further, the technical progress function can be equally apllied to an underdeveloped economy, having low capacity to absorb technical change due to the scarcities of capital and other resources. Thus, kaldor's growth model is more realistic than the earlier neo-classical models because it is equally applicable to developed as well as underdeveloped economies.

Despite these virtues of the kaldor model it is not free certain weaknesses.

The kaldor model does not explain the determination of the rate of growth of the economy, as has been explained in the Harrod-Domar models in terms of the volume of investment, saving income ratio and the capital-output ratio.

Unlike the Harrod-Domar models, this model does not give the reasons for stability or instability in the economic system. Rather, it analyse certain features of the growth process which emphasise 'Convergence and stability.'

L. DUALISTIC DEVELOPMENT THEORIES

It is generally observed that poor countries exhibit some elements of modernisation in one sector and some element of backwardness in the other sector. In many countries, the modern money economy has developed along with the traditional indigenous economy, resulting in what is called "Dual Economy." Such an economy exhibits a contrast between economic and social organisation of the modern advanced sector and that of the indigenous backward sector. The existence of these two sectors creates a problem known as the "problem of dualism." Since the future development of any country requires the spread and expansion of the modern sector, any effort to accelerate the country's rate of development must deal with the problem of dualism.

Dualism is of two kinds :

A. Social Dualism

B. Technological Dualism

Dr. J.H. Boeke has been the leading exponent of the theory of social dualism. He was a civil servant in Netherlands and the concepts of social dualism is the result of his experience as a civil servant. Though his theory was largely based on Indonesian experience, Boeke thought that it had general application. He has given a formal definition of social dualism in the following words. "Social dualism is the clashing of an improted social system with an indigenous social system of another style. Most frequently the imported system is high capitalism. But it may be socialism or communism jush as well, or a blending of them." Social dualism, he further adds, is "a form of disintegration which came into existence with the appearance of capitalism in pre-capitalist countries." He belives that dualism arises from a clash between the social systems of East and West. To substantiate his view point Boeke quotes Rudyard Kipling's famous phrase "East is East and West and never the twain shall meet." This phrase makes the point very clear that "dualistic'" economies are a result of the clash between the Eastern and the western social systems. This clash further results in social dualism arising in less developed countries.

Technological Dualism : As an alternative to Boeke's social dualism, *Professor Higgins* has developed the theory of technological dualism. Technological dualism implies the use of different production functions in the advanced sector and the traditional sector of an underdeveloped economy. The existence of such dualism has accentuated the problem of structural or technnological unemployment in the industrial sector and disguised unemployment in the rural sector. Higgin's theory of technological dualism is related to limited productive employment opportunities found in the two sectors of an underdeveloped economy because of market imperfections, different factor endowments and production function.

To explain the theory of technological dualism, Higgins takes two goods, two factors of production, two sectors with their factor endowments and production functions. Of the two sectors, one is the traditional sector and the other is the modern sector.

The traditional or rural sector is engaged in the production of agricultural products, handicrafts and operates small industries. Production in this sector is carried on with a wide range of techniques and alternative combinations of two factors of production, *viz*, labour and capital. As such this sector has variable technical coefficients of production. The techniques of production are generally labour-intensive because of the excessive supply of labour and employment-oriented projects.

On the other hand, the modern industrial sector is composed of heavy industries, plantations, mines, oil fields, etc. The production in this sector can be carried on with limited techniques because the technical coefficients are generally fixed. The production process are relatively capital-intensive in the sense that large amounts of capital are used with a small amount of labour. The situation of this sector can be explained with the help of the following figure 1.14.

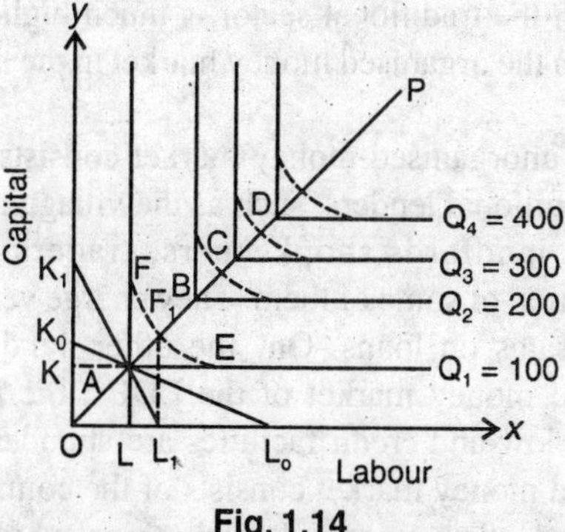

Fig. 1.14

It represents the production function in the industrial sector. Units of labour are measured on the x-axis and units of capital are measured on the Y-axis. Q_1 is an isoquant representing a combination OK units of capital and OL units of labour,producing 100 units of output. Q_2,Q_3 and Q_4 represent higher levels of output, *viz,* 200, 300 and 400 units respectively. Higher level of output is possible by increasing the amounts of labour and capital in the same proportions. The points A, B, C and D show the fixed combinations of labour and capital to produce different levels of output. The line OP joining the pionts A, B, C, C and D is the expansion path and its slope represents the constant proportion in which labour and capital are combined. The production process is capital-intensine and it is shown by the line K_1 L_1. This line shows that OK units of capital are combined with OL units of capital are combined with OL units of labour, producing Q_1 (*i.e.,* 100 units) level of output. 'A' is the piont of equilibrium because at this point the isocost line K_1 L_1 touches the isoquant curve Q_1 and as such the industrial sector will use OL units of labour and OK units of capital for producing an output Q_1, i.e., 100 units. If OL_1 units of labour are available, the excess labour supply will have no effect on production techniques because the technical coefficients are fixed. LL_1 units of labour will remain unemployed. It is only through the incresase of capital stock to the extent of EF_1 that LL_1 units of labour can be absorbed in this sector; other wise they must seak employment in the raural sector. However, the increase in employment will be relatively less than the increase in investment with the expansion of the industrial sector along the expansion path OP.

In actual working, the technical coefficients are not rigidly fixed; rather they are flexible. The dotted protion of the isoquant curves indicates a situation in which there is actually some flexibility in factor proportions. It can be easily seen that small changes in the factor endowments would not bring any marked change in the techniques of production by entrepreneurs. But if substantial changes in factor endowments take place as shown byK_0 L_0, a more labour-intesive technique would be useful.

Having discussed the production function in the industrial sector, Higgins explains the production function in the agricultural sector, where the technical coefficients are variable. This is explained in the following figure 1.15 OX is labour and OY is capital : Q_1, Q_2 and Q_3 are the isoquant curves on the assumption that technical coefficients are available and a wide range of techniques and combination of labour and capital will given the same output. The combination of labour and capital will actually depend on factor endowments and their relative prices. Here capital includes improved land.

We begin with production at Q_1 in each sector. An increase in the output of the industrial sector, along OP results in a population explosion. Since the technical coefficients are fixed in that sector, the

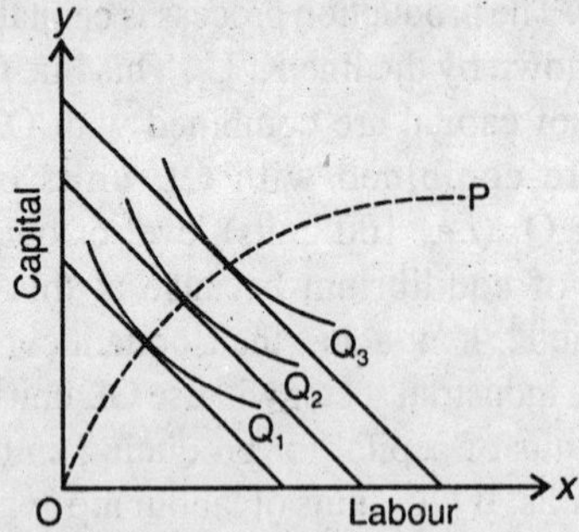

Fig. 1.15 : *The Agriculture Sector*

employment opportunities do not keep pace with the increase in population. Hence, the increased population will have to seek employment in agriculture or some other "variable coefficient" sector and the migration of labour from industry to agriculture starts.

At the beginning of production operations, no factor of production is aboundant. But as migration continues, it may be possible to develop extensive cultivation in order to keep the labour-land ratio constant. Since land is fixed in supply the cultivation opportunities for each family is limited. Though for a short period the optimal combination of labour and capital (in this case improved land) may be possible as output rises from Q_1 to Q_2, eventually land becomes a scarce factor and labour an abundant factor. Since technical coefficients are available in this sector, production process would be more labour-intensive. Finally a point would be reached when all available land would be cultivated by these highly labour-intensive techniques. The marginal product of labour falls to zero and disguised unemployment emerges. Under these circumstances, there would be no incentives for the farmers either to make more envestment or to introduce labour-saving innovations. As a result, the methods of production would be largely labour-intensive and levels of technique, man-hour productivity, and economic and social welfare would remain low in the rural sector.

Disguised unemployment is aggravated by technical progress in the long-run. The high wage rates put up by the trade unions or by goverment policies add further fuel. When industrial wage rates are high, relative to the productivityof the workers in the industrial sector, the entrepreneurs are left with no option but to introduce labour-saving devices. Such devices further diminish the capacity of the industrial sector to provide employment and absorb the growing population. Higgins argues that in the last two centuries there had been little or no technical progress in agriculture, while in the industrial sector rapid technological progress took place. Hence, it can be concluded that technological dualism accentuates the problem of unemployment in underdevelopment countries because of fixed factor proportions in the industrial sector and growing population in the rural sector.

Financial Dualism

Professor Myint has developed the theory of financial dualism. Financial dualism refers to the co-existence of different interest rates between the organised and unorganised money markets in the LDCs. The rate of interest in the unorganised money market in the traditional sector is much higher than the rate in the organised money market in the modern sector.

The unorganised money market consists of the non-institutional lenders, such as the village money-lenders, landlords,shopkeepers, traders or the combination of some of them. They charge very high interest rates on loans. On the other hand in the organised money market of the LDCs, the interest rates are low and credit facilities are abundent. The organised money market consists of the commercial banks and other financial institutions which lend short-term credit at low interest rates to the modern business sector consisting of the big foreign-owned enterprises in the export industries, the government and the larger-scale modern manufacturing enterprises.

M. ROSTOW'S GROWTH MODEL

Professor W.W. Rostow has sought an historical approach to the process of economic development. He refers to five stages of economic growth. They are:

1. the traditional society which rests on static equilibrium until it is disturbed by some mechanism.

2. the pre-conditions for the take-off, which involve slow changes, especially in attitudes and organisation

3. the take-off it is a watershed in the life of a society. It involves a rapid increase in the rate of change as to involve discontinuity. The period of take-off is the interval when the old blocks to steady growth are finally overcome.The changes during this period are characterised by a wave-like expansion.

4. the drive to maturity it is a period of sustained growth extending over four decades after the end of take-off.

5. the age of mass consumption-during this period, the leading sectors of the economy shift towards the durable consumer goods and a large share of the population acquires a high level of lilving.

Criticism

1. Traditional Society not Essential For Developmet.

2. Overlapping in the Stages.

3. The Stage of Drive to Maturity Puzzling and Misleading.

4. The Stage of High Mass Consumption not Chronological

N. MRS. JOAN ROBINSON'S GROWTH MODEL (CAPITAL ACCUMULATION MODEL)

In all the classical theories of economic growth, a good deal of attention was devoted to the analysis of the part played by population, savings, technology and social institutions in the growth of the capitalist economy. So modern economists have accepted these classical ideas of economic growth and presented then in the form of growth models by using the Keynesian and the Harrod-Domar technology. Such growth models are referred to as neo-classical growth models, and Mrs. Joan Robinson's model is one such. An important feature of the neo-classical models is that they invariably incorporate the population factor in the explanation of growth. Mrs. Joan Robinson's model, which deals with a developing economy, clearly brings out the effect of population on the rate of capital accumulation and growth of output. Her model is based on two fundamental factors :

(i) the capital formation is conditioned by the manner in which income is distributed in the economy, and

(ii) the rate at which labour is utilised is a function of the supply of capital and supply of labour.

Assumptions

Mrs. Robinson's model is based upon the following asumptions :

a. There is a laissez-faire closed economy.

b. In such an economy capital and labour are the only productive factors.

c. In order to produce a given output, capital and labour are employed in fixed proportions.

d. There is neutral technical progress.

e. There is no shortage of labour and entrepreneurs can emply as much labour as they wish.

f. There are only two classes-the workers and the entrepreneurs-between whom the national income is distributed.

g. Workers save nothing and spend their wage income on consumption.

h. Entrepreneurs consume nothing but save and invest their entire income (from profits) for capital formation.

i. Total wage-bill is the real wage-rate multiplied by the number of workers.

j. Total profit is the profit-rate multiplied by the amount of capital.

k. Total national income is the sum of total wage-bill and total profit.

Symbolically, the total national income may be expressed as

$$Y = Wn + PK$$

where Y = total income, net
W = wage-rate, real
P = profit rate
K = capital
N = the number of workers employed

The profit rate, according to Mrs. Joan Robinson, is the most strategic factor in the theory of capital accumulation. Symbolically, the rate of rate of profit would be

$$p = \frac{Y - wN}{K}$$

Divided by N.

$$p = \frac{\frac{y}{n} - \frac{wN}{N}}{\frac{K}{N}} = \frac{\frac{Y}{N} - w}{\frac{K}{N}}$$

by putting $\frac{Y}{N} = l$ and θ (theta), we have $p = \frac{l - w}{Q}$

Thus, the profit ratio is the ratio of labour productivity minus the total real wage bill to the amount of capital utilised per unit of labour. In other words, the profit rate *(p)* depends on income *(y)*, labour productivity *(l)*, the real wage rate *(w)* and the capital-labour ratio θ.

On the expenditure side, net national income (Y) equals consumption expenditure (C) plus investment expediture (I),

$$Y = C + I$$

Since Joan Robinson assumes zero saving out of wages but attributes saving to entrepreneurs, profits are meant for investment only, we have

$$S = I$$

This saving-investment relation may be shown as :

$$S = PK$$

and $I = \Delta K$[Δk is increase in real capital]

$$\therefore PK = \Delta K [\because S = I] \text{ or } P = \frac{\Delta K}{K} = \frac{l - W}{Q}$$

The growth rate of capital (Δk/k) being equal top, it depends on the ratio of the net return on capital relative to the given stock of capital. If inome remains constant and the wage rate decreases or income increased and the wage rate remains constant, the profit rate would tend to increase. The profit rate can also increase if the capital-labour ratio falls. In this way the entrepreneurs maximize profits.

Besides the growth rate of capital $\left(\frac{\Delta K}{K}\right)$, another factor which determines the growth rate of an economy is the growth rate of population $\left(\frac{\Delta N}{N}\right)$. An increase in population and labour force un accompanied by an increase in capital would reduce labour productivity. If real wages are hold constant, the reduction in labour productivity would lower the rate of profit. A lowering of the rate of profit would adversely affect the supply of capital and thus, widen the different between capital and labour supply.

An increase in labour supply without a proportionate increase in capital supply would cause unemployment in the economy. To maintain full employment of labour resources it is essential, according to this model, that the growth rate of population (labour supply) should be equal to the growth rate of capital,

$$i.e., \frac{\Delta N}{N} = \frac{\Delta K}{K}$$

if the growth rate of population is equal to the growth rate of capital, *i.e.* $\frac{\Delta N}{N} = \frac{\Delta K}{K}$; there will be full employment of both labour and capital in the economy. Mrs. Joan Robinson calls this the *Golden Age.*

The Golden Age is explained diagrammatically in figure 1.16. Capital-labour ratio $\frac{K}{N}$ or Q is measured along the horizontal axis and per capita output on the vertical axis. The growth rate of labour force is taken to the left of O along the horizontal axis. The curve OP shows the production function. Every point on this curve shows the ration of capital to labour. In order to final out the capital-labour ratio and the wage profit rerlation, we draw a tangent NT which touches the production function OP at point G and cuts the vertical axis at W. Point G shows the capital-labour raito for the golden age which is measured by OK. Per

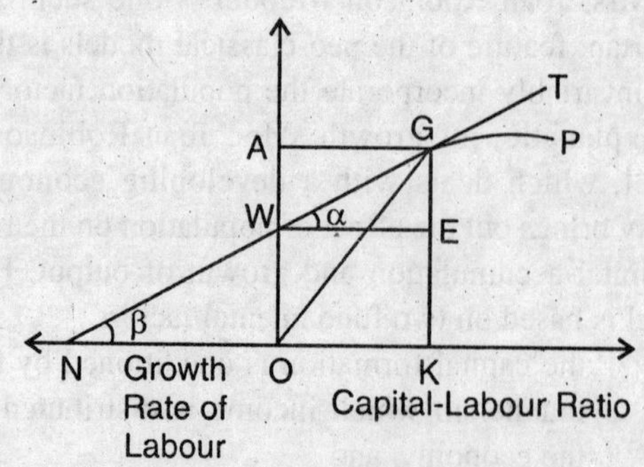

Fig. 1.16

capita output is OA, out of this OW is paid as wages and WA or EG is the surplus which is the rate of profit on capital.

This figure also proves that the growth rate of capital $\left(\frac{\Delta K}{K}\right)$ equals the growth rate of labour $\left(\frac{\Delta N}{N}\right)$. $\frac{EG}{EW}$ reflects $\frac{\Delta K}{K}$ and $\frac{OW}{ON}$ reflects $\frac{\Delta N}{N}$. Thus

$$\frac{EG}{EW}=\frac{OW}{ON} \ [\because \tan\alpha = \tan\beta\ ]$$

If an account of disequilibrium, the economy goes off the path of the Golden Age, there is every possibility of its returning to this path under certain conditions.

If $\frac{\Delta N}{N} > \frac{\Delta K}{K}$; *i.e.*, if the rate of growth of populaion exceeds the rate of growth of capital, a return to the Golden Age would be possible under certain conditions. The excess of labour supply would lower the money wage-rate, and assuming that prices do not change, the real wages would also be reduced. The reduction in real wages would increase the amount of profits which, in turn, would stimulate the rate of growth of capital, and would enable it to catch up with the increase in population. The parity between the two rates would be restored. Ultimately, the economy would come back to the position of the Golden Age. This return would be possible only if the real wages declines. If the real wages do not decline, either because the money wage-rate, are rigid, or because prices decline in the same proportion as the money wage-rate, the Golden Age would not be restored. On the contrary, than would be increasing unemployment in the economy. Generally speaking, a rise in prices helps to promote capital formation.

On the contrary, if the rate of growth of capital exceeds the rate of growth of populations *i.e.*, $\frac{\Delta K}{K} > \frac{\Delta N}{N}$, there is a possibility of Golden Age equilibrium being restored through technological improvements leading to higher capital-output ratio. This would absorb the excess capital and restore the parity between the rate of growth of capital and the rate of growth of population. Any way parity between the growth rate of capital and growth rate of population is an essential prerequisite for the attainment of the Golden Age.

Mrs. Robinson makes a distinction between the desired rate of growth and the possible rate of growth. The desired growth rate is the rate of accumulation which makes the firm satisfied with the situation in which it finds itself. The desired growth rate is determined by the rate of profit caused by the rate of accumulation and the rate of accummulation induced by that rate of profit. She uses the following figure 1.17 to explain it.

The curve A represents the expected rate of profit as a function of the rate of accumualation. The curve I represents the rate of accumulation as a function of the rate of profit. In a situation to the right of point D, the expected rate of profit is less than the rate of accumulation. Any further investment is not likely to be profitable and the rate of accumulation will fall. Between the points S and D the accumulation is less than the expected rate of profit. Therefore, there will be a tendency to increase investment and the rate of accumulation will rise to point D. This point D represents the desired growth rate.

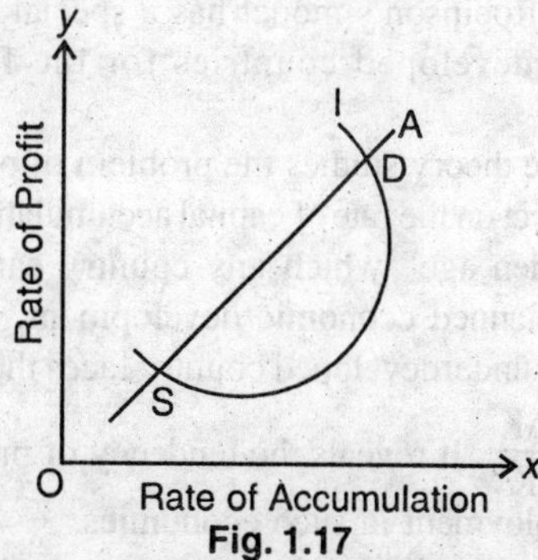

Fig. 1.17

On the other hand, the possible growth rate depends on the physical conditions resulting from the growth of population and technical knowledge.

When the desired growth rate equals the possible growth rate at near full employment, the economy is in a golden age.

The real wage rate is rising with incresing ouput per head due to technological progress. But the rate of profit on capital remains constant, and techniques of production appropriate to the rate of profit are chosen.

Mrs. Robinson's model with its stress on parity between the growth rate of capital and the growth rate of population, conforms closer to the realities of an underdeveloped economy. Mrs. Robinson's main contribution lies in the fact that she has integrated the classical value and distribution theory with the Keynesian saving investment theory.

Defects

1. The model is based on the assumption of a closed economy. This is an unrealistic assumption.
2. The role of institutional factors as one of the determinants of economic growth is neglected.
3. The model is based on the unrealistic assumption of constant prices.
4. Mrs. Robinson assumes that capital and labour are employed in fixed proportions; this is unrealistic because in a dynamic economy there are no fixed coefficients of production. Substitutability between factors takes place through times, the degree of substitutability being dependent upon the nature of technological changes.

Its Applicability to Underdeveloped Countries

Mrs. Robinson's model has a special attraction for underdeveloped countries for the following reason:

1. The theory studies the problem of population and its effect on the rate of capital accumulation. There is a "golden age" which any country can achieve through planned economic development.
2. An underdeveloped country faces the problem if $\frac{\Delta N}{N} > \frac{\Delta K}{K}$. It reveals the tendency of progressive underemployment in such economies.
3. In an underdeveloped economy, the rate of capital accumulation is always less than its potential growth ratio; that is why it is backward and possesses surplus labour force. It, therefore rests with the planning authority to increase the rate of accumulation to the level of the growth ratio of the economy. An underdeveloped country cannot, however, match the two by following the 'capitalist rules of the game.' On the contrary, it devolves on the planning authority to take the initiative in controlling and regulating not only private investment, but also public investment in such countries.

O. INVESTMENT CRITERIA IN ECONOMIC DEVELOPMENT

The problem of investment criteria involves the principles underlying the allocation of scarce investment resources in a rational manner so as to maximise the national income in an underdeveloped economy. It is a commonly known fact that private enterprise in such economies is motivated by profit maximisation. Very often private investment decisions are for projects that are not conducive to economic development. It is, therefore, felt that only a public authority can make decisions to allocate scarce investment resources and to influence the direction of private investment towards development oriented projects. For this, the choice before the public authorities is between techniques of a higher or lower capital intensity. Towards this end, economists have propounded a number of investment criteria which are discussed below.

The Capital-Turnover Criterion

The capital turnover criterion is known by various names *viz*, the rate of turnover criterion, the maximisation of output per unit of capital criterion or the ratio of output to capital criterion (minimum capital intesity or minimum capital-output ratio criterion). This criterion is attributed to **J.J. Polak and N.S. Buchanon.** The logic involed is that since capital is scarce in underdeveloped countries, that technique should be chosen which yields the maximum output per units of capital employed. In other words, for maximising output, investment projects with a high rate of capital turnover (*i.e.,* of a low capital output ratio) should be selected, Quick-yielding projects with a low capital intensity make it possible for scarce capital resources to be realized soon enough for reinvestment into other projects.

The Social Marginal Productivity Criterion

The social marginal productivity (SMP) criterion was first put forward by **A.E. Kahn** and later **Hollis B. Chenery** improved upon it. It is based on the conventional marginal productivity approach. As more and more capital is employed in any project in combination with given amounts of other inputs, its marginal product will after a time start falling tell the marginal productivity of capital in different uses is equalised. The aim is to allocate limited investment resources in such a way as to maximise the national output. In other words, they should be utilised in the most productive projects kahn states that this criterion takes "in to account the total net contribution of the marginal unit to national product and not merely that portion of contribution (or of its costs) which may accrue to the private investor." Thus, it is applicable to the economy as a whole and not to individual investment projects.

The Reinvestment Criterion

The reinvestment criterion is advanced by **Galenson** and **Leibenstein.** It is also known as the rate of surplus criterion or the marginal per capital invesment quotient. The latter is defined as the "net productivity per worker minus consumption per worker." Galenson and Leibenstein emphasize the maximisation of per capita output in the future rather than in the present. This is possible when the rate of saving is maximised leading to the reinvestment of income. Assuming that national income is divided into wages and profits, the former are spent on consumption and the latter are saved for the purpose of investment. The larger the volume of profits, the higher will be rate of savings, as a result the larger will be the amount of capital available per head and the higher will be the growth rate of output which will lead to increased output per head in the future. In the early phase of development a "critical minimum effort" is required on the part of underdeveloped countries to increase the proportion of profits to national income and to restrict consumption per head. This would lead to larger savings and larger reinvestible surplus. Given the quality and quantity of labour force. It is the capital-labour ratio that determines per capita output. Galenson and Leibenstein use the following formules to determine the rate of investible surplus *(r)*

$$r = \frac{p - e.w}{c}$$

Where p = product per machine

e = number of ment per machine

w = real wage rate

c = cost of machine

The Time Series Criterion

A.K. Sen has put forward the "time series" criterion. The criterion seaks to maximise output within a given period of time. Given the capital-output ratio and the rate of savings, the time path of two techniques (Capital intensive and labour-intensive) can be drawn and it can be found out which of the techniques yields the highest returns over the time-horizon.

Conclusion

The various investment criteria discussed above are not different in their ultimate objective, that of the maximisation of national output. Only the approach routes differ. The different components of national income (consumption, saving and investment) are used by economists to maximise the total output by giving more or less importance to one or the other. Some investment criteria aim at maximising total output at a point of time while others over a period of times. But all critenria are incomplete because they neglect the influence of such factors as population growth, tastes,technical progress, market conditions, distribution of income, price changes, balance of payments and social and cultural conditions on the level of investment in one way or the other. Contrariwise, they also fail to study the impact of investment on these factors. But despite these apparent theoretical and practical limitations, the various investment criteria are being increasingly made use of in the programming of resource allocation in almost all the developing countries of world including India. It is, however, essential that they must be in keeping with the social and economic objectives of the developing country.

P. TWO-GAP MODEL

Hollis Chenery and other writers have put forth the "two-grip" approach to economic development. The idea is that "saving gap" and "foreign exchange gap " are two separate and independent constraints, on the attainment of a target rate of growth in LDCs. Chenery seas foreign aid as a way of filling these two gaps in order to achieve the target growth rate of the economy.

To calculate the size of gaps, a target growth rate of the economy is postulated along with a given capital-output ratio. A savings grap arises when the domestic savings rate is less than the investment required to achieve the target. For example, if the growth target of national real income is 6 percent per annum and the capital-output ratio is 3:1, than the economy must save 18 percent of its national income to achieve this growth target. If only 12 percent of savings can be mobilised domestically, the savings gap is 6 percent of national income. The economy can achieve can achieve the target gowth rate by filling this savings gap with foreign aid. Similarly a fixed relationship is postulated between targeted foreign exchange requirements and net export earnings. If net export earnings fall short of foreign exchange requirements, a foreign exchange gap appears which can be filled by foreign aid. The two gaps are explained in terms of the national income accounting identities:

$$E - Y \equiv I - S \equiv MX \equiv F$$

Where E = national expenditure
Y = national income and output
I = investment
S = saving
M = imports
X = exports
F = net capital inflow
(I – S) = domestic saving gap
(M – X) = foreign exchange gap

MODELS OF TECHNICAL CHANGE

NEUTRAL AND NON-NEUTRAL TECHNICAL CHANGE

A technical change is said to be neutral when it is neither capital-saving nor labour-saving. On the contary, non-neutral technical change is either capital-saving or labour-saving. In the literature on growth economies, the two important definitions, pertaining to neutral and non-neutral technical change are by Hicks and Harrod.

HICKS NEUTRALITY

According to *Hicks,* an invention is said to be neutral when it raises the marginal productivities of labour and capital in the same proportion. In other words, a technical change is neutral if the ratio of the marginal product of capital to that of labour remains unchanged at a constant capital-labour ratio. Hicks-neutral technical change is explained in fig 1.18.

A technical change is *labour-saving* if it raises the marginal product of capital relative to that of labour, at a constant capital-labour ratio. The given output would now require less labour relatively to capital. Technical change implies that a given output can be produced with fewer inputs of labour and capital than before so that the isoquant after the change Q_2 shifts below the original isoquant Q_1 in figure

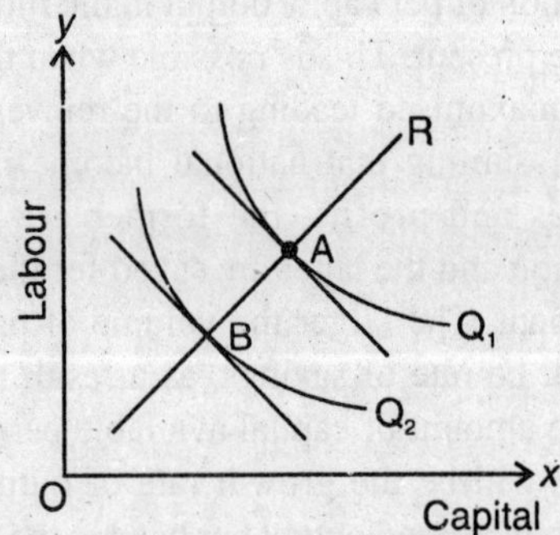

Fig. 1.18 : *Neutral Technical Change*

1.18 and 1.19.

Figure 1.19 depicts the case of labour-saving technical change where Q_1 is the isoquant before the technical progress and Q_2 after the technical progress.

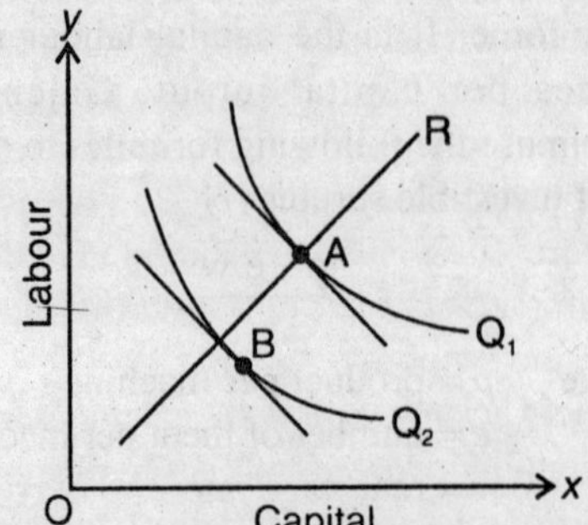

Fig. 1.19 : *Labour Saving Technical Change*

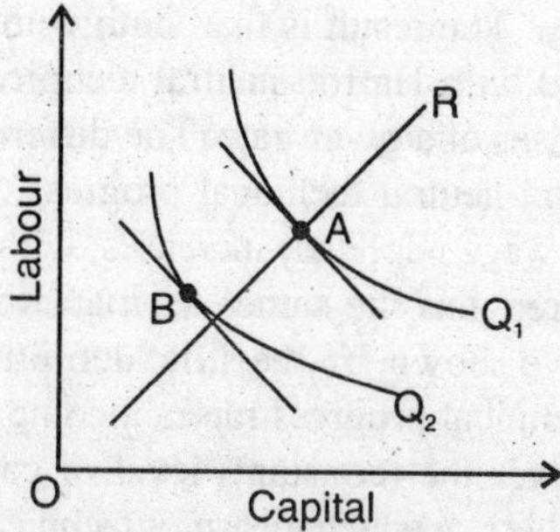

Fig. 1.20 : *Capital Saving Technical Change*

At the point B on the isoquant Q_2 less labour is required relatively to capital for a given capital-labour ratio. This type of technical change is relatively labour saving. If the amount of labour used is reduced absolutely and that of capital rises, then the technical change will be absolutely labour-saving and capital using.

On the other hand, a technical change is *capital-saving* if it raises the marginal product of labour relatively to capital, at a constant capital-labour ratio. The given output will now require less capital relatively to labour. This is illustrated in figure 1.20 where at the point B on the isoquant Q_2 less capital is required relatively to labour after the technical change for a given capital-labour ratio. This type of technical change is relatively capital-saving. If the amount of capital used reduced absolutely and that of labour rises, the techincal change is absolutely capital-saving and labour-using.

The precise manner in which the relative and absolute amounts of labour and capital used will change as the result of the technical change will depend upon the factor-elasticities of substitution and product elasticities of demand. It will depend on the elasticities of substitution between capital and labour in the economy, for these will help to determine what effects the technical change has on the prices of the two factors. It will also depend on the elasticities of demand for the products of the various industries that make up the economy."

Under Hicks-neutral technical progress, the factor shares remain constant if factor proportions and relative remunerations of labour and capital are constant.

Criticism

Hicks-neutrality has been criticised on the ground that it is a rigid type of definition even when a large number of factor of production are involved. Second, the dependence of Hicks-neutrality on demand elasticities, and substitution elasticities make it a cumbersome tool of analysils. Third, **Harrod** has criticised Hicks-neutrality because it is 'quite unrelated to the intrinsic character of the innovation itself' such as the elasticity of demand for products and factors. Lastly the Hicksian neutrality is built within the framewark of *static economic analysis.*

HARROD NEUTRALITY

The alternative definition of neutral technical progress is given by *Harrod* in his *Towards a Dynamic Economics*. According to him, technical change is neutral if at a constant rate of profit (or interest) the capital-output ratio also remain constant. If the rate of profit remains constant after technical change but the capital-output ratio rises, then the technical change is labour-saving. On the other hand, if the capital-output ratio falls with technical change at a constant rate of profit, then.the technical change is capital-saving.

Harrod neutrality is explained with the help of figure 1.21 when capital per man *(k)* is measured along the x-axis and output per man *(q)* along the y-axis OP is the production function before the technical change and OP_1 is the production function after the technical change. The capital-output ratio at point A on the production function OP is $\frac{OK_1}{OY_1}$ and at point B on the production function OP_1 is $\frac{OK_2}{OY_2}$. Since the curve OR passes through both the point A and B, the capital-output ratios at these points are equal, *i.e.*, $\frac{OK_1}{OY_1} = \frac{OK_2}{OY_2}$.

Harrod-neutrality also requires that the rate of profit must remain constant along with a contant capital-output ratio after technical progress. This means that the marginal productivity of capital (or rate of profit) must be the same at points A and B on

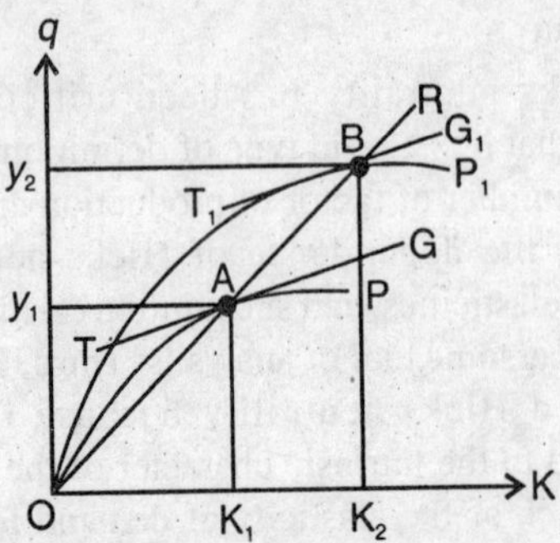

Fig. 1.21 : *Harrod Neutrality*

the production functions OP and OP_1 respectively. This, in turn, requires that the slope of the production function OP at point A must equal the slope of the production function OP_1 at point B. In other words, it means that the tangents at A and B must be parallel to each other. In the figure, the tangent TG at point A is Parallel to the tangenty T_1 G_1 at B. Thus, Harrod-neutral technical change, as shown by the shifting of the production function OP upwards to OP_1, depicts the equality of the capital-output ratio at A and B as represented by the curve OR passing through them, and also the equality of the slopes of the tangents at A and B thereby showing a constant rate of profit.

Hence, Harrod's definition of neutral technical progress is superior to that of Hicks because it is applicable to a dynamic situation rather than to a static situation. As such, it forms an important part of the theory of economic growth because it uses the concept of the capital-output ratio which is indispensable in modern growth analysis. Assuming constant returns to scale, changes in the capital-output ratios can come about only through technical change.

Harrod neutrality can be shown in the form of a production function as

$$Q = F[K, A(t) L]$$

Here Q is a function F of a K and A*(t)* L which means that the given constant returns to scale on equal proportionate rise in capital (K) and in effective labour units [A *(t)* L] must lead to an equal proportionate rise in national output (Q). With the rate of interest being constant, the efficiency of labour increase in the whole economy. "With population growth, there is an increase in the number of men at work, Harrod-neutral technical progress increases the amount of work each man can do. The result is that, both with population growth and with Harrod-neutral technical progress, the GNP rises at a given rate. The difference is that, with Harrod-neutral technical progress, income per head (real wage per head) increases; with population growth it remains the same. As Joan Robinson and Uzawa have shown, on the strict definition, Harrod-neutral technical progress raises income at the same rate whatever the (constant) level of capital-output ratio. It is this rate which measures technical progress." This formulation of Harrod neutrality has been described as 'pure labour augmenting technical progress.' Solow has, however, shown that Harrod-neutrality can be purely 'capital augmenting technical progress' with the production function

$$Q = F[A(t) K, L]$$

Here A *(t)*, the index of technical progress, has been prefixed to K instead of to L, unlike as in the labour augmentation case.

Economists have shown on the basis of Joan Rabinson's analysis that technical progress is both Hicks-neutral and Harrod-neutral if the elasticity of substitution between labour and capital is unity and there is no change in the distribution of income. There is neutral technical change in Hick's sense if with given labour force capital remains unchanged and the distribution of income is the same. It is Harrod neutral if with given labour force, capital increases in the same proportion as national output and the distribution of income is the same.

DISEMBODIED AND EMBODIED TECHNICAL CHANGE

Disembodied Technical Change

In 1956, *Abramkovitz* wrote the first paper followed by *Kendrick* and *Solow* in an attempt to measure the contribution of technical change to economic growth. They treated technical change as '*disembodied.' Disembodied technical change is purely organisational which permits more output to be produced from unchanged inputs, without any new investment.* Disembodied technical change refers to any kind of shift in the production function that leaves the balance between capital and labour undisturbed in the long run. The production function for such technical change is

$$Q = F(K, L, t) \quad ...(1)$$

where Q = output
K = capital input
L = labour input
t = technical change

Taking Hicks-neutral technical change as the basis, solow postulated the production function in the special form as

$$Q = A(t) F(K, L) \quad ...(2)$$

Where $A(t)$ is an index of technical change or measures the cumulated effects of shifts over time. "Such a production function implies that technical progress is organisational in the sense that its effect on productivity does not require any change in the quantity of the inputs. Existing inputs are improved or used more effectively."

The growth rate of output (Q/Q) is equal to the rate of technical change (A/A) plus a weighted average of the growth rate of capital (K/K) and the growth rate of labour (L/L). Assuming linear homogeneous production function, these weights add to one and we have,

$$\frac{Q}{Q} = \frac{A}{A} + at\frac{K}{K} + (1 - at)\frac{L}{L} \quad ...(3)$$

where dots indicate time derivates and at is the capital elasticity of output.

Embodied Technical Change- Vintage Approach.

In an alternative model entitled Investment and Technical Progress (1960), solow himself modified the residual approach based on disembodied technical change in which capital stock is regarded as homogeneous and technical change floats down from the outside. "In this model new capital accumulation is regarded as the vehicle to technical progress. Technical progress increases the productivity of machines built in the previous period, but it does not increase the productivity of machines already in existence. Technical progress is 'embodied' in new machines. Machines unalterably embody the technology of their date of construction. Machines built at different dates...... are therefore qualitatively dissimilar, and cannot in the general case be aggregated into a single measure of capital. A separate production function is needed for each vintage. Total output is the sum of output of all the vintage in use."

Its Appraisal

Unlike the model of disembodied technical change in which the capital stock is assumed to be completely homogeneous, in the model of embodied technical change new machines are better than old machines and technological progress is embodied in the new machines. In the former approach, capital-labour ratios change at all times along the Cobb-Douglas production function. But in the latter approach, once a machine is constructed it has fixed labour requirements. In other words, each machine is designed to be worked with a given crew of men, and the size of the crew cannot thereafter be changed.'

ECONOMIC PLANNING

MEANING

Economic planning is the deliberate control and direction of the economy by a central authority for the purpose of achieving definite targets and objectives within a specified period of time.

PLAN FORMULATION AND REQUISITES FOR SUCCESSFUL PLANNING

The formulation and success of a plan require the following :

1. Planning Commission
2. Statistical Data
3. Objectives
4. Fixation of Targets and Priorities
5. Mobilisation of Resources
6. Balancing in the plan
7. In corrupt and Efficient Administration
8. Proper Development Policy
9. Economy in Administration
10. Public Cooperation

VARIOUS TYPES OF PLANNING

1. Planning by Direction and Planning by Inducement

Planning by direction is an integral part of a socialist society. It entails complete absence of laissez-faire. There is one central authority which plans, directs and orders the execution of the plan in accordance with pre-determined targets and priorities such planning is comprehensive and encompasses the entire economy.

Planning by inducement is democratic planning. It means planning by manipulating the market. There is no compulsion but persuasion. There is freedom of enterprise, freedom of consumption and freedom of production. But these 'freedoms' are subject to state contral and regulation. People are induced to act in a certain way through various monetary and fiscal measures. If the planning authority wishes to encourage the production of a commodity, it can give subsidy to the firms. And if it finds scarcity of goods in the market, it can introduce price control and rationing. In order to increase the rate of capital formation, the planning authority can then undertake public investment and/or encourage private investment. It can adopt a suitable monetary policy and at the same time a taxation policy which encourages investment and discourages consumption.

Thus planning by inducement is able to achieve the same results as âre lkely to be achieved in planning by direction but with less sacrifice of individual liberty.

2. Financial and Physical Planning

Financial planning refers to the technique of planning in which resources are allocated in terms of money while physical planning pertains to the allocation of resources in terms of men, materials and machinery.

3. Perspective Planning and Annual Planning

The phrase 'perspective planning' refers to long-term planning in which long range targets are set in advance for a period of 15, 20 or 25 years. A perspective plan, according to the Indian Planning Commission, "is a blue print of developments to be under taken over a longer period." A perspective plan, however, does not imply one plan for the entire period of 15 or 20 years. In reality, the broader objectives and targets are to be achieved within the specified period of time by dividing the perspective plan into several short-period plans of four, five or six years.

4. Indicative Planning and Imperative Planning

Indicative planning prevails in *France*. This type of planning is not imperative but flexible. Planning in socialist countries is comprehensive in which the planning authority decides about the amount to be invested in each sector, in fixation of prices quantities of products and factors, and the types and quantities of products to be produced. There being rigidity in this type of planning if there is some distortion in one sector, it adversely affects the entire economy which cannot be remedied immediately. The French system of planning is free fromall such troubles because it is based on the principle of decentralisation in the operation and execution of the national plans. It is known as indicative or soft planning, as distinct from comprehensive or imperative planning.

In indicative planning the private sector is neither rigidly controlled nor directed to fulfil the targets and priorities of the plan. Even then, the private sector is expected to fulfil the targets for the success of the plan. The state provides all types of facilities to the private sector but does not direct it, rather indicates the areas in which it can help in implementing the plan.

On the other hand, under imperative planning all economic activities and resources of the economy operate under the direction of the state. There is complete control over the factors of production by the state. The entire resources of the country are used to the maximum in order to fulfil the targets of the plan. There is no consumer's sovereignty in such planning. The consumers get commodities in fixed quantities at fixed prices. Often the commodities are rationed. Production of commodities is in accordance with government policies. What and how much to produce—such decisions are taken by the managers of firms and factories on the direction of the planning commission or a central planning is in operation in China and Russia.

5. Rolling and Fixed Plans

Professor Myrdal was the first economist to

advocate a rolling plan for developing countries in his book *India Economic Planning in its Broader Setting*. It was introduced in Indian planning by the Janta Government on April 1, 1978 and was given up on April 1, 1980 with the comming to power of the India Government.

In a rolling plan, every year three new plans are made and acted upon. *First,* there is a plan for the current year which includes the annual budget and the foreign exchange budget. *Second*, there is a plan for a number of years, say three, four of five. It is changed every year in keeping with the requirements of the economy. It contains targets and techniques to be followed during the plan period, along with price relationships and price policies. *Third,* a perspective plan for 10,15 or 20 or even more years is presented every year in which the broader goals are stated and the outlines of future development are forecast.

The concept of rolling plan is devised to overcome the rigidities encountered in the fixed five year plans. In the rolling plan there are plan targets, projections and allocations that are not fixed for the five-year period but are liable to revision every year in keeping with the changing conditions of the country. It not only provides greater flexibility but also a cleaner perspective and a better view of the priorities.

In contrast to the rolling plan, there is a fixed plan for four, five, six or seven years. A fixed plan lays down definite aims and objectives which are required to be achieved during the plan period. For this purpose, physical targets are fixed along with the total outlay. Physical targets and financial outlays are seldom changed except under emergencies.

6. Centralised and Decentralised Planning

Planning may be centralised or decentralised. This division is made from the view point of the execution of plans. Under centralised planning, the entire planning process in a country is under a central planning authority. This authority formulates a central plan, fixes objectives, targets and priorites for every sector of the economy. It takes all investment decisions in accordance with the goals and targets of the paln. The principal problems of the economy-what and how much is to be produced, how, when and where it is to be produced, and to whom it is to be allocated-are exclusively decided by this authority. The central planning authority controls every aspect of the economy.

On the other hand, decentralised planning refers to the execution of the plan from the grass roots. Under it, a plan is formulated by the central planning authority in consultation with the different administrative units of the country. The central plan in corporates plans under the central schemes and plans for the states under a federal set-up. The state plans in corporate district and village level plans. Similarly, plans for different industries are formulated in consultation with representatives of industries. But individual firms are free to take independent decisions about investment and output policies and so are individual farmers. Under decentralised planning, prices of goods and services are primarily determined by the market mechanism despite government control and regulation in certain fields of economic activity. There is freedom of consumption, production and enterprise under it. However the planning authority recommends to the central and state governments to provide certain incentives to the private sector. It also lays down areas of public sector activities.

Decentralised planning is superior to centralised planning in that it provides economic freedom and flexibility to the economy. But its dependence on the market mechanism leads to shortages or surplulses in the production of goods and services. They are likely to create problems for the government because adjustment are difficult to make.

GROWTH MODELS IN INDIAN PLANNING

The five-year plans in India have been based on various growth models. We analyse below the main analytical features of the growth models used in India Planning. *The First Plan Model* : The model for the first five-year plan set out in 1952 was based on a simple application of *Harrod-Domar* growth model.

$$\frac{\Delta I}{I} = \sigma \alpha$$

where I = annual rate of investment

σ = potential social productivity of investment

α = marginal propensity to save

ΔI = increase investment

The Second Plan Model : The Second Five year plan was based on the *Mahalanobis Four-Sector Model.* This model divided the Indian economy into four sectors: the capital goods sector, the consumer goods sector,the small or household consumer goods producing sector including agriculture and the services producing sector. The basic strategy was "to increase investments in heavy industries and also expenditure on services, to increase purchasing power and create fresh demand, and on the other hand, to increase the supply of consumer goods by increasing investment and production as much as possible in the small and house hold industries to meet the new demand......Planning would be, thus, essentially a feed back process of matching a continuously increasing (planned) demand by a continuously increased (planned) production, giving rise to a steadily expanding economy." The implications of the model were to create larger employment opportunities, build a strong capital base capacity within the economy.

The Third Plan Model : The Third Plan was based almost on the same model as the second plan, but there was greater inter-industry consistency in its formulation. The Plan Model emphasized inter-dependence of agriculture and industry, of economic and skocial development of national and regional development, and of the mobilisation of domestic and external resources.

The Fourth Plan Model : A Consistency Model for India's Fourth Plan by *Alan S. Manne Ashok Rudra* and and others was built in 1965 to provide a frame work for the setting of actual plan targets. With 1960 as the base year, and 1970 as the terminal year, it was a 30-sector consistency model based on the conventional *Leontif Inter-industry "open system.*

The Fifth Plan Model : The Fifth Five-year Plan model was based the document "Technical Note on the Approach to the Fifth Plan of India 1974-79," prepared by the perspective Planning Division of the India Planning Commission.

The Sixth Plan Model : The sixth plan model was based on the "Technical Note of the Sixth Plan." prepared by the perspective planning Division of the planning commissions. The macro-structure of the model had been prepared on 89-sector classifications of the input-output table.

EXERCISE

1. Which one of the following is not true in case of Harrod Model ?
A. APC and MPC are different
B. Investment depends upon current increase in income
C. Capital and labour are not substitutable
D. It is a demand oriented model

2 In Solow's model of growth, the output per capita is a function of
A. labour-capital ratio
B. rate of change of capital-labour ratio
C. capital output ratio
D. technical progress

3. For Hick's technical progress, consider the following statements and choose the correct answer from the code given below :
Statements :
a. The capital-labour ratio is constant
b. It occurs in short period
c. It can be labour saving or labour using
d. It can only be neutral.
Code :
A. *a,b* and *c* are true
B. *b* and *d* are true
C. only *b* is true
D. *b* and *d* are true

4. Which of the following is an obstacle to economic development ?
A. Low rate of capital formation
B. Vicious circles of poverty
C. Socio cultural barriers
D. All of the above

5. The classical model of economic development emphasises
A. Laissez-Fair policy
B. Capital accumulation

C. Both (A) and (B)
D. None of these

6. Harrod model does not talk about
A. Actual growth rate
B. Critical minimum growth rate
C. Warranted growth rate
D. Natural growth rate

7. Entrepreneurship is most closely associated with
A. Inventions B. Innovations
C. Management D. Public Administration

8. Lewis theory explains the process of development considering a—sector economy
A. One B. Two
C. Four D. None of these

9. "A country is poor because it is poor" are the words of
A. Singer B. Nurkse
C. Hicks D. Myrdal

10. According to kuznets, during the process of development the income inequalities tend to
A. increase
B. decrease
C. increase first and then decrease
D. decrease first and then increase

11. A technical change which permits more output to be produced from unchanged inputs is considered to be
A. embodied
B. disembodied
C. both, embodied and disembodied
D. None of these

12 An underdeveloped economy is generally characterised by a
A. high ratio of commercial farming to subsistence farming
B. high ratio of industrial output to total output
C. high utilization of existing capital in the economy
D. coexistence of underutilised labour will unexploited national and other resources

13. Which one of the following statements correctly defines the term Natural Rate of Growth ?
A. It is the minimum rate at which output can be advanced with full employ of labour
B. It is the natural rate at which output can be advanced with full employment of labour
C. It is the maximum rate at which output can be advanced with full employment of labour
D. It is the actual rate at which output can be advanced withfull employment of labour

14. In the Lewis model of economic development, the capitalist sector generates and reinvests surplus and in turn, absorbs labour withdrawn from the subsistence sector. The process continues till
A. MP_L in the capitalist sector is greater than O
B. MP_L in the capitalist sector is less than MP_L in the subsistence sector
C. MP_L in the capitalist sector is greater than wage rate in that sector and MP_L in the subsistence sector is now positive
D. $MP_L = AP_L$ in the capitalist sector

15. Match List-I with List-II and select the correct answer using the codes given below the lists :

List-I
(Doctrinc)
(a) Neo-classical theory of economic growth
(b) Big-push theory of economic development
(c) Critical minimum effort thesis
(d) Social Dualism

List-II
(Name of Economist)
1. Leibenstein
2. J.H. Boeke
3. Hirsch man
4. Rosentein Rodan
5. Meade

Codes :	*(a)*	*(b)*	*(c)*	*(d)*
A.	2	3	4	5
B.	5	4	1	2
C.	3	5	2	1
D.	1	3	5	2

16. Consider the following statements :
According to Nurkse, disguised unemployment is a source of capital formation in an underdeveloped economy, if all unproductive workers are
1. maintained by productive workers
2. provided assets through loans
3. mobilised on works immediately raising productivity

Of the above statements
A. 1,2 and 3 are correct

B. 1 and 2 are correct
C. 1 and 3 are correct
D. 2 and 3 are correct

17. Consider the following statements regarding indicative planning :
1. It was followed in USSR.
2. It was used in France.
3. It has been used in all the Five year Plans of India.
4. It is being used in India's Eight Five year Plan

Of these statements
A. 1 and 2 are correct
B. 1, 2 and 4 are correct
C. 2 and 4 are correct
D. 2, 3 and 4 are correct

18. Consider the following statements :
1. Disguised unemployment is present only in agriculture.
2. Disguised unemployment is a major cause of the low standard of living in the rural areas of India.
3. Disguised unemployment can be useful in India's developmental process as a source of potential saving.
4. Disguised unemployment occurs because people in village do not have motivation to work.

Of these statements
A. 1, 2 and 3 are correct
B. 2 , 3 and 4 are correct .
C. 2 and 3 are correct
D. 1 and 2 are correct

19. The concept of "economic growth" is:
A. uni-dimensional in nature measuring growth in national income
B. multi-dimansional in corporating non-economic aspects also
C. related to development but not to deprivation
D. related to resource development but not to human development

20. Now a days we talk about "sustainable development" which relates to:
A. control of population to suit natural resources
B. development for sufficiency and efficiency which is bio-friendly
C. development which is within the central and state budgetary resources
D. development which takes into account the taxable capacity of people

21. The best indicator of economic development is
A. rising savings
B. rising investment
C. rising capital-output ratio
D. rising levels of living

22 Growth in developed countries is now mostly the result of
A. rising labour productivity
B. rising capital accumulation
C. innovation and technology
D. government assistance in exports

23. In Harrod-Domar models, "over production" is a condition where
A. all producers are producing too much
B. all producers are producing less than the warranted output
C. all producers are producing higher than the warranted output
D. where excess capacity has been created

24. In Domar's model
A. investment is needed to increase demand as well as supply
B. there is great emphasis on increasing the capital-output ratio
C. the classical economics is completely rejected
D. the keynesian economics is completely rejected

25. The development process under capitalism has been described as '*creative destruction*' by
A. Karl Marx B. A.N. Hansen
C. R. Luxemburg D. J. Schumpeter

26. In Harrod model :
A. if the actual growth rate is higher than the warranted growth rate, there will be inflation
B. if the actual growth rate is higher than the warranted growth rate, there will be deflation
C. the economy will be in equilibrium when actual and warranted growth rates are equal
D. higher growth is the consequence of economising on labour

27. In Domar's model
A. investment is the solution for both inflation and deflation
B. higher investment is solution only to control inflation
C. higher investment is solution only to control deflation
D. a high growth rate is preferable to a relatively lower compound growth rate

28. In Harrod model, investment demand is a function of which of the following
A. national income
B. rate of change in price level
C. rate of change in national income
D. interest rate

29. Who among the following Economists held the behaviour of population as an obstacle to economic growth in initiating the process of economic growth
A. P.N. Rosenstein Rodan
B. W.W. Rostow
C. R. Nurkse
D. H. Leibenstein

30. A number of indivisibilities hinder the process of economic growth in the initial stages. This view was emunciated by
A. R. Nurkse
B. H.W. Singer
C. P.N. Rosenstein Rodan
D. W.W. Rostow

31. Development process has been viewed as a 'chain of disequilibria' by
A. P.N. Rosenstein Rodan
B. R. E. Baldwin
C. H. Leibenstein
D. A.O. Harschman

32 The growth of population has a bearing on the
A. natural rate of growth
B. actual rate of growth
C. warranted rate of growth
D. all the above

33. Nurkse was of the opinion that developing countries will have serious and adverse effect on their balance of payments due to
A. backwash effect
B. demonstration effect
C. multiplier effect
D. spread effect

34. Who among the following Economists held that a growing economy is essentially unstable
A. R.F. Harrod B. D. Ricardo
C. R. M. Solow D. T. Swau

35. In developing economies, investment is limited due to in sufficiency of demand. Who among the following Economists, has criticised this view
A. E. D. Domar B. R.F. Harrod
C. R. Nurkse D. J. Viner

36. In developing economies, surplus labour exists in the sense that each labour is working for hours less than the normal working hours. This view has been expressed by
A. J. Robinson B. M. Dobb
C. R. Nurkse D. A.K. Sen

37. In Harrod's model of economic growth, G_a is actual rate of growth G_w is warranted rate of growth and G_n is natural rate of growth. Steady rate of growth is ensured when
A. $G_a = G_n$ B. $G_w = G_n$
C. $G_a = G_w$ D. $G_w > G_n$

38. Who among the following Economists, developed the 'theory of circular causation
A. G. Myrdal B. R. Nurkse
C. J. Robinson D. J.R. Hicks

39. **Assertion (A) :** The neo-classical growth theory believes that there is substantial difference in the growth pattern of less developed countries and the developed countries.
Reason (R) : This is mostly due to the market failure in the less developed countries caused by a variety of imperfections existing in such economies.
A. Both A and R are individually true and R is the correct explanation of A.
B. Both A and R are individually true but R is a *not* the correct explanation of A.
C. A is true but R is false.
D. A is false but R is true

40. The process of economic development refers to
A. growth of national income over time
B. growth of per capita income and standards of living

C. full employment of the entire population
D. growth of national income with structural changes in the economy

41. Match List-I (concepts) with List-II (Economists) and select the correct answer using the codes given below the lists.

(List-I)
(Concepts)
(a) Critical minimum effort
(b) Unlimited supply of labour
(c) Theory of balanced growth
(d) Warranted growth rate

(List-II)
(Economists)
1. Rosenstein Rodan
2. Harrod-Domars
3. W.A. Lewis
4. H. Leibenstein

Codes :	*(a)*	*(b)*	*(c)*	*(d)*
A.	1	2	4	3
B.	4	3	1	2
C.	1	3	4	2
D.	4	2	1	3

42 Marx refers to the concept of organic composition of capital. Which one of the following ratios stands for this (where c is constant capital, V is variable capital and S is surplus value)?

A. $\frac{C}{V+S}$ B. $\frac{C}{V}$

C. $\frac{C}{(C+V)}$ D. $\frac{(C+V)}{V}$

43. The 'Big push' strategy of development was first advocated by
A. Rosenstein Rodan
B. Simon Kuznets
C. W.A. Lewis
D. A.O. Hirschman

44. Assertioin (A) : Non-economic factors play an important role in the process of economic development.

Reason (R) : Accumulation of capital takes the form of human capita formation also.
A. Both A and R are true and R is the correct explanation of A.
B. Both A and R are true but R is *NOT* a correct explanation of A.
C. A is true but R is false.
D. A is false but R is true.

45. Assertion (A) : Per capita income figures are poor tools of ordinal ranking of countries with respect to the real well being.

Reason (R) : A good portion of the national income in poor countries is unreported.
A. Both A and R are true and R is the correct explanation of A.
B. Both A and R are true but R is *NOT* a correct exlanation of A.
C. A is true but R is false.
D. A is false but R is true.

46. Human Development Index (HDI) is a composite index of
A. health, literacy and employment
B. national income,size of population and the general price level
C. national income, per capita income and per capita consumption
D. physical resources, monetary resources and population size

47. According to the Harrod-Domar model, the warranted rate of growth, given the incremental capital-output raio, depends on the
A. rate of growth of labour force
B. marginal productivity of investment
C. marginal efficiency of capital
D. saving-income ratio

48. According to J.R. Hicks, technical progress is said to be neutral if it raises
A. the marginal physical productivity of labour and capital in the same proportion
B. the average productivity of labour and capital in the same proportion
C. the wage rate and the interest rate in the same proportion
D. the interest-rate and the profit-rate in the same proportion

49. According to kuznets, during process of development the income inequalities tend to
A. decrease
B. increase
C. increase first and then decrease
D. decrease first and then increase

50. Perfectly elastic supplies of labour play a crucial role in

A. Malthus' model of growth
B. Kuznets' model of growth
C. The Prebisch hypothesis
D. Lewis model of growth

51. Consider the following statements : The correct order of specific stages of demographic transition associated with economic development is

1. low birth rate with low death rate.
2. high birth rate with high death rate.
3. high birth rate with low death rate.

Which of the above statements are correct ?

A. 1, 2, 3 B. 2, 1, 3
C. 2, 3, 1 D. 3, 2, 1

52 Consider the following statements for the Balanced Growth theory propounded by Ragnar Nurkse and select the correct answer from the code given below :

Statements :

(a) A package of industries be developed by private initiative
(b) A package of industries be developed by state initiative.
(c) If needed foreign capital be used to augment the capital supply
(d) Agriculture and industry be used together

Code :

A. *a, b* and *c* are correct
B. *a* and *c* are correct
C. *b* and *d* are correct
D. *b, c* and *d* are correct

53. Assertion (A) : In the unbalanced theory of growth, different sectors grow at different rates.

Reasons (R) : This allows utilization of interdependence of economic sectors.

Code :

A. Both A and R are true and R is correct explanation of A.
B. Both A and R are true but R is not the correct explanation of A.
C. A is true but R is false
D. A is false but R is true

54. "Development is a continuous and spontaneous change in the stationary state which forever atters and displaces the equilibrium state previously existing; while growth is a gradual and steady change in the long run which comes about by a gradual increase in the rate of savings and population", is the well-known definition of development and growth attributed to

A. C.P. Kindelberger
B. U. Hicks
C. J. A. Schumpeter
D. Ragner Nurkse

55. Consider the following statements :
According to Joan Robinson, "*golden age*" refers to a situation where

1. there is full employment at a high standard of living
2. there is full utilisation of capacity
3. the rate of growth of population is higher than the rate of growth of the economy
4. the per capita income increases at an increasing rate

Of these statements

A. 3 and 4 are correct
B. 1 and 4 are correct
C. 1 and 3 are correct
D. 1 and 2 are correct

56. Consider the following :
The process which enables

1. individuals of a country to accumulate more capital.
2. increasing the knowledge, skill and capacities of the people of the country.
3. accumulation of tangible wealth.
4. accumulation of intangible wealth.

Human capital formation as a concept is better explained in terms of

A. 1, 2 and 4 B. 1, 2 and 3
C. 3 and 4 D. 2 and 4

57. According to Hirschman, '*convergent*' series comprises investment projects that appropriate more external economies than they create and '*divergent*' series comprises investment projects that create more external economies than what they appropriate. In terms of this, investments in power and transport as

A. convergent series
B. divergent series
C. respectively convergent and divergent series

D. both (A) and (B)

58. Match List-I (Investment criteria) with List-II (Authors) and select the correct answer using the codes given below the lists :

List-I

(a) Capital turnover criterion

(b) Social marginal productivity criterion

(c) Time series criterion

(d) Ratio of reinvestment criterion

List-II

1. Galenson-Leibenstein
2. A.K. Sen
3. Kahn-Chenery
4. Buchanan-Polak

Codes :	*(a)*	*(b)*	*(c)*	*(d)*
A.	4	3	2	1
B.	4	2	3	1
C.	1	2	3	4
D.	1	3	2	4

59. The original interpretation of balanced growth relates to

A. large-scale expansion of activities to over come divergence between private and social benefits

B. all sectors growing at the same rate

C. equal amount to investment in all sectors

D. absence of shortages or excesses

60. The vicious circle of poverty can be broke with synchronised application of capital rather than investment in any single line production taken by itself. In this statement '*single line of production*' implies

A. investment in the production of particular type of commodity

B. specialising in a particular process of production

C. investment in a particular region of the economy

D. none of these

61. Match List-I with List-II and select the correct answer using the codes given below the lists :

List-I

(a) P.N. Rosenstein Rodan

(b) H. Leibenstein

(c) R. Nurkse

(d) W.W. Rostow

List-II

1. The critical minimum effort
2. The big push theory
3. Take-off into self-sustained growth
4. Vicious circle of poverty

Codes :	*(a)*	*(b)*	*(c)*	*(d)*
A.	2	1	4	3
B.	3	4	2	1
C.	3	1	4	2
D.	2	4	1	3

62. Consider the following statements :

'Economic Development' is a

1. continuous process
2. short-term process
3. long-term process

Of these statements

A. 2 alone is correct

B. 1 and 3 are correct

C. 3 alone is correct

D. 1 and 2 are correct

63. The index which combines social indicators of life expectancy and literacy with a measure of basic income adjusted to reflect purchasing power sufficient to raise the people above the poverty line is called

A. Basic Needs Index

B. Purchasing Power Index

C. Human Development Index

D. Welfare Index

64. A production possibility frontier (PPF) is shown in the given diagram. A less developed country (LDC) will be

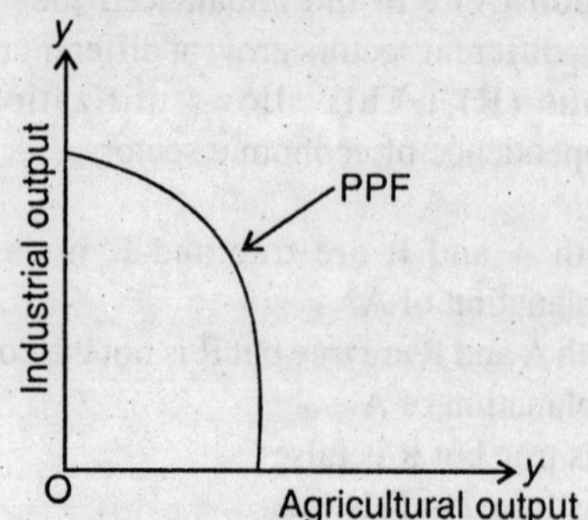

A. inside the PPF

B. on the PPF

C. above the PPF

D. at a point which coincides with the origin

65. In W.W. Rostow's 'stages of Growth' the Drive to Maturity stage

A. follows take-off stage
B. starts development
C. completes development
D. follows High Mass Consumption stage

66. Capital deepening is a process in which

A. output remains constant
B. capital intensity remains constant
C. technology changes with an increase in output per worker.
D. none of these

67. Match List-I with List-II and select the corrct answer using the codes given below the lists :

List-I

(a) Absorptive capacity of capital
(b) Technological dualism
(c) Permissive and compulsive sequences
(d) Physical Quality of Life Index

List-II

1. A.D. Hirschman
2. M. Kalecki
3. B. Higgins
4. D. Morris

Codes :	*(a)*	*(b)*	*(c)*	*(d)*
A.	2	3	4	1
B.	2	3	1	4
C.	3	2	1	4
D.	3	2	4	1

68. Consider the following statements :
On the supply side, the argument for a Big Push theory is tied up with assumed existence of

1. small size of market
2. externalities
3. indivisibilities
4. high growth of population

Of these statements

A. 1 and 2 are correct
B. 1, 3 and 4 are correct
C. 2, 3 and 4 are correct
D. 2 and 3 are correct

69. According to Friedrich List, the different stages of development follow the sequence

A. pastoral, agriculture, agricultural manufacturing
B. savage, agriculture, agricultural manufacturing
C. agriculture, agricultural manufacturing, industry
D. savage, pastoral, agriculture, agricultural manufacturing, commerce

70. Match List-I with List-II and select the corrct answer using the codes given below the lists :

List-I

(a) Economic Growth and Structure
(b) Readings in the Theory of Income Distribution
(c) An essay Marxian Economics
(d) The Theory of Geographical Location of Economic Activity

List-II

1. Fellner
2. Kuznets
3. W.H. Dean
4. Joan Robinsons

Codes :	*(a)*	*(b)*	*(c)*	*(d)*
A.	2	1	4	3
B.	2	1	3	4
C.	1	2	3	4
D.	1	2	4	3

71. Generally speaking the optimum population of a country refers to the size of the population which

A. maximises output per head
B. maintains constant rate of growth of population
C. leads to an increase in the proportion of workers in the industry
D. provides gainful employment to the rural population

72 The most important objective of development planning is to

A. ensure a greater degree of economic equality
B. ensure a higher degree of economic growth and development
C. make available larger provisions for capital formation and investment
D. provide greater opportunities for full employment

73. Consider the following statements:
Mahalanobis model of planning can be

described as a
1. sectoral planning model
2. bi-sector model
3. consistency model
4. growth model
Of these statements
A. 1 and 2 are correct
B. 2 and 3 are correct
C. 1 and 3 are correct
D. 3 and 4 are correct

74. **Assertion (A) :** According to schumpeter, development is a spontaneous and discontinuous change in the channels of the circular flow.
Reason (R) : The entrepreneur is the agent of this change.
A. Both A and R are true and R is the correct explanation of A.
B. Both A and R are true but R is *not* a correct explanation of A.
C. A is true but R is false.
D. A is false but R is true.

75. Which one of the following pairs is *not* correctly matched ?

Author	***Book***
A. Siman Kuznets	Asian Drama
B. J. Robinson	Essays on the Theory of Economic Growth
C. Karl Marx	Das Capital
D. Arthur W. Lewis	Theory of Economic Growth

76. The mercantilist theory of economic growth is primarily conerned with an increase in the
A. Volume of money in circulation through the import of gold
B. Size of population
C. State intervention for the creation of conditions for efficient entrepreneurial functions
D. Surplus in the balance of trade

77. Assuming capital-output ratio to be 3:1 and population grown to be 2.5% per annum, a 10.5% increase in investment will lead to an increase in per capita income to the extent of
A. 0% B. 1.0%
C. 3.0% D. 7.0%

78. Harrod's natural rate of growth is
A. the rate of growth which the increase of population and technical improvement allow
B. the rate of growth which will satisfy profit makers that they have done the right thing
C. the actual rate of growth
D. the increase in the rate of capital accumulation

79. "Economic Development with Unlimited Supplies of labour" is a model of development enunciated by
A. A. O. Hirschman B. W. W. rostow
C. W. A. Lewis D. Holis Chenery

80. Leibenstein in his Critical Minimum Effort thesis treats population as a factor that is
A. income – generating
B. income– depressing
C. investment – inducing
D. market – expending

81. The First Five Year Plan of the Government of India was based on
A. Leontief input – output model
B. Harrod – Domar model
C. Mahalanobis two – sector model
D. Mahalanobis four – sector model

82 *'Economic Drain'* theory was popularised by
A. Dadabhai Naoroji
B. Vera Anstey
C. V. V. Bhatt
D. None of these

83. According to Fisher-Clark thesis which one of following is the correct sequence of shift of resources from one sector to the other for the continuity of development?
A. Agriculture → Services → Manufacturing
B. Agriculture → Manufacturing → services
C. Manufacturing → Services → Agriculture
D. Manufacturing → Agriculture → Services

84. Consider the following statements:
In the estimates of growth of the United states, 'residual growth' is attributed by Denison to
1. technological improvement
2. growth of capital
3. growth of labour
4. combined growth of labour and capital.

Of these statement

A. 1 alone is correct
B. 1 and 2 are corret
C. 1, 2, and 3 are correct
D. 1, 2, 3, and 4 are correct

85. **Assertion (A):** Technological change is regarded as an important factor in the process of economic growth

Reason (R): Changes in the technology lead to increases in the productivity of labour, capital and other factors of production

Codes:

A. Both A and R are true and R is the correct explanation of A
B. Both A and R are true but R is *not* the correct explanation of A
C. A is true but R is false
D. A is false but R is true

86. Which one of the following growth models was the basis of the planning strategy during the second and third Five-year plans of India?

A. Harrod-Domar Growth Model
B. The Mahalanobis Two-Sector model
C. Alan manne and Ashok Rudra's 30-sector consistency model
D. Kaldor's model of growth

87. Which of the following was/were assumed in the neo classical growth model as propounded by solow?

1. A variable savings rate
2. A constant population growth rate
3. A variable capital-output ratio

Select the correct answer using the codes given below.

Codes:

A. 1 alone B. 1 and 2
C. 3 alone D. 2 and 3

88. Despite being a high saving economy, a developing country may still NOT grow fast primarily due to

A. week administrative machinery
B. illiteracy
C. high population density
D. high capital-output ratio

89. Hick's neutral technical change implies that

A. the unit isoquant undergoes a parallel sift upwards
B. the unit isoquant undergoes a parallel shift downwards
C. curvature of the unit isoquant changes
D. None of the above

90. Capital deepening means

A. using larger amount of labour as campared to capital
B. using more of the same type of capital due to increase number of workers
C. increase in capital per worker in already existing production
D. using more of human capital

91. Which one of the following pairs of Economists and doctrines they advocated, is correctly matched?

A. A. W. Lewis..."Big Push" theory
B. A. O. Hirschman...strategy of unbalanced growth
C. Rosenstein Rodan...stages of economic growth
D. W. W. Rostow... Theory of development with unlimited supplies of labour

92 If the marginal productivity of labour in agriculture is zero, then the labour supply curve for industry as assumed by Arthur Lewis will be

A. upward rising
B. perfectly in elastic
C. backward bending
D. perfectly elastic

93. Consider the following statements:

The Knife-edge problem in the Harrod-Domar growth model implies a constant

1. rate of population
2. output
3. rate of saving
4. capital-output ratio

Of these statements

A. 4 alone is correct
B. 1 and 2 are correct
C. 1, 2 and 3 are correct
D. 1, 3 and 4 are correct

94. In the analysis by Hirschman, the industry with the highest combined linkages turned out to be

A. Cement B. Textiles
C. Iron and Steel D. Food processing

95. The utilisation of disguised unemployment as a source of savings potential in underdeveloped countries was suggested by

A. R. Nurkse B. P. Baran
C. R. Harrod D. W.W. Rostow

96. Match list I (Authors) with list II (concepts) and select the correct answer using the codes given below the lists

List I	*List II*
(*a*) Domar	1. Golden Age
(*b*) Rosenstein-Rodan	2. Big-Push
(*c*) Rostow	3. Stages of growth
(*d*) Joan Robinson	4. Required rate of growth

Codes :	(*a*)	(*b*)	(*c*)	(*d*)
A.	4	2	3	1
B.	2	4	3	1
C.	2	4	1	3
D.	4	2	1	3

97. Match List I (Authors) with List II (Theories) and select the correct answer using the codes given below the Lists.

List I	*List II*
(*a*) *Slow*	1. Neutral technological change, under which, despite the change in output, the capital labour ratio remains constant.
(*b*) Hicks	2. Neutral technological change, under which the labour output ratio remains constant, so that the factor proportions are baised in favours of saving capital
(*c*) Harrod	3. Neutral technological change, under which, the capital output ratio remains constant, so that the factor proportions are baised in favour of saving labour

Codes :	(*a*)	(*b*)	(*c*)
A.	2	1	3
B.	1	2	3
C.	3	2	1
D.	3	1	2

98. The two-gap theory as applied to development planning refers to

A. inflationary gap and investment gap
B. saving gap and deflationary gap
C. foreign exchange gap
D. saving constraint and foreign exchange constraint

99. Demographic transition refers to

A. migration of population from rural to urban areas
B. change in the male/female ratio of the population
C. shift from a stable population at high birth and death rates to one of low birth and death rates
D. shift from high birth and low death rates to low birth and low death rates

100. Which one of the following is NOT an assumption of the Harrod-Domar model?

A. Fixed capital-output ratio
B. Variable marginal and average propensity to save
C. Closed economy
D. Capital is the only factor of production

101. The 'Hindu Rate of Growth'

A. refers to growth of Hindu population
B. is the term used by Raj Krishna to represent the nature of the growth of Indian economy at around 3.5 percent per year
C. is the term coined by Amartya Sen to represent the nature of the growth of the Indian economy at around 3.5 percent per year.
D. is the term coined by V. K. R. V. Rao to decide the nature of the growth of the Indian economy at around 4 percent

102. Disguised unemployment in the agricultural sector of India exists due to the

A. dependence of agriculture on the monsoons
B. abolition of Zamindari
C. heavy pressure of population on land
D. absence of trade unions in the agricultural sector

103. The concept of unbalanced growth has not been advocated by

A. H. W. Singer B. A. Lewis
C. A. O. Hirschman D. C. P. Kindleberger

104. The idea of balanced growth is related to the classical

A. idea of the nature of economic science

B. idea of full employment equilibrium
C. law of markets
D. school of thought

105. The difficulties of comparing growth of different countries are
A. Lack of empirical data
B. Choice of a common denominator
C. Assigning weights to the various items of output
D. All of these

106. Investment projects should be capital intensive because they would lead to greater saving and investment in future advocated by
A. H. Leibenstein
B. M. Leibenstein and W. Galenson
C. W. Galenson
D. W. Galenson and R. Nurkse

107. According to Lewis the subsistence sector is that part of the economy which
A. Makes use of reproducible capital
B. Does not make use of reproducible capital
C. Employs labour for wages in mines, factories, plantations for earning profits
D. None of the above

108. Myrdal builds his theory of economic development around the idea of
A. Regional inequalities on the national plane
B. Regional inequalities on the international plane
C. Both A and B
D. None of the above

109. If you like to increase the rate of economic development of a country, increase in which of the folllowing would you suggest
A. Government expenditure
B. Standard of living
C. Consumption
D. Saving

110. All underdeveloped countries are
A. Not developing at all
B. Developing but slowly
C. Developing at different rates
D. Receding backwards

111 To break the vicious circle on the demand side of capital, Nurkse has pleaded for
A. Balance growth
B. Unbalanced growth
C. Agricultural growth
D. Industrial growth

112. Incremental capital-output ratio (ICOR) is defined as
A. $\frac{\text{Increment in capital}}{\text{Increment in output}}$
B. $\frac{\text{Increment in output}}{\text{Increment in capital}}$
C. $\frac{\text{Increment in income}}{\text{Increment in consumption}}$
D. $\frac{\text{Increment in saving}}{\text{Increment in consumption}}$

113. The criticism of the balanced growth theory is mainly based on the considerations of
A. Market-size
B. External economies
C. Scarcity of resources
D. Large population

114. Unbalanced growth hypothesis is formulated on the assumption that
A. Expansion takes place simultaneously on several routes
B. Supplies of capital and labour are fixed
C. There are unlimited supplies of labour and capital
D. Underdeveloped countries impose ceiling on their rates of growth

115. Balanced growth, which is associated with Nurkse and Rosentein Rodan, means
A. Equal increase in resources allocated
B. Equal percentage growth in output
C. Different parts of the economic growth in harmonious manner
D. Different fields of growth at a natural rate

116. Who of the following supported the theory of balanced growth?
A. Ragnar Nurkse B. Hans Singer
C. Hirschman D. None of the above

117. Who has suggested that economic development of developing countries can be accelerated by weakening the '*back wash effects*' and strenghthening the '*Spread effects*'?
A. N. Kaldor B. J. Robinson
C. G. Myrdal D. J. H. Boeke

118. If the capital-output ratio is 3 percent, the savings rate 5 percent and the economy is growing at 4 percent in simple terms and 1.5 percent in per capita terms, what is the percentage of the rate of population growth?

A. 1.5 B. 2.5
C. 3.5 D. 4.5

119. Lewis means by an unlimited supply of labour

A. The supply of labour is more than the demand for labour
B. Infinite labour is available at whatever wage determined by the market
C. The supply of labour at the subsistence wage is greater than the demand for labour
D. The economy adopts only labour intensive techniques of production
E. None of the above

120. Which one of the following is not an assumption of Neoclassical's Growth theory?

A. Perfect competition in commodity and factor markets
B. Factor payment equal their marginal revenue productivity
C. A capital-output ratio.
D. Full employment in the economy

121. Foreign aid is needed to

A. Supplement the domestic savings of developing nations
B. Assure the capital imports needed for development
C. Prevent the absolute gap between rich and poor nations from widening further
D. All of the above

122. "Under–developed countries are the slums of the world economy" is the statement given by

A. David Ricardo B. G. Myrdal
C. Cairncross D. Arthuer Lewis

123. Dualistic economy is one where

A. Public and private sectors exist side by side
B. Modern industrial sector and traditional subsistence sector exist side by side
C. Agriculture and industrial sectors are equally developed
D. Indigeneous industries are developed in collaboration with foreign companies

124. Fei– Ranis theory of economic development is based on

A. Balanced growth during the take off process
B. Importance of agricultural product in capital accumulation in under developed countries
C. Dualistic approach to development
D. All of the above

125. According to myrdal, the main cause of regional inequalities in the under developed countries has been

A. Weak backwash effects and strong spread effects
B. Weak back–wash and spread effects
C. Strong back–wash and spread effects
D. Strong back–wash and weak spread effects

126. The technique of input–output analysis has been popularised by

A. Nurkse B. Samuelson
C. Leontief D. Lange

127. According to solow, the long–run rate of growth on an advanced economy equals Harrod's

A. Warranted rate of growth
B. Actual rate of growth
C. Natural rate of growth
D. None of the above

128. In terms of Harrod–Domar growth model, for achieving a postulated rate of growth an economy requires

A. Increase in the investment ratio
B. Reducing the capital–output ratio
C. Restricting the growth of population
D. All of the above

129. Harrod–Domar model of economic development presupposes—in the economy.

A. Low level of consumption
B. High level of consumption
C. Unemployment
D. Full employment

130. Who believed that the people in less developed contries are not economically motivated towards work and does not respond to normal monetary incentive?

A. A. Marshall B. D. Ricardo
C. J. H. Boeke D. R. Nurkse

131. With economic growth there is

A. A shift away from agriculture
B. A shift away from manufacturing

C. A shift in favour of agriculture
D. A shift away from services

132. The rate of growth of national income is equal to

A. $\frac{\text{National income}}{\text{growth of population}}$

B. $\frac{\text{Investment ratio}}{\text{Capital output ratio}}$

C. $\frac{\text{Capital output ratio}}{\text{Investment ratio}}$

D. None of these

133. An economy will face depression if the
A. Warranted rate of growth is higher than the actual rate of growth
B. Actual rate of growth is higher than the warranted rate of growth
C. Natural rate of growth is higher than the actual rate of growth
D. Actual rate of growth is higher than the natural rate growth

134. The condition of steady growth, in terms of rate of growth, in the Harrod growth model is
A. Actual growth rate = Warranted growth rate
B. Actual growth rate = "Take off" growth rate
C. actual growth rate = Natural grown rate
D. Warranted growth rate = Natural growth rate

135. According to the Hicksion theory, growth is checked when
A. Rate of growth of actual output exceeds rate of growth of ceiling output
B. Rate of growth of actual output is less than the rate of growth of ceiling output
C. Rate of growth of actual output is equal to the rate of growth of ceiling output
D. None of the above

136. According to Colin Clark the third and final stage of development is characterised by the predominance of
A. Manufacturing sector
B. Services sector
C. Agriculture sector
D. Exports sector

137. With economic growth the share of the secondary sector in National Product
A. Rises
B. Falls
C. Remains constant
D. Does not necessarily rise

138. The idea of a 'Big Push' is associated with which of the following theories?
A. Economic development with unlimited supply of labour
B. Theory of Balanced growth
C. Theory of Unbalanced growth
D. None of the above

139. Accumulation of capital involves:
A. Increase in real saving
B. Mobilisation of saving
C. Investment of saving
D. All of the above

140. Boeke, the originator of the theory of Sociological Dualism was
A. An English Civil Servant
B. A French Civil Servant
C. A Dutch Civil Servant
D. None of the above

141. In Harrod growth model, the rate of advance with the increase in population and technological change allow over the long period of time is called the
A. Warranted Growth Rate
B. Actual Growth Rate
C. Natural Growth Rate
D. "Take–off" Growth Rate

142. The 'Theory of Stages of Growth' is associated with the name
A. Simon Kuznets B. Colin Clark
C. Paul Samuelson D. W.W. Rostow

143. The concepts of 'forward linkage' and 'backward linkage' were used mainly in the developmental theory propounded by
A. Myrdal B. Hirschman
C. Boeke D. Leibenstein

144. The phrase 'demonstration effect', was coined by
A. J.K. Galbraith
B. J.M. Keynes
C. James Dussenberry
D. Joan Robinson

145. The stage of growth in which (1) basic needs are no longer a problem, and (2) there is popular consumption of durable goods is known as
A. The age of high mass consumption

B. The drive to maturity
C. The take–off
D. The pre–conditions for change

146. One of the conditions of take–off, as laid down by Rostow is
A. Rise in the rate of productive investment
B. One or more manufacturing sector with high rate of growth
C. Changes in social and institutional frame work
D. All of the above

147. In Rostow's theory, the drive to maturity
A. Starts the development process
B. Completes the development process
C. comes before the take–off
D. Follows the take–off

148. Which one of the following is not an assumption of Harrod-Domar models?
A. MPS is greater than APs
B. MPS remains constant
C. There is no depreciation of capital goods
D. None of the above

149. The Harrod-Domar growth model suggests that growth is
A. Directly related to savings and inversely related to the capital-output ratio
B. Directly related to the capital-output ratio and inversely related to savings
C. Indirectly related to savings and the capital-output ratio
D. Directly related to savings and the capital-output ratio

150. The 'warranted growth' rates as defined by Harrod is the
A. Full capacity growth rate of income of an economy
B. Rates which producers will be content with what they are doing
C. Path on which the supply and demand for goods and services will remain in equilibrium given the propensity to save
D. All the above

151. The basic rationale of the theory of "big push" is based upon the idea of
A. Internal economics
B. External economics
C. Size of population
D. None of the above

152 In both the laspeyres and Paasche indices
A. The growth components are the same
B. The weighting factors are the same
C. Both growth and weight factors are the same
D. The growth component in the Laspayres index is larger for countries at the start of the industrialisation process

153. According to Domar's model, in order to maintain full employment the growth rate of net autonomous investment must be equal to
A. Growth rate of savings
B. Marginal propensity to save
C. Marginal propensity to save and productivity of capital
D. Growth rate of population

154. Rostow's condition for a country to achieve the take-off stage was a rise in the proportion of net investment to over
A. 7% B. 5 – 10%
C. 12% D. 14%

155. Nurkse says in the context of an under developed country inducement to invest is limited by
A. The size of the market
B. Lack of investment opportunities
C. Lack of savings
D. The policy of the government

156. The concept of technological dualism has been put forward by
A. B. Higgins B. J. H. Boeke
C. A. Lewis D. R. Rodan

157. Who put forward the theory of 'financial dualism'?
A. J.H. Beoke B. B. Higgins
C. A. Lewis D. H. Myint

158. Which one of the following countries was the first to reach the age of high mass consumption in 1920'S?
A. Japan B. U.S.A
C. Soviet Union D. Great Britain

159. Disguised unemployment generally means
A. Large number of people remaining unemployed
B. Alternative employment is not available
C. MP_L is zero

D. None of the above

160. In the Lewis' theory, capitalist surplus results because the marginal productivity of labour in the capitalist sector is

A. Higher than the capitalist wage
B. Higher than that in the subsistence sector
C. Positive
D. Ever increasing

161. Which one of the following is not the one of the indivisibilities as prescribed by Rodan for launching economic development?

A. Indivisibilities in the Production Function
B. Indivisibilities in the Consumption Function
C. Indivisibilities of Demand
D. Indivisibilities in the supply of savings

162 Which among the following has the highest forward linkage?

A. Foodgrains B. Guns
C. Iron Ore D. Machinery

163. The actual growth rate is defined by Harrod as the rate which is

A. Determined by the saving ratio and marginal capital-output ratio
B. The full capacity growth rate of income of an economy
C. The welfare optimum rate
D. None of the above

164. Who believed that a deliberate unbalancing of the economy according to a predesigned strategy is the best way to achieve economic growth

A. Rosenstein Rodan
B. A. O. Hirschman
C. J. Schumpeter
D. J.H. Boeke

165. In Lewis' Theory, capital formation dependes upon

A. Capitalist surplus
B. Bank credit
C. Both of (A) and (B)
D. None of the above

166. The 'critical minimum effort' theory is due to

A. H. Leibenstein B. Rosenstein Rodan
C. W. A. Lewis D. J. H. Boeke

167. The classical model of economic development considers:

A. Profits as incentive to investment
B. Tendency of profits to decline with larger capital accumulation
C. Both A and B
D. None of the above

168. "Golden age" corresponds to a situation where

A. Natural rate of growth exceeds warranted rate of growth
B. Actual rate of growth exceed warranted rate of growth
C. Warranted rate of growth exceeds natural rate of growth
D. Natural, warranted and the actual rate of growth of national income are all equal

169. The 'Financial dualism' refers to coexistence in the less developed countries of

A. Commercial banks and non bank financial institutions
B. Scheduled and non-scheduled commercial banks
C. Stock exchange and new issue market
D. None of the above

170. Harrod-Domar models of economic growth are based on the experiences of

A. Underdeveloped economics
B. Developing economics
C. Advanced capitalist economics
D. Socialist economics

171. Which one of the following represents, at least in part, investment in human capital?

A. Formal education
B. On the Job training
C. Better health care
D. All of the above

172 Who was the first economist to advocate a Rolling plan for developing countries?

A. A. K. Sen
B. G. Myrdal
C. P. C. Mahalanobis
D. Rosenstein Rodan

173. Prespective planning refer to

A. Annual planning
B. Five-yearly planning
C. Long term planning
D. None of the above

174. Economist who first defined the conept of *Shadow Prices* is

A. Rosenstein-Rodan
B. H. Leibenstein
C. J. Tinberger
D. G. Myrdal

175. Solow's model or long run growth is a major improvement over that of
A. Harrod-Domar B. J. Robinson
C. J. E. Meade D. None of the above

176. Centralised planning refers to
A. Complete governmental control over the economy
B. Planning specific projects
C. The provision of the general frame work for the Five-year plans
D. The provision of economic projections and voluntary guidelines .

177. The book entitled "The Accumulation of Capital" has been written by
A. J. Robinson B. N. Kaldor
C. J. E. Meade D. Rosenstein Rodan

178. A consistency Model for India's Fourth plan was designed by
A. P. C. Malhalanobis
B. K. N. Raj and A. K. Sen
C. A. S. Manne and A. Rudra
D. All of the above

179. Which one of the following is not included by J. E. Meade in the three principal means whereby an economy can grow
A. Capital accumulation
B. Foreign trade
C. Growth of working population
D. Technical progress

180. The term 'golden age' as used by Joan Robinson refers to
A. Primitive economics
B. The situation of smooth and steady growth with full employment
C. The economy which uses gold coins
D. All of the above

181. When the planning authority formulates the central plan, fixes objectives, targets and priorities for every sector of the economy, the system of planning is known as
A. Physical B. Financial
C. Centralised D. decentralised

182 Shadow prices are particularly useful in
A. Consumer's purchase decision
B. Firm's sale decisions
C. Project evaluation and cost benefit analysis
D. None of the above

183. Indicative planning refers to
A. Complete government control over the economy
B. Planning of specific projects
C. The provision of five year plans
D. The provision of economic projections and voluntary guidelines

184. The capital-output ratio in a country during different phases of growth
A. Changes widely
B. Remains uniform and unchanged
C. Changes with in narrow limits
D. Declines Secularly

185. The second Five-year plan of India was based on Mahalanobis Model. It is considered as.....sector economy
A. One B. Two
C. Four D. None of the above

186. Kahan was among the first to include in his model
A. The importance of exports for a developing country
B. An estimate of the difference between private and social costs and benefits
C. The marginal per capita reinvestment quota
D. None of the above

187. Meade's model of economic growth is designed to show the way in which the simplest form of economic system would behave during the process of
A. Stagnation
B. Inflation
C. Equilibrium growth
D. Disequilibrium growth

188. According to Nurkse Vicious circles of poverty in UDCs operates—
A. On supply side only
B. On demand side only
C. On both demand and supply side
D. Because of lack of resources

189. Which one of the following is not one of the

most commonly used practical rules for project appraisal

A. Minimising incremental capital output ratio
B. Linear programming
C. Maximising social marginal productivities
D. Maximising investment rates

190. The 'technological dualism' in under-developed countries could be broken through by

A. A gradualist approach of development
B. Family planning
C. Planning for increased productivity in the rural sector
D. None of the above

191. The ' back wash effect' refers to the fact that when a particular region develops economically then

A. All the regions, automatically develop
B. Some other regions, particularly the backward ones, lose
C. No other region loses anything
D. None of the above

192 The '*critical growth rate*' of Prof. Meade is one where

A. The growth rate of capital stock equals the growth rate of output
B. The growth rate of savings equals the growth rate of output
C. The growth rate of consumption equals the growth rate of output
D. None of these

193. Balanced growth is preferred because all sectors of economy are

A. Underdeveloped
B. Inter-related
C. Independent of each other
D. None of the above

194. Rostow speaks of a period in a country's economic growth where "both the basic structure of the economy and the social and political structure of the society are transformed in such a way that a steady rate of growth can be there after sustained". The period he refers to in this passage is called

A. Pre-conditions for change
B. The take-off
C. The drive to maturity
D. The age of high mass consumption

195. 'Division of Labour' is optimally exhibited in

A. Large scale production
B. Highly mechanised production
C. High cost of product
D. Hard manual labour involving jobs

196. 'Innovation' according to kuznet, is

A. Application of new knowledge to production process
B. Improvement of efficiency of machines
C. Discovery of new consumption needs
D. Improvement of marketing techniques

197. Saving is

A. The major determinants of growth
B. The only determinants of growth
C. One of the determinants of growth
D. Not concerned with growth

198. In most underdeveloped countries, the markets are

A. Imperfect B. Perfect
C. Not in existence D. Very small

199. A country can meet its deficiency of capital through

A. Internal savings
B. Foreign capital
C. Diversion of savings to productive uses
D. All of the above

200. Economic development can be measured with the help of

A. Increase in GNP
B. Increase in NNP
C. Increase in per capita income at current prices
D. Increase in per capita income at constant prices.

201. Economic development of a country depends on

A. Natural resources
B. Capital formation
C. Size of the market
D. All of these

202 The classical theory of economic development failed to take into account

A. The role of the state
B. Technical innovation
C. Distribution of income

D. None of the above

203. The vicious circle of poverty points out the connection between

A. Income and population
B. Investment and technology
C. Productivity and income
D. Savings and capital

204. The term underdevelopment implies

A. Social institutions are very backward
B. Low per capita real income
C. High level of economic and technological backwardness
D. High population growth

205. Which of the following is a necessary condition for the high rate of modern economic growth?

A. Continuous technological progress
B. Development of urban centres
C. High rate of population growth
D. Expansion of money supply into the economy

206. Economic growth in underdeveloped economies is accompanied by—

A. High rate of growth of population and small change in occupational structure
B. Increased rate of capital formation and decreasing death rate
C. Sustained rise in product per capita and high population growth rate
D. All of the above

207. The economist who questioned the economic aptitude of people in under developed economics was

A. Ricardo B. Boeke
C. Myint D. Scitovsky

208. Inequalities of income are marked in under developed countries in—

A. Agricultural sector
B. Manufacturing sector
C. Service sector
D. All of these

209. The larger the proportion of captital formation in a country

A. The higher is the rate of growth
B. The lower is the rate of growth
C. The constant is the rate of growth
D. Nothing can be said about therate of growth

210. Capital accumulation

A. Facilitates capital widening
B. Makes capital deepening possible
C. Encourages introduction of new technology
D. Affects the proficiency of labour
E. All of the above

211. Capital out put ratio refers to

A. Units of capital required to produce consumer goods
B. Units of capital required to produce one unit of output
C. Amount of capital required to instal a capital asset
D. None of these

212 Kuznet's preference for real G N P over real per capital G N P as a measure of economic growth arises from—

A. The desirability to concentrate on growth of output alone
B. The need to combine output growth and population growth
C. The desirability to concentrate on the factors speeding economic growth and to analyse the population problem separately
D. All of these

213. The capital output ratio

A. Is the most important determinant of growth rate
B. Is not at all relevant for growth rate
C. Is one of the important determinants of growth
D. Is an active agent of growth

214. The crucial determinant of the size of the market is—

A. Monetary expansion
B. Inducement for investment
C. Productivity
D. Savings

215. Which of the following is a social factor that hinders economic development?

A. Lack of effective demand
B. Capital deficiency
C. Lack of skilled personel
D. Rigid religious attachments and conservatism

216. Out of the given possibilities below, the most

favourable capital — output ratio for a country is
A. 6 : 1 B. 5 : 1
C. 4 : 1 D. 3 : 1

217. For economic development, schumpeter gives importance to
A. Creditors B. Entrepreneurs
C. Innovation D. Inventions

218. According to simon kuznets, the criterion of economic growth is provided by the
A. More advanced economies and the more recent times
B. Poor economies and the acient times
C. Petroleum producing countries and their old history
D. None of the above

219. K.N. Raj and A.K.Sen's modal provides alternative patterns of economic growth under the conditions of
A. Expanding exports
B. Stagnant exports
C. Stagnant imports
D. Both (A) and (B)

220. Ricardo predicted the economy would end in a stationary state because
A. People would tire of working
B. The economy would run out of gold
C. Innovation would dry up
D. The economy would run out of arable land

221. The size of the market for a product means
A. The number of potential buyers of the product
B. The number of people in a particular area
C. The geographical area served by the producers
D. The number of sales of the product recorded annually

222. Which of the following is an example of economic overhead?
A. Schools B. Sanitary facilities
C. Hospitals D. Roads and railways

223. The occupational distribution of labour is
A. The same indeveloped and underdeveloped countries
B. Different indeveloped and developed and underdeveloped countries
C. Only a shade different in developed and underdeveloped countries
D. Nothing can be said

224. Which of the following represents at least in part investments in human capital
A. Formal education
B. On-the-job training
C. Better health care and nutrition
D. All of the above

225. Economic growth in underdeveloped economics is accompanied by
A. High rate of growth of population and small change in occupational structure
B. Increased rate of capital formation and decreasing death rate
C. Sustained rise in product per capita and high population growth rate
D. All of the above

226. Social marginal productivity theory
A. Over comes all of the weaknesses of marginal productivity theory
B. Is no different from marginal productivity theory
C. Accounts for all the interconnections in the economies including externalities
D. Is subjective and does not supplant the need for linear programming and input-output analysis

227. The economist who was most interested in population was
A. Smith B. Ricardo
C. Malthus D. Myint

228. Theory of social marginal productivity was proposed by
A. J. Robinson B. R. M. Solow
C. A. M. Khan D. Rosenstein-Rodan

229. The man who connected economic development with the evolution of credit was
A. Hildebrand B. Bucher
C. Boeke D. List

230. With the passage of time, the gap in the outcome based on simple rate of growth and that based on compound rate of growth gets
A. Widened B. Constant
C. Narrowed D. None of these

231. "A circular constellation of forces tend to act and react upon one another insuch a way as to

keep a poor country in a state of proverty" is a description of
A. Underdevelopment
B. Deeprooted proverty
C. Stagnation
D. Vicious circle of poverty

232 According to the time pattern of modern economic growth, an increasing preference for Leisure shows that
A. per apita income growth will shortly slow down
B. per capita income will continue to grow at an increasing rate
C. per capita income growth will be retarding eventually
D. None of there is likely to take place.

233. Ricardo, Marshall and schumpeter had one thing in common on with keynes that was
A. Quasi-rent is universal
B. Rent in universal
C. profit rate would be pushed to minimal levels in the absence of technical change
D. In the stationary state there will be full employment.

234. Galenson and leibenstein advocted investment projects that are
A. Labour intensive because they will help the working class
B. Capital intensive because this is the only way the economy can become competitive internationally
C. Labour intensive because they will stimulate consumer demand
D. Capital intensive because they will lead to greater saving and investment in the future

235. Who has suggested the utilization of "disguised unemployment" as a source of savings potential in underdeveloped countries?
A. Ragnar Nurkse B. W. A. Lewis
C. K. K. Kurihara D. Gunnar myrdal

236. The statement, 'the division of labour is limited by the extent of the market' is due to-
A. Adam Smith B. J. B.Say
C. David Ricardo D. Alfred Marshall

237. The economist who stressed that the role of the entrepreneur in development was
A. Hirschman B. Nurkse
C. Rosentien Rodan D. Schumpeter

238. Out of the following economists, which two have expressed similar ideas
A. Scitovsoky and Hilderbrand
B. Kindleberger and Rosenstein
C. Hirchman and Nurkse
D. Smith and myint

239. The 'spread effect' refers of the fact that when a particular region develops economically then
A. It may favourably affect the development of certain other regions
B. The cost its development is spread over the adjoining regions
C. The cost of its development is spread over the entire nation
D. None of the above

240. Who propounded the theory fo "Economic Development" as a harmonious and cumulative process?
A. Prof. W. A. Lewis
B. Prof. R. Nurkse
C. Prof. J. Schumpeter
D. Prof. O. V. Hirschman

ANSWERS

1	2	3	4	5	6	7	8	9	10
A	A	A	D	C	B	B	B	B	A
11	**12**	**13**	**14**	**15**	**16**	**17**	**18**	**19**	**20**
B	D	C	C	B	A	B	A	B	B
21	**22**	**23**	**24**	**25**	**26**	**27**	**28**	**29**	**30**
D	C	C	A	D	A	A	A	D	C
31	**32**	**33**	**34**	**35**	**36**	**37**	**38**	**39**	**40**
D	A	B	D	C	D	B	A	A	D

41	42	43	44	45	46	47	48	49	50
B	B	A	B	A	A	D	A	B	D
51	**52**	**53**	**54**	**55**	**56**	**57**	**58**	**59**	**60**
C	C	A	C	D	D	B	B	C	A
61	**62**	**63**	**64**	**65**	**66**	**67**	**68**	**69**	**70**
A	B	C	A	A	C	B	D	D	B
71	**72**	**73**	**74**	**75**	**76**	**77**	**78**	**79**	**80**
A	B	A	A	A	D	B	A	C	A
81	**82**	**83**	**84**	**85**	**86**	**87**	**88**	**89**	**90**
B	A	B	A	A	B	D	D	B	C
91	**92**	**93**	**94**	**95**	**96**	**97**	**98**	**99**	**100**
B	D	D	C	A	A	A	D	D	B
101	**102**	**103**	**104**	**105**	**106**	**107**	**108**	**109**	**110**
B	C	B	B	D	B	B	C	A	C
111	**112**	**113**	**114**	**115**	**116**	**117**	**118**	**119**	**120**
A	A	C	B	C	A	C	B	C	C
121	**122**	**123**	**124**	**125**	**126**	**127**	**128**	**129**	**130**
D	C	B	D	D	C	C	D	D	C
131	**132**	**133**	**134**	**135**	**136**	**137**	**138**	**139**	**140**
A	B	A	A	A	B	A	B	D	C
141	**142**	**143**	**144**	**145**	**146**	**147**	**148**	**149**	**150**
C	D	B	C	B	D	D	A	A	D
151	**152**	**153**	**154**	**155**	**156**	**157**	**158**	**159**	**160**
B	A	C	B	B	A	D	B	C	A
161	**162**	**163**	**164**	**165**	**166**	**167**	**168**	**169**	**170**
B	C	A	B	C	A	C	D	A	C
171	**172**	**173**	**174**	**175**	**176**	**177**	**178**	**179**	**180**
D	B	C	C	A	A	A	C	B	B
181	**182**	**183**	**184**	**185**	**186**	**187**	**188**	**189**	**190**
C	C	D	C	C	B	C	C	B	C
191	**192**	**193**	**194**	**195**	**196**	**197**	**198**	**199**	**200**
B	A	B	B	A	C	C	A	D	A
201	**202**	**203**	**204**	**205**	**206**	**207**	**208**	**209**	**210**
D	A	C	B	A	D	B	D	A	E
211	**212**	**213**	**214**	**215**	**216**	**217**	**218**	**219**	**220**
B	C	C	C	D	D	C	A	B	D
221	**222**	**223**	**224**	**225**	**226**	**227**	**228**	**229**	**230**
A	D	B	D	D	C	C	C	C	A
231	**232**	**233**	**234**	**235**	**236**	**237**	**238**	**239**	**240**
D	C	C	D	A	A	D	B	A	C

UNIT V : STATISTICAL METHODS

MEASURES OF CENTRAL TENDENCY OR STATISTICAL AVERAGES

There are five alternative measures of central tendency. They are:

1. Arithmetic Mean (A.M.)
2. Median
3. Mode
4. Geometric Mean (G.M.)
5. Harmonic Mean (H.M.)

ARITHMETIC MEAN

Arithmetic mean of given set of observations is their sum divided by the number of observations. For example, the arithmetic mean of 5, 8, 10, 15, 24, and 28 is

$$\frac{5+8+10+15+24+28}{6}=\frac{90}{6}=15$$

Calculation

Arithmetic mean can be calculated in the following manner:

A. Arithmetic Average in Individual Series

(*i*) Direct method

$$\overline{X} = \frac{\Sigma X}{N}$$

where:

$\overline{X}$ = Arithmetic Average or Mean

Σ = Sum of values and read as summation

X = Values of variable X

N = Number of items

(ii) Short cut method

$$\overline{X} = A+\frac{\Sigma dx}{N}$$

where

$\overline{X}$ = Arithmetic mean

A = Assumed Mean

Σdx = Total of deviations of the values of variables from an assumed mean

N = Number of is observations

B. Arithmetic Average in Discrete Series

(i) Direct Method $\overline{X}=\frac{\Sigma fx}{N}$

where

Σfx = Total of products of the frequencies (*f*) and the variable X

N = Total of frequencies, *i.e.*, $N = \Sigma f$

(ii) Shortcut Method

$$\overline{X} = A+\frac{\Sigma fdx}{N}$$

Σfdx = Total of products of the frequencies (*f*) and the deviations of the values of variables from an assumed mean (*dx*)

N = Total of frequencies

C. Arithmetic Average in Continuous Series

(i) Direct Method

$$\overline{X} = A+\frac{\Sigma fm}{N}$$

where

M = Mid–point

Σfm = Total of products of frequencies (*f*) and the mid point (*m*)

(ii) Short-cut Method

$$\overline{X} = A+\frac{\Sigma fdx}{N}$$

where

Σfdx = Total of products of frequencies (*f*) and the deviations of the values of mid–points from an assumed mean (*dx*)

(iii) Step–Deviation Method

$$\overline{X} = A + \frac{\Sigma fdx}{N} \times i$$

where Σfdx = Total of products of frequencies and the deviation from assumed mean by step-deviation

i = Magnitude of class-intervals

D. Charliers Accuracy Check

$$\Sigma[f(dx+1)] = \Sigma fdx + \Sigma f$$

E. Combined Mean

$$\overline{X}_{12} = \frac{N_1\overline{X}_1 + N_2\overline{X}_2}{N_1 + N_2}$$

where

$\overline{X}_{12}$ = Combined Mean

N_1 = Number of items of the first group

N_2 = Number of items of the second group

$\overline{X}_1$ = Arithmetic Average of the first group

$\overline{X}_2$ = Arithmetic Average of the second group

F. Weighted Mean

$$\overline{X}_w = \frac{\Sigma WX}{\Sigma W}$$

where X_w = Weighted mean

ΣWX = Total of products of weights and the variables X

ΣW = Total of weights

Mathematical Properties of Arithmetic Mean

Arithmetic mean possesses some very interesting and important mathematical properities as given below:

Property-1

The algebraic sum of the deviations of the given set of observations from their arithmetic mean is zero.

Mathematically, $\Sigma(X - \overline{X}) = 0$

or for a frequency distribution

$$\Sigma f(X - \overline{X}) = 0$$

Property-2

If n_1 and n_2 are the sizes and $\overline{X}_1, \overline{X}_2$ are the respective means of two series then the mean $\overline{X}$ of the combined series of size $n_1 + n_2$ is given by :

$$\overline{X} = \frac{n_1\overline{X}_1 + n_2\overline{X}_2}{n_1 + n_2}$$

The above result can be generalised to the case of more than two series. If we have k series with respective sizes $n_1, n_2, \dots n_k$ and means $\overline{X}_1, \overline{X}_2, \dots\dots \overline{X}_k$ respectively, then the mean $\overline{X}$ of the combined series of size $n_1 + n_2 + \dots + n_k$ is given by:

$$\overline{X} = \frac{n_1\overline{X}_1 + n_2\overline{X}_2 + n_3\overline{X}_3 + \dots\dots + n_k\overline{X}_k}{n_1 + n_2 + \dots\dots + n_k}$$

Property–3

The sum of the squares of deviations of the given set of observations is minimum when taken from the arithmetic mean.

Mathematically, for a given frequency distribution, the sum

$$S = \Sigma f(X - A)^2$$

which represents the sum f the squares of deviations of given observations from any arbitary value 'A' is minimum when.

$$A = \overline{X}$$

Property–4

If all the observations of a series are added, subtracted, multiplied or divided by a constant, the mean is also added, subtracted, multiplied or divided by the same constant.

Property–5

The weighted arithmetic mean of first *n* natural numbers whose weights are equal to the corresponding numbers is equal to

$$\left(\frac{2n+1}{3}\right)$$

Property–6

The arithmetic mean of first *n* natural numbers is equal to the arithmetic mean of its first and last term.

$$\overline{X} = \frac{1+2+3+\dots\dots+n}{n}$$

$$= \frac{n(n+1)}{2} \cdot \frac{1}{n} = \frac{n+1}{2}$$

MERITS AND DEMERITS OF ARITHMETIC MEAN

Merits

1. It is rigidly defined.

2. It is easy to understand and calculate.

3. It is based on all the observations.

4. It is least affected by the fluctuations of sampling.

5. It does not require the arranging the data.

Demerits

1. The strongest draw back of arithmetic mean is that it is very much affected by extreme observations. Two or three very large values of the variable may unduly affect the value of the arithmetic mean.

2. Arithmetic mean can not be used in the case of open end classes such as less than 10, more than 70 etc.

3. It cannot be determined by inspection nor can it be located graphically.

4. Arithmetic mean cannot be used if we are dealing with qualitative characteristics which can not be measured quantitatively such as intelligence, honesty, bequty etc. In such cases median is the only average to be used.

5. Arithmetic mean can not be obtained if a single observation is missing or last or is illegible unless we drop it out and compute the arithmetic mean of the remaining values.

6. In extremely asymmetrical (skewed) distribution, usually arithmetic mean is not representative of the distribution and hence is not a suitable measure of location.

MEDIAN

Median is the central value of the variable when the values are arranged in ***ascending*** or ***descending*** order of magnitude.

According to connor—"The median is that value of the variable which divides the groups in to two equal parts, one part camprising all the values greater and the other, all values less than median."

Calculation—Median may be, calculated in the following manner;

A. Calculation of Median in Individual Series

$$\text{M} = \text{Size of} \left(\frac{\text{N}+1}{2}\right) \text{th item}$$

where

M = Median

N = Number of items

2. Calculation of Median in Discrete Series

$$\text{M} = \text{Size of} \left(\frac{\text{N}+1}{2}\right) \text{the item}$$

where

M = Median

N = Total of frequencies

3. Calculation of Median in Continuous Series

$$\text{M} = \text{Size of} \left(\frac{\text{N}}{2}\right) \text{th item}$$

$$\text{M} = \text{L}_1 + \frac{i}{f}(m-c)$$

where

L = Lower limit of median group

i = Difference of lower and upper limit of median group

f = Frequency of median group

m = Median number $= \left(\frac{\text{N}}{2}\right)$ th item

c = Cumulative frequency of the group preceeding the median group

If data are arranged in descending order then we apply the following formula—

$$\text{M} = \text{L}_2 - \frac{i}{f}\left(\frac{\text{N}}{2} - c\right)$$

where

L_2 = Upper limit of the median group

MERITS AND DEMERITS OF MEDIAN

Merits

1. It is rigidly defined

2. Median is easy to understand and easy to calculate for a non–mathematical person.

3. Since median is a positional average, it is not affected at all by extreme observations and as such is very useful in the case of Skewed distributions, J–Shaped or inverted J–Shaped distribution such as the distribution of wages, incomes and wealth. So in case of extreme observations, median is a better average to use than the arithmetic mean since the latter gives a distorted picture of the distribution.

4. Median can be computed while dealing with a

distribution with open end classes.

5. Median can sometimes be located by simple inspection and can also be computed graphically.

6. Median is the only average to be used while dealing with qualitative characteristics which cannot be measured quantitatively but can still be arranged in ascending or descending order of magnitude e.g., to find the average intelligence, average beauty, average honesty etc., among a group of people.

Demerits

1. In case of even number of observations for an ungrouped data, median cannot be determined exactly. We merely estimate it as the arithmetic mean of the two middle terms.

2. Median, being a positional average, is not based on each and every item of the distribution. It depends on all the observations only to the extent whether they are smaller than or greater that it; the exact magnitude of the observations being immoterial.

3. It does not lead itself to algebric treatment.

4. It is affected by fluctuations of items.

5. It is less stable measure of central tendency than the mean.

6. In the case of continuous series, it cannot be calculated exactly.

PARTITION VALUES

The values which divide the series into a number of equal parts are called the *partition values.* Thus, median may be regarded as a particular partition value which divides the given data into two equal parts.

QUARTILES

The values which divide the given data into four equal parts are known as *quartiles* obviously there will be three such points θ_1, θ_2 and θ_3 such that $\theta_1 \leq \theta_2 \leq \theta_3$,termed as the three quartiles. θ_1, known as the lower or *first quartile* is the value which has 25% of the items of the distribution below it and consequently 75% of the items are greater than it.θ_2, known as the *second quartile,* coincides with the median and has an equal number of obervations above it and below it θ_3, known as the upper or *third quartile,* has 75% of the observations below it and consequently 25% of the observations obove it.

To compute θ_1, the following steps are required:

(i) Find $\frac{N}{4}$ where $N = \Sigma f$

(ii) See the cumulative frequency *(c.f.)* just greater than N/4

*(iii)*The corresponding value of & observation gives the value of θ_1. In case of continuous frequency distribution, the corresponding class contains θ_1 and the value of θ_1 is obtained by the interpolation formula:

$$\theta_1 = l + \frac{h}{f}\left(\frac{N}{4} - C\right)$$

where

l = lower limit of the class containing θ_1

f = frequency of the class containing θ_1

h = magnitude of the class containing θ_1

c = cumulative frequency *(c.f)* of the class preceding the class containing θ_1

Similarly to compute θ_3, see the *c.f.* just greater than $\frac{3N}{4}$. The corresponding value of items gives θ_3. In case of continuous frequency distribution, the corresponding class contains θ_3 and value of θ_3 is given by the formula:

$$\theta_3 = l + \frac{h}{f}\left(\frac{3N}{4} - C\right)$$

where

l = lower limit of the class containing θ_3

h= magnitude of the class containing θ_3

f= frequency of the class containing θ_3

c= c.f. of the class preceding the class containing θ_3

DECILES

Deciles are the values which divide the series into ten equal parts. Obviously there are nine deciles $D_1, D_2, D_3....D_9$ such that $D_1 \leq D_2 \leq ...... \geq D_9$. Incidentally D_5 coincides with the median.

The method of computing the deciles D_i, *(i* = 1, 2,...9*)* is the same as discussed for θ_3 and θ_3. To compute the *i*th decile D*i*, (*i* = 1, 2, 3, ...9). See the c.f. just greater than $\frac{iXN}{10}$. The corresponding value of item is D*i*. In case of continuous frequency distribution the corresponding class contains D*i* and its value is obtained by the formula

$$Di = l + \frac{h}{f}\left(\frac{i \times N}{10} - C\right)$$

$$i = 1, 2, 3, ...9$$

where

l = lower limit of the class containing Di

f = frequency of the class containing Di

h= magnitude of the class containing Di

c= $c.f.$ of the class preceding the class containing Di

PERCENTILES

Percentiles are the values which divide the series into 100 equal parts. Obviously, there are 99 percentiles $P_1, P_2, ...P_{99}$ Such that $P_1 \leq P_2 \leq .... \leq P_{99}$. The ith percentile Pi, (i = 1, 2, ...99) is the value of item corresponding to $c.f.$ just greater than $\frac{i \times N}{100}$. In case of continuous frequency distribution, the corresponding class contains Pi and its value is obtained by the formula

$$Pi = l + \frac{h}{f}\left(\frac{i \times N}{100} - C\right)$$

$$i = 1, 2, 3, ...99$$

where

l = lower limit of the class containing Pi

h= magnitude of the class containing Pi

f= frequency of the class containing Pi

c= $c.f.$ of the class preceding the class containing Pi

In particular, we shall have:

$P_{25} = Q_1$

$P_{50} = D_5$

$P_{75} = Q_3$

$D_1 = P_{10}, D_2 = P_{20}, D_3 = P_{30}, ...D_9 = P_{90}$

MODE

Mode is the value which occurs frequently in a set of observations and around which the other items of the set cluster densely. In other words, mode is the value of a series which is predominant in it. In the words of Croxton and Cowden, "The mode of a distribution is value at the point around which the items tend to be most heavily concentrated. It may be regarded as too most typical of a series of values."

Computation of Mode

The value of mode is obtained by the following formula:

$$\text{Mode} = L_1 + \frac{f_1 - f_0}{2f_1 - f_0 - f_2} \times i$$

where

L = lower limit of the modal class

f_1 = frequency of the modal class

f_0 = frequency of the class preceding the modal class

f_2 = frequency of the class succeeding the modal class

i = class interval of modal class

When mode is ill–defined the value of mode may be caluculated with the help of following formula:

Mode = 3 Median – 2 Mean

MERITS AND DEMERITS OF MODE

Merits

1. Mode is easy to calculate and understand. In some cases it can be located merely by inspection. It can also be estimated graphically from a his to gram.

2. Mode is not all affected by extreme observations and as such is preferred to arithmetic mean while dealing with extreme observations.

3. It can be conveniently obtained in the case of open end classes which do not pose any problems here.

Demerits

1. Mode is not rigidly defined.

2. Since mode is the value of X corresponding to the maximum frequency, it is not based on all the observations of the series.

3. Mode is not suitable for further mathematical treatment.

4. As compared with mean, mode is affected to a greater extent by the fluctuations of sampling.

Empirical Relation Between Mean (M), Median (M_d) and Mode (M_0)

In case of a *symmetrical distribution* mean, median and mode, coincide. Thus

$$Mean = Median = Mode$$

However, for a *moderately asymmetrical (non-symmetrical or Skewed)* distribution, mean and mode usually lie on the two ends and median lies in between than and they obey the following important empirical relationships given by Prof. Karl Peason.

Mode = Mean – 3(Mean – Median) ...(1)

$\Rightarrow$ Mean – Mode = 3(Mean – Median)

$\Rightarrow$ Mean – Median = $\frac{1}{3}$ (Mean – Mode)

Thus we see that the difference between mean and mode is three times the difference between mean and median. In other words, median is closer to mean than Mode. The above relation between mean (M), median (M*d*) and mode (M*o*) can be exhibited diagrammatically as follows:

Relationship Between Arithmetic Mean, Median and Mode

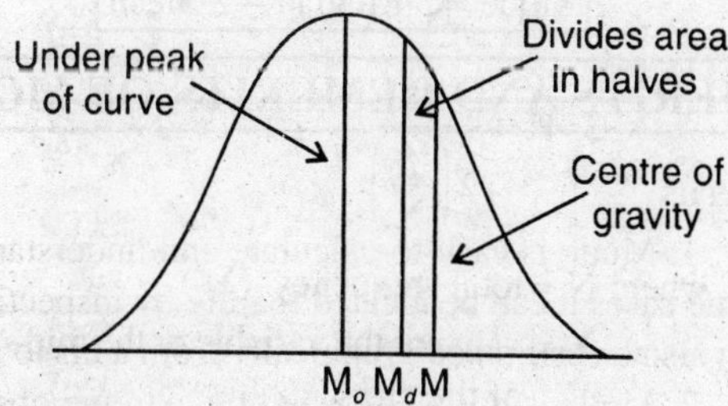

Remarks

1. Equation (1) may be rewritten to give:

Mode = Mean – 3 Mean + 3 Median

Mode = 3 Median – 2 Mean ... (2)

This formula is specially useful to determine the value of mode in case of bimodal or multimodal distributions.

2. If we know any two of the three values M, M*d* and M_0 the third can be estimated by using the formula (2).

3. For a positively Skewed distribution, mean will be greater than median and median will be greater than mode *i.e.*

$$M > M_d > M_0 \Rightarrow M_0 < M_d < M$$

However, in a negatively Skewed distribution the order of the magnitudes of the three averages will be reversed *i.e.* for negatively Skewed distribution we have

$$M_0 > M_d > M \Rightarrow M < M_d < M_0$$

GEOMETRIC MEAN

The geometric mean (usually abbreviated as G.M.) of a set of *n* observations is the *n*th root of their product. Thus if X_1, X_2, ...,X_n are the given *n* observations then their G.M. is given by

$$\text{G.M.} = \sqrt[n]{X_1.X_2.X_3........X_n}$$

$$= (X_1.X_2.X_3.........X_n)^{1/n} \quad ...(3)$$

If *n* = 2, *i.e.*, if we are dealing with two observations only then G.M. can be computed by taking the square root of their product. For example G.M. of 4 and 16 is

$$\text{G.M.} = \sqrt{4 \times 16} = \sqrt{64} = 8$$

But if the number of observations is greater than 2, than the computation of the *n*th root is very tedious. In such a case the calculations are facilitated by making use of the logarithms. Taking logarithm of both sides in (3), we get

$$\log(\text{G.M.}) = \frac{1}{n} \log (X_1.X_2......X_3)$$

$$= \frac{1}{n} (\log X_1 + \log X_2 + ...\log X_n)$$

$$= \frac{1}{n} \Sigma \log X \quad ...(4)$$

Thus, we see that the logerithm of the G.M. of a set observations is the arithmetic mean of their logarithms.

Taking Antilog of both sides in (4) we finally obtain,

$$\text{G.M.} = \text{Antilog}\left[\frac{1}{n}\Sigma \log X\right]$$

Calculation of Geometric Mean in Case of Discrete Series

$$\text{G.M.} = \text{Antilog}\left[\frac{1}{n}\Sigma f \log X\right]$$

where

$\Sigma f \log X$ = Sum of the products of frequencies (*f*) with logarithms of variable log X

n=Total of frequencies (Σf)

Calculation of Gemoetric Mean in Case of grouped or continuous frequency distributions

$$\text{G.M.} = \text{Antilog}\left[\frac{\Sigma f \log m}{n}\right]$$

where

$\Sigma f \log m$ = Sum of the products of frequencies (f) with logarithms of mid–points ($\log m$)

n = Total of frequencies (Σf)

Weighted G.M. = Antilog $\left[\frac{\Sigma w \log x}{\Sigma w}\right]$

where $\Sigma w \log x$ = Sum of the products of weights (w) with logarithms of variable log X

Σw = Total of weights

MERITS AND DEMERITS OF GEOMETRIC MEAN

Merits

1. Geometric mean is rigidly defined.
2. It is based on all the observations.
3. It is suitable for further mathematical treatment. If G_1 and G_2 are the geometric means of two series of sizes n_1 and n_2 respectively, then the geometric means G of the combined series of size $n_1 + n_2$ is given by

$$\log G = \frac{n_1 \log_1 + n_2 \log G_2}{n_1 + n_2}$$

4. Unlike arithmetic mean which has a bias for higher values, geometric mean has bias for smaller observations
5. As compared with mean, G.M. is affected to a lesser extent by extreme observations.
6. It is not affected much by fluctuations of sampling.

Demerits

1. Because of its abstract mathematical character, geometric mean is not easy to understand and to calculate for a non–mathematical person.
2. If any one of the observations is zero, geometric mean becomes zero and if any one of the observations is negative, geometric mean becomes imaginary regardless of the magnitude of other items.
3. It cannot be calculated if some of values in a series are not known.

HARMONIC MEAN

If $X_1, X_2, ...X_n$ is a given set of n observations, then their harmonic mean affreviated as H.M. or simply it is given by:

$$H = \frac{1}{\frac{1}{n}\left[\frac{1}{X_1} + \frac{1}{X_2} + ... + \frac{1}{X_n}\right]}$$

$$= \frac{1}{\frac{1}{n}\left[\Sigma\left(\frac{1}{X}\right)\right]} = \frac{n}{\Sigma\left(\frac{1}{X}\right)}$$

In other words, Harmonic Mean is the reciprocal of the arithmetic mean of the reciprocals of the given observations.

In case of frequency distribution we have:

$$\frac{1}{H} = \frac{1}{N}\left[\frac{f_1}{X_1} + \frac{f_2}{X_2} + ... + \frac{f_n}{X_n}\right]$$

$$\Rightarrow \frac{1}{H} = \frac{1}{N}\Sigma\left(\frac{F}{X}\right)$$

$$\Rightarrow H = \frac{N}{\Sigma\left(\frac{f}{X}\right)}$$

where N = total frequency (Σf)

X = value of the variable or the mid–value of the class

(In case of grouped or continuous frequency distribution)

f = corresponding frequency of X

MERITS AND DEMERITS OF HARMONIC MEAN

Merits

1. Harmonic mean is rigidly defined.
2. It is based on all the observations.
3. It is suitable for further mathematical treatment. If H_1 and H_2 are the harmonic means of two series of sizes N_1 and N_2 respectively, then the harmonic mean H of the combined series of size $N_1 + N_2$ is given by

$$\frac{1}{H} = \frac{1}{N_1 + N_2}\left[\frac{N_1}{H_1} + \frac{N_2}{H_2}\right]$$

4. It is not affected very much by fluctuations of sampling.

5. It is the most suitable average for measuring the time, speed, etc.

Demerits

1. It is not easy to understand and calculate.
2. Its value cannot be obtained if any one of the observations is zero.
3. It is less popular.
4. It cannot we calculated if some of the values in a series we are not know.

Relation Between Arithmetic Mean, Geometric Mean and Harmonic Mean

The arithmetic mean (A.M.), the geometric mean (G.M.) and the harmonic mean (H.M.) of a series of n observations are connected by the relation

$$\text{A.M.} \geq \text{G.M.} \geq \text{H.M.} \qquad \ldots(1)$$

the sign of equality holding if and only if all the n observations are equal.

We shall establish the result (1) for two numbers only, although the result holds in general for n observations.

Let a and b be two real positive numbers *i.e.* $(a > 0, b > 0)$.

Then

$$\text{A.M.} = \frac{a+b}{2} \text{ and G.M.} = \sqrt{ab}$$

$$\text{and H.M.} = \frac{1}{\frac{1}{2}\left[\frac{1}{a}+\frac{1}{b}\right]} = \frac{2ab}{a+b} \qquad \ldots(2)$$

we have

$$\text{A.M.} - \text{G.M.} = \frac{a+b}{2} - \sqrt{ab} = \frac{a+b-\sqrt{ab}}{2}$$

$$= \frac{1}{2}\left(\sqrt{a}-\sqrt{b}\right)^2$$

Since the square of *a* real quantity is always non–negative, we have

$$\left(\sqrt{a}-\sqrt{b}\right)^2 \geq 0$$

$$\therefore \quad \text{A.M.} - \text{G.M.} \geq 0$$

$$\Rightarrow \quad \text{A.M.} \geq \text{G.M.} \qquad \ldots(3)$$

the sign of equality holds if and only if

$$\sqrt{a}-\sqrt{b} = 0$$

$$\Rightarrow \quad \sqrt{a} = \sqrt{b}$$

$$\Rightarrow \quad a = b$$

i.e., if and only if the two numbers are equal.

Again from (2) we get

$$\text{G.M.} - \text{H.M.} = \sqrt{ab} - \frac{2ab}{a+b}$$

$$= \sqrt{ab}\left(1-\frac{2\sqrt{ab}}{a+b}\right)$$

$$= \sqrt{ab}\left(\frac{a+b-2\sqrt{ab}}{a+b}\right)$$

$$= \frac{\sqrt{ab}\left(\sqrt{a}-\sqrt{b}\right)^2}{a+b} \geq 0$$

Since $a > 0$, $b > 0$ and square of a real quantity is always non–negative

$$\therefore \quad \text{G.M} - \text{H.M.} \geq 0$$

$$\Rightarrow \quad \text{G.M.} \geq \text{H.M.} \qquad \ldots(4)$$

the sign of equality holds if and only if

$$\sqrt{a}-\sqrt{b} = 0$$

$$\Rightarrow \quad a = b$$

Thus, combining the results in (3) and (4) we get

$$\text{A.M.} \geq \text{G.M.} \geq \text{H.M.}$$

the sign of equality holds if and only if the two numbers are equal.

Remark—For two numbers we also have

$$G^2 = A \times H$$

where A, G and H represent arithmetic mean, geometric mean and harmonic mean respectively.

Proof: Let $a > o$, $b > 0$ be two positive numbers. Then from (2) above we get

$$A \times H = \frac{a+b}{2} \cdot \frac{2ab}{a+b} = ab = G^2$$

DISPERSION

Averages or the measures of central tendency give us an idea of the concentration of the observations about the central part of the distribution. In spite of their great utility in statistical analysis, they have their own limitations. If we are given only the average of a series of observations, we cannot form complete idea about the distribution since there may exist a number of distributions whose averages are same but which may differ widely from each other in a number of ways. The following example will illustrate this view point.

Consider the following ten observations on a certain variable:

5, 5, 5, 5, 5, 5, 5, 5, 5, 5.

Clearly A.M. = 5, and all deviations from A.M. are zero . Therefore, there is no dispersion at all.

Another example has following observations on the variable:

4, 3, 6, 5, 7, 4, 8, 8, 2, 3.

The A.M. is again equal to 5, but the nature of distribution of values is quite different in this case.

Therefore, knowledge of the central value alone is not enough to appreciate the nature of distribution of values. In one case the values may have wide disparity whereas in the other case they may be close to the central value. The frequency curves shown in the figure 1–1 may help to illustrate this point graphically.

Both in case of I and II the distributions have the same A.M. but in case I there is larger dispersion of values than in II.

From the above illustration it is obvious that the measures of central tendency are in adequate to

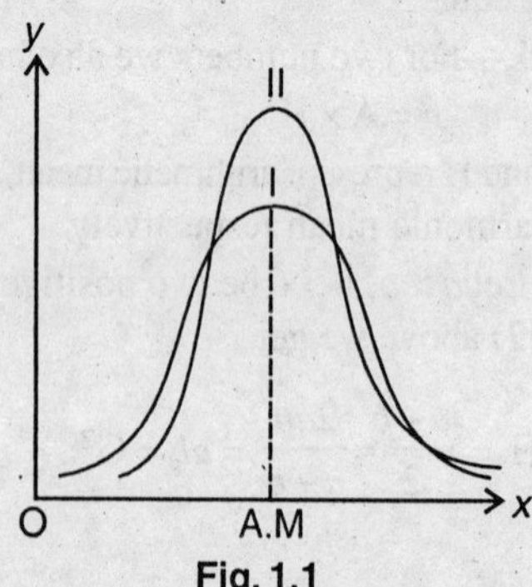

Fig. 1.1

describe the distribution completely. Thus, the measures of central tendency must be supported and supplemented by some other measures . One such measure (v) Dispersion.

According to Connor "Dispersion is the measure of the extent to which the individual items vary

Measures of Dispersion

The various measures of dispersion are

1. Range
2. Quartile deviation or Semi–Interquartile range
3. Mean deviation
4. Standard deviation
5. Lorenz curve

RANGE

The range is defined as the difference between the highest and lowest values in the series. This is the simplest method of measuring dispersion. Thus

$$\text{Range} = L - S$$

where

L = Largest value

S = Smallest value

Absolute and Relative Measures of Range

Range as defined above is an absolute measure of dispersion and depends upon the units of measurement. Thus if want to compare the variability of two or more distributions with the same units of measurement, we may use the above formula. However, to compare the variability of the distributions given in difference units of measurement we cannot use the above formula but we need a relative measure which is independent of the units of measurement. This relative measure, called the *coefficient of range,* is defined as follows:

$$\text{Coefficient of Range} = \frac{L-S}{L+S}$$

In other words, coefficient of range is the ratio of the difference between two extreme observations (biggest and smallest) of the distribution to their sum.

Merits and Demerits of Range

Merits

1. It is easy to under stand.

2. It is easy to calculate.

3. It can be used in Open–end frequency distribution.

Demerits

1. Range is not based on the entire set of data.

2. Range is very much affected by fluctuations of smapling. Its value varies very widely from sample to sample.

3. It is not possible to find out the range in open–end frequency distribution.

4. It does not present the very accurate picture of the series.

5. It is affected by extreme values.

QUARTILE DEVIATION OR SEMI INTER QUARTILE RANGE

Quartile deviation is obtained by dividing the difference of third quartile and first quartile $(Q_3 - Q_2)$ by 2. Thus

$$\text{Quartile Deviation (Q.D.)} = \frac{Q_3 - Q_1}{2}$$

where

Q_3 = Third Quartile or Upper Quartile

Q_1 = First Quartile or Lower Quartile

Q.D. as defined obove is only an absolute measure of dispersion. For comparative studies of variability of two distributions we need a relative measure which is known as coefficient of Quaritile Deviation and is given by

$$\text{Coefficient of Q.D.} = \frac{Q_3 - Q_1}{Q_3 + Q_1}$$

Remark

The quaritile deviation gives the average amount by which the two quartiles differ from median. For a *symmetrical distribution* we have

$$Q_3 - Q_d = M_d - Q_1$$

$$\Rightarrow \quad M_d = \frac{Q_3 + Q_1}{2} \quad \text{... (1)}$$

i.e., median lies half way on the scale from Q_1 to Q_3. Thus , for a symmetrical distribution we have

$$\text{Q.D.} + Q_1 = \frac{Q_3 - Q_1}{2} + Q_1$$

$$= \frac{Q_3 + Q_1}{2} = M_d \text{ [From (1)]}$$

and $$Q_3 - \text{Q.D.} = Q_3 - \frac{Q_3 - Q_1}{2}$$

$$= \frac{Q_3 + Q_1}{2} = M_d \text{ [From(1)]}$$

In other words, for a symmetrical distribution we have

$$Q_1 = M_d - \text{Q.D.}$$

and $$Q_3 = M_d + \text{Q.D.} \quad \text{... (2)}$$

Since in a distribution 25% of the observations lie below Q_1 and 25% observations lie above Q_3, 50% of the observations lie between Q_1 and Q_3. Therefore, using (2) we conclude that for a symmetrical distribution

$M_d \pm$ Q.D. covers exactly 50% of the observatios.

It may also be pointed out here that the word symmetrical distribution used in obove connection refers to symmetry in the central 50% of the distribution and may be asymmetrical (Skewed) at the tail ends'

MERITS AND DEMERITS OF QUARTILE DEVIATION

Mertis

Quartile deviation is quite easy to understand and calculate. It has a number of obvious advantages over range as a measure of dispersion. For example

(a) As against range which was based on two observations only, Q.D. makes use of 50% of the data and as such is obviously a better measure than range.

(b) Since Q.D. ignores 25% of the data from the beginning of the distribution and another 25% of the data from the top end, it is not affected at all by extreme observations.

(c) Q.D. can be computed from the frequency distributions with open end classes. In fact Q.D. is the only measure of dispersion which can be obtained while dealing a distribution having open end classes.

Demerits

1. Q.D. is not based on all the observations since it ignores 25% of the data at the lower end and 25% of the data at the upper end of the distribution, it

cannot be regarded as a reliable measure of variability.

2. Q.D. is affected considerably by fluctuations of sampling.

3. Q.D. is not suitable for further mathematical treatment.

Thus quartile deviation is not a reliable measure of variability, particularly for distribution in which the variation is considerable.

PERCENTILE RANGE

This is a measure of dispersion based on the difference between certain percentiles. It P_i is the *i*th percentile and P_j is the Jth percentile then the so-called *i–j* percentile range is given by

i–j Percentile Range = $P_j - P_i$ $(i < j)$

and $i-j$ SemiPercentile Range = $\dfrac{P_j - P_i}{2}$ $(i < j)$

The above measures are obsolute measures only. The relative measure of variability based on percentiles is given by

Coefficient of $i-j$ percentile = $\dfrac{P_j - P_i}{P_j + P_i}$

MEAN DEVIATION

Mean deviation is defined as the arithmetic average of the deviations of various items from a measure of central tendency, may it be, mean, median or mode. Generally mean deviations is calculated either from mean or from median. Mode is usually not considered as its value is indeterminate. Between mean and median, the median is supposed to be better than the mean because the sum of the deviations from the median is less than the sum of the deviations from the mean. It is also known as first moment of dispersion.

Computation of Mean Deviation

If $X_1, X_2, ..., X_n$ are n given observations then the mean deviation (M.D.) about an average A, say, is

given by $\text{M.D.} = \frac{1}{n}\Sigma|X - A| = \frac{1}{n}\Sigma|D|$

where $|D| = |X - A|$ read as mod (X – A) is the modulus value or obsolute value of the deviation (after ignoring the negative sign) $d = X - A$ and $\Sigma|d|$ is the sum of these absolute deviations and A is any one of the averages mean (M), median (M_d) and mode (M_0).

In the case of frequency distribution or grouped or continuous frequency distribution, mean deviation about an average A is given by

$$\text{M.D.} = \frac{1}{N}\Sigma f\,|X - A|$$

where

X = value of the variable or mid–value of the class interval

$N = \Sigma f$

A = Mean/Median/Mode

Remarks

1. Usually, we obtain the mean deviation (M.D.) about any one of the three averages mean (M), median (M_d) or mode (M_0). Thus

$$\text{M.D. (about mean)} = \frac{1}{N}\Sigma f|X - M|$$

$$\text{M.D. (about median)} = \frac{1}{N}\Sigma f|M - D_d|$$

$$\text{M.D. (about mode)} = \frac{1}{N}\Sigma f|X - M_0|$$

2. The sum of the absolute deviations (after ignoring the signs) of a given set of observations is minimum when taken about median. Hence *mean deviation is minimum when it is calculated from median.* In other words, mean deviation calculated about median will be less than mean deviation about mean or mode.

3. For a symmetrical distribution the range Mean $\pm$ M.D. (about mean) or $M_d \pm$ M.D. (about median), [$\because M = M_d$ for a symmetrical distribution] covers 57.5% of the observations of the distribution. If the distribution is mode rately (Skewed) the range will cover approximately 57.5% of the observations. Thus a small value of mean deviation would imply that the distribution is uniform since in this case a small interval around the average will contain more than 50% of the observations of the series.

Relative Measures of Mean

The relative measure of dispersion, called the coefficient of mean deviation is given by

Co–efficient of M.D.

$$= \frac{\text{Mean Deviation}}{\text{Average about which it is calculated}}$$

Thus

$$\text{Co–efficient of M.D. about mean} = \frac{\text{M.D.}}{\text{Mean}}$$

$$\text{Co–efficient of M.D. about median} = \frac{\text{M.D.}}{\text{Median}}$$

The co–efficients of mean deviation defined above are pure numbers undependent of the units of measurement and are useful for comparing the variability of different distributions.

MERITS AND DEMERITS OF MEAN DEVIATION

Merits

1. Mean deviation is rigidly defined and is easy to understand and calculate.

2. Mean deviation is based on all the observations and is thus definitely a better measure of dispersion than the range and quartile deviation.

3. As compared with standard deviation it is less affected by extreme observations.

4. Since mean deviation is based on the deviations about an average, it provides a better measure for comparison about the formation of different distributions.

Demerits

1. The strongest objection against mean deviation is that while computing its value we take the absolute value of the deviations about an average and ignore the signs of the deviations.

2. It is not a satisfactory measure when taken about mode or while dealing with a fairly Skewed distribution. As already pointed out, theoretically mean deviation gives the best result when it is calculated about median. But median is not a satisfactory measure when the distribution has great variations.

3. It is rarely used in Sociological studies.

4. It cannot be computed for distributions with open end classes.

5. Mean deviation tends to increase with the size of the sample though not proportionately and not so rapidly as range.

STANDARD DEVIATION

Standard deviation, usually denoted by the letter σ (sigma) of the Greek alphabet was first suggested by *Karl Pearson* as a measure of dispersion in 1893. It is defined as the positive square root of the arithmetic mean of the squares of the deviations of the given observations from their arithmetic mean. Thus, if $X_1, X_2, ..., X_n$ is a set of n observations then its standard deviation is given by

$$\sigma = \sqrt{\frac{1}{n}\Sigma(X-\overline{X})^2}$$

where

$$\overline{X} = \frac{\Sigma X}{n} = \text{arithmetic mean of the given values}$$

Computation of Standard Deviation in Case of Frequency Distribution

In case of frequency distribution, the standard deviation is given by

$$\sigma = \frac{1}{N}\sqrt{\Sigma f(X-\overline{X})^2}$$

where X is the value of the variable or the mid–value of the class (in case of grouped or continuous frequency distribution); f is the corresponding frequency of the value X; $N = \Sigma f$, is the total frequency and

$$\overline{X} = \frac{1}{N}\Sigma fX$$

is the arithmetic mean of the distribution.

Remarks

1. It may be pointed out that although mean deviation could be calculated about any one of the averages (M, M_d or M_0), standard deviation is always computed about arithmetic mean.

2. The value of the *s.d.* depends on the numerical value of the deviations $(X_1-\overline{X}), (X_2-\overline{X}), ..., (X_n-\overline{X})$. Thus the value of σ will be greater if the values of X are scattered widely away from the mean. Thus, a small value of σ will imply that the distribution is *homogeneous* and a large value of σ will imply that it is heterogeneous. In particular *s.d.* is zero if each of the deviations is zero *i.e.,* $\sigma = 0$ if and only if,

$$X_1 - \overline{X} = 0,\ X_2 - \overline{X} = 0, ...X_n - \overline{X} = 0$$

$\Rightarrow X_1 = X_2 = X_3 + ... X_n = \overline{X}$

which is the case if the variable assumes the constant value *i.e.*,

$\sigma = 0$

if $X_1 = X_2 = X_3 = ... X_n = K$ (constant)

MERITS AND DEMERITS OF STANDARD DEVIATION

Merits

1. It is rigidly defined.
2. Its value is very precise.
3. Its calculation is based on all the items of the series.
4. It is least affected by fluctuations in sampling.
5. It tends itself to further algebric treatment.

Demerits

1. It is difficult to calculate.
2. It gives more weight to extreme items.

Remark

Since $X - \overline{X} \le R$ (Range) for all the values X_1, X_2, ...X_n we get

$$\sigma^2 = \frac{1}{N}\Sigma f(X - \overline{X})^2$$

$$= \frac{1}{N}\left[f_1(X_1 - \overline{X})^2 + f_2(X_2 - \overline{X})^2 + ... + f_n(X_n - \overline{X})^2\right]$$

$$\le \frac{1}{N}\left[f_1 R^2 + f_2 R^2 + ... + f_n R^2\right]$$

$$(\because X_1 - \overline{X} \le R, X_2 - \overline{X} \le R, ..., X_n - \overline{X} \le R)$$

$$\therefore \sigma \ge \frac{1}{N}.R^2(f_1 + f_2 + f_3 + ... + f_n$$

$$\Rightarrow \sigma^2 \le \frac{1}{N}.R^2.N \quad [\therefore \Sigma f = N]$$

$$\Rightarrow \sigma^2 \le R^2$$

$$\Rightarrow \sigma\ S.d. \le R^2$$

VARIANCE

Variance is the square of the a standard deviation and is denoted by σ^2. For a frequency distribution variance is given by

$$\text{variance} = \sigma^2 = \frac{1}{N}\Sigma f(X - \overline{X})^2$$

Remark

Variance or standard deviation is independent of the change of origin but not of the scale.

Example 1. Find the mean and standard deviation of the first n natural numbers.

Solution–If the variable X denotes the natural number, then the first n notural numbers are 1, 2, 3..., n

$$\therefore \text{Mean} = \frac{\Sigma X}{n}$$

$$= \frac{1 + 2 + 3 + ... + n}{n} = \frac{n(n+1)}{2}.\frac{1}{n}$$

$$\text{and} \quad = \frac{n+1}{2}$$

$$\text{Variance} = \frac{\Sigma X^2}{n} - \overline{X}^2$$

$$= \frac{1^2 + 2^2 + 3^2 + ... + n^2}{n} - \left(\frac{n+1}{2}\right)^2$$

$$= \frac{n(n+1)(2n+1)}{6}.\frac{1}{n} - \frac{(n+1)^2}{4}$$

$$= \frac{(n+1)}{12}[2(2n+1) - 3(n+1)]$$

$$= \frac{(n+1)}{12}[4n + 2 - 3n - 3]$$

$$= \frac{(n+1)(n-1)}{12} = \frac{(n^2 - 1)}{12}$$

$$\Rightarrow \quad s.d. = \sqrt{\frac{n^2 - 1}{12}}$$

Remark: *For any discrete distribution standard deviation is not less than mean deviation from mean.*

CO-EFFICIENT OF VARIATION

Standard deviation is only an absolute measure of dispersion, depending upon the units of measurement. The relative measure of dispersion based on standard deviation is called the coefficient of standard deviation and is given by

$$\text{Coefficient of Standard Deviation} = \frac{\sigma}{\overline{X}}$$

This is a pure number independent of the units of measurement and thus, is suitable for comparing the variability, homogeneity or uniformity of two or more distributions.

We have already discussed the relative measures of dispersion based on range, quartile deviation and mean deviation. Since standard deviation is by for the best measure of dispersion, for comparing the homogeneity or heterogeneity of two or more distributions we generally compute the coefficient of standard deviation asked other wise.

100 times the coefficient of dispersion based on standard deviation is called the *coefficient of variation,* abbreviated as C.V. Thus,

$$\text{C.V.} = 100 \times \frac{\sigma}{\overline{\overline{X}}}$$

For comparing the variability of two distribution we compute the 'coefficient of variation' for each distribution. A distribution with smaller C.V. is said to be more homogeneous or uniform or less variable than the other and the series with greater C.V. is said to be more heterogeneous or more variable than the other.

RELATION BETWEEN VARIOUS MEASURES OF DISPERSION

For a Normal Distribution we have the following relations between the different measures of dispersion:

1. Mean $\pm$ Q.D. covers 50% of the observation of the distribution.
2. Mean $\pm$ M.D. covers 57.5% of the observations.
3. Mean $\pm\sigma$ includes 68.27% of the observations.
4. Mean $\pm 2\sigma$ includes 95.45% of the observations
5. Mean $\pm\sigma$ includes 99.73% of the observations.
6. Q.D. $= \frac{2}{3}$ S.D. (approximately)
7. M.D. $= \frac{4}{5}$ S.D. (approximately)
8. Q.D. $= \frac{5}{6}$ S.D. (approximately)

Combining the results (6), (7) and (8) we get approximately:

3 Q.D. = 2 S.D.

5 M.D. = 4 S.D.

6 Q.D. = 5 M.D.

$\Rightarrow$ 4 D.S. = 5 M.D. = 6 Q.D.

Thus we see that standard deviation ensures the highest degree of reliability and Q.D. the lowest.

9. we have:

$$\text{Q.D.} : \text{M.D.} : \text{S.D.} :: \frac{2}{3}\sigma : \frac{4}{5}\sigma : \sigma$$

$\Rightarrow$ Q.D. : M.D. : S.D. ::10 :12: 15.

10. Range = 6 S.D. = 6σ

LORENZ CURVE

This is the graphic method of measuring dispersion between two series. It was designed by Dr. Lorenz for measuring in equalities in the distribution of wealth. It is a cumulative percentage curve.

A very distinctive feature of the Lorenz curve consists in dealing with the cumulative values of the variable and the cumulative frequencies rather than its absolute values and the given frequencies. The technique of drawing the curve is fairly simple and consists of the following steps:

(a) The size of the item (variable value) and the frequencies are both cumulated. Taking grand total for each as 100, express these cumulated totals for the variable and the frequencies as percentage of their corresponding grand totals.

(b) Now take coordinate axes, X–axis representing the percentages of the cumulated frequencies (x) and Y–axis representing the percentages of the cummulated values of the variable (y). Both x and y take the value from 0 to100 as shown in the diagram given below.

(c) Draw the diagonal line $y = x$, joining the origin O (0, 0) with the point P (100, 100) as shown in the diagram. The line OP will make an angle of 45° with the X–axis and is called the *line of equal distribution.*

(d) Plot the percentages of the cumulative values of the variable *(y)* against the percentages of the corresponding cumulated frequencies *(x)* for the given distribution and join these points with a smooth free hand curve. Obviously, for any given distribution this curve will never cross the line of equal distribution OP. It will always lie below OP unless the distribution is uniform (equal) in which case it will coincide with OP.

Thus when the distribution of items is not proportionately equal, the variability (dispersion) is indicated and the curve is farther from the line of equal distribution OP. The greater the variability the greater is the distance of the curve from OP.

Let us consider the following Lorenz curve (figure 1.2) for the distribution of income. In this figure, OP is the line of equal distribution of income. If the plotted cumulative percentages lie on this line, there is no variability in the distribution of income of persons. The points lying on the curve OAP indicate a less degree of variability as compared to the points lying on the curve OBP. Variability is still greater, when the points lie on the curve OCP. Thus a measure of variability of the distribution is provided by the distance of the curve of the cumulated percentages of the given distribution from the line of equal distribution.

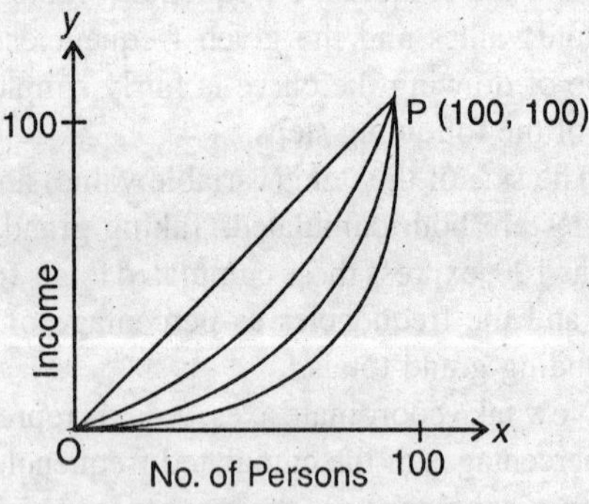

Fig. 1.2 : *Lorenz Curve*

Remarks

1. An obvious disadvantage of the Lorenz curve is that it gives us only a relative idea of the dispersion as compared with the line of equal distribution. It does not provide us any numerical value of the variability for the given distribution. Accordingly it should be used together with some numerical measure of dispersion. However, this should not undermine the utility of Lorenz curve in studying the variability of the distributions particularly relating to income wealth, wages, profits, lands and capital etc.

2. From the Lorenz curve we can immediately find out as to what percentage of persons (frequencies) correspond to a given percentage of the item (variable value).

GINNI'S COEFFICIENT OF CONCENTRATION

Ginni's coefficient of concentration, also known as concentration Ratio is based on his coefficient of mean difference and is defined as:

$$G = \frac{\Delta_1}{2\overline{X}}$$

where

G = Ginni's coefficient of concentration

Δ_1 = Ginni's coefficient of mean difference

$\overline{X}$ = Mean of the given distribution

Ginni's Coefficient of concentration G is a pure number independent of units of measurement and lies between O and 1. G is equal to O in *equal distribution* and its value goes up with increase in the inequality.

In fact, Ginni's coefficient is the ratio of area of concentration to the total area of lower triangle below the line of equal distribution.

SKEWNESS AND KURTOSIS

Two distribution may have the same mean and standard deviation but may differ widely in their overall appearance. It is this difference which shows the presence of Skewness. The *Skewness* refers to '*lack of symmetry*'. It means when a distrbution is asymmetrical (not symmetrical) it is known as a Skewed distribution. Measures of Skewness help us to distinguish between various types of distribution.

According to Simpson and Kafka "Skewness or asymmetry is the attribute of a frequency distribution that extends further on one side of the class with the highest frequency than on the other

We study Skewness to have an idea about the shape of the curve which we can draw with the help of the given frequency distributions. It helps us to determine the nature and extent of the concentration of the observations towards the higher or lower values of the variable. In a symmetrical frequency distribution which is unimodal, if the frequency curve or histogram is folded about the ordinate at the mean, the two halves so obtained will coincide with each other. In other words, in a symmetrical distribution equal distances on either side of the central value will have same frequencies and consequently both the tails, (left and right), of the curve would also be equal in shape and length.

A distribution is said to be Skewed if;

(i) The frequency curve of the distribution is not a symmetric bell shaped curve but it is stretched more to one side than to the other. In other words, it has a longer tail to one side (left or right) than to the other. A frequency distribution for which the curve has a longer tail towards the right is said to be positively Skewed and if the longer tail lies towards the left, it is said to be negatively Skewed.

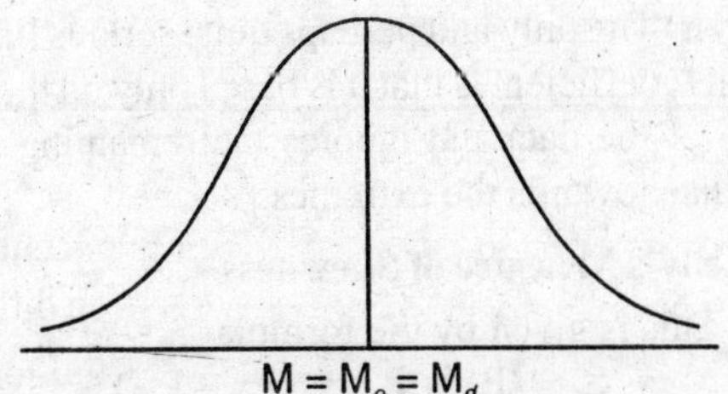

Fig. 1.3 : *Symmetrical Distribution*

(ii) The values of Mean (M), Median(M_d) and mode (M_o) fall at different points *i.e.,* they do not coincide.

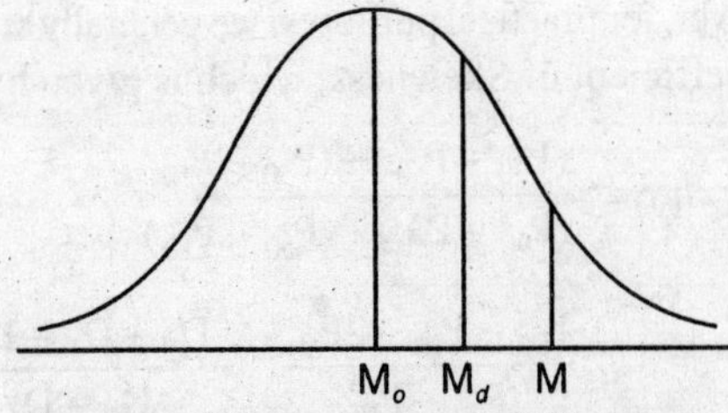

Fig. 1.3 : *Positively Skewed Distribution*

(iii) Quartiles Q_1 and Q_3 are not equidistant from the median *i.e.,*

$$Q_3 - M_d \neq M_d - Q_1$$

(iv) The sum of the positive deviations from the median is not equal to the sum of the negative deviations from the median.

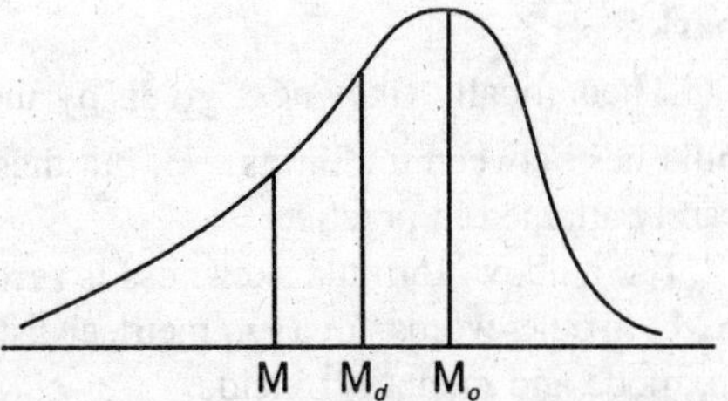

Fig. 1.4 : *Negatively Skewed Distribution*

MEASURES OF SKEWNESS

Absolute Measure of Skewness

a. Skewness = Mean – Mode = $M - M_0$

b. Skewness = 3(Mean – Median) = $3(M\ M_d)$

c. Skewness = $(Q_3 - M_d) - (M_d - Q_1)$

$= Q_3 + Q_1 - 2M_d$

These are the absolute measures of Skewness and are not of much practical utility because of the following reasons:

(i) Since the absolute measures of Skewness involve the units of measurement, they cannot be used for comparative study of the two distributions measured in different units of measurement;

(ii) Even if the distributions are having the same units of measurement, the absolute measures are not recommended because we may come across different distributions which have more less identical Skewness (absolute measures) but which vary widely in the measures of central tendency and dispersion.

Thus for comparing two or more distributions for Skewness we compute the relative measures of Skewness, also commonly known as coefficients of Skewness which are pure numbers independent. *The following are the coefficients of Skewness which are commonly used:*

1. Karl Pearson's Coefficient of Skewness

This is given by the formula:

$$S_k = \frac{\text{Mean} - \text{Mode}}{s.d.}$$

$$= \frac{M - M_0}{s.d.} = \frac{M - (3M_d - 2M)}{s.d.}$$

$$= \frac{3(M - M_d)}{s.d.}$$

Remarks

1. Theoretically Skewness given by the above formula lies between the limits ± 3, but these limits are rarely attained in practice

2. From above formula skewness is zero if $M = M_o = M_d$. In other words, for a symmetrical distribution mean, mode and median coincide.

3. Since *s.d.* is always positive, we have

$S_k > O$, if $M > M_o$

and $Sk > O$, if $M > M_d$

$\because \; 3M_d = M_o + 2M$

$\therefore \; S_k > O$, if $3M_d > M_0 + 2M_o$

$\Rightarrow S_k > O$, if $3M_d > 3M_o$

$\Rightarrow S_k > O$, if $M_d > M_o$

From above equations we conclude that

$$S_k > O, \text{ if } M > M_d > M_o$$

or $$S_k > O, \text{ if } M_o > M_d > M$$

Thus for a positively skewed distribution, the value of the mean is the greatest of the three measures and the value of mode is the least of the three measures.

If the distribution is negatively Skewed, the above inequality is reversed *i.e.*, the inequalities 'greater than' (*i.e.*, >) and 'less than' (*i.e.*, <) are inter changed thus:

$S_k < O$, if $M < M_d < M_o$

or $S_k < O$, if $M_o > M_d > M$

In other words, for a negatively skewed distributions, of the three measures of central tendency mean, median and mode, the mode has the maximum value and the mean has the least value.

2. Bowley's Coefficient of Skewness

Prof. A.L. Bowley's coefficient of Skewness is based on the quartiles and is given by :

$$S_k = \frac{(Q_3 - M_d) - (M_d - Q_1)}{(Q_3 - M_d) + (M_d - Q_1)}$$

$$\Rightarrow \quad S_k = \frac{Q_3 + Q_1 - 2M_d}{Q_3 - Q_1}$$

where

Q_3 = Upper Quartile

Q_1 = Lower Quartile

M_d = Median

Remarks

(*a*) Bowley's coefficient of Skewness is also known as Quartile coefficient of Skewness and is especially useful in situations where quartiles and median are used.

(*b*) From Bowley's equation we observe that

$$S_k = O, \text{ if } Q_3 - M_d = M_d - Q_1$$

This implies that for a symmetrical distribution ($S_k = 0$), median is equidistant from the upper and lower quartiles. Moreover, Skewness is positive if:

$$Q_3 - M_d > M_d - Q_1 \Rightarrow Q_3 + Q_1 > 2M_d$$

and skewness is negative if

$$Q_3 - M_d < M_d < Q_1 \Rightarrow Q_3 + Q_1 < 2M_d$$

(*c*) It whould be clearly understood that the values of the coefficient of skewness obtained by Bowley's formula and pearson's formula are not comparable, although in each case, $S_k = O$ implies the obsence of skewness *i.e.*, the distribution is symmetrical. It may even happen that one of them gives positive Skewness while the other gives negative Skewness.

(*d*) The only and perhaps quite serious limitation of this coefficient is that it is based only on the central 50% of the data and ignores the remaining 50% of the data towards the extremes.

3. Kelly's Measure of Skewness

This is given by the formula

$$S_k = (P_{90} - P_{50}) - (P_{50} - P_{10})$$
$$= P_{90} + P_{10} - 2P_{50}$$

But $P_{90} = D_9$ and $P_{10} = D_1$ .Hence,

$$S_k = (D_9 - D_5) - (D_5 - D_1) \quad [\because P_{50} = D_5]$$
$$= D_9 + D_1 - 2D_5$$

But this is an absolute measure of Skewness. However, for practical purposes, we generally compute the coefficient of Skewness, which is given by:

$$S_k\,(\text{Kelly}) = \frac{(P_{90} - P_{50}) - (P_{50} - P_{10})}{(P_{90} - P_{50}) + (P_{50} - P_{10})}$$

$$= \frac{P_{90} + P_{10} - 2P_{50}}{P_{90} - P_{10}} = \frac{D_9 + D_1 - 2D_5}{D_9 - D_1}$$

$\because D_5 = P_{50}$ = Median

$$\therefore S_k\,(\text{kelly}) = \frac{P_{90} + P_{10} - 2M_d}{P_{90} - P_{10}}$$

$$= \frac{D_9 + D_1 - 2M_d}{D_9 - D_1}$$

MOMENTS

Moment is a measure of a force with respect to its tendency to produce rotation. The notion of moments in statistics is analogus to that in mechanics. The strength of tendency depends on the amount of force and the distance from the origin of the point at which the force is exerted.

Moments are calculated with the help of arithmetic mean. Moment calculated from arithmetic mean are called 'central moments' or 'moments about the arithmetic mean.'

In the calculation of moments it deviations are taken from mean the resulting moments are denoted by symbol μ (pronounced as MU).

Moments about Mean

The *r*th moment of X about the mean $\overline{X}$, usually denoted by μ_r is defined as

$$\mu_r = \frac{1}{N}\Sigma f(X-\overline{X})^r$$

where

$r = 0, 1, 2, 3, ...$

putting $r = 0$, in above equation we get

$$\mu_0 = \frac{1}{N}\Sigma f(X-\overline{X})^0$$

$$= \frac{1}{N}\Sigma f = \frac{1}{N}.N$$

$$= 1$$

Putting $r = 1$ in above equation, we get

$$\mu_1 = \frac{1}{N}\Sigma f(X-\overline{X})^1 = 0$$

Because the algebraic sum of deviations of a given set of observations from their mean is zero. Thus *the first moment about mean is always zero*

again taking $r = 2$ we get

$$\mu_2 = \frac{1}{N}\Sigma f(X-\overline{X})^2 = (s.d.)^2$$

Hence *the second mement about mean gives the variance of the distribution.*

Remark—The moments about mean are invariant under change of origin but not of scale.

Sheppard's Correction For Moments

This correction is valid only for symmetrical or slightly asymmetrical continuous distributions and can not be applied in the case of extremely asymmetrical (Skewed) distributions like J–shaped or inverted J–shaped or U–shaped distributions.

KURTOSIS

The 'kurtosis' is the property of 'peakedness' of a frequency distribution.

If the freequency curve has long tails and high peak we call it '*lepto Kurtic*' distribution. On the other hand if the frequency curve has shot and thick tails and is flat topped we call it 'platy kurtic'. A 'mesokurtic distribution' describs the situation in between a lepto kurtic and platykurtic distribution'. Diagrammatically these distributions will be as follows:

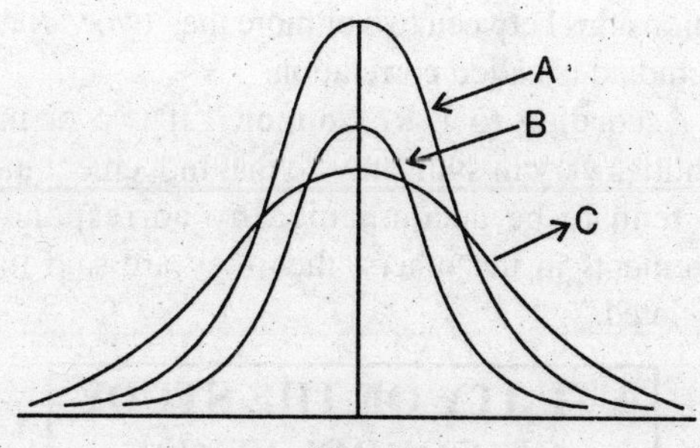

Fig. 1.5

Curve of type B which is neither flat nor peaked is known as Normal curve and shape of its hump is accepted as a standard one. Curve with humps of the form of normal curve are said to have normal kurtosis and are termed as *mesokurtic.* The curves of the type A, which are more peaked than the normal curve are known as *lepto kurtic* and are said to lack kurtosis or to have negative kurtosis. On the other hand, curves of the type C, which are flatter than the normal curve are called platy kurtic and they are said to possess kurtosis in excess or have positive kurtosis.

Measurement of Kurtosis

Karl Pearson gave the following formula for the measurment of kurtosis.

$$\beta_2 = \frac{\mu_4}{\mu_2^2} = \frac{\mu_4}{\sigma^4}$$

where

β_2 = Measure of Kurtosis

μ_4 = Fourth moment of Dispersion
μ_2 = Second moment of Dispersion
σ = Standard Deviation

if $\beta_2 = 3$, the curve is *mesokurtic.*
if $\beta_2 > 3$, the curve is *Lepto Kurtic.*
if $\beta_2 < 3$, the curve is *Platy Kurtic.*

CORRELATION

MEANING OF CORRELATION

The study of relationship between two or more variables is the most important in life. It is a common knowledge that change in are variable will affect the other. For example, when the price of a commodity increases, its demand decreases and on the other hand, when the price of a commodity decreases, its demand increases. The statistical device with the help of which relationships between two or more than two variables are studied is called correlation.

According to L.R. Connor, "If two or more quantities vary in sympathy so that movement in the one tend to be accompanied by corresponding movements in the others, then they are said to be correlated."

UTILITY OF THE STUDY OF CORRELATION

1. With the help of correlation we can measure the degree of relationship existing between the variables.

2. Correlation analysis contribute to the economic behaviour, aids in locating the critically important variable and on which other depend.

POSITIVE AND NEGATIVE CORRELATION

A. Positive Correlation—If both the variables move in the same direction, correlation is said to be positive.

Some examples of series of positive correlation are:

a. Heights and weights.

b. The family income and expenditure on luxury items.

c. Price and supply of a commodity and so on.

B. Nagative Correlation—If both the variables move in opposite direction, the correlations is said to be negative.

Some examples of negative correlation are—

a. Price and demand of a commodity.

b. Volume and pressure of a perfect goes.

c. Sale of woollen garments and the day temperature, and so on.

LINEAR AND NON-LINEAR CORRELATION

The correlation between two variables is said to be linear if corresponding to a unit change in one variable, there is a constant change in the other variable over the entire range of the values. For example, let us consider the following data:

X	1	2	3	4	5
Y	5	7	9	11	13

Thus for a unit change in the value of X, there is a constant change in the corresponding values of Y (2 Units).Mathematically, above data can be expressed by the equation.

$$Y = 2X + 3$$

In general two variables X and Y are said to be linearly related, if these exists a relationship of the form

$$Y = a + bX \qquad \ldots(1)$$

between than. But we know that (1) is the equation of a straight line with slope '*b*' and which an intercept '*a*' on the Y–axis. Hence, if the values of the two variables are plotted as points in XY–plane, we shall get a straight line.

The relationship between two variables is said to be *Non–linear or curvilinear* if corresponding to a unit change in one variable, the other variable does not change at a constant rate but at fluctuating rate. In such cases if the data are plotted on the XY–plane we do not get a straight line curve mathematically speaking, the correlation is said to be non–linear it the slope of the plotted curve is not constant such phenomena are common in the data relating to economics ans social sciencs.

Degree of Correlation

Degree	*Positive*	*Negative*
Perfect	+1	–1
High	Between + .75 and +1	Between – .75 and – 1
Moderate	Between + .50 and + .75	Between – .50 and –.75
Low	Between 0 and + .50	Between 0 and – .50
Absence	0	0

METHODS OF STUDYING CORRELATION

The commonly used methods for studying the correlation between two variables are:

1. Scatter Diagram Method
2. Karl Pearson's coefficient of correlation
3. Ran King Method
4. Concurrent Deviations Method

Scatter Diagram Method

The scatter diagram implies the plotting of values of two variables on graph paper and then observe the, movements. The following points may be borne in mind in interpreting the scatter diagram regarding the correlation between the two variables:

(i) If the points are very dense *i.e.,* very close to each other, a fairly good amount of correlation may be expected between the two variables. On the other hand, if the points are widely scattered, a poor correlation may be expected between then.

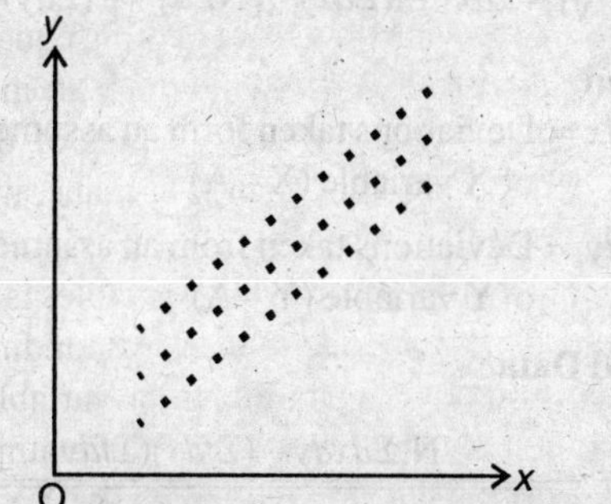

Fig. 1.6 : *High Degree of Positive Correlation*

(ii) If the points on the scatter diagram reveal any trend (either upward or downward), the variables are said to be correlated and if no trend is revealed, the variables are un correlated.

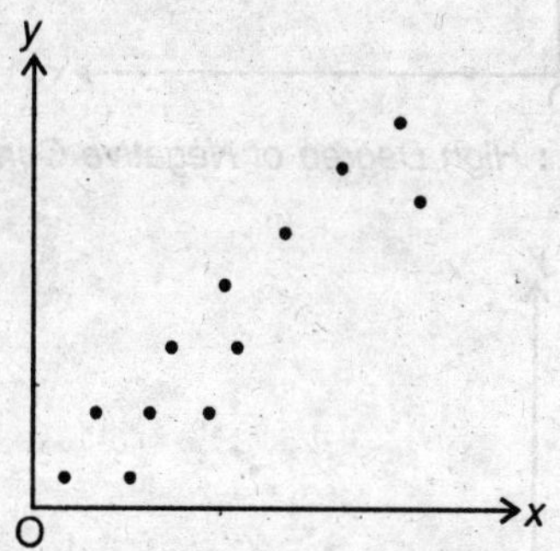

Fig. 1.7 : *Low Degree of Positive Correlation*

(iii) If there is an upward trend rising from lower left hand corner and going upward to the upper right hand corner, the correlation is positive since this reveals that the values of the two variables move in the same direction. If, on the other hands, the points depict a downward trend from the upper left hand corner to the lower right hand corner, the correlation is negative since in this case the values of the two variables move in the opposite directions.

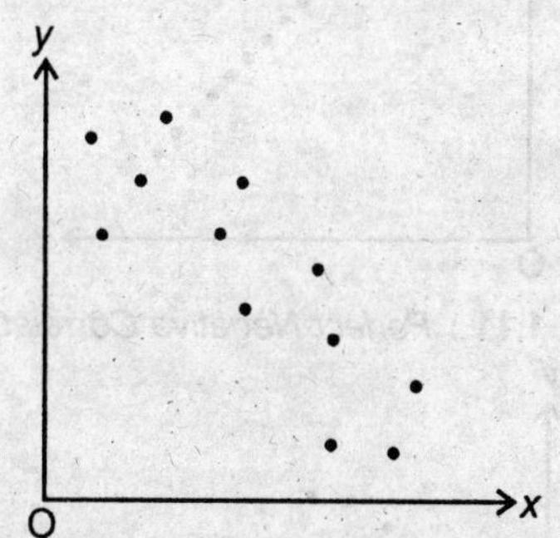

Fig. 1.8 : *Low Degree of Negative Correlation*

(iv) In particulars if all the points lie on a straight line starting from the left bottom and going up towards the right top, the correlation is perfect all positive, and if all the points lie on a straight line starting from left top and coming down to right bottom, the correlation is perfect and negative.

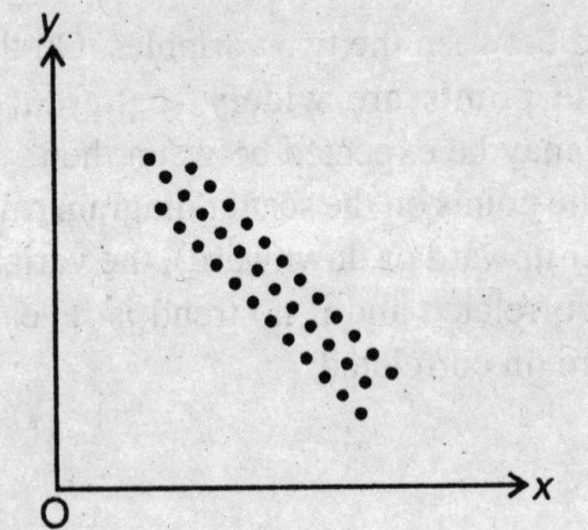

Fig. 1.9 : *High Degree of Negative Correlation*

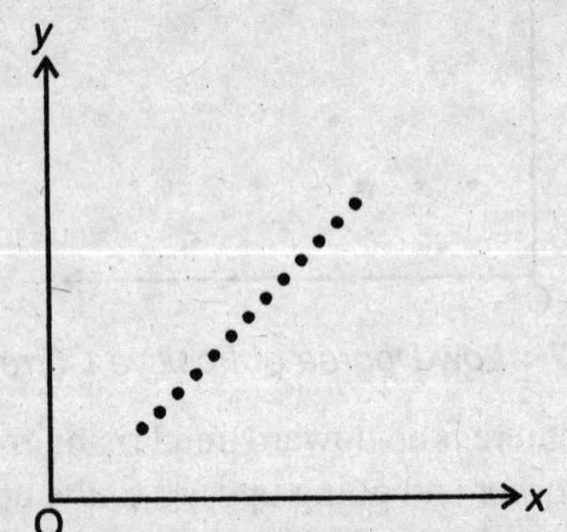

Fig. 1.10 : *Perfect Positive Correlation*

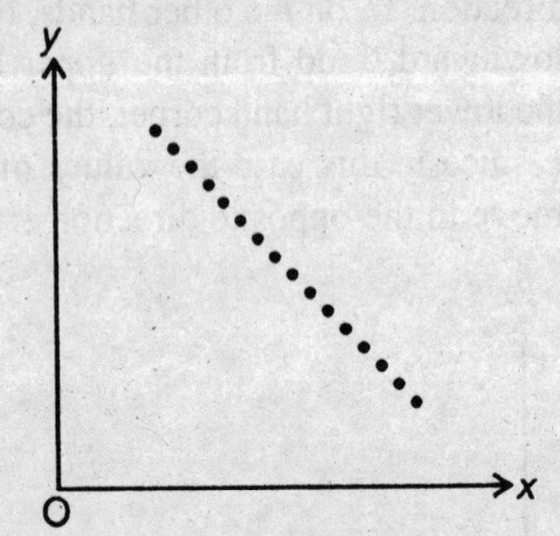

Fig. 1.11 : *Perfect Negative Correlation*

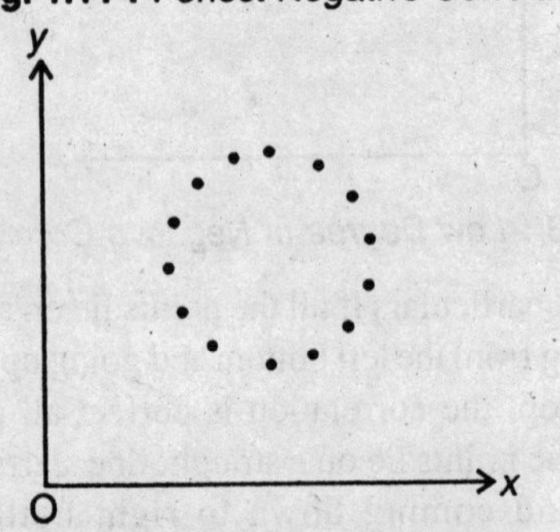

Fig. 1.12 : *No Correlation*

KARL PEARSON'S COEFFICIENT OF CORRELATION

A mathematical method for measuring the intensity or the magnitude of linear relationship between two variables was suggested by *Karl Pearson,* a great British Bio–metriciam and statistician and is by for the most widely used method in practice.

Karl Pearson's coefficient of correlation is calculated by applying the following formula:

Ungrouped Data

When deviations are taken from am actual mean

$$r = \frac{\Sigma xy}{N.\sigma x\,\sigma y}$$

where

r = Karl Pearson's Coefficient of Correlation

$x = (x - \bar{x})$

$y = (y - \bar{y})$

σx = Standard Deviation of x series

σy = Standard Deviation of y series

N = Number of pairs of item

An alternate formula of the above is:

$$r = \frac{\Sigma xy}{\sqrt{\Sigma x^2 . \Sigma y^2}}$$

where

Σx^2 = Total of squares of deviations taken from an actual mean of X series

Σy^2 = Total of squares of deviations taken from an actual mean of Y – series

When deviations are taken from an assumed mean

$$r = \frac{N\Sigma dx.dy - (\Sigma dx)(\Sigma dy)}{\sqrt{[N\,\Sigma dx^2 - (\Sigma dx)^2][N\Sigma dy^2 - (\Sigma dy)^2]}}$$

where

dx = Deviations taken form an assumed mean of X variable (X – A)

dy = Deviations taken from an assumed mean of Y variable (Y – A)

Grouped Data

$$r = \frac{N.\Sigma dxdy - (\Sigma fdx)(\Sigma fdy)}{\sqrt{[N\Sigma fdx^2 - (\Sigma fdx)^2][N\Sigma fdy^2 - (\Sigma fdx)^2]}}$$

PROPERTIES OF CORRELATION COEFFICIENT

Property–1

Pearsonian correlation coefficient can not exceed 1 numerically. In other words it lies between –1 and + 1. Symbolically,

$$-1 \leq r \leq 1$$

In other owrds, $r = +1$ implies perfect positive correlation between the variables and $r = -1$ implies perfect negative correlation between the variables.

Property–2

Correlation coefficient is independent of the change of origin and scale.

Property–3

Two independent variables are uncorrelated but the converse is not ture.

Rank Correlation Method

Sometimes we come across statistical series in which the variables under consideration are not capable of quantitative measurement but can be arranged in serial order. This happens when we are dealing with qualitative characteristics scuh as honesty, beauty, character, morality, etc., which cannot be measured quantitatively but can be arranged serially. In such situations Karl Pearson's coefficient of correlation cannot be used as such. *Charles Edward Spearman,* a British Psychologist, developed a formula in 1904 which consists in obtaining the correlation coefficient between the ranks of n individuals in the two attributes under study.

Suppose we want to find if two characteristics A, say, intelligence and B, say, beauty are related or not Both the characteristics are in capable of quantitative measurement, but we can arrange a group of n individuals in order of merit (ranks) *w. r. t.* proficiency in the two characteristics. Let the random variables X Y denote the ranks of the individuals in the characteristics A and B respectively. If we assume that there is no tie, *i.e.,* if no two individuals get the same rank in a characteristic then, obviously, X and Y assume numerical values ranging from 1 to n

Spearman's rank correlation coefficient, is given by the formula

$$rk = 1 - \frac{\Sigma d^2}{n(n^2 - 1)}$$

where

d = Differences in ranks

n = Number of pairs of items

Remark

Spearman's rank correlation coefficient lies between – 1 and + 1, *i.e.,*

$$-1 \leq rk \leq 1$$

Concurrent Deviation Method

This method is one of the ways of calculating the coefficient of correlation. It is the simplest method of studying correlation. This method is based on the signs of the deviations (*i.e.,* direction of the change) of the values of the variable from its preceding value and does not take into account the exact magnitude of the values of the variables. Thus, we put a plus (+) sign, minus (–) sign or equality (=) sign for the deviation if the value of the variable is greater than, less than or equal to the preceding value respectively. The deviations in the values of two variables are said to be concurrent if they have the same sign, *i.e.,* either both deviations are positive or both are negative or both are equal. The formula used for computing correlation coefficient r by this method is given by

$$r = \pm\sqrt{\pm\left(\frac{2c - n}{n}\right)}$$

where c is the number of pairs of concurrent deviations and n is the number of pairs of deviations. In the above formula plus/minus $-1 \leq r \leq 1$, the quantity inside the square not must be positive, other wise r will be imaginary which is not possible.

Thus if $(2c - n)$ is positive, we take positive sign in and outside the square root in the above equation and if $(2c - n)$ is negative, we take negative sign in and outside the square root in the above equation.

Note—It should be clearly noted that here n is not the number of pairs of observations but it is the number of pairs of deviations and as such it is one less than the number of pairs of observations.

ASSUMPTIONS UNDERLYING KARL PEARSON'S CORRELATION COEFFICIENT

Pearsonian correlation coefficient r is based on the following assumptions:—

(i) The variables X and Y under study are linearly related. In other words, the scatter diagram of the data will give *a* straight line curve.

(ii) Each of the variables is being affected by a large number of independent contributory causes of such a nature as to produce normal distribution.

(iii) The forces so operating on each of the variable series are not independent of each other but are related in a causal fashion

PROBABLE ERROR

After computing the value of the correlation coefficient the next step is to find the extent to which it is dependable. Probable error of correlation coefficient, usually denoted by P.E. *(r)* is an old measure of testing the reliability of an observed value of correlation coefficient in so far as it depends upon the conditions of random sampling.

If r is the observed correlation coefficient in a sample of n pairs of observations then its standard error, usually denoted by

S.E. *(r)* is given by

$$\text{S.E.}(r) = \frac{1-r^2}{\sqrt{n}}$$

Probable error of the correlation coefficient is given by

$$\text{P.E.}(r) = 0.6745 \times \text{S.E.}(r)$$

$$= 0.6745 \, \frac{1-r^2}{\sqrt{n}}$$

Reason for taking the factor 0.6745 is that in a normal distribution 50% of the observations lie in the range $M \pm 0.6745\sigma$, where M is the mean and σ is the S.d.

Use of Probable Error

1. The probable error of correlation coefficient may be used to determine the limits within which the population correlation coefficient may be expected to lie.

Limits for population correlation coefficient are

$$r \pm \text{P.E.}(r) \qquad \ldots(1)$$

This implies that if we take another random sample of the same size n from the same population from which the first sample was taken, then the observed value of the correlation coefficient, say, r_1 in the second sample can be expected to lie within the limits given in (1).

2. P.E. *(r)* may be used to test if an observed value of sample correlation coeffiicient is significant of any correlation in the population. The following guide – lines may be used.

(a) If $r <$ P.E. *(r) i.e.,* if the observed value of r is less than its P.E then correlation is not at all significant.

(b) If $r < \sigma$ P.E. *(r), i.e.,* if observed value of r is greater than σ times its P.E. then r is definitely significant.

(c) In other situations, nothing can be concluded with certainly.

Remarks

P.E. can be used only under the following conditions:

(i) The data must have been drawn from a normal population.

(ii) The conditions of random sampling should prevail in selecting sampled observations.

COEFFICIENT OF DETERMINATION

Coefficient of correlation between two variable series is a measure of linear relationship between them and indicates the amount of variation of one variable which is associated with or is accounted for by another variable. A more useful and readily comprehensible measure for this purpose is the coefficient of determination which gives the percentage variation in the dependent variable that is accounted for by the independent variable. In other words, the coefficient of determination gives the ratio of the explained variance to the determination is given by the square of the correlation coefficient, *i.e.,* r^2. Thus,

Coefficient of determination

$$= r^2 = \frac{\text{Explained Variance}}{\text{Total Variance}}$$

The coefficient of determination is a much useful and better measure for interpreting the value of r.

For example if the value of $r = 0.8$, we cannot conclude that 80% of the variation in the relative series (dependent variable) is due to the variation in the subject series (independent variable). But the coefficient of determination in this case is $r^2 = 0.64$ which implies that only 64% of the variation in the relative series has been explained by the subject series and the remaining 36% of the variation is due to other factors.

By the same argument while comparing two correlation coefficient, one of which is 0.4 and the other is 0.8 it is misleading to conclude that the correlation in the second case is twice as high as correlation is the first case. The coefficient of determination clearly explains this view point, since in the case $r = 0.4$, the coefficient of determination is 0.16 and in the case $r = 0.8$, the coefficient of determination is 0.64, from which we conclude that correlation in the second case is four times as high as correlation in the first case.

Remarks

1. The above discussion implies that—

"The closeness of the relationship between two variables as determined by correlation coefficient r is not proportional"

2. The following table gives the values of the coefficient of determination (r^2) for different values of r.

r	r^2
0.1	0.01
0.2	0.04
0.3	0.09
0.4	0.16
0.5	0.25
0.6	0.36
0.7	0.49
0.8	0.64
0.9	0.81
1.0	1.00

It may be seen from the above table that as the value of r decreases, r^2 decreases very rapidly except in two particular cases $r = 0$ and $r = 1$ when we get $r = r^2$.

3. Coefficient of determination is always non–negative and as such it does not tell us about the direction of the relationship (whether it is positive or negative) between the two series.

4. Coefficient of Non–Determination—The ratio of the unexplained variation to the to the total variation is called the coefficient of non–determination. It is usually denoted by K^2 and is given by the formula:

$$K^2 = \frac{\text{Un}-\text{explained Variance}}{\text{Total Variance}}$$

$$= 1 - \frac{\text{Explained Variance}}{\text{Total Variance}}$$

$$= 1 - r^2$$

5. Coefficient of Alienation—The coefficient of alienation is given by the square root of the coefficient of non – determination, *i.e.,* by K as given below

$$K = \pm\sqrt{1 - r^2}$$

REGRESSION

Regression analysis, in the general sense, means the estimation or prediction of the unknown value of the variable from the known value of the other variable.It is one of the very important statistical tools which is extensively used in almost all sciences–natural; social and physical. It is specially used in business and economics to study the relationship between two or more variables that are related casually and for estimation of demand and supply curves. Cost functions, production and consumption functions, etc.

Prediction or estimation is one of the major problems in almost all spheres of human activity. The estimation or prediction of future production, consumption, prices, investments, sales, profits, income, etc, are of paramount importance to a businessman or economist. Regression analysis is one of the very scientific techniques for making such predictions. In the words of M.M.Blair "Regression analysis is a mathematical measure of the average relationship between two or more variables in terms of the original units of data."

In regression analysis there are two types of variables. The variable whose value is influenced or is to be predicted is called dependent ariable and the variable which influences the values or is used for prediction, is called independent variable. In regression analysis independent variable is also known as regresser or predictor or explanator while the dependent variable is also known as regressed or explained variable.

LINES OF REGRESSION

Line of regression is the line which gives the best estimate of one variable for any given value of the other variable. In case of two variables x and y, we shall have two lines of regression, one of y on x and the other of x on y.

1. Line of Regression of y on x

Line of regression of y on x is the line which gives the best estimate for the value of y for any specified value of x. Hence, the equation of line of regression of y on x is

$$y = a + bx \text{ or } y - \bar{y} = r.\frac{\sigma y}{\sigma x}(x - \bar{x})$$

where

$\bar{x}$ = Arithmetic Mean of x – series

$\bar{y}$ = Arithmetic Mean of y – series

σx = Standard Deviation of x – series

σy = Standard Deviation of y – series

r = Coefficient of Correlation between two Variables x and y.

2. Line of Regression of x on y

Line of regression of x on y is the line which gives the best estimate for the value of x for any specified value of y.

Mathematically

$$x = A + By \text{ or } x - \bar{x} = r.\frac{\sigma x}{\sigma y}(y - \bar{y})$$

Remarks

1. Both the lines of regression passes through the point $(\bar{x}, \bar{y})$. In other words, the mean values $(\bar{x}, \bar{y})$ can be obtained as the point of intersection of the two regression lines.

2. There are always two lines of regression. In a particular case of perfect correlation, positive or negative *i.e.*, $r = \pm 1$, the equation of line of regression of y on x becomes

$$y - \bar{y} = \pm\frac{\sigma y}{\sigma x}(x - \bar{x})$$

$$\Rightarrow \quad \frac{y - \bar{y}}{\sigma y} = \pm\left(\frac{x - \bar{x}}{\sigma x}\right) \quad \ldots(1)$$

Similarly, the equation of the line of regression of x on y becomes:

$$x - \bar{x} = \pm\frac{\sigma x}{\sigma y}(y - \bar{y})$$

$$\Rightarrow \quad \frac{y - \bar{y}}{\sigma y} = \pm\left(\frac{x - \bar{x}}{\sigma x}\right) \quad \ldots(2)$$

Both the equations are same.

Hence in case of perfect correlation ($r = \pm 1$) both the lines of regression coincide. Therefore, in general we always have two lines of regression except in the particular case of perfect correlation when both the lies coincide and we get only one line.

ANGLE BETWEEN THE REGRESSION LINES

The equations of the lines of regression of y on x and x on y are respectively:

$$y - \bar{y} = r.\frac{\sigma y}{\sigma x}(x - \bar{x}) \quad \ldots(1)$$

and $$x - \bar{x} = r.\frac{\sigma x}{\sigma y}(y - \bar{y})$$

$$\Rightarrow \quad y - \bar{y} = \frac{\sigma y}{r.\sigma x}(x - \bar{x}) \quad \ldots(2)$$

This the slopes of lines (1) and (2), are respectively:

$$M_1 = \frac{r\sigma y}{\sigma x} \text{ and } M_2 = \frac{\sigma y}{r\sigma x}$$

if Q is the angle between the two lines of regression then

$$\tan\theta = \frac{m_1 - m_2}{1 + m_1 m_2}$$

$$= \frac{\frac{r\sigma y}{\sigma x} - \frac{\sigma y}{r\sigma x}}{1 + r.\frac{\sigma y}{\sigma x}.\frac{\sigma y}{r.\sigma x}}$$

$$= \frac{\frac{\sigma y}{\sigma x}\left(r - \frac{1}{r}\right)}{\left(\frac{\sigma x^2 + \sigma y^2}{\sigma x^2}\right)}$$

$$= \frac{\sigma x \sigma y}{\sigma x^2 + \sigma y^2} \cdot \left(\frac{r^2 - 1}{r}\right)$$

$$\Rightarrow \qquad \theta = \tan^{-1}\left\{\frac{\sigma x \sigma y}{\sigma x^2 + \sigma y^2}\left(\frac{r^2 - 1}{r}\right)\right\}$$

if $r = \pm 1$ then

$\theta = \tan^{-1}(0)$

$\Rightarrow \qquad \theta = 0$ or π

i.e., the two lines are either coincident ($\theta = 0$) or they are paralled ($\theta = \pi$). But since both the lines of regression intersect at the point $(\bar{x}, \bar{y})$, they cannot be parallel. Hence in case of perfect correlation, positive or negative, the two lines of regression coincide.

if $r = 0$, then

$\theta = (\infty) = \pi/2 = 90°$

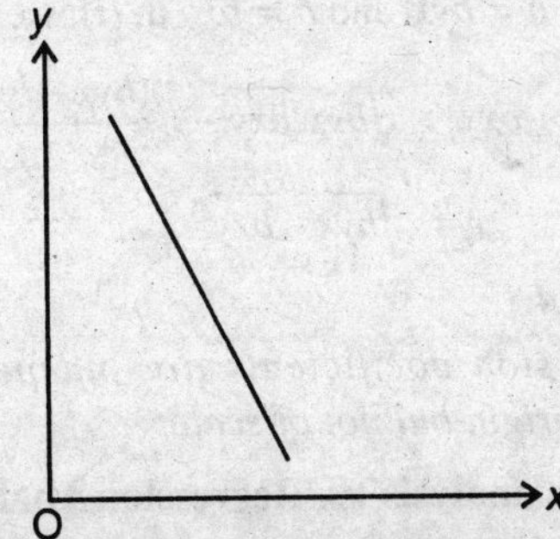

Fig. 1.13 : *Two Regression Lines Coincide (If r = −1)*

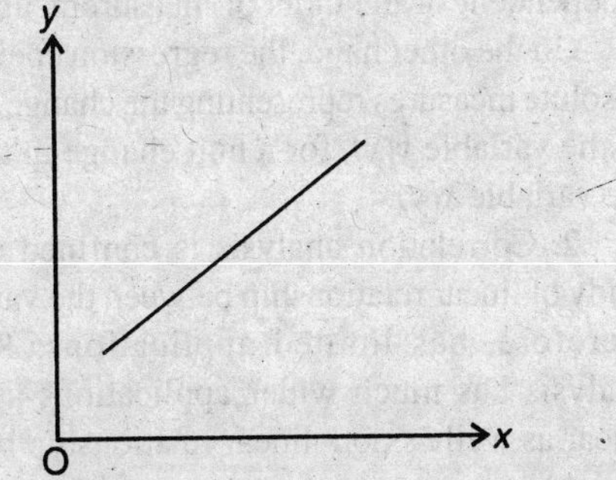

Fig. 1.14 : *Two lines coincide (If r = +1)*

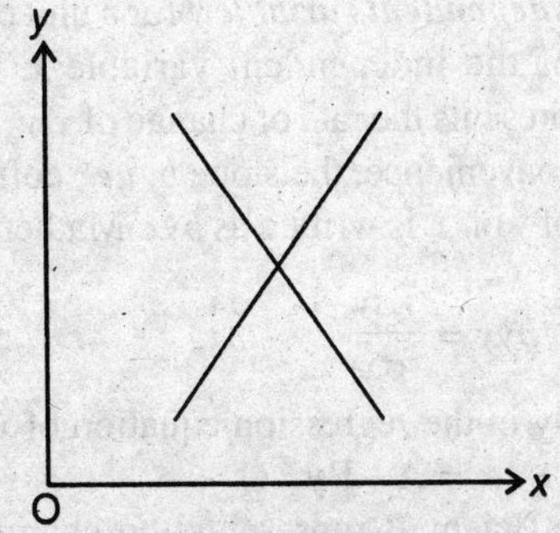

Fig. 1.15 : *Two Lines Perpendicular (If r = 0)*

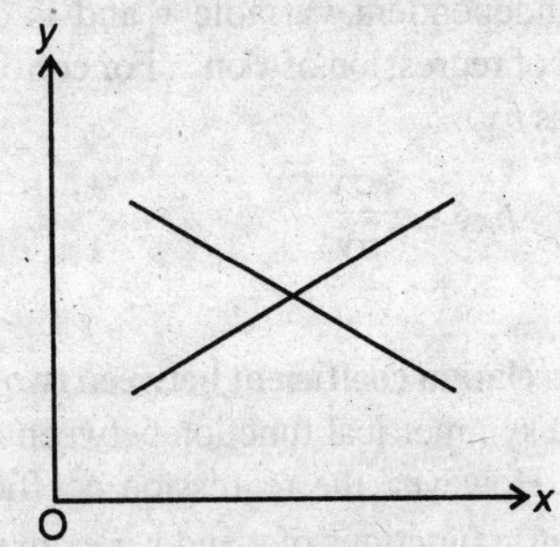

Fig. 1.16 : *Two lines Apart (Low Degree of Correlation)*

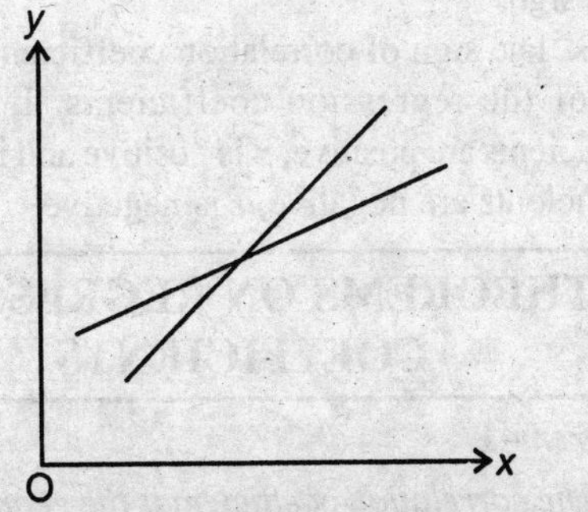

Fig. 1.17 : *Two Line Closer (High Degree of Correlation)*

i.e., if the variables are uncorrelated, the two lines of regression become perpendicular to each other.

COEFFICIENTS OF REGRESSION

Let us consider the line of regression of *y on* x,

$$y = a + bc$$

The coefficient *'b'* which is the slope of the line of regression of *y* on *x* is called the coefficient of regression of *y* on *x*. ***It represents the increment in the***

value of the dependent variable y for a unit change in the value of the independent variable *x*. In other words, it represents the rate of change of *y w.r.t. x*. For notational convenience, the slope *b*, *i.e.*, cofficient of regression of *y* on *x* is written as *byx*. Mathematically

$$byx = \frac{r\sigma y}{\sigma x}$$

similarly in the regression equation of *x* on *y*

$$x = A + By$$

the coefficient B represents the change in the value of dependent variable *x* for a unit change in the value of independent variable *y* and is called the coefficient of regression of *x* on *y*. For convenience, it is written as *bxy*.

$$bxy = \frac{r\sigma x}{\sigma y}$$

Remarks

1. Correlation coefficient between two variables *x* and *y* is a symmetrical function between *x* is *y*, *i.e.*, *rxy* = *ryx*. However, the regression coefficients are not symmetric functions of *x* and *y*, *i.e.*, $byx \neq bxy$.

2. Both the regression coefficients must have the same sign.

3. The sign of correlation coefficient is same as that of the regression coefficients. If regression coefficients are positive, *r* is positive and if regression coefficients are negative, *r* is negative.

THEOREMS ON REGRESSION COEFFICIENTS

Theorem–1

The correlation coefficient is the geometric mean of the regression.

Coefficients *i.e.*,

$$r = \sqrt{byx.bxy}$$

Proof. We have

$$bxy = r.\frac{\sigma x}{\sigma y} \qquad \ldots (i)$$

and $$byx = r.\frac{\sigma y}{\sigma x} \qquad \ldots (ii)$$

Multiplying *(i)* and *(ii)* we get

$$r^2 = byx.\,bxy$$

$$\Rightarrow \qquad r = \pm\sqrt{byx.bxy}$$

which establishes the result.

Theorem–2

If one of the regression coefficients is greater than unity, the other must be less than unity:

Proof: Let $byx > 1$

$$\Rightarrow \qquad \frac{1}{bxy < 1} \qquad \ldots (i)$$

we have

$$byx\,.\,bxy = r^2 \leq 1 \Rightarrow bxy \leq \frac{1}{byx} < 1 \text{ From } (i)$$

Hence if one of the regression coefficients is greater than one, the other must be less than one.

Theorem–3

The arithmetic mean of the regression coefficients is greater than the correlation coefficient.

Proof. We know that for any two real distinct positive numbers *a* and *b*:

$$\text{A.M.} > \text{G.M.} \Rightarrow \frac{a+b}{2} > \sqrt{ab} \qquad \ldots (i)$$

Taking $a = byx$ and $b = bxy$ in *(i)*, we get

$$\frac{1}{2}(byx + bxy) > \sqrt{byx.bxy} \Rightarrow \frac{(byx + bxy)}{2} > r$$

$$\because \qquad r = \sqrt{byx - bxy}$$

Theorem – 4

Regression coefficients are independent of change of origin but not of scale:

Correlation analysis *Vs.* Regression Analysis

1. Correlation coefficient *rxy* is a relative measure of the linear relationship between *x* and *y* and is independent of the units of measurement.

On the other hand, the regression coefficients are absolute measures representing the change in the value of the variable *y(x)*, for a unit change in the value of the variable *x(y)*.

2. Correlation analysis is confined only to the study of linear relationship between the variables and, therefore, has limited applications. Regression analysis has much wider applications as it studies linear as well as non–linear relationship between the variables.

3. Correlation need not imply cause and effect relationship between the variables under study. However, regression analysis clearly indicates the cause and effect relationship between the variables.

INDEX NUMBERS

MEANING

An index number is as its name suggests, an indicator of the general trend of a set of figures. Index numbers are devices for measuring the net amount of change in a group of related variables over a certain period of time. Index numbers are used to measure changes in industrial output, fluctuations in the level of business or variations in the size of agricultural output etc.

The important definitions of index numbers are given below:

According to croxton and Cowden, "Index numbers are devices for measuring differences in the magnitude of a group of related variables."

According to Blair, "Index numbers are a specialised type of averages.

USES OF INDEX NUMBERS

Following are the main uses of Index Numbers;

1. Index numbers are used to measure the changes in the price level over a period of time.

2. Index numbers are used to reduce complex forms of measurement to simple numbers.

3. Index numbers are also used for the purpose of forecasting.

4. Index numbers are also compelled to compare physical changes over a period of time. Such changes relate to industrial production, sales, volume of imports or exports, etc.

5. Since the index numbers study the relative changes in the level of a phenomenon at different periods of time, they are specially useful for the study of the general trend for a group phenomens in a time series data.

TYPES OF INDEX NUMBERS

1. Price Index Numbers
2. Quantity Index Numbers
3. Value Index Numbers

METHODS OF CONSTRUCTING INDEX NUMBERS

The various methods for constructing index numbers are given below:

1. *Fixed Base Method*

$$\text{Price Relatives (R)} = \frac{P_1}{P_0} \times 100$$

where

P_1 = Price of the current year

P_0 = Price of the base year

2. *Simple Aggregative Method*

$$P_{01} = \frac{\Sigma P_1}{\Sigma P_0} \times 100$$

where

P_{01} = Price index of the current year

ΣP_1 = Total of current year prices

ΣP_0 = Total of base year prices

Remark

Based on this method, the quantity index is given by the formula

$$Q_{01} = \frac{\Sigma q_1}{\Sigma q_0} \times 100$$

where Σq_0 and Σq_1 are the quantities of all the selected commodities consumed in the base year and the current year respectively.

3. *Simple Average of Price Relatives Methods*

$$P_{01} = \frac{\Sigma\left(\frac{P_1}{P_0} \times 100\right)}{N}$$

where N stands for number of items or commodities.

4. *Weighted Aggregate Method*

$$P_{01} = \frac{\Sigma WP_1}{\Sigma WP_0} \times 100$$

where w is the weight attached to a commodity. By using different systems of weighting we get a number of formulas. Some of the important formulas are given below:

Laspeyre's Price Index or Base Year Method

Taking base year quantities as weights, *i.e.*, $w = q_0$ we get Laspeyre's Price Index given by:

$$P_{01} = \frac{\Sigma P_1 q_0}{\Sigma P_0 q_0} \times 100$$

where

P_1 = Current Year Price
q_0 = Base Year Quantity
P_0 = Base Year Price
q_1 = Current Year Quantity

This formula was devised by French Economist Laspeyre in 1871.

Paasche's Price Index

If we take current year quantities as weights we obtain Paasche's Price Index which is given by:

$$P_{01} = \frac{\Sigma P_1 q_1}{\Sigma P_0 q_0} \times 100$$

This formula was given by German statistician Paasche in 1874.

Dorbish – Bowley Price Index

This index is given by the arithmetic mean of Laspeyre's and Paasche's price index numbers and we have:

$$P_{01} = \frac{1}{2}\left[\frac{\Sigma P_1 q_0}{\Sigma P_0 q_0} + \frac{\Sigma P_1 q_1}{\Sigma P_0 q_1}\right] \times 100$$

This is also sometimes known as L – P formula.

Fisher's Price Index

Irving Fisher advocated the geometric mean of Laspeyre's and Paasche's price index numbers and is given by:

$$P_{0-1}\left[\frac{\Sigma P_1 q_0}{\Sigma P_0 q_0} \times \frac{\Sigma P_1 q_1}{\Sigma P_0 q_1}\right] \times 100$$

Fisher's index is termed as an Ideal index since it satisfies time reversal and factor reversal tests for the consistency of index numbers

Marshall Edgeworth Price Index

Taking the arithmetic cross of the quantities in the base year and the current year as weights *i.e.*, $w = \frac{(q_1 + q_1)}{2}$, we obtain the Marshall – Edgeworth formula given by

$$P_{01} = \frac{\Sigma P_1 . \frac{(q_0 + q_1)}{2}}{\Sigma P_0 . \frac{(q_0 + q_1)}{2}} \times 100$$

$$= \frac{\Sigma P_1 (q_0 + q_1)}{\Sigma P_0 (q_0 + q_1)} \times 100$$

$$= \left[\frac{\Sigma P_1 q_0 + \Sigma P_1 q_1}{\Sigma P_0 q_0 + \Sigma P_0 q_0)} \times 100\right]$$

Walsch Price Index

Instead of taking the arithmetic mean of base year and current year quantities as weights, if we take their geometric mean, *i.e.*, $w = \sqrt{q_0 q_1}$, then we obtain Walsch Index given by the formula:

$$P_{01} = \frac{\Sigma P_1 \sqrt{q_0 q_1}}{\Sigma P_0 \sqrt{q_0 q_1}} \times 100$$

Kelly's Price Index or Fixed Weights Index

This formula, named after L.Kelly, requires the weights to be fixed for all periods and is also sometimes known as aggregative index with fixed weights and is given by the formula:

$$P_{01} = \frac{\Sigma P_1 q}{\Sigma P_0 q} \times 100$$

where the weights are the quantities *(q)* which may refer to some period (not necessarily the base year or the current year) and are kept constant for all periods.

Value Indices

Value index numbers are obtained on expressing the total value (or expenditure) in any given year as *a* percentage of the same in the base year symbolically, we write

$$V_{01} = \frac{\text{Total value in current year}}{\text{Total value in base year}} \times 100$$

$$\Rightarrow \quad V_{01} = \frac{\Sigma P_1 q_1}{\Sigma P_0 q_0} \times 100$$

Remarks

1. In general, Laspeyre's price index is greater

than Paasche's price index. In other words, Laspeyre's price index has an upward bias in general, with rise in price.

But if the correlation coefficients between the price relatives and quantity relatives is positive (a phenomenon which is rarely observed in economics), then Laspeyre's price index is less than Paasche's price index.

2. Fisher's ideal index number lies between Laspeyre's and Paasche's index numbers

Proof : Let us consider two real positive numbers a and b such that $a > 0$.

Let $a > b$

$\Rightarrow a^2 < ab$ (multiplying by $a > 0$)

$$\Rightarrow \quad a < \sqrt{ab} \qquad \ldots (1)$$

($\because a > 0$, negative sign is rejected)

Also $a < b$

$\Rightarrow ab < b^2$ (Multiplying by $b > 0$)

$$\Rightarrow \quad \sqrt{ab} < b \qquad \ldots (2)$$

$$(\because b > 0)$$

Hence, from equation (1) and (2)

$$a < \sqrt{ab} < b$$

This, the geometric mean of two real positive numbers lies between than. Hence Fisher's ideal index which is the geometric mean of Laspeyre's and Paasche's index numbers lies between them. More precisely,

if $P_{01}^{La} < P_{01}^{Pa}$

there $P_{01}^{La} < P_{01}^{F} < P_{01}^{pa}$

and if $P_{01}^{po} < P_{01}^{La}$

then $P_{01}^{pa} < P_{01}^{F} < P_{01}^{La}$

and if $P_{01}^{La} = P_{01}^{Pa}$

then $P_{01}^{Pa} = P_{01}^{La} = P_{01}^{F}$

3. *Marshall – Edgeworth index also lies between Laspeyre's and Paasche's indices.Rather we have*

if $P_{01}^{La} < P_{01}^{Pa}$

then $P_{01}^{La} < P_{01}^{F} < P_{01}^{ME} < P_{01}^{Pa}$

and if $P_{01}^{Pa} < P_{01}^{La}$

than $P_{01}^{Pa} < P_{01}^{F} < P_{01}^{ME} < P_{01}^{La}$

TESTS OF CONSISTENCY OF INDEX NUMBER FORMULA

1. Unit Test—This test requires that the index number formula should be independent of the units in which the prices or quantities of various commodities are quoted. All the formulae discussed above except the index number based on simple Aggregate of prices (Quantities) satisfy this test.

2. Time Reversal Test—The time reversal tests proposed by *Prof. Irving Fisher* requires the index number formula to possess time consistency by working both forward and back ward *w.r.t.* time.

In other words, if the index numbers are computed for the same data relating to two periods by the same formula but with the bases reversed, then the two index numbers so obtained should be the reciprocals of each other. Mathematically, we should have (omitting the factor 100),

$$P_{01} \times P_{10} = 1$$

or more generally

$$P_{ab} \times P_{ba} = 1$$

where

P_{ab} = Price index (without factor 100) for year '*b*' with year '*a*' as base

P_{ba} = Price index (without factor 100) for year '*a*' with year '*b*' as base

Time reversal test is satisfied by the following index number formulae:

(*i*) Marshall – Edge worth formula

(*ii*) Fisher's ideal formula

(*iii*) Walsch formula

(*iv*) Kelly's fixed weight formula

(*v*) Simple aggregate index

(*vi*) Simple Geometric mean of Price Relatives formula

(*vii*) Weighted Geometric mean of Price Relatives formula with fixed weights

Remark

Laspeyre's and Paasche's index numbers do not satisfy this test.

Let us verify this test for Keily's fixed weight formula. We have (without factor 100)

$$P_{10}^{k} = \frac{\Sigma WP_1}{\Sigma WP_0}$$

and $P_{10}^{k} = \dfrac{\Sigma WP_0}{\Sigma WP_1}$

$$\therefore P_{01}^{k} \times P_{10}^{k} = \frac{\Sigma WP_1}{\Sigma WP_0} \times \frac{\Sigma WP_0}{\Sigma WP_1} = 1$$

Hence Kelly's fixed weight formula satisfies time reversal test.

3. **Factor Reversal Test**—This is the second of the two important tests of consistency proposed by Prof. Irving Fisher. This implies that if the price and quantity indices are obtained for the same data. same base and current periods and using the same formula, then their product (without the factor 100) should give the true value ratio, since price multiplied by quantity gives total value. Symbolically, we should have (without factor 100),

$$P_{01} \times Q_{01} = \frac{\Sigma P_1 q_1}{\Sigma P_0 q_0}$$

where

$\Sigma P_1 q_1$ and $\Sigma P_0 q_0$ denote the total value in the current and base year respectively.

Fisher's formula satisfies the factor reversal test. In fact Fisher's index is the only index satisfying this test and none of the formulae discussed above satisfies this test.

Remark—Since Fisher's index is the only index which satisfies both the time reversal and factor reversal tests, it is sometimes tremed as Fisher's Ideal Index.

4. Circular Test— Circular test, first suggested by Westergaard, is an extension of time reversal test for more than two periods and is based on the shiftability of the base period. This requires the index to work in a circular manner add this property enables us to find the index numbers from period to period without referring back to the original base each time. For, three periods *a, b, c,* the test requires:

$P_{ab} \times P_{bc} \times P_{ca} = 1,\ a \neq b \neq c$

or, $P_{01} \times P_{12} \times P_{20} = 1$

For instance

$$P_{01}^{La} \times P_{12}^{La} \times P_{20}^{La} = \frac{\Sigma p_1 q_0}{\Sigma p_0 q_0} \times \frac{\Sigma p_2 q_1}{\Sigma p_1 q_1} \times \frac{\Sigma p_0 q_2}{\Sigma p_2 q_2} \neq 1$$

Hence Laspeyre's index does not satisfy the circular test. Similarly, it can be verified that none of Pasche's, M – E's , Walsch's, and Fisher's indices satisfies this test. In fact, circular test is not satisfied by any of the weighted aggregative formula with changing weights, *i.e.,* if the weights used in the construction of index numbers P_{01}, P_{12} and P_{20} change. This test is satisfied only by the index number formulae based on:

(i) Simple geometric mean of the price relatives

(ii) Kelly's fixed base method

Remark— The circular test can be generalised to the case of more than three periods to give:

$P_{01} \times P_{12} \times P_{23} \times .... \times P_{n,o} = 1$

where the indices are, considered without the factor 400.

(i) Conversion of Fixed Base to Chain Base

Chain Index No

$$= \frac{\text{Current year fixed base index No.}}{\text{Previous year fixed base index No.}} \times 100$$

(ii) Conversion of Chain Base to Fixed Base

Fixed Base Index No.

$$= \frac{\text{Current year's chain base index No.} \times \text{Previous year's fixed base index No.}}{100}$$

COST OF LIVING INDEX NUMBER

The wholesale price index numbers measure the changes in the genral level of prices and they fail to reflect the effect of the increase or decrease of prices on the cost of living of different classes or groups of people in a society. Cost of living index numbers, also termed as '*Consumber Price Index Numbers,* or Retail Price Index Numbers' are designed to measure the effects of changes in the prices of a basket of goods and services on the purchasing power of a particular section or class of the society during any given (current) period *w.r.t.* same fixed (base) period. They reflect upon the average increase in the cost of the commodities consumed by a class of people so that they can maintain the same Standard of living in the current year as in the base year.

Construction of Cost of Living Index Numbers

The cost of living index numbers are constructed by the following methods:

(i) Aggregate Expenditure Method or Weighted Aggregate Method

In this method, the quantities consumed in the

base year are used as weights. Thus in the usual notations

$$\text{Cost of Living Index} = \frac{\Sigma p_1 q_0}{\Sigma p_0 q_0} \times 100$$

$$= \frac{\text{Total expenditure in current year}}{\text{Total expenditure in base year}} \times 100$$

(ii) Family Budget Method or Method of Weighted Relatives

In this method the cost of living index is obtained on taking the weighted average of price relatives, the weights being the values of the quantities consumed in the base year. Thus, if we write

$$I = \text{Price Relative} = \frac{P_1}{P_0} \times 100$$

and $\qquad w = p_0 q_0$

$$\text{then cost of Living Index} = \frac{\Sigma WI}{\Sigma W}$$

Substituting the values of W and I we get

$$\text{Cost of Living Index} = \frac{\Sigma p_0 q_0 \left(\frac{p_1}{q_0} \times \right)}{\Sigma p_0 q_0}$$

$$= \frac{\Sigma p_1 q_0}{\Sigma p_0 q_0} \times 100$$

Remark—Thus we see that the cost of living Index numbers obtained by both the methods are same.

Uses of Cost of Living Index Numbers

1. Cost of living index numbers are used to determine the purchasing power of money and for computing the real wages (income) from the nominal or money wages (income). we have

Purchasing Power of Money

$$= \frac{1}{\text{Cost of Living Index No.}}$$

$$\text{Real Wages} = \frac{\text{Money Wages}}{\text{Cost of Living Index}} \times 100$$

Thus, cost of living index number enables us to find if the real wages are rising or falling, the money wages remaining unchanged.

2. The government and many big industrial and business units use the cost of living index numbers to regulate the dearness allowance (D.A.) or grant of bonus to the employees in order to compensate them for in creased cost of living due to price rise.

Limitations of Index Numbers

Although index numbers are very important tools for studying the economic and business activity of a country, they have their limitations and as such should be used and interpreted with caution. The following are some of their limitations:

1. Since index numbers are based on the sample data, they are only approximate indicators and may not exactly represent the changes in the relative level of a phenomenon.

2. There is likelihood of error being introduced at each stage of the construction of the index numbers, namely,

(i) Selection of commodities.

(ii) Selection of the base period.

(iii) Collection of the data relating to prices and quantities of the commodities

(iv) Choice of the formula – the system of weighting to be used.

(v) The average to be used for obtaining the index for the composite group of commodities.

THEORY OF PROBABILITY

Meaning of Probability

In every day life we talk about probability of occurrence of various events. Whenever there is an element of uncertainty about the occurrence of some event one makes a probability statement. For example, the probability that India will win a cricket mach against West Indies is 30% or 0.30; the probability that it will rain tonight is 80% or 0.80, etc.

The concept of probability originally developed in the 17th century with the games of chance, line games of cards, tossing of coins and dies etc.

Let us illustrate the concept of probability with the help of the classical example of coin tossing experiment. Suppose a coin is tossed, what is the probability that it will turn up head? Perhaps the immediate answer it $\frac{1}{2}$, provided it is an ideal coin and it is not worn out or biased in any way. The argument will be that there are only two possible ways in which the coin can be tossed (either head or tail will turn up), and the coin being an ideal one both head and tail are equally likely. Therefore, the odds are fifty – fifty, *i.e.*, the probability of getting head is $\frac{1}{2}$ and so is the probability of getting tail. This is, in fact, the classical approach to obtaining the probability of occurrence of an event.

According to La Place—"Probability is the ratio of favourable events to the total number of equally likely events."

Symbolically

$$P = \frac{\text{Number of favourable cases}}{\text{Total number of equally likely cases}}$$

where

P = Probability that the event will take place.

Similarly,

$$q = \frac{\text{Number of cases not favourable}}{\text{Total number of equally likely cases}}$$

In simple words, probability can be defined in the following manner.

The probability of the happening of any one of the several equally likely events is the ratio of the number of cases favourable to it to the total number of possible cases.

Mathematical Definition

If there are n mutually exclusive and equally likely cases and of these n cases, there are p cases favourable and q cases unfavourable to some event, then the probability of occurance of the event is denoted by

$$P = \frac{p}{n}$$

The probability of non–occurance of the event is denoted by

$$Q = \frac{q}{n}$$

where P = Chance of success

Q = Chance of failure

Examples: 1. A uniform die is thrown at random. Find the probability that the number on it is 5.

Solution. As we know a die has six sides with 1, 2, 3, 4, 5 and 6 written on them. Since it is an ideal die all the six sides are equally likely to turn up. Also, only one of the sides will turn up at a time and thus the six possible ways are mutually exclusive. The number 5 can turn up in only one possible way. Therefore, the required probability is 1/6.

2. Suppose an ideal die is tossed twice. What is the probability that 6 will appear on both occasions?

Solution. There are 36 (= 6 × 6) possible ways in which the die can be thrown twice we may get 1 in the first toss and also 1 in the second, or, 1 in the first and 2 in the second, or, 1 in the first and 3 in the second and so on. Let us list the number of possible outcomes as follows:

(1, 1) (1, 2) (1, 3) (1, 4) (1, 5) (1, 6)
(2, 1) (2, 2) (2, 3) (2, 4) (2, 5) (2, 6).
(3, 1) (3, 2) (3, 3) (3, 4) (3, 5) (3, 6)
(4, 1) (4, 2) (4, 3) (4, 4) (4, 5) (4, 6)
(5, 1) (5, 2) (5, 3) (5, 4) (5, 5) (5, 6)
(6, 1) (6, 2) (6, 3) (6, 4) (6, 5) (6, 6)

All these ways are equally likely and mutually exclusive. There is only one possible way in which we get 6 in both the first and the second toss. Therefore, the required probability is $\frac{1}{36}$,

3. In the above example, what is the probability of getting a sum of 10?

Solution. What is required is that the sum of the two numbers shown on the die in two tosses should be 10. This is possible in only three ways:

Either we get 5 in the 1st toss and 5 in the 2nd. or, we get 4 in the 1st toss and 6 in the 2nd. or, we get 6 in the 1st toss and 4 in the second.

Thus the required probability is

$$= \frac{3}{36} = 1/12$$

4. If a coin is tossed two times, what is the probability of getting head at least once?

Solution. The total number of equally likely and mutually exclusive ways is, now, 4:

(H, H) (H, T) (T, H) (T, T)

and the number of favourable way (*i.e.*, the number of ways in which head appears at least once) is 3.

Therefore, the required probability is $\frac{3}{4}$.

5. What is the chance of drawing a queen in a draw from a pack of 52 cards?

Solution. Total number of cases = 52

Total number of queen = 4

$\therefore$ The probability of drawing a queen is

$$= \frac{4}{52} = \frac{1}{13}$$

6. A bag contains 10 black and 20 white balls. What is the probability of drawing:

a. a black ball, and

b. a white ball.

Solution. Total number of balls = 10 + 20 = 30

a. Probability of drawing a black ball is

$$P = \frac{\text{Number of Black Balls}}{\text{Total Numbers of Balls}}$$

$$= \frac{10}{30} = \frac{1}{3}$$

b. Probability of drawing a white ball is

$$P = \frac{\text{Number of White Balls}}{\text{Total Number of Balls}}$$

$$= \frac{20}{30} = \frac{2}{3}$$

Mutually Exclusive Events

Two or more events are said to be mutually exclusive if the hoppening of any one of them excludes the happening of all others in the same experiment.

For example, in toss of a coin the events 'head' and 'tail' are mutually exclusive because if head comes, we cannot get tail and if tail comes we cannot get head.

Equally Likely Cases

The outcomes are said to be equally likely or equally probable if none of them is expected to occur in preference to other. Thus, in tossing of a coin, all the out comes, namely, H and T are equally likely if the coin is unbiased.

Independent Events

Events are said to be independent of each other if happening of any one of there is not affected by and does not affect the happening of any one of others.

For example, in tossing of a die repeatedly the event of getting '5' in 1st throw is independent of getting '5' in second, third or supsequent throws.

Remark

The two events A and B are said to be disjoint or mutually exclusive if they cannot happen simultaneously *i.e.*, if their intersection is a null set. Thus if A and B are disjoint events, there

$$A \cap B = \phi \Rightarrow P(A \cap B) = P(\Phi) = 0$$

Thus $P(A \cap B) = 0$, provides us with a criterion for finding if A and B are mutually exclusive.

Addition Rule of Probability

The probability of occurrence of at least one of the two events A and B is give by:

$$P(A \cup B) = P(A) + P(B) - P(A \cap B)$$

where

P (A) = Probability of occurrence of an event A

P (B) = Probability of occurrence of an event B

$P(A \cap B)$ = Probability of simultaneous occurrence of A and B

$P(A \cup B)$ = Probability of occurrence of at least one of the two events A and B

Addition Rule of Probability for Mutually Exclusive Events

If two events A and B are mutually exclusive (*i.e.*, only one of them can occur at a time) and P (A) and P (B) are the probabilities of occurrence of a and B, respectively; then

$$P(A \cup B) = P(A) + P(B)$$

Multiplication Rule of Probability

The probability of simultaneous happening of two events A and B is given by :

$$P(A \cap B) = P(A) . P(B/A) ; P(A) \neq 0$$

$$\text{or } P(B \cap A) = P(B) . P(A/B) ; P(B) \neq 0$$

where P (B/A) is the conditional probability of happening of B under the condition that A has happened and P (A/B) is the conditional probability of happening of A under the condition that B has happened.

Remark—*Multiplicative Rule for Independent Events.*

If A and B are independent so that the probability of occurrence or non–occurrence of A is not affected by the occurrence or non–occurrence of B, we have

$$P(A/B) = P(A) \text{ and } P(B/A) = P(B)$$

Hence

$$P(A \cap B) = P(A).P(B)$$

Thus, the probability of simultaneous happening of two independent events is equal to the product of their individual probabilities.

Generalisation

The multiplication law of probability can be extended to more than two events. Thus, for there events A, B and C we have

$$P(A \cap B \cap C) = P(A).P(B/A)\,P(C/A \cap B)$$

In particular, if A, B and C are *independent events* there

$$P(A \cap B \cap C) = P(A).P(B).P(C)$$

i.e., the probability of the simultaneous happening of *n* independent events is equal to the product of their individual probabilities.

Theorem:

$$P(\overline{A}) = 1 - P(A)$$

where

$P(\overline{A})$ = Probability of event A does not happen

P (A) = Probability of event A happens

Theorem:

(i) $P(\overline{A} \cap B) = P(B) - P(A \cap B)$

where

$P(\overline{A} \cap B)$ = Probability of A does not happen but B happens

(ii) $P(A \cap \overline{B}) = P(A) - P(A \cap B)$

(iii) $P(\overline{A} \cap \overline{B}) = 1 - P(A \cup B)$

$$= 1 - [P(A) + P(B) - P(A \cap B)]$$

$$= 1 - P(A) - P(B) + P(A \cap B)]$$

where a and B are independent event.

$\because P(A \cap B) = P(A).P(B)$

$\therefore P(\overline{A} \cap \overline{B}) = 1 - P(A) - P(B) + P(A).P(B)$

$$= 1 - P(A) - P(B)\,[1 - P(A)]$$

$$= [1 - P(A)]\,[1 - P(B)] = P(\overline{A}).P(\overline{B})$$

Examples: 1. A card is drawn from a will shuffled pack of playing cards. Find the probability that it is either a diamond or a king.

Solution. Let A denote the event of drawing a diamond and B denote the event of drawing a king from a pach of cards.

Then we have

$$P(A) = \frac{13}{52} = \frac{1}{4}$$

and $$P(B) = \frac{4}{52} = \frac{1}{13}$$

and we want $P(A \cup B)$

Now $P(A \cup B) = P(A) + P(B) - P(A \cap B)$

$$= \frac{1}{4} + \frac{1}{3} - P(A \cap B) \qquad \ldots(i)$$

There is only one case favourable to the event $A \cap B$, namely, king of diamond. Hence

$$P(A \cap B) = \frac{1}{52}$$

Substituting in *(i)*, we get

$$P(A \cup B) = \frac{1}{4} + \frac{1}{13} - \frac{1}{52}$$

$$= \frac{13 + 4 - 1}{52} = \frac{16}{52} = \frac{4}{13}$$

2. In a certain college, the students engage in various sports in the following proportions:

Football (F) : 60% of all students

Basket ball (B) : 50% of all students

Both Football and Basketball : 30% of all students.

If a student is selected at random, what is the probability that he will:

(i) play football or basketball?

(ii) play neither sports?

Solution: Let A denote the event that the student is engaged in Football and B denote the event that he is engaged in Basketball. Then we are given;

$$P(A) = 0.60$$

$$P(B) = 0.50$$

and $P(A \cap B) = 0.30$

(i) The probability that a student selected at random plays Football or Basketball is given by:

$$P(A \cup B)\ P(A) + P(B) - P(A \cap B)$$

$$= 0.60 + 0.50 - 0.30 = 0.80$$

(ii) The probability that the student plays neither Football nor Basketball is given by:

$P(\overline{A} \cap \overline{B})$ 1 – P [the plays at least one of the two games

$$= 1 - 0.80 = 0.20$$

3. Probability that a man will be alive 25 years hence is 0.3 and the probability that his wife will be alive 25 years hence is 0.4. Find the probability that 25 years hence.

(i) both will be alive

(ii) only the man will be alive

(iii) only the woman will be alive

(iv) at least one of there will be alive

Solution. Let us define the following events:

A: The man will be alive 25 years hence,

B: His wife will be alive 25 years hence,

we are given

$$P(A) = 0.3$$

and $P(B) = 0.4$

(i) The probability that 25 years hence both man and his wife will be alive is

$$P(A \cap B) = P(A) . P(B)$$

(∴ A and B are independent)

$$= 0.3 \times 0.4 = 0.12$$

(ii) The probability that 25 years hence only the man will be alive is

$$P(A \cap \overline{B}) = P(A) . P(\overline{B})$$
$$= P(A) . [1 - P(B)]$$
$$= 0.3 \times (1 - 0.4) = 0.3 \times 0.6 = 0.18$$

(iii) The probability that only the woman will be alive 25 years hence is

$$P(\overline{A} \cap B) = P(\overline{A}) \times P(B)$$
$$= [1 - P(A)] \times P(B)$$
$$= (1 - 0.3) \times 0.4 = 0.7 \times 0.4 = 0.28$$

(iv) The probability 'p' that 25 years hence at least one of them will be alive is

$$p = 1 - P\text{ (None will be alive)}$$
$$= 1 - P(\overline{A} \cap \overline{B})$$
$$= 1 - P(\overline{A}) \times P(\overline{B})$$
$$= 1 - (1 - 0.3) \times (1 - 0.4)$$
$$= 1 - 0.7 \times 0.6 = 1 - 0.42 = 0.58$$

4. The probability that a person stopping at a petrol pump will get his tyres checked is 0.12, the probability that he will get his oil checked is 0.29, and the probability that he will get both checked is 0.07.

(i) What is the probability that a person stopping at this pump will have neither his tyres nor oil checked?

(ii) Find the probability that a person who has his oil checked will also have his tyres checked.

Solution. Let A denote the event that a person stopping at a petrol pump will have his tyres checked, and B denote the event that he will get his oil checked. There we are given:

$$P(A) = 0.12$$
$$P(B) = 0.29$$
$$P(A \cap B) = 0.07$$

(i) The probability that a person stopping at this pump will have neither his tyres nor oil checked is given by:

$$P(\overline{A} \cap \overline{B}) = 1 - P(A \cup B)$$
$$= 1 - [P(A) + P(B) - P(A \cap B)]$$
$$= 1 - (0.12 + 0.29 - 0.07)$$
$$= 1 - 0.34 = 0.66$$

(ii) Required probability = P (A/B)

$$= \frac{P(A \cap B)}{P(B)}$$

$$= \frac{0.07}{o.29} = 0.24$$

5. There are 5 white and 7 red balls in a bag. A ball is drawn and then replaced. What is the probability that a white and *a* red ball are drawn in that order? What would be the probability if the balls drawn were not put back into the bag?

Solution: Let A denote the event of drawing a white ball and B denote the event of drawing a red ball.

Balls drawn with replacement—If the drawn ball is replaced before the 2nd draw is not affected by the result of the 2nd draw. In other words, A and B are independent events and hence the probability of drawing a white ball and then a red ball in that order is given by:

$$P(A \cap B) = P(A) . P(B)$$

$$= \frac{5}{12} \times \frac{7}{12} = \frac{35}{144}$$

Balls drawn without replacement—If the drawn ball is not replaced before the 2nd draw, then the events a and B are not independent.

$\therefore$ P(A $\cap$ B) = P (A) . P(B/A) $\quad \ldots (i)$

For the 2nd draw, the total number of balls left in the bag is 12 – 1 = 11 and

$\therefore$ P (B/A) = P (drawing *a* red ball when there are 4 white and 7 red balls)

$$= \frac{7}{11}$$

Hence from (1)

$$P(A \cap B) = P(A) . P(B/A)$$

$$= \frac{5}{12} . \frac{7}{11} = \frac{35}{132}$$

Mathematical Expectation

If x is a random variable which can assume any one of the values $x_1, x_2, \ldots x_n$ with respective probabilities $p_1, p_2 \ldots p_n$ there the mathematical expectation of x usuall called the expected value of x and denoted by E (X) is defined as:

$$E(x) = p_1 x_1 + p_2 x_2 + \ldots + p_n x_n = \Sigma p.x$$

where

$$\Sigma p_i = p_1 + p_2 + \ldots p_n = 1$$

More precisely, if x is a random variable with probability distribution $\{x, p(x)\}$, Hence

$$E(x) = \Sigma x . p(x)$$

Remark.

Mathematical expectation of a random variable is nothing but its arithmetic mean.

Theorems on Expectation

Theorem-1

$$E(c) = C$$

where c is *a* constant

Proof: —we have

$$E(c) = \text{Mean of } c$$

$$= \frac{c + c + c + \ldots + c}{n} = \frac{nc}{n} = c$$

Theorem-2

$$E(cx) = C\,E(x)$$

where c is *a* constant

Theorem-3

$$E(ax \times b) = a\,E(x) + b$$

where *a* and *b* are constants.

***Theorem-4.* Addition Rule of Expectation**

If X and Y are random variables then

$$E(X + Y) = E(X) + E(Y)$$

i.e., Expected value of the sum of two random variables is equal to the sum of their expected values.

Corollary.

$$E(ax - by) = AE(X) + bE(Y)$$

when *a* and *b* are constants

Theorem—5 (Multiplication Rule of Expectation)

If X and Y are independent random variables, then

$$E(XY) = E(X) . E(Y)$$

i.e., the expected value of the product of two independent random variables is equal to the product of their expected values.

BINOMIAL DISTRIBUTION

Suppose the variable under study is measured in such away that each observation can be classified into two categories. For example, if a coin is tossed, the result of each throw can be either a head or a tail. Similarly, if a die is thrown we may call getting 5 or 6 a 'success' and getting 1, 2, 3 or 4 a 'failure'. If data on income of households are collected, we may classify each household as 'poor' or 'Not – Poor' on the basis of its income. For example, if the household monthly income is less than or equal to Rs. 500/– it may be classified as 'Poor' and if it is more than Rs.500/– we may call it 'Not – Poor.'

In Binomial Distribution it is necessary that each observation is classified into only two categories.

For the sake of convenience we name there two categories as *'success'* and 'failure'.

In Binomial distribution it is necessary that the probability of success (failure) remains the same for each observation or in each trial. Thus the probability of getting head (or tail) must remain the same in each toss; similarly, in case of the die throwing experiment the probability of success (*i.e.,* getting 5 or 6) must remain the same in each throw.

If the probability of success (or failure) changes from trial to trial or if the results of each trial are classified into more than two categories, then the Binomial distribution cannot be used.

Another condition underlying the Binomial distribution is that the trials (or individual observations) should be independent of each other

If n independent observations (or n independent trials) are made, the result of each trial is classified into two categories called 'success' and 'failure' and the probability of success is the same for each observation or in each trial, then the probability of getting x successes in n trials is equal to

$$\frac{n!}{x!(n-x)!}p^x q^{n-x}$$

where

p = probability of success in a single trial

Q = probability of failure in a single trial.

and $p+q=1$

Remark.

Putting $x = 0, 1, 2,......n$ in above equation we get the probabilities of 0, 1, 2, 3,......n successes respectively in n trials, which are tabulated below:

The Binomial Distribution

Numbers of Successes x	Probability
0	q^n
1	$n\,q^{n-1}$
2	$\frac{n(n-1)}{2-1}q^{n-2}p^2$
⋮	⋮
x	$\frac{n(n-1)...(n-x+1)}{x(x-1)...3.2.1}q^{n-x}p^x$
⋮	⋮
n	p^n
Total	1

It should be noted that

1. The variable x (number of success) is discrete it can take only the integral values 0, 1, 2, ..,n.

2. The probabilities specified above

$$q^n,\ nq^{n-1}\ p,...p^n$$

are in fact successive terms in the Binomial Expansim of $(q+p)^n$.

3. The sum of binomial coefficient is 2^n.

4. For n trials the binomial probability distribution consists of $(n+1)$ terms.

For Binomial Distribution

1. *Mean* = $n\,p$

2. *Variance* = $(\text{s.d.})^2 = npq$

3. *Third moments*

$$\mu_3 = npq\,(q-p)$$

4. *Fourth moments*

$$\mu_4 = npq\,[1+3pq\,(n-2)]$$

5. *Moment coefficient of Skewness is*

$$\beta_1 = \frac{(q-p)^2}{npq}$$

6. *Coefficient of Kurtosis is*

$$\beta_2 = 3+\frac{1-6pq}{npq}$$

Remarks

1. Since q is the probability (of failure), we always have $0<q<1$.

$\therefore$ Variance $= np \times q < np$ $\quad (\because 0<q<1)$

$\Rightarrow$Variance < Mean

Hence for the Binomial distribution variance is less than mean

2. Binomial distribution is symmetrical if $p = q$ $0.5 = \frac{1}{2}$. It is positively Skewed if $p < 0.5$ and negatively Skewed if $p > 0{,}5$.

Examples: 1. comment on the following:

For a binomial distribution, mean = 7 and variance = 11

Solution; For a binomial distribution with parameters n and p,

Mean $= np = 7$ ...(1)

and variance $= npq = 11$ ...(2)

Dividing (2) by (1), we get

$$q = \frac{11}{7} = 1.6$$

which is impossible, since q being the propability must lie between 0 and 1. Hence, the given statement is wrong.

2. If the probability of a defective bolt is 1/10, find (*i*) the mean; (*ii*) variance; (*iii*) moment coefficient of Skewness; (*iv*) Kurtosis, for the distribution of defective bolts in a total of 400

Solution: In the usual notations, we have

$$n = 400,\ p = \frac{1}{10} = 0.1,$$

$q = 1 - p = 0.9$

According to Binomial Probability law:

(i) Mean $= np$

$= 400 \times 0.1 = 40$

(ii) Variance $= npq$

$= 400 \times 0.1 \times 0.9$

(iii) The moment coefficient of Skewness

$$\beta_1 = \frac{(q-p)^2}{npq}$$

$$= \frac{(0.8)^2}{36} = \frac{0.64}{36} = 0.1777 = 0.018$$

$$\therefore \quad \gamma_1 = \pm\sqrt{\beta_1} = \sqrt{0.018} = 0.134$$

(iv) Coefficient of Kurtosis is given by:

$$\beta_2 = 3 + \frac{1-6pq}{npq}$$

$$= 3 + \frac{1 - 6 \times 0.1 \times 0.9}{36}$$

$$= 3 + \frac{0.46}{36} = 3 + 0.013 = 3.013$$

Remarks

Since $\beta_1 \neq 0$, the distribution is not symmetrical. But since it is nearly zero, it is moderately symmetrical. $\beta_2 > 3$ implies that the distribution is platy Kurtic.

POISSON DISTRIBUTION (AS A LIMITING CASE OF BINOMIAL DISTRIBUTION)

Poisson distribution was derived in1837 by *simon D. Poisson.* Poisson distribution may be obtained as a limiting case of Binomial probability distribution under the following conditions:

(i) n, the number of trials is indefinitely large

(ii) p, the constant probability of success for each trial is indefinitely small *i.e.,* $p \to 0$.

(iii) $np = m$ is finite

Under the conditions given above the probability of getting x successes is

$$\frac{e^{-n} . m^x}{x!} \qquad \ldots(i)$$

where $x = 0, 1, 2, 3$..........

$m =$ mean $= np$

$e = 2.71828$

and $x! = x(x-1)(x-2) \ldots \times 3 \times 2 \times 1$.

Remarks

1. Poisson distribution is a discrete probability distribution, since the variable can take only integral values 0, 1, 2,... ∞

2. Putting x = 0, 1, 2, 3....in (i) we obtain the probabilities of 0, 1, 2, 3..., successes respectively, which are tabulated below:

Poisson Distribution

No. of Successes (x)	Probability $p(x)$
0	e^{-m}
1	$\frac{e^{-m}.m}{1!}$
2	$\frac{e^{-m}.m^2}{2!}$
3	$\frac{e^{-m}.m^3}{3!}$
⋮	⋮
x	$\frac{e^{-m}.m^x}{x!}$
⋮	⋮
Total	1

3. If we know m, all the probabilities of the poisson distribution can be obtained. m is, therefore, called the parameter of the Poisson distribution.

Constants of Poisson Distribution

The mean of poisson distribution

Mean $= m = np$

and the Variance $= m =$ mean

Hence for the poisson distribution with parameter m, we have

Mean $=$ Variance $= m$

i.e., mean and variance are equal, each being equal to the parameter m.

Other Constants:

The moments (about mean) of the poisson distribution are:

$$\mu_1 = 0$$

μ_2 = Variance = m

$\mu_3 = m$

$\mu_4 = m + 3m^2$

Hence,

$$\beta_1 = \frac{(\mu_3)^2}{(\mu_2)^3} = \frac{m^2}{m^3} = \frac{1}{m}$$

and $$\beta_2 = \frac{\mu_4}{\mu_2{}^2} = \frac{m+3m^2}{m^2} = 3+\frac{1}{m}$$

Remarks

1. As $m \to \infty, \beta_1 \to 0$ and $\beta_2 \to 3$

2. Since $\mu_3 = m > 0$, from above equation we observe that $\beta_1 > 0$. This means that Poission distribution is a positively Skewed distribution. As the value of the parameter m increases, β_1 decreases and thus Skewness is reduced for increasing values of m. In particular as $m \to \infty$ (large values of m), $\beta_1 \to 0$ and consequently the distribution tendes to be symmetrical for large m.

Mode of Poisson Distribution

The poission distribution has mode at X = x, if P $(x) > P(x-1)$ and $P(x) > P(x+1)$.

Case 1. *When m is an integer.* If m is an integer, equal to K, (say), then the Poisson distribution is bi-modal, the two modes being at the points X = k and X = k – 1.

Case 2. *When m is not an integer.*—If m is not an integer than the distribution is unimodal, the unique modal value being the integral part of m. For example, if m = 5.6, then mode is 5, the integral part of 5.6

Utility or Importance of Poisson Distribution

The conditions under which poisson distribution is obtained as a limiting case of the Binomial distribution and also the conditions for the general model underlying.Poisson distribution suggest that poisson distribution can be used to ecplain the behaviour of the discrete random variables where the probability of occurrence of the event is very small and the total number of possible cases is sufficiently large. We give below some practical situations where poisson distribution can be used:

(i) Number of accidents taking place per day on a busy road.

(ii) The number of suicides reported in a particular day or the number of casualties due to a rare disease such as heart attack or cancer or snake bite in a year.

(iii) The number of defective material in a packing manufactured by a good concern.

(iv) To count the number of radio–active disintegrations of a radio–active element per unit of time.

Example 1. Comment on the following:

For a Poisson distribution,

Mean = 8 and Variance = 7

Solution. The given statement is wrong, since for a Poisson distribution mean and variance are equal.

NORMAL DISTRIBUTION

Normal distribution is one of the most important continuous theoretical distributions in statistics. Most of the data relating to economic and business statistics or even in social and physical sciences conform to this distribution.

Normal Curve

The $$y = \frac{1}{\sigma\sqrt{2\pi}} e^{-\frac{1}{2}\frac{(x-m)^2}{\sigma^2}}$$

is called the Normal Curve.

where

m = Mean

σ^2 = Standard deviation

As a special case,we may write $m = 0$ and $\sigma^2 = 1$ there

$$y = \frac{1}{\sqrt{2\pi}} e^{-\frac{1}{2}x^2}$$

is the standard Normal Curve (S.N.C).

Remark

If X is a random variable following normal distribution with mean m and standard deviation σ, then the random variable Z defined as follows:

$$Z = \frac{X - E(X)}{\sigma_x} = \frac{X - m}{\sigma}$$

is called the standard normal variate (S.N.V).

we have

$$E(Z) = E\left(\frac{X-m}{\sigma}\right)$$

$$= \frac{1}{\sigma}E(X-m) \quad [\because E(cx) = CE(x)]$$

$$[\because E(x) = E(x)]$$

$$= \frac{1}{\sigma}E(x) - E(m)$$

$$= \frac{1}{\sigma}[m-m] = 0$$

$$\text{Var}(Z) = \text{Var}\left(\frac{x-m}{\sigma}\right)$$

$$= \frac{1}{\sigma^2}Var(x-m)$$

$$[\because \text{Var}(cx) = c^2\,\text{Var}(x)]$$

$$= \frac{1}{\sigma^2}.\text{Var}(x)$$

because variance is independent of the change of orgine.

$$\therefore \quad \text{Var}(Z) = \frac{1}{\sigma^2}\sigma^2 = 1$$

Therefore, *the standard normal variate (S.N.V.) Z has mean 0 and standard deviation* 1.

Properties of Normal Distribution

1. If the parameters m and σ^2 of the normal curve are specified, the normal curve is fully determined and we can draw it by obtaining the value of *(y)* corresponding to different values of x – the abscissa.

we not that the normal curve

$$y = \frac{1}{\sigma\sqrt{2\pi}}e^{-\frac{1}{2}\frac{(x-m)^2}{\sigma^2}}$$

is bell–shaped and it is symmetric about the Straight line $x = m$.

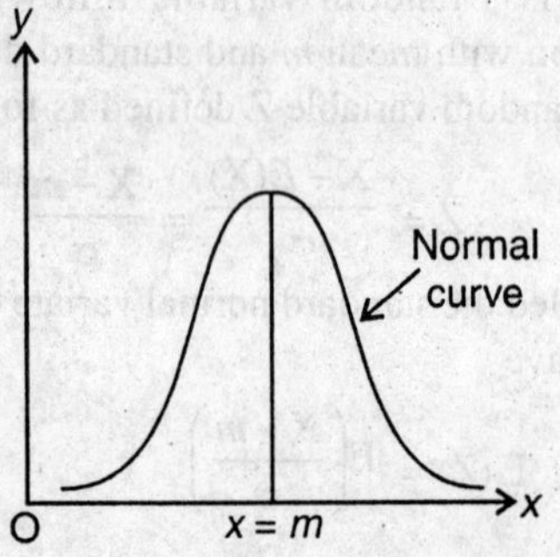

2. The normal curve tends to touch the x – axis only at infinity, *i.e.,* the x – axis is an 'asymptote' to the normal curve. It is a continuous curve stretching from $-\infty$ to $+\infty$.

3. Since the distribution is symmetrical, mean, median and mode coincide. Thus,

Mean = Median = Mode $=m$

4. Since Mean = Median = m, the ordinate at $x = m$, divides the whole area into two equal parts. Further, since total area under normal curve is 1, the area to the right of the ordinate as well as to the left of the ordinate at $x = m$ is 0.5.

5. Also, by virtue of symmetry the quartiles are equidistant from median (m) *i.e.,*

$$Q_3 - M_d = M_d - Q_1 \Rightarrow Q_1 + Q_3 = 2M_d = 2M$$

6. Since the distribution is symmetrical, the moment coefficient of Skewness is given by:

$$\beta_1 = 0$$

7. The coefficient of Kurtosis is given by:

$$\beta_2 = 3$$

8. No portion of the curve lies below the x – axis.

9. Theoretically, the range of the distribution is from $-\infty$ to ∞. But practically, Range = σ_σ.

10. Since the distribution is symmetrical, all moments of odd order about the mean are zero. Thus

$$\mu_1 = \mu_3 = \mu_5 = ... = 0$$

11. X– axis is an asymptote to the curve, *i.e.,* for numerically large value of x (on either side of the point $x = m$), the curve becomes parallel, to the x – axis and is supposed to meet it at infinity.

12. Points of inflexion of the normal curve are at $x = m\,\sigma$ and $x = m - \sigma$.

At the point of inflexion the tangent changes its sign.

13. **Area Property**—One of the most fundamental properties of the normal probability curve is the area property. The area under the normal curve between the ordinates at $x = m - \sigma$ and $x = m + \sigma$ is 0.6826. In other words, the range $m \pm \sigma$ covers 68.26% of the observations.

The area under the normal probability curve between the ordinates at $x = m - 3\sigma$ and $x = m + 3\sigma$ is 0.9973 *i.e.,* the range $m \pm 3\sigma$ covers 99.73% of the observations. Hence, for practical purposes, the range $m \pm 3\sigma$ covers the entire area, which is 1.

Areas Under Normal Curve

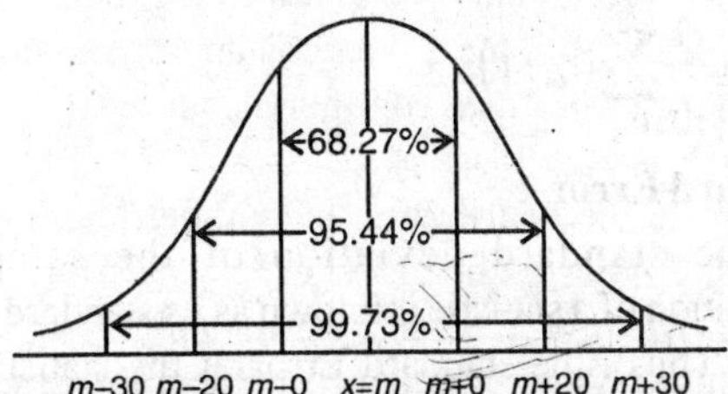

Importance of Normal Distribution

Normal distribution has occupied a very important role in statistics. We enumerate below some of its important applications.

1. Most of the discrete probability distributions (*e.g.* Binomial distribution, Poisson distribution) tend to normal distribution as *n* the number of trials increases. For large values of *n*, computation of probability for discrete distributions becomes quite tedious and time consuming. In such cases, normal distribution can be used with great ease and convenience.

2. Almost all the exact sampling distributions *e.g.*, student's *t* – distribution, snedecor's F – distribution, Fisher's Z – distribution and the Chi square distribution conform to normal distribution for *l*arge degrees of freedom (*i.e.*, as $n \to \infty$).

3. The whole theory of exact sample (small sample) tests, namely, *t*, F, ϕ^2 tests, etc, is based on the fundamental assumption that the parent population from which the samples have been drawn follows Normal distribution.

4. Perhaps, one of the most important applications of the Normal distribution is inherent in one of the most fundamental theorems in the theory of statistics, namely, the Central Limit Theorem.

5. If X is a normal Variate with mean *m* and variance σ^2, then we have proved that

$$P(m-3\sigma < x < m+3\sigma) = P(-3 < z < 3) = 0.9973$$

$$\Rightarrow P[|z| > 3] = 1 - 0.9973 = 0.0027$$

Thus, the probability of standard normal variate going outside the limits ± 3 is practically zero. In other words, in all probability we should expect a standard normal variate to lie between the limits ± 3. This property of the normal distribution forms the basis of entire large sample theory.

6. Normal distribution is used in Statistical Quality Control in Industry for the setting of control limits.

SAMPLING AND CENSUS METHODS

Universe or Population

In any statistical investigation the interest usually lies in studying the various characteristics relating to items or inidividuals belonging to a particular group. This group of individuals under study is known as the population or universe. For example, if an enquiry is intended to determine the average per capita income of the people in a particular city, the population will comprise ass the earning people in that city. On the other hand if we want to study the expenditure habits of the families in that city, then the population will consist of all the house holds in that city. In sampling theory, the population means the larger group from which the samples are drawn.

A population containing a finite number of objects or items in known as finite population, *e.g.*, the students in a college, the day's production in an industrial concern, the population of a city or a twon, etc. On the other hand, a population having an infinite number of objects or with the number of objects so large as to appear parctically infinite, is termed as an infinite population, *e.g.*, the population of temperatures at various points of the the atmosphere; the population of stars in the sky, etc.

Sampling

A finite subset of the population, selected from it with the objective of investigating its properties is called a sample and the number of units in the sample is known as the sample size. Sampling isa tool which enables us to draw conclusions about the characteristics of the population after studying only those objects or itms that are included in the sample.

The main objectives of the sampling theory are:

(*i*) To obtain the optimum results, *i.e.*, the

maximum in formation about the characteristics of the population with the available sources at our disposal in terms of time, money and man power by studying the sample values only.

(ii) To obtain the best possible estimates of the population parameters.

Sampling Distribution

If we draw a sample of size n from a gien finite population of size N, then the total number of possible samples is;

$$N_{C_n} = \frac{N!}{n!(N-n)!} = K, \text{(say)}$$

For each of these K samples we can compute some statistic $t = t(x_1, x_2, ..., x_n)$, in particular the mean $\overline{X}$, the variance S^2, etc., as given below:

Sample Number	*Statistic*		
	t	$\overline{X}$	s^2
1	t_1	$\overline{X}_1$	s_1^2
2	t_2	$\overline{X}_2$	s_2^2
3	t_3	$\overline{X}_3$	s_3^2
⋮	⋮	⋮	⋮
K	t_k	$\overline{X}_k$	s_k^2

The set of the values of the statistic so obtaines, one for each sample, constitutes what is called the sampling distribution of the statistic. For example, the values $t_1, t_2, t_3, ...t_k$ determine the sampling, distribution of the statistic t. In other words, statistic t may be regarded as a random variable which can take the values $t_1, t_2, t_3, ... t_k$ and we can compute the various statistical constants like mean, variance, Skewness, Kurtosis, etc., for its distribution. For example, the mean and variance of the sampling distribution of the statistic t are given by:

$$\bar{t} = \frac{1}{k}(t_1 + t_2 + t_3 + ... + t_k)$$

$$= \frac{1}{k}\sum_{i=1}^{k} t_i$$

where $\bar{t}$ = mean

$$\text{Var}(t) = \frac{1}{k}\left[(t_1 - \bar{t})^2 + (t_2 - \bar{t})^2 + ... + (t_k - \bar{t})^2\right]$$

$$= \frac{1}{k}\sum_{i=1}^{k}(t_i - \bar{t})^2$$

Standard Error

The standard deviation of the sampling distribution of a statistic is known as its standard Error (S.E.). Thus, the standard Error of the statistic t is given by:

$$\text{S.E.}(t) = \sqrt{\text{Var}(t)}$$

$$= \sqrt{\frac{1}{k}\sum_{i=1}^{k}(t_i - \bar{t})^2}$$

Census Versus Sample Enumeration

For any statistical enquiry in any field of human activity, whether it is in business, economics or social sciences, the basic problem is to obtain adequate and reliable data relating to the particular phenomenon under study. There are two methods of collecting the data:

1. The census Method or complete Enumeration.
2. The sample Method or Partial Enumeration.

Census Method

In the census method we resort to 100% inspection of the population and enumerated each and every unit of the population. The census method has its obvious limitations and drawbacks given below:

(i) The complete enumeration of the population requires lot of time, money, manpower and administrative personnel.

(ii) Since the entire population is to be enumerated, the census method is usually very time consuming.

Remark

Census method is recommended in the following situations:

(a) If the information is required about each and every unit of the population, there is no way but to resort to 100% enumeration.

(b) If the size of item is small.

Sample

In the sample method we inspect only a selected representative and adequate fraction (finite subset) of the population and after analysing the results of the sample data we draw conclusions about the characteristics of the population. Prof. R.A. Fisher sums up the advantages of sampling techniques over complete census in just four words: Speed, Economy, Adaptability and scientific Approach. We summarise below the merits of the sample method over the census method:

1. Speed *i.e.,* less time
2. Economy *i.e.,* Reduced cost of the Enquiry
3. Administrative convenience
4. Greater Scope

Limitations of Sampling

The merits of smple surveys over complete enumeration can be realised only if:

(i) the sample is drawn in a scientific manner,
(ii) the appropriate sampling design is used,
(iii) the sample size is adequate.

In spite of the above merits of the sample survey over census, the sampling procedure has its limitations and problems which are enumerated below:

1. If a sample survey is not properly planned, the results obtained will not be reliable and quite often might even be misleading.

2. An efficient sampling scheme requires the services of qualified, skilled and experienced personnel and more sophisticated equipment and statistical techniques for the planning and execution of the survey and for the collection, processing and analysis of the sample data. In the absence of these the results of the survey may not be reliable.

3. Sometimes the sample survey might require more time, money and labour than a complete census.

4. Sampling procedure cannot be used if we want to obtain information about each and every unit of the population.

Principal Steps in Sample Survey

The following are the principal steps in the planning and execution of the sample surveys:

1. Objectives and Scope of the Survey
2. Difining the Population to be Sampled
3. Sampling Units
4. Data to be Collected
5. The Questionnaire or Schedule
6. Method of Collecting Information
7. Selection of Proper Sampling Design
8. Organisation of Field Work
9. Summary and Analysis of the Data

Measures of Statistical Errors (Absolute and Relative Errors)

A measure of the statistical errors is provided by absolute and relative errors.

Absolute Error—An absolute error (A.E.) is the difference between the ture value of any particular observed item and its estimated or approximated value. Symbolically, we may write—

$$\text{A.E.} = |a - e|$$

where

$$\text{A.E.} = \text{absolute error}$$
$$a = \text{actual value}$$
$$e = \text{estimated value}$$
$$|a - e| = \text{modulus value of } (a - e)$$

For example, if a value 5487350 is approximated to the nearest lakh, it can be taken as 55 lakhs. Thus,

$$\text{A.E.} = |a - e|$$
$$= |5487350 - 5500000|$$
$$= |-12650| = 12650$$

The Magnitude of the absolute error is quite independent of the magnitude of the actual value. For example, in the above case AE remains same for all those values which have the digit in the 10 thousand place greater than 5. Consequently, absolute errors cannot be compared meaningfully. For example, the above error of 12,650 in a value of 5487350 may be quite insignificant or immaterial as compared with an absolute error of 10 in a value of 500. Moreover, these errors are in the units of measurement and as such AEs in different units cannot be compared meaningfully. In order to facilitate comparison of the errors, they are reduced to pure numbers which are independent of the units of measurement. This is done by calculating the Relative Error (R.E.) which is defined as the ratio of the absolute error to the actual value. Symbolically,

$$\text{RE} = \frac{\text{AE}}{\text{Actual value}} = \frac{|a - e|}{a}$$

Thus in the above example, RE which relates the magnitude of the error to the magnitude of the true value, is given by

$$RE = \frac{12650}{5487350} = 0.0023$$

The rėlative error may also be expressed as percentage.

$$\text{Percentage RE} = \frac{12650}{5487350} \times 100$$

In statistical analysis, relative error is a much more useful measure than the absolute error as it provides a useful coefficient (a pure number independent of units of measurement) for comparing the degree of the error of different sets of data.

Types of Sampling

Some of the important types of sampling are given below:

1. Simple Random Sampling
2. Stratified Random Sampling
3. Systematic Sampling
4. Multistage Sampling
5. Quota Sampling

Simple Random Sampling

Simple random sampling is the techniques in which "sample is so drawn that each and every unit in the population has an equal and independent chance of being included in the sample."

If the unit selected in any draw is not replaced in the population before making the next draw, then it is known as simple random sampling without replacement and if it is replaced back before making the next draw, then the sampling plan is called simple random sampling with replacement.

A very important and interesting feature of simple random sampling without replacement is that, "the probability of selecting a specified unit of population at any given draw is equal to the probability of its being selected at the first draw." This implies that in this case from a population of size N, the probability that any sampling unit is included in the sample is 1/N and this probability remains constant throughout the drawing.

Stratified Random Sampling

When the population is heterogeneous with respect to the variable or characteristic under study, then the technique of stratified random sampling is used to obtain more efficient results. **Stratification** means division into layers or goups.

The criterion used for the stratification of the universe into various strata is know as stratifying factor. In general geographical sociological or economic characteristics from the basis of stratification of the given population. Some of the commonly used stratifying factors are age, sex, income, occupation, educational level, geographic area, economic status, etc. In many fields of highly skewed distributions, stratification is very effective and valuable tool.

Systematic Sampling

Systematic sampling is slight variation of the simple random sampling in which only the first sample unit is selected at random and the remaining units an automatically selected in a definite sequence at equal spacing from one another. This technique of drawing samples is usually recommended if the complete and up-to-date list of the sampling units, *i.e.*, the frame is available and the units are arranged in some systematic order such as alphabetical, chronological geographical order, etc. This requires the sampling units in the population to be ordered in such a way that each item in the population is uniquely identified by its order, for example the names of persons in a telephone directory, the list of voters etc.

Cluster Sampling

In this case the total population is divided, depending on problem under study, into some recognisable subdivisions which are termed as clusters and a simple random sample of these clusters is drawn.

For example, if we are interested in obtaining the income or opinion data in a city, the whole city may be divided into N different blocks or localities (which determine the clusters) and a simple random sample of *n* blocks is drawn. The individuals in the selected blocks determine the cluster sample.

Multistage Sampling

As the name suggests, multistage sampling refers to a sampling technique which is carried out in various stages. For example, if we are interested in obtaining a sample of, say, n households from a particular state the first stage units may be districts, the second stage units may be villages in the districts and third stage units will be households in the villages. Each stage thus results in a reduction of the sample size.

Quota Sampling

Quota sampling may be looked as a special form of stratified sampling. In this method, the investigator is told in advance the number of the sample units he is to examine or enumerate from the stratum assigned to him. In the language of stratified sampling, the quota of the units to be examined by the investigator from the stratum assigned to him is fixed for each investigators. The sampling quotas may be fixed according to some specified characteristic such as income group, sex, occupation, political or religious affiliations, etc. The choice of the particular units or individuals for investigation is left to the investigators themselves.

SAMPLING DISTRIBUTION OF PROPORTION

We talk of population proportion or sample proportion, if the characteristic under study is an attribute. An attribute is a quality characteristic which cannot be measured quantitatively, *e.g.*, beauty, honesty, intelligence, colour, habit, etc. In a number of situations it may not be possible to measure the characteristic under study yet it may be possible to classify the given population into various classes w.r.t. the given attribute. If we classify the population into only two classes w.r.t. an attribute the classification is termed as **dichotomous classification** and if the population is divided into more than two classes, it is termed as mainfold classification. Here we shall confine our attention to the cases where the population can be classified only into two mutually exclusive and exhaustive classes, say, C or C' according as the given unit possess or does not possess the attribute respectively.

Let us consider a population consisting of N units and let the number of units possessing the attribute under study be 'a', say. Then in a dichotomous classification, the number of units which do not possess the given attribute is $(N - a)$.

Then

P = Proportion of units (in the population) possessing the given attribute = a/N

Q = Proportion of population units which do not possess the given attribute

$$= \frac{N-a}{N}$$

$$= 1 - \frac{a}{N}$$

$$\Rightarrow \quad Q = 1 - P$$

In sampling theory, the possession of an attribute by a sampling unit is termed as a **success** and non-possession as a **failure**. Therefore, P and Q may be interpreted as representing the proportion or probability of success and failure respectively in the population.

TESTING OF HYPOTHESIS

As already stated, the inductive inference is based on deciding about the characteristics of the population on the basis of sample study. Such decisions involve, an element of risk, the risk of taking wrong decisions. For example, a pharmaceutical concern may be interested to find if a new drug is really effective for the particular ailment, say, in reducing blood pressure or inducing sleep; we may want to decide whether a given foodstuff is really effective in increasing weight; or which of the two brands of a particular product, say, foodstuffs, fertilisers, etc, is more effective. It is here that the modern theory of probability plays a very vital role in decision making and the branch of statistics which helps us in arriving at the criterion for such decisions is known as **testing of hypothesis.**

A test of a statistical hypothesis is a two-action decision after observing a random sample from the given population, the two actions being the acceptance or rejection of the hypothesis under consideration. The truth or falsity of a statistical hypothesis is thus based on the information contained in the sample which may be consistent or inconsistent with the hypothesis and accordingly, the hypothesis may be accepted or rejected. It should be clearly borne in mind that the **acceptance of a statistical hypothesis is due to in sufficient evidence provided by the sample to reject it and does not necessarily imply that it is true.**

TESTS OF SIGNIFICANCE

From the knowledge of the sampling distribution of a staristic, it is possible to find the probability that a sample statistic would differ from a given hypothetical value of the parameter or from another sample value, by more than a certain amount and hence to answer the question of significance. Accordingly, a procedure to assess the significance of a statistic or difference between two independent statistics is known as **test of significance**. We say that.' (*i*) The difference between a statistic and the corresponding population parameter, or (*ii*) The difference between two independent statistics, is not significant if it can be attributed to the fluctuations of sampling, otherwise it is said to be significant.

Null Hypothesis : The random selection of the samples from the given population makes the tests of significance valid for us. For applying any test of significance we first set up a hypothesis — a definite statement about the population parameter (*s*). Such a statistical hypothesis, which is under test, is usually a hypothesis of no difference and hence is called **Null Hypothesis**. It is usually denoted by Ho. In the words of **Prof. R.A. Fisher** "Null hypothesis is the hypothesis which is tested for possible rejection under the assumption that it is true."

The following points may be borne in mind in setting the null hypothesis:

1. If we want to test the significance of the difference between a statistic and the parameter or between two sample statistics then we set up the null hypothesis H_0 that the difference is not significant. This means that the difference is just due to fluctuations of sampling.

For example, if we want to test if a particular drug is effective, we shall take a neutral attitude and set-up the hypothesis that it is not effective. For testing if out of the two foodstuffs, one is better than the other, we shall set-up the hypothesis that there is no difference between them.

2. If we want to test any statement about the population, we set up the null hypothesis that it is true. For example, if we want to find if the population mean has specified value H_0: $\mu = \mu_0$.

Types of Errors in Testing of Hypothesis

As already stated, the inductive inference consists in arriving at a decision to accept or reject a null hypothesis (H_0) after inspecting only a sample from it. As such an element of risk—the risk of taking wrong decisions is involved. In any test procedure, the four possible mutually disjoint and exhaustive decisions are :

1. Reject H_0 when actually it is not true, *i.e.*, when H_0 is false.
2. Accept H_0 when it is true.
3. Reject H_0 when it is true.
4. Accept H_0 when it is false.

The decisions in (1) and (2) are correct decisions while the decisions (3) and (4) are wrong decisions. These decisions may be expressed in the following dichotomous table.

		Decision from sample	
		Reject H_0	Accept H_0
True State	H_0 True	Wrong [Type I Error]	Correct
	H_0 False	Correct	Wrong [Type II Error]

Thus, in testing of hypothesis we are likely to commit two types of errors. The error of rejecting H_0 when H_0 is true is known as **Type I Error** and the error of accepting H_0 when H_0 is false, is known as **Type II Error.**

Level of Significance

The maximum size of the type I error, which we are prepared to risk is known as the level of significance. It is usually denoted by α and is given by:

P [Rejecting H_0 when H_0 is true] = α

Commonly used levels of significance is practice are 5% and 1%. If we adopt 5% level of significance, it implies that in 5 samples out of 100 we are likely to reject a correct H_0. In other words this implies that we are 95% confident that our decision to reject H_0 is correct. Level of significance is always fixed in advane before collecting the sample information.

Procedure of Testing of Hypothesis

We now summarise below the various steps in

testing of a statistical hypothesis in a systematic manner.

Step 1. Set up the Null Hypothesis H_0.

Step 2. Set up the Alternative Hypothesis H_1. Any hypothesis which is complementary to the null hypothesis is called an **alternative hypothesis**. This will enable us to decide whether we have to use a single tailed (right or left) test or two-tailed test.

Step 3. Choose the appropriate level of significance (α) depending on the reliability of the estimates and permissible risk. This is to be decided before sample is drawn, *i.e.*, α is fixed in advance.

Step 4. Compute the test statistic

$$Z = \frac{t - E(t)}{S.E.(t)}$$

under the null hypothesis. Some of the commonly used distributions in obtaining the test statistic or test criterion are normal, chi-square, *t* and F tests.

Step 5. We compare the computed value of Z in step (4) with the significant value Z_α at given level of significance, 'α'.

If $|Z| < Z_\alpha$, *i.e.*, if calculated value of Z is less than Z_α we say it is not significant. By this we mean that the difference $[t - E(t)]$ is just due to fluctuations of sampling and the sample data do not provide us sufficient evidence against the null hypothesis which may, therefore, be accepted.

If $|Z| > Z_\alpha$, *i.e.*, if the computed value of test statistic is greater than the critical or significant value, then we say that it is significant and the null hypothesis is rejected at level of significance α or confidence coefficient $(1 - \alpha)$.

CHI-SQUARE (χ^2) TEST

The square of a standard normal variable is called a chi-square variate with 1 degree of freedom. Thus if X is a random variable following normal distribution with mean μ and standard deviation σ then $(X - \mu)/\sigma$ is a standard normal variate.

$$\therefore \quad \left(\frac{x-\mu}{\sigma}\right)^2$$

is a chi-square (abbreviated by the letter χ^2 of the Greek alphabet) variate with 1 *d.f.*

Application of the χ^2 - distribution

Chi-square distribution has a number of applications, some of which are enumerated below:

1. Chi- square test of goodness of fil.

2. Chi-square test for independence of attributes.

3. To test if the population has a specified value of the variance σ^2.

Conditions for the validity of Chi-square Test

The Chi-square test can be used only if the following conditions are satistied.

1. N, the total frequency, should be reasonably large, say greater than 50.

2. The sample observations should be independent. This implies that no individual item should be included twice or more in the sample.

3. No theretical frequency should be small. Small is a relative term. Preferably each theoretical frequency should be larger than 10 but in any case not less than 5. If any theoretical frequency is less than 5 then. We cannot apply χ^2 - test as such.

4. The given distribution should not be replaced by relative frequencies or proportions but the data should be given on original units.

Degrees of Freedom

As the name suggests the degree of freedom, abbreviated as *d.f.*, denotes the extent of independence (freedom) enjoyed by a given set of observed frequencies. Degrees of freedom are usually denoted by the letter ν of the Greek alphabet. Suppose we are given a set of *n* observed frequencies which are subjected to *k* independent constraints, then

d.f. = (Number of frequencies) – (Number of independent constraints on them)

$\Rightarrow \nu = n - k$

Thus if we are given *n* frequencies subject to the linear constraint, then for the application of χ^2– test, $\nu = n - 1$.

Degrees of freedom for $r \times s$ contingency Table

For $r \times s$ contingency table, the total number of frequencies is $n = r \times s = rs$. There *n* frequencies are subjected to the following linear constraints:

(*i*) *r* row totals $(A_1), (A_2), \ldots, (A_r)$ are fixed.

(*ii*) *s* column totals $(B_1), (B_2) \ldots, (B_s)$ are fixed.

Thus there are $r + s$ constraints on the cell frequencies but these $(r + s)$ constraints are not independent since we have:

$$\sum_{i=1}^{r}(A_i) = \sum_{J=1}^{s}(B_J) = N$$

Thus the number of independent constraints is $k = r + s - 1$

Hence for $r \times s$ contingency table, *d.f.* are :

$$\begin{aligned} v &= n - k \\ &= rs - (r + s - 1) \\ &= rs - r - s + 1 \\ &= (r - 1) \times (s - 1) \end{aligned}$$

Hence for 2×2 contingency table, *d.f.* $= (2 - 1) \times (2 - 1) = 1$; for 3×4 contingency table *d.f.* $= (3 - 1) \times (4 - 1) = 2 \times 3 = 6$ and so on.

2 × 2 Contingency Table

Under the null hypothesis of independence of attributes, the value of χ^2 for the 2×2 contingency table.

			Total
	a	b	$a + b$
	c	d	$c + d$
Total	$a + c$	$b + d$	$N = a + b + c + d$

is given by

$$\chi^2 = \frac{N(ad - bc)^2}{(a + c)(b + d)(a + b)(c + d)}$$

where $N = a + b + c + d$, is the total frequency and figures in brackets in the denominator are row and column totals.

Yates Correction For Continuity for 2 × 2 Table

If any cell frequency in 2×2 table is less than 5, then for the application of χ^2 – test. It has to be pooled with the preceding or succeeding frequency so that total is greater than 5. This results in the loss of 1 *d.f.* Since for 2×2 table *d.f.* $= (2 - 1) \times (2 - 1) = 1$; the degrees of freedom left after adjusting for pooling are $v = 1 - 1 = 0$, which is absurd [χ^2 must have at least 1 *d.f.*]. In such a situation *i.e.* when any cell frequency in 2×2 table is less than 5, we apply the correction due to **F. Vates** (1934) and popularly known as the yates correction for 'continuity'. This consists in adding 0.5 to the cell frequency which is less than 5 and adjusting the remaining frequencies accordingly, since row and column totals are fixed and then applying χ^2-test without pooling.

The value of the χ^2 for 2×2 table.

a	b
c	d

after applying yates correction is:

$$\chi^2 = \frac{N\left[|ad - bc| - N/_2\right]^2}{(a + c)(b + d)(a + b)(c + d)}$$

where $|ad - bc|$ is the absolute or modulus value of the deviation $ad - bc$ after ignoring negative sign, if any.

Remark

1. Yates correction for continuity can be applied only in the case of 2×2 table.

2. If N is sufficiently large, the value of χ^2 is not effected much by yates correction.

χ^2 - Test for the Population Variance

Suppose we want to test if the given **normal** population has a specified variance $\sigma^2 = \sigma^2$, say.

We set up the null hypothesis $H_0 : \sigma^2 = \sigma_0^2$. If $x_1, x_2, x_3, \ldots, x_n$ is a random sample of size n from the given population then under the null hypothesis H_0, the statistic.

$$\chi^2 = \frac{\sum_{i=1}^{n}(x_i - \bar{x})^2}{\sigma_0^2}$$

$$\Rightarrow \quad \chi^2 = \frac{ns^2}{\sigma_0^2} \quad \ldots(1)$$

Follows χ^2 - distribution with $(n - 1)$ *d.f.*, where

$$S^2 = \frac{1}{n}\sum_{i=1}^{n}(x_i - \bar{x})^2$$

denotes the sample variance.

By comparing the value of χ^2 obtained in (1) with the tabulated value for $(n - 1)$ *d.f.* at certain level of significance, we may accept or reject the null hypothesis at that level of significance.

Remarks : This test can be applied only if the population is normal.

APPLICATIONS OF *t*-DISTRIBUTION

The *t*-distribution has a number of applications in statistics.

1. *t*-test for significance of single mean, population variance being unknown.

2. *t*-test for the significance of the difference

between two sample means, the population variances being equal but unknown.

3. t-test for significance of an observed sample correlation coefficient.

Suppose we are interested to test:

a. If the given normal population has a specified value of the population mean, say, μ_0.

b. If the sample mean $\bar{x}$ differs significantly from specified value of population mean.

c. If a given random sample $x_1, x_2, \ldots, x_n$ of size n has been drawn from a normal population with specified mean, μ_0.

Basically, all the three problems are same. We set up the corresponding null hypothesis as follows:

a. $H_0 : \mu = \mu_0$, *i.e.*, the population mean is μ_0.

b. H_0 : There is no significant difference between the sample mean and the population mean. In other words, the difference between $\bar{x}$ and μ is due to fluctuations of sampling.

c. H_0 : The given random sample has been draw from the normal population with mean μ_0.

Under H_0 the test-statistic is

$$t = \frac{\bar{x} - \mu_0}{s/\sqrt{n}} \qquad \ldots 1$$

$$= \frac{\bar{x} - \mu_0}{\sqrt{s^2/n}}$$

where $\bar{x} = \frac{1}{n}\sum x$

and $S^2 = \frac{1}{n-1}\sum (x - \bar{x})^2$

and it follows student's t-distribution with $(n - 1)$ degrees of freedom.

We compute the test-statistic (1) under H_0 and compare it with the tabulated value of t for $(n - 1)$ *d.f.* at certain level of significance. If calculated $|t|$ is greater then tabulated 't', we say it is significant and H_0 is rejected and if calculated $|t|$ is less than tabulated t, H_0 may be accepted at the level of significance adopted.

Assumptions for Student's t-test

The following assumptions are made in the student's t-test.

A. The parent population from which the sample is drawn is normal.

B. The sample observations are independent, *i.e.*, the given sample is random.

C. The population standard deviation σ is unknown.

FISHER'S TRANSFORMATION

Fisher's Z-transformation has the following applications in statistics.

A. To test if the correlation coefficient in the population has a specified value.

B. To test if two independent sample correlation coefficients r_1 and r_2 differ significantly.

F-STATISTIC

F-statistic is the ratio of two independent chi-square variates divided by their respective degrees of freedom.

Applications of F-distribution

F-distribution has a number of applications in statistics, some of which are given below:

1. F-test for Equality of Population variances.
2. F-test for testing the significance of an observed sample multiple correlation.
3. F-test for testing the significance of an observed sample correlation ratio.
4. F-test for testing the linearity of regression.
5. F-test for testing the equality of several population means, *i.e.*, for testing $H_0 : \mu_1 = \mu_2 = \ldots = \mu_k$, (say), for k normal populations.

Relation between t and F Distributions

If a statistic t follows student's t-distribution with n *d.f.* then its square (t^2) follows Snedecor's F-distribution with $(1, n)$ *d.f.* Symbolically,

$$t \sim tn \Rightarrow t^2 \sim F(1, n)$$

With the help of this relation, all the applications of t-distribution may be taken as applications of F-distribution. For example, for testing the significance of sample mean, we may consider the test statistic

$$F = t^2 = \left[\frac{\bar{x} - \mu}{s/\sqrt{n}}\right]^2 \sim F(1, n)$$

and apply F-test.

Relation between F and χ^2 Distributions

In F-distribution with (n_1, n_2) *d.f.* if we put

$$n_1 F = \chi^2$$

$$\Rightarrow \quad F = \chi^2/n_1$$

and let $n_2 \to \infty$, then we get chi-square distribution with n_1 *d.f.*

EXERCISE

1. X measures Wages in Rupees
   (a) Unit of its average is Rs. and unit of variance is Rs.
   (b) Unit of its average is Rs. and unit of variance is Rs. square
   (c) Unit of its average is Rs. but variance does not have any unit
   (d) Unit of its average is Rs. but unit of variance is square not of Rs.
2. In order to apply correctly the χ^2-test for goodness of fit, which of the following assumption is correct?
   (a) The observed and theoretical distribution contain the same number of elements
   (b) No expected frequency be less then five
   (c) The observed values are taken from a random sample
   (d) All of the above
3. If a boy cycles 8 km at the speed of 8 km per hour, and walks another 8 km at the speed of 2 km per hour. His average speed per hour is
   (a) 5 km (b) $\frac{16}{5}$ km
   (c) 4 km (d) 6 km
4. Two events are said to be independent, as per the theory of probability, if the occurrence of one
   (a) affects the probability of another
   (b) does not effect the probability of another
   (c) prevents the occurrence of another
   (d) makes the probability of occurrence of other as zero.
5. The Fisher index number is
   (a) GM of Laspeyres and Paasche index numbers
   (b) AM of Laspeyres and Paasche index numbers
   (c) HM of Laspeyres and Paasche index numbers
   (d) GM of Laspeyres and Marshall-Edge worth index numbers
6. Given the following numbers
   2, 8, 6, 5, 0, 9, 7, 11.
   The product of their arithmetic and geometric means is
   (a) 64 (b) 16
   (c) 0 (d) 6
7. Given the following two regression equations
   $y - 0.5 = \beta_1 x$
   $x + 10 = \beta_2 y$
   then the coefficient of correlation between x and y is
   (a) $\sqrt{\beta_1 \beta_2}$ (b) $\sqrt{\beta_1 \beta_2} + 0.5$
   (c) $\sqrt{\beta_1 \beta_2} + 10.0$ (d) $\sqrt{\beta_1 \beta_2}$
8. A commuter drives 10 miles on first day at a speed of 60 km/hour, the second day at 15 km/hour and third day 10 km/hour. The mean speed of the commuter is
   (a) 16.32 (b) 42.50
   (c) 36.35 (d) 22.10
9. The sum of squares of deviation of 20 observations from their mean is 720 and the mean is 60. The coefficient of vatriation is
   (a) 5% (b) 10%
   (c) 15% (d) 20%
10. If x is a random variable and 'a' and 'b' are constants, then Var $(ax + b)$ is
    (a $(a + b)$ Var (x) (b) $(a^2 + b^2)$ Var (x)
    (c) ab Var (x) (d) a^2 Var (x)
11. The probability of drawing a 'spade' from a well shuffled packet of cards is
    (a) $\frac{1}{52}$ (b) $\frac{4}{52}$
    (c) $\frac{1}{4}$ (d) $\frac{2}{3}$
12. The coefficient of correlation between two series x and y is found to be 0.80. If all the values of x and y are reduced by 50 percent, the correlation coefficient will be
    (a) 0.80 (b) 0.40
    (c) 0.60 (d) 0.20
13. For a Poisson's distribution with $n = 200$, $p = 0.02$, the mean is
    (a) 20 (b) 40
    (c) 4 (d) 10
14. The value of χ^2 in a 2 × 4 contingency table is computed as 4.0. The Null hypothesis that then no associationship will be accepted at 5% level

of significance, if this computed value is less than or equal to the value of χ^2 from the table at ..... degrees of freedom.

(a) 8 (b) 6
(c) 4 (d) 3

15. The significance of the difference between two means of the populations, when σ^2 values are known and equal, is tested by

(a) Z-test (b) *t*-test
(c) F-test (d) χ^2-test

16. The portion of the total area covered in a normal curve under $\bar{x} \pm 2.54\ \sigma$ is

(a) 85% (b) 95%
(c) 99% (d) 90%

17. If A and B are dependent events, then

(a) $P(A/B) = \dfrac{P(A).P(B/A)}{P(A)}$

(b) $P(A/B) = P(A).P(B/A)$

(c) $P(A/B) - P(B).P(A/B)$

(d) $P(A/B) = \dfrac{P(A).P(B/A)}{P(B)}$

18. Arithmetic mean of earning of 42 workers in a factory is Rs. 1200 per month. On account of price rise, the workers managed to get 10% hike in their earnings. In addition to this, the management paid Rs. 100 per month to each employee as bonus. The arithmetic mean of total earning of the workers after these changes will be

(a) Rs. 1300 (b) Rs. 1320
(c) Rs. 1420 (d) Rs. 1510

19. If the Karl Pearson coefficient of correlation between *x* and *y* is 0.3, then the coefficient of correlation between—*x* and 2*y* is

(a) –0.6 (b) –0.3
(c) 0.3 (d) 0.5

20. The arithmetic mean of series 'A' is twice that of series 'B' and the standard deviation of series 'B' is twice that of series 'A'. The coefficient of variation of series 'A' in relation to that of series 'B' will be

(a) 1/4 (b) 1/2
(c) same (d) twice

21. The sum of squared deviation is the least when taken from

(a) mode (b) median
(c) arithmetic mean (d) geometric mean

22. Suppose the average weight of 9 persons is 50 kg. Average weight of the first 5 persons is 45 kg, whereas average weight of the last 5 persons is 55 kg. Then the weight of the 5th member will be

(a) 45. 0 kg (b) 47.5 kg
(c) 50.0 kg (d) 52.5 kg

23. Which one of the following statistical measures is NOT affected by extremely large or small values?

(a) Median
(b) Harmonic mean
(c) Standard deviation
(d) Coefficient of variation

24. Given is the following distribution of two variables *x* and *y*:

x : 1	2	3	4	5
y : 3	4	5	6	7

The standard deviation of *y* is

(a) Same as standard deviation of *x*
(b) (the standard deviation of *x*) × 2
(c) (the standard deviation of *x*) + 2
(d) (the standard deviation of *x*) – 2

25. The standard deviation of six numbers 3, 3, 3, 5, 5, 5 is

(a) 1
(b) 4
(c) 0
(d) Cannot be obtained since the unit of measurement is not given

26. If for a sample data: Mean < Median < Mode, then the distribution is

(a) skewed to the right
(b) symmetric
(c) skewed to the left
(d) neither symmetric nor skewwed

27. Let $x = \dfrac{9 - U}{3}$ and $y = V - 4$ and the correlation coefficient between U and V is – 0.93. Then the correlation coefficient between *x* and *y* will be

(a) 0.093 (b) –0.093
(c) –0.93 (d) cannot be derived

28. Which one of the following statements is NOT correct?

Fisher's index

(a) lies between Laspeyres's index (L) and

Paasche's index (P)

(b) is the arithmetic mean of L and P

(c) is the geometric mean of L and P

(d) is equal to L or P if L = P

29. Consider the following statements:

1. Quartile deviation is more instructive range as it discards the dispersion of extreme items
2. Coefficient of quartile deviation cannot be used to compare the degree of variations in different distributions
3. There are 10 deciles for a series which of the above statements is/are correct?

(a) 1, 2 and 3 (b) 2 alone

(c) 3 alone (d) 1 alone

30. Which one of the following indices satisfies both time reversal and factor reversal tests?

(a) Laspeyres' index (b) Fisher's index

(c) Paasche's index (d) Keely's index

31. Given the following data – 1, 2, 3, 4 and 100; the best measure of central tendency is the

(a) arithmetic mean (b) median

(c) mode (d) geometric mean

32. If for a given data, mode = 5, median = 15 and mean = 20, it means that the sample data is

(a) skewed to the right

(b) skewed to the left

(c) symmetric

(d) neither symmetric nor skewed

33. Consider the following statements:

1. Correlation analysis helps in determining the relationship between two or more variables-it does not tell us anything about the cause and effect relationship
2. The ratio of explained variation to the total variation is called the coefficient of correlation
3. Pearsonian coefficient always assumes linear relationship and is unduly effected by the extreme items

Which of the above statements is/are correct?

(a) 2 alone (b) 1 and 2

(c) 1 and 3 (d) 2 and 3

34. The right-hand tail of a frequency distribution is found to the mirror image of the left-hand tail. The distribution is

(a) positively skewed (b) negatively skewed

(c) asymmetric (d) symmetric

35. From the cumulative frequency diagram which one of the following types of average can be estimated?

(a) Geometric Mean (b) Harmonic Mean

(c) Median (d) Mode

36. During one year the ratio of prices of two commodities is 3, whereas during the next year it is 2. For averaging these ratios

(a) arithmetic mean is most appropriate

(b) harmonic mean is most appropriate

(c) geometric mean is most appropriate

(d) all the three, arithmetic, harmonic and geometric means are equally appropriate

37. Consider the following statements:

1. Median is not useful while dealing with skewed distribution such as income distribution or price distribution
2. Median can be determined graphically by drawing only one ogive
3. Mode can be used to describe qualitative phenomenon

Which of the above statements are correct?

(a) 1 and 2 (b) 1 and 3

(c) 2 and 3 (d) 1, 2 and 3

38. The following equation indicates the relationship among average median and mode:

(a) Mode = 3 Median – 2 Mean

(b) Mean = 2 Mode – 3 Median

(c) Median = 3 Mean – 2 Mode

(d) None of these

39. What is the median of 36, 72, 49, 45, 60, 33, 61, 72, 52?

(a) 33 (b) 52

(c) 61 (d) 60

40. In a moderately asymmetrical distribution.

(a) A.M. > G.M > H.M (b) A.M. < G.M < H.M

(c) A.M < G.M > H.M (d) None of these

41. The geometric mean of 8,64 and 512 is

(a) 194 (b) 64

(c) 16 (d) None of these

42. The points of intersection of the 'less than' and the 'more than' ogives correspond to

(a) mean (b) median

(c) geometric mean (d) none of these

43. Histogram is useful to determine graphically the

value of:
(*a*) arithmetic mean (*b*) median
(*c*) mode (*d*) none of these

44. In a series of values if one value is zero, G.M. is
(*a*) positive (*b*) zero
(*c*) indeterminate (*d*) none of these

45. The sum of squared deviations is minimum when taken from
(*a*) mean (*b*) median
(*c*) mode (*d*) none of these

46. Coefficient of quartile deviation is calculated by the formula
(*a*) $\frac{Q_3 + Q_1}{4}$ (*b*) $\frac{Q_3 + Q_1}{2}$
(*c*) $\frac{Q_3 - Q_1}{Q_3 + Q_1}$ (*d*) $\frac{Q_3 + Q_1}{Q_3 - Q_1}$

47. Mean ± 3 σ covers
(*a*) 99.37% items (*b*) 90% items
(*c*) 99.9% items (*d*) 99.73% items

48. Quartile deviation is
(*a*) $\frac{4}{5}\sigma$ (*b*) $\frac{3}{2}\sigma$
(*c*) $\frac{2}{3}\sigma$ (*d*) $\frac{5}{4}\sigma$

49. Coefficient of variation is calculated by the formula:
(*a*) $\frac{\bar{x}}{\sigma} \times 100$ (*b*) $\frac{\sigma}{\bar{x}} \times 100$
(*c*) $\frac{\bar{x}}{\sigma}$ (*d*) $\frac{\sigma}{\bar{x}}$

50. The measure of variation that is least effected by extreme observations is
(*a*) Range (*b*) Mean deviation
(*c*) Standard deviation (*d*) Quartile deviation

51. When coefficient of skewness is zero the distribution is
(*a*) J-shaped (*b*) U-shaped
(*c*) Symmetrical (*d*) L-shaped

52. When $\beta_2 < 3$ the distribution is
(*a*) Leptokurtic (*b*) Platykurtic
(*c*) Mesokurtic (*d*) None of these

53. The second moment about mean is
(*a*) $\frac{\sum(x-\bar{x})^2}{N}$ (*b*) $\frac{(x-\bar{x})^3}{N}$
(*c*) $\frac{(x-\bar{x})^2}{N}$ (*d*) None of these

54. In a negatively skewed distribution
(*a*) Mode > Median > Mean
(*b*) Median > Mode > Mean
(*c*) Mode < Median < Mean
(*d*) None of these

55. Karl Pearson's coefficient of skewness is... Bowley's coefficient of skewness for any skewed distribution.
(*a*) equal to (*b*) less than
(*c*) greater than (*d*) not related to

56. If a frequency distribution is positively skewed, the mean of the distribution is:
(*a*) greater than the mode
(*b*) less than the mode
(*c*) equal to the mode
(*d*) none of these

57. When coefficient of skewness is negative
(*a*) $Q_2 + Q_3 = 2Q_1$ (*b*) $Q_3 + Q_1 < 2Q_2$
(*c*) $Q_3 + Q_1 > 2Q_2$ (*d*) $Q_3 + Q_2 < 2Q_1$

58. The coeficient of correlation is independent of change of
(*a*) Origin (*b*) Scale
(*c*) Both (A) and (B) (*d*) None of these

59. The coefficient of correlation
(*a*) has no limits
(*b*) can be less than one
(*c*) can be more than one
(*d*) varies between ± 1

60. Probable error is
(*a*) 0.6745 S.E. (*b*) 0.6457 S.E.
(*c*) 0.6753 S.E. (*d*) 0.7645 S.E.

61. Coefficient of determination is defined as
(*a*) r^3 (*b*) $1 - r^2$
(*c*) $1 + r^2$ (*d*) r^2

62. If sum of the product of deviations of *x* and *y* series from their means, *i.e.*, Σxy is zero, the coefficient of correlation shall be
(*a*) +1 (*b*) 0
(*c*) −1 (*d*) none of these

63. Mention the correct answers.
The ranks according to two attributes in a sample are given below:

R_1	1	2	3	4	5
R_2	5	4	3	2	1

The rank correlation between them is

(a) 0 (b) +1

(c) −1 (d) None of these

64. If both the regression coefficients are negative, the correlation coefficient would be...

(a) negative (b) positive

(c) zero (d) none of these

65. The under root of two... coefficients gives us the value of correlation coefficient.

(a) regression (b) S.E

(c) S.D (d) None of these

66. Both the regression coefficients cannot be

(a) less than one (b) greater than one

(c) equal to one (d) none of these

67. The regression lines cut each other at the point of

(a) average of x and y (b) average of x only

(c) average of y only (d) none of them

68. Regression coefficient is independent of change of

(a) origin but not of scale

(b) both origin and scale

(c) scale but not of origin

(d) none of these

69. There will be only one regression line in case of two variables if

(a) $r = 0$ (b) $r = \pm 1$

(c) $r = 0.5$ (d) none of them

70. When one regression coefficient is negative the other would be

(a) negative (b) positive

(c) zero (d) none of them

71. Where r is zero the regression lines but each other making an angle of

(a) 45° (b) 60°

(c) 90° (d) none of them

72. The farther the two regression lines cut each other

(a) the greater will be the degree of correlation

(b) the lesser will be degree of correlation

(c) does not really matter

(d) none of them

73. If with a rise of 10% in prices the wages are increased by 20%, the real wage increase is by

(a) 10% (b) more than 10%

(c) less than 10% (d) 20%

74. The circular test is satisfied when

(a) $P_{12} \times P_{23} \times P_{31} = 0$ (b) $P_{12} \times P_{32} \times P_{31} = 1$

(c) $P_{12} \times P_{23} \times P_{31} = 1$ (d) $P_{12} \times P_{23} \times P_{13} = 1$

75. Time reversal test is satisfied when

(a) $P_{01} \times P_{10} = 0$ (b) $P_{01} \times P_{10} = 1$

(c) $P_{02} \times P_{10} > 1$ (d) $P_{01} \times P_{10} < 1$

76. Fisher's ideal index is

(a) arithmetic mean of Laspeyre's and Paasche's index

(b) median of Laspeyre's and Paasche's index

(c) geometric mean of Laspeyre's and Paasche's index

(d) none of these

77. Laspeyre's index is based on

(a) base year quantities

(b) current year quantities

(c) average of current and base year

(d) none of these

78. A good index number is one that satisfies

(a) Unit test

(b) Time test

(c) Time Reversal Test and Factor Reversal Test

(d) None of these

79. Theoretically the best average in the construction of index number is

(a) median (b) geometric mean

(c) mode (d) arithmetic mean

80. Hostorically the first index was constructed in...

(a) 1764 (b) 1844

(c) 1850 (d) 1744

81. ... is known as the 'ideal' formula for constructing index numbers.

(a) Fisher's Ideal Index (b) Laspeyre's Index

(c) Paasche's Index (d) None of these

82. The most important factors causing seasonal variations are

(a) growth of population

(b) technological improvements

(c) weather and social customs

(d) change in fashions

83. The most widely used method of measuring seasonal variations is

(a) Ratio-to-moving average method

(b) Ratio-to-trend method

(c) Link relative method

(d) None of these

84. Cyclical fluctuations are caused by
(a) Wars *(b)* Earth quakes
(c) Floods *(d)* None of these

85. If E(X) is the mathematical expectation of the variable X and C is constant then E(CX) = ?
(a) $E(c) + E(x)$ *(b)* $E(c) \times E(x)$
(c) $CE(x)$ *(d)* None of these

86. $E(x + y) = ?$
(a) $E(x) + E(y)$ *(b)* $E(x) \times E(y)$
(c) $E(x.y)$ *(d)* None of these

87. If A and B are mutually exclusive events, P(AB) = ?
(a) Zero *(b)* P(A) + P(B)
(c) P(A) *(d)* None of these

88. The probability that the throw of two dice yields a total of 5 or 8 is...
(a) 1/4 *(b)* 1/5
(c) 2/5 *(d)* None of these

89. In case of conditional probability (A and B) – ?
(a) P(B) × P(A/B) *(b)* P(B) × P(A)
(c) P(A) + P(B) *(d)* None of these

90. If a card is drawn from a pack of cards the probability of getting either a king or a queen is...
(a) 2/13 *(b)* 5/15
(c) 1/4 *(d)* None of these

91. If an event cannot take place, probability will be
(a) +1 *(b)* –1
(c) 0 *(d)* None of these

92. Addition theorem states that if two events A and B are mutually exclusive the probability of occurrence of either A or B is given by:
(a) P(A) + P(B) *(b)* P(A) × P(B)
(c) P(A) – P(B) *(d)* None of these

93. If two events A and B are independent, the probability that they will both occur is given by:
(a) P(A) + P(B) *(b)* P(A) × P(B)
(c) P(A) – P(B) *(d)* P(A) + P(B) – P(AB)

94. If two events A and B are dependent, the conditional probability of B given A, *i.e.*, P(A/B) is calculated as:
(a) P(AB)/P(B) *(b)* P(A) / P(B)
(c) P(AB) / P(A) *(d)* P(A) / P(AB)

95. If two events A and B are dependent, the conditinal probability of A given B, *i.e.*, P(A/B) is calculated as:
(a) P(B/A)/P(AB) *(b)* P(B)/P(A)
(c) P(AB)/P(A) *(d)* P(AB)/P(B)

96. $^5C_2$ is equal to
(a) 20 *(b)* 10
(c) 30 *(d)* 100

97. Two cards are drawn from a well-shuffled pack of 52 cards. Find the probability that they are both aces if the first is replaced.
(a) $\frac{1}{169}$ *(b)* $\frac{2}{52}$
(c) $\frac{1}{221}$ *(d)* None of these

98. The standard deviation of Binomial distribution is:
(a) $\sqrt{npq}$ *(b)* npq
(c) $n^2p^2q^2$ *(d)* np

99. The standard deviation of Poisson distribution is : (m = mean)
(a) m *(b)* $\sqrt{m}$
(c) m^2 *(d)* $1/\sqrt{m}$

100. In case of normal distribution $\overline{x} \pm 2\sigma$ covers
(a) 95.45% *(b)* 95.54%
(c) 94.45% *(d)* 99.73%

101. If in Binomial distribution mean is 10 and standard deviation 2, q will be
(a) 0 *(b)* 1
(c) 0.4 *(d)* 0.8

102. The normal distribution is an approximation to...
(a) Binomial distribution
(b) Poisson distribution
(c) Both *(a)* and *(b)*
(d) None of these

103. In a normal distribution the points of inflexion occur at...
(a) $\overline{X} + \sigma$ *(b)* $\overline{X} + 2\sigma$
(c) $\overline{X} + 3\sigma$ *(d)* None of these

104. The normal distribution with $x = 0$ and $\sigma = 1$ is known as.....
(a) Standard normal distribution

(b) Poisson distribution
(c) Both (a) and (b)
(d) None of these

105. The mean plus and minus 1.96 standard deviation includes... per cent of the items of normal distribution.
(a) 75 (b) 47.5
(c) 74.5 (d) None of these

106. ..... asserts that there is no true difference in the sample and the population in the particular matter under consideration
(a) Null hypothesis (b) Alternate hypothesis
(c) Both (a) and (b) (d) None of these

107. ..... error is committed when the hypothesis is true but out test rejects it.
(a) Type I (b) Type II
(c) Both (a) and (b) (d) None of these

108. ..... errors are made when we accept a null hypothesis which is not true.
(a) Type I (b) Type II
(c) Both (a) and (b) (d) None of these

109. The standard deviation of sampling distribution is called...
(a) Standard error (b) Probable error
(c) Both (a) and (b) (d) None of these

110. Standard error of number of successes is given by:
(a) $\sqrt{\frac{pq}{n}}$ (b) $\sqrt{npq}$
(c) npq (d) n^2p^2

111. Large sample theory is applicable when:
(a) N is > 30 (b) N is < 30
(c) N = 30 (d) None of these

112. Student's '*t*' Distribution was discovered by:
(a) Karl Pearson (b) Laplace
(c) Fisher (d) Gosset

113. The difference of two means in case of small samples is tested by the formula:
(a) $t = \frac{\bar{x}_1 - \bar{x}_2}{s}$ (b) $t = \frac{\bar{x}_1 - \bar{x}_2}{s}\sqrt{\frac{n_1 + n_2}{n_1 - n_2}}$
(c) $t = \frac{\bar{x}_1 - \bar{x}_2}{s}\sqrt{\frac{n_1 n_2}{n_1 + n_2}}$ (d) None of these

114. While testing the significance of the difference of two sample means in case of small samples, the degrees of freedom is calculated by:
(a) $\nu = n_1 + n_2 - 2$ (b) $\nu = n_1 + n_2 - 1$
(c) $\nu = n_1 - n_2 - 2$ (d) $\nu = n_1 - n_2 + 2$

115. Which one of the following average can be computed from a cumulative frequency curve?
(a) Geometric Mean (b) Harmonic Mean
(c) Mode (d) Median

116. If the standard deviation of a variable x is s and if $y = a + bs$, where a and b are constants, the standard deviation of y would be
(a) $a + bs$ (b) bs
(c) $\sqrt{b}.s$ (d) b^2s

117. Which one of the following statistical measures is based on all observations?
(a) Quartile Deviation
(b) Harmonic Mean
(c) Range
(d) Mode

118. Consider the following measures:
1. Correlation coefficient
2. Covariance
3. Coefficient of variation
4. Index number

Which of these are unit-free?
(a) 1 and 2 (b) 1 and 3
(c) 2 and 4 (d) 1, 3 and 4

119. If r is the correlation coefficients between the two variables, then
(a) $0 \le r \le 1$ (b) $-1 \le r \le 0$
(c) $-1 \le r \le 1$ (d) $1 \le r \le 2$

120. If all values of a variable are multiplied by a given number, which one of the following will NOT be affected?
(a) Mean
(b) Median
(c) Range
(d) Coefficient of variation

121. Dispersions are NOT calculated about
(a) Mean (b) Median
(c) Mode (d) Geometric Mean

122. The price index that uses base year quantities as weights is called
(a) Passche's index
(b) Laspeyere's index

(c) Fisher's ideal index

(d) Wholesale price index

123. Assertion (A): Variance is always greater than the standard deviation.

Reason (R): Variance is the square of the standard deviation.

(a) Both A and R are individually true and R is the correct explanation of A

(b) Both A and R are individually true but R is not the correct explanation of A

(c) A is true but R is false

(d) A is false but R is true

124. Formula of linear correlation coefficient (r_{yx}) is:

(a) $r_{yx} = \dfrac{b_{yx} + b_{xy}}{2}$

(b) $r_{yx} = \sqrt{b_{yx} . b_{xy}}$

(c) $r_{yx} = \dfrac{2}{\left(\dfrac{1}{b_{yx}} + \dfrac{1}{b_{xy}}\right)}$

(d) $r_{yx} = \dfrac{W_1 . b_{yx} + W_2 . b_{yx}}{W_1 + W_2}$

ANSWERS

1	2	3	4	5	6	7	8	9	10
(c)	(d)	(c)	(b)	(a)	(c)	(a)	(a)	(b)	(a)
11	12	13	14	15	16	17	18	19	20
(b)	(a)	(c)	(d)	(d)	(c)	(c)	(c)	(c)	(a)
21	22	23	24	25	26	27	28	29	30
(c)	(c)	(a)	(a)	(c)	(c)	(c)	(b)	(c)	(a)
31	32	33	34	35	36	37	38	39	40
(d)	(a)	(c)	(b)	(c)	(c)	(b)	(a)	(b)	(a)
41	42	43	44	45	46	47	48	49	50
(b)	(b)	(c)	(b)	(a)	(c)	(d)	(c)	(b)	(b)
51	52	53	54	55	56	57	58	59	60
(c)	(b)	(a)	(a)	(d)	(a)	(a)	(c)	(d)	(a)
61	62	63	64	65	66	67	68	69	70
(d)	(b)	(c)	(a)	(a)	(b)	(a)	(a)	(b)	(a)
71	72	73	74	75	76	77	78	79	80
(d)	(b)	(c)	(c)	(b)	(c)	(a)	(c)	(b)	(a)
81	82	83	84	85	86	87	88	89	90
(a)	(c)	(a)	(d)	(c)	(a)	(a)	(a)	(a)	(a)
91	92	93	94	95	96	97	98	99	100
(c)	(a)	(b)	(c)	(d)	(b)	(a)	(a)	(b)	(a)
101	102	103	104	105	106	107	108	109	110
(c)	(a)	(a)	(a)	(b)	(a)	(a)	(b)	(a)	(b)
111	112	113	114	115	116	117	118	119	120
(a)	(d)	(c)	(a)	(d)	(b)	(b)	(d)	(c)	(d)
121	122	123	124						
(d)	(b)	(a)	(b)						

UNIT-VI : MATHEMATICAL ECONOMICS

INPUT-OUTPUT ANALYSIS

Input-output is a novel technique invented by **Profession Wassily W. Leontief** in 1951. It is used to analyse inter-industry relationship in order to understand the inter-dependencies and complexities of the economy and thus the conditions for maintaining equilibrium between supply and demand. It is also known as "inter-industry analysis".

The input-output analysis tells us that there are industrial interrelationships and inter-dependencies in the economic system as a whole. The inputs of one industry are the outputs of another industry and vice versa, so that ultimately their mutual relationships lead to equilibrium between supply and demand in the economy as a whole. Coal is an input for steel industry and steel is an input for coal industry, though both are the outputs of their respective industries. A major part of economic activity consists in producing intermediate goods (inputs) for further use in producing final goods (outputs). There are flows of goods in "whirpools and cross currents" between different industies. The supply side consists of large inter-industry flows of intermediate products and the demand side of the final goods. In essence, the input-output analysis implies that in equilibrium, the money value of aggregate output of the whole economy must equal the sum of the money values of inter-industry inputs and the sum of the money values of inter-industry outputs.

Main Features

The input-output analysis is the finest variant of general equilibrium. As such, it has three main elements. **Firstly**, the input-output analysis concentrates on an economy which is in equilibrium. It is not applicable to partial equilibrium analysis. Secondly, it does not concern itself with the demand analysis. It deals exclusively with technical problems of production. Lastly, it is based on empirical investigation.

Assumptions

This analysis is based on the following assumptions:

1. The whole economy is divided into two sectors— "inter-industry sectors" and "final-demand sectors," both being capable of sub-sectoral division.

2. The total ouput of any inter-industry sector is generally capable of being used as inputs by other inter-industry sectors, by itself and by final demand sectors.

3. No two products are produced jointly. Each industry produces only one homogenous product.

4. Prices, consumer demands and factor supplies are given.

5. There are constant returns to scale.

6. There are no external economies and diseconomies of production.

7. The combinations of inputs are employed in rigidly fixed proportions. The inputs remain in constant proportion to the level of output. It implies that there is no substitution between different materials and no technological progress. There are fixed input coefficients of production.

Importance

The concept of input-output is of tremendous practical value and importance.

1. A producer can know from the input-output table, the varieties and quantities of goods which he and the other firms buy and sell to each other. In this way he can make the necessary adjustments and thus improve his position vis-a-vis other producers.

2. It is also possible to find out from the input-output table the interrelations among firms and industries about possible trends towards combinations.

3. The repercussions of a prolonged strike, of a war and of a business cycle can be easily perceived from the input-output table.

4. The input-output model has come to be used for national income accounting "because it provides a more detailed breakdown of the macro aggregates and money flows."

Input-Output Table

The input-output table relates to the economy as a whole in a particular year. It shows the values of the flows of goods and services between different productive sectors especially inter-industry flows.

Let us assume that an economy consists of 4 producing sectors only; and that the production of each sector is being used as an input in all the sectors and is used for final consumption.

Suppose *(i)* x_1, x_2, x_3 and x_4 are total outputs of the 4 sectors;

(ii) F_1, F_2, F_3 and F_4 are the amounts of final demand consumption capital formation and exports for output of these sectors.

(iii) X_{11}, X_{12}, X_{13} and X_{14} are the amounts of product of sector 1st used as an input in 1st, 2nd, 3rd and 4th sectors respectively.

We can now translate the distribution of total product of 4 producing sectors in the following way:

Input-Output Transaction Table

Producing sector No.	*Total output of the sector*	*Input requirements of producing sectors*				*Requirement of for final uses*
		X_1	X_2	X_3	X_4	
1	2	3	4	5	6	7
1	X_1	X_{11}	X_{12}	X_{13}	X_{14}	F_1
2	X_2	X_{21}	X_{22}	X_{23}	X_{24}	F_2
3	X_3	X_{31}	X_{32}	X_{33}	X_{34}	F_3
4	X_4	X_{41}	X_{42}	X_{43}	X_{44}	F_4
Primary Input (Labour)	Total Primary Input = L	L_1	L_2	L_3	L_4	–

We derive two important equations from the above table:

1. Columns 3, 4, 5 and 6 of the above table give us total inputs (from all sectors) utilised by each sector for its production. In other words col. 3 gives the production function of sector 1 and col. 6 represents the production function of sector 4.

$$X_1 = f_1(X_{11}, X_{21}, X_{31}, X_{41}, L_1)$$
$$X_2 = f_2(X_{12}, X_{22}, X_{32}, X_{42}, L_2)$$
$$X_3 = f_3(X_{13}, X_{23}, X_{33}, X_{43}, L_3)$$
$$X_4 = f_4(X_{14}, X_{24}, X_{34}, X_{44}, L_4)$$

In general terms, if there are '*n*' number of producing sectors then the production function of sector *n* will be represented by

$$X_n = f_n(X_{1n}, X_{2n}, X_{3n}, \ldots\ldots ; X_{4n})$$

2. Rows of the table give us the equality between the demand and supply of each product:

$$X_1 = X_{11} + X_{12} + X_{13} + X_{14} + F_1$$
$$X_2 = X_{21} + X_{22} + X_{23} + X_{24} + F_2$$
$$X_3 = X_{31} + X_{32} + X_{33} + X_{34} + F_3$$
$$X_4 = X_{41} + X_{42} + X_{43} + X_{44} + F_4$$
$$L = L_1 + L_2 + L_3 + L_4$$

In general terms, if there are *x* producing sectors:

$$\begin{bmatrix} X_1 = X_{11} + X_{12} + X_{13} \ldots\ldots X_{1n} + F_1 \\ X_2 = X_{21} + X_{22} + X_{23} \ldots\ldots X_{2n} + F_2 \\ \ldots\ldots\ldots\ldots\ldots\ldots\ldots\ldots \\ \ldots\ldots\ldots\ldots\ldots\ldots\ldots\ldots \\ \ldots\ldots\ldots\ldots\ldots\ldots\ldots\ldots \\ X_n = X_{n1} + X_{n2} + X_{n3} \ldots\ldots X_{nn} + F_n \end{bmatrix}$$

and $L = L_1 + L_2 + L_3 + \ldots\ldots L_n$

or $$X_i = \sum_{J=1}^{n} X_{iJ} + F_i$$

and $$L = \sum_{i=1}^{n} L_i$$

where X_i = Total output of ith sector

X_{iJ} = Output of ith sector used as input in Jth sector

and F_i = Final demand for ith sector.

The above identity states that all the output of a particular sector could be utilised either as an input in one of the producing sectors of the economy and/or as a final demand. Basically, therefore, input-output analysis is nothing more than finding the solution of these simultaneous equations.

The Technological Coefficient Matrix

From the assumption of fixed input requirements we see that in order to produce one unit of Jth commodity, the input used of ith commodity must be a fixed amount, which we denote by a_{iJ}, thus $a_{iJ} = x_{iJ}/x_J$. If x_J represents the total output of the Jth commodity (or Jth producing sector) in the input requirement of ith commodity will be equal to $a_{iJ}X_J$ or $X_{iJ} = a_{iJ}X_J$.

As such we can now put the input-output transaction table in terms of technical coefficients as follows:

Purch-asing sector	*Total output of the sector*	*Input requirements of producing sectors* *Purchases* ↓ X_1	X_2	X_3	X_4	*Require-ments for final con-sumption*
Sales →						
1	X_1	$a_{11}X_1$	$a_{12}X_2$	$a_{13}X_3$	$a_{14}X_4$	F_1
2	X_2	$a_{21}X_1$	$a_{22}X_2$	$a_{23}X_3$	$a_{24}X_4$	F_2
3	X_3	$a_{31}X_1$	$a_{32}X_2$	$a_{33}X_3$	$a_{34}X_4$	F_3
4	X_4	$a_{41}X_1$	$a_{42}X_2$	$a_{43}X_3$	$a_{44}X_4$	F_4
Primary input	L	l_1X_1	l_2X_2	l_3X_3	l_4X_4	

It should be noted that all these coefficients are non-negative (≥0).

The above table gives us the total output of each sector in terms of technical coefficients; and if these are '*n*' producing sectors:

$$X_1 = a_{11}X_1 + a_{12}X_2 + a_{13}X_3, \ldots\ldots, a_{1n}X_n + F_1$$
$$X_2 = a_{21}X_1 + a_{12}X_2 + a_{23}X_3, \ldots\ldots, a_{2n}X_n + F_2$$

....

....

$$X_n = a_{n1}X_1 + a_{n2}X_2 + a_{n3}X_3, \ldots\ldots, a_{nn}X_n + F_n$$
$$L = l_1X_1 + l_2X_2 + l_3X_3 + l_4X_4$$

or $$X_i = \sum_{J=1}^{n} a_{iJ}X_J + F_J \quad (i = 1, 2, \ldots..n)$$

and $$L = \sum l_iX_i$$

The equations may be put in matrix notations:

$$\begin{pmatrix} X_1 \\ X_2 \\ .. \\ .. \\ X_n \end{pmatrix} = \begin{pmatrix} a_{11}\ a_{12}\ a_{13} \ldots\ldots a_{1n} \\ a_{21}\ a_{22}\ a_{23} \ldots\ldots a_{2n} \\ \ldots\ldots\ldots\ldots\ldots\ldots \\ \ldots\ldots\ldots\ldots\ldots\ldots \\ a_{n1}\ a_{n2}\ a_{n3} \ldots\ldots a_{nn} \end{pmatrix} \begin{pmatrix} X_1 \\ X_2 \\ .. \\ .. \\ X_n \end{pmatrix} + \begin{pmatrix} F_1 \\ F_2 \\ .. \\ .. \\ F_n \end{pmatrix}$$

or $$X = AX + F$$

and $$L = \sum l_iX_i$$

Closed and Open Input-Output Model

In the above example besider *n* industries, our model contains exogenous sector of final demand which supplies primary imput factors (labour services-which are not produced by *n* industries) and consumes the output of the *n*-producing industries (not as input). Such an input-output model is known as open model. It includes, exogenous sectors in terms of "final demand bill" -along with the endogenous sectors in terms of *n*-producing sectors. Input-output model which has endogenous final demand vector is known as closed input-output model.

Coefficient Matrix in Value Terms

Again if we assume prices of all the outputs to be given, the $_i$th elements of $[a_{iJ}]$ matrix will represent the amount of *i*th commodity in money terms for "a rupee worth" of *J*th commodity. For example, it a_{iJ} = 0.35, it means that 35 paise worth of *i*th commodity is required as an input for producing a rupee worth of *J*th commodity.

Also, in view of the presence of exogenous sector (which supplies primary inputs) the sum of the elements of each input coefficient column $[a_{iJ}]$ must be less than 1. Each column-sum represents the partial input cost (excluding the cost of primary input) incurred in producing a rupee worth of some commodity; If this sum is greater than or equal to one rupee, the production will not be economically justifiable. Symbolically this fact may be stated as:

$$\sum_{i=1}^{n} a_{iJ} < 1 \; (J = 1, 2, \ldots\ldots, n)$$

i.e., either zero or greater than zero. The cost of the primary inputs (which is also termed as value added) needed in producing a unit of *J*th commodity should be

$$\left[1 \sum_{i=1}^{n} a_{iJ} \right]$$

Note here that a_{iJ} are in value terms.

A Numerical Example

Suppose there are only three industries in an

economy and we have to estimate the output of each industry with the given input coefficient matrix and final demand as follows (the coefficient matrix is in value terms):

$$A = \begin{array}{c} \begin{matrix} P & Q & R \end{matrix} \\ \begin{bmatrix} 0.3 & 0.4 & 0.2 \\ 0.2 & 0 & 0.5 \\ 0.1 & 0.3 & 0.1 \end{bmatrix} \end{array}$$

and $$F = \begin{bmatrix} 100 \\ 40 \\ 50 \end{bmatrix} \text{ million rupees.}$$

Here we note that 3-column sums of A are (0.3 + 0.2 + 0.1) = 0.6, (0.4 + 0 + 0.3) = 0.7, and (0.2 + 0.5 + 0.1) = 0.8; which are less than 1 in each case. In other words, (1 – 0.6) = 0.4, (1 – 0.7) = 0.3 and (1 – 0.8) = 0.2 is the maximum amount of primary input which can be used for producing "a rupee worth" of the three commodities (P.Q and R) respectively.

$$\text{Since } A = \begin{bmatrix} 0.3 & 0.4 & 0.2 \\ 0.2 & 0 & 0.5 \\ 0.1 & 0.3 & 0.1 \end{bmatrix}$$

$$\text{and } [I - A] = \begin{bmatrix} +0.7 & -0.4 & -0.2 \\ -0.2 & +1 & -0.5 \\ -0.1 & -0.3 & +0.9 \end{bmatrix}$$

substituting these values in $X = [I - A]^{-1} F$, we get

$$X = \begin{bmatrix} X_1 \\ X_2 \\ X_3 \end{bmatrix} = \begin{bmatrix} 0.7 & -0.4 & -0.2 \\ -0.2 & 1 & -0.5 \\ -0.1 & -0.3 & 0.9 \end{bmatrix}^{-1} \begin{bmatrix} 100 \\ 40 \\ 50 \end{bmatrix}$$

But

$$\begin{bmatrix} 0.7 & -0.4 & -0.2 \\ -0.2 & 1 & -0.5 \\ -0.1 & -0.3 & 0.9 \end{bmatrix}^{-1} = \frac{1}{0.401} \begin{bmatrix} 0.75 & 0.42 & 0.40 \\ 0.23 & 0.61 & 0.39 \\ 0.16 & 2.25 & 0.62 \end{bmatrix}$$

$$\therefore X = \begin{bmatrix} X_1 \\ X_2 \\ X_3 \end{bmatrix} = \frac{1}{0.401} \begin{bmatrix} 0.75 & 0.42 & 0.40 \\ 0.23 & 0.61 & 0.39 \\ 0.16 & 0.25 & 0.62 \end{bmatrix} \begin{bmatrix} 100 \\ 40 \\ 50 \end{bmatrix}$$

$$\therefore X_1 = \frac{1}{0.401} \{0.75 (100) + 0.42 (40) + 0.40 (50)\}$$

$$= \text{Rs. 279 million (approx.)}$$

$$X_2 = \frac{1}{0.401} \{0.23 (100) + 0.61 (40) + 0.39 (50)\}$$

$$= \text{Rs. 167 million (approx)}$$

$$X_3 = \frac{1}{0.401} \{0.16 (100) + 0.25 (40) + 0.62 (50)\}$$

$$= \text{Rs. 142 million (approx.)}$$

The Hawkins-Simon Conditions

Many a time input-output matrix solution may give outputs expressed by negative numbers. If out solution gives negative outputs, it means that more than one tonne (or any unit) of that product is used up in the production of every one tonne of that product; which is definitely unrealistic situation. Such a system is not a viable system. **Hawkins-Simon conditions** guard against such eventualities.

Our basic equation is $X = [I - A]^{-1} F$, in order that this does not give negative numbers as a solution, the matrix [I – A], which in fact is:

$$\begin{pmatrix} 1 - a_{11} & -a_{12} & -a_{13} & \dots & -a_{1n} \\ -a_{21} & (1 - a_{22}) & -a_{23} & \dots & -a_{2n} \\ -a_{31} & -a_{32} & (1 - a_{33}) & \dots & -a_{3n} \\ -a_{n1} & -a_{n2} & -a_{n3} & \dots & (1 - a_{nn}) \end{pmatrix}$$

Should be such that:

1. the determinant of the matrix must always be positive, and

2. the diagonal elements : $(1 - a_{11})$, $(1 - a_{22})$, $(1 - a_{33})$, ... $(1 - a_{nn})$ should all be positive or in other words elements: a_{11}, a_{22}, a_{33} ..... a_{nn} should all be less than one. One unit of output of any sector should use not more than 1 unit of its own output.

These are Hawkins-Simon conditions.

Example

$$\text{Suppose } [A] = \begin{bmatrix} 0.8 & 0.2 \\ 0.9 & 0.7 \end{bmatrix}$$

$$\therefore \quad [I - A] = \begin{bmatrix} 0.2 & -0.2 \\ -0.9 & 0.3 \end{bmatrix}$$

and the values of determinant of [I – A] will be

0.06 – 0.18 = –0.12 which is less than zero.

As such Hawkins-Simon conditions are not satisfied. No solution will be possible in this case.

Example: Given the following transaction matrix, find the gross output so meet the final demand of 200 units of Agriculture and 800 units of Industry:

Producing sectors	*Purchasing sector Agriculture*	*Industry*	*Final demand*
Agriculture	300	600	100
Industry	400	1200	400

Ans. The Input-output table can be re-written as

	Agri	*Ind.*	*Final demand*	*Gross Output*
Agri.	300	600	100	1000
Ind.	400	1200	400	2000

From this table the input coefficients can be easily determined.

The input coefficient, for agriculture are $\frac{300}{1000}$ = 0.3 and $\frac{400}{1000}$ = 0.4 the input coefficients of industry are $\frac{600}{2000}$ = 0.3 and $\frac{1200}{2000}$ = 0.6

The technology matrix then is

$$A = \begin{bmatrix} 0.3 & 0.3 \\ 0.4 & 0.6 \end{bmatrix}$$

The Final Demand vector is $F = \begin{bmatrix} 200 \\ 800 \end{bmatrix}$

$$\text{Now} \quad [I-A] = \begin{bmatrix} 0.7 & -0.3 \\ -0.4 & 0.4 \end{bmatrix}$$

$$[I-A]^{-1} = \frac{1}{0.28-0.12}\begin{bmatrix} 0.4 & 0.3 \\ 0.4 & 0.7 \end{bmatrix}$$

$$= \frac{1}{0.16}\begin{bmatrix} 0.4 & 0.3 \\ 0.4 & 0.7 \end{bmatrix}$$

We know that

$$X = [I-A]^{-1} F$$

$$= \frac{1}{0.16}\begin{bmatrix} 0.4 & 0.3 \\ 0.4 & 0.7 \end{bmatrix}\begin{bmatrix} 200 \\ 800 \end{bmatrix}$$

$$= \frac{1}{0.16}\begin{bmatrix} 80 + 240 \\ 80 + 560 \end{bmatrix}$$

$$= \frac{1}{0.16}\begin{bmatrix} 320 \\ 640 \end{bmatrix}$$

$$\therefore \quad X = \begin{bmatrix} 2000 \\ 4000 \end{bmatrix}$$

Hence the output in the agricultural sector is 2000 units and that in the industry is 4000 units.

Example. In an economy of three industries R,S,T, the data given below (in millions) are available

Producers	*Users R*	*S*	*T*	*Final demand*	*output*
R	80	100	100	40	320
S	80	200	60	60	400
T	80	100	100	20	300

Determine the output if the final demand changes to 60 for R, 40 for S and 60 for T.

Ans. From the data the input coefficients of R are

$$\frac{80}{320}, \frac{80}{320}, \frac{80}{320} \text{ or } \frac{1}{4}, \frac{1}{4}, \frac{1}{4}$$

the input coefficients of S are

$$\frac{100}{400}, \frac{200}{400}, \frac{100}{400} \text{ or } \frac{1}{4}, \frac{1}{2}, \frac{1}{4}$$

the input coefficients of T are

$$\frac{100}{300}, \frac{60}{300}, \frac{100}{300} \text{ or } \frac{1}{3}, \frac{1}{5}, \frac{1}{3}$$

∴ Technology matrix is

$$A = \begin{vmatrix} \frac{1}{4} & \frac{1}{4} & \frac{1}{3} \\ \frac{1}{4} & \frac{1}{2} & \frac{1}{5} \\ \frac{1}{4} & \frac{1}{4} & \frac{1}{3} \end{vmatrix}$$

$$\text{and} \quad X = \begin{bmatrix} X_1 \\ X_2 \\ X_3 \end{bmatrix}, F = \begin{bmatrix} 60 \\ 40 \\ 60 \end{bmatrix}$$

$$\because \quad X = AX + F$$

$$\text{or} \quad (I-A)X = F$$

$$\therefore \quad X = (I-A)^{-1} F, \text{ if } |I-A| \neq 0$$

$$\text{Now}\quad [I-A] = \begin{bmatrix} \frac{3}{4} & -\frac{1}{4} & -\frac{1}{3} \\ -\frac{1}{4} & \frac{1}{2} & -\frac{1}{5} \\ -\frac{1}{4} & -\frac{1}{4} & \frac{2}{3} \end{bmatrix}$$

$$\therefore\quad |I-A| = \frac{23}{240}$$

$$\therefore\quad (I-A)^{-1} = \frac{240}{23}\begin{bmatrix} \frac{17}{60} & \frac{1}{4} & \frac{13}{60} \\ \frac{13}{60} & \frac{5}{12} & \frac{14}{60} \\ \frac{3}{16} & \frac{1}{4} & \frac{5}{16} \end{bmatrix}$$

$$\therefore\quad \begin{bmatrix} X_1 \\ X_2 \\ X_3 \end{bmatrix} = \frac{240}{23}\begin{bmatrix} \frac{17}{60} & \frac{1}{4} & \frac{13}{60} \\ \frac{13}{60} & \frac{5}{12} & \frac{14}{60} \\ \frac{3}{16} & \frac{1}{4} & \frac{5}{16} \end{bmatrix}\begin{bmatrix} 60 \\ 40 \\ 60 \end{bmatrix}$$

$$= \frac{240}{23}\begin{bmatrix} 17+10+13 \\ 13+\frac{50}{3}+14 \\ \frac{45}{4}+10+\frac{75}{4} \end{bmatrix}$$

$$= \frac{240}{23}\begin{bmatrix} 40 \\ \frac{131}{3} \\ 40 \end{bmatrix}$$

$$\therefore\quad X_1 = \frac{240}{23}\times 40 = 417.39$$

$$X_2 = \frac{240}{23}\times\frac{131}{3}$$

$$= 455.65$$

$$X_3 = \frac{240}{23}\times 40$$

$$= 417.39$$

Example : You are given the following transactions matrix for a two section economy.

Producing sectors	*Purchasing sector 1*	*2*	*Final Demand*	*Gross output*
1	4	3	13	20
2	5	4	3	12
Primary Inputs	11	5		

1. Write the technoloty matrix.

2. Re write the new transactions matrix when the final demand for the output of sector 1 increases to 23 units.

Ans. From the question we get the transaction Matrix to be

$$[X_{12}] = \begin{bmatrix} 4 & 3 \\ 5 & 4 \end{bmatrix}$$

The technology Matrix can be derived from above given the gross output of each sector.

$$A = [a_{ij}] = \frac{[X_{iJ}]}{X_J} = \begin{bmatrix} \frac{4}{20} & \frac{3}{12} \\ \frac{5}{20} & \frac{4}{12} \end{bmatrix}$$

$$= \begin{bmatrix} 0.2 & 0.25 \\ 0.25 & 0.33 \end{bmatrix}$$

$$\text{Now } [I-A] = \begin{bmatrix} 0.8 & -0.25 \\ -0.25 & 0.66 \end{bmatrix}$$

$$\therefore\quad [I-A]^{-1} = \frac{1}{0.528-0.0625}\begin{bmatrix} 0.66 & 0.25 \\ 0.25 & 0.8 \end{bmatrix}$$

$$= \frac{1}{0.4655}\begin{bmatrix} 0.66 & 0.25 \\ 0.25 & 0.8 \end{bmatrix}$$

$$\because\quad X = [I-A]^{-1}F$$

$$= \frac{1}{0.4655}\begin{bmatrix} 0.66 & 0.25 \\ 0.25 & 0.8 \end{bmatrix}\begin{bmatrix} 23 \\ 3 \end{bmatrix}$$

$$X = \frac{1}{0.4655}\begin{bmatrix} 15.18+0.75 \\ 5.7+2.4 \end{bmatrix}$$

$$X = \frac{1}{0.4655}\begin{bmatrix} 15.93 \\ 8.10 \end{bmatrix}$$

$$X = \begin{bmatrix} 34.22 \\ 17.4 \end{bmatrix}$$

The new transaction matrix is

$$[X_{iJ}] = [Q_{iJ}][X_J] = \begin{bmatrix} 6.844 & 4.35 \\ 8.555 & 5.742 \end{bmatrix}$$

Example : The following is a transaction matrix for a two sector economy.

$$\begin{array}{c} \\ A \\ B \end{array}\begin{array}{c} \begin{array}{cc} A & B \end{array} \\ \begin{bmatrix} 30 & 40 \\ 20 & 10 \end{bmatrix} \end{array} \quad \begin{array}{c} \text{Final demand} \\ 60 \\ 40 \end{array}$$

obtain the technology matrix for the economy. Calculate the total ouput for a final demand of 80 units of A and 40 units of B.

Ans. The transaction matrix can be re-writen as

	A	B	Final demand	Gross output
A	30	40	60	130
B	20	10	40	70

From this table the input coefficients can be determined

The input-coefficient for sector A are

$$\frac{30}{130} = \frac{3}{13} \text{ and } \frac{20}{130} = \frac{2}{13}$$

while the input-coefficient for sector B are

$$\frac{40}{70} = \frac{4}{7}, \text{ and } \frac{10}{70} = \frac{1}{7}$$

∴ The technology matrix is

$$A = \begin{bmatrix} \frac{3}{13} & \frac{4}{7} \\ \frac{2}{13} & \frac{1}{7} \end{bmatrix}$$

$$\text{Now } [I-A] = \begin{bmatrix} \frac{10}{13} & -\frac{4}{7} \\ -\frac{2}{13} & \frac{6}{7} \end{bmatrix}$$

$$= \begin{bmatrix} 0.77 & -0.57 \\ -0.15 & 0.86 \end{bmatrix}$$

$$\therefore \quad [I-A]^{-1} = \frac{1}{0.6622 - 0.0855}\begin{bmatrix} 0.86 & 0.57 \\ 0.15 & 0.77 \end{bmatrix}$$

$$= \frac{1}{0.5767}\begin{bmatrix} 0.86 & 0.57 \\ 0.15 & 0.77 \end{bmatrix}$$

We know that

$$\therefore \quad X = [I-A]^{-1} F$$

The new final demand vector is

$$F = \begin{bmatrix} 80 \\ 40 \end{bmatrix}$$

$$\therefore \quad X = \frac{1}{0.5767}\begin{bmatrix} 0.86 & 0.57 \\ 0.15 & 0.77 \end{bmatrix}\begin{bmatrix} 80 \\ 40 \end{bmatrix}$$

$$X = \frac{1}{0.5767}\begin{bmatrix} 68.8 + 22.8 \\ 12 + 30.8 \end{bmatrix}$$

$$X = \frac{1}{0.5767}\begin{bmatrix} 91.6 \\ 42.8 \end{bmatrix}$$

$$X = \begin{bmatrix} 158.8 \\ 74.22 \end{bmatrix}$$

The new total output will be 158.8 units for sector A and 74.22 units for sector B.

LINEAR PROGRAMMING

Linear Programming is a mathematical device developed by the mathematician **George Dantzing** is 1947 for planning the deversified activities of the U.S. Air Force connected with the problem of supplies to the forces. Linear or mathematical programming also known as activity analysis, has been further developed in its application to the economic theory of the firm, managerial economics, interregional trade, general equilibrium analysis, welfare economics and to development planning.

Meaning

It is mathematical technique for the analysis of optimum decisions subject to certain constraints in the form of linear in equalities. Mathematically speaking, it applies to those problems which require the solution of maximization or minimization problems subject to a system of linear inequalities stated in terms of certain variables. If x and y, the two variables, are the function of z, the value of z is maximized when any movement from that point results in a decreased value of z. The value of z is minimized when even a small movement results in an increased value of z. When cost and price per unit change with the size of output, the problem is not linear and if they do not change with output, the problem is linear. Linear programming may thus be defined as a method to decide the optimum combination of factors to produce a given output or the optimum combination of products to be produced by given plant and equipment.

Assumptions

The linear programming analysis of the firm is based upon the following assumptions.

1. The decision-making body is faced with certain constraints or resource restrictions. They may be credit, raw material and space constraints on its activities. Type of constraints infact depend upon the nature of problem. Mostly they are fixed factors in the production process.

2. It assumes a limited number of alternative production processes.

3. It assumes linear relations among the different variables which implies constant proportionality between inputs and output within a process.

4. Input-output prices and co-efficients are given and constant. They are known with certainty.

5. The assumption of additivity also under lies linear programming techniques which means that the total resources used by all firms must equal the sum of resources used by each individual firm.

6. Linear programming techniques further assume continuity and divisibility in products and factors.

7. Institutional factors are also assumed to be constant.

Lastly, for programming a certain period is assumed. For convenience and more accurate results, the period is generally short, though longer periods are not ruled out.

Mathematical Note : Graphic Solutions

We attempt below a complete description and working of some problems of linear programming mathematically and graphically.

Maximisation of Revenue

Take a firm that produces two products x and y at given prices of Rs. 12 and Rs. 15 respectively for each unit. To produce product x, the form requires 12 units of input A, 6 units of input B and 14 units of input C. Product y requires 4 units of input A, 12 units of B, and 12 units of input C. Total available inputs in each case are 48 units of A, 72 units of B and 84 units of C. The input-output data for this problem is presented in following Table.

Table : INPUT-OUTPUT DATA

	Amount of Inputs Required to Produce One Unit of Output		*Total Inputs Available in Each Case*
Input	*x-Units*	*y-Units*	*Units*
A	12	4	48
B	6	12	72
C	14	12	84
Net Revenue Per Unit of Product	Rs. 12	Rs. 15	–

Every linear programming problem has three parts to start with. They are as follows in terms of our problem stated above.

The Objective Function. The objective function states that if the two products x and y bring the revenue of Rs. 12 and Rs. 15 per unit, how much of these products be produced so that the firm earns the maximum revenue. It can be written as:

Max : $f = 12x + 15y$

The constraints. The above table can now be transformed in the form of equations signifying the constraints or restraints within which the firm operates. These are known as *structural constraints*.

First, we take input A. The maximum available quantity of input A is 48 units. But the amounts of two products (x and y) cannot be greater than 48 units. Mathematically, since $12x + 4y$ cannot be greater than 48 units, the constraints imposed by input A would be $12x + 4y \leq 48$. With the same reasoning we can have the constraints in terms of inequalities for inputs B and C. Thus the three structural constraints in our problem can be written as:

$12x + 4y \leq 48$ ...1

$6x + 12y \leq 72$ ...2

$14x + 12y \leq 84$ ...3

The Non-Negativity Constraints. Then there are the non-negativity constraints in the linear programming problem which assume that there can be no negative values of variables in the solution of the problem. This means that the output of x and y products can be zero or positive, but it cannot be negative. Thus the non-negative constraints of our problem are $x \geq 0$ and $y \geq 0$.

The Graphic Solution

For the graphic solution, we restate our problem:

Maximise $\quad f = 12x + 15y$

Subject to (*i*) $\quad 12x + 4y \leq 48$

$6x + 12y \leq 72$

$14x + 12y \leq 84$

(*ii*) $\quad x \geq 0$ and $y \geq 0$

To represent each inequality graphically we ignore the inequality sign ($\leq$) in our equations and replace it by the equality sign. We write EQuation (1) as $12x + 4y = 48$.

By assuming that the product x is produced only by utilising the entire amount of 48 units of input A, we obtain

$12x + 0 = 48$ (at the maximum)

or $x = 4$ (when $y = 0$)

Similarly, assuming that the product y is produced by utilising the entire amount of 48 units of input A, we have

$0 + 4y = 48$

or $y = 12$ (when $x = 0$)

The equation $12x + 4y = 48$ is represented in figure A by the line AB where OA = $12y$ and OB = $4x$. Any point on AB such as T satisfies the equation $12x + 4y = 48$, while the area below and to the left of the line AB satisfies the inequailty $12x + 4y \leq 48$.

By solving the equation $6x + 12y = 72$ in a similar way, we obtain $x = 12$, and $y = 6$. This is plotted in figure A as the line CD which satisfies this equation where OC = $6y$ and OD = $12x$.

And by solving the equation $14x + 12y = 84$, we obtain $x = 6$, and $y = 7$. Line EF in figure A satisfies this equation when OE = $7y$ and OF = $6x$.

Figrue A shows that all the points in the shaded area bounded by the three lines intersecting each other would satisfy the three inequalities. At point S, line EF intersects line CD, and at T, line CD intersects AB.

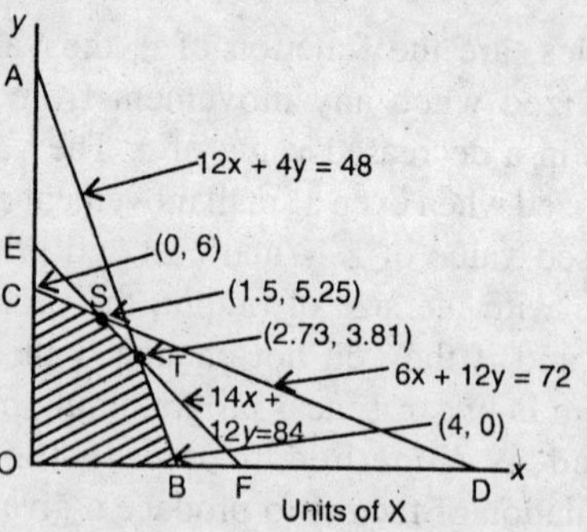

Fig A

Thus the shaded area OBTSC which lies below and to the left of the three lines intersecting at points S and T satisfies the inequalities of the three equations. This shaded area is called the feasible region of production and every point within the region or on the boundary of the region represents the feasible solution to our problem.

Out of the various points BTSC which represents the feasible solution, we have to find out the optimal point that would maximise the revenue of the firm.

We know the coordinates of points B and C from Equations (1) and (2), where by OB = $4x$, and OC = $6y$. In order to determine the coordinates of point T, we treat Equations (1) and (3) as simultaneous equations and solve them as

$$12x + 4y = 48 \quad \ldots 1$$

$$14x + 12y = 84 \quad \ldots 3$$

By multiplying Equation (1) by 3 and subtracting Equation (3) from it, we have

$$36y + 12y = 144$$

$$\underline{\overset{-}{14x} + \overset{-}{12y} = \overset{-}{84}}$$

$$22x = 60$$

$$x = 2.73$$

By substituting this value of x in Equation (1). we obtain

$$12 \times 2.73 + 4y = 48$$

$$32.76 + 4y = 48$$

$$4y = 48 - 32.76$$

$$\text{or } 4y = 15.24$$

$$y = 3.81$$

Thus the coordinates of point T are $x = 2.73$ and $y = 3.81$. Similarly, we can solve the coordinates of point S with Equations (3) and (2) which arrive at x = 1.5 and y = 5.25

At B, we have x = 4 and y = 0 and substituting these in the objective function $f = 12x + 15y$, we have

$12 \times 4 + 15 \times 0 = 48$ ...4

At T, we have x = 2.73 and y = 3.81 and similarly obtain

$12 \times 2.73 + 15 \times 3.81 = 89.91$ ...5

At S, we have x = 1.5 and y = 5.25 and we obtain

$12 \times 1.5 + 15 \times 5.25 = 96.75$ ...6

At C, we have x = 0 and y = 6 and we get

$12 \times 0 + 15 \times 6 = 90$ ...7

From the above Equations (4), (5), (6) and (7) we find the Equation (6) gives the maximum revenue of 96.75. This shows that given the prices of the two products x and y and given the amounts of inputs, the total revenue of the firm is maximised at point S. S is thus the optimal point subject to the given constraints.

Profit Maximisation

Let us take another linear programming problem relating to the maximisation of profits. Suppose there is a small manufacturer who produces two products x and y on two different machines, A and B. Product x requires 3 hours on machine A and 2 hours on machine B, whereas product y requires 3 hours on machine A and 4 hours on machine B. Machine A can be operated for 18 hours a day while machine B can be operated for 16 hours a day. The producer earns a profit of Rs. 30 on each unit of product x and Rs. 40 on each unit of product y. How many units of each product should be manufacture per day so as to have the maximum profit?

For a better understanding the problem is presented in the following Table.

TABLE : DATA FOR PROFIT MAXIMISATION PROBLEM

Machine	*Product* x	y	*Total Working Time*
A	3 hours	3 hours	18 hours
B	2 hours	4 hours	16 hours
Profit from each	Rs. 30	Rs. 40	

For the graphic solution, this linear programming problem can be restated as:

Maximise $P = 30x + 40y$

Subject to

(*i*) $3x + 3y \leq 18$

or $x + y \leq 6$

and $2x + 4y \leq 16$

or $x + 2y \leq 8$

(*ii*) $x \geq 0$, and $y \geq 0$.

By solving the equation $x + y = 6$ we have $x = 6$ and $y = 6$. This is shown as line AB in figure B, where OA = 6y and OB = 6x.

Similarly by solving the equation $x + 2y = 8$, we have $x = 8$ and $y = 4$. This is shown as line CD in figure B, where OC = 4y and OD = 8x.

The shaded area OBPC satisfies all the conditions of these two equations and is the feasibility region. Every point in this region satisfies the mathematical inequalities.

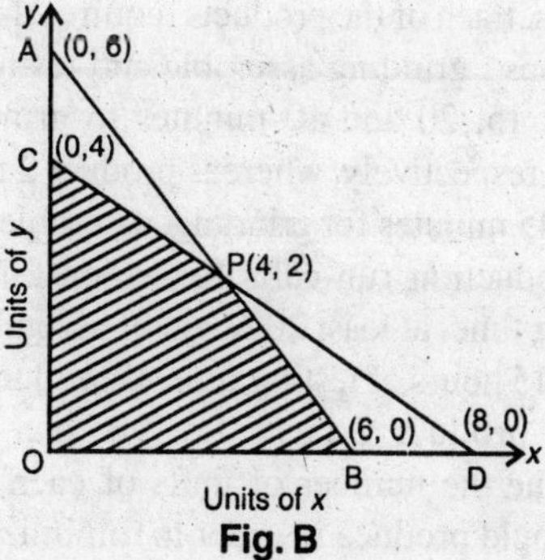

Fig. B

In order to find out which of the corner points O, B, P or C represents the feasible solution when the profit is maximised. We treat the two equations as simultaneous equations and solve them as under:

$$x + y = 6 \quad ...(i)$$
$$x + 2y = 8 \quad ...(ii)$$

By multiplying equation (*i*) by 2 and subtracting equation (*ii*) from it, we get

$$2x + 2y = 12$$
$$x + 2y = 8$$
$$- \quad - \quad -$$
$$x = 4$$

Substituting the value of x = 4 in equation (1), we have

$$4 + y = 6$$
$$y = 2$$

Thus the coordinates of point P are $x = 4$ and $y = 2$. As already calculated above the coordinates of point B are $x = 6$ and $y = 0$ and the coordinates of point C are $x = 0$ and $y = 4$.

In order to get the maximum profit we calculates the profit at the corners of the feasibility region, *i.e.*, O, B, P and C with the help of the values of these coordinates. Profit at point O is zero.

Profit at point B = $30 \times 6 + 40 \times 0 = 180$

Profit at point P = $30 \times 4 + 40 \times 2 = 200$

Profit at point C = $30 \times 0 + 40 \times 4 = 160$

Thus the manufacturer will earn Rs. 200 as the maximum profit (at point P) by producing 4 units of x and 2 units of y per day. The optimal solution is, therefore, $x = 4$, $y = 2$ and Profit = Rs. 200 (maximum).

Minimisation of Cost

Example : A small-scale manufacturer has production facilities for producing two different products. Each of the products requires three different operations : grinding assemble and testig. Product 1 requires 15, 20 and 10 minutes to grind, assemble and test respectively, whereas product 2 requires 7.5, 40 and 45 minutes for grinding, assemble and testing. The production run calls for at least 7.5 hours of grinding time, at least 20 hours of assemble time and at least 15 hours of testing time. If product 1 costs Rs. 60 and product 2 costs Rs. 90 to manufacture, determine the number of units of each product the firm should produce in order to minimize the cost of operations.

Ans. Mathematically, this problem may be formulated as follow:

Minimize Total Cost, $C = 60x + 90y$

Subject to $15x + 7.5y \geq 450$

$20x + 40y \geq 1200$

$10x + 45y \geq 900$

$x, y \geq 0$

The variables x, y indicates, respectively number of units of product 1 and number of units of product 2.

Graphical solution requires setting the first three inequalities as equalities and solving for extreme values of x and y in each case and then plotting the linear constraints. The feasible region is the shaded area above ABCD in the figure.

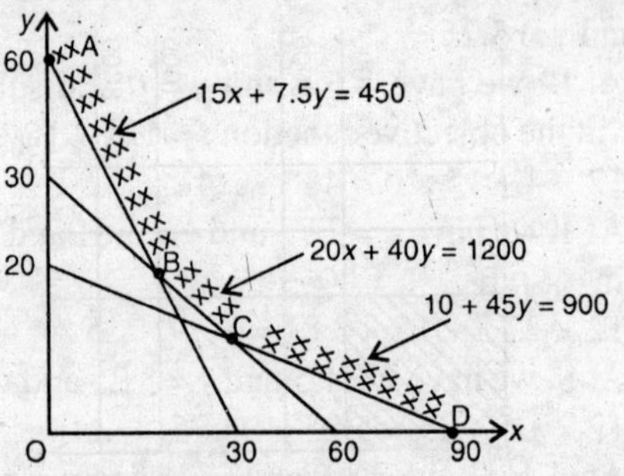

The coordinates of the four vertices of unbounded convex region are given by A (0, 60), B(20, 20), C(36, 12) and D(90, 0).

We evaluate the objective function $C = 60x + 90y$ at each solution points;

C(A) = 5400

C(B) = 3000

C(C) = 3240

C(D) = 5400

Hence the optimum solution is at the point B(20, 20) *i.e.*, the production of 20 units each of products 1 and 2, minimizes the cost.

Example : A company manufactures two products x and y using four major departments Q, R, S and T. The capacity limits of those departments are given in the table below:

Department	*Capacity for the production of* x	y
Q	4000	Nil
R	5000	5000
S	7000	4000
T	8000	3000

Solve graphically for the optimal production level if both the products sell at Rs. 40 per unit and the average costs of the two products x and y are Rs. 14 and Rs. 20 respectively.

Ans. Mathematically, the problem appears as:

Maximize $Z = (40 - 14)x + (40 - 20)y$

Subject to $x \leq 4000$

$x \leq 5000$, $y \leq 5000$

$x \leq 7000$, $y \leq 4000$

$x \leq 8000$, $y \leq 3000$

and $x, y \geq 0$

Graphically the problem appears as:

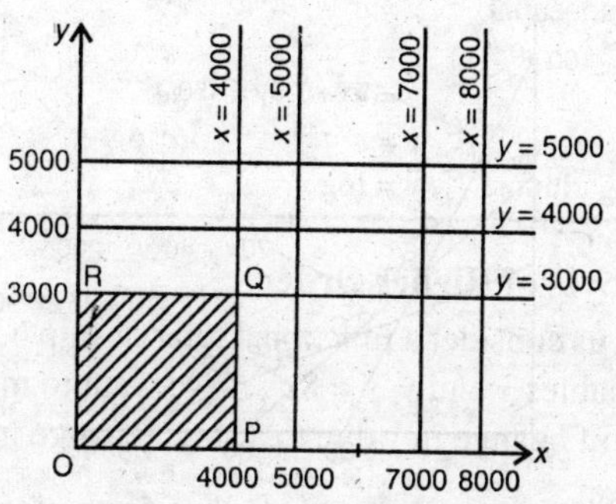

The solution to LPP lies on any corner of the feasible region OPQR. We evaluate the objective functions at each corner.

Corner	*Co-ordinates*	*Value of objective function* (Z = 26x + 20y)
O	(0, 0)	Z = 0
P	(4000, 0)	Z = 104000
Q	(4000, 3000)	Z = 164000
R	(0, 3000)	Z = 60000

Therefore the optimal solution occurs at point Q (4000, 3000).

DIFFERENTIAL CALCULUS

Rules of Differentiation

Rule 1. Functions in power terms (ax^n).

Let us suppose that the functional relationship between x and y is of the form: $y = ax^n$, where a is some contant term.

In this case $\frac{dy}{dx} = anx^{n-1}$

Thus our first rule of differentiation about power terms is as under:

$$\text{If } y = ax^n,\ \frac{dy}{dx} = anx^{n-1}$$

Rule 2. Differentiation of a constant.

Suppose the functional relationship is of the form: $y = C$ (C being constant)

We can write this as $y = Cx^\circ$ (since $x^\circ = 1$)

Applying Rule 1,

$$\frac{dy}{dx} = C(o)\,(x)^{0-1} = 0$$

$$\text{If } y = c;\ \text{then } \frac{dy}{dx} = 0$$

Rule 3. Differentiation of sum and differences

Let $y = 7x^3 + 5x^5 - 3x^6 + 8$

We obtanin $\frac{dy}{dx}$ by differentiating each term separately by applying rules 1 and 2.

$$\frac{dy}{dx} = \frac{d}{dx}\left(7x^3\right) 6 \frac{d}{dx}\left(5x^5\right) - \frac{d}{dx}\left(3x^6\right) + \frac{d}{dx}(8)$$

$$= 21x^2 + 25x^4 - 18x^5$$

$$\text{If } y = u + v + w;\quad \text{then } \frac{dy}{dx} = \frac{du}{dx} + \frac{dv}{dx} + \frac{dw}{dx}$$

Rule 4. Differentiation of a product

$$\text{If } y = UV;\ \text{then } \frac{dy}{dx} = V.\frac{du}{dx} + U.\frac{dv}{dx}$$

More generally, If y is expressed as a product of four functions of x, *i.e.*, if $y = SUVW$, then;

$$\frac{dy}{dx} = SUV\frac{dw}{dx} + SUW.\frac{dv}{dx} + SWV.\frac{du}{dx} + UVW.\frac{ds}{dx}$$

Rule 5. Differentiation of a quotient.

If $\quad y = \frac{U}{V}$

$$\text{then } \frac{dy}{dx} = \frac{V.\left(\frac{du}{dx}\right) - U.\left(\frac{dv}{dx}\right)}{V^2}$$

Rule 6. Differentiation of a function of a function (chain rule).

Let us suppose that consumption is not related to total utility directly but indirectly via income (I).

And our problem is what will be the change in total utility if consumption changes by one unit. Here we have to apply the rule for differentiation of a function of a function.

Assume that $y = \frac{I}{2}$, and $I = \frac{x}{5}$.

Take the expression $I = \frac{x}{5}$; here differentiating I w.r.t. x(which represents change in I due to a small change in x), we get

$$\frac{dI}{dx} = \frac{1}{5} \quad ...1$$

Also when $y = \frac{I}{2}$, then $\frac{dy}{dI} = \frac{1}{2}$

Thus now we have two derivatives,

$\frac{dI}{dx} = \frac{1}{5}$ and $\frac{dy}{dI} = \frac{1}{2}$

But we need the change in y with small change in x, *i.e.*, we need $\frac{dy}{dx}$. The result can be obtained by the following rule:

$$\frac{dy}{dx} = \frac{dy}{dI}.\frac{dI}{dx}$$

$$= \frac{1}{2}.\frac{1}{5} = \frac{1}{10}$$

This particular way of getting the desired derivative in case of a function of a function is known as Chain Rule.

Sl. No.	Form of function	Function	Derivative (dy/dx)
1.	Power terms	$y = ax^n$	anx^{n-1}
2.	Constant	$y = C$	O
3.	Sum and differences	$y = U \pm V$	$\frac{dU}{dx} \pm \frac{dV}{dx}$
4.	Product	$y = UV$	$V.\frac{d(U)}{dx} + U.\frac{d(V)}{dx}$
5.	Quotient	$y = \frac{U}{V}$	$\frac{V.\frac{d(U)}{dx} - U.\frac{d(V)}{dx}}{V^2}$

Some Standard Results

Sl. No.	Form of function	Function	Derivative (dy/dx)
1.	Trigonometric	$y = \sin x$	$\cos x$
		$y = \cos x$	$-\sin x$
		$y = \tan x$	$\sec^2 x = \frac{1}{\cos^2 x}$
		$y = \cot x$	$-\text{cosec}^2 x = \frac{1}{\sin^2 x}$
		$y = \sec x$	$\sec x . \tan x$
		$y = \text{cosec}\, x$	$-\text{cosec}\, x. \cot x$
2.	Exponential	$y = e^x$	e^x
		$y = e^{-x}$	$-e^{-x}$
		$y = e^{ax}$	ae^{ax}
		$y = a^x$	$a^x \log_e a$
3.	Logarithmic	$y = \log x$	$1/x$

Derivatives of Higher Order

Let us consider a functional relationship between two variables x and y, $y = 8x^4$; if we want to measure the rate of change in y due to a small change in x, we find $\frac{dy}{dx}$ of this expression which is given by:

$$\frac{dy}{dx} = 32\,x^3$$

This expression $32x^3$ can once again be differentiated as

$$\frac{d}{dx}(32x^3) = 96\,x^2,$$

which is in fact the derivative of $\frac{dy}{dx}$. In the terminology of calculus we call this expression ($96x^2$) as the second differential coefficient of $y = 8x^4$. To represent this symbolically, we write

$$\frac{d^2y}{dx^2} = 96x^2.$$

More specifically, as $\frac{dy}{dx}$ measures the rate at which y is changing w.r.t. small changes in x; similarly $\frac{d^2y}{dx^2}$ measures the rate at which $\frac{dy}{dx}$ is changing w.r.t. small changes in x. In other words, $\frac{dy}{dx}$ measures the rate of change in $y = 8x^4$ as x changes, while $\frac{d^2y}{dx^2}$ measures the rate of change of the rate of change (that is $32x^3$) as x change.

Some-notations

The successive differential coefficients or derivatives of the original functions are also conveniently denoted in a particular short form as follows:

If the given function is denoted by symbol : y $f(x)$; then

First differential coefficient or first derivative is

denoted by $f'(x)$.

Second differential coefficient or second derivative is denoted by $f''(x)$.

Third differential coefficient or third derivative is denoted by $f'''(x)$

Sign of Derivative and Nature of Function

1. If $\frac{dy}{dx} > 0$, *i.e.*, when first derivative of the given function is positive, the curve rises fro left to right.

2. If $\frac{dy}{dx} < 0$, *i.e.* when first derivative of the given function is negative, the curve falls from left to right.

3. If $\frac{dy}{dx} = 0$, *i.e.*, when first derivative of the given function is zero, the curve remains stationary for a moment and then changes its course. Therefore, this point is minimum, maximum or point of inflexion.

Second Derivative and Nature of Curve

The first derivative refers to the absolute valuc of function and the second derivative refers to the slope of the curve. Thus with the help of second derivative we are able to decide about the rising and falling nature of the curve.

We consider the following four possible cases:

Case 1. $f'(x) > 0$ and $f''(x) > 0$

This would mean that the value of function is increasing at an increasing rate or that the slope of the curve at this point is positive and increasing as the value of x increases. In this case the curve is concave upwards.

Case 2. $f'(x) > 0$ and $f''(x) < 0$

This would mean that the value of function is increasing at a decreasing rate or that the slope of the curve is positive but decreasing as the value of x increases. In this case the curve is concave downwards.

Case 3. $f'(x) < 0$ and $f''(x) < 0$

This means that the value of function is decreasing at a decreasing rate or that the slope of the curve must be negative and decreasing as x increases. (Note that this means that the negative slope of the curve tends to become steeper and steeper as the value of x increases). In this case the curve is concave downwards.

Case 4. $f'(x) < 0$ and $f''(x) > 0$

This means that the value of function is decreasing at an increasing rate or that the slope of the curve is negative but increasing as the value of x increases. Remember that this means that the negative slope tends to become less steep as x increases. In this case the curve is concave upwards.

Conditions for Maximum-Minimum Values

A. Conditions for minimum Value

1. First order condition (Necessary condition) $\}$ $f'(x) = 0$

2. Second order condition (sufficient condition) $\}$ $f''(x) > 0$

B. Condition for maximum value

1. First order condition (Necessary condition) $\}$ $f'(x) = 0$

2. Second order condition (Sufficient condition) $\}$ $f''(x) < 0$

Note that first order condition is the same for both maximum and minimum values.

C. In certain cases when $f''(x) = 0$, the above conditions fail to give the maximum or minimum values of the given function.

If $f''(x) = 0$, it means there may be a point of inflexion.

Application of Derivatives in Economic Theory

Example : Show that marginal revenue can always be expressed as $\left(p + x\frac{dp}{dx}\right)$. Deduce that the gradient of the demand curve is numerically equal to p/x at the output where MR is zero.

Ans. The demand function is $p = f(x)$.

$$\text{TR} = px$$
$$= x.f(x)$$

$$\text{MR} = \frac{d(\text{TR})}{dx}$$

$$= \frac{d}{dx}\{xf(x)\}$$

$$= x\frac{d}{dx}[f(x)] + f(x)\frac{d}{dx}(x)$$

$$\text{MR} = x\frac{dp}{dx} + p.$$

when MR = 0 putting in (*i*) we have

$$\frac{dp}{dx} = -\frac{p}{x}$$

But $\frac{dp}{dx}$ is the slope of the demand curve, hence when MR = O the slope of the demand curve is

$$\frac{dp}{dx} = -\frac{p}{x}$$

which is numerically equal to p/x if the sign is ignored.

Example : The total cost function is $\pi = \sqrt{ax + b + c}$. Find an expression for marginal cost and show that it decreases as output increases.

Ans. $\pi = \sqrt{ax + b + c}$

$$\therefore \quad \text{MC} = \frac{d(\pi)}{dx}$$

$$\Rightarrow \quad \text{MC} = \frac{d}{dx}\left(\sqrt{ax + b + c}\right)$$

$$\Rightarrow \quad \text{MC} = \frac{d\left(\sqrt{ax + b}\right)}{dx} + \frac{d(c)}{dx}$$

$$\Rightarrow \quad \text{MC} = \frac{a}{2\sqrt{ax + b}}$$

$$\frac{d(\text{MC})}{dx} = -\frac{1}{4}(ax + b)^{3/2} < 0$$

Since the first derivative of the MC curve is negative it means that as x increases MC falls.

Example : If the demand law is $x = \frac{20}{p+1}$, find e_d with respect to price at the point, where $p = 3$.

Ans. We are given

$$x = \frac{20}{p+1}$$

$$\therefore \quad \frac{dp}{dx} = \frac{-20}{(p+1)^2}$$

$$\text{At } p = 3, \quad \frac{dx}{dp} = \frac{-20}{(4)^2} = \frac{-5}{4}$$

$$\therefore \quad ed = \frac{p}{x}\cdot\frac{dx}{dp} = \frac{3}{5} \times \frac{-5}{4} = \frac{-3}{4}$$

$$|e_d| = \frac{3}{4}$$

Example : Show that the demand curve $p = \frac{a}{x+b} - c$ is downward sloping and convex from below. Do the same properties hold for the marginal revenue curve.

Ans. Condition for demand curve to be downward sloping is

$f'(x) < 0$

and condition for demand curve to be convex from below is $f''(x) > 0$

$$\because \quad p = \frac{a}{x+b} - c$$

$$\therefore \quad \frac{dp}{dx} = -\frac{a}{(x+b)^2} < 0$$

hence demand curve is down ward sloping.

$$\frac{d^2 p}{dx^2} = \frac{2a}{(x+b)^3} > 0$$

hence demqand curve is convex from below

$$\because \quad \text{MR} = \frac{d(\text{TR})}{dx} = \frac{ax}{x+b} - cx$$

$$\frac{d(\text{MR})}{dx} = \frac{(x+b)(a) - ax}{(x+b)^2} - c$$

Since $\frac{d(\text{MR})}{dx} > 0$, It is upward sloping.

and $\frac{d^2(\text{MR})}{dx^2} = \frac{-2cx - 2bc}{(x+b)^4} < 0$

hence it is concave from below assuming $a > 0$, $b > 0$. Thus the same properties do-not hold true.

Example : A firm has the following total cost and demand functions.

$$\text{C} = \frac{1}{2}\text{Q}^3 - 7\text{Q}^2 + 111\text{Q} + 50\text{Q}$$

and $\text{Q} = 100 - p$

Find profit maximising level of output; also find profit at this level of output.

Ans. We are given $\text{Q} = 100 - p$

or $p = 100 - \text{Q}$

Assuming that the profit maximising level of

output is Q,

$$\therefore \quad TR = Q \times p$$
$$= Q(100 - Q)$$
$$= 100Q - Q^2$$

Profit $\quad \pi = TR - TC$

$$= \left(100Q - Q^2\right) - \left(\frac{1}{2}Q^3 - 7Q^2 + 111Q + 50\right)$$

$$= \frac{1}{3}Q^3 + 6Q^2 - 11Q - 50$$

First order condition for maximising total profit:

$$\frac{d\pi}{dQ} = -Q^2 + 12Q - 11 = 0$$

$\Rightarrow (Q - 1)(11 - Q) = 0$

$\Rightarrow$ profit will be maximum when either Q = 1 or Q = 11. To decide between the two quantities apply second order condition:

$$\frac{d^2\pi}{dQ^2} = -2Q + 12 \text{ which should be } < 0$$

a. Substitute Q = 1, the inequality does not hold good.

b. Substitute Q = 11, the inequality holds good.

Therefore, output level of 11 units is the only profit maximising level. The total profit at this level of output will be

$$\pi = \frac{1}{3}(11)^3 + 6(11)^2 - 11(11) - 50$$
$$= 111.33.$$

In above example, if the firm is assumed to act as monopolist with the object of maxmising net revenue, it fixes the output Q and leaves the price to be determined by the demand conditions; alternatively, the firm can also fix its price and let demand condition determine the approximate output. Let us examine here how the result of the above example is affected if the firm is assumed to fix the price.

When the firm fixes the price:

Given : Total Cost = C

$$= \frac{1}{3}Q^3 - 7Q^2 + 111Q + 50$$

Demand $\quad Q = 100 - p$

Total revenue $= p \times Q$

$$= p(100 - p)$$
$$= 100p - p^2$$

Similarly, TC which is given in terms of Q must now be changed in terms of p.

$$\therefore \quad TC = \frac{1}{3}(100 - p)^3 - 7(100 - p)^2 + 111(100 - p) + 50$$

$$\pi = TR - TC$$
$$= (100p - p^2)$$
$$-\left[\frac{1}{3}(100 - p)^3 - 7(100 - p)^2 + 111(100 - p) + 50\right]$$

First order condition for maximising total profit:

$$\frac{d\pi}{dp} = (100 - 2p) + (100 - p)^2 - 14(100 - p) + 111 = 0$$

$\Rightarrow 8811 - 188p + p^2 = 0$

$(p - 89)(p - 99) = 0$

$\therefore$ either p be fixed at 89 or at 99 units to maximise the net revenue.

If $p = 89$, and since $Q = 100 - p$, $Q = 11$ which is the same level of output as we got by first method.

If $p = 99$, Q = 1 which is not possible as has been explained in first method.

Example : A monopolist firm has the following total cost and demand functions:

$C = aQ^2 + bQ + c$

$p = \beta - \alpha Q.$

what is the profit maximising output level when the firm is assumed to fix the output? Verify that this is the same result as when firm fixes the price.

Ans.

1. When firm fixes the output level.

$$TR = Qp$$
$$= Q(\beta - \alpha Q)$$

$$\therefore \quad MR = \frac{d(TR)}{dQ}$$
$$= \beta - 2\alpha Q$$

$$TC = C = aQ^2 + bQ + c$$

$$\therefore \quad MC = \frac{d(TC)}{dQ}$$
$$= 2aQ + b.$$

Condition for profit maximising output level is MR = MC.

i.e., $\beta - 2\alpha Q = 2aQ + b$

$\beta - b = 2aQ + 2\alpha Q$

$$\therefore \quad Q = \frac{\beta - b}{2(a + \alpha)}$$

Hence, profit maximising level of output is

$$\left\{\frac{\beta - b}{2(a + \alpha)}\right\}.$$

2. When firm fixes the price.

NowTR and TC should be put in terms of price p.

Since $\quad p = \beta - \alpha Q$

$$Q = \frac{\beta - p}{\alpha}$$

$$TR = Qp = \left(\frac{\beta - p}{\alpha}\right) = \frac{\beta p - p^2}{\alpha}$$

$$MR = \frac{d(TR)}{dp}$$

$$= \frac{1}{\alpha}(\beta - 2p)$$

$$TC = a\left(\frac{\beta - p}{\alpha}\right)^2 + b\left(\frac{\beta - p}{\alpha}\right) + c$$

$$MC = \frac{d(TC)}{dp}$$

$$= \left[\frac{-2a\beta + 2ap}{\alpha^2} - \frac{b}{\alpha}\right]$$

For profit maximisation MR = MC

$$\therefore \frac{1}{\alpha}(\beta - 2p) = \left(\frac{-2a\beta + 2ap}{\alpha^2} - \frac{b}{\alpha}\right)$$

This gives, $p = \dfrac{2a\beta + \alpha\beta + \alpha b}{2(\alpha + a)}$

Since the demand function is $p = \beta - \alpha Q$

$$\therefore \frac{2a\beta + \alpha\beta + \alpha b}{2(\alpha + a)} = \beta - \alpha Q$$

or, $$\alpha Q = \beta - \frac{2a\beta + \alpha\beta + \alpha b}{2(\alpha + a)}$$

i.e., $$Q = \frac{\beta - b}{2(\alpha + a)}$$

which is the same level as when firm fixes the output.

Example : For the Cobb-Douglas function

$Q = ak^2L^{1-a}$

where k is capital, L is labour and a is constant, verify that:

$$K\frac{dQ}{dK} + L\frac{dQ}{dL} = Q$$

Ans :

Given : $\quad Q = ak^{\alpha}L^{1-\infty}$

$$\therefore \quad \frac{dQ}{dK} = a^2k^{a-1}L^{1-a}$$

and, $$\frac{dQ}{dL} = a(1-a)k^aL^{-a}$$

$$\therefore k\frac{dQ}{dk} + L\frac{dQ}{dL} = k(a^2k^{a-1}L^{1-a}) + L[a(1-a)K^aL^{-a}]$$

$$= a^2K^aL^{1-a} + a(1-a)k^aL^{1-a}$$

$$= ak^aL^{1-a}[a + (1-a)]$$

$= Q$; hence proved.

Example : The production function of a commodity is given by

$$Q = 40F + 3F^2 - \frac{F^3}{3}$$

where Q is the total output and F is the units of inputs.

(*i*) Find the number of units of input required to give maximum output.

(*ii*) Find the maximum value of marginal product.

(*iii*) Verify that when the average product is maximum, it is equal to marginal product.

Ans.

(*i*) MP of $F = \dfrac{dQ}{dF} = 40 + 6F - \dfrac{3F^2}{3}$

$$= 40 + 6F - F^2$$

For maximum or minimum : $40 + 6F - F^2 = 0$

or, $(F + 4)(F - 10) = 0$

i.e., $\quad F = -4$ or 10

$$\frac{d^2Q}{dF^2} = 6 - 2F$$

when $\quad F = -4$

$$\frac{d^2Q}{dF^2} = 14 > 0$$

and when $F = 10$

$$\frac{d^2Q}{dF^2} = -14 < 0$$

i.e., output is maximum when 10 units of input are used.

(*ii*) $\quad MP_F = \dfrac{dQ}{dF}$

$= 40 + 6F - F^2$

For MP_F to be maximum : $\frac{dQ}{dF}$ should be = 0

or, $6 - 2F = 0$

$F = 3$

$\frac{d^2Q}{dF^2} = -2 < 0$

$\therefore MP_F$ is maximum when F = 3.

(*iii*) $AP = 40 + 3F - \frac{F^2}{3}$

For AP_F to be maximum: $\frac{d(AP)}{dF} = 3 - \frac{2F}{3}$ should be = 0

or, $F = \frac{9}{2}$

and, $\frac{d^2(AP)}{dF^2} = -\frac{2}{3} < 0$

$\therefore$ AP is max. when $F = \frac{9}{2}$.

$AP\left(\text{when } F = \frac{9}{2}\right) = 40 + 3\left(\frac{9}{2}\right) - \frac{81}{12} = \frac{187}{4}$

$= 46.75$

$MP\left(\text{when AP is max } i.e.\ F = \frac{9}{2}\right)$

$= 40 + 27 - \frac{81}{4} = \frac{187}{4} = 46.75$

Hence proved

Technique of Partial Differentiation

The process of taking partial derivative is called partial differentiation and it differs from previously discussed differentiation primarily in that we hold and treat all the independent variables constant except the one which is assumed to vary.

The practical technique of partial differentiation is illustrated by the following example:

Example : Given function is $U = 5x - 6y + 8$ and we are required to find partial derivatives. There can be only two partial derivatives.

1. U with respect to x when y is held constant *i.e.*, $\frac{dU}{dx}$ or f_x

and 2. U with respect to y when x is held constant *i.e.*, $\frac{dU}{dx}$ or f_y.

In case of (1), since y is held constant it is treated as a constant term during differentiation; while in case of (2), since x is held constant it is treated as a constant term during differentiation; thus we have

1. $\frac{dU}{dx} = f_x = 5 - 0 + 0 = 5$ ($-6y$ and $+8$ are treated as constant terms)

2. $\frac{dU}{dx} = f_y = 0 - 6 + 0 = -6$ ($5x$ and $+8$ are treated as constant terms)

Similarly if $z = ax + by + c$ then

$\frac{dz}{dx} = a$ and $\frac{dz}{dy} = 6$

Example : Following are the demand functions for two commodities X_1 and X_2 :

$x_1 = p_1^{-1.7}\ p_2^{0.8}$

$x_2 = p_1^{0.5}\ p_2^{-0.2}$

Determine whether the commodities are complementary or competitive; also find four partial elasticities of demand.

Ans. In order to find the nature of commodity we must find the cross partial derivatives:

$\frac{dx_1}{dp_2}$ and $\frac{dx_1}{dp_1}$

For demand function : $x_1 = p_1^{-1.7} p_2^{0.8}$

$\frac{dx_1}{dp_2} = 0.8\, p_1^{-1.7} p_2^{-0.2}$, which is a positive quantity

Hence $\frac{dx_1}{dp_2} > 0$

For demand function: $x_2 = p_1^{0.5}\ p_2^{-0.2}$

$\frac{dx_2}{dp_1} = 0.5\ p_1^{-0.5} p_2^{-0.2}$ which is also a positive

Hence $\frac{dx_2}{dp_1} > 0$.

Therefore, the commodities X_1 and X_2 are competitive.

Partial elasticities of demand for demand function: $x_1 = p_1^{-1.7} p_2^{0.8}$ are given by

1. $\frac{p_1}{x_1} \cdot \frac{dx_1}{dp_1} = \frac{p_1}{p_1^{-1.7}\ p_2^{0.8}} \left\{(-1.7) p_1^{-2.7}\ p_2^{0.8}\right\} = (-1.7)$

2. $\frac{p_2}{x_1} \cdot \frac{dx_1}{dp_2} = \frac{p_2}{p_1^{-1.7}\ p_2^{0.8}}\left\{(0.8)\ p_1^{-1.7} \cdot p_2^{-0.2}\right\} = (+0.8)$

Elasticities for demand function

$x_2 = p_1^{0.5}\ p_2^{-0.2}$ are given by:

3. $\frac{p_2}{x_2} \cdot \frac{dx_2}{dp_2} = \frac{p_2}{p_1^{0.5}\ p_2^{-0.2}}\left\{(-0.2)\ p_1^{0.5}\ p_2^{-1.2}\right\} = (-0.2)$

4. $\frac{p_1}{x_2} \cdot \frac{dx_2}{dp_1} = \frac{p_1}{p_1^{0.5}\ p_2^{-0.2}}\left\{(0.5)\ p_1^{-0.5}\ p_2^{-0.2}\right\} = (0.5).$

Example : If the utility function is:

$$U = \left(ax_1 + bx_2 + c\sqrt{x_1\ x_2}\right)$$

where x_1 and x_2 are two goods consumed by a person and U is the utility derived therefrom; obtain ratio of marginal utilities.

Ans. $\frac{dU}{dx_1} = a + \frac{1}{2}c\,(x_1x_2)^{-\frac{1}{2}}.x_2$

$$= \frac{2a\sqrt{x_1x_2} + cx_2}{2\sqrt{x_1x_2}}$$

and $\frac{dU}{dx_2} = b + \frac{1}{2}c\,(x_1x_2)^{-1/2}.\ x_1$

$$= \frac{2b\sqrt{x_1x_2} + cx_1}{2\sqrt{x_1x_2}}$$

So that the ratio of marginal utilities of two goods x_1 and x_2 is

$$= \frac{dU/dx_1}{dU/dx_2}$$

$$= \frac{2a\sqrt{x_1x_2} + cx_2}{2b\sqrt{x_1x_2} + cx_1}$$

Example : Find the point where the utility function:

$U = 48 - (x-5)^2 - 3(y-4)^2$

will have maximum or minimum value, if it is subject to $x + 3y = 9$

Ans. Combining the two functions through Lagrange's multiplier λ,

$Z = 48 - (x-5)^2 - 3(y-4)^2 + \lambda(x + 3y - 9)$

First order condition gives the following results:

$$f_x = \frac{dz}{dx} = -2(x-5) + \lambda = 0$$

$$f_y = \frac{dz}{dy} = -6(y-4) + 3\lambda = 0$$

$$f_\lambda = \frac{dz}{d\lambda} = x + 3y - 9 = 0$$

Solving these three equations, we get $x = 3$, $y = 2$ and $\lambda = -4$.

In other words, the given function: $U = 48 - (x-5)^2 - 3(y-4)^2$ will have either maximum or minimum value (since we have considered only first order condition) at point (3, 2) and the value of the given function will be : $48 - (3-5)^2 - 3(2-4)^2 = 32$

Second order conditions for maximiation : Hessian determinant (Maximisation Under Constraints)

Suppose $q = ax^2 + 2hxy + by^2$ which is subject to constraint : $\alpha x + \beta y = 0$

$$\therefore \quad y = -\left(\frac{\alpha}{\beta}\right)x$$

substituting y in q, we get

$$q = ax^2 + 2hx\left(-\frac{\alpha}{\beta}\right)x + b\left(-\frac{\alpha}{\beta}.x\right)^2$$

i.e., $q = \left(a\beta^2 - 2h\alpha\beta + b\alpha^2\right)\frac{x^2}{\beta^2}.$

The value of q will be positive if and only if

$$\begin{vmatrix} 0 & \alpha & \beta \\ \alpha & a & h \\ \beta & h & b \end{vmatrix} < 0,$$

and velue of q will be negative if and only if

$$\begin{vmatrix} 0 & \alpha & \beta \\ \alpha & a & h \\ \beta & h & b \end{vmatrix} > 0,$$

It can be noticed that this determinant is different from the determinant $\begin{vmatrix} a & h \\ h & b \end{vmatrix}$ when the quadratic function was of the form $q = ax^2 + 2hxy + by^2$ and when it was considered without any side condition.

Comparing the two determinants of two different cases, we find that determinant of constrained function contains one extra row and one extra column. Further more, the extra row and column is merely composed of the two coefficients of α and β from the constraint plus a zero element in the principal diagonal.

Since this extra row and column is on the border of the determinant $\begin{vmatrix} a & h \\ h & b \end{vmatrix}$, we call the Hessian of the constraint function

$$= \begin{vmatrix} o & \alpha & \beta \\ \alpha & a & h \\ \beta & h & b \end{vmatrix} \text{ as Bordered Hessian}$$

Example : Given the function : $U = x^2 + y^2 + w^2$ subject to a linear constraint $y + x + w = 1$; find at what point U has a maximum or minimum value. Find also the value of U.

Ans. Combining the function and constraint through Largrange's multiplier λ, we form: $z = x^2 + y^2 + w^2 + \lambda(x + y + w - 1) = 0$

First order condition:

$$f_x = \frac{dz}{dx} = 2x + \lambda = 0$$

$$f_y = \frac{dz}{dy} = 2y + \lambda = 0$$

$$f_w = \frac{dz}{dw} = 2w + \lambda = 0$$

$$f_\lambda = \frac{dz}{d\lambda} = x + y + w - 1 = 0$$

Solving these equations, we obtain

$$x = y = w = \frac{1}{3} \text{ and } \lambda = -\frac{2}{3}.$$

In other words, function U can have either minimum value of maximum value at point $\left(\frac{1}{3}, \frac{1}{3}, \frac{1}{3}\right)$. We apply second order condition to decide about this.

Second order condition:

$$\text{Bordered Hessain } |\overline{H}| = \begin{vmatrix} 0 & 1 & 1 & 1 \\ 1 & 2 & 0 & 0 \\ 1 & 0 & 2 & 0 \\ 1 & 0 & 0 & 2 \end{vmatrix}$$

The principal minors are:

$$|\overline{H}_2| = \begin{vmatrix} 0 & 1 & 1 \\ 1 & 2 & 0 \\ 1 & 0 & 2 \end{vmatrix} = -4 < 0$$

$$|\overline{H}_3| = \begin{vmatrix} 0 & 1 & 1 & 1 \\ 1 & 2 & 0 & 0 \\ 1 & 0 & 2 & 0 \\ 1 & 0 & 0 & 2 \end{vmatrix} = -12 < 0$$

That is, all the principal minors are < 0, therefore, d^2z will have positive value.

Since d^2z possesses positive value, the given function will have minimum value at point $\left(\frac{1}{3}, \frac{1}{3}, \frac{1}{3}\right)$.

$$\therefore \quad U = x^2 + y^2 + w^2$$

$$= \left(\frac{1}{3}\right)^2 + \left(\frac{1}{3}\right)^2 + \left(\frac{1}{3}\right)^2 = \frac{1}{3}$$

The Theory of Consumer Behaviour

Example : Suppose that a consumer has Rs. 90 to be divided between two commodities x and y and suppose the unit price of y is fixed at Rs. 0.20. What will be his demand equation for x if his utility function is : $U = \log Q_x + 2 \log Q_y$ (where Q_x and Q_y are the amounts of x and y consumed by him).

Ans.Condition for utility maximisation is

$$\frac{MU_x}{MU_y} = \frac{P_x}{P_y}$$

$$\because \quad U = \log Q_x + 2 \log Q_y$$

$$\therefore \quad MU_x = \frac{dU}{dQ_x} = \frac{1}{Q_x}$$

$$\text{and} \quad MU_x = \frac{dU}{dQ_y} = \frac{2}{Q_y}$$

substituting all the values in the above condition, we get

$$\frac{\frac{1}{Q_x}}{\frac{2}{2Q_y}} = \frac{P_x}{0.20} \text{ or, } \frac{Q_y}{2Q_x} = \frac{P_x}{0.20}$$

$\therefore 2P_xQ_x = 0.2\,Q_y$ ...1

Substitute the value of Q_y from the given budget constraint:

$P_x.Q_x + P_y.Q_y = 90$

$\therefore \quad 0.2\,Q_y = 90 - Q_xP_x$

$\therefore$ Eq. (1) becomes:

$2p_x\,Q_x = 90 - Q_xp_x$

$Q_x = \frac{30}{P_x}$ is the required demand function.

The Theory of the Firm

Example : A firm's production function is $Q = 5L^{0.7}K^{0.3}$. The price of labour is Rs. 1 per unit and the price of capital is Rs. 2 per unit. Find the minimum cost combination of capital and labour for an output rate of 20.

Ans. The cost equation : $C = L + 2K$.

Production function : $Q = 5L^{0.7}K^{0.3}$

For cost minimisation under the constraint: $Q = 5\,L^{0.7}\,K^{0.3} = 20$

$Z = L + 2K + \lambda[20 - 5L^{0.7}K^{0.3}]$

First order condition gives:

$$\frac{dZ}{dL} = 1 - 3.5\,\lambda L^{-0.3}K^{0.3}$$

$$= 1 - 3.5\,\lambda(K/L)^{0.3} = 0 \quad ...(i)$$

$$\frac{dZ}{dK} = 2 - 1.5\,\lambda L^{0.7}K^{-0.7}$$

$$= 2 - 1.5\,\lambda\,(K/L)^{-0.7} = 0 \quad ...(ii)$$

$$\frac{dZ}{d\lambda} = 20 - 5L^{0.7}K^{-0.3} = 0 \quad ...(iii)$$

Equations (*i*) and (*ii*) give:

$$3.5\left(\frac{K}{L}\right)^{0.3} = \frac{1.5}{2}\left(\frac{K}{L}\right)^{-0.7}$$

i.e., $$\frac{L}{K} = \frac{14}{3} \quad (iv)$$

Equation (*iii*) gives : $L^{0.7}\,K^{0.3} = 4$

i.e., $L.\left(\frac{3}{14}\right)^{0.3} = 4$ [by substituting from (*iv*)]

$$\therefore \quad L = 4\left(\frac{14}{3}\right)^{0.3}$$

$$= 4(4.6)^{0.3}$$

and $$K = \frac{6}{7}\left(\frac{14}{3}\right)^{0.3}$$

$$= 0.86\,(4.6)^{0.3}$$

In other words, the firm should use $\left\{4\left(\frac{14}{3}\right)^{0.3}\right\}$ and $\left\{\frac{6}{7}\left(\frac{14}{3}\right)^{0.3}\right\}$ units of labour and capital respectively for an output rate of 20. This will incur the firm minimum cost (and bring maximum profit).

Example : A firm's production function is $q = 12 - \frac{1}{LK}(L + K)$. The prices of labour, capital and output are Rs. 1,4 and 9 respectively. Find the maximum profit combination of capital, labour and output.

Ans. The cost equation: $C = L + 4K$. Assuming level of output $= q$ that maximises the firm's profit,

$\therefore \pi = 9q - L - 4K.$

For constrained profit maximisation we construct a new function:

$$Z = 9q - L - 4K + \lambda\left[q - 12 + \frac{1}{LK}(L + K)\right]$$

First order condition:

$$\frac{dZ}{dq} = 9 + \lambda = 0$$

$$\frac{dZ}{dL} = -1 - \lambda L^{-2} = 0$$

$$\frac{dZ}{dK} = -4 - \lambda K^{-2} = 0$$

Solving these equations, we obtain

$L = 3,\ K = \frac{3}{2},\ q = 11$ and $\pi = 90$

Example : Given the function : $U = Ax^by^c$; A, b and c are constants.

A. Find the conditions under which this is a linear homogenous function;

B. Apply Euler's theorem if these conditions hold true.

Ans.

A. Let each variable be increased by constant t times, the new function becomes:

$$= A(xt)^b(yt)^c$$
$$= A.t^{b+c}.x^b.y^c$$
$$= t^{b+c}.A.x^b.y^c$$
$$= t^{b+c}(U)$$

In other words, the given function is homogeneous function of $(b + c)$ degree. The given function will be linearly homogeneous when $b + c = 1$.

B. Euler's theorem states:

If $f(x, y)$ is the homogeneous of the kth degree, then $K f(x, y) = x.f_x(x, y) + y.f_y(x, y)$

In our case given function is $U = Ax^by^c$ which is homogeneous of degree $(b + c)$.

$$\text{Hence,}(b+c).U = x\frac{dU}{dx} + y.\frac{dU}{dy}$$
$$= x(A.b.x^{b-1}y^c) + y(A.C.x^b.y^{c-1})$$
$$= x\left(b.\frac{U}{x}\right) + y\left(c.\frac{U}{y}\right)$$

$= U(b + c)$, which proves the theorem.

The Theory of Market Equilibrium

Example : The demand functions of two competitive commodities are:

$$x = 11 - 2p_1 - 2p_2$$
$$y = 16 - 2p_1 - 3p_2$$

and the average cost of production of the commodities are constants, 3 and 1 respectively. Determine prices and quantities that maximise the profit.

Ans. Suppose the monopolist in question produced x and y units of two commodities which are sold at p_1 and p_2 prices.

Total revenue : $TR = p_1x + p_2y$

Total cost : $TC = 3x + y$

Total profit : $\pi = TR - TC$

$$= (p_1x + p_2y) - (3x + y)$$

substituting x and y in terms of p_1 and p_2 from demand functions:

$$\pi = p_1(11 - 2p_1 - 2p_2) + p_2(16 - 2p_1 - 3p_2) - \{3(11 - 2p_1 - 2p_2) + (16 - 2p_1 - 3p_2)\}$$
$$\pi = 19p_1 + 25p_2 - 4p_1p_2 - 2p_1^2 - 3p_2^2 - 49$$

First order condition:

$$\frac{d\pi}{dp_1} = 19 - 4p_2 - 4p_1 = 0 \quad ...1$$
$$\frac{d\pi}{dp_2} = 25 - 4p_2 - 4p_1 - 6p_2 = 0 \quad ...2$$

Solving Eqns. (1) and (2), we get

$$p_1 = \frac{7}{4}$$

and $p_2 = 3$

To ensure that π is maximum at $\left(\frac{7}{4}, 3\right)$, we apply second order condition:

$$\frac{d^2\pi}{dp_1^2} = -4 < 0$$
$$\frac{d^2\pi}{dp_2^2} = -6 < 0$$

Hence this condition is satisfied for maximum value.

Therefore, π is maximum at $\left(\frac{7}{4}, 3\right)$

Since $x = 11 - 2p_1 - 2p_2$

$$\therefore \quad x = \frac{3}{2}$$

and $y = 16 - 2p_1 - 3p_2 = \frac{7}{2}$

$$\pi_{max} = (p_1x + p_2y) - (3x + y)$$
$$= \left[\frac{21}{8} + \frac{21}{2}\right] - \left[\frac{9}{2} + \frac{7}{2}\right] = \frac{41}{8}$$
$$= 5.13$$

That is, the monopolist should fix the prices at $\frac{7}{4}$ and 3 for two commodities x and y to maximise his gross profit, which would be equal to 5.13 units.

Example: the demand functions of two commodities x and y are:

$$p_1 = 8 - 2x$$

and $p_2 = 14 - y^2$

and joint cost function is

$$C = 10 + 4x + 2y$$

Determine the quantities that maximise the profit

of monopolist and also find the maximum profit.

Ans. Profit $\pi = TR - TC$

$= (p_1x + p_2y) - (10 + 4x + 2y)$

$= (8 - 2x)x + (14 - y^2)y - (10 + 4x + 2y)$

$= -y^3 + 12y + 4x - 2x^2 - 10$

First order condition

$$\frac{d\pi}{dx} = 4 - 4x = 0$$

$$\frac{d\pi}{dy} = -3y^2 + 12 = 0$$

So we get $x = 1$ and $y = \pm 2$.

As y cannot be negative, we consider solution: $x = 1, y = 2$.

To ensure the π is maximum at (1, 2), we apply second order condition:

$$\frac{d^2\pi}{dx^2} = -4 < 0$$

$$\frac{d^2\pi}{dy^2} = -6y = -6 \times 2 = -12 < 0$$

At $x = 1$ and $y = 2$; $p_1 = 6$ and $p_2 = 10$

and $\pi_{max} = (p_1x + p_2y) - (10 + 4x + 2y)$

$= 26 - 18$

$= 8$

The producer would fix the output levels of commodities x and y at 1 and 2 respectively to maximise his gross profit; which would be 8 with given prices 6 and 10 of the commodities in the market.

Example : A monopolist firm produces two types of chocolate, X_1 and X_2 at constant average costs of Rs. 2.50 and Rs. 3.00 per kilo respectively. If P_1 and P_2 are prices charged (per kilo) and the market demands are given by,

$$X_1 = 5(P_2 - P_1)$$

$$X_2 = 32 + 5P_1 - 10P_2$$

obtain the levels at which prices will be fixed for the two types of chocolates for maximum joint monopoly revenue.

Find also the prices of two types of chocolates fixed by two independent monopolists and show that they are less than the joint monopoly prices.

Ans. Suppose the monopolist produces x_1 quantity of X_1 chocolate and x_2 quantity of X_2 chocolate.

$\therefore$ Total cost of $x_1 = C_{x1}$

$= AC_{x1} \times x_1$

$= 2.50x_1$

Total Revenue of $x_1 = R_{x1}$

$= P_1 \times x_1$

$= P_1 \times 5(P_2 - P_1)$

$\therefore$ Profit from $x_1 = R_{x1} - C_{x1}$

$\pi_{x1} = 5P_1(P_2 - P_1) - 2.50x_1$

$\pi_{x1} = 5P_1(P_2 - P_1) - 2.50\,\{5(P_2 - P_1)\}$

$\pi_{x1} = 5P_1P_2 - 5P_1^2 - 12.50\,P_2 + 12.50\,P_1$

Again Total cost of x_2 is $C_{x2} = AC_{x2} \times x_2$

$= 3x_2$

Total Revenue of x_2 $(R_{x2}) = P_2 \times x_2$

$R_{x2} = P_2(32 + 5P_1 - 10P_2)$

$\therefore$ Profit from x_2 $(\pi_{x2}) = R_{x2} - C_{x2}$

$\pi_{x2} = P_2(32 + 5P_1 - 10P_2) - 3(32 + 5P_1 - 10P_2)$

$\pi_{x2} = 32P_2 + 5\,P_1P_2 - 10P_2^2 - 96 - 15\,P_1 + 30\,P_z$

Gross (Joint) Profit $\pi = \pi_{x1} + \pi_{x2}$

i.e., $\pi = 10P_1P_2 - 2.50P_1 + 49.50\,P_2 - 5P_1^2 - 10P_2^2 - 96$

To maximise gross profit : (Assuming that he fixes prices to maximise profit)

$$\frac{d\pi}{dP_1} = 0 \text{ and } \frac{d^2\pi}{dP_1^2} < 0$$

and $$\frac{d\pi}{dP_2} = 0 \text{ and } \frac{d^2\pi}{dP_1^2} < 0$$

$$\frac{d\pi}{dP_1} = 10P_2 - 2.50 - 10P_1 = 0 \quad ...(i)$$

$$\frac{d\pi}{dP_2} = 10\,P_1 + 49.50 - 20\,P_2 = 0 ...(ii)$$

Solving Eqns. (*i*) and (*ii*), we get

$P_1 = 4.45$ and $P_2 = 4.70$

If there had been 2 monopolists each producing the chocolate independently, then

π_{x1} will have to be maximised assuming that the other monopolists will not change his price, *i.e.*, P_2 will be taken as constant.

$\pi_{x1} = 5\,P_1P_2 - 5P_1^2 - 12.50P_2 + 12.50\,P_1$

$$\frac{d\pi_{x1}}{dP_1} = 5P_2 - 10P_1 + 12.50 = 0 \quad ...(iii)$$

Again, $\pi_{x2} = 32\,P_2 + 5P_1P_2 - 10P_2^2 - 96 - 15P_1 + 30\,P_2$

Assuming that P_1 remains constant, for maximising π_{x2}, we get

$$\frac{d\pi_{x2}}{dP_2} = 62 + 5P_1 - 20P_2 = 0 \qquad ...(iv)$$

Solving Eqns. (*iii*) and (*iv*), we get

$P_1 = 3.2$ and $P_2 = 3.9$ (approx)

Thus it can be observed that prices in the present case are less than the joint monopoly prices.

Discriminating Monopoly

Example : Under discriminating monopoly the demand curve of a monopolist is made up of two parts:

$$P_1 = 140 - 7q_1$$

$$\text{and} \quad P_2 = 90 - \frac{q_2}{2}$$

Total cost curve is given : $C = 20 + 2q + 3q^2$ ($q = q_1 + q_2$)

Assuming that the firm maximises profit, determine the prices it will set in the two markets.

Ans. Let TR_1 and TR_2 represent the total revenues in the markets I and II respectively.

$$TR_1 = P_1q_1$$

$$\Rightarrow \quad TR_1 = 140\,q_1 - 7q_1^2$$

$$\therefore \quad MR_1 = \frac{d(TR_1)}{dq_1}$$

$$\Rightarrow \quad MR_1 = 140 - 14q_1$$

$$TR_2 = P_2q_2$$

$$\Rightarrow \quad TR_2 = 90\,q_2 - \frac{q_2^2}{2}$$

$$\therefore \quad MR_2 = \frac{d(TR_2)}{dq_2}$$

$$\Rightarrow \quad MR_2 = 90 - q_2$$

$$\text{and} \quad MC = \frac{d(c)}{dq}$$

$$= 2 + 6q$$

Condition for profit maximisation for discriminating monopoly is $MR_1 = MR_2 = MC$; but since MC involves q in its function ($MC = 2 + 6q$), we shall not be able to calculate the value of q_1 and q_2 using this condition directly. We follow the method by which we first obtain the value of q and then of q_1, q_2, p_1 and p_2.

$$MR_1 = 140 - 14q_1 \text{ and } MR_2 = 90 - q_2$$

$$\therefore \quad q_1 = 10 - \frac{MR_1}{14}$$

$$\text{and} \quad q_2 = 90 - MR_2$$

$$q = q_1 + q_2 = 100 - \frac{MR_1}{14} - MR_2$$

$$q = 100 - \frac{15}{14} MR \; [\because MR_1 = MR_2 = MR]$$

For profit maximisation MR = MC,

$$\text{i.e.,} \quad q = 100 - \frac{15}{14}(MC)$$

$$\text{or,} \quad q = 100 - \frac{15}{14}(2 + 6q)$$

$$(\because MC = 2 + 6q)$$

$$\text{or,} \quad q = \frac{685}{52}$$

i.e., for profit maximisation the total output to be sold in the two markets should be $= \frac{685}{52}$ units

$$MC = 2 + 6q$$

$$\Rightarrow \quad MC = 2 + 6\left(\frac{685}{52}\right)$$

$$\Rightarrow \quad MC = \frac{2107}{26}$$

For profit maximisation $MR_1 = MC$

$$\text{i.e.,} \quad \frac{2107}{26} = 140 - 14q_1$$

$$\text{or,} \quad q_1 = \frac{1533}{364}$$

$$\text{Also,} \quad P_1 = 140 - 7q_1$$

$$\therefore \quad P_1 = 140 - 7\left(\frac{1533}{364}\right)$$

$$\Rightarrow \quad P_1 = \frac{5747}{52}$$

$$\text{Again,} \quad MR_2 = MC$$

$$\text{i.e.,} \quad \frac{2107}{26} = 90 - q_2$$

$$\text{or,} \quad q_2 = \frac{233}{26},$$

$$\text{and} \quad P_2 = 90 - \frac{q_2}{2}$$

$$\Rightarrow \quad P_2 = 90 - \frac{233}{52}$$

$$\Rightarrow \quad P_2 = \frac{4447}{52}$$

Duopoly

Example : Suppose there are only two firms in an industry producing a homogeneous product. Market demand function is $P = 140 - 0.6\ Q$ and the cost functions of the duopolists are $C_1 = 7Q_1$ and $C_2 = 0.6Q_2^2$. we are required to find the equilibrium output of each duopolist ignoring their interdependence.

Ans.

a. Profit of duopolist can be obtained as under:

$$\pi_1 = PQ_1 - C_1$$

$$\Rightarrow \quad \pi_1 = \{140 - 0.6(Q_1 + Q_2)\}\ Q_1 - 7Q_1$$

and $\pi_2 = PQ_2 - C_2$

$$\Rightarrow \quad \pi_2 = \{140 - 0.6\ (Q_1 + Q_2)\}\ Q_2 - 0.6Q_2^2$$

Since $Q = Q_1 + Q_2$

$$\therefore \quad \pi_1 = 133Q_1 - 0.6Q_1^2 - 0.6Q_1Q_2$$

and $\pi_2 = 140Q_2 - 1.2Q_2^2 - 0.6Q_1Q_2$

1st order condition.

$$\frac{d\pi_1}{dQ_1} = 133 - 1.2Q_1 - 0.6Q_2 = 0$$

and $\frac{d\pi_2}{dQ_2} = 140 - 2.4Q_2 - 0.6Q_1 = 0$

Thus we have two equations:

$1.2\ Q_1 + 0.6\ Q_2 = 133$ ...1

$0.6\ Q_1 + 2.4\ Q_2 = 140$ ...2

The equilibrium output is given by their point of intersection; thus solving them for Q_1 and Q_2, we obtain:

$$Q_1 = 93.3$$

and $Q_2 = 35.0$

$$\pi_1 = 5227$$

and $\pi_2 = 1471$

The second order conditions are satisfied for this solution:

$$\frac{d^2\pi_1}{dQ_1^2} = -1.2 < 0$$

and $\frac{d^2\pi_2}{dQ_2^2} = -2.4 < 0$

b. Consider mutual collusion.

If duopolists recognize their mutual interdependence and agree to act unitedly in order to maximise their total profit jointly, It becomes a case of monopoly.

Let us solve the above example with this assumption.

Since gross profits of both together are to be maximised, therefore, the objective function becomes:

$$\pi = \pi_1 + \pi_2$$

$$\Rightarrow \quad \pi = (133\ Q_1 - 0.6\ Q_1^2 - 0.6\ Q_1Q_2) + (140\ Q_2 - 1.2\ Q_2^2 - 0.6\ Q_1Q_2)$$

Now we have to maximise π with respect to Q_1 and Q_2

1st order conditions

$$\frac{d\pi}{dQ_1} = 133 - 1.2\ Q_1 - 1.2\ Q_2 = 0 \quad ...3$$

$$\frac{d\pi}{dQ_2} = 140 - 2.4\ Q_2 - 1.2\ Q_1 = 0 \quad ...4$$

Solving (3) and (4) we obtain $Q_1 = 105$ and $Q_2 = 5.8$

Output : $Q_1 = 105$ and $Q_2 = 5.8$

Price : $P = 140 - 0.6\ (Q_1 + Q_2) = 73.5$

Profit : $\pi_1 = 133\ Q_1 - 0.6\ Q_1^2 - 0.6\ Q_1Q_2 = 6741$

$\pi_2 = 140\ Q_2 - 1.2\ Q_2^2 - 0.6\ Q_1Q_2 = 169.4$

On comparison with the situation when duopolist ignored their interdependence, we observe that in the present situation the profits of the 1st duopolist have increased (from 5227 to 6741 = 1514) while that of 2nd duopolist have been reduced [from 1471 to169.4 = –1301.6].

But still the collusion appears to be profitable to both, since the reduction in the profit of 2nd duopolist (= –1301.6) is less than the corresponding increase in the profit of 1st duopolist (= 1514).

Thus the profit of both together has increased to 6910.4 from 6698 in the previous situation. Naturally, therefore, mutual distribution of profit will put each of them on higher indifference curve.

INTEGRATION

If x is the differential coefficient of F(x); we say that $\int f(x)\,dx = F(x) + C$ is an indefinite integral; because C is unknown here. But if integral of $f(x)$ exists for all values of x from a to b, we define

$$\int_a^b f(x)\,dx = F(b) - F(a)$$

as a definite integral of $f(x)$ between limits a and b, a is the lower limit and b is the upper limit.

Basic Rules of Integration

Rule 1. Power Rule

$$\int x^n\,dx = \frac{1}{n+1}x^{n+1} + c$$

Rule 2. Exponential Rule

$$\int e^x\,dx = e^x + c$$

Rule 3. Logarithmic Rule

$$\int \frac{1}{x}.\,dx = \log x + c$$

Rule 4. Integral of sum

Integral of sum of a number of functions is equal to the sum of their separate integrals.

Example

$$\int (x^3 - x + 1)\,dx = \int x^3\,dx - \int x\,dx + \int 1\,dx$$

$$= \left(\frac{x^4}{4} + C_1\right) - \left(\frac{x^2}{2} + C_2\right) + (x + C_3)$$

$$= \frac{x^4}{4} - \frac{x^2}{2} x + C$$

Note. In the find answer we have added up all the constants into a single constant C.

Rule 5. Integral of a multiple

If a function is multiplied by a constant number, this number will remain a multiple of the integral of the function.

Example: $\int 4x^3\,dx = 4\int x^3\,dx$

$$= \frac{4x^4}{4} + C = x^4 + C$$

Important steps in evaluating a definite integral: $\int_a^b f(x)\,dx$.

1. Find the indefinite integral $\int f(x)\,dx = F(x) + c$

2. Substitute for x in this integral the upper limit b, *i.e.*, $= F(b) + c$

3. Substitute for x the lower limit a, *i.e.* $= F(a) + c$.

4. Substract (2) from (3), *i.e.* $F(a) + C$ from $F(b) + c$.

Applications

Example : Given the marginal cost function $f'(x)$, find the total cost function when fixed cost is 50 units and $f'(x) = 2 + x + x^2$; x being output produced.

Ans. Total cost $= \int f'(x)\,dx$

$$= \int (2 + x + x^2)\,dx$$

$$= 2x + \frac{x^2}{2} + \frac{x^3}{3} + c$$

But since fixed cost = 50, *i.e.*, total cost when output $x = 0$ is 50.

$\therefore$ $f(o) = o + o + c$

$= 50$

$\therefore$ $c = 50$

Hence the total cost function is $f(x)$ $2x + \frac{x^2}{2} + \frac{x^3}{3} + 50$.

Example : If the marginal cost function is $f'(q) = 2 + 3\sqrt{q} + \frac{5}{\sqrt{q}}$, find total cost function F(q) when F(1) = 21.

Ans. Total cost – $F(q) = \int f'(q)\,dq$

$$= \int \left(2 + 3\sqrt{q} + \frac{5}{\sqrt{q}} \right) dq$$

Total cost : $TC = 2q + 3\frac{q^{3/2}}{3/2} + 5.\frac{q^{1/2}}{1/2} + C$

$= 2q + 2q^{3/2} + 10q^{1/2} + C$

when $q = 1$: $F(q)$ is given to be 21.

$\therefore \quad 21 = 2(1) + 2(1)^{3/2} + 10(1)^{1/2} + C$

$\Rightarrow \quad 21 = 14 + C$

$\Rightarrow \quad C = 7$ (which is fixed cost)

$\therefore$ Total cost function $F(q) = 2q + 2q^{3/2} + 10q^{1/2} + 7$

Example : If the marginal revenue function is—

$$P_m = \left\{ \frac{ab}{(x+b)^2} - C \right\}$$

show that $P = \left\{ \frac{a}{x+b} - C \right\}$ is the demand law.

Ans. Let R be the total revenue, P is the price and x is the total output.

$\therefore R = P.x$ and $MR = \frac{dR}{dx}$

we are given that :

$$MR = P_m = \frac{dR}{dx} = \left\{ \frac{ab}{(x+b)^2} - C \right\}$$

$\therefore$ Total Revenue (R) $= \int \frac{dR}{dx} dx$

$$\Rightarrow \quad R = \int \left\{ \frac{ab}{(x+b)^2} - C \right\} dx$$

$$\Rightarrow \quad R = ab.\frac{(x+b)^{-1}}{-1} - Cx + A$$

(A = constant)

But $\quad R = P.x$

$$\therefore \quad P.x = \frac{-ab}{x+b} - cx + A \quad ...1$$

we know that if output $x = 0$ revenue must also be zero. Therefore, by substituting $R = 0$ and $x = 0$ in (1) we get

$$O = \frac{-ab}{b} + A,$$

$\Rightarrow \quad A = a$

Now Eqn. (1) will be

$$R = \frac{-ab}{x+b} - cx + a = P.x$$

$$\Rightarrow \quad P.x = \left\{ a - \frac{ab}{x+b} \right\} - Cx$$

$$\Rightarrow \quad P.x = \frac{ax}{x+b} - Cx$$

$$\Rightarrow \quad P = \frac{a}{x+b} - C$$

Example : If $MR = 16 - x^2$, find the maximum total revenue. Also find the total and average revenue and demand.

Ans. Given $MR = 16 - x^2$

we know that TR is maximum when $MR = 0$

$\therefore \quad 16 - x^2 = 0$

$\Rightarrow \quad x = \pm 4.$

Hence total revenue (TR) is maximum when output is 4 units. Our problem now is to find the maximum total revenue which happens when output is 4 units.

$$\therefore \quad TR = \int_0^4 (MR).dx$$

$$= \int_0^4 (16 - x^2).dx$$

$$= \left[16x - \frac{x^3}{3} \right]_0^4 = \frac{128}{3}$$

$\frac{128}{3}$ is the maximum total revenue.

(*ii*) Total revenue (R) $= \int (16 - x^2)\, dx$

$$= 16x - \frac{x^3}{3} + C$$

When $x = 0$, revenue must also be zero.

$\therefore \quad C = 0$

$\therefore R = \left(16x - \frac{x^3}{3} \right)$ which is the required total revenue.

(*iii*) Average revenue $= \frac{TR}{output}$

$= \frac{R}{x}$

$= \frac{16x - x^3/3}{x}$

$= \left(16 - \frac{x^2}{3}\right)$ is the required average revenue.

Example : The marginal cost and revenue of a firm are given as:

MC = 4 + 0.08x, MR = 12

Compute the total profit, given that total cost is zero at zero level of output.

Ans. For profit maximisation

$$MC = MR$$

i.e., $4 + 0.08x = 12$

or, $0.08x = 8$

$x = 100$

Since MR = 12 = constant, hence there is perfect competition.

$\therefore$ P = MR = 12

and Total Revenue = $12x$

Total cost $= \int (4 + 0.08x)\,dx$

$= 4x + \frac{0.08x^2}{2} + A$

$= 4x + 0.04x^2 + A$

$\therefore$ Total cost = 0 when $x = 0$

$\therefore$ A = 0 and TC = $4x + 0.04x^2$

Hence total profit = TR – TC

$= 12x - (4x + 0.04x^2)$

$= 8x - 0.04x^2$

= 400 (when output (x) = 100)

Example : If the demand function is P = 35 – 2x – x^2, and the demand x is 3; what will be the consumer's surplus?

Ans. Given demand function is

P = 35 – 2x – x^2

For x = 3, P = 20

Therefore, CS = Area of the curve below the demand from 0 to 3 minus Area of rectangle (20 × 3) = 60.

$$\therefore \quad C.S = \int_0^3 \left(35 - 2x - x^2\right) dx - 60$$

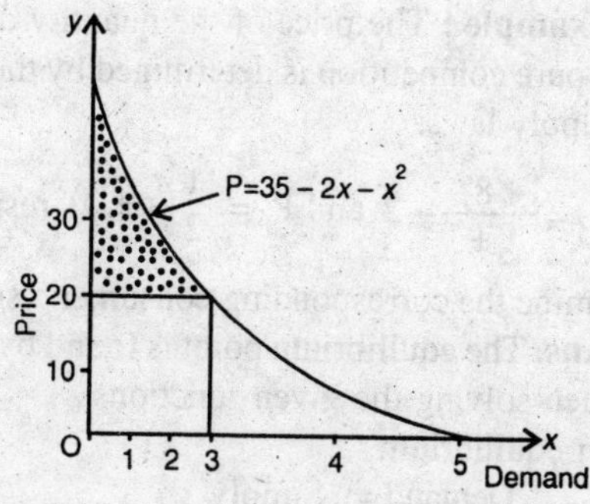

$$= \left[35x - x^2 - \frac{x^3}{3}\right]_0^3 - 60$$

$= 105 - 9 - 9 - 60$

= 27 units

Example : If the demand law is P = 85 – 4x – x^2, find consumer surplus: (*a*) If x = 5 and (*b*) If P – 64

Ans.

(*a*) If x = 5

P will be = 40

$$\therefore \quad C.S. = \int_0^5 \left(85 - 4x - x^2\right) dx - (40 \times 5)$$

$$\Rightarrow \quad C.S. = \left[85x - 2x^2 - \frac{x^3}{3}\right]_0^5 - 200$$

$$\Rightarrow \quad C.S. = \left[333\frac{1}{3}\right] - 200$$

$$\Rightarrow \quad C.S. = 133\frac{1}{3} \text{ Units}$$

(*b*) If P = 64, then

$64 = 85 - 4x - x^2$

i.e., either x = 3 or x = –7 (which has no meaning)

$$\therefore \quad C.S. = \int_0^3 \left(85 + 4x - x^2\right) dx - (64 \times 3)$$

$$= \left[85x - 2x^2 - \frac{x^3}{3}\right]_0^3 - 192$$

$= 228 - 192$

= 36 units

Example : The price of the quantity demanded under pure competition is determined by the demand and supply laws:

$$P_d = \frac{8}{x+1} - 2 \text{ and } P_s = \frac{1}{2}(x+3) \text{ respectively.}$$

Determine the corresponding consumer's surplus.

Ans. The equilibrium point is found by equating and then solving the given functions.

In equilibrium

Demand = Supply

$$\therefore \left(\frac{8}{x+1}\right) - 2 = \frac{x+3}{2}$$

or $x^2 + 8x - 9 = 0$

$\therefore x = 1$ or $x = -9$

At $x = 1$, P will be 2.

$$\therefore \quad \text{C.S.} = \int_0^1 \left(\frac{8}{x+1} - 2\right) dx - (2 \times 1)$$

$$\Rightarrow \quad \text{C.S.} = [8 \log (x+1) - 2x]_0^1 - 2$$

$$\Rightarrow \quad \text{C.S.} = 8 \log 2 - 2 - 2$$

$$\therefore \quad \text{C.S.} = 8(0.693) - 4$$

$$= 1.54$$

Example : The demand ans supply laws are $P_d = (6-x)^2$ and $P_s = 14 + x$ respectively. Find the consumer's surplus if (*i*) the demand and price are determined under pure competition, and (*ii*) the demand and price are determined under monopoly (so as to maximise the profit) and the supply function is identified with the marginal cost function.

Ans. Under pure competition: Market equilibrium conditions are found by equating demand and supply

i.e., $(6 - x)^2 = 14 + x = P$

i.e., $P = 16$ for $x = 2$

$$\therefore \quad \text{C.S.} = \int_0^2 \left(36 - 12x + x^2\right) dx - (16 \times 2)$$

$$= \left[36x - 6x^2 + \frac{x^3}{3}\right]_0^2 - 32$$

$$= \frac{56}{3} \text{ Units}$$

(*ii*) To find demand and price under monopoly, we have

$$\text{TR} = P_d \times x$$

$$\Rightarrow \quad \text{TR} = (36 - 12x + x^2)\, x$$

$$\Rightarrow \quad \text{TR} = 36x - 12x^2 + x^3$$

$$\therefore \quad \text{MR} = \frac{d(\text{TR})}{dx} = 36 - 24x + 3x^2$$

Supply price : $P_s = 14 - x$

But since supply price is to be identified with MC

$\therefore \quad 14 + x = \text{MC}$

To maximise profit, MC = MR

$\therefore 36 - 24x + 3x^2 = 14 + x$

or $(x - 1)(3x - 22) = 0$

i.e., either $x = 1$ or, $x = \frac{22}{3}$

Therefore, at $x = 1$, $P_d = 25$

$$\therefore \quad \text{C.S.} = \int_0^1 \left(36 - 12x + x^2\right) dx - (25 \times 1)$$

$$= \frac{16}{3} \text{ units}$$

Similarly find C.S. at $x = \frac{22}{3}$

Example : The marginal cost function for a firm is $100 - 10x + 0.1x^2$, where x is the output. Obtain the total cost function of the firm under the assumption that its fixed cost is Rs. 500.

Ans. $\because \text{MC} = 100 - 10x + 0.1x^2$

$$\therefore \quad \text{TC} = \int \left(100 - 10x + 0.1x^2\right) dx$$

$$= 100x - 5x^2 + \frac{x^3}{30} + C$$

$\because$ Fixed cost = 500

$$\therefore \quad \text{TC} = 100x - 5x^2 + \frac{x^3}{30} + 500$$

$$\Rightarrow \quad \text{TC} = \frac{x^3}{30} - 5x^2 + 100x + 500$$

Example : The demand function for a commodity is P = 20 – 3D. The supply function on this market is P = 2D. Find consumer's surplus.

Ans. Given P = 20 – 3D, and

P = 2D is the supply function

$\therefore$ Equilibrium price P = 8 and D = 4

$$\therefore \quad \text{C.S.} = \int_0^4 (20 - 3D)\, dD - (8 \times 4)$$

$$= \left[20D - \frac{3D^2}{2}\right]_0^4 - 32 = 24.$$

Example : The marginal cost function for some product is $(1 + 2x + 6x^2)$ where x is the output. Find the total cost function if the fixed cost is Rs. 100 when the output is zero.

Ans. $\quad \text{MC} = 1 + 2x + 6x^2$

$$\therefore \quad \text{TC} = \int \left(1 + x + 6x^2\right) dx$$

$$= x + \frac{x^2}{2} + 2x^3 + c$$

Since fixed cost is given to be 100

$$\therefore \quad \text{TC} = 2x^3 + \frac{x^2}{2} + x + 100$$

Example : An individual's preference scale for the goods x and y is defined by the marginal rate of substitution of y for $x = \frac{x-a}{y-b}$. Show that

$\text{U} = (x-a)^2 + (y-b)^2$

is the form of the utility function.

Ans. MRS between y and x is given by

$$\frac{dy}{dx} = \frac{x-a}{y-b}$$

$$\therefore \; dy + \left(\frac{x-a}{y-b}\right) dx = 0$$

$(y-b)dy + (x-a)\, dx = 0$

Integrating, we have

$$\left(\frac{y^2}{2} - by\right) = -\left(\frac{x^2}{2} - ax\right) + c$$

$$y^2 - 2by = -(x^2 - 2ax) + 2c$$

or, $\quad (y-b)^2 = -(x-a)^2 + 2c - a^2 - b^2$

$\therefore (y-b)^2 + (x-a)^2 = \text{U}$ (some constant)

$\Rightarrow \quad \text{U} = (y-b)^2 + (x-a)^2$

is the form of utility function.

Example : It is known that the elasticity of a demand curve, $x = \phi(\text{P})$ is of the form $(a - b\text{P})$, where a and b are given constants. Find the demand curve.

Ans. We know that elasticity of demand

$$= \frac{\%\text{ change in demand}}{\%\text{ change in price}}$$

$$= \frac{d\frac{\text{D}}{\text{D}}}{\frac{dp}{p}} = \frac{d\text{D}}{d\rho} \cdot \frac{\rho}{\text{D}}$$

But in this example,

$$\frac{d\text{D}}{d\rho} \cdot \frac{\rho}{\text{D}} = (a - b\rho)$$

$$\frac{d\text{D}}{\text{D}} = \left(\frac{a - b\rho}{\rho}\right) d\rho$$

or, $$\int \frac{d\text{D}}{\text{D}} = \int \left(\frac{a - b\rho}{\rho}\right) d\rho$$

or, $\quad \log \text{D} = a \log \rho - b\rho + \text{C}$

$\text{D} = e^{a \log \rho - b\rho + \text{C}}$

$\Rightarrow \quad \text{D} = e^{\log (\rho)a - b\rho + \text{C}}$

$\Rightarrow \quad \text{D} = \text{P}^a . e^{-b\rho + \text{C}} = \rho^a . e^{\text{C} - b\rho}$

This is the required demand curve.

Example : Demand and supply functions for tea are given by:

$$x_d = \left\{120 - 2\rho + 5\frac{d\rho}{dt}\right\} \text{ kg. per week, and}$$

$$x_s = \left\{3\rho - 30 + 50\frac{d\rho}{dt}\right\} \text{ kg. per week;}$$

where ρ is the price at time t.

If the initial price is 36 paise kg., find the condition for equilibrium (dynamic).

Ans. At equilibrium D = S

$$\therefore \; 120 - 2\text{P} + 5.\frac{d\rho}{dt} = 3\rho - 30 + 50.\frac{d\rho}{dt}$$

$$45.\frac{d\rho}{dt} + 5\rho - 150 = 0$$

$$9.\frac{d\rho}{dt} + \rho = 30$$

or, $$\frac{d\rho}{dt} + \frac{\rho}{9} = \frac{10}{3}$$

This is the differential equation of the form $\frac{dy}{dx} + ay = b$ of which the solution is,

$$y = \frac{b}{a} + \left(y(o) - \frac{b}{a}\right)e^{-ax}$$

Here $a = \frac{1}{9}$ and $b = \frac{10}{3}$

Solution of this differential equation will therefore be

$$P(t) = \frac{10}{3}.9 + [\rho(o) - 30]e^{-t/9}$$

$$P(t) = 30 + [\rho(o) - 30]e^{-t/9}$$

Initial price, *i.e.*, at $t = 0$, $\rho(o) = 36$ (given)

$$\therefore \quad \rho(t) = 30 + (36 - 30)e^{-t/9}$$

$$= 30 + 6e^{-t/9}$$

is the time-path of price for tea.

What will be the price after 10 weeks?

It will be: $\rho(10) = 30 + be^{-10/9}$

The Cobweb Model

The basic Cobweb model assumes that today's demand for any commodity is a function of the present price (P_t) while today's supply depends upon yesterday's decisions about the output. Hence, output is naturally influenced by yesterday's price (ρ_{t-1}).

To put this in symbolic form:

Demand function : $X_{Dt} = a + \alpha\rho_t$

Supply function : $X_{st} = b + \beta\rho_{t-1}$

thus both demand and supply functions are assumed to be linear.

For equilibrium

$X_{Dt} = X_{St}$

or, $a + \alpha\rho_t = b + \beta\rho_{t-1}$

Let $\bar{\rho}$ be the equilibrium price

$$\therefore \quad \rho_t = \bar{\rho} \text{ for all } t\text{'s} \quad \ldots 1$$

$$a + \alpha\bar{\rho} = b + \beta\bar{\rho} \quad \ldots 2$$

$$\Rightarrow \quad \bar{\rho} = \frac{b-a}{\alpha - \beta}$$

Subtracting (2) from (1), we get

$$\alpha(\rho_t - \bar{\rho}) = \beta(\rho_{t-1} - \bar{\rho})$$

$$\therefore \quad \alpha\rho_t = \beta(\rho_{t-1})$$

$$\Rightarrow \quad \rho_t = \frac{\beta}{\alpha}(\rho_{t-1})$$

which represents the first order difference equation. The complementary function of this equation will be

$$\rho_t = \rho_o\left(\frac{\beta}{\alpha}\right)^t$$

$$\text{or} \quad (\rho_t - \bar{\rho}) = (\rho_o - \bar{\rho})\left(\frac{\beta}{\alpha}\right)^t$$

$$\rho_t = \bar{\rho} + (\rho_o - \bar{\rho})\left(\frac{\beta}{\alpha}\right)^t \quad \ldots 3$$

ρ_o is the initial price.

Now we have

(*i*) $\bar{\rho} = \frac{b-a}{\alpha - \beta}$, which is the equilibrium price of the model. This being a constant term, it gives a stationary equilibrium price.

(*ii*) The term $(\rho_o - \bar{\rho})$ depicts the scale effect. If $(\rho_o - \bar{\rho}) > 0$, the time-path, as said above, will blow up. If $(\rho_o - \bar{\rho}) < 0$, the time-path will start from below the equilibrium price.

The magnitude of $(\bar{\rho} - \rho_o)$ determines how far above or below ρ_o the time-path starts.

(*iii*) The crucial factor is $\left(\frac{\beta}{\alpha}\right)^t$ when β and α are the slopes of the supply and demand curves. Since the demand curve is generally negatively sloped;

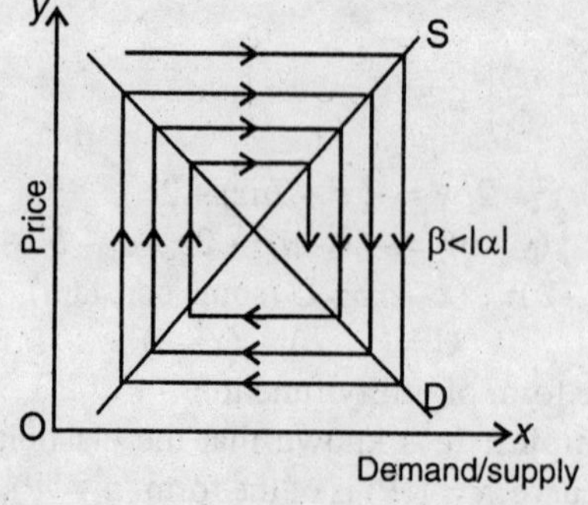

Fig. 1

$\therefore \qquad \alpha < 0$

and since supply curve is positively sloped,

$\therefore \qquad \beta > 0$

$$\therefore \frac{\beta}{\alpha} = \frac{(+)\text{ sign}}{(-)\text{ sign}} = (-)\text{ sign.}$$

Hence the time-path must always be oscillatory. Three possibilities arise:

1. If $\beta > |\alpha|$, then $\frac{\beta}{|\alpha|} > 1$, then there will be explosive oscillations (Fig. 2).

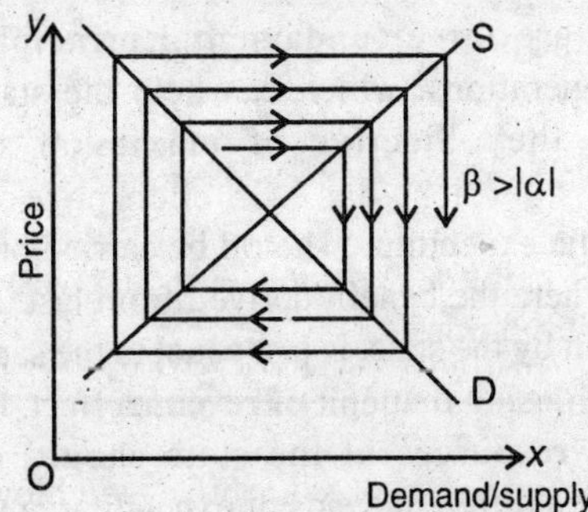

Fig. 2

2. If $\beta = |\alpha|$, then $\frac{\beta}{|\alpha|} = 1$, then there will be regular oscillations (Fig. 3).

3. If $\beta < |\alpha|$, then $\frac{\beta}{|\alpha|} < 1$, then there will be damped oscillations (Fig. 1)

Thus the dunamic equilibrium can only be obtained in the third case when $\beta < |\alpha|$ or when **the demand curve is steeper than the supply curve.**

Time-path of output X: This can be obtained by substituting the value of p_t in the demand equation or the supply equation.

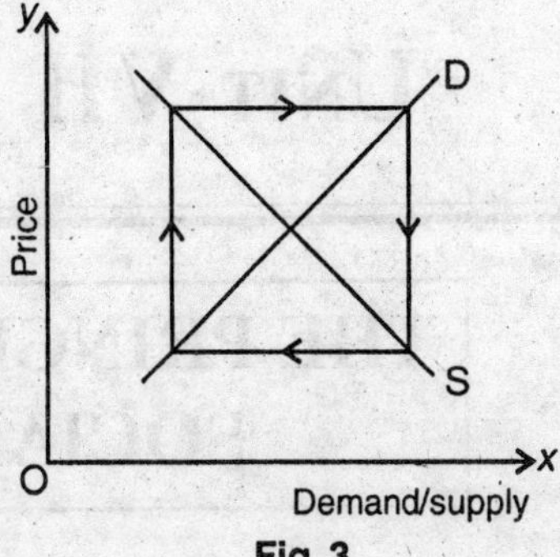

Fig. 3

Thus the disequilibrium price ρ oscillates over successive periods around the equilibrium price $\overline{\rho}$ and converges to $\overline{\rho}$ if and only if $|\beta| < |\alpha|$, or if and only if D is steeper than S around the point of intersection.

Example : Given the following demand and supply functions, find equilibrium price and determine whether the equilibrium is stable.

a. $x_{dt} = 18 - 3P_t$

$x_{st} = -3 + 4P_{t-1}$

b. $x_{dt} = 19 - 6P_t$

$x_{st} = 6P_{t-1} - 5$

Ans.

a. Slope of demand curve = $|\alpha| = 3$

Slope of supply curve = $|\beta| = 4$

Since $\beta > \alpha$

∴ There will be explosive oscillations and equilibrium will be unstable.

Equilibrium price : $\overline{\rho} = 3$

b. Slope of demand curve = $|\alpha| = 6$

Slope of supply curve = $|\beta| = 6$

Since $\beta = \alpha$

∴ There will be regular oscillations and the equilibrium will be unstable.

Unit-VII : Public Finance

THE PRINCIPLE OF MAXIMUM SOCIAL ADVANTAGE

Public revenue and public exdpenditure are two important financial operations of a state. These two financial operations of the state must be governed by some fundamental principles, so that they may result in maximum social benefit. **Prof. Pigou** and **Prof. Dalton** were the two prominent economists, who were responsible for formulating and popularising this fundamental principle of public finance.

The principle says that the state should collect revenue and spent the money so as to maximum the welfare of the people. When the state imposes taxes, some disutility is created. On the other hand, when the state spends the money, there is some gain in utility. The state should so adjust the revenue and expenditure that the surplus of utility is maximised and disutility is minimised. It should be noted here that the individual welfare of all the people cannot be maximised, if the welfare of some may even decrease; but if the welfare of large majority of the people increases, the net welfare of the society as a whole would be greater. To state it in the words of Prof. Dalton—"As a result of these operations of public finance, changes take place in the amount and in the nature of wealth which is produced, and in the distribution of that wealth among individuals and classes. Are these changes in their aggregate effects socially advantageous? If so, the operations are justified, if not, not. The best system of public finance is that which secures the maximum social advantage from the operations, which it conducts." **Prof. Dalton** called this principle as the principle of **Maximum Social Advantage** and **Prof. Pigou** called it as the Principle of Maximum Aggregate Welfare.

How Maximum Social Advantage is Achieved

There are three fundamental principles of financial operations, which can help the state for achieving the objective of maximum social advantage.

1. Public expenditure should be carried on upto the point where the benefit derived from last unit of money spent by the state, is just equal to the sacrifice imposed in raising that unit of revenue.

2. The resources of the state should be so distributed on different heads of expenditure that the marginal return of satisfaction from each of them is the same.

3. The taxes should be so distributed that the marginal utility of the money pain in taxation is equal to all tax pagers.

The above proposition of maximum social advantage can be depicted graphically also. Through this graph the optimum tax and expenditure activity of the state can be determined. In the diagram let public expenditure and taxation be measured along the *x*-axis and let the social benefit and cost be measured along *y*-axis. The quantities measured along *y*-axis will be positive if measured above *x*-axis and negative if measured below *x*-axis. As a result, the curve showing the marginal social benefit from public expenditure will lie above the *x*-axis and the curve showing marginal disutility from taxation will lie below *x*-axis. In the diagram, the curve BB' shows the marginal social benefit accruing to the society from different amounts of the public expenditure. The curve DD' shows the marginal social cost to the society from the taxation levied by the state. The difference between BB' and DD' indicates the net social benefit or advantage (that is the excess of the benefit over the cost to the society), and is depicted by the curve NN'. We find that when an amount OM is taxed and spent by the state, then the marginal social benefit and marginal social disutility are equated (MP being equal to MQ). Till then, the gain to the society is more than the loss. It is here that the state should stop expanding its activities. The net gain to the society (or the maximum possible social advantage) is equal to the shaded area ONM.

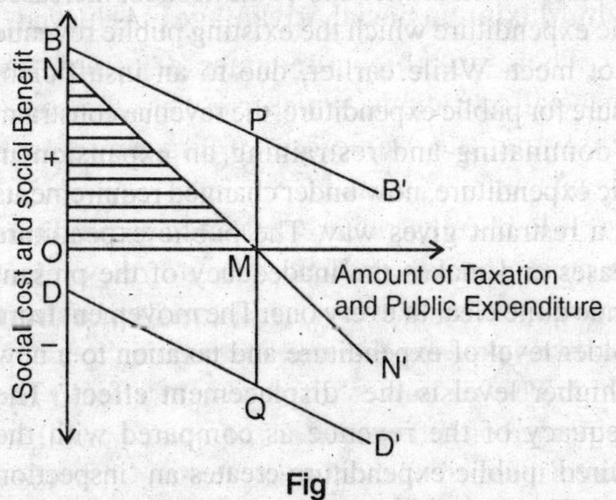

Fig

If the state stops its public finance operations at a figure less than OM, the society will be foregoing a possible gain. If the operations are expanded beyond OM, the total net benefit will again start falling.

Limitations

The principle of maximum social advantage is the fundamental principle of public finance and it is supposed for granted to be the guiding principle of the state's financial activity, yet there are certain limitations and difficulties in the way of practical application of this principle.

In the first place it is very difficult for the state to balance the marginal disutilities caused by the imposition of a tax with the marginal utility of a public expenditure. Even an individual finds it difficult to do so often in his daily practical life, when the disutility of the sacrifice equals the utility of his income. And, this difficulty is much greater for the state, because actual government spending and taxing is done by a larger number of public employees at different places and in different departments. **Secondly**, the state can speculate about the future and try to see the coming event, but it is very difficult to estimate on the basis of there speculations, that expenditure made by the public authorities will yield higher utilities than the disutilities caused at present. Hence, it is very difficult, if not quite impossible for the state to balance marginal disutility of taxation with the marginal utility of expenditure. The success of the state in maximising the net social advantage lies in her ability to correctly foresee all these results of her financial activities. And it requires a sensitive and intelligent mind to be able to do so.

PUBLIC EXPENDITURE

Public Expenditure is the expenditure incurred by public authorities-central, state and local governments-either for the satisfaction of collective needs of the citizens or for promoting their economic and social welfare. The volume of public expenditure has been increasing in almost all countries of the world, because of the continuous expansion in the activities of state and other public bodies on several fronts. A theory of public expenditure in the nineteenth century was not very necessary because the scope of the functions of government was restricted. In the twentieth century the development of the functions of the state in social matters, *e.g.*, in education, public health and in commercial and industrial undertakings, such as railways, irrigation and similar projects have increased public expenditure in a large degree.

Reasons For the Growth of Public Expenditure

1. Increase in the Activities of the state
2. Industrial Development
3. Social Security Measure
4. Nationalisation of Industries and Trade
5. Development of Agriculture
6. Rising Trend of Prices
7. Problems of Defence
8. Urbanisation

9. Economic Development

Wagner's Views on Public Expenditure

The German economist, Adolph Wagner, argued that a nation, as it experience economic development and growth, will experience an increase in the activities of the public sector. According to Wagner there are in herent tendencies for the activities of different layers of a government (such as central and state governments) to increase both intensively and extensively.

A number of early economists discussed the relationship between the level of development and public expenditure. However, Wagner was the first to butteress such remark with an extensive theoretical foundation.

To justify his generalisation that the share of public consumption expenditure would increase, Wagner divided public expenditure into two categories, expenditures for internal and external security and expenditures for "cultural and welfare" which should include education, health, transportation, banking and the like expenditures for external security would increase in a growing economy as the nature of the use of force by the state changes from simple aggression to prevention of attack and as armies use more capital equipment. For internal security Wagner Foresaw greater expenditure because of greater friction between economic units and people as urbanisation progressed.

Canons of Public Expenditure

Like cannons of taxation, people have propounded canons of public expenditure also which should govern the public expenditure decision. some of these canons are in the nature of administrative safeguards while others are expected to be of help to the economy and society in their diverse objectives. Some important cannons of public expenditure are—

1. Cannon of Benefit
2. Cannon of Economy
3. Cannon of Sanction
4. Cannon of Surplus
5. Cannon of Elasticity
6. Cannon of Equitable Distribution
7. Cannon of Productivity

Wiseman-Peacock Hypothesis

The another thesis of the growth of public expenditure was put forth by **Wiseman and Peapock** in their study of public expenditure in UK for the period 1890-1955. The main thesis of the authors is that public expenditure does not increase in a smooth and continuous manner, but in Jerks or steplike fashion. At times some social or other disturbance takes place which at once shows the need for increased public expenditure which the existing public revenue cannot meet. While earlier, due to an insufficient pressure for public expenditure, the revenue constraint was dominating and restraining an expansion in public expenditure, now under changed requirements such a restraint gives way. The public expenditure increases and makes the inadequacy of the present revenue quite clear to every one. The movement from the older level of expenditure and taxation to a new and higher level is the 'displacement effect.' The inadequacy of the revenue as compared with the 'required' public expenditure creates an 'inspection effect.' The government and the people review the revenue position and the need to find a solution of the important problems that have come up and agree to the required adjustments to finance the increased expenditure. They attain a new level of 'tax tolerance.' They are now ready to tolerate a greater burden of taxation and as a result the general level of expenditure and revenue goes up. In this way, the public expenditure and revenue get stabilized at a new level till another disturbance occurs to cause a 'displacement effect.' Since each major disturbance leads to the government assuming a larger proportion of the total national economic activity, the net result is the 'concentration effect.' The concentration effect also refers to the apparent tendency for central government economic activity to grow faster than that of the state and local level governments. British data are consistent with this finding, but its application to other countries needs verification.

THE PUBLIC BUDGET

A budget is the statement of the financial plan of a government. It indicates the revenue and expenditure of the last completed financial year, the probable revenue and expenditure estimates for the current year, *i.e.*, not completed and the estimates of the anticipated revenue and proposed expenditure for the next financial year.

In the constitution of India, a budget has been referred to as the annual financial statement of the estimated receipts and expenditure of the government of India or of a state government, in respect of a financial year. **Article 112** of the constitution of India states that "an annual financial statement" will be placed before both Lok Sabha, and Rajya Sabha, while Article 202 of the constitution states that a similar financial statement for each state will be placed before the Legislature of that state.

Revenue and Capital Budgets

In many countries, the budget is divided into revenue and capital accounts. Revenue account covers those items which are of recurring nature; while capital account covers those items which are in the nature of the acquiring and disposing of capital assets.

In India, the constitution demands that the budget must distinguish expenditure on Revenue Accounts from other expenditure. Accordingly, the budget is necessarily presented into two parts, namely, **Revenue Budget** and **Capital Budget**. Revenue Budget consists of the revenue receipts — both tax revenue and non-tax revenue — and the expenditure met out of revenue receipts. The non-tax-revenue receipts include revenue from currency, coinage and mint, interest receipts, dividends, profits revenue from general services (such as police, jails, public works etc.), revenue from social and community services (such as education, health, housing, broadcasting and so on), and revenue from economic services (such as agriculture and allied services, industry and mines, transport and communications, etc.)

Capital Account receipts, on the other hand, include market loans, borrowings from the RBI, etc., through the sale of Treasury Bills, loans from foreign governments and institutions, and repayment of loans by state governments and others to the central government. Capital disbursements would include expenditure on acquisition of various physical assets like land, buildings, machinery and equipment, investments in shares and debentures and loans to state governments and other bodies.

Zero-Base Budgeting

Zero-base budgeting (ZBB) is an innovative technique to guard against wastage in public expenditure. The technique works not through auditing which is a post — operative check, but through an examination of the very rational of an expenditure item under consideration. In a more practical way, ZBB means the evaluation and prioritisation of all programmes at different levels of efforts. To be more simple, each department is required to justify its budget requests from the bottom up, evaluating alternative programme packages and ranking programmes so as to select the best alternative and allocate resources accordingly. Thus, no consideration is given to the post or existing at present, any programme may be included or excluded. The Budget is considered as a whole and a fresh, *i.e.*, from zero-Base.

In the sphere of public budgeting, ZBB was first tried by **Mr. Jimmy Carter** in1973 when he was the Governer of Georgia, with proper remoulding. Later on its was adopted by a number of states in the U.S.A.

Performance Budgeting

Performance Budgetting is generally understood as a system of presentation of public expenditure in terms of functions, programmes, performance units, viz., activities, projects, etc., reflecting primarily the government out-put and its cost.

The U.S. Bureau of the Budget defines a performance budget in these words, "As performance budget in one which presents the purpose and objectives for which funds are required, the cost of the programmes proposed for achieving those objective and quantitative data measuring the accomplishment and work performed under each programme."

Under Performance Budgeting System the over all budget is divided into functions based on the major purpose of government and then sub divided into programme and activities, funds are granted for doing a specific quantity of work. Performance budgeting implies that the budget statement should indicate the actual achievement expected by a Ministry over a period of time from certain amount of expenditure.

Thus, the process of performance budgeting is not merely a technique, it constitutes a new approach to budget formation and execution. Since the cost and benefits indicated side by side, this technique helps in the decision-making regarding allocations of funds.

Types of Deficits

1. Revenue Deficits. Revenue Deficit = Revenue Expenditure-Revenue Receipts

Current revenue expenditure of the central government is composed of plan and non-plan expanditure, and current-revenue receipts include net tax revenue and non-tax revenue of the central government.

2. Budget Deficit. Budget Deficit = Total Expenditure-Total Receipts

The total expenditure of the central governments always exceeded its total revenue which is known as budget deficit or overall budgetary deficit.

3. Fiscal Deficit. In simple terms, fiscal deficit is budgetary deficit plus market borrowings and other liabilities of the government of India.

∴ Fiscal Deficit = Revenue receipts (Net tax revenue + Non-tax revenue) + Capital receipts (only recoveries of loans and other receipts)– Total expenditure (Plan and non-plan)

4. Primary Deficit. The excess of fiscal deficit over payments of interest is called primary deficit.

5. Monetised Deficit. The increase in net RBI credit for central government is called monetised deficit. It includes:

A. Net increase in holdings of treasury bills of RBI.

B. Contribution of RBI in market borrowings of the govt.

PUBLIC REVENUE

Like any other economic unit, a governemtn also needs funds to finance its activities. Such funds are raised from various sources. It is difficult to give a complete list of all the sources of public revenue, but the important and common sources of public revenue would include taxes, income from currency, market borrowings, sale of public assets, income from public undertakings, fees, fines, gifts and donations, etc.

What is a Tax?

A tax is a compulsory levy and those who are taxed have to pay the sums irrespective of any corresponding return of services or goods by the government. In other words, a tax-payer does not receive a definite and direct quid pro quo from the government. Note the word *direct* here. It is not a price paid by the tax-payer for any definite service rendered or a commodity supplied by the government. The tax-payers do get many benefits from the government but no tax-payer has a right to any benefit from the public expenditure on the ground that he is paying a tax.

The Base of Tax

The base of a tax is the legal description of the object with reference to which the tax applies. For example, the base of an excise duty is the production or packing or processing of a specific goods; the base of an income tax is the income of the assessee defined and estimated in terms of certain rules laid down for this purpose. Note that the base of each tax has to be defined legally and it is to be quantified for the purpose of determining the tax liability of an individual tax-payer. Each tax-payer is considered a legal entity for this purpose. It should be noted that a tax base may have a time dimension also. For example, income-tax is usually on an annual basis and the law has to decide whether income would be taxed on the basis of accrual or receipt. The authorities, while determining a tax base, are expected to give due consideration to various questions like those of cost of collection, administration and effects of that tax. With the passage of time, a tax base under consideration may grow or may shrink. For example, as production of excisable goods increases, the base of excise duties would be termed to have grown. Also, by low, new items may be brought under particular taxation, or the relevant provisions, definitions and rules etc. may be changed to extend the coverage or base of a tax. Thus, if new items are brought under excise duties, we shall say that the coverage of excise taxation has been extended and the base of excise taxation has been widened.

Buoyancy and Elasticity of a Tax

These terms denote the factors responsible for an increase in the yield of a tax over time. If a tax revenue increases with the growth of its base, but without an extension of the tax coverage or an upward revision of the tax rates, then the tax is said to be buoyant. It has an inherent tendency to yield more tax revenue with the growth of the base. Thus, for example, with given rates of income-tax and the definition of taxable income, if yield from income-tax increases as national income increases, it would be termed a buoyent tax. Similarly, excise duties are levied on production of specified goods. If new items are not brought under these duties and the rates of existing duties remain unchanged, but the revenue from excise duties increases with an increase in the production of excisable items, we have a case of buoyancy of excise duties. Numerically, the buoyancy of a tax is measured as a ratio of the proportionate increase in tax revenue to a proportionate increase in the tax base.

The yield of a tax may also go up on account of extension of its coverage or a revision of its rates. Such a characteristic of a tax is referred to as its elasticity. In other words, elasticity of a tax refers to its responsiveness to steps taken up authorities in increasing its yeild through an extension of its coverage or revision of its rates. Numerically, the elasticity of a tax would be measured by as a ratio of the proportionate change in its yield to the proportionate change in its yield to the proportionate change in its coverage or rates.

Principles of Taxation

A good tax system is one which is designed on the basis of an appropriate set of principles, such as equality and certainty. Adam Smith was probably the first economist, who stated the general principle of taxation or rules of taxation (which he called the canons of taxation).

The four canons of taxation as prescribed by **Adam Smith** are the following:

1. Canon of Equality
2. Cannon of Certainty
3. Cannon of Convenience
4. Cannon of Economy

Some writers, like Bastable, have added a few more canons of taxation to Adam Smith's four.

5. Canon of Productivity
6. Canon of Elasticity
7. Canon of Diversity
8. Canon of Simplicity
9. Canon of Co-ordination

Different Approaches to the Division of Tax Burden

Financial Approach

There are various theories with regard to the distribution of burden of taxation among the people. One of them is often called the financial theory, which embodied in principle attributed to collect, Pluck the goose with as little squealing as possible. It aims at obtaining maximum amount of revenue rather than on proper distribution of burden of taxation. The greatest danger of this theory is that the burden of taxation may fall mainly on weak and voiceless people rather than on rich and vocal.

Cost-of-Service Approach

This is one of the oldest principles advocated for the distribution of the tax burden. According to this thoery, the basis of taxation should be the cost incurred by government on different services for the benefit of the individual tax-payers. Each tax-payer has to pay the tax equal to the cost of service to him. It means, the higher the cost, the higher should be the tax rate and *vice versa*. The government acts like a producer of a commodity, who charges the price from his customers equal to the amount of cost of production of the commodity.

However, this principle cannot be accepted as the basis of taxation because of several reasons. In the first place, it is very difficult to estimate the cost of service to every individuals, *e.g.*, the government can estimate total expenditure on the defence of the country, but it is difficult to estimate the expenditure incurred by the government on the defence for a particular individual. Secondly the basis of cost of service principle is not fair in a welfare state. If cost is taken as the basis of taxation, the government may not perform various functions which may be very much desirable for the welfare of the country as a whole, *e.g.*, relief in times of drought, flood and earthquake, free education and free medical facilities, etc. Hence, the cost of service principles cannot be accepted as the basis of taxation. Moreover, this principle is not in accordance with the character of a tax. A tax is a compulsory payment and there is no quid-pro-quo in return of the payment of a tax. But according to this theory, the payment of a tax is, in return of the cost of service.

The Benefits-Received Theory

According to this theory, the burden of taxation should be divided among the people in proporiton to the benefits received from the state. The persons receiving equal benefits from the state should pay equal amount as taxes and those who received greater benefits should pay more as taxes than those getting less benefit. The benefit principle is very much similar to the cost of service principle, the former looks at the problem from the side of demand while the latter looks at it from the side of supply.

Ability-to-Pay Approach

This approach considers the tax liability in its true form-a compulsory payment to the state without *quid pro quo*. It does not assume any commercial or semi-commercial relationshjip between the state and the citizens. According to this approach, a citizen is to pay taxes because he can, and his relative share in the total tax burden is to be determined by his relative paying capacity.

How to Measure Ability to Pay

The theory of ability of pay, however, involves the fundamental problem, as how to measure the ability to pay of a person. There are two approaches which have so far been advanced for this purpose — the subjective approach and the objective approach. In the **Subjective approach**, the sacrifice theory has been evolved to measure ability to pay. In the **objective approach**, the faculty theory has been evolved to measure ability to pay.

Objective Indices of Ability-to-Pay

1. Property as an Index of Ability-to-Pay.

2. Consumption Expenditure as the Index of Ability

3. Income as the Index of Ability-to-Pay.

Subjective Indices of Ability-to-Pay

The subjective approach is based on the psychological or mental reactions of the tax payers. In the subjective approach, we estimate the burden felt by the tax-payer or the sacrifice undergone by him. Each tax-payer should make equal sacrifice, if tax burden is to be justly distributed. In other words, the equal sacrifice approach maintains that each tax-payer should be subjected to the 'same' or 'equal' sacrifice. Equal sacrifice principle has three aspects:

A. Equal absolute sacrifice

B. Equal proportional sacrifice

C. Equal marginal sacrifice

A. Equal Absolute Sacrifice : This means that different tax-payers are made to sacrifice the same amount of utility by way of taxes. To put it differently, the difference between the aggregate utility from income before tax and the utility of income after tax is the same for every tax-payer. Symbolically, $U(y) - U(y - T)$ should be the same for all, where U is the total utility, y is the income before tax and $(y - T)$ is the income after tax. Thus,

$$[U(y) - U(y - T)]_A = [U(y) - U(y - T)]_B \text{ and so on.}$$

B. Equal Proportional Sacrifice : In this case, each tax-payer is supposed to sacrifice the same percentage of the total satisfaction which he would have derived from his income. It means that the satisfaction lost in terms of tax payment bears the same proportion to the satisfaction from the pre-tax income in each case. It implies that the loss of utility, as a result of tax, should be proportional to the total income of the tax payers. Here an individual with higher incomes will pay more as a tax than those who have lower incomes. But the ratio of sacrifice to the income will be the same for all tax-payers. This can be expressed as—

$$\left[\frac{U(y)-U(y-T)}{U(y)}\right]_A = \left[\frac{U(y)-U(y-T)}{U(y)}\right]_B \text{ and}$$

so on.

C. Equal Marginal Sacrifice or the Least Aggregate Sacrifice : According to this theory, the tax burden should be apportioned in such a way that the marginal utility of income left after tax with any tax payer would be the same. Symbolically, for each tax-payer.

$$\left[\frac{dU(y-T)}{d(y-T)}\right]_A = \left[\frac{dU(y-T)}{d(y-T)}\right]_B$$

should be the same.

Can	*Nature of Tax Structure*	*Burden of Taxation Higher Income Group*	*Lower Income Group*
1. Equal Absolute Sacrifice	Less Progressive	Lowest	Higher
2. Equal Proportional Sacrifice	More Progressive than absolute equal Sacrifice	Higher	Lower
3. Equal Marginal Sacrifice	Highly Progressive Taxation	Highest	Lowest

Incidence of Taxes

The burden of a tax does not always lie on the person from whom it is collected. In many cases it is borne by other people also. Thus, the person who initially pays the tax may not be actually bearing its money burden as such. Hence, it is necessary to know who bears the immediate burden of a tax and who bears the ultimate burden of the tax. The problem of determining the ultimate burden of a tax is the problem of determining the incidence of the tax.

Impact of a tax is its first point of contact with the tax-payers. It is upon those who bear the first responsibility of paying it to the authorities, that is those who have the statutory responsibility of paying it to the government. Incidence of a tax, on the other hand, is defined as its final resting place. To put it differently, the incidence of a tax is upon those economic units which finally bear the money burden of it and which are not able to pass it on to others. Incidence lies upon that final source from which the tax money comes.

Effects of a Tax

When a tax is imposed and collected, it involves certain responses from the tax-payers, and the economy. Such responses can be of great variety and can profoundly influence the working of the economy in terms of production, growth, saving, investment, choice of techniques of productions, regional in balances, in equalities of income and wealth, and so on. These responses and their results are collectively called the **effects of that tax**. The effects of a tax, therefore, stand apart, both conceptually, and analytically, from both the impact and the incidence of the tax. While the impact of a tax is its first point of contact with the tax-payers and while incidence is its final resting place, its effects will be the resultant responses and changes in the economy. These effects can be the result of the fact of tax imposition itself and they could also follow from the process of shif its incidence.

Demand and Supply Theory of Tax Shifting

This is the most acceptable approach in explaining the incidence of a tax. Tax incidence can be shifted only through sale/purchase transactions and only through a revision of the prices. A price revision is possible and is determined by the relative values of demand and supply elasticities. A tax can, therefore, be shifted only through a shift in the demand and/or supply curves and the sharing of the incidence will be determined by the demand and supply elasticities. The general rule is that irrespectives of whether the statutory liability of a tax (the impact of the tax) rests upon the buyer or the seller, the share of the tax borne by the seller will be the larger according as the elasticity of demand is larger; and the share of the tax borne by the buyer will be the larger according as the elasticity of supply is larger. Actually, the tax burden will be shared between the buyer and the seller in the ratio of the elasticities of supply and demand.

Let us illustrate this statement by first taking the case of a single commodity which has been subjected to a specific (per unit) tax. Let us assume that the impact of the tax is upon the sellers. Let the original demand and supply curves for the commodity by DD' and SS'. With the imposition of a tax SS_1 per unit upon the commodity, the supply curve shifts to S_1S_1' and the price of the commodity rise from PM to P'M'. However, out of this P'M', the sellers get only Am', the balance being collected by the government by way of tax. In other words, the incidence upon the sellers is equal to BA per unit. On the other hand, the buyers are paying now P'M' instead of PM, an increase of P'B per unit which is the incidence upon them.

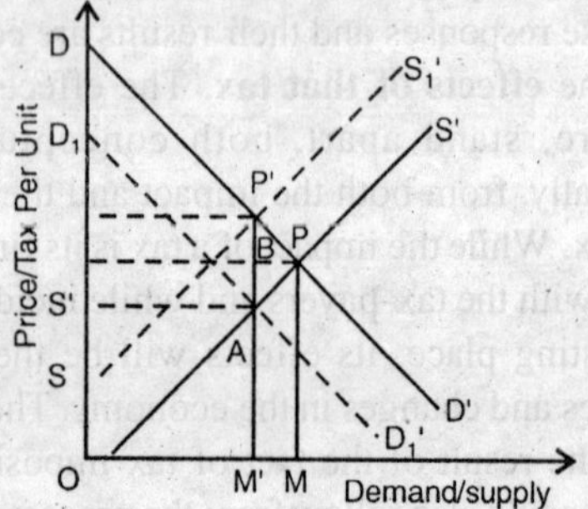

It can be shown that this division of the tax P'A between the two shares P'B and BA is in the ratio of the elasticity of supply to the elasticity of demand. The elasticity of demand is given by proportionate change in demand divided by the proportionate change in the price to the buyers. That is to say, the elasticity of demand E_α is given by

$$E_d = \frac{\frac{MM'}{OM}}{\frac{P'B}{PM}}$$

Similarly, the elasticity of supply is given by the proportionate change in supply divided by the proportionate change in price to the sellers. That is to say the elasticity of supply, E_s is given by

$$E_s = \frac{\frac{MM'}{OM}}{\frac{BA}{PM}}$$

Therefore,

$$\frac{E_s}{E_\alpha} = \left(\frac{MM'}{OM} \Big/ \frac{BA}{PM}\right) \Big/ \left(\frac{MM'}{OM} \Big/ \frac{P'B}{PM}\right)$$

$$= \frac{P'B}{BA}$$

$$= \frac{\text{Incidence on Buyers}}{\text{Incidence on Sellers}}$$

If the tax is imposed upon the buyer, the demand curve would shift left and down wards to D_1D_1. The buyers would then pay a price of AM^1 to the sellers and a tax P'A per unit to the authorities. The resultant incidence on the two parties will ramain unchanged. The formula

$$\frac{\text{Buyers's Share of Incidence}}{\text{Sellers's Share of Incidence}} = \frac{E_s}{E_d}$$

Shows that as the elasticity of supply increases in relation to elasticity of demands the incidence will be more on the buyer and vice versa. Thus, if the commodity taxed is being produced under constant returns, it follows that the supply curve will run parallel to *x*-axis, and the elasticity of supply will tend to be infinity. In that case the incidence of the tax will lie wholly on the buyer. This will happen even when the tax is imposed upon the buyer (in which case the demand curve will shift downwards). Figure A illustrates this phenomenon and it is seen that here the points A and B coincide, so that P'B = P'A.

The tax will be fully borne by the buyers if the demand elasticity is zero (in the ratio E_s / E_d, the denominator becomes zero, see Fig. B). Here the demand curve will run parallel to *y*-axis and an upward shift in the supply curve will automatically mean an

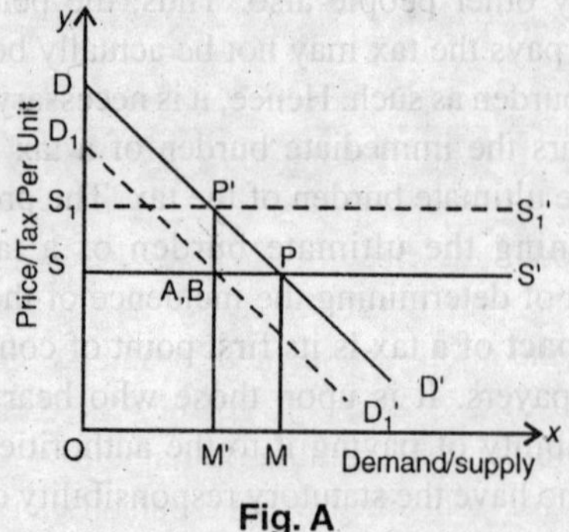

Fig. A

equivalent increase in the price being paid by the buyer. If the tax is ad valorem, say *t* per cent, the price will increase by exactly *t* per cent because the quantity demanded and supplied remains unchanged.

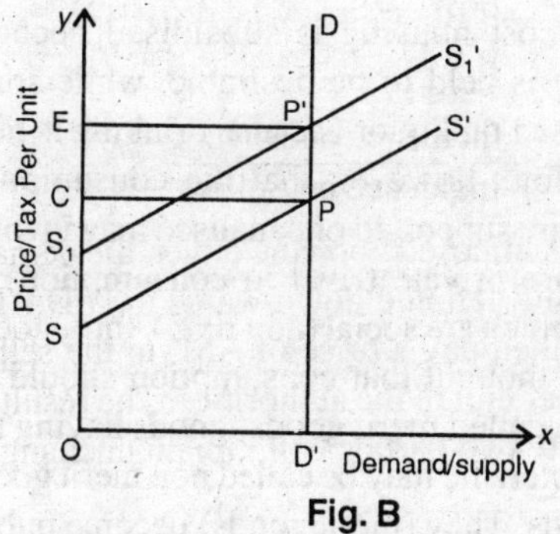

Fig. B

It can be shown in the same way that if the elasticity of supply is zero, or if the elasticity of demand is perfect, the sellers will bear the full incidence of the tax (see figs. C and D).

Conclusion

1. If the elasticity of supply is equal to the elasticity of demand, *i.e.*, $e_s = e_d$; the burden of the tax is equally divided between buyers and sellers, and the price of the commodity will rise by half the amount of tax.

2. When the degree of elasticity of supply is greater than the elasticity of demand, *i.e.*, $e_s > e_d$, the burden of tax will fall upon the buyers in higher proportion than the sellers, and the rise in price will be more than fifty per cent of the amount of the tax per unit.

3. When the degree of elasticity of supply is less than the elasticity of demand, *i.e.*, $e_s < e_d$, the burden of the tax will fall upon the seller in higher proportion than the buyers, and the rise in price will be less than

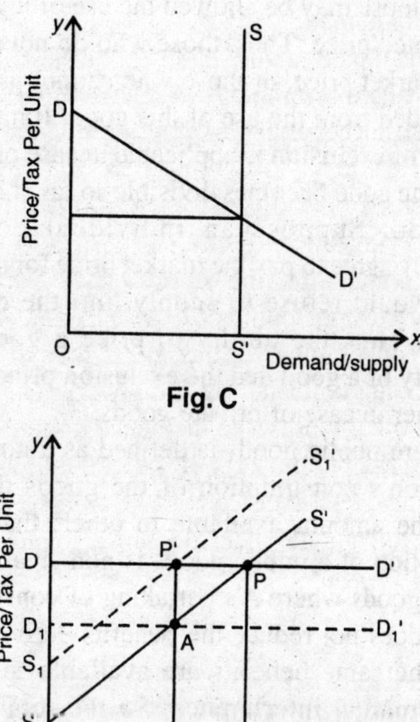

Fig. D

fifty per cent of the tax per unit.

4. If the demand for a commodity is perfectly elastic and its supply is inelastic, the entire burden of the tax will be upon the seller.

5. If the demand for commodity is perfectly in elastic and its supply is elastic, the entire burden of the tax will be upon the buyer.

6. If the supply of a commodity is perfectly elastic and the demand is relatively in elastic the entire burden of the tax will be upon the buyer.

7. If the supply of a commodity is perfectly inelastic and the demand is elastic, the entire burden will be upon the seller.

THE THEORY OF SOCIAL AND PRIVATE GOODS

Private Goods have been defined as "Private goods yield utility (satisfaction) only to the person consuming the good, it is denied to others, only the person who drinks a cup of coffee, for example, benefits from the consumption of that cup of coffee. And the coffee consumed by one person cannot be consumed by any one else. The space in which a person parks his car given satisfaction only to the person whose car is parked there at that time. And during that time, the space is denied to other. Thus, private goods are said to be rival in consumption.

Again, a private goods is priced in the market

and only those may be allowed the use of it who pay its stipulated price. Thus, those who do not agree to pay its market price, or those who cannot pay for it, are excluded from the use of this good. It means the principle of **exclusion** is applicable in case of private goods. The good becomes divisible so far at its use is concerned. Suppose an individual does not voluntarily agree to pay the market price for milk, the market would refuse to supply him the required quantity. Thus the ability to price a goods, the divisibility of a good and the exclusion principle, all go together in case of private goods.

A pure public goods is defined as a goods that one person's consumption of the goods does not reduce the amount available to other; that is, the consumption of a public goods is non-rival. That is they are goods where A's partaking of consumption benefits does not reduce the benefits derived by all othes. The same benefits are available to all and without mutual interference. So the total supply available to the community can be made available to each person in community. For example, a television signal that is available to one person can be made available to all persons in the area within the range of the signal. And one viewer's use of the signal does not reduce the amount of entertainment for others. A dam that controls flooding, benefits everyone in the flood region, and the benefit enjoyed by one property owner does not reduce the benefit available to others. It means a pure public goods is **indivisible**.

Merit Goods : Some goods are considered 'meritorious' while other are held undesirable. For instance, low cost housing is subsidised because decent housing is held to be desirable, while some taxes are imposed on liquor because drinking is held undesirable. Note, however, that the consumption choices which are supported or penalised may involve goods which are private (rival in consumption) as well as goods which are social (non rival). thus, goods for which it is thought that consumption should be encouraged are called merit goods; goods having the opposite characteristic may be called non merit goods or demerit goods. They (merit goods) become public goods if considered so meritorious that their satisfaction is provided for through the public budget, over and above what is provided for through the market and paid for by private buyers.

Difference Between Public Goods and Merit Goods

The Public goods satisfy the conditions of non-excludability, indivisibility and non-rival nature of consumption of goods while these are not the necessary conditions for merit goods, *i.e.*, they may apply or may not apply.

PUBLIC DEBT

Public debt arises due to borrowing by the government. The government may borrow from banks, business organisations, business houses and individuals. The borrowings of the government may be within the country or from outside the country or both. The public debt is generally in the form of bonds (or treasury bills. if the loans are required for a short period), which carries with them the promises of the government to pay interests, to the holders of these bonds at stipulated rate of interest at regular intervals, or lump sum at the end, in addition to the principal which has to be repaid at the stated time.

Objectives of Public Debt

1. To Cover Budget Deficits

2. Rapid Expansion in the States Functions

3. In Times of Depression

4. To Curb Inflation

5. To Finance Development Plan

6. To Finance Public Enterprises

7. Creation of Social Overhead Capital

8. Expansion of Education of Health Services

9. To Finance War

Internal and External Debts

Internal debt refers to the public loans floated within the country, while external debt refers to the obligations of country to foreign governments or foreign nationals or international institution. The payment of interest on foreign debt reduces the net income of the debtor country by transferring a part of its income abroad, the payment of interest on internal debt has no such effect. The country's national income is the same whether the interest on internal debt is left with the tax-payers or is taken from them as taxes and paid out as interest on internal loan.

Factors on which the Effects of Public Debt Depend

The effects of public debt depend upon such factors as the sources of borrowing, the purpose for which borrowing is done, the terms and conditions under which the debt is floated, the volume of the existing public debt, the interest rates, the types of loan employed and the general economic condition of the community.

Effects of the Public Debt Upon the Economy

1. Effects on Consumption
2. Effects on Production
3. Effects on Distribution
4. Effects on Private Sector
5. Effects on the cost of Production
6. Effects of Public Debt on Investment
7. Effects of Public Debt on Working of the Money Market
8. Effects of Public Debt on Resource Allocation and National Income

Public Debt Management

The objective of the management of public debt refers to the aim that the method of borrowing funds and the repayment of loans by the government should not have any adverse effect upon the economic situation of the country. Moreover, the methods of borrowing funds and repayment of loans should help to maintain economic stability, *i.e.*, It should reduce inflationary or deflationary effects upon the economy, and should make available the needed funds to the government. Therefore, all those methods which are adopted by the government to achieve these obejectives, through the process of borrowing funds and repayment of loans, come under public debt management.

Principles of Public Debt Management

1. The Interest Cost of Servicing Public Debts must be Minimised

2. Satisfaction of the Needs of Investors

3. Public Debt Policy must be co-ordinated with Fiscal and Monetary Policy

Redemption of Public Debt

Redemption means repayment of a loans. All government loans, excepting permanent investment in self supporting industries, should be repaid promptly.

Advantages of Debt Redemption

1. It saves the government from bankruptcy.

2. It discourages extravagant expenditure of the government.

3. It maintains the confidence of the lenders.

4. It would be easy for the government to float loan in future.

5. It reduces the cost of debt management.

FISCAL POLICY

Fiscal Policy relates to the governmental decision-making with respect to (1) taxation (2) government spending (3) government borrowing and (4) the management of the government debt.

Classical Concept of Fiscal Policy

Classical economists believed in the policy of *laissez faire*. They believed that supply creates its own demand and, therefore, general over production or involuntary unemployment is well nigh impossible. They believed that a free operation of market forces would achieve full employment and ensure an optimum allocation of resources in an economy. Thus, according to classical economists, full employment is supposed to reach automatically and there is no necessity of any interference.

Modern Concept of Fiscal Policy

The classical concept of fiscal policy has not been accepted by the modern economists like Keynes and Lerner. They believed that the government has to pay a positive role so as to regulate and control the economy by means of taxes and expenditure, which they called as the principle of functional finance.

Modern economists rejected the concept of classical economists, that supply creates it own demand and, therefore, there is no possibility of unemployment, and the equilibrium in the economy is automatically achieved due to the market forces. Contrary to this, Keynes believed that in an advanced economy, the propensity to consume tends to diminish as income increases, in other words, propensity to save increases with the increase in income. Hence, a larger proportion of the additional incomes is saved and not spent. The tendency of less consumption and larger savings results in lowering the demand for goods and services produced at that time; hence dis-equilibrium occurs in the economy. Thus, to maintain income and employment at the present level, it is necessary to offset the effects of decrease in demand for output due to decrease in consumption by a corresponding increase in public expenditure. Hence, if unemployment is to be avoided, the gap between the income and expenditure must be filled either by government expenditure or by increasing the propensity to consume. For instance, during the period of depression, the effective demand is not enough to absorb the available supply of goods and services, resulting in umemployment and under-employment. Therefore, according to modern economists, to maintain full employment and income, it is the duty of the government to increase public expenditure directly by under taking public works programmes on large scale and thereby inducing people to spend more.

Thus, modern fiscal policy is the policy of government under which the government uses its expenditure and revenue programmes to produce desirable of the increase in aggregate production and employment. In other words, the modern fiscal policy is a technique to attain and maintain full employment by manipulating public expenditure and revenue in such a way so as to keep an equilibrium between effective demand and supply of goods and services at that time. Thus, modern fiscal policy is nothing but the application of the principle of functional finance.

Functional Finance

The concept of functional finance was first stated by Keynes and was developed by **Prof. AP. Lerner. Prof. Lerner** believed that Fiscal measures should be judged only by their effects. The way is which the fiscal measures work in the economy is called as functional finance by Prof. Lerner. The central idea is that the government's Fiscal policy involves government spending, and taxing, spending and borrowing of loans, issue of new money and wirhdrawl of money from circulation should all be viewed with the consideration of their impact upon the national economy as a whole and not to any established doctrine of finance, just as the doctrine of sound finance was established by classical economists. **Hence, Judging a Fiscal policy by its effects or the way in which it functions in an economy is called as functional finance.**

Balanced Budget

The budget is the most important instrument of fiscal policy, since the necessary finance is obtained and the public expenditure is made through budget. A government budget is said to be balanced when its tax revenues and expenditures are equal. When the budget is not balanced, there is either a deficit or surplus budget and it is said to be an unbalanced budget in either case. The value of multiplier is more than 1 in case of unbalanced budget, it is1 in case of balanced budget and less than 1 in case of surplus budget.

EXERCISE

1. Cannon of equity in taxation is generally considered to be satisfied by
   (a) Proportional taxation
   (b) Progressive taxation
   (c) Regressive taxation
   (d) Lump sum tax

2. Which one of the following is **NOT** a source of the state tax revenue?
   (a) Land revenue
   (b) Motor vehicles tax
   (c) Entertainment tax
   (d) Corporate tax

3. The receipts from disinvestment of public sector undertakings are shown under which one of the

following sub-heads in the budget of the Government of India?
(*a*) Revenue receipts
(*b*) Non-tax revenue receipts
(*c*) Non-debt capital receipts
(*d*) Debt capital receipts

4. The Principle of Maximum Social Advantage is concerned with
(*a*) Taxation only
(*b*) Expenditure only
(*c*) Public debt only
(*d*) Both taxation and public expenditure

5. Justice in taxation is best exsured by applying the principle of
(*a*) equal absolute sacrifice
(*b*) equal proportional sacrifice
(*c*) equal marginal sacrifice
(*d*) quid pro quo

6. Tobin tax is a tax on
(*a*) exports
(*b*) imports
(*c*) transactions in foreign exchange
(*d*) sales

7. Budgetary deficit does NOT take into account
(*a*) revenue deficit
(*b*) capital budget deficit
(*c*) balance of payment deficit
(*d*) interest payment on public debt

8. **Assertion (A)** : In developing countries, government borrowing is preferred over taxation in financing public expenditure.
Reason (R) : Taxation would require a curtailment in current consumption.
(*a*) Both A and R are true and R is the correct explanation of A
(*b*) Both A and R are true but R is not a correct explanation of A
(*c*) A is true but R is false
(*d*) A is false but R is true

9. which of the following taxes is an exclusive source of revenue for the state governments?
(*a*) Excise duties (*b*) Customs duties
(*c*) Land revenue (*d*) Wealth tax

10. Which one of the following is **NOT** a source of the 'Union Tax revenue'?
(*a*) Property taxes (*b*) Wealth tax
(*c*) Corporate taxes (*d*) Customs duties

11. Given a proportional income tax structure and balanced budget, an autonomous increase in investment will increase the level of equilibrium income and the budget will
(*a*) still be in balance
(*b*) have a surplus
(*c*) have a deficit
(*d*) the outcome is uncertain

12. Provision of social goods possess problem because
(*a*) Such goods tend to be non-rival in consumption
(*b*) Consumption preferences with respect to such goods are not revealed
(*c*) Market mechanism is not well suited for the provision of such goods
(*d*) All the above

13. The imposition of a Selective Sales Tax will raise the price of the taxed product by equal amount if it is produced under
(*a*) constant cost
(*b*) increasing cost
(*c*) decreasing cost
(*d*) imperfect competition

14. Fiscal and Monetary Policies are intended to combat
(*a*) Structural unemployment
(*b*) Frictional unemployment
(*c*) Cyclical unemployment
(*d*) Both (*a*) and (*b*)

15. Assuming a declining marginal utility of money schedule, which one of the following principles will call for "maximum progression"?
(*a*) Principle of equal absolute sacrifice
(*b*) Principle of equal proportional sacrifice
(*c*) Principle of equal marginal sacrifice
(*d*) None of the above

16. In a many person economy with a public and a private goods, revenue allocation will be optimal at the point where
(*a*) the marginal rate of substitution (MRS) is equal to the marginal rate of transformation (MRT) for each individual considered separately
(*b*) the summation of the MRS is equal to the MRT

(c) the MRS is not equal to the MRT since we are dealing with a public goods
(d) none of the above conditions obtain

17. If supply is perfectly inelastic, then the short run impact of a specific sales tax would be to shift the tax burden
(a) entirely on to the consumers
(b) entirely on to the producers
(c) equally between the producers and the consumers
(d) on the other goods where the supply condition may be more elastic

18. Consider the following statements:
1. In the context of the classical model loan finance may be a means of transferring the burden to the future generation.
2. Foreign borrowing permits financing public programmes without placing a burden on the persent generation.
3. Foreign borrowing is not burden some to the future generations even if the funds are used unproductively.
Of the above statements
(a) 1 alone is correct
(b) 1 and 2 are correct
(c) 2 and 3 are correct
(d) 1 and 3 are correct

19. **Octrio** is levied and collected by:
(a) Centre (b) State Government
(c) Local bodies (d) All the above

20. The One Rupee currency note bears the signature of the
(a) Governor, Reserve Bank of India
(b) The Minister for Finance
(c) Chair man, State Bank of India
(d) None of the above

21. Stagflation means
(a) Inflation with recession
(b) Recession and stagnation
(c) Inflation galloping like a stag
(d) Inflation and increasing output

22. The effect of deficit financing is
(a) Always inflationary
(b) Never inflationary
(c) Sometimes inflationary and sometimes not so depending on the response of output and the dose of deficit financing
(d) Always inflationary unless acompanied by effective counteracting measures

23. The Economist on whose suggestions the Wealth Tax, Gift TAx and Expenditure Tax were introduced in India is
(a) V.K.R.V. Rao (b) Kaldor
(c) Galbraith (d) None of the above

24. Agricultural Income Tax is
(a) Levied and appropriated by the respective states
(b) Levied and collected by the Union, but given over to the respective states
(c) Levied by the Union, but collected and appropriated by the respective states
(d) None of the above

25. The MODVAT scheme of taxation benefits
(a) Those manufacturers who import components
(b) Those manufacturers who depend on indigenous material
(c) It is neutral between the above two
(d) Those manufacturers who are importing technology

26. Indirect tax are objectionable because they
(a) Are hard to collect
(b) Are regressive
(c) Do not raise enough revenue
(d) Are particularly hard on the rich

27. All the revenues received, loans raised and money received in repayment of loans by the Union government go into
(a) Consolidated Fund of India
(b) Contingency Fund of India
(c) Public Account of India
(d) Prime Minister's Relief Fund

28. Loans of Public enterprises is a part of
(a) Capital expenditure
(b) Revenue expenditure
(c) Both revenue and capital expenditure
(d) None of the above

29. Interest payment is an item of
(a) Revenue expenditure
(b) Capital expenditure
(c) Plan expenditure
(d) None of the above

30. In India, the states get maximum income from
(a) Sales Tax
(b) Land Revenue
(c) Agricultures income tax
(d) State excise duties

31. In order to reduce inequalities, the government should adopt
(a) Proportional system of taxation
(b) Progressive system of taxation
(c) Regressive system of taxation
(d) None of the above

32. Market borrowings of the Central Government are included in
(a) Capital receipts
(b) Non-tax revenue
(c) Tax revenue
(d) None of the above

33. MODVAT means
(a) Modified Value Added Tax
(b) Moderate Value Added Tax
(c) Modest Value Added Tax
(d) Modern Value added Tax

34. Which one of the following taxes is not levied by the State Governments
(a) Agriculatural Income Tax
(b) Profession Tax
(c) Excise on Liquor
(d) Corporation Tax

35. Who appoints the Finance Commission
(a) President of India
(b) Prime Minister of India
(c) Chairman of the Rajya Sabha
(d) Speaker of the Lok Sabha

36. Excise duties, which are the biggest source of revenue of the Union Government, are levied on
(a) Sale of goods
(b) Production of goods
(c) Consumption of goods
(d) Resale of goods

37. Which of the following is not a direct tax?
(a) Income Tax *(b)* Wealth Tax
(c) Expenditure Tax *(d)* Entertainment Tax

38. The incidence of which of the following will entirely be on the monopolist—
(a) lump-sum tax
(b) specific tax
(c) regulated monopoly pricing
(d) none of the above

39. If supply is perfectly inelastic and demand is highly elastic, then in the short run the incidence of a specific sales tax will be—
(a) entirely on the consumes
(b) entirely on the sellers
(c) equally distributed between the consumers and the sellers
(d) more on the consumers than on the sellers

40. Provision of social goods poses problems because
(a) such goods tend to be non-rival in consumption
(b) individual consumer preferences with respect to these goods is not revealed.
(c) market mechanism is not well suited for the provision of such goods
(d) all the above

41. Which one of the following is not an objective of fiscal policy:
(a) economic growth
(b) economic stability
(c) maximisation of emloyment level
(d) regulating of financial institutions

42. The concept of Zero-Based-Budget (ZBB) was given by
(a) R.A. Musgrave *(b)* J.M. Keynes
(c) Peter A. Pyhr *(d)* A.H. Hansen

43. Which of the following concepts of Budget deficit has become practically redundant in India
(a) Fiscal Deficit *(b)* Budgetary Deficit
(c) Primary Deficit *(d)* Revenue Deficit

44. The tax-multiplier is generally—
(a) greater than the government expenditure multiplier
(b) equal to the government expenditure multiplier
(c) less than the government expenditure multiplier
(d) equal to the investment multiplier

45. Which of the following statements regarding incidence of tax is true:
(a) the incidence of a tax on imports is totally borne by the consumers in the importing country.

(b) the incidence of a tax on exports is totally on the producer
(c) the incidence of taxes on imports and exports is shared equally by the producer and users in the importing country
(d) the incidence of taxes on imports and exports is shared by producers and users in the inverse proportion to the elasticities of their respective demand

46. The difference between Total Public Revenue and Total Public Expenditure in a particular year is termed as
(a) Primary deficit (b) Revenue deficit
(c) Budgetary deficit (d) Fiscal deficit

47. The tax which is not shared by states is—
(a) Sales tax (b) Income tax
(c) Corporation tax (d) Central Excise duty

48. Which one of the following is not an objective of fiscal policy?
(a) Economic growth
(b) Price stability
(c) Maximization of employment level
(d) Regulating of financial institutions

49. Which of the following does not measure income inequality?
(a) Lorenz curve
(b) Per capita income
(c) Ginni's coefficient
(d) Percentage of population in different income groups

50. Black money in India—
(a) Raises prices alone
(b) Encourage lavish consumption alone
(c) Causes only loss of revenue to government
(d) Effects all the above three

51. Agricultural income tax is a source of revenue to—
(a) Central Government
(b) State Government
(c) Local Administration
(d) Central and State Government

52. The chairman of the 12th Finance Commission is—
(a) Dr. C. Rangarajan (b) Raja J. Chalia
(c) T.S. Papola (d) Y.K. Alagha

53. It is generally believed that a rise in the tax rate would normally lead to a rise in the revenue. But there is also a view the reduced rates on income tax would lead to a significant rise in income tax revenue. This later view has been attributed to
(a) Arthur Laffer (b) Robert Lucas
(c) Herbert Simon (d) J.B. Say

54. After allowing for state's share of taxation which one of the following tax revenues brings in the largest amount of revenue to the Central Government?
(a) Corporation tax (b) Income tax
(c) Custom duties (d) Union Excise duties

55. Match list I with list II and select the correct answer using the codes given below the lists—

List I	List II
A. Service tax	1. Central government
B. Stamp duty	2. State government
C. Property tax	
D. Sales tax	

Codes:	A	B	C	D
(a)	1	2	2	–
(b)	1	2	–	2
(c)	–	1	2	–
(d)	–	1	–	2

56. As per the recommendations of the Finance Commission, besides income tax, the net proceeds of which of the following tax (es) is/are to be shared between the centre and the states?
1. Additional duties of excise
2. Wealth tax on agricultural properties
3. Union Excise Duties
Select the correct answer using the codes given below—
Codes :
(a) 1, 2 and 3 (b) 3 only
(c) 1 and 2 (d) 2 and 3

57. Assertion (A) : The burden of Union taxation is borne mainly by the lower and middle income groups in India.
Reason (R) : The tax structure is such that taxes on commodities is predominant
(a) Both A and R are true and R is the correct explanation of A
(b) Both A and R are true but R is NOT a correct explanation of A

(c) A is true but R is false
(d) A is false but R is true

58. Match list I (Nature of deficit) with list II (How it is calculated) and select the correct answer by using the codes given below the lists:

List I	List II
A. Fiscal deficit	1. (Revenue and interest receipts) minus (Revenue expenditure)
B. Revenue deficit	2. (Revenue receipts + Recovery of loans and other receipts) minus (Total expenditure)
C. Budgetary deficit	3. Receipts minus disbursements in capital account
D. Capital deficit	4. (Total receipts) – (Total disbursements)

Codes:	A	B	C	D
(a)	1	2	4	3
(b)	2	1	4	3
(c)	2	1	3	4
(d)	1	2	3	4

59. Consider the following statements—
The incidence of corporate income tax under competition depends upon
1. the elasticity of substitution between factors in the non-corporate sector industries.
2. the income elasticity of demand for the output of the corporate sector industries.
3. the elasticity of substitution in demand between the outputs of the corporate sector and non-corporate sector industries
4. the difference between the factor proportions in the corporate and non-corporate sectors.
Of these statements
(a) 1 and 4 are correct
(b) 1,3 and 4 are correct
(c) 2,3 and 4 are correct
(d) 1,2 and 3 are correct

60. Which of the following is/are included in the capital budget of the Government of India?
1. Borrowings from the RBI
2. Loans received from foreign governments
3. Expenditure on acquisition of assets like roads, buildings, machinery etc.
4. Loans and advances granted to the states and Union Territories.
Select the correct answer using the codes given below:
Codes:
(a) 1, 2 and 4 (b) 2 and 3
(c) 1 alone (d) 1, 2, 3 and 4

61. Assertion (A) : A progressive income tax is based on equimarginal sacrifice.
Reason (R) : Higher the income, lower will be the marginal utility of money for the tax payer.
(a) Both A and R are true and R is the corrrect explanation of A
(b) Both A and R are true but R is **NOT** a correct explanation of A
(c) A is true but R is false
(d) A is false but R is true

62. Consider the following statements—
The two main objectives of fiscal policy in developing countries are
1. rapid economic growth
2. price stability
3. full employment
4. equitable distribution
Of these statements
(a) 1 and 2 are correct
(b) 2 and 3 are correct
(c) 2 and 4 are correct
(d) 1 and 4 are correct

63. The whole burden of a tax will be borne by the sellers, if
(a) the demand for a commodity is inelastic and supply is perfectly elastic
(b) the elasticity of demand for a commodity is same as the elasticity of supply of the commodity
(c) the demand for a commodity is perfectly elastic and supply is inelastic
(d) the elasticity of demand for a commodity is less than the elasticity of supply of that commodity

64. Which one of the following pairs is correctly matched?
(a) Fiscal deficit — G.D.P
(b) Primary deficit — Money supply
(c) Monetised deficit — Interest payments
(d) Budget deficit — Revenue expenditure and receipts on Revenue Account

65. Which one of the following dealt exslusively

with taxation of agricultural wealth and income in India?
(a) John Mathai Committee 1953
(b) Kaldor's Report 1956
(c) Wanchoo Committee 1971
(d) Raj Committee 1972

66. Which one of the following is not the reason for rising debt over the last two decades in India?
(a) The failure to generate adequate resources from internal sectors for financing development plans
(b) The need for foreign aid in the form of technologial assistance to carry out different development projects
(c) Failure to increase exports sufficiently
(d) Decrease in the cost of foreign debt

67. Which one of the following types of revenues is not shared by the Central Government with the State Governments?
(a) Central Sales Tax (b) Income Tax
(c) Excise Duty (d) Customs Duty

68. Which one of the following sources is not considered as a source of government revenue?
(a) Taxes
(b) Surplus of public enterprises
(c) Transfer payments
(d) Mobilisation of internal loans and deposits

69. **Assertion (A) :** Public Finance is a normative science.
Reason (R) : The objective of Fiscal operation implies proper allocation of resources, distribution of income, full employment and stability with grown.
(a) Both A and R are true and R is the correct explanation of A
(b) Both A and R are true but R is not correct explanation of A
(c) A is true but R is false
(d) A is false but R is true

70. Zero-Based Budgeting (ZBB) lays emphasis on
1. Unlimited deficit financing
2. Preparing new budget right from the scratch
3. Preparing the budget neglecting history of expenditure
(a) 1, 2 and 3 (b) 1 and 3
(c) 2 and 3 (d) 1 and 2

71. Which one of the following taxes is levied by the states and shared with the Union Government?
(a) Irrigation tax
(b) Agriculture income tax
(c) Entertainment tax
(d) None of the above

72. Which of the following taxes is levied by the State Government only
(a) Entertainment tax
(b) Wealth tax
(c) Income tax
(d) Corporation tax

73. In the Indian context deficit financing means
(a) An excess of government's revenue over expenditure
(b) An excess of government's current expenditure over its current revenue
(c) An excess of government's total expenditure over its total revenue
(d) None of these

74. Food and Fertilizer subsidies are included in
(a) Capital expenditure
(b) Revenue expenditure
(c) Plan expenditure
(d) All of the above

75. Which one of the following taxes is levied by the centre but wholly assigned to the states
(a) Personal Income tax
(b) Excise on drugs and narcotics
(c) Railway passenger tax
(d) Gift tax

76. Expenditure on 'general services' is
(a) Revenue Expenditure
(b) Capital Expenditure
(c) Plan Expenditure
(d) None of the above

77. The basis of corporate tax is
(a) Total turnover of the company
(b) Profit after distribution of dividend
(c) Profit before distribution of dividend
(d) Capital employed in the company

78. If external debt of country rises faster than its interest obligations, it is a case of
(a) Liquidity trap (b) Debt trap
(c) Poverty trap (d) Export led growth

79. Central assistance for state and UT Plan is a part of
(*a*) Plan expenditure
(*b*) Non-Plan expenditure
(*c*) Revenue expenditure
(*d*) None of the above

80. Loans of foreign governments is
(*a*) Revenue expenditure
(*b*) Capital expenditure
(*c*) Both revenue and capital expenditure
(*d*) Neither revenue nor capital expenditure

81. India's Fiscal policy since independence has centered around
(*a*) More borrowings (*b*) Higher taxation
(*c*) Deficit financing (*d*) All the three

82. Fiscal policy in a developing country like India aims at
(*a*) Widening the tax base
(*b*) Mopping up most of the surpluses through taxation
(*c*) Achieving socio-economic objectives of the state
(*d*) All of these

83. The revenue of the state governments are raised from the following sources except one, which is that
(*a*) Land revenue
(*b*) Agricultural income tax
(*c*) Entertainment tax
(*d*) Expenditure tax

84. As a source of revenue, a tax on a commodity will be more successful if
(*a*) the higher the percentage of the tax
(*b*) the lower the percentage of the tax
(*c*) the more elastic the supply and demand for the commodity
(*d*) the more inelastic the supply and demand for the commodity

85. The long term Fiscal Policy formulated in the context of the Seventh Five Year Plan lays emphasis on
(*a*) Tackling problem of poverty and unemployment
(*b*) Reforming tax system
(*c*) Capital formation by increasing money income and reducing consumption
(*d*) Making taxes easily comprehensible to the tax payers

86. The Agricultural Holding Tax (AHT) was recommended by a committee headed by
(*a*) C.H. Hanumantha Rao
(*b*) M.L. Dantwala
(*c*) R.J. Chelliah
(*d*) K.N. Raj

87. **Assertion (A) :** Indirect taxes contribute a major part of the total Taxation Revenue in India.
Reason (R) : These taxes cannot be evaded.
(*a*) Both A and R are true and R explains A
(*b*) Both A and R are true but R does not explains A
(*c*) A is true but R is false
(*d*) A is false but R is true

88. Debt-Service Ratio is a ratio of—
(*a*) GDP which is to be paid as debt
(*b*) Total debt which is to be paid in the form of interest burden
(*c*) Export earnings which are to be paid by way of interest and principal
(*d*) None of these

89. The relationship between tax collections and tax rates has been expressed by
(*a*) Lorenz Curve (*b*) Engel's Law
(*c*) Laffer Curve (*d*) Indifference Curve

90. Fiscal deficit in the Union Budget means—
(*a*) the sum of budgetary deficit and net increase in internal and external borrowings
(*b*) the difference between current expenditure and current revenue
(*c*) the sum of monetised deficit and budgetary deficit
(*d*) net increase in Government's borrowing from the RBI

91. Since the introduction of '**Ways and Means Advances**' mechanism by the Union government vis-a-vis the RBI, one of the following has become redundant—
(*a*) Monetised deficit (*b*) Revenue deficit
(*c*) Budgetary deficit (*d*) Primary deficit

92. M O D V A T is different from V A T in the sense that—
1. under M O D V A T, tax is levied only on value addition while under V A T, excise is

imposed on final value and then rebate is given on inputs.

2. M O D V A T is only at the production stage while V A T extends both to production and distribution stage

3. Under M O D V A T, excise is levied on final value and then rebate is given on inputs while under V A T, tax is levied only on value addition

4. M O D V A T implies rationalization of excise duty only while V A T implies rationalization of excise, sales and turn over taxes etc. also

Choose correct answer from—

(a) 1, 2 and 4 (b) 1, 3 and 4
(c) 2, 3 and 4 (d) 1, 2, 3 and 4

93. Which of the following does not help to broaden the Tax Base—

(a) M A T
(b) V A T
(c) Zero-Based-Budgeting
(d) Tax on Agricultural Income

94. All Taxes come under—

(a) capital receipts (b) revenue receipts
(c) public debt (d) public expenditure

95. The merit of zero-based budgeting is that—

(a) Tax liability is reduced
(b) Profits go up
(c) Deficit Financing becomes zero
(d) Expenditure is rationalized

96. When the rate of tax goes up with increase in income is called—

(a) Proportional tax (b) Regressive tax
(c) Progressive tax (d) Presumptive tax

97. A budgetary deficit means—

(a) Total expenditure is more than total revenue
(b) Current expenditure is more than current revenue
(c) Capital expenditure is more than capital revenue
(d) Total expenditure is more than current revenue

98. The main source of revenue of the Union Government in ascending order of importance are—

1. Income Tax
2. Corporate Tax
3. Customs Duties
4. Excise Duties

(a) 3, 2, 4, 1 (b) 2, 4, 3, 1
(c) 2, 1, 3, 4 (d) 1, 2, 3, 4

99. When the ratio of indirect taxes to total taxation revenue is very high, it leads to—

1. rise in the price level
2. higher taxation burden on the rich
3. higher taxation burden on the poor
4. fall in tax revenues

(a) 1 and 2 (b) 1 and 3
(c) 1, 2 and 4 (d) 1, 3 and 4

100. Which of the following is not a part of Fiscal Policy?

(a) Subsidy under the Public Distribution System
(b) Control of population
(c) Imposition of taxation
(d) Issue of bonds by Government

101. Ad Valorom means—

(a) According to value
(b) According to weight
(c) According to size
(d) According to advertisement costs

102. Which of the following come under Non-Plan expenditure—

1. Subsidies
2. Interest Payments
3. Defence Expenditure
4. Maintenance expenditure for the infra-structure created previous plans

Choose the correct answer using the codes given below—

(a) 1 and 2 (b) 1 and 3
(c) 2 and 4 (d) 1, 2, 3 and 4

103. When the ratio of direct taxes to GDP goes on increasing, the economy is said to be moving more and more towards—

1. Unequal distribution of income
2. Progressive tax structure
3. Equal distribution of income
4. Proportional tax structure

Select your answer from the following—

(a) 1, 2, 3, 4 (b) 1, 4
(c) 2, 3 (d) 1, 2

104. Which of the following is not an indirect tax?

(a) Land Revenue (b) Sales Tax

(c) Custom Duties (d) Entertainment Tax

105. In India, federal financial assistance to states is given on the basis of
(a) the tax effort of the states
(b) the revenue collection of the states
(c) population, tax effort and special problems of the states
(d) the demands of the states

106. Which one of the following sources of central revenue belongs to the category of indirect taxes?
(a) Corporation Tax (b) Customs
(c) Wealth Tax (d) Interest Receipts

107. Exemption from the entertainment tax is granted if the entire proceeds are devoted to
1. postal savings
2. shares in new industrial undertakings
3. charitable purposes
4. redemption of debt
Select the correct answer using the codes given below—
Codes:
(a) 1 and 2 (b) 1 and 3
(c) 2 and 3 (d) 3 and 4

108. The most expensive head under public revenue expenditure in the Union Budgets of India of the last decade has been—
(a) defence (b) interest payments
(c) subsidies (d) social services

109. Which of the following effects of deficit financing of the central Government effects the common man most adversely?
(a) Forced savings
(b) Credit creation by banks
(c) Inflationary rise in prices
(d) Changes in the pattern of social investment

110. The rapid increase of public debt of the Central Government of India since 1950-51 has been due to
(a) uncontrolled inflation
(b) mounting shares of state governments from revenues raised by the central government
(c) mounting costs of financing public expenditure
(d) rising population

111. "Maximum Social Welfare" in public finance is attained when—
(a) marginal disutility of taxation is greater than the marginal utility of public expenditure
(b) marginal disutility of taxation is less than the marginal utility of public expenditure
(c) marginal disutility of taxation is equal to marginal utility of public expenditure
(d) taxation and public expenditure are at the lowest level

112. Which of the following pairs are examples of direct tax?
1. Income tax and wealth tax
2. Sales tax and Excise duty
3. Capital gains tax and Corporation tax
Select the correct answer using the codes given below—
Codes:
(a) 1 and 3 (b) 1 and 2
(c) 2 and 4 (d) 2 and 3

113. Consider the following statements Non-Plan Revenue Expenditure includes expenditure incurred on
1. interest payments
2. maintenance of capital assets
3. flood control
of these statements
(a) 2 and 3 are correct
(b) 1 and 2 are correct
(c) 1 and 3 are correct
(d) 1, 2 and 3 are correct

114. Consider the following statements—
The division of incidence of a tax between buyers and sellers is governed by
1. elasticity of demand and supply
2. cost conditions
3. market structure
of these statements
(a) 1 and 2 are correct
(b) 2 and 3 are correct
(c) 1 and 3 are correct
(d) 1, 2 and 3 are correct

115. Capital gains mean
(a) increase in the sales on which capital is invested
(b) increase in the value of the property owned
(c) gross profit earnings on a capital asset

(*d*) marginal efficiency of capital

116. Consider the following statements

A government may cover up the deficit by—

1. withdrawing its cash balances from the central bank of the country.

2. borrowing from the central bank and commercial banks

3. printing new money

of these statements

(*a*) 1 and 2 are correct

(*b*) 1 and 3 are correct

(*c*) 2 and 3 are correct

(*d*) 1, 2 and 3 are correct

117. Which one of the following is the most important source of revenue of state governments in India?

(*a*) Land revenue

(*b*) State excise duties

(*c*) Sales tax

(*d*) Stamps and registration fees

118. Assertion (A) : More reliance should be placed on progressive income taxes.

Reason (R) : It is in accordance with the principles of equity.

(*a*) Both A and R are true and R is the correct explanation of A

(*b*) Both A and R are true but R is NOT a correct explanation of A

(*c*) A is true but R is false

(*d*) A is false but R is true

119. The burden of a tax on monopoly profit will be

(*a*) entirely on the producer

(*b*) entirely on the consumer

(*c*) equally distributed among the producer and the consumer

(*d*) more on the consumer than on the producer

120. The incidence of a sales tax will be on the sellers when

(*a*) the demand for the commodity is perfectly elastic

(*b*) the demand for the commodity is perfectly inelastic

(*c*) the demand curve is a rectangular hyperbola

(*d*) the demand forth commodity is moderately elastic

121. Match list I (Tax) with list II (Imposed and collected by) and select the correct answer using the codes given below the list—

List I	**List II**
A. Corporation Tax	1. State
B. Sales Tax	2. Municipal corportation
C. House Tax	
D. Wealth Tax	3. Government of India

Codes:	A	B	C	D
(*a*)	3	1	2	3
(*b*)	2	1	1	3
(*c*)	2	3	3	2
(*d*)	3	2	2	1

122. Assertion (A): Indirect taxes are generally regressive in character.

Reason (R): They are imposed uniformly on all tax payers irrespective of their incomes.

(*a*) Both A and R are individually true and R is the correct explanation of A

(*b*) Both A and R are individually true but R is not the corect explanation of A

(*c*) A is true but R is false

(*d*) A is false but R is true

123. Which one of the following pairs is not correctly matched in the Indian context?

(*a*) Cash Reserve Ratio — Monetary Policy

(*b*) Non-performing Assets — Profitability of Commercial banks

(*c*) Market-determined rate of interest — Post Office deposits

(*d*) Administered rate of interest — Public Provident Fund

124. Assertion (A): In developing countries, government borrowing is preferred over taxation in financing public expenditure.

Reason (R): Taxation would require a curtailment in current consumption.

(*a*) Both A and R are true and R is the correct explanation of A

(*b*) Both A and R are true but R is not a correct explanation of A

(*c*) A is true but R is false

(*d*) A is false but R is true

125. Match list-I with list-II and select the correct answer using the codes given below the lists:

List I	List II
A. New Economic Policy	1. Controlling bank credit
B. Monetary Policy	2. Deficits and debt management
C. Trade Policy	3. Globalisation
D. Fiscal Policy	4. Liberalisation

Codes:

	A	B	C	D
(a)	4	1	3	2
(b)	3	2	4	1
(c)	4	2	3	1
(d)	3	1	4	2

ANSWERS

1	**2**	**3**	**4**	**5**	**6**	**7**	**8**	**9**	**10**
(b)	*(d)*	*(b)*	*(d)*	*(c)*	*(c)*	*(c)*	*(a)*	*(c)*	*(a)*
11	**12**	**13**	**14**	**15**	**16**	**17**	**18**	**19**	**20**
(a)	*(d)*	*(a)*	*(d)*	*(b)*	*(a)*	*(b)*	*(b)*	*(c)*	*(d)*
21	**22**	**23**	**24**	**25**	**26**	**27**	**28**	**29**	**30**
(a)	*(c)*	*(b)*	*(a)*	*(b)*	*(b)*	*(a)*	*(a)*	*(a)*	*(a)*
31	**32**	**33**	**34**	**35**	**36**	**37**	**38**	**39**	**40**
(b)	*(a)*	*(a)*	*(d)*	*(a)*	*(b)*	*(d)*	*(a)*	*(b)*	*(d)*
41	**42**	**43**	**44**	**45**	**46**	**47**	**48**	**49**	**50**
(d)	*(c)*	*(b)*	*(c)*	*(d)*	*(b)*	*(c)*	*(d)*	*(b)*	*(d)*
51	**52**	**53**	**54**	**55**	**56**	**57**	**58**	**59**	**60**
(b)	*(a)*	*(a)*	*(d)*	*(b)*	*(b)*	*(a)*	*(b)*	*(d)*	*(d)*
61	**62**	**63**	**64**	**65**	**66**	**67**	**68**	**69**	**70**
(a)	*(c)*	*(c)*	*(a)*	*(d)*	*(d)*	*(d)*	*(c)*	*(a)*	*(c)*
71	**72**	**73**	**74**	**75**	**76**	**77**	**78**	**79**	**80**
(d)	*(a)*	*(c)*	*(b)*	*(c)*	*(a)*	*(a)*	*(b)*	*(b)*	*(b)*
81	**82**	**83**	**84**	**85**	**86**	**87**	**88**	**89**	**90**
(c)	*(d)*	*(d)*	*(d)*	*(b)*	*(d)*	*(c)*	*(b)*	*(c)*	*(a)*
91	**92**	**93**	**94**	**95**	**96**	**97**	**98**	**99**	**100**
(a)	*(a)*	*(c)*	*(b)*	*(d)*	*(c)*	*(a)*	*(d)*	*(b)*	*(b)*
101	**102**	**103**	**104**	**105**	**106**	**107**	**108**	**109**	**110**
(a)	*(d)*	*(c)*	*(a)*	*(c)*	*(b)*	*(d)*	*(b)*	*(c)*	*(c)*
111	**112**	**113**	**114**	**115**	**116**	**117**	**118**	**119**	**120**
(c)	*(a)*	*(d)*	*(c)*	*(b)*	*(d)*	*(c)*	*(a)*	*(a)*	*(a)*
121	**122**	**123**	**124**	**125**					
(a)	*(a)*	*(c)*	*(a)*	*(a)*					

UNIT-VIII : INTERNATIONAL ECONOMICS

THEORIES OF INTERNATIONAL TRADE

International trade deals with business transactions that take place between citizens of different nations and with considerations of commercial diplomacy that spring from such business transactions. Consequently, international trade may be defined as the exchange of goods and services among the citizens of independent or sovereign states or countries. It consists of the exchange by each country of its low-priced goods and services for those goods and services which can be secured at lower prices from abroad than the prices at home.

A. ABSOLUTE COST ADVANTAGE THEORY OF ADAM SMITH

In Smith's model of international trade, every one will be better off without making any one worse off. As such each country will gain by trading. Taking the case of two individual producers, a tailor and a shoe-maker, tailor does not make his own shoes; he exchanges a suit with shoes. Thereby both the shoe-maker and the tailor gain. In the same manner, Smith argued, a whole country can gain by trading with other countries.

If it takes 10 labour units to manufacture 1 unit of good A in country I but 20 labour units in country II, and if it takes 20 units of labour to manufacture 1 unit of good B in country I but only 10 labour units in country II, then both countries can gain by trading.

If the two countries exchanged the 2 goods at a ratio of 1 to 1, so that 1 unit of good A is exchanged for 1 unit of good B, country I could get 1 unit of good B by sacrificing only 10 units of labour, whereas it would have to give up 20 units of labour if it produced the good itself. Likewise, country II would have to sacrifice only 10 units of labour to get 1 unit of good A, whereas it would have to give up 20 units of labour if it produced it itself. The implication of this is clearly that both countries could have more of both goods, with a given effort, by trading.

This was a simple and powerful illustration of the benefits of trade, and on it Adam Smith rested his plea for non-interference for free trade as the best policy for trade between nations. Smith's argument seems convincing, but it is not very deep. It was left to Torrens and Ricardo to produce the stronger and more subtle argument for the benefits of trade contained in the theory of comparative advantage.

B. DAVID RICARDO AND THE THEORY OF COMPARATIVE COST ADVANTAGE

While it is true that a large part of world trade rests upon absolute differences in costs, such differences in costs cannot explain trade that takes place between two such countries one of which can produce both commodities at a cheaper cost than the other country but she can produce one commodity more cheaply. To express the same idea differently : Why does trade take place when one country produces both goods at an absolutely lower unit cost than the other but her cost is comparatively lower in the production of one good, *i.e.*, the country commands comparative cost advantage in the production of only one good although she possess absolute cost advantage in the production of both the goods? It was David Ricardo who first explained the basis of trade under such situations. According to Ricardo, "Each country will specialise in the production of those commodities in which it has greater comparative advantage or least comparative disadvantage. Thus a country will export those commodities in which its comparative advantage is the greatest, and import those commodities in which its comparative disadvantage is the least."

Assumptions of the Theory

The Ricardian theory is based on the following assumptions :

1. Labour is the only factor of production.
2. All labour units are homogeneous.
3. Labour is perfectly mobile within the country but is perfectly immobile between different countries.
4. Production of two goods takes place under constant cost conditions so that the unit cost ratios of the two goods are constant.
5. Trade takes place between only two countries and in two commodities produced by labour alone. In other words, Ricardian theory is a $2 \times 2 \times 1$ trade model.
6. Prices of the two commodities are determined by labour cost, *i.e.*, the number of labour units employed to produce each.
7. Technological knowledge is unchanged.
8. There is free trade between the two countries, there being no trade barriers or restrictions in the movement of commodities.
9. No transport costs are involved in carrying trade between the two countries.
10. All factors of production are fully employed in both the countries.

Given these asssumptions, Ricardo enunciated the "principle of comparative costs," also called the "principle of comparative cost advantage" by taking the example of two countries England and Portugal and of two commodities wine and cloth. In his celebrated example, Portugal produces both wine and cloth at an absolutely lower cost than does England, *i.e.*, she possesses absolute advantage over England in the production of the both goods. Her comparative advantage is, however, greater in the production of wine than in the production of cloth. Conversely, England is inefficient in the production of both wine and cloth as her absolute real cost of production of both wine and cloth is higher compared with that of Portugal. However, her inefficiency is less marked in the production of cloth than in the production of wine. Under such a situation, it would be mutually advantageous for both the countries if Portugal concentrated only on the production of wine and exchanged her surplus wine against England's surplus cloth and England concentrated only on the manufacture of cloth exchanging her surplus production of cloth for the Portuguese wine. We may now reproduce Ricardo's celebrated example of Portugal and England by means of the following table:

	Per Unit Cost (in labour hours) of	
Country	*Wine*	*Cloth*
Portugal	80	90
England	120	100

According to the above cost data, one unit of wine costs 80 labour hours and one unit of cloth costs 90 hours of labour in Portugal. The corresponding cost of producing 1 unit of wine and 1 unit of cloth in England is 120 and 100 hours of labour. It is, therefore, obvious that Portugal commands absolute superiority over England in the production of both the goods. This absolute superiority of Portugal is, however, more marked (greater) in the production of wine than in the production of cloth. She has, therefore, a comparative cost advantage in the production of wine because here her cost ratio difference (or productivity) is relatively higher than it is in the case of cloth, *i.e.*, $80/120 < 90/100 < 1$. It means that Portuguese labour's productivity in wine is 1.5 times (120/80) that of the productivity of English labour while her labour's productivity in cloth is only 1.1 times (100/90) that of the English labour. Since both 1.5 and 1.1 are greater than 1, it follows that Portugal's labour is more efficient or productive than England's labour in both the branches of production. It is, however, equally true that, since 1.5 is greater than 1.1, Portuguese labour is relatively more efficient or productive in wine than in cloth. In other wods, Portugal possesses a comparative advantage over England in the production of wine relative to the production of cloth. Conversely, England suffers from a greater disadvantage in wine than in cloth.

But how can it be said that in the situation

envisaged by Ricardo both countries will gain from trade? Returning to Ricardo's example, in the absence of trade 1 unit of wine will exchange for 0.88 unit of cloth in Portugal while in England 1 unit of wine will exchange for 1.2 units of cloth. If trade between the two countries begins, it is to the advantage of Portugal to export wine to England where 1 unit of it is exchanged for 1.2 units of cloth. Assuming perfect interindustry labour mobility within the country, Portugal will produce wine instead of cloth. Conversely, it will be to the advantage of England to specialise in the manufacture of cloth because she can obtain wine at a cheaper cost from Portugal by exchanging cloth against wine. There exists sufficient inducement for both the countries to engage in trade. Portugal would gain by trading off her surplus wine against English cloth so long as she can get more than 0.88 unit of cloth for 1 unit of wine while England would gain so long as she is asked to give less than 1.2 units of cloth for 1 unit of wine. Consequently, any exchange ratio between 0.88 and 1.2 units of cloth for 1 unit of wine will be acceptable to both the countries making trade possible between them. The theory of comparative cost advantage leads to the conclusion that each country will specialise in the production of that good in which it enjoys comparative cost advantages as by doing so it will be able to obtain a greater total product-mix from its given endowment of factors of production. Ricardo did not, however, explain where the actual exchange ratio between 0.88 and 1.2 units of cloth for 1 unit of wine will be fixed. In fact, there are possible a vast myriad of exchange ratios between the range of 0.88 and 1.2.

Its Criticism

The principle of comparative advantage has been criticised on the following grounds.

1. Unrealistic Assumption of Labour Theory of Value
2. Static Assumption of Fixed Proportions
3. Unrealistic Assumption of Constant Costs
4. Two-country Two-commodity Model is Unrealistic
5. Unrealistic Assumption of Free Trade
6. Neglects the Role of Technology
7. Unrealistic Assumption of Full Employment
8. Consider only Supply Side of International Trade

C. MODERN THEORY : HECKSCHER-OHLIN THEORY

Bertin Ohlin in his famous book "Interregional and International Trade" criticised the classical theory of international trade and formulated the General Equilibrium or Factor Endowment Theory of International Trade. It is also known as the *Modern Theory of International Trade* or the Hecksher-Ohlin Theorem. In fact, it was Eli Hecksher, Ohlin's teacher, who first propounded the idea in 1919 that trade results from differences in factor endowments in different countries, and Ohlin carried it forward to build the modern theory of international trade.

Assumptions of the Theory

1. It is a 2 × 2 × 2 model, *i.e.*, there are two countries (A and B), two commodities (X and Y) and two factors of production (capital and labour).
2. There is perfect competition in commodity as well as factor markets.
3. There is full employment of resources.
4. There are quantitative differences in factor endowments in different regions, but qualitatively they are homogeneous.
5. The production function of the two commodities have different factor intensities, *i.e.*, labour-intensive and capital-intensive.
6. The production functions are different for different commodities, but are the same for each good in both countries. It means that the production function of commodity X is different from commodity Y. But the technique used to produce commodity X in both countries is the same, and the technique used to produce commodity Y in both countries is the same.
7. There is perfect mobility of factors within each region but internationally they are immobile.
8. There are no transport costs.
9. There is free trade between the two countries.

10. There are constant returns to scale in the production of each commodity in each region.
11. There is no change in technological knowledge.

Given these assumptions, Ohlin contends that the immediate cause of international trade is the difference in relative commodity prices caused by differences in relative demand and supply of factors (factor prices) as a result of differences in factor endowments between two countries. Fundamentally the relative scarcity of factors-the shortage of supply in relation to demand-is essential for trade between two regions. Commodities which use large quantities of scarce factors are imported because their prices are high, while those using abundant factors are exported because their prices are low.

Factor Abundance in Terms of Factor Prices

Ohlin explains richness in factor endowment in terms of factor prices. According to his definition, country A is abundant in capital if $\left(\frac{P_C}{P_L}\right)_A < \left(\frac{P_C}{P_L}\right)_B$, where P_C and P_L refer to prices of capital and labour and the subscripts A and B denote the two countries. In other words, if capital is relatively cheap in country A, the country is abundant in capital, and if labour is cheap in country B, the country is abundant in labour. Thus country A will export the capital-intensive good and country B will export the labour-intensive good.

Factor Abundance in Physical Terms

Another way to explain the Ohlin theorem is in physical terms of factor abundance. If country A is relatively capital-abundant and country B is relatively labour abundant, then measured in physical amounts $\left(\frac{C_A}{L_A}\right) > \frac{C_B}{L_B}$, where C_A and L_A are the total amounts of capital and labour respectively in country A and C_B and L_B are the total amounts of capital and labour respectively in country B.

Its Superiority Over the Classical Theory

Ohlin's theory is an improvement over the classical theory of international trade in many respects.

1. Ohlin's theory is superior to the classical theory in that it regards international trade as a special case of interregional or inter-local trade as distinct from the classical theory which considers international trade totally different from domestic trade.
2. The Ohlin model takes two factors-labour and capital-as against the one factor (labour) classical model, and is thus superior to the latter.
3. Again, the Ohlin theory is superior to the Ricardian theory in that it regards differences in factor supplies as basic for determining the pattern of international trade while the latter theory takes no notice of it.
4. The Ohlin model is more realistic because it is based on the relative prices of factors which in turn influence the relative prices of goods, while the Ricardian theory considers the relative prices of goods only.

Its Criticism

Ohlin's theory has been criticised on the following grounds.

1. Two-by-two-by-two Model is Unrealistic.
2. Static Theory
3. Factors not Homogeneous
4. Production Techniques not Homogeneous
5. Leontief Paradox has Falsified the Theory

LEONTIEF PARADOX

The most interesting empirical test of the Heckscher-Ohlin theorem that has been made so far is the study undertaken by Wassily Leontief in the early 1950s. Leontief tests his hypothesis with the help of an input-output table for the United States for 1947. He attempted to verify the empirical validity of the Heckscher-Ohlin theorem that a capital abundant country would export relatively capital intensive goods and in turn import more labour intensive goods. In context of U.S.A. economy, the Heckscher-Ohlin model tells that this country specialised in export of those good which use more capital than labour and import relatively labour intensive goods. But by Leontief's practical test, it was found that U.S.A. exported more of labour intensive goods and imported more of capital intensive goods, a situation that was in direct contrast to its relative factor endowment position. As such Leontief's result came as a great surprise to many economists of the world. Some economists criticised Leontief's findings on the ground that 1947 was not the right year for testing the theory as during this year the economy was beset with the post war disorganisation of production. In defence to criticisms Leontief stated that America's participation in international division of labour was based on its specialisation in labour intensive rather than capital intensive lines of production. In other words the country resorts to foreign trade in order to economise its capital and dispose of its surplus labour, rather than the reverse. It was also argued that the U.S. export industries employed more skilled labour and are thus human capital intensive rather than physical capital intensive. Abundance of human capital in the U.S. economy explains its exports of labour intensive goods.

HABERLER'S THEORY OF OPPORTUNITY COST

The Opportunity Cost Theory, propounded by *Prof. Gottfried Haberler* in 1883, has been applied to the theory of international trade as a substitute for the doctrine of comparative cost expressed in terms of labour cost or real cost. Haberler's theory explains that if a country can produce either commodity X or Y, the opportunity cost of commodity X is the amount of the other commodity Y that must be given up in order to get one additional unit of commodity X . To explain this theory let us take examples of two countries say England and Russia. Suppose with the given resources England can produce 30 kgs. of wheat and no cloth or 90 metres of cloth and no wheat. Russia on the other hand with its resources can produce 60 kgs. of wheat and no cloth or 90 metres of cloth and no wheat. The opportunity cost of wheat is the production of cloth foregone, *i.e.*, it is the amount of one commodity given up to get the other commodity. Thus in England opportunity cost is

$$30W = 90C$$

$$\Rightarrow \quad 1W = 3C$$

and in Russia opportunity cost is

$$60W = 90C$$

$$\Rightarrow \quad 1W = 1.5C$$

The production possibilities of wheat and cloth in England and Russia and their opportunity cost can be shown in the following figures.

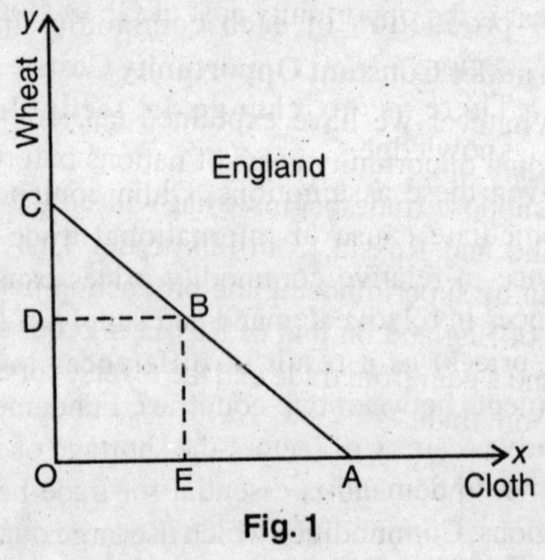

Fig. 1

Since, with all its resources England can produce either OC of wheat or OA of cloth, the line CA is the production possibility curve in figure 1. The point B on production possibility line CA, shows that England can produce OD of wheat and OE of cloth. Hence CD of wheat is the opportunity cost of OE of cloth in England, in the same way as OC of wheat is the opportunity cost of OA of cloth. Since the production possibility curve AC is a straight line. It bears a constant slope. It shows the constant opportunity cost of wheat in terms of cloth and cloth in terms of wheat.

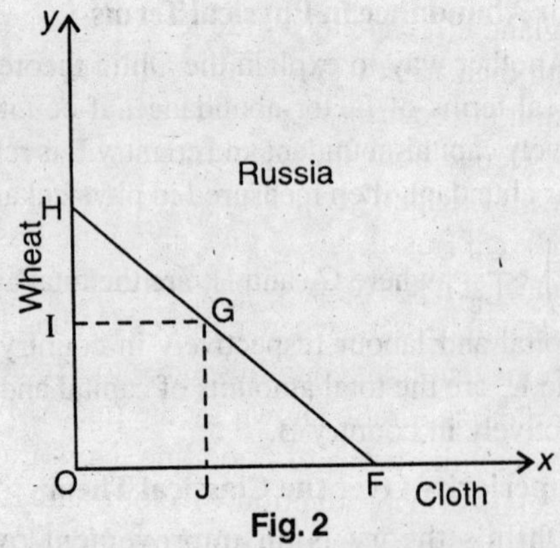

Fig. 2

In the same way FH is the production possibility curve of Russia. At point G Russia can produce OI of wheat and OJ of cloth. Hence IH of wheat is the opportunity cost of OJ of cloth in the same way as OH of wheat is the opportunity cost of OF of cloth.

Trade under Constant Opportunity Costs

Whatever we have explained earlier, was the individual opportunity costs of nations before trade. Now suppose trade begins what will be the gain to England and Russia from this trade. This we can explain by superimposing the production possibility curve of England on that of Russia in order to know England's gain from trade and the reverse for Russia's gain from trade.

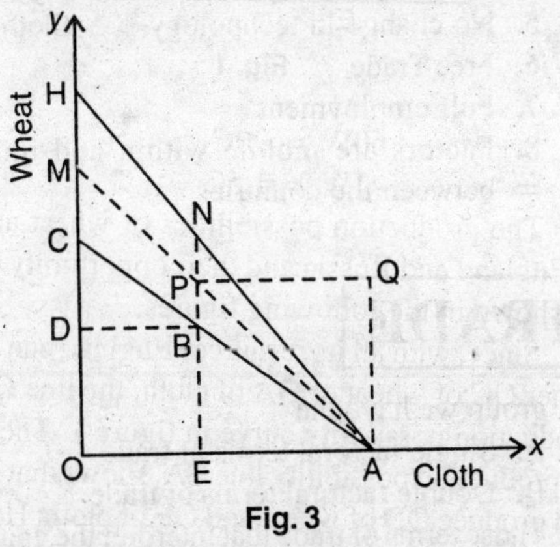

Fig. 3

From the above figure it is clear that the production possibility curve of Russia (AH) is higher than that of England. It reveals that Russia has to sacrifice more of wheat per unit of cloth within the country than England has to do within her country. Thus, Russia will be willing to import cloth from England if it can pay a little less of wheat per unit of cloth than what it has to give up (opportunity cost) within the country to produce a unit of cloth.

Hence both these countries will be willing to trade if England gets a little more of wheat per unit of cloth and Russia has to give up a little less of wheat than what it has to give up at home. Thus the terms of trade will be some where between CA and HA. Let us assume that both countries agree to exchange wheat for cloth at a ratio shown by the line AM which we may call the terms of trade line. Now England will specialise in production of cloth and Russia will specialise in production of wheat. Now England will produce OA of cloth from which OE amount will be kept for domestic consumption and will export EA of cloth for PB amount of wheat which it imports from Russia. Thus England gets an additional amount of wheat PB through specialisation and trade. Hence after trade PQ=EA are England's export and PE = QA are its imports. In the similar process Russia too gains from specialisation and trade through its exports of wheat sacrificing the units of production of cloth.

Trade Under Increasing and Decreasing Opportunity Cost Conditions

The implicit assumption behind the straight line production possibility curve is that all the factors used in production process and equally efficient both in production of wheat and cloth. But the fact is that all factors are not equally efficient in production of both these goods. So the slope of the production possibility curve cannot be a straight line. It is also not possible that both the commodities may be produced either under decreasing opportunity costs or under increasing opportunity costs. Rather the situation may be where wheat is being produced under decreasing opportunity costs and cloth under increasing opportunity costs. This can be shown with the following figure.

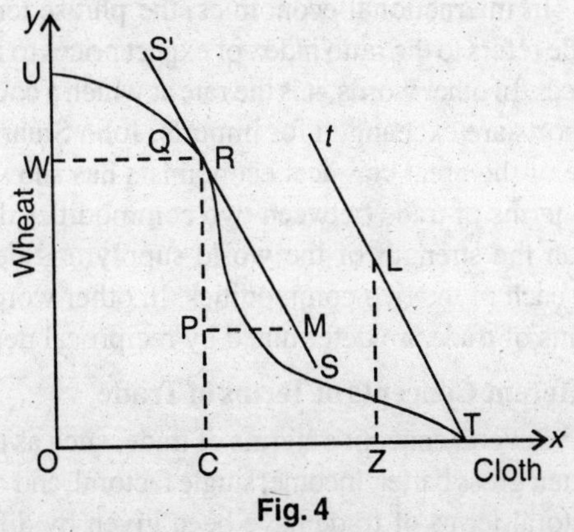

Fig. 4

In figure UT is the PPC of England. This curve is concave in the portion UQ showing increasing opportunity costs and convex in region QT showing decreasing opportunity cost. The point dividing the curve UT into these segments is called the point of inflection. In region UQ international terms of trade line is tangent to point R where both wheat and cloth are being produced under increasing opportunity cost. Russia is producing OC of cloth and OW of wheat. Its consumption point is at M whereby it imports PM of cloth and exports PR of wheat. Since point M is outside the production possibility curve, the country is better off trading with the other country. When the production of cloth starts under decreasing opportunity costs due to internal economics and the PPC becomes convex in the region QT of the UT curve. Consequently as more and more of cloth is produced costs of production diminishes. Now the country (England) reaches point T when it completely specialises in production of cloth. Assuming that the international terms of trade remain the same as before we draw Tt parallel to SS' so that the new consumption point is T. The country will now export ZT of cloth and import LZ of wheat. The country gains more from trade at L than point M. This is possible so long as the terms of trade line Tt is to the right of SS'.

Assumptions

Haberler makes the following assumptions for his theory.

1. There are only two countries, two factors of production, labour and capital and two commodities, say X and Y.
2. There is perfect competition in both the factor and commodity markets.
3. The price of each commodity equals it marginal money costs.
4. The supply of each factor is fixed.
5. No change in technology.
6. Free Trade
7. Full employment
8. Factors are mobile within and immobile between the countries.

TERMS OF TRADE

The terms of trade is one of the measurements of the gains from international trade to a particular country.

In international economics, the phrase terms of trade refers to the ratio index of export prices to import prices. In other words, it is the rate at which a country's exports are exchanged for imports. John Stuart Mill, one of the great classical economists has shown that the terms of trade between two commodities depend upon the strength of the world supply and demand for each of the two commodities. In other words, the terms of trade are determined by reciprocal demand.

Different Concepts of Terms of Trade

Several concept of terms of trade, such as the net barter, gross barter, income, single factoral, and double factoral terms of trade have been given by different writers. These several concepts have been put by **Meier** under the following three broad groups.

1. Those terms of trade that relate to the real ratio of international exchange between the commodities. In this group we have the
   A. Net barter terms of trade
   B. Gross barter terms of trade
   C. Income terms of trade
2. Those terms of trade that relate to their interchange between the productive resources. In this group we have the
   A. Single factoral terms of trade
   B. Double factoral terms of trade
3. Those terms of trade that interpret the gains from trade in terms of the utility analysis. In this group we have the
   A. Real cost terms of trade
   B. Utility terms of trade

Net Barter or Commodity Terms of Trade

While discussing the terms of trade, **Frank William Taussing** introduced the concept of the net barter or commodity terms of trade. His net barter terms of trade, popularly called 'the commodity terms of trade,' is the ratio between import prices and export-prices and can be written as

$$T_C = \frac{P_x}{P_m}$$

Where

T_c = net barter terms of trade
P_x = price of export commodity
P_m = price of import commodity

When this concept of net barter terms of trade is applied to more than one export and import commodity we use the export price and the import price indices instead of using the prices of particular export and import goods. Consequently, a change in the net barter terms of trade would be written as

$$T_c = \frac{P_{x_1}/P_{x_0}}{P_{M_1}/P_{M_0}}$$

$$= \frac{P_{x_1}}{P_{M_1}} \cdot \frac{P_{M_0}}{P_{x_0}}$$

Where

T_C = net barter terms of trade

P_{x_1} = price index of exports for any given year

P_{M_1} = price index of imports for any given year

P_{x_0} = price index of exports for base year

P_{M_0} = price index of imports for base year

As the price index of imports and exports for the base year will always be equal to 100, the term P_{M_0} / P_{x_0} in the formula will be equal to 100/100 = 1. Consequently, the net barter terms of trade will, therefore, move in accordance with the movement of any given year's price indices of imports and exports. Let us suppose that the price index of imports and exports in India in the base year 1960 is 100 and in 1988 the price indices of imports and exports are 120 and 160 respectively. Consequently, the net barter terms of trade will be

$$T_C = \frac{160}{120} \cdot \frac{100}{100}$$

$$= 1.33$$

This means that in 1988 the net barter terms of trade show an improvement of 33 percent over the base year.

Gross Barter Terms of Trade

Introduced by **Taussing**, the gross barter terms of trade is the ratio of the total physical quantity of imports to the total physical quantity of exports of a country, greater this ratio the more favourable being the gross barter terms of trade. Taussing introduced this concept to correct the commodity or net barter terms of trade for unilateral transactions, or unrequited exports or imports such as tributes, gifts, immigrant's remittance etc. The gross barter terms of trade can be expressed as

$$T_G = \frac{Q_M}{Q_x}$$

where

T_G = gross barter terms of trade

Q_M = total quantity of imports

Q_x = total quantity of exports

For comparing changes in the gross barter terms of trade between two time periods we use the index numbers of the quantities of exports and imports in the two time periods instead of the quantities alone. The ratio is expressed as

$$T_G = \frac{Q_{M_1}}{Q_{x_1}} \cdot \frac{Q_{x_0}}{Q_{M_0}}$$

where the terms Q_x and Q_M stand for the index of quantity of exports and imports of the country and the subscripts 0 to 1 stand for the base year and the given year respectively.

Income Terms of Trade

Dorrance and Staehle refined the concept of the commodity terms of trade and developed a new concept known as the 'income terms of trade.' The income terms of trade is the ratio of the value of exports divided by the price index of imports and can be written as

$$T_I = \frac{P_x Q_M}{P_M}$$

where T_I = income terms of trade

P_x = price of exports

P_M = price of imports

Q_M = quantity of exports

It is obvious from the formula that given the import prices, if the export prices rise and the volume of country's exports fall equally, the net barter terms of trade will improve while the income terms of trade will show no change.

Unilateral or Single Factoral Terms of Trade

With changing factor productivity, the concept of the net barter terms of trade is distinctly misleading as a measure of the gains for a country from trade without keeping in view the improvement in factor productivity which results from trading. The concepts which used the commodity technical coefficient index were developed by **Jacob Viner**. The concepts developed by him are known as the 'single factoral' terms of trade.

The single factoral terms of trade is the ratio of

the export price index and the import price index adjusted for changes in the productivity of a country's factors of production engaged in the production of export commodities. If the commodity terms of trade index is multiplied by the reciprocal of the export commodity technical coefficients index, the resultant index is known as the 'single factoral terms of trade' which can be expressed as

$$T_S = \frac{P_x}{P_M}.Z_x$$

where T_S = single factoral terms of trade

$\frac{P_x}{P_M}$ = net barter terms of trade

Z_x = index of factor productivity in exports

Bilateral or Double Factoral Terms of Trade

The concept of the double factoral terms of trade takes account of the productivity of factors of production entering into the production of country's exports as well as of the productivity of foreign factors of production producing country's imports. The concept of double factoral terms of trade can be expressed as

$$T_D = \frac{P_x}{P_M}.\frac{Z_x}{Z_M}$$

where T_D = double factoral terms of trade

Z_M = index of factor productivity in imports

Z_x = index of factor productivity in exports

P_x = price index of exports

P_M = price index of imports

Real Cost Terms of Trade

The real cost terms of trade are obtained by multiplying the single factoral terms of trade with the index of the amount of disutility per unit of the productive resources employed in producing the exports. The real cost terms of trade can be symbolically expressed as

$$T_R = T_S.R_x$$

$$= \frac{P_x}{P_M}.Z_x.R_x$$

where T_R denotes the real cost terms of trade and R_x stands for the index of the amount of disutility suffered per unit of productive resources employed in producing exports. The terms R_x, P_M and Z_x have the same meaning as they have in the formula of the single factoral terms of trade.

Utility Terms of Trade

The utility terms of trade are obtained by multiplying the real cost terms of trade with the index of the relative desirability or utility of imports as compared to the goods that could have been produced for home consumption with those factors of production which are now used in the production of export goods (U_M). The utility terms of trade may be written as

$$T_U = T_R.U_M$$

$$= \frac{P_x}{P_M}.Z_x.R_x.U_x$$

Factors Affecting the Terms of Trade

The major factors which affect the terms of the trade of a country are:

1. Economic growth
2. Shifts in the demand for exports and/or import
3. Tariff
4. Devaluation
5. Availability of Substitutes

ECONOMIC GROWTH AND TERMS OF TRADE

Economic growth of a country causes an outward shift in the production possibilities curve allowing the larger aggregate output. The upward shift in the production possibilities curve may have occurred due to increase in the availability of factors of production and technological improvements allowing the production of larger aggregate output with the given quantity of resources. The influence of economic growth in the terms of trade will depend upon the pattern of country's economic growth. If growth is neutral, the terms of the trade will remain unaffected. If growth is ultra-export biased the country will produce more quantity of the export goods and positively less quantity of the import goods. This condition will necessarily worsen the terms of trade of the country. On the other hand, if growth is ultra-import-biased, the production of import commodities will increase so much that the production of the export commodities will decrease in absolute terms and the terms of trade will be favourable for the country.

If the country is significantly large to influence the international terms of trade by her action, then even with the neutral trade biased growth there exists the possibility that the terms of trade may turn so strongly against the growing country that she will actually wind up on a lower indifference curve than she could attain without economic growth. **Jagdish Bhagwati** has described it as a case of "**immiserizing growth**".

DEVALUATION AND TERMS OF TRADE

Devaluation lowers the value of the home currency expressed in terms of the currency of foreign country. After the foreign exchange value of the home currency has been lowered as a result of devaluation, it is natural to think that the terms of trade of the currency devaluing country will deteriorate because the prices of country's exports fall in terms of the foreign currency while prices of her imports rise in terms of the local currency. But this is not a bare fact. As a matter of fact, the effects of devaluation depend upon the elasticities of demand for and supply of imports and exports of the country. The tendency of devaluation is to improve the terms of trade if the product of the demand elasticities for the country's imports and exports is greater than the product of the supply elasticities of her imports and exports.

In general, if the elasticities of supply of exports and imports are large in proportion to the elasticities of demand for exports and imports, devaluation of a country's currency will worsen its terms of trade and revaluation will improve its terms of trade. Expressed differently, if the product of the supply elasticities is greater than the product of the demand elasticities, devaluation will cause deterioration in the country's terms of trade and vice-versa. If the elasticities of supply of exports and imports are equal to the elasticities of demand for exports and imports so that the product of the supply elasticities equals the product of the demand elasticities, the country's terms of the trade will remain unchanged consequent upon devaluation. This relationship between the terms of trade and devaluation can be stated thus:

A. Terms of trade will improve due to currency devaluation if $\mathbf{D_x . D_M > S_x . S_M}$

B. Terms of trade will deteriorate due to currency devaluation if $\mathbf{D_x . D_M < S_x . S_M}$

C. Terms of trade will remain unchanged due to currency devaluation if $\mathbf{D_x . D_M = S_x . S_M}$

UNDERDEVELOPED COUNTRIES AND TERMS OF TRADE

For world's most underdeveloped countries which are caught in the vicious trap of low income, low employment and low technical know-how, foreign trade is life and blood of the economy. Consequently, '*Trade or Perish*' is an appropriate slogan in the context of the need of their rapid economic development. It is, however, argued by the spokesmen of the underdeveloped countries that international trade which had served as an engine of economic growth for the open lands in the nineteenth century is no more an engine of economic growth for them today. According to the less developed countries, today they face unfavourable conditions which are very different from the favourable ones faced by the open lands in the nineteenth century. **Raul Prebisch insists that the terms of trade of the less developed countries have been secularly deteriorating.**

In his well-known work '*Towards a New Trade Policy for Development*' Raul Prebisch maintains that there is a long-run tendency for the prices of the primary products to deteriorate relative to the prices of manufactured goods. Prebisch's argument is based on the fact that the underdeveloped countries are net producers of primary products such as coffee, copper, tea, rich, sugar, fats, etc. These products are roughly the same goods today that these were 50 years ago. On the other hand, the quality of manufactured goods produced by the developed countries such as the automobiles, radios, petroleum refinery, equipments, trucks, etc., has improved tremendously. Consequently, in the world markets these goods fetch higher prices relative to those fetched by the primary products.

Singer gives a different explanation for the deteriorating terms of the trade of the primary products producing countries. According to him, the fruits of technical progress can either be retained by the producers in terms of the high incomes or passed on to the consumers in the form of low prices. The fruits of technical progress in the underdeveloped countries have been passed on to the consumers in the developed countries in the form of lower prices of primary products whereas these have been retained by the producers in the developed countries in the form of higher incomes of producers. Singer does not give any explanation in support of his argument. A.M. McLeod, however, states that it has happened due to the presence of greater degree of monopolistic control prevalent in the production of finished goods in the developed countries. The less developed countries more or less produce the same (identical) goods and search the markets for these goods abroad. As these countries are less organised they compete among themselves for the export markets for their products and in the process give away a substantial part of their gains in productivity to the developed countries in the form of fall in the prices of their exports.

BALANCE OF PAYMENTS

The balance of payments of a country is a statistical record kept in the form of a balance sheet comprising of all her foreign economic transactions during any given period of time. It presents a summary account of all international transactions of a country during a certain given period of time.

Since the balance of payments is a systematic record of a country's total money receipts from and payments to abroad, the difference between receipts and payments is the surplus or deficit. A country's total money receipts are the receipts or payments that accrue to its residents while the total payments refer to the payments made by the residents of a country. Dividing resident's total receipts, R, and their total payments, P, into their domestic and foreign components and if the domestic receipts and domestic payments are identical, then the international balance of payments, B, of a country can be expressed as

$$\begin{aligned} B &= R - P \\ &= (R_d + R_f) - (P_d + P_f) \\ &= R_f - P_f \text{ (since } R_d = P_d) \end{aligned}$$

For an open economy, the total receipts may differ from the total payments and their difference represents the difference between foreign receipts (R_f) and foreign payments (P_f). The positive difference is termed as a surplus while the negative difference is termed as a deficit in the balance of payments of a country.

The balance of payments of a country is not a balance-sheet showing a country's foreign assets and liabilities at any given point of time. It shows for any given period of time the flow of a nation's total receipts from abroad and its total payments made to abroad. Following the conventional rules of double entry accounting, a nation's total payments and total receipts for any given period of time must be in balance. Further more, one nation's receipts are payments for others while the receipts of other nations are payments for the nation.

Usually, a country's balance of payments distinguishes between items on the current and capital accounts. In the current account are included all kinds of exports and imports of goods and services, interest and dividend payments, private gifts and so on. The capital account, sub-divided into short term capital transfers, lists the imports and exports of all kinds of debt instruments and corporate stocks as well as imports and exports of monetary gold. The following table explains the different items included under various subheads in the balance of payments of a country.

Components of Balance of Payments

Receipts (Credits)	*Payments (Debits)*
1. Exports of goods	1. Imports of goods
2. Exports of services	2. Imports of services
3. Unrequited receipts (gifts, indemnities, etc.,) from foreigners)	3. Unrequited payments (gifts, indemnities, etc. to foreigners)

4. Capital receipts (borrowings from, capital repayments by, or sale of assets to, foreigners)	4. Capital payments (lending to, capital repayments to, or purchase of assets from, foreigners)

BALANCE OF PAYMENTS AND BALANCE OF TRADE

The concepts of balance of trade and balance of payments are often misunderstood. Economists frequently say that while the balance of payments includes the balance of trade, the balance of trade does not include the balance of payments. A country exports and imports many **visible** goods and **invisible** services. **Invisible services** include tourism, shipping and other transport services, banking and insurance services for whose exports and imports payments are made and received by the country in international trade. A country's balance of trade refers to the value of imports and exports of commodities only. The balance of payments is, however, more comprehensive including as it does the total debits and credits relating to all the items on account of which a country makes payments to and receives payments from rest of the world. In short, the balance of trade is only a part of the balance of payments.

Equilibrium and Disequilibrium

The balance of payments of a country is said to be in equilibrium when the demand for foreign exchange is exactly equivalent to the supply of it. The balance of payments is in disequilibrium when there is either a surplus or deficit in the balance of payments. When there is a deficit in the balance of payments, the demand for foreign exchange exceeds the supply for it.

Correction of Disequilibrium

A country may not be bothered about a surplus in the balance of payments; but every country strives to remove, or at least to reduce a balance of payments deficit. A number of measures are available for correcting the balance of payments disequilibrium. We outline below the important measures for correcting the dis-equilibrium caused by a deficit in the balance of payments.

A. Monetary measures
B. Trade measures
C. Miscellaneous

A. Monetary Measures

The important monetary measures are outlined below:

Monetary Contraction

The level of aggregate domestic demand, the domestic price level and the demand for imports and exports may be influenced by a contraction or expansion in money supply and correct the balance of payments disequilibrium. The measure required is a contraction in money supply. A contraction in money supply is likely to reduce the purchasing power and there by the aggregate demand. It is also likely to bring about a fall in domestic prices. The fall in the domestic aggregate demand and domestic prices reduce the demand for imports. The fall in domestic prices is likely to increase exports. Thus, the fall in imports and the rise in exports would help to correct the disequilibrium.

Devaluation

Devaluation means a reduction in the official rate at which one currency is exchanged for another currency. A country with a fundamental disequilibrium in the balance of payments may devalue its currency in order to stimulate its exports and discourage imports to correct the disequilibrium.

The balance of payments deficit of a country will be eliminated as a consequence of devaluation, *i.e.*, the position of the country's balance of payments will improve if the price elasticities of demand for the currency devaluing country's imports and exports are high and at any rate in order to effect improvement in the country's balance of payments the combined absolute value of the two demand elasticities must be greater than one, *i.e.*,

$$e_x + e_m > 1$$

Where the terms e_x and e_m respectively represent the price elasticity of demand for exports, and imports, of the currency devaluing country.

Exchange Control

Exchange control is a popular method employed to influence the balance of payments position of a country. Under exchange control, the government or central bank assumes complete control of the foreign exchange reserves and earnings of the country. The recipients of foreign exchange such as exporters, are required to surrender foreign exchange to the government/central bank in exchange for domestic currency. By the virtue of its control over the use of foreign exchange the government can control the imports.

B. Trade Measures

Trade measures include export promotion measures and import control measures.

Exports may be encouraged by reducing or abolishing export duties, providing an export subsidy and encouraging export production and export marketing by offering monetary, fiscal, physical and institutional incentives and facilities.

Imports may be controlled by imposing or enhancing import duties, restricting imports through import quotas and licensing and even by prohibiting altogether the import of certain non-essential items.

C. Miscellaneous Measures

Apart from the measures mentioned above, there are a number of other measures that can help to make the Balance of Payments position more favourable, such as obtaining foreign loans, encouraging foreign investment in the home country, development of tourism to attract foreign tourists, providing incentives to enhance inward remittances, developing import substituting industries, etc.

THE IMPORT FUNCTION

Imports are an increasing function of income. This functional relationship can be expressed in the following way

$$M = M(y)$$

A country's average propensity to import is defined as the total imports divided by the total national income, *i.e.*

$$API = \frac{M}{Y}$$

The marginal propensity to import measures how much of a change in the national income is spent on imports. Using algebraic terms it is defined as $\frac{\Delta M}{\Delta Y}$.

THE FOREIGN TRADE MULTIPLIER

In equilibrium

$$Y = C + I + X - M \quad ...(1)$$

Where Y = national income

C = consumption

I = investment

X = exports

M = imports

We can rewrite equation (1) as

$$\Delta Y = \Delta C + \Delta I + \Delta X - \Delta M$$

$$\Rightarrow \quad \Delta Y = c\Delta Y + \Delta I + \Delta X - m\Delta Y$$

$$\Rightarrow \Delta Y[1 - c + m] = \Delta I + \Delta X$$

$$\Rightarrow \quad \Delta y = \frac{1}{1 - c + m}(\Delta I + \Delta X) \quad ...(2)$$

Where c = MPC

m = MPI

From equation 2 we see that the effect of a change in exports on the national income equals the change in exports multiplied by the expression $1/(1 - c + m)$, which is the foreign trade multiplier.

DEVALUATION

By devaluation of a country's currency unit is meant the decrease in the external value of a unit of that currency expressed in terms of gold, SDR or foreign currency by government edict. A country may reduce the foreign exchange value of her currency unit for more than one reason, *e.g.*, to create surplus in her balance of payments by means of dumping her goods abroad, or to remove deficit in her external balance of payments. In short, devaluation means an act of officially reducing the external value of the currency unit of the country and appreciation to the extent of devaluation in the external value of the currency unit of the country in whose relationship the country has devalued her currency.

Methods of Removing Balance of Payments Deficit

The conditions under which devaluation would cause an improvement in the balance of payments position of the currency devaluing country have been discussed by Lerner, Robinson, Meade and others. The extent to which deficit of the external balance of payments of the currency devaluing country can be corrected through devaluation depends upon the price elasticities of demand and the price elasticities of supply of her exports and imports. Considering first the price elasticity of demand for the exports of the country, if the price elasticity of demand for the exports of the currency-devaluing country is less than unity in absolute value, devaluation will not reduce deficit of the balance of payments of the country; rather the balance of payments deficit of the country would increase as a consequence of devaluation.

If the price elasticity of demand for the exports of the country is less than unity, a given percentage fall in the rate of exchange, say of 20 percent, will cause less than 20 per cent (say only 10 per cent) increase in the total quantity of exports of the country. This is the positive quantity effect of devaluation. But while the total quantity of exports increases by 10 per cent the total foreign exchange earnings or total value of exports of the country will be less than the pre-devaluation total value of exports because while the total quantity of exports has increased by 10 per cent, the foreign currency price per unit of export goods has fallen by 20 per cent. The negative price factor more than offsets the positive quantity factor reflected in the increase of the total quantity of exports, making the net effect on the total foreign exchange earnings of the country through exports negative. It has been illustrated in figure 5 where the two countries taken are India and America with India devaluing her currency rupee in order to correct her external balance of payments deficit. In this figure, the demand and supply of India's exports have been shown on the *x*-axis and price expressed in the US dollars has been shown on the Y-axis. D_xD_x is inelastic demand curve for India's exports while AS_x is perfectly elastic supply curve of Indian exports.

Before devaluation of the Indian rupee, the dollar price of export was OA, the total quantity exported was OQ_1 and the total foreign exchange (dollars)

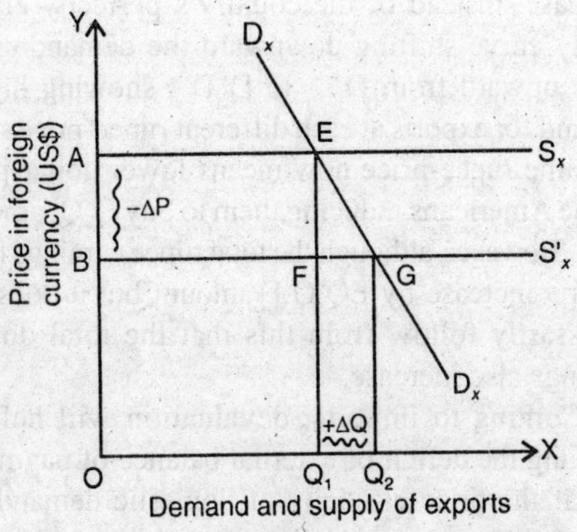

Fig. 5

earned by the country through the exports was $OQ_1 \times OA$ (= rectangle AOQ_1E). Consequent on devaluation of the rupee, the dollar (foreign currency) price of Indian exports falls by AB from OA to OB showing that the dollar price in percentage terms has fallen by the full extent of devaluation. Consequently, the supply curve of India's exports As_x shifts downward to the position of BS'_x while the total quantity of exports increases by Q_1Q_2 (=ΔQ) from OQ_1 to OQ_2. The new total foreign exchange revenue (total dollar earnings) is $OQ_2 \times OB$ (= rectangle BOQ_2G). The net change in the total foreign exchange earnings of the country due to devaluation will be positive (increase) or negative (decrease) according as ABFE is smaller or greater than rectangle Q_1Q_2 GF. In this case, the demand for India's exports being inelastic, rectangle ABFE > rectangle Q_1Q_2 GF. Consequently devaluation increases rather than decrease the deficit of India's balance of payments. It, therefore, follows that although currency devaluation will always lead to an increase in the total quantity of exports of the currency-devaluing country (unless the price elasticity of demand for her exports is zero), it does not, however, necessarily follow from this that it will always also lead to an increase in the total foreign exchange earnings of the country from exports.

Figure 6 shows the position of total export earnings in terms of rupees (domestic currency). It is obvious that the total rupee-earnings will always increase as result of devaluation even when the foreign demand for country's exports is inelastic. In this case, instead of the country's perfectly elastic supply curve shifting downward the demand curve shifts upward from D_xD_x to $D'_xD'_x$, showing higher demand for exports at each different rupee-price since the same rupee-price now means lower dollar-price for the Americans inducing them to buy Q_1Q_2 amount more. However, although the total rupee earnings from exports increase by EQ_1Q_2F amount but it does not necessarily follow from this that the total dollar-earnings also increase.

Coming to imports, devaluation will help in reducing the deficit of external balance of payments only if the price elasticity of domestic demand for imports is greater than unity ($e_m > 1$) because in that situation a given percentage increase in the price of imports measured in terms of the domestic currency would cause more than proportionate fall in the quantity of imports as shown in figure 7 when the demand for and supply of imports have been shown on the X-axis and the price of imports expressed in domestic currency has been shown on the Y-axis. D_mD_m is the demand curve for imports while AS_m is the perfectly elastic supply curve for imports. Before devaluation, the rupee-price of imports was OA and the total imports were OQ_1 giving the total rupee value of imports represented by rectangle OQ_1EA (= OA × OQ_1). As a consequence of devaluation, although the price of imports in foreign currency (dollars) remains unchanged, since the supply curve for imports is expressed in terms of the domestic currency, it shifts upward by the full amount of the difference between the pre-devaluation and post-devaluation rupee-price. The new supply curve is now BS'_m. Consequently, the total amount of imports decreases by Q_1Q_2 from OQ_1 to OQ_2. However, after devaluation India pays higher price OB for her imports. The total rupee-cost of imports is now OQ_2GB. The improvement in the balance of payments resulting from decrease in total imports consequent on devaluation of the rupee would depend on the relative sizes of rectangle Q_2Q_1EF and ABGF. If the elasticity of demand for imports is greater than unity, then rectangle Q_2Q_1EF will be larger than rectangle ABGF. Consequently, the balance of payments position of the country, in so far as imports are concerned, will improve due to devaluation.

Figure 8 shows the effect of devaluation on the total imports and total foreign exchange bill which must fall unless the demand for imports is perfectly inelastic. However, although the total dollar payments obligation is reduced from OQ_1EA to OQ_2FA but it does not necessarily follow from this that the total rupee-payments burden of the country will also fall. It will fall only if the demand for imports is elastic, *i.e.*, if the elasticity of demand for imports is greater than unity. There will be no change in the total-rupee payments burden if the elasticity of demand for imports is unity and the burden will increase in the event of the elasticity of demand for imports being less than unity.

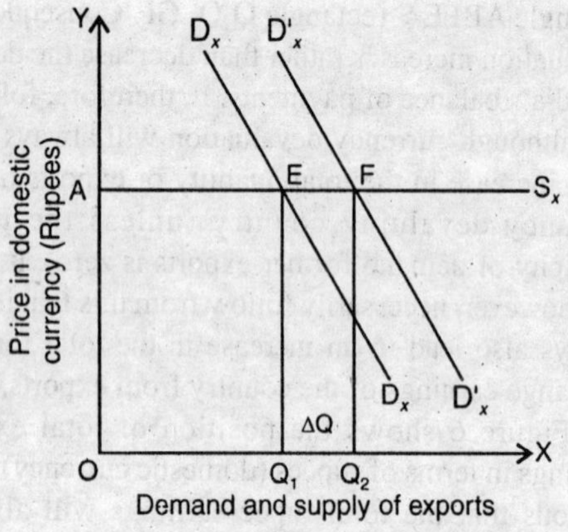

Fig. 6

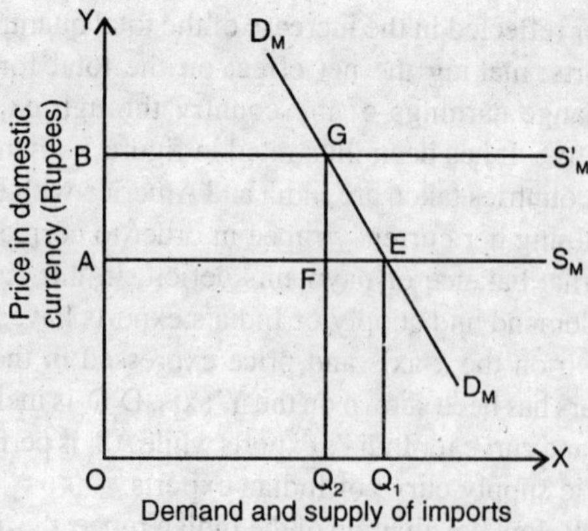

Fig. 7

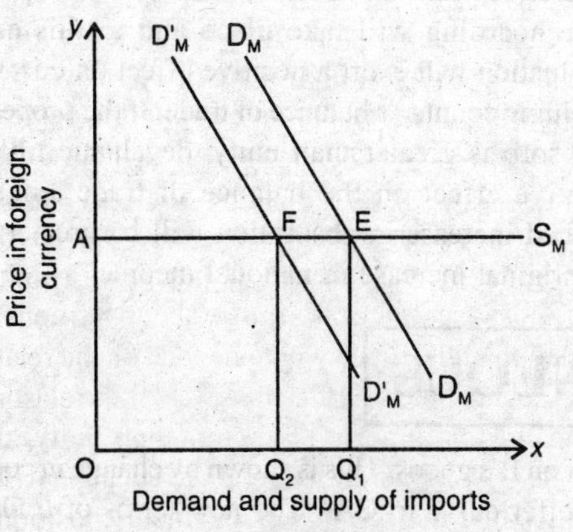

Fig. 8

It can be proved by means of a formula that under conditions of perfectly elastic supply of imports and exports, if a country devalues her currency in order to remove her external balance of payments deficit, the sum of the price elasticities of demand for the currency devaluing country's exports and imports should be greater than unity in absolute value, *i.e.*, $e_x + e_m > 1$. This is the well-known **Marshall-Lerner Condition**. If $e_x + e_m = 1$, no improvement in the balance of payments deficit of the country will result from devaluation. If $e_x + e_m < 1$, devaluation will increase rather than decrease the balance of payments deficit of the country.

ABSORPTION APPROACH

An alternative approach to the effects of devaluation formulated in macro terms, as against the elasticity approach formulated in micro terms, is the absorption approach. This approach as first developed by **Sidney Alexander** in his famous paper published in 1952. According to the absorption approach, the balance of trade can be treated as the difference between national income (Y) and total expenditure (E) or absorption so that

$$B = Y - E \qquad ...(1)$$

Where B = balance of trade

E = total expenditure

Designating total expenditure (E) or total demand as total absorption (A), the above equation can be rewritten as

$$B = Y - A \qquad ...(2)$$

Since total absorption is composed of the demand created for all purposes, it includes the demand for consumption and investment purposes. Thus, for a three-sector economy

$$A = C + I + G \qquad ...(3)$$

Devaluation will affect the balance of trade either by affecting the real national income, Y, or by affecting the total absorption, A. Thus, the change in the balance of trade may be expressed as

$$dB = dY - dA \qquad ...(4)$$

Total absorption can be separated in two parts. First, any change in real income (Y) will cause a change in absorption (consumption demand) which will be equivalent to the change in real income (dY) multiplied by the propensity to absorb (C). Secondly, devaluation will directly affect absorption which will depend, among other things, on the level of real income at which devaluation takes place. Let us call this direct effect on absorption as D. Consequently

$$dA = CdY + dD \qquad ...(5)$$

By substituting equation (5) for the term dA in equation (4) we obtain

$$dB = (1 - C)\, dY - dD \qquad ...(6)$$

Equation (6) states that the effects of a devaluation on the balance of trade depend on first, the effect of devaluation on real income (Y), second, the propensity to absorb (C), and third, the effect on direct absorption (D).

If there are enough unemployed resources in the currency-devaluing country (as is generally true of most developing countries) production can increase in the short period following the devaluation. The process of expansion will start from expansion in exports which will raise real national income through the multiplier process. The increase in exports will, however, depend on the extent to which export's prices in the currency-devaluing country rise and the extent to which rest of the world is willing to absorb the exports from the currency-devaluing country.

The net effect of the increase in real national income on the balance of trade does not, however, comprise the total increase in real income or production; it comprises the difference between the increase in real income and the induced increase in total absorption. This difference between increase in real production and real absorption may be called real hoarding (saving). The effect of devaluation on the balance of trade is, therefore, equal to the amount of real hoarding which takes place in the economy and which is determined by the propensity to hoard (1 – C). As long as C, the propensity to absorb, is positive and less than unity, the propensity to hoard will also be positive and less than unity. Consequently, some hoarding will take place and to this extent devaluation will exert a positive effect on currency-devaluing country's balance of trade. If the propensity to absorb is greater than unity, devaluation have a negative effect on the balance of trade since the induced increase in absorption will be greater than the original increase in national income.

MISCELLANEOUS

THE OPTIMUM TARIFF

Usually, the imposition of a tariff improves the terms of trade of the imposing country, reduces the volume of trade, and may improve the country's welfare. The improvement in the terms of trade is the positive effect of a tariff and the reduction in the volume of trade is the negative effect of a tariff. It is only when the positive effect of a tariff is larger than its negative effect that there is improvement in the welfare of a country. The tariff that maximises a country's welfare, is called the **optimum tariff**.

The optimum tariff is explained with the help of figure A where OA is the offer curve of country A and OB is the offer curve of country B. C_a is the community indifference curve of country A. Under free trade the terms of trade between the two countries are given by the ray OT from the origin. Consequently, they are in equilibrium at point T where their offer curves intersect each other. Suppose country A imposes a tariff on B's goods. This is shown by change in country A's offer curve to OA′. The new terms of trade are given by the ray OT' and T' is the new equilibrium point determined by country B's original offer curve and country A's new offer curve OA'. This tariff which has changed country A's offer curve OA to OA' is the optimum tariff of this country.

The point T' where country A'*s* community indifference curve C'_a is tangent to country B'*s* offer curve, is the point where the tariff is the optimum. The welfare of the people in country A is greater at point T' than at point T. This is because at T' they are at the C'*a* indifference curve which is above the C*a* indifference curve. Thus this is the optimum tariff.

The tariff imposing country can gain from the optimum tariff only if the offer curve of the other trading country is less than perfectly elastic. If the offer curve of the other country is infinitely elastic, levying a tariff will not increase the welfare of the tariff-imposing country. This is illustrated in figure

Fig. A

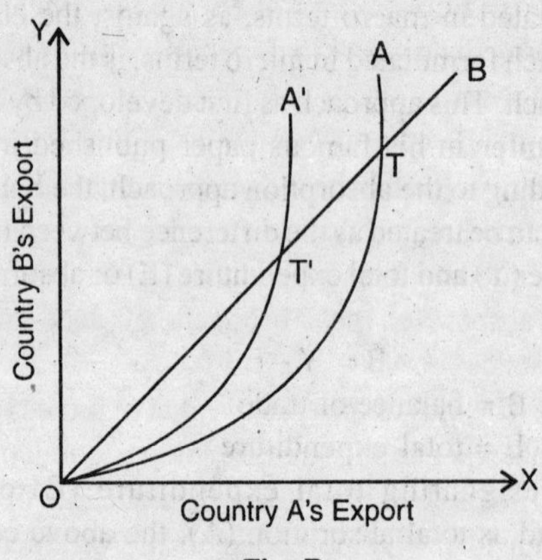

Fig. B

B where the offer curve of country B is shown as the straight line curve OB and OA is the offer curve of country A. Under free trade, the terms of trade are given by OT and the equilibrium is established at point T where the two offer curves intersect each other. When country A imposes a tariff, its offer curve shifts to OA'. The new equilibrium is set at T. In this case, the terms of trade remain unchanged, while the volume of trade is reduced from point T to T'. Here the positive effect of tariff is zero while the negative effect is stronger. Therefore, the optimum tariff is zero.

Prof. Kindleberger has devised a formula to measure the rate of optimum tariff which is

$$T = \frac{1}{e-1}$$

where T = optimum tariff rate
e = point elasticity of the offer curve of the other country.

By applying this formula to the above case of a straight line offer curve having infinite elasticity, the optimum tariff is $1/(\infty - 1) = 0$. Thus the higher the elasticity of the offer curve of other country, the lower the level of the optimum tariff of a country and vice versa.

Effective Rates of Protection

Expirical estimates have shown that a large share and perhaps most of international trade consists of trade in intermediate goods which are used as inputs in the production of other goods. Most of trade theory, however, has been concerned only with trade in final goods. Economists have viewed the neglect of intermediate goods in trade theory differently. Jagdish Bhagwati suggests, for instance, that it constitutes one of the central limitations of trade theory, while Murray Kemp has argued that the neglect of intermediate products in the earlier literature can be defended on the grounds that most results derived in the absence of these products are also valid in their presence.

The idea of the effective rate of protection (E.R.P.) is that when inputs are taken into account the nominal tariff of a good may differ from the rate of protection given to the value added in the production of the good. According to the proponents of the theory, it is the protection to the value added that is of importance, not the nominal tariff on the final good.

Assume that the final tariff on a good is 10 percent and that inputs (raw material, intermediate goods, etc.) used in the production of the good amount to 50 per cent of the value of production and that these inputs are imported without duty. The effective rate of protection accorded to value added is then 20 per cent, not 10 per cent as the manifest duty implies.

The formula for the Effective Rate of Protection

$$r = \frac{v' - v}{v}$$

where r = rate of effective protection
v' = value added per unit of output with protection
v = value added per unit of output without protection

Thus we can illustrate the concept with the following example:

	Free Trade	*With Protection*
Input	0.50	0.50
Value added	0.50	0.60
Unit price of final output	1.00	1.10

Thus the effective rate of protection

$$r = \frac{0.60 - 0.50}{0.50}$$
$$= 0.20$$
$$= 20 \text{ per cent}$$

Trade Creation and Trade Diversion

The pioneering study of the theory of customs unions was made by **Jacob Viner**. In the beginning, customs unions had been viewed favourably. The reasoning was as follows: free trade maximizes welfare; customs unions are a move toward free trade; therefore, they will increase welfare even though they might not maximize it.

Viner showed this conclusion to be incorrect. He introduced, instead, the key concepts of **trade creation** and **trade diversion**. They might best be illustrated by table-1. The table measures the production cost of a commodity in three countries.

Table-1 : Production cost of commodity X in three countries

	Country A	B	C
Production cost	50	40	30

Let us disregard transportation cost, etc., so that production cost completely determines the supply price of the good and tariffs are the only source of diversion between price and cost. If country A has a tariff of 100 percent on X, there will be no imports of the good, but domestic producers will dominate the home market. If A had levied a lower tariff, say 50 per cent, and it was non-discriminatory, it would have imported the good from the lower cost source, country C, and the price in A's home market would be 45.

Let us now assume that A and B form a customs union. A will then, instead, import X from B and the price in A's market will be 40. Imports will be switched from the low-cost supplier, C, to the high-cost supplier B. This is an example of **trade diversion.** Trade diversion takes place when imports from a more efficiently producing country are switched to a less efficiently producing country because of the customs union. Trade diversion will lead to a lowering of welfare, as it entails a less efficient allocation of resources.

We must mention here that this analysis assumes that the countries involved are fully employed both before and after the formation of the customs union. In this sense the analysis is of a neoclassical type. This being the case, it is natural to let the analysis primarily be concerned with the effects on the allocation of resources and the welfare implications of these effects.

This kind of analysis gives rise to three possibilities. **First,** neither of the two countries forming the union produces the good in question. The customs union would then be of no significance, as both countries would import the good from a third country just as they did before forming the union. **Second,** one of the countries forming the union produces the good inefficiently. The union partner would then import from the cheaper source and there will be a case of trade diversion. **Third,** both countries forming the customs union produce the good, in which case one of the countries would be more efficient than the other. The market in both countries will then be secured for the more efficient industry and there will be **trade creation.**

Spot and Forward Foreign Exchange Rates

There are the spot rate of exchange and the forward rate of exchange ruling in the foreign exchange markets. The spot rate of exchange is the rate or price expressed in terms of the home currency which is payable for spot delivery of a specified type of foreign exchange. The forward rate of exchange is the rate or price at which a transaction will be consummated at some specified time in future.

Arbitrage

An arbitrageur is a dealer or trader who by taking advantage of "inconsistencies" in the buying and selling prices quotes in different parts of the foreign exchange market makes profit. Unlike the risky activities of a speculator, the activities of an arbitrageur are free from exchange risk because he never takes an uncovered position in the foreign currency. The arbitrageur may trade either in spot or in forward foreign exchange or he may even simultaneously trade in both the spot and forward foreign exchange.

Theories of Foreign Exchange Rate

1. The Mint Par Parity Theory : This theory is associated with the working of the international gold standard. Under this system, the currency in use was made of gold or was convertible into gold at a fixed rate. The value of the currency unit was defined in terms of certain weight of gold, that is, so many grains of gold to the rupee, the dollar, the pound, etc. The central bank of the country was always ready to buy and sell gold at the specified price. The rate at which the standard money of the country was convertible into gold was called the mint price of gold. If the official British price of gold was 6 per ounce and of the US price of gold 35 per ounce, they were the mint prices of gold in the respective countries. The exchange rate between the dollar and the pound would be fixed at $\frac{36}{£6}$ = \$6. This rate was called the mint parity or mint par of exchange because it was based on the mint price of gold. Thus under the gold standard, the normal or basic rate of exchange was equal to the ratio of their mint par values (R = $/£).

2. The Purchasing Power Parity Theory : The purchasing power parity theory was developed by **Gustav Cassel** in 1920 to determine the exchange rate between countries on the basis of inconvertible paper currencies. The theory states that equilibrium exchange rate between two inconvertible paper currencies is determined by the equality of their purchasing power. In other words, the rate of exchange between two countries is determined by their relatives price levels.

Cassel's purchasing power parity theory became very popular among economists during 1914-1924 and was widely accepted as a realistic explanation of the determination of foreign exchange rate under inconvertible paper currencies. But it has been severely criticised for its weak theoretical base.

EXERCISE

1. In which of the following year, the Articles of Agreement of IMF were changed for the first time?

(*a*) 1969 (*b*) 1975
(*c*) 1980 (*d*) 1985

2. The value of the foreign trade multiplier is equal to

(*a*) $\frac{1}{mpm + mps}$ (*b*) $\frac{1}{mpm - mps}$

(*c*) $mpm + mps$ (*d*) $\frac{1}{mpm}$

3. The devaluation according to Marshall and Learner conditions will not be helpful, if the sum of the elasticities of exports and imports is

(*a*) equal to unity (*b*) greater than unity
(*c*) less than unity (*d*) zero

4. Under the system of fluctuating exchange rates regime, the adjustment in the balance of payments is brought about by the changes in

(*a*) Prices (*b*) Exchange rate
(*c*) Income (*d*) Prices and income

5. The members of the NAFTA are

(*a*) USA, Canada, Mexico
(*b*) USA, Canada, India
(*c*) USA, Canada, Japan
(*d*) USA, UK, India

6. Consider a Ricardian economy that is endowed with 45 units of labour. It can produce two goods: Gajar-Halwa and Kulfi. One unit of labour can produce 4 kilos of Gajar-Halwa or 6 kilos of Kulfi. The international price of Gajar-Halwa in terms of Kulfi is 2. In free trade, this country will produce

(*a*) 15 kilos of Kulfis
(*b*) 130 kilos of Kulfis
(*c*) 180 kilos of Gajar-Halwa
(*d*) 270 kilos of Gajar-Halwa

7. If protection is given to a small import competing industry, consumer surplus and domestic profits will, respectively.

(*a*) rise, rise (*b*) fall, fall
(*c*) rise, fall (*d*) fall, rise

8. Which one of the following conditions is NOT assumed by the factor price equalisation theorem?

(*a*) The countries are characterised by different factor endowments
(*b*) The countries are characterised by different production functions
(*c*) The industries are characterised by different factor intensities
(*d*) Each country will export the commodity which uses its abundent factor relatively intensively

9. India is large exporter of tea and a small exporter of bicycles. In this context, which one of the following is true?

(*a*) An export subsidy to tea would improve India's terms of trade in the world tea market.
(*b*) An export subsidy to tea would worsen India's terms of trade in the world tea market.
(*c*) An export subsidy to bicycles would improve India's terms of trade in the world bicycle market.
(*d*) An export subsidy to bicycles would worsen

India's terms of trade in the world bicycle market.

10. There are two countries. Sugarland and Saltland. Each country produces sugar and salt. The former exports sugar and the latter, salt. Starting from a free trade equilibrium, a tariff on salt by sugarland would affect the offer curves and the relative price of sugar from sugarland's perspective in which one of the following ways?

(*a*) Shift the offer curve of saltland, increase the price of sugar.

(*b*) Shift the offer curve of saltland, decrease the price of sugar.

(*c*) Shift the offer curve of sugarland, increase the price of sugar.

(*d*) Shift the offer curve of sugarland, decrease the price of sugar.

11. Consider the following diagram in the context of India importing edible oil:

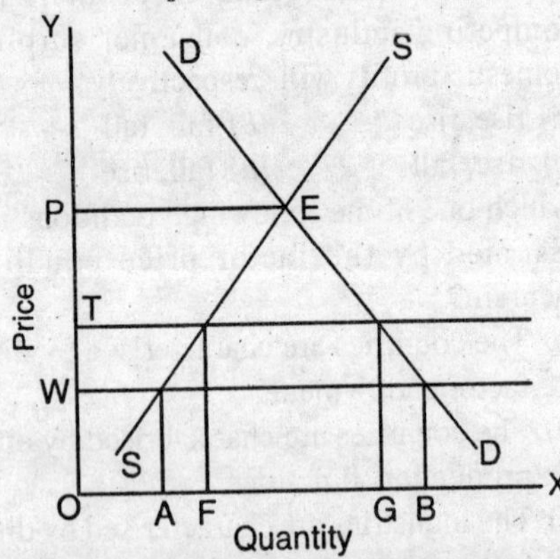

Before trade, demand curve DD and supply curve SS intersect at E to give domestic price OP, which is higher than world price OW. At world price OW:

demand for edible oil = OB

domestic supply of edible oil = OA

import of edible oil = AB

Assume that a tariff is levied on import of edible oil. Price rises to OT.

The following inferences may be drawn from the diagram regarding the effect of tariff. The import tariff.

1. reduces consumption
2. increases production
3. decreases the volume of trade

Select the correct answer using the codes given below:

Code :

(*a*) 1, 2 and 3 (*b*) 1 and 2

(*c*) 2 and 3 (*d*) 1 and 3

12. The country can improve its balance of payments by devaluation when the sum of elasticities of demand for exports and imports is

(*a*) greater than unity (*b*) equal to unity

(*c*) less than unity (*d*) zero

13. The Purchasing Power Parity (PPP) theory of the exchange-rate implies that the currency of a counrty A would depreciate against that of country B if

(*a*) the inflation rate in A exceeds that in B

(*b*) the normal interest-rate in A exceeds that in B

(*c*) the growth rate of GDP in B exceeds that in A

(*d*) foreign direct investment moves from B to A

14. In a freely floating exchange rate system.

(*a*) the current account and capital account add to zero.

(*b*) each account can individually be equal to zero.

(*c*) exchange rate is determined by market forces.

(*d*) all the above statements are correct.

15. In the diagram showing the demand and supply curves for dollars, the Central Authority wants to maintain the exchange rate (rupees per dollar) at E_2.

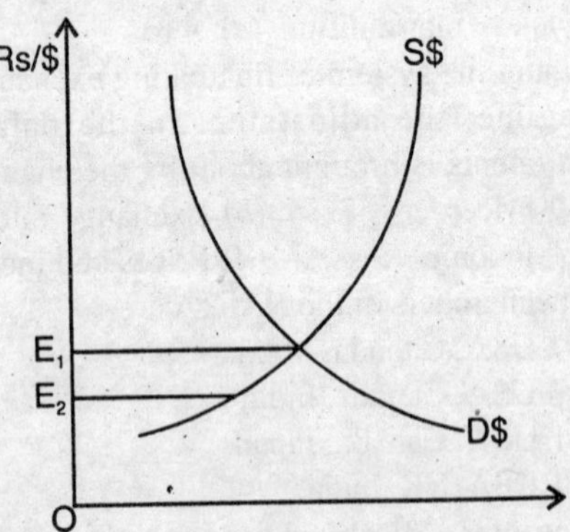

Demand/Supply of Dollars

Then the Central Authority will need to

(*a*) buy dollars and sell rupees

(*b*) sell dollars and buy rupees

(*c*) reduce tariff on imports

(d) impose a tax on exports

16. Which one of the following is NOT permissible under India's current account convertibility?

(a) Residents holding foreign exchange accounts.

(b) Foreigners holding accounts in Indian banks.

(c) Exporters holding foreign currency accounts.

(d) Free movement of short term capital.

17. During the last visit to India, Bill Gates travelled by the government owned airline. He also watched cricket at Bangalore and for the growth of the game, donated one million dollars to the Karnataka Fund for Cricket (KFC). The amount he paid for the air ticket and his donation to KFC would be classified as

(a) service exports and unilateral transfers to India respectively.

(b) unilateral transfers to India in both the cases respectively.

(c) service imports and service exports respectively.

(d) merchandise imports and service imports respectively.

18. In a flexible exchange-rate system, an increase in the domestic interest rate would tend to

(a) improve the current account and worsen the capital account.

(b) improve both the current and capital accounts.

(c) worsen both the accounts.

(d) worsen the current account and improve the capital account.

19. In the current international monetary system the Indian rupee is pegged to

(a) U.S. dollar (b) U.K. pound

(c) Euro (d) A basket of currencies

20. **Assertion (A) :** Compared to no trade, there are production and consumption gains to a country from free trade.

Reason (R) : The magnitude of gain from trade is independent of the magnitude of price change from no trade.

(a) Both A and R are true and R is the correct explanation of A.

(b) Both A and R are true but R is NOT a correct explanation of A.

(c) A is true but R is false.

(d) A is false but R is true.

21. **Assertion (A) :** Suppose, Pakistan forms a FTA (Free Trade Area) with its neighbouring countries including India, and before the formation of this FTA, Pakistan used to import a certain kind of jewellery from South Africa but now imports this from India. This is called trade diversion.

Reason (R) : Now there is a lot of FDI (Foreign Direct Investment) by India in Pakistan, which was non-existent before. This is called trade creation.

(a) Both A and R are true and R is the correct explanation of A.

(b) Both A and R are true but R is NOT a correct explanation of A.

(c) A is true but R is false.

(d) A is false but R is true.

22. **Assertion (A) :** A country's balance of Payments is always equal to zero.

Reason (R) : If a country has a deficit in the balance of payments account, this must be financed by change in reserve, long term capital movements or long term borrowing.

(a) Both A and R are true and R is the correct explanation of A.

(b) Both A and R are true but R is NOT a correct explanation of A.

(c) A is true but R is false.

(d) A is false but R is true.

23. Which one of the following statements is NOT correct?

(a) Free Trade Area among a group of countries means that they eliminate import tariffs against one another but maintain their original tariff levels against the rest of the world.

(b) Customs Union among a group of countries means than they eliminate import tariffs against one another, coordinate their macro-policies and impose a common tariff wall against the rest of the world.

(c) In a common market the member countries eliminate import tariffs against one another, allow free mobility of factors between them and maintain a common tariff wall against the rest of the world.

(d) In an Economic Union, the member countries eliminate import tariffs against one another, allow free mobility of factors between them,coordinate their macro-policies and maintain a common tariff wall against the rest of the world.

24. For a large trading country, the optional tariff argument is based on the proposition that a tariff on imports

(a) lowers the country's terms of trade.

(b) improves the country's terms of trade.

(c) leaves the country's terms of trade unchanged.

(d) fails to protect the import competing industries.

25. Suppose, a country has adopted a freely floating exchange rate system. Then, ceteris paribus, if the price level in the country rises, it leads to a

(a) rise in the demand for the country's currency and the currency depreciates.

(b) rise in the demand for the country's currency and the currency appreciates.

(c) fall in the demand for the country's currency and the currency appreciates.

(d) fall in the demand for the country's currency and the currency depreciates.

26. Which one of the following pairs is correctly matched?

(a) MFA	:	Agricultural Free Trade
(b) UNCTAD	:	Free Trade Area
(c) IMF	:	Balance of Payments Difficulties
(d) MFN	:	Direct Foreign Investment

27. The terms of trade refer to—

(a) the excess of import expenditures over export earnings.

(b) trade agreements.

(c) the ratio between export prices and import prices.

(d) the terms and conditions on which a country is offered loan in the event of balance of payments difficulties.

28. The Government of India announces a new NRI deposit scheme. This offers a very high interest rate, compared to the interest rates abroad, on foreign currency deposits by NRIs in Indian Commercial Banks. Many NRIs in the US do invest under this scheme. Under a flexible exchange rate system, this would tend to

(a) depreciate the value of Indian rupee against US dollar.

(b) appreciate the value of Indian rupee against US dollar.

(c) deplete the foreign exchange reserve of India.

(d) leave the value of rupee against US dollar unchanged.

29. India is a net exporter of hand-made carpets and an importer of high-tech products like computer memory chips and printers. This pattern of Indian trade is explained by the

(a) Ricardian theory

(b) Hecksher-Ohlin theory

(c) Labour theory of value

(d) Purchasing power parity theory

30. Presently, India's exchange rate policy towards current account and capital account transactions is that the rupee is

(a) fully convertible for current account transactions, but not for capital account transactions.

(b) fully convertible for capital account transactions, but not for current account transactions.

(c) fully convertible for both capital and current account transactions.

(d) not convertible for either type of transactions.

31. Mr. Ramprakash travelled to England for medical operation. He had to bear the cost of his air travel by Air India as well as the cost of hospitalisation. In this context, which one of the following is true in terms of entry in India's balance of payments transactions?

(a) The cost of hospitalisation is included in service imports but the cost of air travel is not.

(b) The cost of air travel is included in service imports but the cost of hospitalisation is not.

(c) Both expenditures are included in the category of service imports.

(d) Both expenditures are included in service exports.

32. Suppose that the world economy consists of two

countries, 'Home' and 'Foreign'. A tariff imposed by the Home on its imports from the Foreign shifts.

(a) Home's offer curve to the right
(b) Foreign's offer curve to the right
(c) Home's offer curve to the left
(d) Foreign's offer curve to the left

33. In the context of a small, competitive currency, an increase in import tariff causes

(a) a consumption dead weight loss in terms of welfare since consumers now pay a higher price for the product.
(b) a production dead weight gain in terms of welfare since domestic producers gain from tariff protection.
(c) an overall welfare gain.
(d) a trade gain since the amount imported decreases.

34. In the two-good Ricardian trade model, complete specialisation in production occurs in free trade equilibrium because

(a) the production possibility frontier satisfies increasing opportunity cost.
(b) there are diminishing returns to the factor of production.
(c) there are increasing returns to the factor of production.
(d) the production possibility frontier satisfies constant opportunity cost.

35. Special Drawing Rights (SDRs) is the currency of IMF. This is in the form of

(a) paper currency
(b) gold
(c) silver and gold both
(d) book-keeping entry only

36. Consider the following statements :
The Brettonwoods conference led to the establishment of

1. IMF
2. IBRD
3. United Nations

Which of the above statements are correct?

(a) 1 and 2 (b) 2 and 3
(c) 1 and 3 (d) 1, 2 and 3

37. A deficit in a country's balance of payments refers to the difference between

(a) autonomous receipts and autonomous payments.
(b) accommodating receipts and autonomous payment.
(c) accommodating receipts and accommodating payments.
(d) autonomous receipts and accommodating payments.

38. What is the correct sequence of the following?

1. Uruguay Round Talks
2. WTO's Seattle Meet
3. Establishment of GATT

Select the correct answer using the codes given below:

Codes:
(a) 1, 2, 3 (b) 3, 1, 2
(c) 3, 2, 1 (d) 2, 3, 1

39. Which one of the following treaties was covered by the Uruguay Round Negotiations:

(a) General agreement on trade in services.
(b) Trade-related intellectual property rights.
(c) Trade-related investment measures.
(d) All of the above.

40. The Heckscher-Ohlin theory of trade pattern assumes

(a) perfect competition in the product markets but not in the factor markets.
(b) perfect competition in the factor markets but not in the product markets.
(c) perfect competition in both product and factor markets.
(d) unemployment in the labour market.

41. **Assertion (A) :** The open-economy Keynesian multiplier is less than the closed economy Keynesian multiplier.
Reason (R) : The marginal propensity to import is always greater than the marginal propensity to consume.

(a) Both A and R are true and R is the correct explanation of A.
(b) Both A and R are true but R is NOT a correct explanation of A.
(c) A is true but R is false.
(d) A is false but R is true.

42. **Assertion (A) :** Intellectual property rights were brought into the Uruguay Round Trade Negotiations.
Reason (R) : International trade restrictions can

be used to discourage the violation of intellectual property rights.

(a) Both A and R are true and R is the correct explanation of A.

(b) Both A and R are true but R is NOT a correct explanation of A.

(c) A is true but R is false.

(d) A is false but R is true.

43. Which of the following does **not** form a part of the foreign exchange reserves of India?

(a) Gold

(b) SDRs

(c) Foreign currency assets

(d) Foreign currency and securities held by the banks and corporate bodies.

44. Match List I (Institution) with List II (Main objective) and select the correct answer using the codes given below the lists:

List I (Institution)	*List II (Main objective)*
A. IMF	1. To promote viable and durable multilateral trading system.
B. UNCTAD	2. To promote harmony between developed and developing countries on trade-related developmental issues.
C. World Bank	3. To promote socio-economic development of the member-countries.
D. WTO	4. To reduce the degree of balance of payments dis-equilibrium of the member countries.

Codes :	A	B	C	D
(a)	4	3	2	1
(b)	1	2	3	4
(c)	4	2	3	1
(d)	1	3	2	4

45. Which one of the following is a possible compromise between the fixed and the flexible exchange rate systems?

(a) Adjustable peg system

(b) Crawling peg system

(c) Managed floating system

(d) All the above three

46. Consider the following statements:

Under the Gold Standard System, represented

1. common unit value.
2. international means of payment.
3. a store of value.

which of these statements are correct?

(a) 1 and 2 (b) 1 and 3

(c) 2 and 3 (d) 1, 2 and 3

47. Match List I with List II and select the correct answer using the codes given below the lists :

List I	*List II*
A. Forward exchange	1. A device of covering exchange risk against the price rise of foreign currency.
B. Hedging	2. A contract to buy and sell foreign exchange against another currency at some fixed rate in the future at a price agreed upon now.
C. Arbitrage	3. The movement of exchange rate between two limits set by the cost of moving gold from one country to another.
D. Specie points	4. A mechanism which makes two markets that are physically separate, into a single market in the economic sense.

Codes :	A	B	C	D
(a)	4	3	2	1
(b)	2	1	4	3
(c)	4	1	2	3
(d)	2	3	4	1

48. Which one of the following is non-debt flow of capital between countries?

(a) Commercial borrowings

(b) Portfolio investment

(c) Short-term borrowings from IMF

(d) Sale and purchase of bonds in the capital markets

49. In respect of the production possibility curve under increasing opportunity costs given above, consider the following statements:

1. The production possibility curve is not identical with price curve as in the case of

constant costs.

2. There would be complete specialisation of a country in a single commodity in a two-commodities and two-countries model.

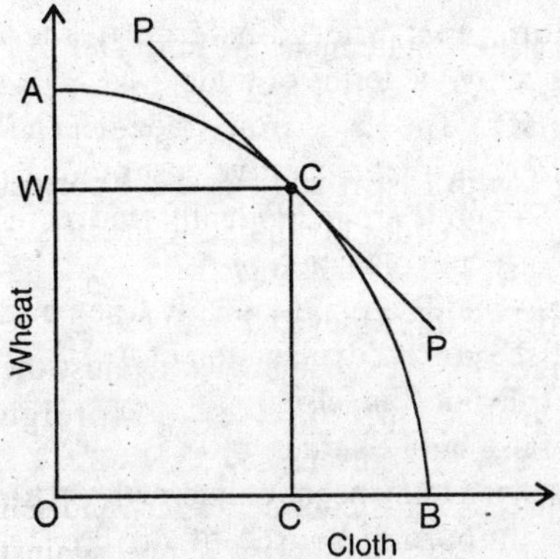

Which of the statements is/are correct?

(*a*) 1 only (*b*) 2 only

(*c*) Both 1 and 2 (*d*) Neither 1 nor 2

50. The diagram shows the demand and supply, DD and SS, curves respectively, for fertilizers in India.

OP = price of fertilisers in India, before trade.

OW = price of fertilizers in world market.

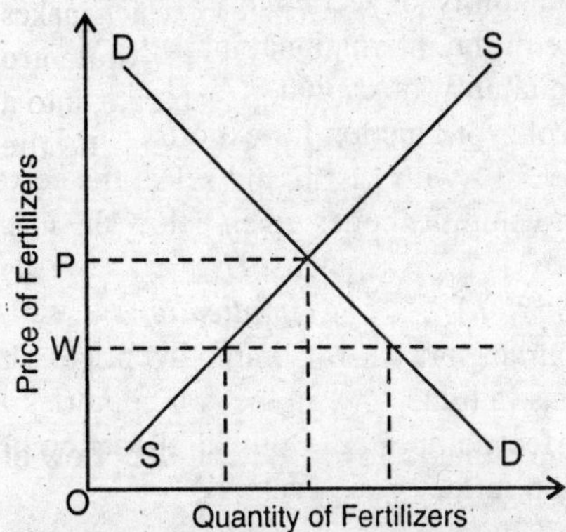

Consider the following statements:

Under free trade

1. prices of fertilizers will be lowered compared to world prices.
2. consumption of fertilizers will increase.
3. imports of fertilizers will be zero.

Which of these statements are correct?

(*a*) 1 and 2 (*b*) 1 and 3

(*c*) 2 and 3 (*d*) 1, 2 and 3

51. Gains in trade results from

(*a*) exporting as much as possible and receiving gold.

(*b*) reallocation of existing goods between the two countries.

(*c*) the fact that exchange brings both specialisation and reallocation of greater output and the increased welfare in each country.

(*d*) one country receiving both imports and gold.

52.

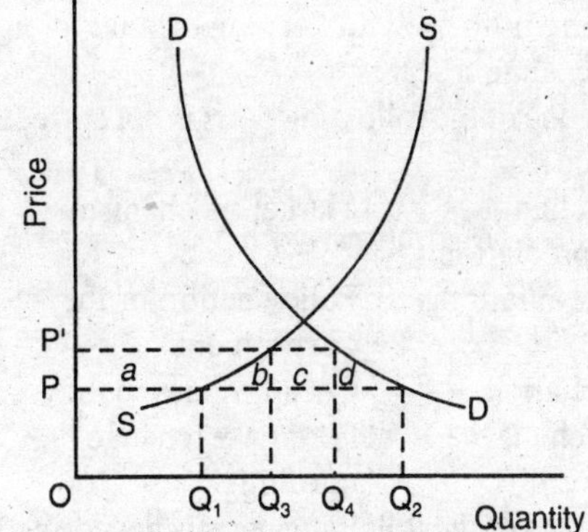

The above graph shows different effects of tariffs in partial equilibrium. Which one of the following indicates the revenue effect of a tariff equal to PP' per unit?

(*a*) Area represented by '*a*'

(*b*) Area represented by '*b*'

(*c*) Area represented by '*c*'

(*d*) Area represented by '*d*'

53. Which of the following statements is not correct in respect of the balance of payments of a country?

(*a*) The current account of balance of payments consists of export and import of goods and the capital account consists of export and import of services, borrowings and lendings.

(*b*) The surplus on current account in the balance of payments must be equal to the deficit on capital account and vice versa.

(*c*) If in the actual balance of payments, the credit and debit do not balance, the balance is usually achieved by adding one item "errors and omissions".

(*d*) The balance of payments of a country must always balance in the accounting sense.

54. The flexible exchange rate has a number of advantages. Which one of the following is not to be considered as such an advantage?
(*a*) The exchange rate moves in a free market to equate demand and supply so that the market does not face the problem of scarcity or surplus of foreign currency.
(*b*) It permits a continued existence of free trade and convertible currencies.
(*c*) It permits a country to follow independent monetary and fiscal policies.
(*d*) There is no need for keeping official foreign exchange reserves.

55. Which one of the following pairs is not correctly matched?

(*a*) Exchange depreciation	Market mechanism
(*b*) Devaluation	Policy action of the government
(*c*) Deflation	Cheap money policy
(*d*) Exchange control	Foreign exchange rationing

56. Which one of the following pairs is not correctly matched?

(*a*) Gross barter terms of trade	— Taussing
(*b*) Purchasing power parity theory	— J.S.Mill
(*c*) Offer curves	— A. Marshall
(*d*) Factor-endowment model	— Heckscher-Ohlin

57. Assertion (A) : Devaluation leads to expenditure switching.
Reason (R) : Devaluation makes imports relatively costhier than domestic goods.
(*a*) Both A and R are individually true and R is the correct explanation of A
(*b*) Both A and R are individually true but R is NOT the correct explanation of A.
(*c*) A is true but R is false.
(*d*) A is false but R is true.

58. Assertion (A) : Special Drawing Rights (SDRs) have the characteristics of an international currency.
Reason (R) : SDRs were introduced to increase international liquidity.
(*a*) Both A and R are individually true and R is the correct explanation of A.
(*b*) Both A and R are individually true but R is NOT the correct explanation of A.
(*c*) A is true but R is false.
(*d*) A is false but R is true.

59. Assertion (A) : The gains from trade are determined by the terms of trade.
Reason (R) : The gains from trade depend on the differences in comparative cost ratios.
(*a*) Both A and R are individually true and R is the correct explanation of A.
(*b*) Both A and R are individually true but R is NOT the correct explanation of A.
(*c*) A is true but R is false.
(*d*) A is false but R is true.

60. In Heckscher-Ohlin theory of international trade, the most important source of difference in relative commodity prices between nations is a differnce in
(*a*) factor endowments
(*b*) technology
(*c*) tastes
(*d*) demand conditions

61. The scope of international trade and division of labour is limited by
(*a*) availability of technology
(*b*) size of the international market
(*c*) availability of capital
(*d*) surplus production for exports

62. Match List I with List II and select the correct answer using the codes given below the lists:

List I *(Assumption)*	*List II* *(Implication)*
A. No transport costs in trade	1. Commodity prices same in the two countries
B. Perfect competition in factor markets	2. Optimal allocation of factors
C. Factor intensities differ between goods	3. Techniques of production different for the two goods
D. Production functions same in both countries	4. Techniques of production same in the two countries
	5. Techniques of production different in the two countries

Codes:	A	B	C	D
(a)	2	1	5	4
(b)	3	4	2	5
(c)	3	2	4	1
(d)	1	2	3	4

63. The tariff which maximises a country's economic welfare is called

(a) protective tariff
(b) discriminatory tariff
(c) non-discriminatory tariff
(d) optimum tariff

64. Match List I with List II and select the correct answer using the codes given below the lists:

List I	List II
A. Classical theory of comparative cost advantage	1. David Ricardo
B. Vent for surplus theory	2. G. Haberler
C. Theory of opportunity cost	3. J.S. Mill
D. Theory of reciprocal demand	4. Adam Smith

Codes:	A	B	C	D
(a)	1	4	2	3
(b)	1	2	3	4
(c)	4	1	2	3
(d)	3	1	2	4

65. A country is said to be relatively well-endowed with capital if the

(a) aggregate value of capital in the country is greater than that of labour and land.
(b) the wage-rental ratio in that country is higher in relation to that in its trading partners.
(c) the interest rate on capital is lower in that country relatively to the interest rate in its trading partners.
(d) the per capita amount of investment in the country had shown a rising trend.

66. Which one of the following transactions represents a credit entry in the current account of a country's balance of payments?

(a) Merchandise imports.
(b) Transportation services rendered by foreign companies.
(c) Expenditure of foreign tourists in a country.
(d) Fees paid to foreign contractors and engineers.

67. Match List I with List II and select the correct answer using the codes given below the lists:

List I	List II
A. Buying and selling of home currency in the foreign exchange market by government or its authorised agency	1. Pegging operation
B. Charging different prices in different markets for an internationally traded commodity	2. Dumping operation
C. The price of imports paid by local purchasers, which is more than their normal value	3. Free on board (*f.o.b.*)
D. Local producers of an export good receiving only the price of the good as it leaves the country	4. Cost, insurance and freight (*c.i.f.*)

Codes:	A	B	C	D
(a)	2	1	3	4
(b)	1	2	4	3
(c)	3	1	2	4
(d)	1	4	3	2

68. Which one of the following pairs is correctly matched?

(a)	Change in imports associated with a given change in income	Average propensity to import
(b)	Value of imports as a percentage of total national income	Marginal propensity to import
(c)	Change in nation's income caused by a change in its exports	Foreign trade multiplier
(d)	When some products contribute much more to growth than others	Balanced growth

69. According to the elasticity approach, for a devaluation to have a positive effect on a country's trade balance, the sum of the elasticities of demand for a country's exports and of its demand for imports has to be equal to

(a) unity (b) less than unity
(c) zero (d) greater than unity

70. Consider the following statements:
Under the gold-standard inflow of gold from the deficit to the surplus nation results in

1. a fall in the interest rate in the surplus nation.
2. a fall in the interest rate in the deficit nation.
3. an outflow of capital from surplus to deficit nation.
4. an outflow of capital from deficit to surplus nation.

Of the above statements

(*a*) 1 and 4 are correct (*b*) 1 and 3 are correct
(*c*) 2 and 3 are correct (*d*) 2 and 4 are correct

71. Direct control refers to

(*a*) interference with the operation of the market forces.
(*b*) price and wage control.
(*c*) trade and exchange control.
(*d*) all of the above.

72. Which of the following items were responsible for most of the increase in international liquidity since World War II?

1. Gold
2. Dollars
3. Other convertible currencies
4. SDRs

Select the correct answer using the codes given below:

(*a*) 1, 2 and 4 (*b*) 1 and 3
(*c*) 2 and 3 (*d*) 2 and 4

73. 'Most Favoured National Clause' under GATT requires

(*a*) Preferential treatment to particular identified countries.
(*b*) preferential treatment only to developing countries.
(*c*) preferential treatment to countries with a balance of payments deficit.
(*d*) preferential treatment to all member countries of GATT.

74. Assertion (A) : Factor price equalisation theorem deals with the effect of trade on factor prices.

Reason (R) : Trade in goods has no effect on factor prices.

(*a*) Both A and R are true and R is the correct explanation of A.
(*b*) Both A and R are true but R is NOT a correct explanation of A.
(*c*) A is true but R is false.
(*d*) A is false but R is true.

75. Assertion (A) : Heckscher-Ohlin theory in validates the classical theory of comparative costs.

Reason (R) : Heckscher-Ohlin theory goes behind the comparative cost theory.

(*a*) Both A and R are true and R is the correct explanation of A.
(*b*) Both A and R are true but R is NOT a correct explanation of A.
(*c*) A is true but R is false.
(*d*) A is false but R is true.

76. Given the usual shapes of LM and IS curves and BOP curve, if there is a shift in the LM curve to the right, the economy will face

(*a*) surplus in the balance of payment and a fall in the rate of interest.
(*b*) Deficit in the balance of payment and an increase in the rate of interest.
(*c*) Surplus in the balance of payment and an increase in the rate of interest.
(*d*) Deficit in the balance of payment and a fall in the rate of interest.

77. If the sum of the elasticities of the exports and imports is less than one, any devaluation will further aggravate the deficit in the BOP. Who has given this view?

(*a*) Marshall and Lerner
(*b*) Harrod and Domar
(*c*) Solow and Swan
(*d*) Hickscher and Ohlin

78. Where the foreign offer curves has an elasticity of one, the optimum tariff will be

(*a*) infinity (*b*) unity
(*c*) less than unity (*d*) zero

79. The Ricardian theory of comparative advantage relates to

(*a*) short-run outcome
(*b*) long-run outcome
(*c*) intermediate outcome
(*d*) all the above

80. Which one of the following assumptions is the most important assumption in the Heckscher-Ohlin theorem of international trade?

(*a*) Two factor model (*b*) Two commodities
(*c*) No tariff (*d*) Constant tastes

81. The country is likely to be better off after export-led growth provided that

(*a*) gains from export-led-growth exceed the

losses from worsening terms of trade.

(*b*) gains from growth off-set the losses from worsening terms of trade.

(*c*) the long-run terms of trade are favourable.

(*d*) the elasticity of demand for imports is less than unity.

82. In a three-country two-commodity model, countries being of unequal sizes, the domestic exchange ratios are as under:

Country	*Domestic Exchange Ratio*
1	$2a : 1b$
2	$1a : 1b$
3	$1a : 2b$

As per this model, the stability in international trade is most likely at the international terms of trade of

(*a*) $2a : 1b$ (*b*) $1a : 1b$

(*c*) $1a : 2b$ (*d*) $0.5a : 1b$

83. Assume that the nominal rate of tariff on imports of final commodity is 30%. The nominal rate of tariff on the imported inputs is 10% and the ratio of imported inputs to the value of the final commodity is 50%. Then the effective rate of tariff will be

(*a*) 50% (*b*) 40%

(*c*) 30% (*d*) 10%

84. The balance of payments of a country is in equilibrium when the

(*a*) demand for the domestic currency is equal to its supply.

(*b*) demand for the domestic currency is the highest.

(*c*) demand for the domestic currency is the lowest.

(*d*) demand as well as supply of the domestic currency are the highest.

85. Dusenberry was of the opinion that less developed countries will have serious and adverse effect on their balance of payments due to

(*a*) backwash effect (*b*) spread effect

(*c*) demonstration effect (*d*) multiplier effect

86. Assertion (A) : A change in the income terms of trade is an indicator of welfare.

Reason (R) : Income terms of trade measure the quantity of imports bought by exports.

(*a*) Both A and R are true and R is the correct explanation of A.

(*b*) Both A and R are true but R is NOT a correct explanation of A.

(*c*) A is true but R is false.

(*d*) A is false but R is true.

87. Match List I with List II and select the correct answer using the codes given below the lists:

List I	**List II**
A. Hamilton-List	1. Trade creation and Trade diversion effects
B. Marshall-Lerner	2. Infant-industry argument
C. F.Y. Edgeworth	3. Elasticity approach
D. Jacob Viner	4. Impoverishing growth

Codes:	A	B	C	D
(*a*)	2	3	1	4
(*b*)	2	3	4	1
(*c*)	3	2	4	1
(*d*)	3	2	1	4

88. In the given diagram, curves *aa* and *bb* represent the isoquants for good A and good B. P_0P_0 represents relative factor prices in country I. P_1P_1 and P_2P_2 represent relative factor prices in country II. Which of the following inferences can be drawn from the data presented in the diagram?

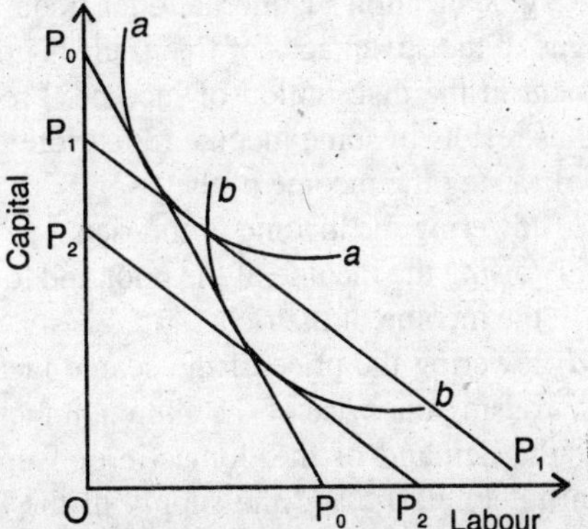

1. Good A is the capital intensive good.
2. Good B is a labour intensive good.
3. Capital is cheap in country I.

Select the correct answer using the codes given below:

(*a*) 1, 2 and 3 (*b*) 1 and 2

(*c*) 2 and 3 (*d*) 1 and 3

89. Match List I with List II and select the correct answer using the codes given below the lists :

List I	List II
A. Supply side of International Trade	1. David Ricardo
B. Demand side of International Trade	2. Bastable and Alfred Marshall
C. Opportunity cost of International Trade	3. G. Haberler
D. Real cost theory of International Trade	4. Alfred Marshall and Edgeworth

Codes:	A	B	C	D
(a)	1	4	2	3
(b)	1	4	3	2
(c)	4	1	2	3
(d)	4	1	3	2

90. The main objective of the World Trade Organization is to secure among others

(a) a general agreement among Common Market countries on technical training and mutual prices of traded goods.

(b) the maintenance of intellectual property rights and patent rights of member countries.

(c) an improvement in the USA's terms of trade in the next decade.

(d) a reduction in tariffs through negotiation, elimination of import quotas and globalization of international trade.

91. One of the advantages of free trade is improvement in the distribution of income. Free trade thus results in some income redistribution by

(a) raising the income of the poor.

(b) lowering the income of the rich.

(c) raising the income of the poor and lowering the income of the rich.

(d) lowering the price of the scarce factor and raising the price of the abundant factor.

92. If the demand of the domestic consumers is infinitely elastic and the supply of the foreign producer is perfectly inelastic, then the whole of the tariff will

(a) be paid by the domestic consumers.

(b) be paid by the foreign producer.

(c) be equally shared by the domestic consumers and the foreign producer.

(d) yield neither revenue nor protection to either of them.

93. The optimum tariff is at a point where the elasticity of the offer curve is

(a) infinity

(b) unity

(c) greater than unity but less than infinity

(d) less than unity

94. The given diagram represents a country producing only two goods 'A' and 'B'. PP represents the production possibility curve. Consider the following statements in this regard:

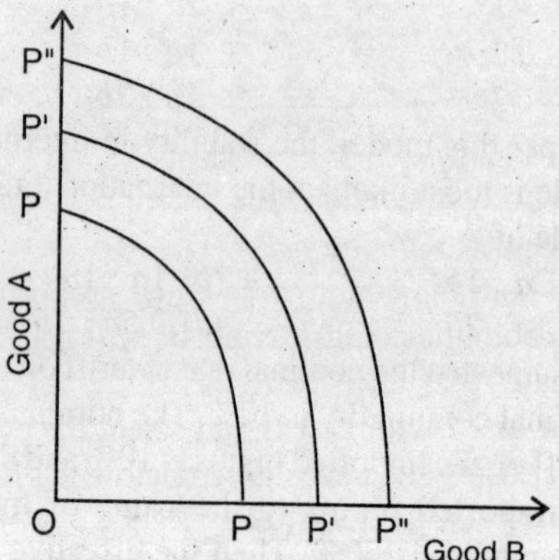

An outward shift of the production possibility curve (to P'P', P"P") will take place due to

1. technological progress.
2. increase in available resources.
3. increase in consumption.

Of these statements :

(a) 1, 2 and 3 are correct *(b)* 1 and 2 are correct

(c) 2 and 3 are correct *(d)* 1 and 3 are correct

95. Which of the following pairs of GATT rounds and the associated years are correctly matched?

1. First Round 1948
2. Kennedy Round 1964-67
3. Tokyo Round 1973-79

Select the correct answer using the codes given below:

(a) 1, 2 and 3 *(b)* 1 and 2

(c) 2 and 3 *(d)* 1 and 3

96. In the given diagram curves I and II represents respectively production–possibility curves of countries A and B. The diagram refers to a two-country, two-commodity model. When free trade opens up, each country specialises on the lines of Ricardian model of trade. At some point of time, the terms of trade are settled at domestic exchange ratio of country 'A'. In this case, gain from international trade will accrue.

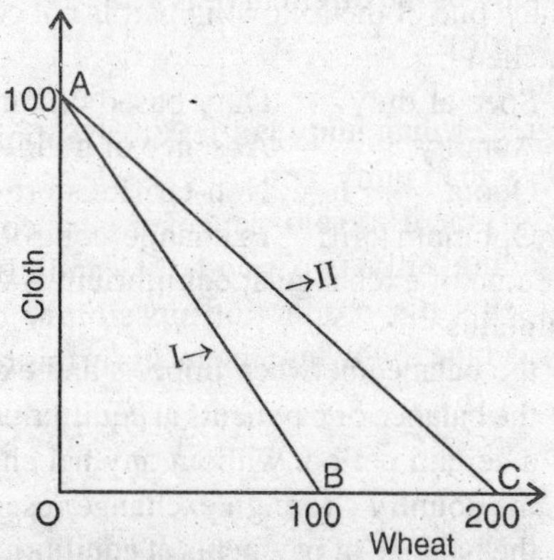

(*a*) Wholly to country 'A'
(*b*) Wholly to country 'B'
(*c*) to both the countries in equal proportions
(*d*) to both the countries but 'B' will gain more than 'A'

97. Match List I with List II and select the correct answer using the codes given below the lists:

List I	*List II*
A. Free trade area	1. No restrictions on trade and factor movement
B. Customs union	2. Trade is free and no customs duties
C. Common market	3. No customs duties; duties on non-members
D. Economic union	4. Advanced stage of integration

Codes:	A	B	C	D
(*a*)	2	1	3	4
(*b*)	3	2	4	1
(*c*)	2	3	1	4
(*d*)	1	3	4	2

98. Match List I with List II and select the correct answer using the codes given below the lists:

List I	List II
A. Unrequited receipts	1. Gifts, reparations received from foreigners
B. Accommodating finance	2. Lending, borrowing and gold transfer
C. Transfer items	3. Commercial imports and exports
D. Autonomous items	4. Currency transfer by monetary authority

Codes:	A	B	C	D
(*a*)	1	4	2	3
(*b*)	4	1	2	3
(*c*)	1	4	3	2
(*d*)	4	1	3	2

99. For a closed economy having no foreign trade which one of the following is correct?
(*a*) GDP = GNP (*b*) GDP > GNP
(*c*) GDP < GNP (*d*) None of these

100. The Singer-Prebisch theory maintains that
(*a*) less developed countries suffer a welfare loss from secular decline in terms of trade due to primary product exports.
(*b*) Less developed countries always gain in trade when they trade with developed countries.
(*c*) Less developed countries lose in terms of welfare but gain in terms of foreign exchange
(*d*) Dependence upon trade for development is not harmful to less developed countries.

101. Denoting the price of capital and labour by P_K and P_L respectively and countries by A and B, if

$$\left(\frac{P_K}{P_L}\right)_A > \left(\frac{P_K}{P_L}\right)_B$$

(*a*) Country B is relatively labour abundant.
(*b*) Country A is relatively labour abundant.
(*c*) Country A is relatively capital abundant.
(*d*) relative fctor abundance is indeterminate.

102. The terms of trade for a country will improve as a result of currency devaluation (where S_x = export elasticity of supply, S_m = import elasticity of supply, D_x = export elasticity of demand, D_m = import elasticity of demand) if
(*a*) $S_x.S_m > D_x.D_m$ (*b*) $D_x.D_m > S_x.S_m$
(*c*) $D_x.D_m = S_x.S_m$ (*d*) $\frac{S_x.S_m}{D_x.D_m} < 1$

103. Consider the following statements :
The equivalence between the effects of a tariff and a quota which limits imports by the same amount depends on the assumption that,
1. there are competitive conditions prevailing abroad.
2. there is perfect competition among quota holders.
3. there is free competition within the domestic

import competing industry.

Of these statements

(a) 1 alone is correct (b) 1 and 2 are correct

(c) 1, 2 and 3 are correct (d) 2 and 3 are correct

104. The three offer curves viz., $\alpha_0, \alpha_1, \alpha_2$ of country α cut the offer curve of β at points *a, b, c* which is equivalent to international terms of trade as shown in the diagram below:

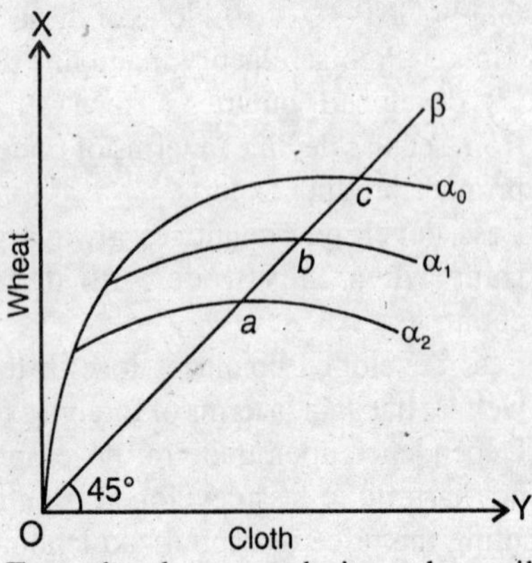

From the above graph, it can be easily deduced that

(a) α reaps all gains from trade at all points viz. *a,b,c*

(b) α reaps all gains from trade at point *c* only

(c) both α and β share gains from trade reciprocally

(d) both α and β gain from trade, but α gains more than β

105. Consider the following statements :

Foreign indirect investment includes

1. Global Depository Receipts and Foreign Currency Convertible Bonds.
2. Foreign Institutional Investment.
3. Non-resident External Deposits.
4. Investment of a Multinational company in a domestic power project.

Of these statements :

(a) 1 and 2 are correct

(b) 1 and 3 are correct

(c) 1, 2 and 4 are correct

(d) 2, 3 and 4 are correct

106. Which one of the following pairs is not correctly matched

(a) Taussing — Barter terms of trade

(b) Prebisch — Deteriorating terms of trade

(c) Marshall — Offer curves

(d) Walras — Dumping conditions

107. Which one of the following pair is not correctly matched?

(a) Special duty — Duty based on quantity

(b) Autarky — Absence of trade

(c) Quota — Non-tariff distortion

(d) Optimum tariff — Exchange control

108. The rate of exchange at equilibrium is one that maintains

(a) the balance between imports and exports

(b) the balance of payments at equilibrium, over a certain period, without any net change in the country's foreign exchange reserves

(c) the balance of payments at equilibrium with domestic deflationary policy

(d) Satisfactory foreign-exchange-reserve at the disposal of the monetary authority.

109. Which one of the following pairs is correctly matched?

(a) Lowering of the value of a country's currency — Revaluation

(b) Decline in the value of a country's currency in terms of other currencies — Depreciation

(c) Increase in the value of a country's currency in terms of other currencies — Devaluation

(d) Increase in a country's foreign exchange reserves — Depression

110. Which of the following items may be included in the Current Account part of the Balance of Payments Statement?

1. Merchandise exports.
2. Foreign tourist's expenditure in home country.
3. Foreign short-term investment in home country.
4. Banking, insurance and transport services.
5. Income received on investments abroad.

Select the correct answer using the codes given below:

(a) 1 alone (b) 1, 2, 3 and 4

(c) 1, 2, 4 and 5 (d) 1, 3 and 4

111. Assertion (A) : The Ricardian theory of comparative costs is based on the labour theory of value.

Reason (R) : Labour theory of value holds good in domestic trade, but breaks down when applied to international trade.

(a) Both A and R are true and R is the correct explanation of A
(b) Both A and R are true but R is NOT correct explanation of A
(c) A is true but R is false
(d) A is false but R is true

112. Assertion (A) : Devaluation changes *ipso facto* exchange rates.

Reason (R) : Revaluation is the opposite of devaluation.

(a) Both A and R are true and R is the correct explanation of A.
(b) Both A and R are true but R is NOT a correct explanation of A.
(c) A is true but R is false.
(d) A is false but R is true.

113. Assertion (A) : Customs duties primarily influence commodity prices.

Reason (R) : Quantitative restrictions are designed to determine the amount of goods imported or exported.

(a) Both A and R are true and R is the correct explanation of A.
(b) Both A and R are true but R is NOT a correct explanation of A.
(c) A is true but R is false.
(d) A is false but R is true.

114. Assertion (A) : Marshall-Lerner condition should be fulfilled if devaluation is to be successful.

Reason (R) : Devaluation makes exports costly and imports cheaper.

(a) Both A and R are true and R is the correct explanation of A.
(b) Both A and R are true but R is NOT a correct explanation of A.
(c) A is true but R is false.
(d) A is false but R is true.

115. Assertion (A) : Devaluation can correct the imbalance in the balance of payment.

Reason (R) : Devaluation raises the price of imported goods and reduces the foreign price of exports of the devaluing country.

(a) Both A and R are true and R is the correct explanation of A.
(b) Both A and R are true but R is NOT a correct explanation of A.
(c) A is true but R is false.
(d) A is false but R is true.

116. Assertion (A) : Free international trade necessarily lowers the real wage of the scarce factor of production in terms of any good.

Reason (R) : If the real wage declines in terms of every good, real income must suffer regardless of the tastes and expenditure patterns of the labourers as consumers.

(a) Both A and R are true and R is the correct explanation of A.
(b) Both A and R are true but R is NOT a correct explanation of A.
(c) A is true but R is false.
(d) A is false but R is true.

117. In a word, with only two goods, X and Y, and the full employment of factors, a rise in the price of a commodity, X, leads to

(a) an increase in the real reward of the factor used intensively in the production of X.
(b) a decrease in the real reward of the factor used less intensively in the production of Y.
(c) an increase in the real reward of the factor used less intensively in the production of X.
(d) an increase in the real reward of the factor used more intensively in the production of Y.

118. The infant industry argument is often advocated in the context of

(a) price discrimination
(b) product diversification
(c) protection
(d) resource mobilisation

119. Under which of the following conditions will there be the possibility of trade between two countries whose factor endowments are identical?

(a) When there are differences in tastes and preferences of the consumers in the two countries.
(b) When there are differences in commodity prices in the two countries.
(c) When cost of production of different commodities differs between the two

countries.

(*d*) When production functions of the same goods are identical in the two countries.

120. A tariff will not have any effect on revenue if the duty imposed is

(*a*) 50% (*b*) 100%

(*c*) non-prohibitive (*d*) prohibitive

121. Consider the following statements:

If the offer-curve is a straight line,

1. high tariff rates can improve terms of trade.

2. law tariff rates can improve terms of trade.

3. absence of tariff can improve terms of trade.

Of these statements :

(*a*) 1 alone is correct (*b*) 2 alone is correct

(*c*) 3 alone is correct (*d*) 2 and 3 are correct

122. Dumping aims at flooding a foreign country with

(*a*) high-priced commodities

(*b*) low-priced commodities

(*c*) commodities with similar prices

(*d*) commodities with fluctuating prices

123. Which one of the following is the major characteristic of foreign direct investment (FDI)?

(*a*) It is non-debt creating capital flow.

(*b*) It is portfolio investment in stock market.

(*c*) It is that investment which involves debt servicing.

(*d*) It is investment made by foreign institutional investors in government securities.

124. Over-valuation of currency is NOT desirable, when

(*a*) a country is under the sudden necessity of making large purchases from abroad.

(*b*) a country is under the sudden necessity of acquiring large amounts of foreign currency to pay its debts.

(*c*) the prices in the country are higher than the corresponding prices in other countries.

(*d*) a country wants to boost up its exports and reduce its imports.

125. Which one of the following represents capital account convertibility of a currency?

(*a*) Freedom to transact in foreign currency on account of trade in goods and services.

(*b*) Freedom to transact in foreign currency on account of trade in services only.

(*c*) Freedom to transact in financial assets with foreign countries without restrictions.

(*d*) No restrictions on remittances by nationals of a country to another country.

126. Hot money refers to the

(*a*) Short-term capital movements from one country to another seeking either a higher rate of interest or safety of capital irrespective of the rate of interest.

(*b*) Long-term capital movements from one country to another seeking higher rate of interest.

(*c*) medium-term capital movements from one country to another.

(*d*) Currency which is very much in demand in the foreign exchange market.

127. Which one of the following items is **NOT** included in the current account of India's balance of payments?

(*a*) Short-term commercial borrowings

(*b*) Non-monetary gold movements

(*c*) Investment income

(*d*) Transfer payments

128. Which one of the following items is **NOT** included in the 'invisibles' on current account of the balance of payments of India?

(*a*) Foreign travel

(*b*) Transportation

(*c*) Insurance

(*d*) Loans from foreign banks

129. Consider the following statements:

Devaluation results in a

1. rise in the domestic price of imports.

2. rise in the domestic price of exports.

3. rise in the domestic price of exports and imports.

4. fall in the foreign price of exports.

Which of the above statements are correct?

(*a*) 1, 2 and 3 (*b*) 1 and 2

(*c*) 2, 3 and 4 (*d*) 1 and 4

130. An optimum tariff

(*a*) improve the terms of trade

(*b*) keeps the terms of trade constant

(*c*) lowers the terms of trade

(*d*) reduces the country's welfare level

131. For the Heckscher-Ohlin theory of trade to be valid, the relative factor endowments of two countries should be

(*a*) close to each other

(b) as divergent as possible
(c) identical
(d) none of these

132. Which one of the following statements is **NOT** correct?
(a) Trade between two countries can take place when their supply and demand conditions are identical.
(b) Trade between two countries can take place with different supply conditions and similar demand conditions.
(c) Trade between two countries can take place with identical supply conditions and dissimilar demand conditions.
(d) Trade between two countries can take place with different supply and demand conditions.

133. If the price elasticity of demand for exports is zero, then exports in local currency will
(a) be the same after devaluation.
(b) fall after devaluation.
(c) substantially increase after devaluation.
(d) partially increase after devaluation.

134. **Assertion (A):** Any important policy instrument of economic liberalisation is reduction in import duties on capital goods.
Reason (R): Reduction in import duties would help the local entrepreneurs to improve technology to face the global markets.
(a) Both A and R are true and R is the correct explanation of A.
(b) Both A and R are true but R is not a correct explanation of A.
(c) A is true but R is false
(d) A is false but R is true

135. Consider the following diagram showing OH and OF as the offer curves of two countries, H and F:

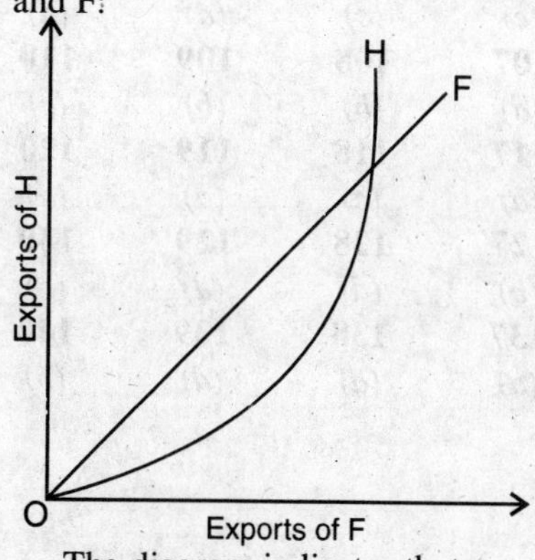

The diagram indicates that
(a) H is a large country.
(b) F is a large country.
(c) Both H and F are large countries.
(d) Both H and F are small countries.

136. Match list-I with list-II and select the correct answer using the codes given below the lists:

List-I	List-II
A. W.T.O.	1. Provides loans to address short term balance of payments problems
B. I.D.A.	2. Multi-lateral trade negotiation body
C. I.M.F.	3. Sanction of soft loans
D. I.B.R.D.	4. Facilitating lending and borrowing for reconstruction and development

Codes:

	(A)	(B)	(C)	(D)
(a)	2	3	4	1
(b)	2	3	1	4
(c)	3	2	4	1
(d)	3	2	1	4

137. Consider the following assumptions:
1. Perfect competition
2. Perfect mobility of factors between countries
3. Constant returns to scale
Which of the above assumptions are associated with Ricardo's Theory of Comparative Costs?
(a) 1, 2 and 3 (b) 1 and 2
(c) 1 and 3 (d) 2 and 3

138. Which one of the following pairs is **NOT** correctly matched?
(a) WTO — Generally forbids the use of quantitative restrictions in trade.
(b) IMF — Provides finance to correct disequilibrium in balance of payments.
(c) SAARC — Promotes trade among South Asian countries.
(d) ASEAN — Economic organisation of all Asian countries.

139. Consider the following statements:
Foreign Portfolio Investment in India means—
1. investment by a foreign firm to start a subsidiary.
2. investment by a foreign firm to take over an

existing firm.

3. foreign investment in shares.
4. foreign investment in bonds.

Which of the above statements are correct?

(a) 1, 2 and 3 (b) 2, 3 and 4
(c) 2 and 3 (d) 3 and 4

140. Consider the following statements:

As per the Trade Related Investment Measures (TRIMs)

1. all restrictions on foreign capital companies are to be scrapped.
2. no restrictions will be imposed on any area of investment.
3. imports of raw materials are to be allowed freely.
4. export of part of the output will be mandatory.

Which of the above statements are correct?

(a) 1, 3 and 4 (b) 1, 2 and 3
(c) 1, 2 and 4 (d) 2, 3 and 4

ANSWERS

1	2	3	4	5	6	7	8	9	10
(a)	(a)	(c)	(d)	(a)	(c)	(d)	(b)	(c)	(c)
11	12	13	14	15	16	17	18	19	20
(a)	(a)	(a)	(c)	(a)	(d)	(a)	(d)	(d)	(b)
21	22	23	24	25	26	27	28	29	30
(c)	(d)	(b)	(b)	(d)	(c)	(c)	(b)	(b)	(a)
31	32	33	34	35	36	37	38	39	40
(a)	(c)	(d)	(d)	(d)	(a)	(a)	(b)	(d)	(c)
41	42	43	44	45	46	47	48	49	50
(a)	(b)	(d)	(c)	(d)	(d)	(b)	(b)	(a)	(a)
51	52	53	54	55	56	57	58	59	60
(c)	(c)	(a)	(c)	(c)	(b)	(a)	(a)	(a)	(a)
61	62	63	64	65	66	67	68	69	70
(b)	(d)	(a)	(a)	(d)	(c)	(b)	(c)	(d)	(c)
71	72	73	74	75	76	77	78	79	80
(d)	(a)	(d)	(b)	(a)	(a)	(a)	(a)	(b)	(a)
81	82	83	84	85	86	87	88	89	90
(a)	(d)	(a)	(a)	(c)	(a)	(b)	(a)	(b)	(d)
91	92	93	94	95	96	97	98	99	100
(d)	(b)	(c)	(b)	(c)	(b)	(c)	(c)	(a)	(a)
101	102	103	104	105	106	107	108	109	110
(b)	(b)	(a)	(a)	(b)	(d)	(d)	(b)	(b)	(c)
111	112	113	114	115	116	117	118	119	120
(a)	(a)	(b)	(c)	(a)	(a)	(a)	(c)	(a)	(d)
121	122	123	124	125	126	127	128	129	130
(a)	(b)	(a)	(d)	(c)	(a)	(b)	(d)	(d)	(a)
131	132	133	134	135	136	137	138	139	140
(b)	(a)	(a)	(a)	(b)	(b)	(a)	(d)	(d)	(b)

UNIT-IX : INDIAN ECONOMY

1. NATIONAL INCOME

- According to the National Income Committee (1949), "A national income estimate measures the volume of commodities and service turned out during a given period counted without duplication". Thus, national income measures the net value of goods and services produced in a country during a year and it also includes net earned foreign income. In other words, a total of national income measures the flow of goods and services in an economy.
- National income is a flow concept not a stock concept.
- In India, National income estimates are related with the financial year (April 1 to 31st March).
- The various concepts of national income are as follows:
  - *(i)* **GNP (Gross National Product):** GNP refers to the money value of total output or production of final goods and services produced by the nationals of a country during a given period of time, generally a year.
  - *(ii)* **NNP (Net National Product):** NNP is obtained by subtracting depreciation value from GNP. NNP can be calculated in two ways: (*a*) at market prices of goods and services and (*b*) at factor cost.
  - *(iii)* **National Income:** When NNP is obtained at factor cost, it is known as National Income. National Income is calculated by subtracting net indirect taxes from NNP at market prices. The obtained value is known as NNP at factor cost or National income.
  - *(iv)* **Personal Income:** Personal income is that income which is actually obtained by nationals. Personal income is obtained by subtracting corporate taxes and payments made for social securities provisions from national income and adding to it government transfer payments, business transfer payments and net interest paid by the government.

Methods of Measuring National Income

- According to Simon Kuznets, national income of a country is calculated by following mentioned three methods:
  - *(i)* **Product Method:** S. Kuznets gave a new name to this method, *i.e.*, product service method. In this method, net value of final goods and services produced in a country during a year is obtained and the total obtained value is called total final product.
  - *(ii)* **Income Method:** In this method, a total of net incomes earned by working people in different sectors and commercial enterprises is obtained.
  - *(iii)* **Consumption Method:** It is also called expenditure method. Income is either spent on consumption or saved. Hence, national income is the addition of total consumption and total savings.
- In India, a combination of production method and income method is used for measuring estimating national income.
- For measuring national income in India, in 1868, the first attempt was made by *Dada Bhai Nauroji.* He, in his book, *"Poverty and Un-British Rule in*

India", estimated Indian per capita annual income at a level of ₹ 20.

- After independence, the Government of India appointed the National Income Committee in August, 1949, under the Chairmanship of Prof. P.C. Mahalanobies, to compile authoritative estimates of national income.
- Estimation and publishing of National Income data by CSO (Central Statistical Organization) is done every year.
- National income includes the contribution of three sectors—primary sector, secondary sector, Tertiary sector.
- Under Primary Sector—Agriculture, Forest, Fisheries and allied sector are included.
- Under Secondary Sector—Manufacturing, Construction, Electricity, Gas and Water Supply are included.
- Under Teritiary Sector—Trade, Transport, Communication, Banking, Insurance, Real Estate, Community and Personal Services are included.
- The contribution of primary sector in GDP was 55.4% in 1950-1951. But now the share of primary sector in national income has come down. In 2017-2018, the contribution of primary sector in GDP was 16.4%.
- The contribution of secondary sector has shown a steady increase from 13.34% in 1950-51 to 31.2% in 2017-18.
- The contribution of tertiary sector indicated a sharp improvement from 29.6% in 1950-51 to about 55.2% in 2017-18.
- At present estimation of national income is based on the base year of 2011-2012.
- The structural change in the composition of national income by industrial origin is the consequence of the process of economic growth initiated during the plans. Since the growth process involved a rapid expansion of manufacturing in the organised sector, the share of manufacturing was bound to indicate a relatively sharp increase. However, agriculture did not indicate a fast rate of growth.

Annual Average of Growth Rate in Various Plans

Five Year Plan	NNI at Constant Price	Per Capita NNI
First Plan (1951-56)	4.6	2.7
Second Plan (1956-61)	4.1	2.1
Third Plan (1961-66)	3.3	1.0
Three Annual Plans (1966-69)	3.5	1.3
Fourth Plan (1969-74)	3.0	0.7
Fifth Plan (1974-79)	5.0	2.7
Annual Plan (1979-80)	–5.9	–8.2
Sixth Plan (1980-85)	5.3	3.1
Seventh Plan (1985-90)	5.8	3.6
Two Annual Plan (1990-92)	2.8	0.8
Eighth Plan (1992-97)	6.5	4.4
Ninth Plan (1997-2002)	5.4	3.4
Tenth Plan (2002-07)	7.6	5.9
Eleventh Plan (2007-12)	7.5	6.0
Twelfth Plan (2012-17)	9.0	—

Source: CSO

2. POPULATION

- Every year 11th July is celebrated as the World Population Day.
- The first census of India was done in 1872 during the reign of Viceroy Lord Mayo. But a series of census (After every ten years) was adopted in 1881 during the reign of Viceroy Lord Ripon.
- 2011 census is the 15th census of India, and the 7th census of free India.
- The entire census of 2011 exercise has been completed by March 15, 2011.
- The term density of population implies the average number of persons living per sq. km. It is denoted in the following way:

  The density of population

$$= \frac{\text{Total population of a certain place}}{\text{Total area of the certain place}}$$

- No. of females in comparison to per 1000 males is known as sex ratio. It is denoted in the following way:

$$\text{Sex Ratio} = \frac{\text{No. of Females}}{\text{No. of Males}} \times 1000$$

- No. of females in age group between 0-6 year, in comparison of per 1000 males of same age group is known as child sex ratio. It is denoted in the following way:

  Child Sex Ratio (0-6 year)

$$= \frac{\text{No. of Females Children (0-6)}}{\text{No. of Males Children (0-6)}} \times 1000$$

- Birth Rate (or crude Birth Rate) is number of the birth per thousand of the population during a period, usually a year. Only live births are included in the calculation of birth rate.
- Death rate signifies the number of deaths in a year per thousand of the population. It is mostly known as crude death rate. Life expectancy is important determinant of death rate. A country having high life expectancy will have a high crude death rate.
- The term fertility refers to the actual bearing of children or 'occurrence of births'. Fertility rate measures the average number of the live births per 1000 women. This rate is one of the most important and useful aids to population projection. It helps in assessing population trends in the economy.
- Percentage of literates between the age of 7 and above of total population is called 'Literacy Rate'.
- The people between the age of 7 and above, who can understand, write and read any language are known as 'literate'.
- An urban area having population of 1,00,000 or above persons is known as a city.
- In the 2011 census, an urban area was defined as follows:
  - (*a*) All places with a municipal corporation, cantonment board or notified towns area committee, etc.
  - (*b*) All other places which satisfy the following criteria:
    - (*i*) Minimum population of 5,000 persons;
    - (*ii*) At least 75 per cent of male working population engaged in non-agricultural pursuits; and
    - (*iii*) A density of population of at least 400 persons per sq. km (1,000 persons per sq. mile).
- From the 1920s onwards, the rate of growth of population picked up. The year 1921 is termed as year of 'great divide'.
- High birth rate supplemented with improved health and medical facilities (which makes death rate fall) pushes the economy towards the state of "population explosion". India faces the same situation at present.
- An increasing difference between birth rate and death rate has created a scene of population explosion in India. This problem in India is not the result of declining death rate alone, which is actually an indicator of social development. But a simultaneous effort for reducing birth rate should have been made, where we have totally failed.
- The framework of the new population policy, 2000 was derived from recommendations of M.S. Swaminathan Committee. Three main objectives of this policy are:
  - (*i*) The immediate objective of this policy is to address the unmet needs of contraception, health infrastructure, health personnel and to provide integrated service delivery for basic reproductive and child healthcare.
  - (*ii*) The medium term objective is to bring the total fertility rates to replacement level by 2010.
  - (*iii*) The long-term objective is to achieve a stable population by 2045.
- The National Commission on Population (NCP) was constituted in May 2000 to review, monitor and give direction for the implementation of the National Population Policy (NPP), 2000.
- The National Commission of Population was reconstituted on 11th April, 2005 with 40 members under the chairmanship of the Prime Minister. Minister of Health and Family Welfare and the Deputy Chairman of the Planning Commission are Vice Chairmen of the Commission. The present membership also includes the Chief Ministers of the states of Uttar Pradesh, Madhya Pradesh, Rajasthan, Bihar, Jharkhand, Kerala and Tamil Nadu.

- According to the census 2011, total population of India is 1,21,08,54,977. Census 2011 makes India the second most populated country in the world.
- The growth rate of the population between 2001 and 2011 is 17.7 per cent. Meghalaya recorded the highest growth rate of 27.9 per cent while Nagaland the lowest –0.6 per cent.
- There were 623.27 million males and 587.58 million females according to Census 2011, making a ratio of 943 males per 1000 females. Kerala is the only state where females outnumber males. The sex-ratio these was 1084 females per 1000 males.
- According to census 2011, five most populous states (in descending order) are: Uttar Pradesh (19.9 crore), Maharashtra (11.2 crore), Bihar (10.4 crore), W. Bengal (9.12 crore) and Andhra Pradesh (8.4 crore).
- According to census 2011, three least populous states (in ascending order) are: Sikkim (6.10 lakh), Mizoram (10.9 lakh) and Arunachal Pradesh (13.8 lakh).
- According to census 2011, three most populous Union Territories (in descending order) are: Delhi, Puducherry and Chandigarh.
- According to census 2011, three least populous Union Territories (in ascending order) are: Lakshadweep, Daman and Diu, Dadra and Nagar Haveli.
- **Population Density:** In 2011, 382 persons were living in per square km area. Bihar was most densely populated state with a population density of 1,106 followed by West Bengal (1,028). Among the Union Territories, Delhi had the density of 11,320 and Chandigarh of 9,258. In Arunachal Pradesh, only 17 people were living in per sq. km area while in Mizoram 52.
- According to census-2011, 73.0 per cent of the country's population are literate. The male literacy rate (80.9%) is far more than the female literacy rate (64.6%). Kerala retains the top spot with 94.0 per cent literacy rate. Bihar is at the bottom with a literacy rate of 61.8 per cent.
- According to census 2011, five states with least sex ratio (in ascending order) are: Haryana (879), Jammu & Kashmir (889), Sikkim (890), Punjab (895), and Uttar Pradesh (912).
- According to census 2011, five states with most decadal growth rate (in descending order) are: Meghalaya (27.9%), Arunachal Pradesh (26%), Bihar (25.4), Jammu & Kashmir (23.6%), and Mizoram (23.5%).

Occupational Pattern 2011 (per cent)

Category	Total Population	Rural Population	Urban Population
Main Worker			
Cultivators	26.44	37.74	2.66
Agricultural Labourers	23.77	32.94	4.46
Household Industry Workers	3.4	2.95	4.36
Other Workers	46.38	26.37	88.52
Marginal Workers			
Cultivators	19.15	21.62	3.77
Agricultural Labourers	48.75	54.48	12.93
Household Industry Workers	5.03	4.58	7.91
Other Work	27.06	19.33	75.38

Census-2011: Area, Population, Density, Decadal Growth Rate

S.N.	State/UTs	Area (sq. km.)	Population 2001	Population 2011	Density 2001	Density 2011	Decadal G. (%) 2001–2011
1.	J&K	222,236.00	10,143,700	1,25,41,302	100	124	23.6
2.	Himachal Pradesh	55,673.00	6,077,900	68,64,602	109	123	12.9
3.	Punjab	50,362.00	24,358,999	2,77,43,338	484	551	13.9
4.	Chandigarh	114.00	900,635	10,55,450	7,900	9258	17.2
5.	Uttarakhand	53483.00	8,489,349	1,00,86,292	159	189	18.8
6.	Haryana	44212.00	21,144,564	2,53,51,462	478	573	19.9
7.	Delhi	1483.00	13,850,507	1,67,87,941	9,340	11320	21.2
8.	Rajasthan	342,239.00	56,507,188	6,85,48,437	165	200	21.3
9.	Uttar Pradesh	240,928.00	166,197,921	19,98,12,341	690	829	20.2
10.	Bihar	94,163.00	82,998,509	10,40,99,452	881	1106	25.4
11.	Sikkim	7,096.00	540,851	6,10,577	76	86	12.9
12.	Arunachal Pradesh	83,743.00	1,097,968	13,83,727	13	17	26.0
13.	Nagaland	16,579.00	1,990,036	19,78,502	120	119	–0.6
14.	Manipur	22,327.00	2,293,896	28,55,794	103	128	31.79
15.	Mizoram	21,081.00	888,573	10,97,206	42	52	23.5
16.	Tripura	10,486.00	3,199,203	36,73,917	305	350	14.8
17.	Meghalaya	22,429.00	2,318,822	29,66,889	103	132	27.9
18.	Assam	78,438.00	26,655,528	3,12,05,576	340	398	17.1
19.	West Bengal	88752.00	80,176,197	9,12,76,115	903	1028	13.8
20.	Jharkhand	79714.00	26,945,829	3,29,88,134	338	414	22.4
21.	Odisha	155,707.00	36,804,660	4,19,74,218	236	270	14.0
22.	Chhattisgarh	135,191.00	20,833,803	2,55,45,198	154	189	22.6
23.	Madhya Pradesh	308,245.00	60,348,023	7,26,26,809	196	236	20.3
24.	Gujarat	196,024.00	50,671,017	6,04,39,692	258	308	19.3
25.	Daman & Diu	112.00	158,204	2,43,247	1,413	2191	53.8
26.	Dadra & N. Haveli	491.00	220,490	3,43,709	449	700	55.9
27.	Maharashtra	307,713.00	96,878,627	11,23,74,333	315	365	16.0
28.	Andhra Pradesh	160,205.00	76,210,007	4,93,86,799	277	308	11.0
29.	Karnataka	191,791.00	52,850,562	6,10,95,297	276	319	15.6
30.	Goa	3,702.00	1,347,668	14,58,545	364	394	8.2
31.	Lakshadweep	32.00	60,650	64,473	1,895	2149	6.3
32.	Kerala	38863.00	31,841,374	3,34,06,061	819	860	4.9
33.	Tamil Nadu	130,058.00	62,405,679	7,21,47,030	480	555	15.6
34.	Puducherry	479.00	974,345	12,47,953	2,030	2546	28.1
35.	Andaman & Nicobar Islands	8249.00	356,152	3,80,581	43	46	6.9
36.	Telangana	114,840.00	—	3,51,93,978	—	307	13.58
	India	**3,287,240.00**	**1,028,737,436**	**1,21,08,54,977**	**325**	**382**	**17.7**

Census-2011: Population and Sex-Ratio

S.N.	State/UTs	Census 2011			Sex-Ratio	
		Population	**Male**	**Female**	**2001**	**2011**
1.	J&K	1,25,41,302	66,40,662	59,00,640	892	889
2.	Himachal Pradesh	68,64,602	34,81,873	33,82,729	968	972
3.	Punjab	2,77,43,338	1,46,39,465	1,31,03,873	876	895
4.	Chandigarh	10,55,450	5,80,663	4,74,784	777	818
5.	Uttarakhand	1,00,86,292	51,37,773	49,48,519	962	963
6.	Haryana	2,53,51,462	1,34,94,734	1,18,56,728	861	879
7.	Delhi	1,67,87,941	89,87,326	78,00,615	821	868
8.	Rajasthan	6,85,48,437	3,55,50,997	3,29,97,440	921	928
9.	Uttar Pradesh	19,98,12,341	10,44,80,510	9,53,31,831	898	912
10.	Bihar	10,40,99,452	5,42,78,157	4,98,21,295	919	918
11.	Sikkim	6,10,577	3,23,070	2,87,507	875	890
12.	Arunachal Pradesh	13,83,727	7,13,912	6,69,815	893	938
13.	Nagaland	19,78,502	10,24,649	9,53,853	900	931
14.	Manipur	28,55,794	14,38,586	14,17,208	974	985
15.	Mizoram	10,97,206	5,55,339	5,41,867	935	976
16.	Tripura	36,73,917	18,74,376	17,99,541	948	960
17.	Meghalaya	29,66,889	14,91,832	14,75,057	972	989
18.	Assam	3,12,05,576	1,59,39,443	1,52,66,133	935	958
19.	West Bengal	9,12,76,115	4,68,09,027	4,44,67,088	934	950
20.	Jharkhand	3,29,88,134	1,69,30,315	1,60,57,819	941	949
21.	Odisha	4,19,74,218	2,12,12,136	2,07,62,082	972	979
22.	Chhattisgarh	2,55,45,198	1,28,32,895	1,27,12,303	989	991
23.	Madhya Pradesh	7,26,26,809	3,76,12,306	3,50,14,503	919	931
24.	Gujarat	6,04,39,692	3,14,91,260	2,89,48,432	920	919
25.	Daman & Diu	2,43,247	1,50,301	92,946	710	618
26.	Dadra & N. Haveli	3,43,709	1,93,760	1,49,949	812	774
27.	Maharashtra	11,23,74,333	5,82,43,056	5,41,31,277	922	929
28.	Andhra Pradesh	4,93,86,799	2,47,38,068	2,46,48,731	978	993
29.	Karnataka	6,10,95,297	3,09,66,657	3,01,28,640	965	973
30.	Goa	14,58,545	7,39,140	7,19,405	961	973
31.	Lakshadweep	64,473	33,123	31,350	948	947
32.	Kerala	3,34,06,061	1,60,27,412	1,73,78,649	1,058	1084
33.	Tamil Nadu	7,21,47,030	3,61,37,975	3,60,09,055	987	996
34.	Puducherry	12,47,953	6,12,511	6,35,442	1,001	1037
35.	Andman & Nicobar Islands	3,80,581	2,02,871	1,77,710	846	876
36.	Telangana	3,51,93,978	1,77,04,078	1,74,89,900	—	988
	India	**1,21,08,54,977**	**62,32,70,258**	**58,75,84,719**	**933**	**943**

Census 2011: Literacy

S. No.	State/Union Territories	Total Population	Total Literacy	Male Literacy	Female Literacy	Literacy (%)		
						Total	Male	Female
1.	J&K	1,25,41,302	70,67,233	42,64,671	28,02,562	67.2	76.8	56.4
2.	Himachal Pradesh	68,64,602	50,39,736	27,52,590	22,87,146	82.8	89.5	75.9
3.	Punjab	2,77,43,338	1,87,07,137	1,04,36,056	82,71,081	75.8	80.4	70.7
4.	Chandigarh	10,55,450	8,05,438	4,65,346	3,40,092	86.0	90.0	81.2
5.	Uttarakhand	1,00,86,292	68,80,953	38,63,708	30,17,245	78.8	87.4	70.0
6.	Haryana	2,53,51,462	1,65,98,988	97,94,067	68,04,921	75.6	84.1	65.9
7.	Delhi	1,67,87,941	1,27,37,767	71,94,856	55,42,911	86.2	90.9	80.8
8.	Rajasthan	6,85,48,437	3,82,75,282	2,36,88,412	1,45,86,870	66.1	79.2	52.1
9.	Uttar Pradesh	19,98,12,341	1,43,97,555	6,82,34,964	4,61,62,591	67.7	77.3	57.2
10.	Bihar	10,40,99,452	5,25,04,553	3,16,08,023	2,08,96,530	61.8	71.2	51.5
11.	Sikkim	6,10,577	4,44,952	2,51,269	1,93,683	81.4	86.6	75.6
12.	Arunachal Pradesh	13,83,727	7,66,005	4,39,868	3,26,137	65.4	72.6	57.7
13.	Nagaland	19,78,502	13,42,434	7,23,957	6,18,477	79.6	82.8	76.1
14.	Manipur	28,55,794	17,68,181	9,60,015	8,08,166	79.2	86.1	72.4
15.	Mizoram	10,97,206	8,48,175	4,38,529	4,09,646	91.3	93.3	89.3
16.	Tripura	36,73,917	28,04,783	15,01,369	13,03,414	87.2	91.5	82.7
17.	Meghalaya	29,66,889	17,85,005	9,13,879	8,71,126	74.4	76.0	72.9
18.	Assam	3,12,05,576	1,91,77,977	1,05,68,639	86,09,338	72.2	77.8	66.3
19.	West Bengal	9,12,76,115	6,15,38,281	3,38,18,810	2,77,19,471	76.3	81.7	70.5
20.	Jharkhand	3,29,88,134	1,83,28,069	1,08,82,519	74,45,550	66.4	76.8	55.4
21.	Odisha	4,19,74,218	2,67,42,595	1,50,89,681	1,16,52,914	72.9	81.6	64.0
22.	Chhattisgarh	2,55,45,198	1,53,79,922	88,07,893	65,72,029	70.3	80.3	60.2
23.	Madhya Pradesh	7,26,26,809	4,28,51,169	2,51,74,328	1,76,76,841	69.3	78.7	59.2
24.	Gujarat	6,04,39,692	4,10,93,358	2,34,74,873	1,76,18,485	78.0	85.8	69.7
25.	Daman & Diu	2,43,247	1,88,406	1,24,643	63,763	87.1	91.5	79.5
26.	Dadra & N. Haveli	3,43,709	2,23,230	1,42,521	80,709	76.2	85.2	64.3
27.	Maharashtra	11,23,74,333	8,15,54,290	4,52,57,584	3,62,96,706	82.3	88.4	75.9
28.	Andhra Pradesh	4,93,86,799	2,97,72,532	1,65,01,990	1,32,70,542	67.0	74.9	59.1
29.	Karnataka	6,10,95,297	4,06,47,322	2,25,08,471	1,81,38,851	75.4	82.5	68.1
30.	Goa	14,58,545	11,65,487	6,15,823	5,49,664	88.7	92.6	84.7
31.	Lakshadweep	64,473	52,553	28,023	24,530	91.8	95.6	87.9
32.	Kerala	3,34,06,061	2,81,35,824	1,37,04,903	1,44,30,921	94.0	96.1	92.1
33.	Tamil Nadu	7,21,47,030	5,18,37,507	2,80,40,491	2,37,97,016	80.1	86.8	73.4
34.	Puducherry	12,47,953	9,57,309	4,97,378	4,59,931	85.8	91.3	80.7
35.	Andaman & Nicboar Islands	3,80,581	2,94,281	1,64,377	1,29,904	86.6	90.3	82.4
36.	Telangana	3,51,93,978	2,07,84,228	1,17,49,253	90,34,975	66.4	74.9	57.9
	India	**1,21,08,54,977**	**76,34,98,517**	**43,46,83,779**	**32,88,14,738**	**73.0**	**80.9**	**64.6**

States & UTs Rankings (in descending order) based on Census 2011

Rank in 2011	State/Union Territories	Census 2011	Total Population of India (%) 2011	2001
1.	Uttar Pradesh	19,98,12,341	16.51	16.16
2.	Maharashtra	11,23,74,333	9.28	9.42
3.	Bihar	10,40,99,452	8.60	8.07
4.	West Bengal	9,12,76,115	7.54	7.79
5.	Madhya Padesh	7,26,26,809	6.00	5.87
6.	Tamil Nadu	7,21,47,030	5.96	6.07
7.	Rajasthan	6,85,48,437	5.66	5.49
8.	Karnataka	6,10,95,297	5.05	5.14
9.	Gujarat	6,04,39,692	4.99	4.93
10.	Andhra Pradesh	4,93,86,799	4.08	7.41
11.	Odisha	4,19,74,218	3.47	3.58
12.	Telangana	3,51,93,978	2.91	—
13.	Kerala	3,34,06,061	2.76	3.10
14.	Jharkhand	3,29,88,134	2.73	2.62
15.	Assam	3,12,05,576	2.58	2.59
16.	Punjab	2,77,43,338	2.29	2.37
17.	Chhattisgarh	2,55,45,198	2.11	2.03
18.	Haryana	2,53,51,462	2.09	2.06
19.	Delhi	1,67,87,941	1.39	1.35
20.	Jammu & Kashmir	1,25,41,302	1.04	0.99
21.	Uttarakhand	1,00,86,292	0.83	0.83
22.	Himachal Pradesh	68,64,602	0.57	0.59
23.	Tripura	36,73,917	0.30	0.31
24.	Meghalaya	29,66,889	0.25	0.23
25.	Manipur	28,55,794	0.23	0.22
26.	Nagaland	19,78,502	0.16	0.19
27.	Goa	14,58,545	0.12	0.13
28.	Arunachal Pradesh	13,83,727	0.11	0.11
29.	Puducherry	12,47,953	0.10	0.09
30.	Mizoram	10,97,206	0.09	0.09
31.	Chandigarh	10,55,450	0.09	0.09
32.	Sikkim	6,10,577	0.05	0.05
33.	A & N Islands	3,80,581	0.03	0.03
34.	Dadra & N. Haveli	3,43,709	0.03	0.02
35.	Daman and Diu	2,43,247	0.02	0.02
36.	Laskhadweep	64,473	0.01	0.01
	India	**1,21,08,54,977**	**100.0**	**100.00**

Population of Age Group (0-6) Rankings (in descending order) based on Census-2011

Rank	State/UTs	Population	Male	Female
1.	Uttar Pradesh	3,07,91,331	1,61,85,581	1,46,05,750
2.	Bihar	1,91,33,964	98,87,239	92,46,725
3.	Maharashtra	1,33,26,517	70,35,391	62,91,126
4.	Madhya Pradesh	1,08,09,395	56,36,172	51,73,223
5.	Rajasthan	1,06,49,504	56,39,176	50,10,328
6.	West Bengal	1,05,81,466	54,10,396	51,71,070
7.	Gujarat	77,77,262	41,15,384	36,61,878
8.	Tamil Nadu	74,23,832	38,20,276	36,03,556
9.	Karnataka	71,61,033	36,75,291	34,85,742
10.	Jharkhand	53,89,495	27,67,147	26,22,348
11.	Odisha	52,73,194	27,16,497	25,56,697
12.	Andhra Pradesh	52,22,384	26,86,453	25,35,931
13.	Assam	46,38,130	23,63,485	22,74,645
14.	Telangana	39,20,418	20,28,497	18,91,921
15.	Chhattisgarh	36,61,689	18,59,935	18,01,754
16.	Kerala	34,72,955	17,68,244	17,04,711
17.	Haryana	33,80,721	18,43,109	15,37,612
18.	Punjab	30,76,219	16,65,994	14,10,225
19.	Jammu & Kashmir	20,18,905	10,84,355	9,34,550
20.	Delhi	20,12,454	10,75,440	9,37,014
21:	Uttarakhand	13,55,814	7,17,199	6,38,615
22.	Himachal Pradesh	7,77,898	4,07,459	3,70,439
23.	Meghalaya	5,68,536	2,88,646	2,79,890
24.	Tripura	4,58,014	2,34,008	2,24,006
25.	Manipur	3,75,357	1,94,484	1,80,873
26.	Nagaland	2,91,071	1,49,785	1,41,286
27.	Arunachal Pradesh	2,12,188	1,07,624	1,04,564
28.	Mizoram	1,68,531	85,561	82,970
29.	Goa	1,44,611	74,460	70,151
30.	Puducherry	1,32,858	67,527	65,331
31.	Chandigarh	1,19,434	63,536	55,898
32.	Sikkim	64,111	32,761	31,350
33.	Dadra and Nagar Haveli	50,895	26,431	24,464
34.	Andman and Nicobar Island	40,878	20,770	20,108
35.	Daman and Diu	26,934	14,144	12,790
36.	Lakshadweep	7,255	3,797	3,458
	India	**16,45,15,253**	**8,57,72,254**	**7,87,62,999**

State & UTs Rankings (in descending order) based on Decadal Growth (2001-2011)

Rank	State/UTs	Decadal Growth
1.	Dadra & Nagar Haveli	55.9
2.	Daman and Diu	53.8
3.	Manipur	31.79
4.	Puducherry	28.1
5.	Meghalaya	27.9
6.	Arunachal Pradesh	26.0
7.	Bihar	25.4
8.	Jammu and Kashmir	23.6
9.	Mizoram	23.5
10.	Chhattisgarh	22.6
11.	Jharkhand	22.4
12.	Rajasthan	21.3
13.	NCR Delhi	21.2
14.	Madhya Pradesh	20.3
15.	Uttar Pradesh	20.2
16.	Haryana	19.9
17.	Gujarat	19.3
18.	Uttarakhand	18.8
19.	Chandigarh	17.2
20.	Assam	17.1
21.	Maharashtra	16.0
22.	Tamil Nadu	15.6
23.	Karnataka	15.6
24.	Tripura	14.8
25.	Odisha	14.0
26.	Punjab	13.9
27.	West Bengal	13.8
28.	Telangana	13.5
29.	Himachal Pradesh	12.9
30.	Sikkim	12.9
31.	Andhra Pradesh	11.0
32.	Goa	8.2
33.	A & N Islands	6.9
34.	Lakshadweep	6.3
35.	Kerala	4.9
36.	Nagaland	–0.6
	India	**17.7**

Child Sex-Ratio in State/UTs based on 2011

Rank	State/UTs	Decadal Growth
1.	Arunachal Pradesh	972
2.	Mizoram	970
3.	Meghalaya	970
4.	Chhattisgarh	969
5.	A & N Islands	968
6.	Puducherry	967
7.	Kerala	964
8.	Assam	962
9.	Tripura	957
10.	Sikkim	957
11.	West Bengal	956
12.	Jharkhand	948
13.	Karnataka	948
14.	Goa	942
15.	Odisha	941
16.	Tamil Nadu	943
17.	Nagaland	943
18.	Andhra Pradesh	939
19.	Bihar	935
20.	Telangana	933
21.	Manipur	930
22.	Dadra & Nagar Haveli	926
23.	Lakshadweep	911
24.	Madhya Pradesh	918
25.	Himachal Pradesh	909
26.	Daman & Diu	904
27.	Uttar Pradesh	902
28.	Maharashtra	894
29.	Uttarakhand	890
30.	Gujarat	890
31.	Rajasthan	888
32.	Chandigarh	880
33.	Delhi	871
34.	Jammu & Kashmir	862
35.	Punjab	846
36.	Haryana	834
	India	**918**

State/UTs Rankings based on Population Density as per Census 2011 & 2001

Rank in 2011	State/UTs	Census-2011	Density (per sq. km) 2011	Density (per sq. km) 2001	Rank in 2001
1.	NCR Delhi	1,67,87,941	11320	9,340	1
2.	Chandigarh	10,55,450	9258	7,900	2
3.	Puducherry	12,47,953	2547	2,034	3
4.	Daman and Diu	2,43,247	2191	1,413	4
5.	Lakshadweep	64,743	2149	1,895	5
6.	Bihar	10,40,99,452	1106	881	6
7.	West Bengal	9,12,76,115	1028	903	7
8.	Kerala	3,34,06,061	860	819	8
9.	Uttar Pradesh	19,98,12,341	829	690	9
10.	Dadra & Nagar Haveli	3,43,709	700	449	10
11.	Haryana	2,53,51,462	573	478	11
12.	Tamil Nadu	7,21,47,030	555	480	12
13.	Punjab	2,77,43,338	551	484	13
14.	Jharkhand	3,29,88,134	414	338	14
15.	Assam	3,12,05,576	398	340	15
16.	Goa	14,58,545	394	364	16
17.	Maharashtra	11,23,74,333	365	315	17
18.	Tripura	36,73,917	350	305	18
19.	Karnataka	6,10,95,297	319	276	19
20.	Gujarat	6,04,39,692	308	258	21
21.	Andhra Pradesh	4,93,86,799	308	277	20
22.	Telangana	3,51,93,978	307	—	—
23.	Odisha	4,19,74,218	270	236	22
24.	Madhya Pradesh	7,26,26,809	236	196	23
25.	Rajasthan	6,85,48,437	200	165	24
26.	Uttarakhand	1,00,86,292	189	159	25
27.	Chhattisgarh	2,55,45,198	189	154	26
28.	Meghalaya	29,66,889	132	103	27
29.	Manipur	28,55,794	128	103	28
30.	Jammu & Kashmir	1,25,41,302	124	100	29
31.	Himachal Pradesh	68,64,602	123	109	30
32.	Nagaland	19,78,502	119	120	31
33.	Sikkim	6,10,577	86	76	32
34.	Mizoram	10,97,206	52	42	33
35.	A & N Islands	3,80,581	46	43	34
36.	Arunachal Pradesh	13,83,727	17	13	35
	India	**1,21,08,54,977**	**382**	**325**	

State/UTs Rankings based on Sex-ratio (in descending order) as per Census-2011

Rank	State/UTs	Sex Ratio
1.	Kerala	1,084
2.	Puducherry	1,037
3.	Tamil Nadu	996
4.	Andhra Pradesh	993
5.	Chhattisgarh	991
6.	Meghalaya	989
7.	Telangana	988
8.	Manipur	985
9.	Odisha	979
10.	Mizoram	976
11.	Karnataka	973
12.	Goa	973
13.	Himachal Pradesh	972
14.	Uttarakhand	963
15.	Tripura	960
16.	Assam	958
17.	West Bengal	950
18.	Jharkhand	948
19.	Lakshadweep	946
20.	Arunachal Pradesh	938
21.	Nagaland	931
22.	Madhya Pradesh	931
23.	Maharashtra	929
24.	Rajasthan	928
25.	Gujarat	919
26.	Bihar	918
27.	Uttar Pradesh	912
28.	Punjab	895
29.	Sikkim	890
30.	Jammu and Kashmir	889
31.	Haryana	879
32.	A & N Islands	876
33.	Delhi	868
34.	Chandigarh	818
35.	Dadra & Nagar Haveli	774
36.	Daman and Diu	618
	India	**943**

State/UTs Rankings based on Literacy as per Census 2011

Rank	State/UTs	Literacy Rate
1.	Kerala	94.0
2.	Lakshadweep	91.8
3.	Mizoram	91.3
4.	Goa	88.7
5.	Tripura	87.2
6.	Daman and Diu	87.1
7.	A & N Islands	86.6
8.	NCR Delhi	86.2
9.	Chandigarh	86.0
10.	Puducherry	85.8
11.	Himachal Pradesh	82.8
12.	Maharashtra	82.3
13.	Sikkim	81.4
14.	Tamil Nadu	80.1
15.	Nagaland	79.6
16.	Manipur	79.2
17.	Uttarakhand	78.8
18.	Gujarat	78.0
19.	West Bengal	76.3
20.	Dadra & Nagar Haveli	76.2
21.	Punjab	75.8
22.	Haryana	75.6
23.	Karnataka	75.4
24.	Meghalaya	74.4
25.	Odisha	72.9
26.	Assam	72.2
27.	Chhattisgarh	70.3
28.	Madhya Pradesh	69.3
29.	Uttar Pradesh	67.7
30.	Jammu & Kashmir	67.2
31.	Andhra Pradesh	67.0
32.	Jharkhand	66.4
33.	Telangana	66.4
34.	Rajasthan	66.1
35.	Arunachal Pradesh	65.4
36.	Bihar	61.8
	India	**73.0**

State/UTs Rankings based on Male Literacy as per Census 2011

Rank	State/UTs	Literacy Rate
1.	Kerala	96.1
2.	Lakshadweep	95.6
3.	Mizoram	93.3
4.	Goa	92.6
5.	Tripura	91.5
6.	Daman and Diu	91.5
7.	Puducherry	91.3
8.	NCR Delhi	90.9
9.	A & N Islands	90.3
10.	Chandigarh	90.0
11.	Himachal Pradesh	89.5
12.	Maharashtra	88.4
13.	Uttarakhand	87.4
14.	Tamil Nadu	86.8
15.	Sikkim	86.6
16.	Manipur	86.1
17.	Gujarat	85.8
18.	Dadra & Nagar Haveli	85.2
19.	Haryana	84.1
20.	Nagaland	82.8
21.	Karnataka	82.5
22.	West Bengal	81.7
23.	Odisha	81.6
24.	Punjab	80.4
25.	Chhattisgarh	80.3
26.	Rajasthan	79.2
27.	Madhya Pradesh	78.7
28.	Assam	77.8
29.	Uttar Pradesh	77.3
30.	Jharkhand	76.8
31.	Jammu and Kashmir	76.8
32.	Meghalaya	76.0
33.	Andhra Pradesh	74.9
34.	Telangana	74.9
35.	Arunachal Pradesh	72.6
36.	Bihar	71.2
	India	**80.9**

State/UTs Rankings based on Female Literacy as per Census 2011

Rank	State/UTs	Literacy Rate
1.	Kerala	92.1
2.	Lakshadweep	89.3
3.	Mizoram	89.3
4.	Goa	84.7
5.	Tripura	82.7
6.	A & N Islands	82.4
7.	Chandigarh	81.2
8.	NCR Delhi	80.8
9.	Puducherry	80.7
10.	Daman and Diu	79.5
11.	Nagaland	76.1
12.	Himachal Pradesh	75.9
13.	Maharashtra	75.9
14.	Sikkim	75.6
15.	Tamil Nadu	73.4
16.	Meghalaya	72.9
17.	Manipur	72.4
18.	Punjab	70.7
19.	West Bengal	70.5
20.	Uttarakhand	70.0
21.	Gujarat	69.7
22.	Karnataka	68.1
23.	Assam	66.3
24.	Haryana	65.9
25.	Dadra & Nagar Haveli	64.3
26.	Odisha	64.0
27.	Chhattisgarh	60.2
28.	Madhya Pradesh	59.2
29.	Andhra Pradesh	59.1
30.	Telangana	57.9
31.	Arunachal Pradesh	57.7
32.	Uttar Pradesh	57.2
33.	Jammu & Kashmir	56.4
34.	Jharkhand	55.4
35.	Rajasthan	52.1
36.	Bihar	51.5
	India	**64.6**

Census-2011: Rural and Urban Population

S. No.	State/UTs	Rural Population	Urban Population	Percentage of Rural Population	Percentage of Urban Population
1.	J&K	91,08,060	34,33,242	72.6	27.4
2.	Himachal Pradesh	61,76,050	6,88,552	90.0	10.0
3.	Punjab	1,73,44,192	1,03,99,146	62.5	37.5
4.	Chandigarh	28,991	10,26,459	2.7	97.3
5.	Uttarakhand	70,36,954	30,49,338	69.8	30.2
6.	Haryana	1,65,09,359	88,42,103	65.1	34.9
7.	Delhi	4,19,042	1,63,68,899	2.5	97.5
8.	Rajasthan	5,15,00,352	1,70,48,085	75.1	24.9
9.	Uttar Pradesh	15,53,17,278	4,44,95,063	77.7	22.3
10.	Bihar	9,23,41,436	1,17,58,016	88.7	11.3
11.	Sikkim	4,56,999	1,53,578	74.8	25.2
12.	Arunachal Pradesh	10,66,358	3,17,369	77.1	22.9
13.	Nagaland	14,07,536	5,70,966	71.1	28.9
14.	Manipur	20,21,640	8,34,154	70.8	29.2
15.	Mizoram	5,25,435	5,71,771	47.9	52.1
16.	Tripura	27,12,464	9,61,453	73.8	26.2
17.	Meghalaya	23,71,439	5,95,450	79.9	20.1
18.	Assam	2,68,07,034	43,98,542	85.9	14.1
19.	West Bengal	6,21,83,113	2,90,93,002	68.1	31.9
20.	Jharkhand	2,50,55,073	79,33,061	76.0	24.0
21.	Odisha	3,49,70,562	70,03,656	83.3	16.7
22.	Chhattisgarh	1,96,07,961	59,37,237	76.8	23.2
23.	Madhya Pradesh	5,25,57,404	2,00,69,405	72.4	27.6
24.	Gujarat	3,46,94,609	2,57,45,083	57.4	42.6
25.	Daman & Diu	60,396	1,82,851	24.8	75.2
26.	Dadra & N. Haveli	1,83,114	1,60,595	53.3	46.7
27.	Maharashtra	6,15,56,074	5,08,18,259	54.8	45.2
28.	Andhra Pradesh	3,99,70,761	1,46,10,410	66.6	33.4
29.	Karnataka	3,74,69,335	2,36,25,962	61.3	38.7
30.	Goa	5,51,731	9,06,814	37.8	62.2
31.	Lakshadweep	14,141	50,332	21.9	78.1
32.	Kerala	1,74,71,135	1,59,34,926	52.3	47.7
33,	Tamil Nadu	3,72,29,590	3,49,17,440	51.6	48.4
34.	Puducherry	3,95,200	8,52,753	31.7	68.3
35.	Andman & Nicobar Islands	2,37,093	1,43,488	62.3	37.7
36.	Telangana	2,15,85,313	1,36,08,665	61.33	38.64
	India	**83,37,48,852**	**37,71,06,125**	**68.9**	**31.1**

3. POVERTY

- Poverty can be defined as a social phenomenon in which a section of society is unable to fulfil even the basic necessities of life.
- The term 'poverty' has been defined in different societies in a different ways but all of them are conditioned by the vision of minimum or good life living in society.
- The concept of poverty in the U.S.A. would be significantly different from that in India because the average person is able to afford a much higher level of living in the United States.
- There is an effort in all definitions of poverty to approach the average level of living in a society and as such these definitions reflect the existence of inequalities in a society and the extent to which different societies are prepared to tolerate them.
- In India, the generally accepted definition of poverty emphasises minimum level of living rather than a reasonable level of living.
- Several economists and organisations have given different estimates of poverty. Most of them estimated poverty line on the basis of an average number of persons below the calories intake of 2250 per capita per day, according to the report of 'Task Force on Minimum Needs and Effective Consumption Demand'.
- An expert group of planning commission, defined poverty line on a nutritional norm of per capita daily intake of 2400 calories in rural areas and 2100 calories for urban areas. A person who fails to obtain this minimum level of calories is treated as being below the poverty line.
- There are two types of common standards in economic literature for the measurement of poverty:
  1. **Absolute Poverty:** In the absolute standard, minimum physical quantities of cereals, pulses, milk, butter, etc. are determined for a subsistence level and then the price quotations converted into monetary terms the physical quantities. Aggregating all of the quantities included, a figure expressing per capita consumer expenditure is determined. The population whose level of income or expenditure below the figure, is considered to be below the poverty line.
  2. **Relative Standard:** According to the relative standard, income distribution of the population in different fractile groups is estimated and a comparison of the levels of living of the top 5 to 10 per cent with the bottom 5 to 10 per cent of the population reflects the relative standards of poverty.
- The defect of the relative standard approach is that it indicates the relative position of different segments of the population in the income hierarchy. Even in affluent societies, such pockets of poverty exist. But for underdeveloped countries, it is the existence of mass poverty that is the cause for concern.
- The Planning Commission, the nodal agency for estimating the number and proportion of people living below the poverty line at national and state levels, separately for rural and urban areas, makes poverty estimates based on a large sample survey of household consumption expenditure carried out by the National Sample Survey Office (NSSO) approximately every five years.
- For estimation and review of poverty, the Planning Commission constituted an expert group under the chairmanship of Prof. Suresh D. Tendulkar in December 2005, which submitted its report in December 2009.
- The recomputed poverty estimates for the years 1993-94 and 2004-05 as recommended by the Tendulkar Committee have been accepted by the Planning Commission.
- As per the Tendulkar Committee Report, the national poverty line at 2004-05 prices was a monthly per capita consumption expenditure of ₹ 446.68 in rural and ₹ 578.80 in urban areas in 2004-05.

Poverty Line

Committee	Year	Per capita Expenditure per day (₹)		Per capita Average Montly Expenditure (₹)		All India Poverty Line (Average Monthly Expenditure per Family of 5)	
		Rural	Urban	Rural	Urban	Rural	Urban
Rangarajan	2011-12	32.4	46.9	972	1407	4760	7035
	2009-10	26.7	39.9	801	1198	4005	5990
Tendulkar	2011-12	27.2	33.3	816	1000	4080	5000
	2009-10	22.4	28.7	673	860	3365	4300

Various Employment Generations Programmes

S.N.	*Programme*	*Year of beginning*	*Objective*
1.	Community Development Programme (CDP)	1952	Overall development of rural areas with people's participation.
2.	Green Revolution	1966-67	To increase the foodgrains, specially wheat production.
3.	Drought-Prone Area Programme (DPAP)	1973	To try an expedient for protection from drought by achieving environmental balance and by developing the ground water.
4.	Command Area Development Programme (CADP)	1974-75	To ensure better and rapid utilisation of irrigation capacities of medium and large projects.
5.	Twenty Point Programme (TPP)	1975	Poverty eradication and raising the standard of living.
6.	Antyodaya Yojana	1977-78	To make the poorest families of the village economically independent (only in Rajasthan State).
7.	Training Rural Youth for Self-Employment (TRYSEM)	Aug., 15, 1979	Programme of training rural youth for self-employment.
8.	Integrated Rural Development Programme (IRDP)	Oct., 2, 1980	All-round development of the rural poor through a programme of asset endowment for self-employment.
9.	National Rural Employment Programme (NREP)	1980	To provide profitable employment opportunities to the rural poor.
10.	Development of Women and Children in Rural Areas (DWCRA)	Sept. 1982	To provide suitable opportunities of self-employment to the women belonging to the rural families who are living below the poverty line.
11.	Comprehensive Crop Insurance Scheme	Aprl 1, 1985	For insurance of agricultural crops.
12.	Council for Advancement of People's Action and Rural Technology (CAPART)	Sept. 1, 1986	To provide assistance for rural prosperity.
13.	Jawahar Rozgar Yojana	April 1989	For providing employment to rural unemployed.
14.	Nehru Rozgar Yojana	Oct. 1989	For providing employment to urban unemployed.
15.	Supply of Improved Toolkits to Rural Artisans	July 1992	To supply modern toolkits to the rural craftsmen except the weavers, tailors, embroiders and tobacco labourers who are living below the poverty line.

S.N.	Programme	Year of beginning	Objective
16.	Employment Assurance Scheme (EAS)	Oct., 2, 1993	To provide employment of at least 100 days in a year in villages.
17.	District Rural Development Agency (DRDA)	1993	To provide financial assistance for rural development.
18.	Mahila Samridhi Yojana	2 Oct., 1993	To encourage the rural women to deposit in Post-office Saving Account.
19.	Ganga Kalyan Yojana	1997-98	To provide financial assistance to farmers for exploring and developing ground and surface water resources.
20.	Kasturba Gandhi Education Scheme	Aug., 15, 1997	To establish girls schools in districts having low female literacy rate.
21.	Swarna Jayanti Shahari Rozgar Yojana (SJSRY)	Dec., 1997	To provide gainful employment to urban unemployed and under-employed poor through self-employment or wage-employment.
22.	Bhagya Shree Bal Kalyan Policy	Oct., 19, 1998	To uplift the girls conditions.
23.	Rajrajeshwari Mahila Kalyan Yojana	Oct., 19, 1998	To provide insurance protection to women.
24.	Swarna Jayanti Gram Swarozgar Yojana	April 1999	For eliminating Rural poverty and unemployment and promoting self-employment.
25.	Jan Shree Bima Yojana	Aug., 10, 2000	Providing Insurance Security to people living below poverty line.
26.	Antyodaya Anna Yojana	Dec., 25, 2000	To provide food security to poor.
27.	Ashraya Bima Yojana	June 2001	To provide compensation to labourers who have lost their employment.
28.	Pradhan Mantri Gram Sadak Yojana (PMGSY)	Dec., 25, 2000	To line all villages with Pacca Road.
29.	Mahatma Gandhi National Rural Employment Guarantee Act (MNREGA)	Feb., 2, 2006	To provide at least 100 days wage-employment in rural areas.
30.	Pradhan Mantri Kaushal Vikas Yojana	March 2015	To Provide skill training to youth.
31.	Pradhan Mantri Jeevan Jyoti Bima Yojana	2015-16	Renewable one year life cover of ₹ 2 lakh to all savings bank account holders in the age group of 18-50 years covering death due to any reason for a premium of ₹ 330 per annum per sub-scriber.
32.	Pradhan Mantri Suraksha Bima Yojana	2015-16	Renewable one year accidental death cum disability to all savings bank account holders in the age group of 18-70 years for a premium of ₹ 12 per annum per subscriber.
33.	Atal Pension Yojana	2015-16	Pension to the labourers of unorganized sector
34.	Deen Dayal Upadhyay Grameen Kaushlya Yojana	Sep. 24, 2015	Skill development of rural youth.
35.	Atal Innovation Mission	2015-16	Atal Innovation Mission and Self Employement and Talent Utilisation.

S.N.	*Programme*	*Year of beginning*	*Objective*
36.	Swachh Bharat Mission	Oct. 2, 2014	Providing access to clean toilet to all rural households and initiating solid and liquid waste management activities in all gram panchayats.
37.	Pandit Deen Dayal Upadhyay Shramev Jayate Scheme	Oct. 16, 2014	To improve employability, skill development and other conveniences for labour.
38.	Shyama Prasad Mukherjee Rurban Mission	Sept. 16, 2015	Setting up 300 village clusters by 2019-20 across the country with all possible urban amenities.
39.	HriDay	2015-16	Heritage City Development and Augmentation Yojana to preserve and rejuvenate the rich cultural heritage of the country through the identified 12 cities.
40.	PRASAD	2015-16	National Mission on Pilgrimage Rejuvenation and Spiritual Augmentation Drive (PRASAD).
41.	'Housing for all by 2022'	June 18, 2015	Providing affordable housing in Urban Areas.
42.	Pradhan Mantri Awas Yojana	June 25, 2015	Providing housing facilities in rural areas.
43.	Startup India, Standup India	16 Jan., 2016	To provide Support to all start-up businesses in all aspects of doing business in India.
44.	Pradhan Mantri Ujjwala Yojana	May 1, 2016	Launched to Provide free LPG connection to women from below poverty line families.
45.	Urja Ganga Yojana (UGY)	Oct. 24, 2016	To provide the accessibility of approx, 5 Lakh LPG gas cylinders within next 5 years.
46.	Pradhan Mantri Surakshit Matritva Abhiyan	June 9, 2016	To improve the quality and coverage of Antenatal care with Diagnostics and counselling Services as part of Reproductive Maternal Neonatal Child and Adolescent Health.
47.	Pradhan Mantri Vittiya Saksharta Abhiyan (PMVSA)	Dec. 1, 2016	To go for cashless transaction and payment modes like using credit or debit cards or the payment wallets to reduce the malpractice in the country.
48.	Digi Dhan Vyapar Yojana (DDVY)	Dec. 15, 2016	To increase the "Cashless Transactions".
49.	Pradhan Mantri Garib Kalyan Yojana (PMGKY)	Dec. 2016	To improve the financial position of the poor people.
50.	Atal Amrit Abhiyan (AAA)	Dec. 25, 2016	To provide health insurance against 437 illnesses including 5 critical diseases.

4. AGRICULTURE

- Agriculture is an important sector of the economy. Though the share of agriculture in national income has come down since the inception of planning era in the economy but still it has substantial share in GDP.
- In terms of composition, out of the total share of 16.4 per cent that agriculture and allied sector had in GDP in 2017-18.
- Agriculture in our country provides livelihood to about 49% of the population.
- Gross Capital Formation (GCF) in Agriculture and Allied sector relative to GVA in this sector has been snowing a fluctuating trent from 18.3 per cent in 2011-12 to 16.2 per cent in 2014-15.
- Agriculture provides raw materials to various industries and other agro-based industries. Cotton and Jute textile industries, Sugar, Vanaspati industry etc. are directly dependent on agriculture.
- India's foreign trade is deeply associated with Agriculture Sector. Value of agriculture exports to total exports of the country was 13.8 per cent in 2013. But the share of agriculture has come down in foreign trade at present. Share of agriculture in foreign trade was 10 per cent in 2017-18.

Land Reform Programmes

- Land reform programme in India include:
  - (*i*) Elimination of intermediaries.
  - (*ii*) Tenancy Reform.
  - (*iii*) Determination of ceiling of holding per family and to distribute surplus land among landless people.
  - (*iv*) Consolidation of holdings.
- The legislation for abolition of intermediaries was aimed at providing land to the tiller.
- Measures of tenancy reform pertain to—
  - (*i*) Regulation of rent
  - (*ii*) Security of tenure
  - (*iii*) Confirment of ownership on tenants.
- Land ceiling laws were first enacted in the 50s and 60s. It was further revised in 1972. Family ceiling were lowered to 5 hectares for irrigated land with two crops, 7.5 hectares for irrigated land with one crops and 12 hectares for other lands.

Irrigation

- The planning commission has introduced a new classification of irrigation schemes:
  1. **Major Irrigation Schemes**—Those with culturable command areas (CCA) more than 10,000 hectares.
  2. **Medium Irrigation Schemes**—Those with culturable command areas (CCA) between 2,000 to 10,000 hectares.
  3. **Minor Irrigation Scheme**—Those with culturable command area (CCA) upto 2,000 hectares.
- **Accelerated Irrigation Benefits Programme (AIBP):** The Central Government initiated the Accelerated Irrigation Benefit Programme (AIBP) from 1996-97 for extending assistance for the completion of incomplete irrigation schemes. Under this programme, projects approved by the Planning Commission are eligible for assistance.
- **Micro Irrigation:** A centrally sponsored scheme on Micro Irrigation (MI) was launched in Tenth Plan for promoting water use efficiency by adopting drip and sprinkler irrigation. All states and Union Territories and all horticulture as well as agricultural crops are covered under the scheme. The National Committee on Plasticulture Applications in horticulture (NCPAH) provides the required technical guidance in association with Precision Farming Development Centers (PDFCs) at 22 locations. The PRI's are involved in selecting the beneficiaries. Since its inception, about 10 lakh hactares has been covered under drip and sprinkler irrigation.
- **Sprinkler/Drip Irrigation:** Under Sprinkler/Drip Irrigation System water is sprinkled evenly on total agriculture ground through a pipe network cropped area. Empircal studies show that this system of drip irrigation saves 30% to 40% water as compared to irrigation with traditional method,

i.e., surface irrigation. This new system of irrigation also ensures 20-25% more productivity per hectare.

- **Source of Irrigation:** There are three main sources of irrigation in India:

  Canals: Canals water apporoximately 24% of irrigation in India. This include large areas in Punjab, Haryana, Uttar Pradesh, Bihar and some parts of the Southern States.

  Well & Tubewells: Wells and Tubewell irrigate around 62% of the irrigated land in India. Wells and Tubewells are now spread over large area of Punjab, Uttar Pradesh, Bihar, Rajasthan, Tamil Nadu and Haryana.

  Tanks: Tank irrigation is resorted to mostly in Tamil Nadu, Andhra Pradesh, and some parts of West Bengal and Bihar. Tanks irragate arround 3% of the irrigated land.

- In agriculture, new technology was tried in 1960-61 as a pilot project in seven districts and was called Intensive Agricultural District Programme (IADP). Later, the high-yielding varieties programme (HYVP) was also added and the strategy was extended to cover the entire country. This strategy has been called by various names—modern agricultural technology, seed-fertilizer-water technology or simply Green revolution.

Achievements of the New Agricultural Strategy

(*i*) Increase in the production of cereals.
(*ii*) Increase in the production of commercial crops.
(*iii*) Significant changes in the crop pattern.
(*iv*) Boost to agricultural production and employment.

Agricultural Prices

- **Minimum Support Prices (MSP):** Keeping in view the interests of the farmers as also the need of self reliance, Govt. has been announcing minimum support price. The main objectives of announcing MSP are:
  1. To prevent fall in price in the situation of over production.
  2. To protect the interest of farmers by ensuring them a minimum price for their crops in the situation of a price fall in the market.
- **Procurement Prices:** The price at which government buys surplus from the farming coming in the market. The minimum support price and the procurement price may be the same.
- **Issue Prices:** The prices at which fair price shops sell cereals like wheat rice etc.

National Policy for Farmers 2007

Taking into account the recommendations of the National Commission on Farmers and after consulting the State Governments. Government of India has approved the National Policy for Farmers, 2007. The National policy for farmers, among other things, has provided for a holistic approach to development of the farm sector. The broad areas of its coverage include:

(*i*) Focus will be on the **economic well-being of the farmers** in addition to production and productivity.

(*ii*) **Asset reforms:** To ensure that a farmer household in villages either possesses or has access to a productive asset or marketable skill.

(*iii*) **Water use efficiency:** The concept of maximizing yield and income per unit of irrigation water in all the crop production programmes would be accorded priority with stress on awareness and efficiency of water use.

(*iv*) **New technologies** like bio-technology, information and communication technology (ICT), renewable energy technology, space aplications and nano-technology would be encouraged for improving productivity per unit of land and water on a sustainable basis.

(*v*) **National Agricultural Bio-security System** would be established to organize a coordinated agricultural bio-security programme.

Major Crops and Their Seasons

The Indian crops can be devided into two major groups:

1. **Kharif Crops:** This crop is sown in the month of July and harvested in October every year. Kharif crop includes—Rice (Paddy), Jowar, Bajra, Maize, Cotton, Sugarcane, Seasamum, Soyabean, and Groundnut etc.

2. **Rabi Crop:** This crop is sown in October end and harvested in March/April every year. Rabi crop includes—Wheat, Jowar, Barley, Gram, Tur, Rapseed, and Mustard etc.
3. **Zayad Crop:** In some parts of the country a crop, known as Zayad crop is sown during March to June every year. Zayad crops include—Melon, Watermelon, Vegetables, Cucumber, Moong, and Urad etc.

Commercial Crops

Commercial crops are those crops which are produced for trade purpose and earning money and not for self-consumption by the farmers. These commercial crops include:

(*i*) **Oilseeds crops:** Groundnut, Mustard, Sesamum, Rapeseed, Linseed, Castor, Sunflower, Nigenseed and Soyabean etc.
(*ii*) **Sugar Crops:** Sugarcane and Beat.
(*iii*) **Fibre Crops:** Jute, Mesta, Sunhemp and Cotton.
(*iv*) **Narcotic Crop:** Tobacco.
(*v*) **Beverage Crops:** Tea, Coffee.

National Mission on Oilseeds and Oil Palm: National Mission on Oilseeds and Oil Palm (NMOOP) envisages increase in production of vegetable oils sourced from oilseeds, oil palm and tree borne oilseeds from 7.06 million tonnes to 9.51 million tonnes by the end of 12th Plan (2016-17). The Mission is being implemented through three mini missions with specific target.

The strategy to implement the proposed mission will include increasing seed replacement ratio with focus on varietal replacement; increasing irrigation coverage under oilseeds from 26 per cent to 36 per cent; diversification of area from low yielding cereals crops to oilseeds crops; inter-cropping of oilseeds with cereals/pulses/sugarcane; use of fallow land after paddy potato cultivation; expansion of cultivation of oil palm in watersheds and wastelands; increasing availability of quality planting materials of oil palm.

National Mission for Sustainable Agriculture: (NMSA) as a programmatic intervention made operational from the year 2014-15 aims at making agriculture more productive, sustainable and remunerative and climate resilient by promoting location specific integrated / composite farming systems; soil and moisture conservation measures; comprehensive soil health management; efficient water management practices and mainstreaming rainfed technologies.

Various Crops and their producing states

Crops/Groups of Crops	Producing State (In Descending Order)
I. Foodgrains	
Rice	West Bengal, Uttar Pradesh, Punjab
Wheat	Uttar Pradesh, Madhya Pradesh, Punjab
Maize	Maharashtra, Karnataka, Madhya Pradesh
Total Coarse Cereals	Maharashtra, Rajasthan, Karnataka
Gram	Madhya Pradesh, Maharashtra, Rajasthan
Tur	Maharashtra, Karnataka, Madhya Pradesh
Total Pulses	Madhya Pradesh, Maharashtra, Rajasthan
Total Food-grains	Uttar Pradesh, Madhya Pradesh, Punjab
II. Oilseeds	
Groundnut	Gujarat, Rajasthan, Andhra Pradesh
Rapeseed & Mustard	Rajasthan, Madhya Pradesh, Haryana
Soyabean	Madhya Pradesh, Maharashtra, Rajasthan
Sunflower	Karnataka, Odisha, Andhra Pradesh
Total Oilseeds	Madhya Pradesh, Rajasthan, Maharashtra
III. Other Cash Crops	
Sugarcane	Uttar Pradesh, Maharashtra, Karnataka
Cotton	Maharashtra, Gujarat, Telangana
Jute & Mesta	West Bengal, Bihar, Assam

Source: Economic Survey 2017-18

Paramparagat Krishi Vikas Yojana: Government is implementing a cluster based programme to encourage the farmers for promoting organic farming called Paramparagat Krishi Vikas Yojana (PKVY). Under this programme, group of farmers would be motivated to take up organic farming. Fifty or more farmers will form a cluster having 50 acre land to take up organic farming under the scheme. In this way during three years (2015-16 to 2017-18) 10,000 clusters will be formed covering 5.0 lakh acre area under organic farming. There will be no liability on the farmers for expenditure on certification. Every farmer will be provided ₹ 20,000 per acre over three years to meet end to end expenditure— seed to harvesting of crops to transport of produce to the market. Organic farming will be promoted by using traditional resources and the organic products will be linked with the market. It will increase domestic production and certification of organic produce by involving farmers.

MAJOR SCHEMES/PROGRAMMES IN THE AGRICULTURE SECTOR

1. National Food Security Mission (NFSM)

National Food Security Mission (NFSM) was launched in 2007-08 to increase the production of rice, wheat and pulses by 10, 8 and 2 million tonnes, respectively by the end of 11th Plan through area expansion and productivity enhancement; restoring soil fertility and productivity; creating employment opportunities; and enhancing farm level economy. The Mission was continued during 12th Five Year Plan with new target of additional production of 25 million tonnes of foodgrains comprising 10 million tonnes of rice, 8 million tonnes of wheat, 4 million tonnes of pulses and 3 million tonnes of coarse cereals by the end of the 12th Plan.

The major interventions/activities covered under NFSM include cluster demonstrations of rice, wheat, pulses and coarse cereals, distribution of improved varieties/hybrid seeds, need based plant and soil management, farm mechanization, resource conservation techniques/energy management, efficient water/application tools, cropping system based trainings and local initiatives, etc. NFSM-coarse cereals and NFSM-commercial crops are included under revamped NFSM. From 2016-17, NFSM is being implemented in 638 districts of 29 states. From the year 2015-16, the programme is being implemented on a fund sharing ratio of 50 : 50 between Government of India and states. The budget allocation of NFSM in 2015-16 is ₹ 1,300.00 crore (Central share).

2. Macro Management of Agriculture (MMA)

The Macro Management of Agriculture (MMA) scheme was revised in 2008 to improve its efficacy in supplementing / complementing the efforts of the States towards enhancement of agricultural production and productivity and provide opportunity to draw upon their agricultural development programmes relating to crop production and natural resource management, with the flexibility to use 20 per cent of resources for innovative components. The revised MMA Scheme has formula-based allocation criteria and provides assistance in the form of grants to the states/UTs on 90 : 10 basis except in case of the north-eastern States and Union Territories where the Central share is 100 per cent.

Main features of the revised MMA scheme are as follows:

- The practice of allocating funds to States/UTs on a historical basis has been replaced by a new allocation criteria based on gross cropped area and area under small and marginal holdings. The assistance would be provided to the states/UTs as 100% grant.
- The subsidy structure has been rationalized to make the pattern of subsidy uniform under all the schemes implemented by the Department of Agriculture and permissible limit of assistance.
- Two new components have been added namely, (*a*) Integrated Scheme of Oilseeds, Pulses, (*b*) 'Reclamation of Acidic Soil'.
- The permissible ceiling for new initiatives has been increased from the existing 10% to 20% of the allocation.
- At least 33% of the funds have to be earmarked for small, marginal and women farmers.
- Active participation of the Panchayati Raj Institutions (PRIs) of all tiers would have to be ensured in the implementation of the Revised MMA scheme including review, monitoring and evaluation at district and sub-district level.

3. Rashtriya Krishi Vikas Yojana (RKVY)

The RKVY was launched in 2007-08 with an outlay of of ₹25,000 crore for the 11th five year plan. The RKVY aims at achieving the 4% annual growth in the agriculture sector during the 11th five year plan period by ensuring a holistic development of agriculture and allied sectors. The funds under the RKVY is provided to the states as 100 per cent grant by the Central Government. The main objective of the schemes were:

- To incentivise the states to increase public investment to achieve 4% growth in agriculture and allied sector during 11th plan.
- To provide flexibility and autonomy to the states in planning and exceuting agriculture and allied sector schemes.
- To ensure the preparation of plans for the district and the states based on agro-climatic conditions, availability of technology and natural resources.
- To ensure that the local needs/crops priorities are better reflected.
- To achieve the goal of reducing the yield gaps in important crops, through focused interventions.
- To maximize returns to farmers.

4. Integrated Scheme of Oilseeds, Pulses, Oil palm, and Maize (ISOPOM)

The ministry of agriculture has restructured oilseeds, pulses, oil palm and maize development programmes into one centrally sponsored ISOPOM which is being implemented in 14 major states for oilseeds and pulses, 15 for maize, and 9 for oil palm. The pulses component has been merged with the NFSM with effect from 1 April, 2010.

5. National Mission for Sustainable Agriculture (NMSA)

NMSA as a programmatic intervention made operational from the year 2014-15 aims at making agriculture more productive, sustainable and remunerative and climate resilient by promoting location specific integrated/composite farming systems; soil and moisture conservation measures; comprehensive soil health management; efficient water management practices and mainstreaming rainfed technologies.

6. Pradhan Mantri Krishi Sinchai Yojana

With the aim of improving farm productivity, the government has decided to spend ₹ 50,000 crore over the next five years under the Pradhan Mantri Krishi Sinchai Yojana (PMKSY). The major objective of the PMKSY is to achieve convergence of investments in irrigation at the field level, expand cultivable area under assured irrigation (har khet ko pani), improve on-farm water use efficiency to reduce wastage of water, enhance adoption of precision-irrigation and other water-saving technologies (more crop per drop). The scheme is aimed at enhancing recharge of acquifers and introducing sustainable water conservation practices by exploring feasibility of re-using treated municipal water for peri-urban agriculture and attracting greater private investment in precision irrigation. The scheme also aims at bringing ministries, departments, agencies, research and financial institutions engaged in creation/recycling/potential recycling of water under a common platform so that a comprehensive and holistic view of the entire 'water cycle' is taken into account and proper water budgeting is done for all sectors.

7. Mission for Integrated Development of Horticulture

The Mission for Integrated Development of Horticulture (MIDH), was launched during the Twelfth Plan with effect from 2014-15, for the holistic development of the horticulture sector covering fruits, vegetables, mushrooms, spices, flowers, aromatic plants, coconut, cashew, cocoa and bamboo. The MIDH subsumes the National Horticulture Mission (NHM), the Horticulture Mission for North East & Himalayan States (HMNEH), the National Bamboo Mission (NBM), the National Horticulture Board (NHB), the Coconut Development Board (CDB) and the Central Institute for Horticulture (CIH), Nagaland. The Government of India (GOI) contributes 85 per cent of the total outlay for developmental programmes in all the states. From 2015-16, the pattern of assistance is 60 : 40 between the Government of India and NHM states and 90 : 10 for HMNEH states. All states are covered under the MIDH. During 2014-15, a budget provision of ₹ 2,263.00 crore had been made for the MIDH, out of which, an amount of ₹ 1,584.84

crore was released for the NHM and HMNEH components.

Since the inception of the NHM, an area of 24.63 lakh ha has been covered under various horticulture crops. In addition, an area of 5.25 lakh ha of old orchards, has been rejuvenated. 12.04 lakh farmers have been trained under various horticulture activities. 2,923 nurseries have been established for supply of quality planting material to beneficiaries. Under protected cultivation practices, and area of 1.54 lakh ha has been covered. An area of 11.96 lakh ha has been covered under Integrated Pest Management (IPM)/ Integrated Nutrient Management (INM). 816 IPM infrastructures have been established. A total of 45,858 water harvesting structures have been created. To promote apiculture, 6,10,048 bee colonies, with hives have been distributed. Under Horticulture Mechanization, 82,771 mechanical equipments including Plant Protection equipments have been distributed.

8. Pradhan Mantri Fasal Bima Yojana

The Hon'ble Prime Minister of India, Shree Narendra Modi has launched a brand new crop insurance scheme on 13th January, 2016. This crop insurance scheme is called Pradhan Mantri Fasal Bima Yojana (PMFBY) which will be implemented in every state of India, with association with the respective State Governments. This crop insurance scheme will be administered under the Ministry of Agriculture and Farmers' Welfare, Government of India.

The main motto of this new crop insurance scheme is to provide a more efficient insurance support to the farmers of the country and become a financial support to thousands of farmers. Govt. has decided to provide low premium insurance cover to the farmers so that they can sustain even if the yield is damaged.

A major portion of Indian citizens, mostly in rural areas depends on agriculture and farming. So it is very necessary to strengthen their crop insurance scheme so as to prevent them incur heavy losses even if the crops gets damaged due to natural calamities and other unavoidable circumstances. There are several factors that result in poor production of crops in some regions.

Worst case scenario is that the entire crop gets damaged and the cultivators have to go through heavy losses. Most farmers take loans for buying agricultural seeds, fertilizers, irrigation facilities, pesticides and other agricultural machineries for cultivation of crops. But sometimes unavoidable natural disasters like draught, floods, fire, pest attack, etc. strike and destroy the crop yield.

Then farmers choose the path of suicide as they become unable to cope up with the burden of debt. There is an alarming number of farmer suicides in India, which is a burning issue, not only in India, but also throughout the world. As per reports of Home Ministry, reports of near about 3000 farmers' suicide have been registered in India, in the last three years itself. So the Centre has planned to bring back a new crop insurance scheme called Pradhan Mantri Fasal Bima Yojana in the country and rectify the loopholes, present in the existing one.

In the year of 1999, an insurance scheme was launched which was named National Agriculture Insurance Scheme (NIAS). But it had some drawbacks due to which it never became a success and could not stand efficient for the insurance purposes of the farmers. It was implemented only in 14 states of India, which are most affected by weather calamities. States like Madhya Pradesh, Uttar Pradesh, Rajasthan, etc. were in the list of the affected states. As per NIAS, the insurance premium rates were 1.5% and up to 3.5% of the net sum assured for all food crops. These food crops include pulses, cereals, oilseeds, grains, etc. And actuarial premium rates were charged for commercial crops and horticulture crops.

Cotton was the most popular commercial crop at that time, which got largely affected by pest attacks. Later, the NIAS was restructured and modified as MNIAS which stands for Modified NIAS. But MNIAS was implemented in only 6 states of India and thus could not get success. The other failing factors of these past schemes were caps on the sum assured, slow claim process, fraud in the insurance system, etc. Also a major setback of this insurance plan was that those farmers who have taken loan for purchasing agriculture machineries, crop seeds, insecticides and pesticides, etc. were only given the insurance benefit.

So due to all those disadvantages of the earlier insurance scheme, the Govt. has planned for a new crop insurance scheme that will not provide insurance to all farmers from crop damage, but also become a financial support for them. Under this insurance plan, the premium rate will be 2% of the actual sum assured amount for Kharif crops and for the Rabi crops, it will be 1.5% of the total sum assured. The sum assured amount is likely to be increased so as to provide a better insurance cover to the farmers.

For the commercial and horticulture crops, the premium rate will be 5%. Apart from this, the Prime Minister has mentioned that the use of technology will be implemented into the scheme to make it a fast, user friendly, efficient and fraud free system. Better infrastructure will be built to provide irrigation facilities to every farmland of India and fight the drought conditions. More technologies for weather prediction is to be implemented so as to lower the levels of crop damage due to natural calamities. This new crop insurance plan will be functional from the next Kharif season of crop cultivation.

9. Agricultural Credit

The Government has taken many policy initiatives for strengthening of farm credit delivery system for providing credit at affordable rate of interest to support the resource requirments of the agricultural sector. Some sources of agricultural credit are as follows:

- Agricultural credit is disbursed through a Multi Agency network comprising of Commercial Banks (CBs), Regional Rural Bank (RRBs) and Cooperative with their vast network covering allmost all the villages in the country and outreach extending to the remotest part of the country. In addition, on the lines of the Business Correspondent and Business Facilitator model, Banks are using the services of NGOs, SHGs, Joint Liability Groups (JLGs), Micro Finance Institutions and other civil society organisation as intermediates in providing financial and banking services in the rural areas.
- Kisan Credit Card (KCC) scheme was introduced in August, 1998 with major share of crop loans being routed through it. Banks were advised that the credit card should normally be valid for 3 years subject to an annual review.
- The scheme was revised in October 2004. The revised scheme aims at providing adequate and timely credit for the comprehensive credit requirements of farmers under single window, with flexible and simplified procedure, adopting whole farm approach including the short term credit needs, term loan and a reasonable component for consumption needs, through Kisan Credit Card.
- There is coverage of risk of KCC holder against accidental death or permanent disability upto a maximum of ₹ 50,000 and ₹ 25,000 respectively. It has been decided to convert KCCs into Smart Cards to facilitate its operation through ATMs. There are 12.03 crore active KCCs in the country as on 31.3.2013.

Agricultural Insurance

There are various major crop insurance schemes under implementation in the country. Some Insurance schemes are as follows:

1. **National Agricultural Insurance Scheme (NAIS):** With a view to provide insurance coverage and financial support to the farmers in the event of failure of any of the notified crop in the notified areas as a result of natural calamities, pest and diseases; to encourage the farmers to adopt progressive farming practices, high value inputs and higher technology in agriculture and to stabilise farm incomes, particularly in disaster years, NAIS is being implemented in the country from Rabi 1999-2000 season. At present, the scheme is being implemented by 25 states and 2 UTs.
2. **Modified NAIS (MNAIS):** With the aim of further improving crop insurance scheme, the MNAIS is under implementation on pilot basis in 50 districts in the country from the Rabi 2010-11 season. The Salient features of MNAIS are as under:
   - only upfront premium is shared by the Central and State Governments on 50:50 basis and all chains liability would be on the insurance companies.
   - Actuarial premium with subsidy in premium ranging 40% to 75% to all farmers.
   - Unit area of insurance reduced to village/ village panchayat level for major crops.
   - Indemnity for prevented sowing/planting risk and for post harvest losses due to cyclone.

- One account payment up to 25% advance of likely claims as immediate relief.
- Minimum indemnity level of 70% instead of 60%.
- Scheme is available to all the farmers—loanee and non-loanee—irrespective of their size of holding.
- Loanee farmers are covered on compulsory basis in a notified area for notified crops whereas for non-loanee farmers scheme is voluntary.
- Uniform seasonality disciplines both for loanee and non-loanee farmers.
- Participation of private sector insurers for creation of competitive environment for crop insurance.

3. **Weather Based Crop Insurance Scheme (WBCIS):** The WBCIS is being implemented as a central-sector scheme from Kharif 2007 season. The scheme is intended to provide insurance protection to farmers against adverse weather incidence, such as deficit and excess rainfall, high or low temperature and humidity that are deemed to adversely impact crop production. The WBCIS is based on actuarial rates of premium but to make the scheme attractive, premium actually charged from farmers has been restricted to be on a par with NAIS.
4. **Coconut Palm Insurance Scheme (CPIS):** The Department of Agriculture and Cooperation is implementing CPIs on pilot basis during years 2009-10 and 2010-11 in the selected areas of Andhra Pradesh, Goa, Karnataka, Kerala, Maharashtra, Odisha, Tamilnadu and West Bengal. The scheme is being administered by the Coconut Development Board (CDB) through AIC. The scheme propose to cover entire palms in the region selected for implementation, according to eligibility criteria. The Sum Insured (SI) is based on average input cost of the plantation and the age of the specific plant.

Agricultural Marketing

Organised marketing of agricultural commodities has been promoted of regulated markets. Most of the state governments and Union Territories have enacted legislations (APMC Act) to provide for regulation of agricultural produce market. According to the provision of the APMC Acts of the state every APMC is authorised to collect market fees from the buyers/ traders in the prescribed manner on the sale of notified agricultural produce.

The Government of India has circulated model legislation titled "The State Agricultural Produce Marketing (Development and Regulation) Act 2003 to bring about reform in agricultural marketing. Contract farming, direct marketing and public-private partnership in management and development of agricultural markets are the major instruments of change among others.

Infrastructure Requirement

Investment requirement for the development of marketing, storage and cold storage infrastructure in the country has been estimated to be huge and with a view to induce investment in the development of marketing infrastructure as envisaged above, the Ministry has implemented the following plan schemes:

(*i*) ***Grameen Bhandaran Yojana:*** The Government of India, Ministry of Agriculture has launched 'Grameen Bhandaran Yojana' w.e.f. 1st April, 2011. The main objectives of the scheme include creation of scientific storage capacity with allied facilities in rural areas to meet out various requirements of farmers for storing farm produce, processed farm produce, agricultural inputs, etc, and prevention of distress sale by creating the facility of pledge loan and marketing credit.

(*ii*) ***Marketing Research and Information Network:*** The Ministry of Agriculture has launched an ICT based Central Sector Scheme of Marketing Research and Information Network in March 2000 to provide electronic connectivity to important wholesale agricultural markets in the country for collection and dissemination of wholesale prices and other market related information to the farmers and other users through AGMARKNET portal (www.agmarknet.nic.in). As on date, 3026 markets have been linked with AGMARKNET portal from all over the country. These markets are reporting daily prices and arrival in respect of more than 300 commodities and 2000 varieties from more than 1800 market covering all major agricultural and horticultural produce.

(*iii*) ***Development/Strengthening of Agricultural Marketing Infrastructure, Grading and Standardization:*** The Ministry of Agriculture is implementing another Central Sector Scheme for 'Development Strengthening of Agricultural Marketing Infrastructure, Grading and Standardisation' under which, investment subsidy is provided @ 25 per cent on the capital cost of the marketing infrastructure development subject to a maximum of ₹ 60 lakh for each project in case of North-Eastern States, Jammu and Kashmir, Uttarakhand, Himachal Pradesh, hilly area and to SC/ST and their cooperatives.

(*iv*) ***Terminal Market Complex:*** The Department has taken the initiative to promote modern terminal markets for fruits, vegetables and other perishables in important urban centres of the country. These markets would provide state of art infrastructure facilities for electronic auction, cold chain and logistics and operate through primary collection centres conveniently locate in producing areas to allow easy access to farmers.

Food Management

Food Management in India has three basic objectives:

- Procurement of foodgrains from farmers at remunerative prices.
- Distribution of foodgrains to the consumers particularly, the vulnerable sections of the society at affordable prices.
- Maintenance of food buffers for food security and price stability. The instruments for food management are—the Minimum Support Price (MSP) and Central Issue Price (CIP).
- Food Stock are maintained by the Central Government for three purposes:
  (*i*) Meeting the prescribed minimum buffer stock norms for food security.
  (*ii*) For monthly release of foodgrains for supply through Public Distribution System (PDS).
  (*iii*) For market intervention to augment supply so as to help moderate the open market prices.

Miscellaneous

- ***Krishi Shramik Suraksha Yojana:*** The multi-benefit scheme for the agricultural workers, commenced on 1 July, 2001 provides life insurance protection, perodical lumpsum survival benefit and pension to those who were between the age of 18-50 years.
- ***Farm Income Insurance Scheme (FIIS):*** Prime Minister inaugurated this scheme in January 2002. Main features of this scheme are:
  (*i*) Farmers will be protected by ensuring minimum guarnteed income.
  (*ii*) If the actual income of the farmers falls short of the guaranteed income (product of average yield and MSP) of the farmers they would be eligible for compensation to the extent of indemnity from the Agriculture Insurance company of India Ltd (AICI).
  (*iii*) Area approach as in National Agricultural Insurance scheme (NAIS) would be used for actual yield and price measurement of the insured crop.
  (*iv*) Initially the scheme would cover paddy and wheat only.
  (*v*) The scheme would be available for all the states compulsory for farmers availing crop loans.
  (*vi*) NAIS will be withdrawn for the crops covered under FIIS but would continue to be applicable for other crops.
- ***Command Area Development & Water Management Programme (CADWMP):*** The centrally-sponsored Command Area Development (CAD) programme was launched in 1974-75, with the main objectives of improving the utilisation of created irrigation potential and optimising agriculture production and productivity from irrigated lands on sustainable basis, by integrating all functions related with irrigated agriculture through a multi-disciplinary team under an area Development Authority. The CAD Programme was initiated with 60 major and medium irrigation projects.

  The CAD Programme has been restructured and renamed as Command Area Development and Water Management Programme (CADWMP) w.e.f. 1st April, 2004.

5. INDUSTRY

- After independence, the first industrial policy was declared on April 6, 1948 by then Union Industry Minister Mr. Shyama Prasad Mukherjee.
- Under this first industrial policy established a base for Mixed and Controlled Economy in India and clearly divided the industrial sector into private and public sectors.
- Second Industrial Policy Resolution declared on April 30, 1956 with the basic objective of establishing 'Socialistic Pattern of Society' in the country.
- The 1956 Resolution laid down the following objectives for the industrial policy:
  1. To accelerate the rate of growth and to speed up industrialisation;
  2. To develop heavy industries and machine making industries;
  3. To expand public sector;
  4. To reduce disparities in income and wealth;
  5. To build up a large and growing cooperative sector; and
  6. To prevent monopolies and the concentration of wealth and income in the hands of a small number of individuals.
- To control and regulate the process of industrial development in the country, an Act was passed by the parliament in October 1951. Known as the Industries (Development and Regulation) Act, 1951, the Act came into force on May 8, 1952. Though it aimed at both, development and regulation of private sector, its main task over the year has been to concentrate more on the 'regulation aspect'.
- Because of the criticisms indicating the failure of the industrial licensing policy in achieving its objectives, the Government of India announced a number of liberalisation measures in the industrial Licensing Policy announced in 1970, 1973 and 1978. In 1980, the government came forward with an Industrial Policy statement which served as a guideline to various liberalisation measures undertaken all through the 1980s.
- In line with the liberalisation measures announced during the 1980s, the government announced a New Industrial Policy on July 24, 1991. This new policy de-regulates the industrial economy in a substantial manner. The major objectives of the new policy are "to build on the gains already made, correct the distortions or weaknesses that might have crept in, maintain a sustained growth in productivity and gainful employment, and attain international competitiveness." In pursuit of these objectives, the government announced a series of initiatives in respect of the policies relating to the following areas:
  1. **Abolition of Industrial Licencing:** Industrial licensing policy in India has been governed by the Industries (Development and Regulation) Act, 1951. Industrial licensing policy and procedures have been liberalised considerably from time to time. Yet, the industrial licensing policy has all along been resented to by the entrepreneurs as it led to unnecessary governmental interference, delays in investment decisions and bureaucratic red-tapism, corruption etc. Not only this, the industrial licensing policy was also unable to achieve the objectives laid down for it by the government. On account of these considerations, and in order to liberalise the economy and to enable the entrepreneurs to make investment decisions on the basis of their own commercial judgement, the 1991 industrial policy abolished industrial licensing for all but 18. The 18 industries for which licensing was kept necessary, with the passage of time, most of these industries have also been delicensed. As of now, licensing is compulsory for only 5 industries. These are:

(*a*) Distillation and brewing of alcoholic drinks.

(*b*) Cigar, Cigarettes and other substitutes of prepared tobacco.

(*c*) Electronic, Aerospace and all types of defence equipment.

(*d*) Industrial Explosive including match boxes.

(*e*) Hazardous chemicals.

2. **Public Sector's Role Diluted:** The 1956 Resolution had reserved 17 industries for the public sector. The 1991 industrial policy reduced this number to 8. The policy has been liberalised progressively and presently only 3 industries are reserved for the public sector.

   These are:

   (*a*) atomic energy,

   (*b*) the substances specified in the schedule to the notification of the Government of India in the Department of Atomic Energy dated the 15 March, 1995 and

   (*c*) railway transport.

3. **MRTP Limit Goes:** Under the MRTP Act, all firm with assets above a certain size were classified as MRTP firms. Such firms were permitted to enter selected industries only and this also on a case by case approval basis. In addition to control through industrial licensing, separate approvals were required by such large firms for any investment proposals. The new industrial policy therefore scrapped the threshold limit of assets in respect of MRTP and dominant undertakings. These firms will now be at par with others, and not require prior approval from the government for investment in the delicensed industries. The MRTP Act was accordingly amended. The amended Act gave more emphasis to prevention and control monopolistic, restrictive and unfair trade practices so that consumers are adequately protected from such practices.

4. **Industrial location policy liberalised:** In a departure from the earlier locational policy for industries, the new industrial policy provided that in locations other than cities of more than 1 million population, there will be requirement of obtaining industrial approvals from the centre, except for industries subject to compulsory licensing. In cities with a population of more than 1 million, industries other than those of a polluting nature, were required to be located outside 25 kms. of the periphery.

5. **Free Entry to Foreign Investment and Technology:** Presently FDI (Foreign Direct Investment) is permitted upto 100 per cent on the automatic route in most sectors subject to sectorial rules/regulations applicable. FDI is prohibited only in the following sectors:

   (*a*) retail trading except single brand product retailing,

   (*b*) atomic energy,

   (*c*) lottery business, and

   (*d*) gambling and betting.

- The new Index of industrial production (IIP) series with 2011-12 as base years replacing the earlier IIP series with base year 2004-05.
- The new IIP series not only has a more recent base, it has larger and more representative product basket and weights that appropriately reflect the relative importance of the sectors, products and product group.
- There are 682 items included in the IIP of 2004-05 base years. (Previously it was 538).
- The government released the National Manufacturing policy (NMP) on 4 November 2011 for bringing about a quantitative and qualitative change with objectives to (*i*) increase manufacturing sector growth to 12-14 per cent over the medium term; (*ii*) enable manufacturing to contribute at least 25 per cent of GDP by 2022; (*iii*) create 100 million additional jobs in the manufacturing sector by 2022; (*iv*) create appropriate skill sets among the rural migrant and urban poor for their easy absorption in

manufacturing; (*v*) increase domesting value addition and technological depth in manufacturing; and (*vi*) enhance global competitiveness of Indian manufacturing.

- With a view to delegating enhanced financial and operational powers to CPSEs (Central Public Sector Enterprises), the government introduced the Navratna Scheme in July 1997.
- In December 2010, the Government introduced the Maharatna Scheme enhancing financial delegation to CPSEs.
- In December 2004, the government established a Board for Reconstruction of Public Sector Enterprises (BRPSE) to advice on revival/ restructuring of sick and loss-making CPSEs.
- Some of the recent reforms are: reducing the list of industries that can be considered defence industries requiring industrial licence; and amendments in FDI policy which include allowing FDI in defence up to 49 per cent, in railway infrastructure up to 100 per cent and in the insurance and pension sector up to 49 per cent.
- The government has launched several programmes/initiatives such as ease of doing business, Make in India, Invest India, and e-biz Mission Mode Project under the National e-Governance Plan.
- With the objective of making India a global hub of manufacturing, design and innovation, the Make in India initiative, which is based on four pillars — new processes, new infrastructure, new sectors and new mindset — has been taken by the government. The initiative is set to boost entrepreneurship, not only in manufacturing but in relevant infrastructure and service sectors as well.
- The 1991 industrial policy brought the public sector units at par with the private sector units. As a result, the public sector units were also brought within the jurisdiction of Board of Industrial and Financial Reconstruction (BIFR). Thus BIFR was given the responsibility to decide whether a sick public sector unit can be effectively restructured or whether it has to be closed down.
- One of the major initiatives towards the public sector as outlined in the new industrial policy of July 1991 was to bring all public sector enterprises under the system of Memorandum of Understanding (MoU). The system of MoU envisages an arm's length relationship between the PSU and the administrative ministries. It gives clear targets to PSUs and ensures operational autonomy to them for achieving those targets. The MoU system was started in 1987-88.
- The first unit in the public sector, now known as the Visvesvaraya Iron and Steel Works Ltd., started functioning at Bhadravati in 1923.
- During the second five year plan (1956-61) a major task in industry was building up of three steel plants in the public sector—Rourkela Steel Plant in Odisha (then Orissa), Bhilai Steel Plant in Chhattisgarh (then Madhya Pradesh) and Durgapur Steel Plant in West Bengal. The three steel plants came into operation in stage between 1959 and 1962.
- Bokaro steel plant was established in third five year plan.
- Increased production capacity of iron and steel was planned by establishing new steel plants at Salem (Tamil Nadu), Vijai Nagar (Karnataka) and Vishakhapatanam (Andhra Pradesh), during the fourth-five year plan.
- In 1974, the Steel Authority of India Limited (SAIL) was created and was made responsible for the development of steel industry.
- SAIL is also responsible for management of Bhilai, Durgapur, Rourkela, Bokaro and Burnpur steel plants. Besides SAIL has been given responsibility of managing Alloy Steel Plant, Durgapur and Salem Steel Plant.
- On July 14, 1976, the Government took over the ownership of IISCO plant and as a result IISCO also came under the control of SAIL.

- The National Steel Policy (NSP) 2005 has already been approved by Government. The long-term goal of NSP is to ensure that India has a modern and efficient steel industry, capable of standing up to international competition and catering to the growing domestic demand for steel.
- Globally, India is the largest producer and second largest exporter of jute goods. There are 89 jute mills in the country of which 64 are in West Bengal, 3 each in Bihar and Uttar Pradesh, 7 in Andhra Pradesh two each in Assam and Chhattisgarh.
- The government has formulated first ever National Jute policy in 2005 with an objective of increasing production, improving quality, ensuring remunerative prices to the jute farmers and per hectare yield.
- Sugar industry occupies an important place among agriculture based industries. This industry took a shape of a large industry in the beginning of 20th century. Sugar industry is the second largest industry after cotton textile industry among agriculture based industries of the country.
- India is the second largest producer of cement in the world after China. The cement industry was delicensed in 1991.
- The small and medium sector has been defined as micro, small and medium enterprises with effect from October 2, 2006 (the Act defined the medium enterprises for the first time). Further, separate investment limits have been prescribed for manufacturing and service enterprises. The new definition is as follows:

A. Manufacturing Enterprises

(*a*) *A micro enterprise, where the investment in plant and machinery does not exceed ₹ 25 lakh;*

(*b*) *A small enterprise, where the investment in plant and machinery is more than ₹ 25 lakh but does not exceed ₹ 5 crore; and*

(*c*) *A medium enterprise, where the investment in plant and machinery is more than ₹ 5 crore but does not exceed ₹ 10 crore.*

B. Service Enterprises

(*a*) *A micro enterprise, where the investment in equipment does not exceed ₹ 10 lakh;*

(*b*) *A small enterprise, where the investment in equipment is more than ₹ 10 lakh but does not exceed ₹ 2 crore; and*

(*c*) *A medium enterprise, where the investment in equipment is more than ₹ 2 crore but does not exceed ₹ 5 crore.*

- In 2015-16, there were 63 million MSMEs in the country, which provide employment to about 110.9 million persons. Of the total, 67 per cent were in the manufacturing sector and 33 per cent in the service sector.
- Manufacturing enterprises constitute 31.8 per cent of the micro, small, and medium enterprises (MSME) sector and service enterprises account for the remaining 68.2 per cent. About 55.3 per cent of these enterprises are located in rural areas.
- A Cottage Industries Board was set up in 1947 itself. This was split into the following three board during the First Five Year Plan—All India Handloom Board, All India Handicrafts Board, and All India Khadi and Village Industries Board. In addition, three more boards were set up. These were the small scale Industries Board, Coir Board and Central Silk Board. Thus at the end of First Five Year Plan, there were a total of six boards covering the entire field of small-scale and cottage industries.
- Small Industries Development Organisation (SIDO) was set up in 1954. It functions as an apex body in the formulation of policies and co-ordination of institutional activities for sustained and organised growth of small-scale industries. It has a large network of small industries services institutes, branch institutes, toolrooms etc. SIDO has now been renamed as the Micro, Small and Medium Enterprises Development Organisation.

- National Small Industries Corporation Ltd. (NSIC) was set up in 1955 to provide machinery to small-scale units an hire-purchase basis and to assist these units in procuring orders from government departments and offices.
- The programme of District Industries Centre (DICs) was introduced in May 1979. The idea was to establish on agency in each district called the District Industries Centre to provide and arrange a package of assistance and facilities for credit guidance, raw materials, training, marketing etc. including the necessary help to unemployed educated young entrepreneurs in general and custom services.
- Several Schemes were introduced to provide financial assistance to small scale industries. These include—

  (*i*) **SIDF :** The Small Industries Development Fund (SIDF) was set up in 1986. It provides refinance assistance for development, expansion, diversification and rehabilitation of small scale, cottage and village industries and tiny sector in rural areas.

  (*ii*) **NEF :** National Equity Fund (NEF) was set up in 1987. It provides equity type support to small entrepreneurs for setting up new projects in tiny/small scale sector and also assistance for rehabilitation of viable sick units in the small-scale sector.

  (*iii*) **SWS :** Single Window Scheme (SWS) was set up in 1988. It provides working capital loans alongwith term loans for fixed capital to new tiny and small scale units.
- Small Industries Development Bank of India (SIDBI) was set up in 1990. It is a Separate Apex Bank, to provide financial assistance to the small-scale industries.
- Due to the policy of de-reservation, the number of items reserved for the SSI Sector (Small Scale Industry Sector) came down from 836 in July 1969 to 114 in March 2007. At present, only 14 items are reserved for the small-scale sector.
- Since the adoption of the economic reforms programme in 1991, the argument is that the MRTP Act has lost its relevance in the new liberalised and global competitive scenario. In view of this, the government appointed an expert committee headed by SVS Raghavan to examine the whole issue. The Raghavan Committee submitted its Report to the government on May 22, 2000 wherein it proposed the adoption of a new competition law and doing away with the MRTP Act, 1969. Accordingly, the government decided to enact a law on competition. Competition Bill, 2001 was introduced in parliament and passed in December 2002. The Act is called Competition Act, 2002. The Act was amended in September 2007.
- The definition of a sick industrial company was changed by the companies (Second Amendment) Act, 2002. According to this Act, "sick industrial company" means an industrial company which has—

  (*i*) the accumulated losses in any financial year which are equal to 50 per cent or more of its average network during four years immediately preceding such financial year; or (*ii*) failed to repay its debt within any three consecutive quarters on demand made in writing for its repayment by a creditor or creditors of such company.
- By a notification issued on March 20, 1985, the government converted the IRCI (which was a company registered under the companies Act, 1956) into a statutory corporation and it was given the name Industrial Reconstruction Bank of India (IRBI). The authorised capital and paid-up capital of IRBI are ₹ 200 crore and ₹ 50 crore respectively.
- IRBI was reconstituted into a full-fledged all purpose development financial institution with effect from March 27, 1997 and its new name is Industrial Investment Bank of India Ltd. (IIBIL). The head office of IIBIL is situated at Kolkata.

6. LABOUR

- Labour policy in India has evolved in response to specific needs of the situation to suit the requirements of a planned economic development and social justice and has a two fold objective—(*i*) Maintaining Industrial peace and (*ii*) promoting the welfare of labour.
- The Factories Act, 1948 is the principal legislation for regulating various aspects relating to safety, health and welfare of workers employed in factories. This Act is a Central Enactment, which aims at protecting workers employed in factories from industrial and occupational hazards.
- The Factories Act, 1948 prescribes a 48 hours week for adult workers and forbids employment of children below the age of 14 years in any factory.
- The Minimum Wages Act, 1948 was enacted primarily to safeguard the interests of the workers engaged in an unorganised sector who are vulnerable to exploitation due to illiteracy and lack of bargaining power. The Act binds the employers to pay the minimum wages to the workers as fixed under the statute and workers get protected against exploitation.
- Under the provisions of the Minimum Wages Act, 1948 both the Central and State Governments are appropriate Governments to fix, review, revise and enforce the minimum rates of wages for workers employed in the scheduled employments under their respective jurisdictions. All the provisions of the Act equally apply to both male and female.
- The Payment of Wages Act, 1936, which is labour-friendly legislation, ensures primarily timely payment of wages and that no unauthorized deductions are made from the wages of the workers.
- The Central Government, on the basis of figures of the Consumer Expenditure Survey published by National Sample Survey Organization, has enhanced the wage ceiling from ₹ 10,000 to ₹ 18,000 per month from September 2012.
- The payment of Bonus Act, 1965 provides for payment of bonus to employees of the factories and other establishments employing 20 or more persons. The minimum bonus of 8.33% is payable by every industry and establishment under the section 10 of the Act. The maximum bonus including productivity linked bonus that can be paid in any accounting year shall not exceed 20% of the salary/wage of an employee under the Sections 11 and 31A of the Act.
- The Working Journalist and other Newspaper Employees (conditions of service) and Miscellaneous Provisions Act, 1955 regulates conditions of service of working journalists and other persons employed in newspaper establishments. The Act provides for setting up of Wage Board for fixation and revision of rates of wages in respect of working journalists and non-journalists newspaper/news agency employees.
- Child Labour (Prohibition & Regulation) Act, 1986, employment of children below the age of 14 years are prohibited in notified hazardous occupations and processes. The Act also regulates employment of children in non-hazardous occupations and processes. There are at present 16 hazardous occupations and 65 processes, where employment of children is prohibited.
- The issue of 'Bonded Labour came in force first in national politics, when it was included in the old 20-point programme in 1975. To implement this Bonded Labour System (Abolition) ordinance was promulgated. This was later replaced by the Bonded Labour System (Abolition) Act, 1976. The district and sub-district magistrates have been entrusted with certain duties and responsibilities towards implementation of statutory provisions.
- The Social Security Act, 2008, provides the social security of unorganised sector workers. The

'unorganised sector' means an enterprise owned by individuals or self-employed workers and engaged in the production or sale of goods or providing service of any kind whatsoever, and where the enterprise employs workers, the number of such workers is less than ten.

- V.V. Giri National Labour Institute is a premier institution involved with research, training, education, publication, and consultancy on labour and related issues. The institute, established in 1974, at Noida (Uttar Pradesh), is an autonomous body of the Ministry of Labour and Employment, Government of India. The Institute engages in research pertaining to labour and training of labour, administrators concerned with labour. Seminar, workshops and lectures are organised on specific issues from time to time.
- The Central Board for Workers Education (CBWE) was established in 1958 by the Ministry of Labour & Employment, Government of India to implement the workers education scheme at national, regional and unit/village levels for the workers from organized, unorganized and rural sectors. The Board has its headquarters at Nagpur with a network of 50 Regional and Subregional Directorates spread throughout the country. The six Zonal Directorates at Delhi, Guwahati, Kolkata, Chennai, Mumbai and Bhopal monitor the activities of the Regional Directorates within respective zone. The Board has an apex training institute at Mumbai called IIWE.

WORKER'S SAFETY ACT

- The Factories Act, 1948 is the principal legislation for regulating various aspects relating to safety, health and welfare of workers employed in factories. This Act is a Central Enactment, which aims at protecting workers employed in factories from industrial and occupational hazards. The factories employing one thousand workers or more and five hundred workers or more, are required to employ safety officer/s and welfare officer/s respectively.
- Provisions relating to safety, health and welfare of workers employed in docks are contained in the Dock Workers (Safty, Health and Welfare) Act, 1986 and rules and regulations framed there under. The Act came into force on 15th April, 1987.
- Provisions for safety, health and welfare of workers employed in mines are contained in the Mines Act, 1952 and rules and regulations framed there under. These provisions are enforced by the Ministry of Labour and Employment through the Directorate General of Mines Safety. The Directorate General, has its headquarters at Dhanbad.
- The National Safety Council was set up in 1966 to promote safety consciousness among workers to prevent accidents, minimize dangers and mitigate human suffering, arrange programmes, lectures and conferences on safety, conduct educational compaign to increase consciousness among employers and workers and collect educational and information datas, etc.

INDUSTRIAL RELATIONS

- The Industrial Disputes Act, 1947 provides the machinery and procedure for the investigation and settlement of industrial disputes. The Act has been amended vide the Industrial Disputes (Amendment) Act, 2010 and enforced w.e.f. 15th September, 2010.
- The Trade Unions Act, 1926 provides for registration of trade unions of employers and workers, and in certain respects, it defined the law relating to registered trade union. It confers legal and corporate status on registered trade unions. The Trade Unions Act, 1926 is administered by the concerned State Governments. The act has been amended and enforced from 9th January, 2002.
- The Plantations Labour Act, 1951 provides for welfare of plantation labourers and regulates their conditions of work. The Plantations Labour Act, 1951 has been amended and the Plantation Labour (Amendement) Act, 2010 has been enforced w.e.f. 7th June, 2010.
- The 'Rashtriya Swasthya Bima Yojana' for BPL families (a unit of five) in Unorganised Sector

was launched on 1st October, 2007 and became operational w.e.f. 1st April, 2008. Under the scheme, smart card based cashless health insurance cover of ₹ 30,000 per annum on a family is provided. The premium is shared on 75:25 basis by centre and state Government. In case of states of North East region and Jammu & Kashmir, the premium is shared in the ratio of 90:10.

SOCIAL SECURITY

- A beginning in social security in India was made in 1923 when Workmen's Compensation Act was passed. The Act is very wide in coverage and covers many diverse industries including mines, factories, transport, plantations, construction activities, electricity generation etc.
- The Workmen's Compensation Act, 1923, does not apply to those industries or factories where Employee's State Insurance Act, 1948, is in operation.
- The Workmen's Compensation Act was amended in 2000. Under this amendment, the workmen or their family members will get the compensation money at the enhanced rate if they die or get disabled. As a result of the death in the working capacity, the compensation money will be minimum 1,20,000. The maximum limit can be ₹ 9.14 lakhs. In the case of disability, the minimum limit is increased from 90,000 to 1,40,000 rupees. The maximum limit in this case, can go upto 10.97 lakh rupees.
- The Maternity Benefit Act, 1961, regulates the employment of women in certain establishments for certain period before and after child birth (six week before and six weeks after confinement) and provides for maternity and other benefits.
- The Materity Benefit Act, 1961 applies to mines, factories, circus, industry, plantations, shops and establishments employing 10 or more persons except the employees who are covered under the ESI Act, 1948. There is no wage limit coverage under the Act.
- The most important step in the field of social security was taken in 1948 when the Employee's State Insurance (ESI) Act was passed. The Act is applicable to non-seasonal factories using power and employing 10 or more persons and non-power using factories employing 20 or more persons. It covers employees drawing wages not exceeding ₹ 21,000 with effect from 1st Jan, 2017.
- The Employees Provident Funds and Miscellaneous Provision Act, 1952 seeks to provide the financial social security to the employees in the form of provident fund, pension and deposit-linked insurance. It extends to the whole of India except the State of Jammu and Kashmir. It applies to every establishment specified in the schedule and in which 20 or more persons are employed. The object of this Act is to make:
  - (*i*) Some provisions for the future of the industrial workers after the retirement.
  - (*ii*) to provide for the dependants in the case of the employee's death, and
  - (*iii*) to cultivate the spirit of saving among the employees.
- Other important social security schemes are:
  - (*a*) The payment of Gratuity Act, 1972.
  - (*b*) Employee's Deposit Linked Insurance Scheme, 1976.
  - (*c*) Employee's Pension Scheme, 1995.

TRADE UNION

- Trade unions are voluntary organisations of workers formed to protect the interest of workers through collective action.
- In India, the first trade union was formed in 1918.
- There are number of trade unions in India, which are associated with main political parties. Some important trade unions are as follows:
  - (*i*) Bharatiya Mazdoor Sangh (BMS), associated with the Bharatiya Janta Party.
  - (*ii*) Indian National Trade Union Congress (INTUC), associated with the Congress Party.
  - (*iii*) All-India Trade Union Congress (AITUC), associated with the Communist Party of India.

(*iv*) Centre of Indian Trade Unions (CITU), associated with the CPI (M).

- The First National Labour Commission was formed on December 24, 1966.
- The Second National Labour Commission was formed on October 15, 1999 under the Chairmanship of Ravindra Verma.
- Trade Union (Amendment) Act, 2001 was introduced with the following objectives:
  (*i*) To control multiplicity of trade unions.
  (*ii*) Establishing industrial democracy.
  (*iii*) Encourage well managed expansion of trade unions.
- The amended Act was introduced after incorporating the recommendations of Ramanujan Committee. The Act has following important provisions:
  (*i*) Minimum 10% of the total labour force or 100 labourers in an organization (whichever is less) must be required to form trade union.
  (*ii*) No. of members should not be less than of in any condition.
  (*iii*) At least 5 members or one-third (whichever is less) should be the employees of the concern.
  (*iv*) Annual contribution for trade union should not be less than ₹ 12.00

7. ECONOMIC PLANNING

- Economic Planning refers to any directing or planning of economic activity outside the mechanisms of the market. Planning is an economic mechanism for resources allocation and decision-making held in contrast with the market mechanism. Economic Planning can be applied to production, investment, distribution or all three of these functions.
- In the year 1934, Sir M. Visheshvraya wrote a book named 'Planned Economy for India', which was the first attempt in this direction.
- In 1938, the Indian National Congress, under the leadership of Pt. Jawaharlal Nehru, made a National Planning Committee.
- In 1944, eight industrialists of Bombay (Now Mumbai) presented a well-organised plan called 'The Bombay Plan'.
- Inspired by the economic views of Mahatma Gandhi, Shri Sriman Narayan Constructed a plan in 1944 which is known as 'Gandhian Plan'.
- Mr. M.N. Rao, chairman of post-war Reconstruction Committee of Indian Trade Union, introduced a 'People's Plan' in April 1945.
- In January 1950, Shri Jaiprakash Narayan published a plan called 'Sarvodaya Plan'.
- The Planning Commission was constituted on 15th March, 1950, by the Government of India.
- There is no account of Planning Commission in the Indian Constitution. Therefore, it was constituted in the form of an advisory and specialised institution by means of a document of the Government. Consequently, the Government has been changing its nature and organisation from time to time.
- Pt. Jawaharlal Nehru was appointed as the first Chairman of Planning Commission.
- The Prime Minister is the ex-officio chairman of Planning Commission.
- National Development Council (NDC) is a non-statutory body which was constituted to build co-operation between the States and the Planning Commission for economic planning.
- The National Development Council (NDC) was constituted on 6th August, 1952. The Prime Minister is the chairman and the secretary of the Planning Commission remains its secretary.

Niti Aayog

- The government on January 1, 2015 replaced the 65-year-old Planning Commission—a relic of the Socialist era—with a Niti Aayog or National Institution for Transforming India, marking a major shift in policy making by involving states.

The Aayog will recommend a national agenda, including strategic and technical advice on elements of policy and economic matters. It will also develop mechanisms for village-level plans and aggregate these progressively at higher levels of government. To be headed by PM Narendra Modi, the new body will have a governing council comprising CMs of all states and Lt Governors of Union Territories and will work towards fostering co-operative federalism for providing a national agenda to the Centre and states. The membership of states has rendered the National Development Council, a body of CMs that approves five-year Plans, defunct. Former secretary of Defence Research and Development Organisation (DRDO) VK Saraswat and economist Bibek Debroy are appointed as full-time members. The Aayog will have finance minister Arun Jaitley, home minister Rajnath Singh, Railway Minister Piyuch Goyal and agriculture minister Radha Mohan Singh as ex-officio members. Union ministers Nitin Gadkari, Thawar Chand Gehlot and Smriti Irani are special invitees to the panel

First Five Year Plan (1951-1956)

- The First Five Year Plan began on April 1, 1951 and ended on March 31, 1956.
- The plan was based on the model of Harrod-Domer.
- The plan has given highest priority to agriculture, irrigation and power projects.
- The achievements of this plan were more than its targets. The annual compound growth rate of national income was 3.6% (target 2.1%) during the planning period.
- The per capita income growth rate was 1.8% and ICOR was 2.95 during this plan.

Second Five Year Plan (1956-1961)

- Based on the model prepared by Prof. P.C. Mahalnobis, the Second Five Year Plan was started on April 1, 1956 and ended on March 31, 1961.
- The fundamental objective of this plan was to initiate and accelerate the process of industrialisation so that the development of Indian economy takes a firm base.
- The Industrial policy, 1956 (During Second Five Year Plan), was based on the objective of establishing the socialistic pattern of society.
- Large industries including steel plants (Durgapur, Bhilai and Rourkela) were set up. The Locomotive factory at Chittaranjan and Coach factory at Perambur were other major projects of this period.

Third Five Year Plan (1961-1966)

- This plan started on April 1, 1961 and ended on March 31, 1966.
- The basic aim of this plan was to push the economy upto the take-off stage development.
- This plan set as its goal the establishment of a self-reliant and self-generating economy.
- In this plan top priority was given to agriculture but it also laid adequate emphasis on the development of basic industries, which were vitally necessary for rapid economic development of the country.

Annual Plans (1966-1969)

- The Fourth Plan was scheduled to begin from April 1, 1966, but due to the unfortunate failure of third plan, the production in various sector of the economy became stagnant.
- In 1966, the Government of India declared the devaluation of rupee, with a view to increase the exports of the country. However, favourable results couldnot be obtained. Under these circumstances the fourth plan was postponed for sometime and Three Annual Plans were implemented during this period.
- Some of the economists called this period, *i.e.* from 1966 to 1969 as 'Plan Holiday' because no regular planning was done during this period.

Fourth Five Year Plan (1969-1974)

- The Fourth Plan started on April 1, 1969 and ended on March 31, 1974.
- Growth with stability and progress towards self-reliance were the prime objective of the plan.
- The plan aimed at 5.5 per cent average rate of growth in the national income.

Fifth Five Year Plan (1974-1979)

- The Fifth Five Year Plan began on April 1, 1974 which was scheduled to end on March 31, 1979.
- The final draft of the Fifth Plan was prepared and launched by D.P. Dhar proposed to achieve the two main objectives removal of poverty and attainment of self-reliance.
- The plan objective, 'removal of poverty is also known as the slogan 'Garibi Hatao'.
- This plan also gave high priority to bring inflation under control and to achieve stability in economic situation.

Sixth Five Year Plan (1980-1985)

- The Janta Government ended the Fifth Five Year Plan, one year to its term, *i.e.,* only within four years span (1974-78) and introduced a new plan since April 1, 1978. This plan was named as the "Rolling Plan".
- In 1980, the Sixth Plan (Rolling Plan) prepared by Janta Government was abandoned by the Congress Government and a new Sixth Plan was introduced for the period 1980-85.
- The focus of Janta Government's Sixth Plan (Rolling Plan) was enlargement of the employment potential in agriculture and allied activities, whereas the focus of Congress Sixth Plan was to solve the problem of poverty by creating conditions of an expanding economy.

Seventh Five Year Plan (1985-1990)

- The 7th plan began on April 1, 1985 and ended on March 31, 1990.
- This plan emphasised policies and programmes which aimed at rapid growth in foodgrains production, increased employment opportunities and productivity within the framework of basic tenents of planning, *i.e.*, growth, modernisation, self-reliance and social justice.

Eighth Five Year Plan (1992-1997)

- The 8th Five Year Plan which was supposed to start from April 1, 1990 could not be started on scheduled time because of some political changes at the Centre during 1990-92.
- NDC ratified the format of the Plan in one of its meeting held on May 23, 1992. This Plan began on April 1, 1992 which ended on March 31, 1997.
- The Plan has initiated the process of fiscal reforms as also of economic reforms with a view to provide a new dynamism to economy.
- Fundamental objective of this Plan was human development.
- Pradhanmantri Rojgar Yojana (1993) was started during this Plan.

Ninth Five Year Plan (1997-2002)

- The 9th Plan began on April 1, 1997 and ended on March 31, 2007.
- 'Growth with Equity and Distributive Justice' was determined as the main focus of the Ninth Plan. In order to achieve this focus, four fields were identified which are as follows:
  (*i*) Quality of life
  (*ii*) Employment promotion
  (*iii*) Regional imbalance
  (*iv*) Self-dependence

Tenth Five Year Plan (2002-2007)

- The 10th Plan began on April 1, 2002 and ended on March 31, 2007.
- The Plan has not been able to achieve its target of 8 per cent growth of GDP, but has taken the economy to a higher trajectory of growth rate at 7.8 per cent as against 5.5 per cent in the 9th Plan.
- Gross domestic savings averaged 28.2 per cent in 10th Plan as against 23.1 per cent in the 9th plan.
- The economy has been able to reduce its ICOR from a level of 4.3 during the 9th Plan to a level of 4.2 during the 10th Plan.

- Our foreign exchange reserve reached a level of US $ 185 billion in February 2007. This is another indication of the strength of the economy.

Eleventh Five Year Plan (2007-12)

- The 11th Plan began on April 1, 2007 and ended on March 31, 2012.
- The 11th Plan visualises "Faster and more inclusive growth" as its objective.
- 11th Plan has fixed a target of pushing up overall GDP growth to an average rate of 9.0 per cent.

Twelfth Five Year Plan (2012-17)

- The 12th Plan began on April 1, 2012 and ended on March 31, 2017.
- Real GDP Growth Rate of 8.0 per cent.
- Agriculture Growth Rate of 4.0 per cent.
- Manufacturing Growth Rate of 7.1 per cent.
- Industrial Sector Growth Rate of 7.6 per cent.
- Service Sector Growth Rate of 9.0 per cent.
- Generate 50 million new work opportunities.
- Eliminate gender and social gap in school enrolment.
- Reduce Total Fertility Rate to 2.1 by the end of Twelfth Five Year Plan.

8. MONEY AND BANKING

- A money market is not a market for money but it is the market for lending and borrowing of short term funds. It is the market where the short-terms surplus investible funds for bank and other financial institutions are demanded by borrowers comprising of individuals, companies and the Government.
- Capital market is the market for long-term funds. It refers to all the facilities and the institutional arrangements for borrowing and lending term funds (medium-term and long-term funds). It does not deal in capital for purposes of investment.
- In monetary economics, control of money supply usually refers to control of the supply of currency and deposit money.
- The RBI now calculates on four concepts of money supply in India. These are known as money stock measures or measures of monetary aggregate. The four concepts of money supply are:

  M_1 = Currency with the public, i.e. coins and currency notes + demand deposits of the public; also known as narrow money.

  M_2 = M_1 + Post office saving deposits

  M_3 = M_1 + Time deposits of the public with banks; also known as broad money

  M_4 = M_3 + Total post office deposits

- The monetary policy referes to a regulatory policy whereby the central bank (RBI) maintains its control over the supply of monetary for the realisation of general economic goals.
- Among the functions of RBI, one main function is to control and regulate the credit in the country. In India, this function is performed by the Reserve Bank of India (RBI). The measures of credit control can be divided into two types:

  (*i*) Quantitative Credit Control

  (*ii*) Selective Credit Control

- The main objective of quantitative credit control is to establish control over the total quantity of credit in the country. For quantitative credit control, the central bank (RBI) takes the help of bank rate, open market operations, SLR and CRR, whereas publicity, rationing of credit, regulation of consumer credit, moral suasion, variation in margin requirements are the selective credit (qualitative) control methods.

- Reserve Bank of India (RBI) is the central bank of the country.
- Reserve Bank of India was established on April 1, 1935 under Reserve Bank of India Act, 1934 with a authorised capital of ₹ 5 crore.
- The Reserve Bank of India was nationalised on January 1, 1949.
- The general administration and direction of RBI is managed by a Central Board of Directors consisting of 20 members which includes 1 Governor and 4 Deputy Governors.
- The head office of the Reserve Bank of India is in Mumbai.
- SBI functions as an agent of RBI, where there are not any branches of RBI.

Governors of RBI

S.N.	Governors	Period
1.	Sir Osborne Smith	1-4-35 to 30-6-37
2.	Sir James Braid Taylor	1-7-37 to 17-2-43
3.	Sir C. D. Deshmukh	11-8-43 to 30-6-49
4.	Sir Benegal Rama Rau	1-7-49 to 14-1-57
5.	K. G. Ambegaonkar	14-1-57 to 28-2-57
6.	H. V. R. Iyengar	1-3-57 to 28-2-62
7.	P. C. Bhattacharya	1-3-62 to 30-6-67
8.	L. K. Jha	1-7-67 to 3-5-70
9.	B. N. Adarkar	4-5-70 to 15-6-70
10.	S. Jagannathan	16-6-70 to 19-5-75
11.	N. C. Sen Gupta	19-5-75 to 19-8-75
12.	K. R. Puri	20-8-75 to 2-5-77
13.	M. Narasimham	2-5-77 to 30-11-77
14.	Dr. I. G. Patel	1-12-77 to 15-9-82
15.	Dr. Manmohan Singh	16-9-82 to 14-1-85
16.	A. Ghosh	15-1-85 to 4-2-85
17.	R. N. Malhotra	4-2-85 to 22-12-90
18.	S. Venkataramanan	22-12-90 to 21-12-92
19.	Dr. C. Rangarajan	22-12-92 to 21-11-97
20.	Dr. Bimal Jalan	22-12-97 to 6-9-03
21.	Dr. Y. V. Reddy	6-9-03 to 5-9-08
22.	Dr. Duvvuri Subbarao	5-9-08 to 4-9-13
23.	Raghuram Rajan	4-9-13 to 4-9-16
24.	Urjit Patel	4-9-16 to till date

- Functions of Reserve Bank of India:
  - ❖ Issue of Notes.
  - ❖ Bankers to the Government.
  - ❖ Banker's Bank.
  - ❖ Controller of Credit.
  - ❖ Custodian of Foreign Reserves.
  - ❖ Other Functions (function of clearing house arranging credit for agriculture, collecting and publishing the economic data, buying and selling of government securities and trade bills etc.)

Foundation Years of Main Indian Banks

Reserve Bank of India	1935
Nationalisation of RBI	1949
State Bank of India	1955
Nationalisation of 14 Commercial Banks	1969
Nationalisation of 6 other Banks	1980
Regional Rural Bank	1975
Bharatiya Mahila Bank	2013

- **Bank Rate:** Bank Rate is the rate of discount at which the central bank of the country discounts first class bills. It is the rate of interest at which the central bank lends money to the lower banking institutions. Bank rate is a direct quantitative method of credit control in the economy.
- **Cash Reserve Ratio (CRR):** Commercial banks are required to keep a certain amount of cash reserves at the central bank. This percentage amount is called CRR. It influences the commercial bank's volume of credit because variation in CRR affects the liquidity position of the banks and hence their ability to lend.
- **Prime Lending Rate (PLR):** Prime Lending Rate (PLR) is that rate of interest at which bank gives loan to its most reliable customer. This reliability means 'zero risk'. Thus, PLR provides the role of a basic interest rate at which loan is provided to other customers.
- **Repo Rate:** Repo (Repurchase option) rate is a instrument under the Liquidity Adjustment

Facility (LAF) at which RBI lends to commercial banks. In case of inflationary tendencies RBI perceived need to inject liquidity into the system, RBI can reduce the Repo rate which will lead to release of money into the market.

- **Reverse Repo Rate:** Reverse Repo Rate is the rate at which RBI borrows from commercial banks. In case of inflationary tendencies, RBI can hike the Reverse Repo rate to absorb the excess liquidity in the market. It is also a Liquidity Adjustment facility instrument.
- **Statutory Liquidity Ratio (SLR):** Commercial banks are also required to keep (in additon to CRR) a certain percentage of their net demand and time liabilities (NDTL) as liquid assets in the shape of cash, gold or approved securities. As most of the SLR money is kept in treasury bills, government had, in the past, been using SLR as a means to mobilise low cost resources. Its upper limit is 40%.
- The Reserve Bank Act, 1934 and the Banking Regulation Act, 1949 have given the RBI wide powers of supervision and control over commercial and co-operative banks, relating to licensing and establishments, branch expansion, liquidity of their assets, management and method of working, amalgmation, reconstruction and liquidation.
- On the recommendation of the Rural Credit Survey Committee the Imperial Bank of India was converted into the State Bank of India on July 1, 1955. Alongwith it, other 8 (at present 5) banks were converted as its associate banks which form what is named as the State Bank Group. They are as follows:
  1. The State Bank of Bikaner and Jaipur
  2. The State Bank of Hyderabad
  3. The State Bank of Mysore
  4. The State Bank of Patiala
  5. The State Bank of Travancore

  5 associate banks of SBI have been merged with SBI on April 1, 2017.

Reasons for Nationalisation of Banks

(*i*) Removal of control by a few.

(*ii*) Provision of adequate credit for agriculture and small industry and export.

(*iii*) Giving a professional bent to management.

(*iv*) Encouragement of a new class of entrepreneurs; and

(*v*) The provision of adequate training as well as terms of service for bank staff.

- In order to have more control over the banks, 14 large commercial banks whose reserves were more than ₹ 50 crore each were nationalised on 19th July, 1969. These banks are as follows:
  1. The Central Bank of India
  2. Bank of India
  3. Punjab National Bank
  4. Canara Bank
  5. United Commercial Bank
  6. Syndicate Bank
  7. Bank of Baroda
  8. United Bank of India
  9. Union Bank of India
  10. Dena Bank
  11. Allahabad Bank
  12. Indian Bank
  13. Indian Overseas Bank
  14. Bank of Maharashtra
- After one decade, on April 15, 1980 another 6 private sector banks whose reserves were more than ₹ 200 crore each were nationalised. These banks are as:
  1. Andhra Bank
  2. Punjab and Sindh Bank
  3. New Bank of India
  4. Vijaya Bank
  5. Corporation Bank
  6. Oriental Bank of Commerce.
- On 4th September, 1993 the Government merged the New Bank of India with Punjab National Bank and as a result of this the total number of nationalised bank got reduced from 20 to 19. But after the transformation of IDBI into Scheduled Bank on October 2004, the number of nationalise banks has increased to 20.

TYPES OF BANKS

On the basis of functions, the banking institutions in India may be divided into the following types:

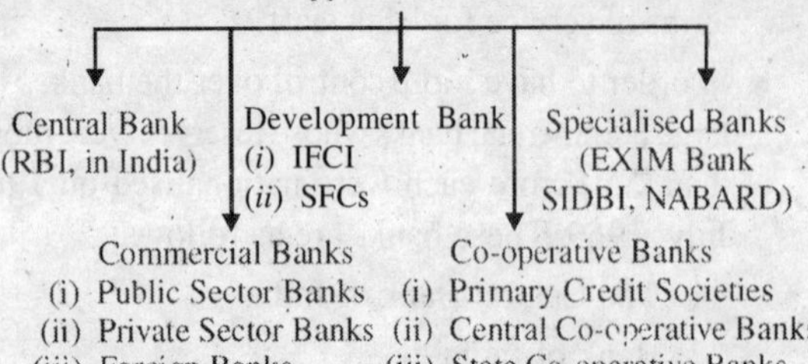

Central Bank

A bank which is entrusted with the functions of guiding and regulating the banking system of a country is known as its Central bank. Such a bank does not deal with the general public. The Reserve Bank of India is the central bank of our country.

Commercial Banks

Commercial Banks are banking institutions that accept deposits and grant short-term loans and advances to their customers. In addition to giving short-term loans, commercial banks also give medium-term and long-term loan to business enterprises.

Development Banks

Business often requires medium and long-term capital for purchase of machinery and equipment, for using latest technology, or for expansion and modernization. Such financial assistance is provided by Development Banks. Industrial Finance Corporation of India (IFCI) and State Financial Corporations (SFCs) are examples of development banks in India.

Co-operative Banks

Co-operative banks in India also perform fundamental banking activities but they are different from commercial banks. Commercial banks have been constituted by an Act passed by parliament while co-operative banks have been constituted by different States under various Acts related to co-operative societies of various states. Co-operative bank organisation in India has three tier set up: 1. State Co-operative Bank is the apex co-operative institution in the state. 2. Central or District Co-operative Bank works at district level. 3. Primary Credit societies which works at the lowest or village level.

CLASSIFICATION OF COMMERCIAL BANKS

The commercial banking institutions of the country can be divided into two groups:

A. Scheduled Banks: Those banks are scheduled banks which have been included in the Schedule (Second) of Reserve Bank Act, 1934. The banks included in this scheduled list should fulfil two conditions:

1. The paid up capital and collected funds of bank should not be less than ₹ 5 lakh.
2. Any activity of the bank should not adversely affect the interest of depositors.

Every scheduled bank enjoys following facilities:

1. Such bank becomes eligible for obtaining debts/loans on bank rate from RBI.
2. Such bank automatically acquires the membership of clearing house.
3. Such banks also get the facility of rediscount of first class exchange bills from RBI.

B. Non-scheduled Banks: Those banks which are not included in the list of scheduled banks are called non-scheduled banks. These non-scheduled banks are not eligible for having loans from RBI for meeting their day-to-day general activities but under emergency conditions these banks can be granted loans by RBI.

FUNCTIONS OF COMMERCIAL BANKS

The functions of commercial banks are of **two** types.

(A) Primary functions; and

(B) Secondary functions.

Primary functions

There are two primary functions of a commercial bank. These are:

(*a*) ***Accepting deposits:*** The most important activity of a commercial bank is to mobilise deposits from the public. People who have surplus income and savings find it convenient to deposit the amounts with banks. Depending upon the nature of deposits, funds deposited with bank also earn interest.

(*b*) ***Grant loans and advances:*** The second important function of a commercial bank is to grant loans and advances. Such loans and advances are given to members of the public and to the business community at a higher rate of interest than allowed by banks on various deposit accounts.

Secondary functions

In addition to the primary functions of accepting deposits and lending money, banks perform a number of other functions, which are called secondary functions. These are as follows:

(a) Issuing letters of credit, travellers cheque, etc.

(b) Undertaking safe custody of valuables, important document and securities by providing safe deposit vaults or lockers.

(c) Providing customers with facilities of foreign exchange dealings.

(d) Transferring money from one account to another; and from one branch to another branch of the bank through cheque, pay order, demand draft.

(e) Standing guarantee on behalf of its customers, for making payment for purchase of goods, machinery, vehicles etc.

(f) Collecting and supplying business information.

(g) Providing reports on the credit-worthiness of customers.

(i) Providing consumer finance for individuals by way of loans on easy terms for purchase of consumer durables like televisions, refrigerators, etc.

(j) Educational loans to students at reasonable rate of interest for higher studies, especially for professional courses.

NON-BANKING FINANCIAL COMPANIES (NBFCS)

Introduction

Non-banking financial companies (NBFCs) are fast emerging as an important segment of Indian financial system. It is an heterogeneous group of institutions (other than commercial and co-operative banks) performing financial intermediation in a variety of ways, like accepting deposits, making loans and advances, leasing, hire purchase, etc.

Differences Between Banks & NBFCs

NBFCs are doing functions akin to that of banks, however there are a few differences:

(*i*) An NBFC cannot accept demand deposits (demand deposits are funds deposited at a depository institution that are payable on demand—immediately or within a very short period—like your current or savings accounts.)

(*ii*) It is not a part of the payment and settlement system and as such cannot issue cheque books to its customers; and

(*iii*) Deposit insurance facility of DICGC is not available for NBFC depositors unlike in case of banks.

Types of NBFCs

The types of NBFCs registered with the RBI are:

1. **Equipment leasing companies:** It is any financial institution whose principal business is that of leasing equipments or financing of such an activity.
2. **Hire-purchase companies:** It is any financial intermediary whose principal business relates to hire purchase transactions or financing of such transactions.
3. **Loan companies:** It means any financial institution whose principal business is that of providing finance, whether by making loans or advances or otherwise for any activity other than its own (excluding any equipment leasing or hire-purchase finance activity).
4. **Investment companies:** It is any financial intermediary whose principal business is that of buying and selling of securities.

NBFCs by their Principal Business

Non-Banking Financial Companies (NBFCs)	Principal Business
Equipment Leasing Companies (EL)	Equipment leasing or financing of such activity
Hire Purchase Finance Companies (HP)	Hire purchase transaction or purchasing or such transactions
Investment Companies (IC) Loan Companies (LC)	Acquisition of securities and trading in such securities to earn a profit Making loans or advances for any activity other than its own; EL/HP/ Housing Finance
Residuary Non-Banking Companies (RNBCs)	Receives deposits under any scheme or arrangement, by whatever name called, in one lump-sum or in instalments by way of contributions or subsriptions or by sale of units or certificates or other instruments, or in any manner
Mutual Benefit Financial Companies (MBFC) *i.e.* Nidhi Companies	Any company which is notified by the Central Government as a Nidhi Company under section 620A of the Companies Act, 1956. It is an NBFC doing the business of lending and borrowing with its members or shareholders.
Miscellaneous Non-Banking Company (MNBC) *i.e.* Chit Fund Companies	Managing, conducting or supervising as a promoter, foreman or agent of any transaction or arrangement by which the company enters into an agreement with a specified number of subscribers that every one of them shall subscribe a certain amount in instalments over a definite period and that every one of such subscribers shall in turn, as determined by lot or by auction or by tender or in such manner as may be provided for in the arrangement, be entitled to the prize amount.

Bandhan Bank

Bandhan Financial Services, a Micro Financial Institution (MFI), on August 23, 2015 started operations as a Scheduled Commercial Bank (SCB). Henceforth it has been named as Bandhan Bank. The banking services were inaugurated by the Union Finance Minister Arun Jaitley in Kolkata. On the inaugural day, the bank started operations with 501 branches in 24 states across the country with 1.43 crore accounts.

With this, Bandhan became the first micro finance company in the country to start operations as a full-fledged commercial bank. It is also the first commercial bank from Eastern India to get RBI clearance since independence. Bandhan started as a Non-Banking Finance Company in 2001 and focused on the lower strata of the especially unorganized sector workers.

Payment Banks

Opening the way for revolutionising cashless payments services in the country, the Reserve Bank of India has granted Payment Bank licences to 11 firms. These 11 applicants that have got 'in principle' approval for setting up payments banks will provide barebones facilities aimed at covering the vast population that has no access to financial services. They will take deposits, convey, remittances and dispense payments to recipients, making them ideal for migrant workers who need to send money home, for instance. These 11 licence obtaining firms include telecom companies Vodafone and Airtel; non-banking financial company Cholamandalam Distribution Services Ltd; large conglomerates Reliance Industries and Aditya Birla Nuvo; and individuals Vijay Shekhar Sharma, founder of Paytm, and Dilip Shanghvi, Managing Director of Sun

Pharmaceuticals. The Department of Posts, FinoPaytech, Tech Mahindra and National Securities Depository Ltd also got place in the list.

Payments banks differ from conventional banks as they are not allowed to lend to customers or issue credit cards. They can, however, accept deposits of up to 1 lakh and can offer current and savings account deposits. They can also issue debit cards and offer internet banking.

Of the 11 companies that were given in-principle nod by RBI to set up Payments Bank in August 2015, three-Tech Mahindra, Cholamandalam Finance and Dilip Shanghvi-IDFC Bank-Telenor JV, have already dropped out.

- Liquidity Adjustment Facility (LAF) is started by RBI in June 2000.
- Liquidity Adjustment Facility (LAF) refers to RBI's policy of Using Repos and Reverse Repos to adjust liquidity on a day to day basis.
- Regional Rural Banks (RRBs) were established since 1975 under the provisions of the RRB Act 1976 with a view to developing the rural economy as well as to creating an alternative channel to 'Co-operatives'.
- With a view to consolidating and strengthening RRBs, the Government of India initiated in September 2005, the process of amalgamation of RRBs in a phased manner.
- RBI introduced a Banking ombudsman scheme in the country on June 14, 1995, for giving a solution for customer's complaints.
- The IDBI which was established as Development Finance Institution under IDBI Act, 1964 has been converted as a banking company (on October 11, 2004)
- Small Industries Development Bank of India (SIDBI) was established as wholly-owned subsidiary of IDBI under the Small Industries Development Bank of India Act, 1989 as the principal financial institution for promotion, financing and development of industries in the Small Scale Sector. Its headquarter is situated at Lucknow.
- ICICI was established in 1955 as public limited company under Indian Companies Act for developing medium and small industries of private sector.
- With effect from May 3, 2002, erstwhile ICICI limited and two of its wholly-owned subsidiaries were merged with ICICI Bank. The appointed date for merger was March 30, 2002.
- In 1987, a National Equity Fund Scheme was started for providing equity assistance to Tiny Small Scale units having capital investment of less than ₹ 10 lakh and working in areas having population less than 5 lakh (15 lakh for hill areas and north-east areas). SIDBI and Central Government contribute 50:50 share in this scheme of SIDBI.
- IRBI was established on March 20, 1985 under Indian Industrial Reconstruction Bank Act, 1984 as a Result of reconstituting Indian Industrial Reconstruction Corporation Ltd. The basic aim of establishing IRBI was to revive sick and closed industrial units and to act as a prime loan and reconstruction agency.
- But now under the new arrangements, IRBI is functioning with the new name IIBIL (Industrial Investment Bank of India Ltd.). IIBIL's head office is situated at Kolkata.
- State Governments have established State Industrial Development Corporations (SIDCs) under their sole ownerships. The objectives of SIDCs include:

  (*i*) To develop industrial areas

  (*ii*) To ensure market facilities

  (*iii*) To establish new development centres.
- EXIM bank in India was established on January 1, 1982 for financing, facilitaing and promoting foreign trade in India. Besides, EXIM Bank also discharge duties of coordinating the activities of various financial institutions, providing finances for export-imports of goods and services.
- Besides India, this bank also manages finances to third world countries for export-import of goods and services.

Establishment Years of Major Financial Institutions in India

❑ Imperial Bank of India	1921
❑ Reserve Bank of India (Nationalisation of RBI took place on January 1, 1949)	April 1, 1935
❑ Industrial Finance Corporation of India (IFCI)	1948
❑ State Bank of India (SBI)	July 1, 1955
❑ Unit Trust of India (UTI)	Feb. 1, 1964
❑ IDBI	July 1964
❑ NABARD	July 12, 1982
❑ IRBI (Now it has been renamed as IIBIL since March 6, 1997)	March 20, 1985
❑ SIDBI	1990
❑ EXIM Bank	January 1, 1982
❑ National Housing Bank (NHB)	July 1988
❑ Life Insurance Corporation (LIC)	September 1956
❑ General Insurance Corporation (GIC)	November 1972
❑ Regional Rural Banks (RRBs)	Oct. 2, 1975
❑ Risk Capital and Technology Finance Corporation Ltd.	March 1975
❑ Technology Development & Information Co. of India Ltd.	1989
❑ Infrastructure Leasing & Financial Services Ltd.	1988
❑ Housing Development Finance Corporation Ltd. (HDFC)	1977

- National Housing Bank (NHB) was established in July 1988 as wholly owned subsidiary of RBI. A major activity of NHB includes extending financial assistance to eligible institutions in the housing sector by way of refinance and direct finance.
- National Bank for Agriculture and Rural Development (NABARD) is the apex banking institution providing finance for agriculture and rural development.
- It was established on July 12, 1982 with the paid-up capital of ₹ 100 crore having 50:50 contribution of Indian Government and RBI. NABARD's head office is situated at Mumbai.
- IDFC (Infrastructure Development Finance Company) was proposed to be established on January 31, 1997, Under Companies Act, 1956, for financing infrastructure sector for the country. The mission of IDFC is to:
  - (*i*) Lead private capital to commercially viable intrastructural projects in India.
  - (*ii*) Provide a strong policy advisory role to government to meet this objective.
  - (*iii*) Develop and strengthen the connectivity of infrastructure projects to markets and institutions.
- Agriculture and Rural Development Banks basically known as Land Mortgage Banks/Land Development Banks have now been

redesignated as Agricultural and Rural Development. These banks provide long term credit to agriculture and rural sector. A two-tier structure is in operation:

⇒ State Co-operative and Rural Development Banks (SCARDBs).

⇒ Primary Co-operative Agriculture and Rural Development Banks (PCARDBs).

- Under an Act passed by the parliament, on September 1, 1956 Life Insurance Corporation (LIC) of India was established with the capital of ₹ 5 crore given by the Government of India. LIC head office is situated at Mumbai.
- General Insurance Company (GIC) was established in November, 1972.
- The insurance sector was opened for private participation with the enactment of Insurance Regulatory and Development Authority Act (IRDA Act), 1999.
- On the recommendation of Malhotra committee, government has permitted privatization of Insurance sector. The committee was constituted in April 1993.

Base Year of Existing Price Indices in India

Price Index	*Base Year*
1. New Wholesale Price Index	2011-12
2. Consumer Price Index for Industrial Workers	2001
3. Industrial Production Index	2011-12
4. Consumer Price Index for Urban Non-manual Employees	1984-85
5. Consumer Price Index for Agriculture Labourers	1986-87

Non-Performing Assets (NPA)

In simple words the assets of the Banks which don't perform (means don't bring any return) are called Non- Performing Assets. In more general sense they are 'bad loans'. Any asset, including a based asset, becomes non-performing when it ceases to generate income for the bank.

However, there is a prescribed definition by the RBI which defines the NPAs as—

- Terms loans on which interest and/or instalment of principal remain overdue for a particular quarter for a period of more than 90 days from the end of that particular quarter.
- The Bills those remain overdue for a period of more than 90 days from the end of a quarter.
- Any amount to be received remains overdue for a period of more than 90 days.
- The Cash Credit Account remains out of order for a period of more than 90 days. Out of order means over the sanctioned limit.

Printing of Securities and Minting in India

- ***India Security Press (Nasik Road) :*** Postal Material, Postal Stamps, Non-postal Stamps, Judicial and Non-judicial Stamps, Cheques, Bonds, NSCs, Kisan Vikas Patras, Securities of State Governments, Public Sector Enterprise and Financial Corporations.
- ***Security Printing Press (Hyderabad) :*** Established in 1982 for meeting the demand for postal material by Southern States. It also fulfils the demand for Union Excise Duty Stamps of the Country.
- ***Currency Notes Press (Nasik Road):*** Since 1991, this press prints currency notes of ₹ 1, ₹ 2, ₹ 5, ₹ 10, ₹ 50, and ₹ 100. (Earlier printing of ₹ 50 and ₹ 100 currency notes was not done here).
- ***Bank Notes Press (Dewas):*** Currency notes of ₹ 20, ₹ 50, ₹ 100 and ₹ 500 are printed here.
- ***Modernised Currency Notes Press:*** Two new modernised currency notes press are established at Mysore (Karnataka) and Salboni (West Bengal).
- ***Security Paper Hoshangabad*** (Established in 1967-68) makes production of Bank and Currency notes paper.
- ***Coins are minted at four places:*** Mumbai, Kolkata, Hyderabad and Noida.

9. CAPITAL MARKET

- Capital Market may be defined as a market dealing in medium and long-term funds. It is an institutional arrangement for borrowing medium and long term funds and which provides facilities for marketing and trading of securities.
- Capital Market Constitutes all long term borrowings from banks and financial institutions, borrowings from foreign markets and raising of capital by issue various securities such as share debentures, bonds etc.
- For trading of securities there are two different segments in capital market. They are:

  1. Primary Market, 2. Secondary Market.

Primary Market

- The primary market deals with new/fresh issue of securities and is, therefore known as new issue market.
- The new issue market primarily consists of the arrangements, which facilitates the procurement of long-term finance by the companies in the form of shares, debentures and bonds. The companies usually issue those securities at the initial stages of their formation and so also later on for expansion and/or modernization of their activities.
- However, the selling of securities is not an easy task, as the companies have to fulfil various legal requirements and decide upon the appropriate timing and the method of issue.
- The new issues seek assistance of various intermedian'es such as merchant bankers, underwriters, stock brokers etc. All these intermediaries form an integral part of the primary market.

Secondary Market

- The secondary market is an association or organisation or a body of individuals established for the purpose of assisting, regulating and controlling the business of buying selling and dealing in securities.
- It may noted that it is called a secondary market because only the securities already issued can be traded on the floor of the stock exchange.
- Secondary market is open only to its members, most of whom are brokers acting as agents of the buyers and sellers of securities.
- The main functions of this market lie in providing liquidity to securities and safety in dealing. It is because of the availability of such facilities that people are ready to invest in securities.

Distinction Between Capital Market and Money Market

Capital Market	Money Market
1. The capital market is related to long term funds.	1. Money market is related to short term fund.
2. The capital market deals in shares, debentures, bonds and government securities.	2. Money market deals in securities like treasury bills, commercial papers, trade bills, deposit certificates etc.
3. The participants in capital market are stockbrokers, underwriters, mutual funds, financial institutions and individual investors.	3. The participants in money market are RBI, commercial banks, NBFCs etc.
4. The capital market is regulated by Securities Exchange Board of India (SEBI).	4. Money market is regulated by RBI.

- Discount Bill Market is one that deals in short-term loans. Treasury Bills and Commercial Bills of Exchange also fall in this category.
- Dividend is the amount which the company distributes to shareholders when the profits of the company are calculated by the board of directors.

- The debenture is a written acknowledgement of money borrowed. It specifies the terms and conditions, such as rate of interest, time of repayment, security offered, etc. These are offered to the public to subscribe in the same manner as is done in the case of shares.
- Share is the smallest unit into which the total capital of the company is divided. For example, when a company decides to raise ₹ 50 crores of capital from the public by issuing shares, then it can divide its capital into units of a definite value, say ₹ 10/or ₹ 100/- each, these individual units are called as its share. In order to tap the savings of different types of people, a company can issue two type of Shares—(*a*) Equity Shares, and (*b*) Preference Shares.
  (*a*) ***Equity Shares:*** Equity shares are shares, which do not enjoy any preferential right in the matter of claim of dividend or repayment of capital. The equity shareholders get dividend only after making the payment of dividends on preference shares. There is no fixed rate of dividend for equity shareholders.
  (*b*) ***Preference Shares:*** Preference Shares are those shares, which carry preferential rights in respect of dividend and return of capital. Before any dividend is paid to the equity shares, the dividend at a fixed rate must be paid on the preference shares. However, this dividend is payable only if there are profits.
- Financial institutions which are engaged in borrowing and lending money are called financial intermediaries. It also includes commercial banks. Financial intermediary is a middle man between manufacturer and whole-seller and retailer and between a retailer and consumer.
- Business in the country's oldest stock exchange, namely the Bombay Stock Exchange (BSE) dating back to 1875, which is also one of the oldest stock exchanges in the world, continued to operate.
- The National Stock Exchange (NSE), which emerged in the mid-1990 and catalysed improvements in trading system to provide the necessary depth and choice to investors, made sustained progress.
- On June 15, 1998 National Stock Exchange has launched two new Reference Rates for the loans of Inter-Bank Call Money Market. These rates are MIBOR (Mumbai Inter Bank Offer Rate) and MIBID (Mumbai Inter-Bank Bide Rate)
- MIBOR will be the indicator of Lending Rate for loans while MIBID will be the lending rate for receipts.

Difference between Shares and Debenture

S.No.	Basis	Shares	Debentures
1.	Status	Shareholders are the owners of the company. They provide ownership capital which is not refundable unless the company is liquidated.	Debentureholders are the creditors of the company. They provide loans generally for a fixed period, which are to be paid back.
2.	Nature of return on investment	Shareholders get dividends. Its amount is not fixed as it depends on the profit of the company.	Interest is paid on debentures at a fixed rate. Interest is payable even if the company is running at a loss.
3.	Rights	Shareholders are the real owners of the company. They have the right to vote and determine the policies of the company.	Debentureholders do not have the right to attend meetings of the company. So they have no say in the management of the company.
4.	Security	No security is required to issue shares.	Generally debentures are secured. So, sufficient fixed assets are required when debentures are to be issued.
5.	Order of repayment	Share capital is paid back only after paying the debentureholders and creditors.	Debentureholders have the priority of repayment over shareholders.
6.	Risk	Risk is high due to uncertainty of returns.	Little risk due to certainty of return.

Difference between equity shares and preference shares

S.No.	Basis of difference	Equity shares	Preference Shares
1.	Choice	It is compulsory to issue these shares.	It is not compulsory to issue these shares.
2.	Payment of dividend	Dividend is paid on these shares only after paying dividend on preference shares.	Dividend is paid on these shares in preference to the equity shares.
3.	Return of capital	In case of winding up of the company the equity share capital is refunded only after the refund of preference share capital.	In case of winding up of the company the capital is refunded in preference over the equity shares.
4.	Voting Right	The equity shareholders enjoy voting rights.	The preference shareholders do not have voting rights.
5.	Accumulation of Dividend	The dividends on equity shares are not accumulated and therefore cannot be carried forward.	The unpaid dividends are accumulated and are carried forward to the future years in case of cumulative preference shares.

Securities and Exchange Board of India (SEBI)

- Securities and Exchange Board of India (SEBI) is an independent statutory regulatory authority.
- SEBI was initially constituted on April 12, 1988 as a non-statutory body through a resolution of the Government for dealing with all matters relating to development and regulation of securities market and investor protection and to advise the Government of all these matters.
- SEBI was given statutory status and powers through an ordinance promulgated on January 30, 1992.
- SEBI is managed by six members—one chairman (nominated by Central Government), two members (officers of Central Ministries), one member (from RBI) and remaining two members are nominated by Central Government.
- The office of SEBI is situated at Mumbai with its regional office at Kolkata, Delhi and Chennai.

Functions of SEBI

- To safeguard the interests of investors and to regulate capital market with suitable measures.
- To regulate the business of stock exchanges and other securities market.
- To regulate the working of Stock Brokers. Sub-brokers, Share Transfer Agents, Trustees, Merchant Bankers, Underwriters, Portfolio Managers etc. and also to make their registration.
- To register and regulate collective investment plans of mutual funds.
- To encourage self-regulatory organisations.
- To eliminate malpractices of security markets.
- To train the persons associated with security markets and also to encourage investors' education.
- To check insider trading of securities.
- To supervise the working of various organisations trading in security market and also to ensure systematic dealings.
- To promote research and investigations for ensuring the attainment of above objectives.

	Recognised Stock Exchanges in India
1.	U.P. Stock Exchange, Kanpur
2.	Vadodara Stock Exchange, Vadodara
3.	Koyambtour Stock Exchange, Coimbatore
4.	Meerut Stock Exchange, Meerut
5.	Mumbai Stock Exchange, Mumbai

6.	Over the Counter Exchange of India, Mumbai
7.	National Stock Exchange, Mumbai
8.	Ahmedabad Stock Exchange, Ahmedabad
9.	Bangalore Stock Exchange, Bangalore
10.	Bhubaneshwar Stock Exchange, Bhubaneshwar
11.	Calcutta Stock Exchange, Kolkata
12.	Cochin Stock Exchange, Cochin
13.	Delhi Stock Exchange, Delhi
14.	Guwahati Stock Exchange, Guwahati
15.	Hyderabad Stock Exchange, Hyderabad
16.	Jaipur Stock Exchange, Jaipur
17.	Canara Stock Exchange, Mangalore
18.	Ludhiana Stock Exchange, Ludhiana
19.	Chennai Stock Exchange, Chennai
20.	M.P. Stock Exchange, Indore
21.	Magadh Stock Exchange, Patna
22.	Pune Stock Exchange, Pune
23.	Capital Stock Exchange Kerala Ltd. Thiruvananthapuram, Kerala

Concept of Depository System

Depository system is that system in which ownership of security is changed by an electronic account entry and physical transaction of securities does not take place. The main functions of depository are as follows:

- To accept deposits for ensuring safe custody of securities.
- To make computerised account entry for ensuring evidence of ownership transfer.
- To keep record of mortgaged securities.

Different countries possess generally two types of depositories:

(*a*) Securities immobilisation system of depositories.

(*b*) Securities dematerialisation system of depositories.

Main Share Price Index in Famous Share Market of the World

BSE (Mumbai)	SENSEX
NSE (Mumbai)	S & P CNX Nifty
New York	DOW JONES
Tokyo	NIKKEI
Frankfurt (Germany)	MID DAX
Hong Kong	HANG SENG
Singapore	SIMEX STRAITS TIMES

10. PUBLIC FINANCE

- Direct Taxes are—Income Tax, Corporation Tax, Wealth Tax, Estate Duty, Gift Tax, Expenditure Tax and Interest Tax.
- Indirect Taxes are—Custom Duties, Union Excise Duties, Sale/Purchase Tax, Advertisements Tax.
- India possesses a federal structure in which a clear distinction is made between the Union and the State functions and sources of revenue.
- Our constitution provides residual powers of the centre. Article 264 and 293 explain the financial relations between the Union and State Government.

A. The List I of Seventh Schedule of Indian Constitution enlists the Union taxes which are as follows:

- Taxes on income other than agriculture income
- Corporation tax
- Custom duties
- Excise duties except on alcoholic liquors and narcotics not contained in medical or toilet preparation
- Estate and succession duties other than on agricultural land
- Taxes on the capital value of assets except agricultural land of individuals and companies

- Rates of stamp duties on financial documents
- Taxes other than stamp duties on transactions in stock exchanges and future markets
- Taxes on sales or purchases of newspapers and on advertisements therein
- Taxes on railway freight and fares
- Terminal taxes on goods or passengers carried by railways, sea or air
- Taxes on the sale or purchase of goods in the course of inter state trade

B. List II of Seventh Schedule enlists the taxes which are within the jurisdiction of the states:

- Land revenue
- Taxes on the sale and purchase of goods, except newspapers
- Taxes on agricultural income
- Taxes on land buildings
- Succession and estate duties on agricultural land
- Excise on alcoholic liquors and narcotics
- Taxes on the entry of goods into a local area
- Taxes on the consumption and sale of electricity
- Taxes on mineral rights (subject to any limitations imposed by the Parliament)
- Taxes on vehicles, animals and boats
- Stamp duties except those on financial documents
- Taxes on luxuries including entertainments, betting and gambling
- Tolls
- Taxes on professions, trades, callings and employment
- Capitation taxation
- Taxes on advertisements other than those contained in newspapers

C. Apart from taxes levied and collected by the states, the constitution has provided for the revenues for certain taxes on the union list to be alloted, partly or wholly to the states. These provisions fall into various categories:

- Duties which are levied by the Union Government but are collected and appropriated by the States. These include stamp duties, excise duties on medical preparations containing alcohol or narcotics.
- Taxes which are levied and collected by the union, but the entire proceeds of which are assigned to the states, in proportion determined by the Parliament.

  These taxes include:

  (*i*) Succession and Estate duty

  (*ii*) Taxes on railway freight and fares

  (*iii*) Terminal taxes on goods and passengers

  (*iv*) Taxes on transactions in stock exchanges and future markets

  (*v*) Taxes on sale and purchase of newspapers and advertisements therein
- Central taxes on income and union excise duties are levied and collected by the union but are shared by it with the states in a prescribed manner.
- Proceeds of additional excise duty on mill made textiles, sugar and tobacco which are levied by the union since 1957 in replacement of state sales taxes on these commodities, are wholly distributed among the states in a manner as to guarantee their former incomes from the displaced sales taxes.
- The central government levies four main taxes, viz; taxes on income (personal income tax and corporation tax), customs duties. Union excise duties and service tax. These taxes account for almost total tax proceeds of the central government.
- The principal tax revenue sources of the state government are the share of the state in the central taxes and duties, commercial taxes land revenue, stamp duties and registration fees and the state excise duties on alcohol and other narcotics, of all commercial taxes, sales tax has been the most important. However, this tax has been now replaced by Value Added Tax (VAT).
- Corporation Tax is the major source of central government revenue.
- Like all other countries, tendency of income tax is progressive in India.

- The Laffer Effect which implies that a reduction in the rate of taxation leads to more than proportionate increase in tax yield.
- In India, the base of income tax is very narrow.
- Minimum Alternative Tax—MAT has been levying on companies.
- Estate Duty was first introduced in India in 1953. It was levied on total property passing on the death of a person. The whole property of the deceased constituted the estate and was considered liable to pay estate duty. Hence, the central government decided to abolish it with effect from April 1, 1985.
- An Annual Tax on wealth was first introduced in May 1957 on the recommendations of Kaldor. It is levied on the excess of net wealth over exemption of individuals, joint Hindu families and companies.
- Excise duties on commodities other than alcoholic liquors and narcotics are levied by the central government.
- The state have exclusive jurisdiction over the excise duties on alcohol and narcotics.
- Service tax was introduced in 1994-95 in a small way to operationalise the principle of neutrality of the tax system to different forms of production and in recognition of the fact that value additions whether in manufacturing or service should form the basis of taxation.
- VAT (Value Added Tax) seeks to tax the value added at every stage of manufacturing and sale, with a provision of refunding the amount of VAT already paid at earlier stages to avoid double taxation. In other words, the tax already paid can be claimed at the next stage of value addition.
- Following the June 18, 2004 decision of the Empowered Committee of State Finance Ministers to implement state-level VAT from April 1, 2005, all states/UTs had introduced VAT to replace the sales tax by December 31, 2005.
- Haryana was the first state to introduce VAT in 2003.
- MODVAT, was introduced in budget of 1986-87.
- Nobel Prize recipient Prof. James Tobin had suggested in 1978 to impose a tax on all transactions in Foreign Money Markets. Tobin was of the opinion that most of transactions of foreign currencies are for speculation and arbitrage benefits which can be used for mobilising enough resources by imposing a tax. This suggested tax was given a name of 'Tobin Tax'.
- CENVAT, was introduced at first in budget of 2000-01.
- Performance Budgetting is generally understood as a system of presentation of public expenditure in terms of functions, programmes, performance units, viz; activities, projects, etc., reflecting primarily the government output and its cost. At first it adopted by USA federal government in 1951.
- Zero-base budgeting (ZBB) is an innovative technique to guard against wastage in public expenditure. The technique works not through auditing which is a post-operative check, but through an examination of the very rational of an expenditure item under consideration.
- In the sphere of public budgeting, ZBB was first tried by Mr. Jimmy Carter in 1973 when he was the Governor of Georgia, Later on it was adopted by a number of states in the USA.
- GST full form is Good and Services Tax in India. GST applies throughout India and is indirect tax. Moreover from now on GST replaces many taxes. Generally state and central Governments levy taxes. But after may meetings, Finance Minister of India and Indian Government Introduced GST on July 1, 2017. Government of India introduced Goods and Services Tax as the Constitution Act 2017.
- Finance Commission is constituted to define financial relations between the Centre and the States. Under the provision of Article 280(1) of the constitution, the President appoints a Finance Commission for the specific purpose of devolution of non-plan revenue resources.

Finance Commission: At a Glance

Finance Commission	*Chairman*	*Operational Duration*
I	K.C. Niyogi	1952-57
II	K. Santhanam	1957-62
III	A.K. Chanda	1962-66
IV	P.V. Rajamannar	1966-69
V	Mahaveer Tyagi	1969-74
VI	Brahma Nand Reddy	1974-79
VII	J.M. Shellet	1979-84
VIII	Y.B. Chawan	1984-89
IX	N.K.P. Salve	1989-95
X	K.C. Pant	1995-00
XI	A.M. Khusro	2000-05
XII	Dr. C. Rangrajan	2005-10
XIII	V.L. Kelkar	2010-15
XIV	Y.V. Reddy	2015-20
XV	N.K. Singh	2020-25

Various Types of Deficits of the Central Government

- Budget may take a shape of deficit when the public revenue falls short to public expenditure. Budget deficit is the difference between the estimated public expenditure and public revenue. The government meets this deficit by way of printing new currency or by borrowing. Some types of deficits are as follows:

- **Revenue Deficits:** Revenue Deficit = Revenue Expenditure-Revenue Receipts

  Current revenue expenditure of the central government is composed of plan and non-plan expenditure, and current-revenue receipts include net tax revenue and non-tax revenue of the central government.

- **Budget Deficit:** Budget Deficit = Total Expenditure—Total Receipts

  The total expenditure of the central governments always exceeded its total revenue which is known as budget deficit or overall budgetary deficit.

- **Fiscal Deficit:** In simple terms, fiscal deficit is budgetary deficit plus market borrowings and other liabilities of the government of India.

  ∴ Fiscal Deficit = Revenue receipts (Net tax revenue + Non-tax revenue) + Capital receipts (only recoveries of loans and other receipts)–Total expenditure (Plan and non-plan)

- **Primary Deficit:** The excess of fiscal deficit over payments of interest is called primary deficit.

- **Monetised Deficit:** The increase in net RBI credit for central government is called monetised deficit. It includes:

  A. Net increase in holdings of treasury bills of RBI.

  B. Contribution of RBI in market borrowings of the govt.

Important Committees: At a Glance

Committees	Constituted Year	Related Area
• **Hanumant Rao Committee**	*28 January, 1997*	Fertilisers
• **Mahajan Committee**	*March 1997*	Sugar Industry
• **R.V. Gupta Committee**	*December 1997*	Agriculture Credit
• **Narsimham Committee (Second)**	*1997*	Banking Reforms
• **Khan Working Group**	*1998*	Development Finance Institutions
• **Chandrate Committee**	*Feb. 1997*	Delisting in Share Market
• **UK Sharma Committee**	*January 1998*	NABARD's role in RRB
• **Ajit Kumar Committee**	*December 1997*	Army Pay Scales
• **CB Bhave Committee**	*October 27, 1997*	Company Information

Committies	Constituted Year	Related Area
• **NN Vohra Committee**	*September 8, 1997*	Relations of Politicians with Criminals
• **Bimal Julka Committee**	—	Working Conditions ATCOS
• **Dhanuka Committee**	—	Simplification of Transfer Rules in Securities Market
• **C. Babu Rajeev Committee**	—	Reforming Ship Act, 1908 and Ship Trust Act, 1963.
• **S.L. Kapoor Committee**	*December 1997*	Credit & Flow Problems of SSIs
• **Dave Committee**	2000	Pension Scheme for Unorganised Sector
• **Mashelkar Committee**	Jan. 2002	Auto Fuel Policy
• **S.N. Verma Committee**	1999	Restructuring the Commercial Banks
• **Y.B. Reddy Committee**	Oct. 2001	Review of Income Tax Rebates
• **Bhurelal Committee**	—	Increase in Motor Vehicle Tax
• **Sapta Rishi Committee**	July 2002	Development of Domestic Tea Industry
• **Abhijit Sen Committee**	July 2002	Long Term Food Policy
• **Kelkar Committee**	—	Tax Structure Reforms
• **J.J. Irani Committee**	—	Company Law Reforms
• **Parekh Committee**	—	Infrastructure Financing

International Organisation: At a Glance

Organisation	Establishment Year	Head quarter	Important Features
1. IMF and IBRD	1945	Washington D.C.	IBRD, IFC, IDA, MIGA are associate institutions of World Bank. Initially IBRD was constituted in 1945. IFC and IDA were established in 1956 and 1960 respectively
2. European Union	Changed form of EEC Established in 1958	Brussels	19 nations have accepted to circulate a common 'EURO' currency since January 1, 1999 (10 nations joined the EU since May 1, 2004)
3. OPEC	1960	Vienna (Austria)	—
4. OECD	1961	Paris	Changed name of OEEC established in 1948
5. ADB	1966	Manila	—
6. ASEAN	1967	Jakarta	Indonesia, Philippines, Malaysia, Singapore, Thailand, Brunei, Vietnam, Laos, Myanmar and Combodia.
7. ACU	1975	Tehran	India, Pakistan, Bangladesh, Nepal, Sri Lanka, Iran, Myanmar, Bhutan and Maldives

8. SAARC	1985	Kathmandu	India, Pakistan, Bhutan, Bangladesh, Sri Lanka, Nepal, Maldives and Afghanistan. SAARC nations started SAPTA since December 7, 1995, but since January 1, 2006 SAPTA has been replaced by SAFTA.
9. G-15	1989	Geneva	A group of 17 developing countries
10. APEC	1989	—	APEC declared to convert Asia pacific region into free trade zone by 2020 A.D. which will be the largest free trade area of the world.
11. NAFTA	1992	—	USA, Canada and Mexico
12. WTO	1995	Geneva	—
13. Mercosur	1995	—	Brazil, Argentina, Paraguay, Uruguay & Venezuela (Free trade zone of south American region)
14. ASEM	1996	—	27 countries of EU, 10 from ASEAN, and 8 other countries including Japan, South Korea and China
15. BRICS	2014	Shanghai China	Brazil, Russia, India, China, South Africa

EXERCISE

1. Which state has maximum branches of public sector commercial banks?
(*a*) U.P. (*b*) Maharashtra
(*c*) Karnataka (*d*) Gujarat

2. In which plan phase of industrialisation was initiated?
(*a*) Fourth (*b*) Third
(*c*) Second (*d*) First

3. Which is the first Export Processing Zone declared as Free Trade Zone in India?
(*a*) Santacruz (*b*) Kandla
(*c*) Falta (*d*) Noida

4. Which institution is known as 'soft loan window' of World Bank?
(*a*) IFC
(*b*) IDA
(*c*) IMF
(*d*) Indian Development Forum

5. 'Backwash Effect' was firstly introduced by—
(*a*) Gunnar Myrdal (*b*) Peter Suderland
(*c*) Arthur Dunkel (*d*) Kindelberger

6. Meera Seth Committee was related to—
(*a*) Development of Handlooms
(*b*) Sex-differentiation in employment
(*c*) Abolition of Child Labour
(*d*) Welfare of working women

7. Finance Commission is appointed by the President under Article—
(*a*) 256 of constitution
(*b*) 280 of constitution
(*c*) 293 of constitution
(*d*) 356 of constitution

8. 'SAPTA' is related to—
(*a*) Education (*b*) Trade
(*c*) Security (*d*) Environment

9. National Income estimates in India is prepared by—
(*a*) Planning Commission
(*b*) RBI
(*c*) Finance Ministry
(*d*) C.S.O.

10. Scheduled bank is that bank which is—
(*a*) Nationalised
(*b*) Not–nationalised
(*c*) Based at foreign country
(*d*) Included in the second schedule of R.B.F

11. The definition of small scale industry in India is based on—
(*a*) Sales of a unit
(*b*) Investment in machines and equipment
(*c*) Market coverage
(*d*) Export capacity

12. Which one of the following committees was set up to review the concept of poverty line?
(*a*) S. Chakravarty Committee
(*b*) K.N. Wanchoo Committee
(*c*) D.T. Lakdawala Committee
(*d*) R.C. Dutt Committee

13. Which one of the folloiwng is not the canon of taxation as stated by Adam Smith?
(*a*) Canon of productivity
(*b*) Canon of convenience
(*c*) Canon of certainty
(*d*) None of these

14. According to 2011 census the state having highest urban population is—
(*a*) U.P. (*b*) Maharashtra
(*c*) Tamil Nadu (*d*) Kerala

15. Which place India holds in milk production?
(*a*) Fourth (*b*) Third
(*c*) Second (*d*) First

16. Who is the chairman of Island Development Authority?
(*a*) President (*b*) Prime Minister
(*c*) Home Minister (*d*) Planning Minister

17. The book 'Politics with Charkha' is written by—
(*a*) Ashok Mehta (*b*) J.B. Kriplani
(*c*) K.G. Mashruwala (*d*) Morarji Desai

18. The base year of the present Wholesale Price Index (WPI) is—
(*a*) 2011-12 (*b*) 1971-72
(*c*) 1980-81 (*d*) 1981-82

19. The base year of present Consumer Price Index (CPI) for industrial labourers is—
(*a*) 2001 (*b*) 1981
(*c*) 1982 (*d*) 1985

20. CAPART is related with—
(*a*) Assisting and evaluating rural welfare programmes
(*b*) Computer hardware
(*c*) Consultant service of export promotion
(*d*) Controlling pollution in big industries

21. Note issuing deptt. of RBI should always possess the minimum gold stock of worth—
(*a*) ₹ 85 crores (*b*) ₹ 115 crores
(*c*) ₹ 200 crores (*d*) None of these

22. Which of the following does not grant any tax rebate?
(*a*) National Saving Certificate
(*b*) Indira Vikas Patra
(*c*) National Saving Scheme
(*d*) Public Provident Fund

23. 13th Finance Commission was constituted under the chairmanship of—
(*a*) C. Rangrajan (*b*) V.L. Kelkar
(*c*) K.C. Pant (*d*) None of these

24. SEBI was established in—
(*a*) 1993 (*b*) 1992
(*c*) 1988 (*d*) 1990

25. The working of SEBI includes—
(*a*) To regulate the dealings of share market
(*b*) To check the foul dealings in share market
(*c*) To control the inside trading of shares
(*d*) All of these

26. The "Ad hoc Treasury Bill System" of meeting budget deficit in India was replaced by 'Ways and means Advances System' which has come into force on—
(*a*) March 31, 1997
(*b*) April 1, 1996
(*c*) April 1, 1997
(*d*) None of these

27. Asian Development Bank has opened its Residential Office in—
(*a*) New Delhi (*b*) Kolkata
(*c*) Mumbai (*d*) Bangalore

28. Which statement of the following is true for IMF?
(*a*) It is not an agency of UNO
(*b*) It can grant loan to any country of the world
(*c*) It can grant loan to state Govt. of a country
(*d*) It grants loan only to member nations

29. Chairman of Tax Reform Committee was—
(a) Pranab Mukherjee *(b)* K.P. Narsimham
(c) S. Janakiraman *(d)* Raja Chelliah

30. Which of the following is public sector organisation?
1. FCI Food Corporation of India
2. FCI Fertilizer Corporation of India
3. Cotton Corporation of India
4. Jute Corporation of India

(a) only 1 and 2 *(b)* only 2, 3
(c) only 3, 4 *(d)* All of these

31. Find the odd one out—
(a) SAIL *(b)* BHEL
(c) ONGC *(d)* ESSAR OIL

32. SAIL was established in—
(a) 1974 *(b)* 1984
(c) 1990 *(d)* 1964

33. Rural women can avail the benefit of Mahila Samriddhi Yojana if they open their account in–
(a) Rural Post Offices
(b) Commercial Banks
(c) Rural Development Bank
(d) Any of the above

34. Pradhan Mantri Gram Sadak Yojana (PMGSY) was launched in—
(a) 2000 *(b)* 1999
(c) 2001 *(d)* 2004

35. The Headquarter of CAPART is situated at—
(a) Mumbai *(b)* Kolkata
(c) New Delhi *(d)* Bangalore

36. The main security guard of International Trade is–
(a) IMF *(b)* World Bank
(c) WTO *(d)* IFC

37. Which is true for existing Economic and Industrial Policies of Indian Govt?
1. FERA was abolished
2. MRTP was abolished
3. Cash compensatory support for exports was abolished
4. Industrial licensing (except a few goods) was abolished

(a) 1, 2, 3 and 4 *(b)* 1, 3 and 4
(c) only 3 and 4 *(d)* only 2 and 3

38. Cheque which is crossed can be encashed only—
(a) Through SBI *(b)* Through the payee
(c) Through any bank *(d)* None of these

39. Post office funds will now be managed in capital market by—
(a) Unit Trust of India Mutual Fund
(b) SBI Mutual Fund
(c) LIC Mutual Fund
(d) Both (a) and (b)

40. One major proposal of New Industrial Policy (1991) was—
(a) NRIs will not be allowed for capital investment in India
(b) All types of industries have been made licence free
(c) Import restrictions of technical know-how for one year
(d) Facility of direct foreign investment upto 51% in high priority industries.

41. 'Closed Economy' is that economy in which—
(a) Only export takes place
(b) Money supply is fully controlled
(c) Deficit financing takes place
(d) Neither export nor import takes place

42. Which one of the following method is not used by N.S.S.O. for the measurement of unemployment in India?
(a) Current Monthly Status
(b) Current Weekly Status
(c) Current Daily Status
(d) Usual Principal Status

43. National Rural Development Institute is situated at—
(a) Shimla *(b)* Hyderabad
(c) Patna *(d)* New Delhi

44. Which of the following have/has not been included in wealth of a nation?
(a) Mines *(b)* Dams
(c) Money Supply *(d)* Animals

45. Which statement of the following is false (according to literacy data of 2011 census)?
(a) Literacy rate was calculated among people having age 6 years or above
(b) During 2001-2011, the number of literate population increased

(c) Indian literacy rate was estimated to be 73%
(d) Kerala was cent-per cent literate state

46. The Headquarter of World Bank is situated at—
(a) Manila (b) Washington D.C.
(c) New York (d) Geneva

47. Which state has a lower literacy rate than country's literacy rate according to 2011 census?
(a) Maharashtra (b) Gujarat
(c) Orissa (d) West Bengal

48. **Assertion (A):** From the point of view of technique of planning, there was little difference between India's 2nd and 3rd plan.
Reason (R): Despite sticking to Mahalanobis model both followed a balanced development approach.
(a) Both A and R are true and R is the correct explanation of A
(b) Both A and R are true but R is not a correct explanation of A
(c) A is true but R is false
(d) A is false but R is true

49. Which pair is not correct?
(a) EXIM Bank—Financing for export-import
(b) RBI—Banker's bank
(c) IDBI—Industrial finance
(d) FCI—Financial assistance to commercial institutions

50. Which of the rate is not determined by RBI?
(a) Bank Rate (b) CRR
(c) SLR (d) PLR

51. Which of the following controls the working of share market in India?
(a) MRTP Act (b) FERA
(c) BIFR (d) SEBI

52. The main foodgrains of India is—
(a) Rice (b) Wheat
(c) Sugarcane (d) Maize

53. Which rank India attains in tobacco production in the world?
(a) First (b) Sixth
(c) Second (d) Fourth

54. Which district of Hindi speaking belt has firstly been declared as fully literate?
(a) Narsinghpur (M.P.)
(b) Palampur (H.P.)
(c) Jhunjhanu (Rajasthan)
(d) Palamu (Jharkhand)

55. Which sector has the maximum quantum of disguised unemployment in India?
(a) Agriculture (b) Industry
(c) Trade (d) Transport

56. 'Food for work programme' was renamed as—
(a) RLEGP (b) IRDP
(c) NREP (d) MNP

57. The proportion of rainfed agriculture to the net sown area in India is about—
(a) 45% (b) 75%
(c) 50% (d) 52.4%

58. India has emerged in the world as the
(a) Second Largest Steel Producer
(b) Third Largest Steel Producer
(c) Fourth Largest Steel Producer
(d) None of these

59. Who is the ex-officio chairman of 'National Child Labour Abolition Authority'?
(a) Prime Minister
(b) Industry Minister
(c) Social Welfare Minister
(d) Labour Minister

60. Employees State Insurance Scheme in India was introduced in—
(a) 1947 (b) 1952
(c) 1955 (d) 1972

61. The goods can be taxed heavily to earn additional revenue if they are—
(a) Highly elastic (b) Unit elastic
(c) Perfectly elastic (d) Inelastic

62. Scheduled Bank is that bank which is—
(a) Nationalised
(b) Not nationalised
(c) Based at foreign country
(d) Included in the second schedule of RBI

63. For which type of fertilizer India is fully dependent on imports?
(a) Nitrogen Fertilizer
(b) Phosphetic Fertilizer
(c) Potash Fertilizer
(d) None of these

64. Which fertilizer is mostly consumed in India?
(*a*) N
(*b*) P
(*c*) K
(*d*) All are used in equal ratio

65. UNO has the maximum dues on—
(*a*) India (*b*) Mexico
(*c*) USA (*d*) Japan

66. Match the following—

List-I	***List-II***
A. Aquaculture	(1) Silk
B. Floriculture	(1) Grapes
C. Sericulture	(3) Flower
D. Viticulture	(4) Fisheries

	A	B	C	D
(*a*)	4	3	2	1
(*b*)	3	4	1	2
(*c*)	3	4	2	1
(*d*)	4	3	1	2

67. The CSO has changed the base year for national income estimates. The new base year is—
(*a*) 1990-91 (*b*) 2011-2012
(*c*) 1994-95 (*d*) 1995-96

68. The Ex-officio Secretary of NDC is—
(*a*) Secretary of Finance Ministry
(*b*) General Secretary of Lok Sabha
(*c*) Secretary of Planning Commission
(*d*) Vice-Chairman of Planning Commission

69. India's National Hydroelectric Power corporation is establishing 'Tamarthi Power Project' in—
(*a*) Bangladesh (*b*) Bhutan
(*c*) Myanmar (*d*) Nepal

70. 'Hydro carbon Vision-2025' is associated with—
(*a*) Storage of petroleum products
(*b*) Euro-I & Euro II
(*c*) Green house effect
(*d*) None of these

71. Which state possesses the maximum percentage of SC population?
(*a*) U.P. (*b*) M.P.
(*c*) Kerala (*d*) Punjab

72. Which country is not the member of IMF?
(*a*) Russia (*b*) Uzbekistan
(*c*) India (*d*) None of these

73. What is 'NIKKEI'?
(*a*) Share Price Index of Tokyo Share Market
(*b*) Name of Japanese Central Bank
(*c*) Japanese name of Country's Planning Commission
(*d*) Foreign Exchange Market of Japan

74. Which statement is correct for Indian Planning Commission?
(*a*) It is not defined in Indian Constitution
(*b*) Members and Vice-Chairman of it do not have fixed working duration
(*c*) Members do not require any minimum education
(*d*) All of these

75. SEBI is a:
(*a*) Statutory body (*b*) Advisory body
(*c*) Constitutional body (*d*) Non-statutory body

76. Who is the Chairman of NDC?
(*a*) Finance Minister (*b*) Prime Minister
(*c*) Planning Minister (*d*) Lok Sabha Speaker

77. NABARD was established on the recommendation of—
(*a*) Public Account Committee
(*b*) Shivaraman Committee
(*c*) Narsimham Committee
(*d*) None of these

78. "World Economic Outlook" report is published by:
(*a*) IMF (*b*) World Bank
(*c*) RBI (*d*) UNCTAD

79. The field given to Rangarajan Committee was—
(*a*) Modernisation of Cloth Industry
(*b*) To probe Share scam
(*c*) To probe Sugar scam
(*d*) To suggest measures for controlling BOP deficit

80. VAT is imposed—
(*a*) Directly on consumer
(*b*) On final stage of production
(*c*) On first stage of production
(*d*) On all stages between production and final sale

81. Kutir Jyoti scheme is associated with—
(*a*) Promoting cottage industry in villages
(*b*) Promoting employment among rural unemployed youth
(*c*) Providing electricity to rural families living below the poverty line
(*d*) All of these

82. The Headquarter of 'Economic and Social Commission for Asia and Pacific' is at—
(*a*) Singapore (*b*) Bangkok
(*c*) Manila (*d*) Hong Kong

83. OTCEI is—
(*a*) Atomic submarine of China
(*b*) Economic policy of USA
(*c*) A Indian Share Market
(*d*) A defence research organisation

84. Which is the most liquid measure of money supply?
(*a*) M_1 (*b*) M_2
(*c*) M_3 (*d*) M_4

85. M_3 measure of money supply does not include—
(*a*) Cash with public
(*b*) Demand deposits with Post offices
(*c*) Demand deposits with Banks
(*d*) Time deposits with Banks

86. Which public sector enterprise has become the largest from annual sales point of view?
(*a*) BHEL (*b*) SAIL
(*c*) IOCL (*d*) Coal India Ltd

87. NITI Aayog was constituted in—
(*a*) 1948 (*b*) 1949
(*c*) 2015 (*d*) 1951

88. Which of the following represents the correct combination of sex-ratio in India in 1951 and 2011?
(*a*) 941, 933 (*b*) 946, 943
(*c*) 946, 927 (*d*) 972, 933

89. Gresham's Law is related to—
(*a*) Consumption and Demand
(*b*) Supply and Demand
(*c*) Circulation of Money
(*d*) Deficit Financing

90. TRYSEM was—
(*a*) a modern technique of agriculture production
(*b*) a code used in space science
(*c*) a programme to train rural youth for self employment
(*d*) none of these

91. Kelkar committee report is related on—
(*a*) Tax Reforms
(*b*) Financial Sector Reforms
(*c*) Trade Reforms
(*d*) Administrative Reforms

92. The process of budget making after re-evaluating every item of expenditure in every financial year is known as—
(*a*) Performance Budgeting
(*b*) Deficit Budgeting
(*c*) Zero Based Budgeting
(*d*) Fresh Budgeting

93. Which place India holds in milk production?
(*a*) Fourth (*b*) Third
(*c*) Second (*d*) First

94. In which production India has attained self-sufficiency?
(*a*) Fertilizers (*b*) Foodgrains
(*c*) Edible oil (*d*) Petroleum

95. What is 'Super 301'?
(*a*) A name of modern computer
(*b*) A new variety of Rice
(*c*) American trade law
(*d*) American treatment name for Aids

96. If the capital stock is always stable, its depreciation will be—
(*a*) High (*b*) Low
(*c*) Zero (*d*) Infinite

97. The proportion of labour in GNP becomes low, due to the following reason—
(*a*) Wages lag behind prices
(*b*) Prices lag behind wages
(*c*) Profit lags behind prices
(*d*) Prices lag behind profit

98. When development in economy takes place the share of tertiary sector in National Income?
(*a*) Declines
(*b*) Increases
(*c*) Remains constant
(*d*) First rises and then falls

99. Which country among following is relatively more industrialised?
(*a*) Bangladesh (*b*) Thailand
(*c*) India (*d*) Pakistan

100. Plan expenditure in India is met by—
(*a*) Internal debt and other resources
(*b*) Assistance from Aid India Club
(*c*) Assistance from IMF
(*d*) Assistance from OECD countries

101. National Income in India is estimated by—
(*a*) NITI Aayog
(*b*) Finance Commission
(*c*) Indian Statistical Institute
(*d*) Central Statistical Organisation

102. Population Density means—
(*a*) No. of persons living per sq. km.
(*b*) No. of persons living per kilometre
(*c*) Ratio of population living below poverty line to total population
(*d*) No. of persons in a village

103. Which tax is collected by Panchayat?
(*a*) Sales Tax (*b*) Custom Duty
(*c*) Land Revenue (*d*) Tax on local fairs

104. Centralised planning was first adopted in the economy of—
(*a*) Russia (*b*) Poland
(*c*) China (*d*) India

105. Which sector got high rate of growth in its co-operative units?
(*a*) Sugar (*b*) Cotton Textile
(*c*) Jute (*d*) Cement

106. Which among the following states is a leading industrialised state?
(*a*) West Bengal (*b*) Orissa
(*c*) Maharashtra (*d*) Madhya Pradesh

107. The first fully literate district outside the Kerala State is—
(*a*) Wardhaman (West Bengal)
(*b*) Chingelpattu (Tamil Nadu)
(*c*) Nasik (Maharashtra)
(*d*) Merkata (Karnataka)

108. The Headquarter of IMF is in—
(*a*) New York (*b*) Washington D.C.
(*c*) London (*d*) Manila

109. Which committee recommended tax on Agriculture Holdings?
(*a*) Bhootlingam Committee
(*b*) Wanchoo Committee
(*c*) Raj Committee
(*d*) None of these

110. Which bank in India performs duties of Central Bank?
(*a*) Central Bank of India
(*b*) State Bank of India
(*c*) Reserve Bank of India
(*d*) Both (*a*) and (*b*)

111. Which part of separated UTI is under SEBI's regulation?
(*a*) UTI-I (*b*) UTI-II
(*c*) Both the above (*d*) None of these

112. Mixed Economy means—
(*a*) Co-existence of small and large industries
(*b*) Promoting both Agriculture and Industries in the economy
(*c*) Co-existence of public and private sectors
(*d*) Co-existence of rich and poor

113. Which statement of the following is true regarding India's foreign trade over past three years?
(*a*) Imports declined
(*b*) Exports declined
(*c*) Imports declined but exports increased
(*d*) Both import and export increased

114. Foreign currency which has a tendency of quick migration is called—
(*a*) Scarce currency (*b*) Soft currency
(*c*) Gold currency (*d*) Hot currency

115. Indian State having the lowest Infant Mortality Rate is—
(*a*) Maharashtra (*b*) Goa
(*c*) Gujarat (*d*) Kerala

116. Which state in India has largest area under production of food grains?
(*a*) Punjab (*b*) Uttar Pradesh
(*c*) West Bengal (*d*) Andhra Pradesh

117. The main objective of TRYSEM was—
(*a*) To train rural youth for self employment
(*b*) To train urban youth for self employment
(*c*) Both of the above
(*d*) None of these

118. Inside Trading is related to—
(*a*) Share Market (*b*) Horse racing
(*c*) Taxation (*d*) Public Expenditure

119. The largest source of National Income in India is—
(*a*) Service Sector (*b*) Agriculture
(*c*) Industrial Sector (*d*) Trade Sector

120. 'Public Sector' means—
(*a*) Government ownership on commerce and trade
(*b*) Capitalist ownership on commerce and trade
(*c*) Private ownership on trade
(*d*) None of these

121. NABARD is—
(*a*) A bank (*b*) A board
(*c*) A block (*d*) A department

122. Indian Green Revolution is the most successful in—
(*a*) Wheat and Potato (*b*) Jwar and Oil Seeds
(*c*) Wheat and Rice (*d*) Tea and Coffee

123. The period of 12th plan in India was—
(*a*) 2000-2005 (*b*) 2001-2006
(*c*) 2012-2017 (*d*) 2003-2008

124. Economic Planning is in—
(*a*) Union list (*b*) State list
(*c*) Concurrent list (*d*) Not any specified list

125. Indian Banks have the maximum foreign branches in—
(*a*) Bangladesh (*b*) U.K.
(*c*) USA (*d*) Sri Lanka

126. Which types of tax helps in reducing disparities of income?
(*a*) Proportionate tax (*b*) Progressive tax
(*c*) Regressive tax (*d*) All of these

127. Which Bank is limited to the needs of agriculture and rural finance?
(*a*) SBI (*b*) IFC
(*c*) NABARD (*d*) RBI

128. 'Golden Handshake Scheme' is associated with—
(*a*) Inviting foreign companies
(*b*) Private investment in public enterprises
(*c*) Establishing joint enterprises
(*d*) Voluntary retirement

129. Which state has the lowest women literary rate in India (2011 census)?
(*a*) Bihar (*b*) Jharkhand
(*c*) U.P. (*d*) Rajasthan

130. Which country is the largest oil producing country of the world?
(*a*) America (*b*) Saudi Arabia
(*c*) Russia (*d*) None of these

131. Which is an indicator of economic under-development and backwardness?
(*a*) High birth rate
(*b*) High illeteracy
(*c*) High pressure of population on agriculture
(*d*) All of these

132. Which of the following took the decision of establishing 'South Asian Development Fund'?
(*a*) ADB (*b*) World Bank
(*c*) SAARC (*d*) IMF

133. During 11th plan the annual growth rate in GDP at factor cost achieved was—
(*a*) 5.5% (*b*) 6.5%
(*c*) 7.5% (*d*) 7.9%

134. TRIPS-'Trade Related Intellectual Property Rights' and TRIMS-'Trade Related Investment Measures' are associated with—
(*a*) Preston Proposal (*b*) Dunkel Proposal
(*c*) Chelliah Committee (*d*) None of these

135. Which is true for Finance Commission?
(*a*) It is a statutory body
(*b*) It is constituted under article 280 of the constitution
(*c*) Mr. K.C. Pant was Chairman of 10th Finance Commission
(*d*) All of these

136. **Assertion (A):** According to National Sample Survey, the proportion of poor is higher in rural India than in urban.
Reason (R): After independence, the growth rate of industry has been lower than that of agriculture.
(*a*) Both A and R are true and R is the correct explanation of A
(*b*) Both A and R are true but R is not a correct explanation of A
(*c*) A is true but R is false
(*d*) A is false but R is true

137. What is the CRR minimum limit for a commercial bank to be deposited with RBI?
(*a*) 3% (*b*) 10%
(*c*) 5% (*d*) 6%

138. Which is not a part of new economic reforms in India?
(*a*) Globalisation (*b*) Centralisation
(*c*) Privatisation (*d*) Liberalisation

139. The official exchange rate of Indian rupee is associated with
(*a*) Pound Sterling
(*b*) Dollar
(*c*) SDR
(*d*) A basket of selected currencies

140. As a result of Green Revolution which foodgrains had a reduced percentage in total foodgrain production?
(*a*) Wheat (*b*) Rice
(*c*) Cereals and Pulses (*d*) None of these

141. Which sector constitutes the maximum share in National Income of India?
(*a*) Primary
(*b*) Secondary
(*c*) Tertiary
(*d*) All the above have equal share

142. Corporate Tax is imposed by—
(*a*) State Government
(*b*) Local Government
(*c*) Central Government
(*d*) Both Centre and State Government

143. The First Finance Commission was constituted in the year—
(*a*) 1947 (*b*) 1950
(*c*) 1951 (*d*) 1952

144. Who has not yet been appointed Chairman of Finance Commission among the following?
(*a*) Amrish Baghchi (*b*) Mahaveer Tyagi
(*c*) N.K.P. Salve (*d*) Brahmanand Reddy

145. MRTP is related to—
(*a*) Monopoly and trade restrictions
(*b*) Inflation control
(*c*) Transport control
(*d*) Foreign Exchange Regulations

146. The basis of determining dearness allowance to employee in India is—
(*a*) National Income
(*b*) Consumer Price Index
(*c*) Standard of Living
(*d*) Per Capita Income

147. The State having the highest literacy rate among woman in India is—
(*a*) Tamil Nadu (*b*) Kerala
(*c*) West Bengal (*d*) Maharashtra

148. IRDP was introduced in the year—
(*a*) 1978-79 (*b*) 1979-80
(*c*) 1980-81 (*d*) 1981-82

149. The industry having the largest investment in Indian Economy is—
(*a*) Tea (*b*) Cement
(*c*) Steel (*d*) Jute

150. The maximum outlay was proposed in 9th plan (among public sectors) in—
(*a*) Agriculture Sector
(*b*) Transport Sector
(*c*) Energy Sector
(*d*) Communications Sector

151. The outlines of second five year plan was made by—
(*a*) B.N. Gadgil (*b*) VKRV Rao
(*c*) P.C. Mahalanobis (*d*) C.N. Vakil

152. The main aim of fifth five year plan was—
(*a*) Poverty elimination
(*b*) Self dependence
(*c*) Both the above
(*d*) None of these

153. NABARD was established in—
(*a*) Fourth Plan (*b*) Fifth Plan
(*c*) Sixth Plan (*d*) Eighth Plan

154. The first type of co-operative societies established in India was—
(*a*) Credit Societies
(*b*) Marketing Societies
(*c*) Agriculture Societies
(*d*) Housing Societies

155. Which currency has got the highest value when compared with Indian Rupee?
(*a*) Marc (*b*) Yen
(*c*) Rial (*d*) Pound sterling

156. The State with the second largest population in India is—
(*a*) Uttar Pradesh (*b*) Bihar
(*c*) West Bengal (*d*) Maharashtra

157. Dalal street is situated at—
(*a*) London (*b*) Paris
(*c*) Mumbai (*d*) New Delhi

158. RBI was nationalised in—
(*a*) 1959 (*b*) 1947
(*c*) 1945 (*d*) 1949

159. R.N. Malhotra committee gave recommendations on the field of—
(*a*) Sick Industries (*b*) Tax Reforms
(*c*) Insurance Sector (*d*) Banking Sector

160. India is not a member of—
(*a*) G-15 (*b*) UNO
(*c*) ASEAN (*d*) Commonwealth

161. Which states have not yet established any RRB?
(*a*) Sikkim and Goa
(*b*) Bihar and Rajasthan
(*c*) Sikkim and Arunachal Pradesh
(*d*) Nagaland

162. On the recommendations of Kelkar committee, no new RRB was established since—
(*a*) April 1987 (*b*) April 1988
(*c*) April 1989 (*d*) April 1990

163. IRBI—Industrial Reconstruction Bank of India was established in—
(*a*) 1975 (*b*) 1985
(*c*) 1990 (*d*) 1992

164. The headquarter of SIDBI is in—
(*a*) Lucknow (*b*) New Delhi
(*c*) Mumbai (*d*) Bangalore

165. LIC of India was established in—
(*a*) 1897 (*b*) 1950
(*c*) 1956 (*d*) 1965

166. Consumer Protection Act (COPRA) was implemended in—
(*a*) 1985 (*b*) 1986
(*c*) 1987 (*d*) 1988

167. Narsimham committee recommended to make banking structure of the country—
(*a*) Two tier (*b*) Three tier
(*c*) Four tier (*d*) Five tier

168. 'Canfina' is associated with—
(*a*) Canara Bank
(*b*) SBI
(*c*) National Housing Bank
(*d*) Standard Chartered Bank

169. Inside Trading is related to—
(*a*) Share Market
(*b*) Horse Market
(*c*) Taxation
(*d*) Public Expenditure

170. Grameen Bank and Micro Credit are associated with—
(*a*) Manmohan Singh (*b*) Bill Gates
(*c*) Md. Yunus (*d*) Aung San Su Ki

171. 20 rupee and above value notes are printed in—
(*a*) Currency Note Press, Nasik Road
(*b*) Bank Note Press, Dewas
(*c*) Security Printing Press, Hyderabad
(*d*) All of these

172. Central Revenue Board was divided into 'Central Excise and Custom Duty Board' and 'Central Direct Tax Board' in—
(*a*) 1950 (*b*) 1958
(*c*) 1963 (*d*) 1975

173. Which direct tax gives maximum net revenue to the Government—
(*a*) Corporate Tax (*b*) Income Tax
(*c*) Wealth Tax (*d*) Gift Tax

174. The view that 'Planning in India should, in future, pay more attention to the people than to commodities' was given by—
(*a*) Amartya Sen (*b*) Yashwant Sinha
(*c*) A.B. Vajpayee (*d*) None of these

175. Operation Flood programme was introduced in—
(*a*) 1951 (*b*) 1970
(*c*) 1975 (*d*) 1985

176. Health Insurance Business is associated with—
(*a*) LIC
(*b*) UTI
(*c*) GIC
(*d*) State Trading Corporation

177. DWCRA is now merged in—
(*a*) JRY (*b*) SJSRY
(*c*) TRYSEM (*d*) SGSY

178. Which state has the highest per capita income?
(*a*) Punjab (*b*) Goa
(*c*) Maharashtra (*d*) Gujarat

179. According to 2011 census, per 1000 male female number is—
(*a*) 939 (*b*) 959
(*c*) 943 (*d*) 927

180. Under Prime Minister's Integrated Urban Poverty Eradication Programme (PMIUPEP) those urban areas were included which had a population—
(*a*) Upto 50,000

(*b*) Between 50,000 and 1 Lakh
(*c*) Between 50,000 to 5 Lakh
(*d*) None of these

181. Name a Poverty Eradication Programme in which Banks played the dominant role—
(*a*) IRDP
(*b*) MNP
(*c*) Rojgar Bima Yojana
(*d*) Jawahar Rojgar Yojana

182. SJSRY belongs to—
(*a*) Urban areas (*b*) Rural areas
(*c*) Semi-urban areas (*d*) All of these

183. What is 'Hawala'?
(*a*) Full details of a subject
(*b*) Illegal transactions of foreign exchange
(*c*) Illegal trading of shares
(*d*) Tax evasion

184. Which plan was suspended one year before the time schedule?
(*a*) First Plan (1951-56)
(*b*) Third Plan (1966-71)
(*c*) Sixth Plan (1980-85)
(*d*) Fifth Plan (1974-79)

185. Which pair is not correct?
(*a*) I Plan (1951-56)
(*b*) III Plan (1966-71)
(*c*) VI Plan (1980-85)
(*d*) X Plan (2002-2007)

186. According to 2011 census, Indian Population was—
(*a*) 98.7 crore (*b*) 100.0 crore
(*c*) 121.08 crore (*d*) 105.7 crore

187. Which Union Territory ensured Lowest Population in 2011 census?
(*a*) Delhi (*b*) Chandigarh
(*c*) Puducherry (*d*) Lakshadweep

188. The Headquarter of Asian Development Bank (ADB) is at—
(*a*) Singapore (*b*) Manila
(*c*) Hong Kong (*d*) Tokyo

189. The Chairman of 10th Finance Commission was–
(*a*) Pranab Mukherjee (*b*) K.C. Pant
(*c*) Mohan Dharia (*d*) Man Mohan Singh

190. The aim of Differentiated Interest Scheme was to provide concessional loans to—
(*a*) Weaker Section of Society
(*b*) Public Sector Industries
(*c*) Public Limited Companies
(*d*) Big Exporters

191. Which Indian plan ensured high growth rate as compared with targetted growth rate?
(*a*) Fifth Plan (*b*) Fourth Plan
(*c*) Second Plan (*d*) Eighth Plan

192. MRTP Act was implemented since—
(*a*) 1970 (*b*) 1968
(*c*) 1969 (*d*) 1967

193. Which committee was constituted for reforms in tax-structure?
(*a*) Narsimham Committee
(*b*) Chelliah Committee
(*c*) Gadgil Committee
(*d*) Kelkar Committee

194. Match list-I with list-II and select the correct answer by using the codes given below the lists:

List-I	***List-II***
A. Balance of Payments & Foreign Investment	(1) Rakesh Mohan
B. Public Sector Enterprises Autonomy	(2) Arjun Sen Gupta
C. Small Scale Industries	(3) Rangarajan
D. Infrastructure Development	(4) Abid Hussain

	A	B	C	D
(*a*)	1	4	2	3
(*b*)	3	2	4	1
(*c*)	1	2	3	4
(*d*)	2	1	4	3

195. Assertion (A): Fiscal deficit is greater than budgetary deficit.
Reason (R): Fiscal deficit is the borrowing from the Reserve Bank of India plus other liabilities of the government to meet its expenditure.
(*a*) Both A and R are true and R is the correct explanation of A
(*b*) Both A and R are true but R is not a correct explanation of A
(*c*) A is true but R is false
(*d*) A is false but R is true

196. Match list-I with list-II and select the correct answer by using the codes given below the lists:

List-I	*List-II*
A. Second Plan	(1) Priority to reducing unemployment and poverty by redistributive schemes
B. Fourth Plan	(2) Rapid industrialization with emphasis on heavy industry
C. Fifth Plan	(3) Perspective Plan for 15 years
D. Sixth Plan	(4) Shift in emphasis towards quick-yielding projects and light industry

	A	B	C	D
(a)	2	4	1	3
(b)	1	2	3	4
(c)	3	4	2	1
(d)	3	4	1	2

197. Which one of the following pairs is not correctly matched?

(a) EXIT policy — Import controls
(b) EXIM scrips — Export subsidy
(c) LERMS — Rupee convertibility
(d) EPZ — Export promotion

198. Assertion (A): Agricultural poduction is characterised by growth and instability in India.

Reason (R): There are marked inter-regional and inter-crop variations in form production in India.

(a) Both A and R are true and R is the correct explanation of A
(b) Both A and R are true but R is not a correct explanation of A
(c) A is true but R is false
(d) A is false but R is true

199. Assertion (A): The industrial structure in India has become non-competitive over time.

Reason (R): The Goverment's licensing and other interventionist policies were devised to benefit the public.

(a) Both A and R are true and R is the correct explanation of A
(b) Both A and R are true but R is not a correct explanation of A
(c) A is true but R is false
(d) A is false but R is true

200. Which one of the following is not correctly matched?

(a) Rural Credit : NABARD
(b) Industrial Finance : SIDBI
(c) Rural poverty : SJSRY
(d) Disguised unemployment : Subsistence agriculture

ANSWERS

1	2	3	4	5	6	7	8	9	10
(a)	*(c)*	*(a)*	*(b)*	*(a)*	*(a)*	*(b)*	*(b)*	*(d)*	*(d)*
11	**12**	**13**	**14**	**15**	**16**	**17**	**18**	**19**	**20**
(b)	*(c)*	*(a)*	*(b)*	*(d)*	*(b)*	*(b)*	*(a)*	*(a)*	*(a)*
21	**22**	**23**	**24**	**25**	**26**	**27**	**28**	**29**	**30**
(b)	*(b)*	*(b)*	*(c)*	*(d)*	*(c)*	*(a)*	*(d)*	*(d)*	*(d)*
31	**32**	**33**	**34**	**35**	**36**	**37**	**38**	**39**	**40**
(d)	*(a)*	*(a)*	*(a)*	*(c)*	*(c)*	*(c)*	*(c)*	*(d)*	*(d)*
41	**42**	**43**	**44**	**45**	**46**	**47**	**48**	**49**	**50**
(d)	*(d)*	*(b)*	*(c)*	*(d)*	*(b)*	*(c)*	*(c)*	*(d)*	*(d)*
51	**52**	**53**	**54**	**55**	**56**	**57**	**58**	**59**	**60**
(d)	*(a)*	*(c)*	*(a)*	*(a)*	*(c)*	*(d)*	*(b)*	*(d)*	*(b)*
61	**62**	**63**	**64**	**65**	**66**	**67**	**68**	**69**	**70**
(d)	*(d)*	*(c)*	*(a)*	*(c)*	*(d)*	*(b)*	*(c)*	*(b)*	*(a)*

71	**72**	**73**	**74**	**75**	**76**	**77**	**78**	**79**	**80**
(d)	*(d)*	*(a)*	*(d)*	*(a)*	*(b)*	*(a)*	*(a)*	*(d)*	*(d)*
81	**82**	**83**	**84**	**85**	**86**	**87**	**88**	**89**	**90**
(c)	*(b)*	*(c)*	*(a)*	*(b)*	*(c)*	*(c)*	*(b)*	*(c)*	*(c)*
91	**92**	**93**	**94**	**95**	**96**	**97**	**98**	**99**	**100**
(a)	*(c)*	*(d)*	*(b)*	*(c)*	*(c)*	*(a)*	*(b)*	*(b)*	*(a)*
101	**102**	**103**	**104**	**105**	**106**	**107**	**108**	**109**	**110**
(d)	*(a)*	*(d)*	*(a)*	*(a)*	*(c)*	*(a)*	*(b)*	*(c)*	*(c)*
111	**112**	**113**	**114**	**115**	**116**	**117**	**118**	**119**	**120**
(b)	*(c)*	*(d)*	*(d)*	*(d)*	*(b)*	*(a)*	*(a)*	*(a)*	*(a)*
121	**122**	**123**	**124**	**125**	**126**	**127**	**128**	**129**	**130**
(a)	*(c)*	*(c)*	*(c)*	*(b)*	*(b)*	*(c)*	*(d)*	*(a)*	*(c)*
131	**132**	**133**	**134**	**135**	**136**	**137**	**138**	**139**	**140**
(d)	*(c)*	*(d)*	*(b)*	*(d)*	*(c)*	*(a)*	*(b)*	*(d)*	*(c)*
141	**142**	**143**	**144**	**145**	**146**	**147**	**148**	**149**	**150**
(c)	*(c)*	*(c)*	*(a)*	*(a)*	*(b)*	*(b)*	*(a)*	*(c)*	*(c)*
151	**152**	**153**	**154**	**155**	**156**	**157**	**158**	**159**	**160**
(c)	*(c)*	*(c)*	*(a)*	*(d)*	*(d)*	*(c)*	*(d)*	*(c)*	*(c)*
161	**162**	**163**	**164**	**165**	**166**	**167**	**168**	**169**	**170**
(a)	*(a)*	*(b)*	*(a)*	*(c)*	*(b)*	*(c)*	*(a)*	*(a)*	*(c)*
171	**172**	**173**	**174**	**175**	**176**	**177**	**178**	**179**	**180**
(b)	*(c)*	*(a)*	*(a)*	*(b)*	*(c)*	*(d)*	*(b)*	*(c)*	*(b)*
181	**182**	**183**	**184**	**185**	**186**	**187**	**188**	**189**	**190**
(a)	*(a)*	*(b)*	*(d)*	*(b)*	*(c)*	*(d)*	*(b)*	*(b)*	*(a)*
191	**192**	**193**	**194**	**195**	**196**	**197**	**198**	**199**	**200**
(d)	*(a)*	*(b)*	*(b)*	*(a)*	*(a)*	*(a)*	*(a)*	*(a)*	*(c)*

UNIT–X : ENVIRONMENTAL ECONOMICS AND DEMOGRAPHY

ENVIRONMENTAL ECONOMICS

INTRODUCTION

Environmental economics is a subfield of economics concerned with environmental issues. Quoting from the National Bureau of Economic Research Environmental Economics program: Environmental Economics undertakes theoretical or empirical studies of the economic effects of national or local environmental policies around the world.

Particular issues include the costs and benefits of alternative environmental policies to deal with air pollution, water quality, toxic substances, solid waste, and global warming. Central to environmental economics is the concept of market failure.

Market failure means that markets fail to allocate resources efficiently. A market failure occurs when the market does not allocate scarce resources to generate the greatest social welfare. A wedge exists between what a private person does given market prices and what society might want him or her to do to protect the environment.

Such a wedge implies wastefulness or economic inefficiency; resources can be reallocated to make at least one person better off without making anyone else worse off. Common forms of market failure include externalities, non-excludability and non-rivalry.

Environmental economics is related to ecological economics but there are differences. Most environmental economists have been trained as economists. They apply the tools of economics to address environmental problems, many of which are related to so-called market failures—circumstances wherein the invisible hand of economics is unreliable.

Most ecological economists have been trained as ecologists, but have expanded the scope of their work to consider the impacts of humans and their economic activity on ecological systems and services, and vice-versa.

This field takes as its premise that economics is a strict subfield of ecology. Ecological economics is sometimes described as taking a more pluralistic approach to environmental problems and focuses more explicitly on long- term environmental sustainability and issues of scale.

Environmental economics is viewed as more pragmatic in a price system; ecological economics as more idealistic in its attempts not use money as a primary arbiter of decisions. These two groups of specialists sometimes have conflicting views which may be traced to the different philosophical underpinnings.

Environmental economics was once distinct from resource economics. Natural resource economics as a subfield began when the main concern of researchers was the optimal commercial exploitation of natural resource stocks.

But resource managers and policy-makers eventually began to pay attention to the broader importance of natural resources It is now difficult to distinguish environmental and natural resource economics as separate fields as the two became associated with sustainability. Many of the more radical green economists split off to work on an alternate political economy.

Environmental economics was a major influence for the theories of natural capitalism and environmental finance, which could be said to be two sub-branches of environmental economics concerned with resource conservation in production, and the value of biodiversity to humans, respectively. The theory of natural capitalism (Hawken, Lovins) goes further than traditional environmental economics by envisioning a world where natural services are considered on par with physical capital.

ENVIRONMENTAL ECONOMICS

Meaning

In the words of D.W. Pearce, "Environmental Economics brings the discipline of economic analysis to environmental issues such as pollution, the rate of use of renewable and non-renewable natural resources, conservation of living species and resources, and the choice of policy to achieve environmental ends."

The mainstream of economics is based on market mechanism. Its primary emphasis is on the market as a supplier of advice about human preferences. It focuses on the rational behaviour of consumers and producers. It studies the micro and macro aspects of the economy. But economics differs from environmental economics.

In economic sense, pollution is termed as any loss of human well being arising from physical environmental change. Pollution may also have short-run or long-run impacts upon the health of human beings. Resource issues, as pointed out by D.W. Pearce, may be interpreted as possible degradation of the human environment. Other forms of degradation may also be added, such as the exploitation of natural resources other than for crop land (for housing/ transport etc.), the exhaustion of non-renewable resources (such as oil and mineral), and the mismanagement of renewable resources.

According to Charles Kolstad, the best division between environmental economics and resource economics is between static and dynamic issues related to the natural world. "Environmental economics involves questions of excessive production of pollution by the market (or insufficient protection of the natural world due to market failure).

Resource economics, on the other hand, is concerned with the production and use of natural resources, both renewable and exhaustible. Renewable resources would include fisheries and forests. Non-renewables would include minerals and energy as well as natural assets."

CONCEPT OF ENVIRONMENTAL ECONOMICS

Environment

The word environment has been derived from the French word 'Environer' which means to surround. Environment includes water, air and land, and their inter-relationships with human beings, other living creatures, plants and microorganisms. Environment provides basic services essential to humanity such as supporting life, supplying materials, energy and absorbing waste products.

The services of environment are used by production and household sector in an economy. These include minerals such as coal, petroleum and a wide assortment of ores that can be processed into metals/metal alloys. Other resources include plant, soil and water components used directly in production processes. Life supporting services are also provided by environment. These are clean air, water and food etc.

Environmental Pollution

A change in the physical, chemical or biological characteristics of the air, water or soil that can affect the health, survival or activities of human beings or other living organisms in a harmful manner. In economics, pollution is termed as any loss of human well-being arising from physical environmental changes.

Natural Resources

Anything obtained from the physical environment to meet human needs relates to natural resources. Basic human needs are fulfilled by materials provided by nature itself. They are air, water, soil, minerals, coal, petroleum, animals and plants.

These stocks of the nature, useful to mankind are called natural resources. In the primitive age, man had used only those resources that supported his life. But the process of economic growth and increase in population have led to mismanagement of natural resources.

There are two types of natural resources:

(*i*) Non-renewable resources

(*ii*) Renewable Resources.

(i) Non-renewable Resources

These resources were formed in millions of years and hence will get exhausted sooner or later. Some of the non-renewable resources are coal, petroleum, natural gas, minerals etc. The stock of these resources is limited. They are susceptible to be degraded in quantity and quality by the human activities.

(ii) Renewable Resources

These resources are present in unlimited quantity in the nature. They are solar radiation, air and water. These are not likely to be exhausted by human activities.

Ecology

Ecology and economics share the same etymology—OIKOS (House). In Ecology, it represents the study of our house, whereas in economics, it ensures the management of that place. Ecology is concerned with the relationship between the physical environment (soil, water and air) and organism environment (plant and animal life etc.).

Ecological economists have analysed the interdependence between the physical environment and economic activities in their models. According to them, some economic activities may be the cause of environmental degradation.

Industrial Ecology

Industrial Ecology is the means by which humanity can deliberately and rationally maintains a desirable carrying capacity, given continued economic, cultural and technological evolution. It is a system in which one seeks to optimize the total material cycle from virgin material, to finished material, to components, to product, to obsolete product and to ultimate disposal. Factors to be optimized include resources, energy and capital.

Industrial ecology redefines waste as a starting material for another industrial process. It also seeks to structure the economy's industrial base along the lines of natural economic systems whose cyclical flows of material and energy are both efficient and sustainable.

Ecosystem

Ecosystem is a term applied to a particular relationship between living organism and their environment. An eco-system has two main components: (*a*) abiotic, and (*b*) biotic. All the non-living components of environment present in an ecosystem are known as abiotic components.

These include the inorganic and organic components and climatic factors. On the other hand, the living organisms of an ecosystem are known as its biotic components which include plants, animals and micro-organisms.

Ecosystems may be affected by anthropogenetic factors. They also face short and long run natural changes imposed from both within and outside the systems such as climatic changes.

Environmental Goods

Environmental goods are public goods. They include air quality, water quality and sun heat etc. Environmental goods are unique in nature. Excess use of these may lead to environmental degradation. For example, due to global climate change, the snow on the peaks of the Himalayas starts losing its density and thickness.

Environmental Pollution as an Economic Problem

Environmental pollution is an economic problem because it requires us to make choices and to resolve conflicts of interests. It is an economic problem because the means by which pollution can be reduced are themselves resources using. Further, it also reduces the value of some resources that society has at its disposal.

It means that pollution is a problem of scarcity in terms of waste disposal capacity. The main problem of choice is how to utilize the scarce resources in relation to society's needs. The market forces will be helpful in determining these scarce resources in most rational manner. The equilibrium will be attained at the equality of demand and supply of environmental quality.

Since resources are scarce they cannot be used to produce all types of goods simultaneously. Therefore, if they were used to produce one thing, they have to be withdrawn from other uses. The problem of choice facing a modem society is whether to maintain environmental quality or to increase industrial production (*i.e.*, automobiles). It creates conflicts of interest between potential gainers and potential losers.

The problem of externalities is an important aspect of environmental quality. The external effects of industrial production may affect the environmental quality. Therefore, the economic problem is the optimal allocation of resources in the context of externalities.

One of the objectives of environmental quality is to restrict those production activities which enhance social costs to society. Environmental quality is largely influenced by human activities in terms of excess exploitation of resources and the production of waste. How much environmental quality is affected by exploitation of resources and production of waste depends on ecological conditions of the economy. More exploitation of it means more pollution.

Environmental pollution as an economic problem is explained in terms of Figure.

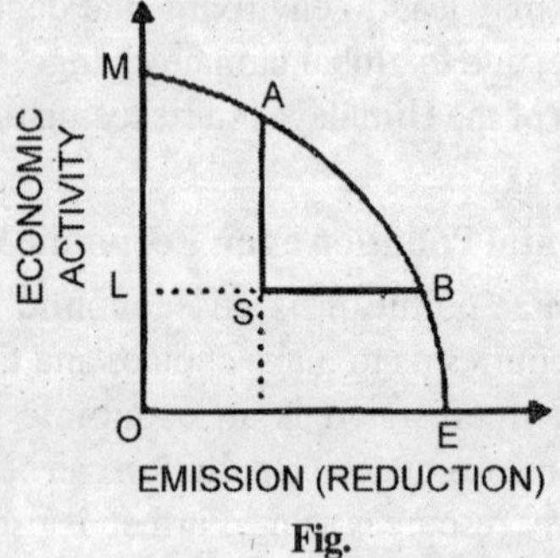

Fig.

It is assumed that the economy is producing two sets of goods, a composite good (M) which is the aggregate of all existing goods and services, and second, an environmental quality good which also represents certain quantity of emission reductions.

The ME curve represents a production frontier which explains the trade-off between economic activity and emission reduction. If the economy moves from point S to point A on the ME curve, it means more production with increase in economic activity without increased emission.

On the other hand, if the economy moves from point S to points B on the ME curve, it means more emission reduction without reducing the economic activity level (L) because point S and point B lie in the same direction.

In this connection, Ian Hodge points out, what we will find is that choices made about the environment depend upon similar factors as do choices made in other areas of economics. Our views of changes in environmental quality depend (as do all prices) upon supply and demand factors: how much of the environment is supplied for particular purposes and how much is demanded. Thus, the forces of supply (production) and demand (preference for clean environment) and market instruments used by the state are important issues in environmental policy.

Economic growth can affect environmental quality under different situations. Environmental quality can increase with economic growth. Thus, increased incomes, for example, provide the resources for public services.

With availability of these services individuals can devote more resources for conservation. Second, environmental quality can initially worsen but then improve as the growth rate rises. Third, environmental quality can decrease when the rate of growth increases.

ENVIRONMENT-ECONOMY LINKAGES

All economic activities either affect or are affected by natural and environmental resources. Activities such as extraction, processing, manufacture, transport, consumption and disposal change the stock of natural resources, add stress to the environmental systems and introduce wastes to environmental media. Moreover, economic activities today affect the stock of natural resources available for the future and have inter-temporal welfare effects. From this perspective, the productivity of an economic system depends in part on the supply and quality of natural and environmental resources.

Natural and environmental resources have three economic roles : waste disposal services, related to the environment's assimilative capacity; natural resource inputs into production; and directly consumed life support services and aesthetic amenities. The natural and environmental resource input function is central to understanding the relationship between economic growth and environment. Water, soil, air, biological, forest and fisheries resources are productive assets, whose quality helps determine the productivity of the economy. Focusing on this role of environment as a producer good highlights the direct effect environmental problems have on economic growth. Thus, economic management impacts on the environment and the environmental quality impacts on the efficient working of the economy. Environmental degradation imposes costs on the economy which results in output and human capital losses.

Lost labour productivity resulting from ill health, foregone crop output due to soil degradation and erosion, lost fisheries output and tourism receipts from coastal erosion or lost soil productivity from deforestation can be some of the manifestations of such reduced output. Moreover, a growing body of epidemiological studies suggest that air and water pollution are taking a heavy toll, particularly of people in the developing world, through ill health and premature mortality. The impact of water and air pollution is particularly adverse to the younger, the very aged and poor. Pollution control, is thus linked to sustainable development and not a luxury good to be afforded after the development process has taken off.

Linkage between Economy and Environment

The environment, both biological and physical, is the source of all natural resources. Some natural resources are renewable (*e.g.*, water, biological resources) while others are non renewable (*e.g.*, geological deposits). The interlinkages between the economy and the environment are summarized in the figure. The economy consists of two sectors: Producers and Consumers, exchange of goods, services and factors of production (Labour and Capital) take place between the two sectors. The

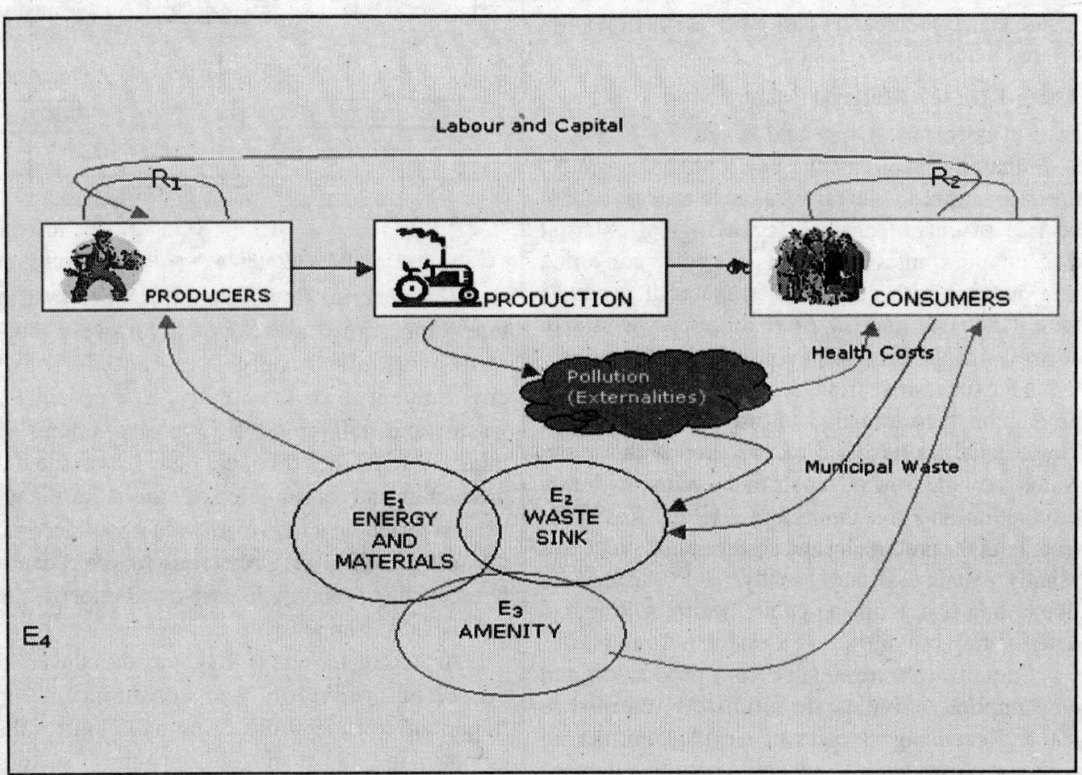

Fig.: *Linkage between Economy – Environment*

environment is shown in two ways: as the three interlinked circles E1, E2 and E3, and the all encompassing boundary labeled E4 .The production sector extracts energy resources (such as oil) and material resources (such as iron ore) from the environment, these are transformed into outputs through the production process, these transformation processes also generate wastes at different stages and often the environment is used as a repository (Sink) for waste products. There is some recycling of resources within the production sector, shown by the loop R1, and within the consumption sector, as shown by the loop R2.

As we can see the environment's first role is as a supplier of resources. Secondly, it acts as a sink or a receptor for waste products. These wastes may result directly from production, as already mentioned or from consumption. When an individual puts out their garbage, or when they drive to work, they are contributing to this form of waste. Finally the environment also serves as an amenity these include scenic beauty, recreation and other aesthetic values offered by the environment.

Ayres-Kneese's Material Balance Model

In the words of Ayres and Kneese, "If waste assimilative capacity of the environment is scarce, the decentralized voluntary exchange process cannot be free of uncompensated technological external diseconomies unless all inputs are fully converted into outputs, with no unwanted material residuals along the way and all final outputs are utterly destroyed in the process of consumption."

The functions of an economy are related to production, consumption and distribution activities. These activities have a direct relation with nature. Nature provides raw materials to the economy for its production and consumption activities. Residuals from both the production and consumption processes usually remain and they usually render disservices like killing fish, reducing public health, soiling and deteriorating buildings due to industrial pollution.

Some wastes (residuals) from production and consumption activities are ultimately returned to nature. Remaining wastages are recycled. Further, all emission of residuals do not cause pollution damage because of assimilative capacity of the environment.

Further, energy that is taken out of the environment must reappear somewhere else in the economic system. Its form may, however, be changed so that it appears as waste products and gases. Moreover, waste energy cannot be recycled but waste materials can be used up to a point. It means that economic activity always affects environment in a direct or indirect manner.

Thus, the law of conservation of matter and energy holds that matter can be transformed to other matter or into energy but can never vanish. All inputs (fuels, raw materials, water and so forth) used in the economy's production processes will ultimately result in an equivalent residual or waste. The model is explained in the Material Flow Diagram (Figure).

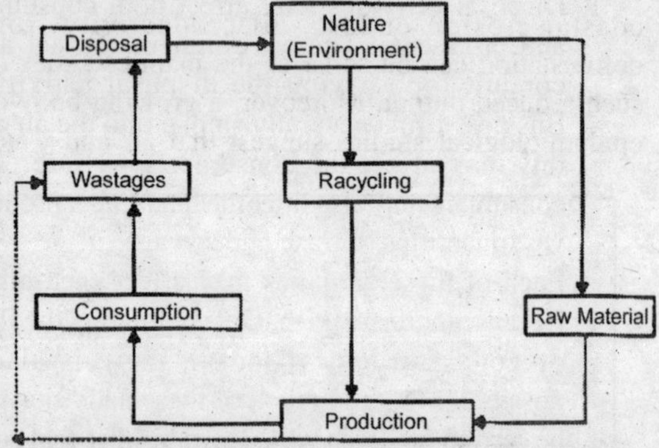

Fig.: *Material Flow Diagram*

The material flow diagram implies that mass inputs must equal mass outputs for every process. Moreover, all resources extracted from the environment must eventually become unwanted wastes and pollutants. This means, among other things, externalities (market failures) associated with production and consumption of materials are actually pervasive and they tend to grow in importance as the economy itself grows. Materials recycled can help but recycling is energy intensive and imperfect, so it cannot fully compensate.

According to John H. Baldwin, the conventional model of production and consumption omits important considerations. This omission results in emphasizing and managing only those sectors of production and consumption that are monetized.

Most real production and consumption of goods and services in the world, especially in developing countries, occur even outside the formal monetized economy. Hence, the materials balance model provides a useful framework for analyzing alternative methods of resource and residuals management.

Thus, economics of the environment may be defined as a study which concerns allocation of resources among alternative uses in such a way that there is an efficient reduction of the waste or residuals in the environment, which lead to an increase in social welfare.

Its implications

The material balance model has important implications:

1. Disposal activities may affect both consumers and producers. The environment can act as a conduit for carrying the disposal activities. Business firms generally smoke into the air and this may affect the consumer's welfare. The consumers may also litter the landscape; produce vast quantities of trash and sewage.
   Each of these activities may affect each other. Because there are no markets regulating the flow of goods through disposal, there is also a possibility that too much of these activities will be carried on. Each will regard his disposal costs as zero and will use the environment so long as this use permits him to improve his own welfare.
2. The environment has a large waste assimilation capacity, but this is not infinite. Too much waste entering the environment rather than being recycled or reused will put too much stress on the assimilative capacity of the environment to handle such waste safety. The result will be a range of pollution and resources degradation impacts, and consequent economic damage cost.
3. With the application of the laws of thermodynamics, economic production and consumption activities always generate some pollution and waste. It requires proper disposal. Moreover, it is not always possible to have 100 per cent recycling. Nevertheless, society does not have a choice over the total quantity of waste that its economic system produces.
4. In a general sense, policy makers can weigh up the social benefits of various productive activities and compare them with the social costs (including disposal) imposed by these activities. Policy makers may then decide to intervene in the economic process in order to change or modify production processes.
5. If a balance can be reached between acceptable levels of materials flows, there will be an increase in output and improvement in environmental quality.
6. From the policy point of view, this approach emphasizes recycle process and less residual-generating production process. It is only possible by modifying an environmental medium through investment in control facilities so as to improve its assimilative capacity. Investments involving public goods such as transportation systems, sewage disposal and river flow regulation are intimately related to the amounts and effects of residuals and must be planned in the light of them.
7. It is important to develop not only measures for the external costs resulting from different concentrations and duration of residuals in the environment but more systematic methods for forecasting emissions of external cost-producing residuals, technical and economic trade-offs between them, and the effects of recycle on environmental quality.
8. The application of the law of thermodynamics to the problem of waste is an important event in integrated residuals management. Residuals are generated by all production and consumption activities. This pervasive nature of the residuals problem, along with the inter-relationships of residuals, economic activities and recycling provides a physical system basis for environmental quality management.
   In other words, it demonstrates that waste generation is pervasive to the economy. In turn, if the çapacity of the environment to assimilate and degrade the waste into harmless form is limited, the externalities arising from the waste will be pervasive. This is in marked contract to the view that externalities are occasional deviations from market perfection.

9. The importance of the materials balance principle lies in the fact that it provides a coherent framework in which an economic analysis of resources use and its implications for the environment can be placed. It draws one's attention to the long-term implications of economic activity, by focusing on the stock-flow relationships implied by that behaviour and its importance in this relationships.

EXTERNALITIES

Externalities are unintentional side effects of an activity affecting people other than those directly involved in the activity. A negative externality is one that creates side effects that could be harmful to either the general public directly or through the environment. An example would be a factory that pollutes as a result of its production process. This pollution may pose health risks for nearby residents or degrade the quality of the air or water. Either way, the owner of the factory does not directly pay the additional cost to address any health issues or to help maintain the cleanliness of the air or water. In some cases, however, the harmed parties can use legal measures to receive compensation for damages.

Positive Externality

A positive externality, on the other hand, is an unpaid benefit that extends beyond those directly initiating the activity. One example would be a neighbourhood resident who creates a private garden, the aesthetic beauty of which benefits other people in the community. Also, when a group voluntarily chooses to create a benefit, such as a community park, others may benefit without contributing to the project. Any individuals or groups that gain additional benefits without contributing are known as "**free riders**".

Negative Externality

Traditionally, both negative and positive externalities are considered to be forms of market failure - when a free market does not allocate resources efficiently. **Arthur Pigou**, a British economist best known for his work in welfare economics, argued that the existence of externalities justified government intervention through legislation or regulation. Pigou supported taxes to discourage activities that created harmful effects and subsidies for those creating benefits to further encourage those activities. These are now known as **Pigovian taxes and subsidies**.

Many economists believe that placing Pigovian taxes on pollution is a much more efficient way of dealing with pollution as an externality than government imposed regulatory standards. Taxes leave the decision of how to deal with pollution to individual sources by assessing a fee or "tax" on the amount of pollution that is generated.

Therefore, in theory, a source that is looking to maximize its profit will reduce, or control, their pollution emissions whenever it is cheaper to do so.

Other economists believe that the most efficient solution to externalities is to include them in the cost for those engaged in the activity. Thus, the externality is "internalized." Under this framework externalities are not necessarily market failures, which weaken the case for government intervention. Many externalities (pollution, free rider benefits) can be internalized through the creation of well-defined **property rights**. Through much of his work, economist **Ronald Coase** showed that taxes and subsidies were typically not necessary as long as the parties involved could strike a voluntary bargain. According to **Coase's theorem,** it does not matter who has ownership, so long as property rights exist and free trade is possible.

Two methods of controlling negative externalities loosely related to property rights include **cap and trade** and **individual transferable quotas** (ITQs). The cap and trade approach sets a maximum amount of emissions for a group of sources over a specific time period. The various sources are then given emissions allowances which can be traded, bought or sold, or banked for future use, but - over the course of the specified period of time - overall emissions will not exceed the amount of the cap and may even decline. Therefore, individual sources, or facilities, can determine their level of production and/ or the application of pollution reduction technologies or the purchase of additional allowances.

Individual transferable quotas are a market-based solution that is often used to manage fisheries. Regulators first determine a total annual catch that will preserve the health of the ecosystem, and then it is divided into individual quotas to prevent overfishing. Each ITQ allows for a certain amount of fish to be caught in any given year. ITQs are transferable, which allows fishing vessel owners to buy and sell their quotas depending on how much they want to catch. The ITQ program also tries to create a commercial fishing industry that is more stable and profitable.

The options for dealing with externalities - positive or negative - are numerous, and often depend on the type of externality. The key is to identify the particular tool or policy alternative that will best move the market toward the most efficient allocation of resources.

MARKET EFFICIENCY

Situation where resources cannot be efficiently allocated due to the breakdown of price mechanism caused by factors such as establishment of monopolies. See also market inefficiency.

A **market failure** occurs when the supply of a good or service is insufficient to meet demand. This results in an inefficient distribution of resources among market participants.

How it works/Example:

Under free market conditions, prices are determined almost exclusively by the forces of supply and demand. Any shift in one of these results in a price change that signals a corresponding shift in the other. Then, the prices return to an equilibrium level. A market failure results when prices cannot achieve equilibrium because of market distortions (for example, minimum wage requirements or price limits on specific goods and services) that restrict economic output. In other words, government regulations implemented to promote social wellbeing inevitably result in a degree of market failure.

Why it Matters:

Economic and social policymakers try to consider the market failures that will result from specific legislation, and, in most cases, they ultimately attempt to minimize market failure by finding a balance between protecting social (or political) interests and maintaining efficient markets.

Market failure happens when the price mechanism **fails to allocate scarce resources efficiently** or when the operation of market forces lead to a **net social welfare loss.**

Market failure exists when the competitive outcome of markets is not satisfactory from the point of view of society. What is satisfactory nearly always involves **value judgments.**

Complete and Partial Market Failure

- **Complete market failure** occurs when the market simply does not supply products at all - we see "missing markets"
- **Partial market failure** occurs when the market does actually function but it produces either the wrong quantity of a product or at the wrong price.

Markets can Fail for Lots of Reasons

1. **Negative externalities** (*e.g.*, the effects of environmental pollution) causing the social cost of production to exceed the private cost
2. **Positive externalities** (*e.g.*, the provision of education and health care) causing the social benefit of consumption to exceed the private benefit
3. **Imperfect information** or **information failure** means that merit goods are underproduced while demerit goods are over-produced or over-consumed
4. The private sector in a free-markets cannot profitably supply to consumers **pure public goods** and **quasi-public goods** that are needed to meet people's needs and wants
5. **Market dominance by monopolies** can lead to under-production and higher prices than would exist under conditions of competition, causing consumer welfare to be damaged
6. **Factor immobility** causes unemployment and a loss of productive efficiency
7. **Equity (fairness) issues:** Markets can generate an 'unacceptable' distribution of income and consequent social exclusion which the government may choose to change

Types of Market Failure

1. **Positive externalities** – Goods/services which give benefit to a third party, *e.g.* less congestion from cycling
2. **Negative externalities** – Goods/services which impose cost on a third party, *e.g.* cancer from passive smoking
3. **Merit goods** – People underestimate the benefit of good, *e.g.* education
4. **Demerit goods** – People underestimate the costs of good, *e.g.* smoking
5. **Public Goods** - Goods which are non-rival and non-excludable – *e.g.* police, national defence.
6. **Monopoly Power** – when a firm controls the market and can set higher prices.
7. **Inequality** – unfair distribution of resources in free market
8. **Factor Immobility** – For example, geographical/ occupational immobility
9. **Agriculture** – Agriculture is often subject to market failure – due to volatile prices and externalities.

Key Terms in Market Failure

1. **Externalities:** These occur when a third party is affected by the decisions and actions of others.
2. **Social benefit:** is the total benefit to society = Private Marginal Benefit (PMB) + External Marginal Benefit (XMB)
3. **Social Cost:** is the total cost to society = Private Marginal Cost (PMC) + External Marginal Cost (XMC)
4. **Social Efficiency:** This occurs when resources are utilised in the most efficient way. This will occur at an output where social marginal cost (SMC) = Social Marginal Benefit. (SMB)

Overcoming Market Failure

1. Tax on Negative Externalities – *e.g.* Petrol tax
2. Carbon Tax *e.g.*, tax on CO_2 emissions
3. Subsidy on positive externalities – why government may subsidies public transport
4. Laws and Regulations – Simple and effective ways to regulate demerit goods, like ban on smoking advertising.
5. Buffer stocks – aim to stabilise prices
6. Government failure – why government intervention may not always improve the situation.

Causes of Market Failure

Some of the major causes of market failure are: 1. Incomplete markets, 2. Indivisibilities, 3. Common Property Resources, 4. Imperfect Markets, 5. Asymmetric Information, 6. Externalities, 7. Public Goods 8. Public Bads.

Public Goods

Another cause of market failure is the existence of public goods. A public good is one whose consumption or use by one individual does not reduce the amount available for others. An example of a public good is water which is available to one person and is also available to others without any additional cost. Its consumption is always joint and equal.

It is non-excludable if it can be consumed by anyone. It is non-rivalrous if no one has an exclusive rights over its consumption. Its benefits can be provided to an additional consumer at zero marginal cost. Thus, public goods are both non-excludable and non-rivalrous. Moreover, environmental quality is generally considered as a public good and when it is valued at market price, it leads to market failure.

The Paretian condition for a public good is that its marginal social benefit (MSB) should equal its marginal social cost (MSC). But the characteristics of a public good are such that the economy will not reach a point of Pareto optimality in a perfectly competitive market. Public goods create externalities.

The externality starts when the marginal cost of consuming or producing an additional unit of a public good is zero but a price above zero is being charged. This violates the Paretian welfare maximization criterion of equating marginal social cost and marginal social benefit. This is because the benefits of a public good must be provided at a zero marginal social cost.

Suppose potable water is supplied by the municipal corporation. There are two individuals A and who use it. Both consume the same quantity of water. But they differ in how much they are willing to pay for any given quantity.

This is illustrated in Figure where D_a and D_b are the demand curves of two individuals A and B respectively. Therefore, demand prices are OP_a and OP_b corresponding to a given quantity OW of water. The curve ΣD is the vertical summation of D_a and D_b curves.

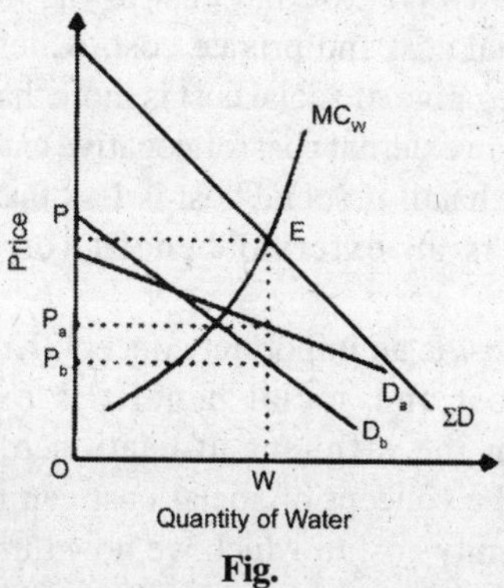

Fig.

The Lindhal equilibrium for a public good exists where the sum of the individual prices equal marginal cost. Therefore,

$$OP = OP_a + OP_b = MCW$$

But each consumer is being charged a different price. This is a case of price discrimination because price OP_a is greater than price OP_b for the same quantity of water OW. Hence, there is market failure.

Public Bads

There are also public bads in which one person experiencing some disutility does not diminish the disutility of another, such as air and water pollution. Public goods and public bads cannot be handled by the institution of private property. K.E. Boulding has explained public bads with the following example: "If someone drives his car into my living room and pollutes it, I can sue him for damages. This is a private bad. But if someone congests the roads or pollutes the air, however, there is not much I can do about it as an individual. This is public bad."

Market failure is a necessary but not a sufficient condition for intervention. To be truly worthwhile, a government intervention must outperform the market or improve its functions. Second, the benefits from such intervention must exceed the costs of planning, implementation, and enforcement, as well as any indirect and unintended costs of distortions introduced to other sectors of the economy by such intervention.

CONCEPT OF MARKET FAILURE

In economics, **market failure** is a situation in which the allocation of goods and services is not efficient. That is, there exists another conceivable outcome where an individual may be made better-off without making someone else worse-off. (The outcome is not Pareto optimal.) Market failures can be viewed as scenarios where individuals' pursuit of pure self-interest leads to results that are not efficient – that can be improved upon from the societal point of view. The first known use of the term by economists was in 1958, but the concept has been traced back to the Victorian philosopher Henry Sidgwick.

Market failures are often associated with time-inconsistent preferences, information asymmetries, non-competitive markets, principal–agent problems, externalities, or public goods. The existence of a market failure is often the reason that self-regulatory organizations, governments or supra-national institutions intervene in a particular market. Economists, especially micro economists, are often concerned with the causes of market failure and possible means of correction. Such analysis plays an important role in many types of public policy decisions and studies. However, government policy interventions, such as taxes, subsidies, bailouts, wage and price controls, and regulations (including poorly implemented attempts to correct market failure), may also lead to an inefficient allocation of resources, sometimes called government failure.

Given the tension between, on the one hand, the undeniable costs to society caused by market failure, and on the other hand, the potential that attempts to mitigate these costs could lead to even greater costs from "government failure," there is sometimes a choice between imperfect outcomes, *i.e.,* imperfect market outcomes with or without government interventions. But either way, if a market failure exists the outcome is not Pareto efficient. Most mainstream economists believe that there are circumstances (like building codes or endangered species) in which it is possible for government or other organizations to improve the inefficient market outcome. Several heterodox schools of thought disagree with this as a matter of principle.

Categories

Different economists have different views about what events are the sources of market failure. Mainstream economic analysis widely accepts a market failure (relative to Pareto efficiency) can occur for three main reasons: if the market is "monopolised" or a small group of businesses hold significant market power, if production of the good or service results in an externality, or if the good or service is a "public good".

Private Cost and Social Cost

Private Cost

Private cost refers to the cost of production incurred and provided for by an individual firm engaged in the production of a commodity. It is found out to get private profits.

This cost has nothing to do with the society. It includes both explicit as well as implicit cost. A firm is interested in minimising private cost.

Social Cost

Social cost refers to the cost of producing a commodity to the society as a whole. It takes into consideration all those costs, which are borne by the society directly or indirectly. Social cost is not borne by the firm. It is rather passed on to persons not involved in the activity in the direct way. Social cost is a much broader concept.

It is found out to get social profits rather than private profits. The production of a commodity by a firm generates advantages (benefits) as well as disadvantages (cost) to other members of society, called external benefits and external costs respectively.

These benefits are available free of cost. For instance, to facilitate easier movement of raw materials and finished products, a producer constructs a road, linking it with a highway. This road may be used by others, who will not pay for the benefits derived. On the similar lines, no producer compensates others for the costs incurred to them as a result of his production.

Water pollution caused by the disposal of wastes into a river (or sea) or air pollution and consequent health hazards by the smoke generation by factories or buses plying in big cities are some other examples.

Noise pollution and accident proneness are some other social costs due to rising traffic in big cities. While computing social costs, market prices of goods and factor of production are adjusted as social and shadow prices.

Social cost is the sum of private cost and external cost. Alternatively, external cost is the difference between social cost and private cost, which may be positive or negative. If social cost is more than private cost, there is an external cost (or negative externality). On the other hand, if social cost is less than private cost, there is an external benefit (or positive externality).

Social cost is an important concept. Knowledge of social cost and social benefit is extremely important in the efficient utilisation of limited resources. The concept of social cost can be linked with opportunity cost to which we now turn.

Social Cost

Social cost in economics may be distinguished from "private cost". Economic theorists model individual decision-making as measurement of costs and benefits. Social cost is also considered to be the private cost plus externalities. Rational choice theory often assumes that individuals consider only the costs they themselves bear when making decisions, not the costs that may be borne by others.

With pure private costs, the costs carried by the individuals involved are the only economically meaningful costs. The choice to purchase a glass of lemonade at a lemonade stand has little consequence for anyone other than the seller or the buyer. The costs involved in this economic activity are the costs of the lemons and the sugar and the water that are ingredients to the lemonade, the opportunity cost of the labour to combine them into lemonade, as well as any transaction costs, such as walking to the stand.

The Difference between Private and Social Costs

This is an important distinction to understand. Private costs to firms or individuals do not always equate with the total cost to society for a product, service, or activity. The difference between private costs and total costs to society of a product, service, or activity is called an external cost; pollution is an external cost of many products. External costs are directly associated with producing or delivering an item or service, but they are costs that are not paid directly by the producer. When external costs arise because environmental costs are not paid, market failures and economic inefficiencies at the local, state, national, and even international level may result.

Let's start by defining private costs, external costs, and social costs. Next, we will briefly examine the impact external costs can have on prices, production, resource allocation, and competition.

Key Concepts

Private Costs + External Costs = Social Costs

If external costs > 0, then private costs < social costs

Then society tends to:

– Price the goods or service too low, and

– Produces or consumes too much of the goods or service.

Different Costs Matter

Private costs for a producer of an item, service, or activity include the costs the firm pays to purchase capital equipment, hire labour, and buy materials or other inputs. While this is straightforward from the business side, it is also important to look at this issue from the consumers' perspective. Field, in his 1997 text, Environmental Economics provides an example of the private costs a consumer faces when driving a car.

The private costs of this (driving a car) include the fuel and oil, maintenance, depreciation, and even the drive time experienced by the operator of the car.

Private costs are paid by the firm or consumer and must be included in production and consumption decisions. In a competitive market, considering only the private costs will lead to a socially efficient rate of output only if there are no external costs.

External costs, on the other hand, are not reflected on firms' income statements or in consumers' decisions. However, external costs remain costs to society, regardless of who pays for them. Consider a firm that attempts to save money by not installing water pollution control equipment. Because of the firm's actions, cities located down river will have to pay to clean the water before it is fit for drinking, the public may find that recreational use of the river is restricted, and the fishing industry may be harmed. When external costs like these exist, they must be added to private costs to determine social costs and to ensure that a socially efficient rate of output is generated.

Social costs include both the private costs and any other external costs to society arising from the production or consumption of a good or service. Social costs will differ from private costs, for example, if a producer can avoid the cost of air pollution control equipment allowing the firm's production to imposes costs (health or environmental degradation) on other parties that are adversely affected by the air pollution. Remember too, it is not just producers that may impose external costs on society. Let's also view how consumers' actions also may have external costs using Field's previous example on driving.

The social costs include all these private costs (fuel, oil, maintenance, insurance, depreciation, and operator's driving time) and also the cost experienced by people other than the operator who are exposed to the congestion and air pollution resulting from the use of the car.

The key point is that even if a firm or individual avoids paying for the external costs arising from their actions, the costs to society as a whole (congestion, pollution, environmental clean up, visual degradation, wildlife impacts, etc.) remain. Those external costs must be included in the social costs to ensure that society operates at a socially efficient rate of output.

There is a distinction to be drawn here between private costs and benefits, and social costs and benefits of production and consumption.

- Private costs refer to the expenditure incurred by producers in using resources to produce output or the costs incurred by consumers in giving up a part of their money income in buying goods and services.
- Private benefits include the profits made by producers in selling goods and services or the utility gained by consumers from consuming goods and services to satisfy needs and wants.
- Social costs refer to the costs imposed or borne y society as a result of private actions. For example,

the pollution caused by private production such as industrial output may be borne by the surrounding community. Markets do not exist for some environmental resources such as clean air or water and property rights for the use of environmental goods are not well defined or may be absent. The price mechanism cannot function without the use of a system of property rights. Property rights give individuals the right of usage and/or ownership over certain resources. They allow market exchange to occur because of three important features:

- Excludability – The owner of a property right has the right to exclude others from enjoying the benefits of using the property.
- Transferability – Property rights are marketable and can be traded in a market.
- Enforceability – Property rights are legally binding and courts can settle disputes and impose penalties on those who violate others property rights.

The problem that arises with many environmental goods, especially common property, is a lack of well defined property rights.

MEASUREMENT OF ENVIRONMENTAL VALUES

Understanding value of Environmental Goods requires understanding of the notion of "values" of environmental goods. There are two types of values: Use Value and Non-use Value.

Use Value: Satisfaction/utility that consumers obtain by directly consuming the goods. (*e.g.*, hiking through the woods).

In case of environmental goods, Use Value could include current use ("I am currently visiting the park), expected use ("I plan to visit the park later this year) and possible use (I might visit the park within next 10 years) Option Value: The value placed on a future ability to use the environment people are willing to pay for an option to use the environment in the future even they are not currently using it.

Non-use Value: It's a gain in person's utility without the person actually using the good directly. For example, one may value the wilderness areas in the Seirra Nevada, Nevada, not because because he/she plans to make use of the wilderness but because others may, and that may make him/her feel good.

There are three basic types of non-use value: Existence value, Altruistic vale and Beques value:

Types of non-use value: Existence value: The value a consumer attaches to knowing something exists (*e.g.*, One-horned rhinoceros in Kaziranaga National Park) Altruistic value: It's a value that the consumers derive from not consuming the goods themselves but from the fact they derive the benefit when someone else gains utility. (*e.g.*, If person A's neighbour derives benefit from his cleaning his front yard, person A obtains utility from the fact that his neighbours are better off.

Types of Non-use Value

Bequest value: It is associated with the well-being of the descendants. For example, if one values passing a wilderness area on to the next generation that wilderness area has a bequest value to the person even if he or she never uses it or intends to use it

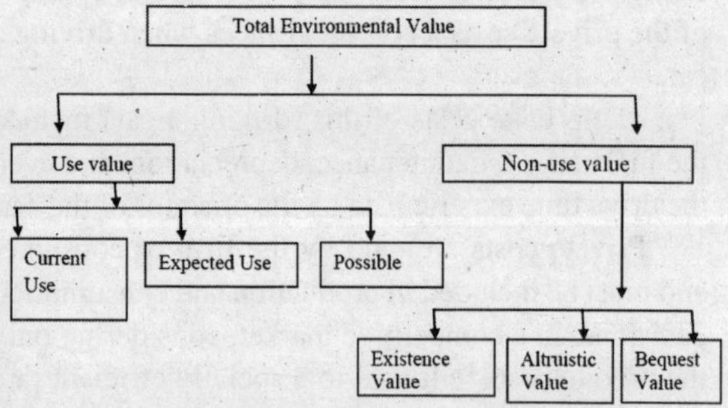

Why do we have to value the environment?

1. No price data exists for non-marketed environmental resources (demand or prices for private goods can be obtained from the market)
2. Need for information on benefits and costs of protecting and restoring the environment to guide policy makings
3. Need information on benefits and costs of protecting and restoring the environment to guide budget allocations

4. Need information to guide compensation setting for victims
5. Need information on external costs of development projects to guide development policies
6. Need information to guide setting of user charges/ fees/taxes for pollution control Need information to guide efficient and fair resource allocation

Methods of Measuring Environmental Values

Revealed Preference

In revealed preference approach real choices of people are observed in some market and information are inferred on the trade-offs between money and the environmental good.

Stated Preference

It basically involves asking people how much an environmental goods is worth.

Table: Methods of valuation of environmental goods

Methods	Revealed Preference	Stated Preference
Direct		Contingent Valuation Contingent Ranking
Indirect	Hedonic Pricing Travel Cost Method Household Production Function Does Response Approached Averting Expenditure/ Avoided Cost Approaches	

HEDONIC PRICING METHOD

Hedonic Pricing (HP) Approach is derived from the characteristic theory of value first proposed by Lancaster (1966) and Rosen (1974). This seeks to explain the value of a commodity as a bundle of valuable characteristics (*e.g.*, the price/rent of house depends on number of rooms, availability of garden in the campus, proximity to shops, noise level in the neighborhood, air quality levels etc.)

HP was first applied to environmental valuation by Ridker and Henning (1967). HP proceeds on three stages: First, hedonic price function is estimated Second, implicit prices are calculated Third, a demand curve for this variable may be estimated.

Dose Response Method

Dose response method involves finding a link between environmental change and production conditions for some marketed goods. Depending on the behavioral assumptions made and the statistical techniques employed, welfare estimates are then calculated using changes in *e.g.*, profits from the production of marketed goods.

For example, Ellis and Fischer (1987) estimated the contribution that wetland protection makes to the production of shell fish. They estimated a production function for Florida blue club off the Florida Gulf Coast which includes wetland club off the Florida Gulf Coast which includes wetland acreage as an input along with labour and capital.

Averting Expenditure Avoided Cost Method

This method tries to measure welfare loss to a household due to increase in averting or preventing expenditure arising out of decrease in environmental quality . The main notion is that a household produces flow of certain services or goods combining various inputs, one of which is environmental quality. For example, a rural household might combine water taken from its well with purification equipment to produce water potable.

Now, if water quality in the well declines, the household must increase its expenditure on other inputs to maintain quality of drinking water constant. This averting expenditure, as Cournot and Potter (1981) showed, can be used to measure welfare loss to the household of the decline in environmental quality. Other examples may include: the value of reduced risks of car accidents (Blomquist 1979), value of reduced risk of death as the result of fitting smoke alarms and noise nuisance from airports (layard 1972).

Travel Cost Method

One of the oldest approaches to environmental valuation proposed in a letter from Harold Hotelling to the US Forest Service in the 1930's, first used by Wood and Trice in 1958, popularized by Clawsen and Knetsch (1966) Premises • People bear cost to visit regions or sites (national park or estate) • Hypothesis : These costs are at least equal to the minimum value of the benefit people get when visiting the sites and their environmental goods or services. Thus, these travel costs can be used as a proxy for the price of visiting outdoor recreational sites . (In other words, the recreational benefits at a specific site can be derived from the demand functions that relate observed user's behaviour to the cost of visit.)

Steps of Analysis

1. Estimate the cost of travel and visit for each regions of origin
2. Questionnaire : visitors trip, expenses and characteristics
3. Estimate of the demand for the site (and environmental goods and services) depending on the cost of travel and visit and other characteristics

Options for Applying the Travel Cost Method

A simple zonal travel cost approach, using mostly secondary data, with some simple data collected from visitors. The zonal travel cost method is applied by collecting information on the number of visits to the site from different distances.

An individual travel cost approach, using a more detailed survey of visitors. The individual travel cost approach is similar to the zonal approach, but uses survey data from individual visitors in the statistical analysis, rather than data from each zone. This method thus requires more data collection and slightly more complicated analysis, but will give more precise results.

Hedonic Travel Cost Model which attempts to place values on the characteristics of recreational resources.

A random utility approach has been used to survey other data with more complicated statistical techniques. The random utility approach assumes that individuals will pick the site that they prefer, out of all possible fishing sites. Individuals make tradeoffs between site quality and the price of travel to the site. Hence, this model requires information on all possible sites that a visitor might select, their quality characteristics, and the travel costs to each site.

The travel cost method is applied by collecting information on the number of visits to the site from different distances. Because the travel and time costs will increase with distance, this information allows the researcher to calculate the number of visits purchased at different prices: the demand function and the consumer surplus, or economic benefits, for the recreational services of the site.

Step 1: The first step is to define a set of zones surrounding the site. These may be defined by concentric circles around the site, or by geographic divisions that make sense, such as metropolitan areas or counties surrounding the site at different distances.

Step 2: The second step is to collect information on the number of visitors from each zone, and the number of visits made in the last year.

Step 3: The third step is to calculate the visitation rates per 1000 population in each zone. This is simply the total visits per year from the zone, divided by the zone's population in thousands.

Step 4: The fourth step is to calculate the average round-trip travel distance and travel time to the site for each zone, using average cost per mile and per hour of travel time. What is the opportunity cost of time?

Step 5: The fifth step is to estimate, using regression analysis, the equation that relates visits per capita to travel costs and other important variables. From this, the researcher can estimate the demand function for the average visitor. In this simple model, the analysis might include demographic variables, such as age, income, gender, and education levels, using the average values for each zone.

Step 6: The sixth step is to construct the demand function for visits to the site, using the results of the regression analysis. The first point on the demand curve is the total visitors to the site at current access costs (assuming there is no entry fee for the site), which in this example is 1600 visits per year.

Step 7: The final step is to estimate the total economic benefit of the site to visitors by calculating the consumer surplus, or the area under the demand curve.

Hedonic Travel Cost Model

On many occasion, we interested in the value of changing characteristics of a site rather than in the value of the site in toto. In this respect, hedonic travel cost model attempts to place values on the characteristics of recreational resources. Hedonic travel cost model was first proposed by Brown and Mendelsohn (1984) and has been applied recently to forest characteristics by Englin and Mendelsohn (1991) and coastal water quality by Bockstael et. al. (1987).

Hedonic Travel Cost Model: Steps: 1. Respondents to a number of sites (*e.g.*, forest) are sampled to determine their zone of origine. The levels of physical characteristics are recorded for each site A travel cost function is estimated for each zone, as

$$C(Z) = c_0 + c_1 z_1 + c_2 z_2 + \ldots c_m z_m \qquad \ldots(1)$$

Where, C(Z) are travel costs, z_1 is distance to site, $z_1 \ldots z_m$ are characteristics and $c_0 \ldots c_m$ are coefficients to be estimated.

Hedonic Travel Cost Model: Steps: A separate regression is performed for each zone of origin such that each will have a vector of coefficients $\{c_0 \ldots c_m\}$. For a given characteristics *m*, the utility maximising individual will choose visits such that the marginal costs of characteristics (the coefficient c_m) is just equal to the marginal benefit to him.

Hedonic Travel Cost Model: Steps: 2. Estimate a demand curve for each characteristics regressing a site characteristic levels (dependent variable) against the predicted marginal cost of that characteristic and socio-economic variables for each zone of origin. A separate regression is run for each characteristic. The expectation is that the coefficient on the marginal cost variable will be negative implying that as the level of characteristics rises people are unwilling to pay as much for each further increment.

Contingent Valuation Method

Contingent Valuation Method (CVM) was first used by Davis (1963) in a study of hunters in Maine and it was widely developed with Bohm (1972), Randal et.al. (1974), Brookshire et. al., (1976) etc. The essence of CVM method involves asking The essence of CVM method involves asking individual to imagine some situation that is typically outside the individual's experience and speculate on how he or she would act in such a situation.

It is called 'contingent valuation' because the valuation is contingent on the hypothetical scenario put to respondents.

1. CVM exercise can be split into five stages:
2. Setting up the hypothetical market
3. Obtaining bids
4. Estimating mean WTP and or WTAC
5. Estimating bid curves
6. Aggregating the data

As Carson (1991) noted, there are six main component of a successful CV study:

1. Define Market Scenario
2. Choose elicitation method
3. Design market administration
4. Design sampling
5. Design of experiment
6. Estimate willingness-to-pay function

COASE'S BARGAINING SOLUTION AND COLLECTIVE

There are two main approaches to solve the environmental externality: (*a*) appropriate government policies, and (*b*) well-defined property rights. Government policies pertain to direct regulation (or, command and control approach), and marketbased approach in the form of economic instruments.

The property rights approach is applicable when either community or individual posses well defined property rights in carrying out the environment related activities. The property rights approach, developed by Ronald Coase in 1960, suggests that an efficient solution to the problem of externality may be arrived at if property rights are welldefined. This solution, popularly known as **'Coase** theorem', states that efficient allocation of resources and solution to Pareto relevant externality is possible under the following assumptions: (*i*) zero transaction costs – the cost involved in the bargaining process between the two parties do not exists, (*ii*) well defined property rights - either of the party or both the parties posses well-defined property rights, (*iii*) perfect competition prevails in the market, iv) no income or wealth effects is imposed with the Coasean solution, and (*v*) no free rider effects — since the parties have well defined property rights. In this situation, let us illustrate the method of bargaining for feasible solution through an example.

Let us consider the case of a polluting factory which dumps its effluents to the nearby river as a result of which the water downstream gets polluted. The water pollution has adverse effects on the health and property of the nearby community who use the river water. Therefore, they want the pollution load released into the river to be zero. It is possible for the factory to adopt pollution abatement measures which can purify the effluents and reduce the pollution load to zero level. Installation of such technology, however, would increase the cost of production for the factory and keeping up with its objective of profit maximization the factory does not want to install pollution abatement measures. Thus, a conflict in interest between the factory and the community is generated.

Let us explain the position through Fig. using the typical economics analogy. On the *x*-axis we measure pollution abatement (that is, removal of pollution) by the factory and on y-axis we measure the level of pollution cost. The nearby community faces a downward sloping pollution abatement cost curve (AB). It indicates that as pollution abatement increases (that is, more amount is pollution is removed or, less amount is pollution is present in the river), there is a decrease in the pollution cost to the community. Thus, when pollution abatement reaches the level 'OB' (that is, all the pollutants are removed from the river), the pollution cost to the community is zero. On the other hand, the factory has an upward sloping pollution abatement cost curve indicating the increasing marginal cost of abatement (OD). When pollution abatement is zero, no pollution cost is borne by the factory. The factory would like to reduce its pollution abatement expenditure while the community would like the pollution level to be zero.

Let us take the situation that the community is holding the property rights for clean environment. Hence, the community can dictate terms to the factory about the pollution load to be released to the river. In this situation, the factory is generating pollution and creating problems for a community that demands zero pollution. For various welfare reasons, the factory cannot be closed down and financial constraints have made the factory to apply limited pollution abatement measures. In this context, negotiation is the only solution to resolve the conflict.

In the negotiation, let us assume that the community can accept a slightly lower level of pollution emission '*n*'. At this level of pollution abatement, however pollution cost to the community is '*h*' and pollution cost to the factory is '*g*'. Hence, through negotiation, the factory is willing to give compensation up to the extent 'gh' to the community (see Fig.). The level of abatement reached through the negotiation in this case is anywhere between the optimum (t) and the maximum (B).

Diagram

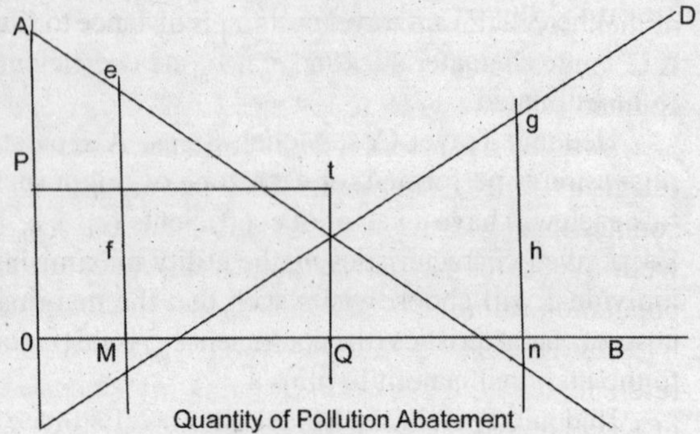

Let us take the other situation where factory has the property rights. Since the polluter has the property rights, the starting point for negotiation is zero level of pollution abatement. Obviously, for welfare reasons, the community would like the pollution level to be reduced by the factory, which in turn implies higher pollution abatement expenditure by the factory. Suppose the community wants the pollution abatement to be '*m*'. At this level, the pollution cost to the community is **'f** while pollution abatement cost to the factory is '*e*'. It is, therefore, viable to the community to pay compensation to the factory to the extent of '*ef*'.

We observe from fig. that it is expensive to abate pollution beyond the level **'q'.** The government can regulate pollution abatement to be fixed at the level '*q*' through command and control measures. Otherwise, it can impose taxes on the polluter (the factory, in this case) to the extent '*t*', which is equivalent to the pollution cost on the community. The Coasean principle, however, provides an alternative to pollution tax. Here, externality can be internalized through well-defined property rights and compensation.

POPULATION THEORIES

It appears that population records were maintained during the times when Egyptian, Chinese, Greek, and ancient Indian civilizations flourished in the world. It also appears that population was counted in Jeddah in 2030 B.C. Greek historian Herodotus makes us believe that in about 400 B.C. Zerxes had the counting of his soldiers before invading Greece. From the records it also appears that among Romans counting of their population for the first time was done in 435 B.C. and thereafter in 470 years, population was counted as many as 69 times.

As so far as ancient India is concerned, from our religious books it appears that population was counted during Ramayana and Mahabharata times as well. We come across frequent references about population counting particularly those who laid their lives during Mahabharata was. Similarly, we also find references about population counting in *Arthasastra* of Kautilya and in later texts as *Ain-i-Akbari*.

Coming to recent times we find that Henry VIII of England got the records of the number of people who were the victims of plague of 1535. He also gotweekly, wills of mortality prepared in which information was provided about those who died during the course of the week. For this purpose, even a press was set up in London. But it may he clearly understood that during that period population counting was not considered as end in itself, but was only means to an end; end being either to know the strength of the armed forces or making an estimate of available man power for invading the enemy, etc. Another important reason and consideration which weighed with them was that they wanted to know how many more persons had been order to pay revenue. Even some religions maintained an account of deaths and births of their followers and those who performed marriages according to their religious traditions.

In the development of demographic studies, since the very initial stages, attention of the society and demographers has been drawn towards population theories. Even Confucius and Chinese thinkers at the very initial stages of development, realized that population explosion could dislocate economic system of a nation. The old writers and thinkers, however, could not clarify how death or birth rates influenced and disturbed economic system. Both Plato and Aristotle believed that a state should have only such population as was essential for economic self-sufficiency and national defence. If less population made a nation dependent on other, then more population was likely to become a burden on society. 17th and 18th century economists also paid attention to this problem. According to them, increase in population as such was not bad. According to them increased population was bound to result in increased wages and labour and also in increased production. But Quemey believed that instead of increase in population there should be increased population. In our own times Smith linked wages with population.

Greek thought on population: Historically both Plato and Aristotle believed that limited population was essential for happy life of a society. Low population will make the society poor. According to them the laws of succession and inheritance should be such that in that there were no sharp variances either in family or properly structure. If someone had no child, he should be permitted to adopt someone as his child. Both of them believed that in order to check abnormal population growth it was idea of communism of wires as a means for checking population. He also did not favour the idea of using artificial means and method for checking population growth.

Population Philosophy during Middle ages: As regards population ideas of the people of middle ages Europe, the whole period can be divided into two parts; namely the period from 400-1200 A.D. and 1200-1500 AD. But on the whole population control philosophy was not favoured. Christian thinkers, during this period took a moral view of the population problem. On the one hand they opposed divorce, killing of children, abortion etc., whereas on the other hand they laid stress on controlling of passions and leading a bachelor's life. These people believed that nature and natural calamities could reduce population to a considerable extent and as such they pleaded that in order to save population and to keep that at a particular level, birth rate should always be high. During this period the muslims and the Mercantilists believed that there should be growth in population because manpower will be available to produce more and more and demands for finished goods for consumption will go up. They wanted to have more births, no matter what the living standard of the people was. According to these people, population could be controlled by the spread of diseases, abortions, late marriages etc.

Many thinkers believed that birth and death rates were predestined and that nothing could be done to check these. Many also believed that growth of population should not be checked because people were real strength of a country. In the words of Samual Forrey 'People and plenty are commonly the begetters. The one of the other, if rightly ordered.' Prof. Child pleaded that increasing population alone could make the people happy and prosperous.

In France, M. Dela Riviere L. said, 'The social order is not the work of man but is on the contrary instituted by the author of all nature himself as all the branches of physical order.' Similarly, Dr. Quesmay also said that, 'Nature order is merely the physical constitution which God himself has given to the universe'. They believed that whatever nature has made for man is essential and that the men should practice celibacy. They also laid stress on the establishment of new colonies. They have also said that in order to increase population, the people should be given suitable rewards as well; if growth rate was very low, so that population growth continued.

Both of them believed that there was direct relationship between population and poverty. Plato also believed that population equilibriums were necessary for maintaining social equilibrium. Other Greek thinkers who discussed population problems included Herodotus, Thucidides and Xenophon. The last mentioned one who is believed to have lived between 440-335 B.C. believed that for division of labour it was essential that there should be more population. He wanted that all restrictions on immigration and emigration should be removed.

Many thinkers in the past believed that in case poverty was to be removed, it was essential that the state should take steps for increasing income of people. One of the methods which state could follow was that all restrictions on the coming of the foreigners in the country should be removed. They should be provided all facilities so that international trade could increase. This will result in increased profit, trade and peace between the two countries. Obviously, it is in peace that income can increase and not in a war situation in any way.

Roman thinkers on population: Romans did not favour city states and instead they believed in the idea of having big states and empires. On the whole they did not bother about the growth of population and roman economists did not spend much time on this problem as well. In the words of Prof. Haney, 'Athenians were thinkers keen and analytical. The Romans were men of action, warriors and statesmen. The former left a philosophy which influenced that ethics and economics of later thinkers, the latter built institution which as profoundly affected law and politics.' They on the whole wanted to have more population because then alone the state could have soldiers to fight and help in the expansion of empire. Cicero, an important Roman thinker bitterly opposed that is complete and perfect. They however, also believed that, 'As it is in the physical order that men thus united in society multiply promptly, by natural and necessary parallel to the multiplication they are reduced to lack of means of subsistence if they do not at the same time, multiply those means of cultivation.' According to them any attempt to check population was only a hindrance on the way of will of God and as such population growth was in the interest of society as a whole. There were some thinkers, however, who believed that if population growth gave strength to the nation then such a growth also created many problems for the country as a whole. On the whole, however, in the past population growth was not condemned in any society as that did not create any problem.

The Mercantilists: Somewhere during 16th century mercantilists came to the front and continued to preach their philosophy for about two centuries. These people were primarily in favour of increased population.

B. Colbert, Charles Devant and John Locke were among many who can be mentioned in this regard. According to them real happiness came with trade, because then alone people could earn wealth. Increase in population can help in the development of trade and industry. More the number of people in a state, more shall it be possible for it to have increased trade and industry. Since more man power will be available therefore, people will be available on less wages and there will be more profits and production. Both the society and individual shall have more income. Many believed that if there was more population then nature automatically checked that and as such there was no need to use artificial means and methods for checking population. More population was also favoured because that was essential for the defence of country that is to say that the nation could have any number of soldiers, if need be.

The Physiocrates: These scholars mostly belonged to France. Among others mention may be made of the names of F. Quesnay, Robert Turgot, Marquis Reviere, etc., by and large. They did not believe that population growth in any way should be checked. They were of the view that population of a state was always a source of strength as well as cause of misery and thus a double-edged sword. But still they did not favour the unnatural means for checking population growth. Malthus formulation on population was a landmark in the history of population theories. He generalizes the relationship between population factors and population growth.

Malthusian Theory

Malthus was undoubtedly important in the history of political, economic and welfare theory and was at the same time a crucial and acknowledged influence in the evolutionary debate, carrying the history of socio-economic theory with a deeper analysis of Darwin's development of evolutionary theory.

Malthusian law that population when left unchecked, increases geometrically (while at most the food supply can increase arithmetically) can be seen as a natural law about man. Indeed, it was evolutionism which brought the distinction between mind and body into question: if man is considered a person for social purposes, he remains an organism from a biological point of view. Looking back once again, one sees Malthus as the source of the view of nature which led to Social Darwinism—The social struggle for existence, the survival of the fittest.

The significance of this view for the history of Evolutionary Theory (is the process by which organisms change over time as a result of changes in heritable physical or behavioral traits as proposed by Darwin) is that it so affronted Malthus's sense of reality that it occasioned his essay. Even though Malthus softened his doctrine in later editions, it altered the image of nature from benign harmony to an inexorable imbalance between nature's supply of sustenance and man's need for both food and sex and became the hallmark for the way he envisioned the Social Theory to be acting as an important catalyst for the development of Evolutionary Theory. To Malthus, Godwin had gone too far in removing man from nature.

Human life would be prolonged indefinitely; both the physical and mental constitution of man would undergo limitless improvement; slavery and war would cease; and the acquired perfections of an individual would naturally be transmitted to the next generation by inheritance, the basis of this all were the improvement in domesticated animals, lending this credence hope. Condorcet posited that the population might exceed the means of subsistence, but this day was far away and posed no threat to the indefinite perfectibility of the human race; by which time there would be some technological way to overcome the said problems.

Malthus observes in the additions made to the essay in 1817 that 'It is probable that having found the bow bent too much one way, I was induced to bend it too much the other, in order to make it straight....But I shall always be quite ready to blot out any part of the work which is considered as a competent Tribunal as having a tendency to prevent the bow from becoming finally straight, and to impede the progress of truth...' and in so doing, rejected this view as well. Malthus concentrates first on the impediments to progress, and thus that the perspective on man's place in nature was radically changed.

This shows how Robert Wallace, Godwin, Condorcet and even Paley, among many others, had acknowledge some version of potential disproportion between population and food supply: yet, the paradigm within which they viewed it prevented them from taking it seriously, and as a genuine prospect for mankind. The problem was absorbed in the general area of optimism, and lingering doubts were put to sleep with the promise of progress overcoming the obstacle should it arise.

Now, we have studied about the history of population theories, in the next section, we will concentrate on the Mercantilist theories.

MERCANTILIST AND RELATED THEORIES

Mercantilism was the theory of trade espoused by the major European power from roughly 1500 to 1800. It advocated that a nation should export more than it imported and accumulate bullion to make up the difference. The exportation of finished goods was favoured over extractive industries like farming.

Mercantile was a reaction against the economic problems of earlier times when states were too weak to guide their economies and when every town or principality levied its own tariffs on goods passing through its borders.

The modern age brought the rise of powerful nation states (Holland, France, Spain and England) and was marked by almost constant welfare. Money (bullion) was needed to support ever-expanding armies and navies. Mercantilist concept developed from this need.

Underlying their theory was the belief that wealth was finite. If one nation hoped to grow richer, it had to do so at the expense of some other nation.

The development of colonies become very attractive during this era. Wealth could be kept by a nation if its colonies provided raw materials to the mother country and the mother country could sell-finished goods to the colonies.

In England, the application of mercantilist theory led to the development of a skilled labour force at home and the creation of a large navy and merchant marine. However, mercantilism also led to inflation and alienation in the colonies.

The theory of mercantilism was put into practice in the English colonies through the Navigation Acts. The Navigation Acts were efforts to put the theory of mercantilism into actual practices.

Mercantilists viewed the economic system as a zero-sum game, in which any gain by one party required a loss by another. Thus, any system of policies that benefited one group would be definition among the other, and there was no possibility of economics being used to maximize the commonwealth or common good. Mercantilists writings were also generally created to rationalize particular practices rather than as investigations into the best policies.

Mercantilist domestic policy was more fragmented into its trade policy. While Adam Smith portrayed Mercantilism as supportive of strict contracts over the economy, many mercantilists disagreed. The early modern era was one of letters patent and government imposed monopolies; some mercantilists supported these, but others acknowledged the corruption and insufficiency of such systems. Many mercantilists also realized that the inevitable results of quotas and price ceilings were black markets. One notion that mercantilists widely agreed upon was the need for economic operation of the working population. Labourers and farmers were to live at the 'margins of subsistence'. The goal was to maximize production, with no concern for consumption. Extra money, free time and education for the lower classes were seen to inevitably lead to vice and laziness and would result in harm to the economy.

The mercantilists saw a large population as a form of wealth that made possible the development of bigger markets and armies. Opposite of mercantilism was the doctrine of physiocracy, which predicted that mankind would outgrow its resources. The idea of Mercantilism was to protect the markets as well as maintain agriculture and those who were dependent upon it.

The Austrian lawyer and scholar Philipp Wilhelm van Horwick, one of the pioneers of Cameralism, detailed a nine-point program of what he deemed effective national economy in his *Austria Over All, If She Only Will* of 1684 which comprehensively sums up the tenets of mercantilism':

- That every little bit of a country's soil be utilized for agriculture, mining or manufacturing.

- That all new materials found in a country be used in domestic manufacture, since finished goods have a higher value than raw material.
- That a large, working population be encouraged.
- The all exports of gold and silver be prohibited, all domestic money be kept in circulation.
- That all imports of foreign goods be discouraged as much as possible.
- That where certain imports are indispensable they be obtained at first hand, in exchange for other materials that can be finished.
- That opportunities be constantly sought for selling a country's surplus manufactures to foreigners, so far as necessary, for gold and silver.
- That no importation be allowed if such goods are sufficiently and suitably supplied at home.

Mercantilism was a system of statism which employed economic fallacy to build up a structure of imperial state power, as well as special subsidy and monopolistic privilege to individuals or groups favoured by the state. Thus, mercantilism held exports should be encouraged by the government and imports discouraged.

SOCIALIST AND MARXIST WRITINGS

Karl Marx (1818-1883) was a German social philosopher, who became founder of modern communism. Marx did not believe that all hardships with which the people were suffering were due to man's tendency to grow in numbers faster than his production of subsistence would permit. On the other hand, he believed that man's tendency to press on the means of subsistence was due to evils of capitalism which would disappear with the emergence of communism. He related population growth with present economic system and for him both were inseparable. To quote him:

It is the working population which, while effecting the accumulation of capital, also produces the means where by it is itself rendered relatively superfluous is turned into a relatively surplus population and it does so to an increasing extent. This is a law of population peculiar to capitalist method of production, and in fact, every method of production that arises in the course of history has its own peculiar, historically valid law of population. It is only for plants and animals that there is law of population in the abstract and that only in so far as man does not interfere with them.

He believed that poverty and unemployment were not due to increased population, but on account of capitalist system which tailed to provide jobs. It was this system which was responsible for real production and uneven distribution of wealth and for providing jobs to only few persons.

Marx did not agree with Malthus's Theory of Population. According to him, Malthus was plagiarist and poured ridicule over him. According to him, the work of Malthus was that of school children. According to Marx, 'His work in the first term was nothing than a school boyish, superficial and parsonic, declamatory with plagiarism from Defoe., Sir James Stuart, Townsend, Franklin Wallace and others, and did not contain single sentence thought out lay Malthus himself.'

According to Marx, in no country of the world does population increases on account of fertility but increases only on account of capitalist policies. The capitalists make labour part of their production and steal something out of that. By installing new machines, a capitalist wants to have maximum surplus value and also spread unemployment out of that as well. In this way, he creates an army of unemployed persons and thus labour wages go on decreasing. The poor population cannot nourish their children due to limited financial means and as such the question of surplus population arises. He thus came to the conclusion that main cause of surplus population was nothing else but wrong policies of the capitalists. There is less production of food supplies from the lands on account of Zamindari system where there is uncertainty about ownership of land. According to him, 'it is working population which, while effecting the accumulation of capital, also provides means whereby it is itself rendered relatively superfluous, is turned into a relative surplus population, and it does so to an ever increasing extent. This is law of population peculiar to the capitalist method of population.'

Marx also believed that in every period of production there is a separate law of population. That law suits that condition alone. Thus, a law of population prevailing in a capitalist society cannot be made applicable to the socialist society and so on.

The socialists, who closely follow Marx include Urianis, Boyarski, Shusharin, Malisher, Riabouekin and Raichko. They all believe that in socialist system there will be full opportunity of employment and as such there will be no section of population which in any way will be surplus. In socialist countries, there is no need to reduce birth rate and that in these countries production is increased by controlling nature and exploiting natural resources. There is no need to check birth rate because the whole system of distribution is rational and to the advantage of the society as a whole. They, therefore, believe that present system of unemployment which prevails in a capitalist society is responsible for increased or over-population.

Marx was of the view that one important cause of population growth was food deficiency, which was due to evils of capitalism. He supported his argument by saying that in communist countries where all were getting proper food, there was no population problems. In none of the communist countries was there compulsory family planning. He was convinced that fertility differentials were due to economic inequalities.

The socialists believe that population in a socialist society will increase slowly than in a capitalist society because of the superior status of women under socialism. Marx was of the view that in a socialist society reproductive behaviour would develop a complete harmony between the individual and the society. The socialists today believe that birth control contributes to the emancipation of women. Modern socialists believe not only in birth control but allow abortion as well.

GROWTH THEORY

Growth theories attempt to explain the conditions that are necessary for development to occur and weigh up the relative importance of particular conditions. Growth theories offers two plausible explanation of growth. One stresses the supply of productive ideas and holds that the individual evolution had to wait until we had thought up enough inventions to lift us into the era of modern growth. It says roughly, that the growth of the living standards depends on the growth of science. The other explanation stresses incentives: Growth could begin only when hard work and business enterprise were free of heavy taxation, of social stigma and of other interference by the government. The first branch of theory is well developed. It is the second that now challenges the growth economist to explain not just growth but the evolution of political and religious initiatives and social attitudes as well. Early theories focussed an understanding economic growth and attempted to find general determinants of growth that could be applied to any instance under consideration. By looking at patterns of growth, the hope was to discover some of the laws or principles which govern growth at all times and in all countries. Modern theories tend to accept the conditions growth change overtime and are often more critical of the attempts to generate one-size-fits all growth theories.

There are several broad categories of growth theories including:

- Linear growth theory
- Structural change theory
- Dependency theory
- New-classical theory
- New-growth theory
- Property rights.

Measurement and Indicators of Demographic Determinants

Fertility: Demographics distinguish between fecundity the underlying biological potential for reproduction, and fertility, the actual level of achieved reproduction. The difference between biological potential and realized fertility is determined by several intervening factors including the following:

- Most women do not begin reproducing immediately upon the onset of puberty, which itself does not occur at a fixed age.
- Some women with the potential to reproduce never do so.
- Some women become widowed and do not remarry.

- Various elements of social behaviour restrain fertility, and
- Many human couples choose consciously to restrict their fertility by means of sexual abstinence, contraception, abortion or sterilization.

The total fertility rate in a specific year is defined as the total number of children that would be born to each woman if she was to live to the end of the child-bearing years and give birth to children in alignment with the prevailing age specific fertility rates. It is calculated by totalling the age specific fertility rates as defined over five year intervals. Assuming no net migration and unchanged mortality, a total fertility rate of 2.1 children per woman ensures a broadly stable population. Together with mortality and migration, fertility is an element of population growth, reflecting both the causes and efforts of economic and social developments. The reasons for the dramatic decline in birth rate during the past few decades include, postponed family formation and child bearing and a decrease in desired family sizes. This indicator is measured in children per woman.

Mortality: As noted above, the science of demography and natural increase in population, has its intellectual roots in the realization that human mortality, while consisting of unpredictable individual events has a statistical regularity when aggregated across a large group. This recognition forms the basis of a life insurance. The basis of their industry is the life-table or mortality table which summarizes the distribution of longevity – observed over a period of years among members of a population.

Overall human mortality levels can best be compared by using the life-table measures including life expectancy at birth, the number of years of life expected of a newborn baby on the basis of different mortality levels for persons of all ages. Life expectancies of premodern populations, with the poor knowledge of sanitation and health care, may have been low as 25–30 years. The largest toll of death was observed in infancy and childhood, perhaps 20 per cent of new born children died in their first 12 months of life and another 30 per cent before they reached five years of age. Life expectancy of females usually exceeds that of males and this female advantage has grown as overall life expectancy has increased. Following may be factors of natural increase in population.

- **The epidemiologic transition:** It is the process by which the pattern of mortality and disease is transformed from one of high mortality among infants and children and episodic famine and epidemic affecting all age groups to one of the degenerative and man-made diseases affecting principally the elderly. It is generally, believed that the epidemiologic transitions prior to the 20th century were closely associated with rising standards of living, nutrition and sanitation. In contrast, those occurring in developing nations have been more or less independent of such internal socio-economic development and more closely tied to organized health care and disease control programme developed and financed internationally. There is no doubt that 20th century declines in mortality in developing countries have been far more rapid than those that occurred in the 19th century.
- **Infant mortality:** Infant mortality is conventionally measured as the number of deaths in the first year of life per 1,000 live births during the same year. Approximately 8 per cent of new born babies die within the first year of life. In developing countries, substantial declines in infant mortality have been credited to improved sanitation and nutrition increased access to modern health care and improved birth spacing through the use of contraception.
- **Infanticide:** The deliberate killing of new born infants has long been practiced in human societies. It seems to have been common in the ancient cultures of Greece, Rome and China and it was practiced in Europe until the 19th century. In many societies practicing infanticide, infants were not deemed to be fully human until they underwent a rite of initiation that took place from a few days to several years after and therefore killing before such initiation was socially acceptable. The purpose of infanticide were various:
  (*i*) Child spacing or fertility control in the absence of effective contraception,

(*ii*) Elimination of illegitimate deformed or orphaned or twin children, and

(*iii*) Sex preferences

With the development and spread of the means of effective feeling regulation, infanticide has come to be strongly disapproved in most societies, though it continues to be practiced in same isolated traditional cultures.

- Mortality among the elderly: During the 1970s and 1980s, in industrialized countries there were unexpectedly large declines in mortality among the elderly, resulting in larger than projected numbers of the very old. The decline in elders' morality rate was the result of improved health and hygiene conditions, good health facilities, improved nutrition and other improved surroundings for the better quality of life.

CONCEPTS OF FERTILITY AND FECUNDITY

Definition of Fertility

Some of the definitions of fertility include:

- According to Lewis and Thomson, fertility is generally used to indicate the actual reproductive performance of a woman or groups of women. The crude birth rate is only one measure of fertility.
- According to Barnard Benjamin, fertility measures the rate at which a population adds to itself by births and is normally assessed by equating the number of births to the size of same section of population, such as the number of married couples to the numbers of the women of child bearing age, which is an appropriate yardstick of potential fertility.
- Medically defined, fertility is the ability to conceive and bear children, the ability to become pregnant through normal sexual activity.
- Barclay stated that fertility is an actual level of performance in a population, based on the number of live births that occur. Fertility can be ascertained from statistics of birth. The study of fertility does not indicate the level of fecundity for which there is no direct measurement.

As a measure, fertility rate is the number of offspring born per mating pair, individual or population. Fertility differs from fecundity, which is defined as the potential for reproduction. A lack of fertility is infertility, while a lack of fecundity would be called sterility.

In demographic context, fertility refers to the actual production of offspring, rather than the physical capability to produce, which is termed fecundity. Demographers measure the fertility rate in a variety of ways, which can be broadly broken into 'period' measure and 'cohort' measures.

Table: Measures of Fertility

I. Period Measure	II. Cohort Measure
1. Crude birth Rate (CBR)	1. Total fertility Rate (TFR)
2. General fertility Rate (GFR)	2. Cross Reproduction Rate (GPR)
3. Child-woman Ratio (CWR)	3. Net Reproduction Rate (NRR)
4. Coale's Index of Fertility (CIF)	Net Reproduction Rate (NRR)

I. Period Measures

1. **Crude birth rate (CBR):** It means the number of live births in a given per year per 1,000 people alive at the middle of the year. One disadvantage of this indicator is that it is influenced by the age structure of the population.
2. **General fertility Rate (GFR):** The number of births in a year divided by the number of women aged 15-44 per 1000. It focuses on the potential mother only and takes the age distribution into account.
3. **Child-woman ratio (CWR):** The ratio of the number of children under 5 to the number of women aged 15-49 per 1000. It is especially useful in historical data as it does not require counting births. This measure is actually a hybrid, because it involves deaths as well as births. This is because of infant morality same of the birth are not included and because of adult mortality, same of the women who gave birth, are not counted either.
4. **Coale's Index of Fertility (CIF):** This is a special device used in historical research.

II. Cohort Measures

1. **Total fertility rate (TFR):** The total number of children a woman would bear during her lifetime if she were to experience the prevailing age specific fertility rates of women. TFR equals the sum of all age groups of times each ASFR rate.
2. **Gross Reproduction Rate (GRR):** The number of girl babies a synthetic cohort will have. It assumes that all of the baby girls will grow up and live to at least age 50.
3. **Net Reproduction Rate (NRR):** The NRR starts with the GRR and adds the realistic assumption that some of the women will die before the age of 49, therefore, they will not be alive to bear some of the potential babies that are now counted in the GRR. NRR is always lower than GRR, but in countries where mortality is very low, almost all the baby girls grow up to be potential mothers, and the NRR is practically the same as GRR. In countries with high mortality, NRR can be as low as 70% of GRR. When NRR = 1.0, each generation of 1000 baby girls grows up and gives birth to exactly 1000 girls. When NRR is less than one, each generation is smaller than the previous one. When NRR is greater than each generation is large than the one before. NRR is a measure of the long-term future potential for growth, but it usually is different from the current population growth rate.

Fecundity

According to Thompson and Lewis, fecundity is a biological potential and the physiological capacity to participate in reproduction. The absence of this potential is known as infecundity or sterility. It is the capacity to conceive or bear children. In every society, a very large proportion of infertile women are also infecund. In the near past, it was believed that an involuntarily childless marriage was almost always due to infecundity of wife, but it is not so the case today.

However, Thompson and Lewis state that childlessness is not proof of infecundity of the wife but may be due to the sterility of either of the wife or the husband and may arise from the fact that the spernatozoa of a particular make cannot fertilise the ova of a particular female to the mutual incapability of the individual's germs cells.

Barcklay has defined fecundity as the potential level of performance of physical capacity for bearing children of the population.

Morbidity and Mortality

Mortality is a stage at which person ceases to live but in morbidity the person is actually alive but this state of mind is such that he is not in a position to perform any solid mental or physical work. If health is understood as state of complete physical, mental and social wellbeing, morbidity is a situation in which one of the above conditions must be essentially missing. In a state of morbidity a person can be deformed, deficient, mentally depressed and so on. Since, in some cases, the diseases or trouble can be diagnosed after a very long time, therefore, the whole affair becomes complex and complicated.

How to Find Morbidity?

A question now arises as to how morbidity should be found. Of course a simple method is to contact either such a person himself or his doctors or persons attending on him, who can speak on his behalf, but there are other methods as well. These include both survey and record methods. The survey method can be both a large survey as well as a small survey. In a survey, an area is picked up and in that efforts are made to find out the type of sickness, system of treatment, number of sick persons and other related information. In some cases, only the head of the family is contacted and from him all information about family is collected. When the surveyor visits the locality once and tries to get all information, this is called single visit survey. But when the some families are visited at periodical intervals and information is again collected and compared that is called periodical visit survey.

A survey can be conducted by the government, governmental financed bodies as well as private bodies. Since surveys are costly and time consuming, therefore, large scale surveys are conducted by government bodies whereas private agencies carry only small scale surveys. Many governmental maintain records about sick persons.

Life Tables

In finding out the mortality rate, life tables play a very big role. In the words of David M. Heer, these provide the most complete picture of mortality in a given population. Life tables help in finding out the average death or birth rate of a society and as such are extensively used by those who are engaged in life insurance. In the words of Thompson and Lewis, 'Such information could be used to calculate the premium any individual as a member of group would need to pay in order to make it possible to guarantee each member of this group a specified sum of money at a given age or his heirs a specified sum upon his death. Since with the help of life tables it becomes possible to know the expected age of a persons in society. It becomes easy for the insurance people to fix rates of premium. In the words of Bogue, 'The life tables is a mathematical model that portrays mortality conditions at a time among a population and provides a basis for measuring longevity.' Such a table is constructed on the basis rate of death. These tables also help in preparing and determining average life expectancy, based on age specific mortality trends. It is possible to compare national and international rates of mortality. These have proved useful for making hypothetical model of population and studying crude death and migration rates. In practice this was done by Lotka A.J. (1925), Coal A. J. and Glass DV. For marriage analysis, life tables were used by Graunt and Makeham.

There are two types of life tables that can be constructed. One of these is timed as period life tables, which according to David M. Heer, 'Summarizes the age sex specific mortality conditions pertaining in a given year or other short time period. The second type of life table is called a cohort or generation life table, which summaries the age sex specific mortality experience of a given birth cohort (a group of persons all born at the same time) for their lifetime and thus a time period of many calendar years.' The life tables help to provide the following information:

(*a*) The probability of death rate during the year for those persons entering and exact age, *x*(*q x*);

(*b*) The number of deaths occurring between exact age x and exact age *x* + 1 (*dx*);

(*c*) The number of survivors to exact age *x* (*l x*);

(*d*) The number of years of life lived by the Cohort between exact age *x* and exact age *x* + 1 (*lx*);

(*e*) The total years of life lived by the Cohort from age × to the end of the human life span (T*x*).

MORTALITY

Mortality is the condition of being mortal, or susceptible to death; the opposite of immortality. Mortality rate is a measure of the number of deaths (in general, or due to a specific cause) in some population, scaled to the size of that population, per unit time. Mortality rate is typically expressed in units of deaths per 1000 individuals per year; thus, a mortality rate of 9.5 in a population of 100,000 would mean 950 deaths per year in that entire population. It is distinct from morbidity rate, which refers to the number of individuals in poor health during a given time period (the prevalence rate) or the number who currently have that disease (the incidence rate), scaled to the size of the population.

One distinguishes:

1. The **crude death rate**, the total number of deaths per year per 1000 people. The crude death rate for the whole world is currently about 8.23 per 1000 per year according to the current CIA World Factbook.
2. The **perinatal mortality rate**, the sum of neonatal deaths and fetal deaths (stillbirths) per 1000 births.
3. The **maternal mortality rate**, the number of maternal deaths due to childbearing per 100,000 live births.
4. The **infant mortality rate**, the number of deaths of children less than 1 year old per 1000 live births.
5. The **child mortality rate**, the number of deaths of children less than 5 years old per 1000 live births.
6. The **standardised mortality rate** (SMR)- This represents a proportional comparison to the numbers of deaths that would have been expected if the population had been of a standard composition in terms of age, gender, etc.
7. The **age-specific mortality rate** (ASMR) - This refers to the total number of deaths per year per 1000 people of a given age (*e.g.* age 62 last birthday).

In regard to the success or failure of medical treatment or procedures, one would also distinguish:

1. The **early mortality rate**, the total number of deaths in the early stages of an ongoing treatment, or in the period immediately following an acute treatment.
2. The **late mortality rate**, the total number of deaths in the late stages of an ongoing treatment, or a significant length of time after an acute treatment.

Note that the crude death rate as defined above and applied to a whole population can give a misleading impression. The crude death rate depends on the age (and gender) specific mortality rates and the age (and gender) distribution of the population. The number of deaths per 1000 people can be higher for developed nations than in less-developed countries, despite life expectancy being higher in developed countries due to standards of health being better. This happens because developed countries typically have a completely different population age distribution, with much higher proportion of older people, due to both lower recent birth rates and lower mortality rates. A more complete picture of mortality is given by a life table which shows the mortality rate separately for each age. A life table is necessary to give a good estimate of life expectancy.

During ancient times and the middle ages, the crude death rate was about 40 deaths per year per 1,000 people.

RATES AND RATIOS

Rates and ratios are frequently used in measuring demographic events. *Rate* refers to the frequency of events. A rate is estimated by taking the number of events in a given period and dividing it by the population at risk during that period. Pressat (1985, p. 194) stated that the term *rate* is also used more loosely to refer to the ratio between a sub-population and the total .... In many other uses of rate, the measure in question would be better termed a ratio, proportion, or probability. The term can be justified only when a dynamic process is being measured, not a static description of a population at a given date, although its use in the latter sense is widespread. In general the word ratio is preferable to rate when the measure is not one relating events to a population at risk.

A ratio is the proportion between a numerator and a denominator that are related (for example, under-five child deaths per 1000 under-five person–years lived in a given year).

Crude Death Rate

The crude death rate (CDR) is defined as the number of deaths in a given period divided by the total population. Although the CDR can be computed for any segment of time, the period usually used is a year, and the denominator used in the rate calculation is the midyear population. The midyear population is the size of the population (or any specified group within the population) at the midpoint of a calendar year. This midpoint is often calculated as the arithmetic mean of the size of the population at the beginning and end of the year. Conventionally, the rate is expressed as a number per 1000 individuals.

In the case of a population under continuous surveillance, with possibly high in- and out-migration rates that may yield a strong variation in population size, the use of exact person–years lived is preferred. Person–years is the sum, expressed in years, of the time spent by all individuals in a given category of the population (Pressat 1985). Specifically, these years express the periods that eligible individuals spent in the DSA. Times or periods spent outside the DSA due to migration or death are excluded.

A crude death rate has four components:

1. A specified measurement period.
2. The numerator; the number of deaths that occurred in a specified geographic area during a given period of time, and
3. The denominator, the total number of people in the population at risk in the same geographic area for the same period of time ("person-years at risk"). The population estimate used is typically the mid-year (July 1) population count estimate for the same year(s) included in the numerator.
4. A constant. The result of the fraction is usually multiplied by some factor of 10 (such as 100,000), so that the rate may be expressed as a whole number.

Infant Mortality

It is usually difficult to estimate the number of person–years lived for children <1 year old (infants).

Consequently, the total number of live births is often used as the denominator to calculate the infant mortality rate. The total number of deaths among children <1 year old in a calendar year is divided by the live births in the same year, multiplied by 1000. Calculating the infant mortality rate in this way makes it more appropriately referred to as a ratio.

Infant deaths are unevenly distributed through the first year of life. A high proportion of infant deaths usually occur in the first month of life. Of these deaths, a high proportion occurs during high proportion occurs during the first day. The conventional infant mortality rate or ratio may usefully be broken up into rates or ratios covering the early stages of life and a rate or ratio for the remainder of the year. The one for the first period is called the neonatal mortality rate or ratio, and that for the second period is called the post neonatal mortality rate or ratio. These concepts are briefly defined in the following paragraphs.

Neonatal mortality is defined as the number of deaths of infants <4 weeks old (or <1 month old) during a year. It is calculated by dividing the deaths of infants <28 days old during a year by the live births in the same year and multiplying by 1000. Early neonatal mortality is calculated by dividing the deaths of infants <7 days old during a year by live births in the same year and multiplying by 1000. Late neonatal mortality is calculated by dividing the deaths of infants 7–28 days old in a year by live births in the same year and multiplying by 1000. Post neonatal mortality is calculated by dividing the deaths of infants 4–51 weeks old during a year by live births in the same year and multiplying by 1000.

Infant mortality can also be expressed as a probability of dying before reaching the age of 1 year. Prenatal mortality is calculated by dividing the sum of stillbirths in the year and the deaths of infants <7 days old during the year by the sum of stillbirths in the year and live births in the same year.

Maternal Mortality Rate and Ratio

The maternal mortality ratio is conventionally defined as the number of deaths due to puerperal (pregnancy-related) factors per 100,000 live births. But strictly speaking, this is referred to as a ratio because the denominator is not the persons at risk of experiencing the event. In view of this, the following are the methods for estimating maternal mortality ratios and rates. The maternal mortality ratio is calculated by dividing the number of pregnancy-related deaths in a specified period by that of live births in the same period and multiplying by 100,000. The maternal mortality rate is calculated by dividing the number of pregnancy-related deaths in a specified period by person–years lived by women of childbearing age and multiplying by 1000.

Maternal mortality can also be estimated by relating maternal deaths to women of reproductive age or to all pregnancies, including stillbirths and abortions.

LIFE TABLES

In actuarial science, a life table (also called a mortality table or actuarial table) is a table which shows, for each age, what the probability is that a person of that age will die before their next birthday. From this starting point, a number of statistics can be derived and thus also included in the table:

- The probability of surviving any particular year of age
- Remaining life expectancy for people at different ages
- The proportion of the original birth cohort still alive
- Estimates of a cohort's longevity characteristics.

Life tables are usually constructed separately for men and for women because of their substantially different mortality rates. Other characteristics can also be used to distinguish different risks, such as smoking status, occupation, and socio-economic class.

Life tables can be extended to include other information in addition to mortality, for instance health information to calculate health expectancy. Health expectancies, of which disability-free life expectancy (DFLE) and Healthy Life Years (HLY) are the best-known examples, are the remaining number of years a person can expect to live in a specific health state, such as free of disability. Two types of life tables are used to divide the life expectancy into life spent in various states: (1) multi-state life tables (also known as increment-decrement life tables) based on transition rates in and out of the different states and to death, and (2) prevelence-based life tables (also known as the

Sullivan method) based on external information on the proportion in each state. Life tables can also be extended to show life expectancies in different labour force states or marital status states.

Life tables are also used extensively in biology and epidemiology. The concept is also of importance in product life cycle management.

It is significant that two seemingly opposed designations have been applied to the same thing; Mortality Table." or the Life Table." Quite in accord with this dual character of the life table, its applications may be broadly classed in two categories—applications relating primarily to mortality and death rates, and applications relating primarily to survivals. In the field of life insurance, we find a corresponding duality of interests related to these two aspects of the life table: insurance for the benefit of others in the event of death of the insured; and insurance in the form of endowments or annuities for the benefit of the insured himself in the case of his survival.

We here are concerned with applications to general demographic problems. In the first category, applications relating more particularly to mortality, we have, first of all, the direct use of the life table as a gauge or measure of the mortality in a given population or group of persons. The crude death rate, for well known reasons, is not a good measure, because it is quite seriously affected by differences in age composition. Standardized death rates, on the other hand, have the disadvantage that they depend' on an arbitrarily selected standard population.

The life table is free from this arbitrary feature, and, of course, with its several columns, exhibiting, for a " cohort " or " generation " traced from birth through life, the number of survivors, the number of deaths, the death rate, and the expectation of life at each' age, such a table gives much more detailed information than a general death rate, whether crude or standardized. There is, however, necessarily a relation between the pictures presented by the life table and the corresponding general death rate.

Only a few applications of the life table to problems in vital statistics can be presented by way of example. The list might be extended to include such topics as the probability of dying from specified causes; the age distribution of deaths from specified causes in a generation of persons traced from birth to the extinction of the entire generation; the proportion of widows and of orphans in the population, and the related problem recently discussed by P. Luzzatto-Fegiz in his article The Occupational Evolution of a Generation; or, to mention one more example, the extinction of a line of descent—a problem which is of interest not only in human vital statistics but also in relation to certain problems in genetics. The fact is that possibilities of such applications are legion. It has not been the purpose of this brief paper to attempt even a summary of this subject, but only by a few landmarks here and there to give some idea of the scope and nature of the field.

Types of life tables

1. An **actuarial life table** assumes the population is subject through life to mortality rates currently observed in the population – it is what is called a current life table. So, it will not describe the actual mortality experience of a real initial population – the mortality rate in a particular age group for the current population (*e.g.* 60-61) cannot be expected to be the same as when those much younger (*e.g.*, the newborn in '0) reach that age. This is clearly a hypothetical population, but the life table is still used as a current approximation for the real population under consideration.
2. A **cohort life table** uses the actual mortality experience of a group of individuals born at the same time then the 'lx's are observed #survivors in this group so the qx's represent actual (*i.e.*, observed) mortality rates.
3. A **clinical life table** relates to a group of individuals whose survival time after some event (*e.g.*, treatment for a particular disease) is of interest x refers to this survival time. The #survivors for appropriate intervals of time (not necessarily of 1 year duration) can be observed, which gives observed 'lx's this is a form of cohort life table, but the individuals are not born at the same time, so time 'zero' might be (for example) when the treatment takes place.

MIGRATION

Human migration is movement (physical or psychological) by humans from one district to another, sometimes over long distances or in large groups. The movement of populations in *modern* times has continued under the form of both voluntary migration within one's region, country, or beyond, and involuntary migration (which includes the slave trade, trafficking in human beings and ethnic cleansing). People who migrate are called migrants, or, more specifically, emigrants, immigrants, or settlers, depending on historical setting, circumstances and perspective.

Types of Migrations

- The **cyclic movement** which involves commuting and a seasonal movement, and nomadism.
- The **periodic movement** which consists of migrant labour, military service, and pastoral farming Transhumance.
- The **migratory movement** that moves from the eastern part of the US to the western part. It also moves from China to southeast Asia, from Europe to North America, and from South America to the middle part of the Americas.
- Rural exodus, migration from rural areas to the cities.

Ravenstein's 'Laws of Migration'

Certain laws of social science have been proposed to describe human migration. The following was a standard list after Ravenstein's proposals during the time frame of 1834 to 1913. The laws are as follows:

1. Every migration flow generates a return or counter migration.
2. The majority of migrants move a short distance.
3. Migrants who move longer distances tend to choose big-city destinations.
4. Urban residents are less migratory than inhabitants of rural areas.
5. Families are less likely to make international moves than young adults.

Other Migration Models

- *Migration occurs because individuals search for food, sex and security outside their usual habitation.*(Idyorough, 2008)
- Zipf's Inverse distance law (1956)
- Gravity model of migration and the Friction of distance
- Buffer Theory
- Stouffer's Theory of intervening opportunities (1940)
- Lee's Push-pull theory (1967)
- Zelinsky's Mobility Transition Model (1971)
- Bauder's Regulation of labour markets (2006) "suggests that the international migration of workers is necessary for the survival of industrialized economies...[It] turns the conventional view of international migration on its head: it investigates how migration regulates labour markets, rather than labour markets shaping migration flows." (from the book description).

Causes of Migrations

Causes of migrations have modified over hundreds of years. Some cases are constant, some of them do not carry the same importance as years ago (*for example: in 18th and 19th centuries labour migration did not have the same character like today*).

In general we can divide factors causing migrations into two groups of factors: Push and pull factors. In general:

- **Push Factors** are economic, political, cultural, and environmentally based.
- **Pull Factors** are economic, political, cultural, and environmentally based.
- **Barriers/Obstacles** of which Nigeria in the 1970s and 1980s is an example.

On the macro level, the causes of migration can be distilled into two main categories: *security dimension of migration* (natural disasters, conflicts, threats to individual safety, poor political prospects) and *economic dimension of migration* (poor economic situation, poor situation of national market).

THEORIES OF MIGRATION

Land Bridge Theory

Also known as the Bering Strait Theory or Beringia theory, the Land Bridge theory has been widely accepted since the 1930s. This model of migration into the New World proposes that people migrated from Siberia into Alaska, tracking big game animal herds. They were able to cross between the two continents by a land bridge called the Bering Land Bridge, which spanned what is now the Bering Strait, during the Wisconsin glaciations, the last major stage of the Pleistocene beginning 50,000 years ago and ending some 10,000 years ago, when ocean levels were 60 meters (200 ft) lower than today. This information is gathered using oxygen isotope records from deep-sea cores. An exposed land bridge, which was at least 1,000 miles wide, existed between Siberia and the western coast of Alaska. In the "short chronology" version, from the archaeological evidence gathered, it was concluded that this culture of big game hunters crossed the Bering Strait at least 12,000 years ago and could have eventually reached the southern tip of South America by 11,000 years ago.

Synopsis

At some point during the last Ice Age, about 17,000 years ago, as the ice sheets advanced and sea levels fell, people first migrated from the Eurasian landmass to the Americas. These nomadic hunters were following game herds from Siberia across what is today the Bering Strait into Alaska, and then gradually spread southward. Based upon the distribution of Amerind languages and language families, a movement of tribes along the Rocky Mountain foothills and eastward across the Great Plains to the Atlantic seaboard is assumed to have occurred at least some 13,000 to 10,000 years ago.

Clovis Culture

Examples of Paleoindian point forms. The 2nd is a Cumberland point, the 3rd is a Clovis point, the 4th a Barnes point, and the 5th a Folsom point. These flaked-stone tools are important archaeological markers of early and Middle Paleoindian cultures in North America.

This big game-hunting culture has been labelled the Clovis culture, and is primarily identified with fluted projectile points. The culture received its name from artifacts found near Clovis, New Mexico, the first evidence of this tool complex, excavated in 1932. The Clovis culture ranged over much of North America and appeared in South America. The culture is identified by distinctive "Clovis point", a flaked flint spear-point with a notched flute by which it was inserted into a shaft; it could then be removed from the shaft for travelling. This flute is one characteristic that defines the Clovis point complex.

Dating of Clovis materials has been by association with animal bones and by the use of carbon dating methods. Recent re-examinations of Clovis materials using improved carbon-dating methods produced results of 11,050 and 10,800 radiocarbon years B.P. (before present). This evidence suggests that the culture flowered somewhat later and for a shorter period of time than previously believed. Michael R. Waters of Texas A&M University in College Station and Thomas W. Stafford Jr., proprietor of a private-sector laboratory in Lafayette, Colorado and an expert in radiocarbon dating attempted to determine the dates of the Clovis period. The heyday of Clovis technology has typically been set between 11,500 and 10,900 radiocarbon years B.P. (The radiocarbon calibration is disputed for this period, but the widely used IntCal04 calibration puts the dates at 13,300 to 12,800 calendar years B.P.). In a controversial move, Waters and Stafford conclude that no fewer than 11 of the 22 Clovis sites with radiocarbon dates are "problematic" and should be disregarded—including the type site in Clovis, New Mexico. They argue that the datable samples could have been contaminated by earlier material. This contention was received as highly controversial by many in the archaeological community.

Clovis-type artifacts seem to disappear from the archaeological record after the hypothesized Younger Dryas impact event roughly 12,900 years before the present. The effects of the event possibly caused a decline in post-Clovis human populations and shifts in culture and behaviour patterns.

Problems with Clovis Migration Models

Significant problems arise with the Clovis migration model. If Clovis people radiated south after entering the New World and eventually reached the southern tip of South America by 11,000 years ago, this leaves only a short time span to populate the entire hemisphere. Another complication for the Clovis-only theory arose in 1997, when a panel of authorities inspected the Monte Verde site in Chile, concluding that the radiocarbon evidence predates Clovis sites in the North American Midwest by at least 1,000 years. This supports the theory of a primary coastal migration route that moved South along the coastline faster than those that migrated inland into the central areas of the Americas. Many excavations have uncovered evidence that subsistence patterns of early Americans included foods such as turtles, shellfish, and tubers. This is quite a change of diet from the big game mammoths, long-horn bison, horse, and camels that early Clovis hunters apparently followed east into the New World.

At the Topper archaeological site (located along the banks of the Savannah River near Allendale, South Carolina) investigated by University of South Carolina archaeologist Dr. Albert Goodyear, charcoal material recovered in association with purported human artifacts returned radiocarbon dates of up to 50,000 years BP. This would indicate the presence of humans well before the last glacial period, nevertheless considerable doubt over the validity of these findings has been raised by many other researchers, and the pre-Clovis Topper dates remain controversial.

Pre-Clovis dates have been claimed for several sites in South America, but these early dates have yet to be verified unequivocally.

Recent discoveries of human coprolites (desiccated feces) found deeply buried in an Oregon Cave, indicates the presence of humans in North America as much as 1,200 years prior to the Clovis culture.

Watercraft Migration Theories

Earlier finds have led to a pre-Clovis culture theory encompassing different migration models with an expanded chronology to supersede the "Clovis-first" theory.

Pacific Coastal Models

Pacific models propose that people reached the Americas *via* water travel, following coastlines from northeast Asia into the Americas. Coastlines are unusually productive environments because they provide humans with access to a diverse array of plants and animals from both terrestrial and marine ecosystems. While not exclusive of land-based migrations, the Pacific 'coastal migration theory' helps explain how early colonists reached areas extremely distant from the Bering Strait region, including sites such as Monte Verde in southern Chile and Taima-Taima in western Venezuela. Two cultural components were discovered at Monte Verde near the Pacific Coast of Chile. The youngest layer is radiocarbon dated at 12,500 radiocarbon years (~14,000 cal BP) and has produced the remains of several types of seaweeds collected from coastal habitats. The older and more controversial component may date back as far as 33,000 years, but few scholars currently accept this very early component.

Other coastal models, dealing specifically with the peopling of the Pacific Northwest and California coasts, have been advocated by archaeologists Knut Fladmark, Roy Carlson, James Dixon, Jon Erlandson, Ruth Gruhn, and Daryl Fedje. In a 2007 article in the Journal of Island and Coastal Archaeology, Erlandson and his colleagues proposed a corollary to the coastal migration theory—the kelp highway hypothesis—arguing that productive kelp forests supporting similar suites of plants and animals would have existed near the end of the Pleistocene around much of the Pacific Rim from Japan to Beringia, the Pacific Northwest, and California, as well as the Andean Coast of South America. Once the coastlines of Alaska and British Columbia had deglaciated about 16,000 years ago, these kelp forest (along with estuarine, mangrove, and coral reef) habitats would have provided an ecologically similar migration corridor, entirely at sea level, and essentially unobstructed.

Australia/Oceania Model

As early as 1787 Chilean naturalist Juan Ignacio Molina mentioned the possibility of South America being populated from south Asia through the "infinite island chains" of the Pacific while north America could have been populated from Siberia. Some anthropologists such as Paul Rivet have proposed that peoples of Oceania or southeast Asia crossed the Pacific Ocean and arrived in South America long before the Siberian hunter-gatherers. These hypothetical Pre-Siberian American Aborigines populated much of South America before being nearly ex-terminated and/or absorbed by the Siberian migrants coming from the north. Some of the theories involve a southward migration from or through Australia and Tasmania, hopping Subantarctic islands and then proceeding along the coast of Antarctica and/or southern ice sheets to the tip of South America sometime during the last glacial maximum.

There have been well-dated stratigraphic studies that point to people entering Australia some 40,000 years ago. At this period, Australia was not connected to another continent, which leads to the assumption that it was reached by watercraft. If Australia was reached in this fashion, some reason that the New World could have been reached in the same way. Proponents of this model have pointed to cultural and phenotypical similarities between the Aboriginals of Australia and the Selknam and Yaghan tribes of southern Patagonia. The theory of Australoid migration to the Americas has earned little scientific support as there is no genetic evidence matching indigenous Australians with South American populations. This model is taught in Chilean schools together with the land bridge model. 97

A recent study claimed that the Mapuche pre-Columbian Araucana chicken came from Polynesia by analysing their DNA; this suggests a more recent contact between the Mapuche and Polynesia. Another recent study has contradicted this claim stating that the DNA found in the chicken bone was closer to post-colonial European chickens.

One of the earliest known sites of human occupation in the Americas, Monte Verde, lies within what was later to become Huilliche territory, although there is currently no demonstrated link between the Monte Verde people and the Mapuche.

Southeast Asians: Paleoindians of the Coast

The boat-builders from Southeast Asia may have been one of the earliest groups to reach the shores of North America. One theory suggests people in boats followed the coastline from the Kurile Islands to Alaska down the coasts of North and South America as far as Chile [2 62; 7 54, 57]. The Haida nation on the Queen Charlotte Islands off the coast of British Columbia may have originated from these early Asian mariners between 25,000 and 12,000. Early watercraft migration would also explain the habitation of coastal sites in South America such as Pikimachay Cave in Peru by 20,000 years ago and Monte Verde in Chile by 13,000 years ago [6 30; 8 383].

"*'There was boat use in Japan 20,000 years ago,' says Jon Erlandson, a University of Oregon anthropologist. 'The Kurile Islands (north of Japan) are like stepping stones to Beringia,' the then continuous land bridging the Bering Strait. Migrants, he said, could have then skirted the tidewater glaciers in Canada right on down the coast.*"

Atlantic Coastal Model

Archaeologists Dennis Stanford and Bruce Bradley champion the coastal Atlantic route. Their Solutrean Hypothesis is also based on evidence from the Clovis complex, but instead traces the origins of the Clovis tool making style to the Solutrean culture of Ice Age Western Europe. They have hypothesized that Solutrean hunters and fishers may have worked their way along the southern margins of the Atlantic sea ice to North America. Their argument is based on technological analysis of the similarities between Solutrean and Clovis flint-knapping techniques. Their book on the Solutrean Hypothesis is scheduled for publishing in 2009.

Other Atlantic migration proponents include the French archaeologist Remy Cottevieille-Giraudet, who in the 1930s suggested a European Cro-Magnon origin of the Algonquian peoples. In 1963, Emerson Greenman proposed a hypothetical Atlantic migration during the Upper Paleolithic, also citing New World similarities with Solutrean tools as well as art. He suggested that the Beothuk people of Newfoundland, among others, may have been at least partial descendants of that migration. According to a research report on Beothuk DNA published in 2007, " the data do not lend credence to the proposed idea that the Beothuk (specifically, Non-osabasut) were of admixed (European-Native American) descent." 98

Problems with Evaluating Coastal Migration Models

The coastal migration models provide a different perspective on migration to the New World, but they are not without their own problems. One of the biggest problems is that global sea levels have risen over 100 metres since the end of the last glacial period, and this has submerged the ancient coastlines which maritime people would have followed into the Americas. Finding sites associated with early coastal migrations is extremely difficult—and systematic excavation of any sites found in deeper waters is challenging and expensive. If there was an early pre-Clovis coastal migration, there is always the possibility of a failed colonization. Another problem that arises is the lack of hard evidence found for a long chronology theory. No sites have yet produced a consistent chronology older than about 12,500 radiocarbon years (~14,500 calendar years), but South America has still seen only limited research on the possibility of early coastal migrations.

AGE SEX STRUCTURE

The most important demographic characteristic of a population is its age-sex structure. Age-sex pyramids (also known as population pyramids) graphically display this information to improve understanding and ease comparison.

A population pyramid, also called age-sex pyramid and age structure diagram, is a graphical illustration that shows the distribution of various age groups in a population (typically that of a country or region of the world), which normally forms the shape of a pyramid.

It typically consists of two back-to-back bar graphs, with the population plotted on the X-axis and age on the Y-axis, one showing the number of males and one showing females in a particular population in five-year age groups (also called cohorts). Males are conventionally shown on the left and females on the right, and they may be measured by raw number or as a percentage of the total population.

PATTERNS OF POPULATION CHANGE

Aside from the total size, the most important demographic characteristic of a population is its age and sex structure, or the proportion of people at each age, by sex. The age-sex structure determines potential for future growth of specific age groups, as well as the total population. For these reasons, the age structure has significant government policy implications. A population of young people needs a sufficient number of schools and, later, enough jobs to accommodate them. Countries with a large proportion of older people must develop retirement systems and medical facilities to serve them. Therefore, as a population ages, needs change from childcare and schools to jobs, housing, and medical care.

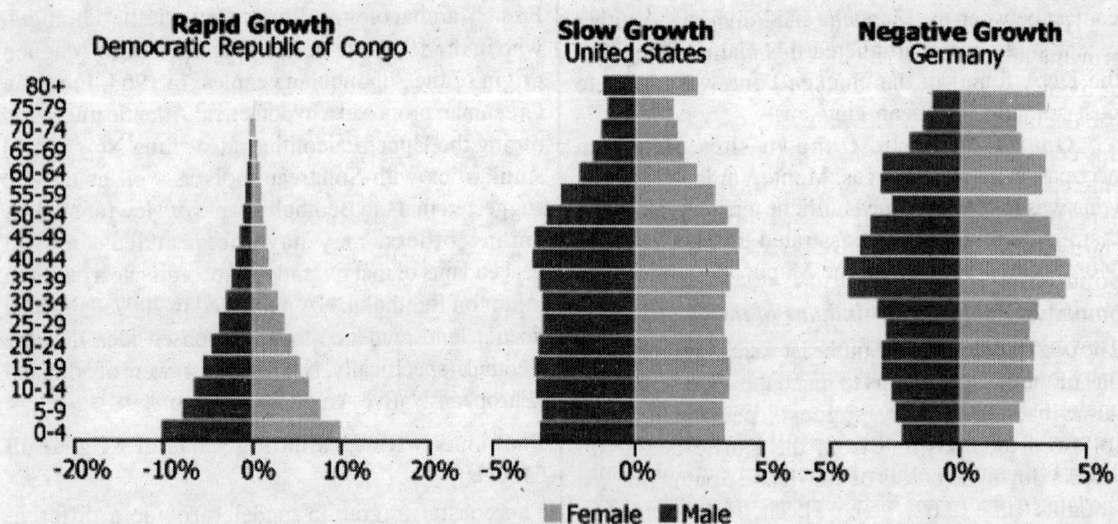

Source: United Nations, *World Population Prospects, The 2006 Revision.*

POPULATION PYRAMIDS

The age-sex structure of a country can be studied through population pyramids. The overall shape of the pyramid indicates the potential for future growth. The four representations of population age-sex structure provide an overall example of what a pyramid for different levels of population growth would look like — rapid growth, slow growth, zero growth, and negative growth. The horizontal bars show the percentage (or in some cases the actual numbers) of males and females in each age group.

The country pyramids shown in "Three Patterns of Population Change" also represent different stages of population growth going on today. The first pyramid, representing the population of the Democratic Republic of Congo, with its wide base and narrow top, is typical of a young population. This shape is the result of high birth rates that feed more and more people into the lowest bars and in turn shrink the relative proportion at the oldest ages. As the death rate declines, more people survive to the reproductive ages and beyond. The births they have further widen the base of the pyramid. This shape is common in many less developed countries that have experienced improvements in life expectancy but continue to have high birth rates. It reflects both a history of rapid population growth and the potential for future rapid growth.

The second age-sex pyramid is typical of a slowly growing population. The United States is an example of a country in slow growth. The United States has had declining fertility and mortality rates for most of this century. With lower fertility, fewer people have entered the lowest bars of the pyramid, and as life expectancy has increased, a greater percentage of the "births" have survived until old age. As a result, the population has been aging, meaning that the proportion of older persons in the population has been growing. This trend was interrupted by the postwar baby boom, 1946-1964, when birth rates climbed again. (The bulge of the baby-boom generation can be seen in the pyramid for ages 40-59 in 2005.) After 1964, birth rates continued their downward trend until the late 1970s. As the last members of the baby boom approached their childbearing years during the 1980s, the number of births rose again, peaking in 1990. These children, the youngest generation, are represented by the slightly widening base of the pyramid. Even though the number of births per woman is lower than ever before, the population continues to grow because of the children and grandchildren of the huge baby-boom generation.

A few countries have reached zero population growth or are experiencing negative growth because of low birth rates and an old age structure coupled with minimal net migration. While Germany's death rate exceeds its birth rate, its population continues to grow because of net migration. Pyramids in which the proportions of the population are fairly evenly distributed among all age groups are representative of many highly industrialized societies. Germany's old population reflects an extended period of low birth and death rates. While fewer children have been born, most of those born survive through to old age. The net effect is zero growth or no natural increase. Germany's pyramid also shows the effect of higher mortality among males. In an industrialized society, females generally outnumber males after age 40. This trend is particularly evident in Germany's oldest age group.

While birth and death rates usually determine the basic pyramid shape, migration also affects it. Typically, most migrants are in the working ages, and often more males than females migrate across national borders. In some Middle Eastern countries a large number of men migrated to work in the oil fields, which caused a bulge in one side of the pyramid, while it took a "bite" out of the pyramid of some of the countries from which they came.

Short-term fluctuations in birth and death rates that produce unusual bites or bulges in population pyramids, such as the baby boom, often can be traced to such historical events as wars, epidemics, economic booms, or depressions. The decline in the birth rate during the Great Depression caused a small bite in the U.S. pyramid for the group born between 1930 and 1934. World Wars I and II caused a deficit of older men in Germany. The impact of these events emphasizes the inter-relationships among population change and economic, social, political, and health factors.

Terms

Age-sex structure: The composition of a population as determined by the number or proportion of males and females in each age category. The age-sex structure of a population is the cumulative result of past trends in fertility, mortality, and migration. Information on age-sex composition is essential for the description and analysis of many other types of demographic data.

Baby boom: A dramatic increase in fertility rates and in the absolute number of births. In the United States this occurred during the period following World War II (1946 to 1964).

Birth rate (or crude birth rate): The number of live births per 1,000 population in a given year. Not to be confused with the growth rate.

Death rate (or crude death rate): The number of deaths per 1,000 population in a given year.

Growth rate: The number of persons added to (or subtracted from) a population in a year due to natural increase and net migration; expressed as a percentage of the population at the beginning of the time period.

Less developed countries: Less developed countries include all countries in Africa, Asia (excluding Japan), and Latin America and the Caribbean, and the regions of Melanesia, Micronesia, and Polynesia.

Life expectancy: The average number of additional years a person of a given age could expect to live if current mortality trends were to continue for the rest of that person's life. Most commonly cited as life expectancy at birth.

More developed countries: More developed countries include all countries in Europe, North America, Australia, New Zealand, and Japan.

Mortality: Deaths as a component of population change.

Net migration: The net effect of immigration and emigration on an area's population in a given time period, expressed as an increase or decrease.

Population pyramid: A bar chart, arranged vertically, that shows the distribution of a population by age and sex. By convention, the younger ages are at the bottom, with males on the left and females on the right.

Rate of natural increase: The rate at which a population is increasing (or decreasing) in a given year due to a surplus (or deficit) of births over deaths, expressed as a percentage of the base population.

Zero population growth: A population in equilibrium, with a growth rate of zero, achieved when births plus immigration equal deaths plus emigration. Zero growth is not to be confused with replacement level fertility.

A great deal of information about the population broken down by age and sex can be read from a population pyramid, and this can shed light on the extent of development and other aspects of the population. A population pyramid also tells the council how many people of each age range live in the area. There tends to be more females than males in the older age groups, due to females' longer life expectancy.

TYPES OF POPULATION PYRAMIDS

There are three key types of population pyramids:

Rapid Growth

This pyramid of the Philippines shows a triangle-shaped pyramid and reflects a high growth rate of about 2.1 per cent annually.

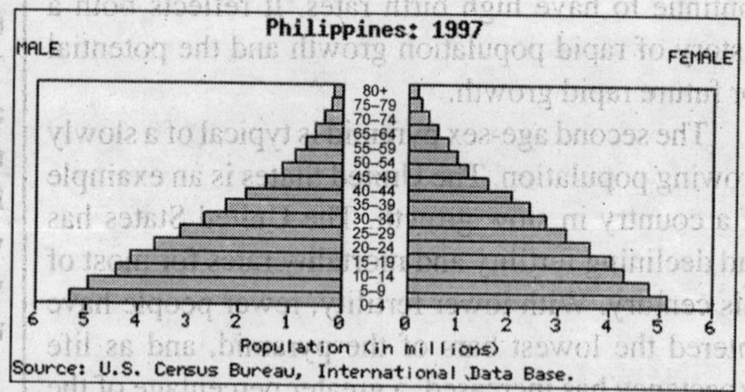

Fig.

Slow Growth

In the United States, the population is growing at a rate of about 1.7 per cent annually. This growth rate is reflected in the more square-like structure of the pyramid. Note the lump in the pyramid between the ages of about 35 to 50. This large segment of the population is the post-World War II "baby boom." As this population ages and climbs up the pyramid, there will be a much greater demand for medical and other geriatric services. An online animated population pyramid from 1950 to 2050 shows the aging of the boomers.

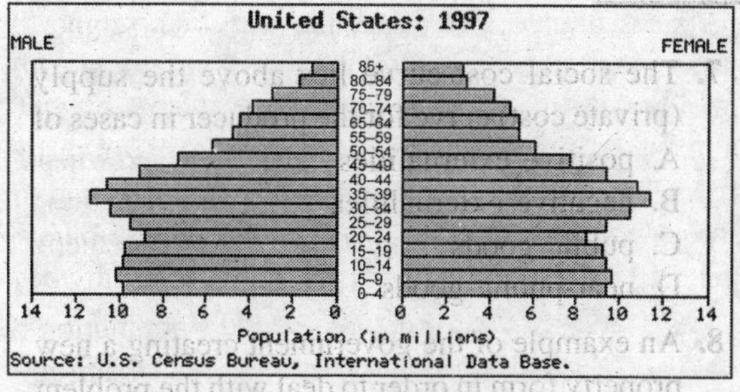

Fig.

Negative Growth

Germany is experiencing a period of negative growth (–0.1%). As negative growth in a country continues, the population is reduced. A population can shrink due to a low birth rate and a stable death rate. Increased emigration may also be a contributor to a declining population.

While all countries' population pyramids differ, three types have been identified by the fertility and mortality rates of a country.

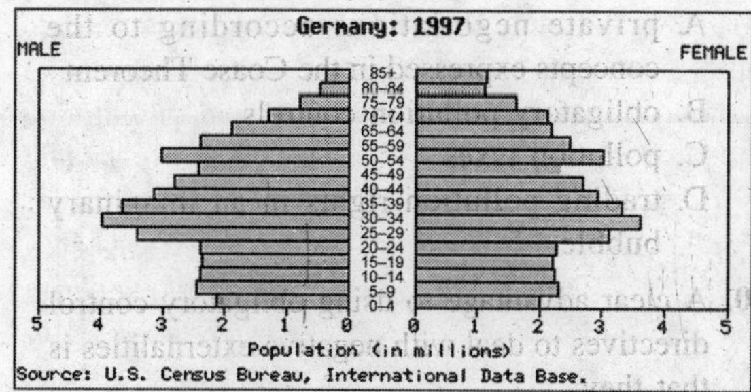

Fig.

Stable pyramid: A population pyramid showing an unchanging pattern of fertility and mortality.

Stationary pyramid: A population pyramid typical of countries with low fertility and low mortality, also called a constrictive pyramid.

Expansive pyramid: A population pyramid showing a broad base, indicate a high proportion of children, a rapid rate of population growth, and a low proportion of older people. This wide base indicates a large number of children. Steady upwards narrowing shows that more people die at each higher age band. This type of pyramid indicates a population in which there is a high birth rate, a high death rate and a short life expectancy. This is the typical pattern for less economically developed countries, due to little access to and incentive to use birth control, negative environmental factors (for example, lack of clean water) and poor access to health care.

Constrictive pyramid: A population pyramid showing lower numbers or percentages of younger people. The country will have a greying population which means that people are generally older.

AGEING OF THE POPULATION

Population ageing is a shift in the distribution of a country's population towards older ages. This is usually reflected in an increase in the population's mean and median ages, a decline in the proportion of the population composed of children, and a rise in the proportion of the population that is elderly. Population ageing is widespread across the world. It is most advanced in the most highly developed countries. However research by the Oxford Institute of Ageing, one of the top institutions looking at global population ageing, has concluded that population ageing has slowed considerably in Europe and will have the greatest future impact in Asia.

Population ageing arises from two (possibly related) demographic effects: increasing longevity and declining fertility. An increase in longevity raises the average age of the population by increasing the numbers of surviving older people. A decline in fertility reduces the number of babies, and as the effect continues, the numbers of younger people in general also reduce. A possible third factor is migration.

Of these two forces, it is declining fertility that is the largest contributor to population ageing in the world today. More specifically, it is the large decline in the overall fertility rate over the last half century that is primarily responsible for the population ageing in the world's most developed countries. Because many developing countries are going through faster fertility transitions, they will experience even faster population ageing than the currently developed countries in the future.

EXERCISE

1. If the social cost of producing chickens is greater than the private cost, then we can be sure that
A. a positive externality exists
B. chicken is healthful and more should be produced
C. a negative externality exists
D. the price of chicken is too low

2. Pollution is an example of market failure because
A. the equilibrium price is higher than the efficient price
B. the equilibrium price is less than the efficient price
C. property rights are poorly distributed
D. the market does not produce enough of the good

3. In order for someone to be a free rider, an activity must be undertaken that
A. arranges for ride-sharing at rush hour
B. creates benefits for people who can't be forced to pay for them
C. beautifies a neighbourhood
D. improves national defense

4. All of the following are goods for which property rights are hard to identify **except**
A. a river running along a field of corn
B. the atmosphere over a field of corn
C. crows that eat the corn on the field
D. a field of corn

5. When there are negative externalities, the price should be adjusted so that it is equal to
A. social cost
B. private cost
C. the amount of the externality
D. zero

6. All of the following are ways to cope with negative externalities **except**
A. public choice
B. obligatory controls
C. pollution taxes
D. creating new property forms

7. The social cost curve lies above the supply (private cost) curve for the producer in cases of
A. positive externalities
B. negative externalities
C. public goods
D. near-public goods

8. An example of the government creating a new property form in order to deal with the problem of a negative externality would be
A. the establishment of the EPA
B. taxing air and water pollution
C. requiring catalytic convertors on automobiles
D. auctioning rights to pollute to electric utility companies

9. Which of the following approaches **would likely fail** to control pollution that is noxious, yet not life-threatening, but affects millions of people (for example, acid rain)?
A. private negotiations according to the concepts expressed in the Coase Theorem
B. obligatory pollution controls
C. pollution taxes
D. trading pollution rights in an imaginary bubble

10. A clear advantage to using obligatory control directives to deal with negative externalities is that they
A. reduce the need for bureaucrats
B. reduce pollution to zero
C. are relatively simple
D. are costless to monitor and enforce

11. If a per unit tax is imposed on a producer of a good with a negative externality, then the tax shifts the producer's
A. marginal cost curve to the right
B. marginal cost curve to the left
C. total fixed cost to the left
D. total fixed cost to the right

12. The private market will not provide enough of a pure public good because of

A. negative externalities
B. obligatory controls over production methods
C. public choice not to produce the good
D. the free rider problem

13. Which of the following is an example of a near-public good?
A. a lighthouse
B. a congested freeway during the morning rush hour
C. a polio vaccination program sponsored by the government
D. national defense

14. Government failure occurs when
A. social cost lies to the left of private cost
B. the good it purchases has a greater negative externality than a positive one
C. the quantity of public goods it purchases is less than the socially optimal quantity
D. it pays a higher price for a public goods than it would pay on the private market

15. Public choice holds that
A. public officials serve the community's interest
B. government failure cannot occur
C. society does not consume enough public goods
D. we should presume self-interested behaviour on the part of public officials

16. Voting fails to generate the efficient quantity of a public goods because
A. lobbying groups use bribes to change people's votes
B. public goods are not depleted by consumption
C. public goods cannot be withheld from consumption
D. voting doesn't accurately reflect the magnitude of benefits from public goods

17. Consumption of a pure public goods
A. depletes the supply of the goods for others
B. increases the supply of the goods
C. denies the opportunity to consume the goods to others
D. neither depletes the goods nor excludes others from consuming it

18. All of the following are examples of obligatory controls **except**
A. the "No Smoking" signs posted in public buildings
B. automobile emissions testing requirements
C. restrictions on the transportation of hazardous wastes
D. trading in pollution rights between electrical utility companies

19. A government-sponsored cash subsidy to people who plant trees will have the effect of
A. decreasing the supply of privately-grown trees
B. result in government failure
C. increasing the demand for trees
D. increasing the supply of trees

20. Suppose that farmers decide individually whether or not to get their own cattle vaccinated against anthrax. Which of the following results?
A. There is market failure because the equilibrium quantity of vaccine is too low.
B. There is market failure because the equilibrium price of vaccine is too low.
C. There is market failure because both the equilibrium price and quantity of vaccine are too high.
D. There is no market failure because the market will tend toward equilibrium.

21. Positive economics
A. does not depend on market interactions.
B. only looks at the best parts of the economy.
C. examines how the economy actually works (as opposed to how it should work).
D. is very subjective.

22. The Coase theorem has problems because
A. generally, bargaining costs are not zero.
B. individuals are not concerned with others.
C. markets always exist.
D. all of the above.

23. Market failure can occur when
A. monopoly power exists in the market.
B. markets are missing.
C. consumers can influence prices.
D. all of the above

24. A public goód is
A. a good that the public must pay for.
B. non-rival in consumption.
C. more costly than a private good.
D. paid for by the government.

25. The economic theory of optimal health care provision says that
A. It is socially optimal for free medical treatment to be provided to everyone
B. Everyone should pay their own medical expenses because they will set marginal cost equal to marginal benefit.
C. Adverse selection can prevent efficient insurance markets from developing even when every-one buys the same insurance.
D. The optimal health care system will ration care: Some people who would benefit from treatment should be denied that treatment.

26. Market mechanisms are unlikely to provide
A. prices.
B. non-rival goods efficiently.
C. supply and demand.
D. None of the above

27. Public goods can be
A. provided privately.
B. provided publicly.
C. subject to free rider problems.
D. all of the above

28. Externalities can be positive because
A. marginal damages do not last over time.
B. utility can be impacted positively as well as negatively.
C. there is no concept for marginal benefit.
D. positive externalities are subsidies.

29. A Pigouvian subsidy
A. cannot exist with externalities.
B. is the same thing as a Pigouvian tax.
C. is measured in terms of Pigouvian dollars.
D. moves production to the socially optimal level of output

30. Which method can help in obtaining a welfare improvement if externalites exist?
A. Pigouvian taxes
B. regulation
C. assigning property rights and permitting bargaining
D. all of the above

31. Marginal damages
A. must always be considered in social marginal costs.
B. must not be considered in social marginal costs.
C. must sometimes be considered in social marginal costs.
D. have nothing to do with social marginal costs.

32. In a public goods context, it is difficult to measure impact on real income because
A. public goods are generally free to the public.
B. they make up a small percentage of total GDP.
C. it is hard to measure how people value the public goods.
D. inflation decreases the value of the goods.

33. A fully funded Social Security plan requires
A. negative generational accounts
B. no taxes since current workers pay for current retirees.
C. future generations to pay for the benefits of current retirees
D. retirees to be paid from investments that have accumulated with interest over their working lives.

34. What are ecosystem goods and services?
A. Ecosystem goods and services are goods and services produced by companies that are "ecologically friendly."
B. Ecosystem goods and services are goods and services that are supplied by ecosystems and directly benefit the wildlife population in an area.
C. Ecosystem goods and services are goods and services that are supplied by ecosystems and directly benefit at least one per cent of the human population.
D. Ecosystem goods and services are goods and services that are supplied by ecosystems and directly benefit at least one person.

35. Which of the following is a way that economic activity can pose a threat to the natural world?

A. Economic activity often means converting wildlife habitat into housing and commercial real estate.

B. Business practices that promote over-harvesting.

C. Economic activity may provide funding for wetland and wildlife reclamation.

D. Both land conversion and overharvesting threaten the environment.

36. Which of the following is NOT one of the categories into which the Millennium Ecosystem Assessment (MA) divides ecosystem services?

A. Provisioning services provide direct benefits

B. Cultural services provide recreational, aesthetic, and spiritual benefits

C. Value-added services that provide opportunities for a site to get on the UNESCO world heritage list

D. Supporting services

37. Which of the following is NOT a main finding of the Millennium Ecosystem Assessment (MA)?

A. It will be difficult to achieve many of the UN Millennium Development Goals if environmental degradation continues at the same rate.

B. Ecosystems have been changing at a slower rate over the last fifty years than in previous time periods.

C. Institutions and policies will have to change significantly in order for the rate of environmental degradation to reverse.

D. Ecosystem health has suffered due to many of the ecosystem changes that have increased the well-being of humans.

38. Which of the following is NOT an example of an economics value foregone by the loss of ecosystem services?

A. The loss of revenue to firms when costs increase due to tougher

B. The loss of vital landscape when coral reefs are destroyed.

C. The loss of pollination of agricultural crops when bees die from pesticides.

D. The loss of recreational activities when a lake is polluted.

39. Which of the following is NOT an example of an economics value foregone by the loss of ecosystem services?

A. The loss of revenue to firms when costs increase due to tougher

B. The loss of vital landscape when coral reefs are destroyed.

C. The loss of pollination of agricultural crops when bees die from pesticides.

D. The loss of recreational activities when a lake is polluted.

40. Which of the following gives an accurate description of institutional arrangements for protecting ecosystems?

A. Tradable entitlement systems treat all land as if it has equal value.

B. Wetlands Banking works to preserve freshwater resources.

C. Costa Rica's PSA Program focuses on forestry ecosystems.

D. Ecotourism creates a revenue stream based on environmental services that can serve to fund protection of those services.

41. Ecotourism _________.

A. projects are all consistent with the definition of ecotourism.

B. was created to provide an income stream from the land to help correct the bias against preserving land.

C. shifts the private preservation bid rent function inward.

D. always helps to conserve the ecology of a protected area.

42. Which one of the following states in India recorded the lowest sex ratio as per 2011 census?

A. Uttarakhand B. Tamil Nadu

C. West Bengal D. Himachal Pradesh

43. Which one of the following groups of states in Indian recorded Sex Ratio higher than 950 according to year 2011 census?

A. Andhra Pradesh, Odishâ, Telengana
B. Andhra Pradesh, Uttar Pradesh, Maharashtra
C. Uttar Pradesh, Punjab, Andhra Pradesh
D. Haryana, Bihar, Andhra Pradesh

44. Match the List-I with List-II and select the **correct** answer from the code given below:

List-I (Demographic terms)	List-II (Explanation)
(*a*) Cohart	(*i*) Birth rate minus death rate
(*b*) Natural increase	(*ii*) A population group unified by a specific common characteristic
(*c*) Total fertility rate	(*iii*) Average number of children that a women will bear through her child bearing years
(*d*) Dependency ratio	(*iv*) Measure in terms of number of dependants against productive age groups

Code:

	(*a*)	(*b*)	(*c*)	(*d*)
A.	(*iii*)	(*iv*)	(*ii*)	(*i*)
B.	(*ii*)	(*i*)	(*iii*)	(*iv*)
C.	(*i*)	(*iv*)	(*iii*)	(*ii*)
D.	(*iv*)	(*ii*)	(*i*)	(*iii*)

45. Which one of the following Total Fertility Rate is required to maintain the world's existing population?
A. 3.4 B. 2.1
C. 1.2 D. 4.2

46. Which one of the following is not included in the Ravenstein's Laws of Migration?
A. Most migrants proceeds step by step
B. Most migrants go for short distance
C. Most migrants move from Urban to Rural areas
D. Most migrants are adults

47. Consider the following statements:
Developing countries have registered increase in population despite significant decline in fertility rates because of:
(*a*) Increase in Life Expectancy Rate
(*b*) Increase in Infant Mortality Rate
(*c*) Falling Death rate
(*d*) Better Living conditions
Tick one of the following code which reflects the above statements?
A. (*a*), (*b*) and (*d*) are correct
B. (*a*), (*c*) and (*d*) are correct
C. (*a*), (*b*) and (*c*) are correct
D. (*b*), (*c*) and (*d*) are correct

48. Which one of the following statements represents Population Pyramid with Wide base?
A. Declining Fertility Rates
B. High Fertility Rates
C. Declining Death Rates
D. High Death Rates

49. Which one of the following depicts correct statement of Population Threshold for any service?
A. Maximum distance that people can travel to use a service
B. Minimum distance required for opening a service
C. Minimum population size required for a service
D. Maximum population size required for a service

50. Which one of the following is responsible for concentration of slum population in India?
A. Commercial plantation activities are dominant.
B. Manufacturing activities in organised sector are dominant.
C. Service activities in organised sector are dominant.
D. Manufacturing and Service activities in non-formal sector are dominant.

51. Who developed the theory of demographic transition?
A. Zelinskey
B. Whittlesey
C. Warren Thompson
D. Ravenstein

52. Match List-I with List-II and select the correct answer from the codes given below:

List-I (General Terms)	List-II (Definitions)
(a) Crude birth rate	1. Births over deaths per thousand of population
(b) General fertility rate	2. Number of deaths per thousand of population
(c) Natural increase of population	3. Ratio between number of births and number of females in productive age
(d) Death rate	4. Ratio between the number of births and total population

Codes:

	(a)	(b)	(c)	(d)
A.	4	3	1	2
B.	1	2	3	4
C.	3	4	2	1
D.	2	1	4	3

53. When 0–14 and 15–44 age groups population of a country is almost identical, the growth of population would be called:

A. Rapid growth B. Slow growth
C. Zero growth D. Negative growth

54. The transition zone between two ecosystems is called:

A. Biotope B. Ecotone
C. Biome D. Habitat

55. How many stages of population growth are involved in demographic transition?

A. 3 B. 4
C. 5 D. 6

56. Which one of the following models is based on the study of human ecology?

A. Burges and Park's concentric zone model
B. Weber's location model
C. Haggerstrand's innovation diffusion model
D. Zelinsky's mobility transition model

57. The census of India (2011) states that maximum density of population is found in which of the following Union Territories?

A. Andaman and Nicobar Islands
B. Lakshdweep Islands
C. Dadra and Nagar Haveli
D. Daman and Diu

58. Which one of the following criteria is used by Census of India 2011 to define the town?

A. Population Growth
B. Population Density
C. Literacy Rate
D. Sex Ratio

59. Which of the following is a major immigrating state of India?

A. Rajasthan B. Uttar Pradesh
C. Bihar D. Maharashtra

60. The density of population is highest in which of the following states of india according to the census of 2011?

A. Bihar B. Punjab
C. Uttar Pradesh D. West Bengal

61. Which one of the following states recorded the lowest decadal growth rate of population according to the 2011 census?

A. Arunachal Pradesh
B. Madhya Pradesh
C. Punjab
D. Nagaland

62. Out of total population of 121 crore, what was the level of urbanisation in 2011 census?

A. 33.16% B. 32.16%
C. 30.16% D. 31.16%

63. Which one of the following measures of central tendency is used to indicate the 'centre of population'?

A. Median B. Mode
C. Mean D. Harmonic mean

64. Which of the concept relates population size to the land area with a view to assess pressure of population upon the resources of the area?

A. Population Growth Rate
B. Population Density
C. Agriculture Density
D. Physiological Density

65. What is the trend of Urbanization in India?

A. Urban population is rising slowly.
B. Urban population is rising rapidly.
C. Growth rate of urban population is lower than total.
D. Urban population is falling.

66. Net population change is determined by

A. Mortality B. Migration
C. Fertility D. Both A and C

67. 'Montreal Protocol' is related to

A. Global Warming
B. Ozone Depletion
C. Air Pollution
D. Water Pollution

68. Which of the following conditions is characterised by the second stage of Demographic Transition?

A. Low birth rate, High death rate
B. High birth rate, High death rate
C. High birth rate, Declining death rate
D. Low birth rate, Low death rate

69. 'Chain migration' is based on :

A. Job opportunities
B. Kinship
C. Proximity to place of earlier Residence
D. Combination of A and C

70. Demographic transition is a framework that explores the historical sequence of changes in

1. Fertility and migration
2. Mortality and age-structure
3. Mortality and migration
4. Age-structure and sex-composition

Codes:

A. 1 and 4 are correct
B. 3 and 4 are correct
C. Only 1 is correct
D. 1 and 2 are correct

71. India's decadal population growth rate has been continuously declining since

A. 1971-81 B. 1981-91
C. 1991-2001 D. 2001-2011

72. Which one of the following stages of demographic transition model predicts "a-high birth but a-low death rate"?

A. First stage
B. Second stage
C. Third stage
D. Late-second stage

73. Match the following:

List-I **(State)**	*List-II* **(Rate of Literacy (%) at 2011 census)**
(*a*) Uttarakhand	(*i*) 69.7
(*b*) Chhattisgarh	(*ii*) 70.0
(*c*) Tamil Nadu	(*iii*) 60.2
(*d*) Gujarat	(*iv*) 73.4

Codes:

	(*a*)	(*b*)	(*c*)	(*d*)
A.	(*i*)	(*ii*)	(*iii*)	(*iv*)
B.	(*ii*)	(*iii*)	(*iv*)	(*i*)
C.	(*iii*)	(*iv*)	(*i*)	(*ii*)
D.	(*iv*)	(*iii*)	(*ii*)	(*i*)

74. Which one of the following groups of states of India reco·ded more than one fourth of total population of the country in the census year 2011?

A. Uttar Pradesh, Assam, Punjab
B. Uttar Pradesh, Madhya Pradesh, Karnataka
C. Uttar Pradesh, Andhra Pradesh, Punjab
D. Uttar Pradesh, Gujarat, Haryana

75. Match the List-I with List-II and select the **correct** answer from the code given below:

List-I (Religious Community)	**List-II (Population Share (%), 2011)**
(*a*) Christian	(*i*) 1.7
(*b*) Buddhist	(*ii*) 0.4
(*c*) Sikhs	(*iii*) 2.3
(*d*) Jains	(*iv*) 0.7

Code:

	(*a*)	(*b*)	(*c*)	(*d*)
A.	(*i*)	(*ii*)	(*iii*)	(*iv*)
B.	(*iv*)	(*iii*)	(*ii*)	(*i*)
C.	(*iii*)	(*iv*)	(*i*)	(*ii*)
D.	(*ii*)	(*i*)	(*iv*)	(*iii*)

76. The percentage of decadal growth of population (2001-2011) is the highest in which of the following states?

A. West Bengal
B. Maharashtra
C. Uttar Pradesh
D. Arunachal Pradesh

77. As per the Indian census, the difference of sex ratio (Females per 1000 males) of the total population in India between 2001 and 2011 was:

A. 5 B. 6
C. 7 D. 8

78. As per Socio-Economic and Cast Census 2011, how many rural families earn their liveli-hood mainly from physical labour?

A. 49% B. 51%
C. 58% D. 65%

79. As per Census 2011 data, which of the following State has the lowest literacy rate in India?

A. Bihar B. Arunachal Pradesh
C. Nagaland D. Sikkim

80. As per the latest census data 2011, the decadal growth rate of Muslim population during 2001-11 is—

A. 23.6% B. 14.2%
C. 24.6% D. 16.8%

ANSWERS

1	2	3	4	5	6	7	8	9	10
C	B	B	D	A	A	B	D	A	C
11	**12**	**13**	**14**	**15**	**16**	**17**	**18**	**19**	**20**
B	D	B	C	D	D	D	D	C	A
21	**22**	**23**	**24**	**25**	**26**	**27**	**28**	**29**	**30**
C	A	D	B	D	B	D	B	D	D
31	**32**	**33**	**34**	**35**	**36**	**37**	**38**	**39**	**40**
A	C	D	D	D	C	B	A	A	D
41	**42**	**43**	**44**	**45**	**46**	**47**	**48**	**49**	**50**
B	C	A	B	B	C	B	B	C	D
51	**52**	**53**	**54**	**55**	**56**	**57**	**58**	**59**	**60**
C	A	C	B	C	A	D	B	D	A
61	**62**	**63**	**64**	**65**	**66**	**67**	**68**	**69**	**70**
D	D	C	B	B	D	B	C	B	D
71	**72**	**73**	**74**	**75**	**76**	**77**	**78**	**79**	**80**
A	B	B	B	C	D	C	B	A	C

UNIT–XI : MISCELLANEOUS

THE THEORY OF INTEREST

In economics, interest has been defined in a variety of ways. Commonly, interest is regarded as the payment for the use or service of capital. In *Mill's* words "Interest is the remuneration for meer abstinence." According to the classical economist, it is only by postponing consumption that capital can be created. Since to abstain from consumption is disagreeable and painful, the lender is paid a reward in the form of interest. When people abstain from consumption they save and thus interest becomes the reward for saving.

The Austrians led by *Jhon Rae* and *Bohm Bawerk* and followed by Fisher in America considered interest to be the 'agio' or the premium for time preference. People prefer present to the future and hence they attach more importance to present goods. In order to induce them to post pone enjoyment of goods in the present to the future, they must be compensated in the form of interest. Interest is thus the difference between the present enjoyment (utility) and the future enjoyment of the same goods.

Gross And Pure Interest

The payment which the borrower makes to the lender excluding the principal is gross interest. It is a composite item which includes the following payments.

1. Pure or Net Interest
2. Reward for Risk–taking
3. Reward for Inconvenience
4. Reward for Management

Pure interest is what remains with the lender after deducting the reward for risk–taking, management and inconvenience from gross interest.

Time Preference Theory

The Time Preference Theory is associated with Irving Fisher who defined interest as an "index of the community's preference for a dollar of present over a dollar of future income." Time preference is the preference that people have for present income over future income of an equal amount and equal certainty. It is tendency on the part of the people to vary the income meant for consumption from time to time by saving and borrowing. Interest is the price that is paid to the people for present income rather than for future income.

The Classical Theory of Interest

According to the classical theory, rate of interest is determined by the supply and demand of capital. The supply of capital is governed by the time preference and the demand for capital by the expected productivity of capital. Both time preference and productivity of capital depend upon waiting or saving.

The demand for capital is inversely related to the rate of interest, and the demand schedule for capital slopes downward from left to right. On the other hand, the supply of capital depends on savings and directly related to the rate of interest. The higher the rate of interest, the larger will be the community savings and more will be the supply of funds. The supply curve of capital thus moves upward to the right.

Determination : Assuming the level of income to be given, the rate of interest is determined by the interaction of the demand curve and the supply curve of capital. This is shown in the figure D and S curves interset at E which is the equilibrium point when OQ quantity of capital is demanded and supplied at OR rate of interest.

If at any time the rate of interest rises above OR to OR_1 the demand for investment funds will fall and the supply of funds will increase. Since the supply of capital is more than the demand the rate of interest will come down to the equilibrium level OR. The opposite will be the case if the rate of interest falls to OR_2. The demand for capital is greater than the supply

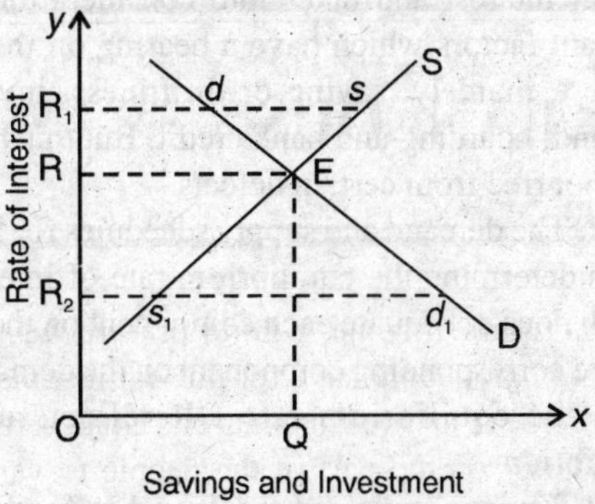

Fig. *Classical Theory : Determination of Interest*

and rate of interest will rise to OR. The ultimate situation is one of equality between saving and investment brought about by the equilibrium or the natural rate of interest. If at any time savings are more than OQ, the rate of interest would fall below OR because the demand for capital remains the same. (Imagine a supply curve below the S curve in the figure, D curve being the same). At the lower rate of interest, people will save less but the demand for investible funds will increase which will tend to raise the rate of interest to the equilibrium level OR.

Criticism

The 'pure' or the real theory of interest of the classicals as enunciated by Marshall and pigou has been severely criticised by Keynes.

1. Income is not a constant but a variable
2. Saving and Investment Schedules are not Independent.
3. Neglects the Effects of Investment on Income
4. Indeterminate Theory
5. Unrealistic Assumption of Full Employment
6. Neglects Monetary Factors
7. No Automatic Eqality between Natural and Market Rates of Interest.

Loanable Funds Theory of Interest

The neo-classical or the loanable funds theory explains the determination of interest in terms of demand and supply of loanable funds or credit. Expounded by Wicksell, the theory was elaborated by Ohlin, Robertson, Pigou and other new–classical economists.

According to this theory, the rate of interest is the price of credit which is determined by the demand and supply for loanable funds.

Demand for Loanable Funds : The demand for loanable funds has primarily three sources : government, businessmen and consumers who need them for purposes of investment, hoarding and consumption. The government borrows funds for constructing public works or for war preparations. The businessmen borrow for the purchase of capital goods and for starting investment projects. Such borrowings are interest elastic and depend mostly on the expected rate of profit as compared with the rate of interest. The demand for loanable funds on the part of consumers is for the purchase of durable consumer goods like scooters, houses, etc. Individual borrowings are also interest elastic. The tendency to borrow is more at a lower rate than at a higher interest rate in order to enjoy their consumption soon. Since this demand for funds is mostly met out of past savings or through dissaving, it is represented by the curve DS in the given figure. The demand curve for investment funds both for the government and the businessmen is shown as curve I, it slopes downward showing that less funds are borrowed at a higher rate and more at a lower rate of interest. Lastly, funds are demanded for the purpose of hoarding are also interest elastic and are shown by the curve H. The lateral summation of these curves H, DS and I gives us the aggregate demand curve for loanable fund ΣD.

Supply of Loanable Funds : The supply of loanable funds comes from savings, dishoardings and bank credit. Private savings, individual and corporate, are the main source of saving. Though personal savings depend upon the income level yet taking, the level of income as given, they are regarded as interest elastic. The higher the rate of interest, the greater will be the inducement to save and vice versa– corporate savings are the undistributed profits of a firm which also depend on the current rate of interest to some extent. Savings are indicated as curve S in the given figure. The second source is the volume of funds coming out of hoards or being added to them. When people dishoard, the idle cash balances become active cash balances in the present period and thus add to the supply of loanable funds. People hoard money because of their preference for liquidity. When the rate of interest rises or when the prices of securities decline, they may like to take advantage of these market movements and thus dishoard money for lending it to others or for purchasing securities. At a higher rate of interest, the individuals possessing idle cash balances will induced to dishoard more money. At very low rates of interest, their parting with liquidity will not be rewarded sufficiently and, therefore they will hold on to money. It is evident that dishoarding is interest elastic and the curve of dishoarding slopes upwards to the right as is shown in this figure by curve DH. Lastly, there is the bank credit as an important source of the supply of loanable funds. Generally speaking, the banks will lend more money at higher rates of interest than at lower ones. Therefore, supply curve of bank money slopes upwards to the right as is shown by the cure M in the figure. If these curves DH, M and S are laterally added up we have the aggregate supply curve Σs of loanable funds.

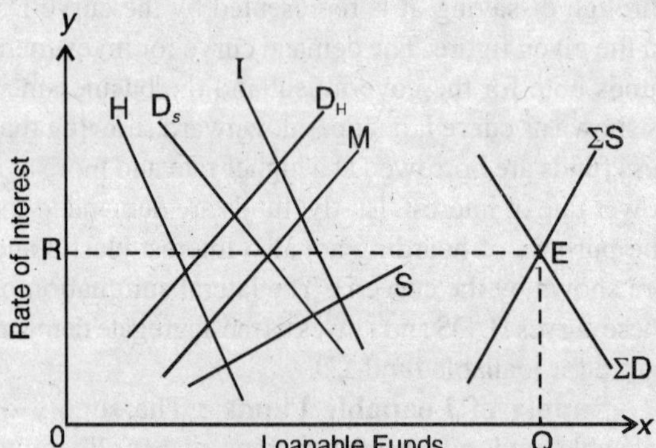

Fig. *Determination of rate of interest through equilibrium between demand and supply of loanable funds.*

The total demand curve for loanable funds ΣD and the total supply curve of loanable funds Σs intersect each other at E and give OR rate of interest. At this rate OQ amount of funds are borrowed and lent.

Critical Evaluation of Loanable Funds Theory

Loanable funds theory is superior to classical theory of interest. It has greatly improved our under standing of the forces working on the supply of and demand for loanable funds. It makes quite comprehensive analysis of the determination of the rate of interest and takes into consideration all the relevant factors which have a bearing on the rate of interest, mamely, saving or thriftiness, investment demand, hoarding and bank credit. But this theory is also not free from certain defects.

1. The demand and supply schedules for loanable funds determine the equilibrium rate of interest OR which does not equate each component on the supply with te corresponding component on the demand side. Thus the equilibrium rate OR reflects unstable equilibrium.

2. Keynes criticised the loanable funds theory on the ground that like classical theory it does not provide a determinate solution to the interest rate determination and involves what is called circular reasoning. According to him, since savings is an important constituent of the supply of loanable funds, the supply of loanable funds curve will vary with the level of income. We, therefore, cannot know the rate of interest unless we know what the level of income is. And we cannot know the level of income unless we know the rate of interest since rate of interest affects investment which in turn determines the level of income.

3. The loanable funds theory states that the supply of loanable funds can be increased by releasing cash balances of savings and decreased by absorbing cash balances into savings. This implies that the cash balances are fairly elastic. But this does not seem to be a correct view because the total cash balances available with the community are fixed and equal the total supply of money at any time. Whenever there are variations in the cash balances, they are infact in the velocity of circulation of money rather than in the amount of cash balances with the community.

4. The loanable funds theory has been criticised for combining monetary factors with real factors. It is not correct to combine real factors like saving and investment with monetary factors like bank credit and dishoarding without bringing in changes in the level of income. This makes the theory unrealistic.

Its Superiority Over the Classical Theory

Despite these weaknesses, the loanable funds theory is better and more realistic than the classical theory on a number of counts.

First, the classical theory is a real theory of

interest and neglects monetary influences on interest. With the inclusion of real as well as monetary factors, the loanable funds theory becomes superior to the classical theory.

Second, the classicists neglect the role of bank credit as a constituent of money supply influencing the rate of interest which is an important factor in the loanable funds.

Third, the classicists also do not consider the role of hoarding. By including the desire to hoard money in the demand for loanable funds, the loanable funds theory becomes more realistic and brings us nearer to Keyne's liquidity preference theory.

Fourth, to the classicists money is merely a 'veil', a passive factor influencing the rate of interest. The loanable funds theory is superior because it regards money as an active factor in the determination of the interest rate.

Keynes's Liquidity Preference Theory of Interest

Keynes defines the rate of interest as the reward of not hoarding but the reward for parting with liquidity for the specified period. In other words, the rate of interest in the Keynesian sense is determined by the demand for and the supply of money. This theory is, therefore, characterised as the monetary theory of interest, as distinct from the real theory of the classicals.

Supply of Money : Of the two determinants of the rate of interest, the supply of money refers to the total quantity of money in the country for all purposes at any time. Though the supply of money is a function of the rate of interest to a degree, yet it is considered to be fixed by the monetary authorities (the supply curve of money is taken as perfectly inelastic).

Demand for Money : For the second determinant the demand for money, Keynes coined a new term "liquidity preference" by which his theory of interest is commonly known. Liquidity preference is the desire to hold cash. The desire for liquidity arises because of three motives : *(i)* the transactions motive *(ii)* the precautionary motive, and *(iii)* the speculative motive.

If the total supply of money is represented by M, we may refer to that part of M held for transactions and precautionary motive as M_1 and to that part held for the speculative motive as M_2. Thus $M = M_1 + M_2$. The money held under the transactions and precautionary motives, i.e., M_1 is completely interest–inelastic unless the interest rate is very high. The amount of money held as M_1, that is, for transactions and precautionary motive, is mainly a function of the size of income. We can write this in a functional form as follows.

$$M_1 = L_1(Y) \qquad ....(i)$$

Where Y stands for income, L_1 for liquidity preference function, and M_1 for money held under the transactions and precautionary motive.

The above functions implies that money held under the transaction and precautionary motive is a function of income.

On the other hand, money demanded for speculative motive (M_2) is primarily a function of the rate of interest. This can be written as—

$$M_2 = L_2(r) \qquad ....(ii)$$

where *r* stands for the rate of interest, L_2 for liquidity preference function for speculative motive.

Since total supply of money $M = M_1 + M_2$. We get from *(i)* and *(ii)* above

$$M = L_1(Y) + L_2(r) \qquad .....(iii)$$

It follows from *(iii)* above that given the supply of money M (and also income) the rate of interest will be determined by the liquidity preference.

Determination of the Rate of Interest

According to Keynes, the demand for money i.e., the liquidity preference and supply of money determine the rate of interest. In the given figure the vertical line QM represents the quantity (supply) of money and LP, the liquidity preference curve. Both intersect at E and the equilibrium rate of interest OR is established. If the supply of money is increased by the monetary authorities, but the liquidity preference remains the same, the rate of interest will fall and vice versa. On the other hand, if the liquidity preference rises, the quantity of money remaining the same, the rate of interest will also rise and vice versa.

In the above figure with the upward shifting of the liquidity preference curve to LP′ the quantity of money QM remaining the same, the rate of interest rises to OR_2 at the equilibrium point E_1. If with the increase in the liquidity preference of LP′, the quantity of money is also increased in the same proportion to Q_1M_1, there is no change in the rate of interest OR, except that the new equilibrium point is E_2. On the

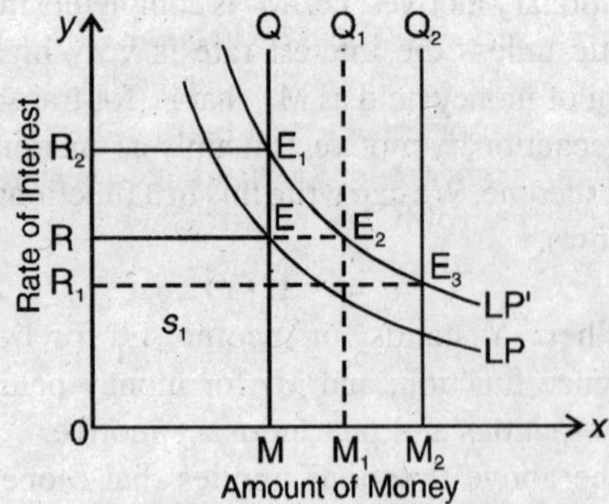

Fig. *Equilibrium between Demand for and Supply of Money*

other hand, if the quantity of money is increased to Q_2M_2, i.e, more than the increase in the demand for money LP′, the rate of interest falls to OR_1 at the equilibrium point E_3. Thus according to the liquidity preference theory rate of interest is determined at a point where the liquidity preferenc schedule equals the available quantity of money schedule.

Its Criticism

1. Keynes ignored real factors in the determination of interest.

2. Keynesian theory is also indeterminate.

3. No liquidity without savings.

4. Notion of Liquidity Trap Wrong.

It follows from above that Keynesian theory of interest is not only indeterminate, but is also an inadequate explanation of the determination of the rate of interest. It treats the interest rate as a purely monetary phenomenon and by neglecting the real factors makes the theory narrow and unrealistic.

Modern Theory of Interest

We have seen above that no single theory of interest rate is adequate and determinate. An adequate theory to be determinate must take into consideration both the real and monetary factors that influence the interest rate. *Hicks* has utilised the Keynesian tools in a method of presentation which shows that productivity, thrift, liquidity preference and money supply are all necessary elements in a comprehensive and determinate interest theory. According to Hansen, "An equilibrium condition is reached when the desired volume of cash balances equal the quantity of money, when the marginal efficiency of capital is equal to the rate of interest and finally when the volume of investment is equal to the normal or desired volume of saving. And these factors are interrelated." Thus in the modern theory of interest., saving, investment, liquidity preference and the quantity of money are integrated at various levels to income for a synthesis of the loanable funds theory with the liquidity preference theory. The four variables of the two formulations have been combined to construct two new curves, the IS curve representing flow variables of the loanable funds formulation (or the real factors of the classical theory) and the LM curve representing the stock variables of liquidity preference formulation. The equilibrium between IS and LM curves provides a equilibrium rate of interest.

New Series of National Accounts Statistics

The Central Statistical Organisation (CSO), mandated to prepare and release estimates of national income, consumption expenditure, saving and capital formation, prepared the first official estimates of national income with base year 1948-49 in 1956. To take into account the structural changes taking place in the economy, the base year has been shifted five times so far to 1960-61, 1970-71, 1980-81, 1993-94 and 1999-2000.

The choice of the latest base year 1999-2000 coincides with the year of the 55th round of the quinquennial survey on employment and unemployment by the National Samply Survey Organisation (NSSO). Besides using the 56th, 57th and 58th rounds of NSSO surveys on Unorganized Manufacturing, Services Sectors and Housing Conditions respectively, the new1999-2000 series also uses All India Livestock Census, 2003, Population Census, 2001 and All India Census of small scale industries, 2001-02. With a widening of the coverage, improvement in procedures and inclusion of long-term survey results, the change in base has resulted in some changes in the GDP estimates according to the New Series.

National Policy for Farmers, 2007

Government of India has approved the National Policy for Farmers, 2007 taking into account the recommendations of the National Commission on Farmers and after consulting the State Governments. The National Policy for Farmers, among other things, has provided for a holistic approach to development of the farm sector. The broad areas of its coverage include :

- *(i)* *Focus* will be on the economic well being of the farmers in addition to production and productivity.
- *(ii)* *Asset reforms :* To ensure that a farmer household in villages either possesses or has access to a productive asset or marketable skill.
- *(iii)* *Water use efficiency* : The concept of maximizing yield and income per unit of irrigation water in all the crop production programmes would be accorded priority with stress on awareness and efficiency of water use.
- *(iv)* *New technologies* like biotechnology, information and communication technology (ICT), renewable energy technology, space applications and nano-technology would be encouraged for improving productivity per unit of land and water on a sustainable basis.
- *(v)* *National Agricultural Bio-security System* would be established to organize a coordinated agricultural bio-security programme.
- *(vi)* *Seeds and Soil Health :* Quality seeds, disease free planting material and soil health enhancement hold the key to raising small farm productivity. Every farmer is to be issued with a soil health passbook containing integrated information on farm soils with corresponding advisories.
- *(vii)* *Support services for women :* Appropriate support services like creches, child care centres and adequate nutrition needed by women working in fields would be funded.
- *(viii)* *Credit & Insurance :* The financial services would be galvanized for timely, adequate and easy reach to the farmers at reasonable interest rates.
- *(ix)* *Gyan Chaupals* at village level with the help of ICT and farm schools in the fields of outstanding farmers to promote farmer to farmer learning would be set up through the State Governments for strengthening extension services.
- *(x)* Necessary steps would be taken to put in place an appropriate *social security scheme* for farmers.
- *(xi)* *Minimum Support Price (MSP)* mechanism to be implemented effectively across the country so as to ensure remunerative prices for agricultural produce.
- *(xii)* *Food Security basket* is to be enlarged to include nutritious millets such as bajra, jowar, ragi and millets, mostly grown in dry land farming areas.

An inter Ministerial Committee has been setup to operationalize the implementation of the policy.

Micro-Irrigation

A Centrally-sponsored scheme of microirrigation was launched in January 2006 to promote water use efficiency by adopting drip and sprinkler irrigation. During 2005-06 and 2006-07, Rs. 280.58 crore and Rs. 460.7 crore, respectively, were released for covering 5.9 lakh ha (3.5 lakh ha under drip and 2.4 lakh ha under sprinkler irrigation system). Up to March 2007 an expenditure of Rs. 366.4 crore was incurred and an area of 3.4 lakh ha under drip and sprinkler irrigation system was covered. Allocation of funds during 2007-08 is Rs. 550 crore for covering 3.6 lakh ha. Rs. 266.7 crore of the allocated amount was released till the end of January 2008.

National Bamboo Mission

A Centrally-sponsored scheme called National Bamboo Mission was launched in 2006-07. An area of 20,500 ha was covered, the existing stock in 4,117 ha was improved and 213 bamboo nurseries were established with an outlay of Rs. 80 crore. A sum of Rs. 70 crore has been allocated for implementation of the scheme during 2007-08 and Rs. 33.6 crore has been released so far.

Eleventh five year Plan at a Glance
Vision for Eleventh Plan

- Trigger a development process which ensures broad based improvement in the quality of life of the people especially the poor, SCs/ STs, OBCs, minorities and women.
- The focus is on Faster and more Inclusively Growth

Growth Targets

- Growth rate of GDP : 9.0 per cent per annum
- Sectorial growth rates:

  Agriculture : 4 per cent per annum

  Industry : 10 per cent per annum

  Services : 9-11 per cent per annum

Monitorable Targets

- 27 monitorable targets at national level of which 13 can be disaggregated at the level of individual States
- 27 monitorable targets divided into six categories: (i) Income and poverty; (ii) Education; (iii) Health; (iv) Women and children; (v) Infrastructure; and (vi) Environment.

Important targests In the above categories are:

- Reduction in head-count ratio of consumption poverty by 10 percentage points .

  Creation of 58 million jobs in five years.
- Increasing the literacy rate for persons of age 7 years or more to 85 per cent by 2011-12.
- Infant mortality rate (IMR) to be reduced to 28 per Thousand.
- Maternal mortality rate (MMR) to be reduced to 1 per 1000 live births.
- Sex ratio for age group 0-6 years to be raised to 935 by 2011-12 and to 950 by 2016-17.
- To ensure electricity connection to all villages and BPL households by 2009 and reliable power by end of the Plan.
- To increase forest and tree cover by 5 percentage points.

Financial Outline

1. Total outlay : Rs. 36,44,718 crore (at 2006-07 prices)

(i) Central Plan Outlay : Rs. 21,56,571 crore

(ii) Outlay of States and Union Territories : Rs. 14,88,147 crore

2. Centre's GBS (Gross Budgetary Support) : Rs. 14,21,711 crore
3. Centre's assistance to States & UTs : Rs. 3,24,851 crore
4. Sectoral allocation of Plan resources :

   Social services: 30.24 per cent

   Energy : 23.43 per cent

   Transport : 15.71 per cent

   Agriculture* : 18.49 per cent

   Industry : 4.21 per cent

* Includes (i) agriculture and allied activities (ii) rural development, (iii) special area programmes, and (iv) irrigation and flood control

Macro economic parameters

GDP growth	: 9 per cent per annum
Investment rate	: 36.72 per cent of GDP
Saving rate	: 34.84 per cent of GDP
Current account deficit	: 1.88 per cent of GDP
ICOR	: 4.1

Main Strategies

- Fostering inclusiveness of farmers through a group approach
- Improving efficiency of investment
- Restructuring agriculture planning
- Tackling the problems of poor infrastructure and skill deficit for better industrial growth
- Making about laws flexible
- Providing more credit to small scale enterprises
- Increasing investment in infrastructure from 5 per cent of GDP in 2006-07 to 9 per cent by 2011-12
- Adding 78,577 MW capacity in power sector
- Adoption of public- private partnership in physical and social infrastructure.
- Commitment to pursue a development process which is environmentally sustainable.
- Gender equity–move beyond empowerment and recognise women as agents of sustained socio-economic growth and change.
- Improvement in governance (critical elements being accountability and transparency).

EXERCISE

1. Bank Rate is the rate :

A. which is reference rate in all countries for interest structure.

B. at which the central bank rediscounts the first class gilt edged securities of the banks.

C. the rate which is given to the depositors of money with bank.

D. the rate which is charged on loans given by banks.

2. The classical theory of money postulates that :

A. more money will secure more growth.

B. more money will secure no growth but only inflation.

C. more money will increase the real and relative prices only.

D. during deflation a reduced velocity will end deflation.

3. Statutory liquidity ratio (SLR) of commercial banks means—

A. the percentage of cash that banks keep with them under rules

B. the bank rate which is reference rate also

C. the ratio of government and other gilt-edged securities to liquid liabilities

D. the "reserve money"

4. If banks want to increase credit creation.

A. they should increase interest rate to have more deposits

B. they should reduce the rate of interest

C. they should have high cash reserves with them

D. they should force investors to create demand for loans

5. Monetary-base is made up of :

A. Required reserves with the central bank and currency with the public

B. Currency with the public and total deposits

C. Reserves of banking system and currency with the public

D. Borrowed reserves and non-borrowed reserves

6. Which combination represents the IS curve?

A. High interest rate and high income level

B. High interest rate and low income level

C. High interest rate and low saving level

D. High interest rate and high investment level

7. If the supply of money exceeds the demand for money by 5%, then by how much does the rate of interest have to fall to restore market equilibrium, assuming interest elasticity of the demand for money to be–0.5% and other things remaining unchanged?

A. 2.5% B. 5%

C. 10% D. 15%

8. As regards changes in interest rates, the most sensitive money market is the :

A. Bill market

B. Un-organised money market

C. Call money market

D. Collateral loan market

9. The Unit Banking System is very popular in

A. England B. Japan

C. India D. U.S.A.

10. In a multi-bank system, with 20% cash reserve ratio, on a receipt of cash deposits of Rs, 100 crores, the banking system as a whole can create deposits to the extent of

A. Rs. 80 crores B. Rs. 100 crores

C. Rs. 320 crores D. Rs. 400 crores

11. The theory of open market operations assumes that :

A. the velocities of both bank deposits and legal tender money have no relationship

B. the legal tender money has a higher velocity than bank deposits

C. the bank deposits have a higher velocity than legal tender money

D. the circulation of bank deposits and legal tender money has constant velocity

12. Consider the following statements :

The success of a policy of variable reserve requirement depends on the

1. maintenance of a fixed reserve ratio by the commercial banks
2. maintenance of little or no excess reserves by the commercial banks
3. presence of a developed money market of the above statements

A. 2 and 3 are correct
B. 1 and 2 are correct
C. 3 alone is correct
D. 1 and 3 are correct

13. The speculative demand for money, according to Keynes, is a function of
A. Rate of interest B. Level of income
C. Level of savings D. Level of output

14. Which of the following instruments for quantitative control of credit are used by Reserve Bank of India?
1. Cash requirement ratio
2. Statutory liquidity ratio
3. Open market operations
4. Margin requirements

Select the correct answer using the following codes. :
A. 1 and 2 B. 2 and 4
C. 1, 2 and 3 D. 3 and 4

15. The time-preference theory of interest is mainly associated with
A. J.M. Keynes B. I. Fisher
C. K. Wicksell D. M. Friedman

16. In the liquidity preference theory of interest of Keynes, money acts as a link between the present and the future in the case of :
A. transactions demand for money
B. precautionary demand for money
C. business demand for money
D. speculative demand for money

17. Match List I (Theory of interest) with List II (Authors) and select the correct answer using the codes given below the lists :

	List-I	*List-II*
(a)	Abstinence theory of interest	1. Knut Wicksell
(b)	Time preference theory of interest	2. Irving Fisher
(c)	Loanable funds theory of interest	3. N.W. Senior
(d)	Liquidity preference theory of interest	4. J.M. Keynes

	(a)	(b)	(c)	(d)
A.	2	3	1	4
B.	3	2	1	4
C.	3	2	4	1
D.	2	3	4	1

18. Open market operations refers to :
A. borrowing by scheduled banks from the RBI
B. lending by commercial banks to industry and trade
C. purchase and sale of government securities by the RBI
D. deposit mobilisation

19. Which of the following pairs are correctly matched?

1.	Interest rate is a real phenomenon	Neo classical economists
2.	Interest rate is a monetary phenomenon	Marshall
3.	Interest rate does not determine the level of saving	Cambridge school
4.	Reduced interest rates always bring with them production processes	Bohm Bawerk
	which are more round about	Bohm Bawerk

Select the correct answer using the codes given below :
A. 1,2 and 3 B. 1, 3 and 4
C. 1, 2 and 4 D. 3 and 4

20. If the rate of interest is greater than zero, it follows that :
A. present goods and future goods always have an equal value
B. present goods are worth less than future goods
C. present consumption is worth more than future consumption
D. present consumption is worth less than future consumption

21. The objective of selective credit controls is mainly to
A. selectively allocate credit to commercial banks
B. selectively allocate credit among borrowers
C. regulate the quantity of demand deposits created by commercial banks
D. regulate the quantity of credit created by commercial banks

22. Speculative demand for money would increase if
A. prices of securities are expected to rise
B. prices of goods are expected to fall

C. the interest rate is expected to be constant
D. the interest rate is expected to rise

23. Under the 'liquidity trap' situation the liquidity preference curve
A. is perfectly inelastic
B. is perfectly elastic
C. intersects the horizontal axis
D. interests the vertical axix

24. The theory that the transactions demand for money also depends on the rate of interest was put forward by
A. Keynes and Pigou
B. Baumol and Tooin
C. Hicks and Solow
D. Samuelson and Meade

25. Interest–elasticity of demand for money, according to classical theroy is
A. one B. zero
C. greater than one D. none of the above

26. IS–LM model relates to
A. Rent B. Interest
C. Wages D. Profits

27. The IS–curve shows
A. a positive relationship between rate of interest and the level of income
B. a negative relationship between rate of interest and the level of income
C. a positive relationship between rate of interest and the level of autonomous investment
D. a negative relationship between rate of interest and level of autonomous investment

28. According to Keynes, the transactions demand for money is mainly a function of
A. Rate of interest B. Profits
C. Wages D. Income

29. According to Keynes, investors prefer holding money rather than bonds when they expect
A. interest rates to remain constant
B. interest rates to rise
C. interest rates to fall
D. bond prices to rise

30. An increase in the supply of money will cause LM schedule to
A. remain unchanged
B. shift to the left
C. shift to the right
D. shift upwards

31. LM curve expresses the ralation of :
A. Higher interest and higher level of real income
B. Lower interest and higher level of real income
C. Higher interest and lower level of real income
D. Both B and C

32 The real rate of interest is defined as the difference between
A. the nominal rate of interest and the expected rate of inflation
B. the nominal rate of interest and market rate of interest
C. the expected rate of interest and the market rate of interest
D. the expected rate of interest and the current rate of inflation

33. Grasham's law relates to :
A. money supply B. money and prices
C. real output D. employment

34. Which of the following items is not included in a country's balance of payments?
A. Import and export duties
B. Shipping services
C. Interest received from abroad
D. Tourists' expenditure

35. According to Keynes, investors prefer holding money rather than bonds when they expect
A. Interest rates to fall
B. Bond prices to rise
C. Interest rates to rise
D. Interest rates to remain constant

36. The most important item of expenditure of the Union Government in India is
A. Subsidies
B. Defence
C. Wages and salaries
D. Interest payments

37. Public Debt constitutes
A. External public debt
B. External liabilities and external commercial borrowings
C. National debt and other miscellaneous debt for which the government is ultimately responsible
D. Both B and C above

38. The direct effect of deficit financing is
A. It leads to extra money supply which in turn pushes up prices
B. It leads to extra money supply which in turn makes market more and more competitive
C. The price situation comes under complete control
D. Demand and supply both increase

39. 'Misery Index' represents
A. Sum of rate of inflation and rate of unemployment
B. Product of rate of inflation and rate of unemployment
C. Proportion of very poor to poor living below the poverty line
D. Both the above B and C

40. Which of the following is the most important source of financing the gross fiscal deficit of the Government of India?
A. Market borrowings
B. Loans from the State Government
C. Loans from the financial institutes
D. Loans from Provident Funds

41. According to Keynes, Investment depends on
A. Size of income and propensity to consume
B. Marginal efficiency of capital and size of income
C. Marginal efficiency of capital and rate of interest
D. Propensity to consume and rate of interest

42. The Reserve Bank of India (RBI) keeps on modifying various rates/ratios to keep the flow of liquidity in the market in a balanced situation. Which of the following rates/ratios/indexes is not directly controlled by the RBI?
A. Cash Reserve Ratio (CRR)
B. Bank Rate
C. Repo rate
D. Reverse Repo Rate
E. Wholesale Price Index (WPI)

43. Many banks have adopted/launched 'Core Banking Solutions' (CBS). Core Banking Solution is ....
A. A marketing strategy adopted by the banks.
B. A new type of ATM useful for rural population
C. A delivery channel for quick and fast delivery
D. A new product launched to help senior citizens only as they are not able to visit branches/ATMs frequently
E. None of these

44. Opening the Savings Bank Account of a minor girl will be called as which of the following in Banking terminology?
A. Retail Banking
B. Merchant Banking
C. Institutional Banking
D. Social Banking
E. Corporate Banking

45. Which of the following terms is not used in Banking Sector?
A. SLR B. NPA
C. Credit Rating D. Fixed
E. PURA

46. Banking Sector will fall under which of the following sectors?
A. Agricultural Sector
B. Service Sector
C. Manufacturing
D. Industrial Sector
E. None of these

47 An account in which trading of shares in their electronic form is done is known as ....
A. Demat Account B. NRI Account
C. NRIO Account D. Current Account
E. None of these

48. Which of the following is not a measure of the Risk Management in Banks?
A. CRR
B. RTGS
C. SLR
D. Deposit Insurance
E. All are the measures of risk management

49. As we all know the value of the Indian rupee has appreciated in the recent past. The value of the Rupee is directly dependent on which of the following?
A. Availability of commodities in the market
B. VAT introduced by the Govt. on various commodities
C. Size of total Forex Reserve of India currently
D. Capital flow in the market during a given period of time
E. None of these

50. Inflation has become a major area of concern in India these days. What measures do the Govt. of India/RBI normally take to control the same?

1. Fixation of Maximum Prices of the Commodities
2. System of Dual prices.
3. Increase in supply of foodgrains.
4. Control on credit and liquidity in market.

A. Only 1 B. Only 2
C. Only 3 D. Only 2, 3 and 4
E. All 1, 2, 3 and 4

51. Which of the following is/are included in 'Deficit Financing' in India?
(The term is used frequently in economic planning)

1. Borrowing from the Reserve Bank of India.
2. Issue of New Currency Notes.
3. Withdrawal of past balances/surpluses etc.

A. Only 1 B. Only 2
C. Only 3 D. All 1, 2 and 3
E. None of these

ANSWERS

1	2	3	4	5	6	7	8	9	10
B	B	C	A	C	B	A	C	D	D
11	**12**	**13**	**14**	**15**	**16**	**17**	**18**	**19**	**20**
B	D	A	C	B	D	B	C	D	C
21	**22**	**23**	**24**	**25**	**26**	**27**	**28**	**29**	**30**
B	D	B	B	B	B	B	D	C	C
31	**32**	**33**	**34**	**35**	**36**	**37**	**38**	**39**	**40**
A	A	A	A	A	D	D	A	A	A
41	**42**	**43**	**44**	**45**	**46**	**47**	**48**	**49**	**50**
C	E	C	A	E	B	A	B	A	D
51									
A									

YOUR SPACE